This book is dedicated to
the Leslie Price Memorial
Library by

Jane and David Pennock

THE
PENGUIN
OPERA
GUIDE

EDITED BY AMANDA HOLDEN

with NICHOLAS KENYON

and STEPHEN WALSH

Preface by SIR COLIN DAVIS

VIKING

VIKING

Published by the Penguin Group
Penguin Books Ltd, 27 Wrights Lane, London W8 5TZ, England
Penguin Books USA Inc., 375 Hudson Street, New York, New York 10014, USA
Penguin Books Australia Ltd, Ringwood, Victoria, Australia
Penguin Books Canada Ltd, 10 Alcorn Avenue, Toronto, Ontario, Canada M4V 3B2
Penguin Books (NZ) Ltd, 182–190 Wairau Road, Auckland 100, New Zealand

Penguin Books Ltd, Registered Offices: Harmondsworth, Middlesex, England

The Viking Opera Guide first published 1993
This abridged edition, with revisions, first published as
The Penguin Opera Guide 1995
1 3 5 7 9 10 8 6 4 2
First edition

Copyright © Amanda Holden, 1993, 1995

Filmset by Datix International Limited, Bungay, Suffolk
Printed in England by Clays Ltd, St Ives plc
Set in 8/9 pt Monophoto Times

A CIP catalogue record for this book is available from the British Library

ISBN 0–670–81293–5

Contents

Preface

BY SIR COLIN DAVIS

The Penguin Opera Guide, like its parent, *The Viking Opera Guide*, is wonderful – practical, entertaining, scholarly. Amanda Holden and her distinguished team of contributors have produced an essential reference book for anyone with an interest in opera, from the ingenue who is merely curious to the most knowledgeable professional.

Opera is part of us all, and its bizarre glory reflects the complexity of our existence. And in the years since I began conducting opera it has flourished as never before. There are audiences everywhere for less well-known works, which prove to have been unworthy of neglect; the repertoire is expanding every year.

This book provides a comprehensive guide to today's richly diverse repertoire. If you're hurrying out to a performance a synopsis can be read in a few minutes; spend a few more and you can read the background to the opera and find points of musical interest. The composers are all introduced with the essentials of their biographical background.

What more could you want? Only the music and the stage.

About this Book

The Penguin Opera Guide consists of roughly 150 articles on opera composers. It is largely derived from its slightly older relation *The Viking Opera Guide* (published in 1993). But the development of opera, as any art form, never stands still; hence the latest works by several living composers have been added.

Each composer article opens with a biographical introduction; entries on their important operatic works then follow in order of composition. Works without separate entries are listed at the end of their articles, with premiere date (dates in brackets signify completion of composition if significantly earlier than the premiere or for an unperformed work); thus each composer's *complete* operatic works are included.

Every opera entry includes the title (in the original language and English translation), genre and duration (to the nearest five minutes for works under an hour and to the nearest fifteen minutes for longer pieces), librettist and source of libretto, composition dates (if apposite) and premiere dates (world premiere followed by UK and US premieres in chronological order). An introduction to the work is followed by a synopsis and – finally – a musical discussion. Operas are given space as merited.

To look up an opera, turn to the Index of Titles, where all the works are listed in their original form and in translation.

Technical terms are to be found in the Glossary. The most familiar musical terms, such as intermezzo and singspiel, have been treated as English words (i.e. printed in roman type and (if German nouns) without initial capital letters). Less familiar foreign terms and expressions remain in italics. Cast lists are (we hope) sensible rather than logical, e.g. we give Emperor and Empress in Richard Strauss's *Die Frau ohne Schatten*, whereas Puccini's *Suor Angelica* keeps the original Italian names. Dates mentioned *en passant* in the text are either of publication (books) or of first performance (musical works).

Contributors are credited by initial, a full biographical index of contributors is at the end of the book.

The term opera is here interpreted in its widest sense, as any dramatic work that can be sung (or at times declaimed or spoken) in a place for performance, set to original music for singers (usually in costume) and instrumentalists. It seemed sensible and natural to include, along with opera in the more usual sense, all related genres – e.g. singspiels, musicals, semi-operas and music theatre.

I am happy to take this opportunity to thank not only the original contributors to *The Viking Opera Guide* but also those who have added the new material for this book. Many thanks also to Rodney Milnes for constant helpful advice and to Judith Flanders and Ravi Mirchandani at Penguin for their continued support. Finally, I cannot sign off without a tribute to my sons, Sam, Joe and Ben; they deserve one for their generosity to me.

Amanda Holden
Highbury, London, 1995

Abbreviations

a	alto	NBC	National Broadcasting Company
arr.	arranged by	n.d.	no date
		no.	number
b	bass	nr	near
b	born (composer headings)		
bar	baritone	orch.	orchestra; orchestrator; orchestrated by
b-bar	bass-baritone	ORTF	Office de Radiodiffusion-Télévision
BBC	British Broadcasting Corporation		Française
boy s	boy soprano; treble	OUP	Oxford University Press
c	contralto	pf	piano
coll.	collaborator; collaboration	prod.	producer; produced by
cond.	conductor; conducted by	pt	part
ct	counter-tenor		
CUP	Cambridge University Press	RAI	Radio Audizioni Italiane
		rev.	revised; revision
d	died		
dir.	director; directed by	*s*	soprano
		S., SS	Saint, Saints
ed.	editor; edited	*satb*	soprano, alto, tenor, bass
ENO	English National Opera	snr	senior
fl.	*floruit* (flourished)	*t*	tenor
		t-bar	tenor-baritone
inc.	incomplete	trans.	translator; translated by
IRCAM	Institut de Recherche et de Coordination Acoustique/Musique (see glossary)	unperf.	unperformed
jnr	junior	vol.	volume
lib.	libretto	WDR	Westdeutscher Rundfunk
mc	mezzo-contralto	WNO	Welsh National Opera
ms	mezzo-soprano		

Glossary

12-note see *serial*

afterpiece a short opera performed after a play or an opera, in 18th-century England

air de cour a French secular song or part-song of the late 16th or early 17th century

aleatoric involving elements of chance ('with dice')

allegretto diminutive of allegro (q.v.) and therefore lively etc. but slightly less so

allegro cheerful, lively: quick

alto the register between soprano and tenor; the alto voice is usually that of a male (falsetto) singer in this register, but the term is also used for choral singers of either sex

andante 'walking': slow but mobile

andantino diminutive of andante (q.v.), usually meaning a little faster but can mean slower; it implies that the music is more modest in scope

antiphonal the term used to describe music performed by a divided group of singers (or players), the two sections often 'answering' one another

appoggiatura literally 'to be leant on': a melodic ornament which carries more accent than the note ornamented

aria Italian for 'air', and the standard term for a distinct solo song in an opera

arioso 'like an aria'; an arioso is usually an accompanied recitative in strict time, but the term can also denote a short, informal aria (q.v.)

arpeggio (from *arpa*, Italian for 'harp'): a chord whose notes are played consecutively instead of simultaneously

atonal having no discernible key or tonality (q.v.)

avant-garde a term describing artists whose techniques and aims are radically different from traditional ones, its common usage dates from the years immediately after the Second World War

azione scenica a part of a play that is set to music

azione teatrale (1) a short one-act opera or piece of musical theatre, with a small cast and orchestra, designed to form part of an evening's entertainment; (2) a staged oratorio

balalaika the Russian peasant lute, with a triangular body and three strings

ballatella a folksong with a dance character

ballet a dance episode in an opera, with or without singing (also the dancers who perform it)

ballet de cour a French courtly entertainment of the 16th and 17th centuries in which an allegory was presented through a mixture of dancing and singing

banda a stage band, usually a group of wind instruments, often a feature of Italian 19th-century opera

bandora a plucked bass string instrument, often used as continuo (q.v.) instrument in 17th-century opera; it had (usually) six metal strings, and a characteristic scalloped body outline

baritone the male voice in the register between tenor and bass

baryton Martin a light baritone voice with near-tenor range of the kind often found in French Romantic opera. Named after the singer Jean-Blaise Martin (1768–1837)

bass (1) the lowest male voice; (2) the lowest part of a musical texture

bass-baritone a bass voice with strong top notes

basse chantante a bass voice of lyric, almost baritone, quality

basset horn a low clarinet (in F) much used by Mozart in his late works

basso continuo the instrument or instruments which, in baroque and early classical music, played the bass line and supporting harmonies; the part was normally notated as a single line of music, with or without figures indicating the chords

basso profondo a bass voice capable of reaching very low notes

bitonality in bitonal music, two distinct keys are felt to be present at the same time

book musical a term used to distinguish a musical with story and continuing characters (i.e. a libretto or book) from a revue (which has neither)

breeches role a male role sung by a woman

brindisi   a drinking song

buffo, buffa   Italian for 'comic' (cf. 'buffoon')

bylina   a traditional Russian epic poem or ballad

cabaletta   a quick, often brilliant, final section of an aria (q.v.), especially in Italian opera

cadence   a harmonic formula at the end of a musical phrase (derived from the convention of melodic fall (Latin *cadere*) in plainsong); cf. 'dying fall'

cadenza   a free solo (vocal or instrumental) passage originally improvised over the penultimate chord of a cadence (q.v.), later sometimes written in by the composer; any such bravura solo

Camerata   the name given to the salon, or intellectual circle, of Count Giovanni de' Bardi in Florence in the 1570s and 1580s; it included the composer Giulio Caccini, through whom the term was later also associated with the 'first' experiments in music drama, by Giulio Caccini and Jacopo Peri, in the 1590s

canon   the exact imitation of one melody by one or more others, each starting later but overlapping the previous one

cantabile   in a singing style

cantilena   melody (or 'small song'), usually applied to sustained phrases of vocal melody

cantus firmus   the fixed structural melody of medieval and Renaissance music, always based on an existing and recognizable tune; thence any simple, slow-moving melody which supports a complicated texture or other parts

canzona   originally a verse form of the troubadour period, the term is now freely used to denote a simple song of popular or quasi-folk character

canzonetta   literally a small 'canzona'; usually denotes a light-hearted song in simple verse form

castrato   the vocal type of the male soprano in 17th- and 18th-century opera, achieved by prepubescent castration

cavatina   a short aria, distinguished in 18th-century opera from the aria proper by its lack of a da capo (q.v.)

chaconne   a slow baroque dance in triple time, designed as a series of variations over a repeating bass line

chain finale   an extended finale in a number of linked sections and without formal (large-scale) reprise (e.g. Act II of Mozart's *Le nozze di Figaro*)

chalumeau   a 17th-century ancestor of the clarinet; the word is also used for the rich low register of the modern clarinet

chromaticism   the presence of notes other than those of the actual scale in use, e.g. in C major the piano's black notes are all chromatic; more generally, the term can refer to complex music with either harsh dissonance or no fixed tonality

ciaccona   Italian for 'chaconne' (q.v.)

cluster   a chord of several adjacent notes such as a child will make with his fist on a keyboard

coll'arco   with the (violin etc.) bow, as opposed to pizzicato (q.v.)

coloratura   Italian for 'colouring'; florid vocal ornamentation, and the type of brilliant and agile voice (usually soprano) suited to such music

common chord   the basic chord of a particular key (the common chord of C major consists of the notes C, E and G)

comprimario   in Italian opera, a sub-principal operatic soloist, not qualifying for full-blown solo arias

concertante   concerto-like: where one or more parts has a solo or virtuoso quality

concertato   a passage in which independent instrumental parts are combined with the voices (e.g. the quartet in Mozart's *Idomeneo*)

concertino   the solo instrumental group, as opposed to the ripieno (q.v.), in baroque music

concerto grosso   the baroque term for a concerto with a solo group as opposed to a single soloist

conte   French for 'tale'

continuo   see *basso continuo*

contralto   the female alto (q.v.); originally also a low-voiced castrato (q.v.)

contrapuntal   consisting of counterpoint (q.v.)

coro   Italian and Spanish for 'chorus'

counterpoint   music which is constructed of two or more independent melodic lines

counter-tenor   the male alto; historically the terms seem to be interchangeable, though there is some support for the idea that the counter-tenor sings without the 'break' into falsetto that characterizes the alto (q.v.; see also *haute-contre*)

csárdás   a Hungarian dance in two sections: slow (*lassú*) and fast (*friss*)

da capo   'from the beginning'; a da-capo form (e.g. aria, q.v.) is in three parts, of which the third is a repeat of the first, shown by a da capo, or 'D.C.', sign at the end of the second

dactyl   in poetry, a metrical 'foot' consisting of one long and two short stresses

descant   a melody sung above the main melody

deus ex machina   'god from a machine': the device in 17th- and 18th-century opera whereby a happy ending is contrived by the sudden appearance of a god or allegorical figure who decrees that all shall be well

development   a musical section in which material already presented is subjected to various elaborative processes

diatonic   diatonic music stays within the chosen major or minor scale

divertissement   (1) a musical episode, of a light or diversionary character though often with its own narrative, in a large-scale drama; (2) a self-contained theatrical entertainment, involving singing, dance and spectacle, celebrating some grand event; both meanings were standard in 17th- and 18th-century France

divisi   Italian word meaning 'divided': divisi cellos, for example, are split into two or more parts

dodecaphonic   see *serial*

dominant   the fifth degree of the major and minor scales (for instance, in the scale of C major, the dominant is G); it has a strong controlling function in the harmonic structure of tonal music

domra   a Russian peasant plucked stringed instrument

Drama für Musik   see *dramma per musica*

dramaturgy   the general principles of drama or stage action

drame lyrique   a genre of Romantic opera, without dialogue but less 'public' and ostentatious than grand opera (q.v.) (Massenet's *Werther* is a well-known example)

dramma giocoso   a comic operatic genre developed by Baldassare Galuppi and Carlo Goldoni, in which serious and comic characters and elements intermingle (the best-known example is Mozart's *Don Giovanni*)

dramma per musica   (1) a play written specifically for setting to music; (2) a term for serious opera in the 18th century, synonymous with opera seria (q.v.)

dumka   a Ukrainian folk idiom adopted by 19th-century composers (famously Dvořák) to produce music of a predominantly melancholy, ruminative character alternating with relatively boisterous music in quick time

écossaise   a (supposedly Scottish) lively folk dance in duple time

enharmonic progression   a change of key hinging on the fact that notes in Western harmony have two or more names (e.g. G sharp = A flat): a chord containing notes common to both keys acts as a pivot from one harmonic centre to another

entr'acte   a musical interlude between acts of a play or opera; a distinct musical work intended for performance in this way

entrée   'entry'; in the 17th and 18th centuries (1) a self-contained group of dances in a ballet de cour (q.v.); (2) an instrumental piece marking the beginning of the divertissement in a tragédie lyrique or an opéra-ballet (q.v.)

falcon   a dramatic and powerful soprano voice with a rich middle register, named after the French singer Cornélie Falcon

falsetto   a method of singing which enables a male singer to reach notes above his usual range

farandole   a 'chain' folk dance from the South of France, usually in six-eight time and a moderate tempo

farsa   'farce'; (1) a musical intermezzo or afterpiece (q.v.) to a comic play (18th-century Italy before 1770); (2) a short independent musical play of a farcical character

fiaba   Italian for 'fable, fairy-tale'

fioritura   'flourish': vocal embellishment

fisarmonica   'bellows harmonica'; the standard Italian word for an accordion

fugal   having all or some properties of a fugue (q.v.)

fugato   a section in which the music proceeds in the manner of a fugue (q.v.)

fugue   a strict, originally instrumental, style in which an initial theme builds up through a series of imitative entries into a piece in several parts

furiant   a quick Bohemian dance with frequently alternating two- and three-beat bars

galant   see *style galant*

galop   a fast 19th-century ballroom dance in duple time

gamelan   the traditional Indonesian orchestra (Bali and Java) consisting mainly of metal percussion, with one or two melody instruments

Gesamtkunstwerk   German for 'total art-work'; in Wagner and others, a work in which all or many art forms are combined

glissando   literally 'sliding': a rapid scale involving a lightning succession of notes produced on a keyboard by drawing the fingers quickly across the keys and on a string instrument by sliding the left hand up or down the finger-board

gopak   a Ukrainian dance in quick duple time

grand opera   (1) the large-scale operatic genre of the early 19th century particularly in France, in which epic historical subjects were staged with enormous forces and great spectacle; (2) opera in general, as opposed to operetta or other forms of sung musical theatre

guerre des bouffons   one of the most famous controversies in French musical history, between the adherents of French and Italian opera respectively; it raged in Paris between 1752 and 1754, when an Italian comic opera troupe (the bouffons in question) performed Pergolesi's *La serva padrona* and triggered off a virulent argument which involved many of the greatest figures of the day, including Rousseau, Diderot and, on the Francophile side, Mme de Pompadour

habanera   ('from Havana') a slow Cuban dance in duple time, with a characteristic dotted rhythm on the first beat

Handlung German for 'plot' or 'action'

haute-contre the very high tenor voice of French 18th-century opera

head voice a vocal technique resonated in the head (rather than in the chest) for the production of a light sound quality; occasionally called 'head tone'

Heldenbariton 'heroic baritone'

Heldentenor German for 'heroic tenor'; the standard term for the powerful tenor voice called for by Wagner

hemiola a rhythmic device in which two three-beat bars are reinterpreted as a single bar of three double-length beats

intermède the French equivalent of the Italian 'intermedio' (2) (q.v.)

intermedio (1) 'intermezzo' (q.v.); (2) the normal term for the short staged pieces often interpolated between the acts of Italian serious plays or operas in the 16th–18th centuries; they were typically comic or light in tone, but court intermedi were lavish affairs with elaborate sets and stage machinery; the early intermedio was part of the ancestry of 17th-century opera, while the later intermedio is generally regarded as the forerunner of 18th-century comic opera

intermezzo (1) a musical (usually orchestral) interlude between operatic scenes; (2) intermedio (q.v.)

intrada instrumental music, either at the start of a work or on the appearance on-stage of a main character

IRCAM Institut de Recherche et de Coordination Acoustique/Musique; the Parisian institute for electronic and computer music, opened in 1976 with Pierre Boulez as its director

kapellmeister originally the master of music in a court chapel; later any musical director, whether working at an ecclesiastical or a theatrical establishment

key see *tonal*

khorovod a traditional Russian 'round dance'

Klangfarbenmelodie 'sound-colour melody'; the term applied to a style of 20th-century composition in which pitch change (i.e. melody) is replaced, or enhanced, by frequent changes of instrumental timbre

kobza a Ukrainian guitar-like plucked stringed instrument

krakowiak a cheerful dance from the Cracow (Kraków) region of Poland, in duple time with frequent syncopations

ländler a leisurely waltz originating in the Landl area of Austria

leitmotif/leitmotiv the 'leading motif' of Wagner's music dramas (though the term was neither invented nor significantly used by him): a theme or musical figure that recurs – altered or unaltered – as a recognizable symbol or reminder of a character or some other element of the plot

Les Six Parisian group of composers brought together by Jean Cocteau at the end of the First World War to promote his idea that art should be practical, anti-earnest, and fun; its members were Georges Auric, Louis Durey, Arthur Honegger, Darius Milhaud, Francis Poulenc and Germaine Tailleferre

lezginka a traditional dance of the Lezghians, a people living in the Caucasus mountains

libretto 'small book': (1) the printed or manuscript literary text of an operatic work; (2) the text of an operatic work

licenza a celebratory conclusion to a stage work, usually written to mark a particular occasion

Liebestod 'love-death': a term applied to the final scene of Wagner's *Tristan und Isolde*, where love finally carries Isolde beyond life to join Tristan in death, in literal fulfilment of the opera's imagery of love as death to the world

lied (plural '*lieder*') the standard German word for 'song', especially art song

loure a ponderous, rather slow French-style jig, often with a short–long upbeat

lyrics words for singing as distinct from spoken dialogue

lyric soprano, tenor, etc. a voice of comparatively light, fluent quality

maestro al cembalo a musician who directs performances from a keyboard instrument

masque the hybrid court entertainment of 16th- and 17th-century England, combining music, dance, spoken poetry and elaborate sets and costumes

mazurka a Polish dance (from Mazovia, near Warsaw), in triple time with the accent on the second or third beat

melisma a melodic phrase sung to a single syllable

melodram see *melodrama* (1)

melodrama (1) a technique found within opera or as an independent genre in which a text is spoken to musical accompaniment, or in the pauses between musical phrases; (2) an exaggerated or sensational drama

melodramma an Italian word for 'opera'

mezza voce 'half-voice'; a direction to sing in a soft, withdrawn tone

mezzo-soprano the female voice between soprano and contralto

Mighty Handful the common English translation of the Russian expression *moguchaya kuchka*: the Russian Five (Mily Balakirev, Aleksandr Borodin, César Cui, Modest Musorgsky, Nikolay Rimsky-Korsakov) who in the 1860s promoted the idea of a national Russian music

minimalism a term borrowed from visual art in the 1960s to describe a kind of music in which a single figure or phrase is made to constitute a long stretch of music through extremely slow tempo or multiple repetition with little or no change

modal modal music confines itself to the notes of a single unchanging scale (or collection), as opposed, for example, to tonal music, which tends to contradict an initial scale by the introduction of foreign (chromatic) notes, often leading to change of key; the effect of modal music is typically rather static. The term is also used, more loosely, to refer to music using the old scales (modes) of church music, or other exotic or ethnic scales, or even unusual invented scales, even where the scales are not rigidly adhered to

modernism the idea that modern art must of necessity be difficult, abrasive, complicated and hard to understand, perhaps because the modern world is those things

modulation the procedure of changing key in tonal (q.v.) music

monody music consisting of only a single melodic line (e.g. plainsong); the vocal music of the early baroque is 'monody' though accompanied, as distinct from the polyphony (q.v.) of contemporary church music

motif a short, characteristic theme that recurs often as a unifying element; see also *leitmotif*

musical apparently short for 'musical comedy' (q.v.), and since the 1920s the normal term for the popular musical play with songs, dances and chorus ensembles

musical comedy see *musical*; now usually applied to the early history of the genre (from about the 1890s), when it diverged from conventional operetta towards the idea of the popular play with music, often with a contemporary bourgeois setting

music drama a highly integrated form of opera in which music, words, stage action and setting work together on an equal footing; the term is often erroneously attributed to Wagner, who in fact rejected it

music-theatre originally a coinage of the 1960s to describe a kind of highly informal opera, often involving speech and dance as well as singing, invariably for a small number of performers, designed to be played in a concert hall, church, or almost anywhere except a theatre; the term soon broadened to include concert works incorporating elements of gesture, and (in the other direction) various kinds of small-scale but otherwise fairly conventional opera. There remains an unstated assumption that music-theatre is somehow more serious and socially/psychologically aware than opera, though the artistic achievement of the genre remains slight

neotonality a fashionable tendency in music since the late 1970s, in which certain aspects of tonality (q.v.)

are once again accepted by so-called avant-garde (q.v.) composers as part of their musical language

number opera an opera clearly divided into distinct pieces or 'numbers' (so-called because they are in fact numbered in the score)

obbligato an important instrumental solo (in opera often forming a duet with the solo voice), so-called because in baroque music such parts were fully written out and had to be played as written, unlike the continuo (q.v.) part, which involved improvisation

Ondes Martenot an electronic instrument named after its inventor, Maurice Martenot, and popular especially with French composers from Varèse to Messiaen; a melody-only keyboard instrument, it makes a sound like an amorous cat

opéra-ballet a hybrid genre most common in the French musical theatre of the 18th century, usually with a number of separate actions illustrating the central idea through singing and dance

opera buffa the genre of Italian comic opera of the 18th and 19th centuries, usually with musical numbers divided by sung recitative

opéra comique opera with dialogue, in the French 18th- and 19th-century tradition; such opera was usually comic in the 18th century, but later the term became purely generic – e.g. Bizet's *Carmen* is an opéra comique

opera semiseria a hybrid genre in which a serious or melodramatic subject is moderated by comic or picturesque elements; it often uses spoken dialogue instead of recitative

opera seria a term now applied to the whole range of Italian-language serious or tragic opera of the 18th and early 19th centuries, especially as defined by the somewhat stereotyped libretti of Pietro Metastasio (1698–1782)

operetta (also '*opérette*') the light romantic opera of the 19th century, usually with spoken dialogue between the musical numbers; in the 20th century it faded almost imperceptibly into musical comedy (q.v.)

ostinato 'obstinate': a figure or pattern repeated over and over

ottocento Italian for 'eight hundred'; used to denote the 19th century

overture (*ouverture*) 'opening': an instrumental piece, often in several sections, introducing an operatic work, played before the curtain rises

pantomima Greek for 'imitating'; a mime section (e.g. in Act I of Mozart's *Idomeneo* accompanying the vision of Neptune calming the sea)

parlando a vocal style that imitates speech

parlando rubato a rhythmically flexible speechlike vocal or instrumental style

parte buffa Italian for 'comic role'

parte di mezzo carattere Italian for the central characters, not defined by either their serious or their comic nature

parte seria Italian for 'serious role'

passacaglia a set of variations over a repeated (actual or implied) bass line; closely related to the *chaconne* (q.v.)

pasticcio a work consisting mainly or entirely of borrowings from existing works by the same or other composers

pastorella a vocal piece about the Christmas story

pedal a pedal (or harmony) note is a held or recurrent (usually bass) note over or around which other parts move freely; the term derives from the organ pedal

pentatonic containing five notes: applied above all to certain scales of folk music. The best-known pentatonic scale is provided by the black notes of the piano

pizzicato plucked (on a string instrument)

polyphony 'many-voiced' music: music made up of several independent vocal (or instrumental) lines

polytonal music is said to be polytonal when two or more key-notes are functioning simultaneously. But from a theoretical point of view the concept is vague, and in practice polytonal harmony is tonal (q.v.) harmony with a lot of added discord, or harmony in which different types of tonal chord are played simultaneously

postlude by extension from prelude, a concluding section usually for instruments alone

post-modernism the 1980s reaction against modernism (q.v.) involving a return to such things as tonality (q.v.), antique styles (often with quotation), and popular aesthetic values

premiere in English usage, the very first performance of a work

prima donna the principal female singer in an operatic cast; in Italian usage it is only one of several such defining terms, including seconda donna, primo uomo (q.v.) and comprimario (q.v.)

primo uomo the principal male singer in an operatic cast

quarter tone the interval between two notes that are half a semitone apart; the semitone (half-step) is the smallest interval on a piano, but smaller ones are obtainable in singing and on other instruments

querelle des bouffons see *guerre des bouffons*

raga a mode or pitch repertoire in Indian music; however, a given raga specifies not just available pitches but also other features, including overall duration and mood

rataplan onomatopoeia for a drum beat; a song which uses this device

recapitulation a formal repeat of an identifiable musical section

recitative the free setting of speech in which the music follows the rhythms and inflexions of the spoken language; in *recitativo secco* the voice is accompanied only by continuo (q.v.) playing a skeleton of chords outlining the harmony; in *recitativo accompagnato* it is accompanied more fully by the orchestra

recitativo accompagnato see *recitative*

recitativo secco see *recitative*

recitativo semplice the original term for what was later dubbed *recitativo secco* (see *recitative*)

regal a small, portable reed organ (16th and 17th centuries)

relative major/minor the pair of keys – one major, the other minor – with the same number of sharps or flats in the key signature: for instance, F major/D minor (one flat); relative keys are always the same interval (a minor third) apart

rescue opera a genre of opera in the French Revolutionary period in which the hero or heroine is rescued in the nick of time from some tyrant or natural disaster through the agency of human self-sacrifice or heroism. Beethoven's *Fidelio* is the best-known example

ripieno the main body of the orchestra (as opposed to the concertino (q.v.)) in baroque music

ritornello the Italian term (French: ritournelle) for an instrumental interlude in an operatic aria (or the orchestral episodes in a concerto grosso); 'ritornello' implies return, and ritornelli were originally in fact refrains, but the term soon became more general, and a ritornello may well consist of new or varied material

ritournelle see *ritornello*

rock music the term used to embrace most types of popular music since the early 1970s

romanesca [*antica*] a 16th-century Italian chord scheme for vocal improvisation (an ancient equivalent of a jazz progression); the bass was later treated as a ground bass

romanza a term used rather generally, sometimes as the title of a simple operatic aria; the English term 'romance', with its sentimental overtones, is roughly parallel

rondeau a form based on a simple alternation of a repeating refrain and changing verses (couplets); also the French version of the more general rondo form (q.v.)

rondo any form based on the alternation of a repeating main section with contrasting episodes; it includes the simple French rondeau (q.v.), but also the more elaborate form often found in symphonic finales

rubato 'robbed' time: a flexibility in musical rhythm

in which a little time is taken which is theoretically given back later

rusalka   a Russian word for a mermaid or water sprite

sarabande   a slow, stately baroque dance in triple time, characterized by an accent on the second beat

scale   a repertoire of notes arranged in ascending or descending order; the steps of a musical scale are normally close together, but in some ethnic or non-European scales slightly larger steps are found. The scale is strictly speaking an abstraction which is thought of as defining the basic 'field' of operation of a piece of music, but it materializes in vocal and instrumental exercises, and also frequently as a melodic feature

scena   Italian for 'scene', but with various other connotations as well: (1) the stage itself; (2) the stage setting; (3) an informal episode as opposed to a formal set piece; also such an episode designed as a separate concert piece

Schauspiel   German for a stage play

scherzando   playful

scherzo   joke; hence a short, light piece of music

Scotch snap   a rhythmic figure with a strongly accented short note followed by a long note, common in Scottish and other folk music

secco   'dry': *recitativo secco* (q.v.) has a very spare chordal accompaniment

Second Viennese School   the group of composers led by Arnold Schoenberg, and including above all his two greatest pupils, Alban Berg and Anton Webern (the First Viennese School being understood as the classical group of composers Haydn, Mozart and Beethoven)

semi-opera   a late-17th- or early-18th-century English work combining spoken dialogue and through-composed operatic scenes, usually having elaborate sets

semiseria   see *opera semiseria*

serenata   Italian for 'serenade', but usually denoting a ceremonial vocal work of a courtly kind, with quasi-dramatic elements

serial   based on a series, or ordered note-row; serial music originally always meant the music of Schoenberg and his school, in which all 12 notes are included in the serial ordering that governs the music (dodecaphony); but any music that uses a fixed order, of whatever number of notes, can properly be described as serial

simile aria   an aria in which the text draws a parallel between the singer's predicament or frame of mind and natural phenomena

sinfonia   Italian for 'symphony'; a name used as a description of the instrumental preludes and interludes of early operas (since these were the only sections where all the instruments 'sounded together'), though it had also a wider currency for instrumental works and became a strict generic term only with the appearance of the classical symphony

singspiel   the German 'ballad' opera form, with songs and spoken dialogue, which evolved into operas such as Mozart's *Die Zauberflöte* and Weber's *Der Freischütz* and survives in the musical plays of Brecht and Weill

skazka   Russian for 'tale'

skočná   a quick Czech dance in duple time of a light and comic nature

solfège   the standard French term for music theory (as studied in schools and conservatories), derived from the note names in wordless vocal exercises (cf. 'tonic sol-fa' do, re, mi, etc.)

sommeil   French for 'sleep': a sleeping (or dreaming) scene found in 17th- and 18th-century French stage music, often involving the classical gods of sleep

sonata   now usually a substantial instrumental work in several movements (or one elaborate one), but earlier applied to any instrumental piece; something sounded (*sonata*) as opposed to sung (*cantata*)

sonata form   the standard name for the particular form in which the first (and sometimes later) movements of the classical sonata and symphony were usually cast; in its textbook format a first theme is followed by a second theme in the key of the dominant (q.v.), a development (q.v.) of this material, and a recapitulation (q.v.) with the second theme now in the home, or tonic, key. In practice this form was much varied

soprano   the highest female voice

soprano falcon   see *falcon*

sostenuto   sustained

soubrette   the stock servant-girl figure of 18th-century opera; she is usually clever, quick and resourceful; the term is sometimes misleadingly extended to describe the kind of voice called for

sousedská   a Bohemian dance in triple time

spieloper   a form of singspiel (q.v.) with songs and dialogue, but with more emphasis on the 'operatic', less on the idea of popular theatre

spinto   Italian for 'pushed' (properly, *lirico spinto*): a lyrical voice with reserves of muscle, as usually called for by the main tenor and soprano roles of late-Romantic Italian opera

sprechgesang   a hybrid vocal delivery, between speech and song, used most famously by Schoenberg and Berg, but developed earlier by Humperdinck in the original version of *Königskinder* (1897). There is no accepted sprechgesang technique, and Schoenberg's account of his requirements is obscure

stile concitato   'excited style': the term used by Monteverdi to describe the musical depiction of anger and aggression

stretta   the final section of an Italian opera aria,

ensemble or act where the music becomes faster (literally, 'tightened')

strophe the basic verse of a strophic poem; a strophic song or aria is one with the same music repeated for each of a series of verses

style galant French for 'gallant style': the light and elegant 18th-century rococo style, as opposed to the serious and elaborate baroque style

subdominant the fourth degree of the major and minor scales (for instance, in the key of C, the note F)

tableau French for 'scene', in the sense of stage setting and subdivision of an act

Tafelmusik German for 'table music': music (usually instrumental) played during a meal

taille an early French word for 'tenor', both vocal and instrumental

tambourin (1) a two-headed Provençal drum, a tabor; (2) a lively Provençal folk dance in duple time accompanied by pipe and tabor; (3) an 18th-century French character piece based on the idiom of the old dance

tam-tam a large orchestral gong

tarantella a quick southern-Italian dance in six-eight time

tenor the standard high male voice (but see *haute-contre* and *counter-tenor*)

tenor altino a high tenor with natural (non-falsetto) production into the soprano register

tenor trial a term used at the Paris Opéra-Comique for a tenor voice with a thin, reedy quality, usually cast in comic roles; named after the 18th-century singer Antoine Trial

tessitura vocal range, but more specifically that range within which a singer's part lies

tetrachord a four-note segment of a scale (for instance the notes C–D–E–F in the scale of C major)

third the interval between a note and the next but one in the standard major or minor scale; there are various sizes of thirds (diminished, minor, major, augmented), depending on the key and context

timbre tone colour

tinta (vocal) colour

tonal tonal music partakes of the system of keys that dominated music and music theory of the 17th to early 20th centuries, and still dominates much popular music; key = tonality (the key-note is known as the tonic)

tonality the relationship between the notes of a musical scale

tragédie lyrique the epic form of serious French opera from Lully to Gluck

transpose to play a passage of music in a key other than that in which it is written, or in which it was previously heard

travesti French for 'disguised', especially as someone of the opposite sex; a person or role so disguised

treble the top (soprano) voice in choral music, and the name of the register it inhabits; the standard term for a child's singing voice

tremolo a rapid oscillation between two notes, or (on instruments capable of this) the rapid repetition of one note

triad the common chord (q.v.); more freely, it can mean any chord of three notes

trial see *tenor trial*

trouser role breeches role (q.v.)

turba Latin for 'crowd'; hence the name of the crowd choruses in Bach's and other baroque Passion settings

tutti Italian for 'all'; hence the sections of a work in which everyone sings and/or plays

tyrolienne a fast triple-time song or dance, related to the traditional ländler (q.v.); Alpine folk music was especially popular throughout Europe and in the US in the early 19th century

unendliche Melodie 'endless melody': metaphorical description of the extended and more or less informal flow of the music of Wagner and his successors

vaudeville a Parisian street song, of the kind that, in the 18th century, formed the basis of the comic musical plays ('comédies en vaudevilles') which borrowed the name; in the first half of the 20th century, vaudeville meant 'variety' or music-hall; the kind of operatic finale in which a single tune is passed from character to character (as in Mozart's *Die Ent-führung aus dem Serail* and Rossini's *Il barbiere di Siviglia*) is also sometimes known as a vaudeville

verismo 'realism', but specifically as applied to the brutal and earthy dramas of late-19th- and early-20th-century Italian opera

veristi the group of Italian composers and writers who wrote verismo (q.v.) works

vibrato the rapid fluctuation of pitch (and sometimes loudness) that gives the voice and certain instruments their main expressive quality; it is also a vehicle for control as well as for the disguising of defects, but can itself get out of control, when it is called 'wobble'

Vorspiel German for 'prelude'

zarzuela a traditional Spanish operetta form combining singing, dialogue and dance

zeitoper 'topical opera', specifically in 1920s Germany, where there was a fashion for operas of modern life

INTRODUCTION

BY RODNEY MILNES

Many an hour may be spent trying to say exactly what opera is, and though no definition ever emerges the time is seldom wasted. The composer Elisabeth Lutyens said it was 'anything that benefits from being staged', an engaging notion but perhaps too all-embracing. Some would paraphrase Beaumarchais and agree that it is something sung because it is not worth saying. In the 1950s the British critic Arthur Jacobs provocatively defined it as 'music by dead composers sung in foreign languages to rich people', which in the palmier days of the 1970s and 1980s people smiled at as a fair description of opera in the first half of the century, though the smile is growing a little thin during a final decade that seems to be looking backwards rather than forwards.

Opera is not simply a sung play, since many of the most popular works – *Fidelio*, *The Tales of Hoffmann*, *Carmen* – contain long stretches of spoken dialogue, and there is more speech in Mozart's *The Magic Flute* than there is in Sondheim's *Sweeney Todd*. The mix is more complicated than that. Orchestral music, solo and choral singing, declamation, dance, design and stage spectacle all have been part of opera since it was officially 'invented' in around 1600. Perhaps 'a drama in which sung music takes the leading role' is the least cumbersome umbrella definition available.

To Dr Johnson, in a famous throwaway remark in his *Lives of the Poets*, it was 'an exotick and irrational entertainment'. He was right in more than one sense, but perhaps not in the way that he meant. In the first part of the 18th century opera was, in Britain, 'exotic' in the literal meaning of the word – it was a form imported from abroad, Italy, and most successfully composed by a German, Handel. But since opera is largely carried by music, the good doctor was being

wiser than he knew. In 1818 Schopenhauer described music as 'a language intelligible with absolute directness, yet not capable of translation into that of our faculty of reason', continuing with the unanswerable statement that 'the composer expresses the profoundest wisdom in a language that his reasoning faculty does not understand'.

It is the very irrationality of opera, combined with the scale of the art – 200 people and more may be involved in preparing and presenting a single performance – that accounts for its overwhelming and sometimes sinister power. How many people rapturously humming along with the Three Tenors in 'Nessun dorma', the World Cup theme-tune of 1990, would stop humming if they knew the action of Puccini's *Turandot*? This opera is a monument to irrationality, an epic fable of splendour and cruelty depicting forces of unreason locked in unresolvable conflict, heedless of the consequences. The chorus can change from collective compassion to slavering sadism without so much as a line of text to motivate them, and the three *commedia dell'arte* ministers, established as the voice of reason, turn without warning into torturers. Opera – music – can be very dangerous.

Of course this irrational power can also be positive if it so chooses. Music is part of all our lives, heightening religious experience, central to the expression of patriotism, vital to outpourings of personal grief or elation. Our attitude to the singing of 'Land of Hope and Glory' at the Last Night of the Proms in London, even to the hand-on-heart fervour of 'The Star-Spangled Banner', may be equivocal, but who can forget the part that music played in the collapse of the Eastern Bloc in the late 1980s – the sight of the people of the Baltic states singing their national music in defiance of occupation? Authoritarian regimes fear music more than almost any other art form – precisely because of its irrationality, its stubborn refusal to submit to reason. The Nazis, while hijacking Wagner for their own ends, went to extraordinary lengths to track down and destroy the music of Kurt Weill – scores, orchestral parts, recordings – not only in Germany but, through diplomatic channels, around the world as well. The greatest single example of benign music, the antithesis to *Turandot* has to be Beethoven's *Fidelio*, a blazing affirmation of the concept of liberty and idealism. Yet the hidden irony remains that the text of this paean to freedom, customarily seen as the acceptable face of the French Revolution, was in fact based on a counter-revolutionary incident. Music, positive or negative, creates and abides by its own rules, as incapable of lying as of telling the whole truth.

If 'opera' as a word – meaning 'work', a shortened form of '*opera in musica*' – came into use around the end of the 16th century, it is misleading to say that this is when opera as we know it was invented. The members of the Florentine Camerata, significantly a literary rather than a musical society, thought that they were reviving in true Renaissance style the glories of the classical Greek theatre. They were probably not far from the truth. We do not know exactly how Greek dramas were performed, but we may be fairly certain that they were not simply spoken. Fragments of notation have survived, and if Aeschylus spent months preparing the chorus for the *Oresteia* he must have been doing more than drumming the words into them. Pitch and rhythm, if not precisely singing, must have played a part, and you have only to listen to recordings of old-style political orators to realize how hazy is the line separating pitched speech from song. Many operatic and extra-operatic attempts have been made to reproduce the practice of Greek drama, of which one of the most interesting was the production of the *Oresteia* directed by Peter Hall with music by Harrison Birtwistle at the National Theatre in London in 1981. By the end of the evening the music was controlling the pacing and shape of the drama, and in his perceptive notice the critic James Fenton concluded with the words, 'what we have here is a closet opera'.

Music was indeed in something of a closet in pre-1600 Western theatre. The Christian Church, faced with the supposed immorality of theatre and its practitioners, frowned upon both before realizing that the power of music could be harnessed to its own use: medieval liturgical drama is one of opera's most significant forerunners. Yet music was always there, in mystery plays, in madrigals strung together to create a narrative dramatic shape, in Shakespeare; in such a context 1600 looks all the more arbitrary a date for the 'invention' of opera. And in the context of music-in-drama since that time – songs in Restoration and 18th-century comedy, pit accompaniment to Victorian melodrama, music cues from those most wordy of playwrights Shaw and Ibsen, or Brecht, in whose plays music is a crucial element – it could be said that a play without music is a far more exotic and irrational creature than any opera. In other words, over the long history of Western drama, opera can be seen simply as mainstream theatre.

In 17th-century Italy opera in its purest form was indeed a sung play. The music embellished the words, made them more expressive. Librettists were the senior partners, and wrote the prefaces to published word-books. But music soon took over. In 1651 we read of a librettist saying he has inserted arias – or songs – in his drama to please the public, and in 1669 another librettist admits he has done the same thing to please singers. Vocal artistry was putting in its bid for dominance. Audiences in Rome and Naples developed a taste for stage spectacle, a taste that spread as opera became more and more associated with court entertainments – the grander the spectacle, the grander the court. Dance was more prominent in French opera (and remained so for over 200 years), and speech in English opera, so much so that it was dubbed 'semi-opera'. The mix was already developing.

And so was the form. The libretti set by Italian composers in the 17th century were thoroughly Shakespearian in their mixture of comedy and tragedy. As the century proceeded, the comedy – full of cross-dressing and innuendo – became increasingly coarse, leading to one of the first of the many reform movements that have punctuated the history of opera. The Arcadian Society of Rome, founded in 1690, aimed 'to reawaken good taste in literature', and the librettist Apostolo Zeno, one of its members, and his successor Pietro Metastasio helped crystallize the strict form of opera seria, a somewhat relentlessly 'improving' affair of high moral content without a whiff of humour. The strictness of the form involved a string of solo arias for (usually) six characters separated by recitative. More than any other composer, Handel managed consistently to breathe dramatic life and human warmth into these seemingly arid texts. Comedy developed separately as opera buffa until towards the end of the century such masters as Mozart and Rossini reunited the tragic and the comic in a genuinely Shakespearian blend.

Virtuoso singers dominated opera seria: sopranos like Cuzzoni, notoriously ill-favoured but, according to one enthusiastic galleryite, with 'a nest of nightingales in her belly', and the virtuoso castrati who were the Pavarottis and Domingos of their day. With such dominance (and huge fees) came abuse of the music – Handel threatened to throw Cuzzoni out of a window if she refused to sing what he had written for her – and treatment of drama as a mere excuse for extravagant vocal display. Hence the second great reform movement: Gluck's pursuit of 'bella simplicità'. In his preface to *Alceste* (1769) he wrote that his aim was to get rid of 'those abuses which, introduced either by the vanity of singers or the too great complaisance of composers, have for so long disfigured Italian opera'. Gluck's music is indeed of 'beautiful simplicity', and in its absence of frills extremely difficult to sing. His operas tend to be about what is noblest in the human race – forbearance, self-denial, loyalty – and are thus notoriously risky box-office; audiences on the whole seem to prefer to go to the theatre for rape, incest, torture and murder – the sort of thing they don't get enough of at home.

Strictness of form took longer to temper, not least because it was a help at a time when composers were freelance rather than salaried by a court or nobleman, and so needed to write at speed in order to earn a living from tight-fisted and demanding impresarios. If Rossini knew that arias and duets came in three parts (fast, slow, faster), or the young Verdi accepted that in melodramma each character required a two-part aria –

cavatina (slow) and cabaletta (fast) – and once they had been given them plus, perhaps, the odd duet, it was time for a finale – concertato (slow) and stretta (fast) – then half the work was done. On such principles was founded the to us incredible speed with which these composers wrote their operas. It is fascinating to study the way that Verdi, in a composing life of over 50 years, used, adapted, loosened but never quite abandoned traditional Italian operatic form.

In Germany the profusion of princely states and rich self-governing cities with an interest in patronage meant that composers in the early part of the 19th century were under less pressure: Weber, one of opera's great innovators, was not so prolific as his Italian contemporaries, though the length of Wagner's operas and the care with which he composed them caused him severe cash-flow problems until he found a royal patron in Ludwig II of Bavaria. Weber built on a tradition of German opera created in the 18th century and in part formed by Mozart, folk-based but also founded on a more complex contribution from the orchestra – heritage of the classical symphonic tradition – than the Italians attempted. Wagner saw himself as a great innovator, but in fact developed the techniques of others – Gluck's and Bellini's endless melody, Weber's instrumental ingenuity and system of reminiscence motives, Beethoven's symphonic method and Liszt's harmonic freedom. Admittedly Wagner developed such things far beyond anything hitherto attempted, but he did not invent them.

There was an easy co-existence between the serious and the comic at the end of the 18th century and in the explosion of opera in the aftermath of the French Revolution. To some the juxtaposition of comic and heroic music in *Fidelio* is unsettling, and only recently has the brilliance of Rossini's *The Thieving Magpie*, at once rustic, near-farcical and bleakly tragic, been recognized. It belongs in principle if not in name to the genre of opera semiseria, in which villains were often portrayed as comic characters – an interesting way of helping people to deal with evil. But following the Congress of Vienna in 1815, which virtually re-established the *ancien régime*, and even more so after the failed uprisings of 1848, opera seemed to revert to being either comic or serious, with rare exceptions such as Donizetti's *L'elisir d'amore* and *Don Pasquale*. Verdi either wrote tragic operas (24) or comedies (2), with only the massively Shakespearian *La forza del destino* attempting to combine the two. Comedy is, after all, the most subversive of art forms, because if audiences are laughing they don't realize that they are being got at. Offenbach, that anarchic and lethal satirist, both entertained Louis Napoleon's Second Empire and, in the sense that he celebrated its frivolous, empty amorality, helped to destroy it.

The 19th century also saw the emergence of national schools. In Russia opera had largely been an exotic import, but in the hands of composers like Rimsky-Korsakov, Musorgsky and other members of the well-named 'Mighty Handful' it became so fervently nationalist that even Tchaikovsky was regarded with suspicion for supposedly being influenced by the West. In what is now the Czech Republic, the school was inextricably bound up with the growing nationalist movement – the building of the National Theatre in Prague was seen virtually as a declaration of independence from the Habsburg Empire. Neither school paid any heed to accepted form, which both limited the extent to which their operas were performed elsewhere and, especially in the case of Russian exoticism, added spice to existing schools. It would be rash to speak of a specifically French school, since the best opera in Paris was composed by foreigners, albeit usually to libretti in French, in the first half of the century – Cherubini, Rossini, Meyerbeer, Donizetti – but the emergence of Gounod, Bizet and Massenet re-established the supremacy the French language had enjoyed in the time of Rameau as a vehicle for dramatic music, and exerted a great influence on the younger generation of Italian composers – such *veristi* as Mascagni and Leoncavallo – who, overshadowed by the colossus of Verdi, looked abroad for inspiration.

This brief history of opera is of course oversimplified, the merest outline, but it brings us to the start of our own century in a healthy state – wide and varied output, audiences eager for it. But one of the unwritten laws of opera is that it is always in a state of crisis: there are no singers any more, or conductors,

or composers – take your pick. The current crisis is apparently that no successful operas – operas that enter the repertory – have been written since 1924, the date that Puccini was prevented by death from completing *Turandot*. Opera, so it is said, is therefore dead, a museum art form. People who say this tend also to try to erect an artificial barrier between literal, representational productions (good) and more adventurous, expressionist stagings (bad), which is nonsense: productions either work or don't work, regardless of their style, and that is all there is to it.

The larger 'opera is dead' proposition is also nonsense. Consider the case century by century. The 17th century produced one great opera composer: Monteverdi. The 18th produced Mozart, Handel, Gluck, Rameau. The productive 19th did well with Rossini, Verdi, Wagner, Bizet – all central to the repertory – not to mention Musorgsky, Tchaikovsky, Donizetti and Berlioz. The twentieth century, with Janáček, Britten, Strauss, Shostakovich and Puccini, to mention those whose works no serious opera company can afford to ignore, is not exactly bleak. Add Stravinsky, Weill, Poulenc, Tippett, Henze, Gershwin, and, if our century is an operatic corpse, then it is an extraordinarily lively one.

Yet it would be absurd to deny an element of crisis in the field of composition. Again, to oversimplify wildly, Wagner pushed the accepted language of Western music – tonality – as far as it could go. What next? Schoenberg, maybe one of the less approachable of great composers but great none the less, devised his own system of composition, the 12-note series. Some of his contemporaries – Schreker, Zemlinsky, Krenek – nudged Wagnerian frontiers forward a step into expressionism. Others – Busoni, Stravinsky – took one step back and two forward into neoclassicism. All travelled in the direction of making music more 'difficult' to listen to. An artificial barrier was inevitably erected between serious music and popular music, between high art and low art, reflecting the equally artificial separation that had appeared between comedy and tragedy in the 18th and 19th centuries.

High art was sustained in Germany, now accepted as the heartland of operatic creativity, by a generously subsidized system of repertory theatres and the subscription audiences they attracted. But in the late 1920s a composer as successful and established as Weill made a conscious decision temporarily to abandon this and write for (but not down to) the equivalent of the West End and Broadway (*The Threepenny Opera, Happy End*); and in 1931 he even adapted his *Mahagonny* opera for a run on Berlin's Kurfürstendamm (conducted by Zemlinsky) and in Vienna. Before the significance of this development could be evaluated, the Nazis took power in Germany in 1933 and creative operatic activity to all intents and purposes ceased. (The reverberations from this arbitrary interruption of natural artistic development are only now starting to subside.) Weill emigrated to the USA and composed for Broadway, throwing down the gauntlet in a 1940 newspaper interview: 'Schoenberg has said he is writing for a time 50 years after his death. But the great classical composers . . . wanted those who heard their music to understand it, and they did. For myself, I write for today. I don't give a damn about writing for posterity.'

That is just one example, one symptom, of the crisis. Germany was most certainly the centre of music criticism, and critical orthodoxy has supported the concept of progress, even at the risk of alienating 'ordinary people' (whoever they may be) from the opera house. That critical orthodoxy is only now relaxing its grip. A composer like Poulenc was written off because he fitted in to no recognizable school and wrote tonal music in the 1950s, and even Britten was regarded with intense suspicion in the years immediately after his death, because his music was popular with audiences. To the critical orthodoxy, Stockhausen was all: he writes extremely beautiful music, but one doesn't exactly come out of the theatre whistling his tunes in the way that one does Rossini's, Wagner's or – I am not joking – Schoenberg's. Puccini was still not being taken seriously 60 years after his death: only now are people starting to examine the scores of the composer whom the musicologist Julian Budden has described as 'Wagner's best Italian pupil' (the motivic structure of *Tosca* is near-unfathomably complex).

The relaxation of this orthodoxy allows us to revel without guilt in the plurality of the 20th-century operatic experience: Schoenberg and Stockhausen, but also Britten (who fre-

quently used serial techniques but didn't feel the need to advertise the fact). The 1980s and 1990s saw composers as diverse as Birtwistle and Sondheim at full stretch. Why should appreciation of one preclude enjoyment of the other? Eyebrows were raised when the Royal National Theatre in London staged *Carousel*, a little masterpiece of 20th-century musical theatre, but not when the Lincoln Center followed suit. (Puccini and Weill, both of whom knew good material when they saw it, tried unsuccessfully to get the rights to the play on which it is based before Richard Rodgers succeeded.) Even before Weill went to Broadway and paved the way for Bernstein and Sondheim, Jerome Kern had demonstrated in *Show Boat* that it was possible to write good musical comedy about things that matter.

This plurality is matched by a perceptible post-modernist school of composition. Philip Glass and John Adams have enjoyed phenomenal public and (in the USA) critical success. Corigliano's *The Ghosts of Versailles* has been revived at the Met, and restaged in Chicago. In the UK the absorbing complexity of Birtwistle is complemented by the astringent economy and wit of Judith Weir. In Europe Berio and Henze also bridge the 'high art'/'popular art' gap, and Sallinen has fashioned an unmistakably Nordic musical language that speaks to audiences beyond his native Finland. Opera is most certainly alive and well.

Why does opera exert such power over audiences? Music speaks its language 'intelligible with absolute directness' all the more powerfully because it may not – almost certainly does not – say the same thing to any two listeners. An audience of anything between a few hundred in an 18th-century court theatre and 20,000 in the Verona Arena is undergoing both a communal experience and an utterly personal one: the composer is speaking directly and intimately to each individual, yet the sum of individuals responds collectively. It is no coincidence that the origins of opera, and theatre itself, lie in religious festivals in classical Greece: the power of a theatrical performance is not unlike that of religious observance.

The way that the combination of words and notes works has obviously developed in the 400-odd years since opera was 'invented'. At first music performed the primary function of intensifying the meaning and feeling of the text through its own basic signals: for example, we are conditioned to finding fast music in a major key cheerful, slow music in the minor sad. If that sounds simple, listen to how a master like Monteverdi makes it extremely complex, or how Handel takes a human emotion and through music quadruples its power, sometimes – especially when depicting despair – to near-breaking point on the part of both singer and listener. The process of intensification pure and simple, though, like Wilde's truth, it is neither, lasted into the nineteenth century and the bel-canto era: in the hands of a great singer like Callas or Caballé the melodic lines of Bellini and Donizetti do not just add to but transcend the sometimes homespun words of the libretto.

But meanwhile another element had been brought into play. Gluck is popularly credited with being the first composer to make music and words contradict each other. In *Iphigénie en Tauride* (1779) Orestes, pursued by the Furies, seems to experience a brief moment of peace, but under the smooth, sustained, legato vocal line of 'Le calme rentre dans mon coeur' – 'Calm returns to my heart' – the violas play a syncopated, agitated rhythm. In one of the great *ben trovato* stories of operatic history, Gluck was asked by a viola player why this was, and replied, 'Because he is lying – he has killed his mother.' Thus was a whole new world of musico-dramatic communication opened up, and the web of vocal line, word and orchestral accompaniment grew ever more complex through the 19th and early 20th centuries.

Sometimes it is simply a matter of unexpected juxtaposition: the sweet tunefulness of Weill's songs for *The Threepenny Opera* and the cynical obscenity of Brecht's words add up to an unsettling whole: for one thing, you can't help singing the tunes, and the words are hence implanted indelibly in your mind – very subversive. More constructively, once a musical idea – a rhythm, a melodic fragment, even a solo instrument – has been associated with an extra-musical idea or character, the possibilities are endless. The entry of the giants in Wagner's *Das Rheingold* is accompanied by a simple, instantly memorable musical phrase; for the remaining 15 or so hours of the *Ring* cycle that phrase can recur either in its original form or adapted harmonically, at different speeds or with different intervals, yet each time the stimulus fed to the listener's brain conveys 'Giants', whatever may be happening on stage. In comedy such techniques can bring many a wry smile. The stately field marshal's wife in Strauss's *Der Rosenkavalier* remarks that she has a headache, but a passing orchestral phrase already associated with her energetic night of love hints that the seat of pain may lie elsewhere.

In Weber's *Der Freischütz* the hero Max hesitates before entering the Wolf's Glen, well aware of the terrors that lie in store there: why does he suddenly change his mind and go down? A five-second reminiscence in the orchestra of the song with which his social inferiors mocked his failure to win a shooting match earlier in the day tells us – and it would take twice as long to explain his change of mind in words (one of the many functions of music in drama is to save time). Opera-goers may not notice this the first or even the second or tenth time they hear it, but it will have penetrated their subconscious, which is on the whole how opera works.

Half the fascination of opera, then, lies in the sheer complexity of its means of communication – and always remember that its main strand, music, is abstract, 'not capable of translation' into reason. That is why we go again and again to hear the same work: the same music may say something different each time. And, with so complex a means of communication at their disposal, composers are not going to waste their time on trivia: they deal with Big Subjects. Has ordinary human behaviour ever been subjected to more analytical, less flattering examination than by Monteverdi and Busenello in *L'incoronazione di Poppea*? I hope not. Or with more wisdom and compassion than by Mozart and da Ponte in *Così fan tutte*? I doubt it. Or has the malignancy of fate, the hopelessness of the human condition, been more powerfully conveyed than in the operas of Verdi? Surely not. At the other end of the scale is Wagner's sinisterly prophetic *Ring* cycle, which presents the whole of human philosophical and political experience and seems not yet to have finished – I reckon we have got about as far as the middle act of *Götterdämmerung*.

Opera is extremely expensive to perform. Being so labour-intensive, how could it be otherwise? The expense was once borne by courts and princes, for reasons of status or in some cases (notably that of Gustaf III of Sweden) genuine love of the art, and later by city states and the high bourgeoisie for a similar combination of reasons. Yet it has also always had genuine popular appeal: between 1637 and 1699 12 opera houses opened in Venice. In 1819 three different productions of *Der Freischütz* ran simultaneously in London. Verdi was astonishingly popular in San Francisco in the gold-rush years from 1850 onwards. Going to a provincial Sunday matinée in Italy today with the butcher, the baker, the candlestick-maker and their wives and children all set on having a really good time is still an education for the most blasé opera buff, one that banishes for all time the notion of opera as necessarily élitist.

Such popularity may never have been consistently matched outside the country that gave opera birth, but other European governments have recognized that the provision of art of all kinds is part of their duty to their citizens, aimed at the general improvement of society (if you listen regularly to *The Magic Flute* you may be less inclined to go out and mug old-age pensioners). This has been especially true of the Nordic countries, and of Germany and France. Even the not notoriously art-loving UK embraced the concept when the Arts Council was set up after the Second World War. Whatever the faults of the former Eastern Bloc countries, they poured money into the theatre as though it were as essential as schools and hospitals, and in the baby-and-bathwater aftermath of the Bloc's collapse subsidies have been drastically reduced. Some western European governments have followed suit, especially in the UK, where government policy aims at emulating the US system of private sponsorship for opera but without providing the tax incentives to make it work. Too many opera-house managements have been forced by falling government subsidies to raise seat prices to socially unrealistic levels simply to keep their doors open, and to play safe by concentrating on the most popular works. The endeavours

of the 20th-century composers mentioned above are scarcely being given a fair chance, and there is a very real danger that, despite all that has been achieved in the last 50 years by way of widening both the repertory and the audience base, opera will once more become 'music by dead composers sung in foreign languages to rich people'.

As I have said, opera is always in a state of crisis. In addition to the above, as we approach the end of the 20th century, there is looming a crisis of communication. Throughout history opera has been sung in the language of the audience. Exceptions have proved the rule; Italian was the official language in Handel's day (until he turned to English music drama and dramatic oratorio), and at the Viennese court, for which Mozart composed, opera was sung in Italian even though the emperor Joseph II also sponsored the creation of German operas. But Mozart's Italian libretti were automatically and immediately translated into German for performance away from court circles. Britten's early vocal scores were published with a German translation already in place, since Germany was the likeliest country outside Britain in which they would be performed. When in 1894 the Paris Opéra decided to honour Verdi by presenting the French premiere of *Otello* in Italian, the management received an angry letter of protest from the composer, and Verdi got his way – *Otello* was sung in a French translation by Boito and Camille du Locle.

In the last 40 years, or a tenth part of operatic history, there has been a movement worldwide towards performance in the original language, partly for the convenience of singers (and hence managements) at a time when the jet aeroplane has given them extra mobility, and partly from a residual snobbery maintaining that opera probably isn't any good unless it's impossible to understand (it's certainly less troublesome that way). Centuries-old common sense about the immediacy of communication between composers and audiences has counted for nothing, and very few companies still perform exclusively in the language of their audience. This is one of opera's less amiable dottinesses, and would never be countenanced in any other form of theatre.

More than dotty, indeed dangerous, is the

development since 1983 of projected titles, not only for operas sung in foreign languages, but for those sung in the language of the audience as well. In the preparation of title-texts, libretti, some of them of the highest literary quality, are filleted, censored, reduced to novelettish banality. Worse, they encourage audiences to stop listening to words altogether: in titled English-language performances of comedy audiences laugh at a projected line, not at the same line when it is sung. The very heart-beat of operatic communication, the immediate assimilation by the brain of simultaneous word and note, is under dire threat. What those who favour the practice will not accept is that they are being given second-best, that they are being treated as passive consumers at the level of those at whom television commercials are aimed. And passivity is what is required from society in an age when political debate is reduced to the sound-bite, and when it is assumed that human attention-span is no greater than 40 seconds. Are audiences for opera content to be treated with such condescension, if not contempt?

Therein lies one of the many paradoxes of opera. On the one hand it is potentially one of the most popular, all-embracing forms of human expression, based on a universal language that all can understand if not reason with. On the other it is in its very complexity enormously demanding, requiring an active response from each listener, something more than wallowing in a warm bath of beautiful sound. Among the many topics of operatic conversation is the debate as to whether words or notes, splendid decor or orchestral sound, expensive singers or production, are the most important element in opera – Strauss wrote a whole piece, *Capriccio*, around the subject. Of course the most important element is the audience: how it responds, what happens to it, whether it resolves to go forth and do likewise (not, one hopes, after a performance of *Salome*) or to rush out of the theatre and burn down the nearest post office, as reputedly was the case after a performance of Auber's *La muette de Portici* in Brussels in 1830, leading to Belgian independence later the same year. Opera can indeed threaten the established order: the very name 'Verdi' became a rallying cry of the Risorgimento, and one of Weill's tunes, 'J'attends un navire', was used as a signal by the French Resistance in the Second World War.

We are all that audience. The works of the greatest opera composers are described in the pages that follow. They are of bewildering variety, treating of every facet of human endeavour, aspiration and failure, determination and success. They are created by artists who wanted and still want to change the world, whether by lecturing the rulers of the Age of Enlightenment on how they were expected to behave, by fomenting revolution, by anticipating the discoveries of Freud by decades, or simply by entertaining their audiences with comedies that are often as subversive as they are funny.

There is a world of enchantment, danger and diversion in this book. Enter it, absorb it, and then ponder well what you are to do with its content. Its future is in your hands.

The Penguin Opera Guide

A

JOHN ADAMS
John Coolidge Adams; *b* 15 February 1947, Worcester, Massachusetts, US

Together with Philip Glass, Adams is a leading composer of the so-called minimalist opera of the late 20th century. But his development owes more to that other well-known American minimalist, Steve Reich; additionally, Adams has moved further away even than Reich from minimalism as previously understood.

While only ten years younger than Glass, Adams could be said to have become the foremost figure in a second generation of composers inspired by the early explorations of repetition, long-held sounds and clearly audible structural processes undertaken by La Monte Young and Terry Riley around 1960. They built their experimental work on a solid conventional training in Western classical music and Adams has allied himself more consistently with this heritage, though he has more recently become more interested in the wide range of other musics – non-Western, jazz, rock – from which the minimalist approach in part derived. Following Adams's move from the East Coast to the West in 1972, his music first became more experimental – notably during the earlier part of his period as a teacher at the San Francisco Conservatory (1972–82) – and then increasingly related to the styles and techniques of a range of 19th- and early 20th-century Romantic composers. His invention in the mid-1980s of an operatic style owing at least as much to earlier operatic and even oratorio traditions as to avant-garde genres of music-theatre and performance art thus appears quite natural. And it is by bringing a new vigour and purpose to composing music for drama that does not avoid a clear narrative basis that Adams has found his full maturity.

Adams's style from as far back as the late 1970s is, in fact, characterized by its individual development of a repetitive idiom in which direct emotional expression is, unusually, not avoided, and in which allusions to – or even direct quotations from – other musics have played an increasingly significant part; *Shaker Loops* for string septet (1978) represents the emergence of this style. An avoidance of extensive reliance on tuned percussion or keyboard instruments (mainstays of at least the earlier Reich and Glass) is significant, Even more important is an increasing concern with melody, harmonic motion and regular metre (which Adams shares with these composers but takes even further).

The development of this approach has taken him naturally to opera. Here he has been aided by the American poet Alice Goodman, who has provided him with texts closely reflecting Adams's own musical approach in their combination of everyday language with references to great literature of the past (particularly in *The Death of Klinghoffer*). But he has also been strongly influenced and assisted by the American director Peter Sellars – who has provided the initial ideas for the two operas Adams has so far composed, as well as directing them using his own particular blend of past and present – and, to a lesser extent, by the American choreographer Mark Morris.

Nixon in China
Opera in three acts (2h 30m)
Libretto by Alice Goodman
PREMIERES 22 October 1987, Brown Theater, Wortham Center, Houston; UK: 1 September 1988, Playhouse Theatre, Edinburgh
CAST Chou En-lai *b*, Richard Nixon *b*, Henry Kissinger (also Lao Szu) *b*, Nancy T'ang (First Secretary to Mao) *ms*, Second Secretary to Mao *ms*, Third Secretary to Mao *ms*, Mao Tse-tung *t*, Pat Nixon *s*, Chiang Ch'ing (Madame Mao Tse-tung) *s*, Wu Ching-hua *dancer*, Hung Chang-ching (Party Representative) *silent; satb* chorus of Chinese militia, guests at banquet, citizens of Peking, trio of citizens (also singing the roles of participants in *The Red Detachment of Women* and the voice of Ching-hua); dancers in *The Red Detachment of Women*

Peter Sellars's idea of basing an opera on the American president Richard Nixon's visit to the Chinese chairman Mao Tse-tung in February 1972 resulted in his close collaboration with the librettist Alice Goodman and the choreographer Mark Morris and Adams himself. The original Sellars production toured to New York, Washington, Amsterdam, Edinburgh and Los Angeles and was televised.

SYNOPSIS
Act I Nixon – with an entourage that includes his wife Pat and Dr Henry Kissinger – arrives at Peking airport

for his historic visit to China in February 1972. His first audience with Chairman Mao finds the Chinese leader philosophical and inscrutable, but a banquet the same evening brings the two sides together more successfully.

Act II   Pat Nixon goes sightseeing and the Nixons watch a performance of the ballet *The Red Detachment of Women*, presided over by Madame Mao, in the course of which fact and fiction become hopelessly confused; the singer playing Kissinger is required to take a leading role in the ballet's action.

Act III consists of one long scene in which the six main protagonists, on the Americans' last night in Peking, ruminate on the events that have taken place and on their significance for themselves as individuals more than as political figures.

Nixon in China demonstrates, in a more extended form than ever before in Adams's music, the move from stylistic allusion – to Romantic music in particular – to actual quotation. Also notable is the integration of musical and dramatic incident and the related use of music for characterization. As the action develops following the performance of *The Red Detachment* ballet in Act II, for instance, an arpeggio figure is quickly speeded up and soon develops into the perfect complement to the onset of a tropical storm.

The increasing emphasis on the protagonists as real people, in an opera that could easily have developed purely as a political pageant in poster colours, is most clearly demonstrated in the final act. And it is here that another expansion of Adams's style is to be found: the virtual abandonment of minimalist repetition and its replacement by a new, highly lyrical manner, predominantly slow but highly sensitive to the ebb and flow of action and, especially, text. Emphasis is placed firmly on a natural and free-flowing setting of Goodman's libretto, underpinned by a harmonic language of great variety and subtlety.

The Death of Klinghoffer

Opera in a prologue and two acts (2h 30m)
Libretto by Alice Goodman
PREMIERES   19 March 1991, Théâtre de la Monnaie, Brussels; US: 5 September 1991, Brooklyn Academy of Music, New York; UK: 23 April 1995, Free Trade Hall, Manchester (concert)
CAST   Alma Rumor *ms*, Jonathan Rumor *t*, Harry Rumor *b*, Captain *b*, Swiss Grandmother *s*, First Officer *b*, Molqi *t*, Mamoud *b*, Austrian Woman *s*, Leon Klinghoffer *b*, 'Rambo' *b*, British Dancing Girl *s*, Omar *ms*, Marilyn Klinghoffer *c*; dancers (both ensemble and solo, including the doubling of some of the solo singing roles); *satb* chorus

As with the same team's previous opera, *The Death of Klinghoffer* is based on a recent world event: in this case, the hijacking, in 1985, of the cruise liner *Achille Lauro* by Palestinian terrorists and their eventual murder of a paralysed American Jewish tourist. Goodman drew for her libretto on the Bible and the Koran, as well as on her own personal transmutations of

everyday language. The original production by Sellars was shared among opera houses in Lyons, Vienna, New York, Los Angeles and San Francisco.

SYNOPSIS
A lengthy prologue portrays a wealthy American family relaxing at home and talking about travel abroad; this is preceded by a Chorus of Exiled Palestinians and followed by a Chorus of Exiled Jews.

Act I   The cruise liner *Achille Lauro* has been hijacked just a few hours out of Alexandria. The purpose of the hijackers is at first unclear. The hostages are rounded up; the ship's captain is guarded by Mamoud, and both soon start to reflect on their situation.

Act II   The liner awaits permission to enter the Syrian port of Tartus. The passengers have now been moved on deck, but the wheelchair-bound Leon Klinghoffer is forced to remain apart. The Palestinians begin to quarrel. Klinghoffer is shot. The captain and the hijackers come to an arrangement which will allow the ship to return to Alexandria, where the Palestinians will be able to disembark. Klinghoffer's body is thrown overboard. After their arrival in port, the captain tells Mrs Klinghoffer of her husband's death.

As in the final act of *Nixon in China*, *Klinghoffer* takes as its main subject matter the private thoughts and emotions of its characters, The two main acts allow the action to unfold via a libretto consisting mainly of individual statements and meditations. The opera thus falls into a sequence of arias and choruses inspired, according to Sellars, by Bach's Passions. The arias offer reflections of the individual protagonists in the *Achille Lauro* drama, with the captain of the ship emerging as the character with whom one might most readily sympathize. In this opera, however, unlike *Nixon*, Sellars and his associates deliberately eschew attempts at characterization, in order to focus more strongly on the issues and make the audience question their own preconceptions.

Musically, the opera continues for the most part the approach first observed in the final act of *Nixon*. Occasional use is made of what the composer himself calls his 'trickster' style – the other aspect of Adams's recent development in his non-operatic works – as in the aria for a British dancing girl at Act II, which draws on popular styles in a more overtly minimalist way. But, for the most part, the music is more reflective and sometimes more dissonant, responding acutely to the nuances of Goodman's text but still providing virtuosic orchestration, aided in the premiere production by a specially devised sound-distribution system. The use of video to provide close-up views added a further dimension. Even more than *Nixon, The Death of Klinghoffer* suggests that Adams may ultimately remove from his style all traces of minimalism as previously practised.

K.P.

EUGEN D'ALBERT

Eugen [Eugène] Francis Charles d'Albert; *b* 10 April 1864, Glasgow; *d* 3 March 1932, Riga, Latvia

D'Albert's mother came from Newcastle and his father, a composer and ballet master, was of French nationality though born in Hamburg. He studied composition with Arthur Sullivan and Ebenezer Prout and, having taught himself German, developed an obsession with Germany and its music. He became devoted to Wagner, whose music he heard in London conducted by Hans Richter. Richter recognized d'Albert's talents and brought him to Vienna, where he introduced him to Brahms and, more significantly, to Liszt, who took him on to Weimar as a pupil. Within a few years d'Albert was established as one of the foremost concert pianists of his day, and he travelled throughout Europe and to America. In 1895 he was appointed hofkapellmeister in Weimar and hofpianist to the king of Saxony. Though performance was the mainstay of his life, composition became more important in later years. D'Albert published songs, concertos, a symphony and string quartets. He also edited piano classics and transcribed Bach organ works for piano. Between 1893 and his death in 1932 he composed twenty operas; only the seventh, *Tiefland*, has endured. The first three show the strong influence of Wagner. As a composer he never achieved the fame he had earned as a concert pianist. D'Albert, six times married, had a temperamental personality, and his music is either highly passionate or delightfully humorous.

None of d'Albert's later operas achieved the success of *Tiefland*. Several are based on the theme of confrontation, which underlies *Tiefland*, including *Revolutionshochzeit* (set during the French Revolution) which d'Albert considered to be his finest work.

Tiefland

The Lowlands
Musikdrama in a prologue and two acts (2h 15m)
Libretto by Rudolf Lothar, based on the Catalan play *Terra Baixa* by Àngel Guimerà (1896)
Composed 1902; rev. 1904–5
PREMIERES 15 November 1903, Neues Deutsches Theater, Prague (without prologue); rev. version: 16 January 1905, Stadttheater, Magdeburg; US: 23 November 1908, Metropolitan. New York; UK: 5 October 1910, Covent Garden, London
CAST Sebastiano *bar*, Tommaso *b*, Moruccio *bar*, Marta *s*, Pepa *s*, Antonia *s*, Rosalia *c*, Nuri *s*, Pedro *t*, Nando *t*, Priest *silent*; *satb* chorus of peasants

Tiefland's opening bears a striking resemblance to Leoncavallo's *Pagliacci*. D'Albert had already been impressed by Mascagni's operas, and the influence of these two composers had changed the flavour of his music from that of the Germanic north to the verismo style of the Italianate south.

SYNOPSIS

Prologue Pedro, a simple mountain shepherd, dreams of marriage. The local landowner, Sebastiano, arrives with his mistress, Marta. As he has decided to marry a rich girl, he orders Marta to marry Pedro, who agrees to leave the mountains for life in the village below.

Act I The village girls gossip about Marta's marriage. Sebastiano, meanwhile, tells the unhappy Marta that he expects her to continue as his mistress after her marriage. After the wedding Pedro lovingly gives Marta a silver coin, which he received from Sebastiano when he killed a wolf with his bare hands. Marta, though touched, insists they sleep in separate rooms. But when she sees a signal that Sebastiano is in her room, she stays with Pedro.

Act II The next day Tommaso, the wise old man of the village, advises Marta to tell her husband the truth. Pedro, teased by the village girls who know Sebastiano has made a fool of him, decides to return to the mountains. But Marta, now in love with him, begs him to take her with him and admits that she has been Sebastiano's mistress. When Sebastiano, whose marriage has been called off, returns for Marta he is challenged by Pedro, who strangles him.

The unique success of *Tiefland*, like that of *Carmen*, with which it shares both the sexual antagonism and the thrilling passion of fatal love, lay in its earthy drama. Though the music includes simple melodies which set the rustic and wedding scenes, it is generally thickly orchestrated and overladen with musico-dramatic clichés. Its best qualities are revealed in the two narratives, Marta's dream and Pedro's tale of his fight with the wolf, and at the shattering climax when the shepherd strangles his master. The opera shows how well the Anglo-German d'Albert had assimilated hot-blooded drama through *Pagliacci* and *Cavalleria rusticana*, and how he would in turn influence Puccini's conclusion to *Il tabarro*. In the 36 years between the Prague premiere of *Tiefland* in 1903 and the outbreak of the Second World War the opera was performed in 38 cities, even proving popular with the British occupation forces in Cologne in 1919.

Other operas: *Der Rubin*, 1893; *Ghismonda*, 1895; *Gernot*, 1897; *Die Abreise*, 1898; *Kain*, 1900; *Der Improvisator*, 1902; *Flauto solo*, 1905; *Tragaldabas*, 1907; *Izeÿl*, 1909; *Die verschenkte Frau*, 1912; *Liebesketten*, 1912; *Die toten Augen*, 1916; *Der Stier von Olivera*, 1918; *Revolutionshochzeit*, 1919; *Scirocco*, 1921; *Mareike von Nymwegen*, 1923; *Der Golem*, 1926; *Die schwarze Orchidee*, 1928; *Mister Wu* (inc.; completed by Leo Blech), 1932

C.F.

LOUIS ANDRIESSEN

b 6 June 1939, Utrecht, Netherlands

Andriessen established himself as one of the most distinctive voices in European new music during the 1980s, with a series of instrumental works that brought together elements of American minimalism, jazz, rock and neo-classical Stravinsky within a sound world that was abrasive, heavily amplified, and dominated by woodwind and brass. He has deliberately set himself apart from the bourgeois musical establishment, and his scores avoid conventional orchestral trappings, though his interest in music-theatre has led him to an inevitable compromise with the world of opera.

The son of the composer Hendrik Andriessen, Louis studied with his father at Utrecht Conservatory, then with Kees van Baaren in The Hague before working in Milan and Berlin with Berio. From his earliest published works, Andriessen adopted a critical and questioning attitude to musical orthodoxy, and from the late 1960s onwards his music became explicitly political; in 1969 he was one of a group of five Dutch contemporaries (with Ton de Leeuw, Mischa Mengelberg, Peter Schat and Jan van Vlijmen) who composed the anti-imperialist opera *Reconstructie*. In the 1970s Andriessen founded two performing groups, Hoketus and Die Volharding, for which many of his subsequent pieces have been composed. Though his output has included a series of music-theatre pieces – *Mattheus Passion* (1976), *Orpheus* (1977), *George Sand* (1980) and *Doctor Nero* (1984) – it was with the 1989 premiere of *De Materie*, in a striking production by Robert Wilson, that Andriessen established himself as a major dramatic composer. *De Materie* is designed for both concert hall and opera house, and can be seen as part of a series of instrumental and vocal scores composed over the previous ten years, but *Rosa* (1994), a collaboration with the film-maker Peter Greenaway, is explicitly a narrative-driven theatre work.

De Materie

Matter
Music-theatre in four parts (1h 45m)
Composed 1985–8
Libretto by the composer, based upon the Dutch
Declaration of Independence and the writings of David
Gorlaeus, Nicolaes Witsen, Hadewych, Piet Mondrian,
M. H. J. Schoenmakers, Marie Curie and Willem Kloos
PREMIERES 1 June 1989, Muzeiktheater, Amsterdam;
UK: 3 July 1994, Queen Elizabeth Hall, London
(concert)

The four parts of *De Materie* are linked by their subject matter: all deal with an aspect of the relationship between human spirit and matter, and all but one of the texts are taken from Dutch sources. Part 1 combines extracts from a treatise on shipbuilding and Gorlaeus's atomic theory of matter with the Dutch Treaty of Independence from Spain; Part 2, *Hadewych*, sets the 12th-century mystic's erotic descriptions of religious experience as an aria for solo soprano. Part 3, *De Stijl*, is a portrait of the painter Mondrian, using extracts from the artist's diaries and Schoenmakers' theoretical writings on painting, while Part 4 sets fragments of sonnets by Willem Kloos and physicist Marie Curie's memories of her dead husband.

De Materie's equivalent role as a concert work is reflected in its musical shape, which outlines a symphony, with the sensuous rapture of *Hadewych* as the slow movement and the boogie-woogie-inspired athleticism of *De Stijl* (reflecting Mondrian's love of dance and jazz and his infatuation with New York) as scherzo. Music and action always pursue independent trajectories, and, though Wilson's stage images attracted as much attention as Andriessen's music at the premiere, subsequent concert performances have confirmed the power of the score and its complex yet highly coherent organization.

Rosa

A horse drama in twelve scenes (1h 30m)
Libretto by Peter Greenaway
PREMIERE 2 November 1994, Muzeiktheater, Amsterdam

Andriessen's collaboration with Greenaway recounts the mysterious murder in 1957 of the fictional composer Juan Manuel de Rosa, who lives in a Uruguayan abattoir with his fiancée Esmeralda and his horse, which he keeps imprisoned in a treadmill. Esmeralda takes second place in Rosa's affections to the horse, and, in her desperate efforts to win his love, turns herself into a horse, daubed with black paint and walking on all fours. Rosa achieves ever greater fame as a composer of film scores for Hollywood westerns, until one day two mysterious cowboys arrive at the abattoir to shoot Rosa and his horse dead. The remaining scenes of the opera are taken up with the investigation of the murder and with Esmeralda's subsequent degradation – she is incarcerated within the carcass of Rosa's horse and eventually burned to death. As the audience leaves the auditorium, a jazz singer recites an index of all the words and phrases crucial to the solution of the murder.

Though Greenaway's scenario is consistently violent and sexually graphic, and his staging of the premiere was an extraordinary *tour de force* of film and theatrical techniques, Andriessen's music is never subsidiary. The expressive range of his music in *Rosa* seems greater than ever before, from the hocketing saxophone lines of the opening, through moments of luscious, reflective harmony for Esmeralda's set pieces, to the virtuoso pastiches of film music, which are recapitulated in the final scene as an ironic peroration.

A.J.C.

DOMINICK ARGENTO

b 27 October 1927, York, Pennsylvania, US

Argento is one of the most successful American opera composers of his generation. His parents came from Italy and his music has its roots in the tradition of Italian opera. He has said, 'I want my work to have emotional impact: I want it to communicate, not obfuscate.'

At first self-taught, in 1947 Argento went to the Peabody Conservatory in Baltimore and, in 1951, to Florence where he studied with Dallapiccola and encountered serial techniques. Soon after his return to the US Argento's first opera, *Sicilian Limes*, was produced; this was later withdrawn.

From 1955 to 1957 Argento studied at the Eastman School, Rochester, New York, with Howard Hanson, Bernard Rogers and Alan Hovhaness. Here his second opera, *The Boor* – based on Chekhov – was premiered in the 1957 Festival of American Music. It was praised for its idiomatic handling of traditional operatic techniques of aria, ensemble and dramatic pacing and has been widely performed throughout the US and abroad. Back in Florence on a Guggenheim Fellowship, Argento began *Colonel Jonathan the Saint*, which was a failure when it was eventually premiered at Denver (1971).

In 1958 Argento took a teaching post at Minnesota University. Here, along with his librettist and director John Olon-Scrymgeour, he founded Center Opera (later called Minnesota Opera) which was launched with Argento's *The Masque of Angels*. In the mid-1960s Argento worked with Tyrone Guthrie and Douglas Campbell, writing incidental music for several plays. His most popular work came in 1971 – the chamber extravaganza *Postcard from Morocco*.

The Voyage of Edgar Allan Poe was an American Bicentennial commission, to a libretto by C. M. Nolte, based on the later years of Poe's madness. Minnesota Opera gave the premiere, then took its production to Baltimore. The plot was felt to be confused, but Andrew Porter wrote of 'touching lyrical passages' and found the opera 'intelligent, accomplished, imaginative'.

Generally melodious and harmonious, Argento's music belongs to no particular contemporary trend. It has enjoyed considerable success in America, but apart from isolated performances in Britain (especially at the Aldeburgh Festival) it has made little impact abroad.

Postcard from Morocco

Opera in one act (1h 30m)
Libretto by John Donahue
PREMIERES 14 October 1971, Center Opera Company, Minneapolis; UK: 28 July 1976, King's College, London

Postcard from Morocco is set in 1914 at a railway station in Morocco, where a group of travellers is stranded. After various deceptively light-hearted incidents, one of the travellers is tricked into revealing himself when he opens his suitcase. Matching the episodic nature of the libretto, with its sequence of dreams and reminiscences, Argento's music – scored for seven singers and eight instrumentalists – is eclectic, with hints of Stravinsky and Britten.

Other operatic works: *Sicilian Limes* (withdrawn), 1954; *The Boor*, 1957; *Colonel Jonathan the Saint*, (1960), 1971; *Christopher Sly*, 1963; *The Masque of Angels*, 1964; *The Shoemaker's Holiday*, 1967; *A Waterbird Talk*, (1976), 1977; *The Voyage of Edgar Allan Poe*, 1976; *Miss Havisham's Fire*, 1979; *Miss Havisham's Wedding Night*, 1981; *Casanova's Homecoming*, 1985; *The Aspern Papers*, 1988; *The Dream of Valentino*, 1994

P.D.

DANIEL AUBER

Daniel-François-Esprit Auber; *b* 29 January 1782, Caen, France; *d* 12 May 1871, Paris

In his long life Auber composed fluently and prolifically for the French operatic stage, especially in the field of opéra comique. With Adolphe Adam, he took on the mantle of Adrien Boieldieu and Ferdinand Hérold, and passed it on in turn to Ambroise Thomas and Jacques Offenbach.

His first efforts in composition were Italian airs, French romances and concertos for violin and cello. He studied with Cherubini, whom he was later to succeed as director of the Paris Conservatoire. From 1811 for 60 years he was engaged in operatic enterprises, his first success being *Le séjour militaire*, a one-act comedy played at the Opéra-Comique in 1813. *Leicester*, in 1823, began a long collaboration with Eugène Scribe, whose versatility and fecundity brought a stream of successes in the coming years. Their most impressive work is *La muette de Portici*, a grand opera that served as a model for the Meyerbeerian genre. Yet Auber made few later attempts at serious opera and confined himself principally to the lighter forms. *Fra Diavolo, Le domino noir, Les diamants de la couronne*, and many others, held the stage throughout the century. His melodies are attractive and popular, his orchestral textures piquant and simple. He never explored the harmonic avenues suggested in *La muette de Portici*; he eschewed the sentimental. In his later years he reached his peak with *Haydée*, based on a story by Mérimée, and in *Manon Lescaut*, in which he anticipated the better-known settings of Prévost's novel by Massenet and Puccini.

Masaniello, ou La muette de Portici

Masaniello, or The Dumb Girl of Portici
Opera in five acts (2h 30m)
Libretto by Eugène Scribe and Germain Delavigne, after Raimond de Moirmoiron's *Mémoires sur la révolution de Naples de 1647*
PREMIERES 29 February 1828, Opéra, Paris; UK: 4 May 1829, Drury Lane, London; US: 9 November 1829, Park Theater, New York
CAST Elvire *s*, Masaniello *t*, Alphonse *t*, Lorenzo *t*, Pietro *b*, Borello *b*, Moreno *b*, Selva *b*, *ms*, Fenella *dancer*; *satb* chorus of fishermen, soldiers, the court, Neapolitans

La muette de Portici was one of the earliest and most influential of French grand operas, even though its composer's *métier* was truly in opéra comique. It preceded Rossini's *Guillaume Tell* by a year and had a pronounced influence on both Meyerbeer and Wagner. It set Scribe on the course of his later career more clearly perhaps than Auber, for the libretto contains many of the elements that became standard at the Opéra in the next 30 years, notably a foreground of personal dilemma against a background of political tension in a specified historical and geographical setting. The five acts contain ample ensembles, choruses and ballets.

SYNOPSIS
The opera is set in Naples in 1647 at the time of Masaniello's revolt against Spanish rule.

Act I As Alphonse, the son of the Spanish viceroy, marries Elvire, a Spanish princess, he is denounced by Fenella, a dumb girl, as her seducer.

Act II At Portici, Masaniello, Fenella's brother, gives the signal for insurrection.

Act III They take the rebellion to Naples.

Act IV In their flight Alphonse and Elvire are unknowingly sheltered by Masaniello himself.

Act V Masaniello is eventually killed after saving his royal guests. At the final curtain Fenella leaps into the crater of Vesuvius.

Apart from the vivacity and ingenuity of the music, the opera's strength lies in its touching treatment of the dumb heroine, whose thoughts are transmitted throughout in mime with expressive orchestral accompaniment. There is much Neapolitan colour in the music, and the chorus is prominently featured, especially in the big ensembles. The opera was successful in the 19th century, although little more than the overture (with its tremendous opening on a diminished seventh) has been played in the twentieth. When played in Brussels in 1830 it is said to have sparked off the revolt that led to Belgian independence.

Fra Diavolo, ou L'hôtellerie de Terracine

Fra Diavolo, or The Inn at Terracina
Opéra comique in three acts (2h)
Libretto by Eugène Scribe, based on a historical character
of *c.* 1810
PREMIERES 28 January 1830, Opéra-Comique, Paris; UK: 1 February 1831, Drury Lane, London; US: 16 September 1831, Chestnut St Theater, Philadelphia
CAST Fra Diavolo *t*, Lord Cokbourg *b* (or *t*), Lady Pamela *ms*, Lorenzo *t*, Mathéo *b*, Zerline *s*, Beppo *t*, Giacomo *b*, Francesco *silent*; *satb* chorus of inhabitants of Terracina, servants, soldiers

The most successful of Auber's many opéras comiques, *Fra Diavolo* uses a historical Italian bandit (Michele Pezza) as a model for a comic character who masquerades as a marquis and preys on travellers around Naples. His victims are an English milord and lady named Cockburn (rendered by Scribe as 'Cokbourg') staying at an inn at Terracina.

SYNOPSIS
Act I Zerline, daughter of the innkeeper Mathéo, is to marry a rich peasant, Francesco, but really she loves Lorenzo, a poor soldier. Lorenzo has instructions to find the bandit Fra Diavolo. Lord and Lady Cokbourg arrive at the inn, having been robbed. A mysterious marquis (in fact Fra Diavolo) steals Lady

Pamela's diamonds from around her neck. Lorenzo retrieves some of the missing goods and is rewarded with enough money to enable him to marry Zerline.

Act II The 'marquis' steals into Zerline's bedroom and there confronts Lorenzo, who takes him for a rival in love.

Act III A trap is set for Fra Diavolo and his two clumsy henchmen. The English travellers realize that the 'marquis' was a bandit after all. Zerline is able to marry Lorenzo.

The dashing bandit was a winning operatic idea and the two subsidiary bandits, Giacomo and Beppo, provided characters for Laurel and Hardy's *Fra Diavolo* in 1933.

The music has a lively spring, with Auber's abundant melodic gift always in evidence. The military music is plain, too dependent on the percussion, but there are some excellent individual numbers. The duet for the milord and his lady is a neat adaptation of the traditional 'couplets' formula, and the quintet that follows in Act I is original and witty, with an enchanting 'oompah' effect in the voices. Diavolo's recitative and aria at the beginning of Act III is a *tour de force*, offering scope for vocal antics of every kind. While Rossini's mannerisms are to be heard here and there, there are also chromatic touches that anticipate Smetana.

Other operas: *L'erreur d'un moment*, 1811; *Jean de Couvain*, 1812; *Le séjour militaire*, 1813; *Le testament et les billets doux*, 1819: *La bergère châtelaine*, 1820; *Emma, ou La promesse imprudente*, 1821; *Leicester, ou Le château de Kenilworth*, 1823; *La neige, ou Le nouvel Eginard*, 1823; *Vendôme en Espagne*, 1823; *Les trois genres*, 1824; *Le concert à la cour, ou La débutante*, 1824; *Léocadie*, 1824; *Le maçon*, 1825; *Le timide, ou Le nouveau séducteur*, 1826; *Fiorella*, 1826; *La fiancée*, 1829; *Le Dieu et la bayadère*, 1830; *Le philtre*, 1831; *La marquise de Brinvilliers*, 1831; *Le serment, ou Les faux-monnayeurs*, 1832; *Gustav III, ou Le bal masqué*, 1833; *Lestocq, ou L'intrigue et l'amour*, 1834; *Le cheval de bronze*, 1835; *Actéon*, 1836; *Les chaperons blancs*, 1836; *L'ambassadrice*, 1836; *Le domino noir*, 1837; *Le lac des fées*, 1839; *Zanetta, ou Jouer avec le feu*, 1840; *Les diamants de la couronne*, 1841; *Le duc d'Olonne*, 1842; *La part du diable*, 1843; *La sirène*, 1844; *La barcarolle, ou L'amour de la musique*, 1845; *Les premiers pas*, 1847; *Haydée, ou Le secret*, 1847; *L'enfant prodigue*, 1850; *Zerline, ou La corbeille d'oranges*, 1851; *Marco Spada*, 1852; *Jenny Bell*, 1855; *Manon Lescaut*, 1856; *La circassienne*, 1861; *La fiancée du roi de Garbe*, 1864; *Le premier jour de bonheur*, 1868; *Rêve d'amour*, 1869

H.M.

B

MICHAEL BALFE

Michael William Balfe; *b* 15 May 1808, Dublin;
d 20 October 1870, Rowney Abbey, Hertfordshire, England

Balfe was the most prolific British opera composer of
his generation and arguably the most popular of the
19th century. His works enjoyed great success both in
Britain and widely abroad.

After early training in Dublin and London, Balfe
spent some years in Italy and Paris, gaining the support of Rossini and Cherubini as he developed his
career as an opera singer and composer. In 1833 he
came to London and in 1835 achieved an overnight
success with his first English opera, *The Siege of
Rochelle*. His subsequent commissions included *Falstaff* for Her Majesty's Theatre, then among the most
prestigious Italian opera houses in Europe. Balfe made
an attempt as a manager himself, but after the venture's failure transferred his attention to Paris. Drury
Lane reopened as the English Opera House in 1843
and that autumn saw the premiere there of Balfe's
best-known opera, *The Bohemian Girl*. Its popularity
outstripped that of all other English works of the
period. Balfe continued to divide his time between
London and Paris; in 1843, 1844 and 1845 he produced a new opera in each capital, including *L'étoile
de Séville* for the Paris Opéra, the Continental Mecca
for opera composers – a unique achievement for a
British musician. In *The Daughter of St Mark*, Balfe
made his second attempt to overcome the traditional
national prejudice against all-sung opera (*Catherine
Grey*, of 1837, also excluded spoken dialogue), but
this did not score a success.

In addition to composing and continuing to sing –
he was London's first Papageno in 1838 – Balfe
became conductor at Her Majesty's in 1846, working
with Verdi when he came to prepare *I masnadieri* the
following year. Renewed managerial failure brought
English opera virtually to a halt and Balfe again
sought his fortune abroad, travelling to Berlin,
Vienna, St Petersburg, and Trieste, where *Pittore e
duca* appeared in 1854. Its libretto was by Piave,
Verdi's librettist. In 1856 Balfe returned to London
after four years' absence. The final phase of his composing career lasted from 1857 until 1864. Written
with a new management and superior singers in mind,
the operas of this period are more expansive, though
not free from the carelessness over word-setting and

dramatic effect that mars his earlier work. He emerged
from his retirement in 1868 for a Parisian revival of
The Bohemian Girl.

Balfe may have lacked the dramatic imagination of
great opera composers, but he nevertheless led the
attempt to institute English opera as a substantial
musical form, and his international reputation served
to raise the status of British composers. His talent was
primarily melodic, and stylistically he was essentially
Italianate. Having been the source of his rise to fame,
these features also contributed to his decline. Within a
few years of his death, the increasing support for
Wagner led to an altered view of Balfe's operas, from
which they have yet to recover.

The Bohemian Girl

Opera in three acts (3h)
Libretto by Alfred Bunn after Jules-Henri Vernoy de Saint-
Georges's and Mazilier's ballet *The Gypsy* (1839), based in
turn on Miguel de Cervantes's novel *La gitanilla* (1613)
PREMIERES 27 November 1843, Drury Lane, London; US:
25 November 1844, New York
CAST Count Arnheim *bar*, Thaddeus *t*, Florestein *t*,
Devilshoof *b*, Arline *s*, Queen of the Gypsies *s*, *s*, *t*, *b*; *satb*
chorus of Austrians and gypsies

Like many English operas of the period, *The Bohemian
Girl* was based by Bunn, the manager of Drury Lane,
on a French source, in this case a ballet.

SYNOPSIS

The opera is set near Pressburg (now Bratislava) at
the end of the 18th century.

Act I Following festivities in praise of the Austrian
emperor, Arline, the six-year-old daughter of Count
Arnheim, is kidnapped.

Act II Twelve years later. Arline has been brought
up in a gypsy camp. Here she falls in love with Thaddeus, a proscribed Polish soldier who has been forced
to take refuge in the camp. But this enrages the gypsy
queen, who herself loves Thaddeus, and she engineers
a trumped-up charge in order to remove her rival. At
her trial Arline is recognized by her father, the judge.

Act III The thwarted gypsy queen plans Thaddeus's death, but is herself killed. The hero is accepted
by Count Arnheim, and general rejoicing brings the
opera to an end.

True to the English tradition, the opera includes

spoken dialogue, and there is little recitative. The music is characteristic of Balfe and, stylistically, owes much to Rossini. Its effect derives not from dramatic intensity but from melodic charm. This emerges strongly in the ballads, the simple songs typical of English opera of the period. 'I dreamt that I dwelt in marble halls' and 'When other lips and other hearts', for the heroine and hero respectively, are two of Balfe's best-known examples. Their apparent effortlessness belies the time and concern he lavished on them – far more, clearly, than he devoted to details of word-setting and dramatic impact. However, it should be remembered that the sales of such ballads provided an important source of income for the composer.

Other operas: *I rivali di se stessi*, ?1829; *Un avvertimento ai gelosi*, ?1830; *Enrico IV al passo della Marna*, 1833; *The Siege of Rochelle*, 1835; *The Maid of Artois*, 1836; *Catherine Grey*, 1837; *Joan of Arc*, 1837; *Diadesté*, 1838; *Falstaff*, 1838; *Këolanthé*, 1841; *Le puits d'amour*, 1843; *Les quatre fils Aymon*, 1844; *The Daughter of St Mark*, 1844; *The Enchantress*, 1845; *L'étoile de Séville*, 1845; *The Bondman*, 1846; *The Maid of Honour*, 1847; *The Sicilian Bride*, 1852; *The Devil's In It*, 1852; *Pittore e duca*, 1854; *The Rose of Castille*, 1857; *Satanella, or The Power of Love*, 1858; *Bianca, or The Bravo's Bride*, 1860; *The Puritan's Daughter*, 1861; *Blanche de Nevers*, 1862; *The Armourer of Nantes*, 1863; *The Sleeping Queen*, 1864; *The Knight of the Leopard* (inc.; completed by Michael Costa), 1874

G.B.

SAMUEL BARBER

b 9 March 1910, West Chester, Pennsylvania, US;
d 23 January 1981, New York

Barber was one of the most successful American composers of the mid 20th century. Confidently conservative in style, his romantic music has stood its ground through changes of fashion and seems as enduring as that of Copland or Gershwin, although it is less distinctively American in style.

Barber's family background was conducive to his musical development. His mother was a good pianist and his aunt, the opera singer Louise Homer, was married to a composer. Barber began composing when he was seven and his first attempts at an opera date from three years later. In 1924 Barber became a student of singing, piano and conducting as well as composition at the newly founded Curtis Institute in Philadelphia. There he met Gian Carlo Menotti, who became an essential colleague, librettist and near-life-long companion. After graduating, Barber went to study singing in Vienna, gave recitals and radio broadcasts and recorded his own *Dover Beach* (composed 1931), for voice and string quartet.

At Curtis, Barber received a thorough traditional grounding in composition from Rosario Scalero. His student works were polished and well received, enabling him to gain awards for European travel. He soon attracted the attention of major conductors such as Artur Rodziński and Arturo Toscanini. The latter conducted the first performance of the famous *Adagio* for strings (arranged from the String Quartet, 1936) which has become a classic.

All this augured well for Barber's progression to opera, as did his early orchestral pieces related to dramatic subjects, such as the *School for Scandal* overture and the *Music for a Scene from Shelley*, as well as his ballets, *Medea* (1946) and *Souvenirs* (1952). Barber was concerned to communicate directly. In a late interview he said, 'There's no reason music should be difficult for an audience to understand, is there?'

Vanessa

Opera in four acts (2h)
Libretto by Gian Carlo Menotti, based on a story in *Seven Gothic Tales* by Isak Dinesen (Karen Blixen) (1934)
Composed 1956–7, rev. 1964
PREMIERES 15 January 1958, Metropolitan, New York; rev. version: 13 March 1965, Metropolitan, New York
CAST Vanessa *s*, Erika *ms*, The Old Baroness *c*, Anatol *t*, The Old Doctor *bar*, Nicholas *b*, Footman *b*; *satb* chorus of servants, guests, peasants, children, musicians

Menotti, as a seasoned man of the theatre, contributed significantly as both librettist and director of *Vanessa*. Elegant sets and costumes were designed by Cecil Beaton, and the casting – as can readily be confirmed in the original recording – was superb. Barber had written *Knoxville: Summer of 1915* (1948) for Eleanor Steber and she was chosen for the title role (Callas had refused it on the grounds that the work had no melody and she could not be expected to fall in love with a man who had slept with the mezzo-soprano). Menotti's plot has overtones of Ibsen, which suited Barber's nostalgic side and inspired arias, dances and dramatic moments in his strongest vein.

Remarkably for a first opera, *Vanessa* was a resounding success. Winthrop Sargeant considered it a 'near masterpiece in the genre' and Paul Henry Lang predicted that its impeccable vocal writing and sumptuous orchestration would be an 'eye-opener for Europeans'. Although there were reservations about its derivative nature when it was performed at the Salzburg Festival later in 1958, *Vanessa* seems likely to survive.

SYNOPSIS

The action takes place at Vanessa's country house in an unspecified northern country, *c*. 1905.

Act I Vanessa, her mother the baroness and her niece Erika are waiting for the return of Vanessa's lover, Anatol, who left 20 years ago. Instead the son of her lover, also called Anatol, arrives; his father is dead.

Act II Anatol and Vanessa are becoming increasingly attached although Anatol had seduced Erika on the night of his arrival. Erika decides to give him up.

Act III At a splendid ball Anatol and Vanessa pledge their love in public: Erika collapses.

Act IV Erika, pregnant by Anatol, is recovering after attempting suicide. Vanessa and Anatol, married, prepare to leave for Paris. Erika settles down to wait for Anatol indefinitely, as had Vanessa at the start of the opera.

Although Barber sticks to the traditional forms of opera (arias, duets, ensembles, etc.) his musical language is far-ranging, encompassing folklike and parodistic elements within the predominantly lyrical whole. Barber and Menotti revised the opera to a three-act version in 1964, but the original version is more commonly performed.

Antony and Cleopatra

Opera in three acts (2h)
Libretto by Franco Zeffirelli, after the play by William Shakespeare (1606–7)
Composed 1966, rev. 1975
PREMIERES 16 September 1966, Metropolitan, New York; rev. version: 6 February 1975, Juilliard School of Music, New York; UK: 27 March 1982, Logan Hall, London (concert)
CAST Cleopatra s, Octavia spoken role, Charmian ms, Iras c, Antony bar, Caesar t, Agrippa b, Enobarbus b, Eros t or bar, Dolabella bar, Thidias t or bar, Maecenas spoken role, Caesar's Soldier bar, Rustic bar or b, Messenger t, Soothsayer b, Eunuch spoken role, Alexas b, 4 guards t, bar, 2 b, 2 Soldiers 2 b, Watchman spoken role; satb chorus; dancers

Barber's Antony and Cleopatra was commissioned for the opening of the new Metropolitan Opera House at Lincoln Center – a public ordeal that proved as damaging to the work's future as the Coronation gala performance in 1953 was to Britten's Gloriana. Although the singers were much admired, Zeffirelli's production was felt to be over-elaborate. Desmond Shawe-Taylor reported that Barber's music, 'rich in substance and sometimes very engaging, was being submerged beneath the glitter and complexity of the spectacle', on- and offstage. The opera was regarded as a failure. Even after the 1975 revival produced by Menotti, Andrew Porter pointed out the difficulties of word-for-word Shakespeare setting and thought that the music 'did not rise to the size of the subject'. The impact of this apparent failure on Barber was disastrous and may have contributed to the decline of his health. But the recording by Leontyne Price and more recent radio broadcasts suggest that there is unrealized potential in Antony and Cleopatra.

Other opera: A Hand of Bridge, 1959

P.D.

BÉLA BARTÓK

Béla Viktor János Bartók; b 25 March 1881, Sînnicolau Mare, Romania (formerly Nagyszentmiklós, Hungary); d 26 September 1945, New York

Bartók wrote only one opera, but it is the major work of his early maturity. Duke Bluebeard's Castle would doubtless have had successors but for the obstacles it encountered; these not only deterred him from writing for the stage but for a time blocked his creative faculty altogether. In 1911, at the time of its composition, Bartók was becoming established as a leading figure in Hungarian music, albeit through performance of early works which were no longer representative of his current style. In 1910 the first performance

of his First String Quartet, together with the experimental Bagatelles and the First Romanian Dance for piano, had been greeted with incomprehension verging on hostility, and when he entered his new opera for a competition sponsored by the Budapest Lipótváros Club it was rejected as unperformable and denied a prize.

The opera is nevertheless the most integrated of all Bartók's works written before the First World War and the first to show a completely personal synthesis of the various strains in his music up to that time. Seven years earlier he had been writing chamber works in a post-Brahmsian manner. Then, in about 1905, he made his first contact with the ancient peasant music of Hungary, a music remote from the Hungarian style copied by Brahms, Liszt and others; and a year or two later he came across the latest piano music of Debussy (the Estampes and Images). The Bagatelles of 1908 show in rather anecdotal form some of the effects of these encounters. Folktunes with drumming accompaniments alternate with pieces using streams of common chords or series of irregular scale patterns that seem to mimic the modal scales of peasant music. In the first Bagatelle the left and right hands play in different keys, a semitone apart. But the First String Quartet written at about the same time, sticks to a lyrical manner not wholly remote from the Expressionism of contemporary Viennese music, though with folksong ingredients too. In the opera, which was Bartók's first major work for voices, these apparently incompatible elements fused to create a unique masterpiece of Hungarian Symbolism.

Duke Bluebeard's Castle

A kékszakállú herceg vára
Opera in one act (1h)
Libretto by Béla Balázs, after the story by Charles Perrault (1697)
Composed March–September 1911; ending rev. 1912, 1918, 1921
PREMIERES 24 May 1918, Budapest Opera; US: 8 January 1946, Dallas (concert); 2 October 1952, City Opera, New York; UK: 16 January 1957, Rudolf Steiner Hall, London
CAST Prologue (The Bard) speaker, Judith s, Kékszakállú (Duke Bluebeard) bar, Bluebeard's 3 Former Wives silent

Balázs's play owes a good deal to Maurice Maeterlinck's Ariane et Barbe-bleue, set by Dukas in 1907, and was apparently written in the same spirit as that play – that is, without commission but in the conscious hope that it would be set as an opera: 'I wrote [it] for Béla Bartók and Zoltán Kodály because I wanted to give them an opportunity to write works for the stage.' It treats the well-known legend of Bluebeard in Symbolistic fashion as an allegory of the incommunicable privacy of our inmost selves, and hence as a tragedy of Expressionism well adapted to the dying years of Romanticism. It must have had special resonance for Bartók, an intensely withdrawn but passionate man who had, moreover, recently married (the opera is dedicated to his wife, Márta Ziegler).

Duke Bluebeard's Castle had to wait until after the success of Bartók's ballet The Wooden Prince (1917) for its first production, and after 1918 there were no further Hungarian productions for nearly 20 years because the reactionary regime of Admiral Horthy would not allow the socialist Balázs's name to be credited, and Bartók would not allow performances if it were not. Recent revivals have shown, however, that the work's supposed untheatricality is a myth; static it may be, but the strong visual imagery more than compensates.

SYNOPSIS

The short spoken prologue (often omitted in performance) hints that the well-known tale is to be retold as a parable of the inner self; the curtain then rises on a 'vast, circular Gothic hall' with seven large doors. When Bluebeard and Judith enter through another door at the top of the stairs, the 'dazzling white opening' is the only light in the darkened hall.

A short orchestral introduction sets the gloomy scene. Judith, who is still in her wedding dress, has married Bluebeard against her family's wishes. She finds his castle cold and dark and the walls ooze moisture. Bluebeard reminds her that she could have married into a 'brighter castle, girt with roses', but she insists that she will bring brightness to his castle. An orchestral transition clearly supports Bluebeard's denial of this possibility.

Judith now notices the seven doors and demands that they be unlocked. She hammers on the first door, and as she does so a deep sigh is heard from behind it 'like the wind in a long, low corridor'. As the door swings open to reveal Bluebeard's torture chamber a blood-red light glares on to the stage. Undeterred, Judith insists on opening the second door. This time Bluebeard's armoury is revealed in 'a lurid reddish-yellow light'. Once again the 'blood' motif intrudes, as Judith sees blood on the weapons. But as she presses Bluebeard for the remaining keys, he senses the joy of release from oppressive secrets. He allows her three more keys. The doors open to display first his treasury and then his garden, bathed in a blue-green light. Yet again, the image of blood returns as Judith sees spots of red on the flowers. Finally the fifth door opens on to Bluebeard's vast and beautiful domains, portrayed in the grandest and loudest music in the whole work.

This is the architectural centre of the opera, and its climax of light. The mood now returns gradually to the gloom and darkness of the start. Bluebeard tries to distract Judith from the remaining two doors, but she persists. She sees blood even on the lands that for him are radiant with light. Reluctantly he yields the sixth key, and as she turns it in the lock another deep sigh warns of sinister revelations, and a shadow passes over the hall. The door conceals a silent lake of tears. Judith now exerts her feminine guile to coax the final key out of Bluebeard. She questions him about his past lovers and suddenly guesses that the blood on his possessions signifies that he has murdered them all. Bluebeard gives her the key. The seventh door opens (at this point doors five and six should swing shut), and his three former wives, richly adorned, process slowly out. The first, he says, he met in the morning, the second at midday, the third in the evening. 'You', he tells Judith as the three women vanish back through the door, 'I met at night.' He dresses her in the crown, mantle and jewels she herself brought from the treas-ury (the third door closes as he does so), and she slowly follows the other wives through the seventh door, which closes behind her. 'The darkness of night creeps back across the stage, and engulfs Bluebeard.'

In musical style, *Duke Bluebeard's Castle* is still an early work which shows Bartók's debt to German and Austrian late-Romanticism. But it also reveals influences that were to help turn him into an abrasive modernist. Debussy is an obvious model for passages such as the massive parallel chords at the opening of the fifth door (cf. *La cathédrale engloutie* in the first book of *Préludes*, published in 1909), while echoes of Richard Strauss's *Ein Heldenleben*, a work Bartók had once transcribed for piano, are unmistakable in the biting semitone clashes of the 'blood' motif. Yet *Bluebeard* is hardly a derivative score. It has an individuality that comes partly, perhaps, from Bartók's study of Hungarian folk music, with its strange modal scales, which seem to rub off on the opera's harmony as well as on its melody. The sharpened fourth note, which produces the interval C–F♯, is a common feature of the folksongs Bartók was collecting at this time, as is the descending perfect fourth, and both leave their mark on the very opening of the opera. Also typical of Hungarian peasant music are rhythmic details such as the decorated first beat, which produces the characteristic 'snap' or 'turn', and the so-called parlando rubato style of word-setting, which ensures that the incessant Hungarian accent on the first syllable rarely becomes monotonous, though it makes translation hard. Balázs himself modelled his regular octosyllabic lines on peasant verse.

Balázs's imagery, on the other hand, aligns him with modern Expressionism, with its strong colour symbolism; and with the German art nouveau, or *Jugendstil*, of which images of blood, flowers, castles and crowns were the stock in trade. Bartók adapts the gentle colourings of Debussian Impressionism to provide vivid but not-so-gentle musical equivalents of this imagery. In this respect *Bluebeard* is a kind of stage tone poem. It also has a strong built-in symbolism of its own, based on the opposition of keys and tonal centres. The score follows the arch form of the libretto. The darkness–light–darkness cycle is exactly matched by the tonal scheme, F♯–C–F♯, with its centre at the opening of the fifth door, and its ending in the 'darkness' music of the start. Bartók's later instrumental music offers many more instances of this type of plan: the first movement of the *Music for Strings, Percussion and Celesta* (A–E♭–A), its third movement, and the larger arch structures of the Third and Fourth String Quartets. The actual key symbolism of *Bluebeard*, however, is unique in Bartók. F♯ stands for Bluebeard's world, while the outside world represented by Judith inhabits the region of F and C. But the symbolism is made ambiguous. For example, the C major of the fifth door is Bluebeard's pretence at normality, while Judith sees the shadow of blood on it (F♯). Bluebeard's first note is F♯; Judith's is F, but the wives are in C minor, though now belonging exclusively to his world. Bluebeard's last two notes are F♯ and C, and the last orchestral note C♯. The same ambiguity is constantly present in the harmony, which achieves psychological depth by mixing elements rather than segregating them.

S.W.

LUDWIG VAN BEETHOVEN
b 16 December 1770, Bonn; *d* 26 March 1827, Vienna

Amid the abundance and supreme self-confidence of Beethoven's *oeuvre*, his solitary opera cuts a strangely isolated and equivocal figure. In large-scale instrumental forms, Beethoven wrote prolifically and with a mastery surpassed by none. Yet he achieved only one opera – and this not from any lack of interest in writing for the theatre. (Music for the stage forms a surprisingly large part of his output – *Egmont* and the *Prometheus* ballet music are only the most obvious examples – and at intervals throughout his career we find him searching for a congenial opera libretto.) Moreover, that one opera took more than ten years to reach its final shape and went through three separate versions and no fewer than four overtures. Compared with the speed and assurance with which he wrote the 'Eroica' Symphony, the Violin Concerto, the Rasumovsky Quartets, this degree of uncertainty suggests a clear distinction between a composer in his element in the symphonic medium and out of it in the operatic one.

So the argument frequently goes. *Fidelio* has regularly fallen foul of academic commentators. It is as if the work's detractors needed to free themselves of the burden of Beethoven's greatness by finding some field of composition in which he was not a master but could, on the contrary, be criticized and even patronized with impunity. Yet looked at without prejudice (including the prejudice against opera with spoken dialogue), *Fidelio* in its final form is as characteristic and as powerfully wrought as anything Beethoven wrote. It took him longer to get right not only because to begin with he lacked experience of the operatic medium but also because the subject – the unjustly imprisoned man, the fearless, dedicated woman – moved him too much and struck such resounding chords in the depth of his being. But he got it right in the end.

Fidelio, oder Die eheliche Liebe
Fidelio, or Married Love
Opera in two acts (19 scenes) (2h 15m)
Libretto by Joseph Sonnleithner and Georg Friedrich Treitschke, after Jean-Nicolas Bouilly's libretto *Léonore, ou L'amour conjugal* for Pierre Gaveaux (1798)
Composed 1804–5, rev. 1806 and 1814
PREMIERES original three-act version: 20 November 1805, Theater an der Wien, Vienna; first rev. version, in two acts: 29 March 1806, Theater an der Wien; second rev. version: 23 May 1814, Kärntnertortheater, Vienna; UK: 18 May 1832, King's Theatre, Haymarket, London; US: 9 September 1839, Park Theater, New York
CAST Leonore (Fidelio) *s*, Florestan *t*, Rocco *b*, Marzelline *s*, Jaquino *t*, Don Pizarro *bar*, Don Fernando *b-bar*, First Prisoner *t*, Second Prisoner *bar*; *satb* chorus of officers, soldiers, state prisoners, people

Vienna first heard the rescue operas of the French Revolution school in the spring of 1802. These opéras comiques – i.e. operas with spoken dialogue, of which Cherubini's *Lodoïska* and *Les deux journées* were the prime examples – startled the Viennese by their dramatic force, realism and topicality and, for the next few years, dominated the Viennese stage. They made a profound impression on Beethoven, whose orchestral style, not only in *Fidelio* but generally, shows clear signs of the influence of Cherubini's massive, driving tuttis, insistent rhythms, incisive accents and cross-accents, and strong dynamic contrasts. By early 1803 he had signed a contract with the Theater an der Wien.

For some reason it was for a work not after the current French model but on an ancient Roman subject, entitled *Vestas Feuer*, the libretto by Emanuel Schikaneder (perhaps Beethoven accepted it because of his admiration for *Die Zauberflöte*). He composed a couple of scenes – musical material from one of them was later used for the *Fidelio* duet 'O namenlose Freude!' – but by the end of 1803 he had abandoned it and turned to a French libretto by Jean-Nicolas Bouilly (librettist of *Les deux journées*), which had been set a few years earlier by the French composer Pierre Gaveaux (and which both Ferdinando Paer and Simon Mayr set at about the same time as Beethoven).

The plot was based on an actual event that had happened not long before in France during the Terror: a woman disguising herself as a man in order to free her husband from a gaol where he was being held as a political prisoner. The poet Joseph Sonnleithner made a German version, and Beethoven worked on it during 1804 and the first half of 1805. Composition coincided with his abortive love affair with Josephine von Brunsvik, and there is little doubt that his longing for a woman who would commit herself unreservedly to him gave added intensity to his portrait of Leonore, just as his self-identification with the lonely, persecuted Florestan – immured in the darkness of his cell, as Beethoven felt himself imprisoned in his growing deafness – contributed to the extraordinary force and vividness of the dungeon scene.

Despite its many beauties the first version of *Fidelio* (usually known as *Leonore*, the title Beethoven wanted to give the work) was not a success when it was performed in November 1805. Vienna was occupied by Napoleon's army. Most of Beethoven's supporters were absent, having fled the city, and by the time they came back the opera had been taken off. But it was also felt that the work had failed because it was too long, in particular because the early scenes dragged. For the revival in March–April 1806 Beethoven was persuaded, by Stephan von Breuning and others, to make cuts, some of them quite drastic. In this form (in two acts instead of three) it was more successful, but Beethoven, in dispute with the management, withdrew his score after only two performances.

It was not heard again for eight years. (A Prague production planned for 1807 came to nothing. It was probably for this production that Beethoven wrote the overture known as *Leonore No. 1*.) In 1814, when his fame (thanks to the enormously popular orchestral extravaganza *Wellington's Victory*) was at its height in Vienna, the Kärntnertortheater asked permission to revive *Fidelio*. He agreed, but insisted on a thorough revision. This time the opera was a triumphant success. The remodelling of the libretto was carried out by Georg Friedrich Treitschke, the theatre's stage manager and resident poet, in close collaboration with the composer. Treitschke removed several numbers from Act I and provided texts for a new final scene for the act, a new recitative ('Abscheulicher!') before the great aria 'Komm', Hoffnung' in which Leonore reasserts her faith in her heroic mission, a new final section for Florestan's scena, and a rewritten opening to the final scene of the opera (which was moved to the castle parade ground). It is to this revision that we owe two of the most exalted passages in the work: the farewell to the light of day sung by the prisoners as they return to their cells at the end of Act I (replacing the blustering, conventional original number) and Florestan's radiant vision of his wife.

In addition, the whole score was subjected to minute overhaul. *Fidelio* is a shorter opera than *Leonore*, not only because there are fewer numbers but because of a general tightening up. The excessive repetitions that marred the original score, especially in the domestic scenes of Act I, were stripped away. (Its prolixity is one reason why *Leonore*, though sometimes revived, cannot seriously be regarded as a valid alternative to *Fidelio*.) But the changes go deeper than simple abbreviation. Again and again Beethoven altered the declamation or the rhythmic emphasis, so that the voice part made its point more tellingly and the rhythms became more varied and vital. To take only the most striking example, the dungeon quartet was transformed; though most alterations may be small, the cumulative effect is crucial. Already a very powerful piece of dramatic music in 1805, it becomes overwhelming in its final form.

A few changes made in 1806 were retained; but some of the most extreme were rejected. In particular, both the dungeon trio and the great ensemble of thanksgiving in the final scene were reshaped, ending up the same length as in the hurriedly cut version of 1806 but now perfectly formed, no longer mutilated.

The work's key structure was also changed. In *Leonore* C major, the key of freedom and salvation, was established at the outset as the home key; in *Fidelio* it emerges gradually. The new overture (*Fidelio*) is in E (the key of Leonore's aria). During the first act Bb, the prison key, becomes increasingly prominent, and the second act begins in its dominant minor, F. C is touched on from time to time, but as a foreign key, though often at moments of transcendent meaning (the sacrament of bread in the dungeon trio, Leonore's holy resolve to save the prisoner even if he is not her husband). It is only in the final scene that its triumph is finally achieved. This new evolutionary treatment of tonality is an aspect of the more flexible and dramatic conception of opera that Beethoven had acquired by the time he revised his score.

Even more important, he reduced the weight of his orchestration. The original version is much more thickly scored, less epic in sound, more lyrical, more Romantic. For example, in *Leonore* the introduction

to the dungeon scene makes an almost Wagnerian effect. Beethoven's revision, which also shortened it by nine bars, altered its character profoundly. The texture was thinned out: string tremolos were confined to four bars, the trombones were removed altogether. So were the trumpets; they were now kept back until the quartet, to blaze forth the more brilliantly at the moment when the prisoner defies his assassin. Horns and timpani were left on their own to evoke a far more awesome sense of cold, vaulted darkness; in this austerer texture, too, the melodic cries in octave doublings on the woodwind which sound from the surrounding gloom stand out more sharply. This leaner, starker but also more glowing sonority is characteristic of the final version as a whole; it is true to the original idea behind the opera as the luxuriance of 1805 was not. The grief and passion and heroism of the drama, the sense of feelings stretched almost to breaking point, the central concept of human suffering in the context of divine providence, achieved their destined sound in 1814.

SYNOPSIS

Florestan, who disappeared two years ago and is believed dead, has been incarcerated secretly by his political enemy Don Pizarro. Florestan's wife, Leonore, in search of him, disguises herself as a young man and, under the name Fidelio, enters the service of the prison where Pizarro is governor.

Act I   The prison courtyard on a fine spring morning. Marzelline, the gaoler's daughter, is ironing. Jaquino the turnkey, in the intervals of dealing with packages arriving at the postern gate, tries to get her to name a day for their wedding, but she rebuffs him ('Jetzt, Schätzchen, jetzt sind wir allein'). She used to like Jaquino, but everything has changed; now her dream is of married bliss with Fidelio ('O wär'ich schon mit dir vereint'). Rocco, the gaoler, enters, followed by Fidelio (Leonore), who is carrying heavy chains from the blacksmith. Rocco praises Fidelio's zeal, and hints broadly that he understands the reason for it. They all reflect on what this new turn of events means for them ('Mir ist so wunderbar'). Rocco offers Fidelio his daughter's hand, but points out that a sound marriage depends as much on money as on love ('Hat man nicht auch Gold beineben'). Leonore begs Rocco, as a mark of trust, to let her help him in the cells. Rocco agrees to ask the governor, though there is one cell, occupied by a prisoner on starvation rations, where he will never be allowed to take Fidelio. Pizarro arrives with an armed escort. One of the letters he is given warns him that the minister, Don Fernando, has heard rumours of injustice and is coming to inspect the gaol. Pizarro decides to kill Florestan ('Ha! welch' ein Augenblick!'). He posts a trumpeter on the tower overlooking the road from Seville, and orders Rocco to prepare the unnamed prisoner's grave. Leonore overhears their conversation. Appalled by Pizarro's inhuman cruelty, she reaffirms her faith in the power of love ('Abscheulicher! . . . Komm', Hoffnung'). Leonore persuades Rocco to let the prisoners out into the garden. With Jaquino she unlocks the cell doors, and the prisoners emerge wonderingly into the light of day ('O welche Lust!'). Rocco returns with the news that Fidelio is to be allowed to help dig the grave of the mysterious prisoner. Leonore weeps at the thought that it may be her husband's, but convinces Rocco that it is her duty to go with him. Pizarro, discovering that the prisoners have been let out, angrily orders them back, and they return to their cells ('Leb' wohl, du warmes Sonnenlicht').

Act II A deep dungeon. Florestan sits in darkness lit by a small lamp; he is chained to a stone, but his spirit is unbroken. Half delirious with hunger, he has a vision of an angel in the likeness of Leonore, surrounded by bright light and leading him to freedom ('Gott! welch' Dunkel hier! . . . In des Lebens Frühlingstagen'). He rises to follow it but the chain drags him back and he collapses unconscious. Rocco and Leonore enter the dungeon and, while the prisoner sleeps (his face invisible), clear the opening of a disused cistern. Leonore resolves to save the man whoever he is. When Florestan wakes, she recognizes him. Rocco gives him a little wine, and is persuaded by Leonore to overlook orders and let her give him some bread ('Euch werde Lohn'). At a signal from Rocco, Pizarro appears. He is about to stab Florestan when Leonore springs forward and shields him, crying 'Töt' erst sein Weib!' ('First kill his wife!'). She draws a pistol. At that moment, far above, a trumpet sounds. It sounds a second time, louder, as Jaquino calls out from the top of the steps that Don Fernando has arrived. Alone, Leonore and Florestan, reunited, thank God for their deliverance ('O namenlose Freude!'). The parade ground of the fortress. Don Fernando addresses the people: he has come to free them from tyranny. Pizarro is taken away by guards. Leonore unlocks Florestan's chains and all give thanks to God who did not forsake them ('O Gott! welch' ein Augenblick!'). Led by Florestan, the released prisoners and the people join in a hymn of praise to the noble woman who saved her husband's life ('Wer ein holdes Weib errungen').

The mixture of domestic comedy and heroic melodrama, which Beethoven took from Cherubini and which remains central to the work even in the shortened final version, has worried many commentators. But it is fundamental to the whole conception, which is that love, devotion, courage, faith are not exclusively 'operatic' qualities, to be presented only in lofty romantic settings, but human attributes that may flower in the most humdrum surroundings. It is right that Fidelio should begin with Marzelline ironing, that Leonore's first words – spoken, not sung – should concern the cost of repairs carried out by the blacksmith, and that we learn of her perilous quest only by degrees. The process by which the singspiel atmosphere of the early scenes is gradually left behind and the musical language deepens and intensifies in preparation for the great dungeon scene – a process that culminates in the mysterious final bars of Act I – is the work of a master of music drama, however heterodox.

For the same reasons the two huge Leonore overtures of 1805 (No. 2) and 1806 (No. 3), virtual symphonic poems that anticipate the heroic issues of the opera, make way for a much shorter piece, a true prelude to the action – to quote Tovey, 'dramatic, brilliant, terse, and with an indication of some formidable force in the background'. The practice of playing the Leonore No. 3 overture between the dungeon scene and the finale – a practice, still not uncommon, that goes back at least to the middle of the 19th century and therefore antedates Mahler, who is often said to have originated it – is wrong on at least two counts. It imposes an alien sound on Fidelio – the heavier 1805–6 orchestration that Beethoven deliberately changed in 1814 – and it destroys the effect that is created by going straight from the sublimities of the Leonore–Florestan duet to the festive, breezy march that begins the finale.

To bring us back to earth again in the final scene of the opera, after the torrential force of the dungeon quartet and the incandescence of the ensuing duet, is a stroke of the highest realism. But realism cannot have the last word. The opera ends in a mighty hymn to liberty and the noble, all-enduring woman, sung by the whole company, soloists and chorus, in a blazing C major that dissolves the personal drama into a vision of universal love. This conclusion has been criticized as being more cantata than opera. But Fidelio could not end in any other way. That has been the message of the work from the moment that Leonore's aria was followed immediately by the prisoners' chorus. The final progression from the particular to the universal is the natural and logical conclusion. It brings to flower the seed of selfless love planted in the darkness of the dungeon (and in the key of C major) at the most apparently hopeless point of Leonore's quest, as she digs the grave of the man who may be her husband – the discovery that ultimately it does not matter who he is: even if he is not Florestan and her journey has been in vain, 'I will loose your chains whoever you are, unhappy man, by God I will save you and set you free.'

D.A.C.

VINCENZO BELLINI

Vincenzo Salvatore Carmelo Francesco Bellini;
b 3 November 1801, Catania, Sicily; d 23 September 1835, nr Puteaux, Paris

Together with Rossini, Donizetti and Verdi, Bellini is one of the four great figures of Italian Romantic opera whose work remains fundamental to the repertoire of all Italian and most international opera houses. Less prolific and less versatile than the other three, he nevertheless produced in the late 1820s a group of operas that were seminal in establishing in Italy a distinctively Romantic musical language; and in the masterpieces of the early 1830s – La sonnambula (1831), Norma (1831) and I puritani (1835) – he brought the art of bel-canto opera to its apogee.

Bellini's early musical education was at the hands of his father Rosario and his grandfather Vincenzo Tobia, both professional musicians in Catania. In 1819, he was enrolled as a pupil at the Conservatorio di San Sebastiano in Naples, where, from 1822, the teaching of Niccolò Zingarelli, the director, exerted a lasting influence. Zingarelli introduced Bellini to the best of the Neapolitan masters of the past, and to the instrumental music of Haydn and Mozart, but his shrewdest pedagogical stroke was to invite him to put away his contrapuntal studies and concentrate on refining his skills as a melodist, listening to the dictates of his heart and striving to express them in pure and simple song. Zingarelli apparently felt it necessary to 'protect' his students from Rossini, whose music dominated the repertoire in the public theatres of the city, and it was only as a final-year student, in 1824, that Bellini first heard a Rossini opera (*Semiramide*). Nevertheless, relations between Bellini and Zingarelli remained exceptionally affectionate: the old maestro followed his young protégé's career with pride, and in due course was thanked in princely fashion with the dedication of *Norma*.

It was customary each year to give one of the outstanding students the experience of composing a short opera and staging it in the conservatory theatre. Bellini's début, *Adelson e Salvini*, came early in 1825, and was so successful that he was commissioned to compose a full-length opera (*Bianca e Gernando*) for the Teatro San Carlo the following year. The impresario there, Domenico Barbaja, was also involved in the running of La Scala in Milan. Inevitably, therefore, Bellini's success in Naples led to his being invited to go north and compose his third opera, *Il pirata* (1827), for La Scala, to a libretto by Felice Romani, the most admired theatre poet of the age. The two men got along famously, and their partnership was to prove one of the most remarkable in operatic history: all seven of the remaining operas Bellini composed in Italy had Romani libretti, and all but *Zaira* (1829) and *Beatrice di Tenda* (1833) triumphed gloriously. Their first works together, *Il pirata* and *La straniera* (1829), bizarre and violent in plot and set to music of matching emotional abandon, marked the beginning of full-blooded Romanticism in Italian opera. But tragedy in the most elevated classical style also came within their range (*Norma*); and so did sentimental tenderness (*La sonnambula*).

Until the early months of 1833, Bellini had enjoyed a prodigiously successful Italian career, and by now his fame had spread throughout Europe and reached America. From an early date he could and did demand high fees for his operas, not simply out of greed, but because he was, for Italy, a new kind of composer, one who felt a need for a greater measure of independence than did most of his predecessors; he liked to work slowly, and was disinclined to assume the kind of official teaching or administrative posts they had virtually always filled. The fiasco of *Beatrice di Tenda* in March 1833 and the attendant breakdown of his partnership with Romani was a severe blow. At the same time his personal life was in a state of upheaval; a longstanding love affair with Giuditta Turina, having been discovered by her husband, had become a source of embarrassment and inconvenience. An invitation to visit London to help produce three of his operas was probably doubly welcome therefore. After a successful trip, he made no hasty return to Italy, but lingered in Paris, traditionally a Mecca for Italian composers.

Bellini's last opera, *I puritani*, was composed for the Théâtre Italien. Like so many Italians before him, he found it enormously stimulating to compose for Paris: the scope of his work seemed to expand, its manner to become more urbane and cosmopolitan. During the composition he was often with Rossini, who, though he no longer held an official position at the Théâtre Italien, remained the presiding genius of operatic life in Paris. A relationship that began, as far as Bellini was concerned, out of calculated self-interest developed into one of genuine mutual respect, and Bellini benefited much from the older composer's advice. But working on the opera showed him more clearly than ever how badly he needed a librettist of Romani's calibre, and in the last year of his life he made energetic attempts to re-establish a working relationship with his old comrade-in-arms. The success of *I puritani* gave Bellini a position in Parisian musical life 'second only to Rossini' (letter to Francesco Florimo, 21 September 1834); but there is no reason to doubt that, but for an untimely and wretched death from acute gastro-enteritis, complicated by an abscess of the liver, he would soon have returned to Italy.

Il pirata
The Pirate

Melodramma (opera seria) in two acts (2h 30m)
Libretto by Felice Romani, after the melodrama *Bertram, ou Le pirate* (1826) by Raimond (Isidore J. S. Taylor), itself a translation of Charles Robert Maturin's drama *Bertram, or The Castle of Saint Aldobrand* (1816)
PREMIERES 27 October 1827, La Scala, Milan; UK: 17 April 1830, King's Theatre, London; US: 5 December 1832, Richmond Hill Theater, New York
CAST Ernesto *b*, Imogene *s*, Gualtiero *t*, *s*, *t*, *b*; *satb* chorus of fisherfolk, pirates, courtiers, ladies and maidens

The first of seven operas composed by Bellini in collaboration with Felice Romani, *Il pirata* has good claim to be regarded as the earliest full-bloodedly Romantic opera to appear in Italy. It was by now clear that Bellini's was the most individual voice among the post-Rossinian generation of composers, and the huge success enjoyed by *Il pirata* laid the foundation for his international fame. The part of Gualtiero was written for Giovanni Battista Rubini, who, like many of the great singers of the period, was at first disconcerted by the apparent simplicity of Bellini's music, but soon became a passionate admirer and one of the composer's most trusted collaborators.

SYNOPSIS

Thirteenth-century Sicily. Gualtiero, count of Montaldo, and Ernesto, duke of Caldora, both love Imogene, but are supporters of rival factions in the power struggle for the Sicilian throne between Manfred and Charles of Anjou. After the death of Manfred and the Angevin victory, Gualtiero is driven into exile, where he resorts to a life of piracy, while Ernesto blackmails Imogene into marrying him by threatening the life of her father – like Gualtiero a supporter of Manfred.

Act I After some years of buccaneering, Gualtiero's ships are pursued by a punitive expedition led by Ernesto; they are scattered and, during a storm, shipwrecked on the coast near Ernesto's castle. In accordance with Caldoran custom Imogene offers hospitality to the shipwrecked mariners; she recognizes Gualtiero.

Act II   Though long absence has done nothing to lessen their love, Gualtiero is unable to persuade Imogene to abandon her lawful husband and the child she has borne him. Discovered by Ernesto, Gualtiero kills him in a duel and then surrenders himself. Imogene despairs. (In the libretto there follows a final scene which Bellini did set, but cut again, apparently before it was performed: Gualtiero's pirate band attempt to rescue him; but he refuses to rejoin them and kills himself.)

Contemporaries particularly admired the way in which Bellini resisted the temptation to emulate Rossini's brilliant style, cultivating instead a type of melody that was sometimes so simple, and followed the inflexions of the text so closely, that it seemed almost to 'speak'. The coloratura that Rossini had scattered so prodigally is now reserved for specific points of expression, such as the lacerating despair of Imogene's final cabaletta ('O sole! ti vela'). Bellini's simpler melodic style is matched by a fondness for symmetrically balanced aria forms, with a clearly audible reprise at the point of climax; the pattern he preferred in *Il pirata* (AA'BA') remained the favourite of Italian composers until the 1850s. Bellini's and Romani's genius for extracting dramatic capital from the theatrical conventions within which they worked is clearest in their handling of the chorus, which is never used merely decoratively: it serves either as a means of creating dramatic atmosphere (the opening storm scene has often been seen as a precursor of that in Verdi's *Otello*) or to make explicit the dramatic context within which the soloists find themselves. It is a remarkable fact that all the arias involve the chorus.

La straniera
The Stranger
Melodramma in two acts (3h)
Libretto by Felice Romani, after Charles-Victor Prévost d'Arlincourt's novel *L'étrangère* (1825)
PREMIERES 14 February 1829, La Scala, Milan; UK: 23 June 1832, King's Theatre, London; US: 10 November 1834, Italian Opera House, New York
CAST Alaide (La Straniera) *s*, Isoletta *ms*, Arturo, Count of Ravenstal *t*, Baron Valdeburgo *bar*, *t*, 2 *b*; *satb* chorus of ladies, knights, fishermen, gondoliers, monks, hunters, guards and vassals

Bellini's first experience of Milan audiences had persuaded him that nothing suited the city so well as originality and boldness. *La straniera*, a setting of a libretto he rightly described as 'abounding in novel situations', accordingly became his most radically Romantic opera, demanding new types of skill from the performers. 'In this opera it is not just a matter of singing,' wrote Romani. 'It is a matter of passion, of soul, of imagination: here is love in all its transports, sorrow with all its sighs, disaster in all its pallor.' Unable to have Rubini – whose singing had contributed so much to the success of *Il pirata* – in his cast, Bellini wrote the tenor part for the young Domenico Reina; towards the end of the year he revised it for a

revival in Naples in which Rubini was to sing, but it enjoyed little success in this form.

SYNOPSIS
The action is set in Brittany, the castle of Montolino and its vicinity, in *c.* 1300. Agnese, queen of France (disguised as Alaide), has been banished to Brittany under the guardianship of her brother Leopoldo (disguised as Valdeburgo), because of the pope's insistence that the king honour an earlier marriage contract.

Act I   Alaide has escaped, and lives in solitude on the shores of Lake Montolino as *la straniera*, a mysterious recluse, suspected of witchcraft by the local people. But Arturo, shortly to be married to Isoletta, daughter of the lord of Montolino, has fallen in love with her. Witnessing a secret meeting between Alaide and Valdeburgo, he challenges the latter to a duel. Valdeburgo slips, apparently drowning, and Alaide is accused of his murder.

Act II   Arturo is prepared to take the blame for the death of Valdeburgo, who however now appears. On the death of the new queen, Alaide / Agnese is summoned back to take her place as rightful wife of the king of France, but not before Arturo, maddened by his passion and the revelation of Alaide's true identity, has stabbed himself to death in the middle of his own wedding to Isoletta.

The premiere of *La straniera*, hugely successful with the public, prompted much debate over the dilemma posed by one critic of the time: 'We do not know whether we should describe the style he has adopted as sung declamation or declamatory song.' For while the melodies in aria and ensemble are even plainer than in *Il pirata*, the recitatives are now full of passages of expressive cantabile singing. As it happened, the contrast with Rossini's florid song was highlighted at the premiere, since the new opera had been preceded by a run of Rossini performances.

The number of arias is small in relation to the ensembles: Arturo himself – and Bellini explained this in terms of the violent instability of his character – has no aria at all. But Valdeburgo's music, composed for Antonio Tamburini, introduces a warmly cantabile quality into Bellini's writing for the baritone voice that had no precedent in Italian opera. The imaginative handling of the chorus and the frequent boldness of modulation testify to Bellini's readiness to explore sonority, texture and colour as means of dramatic expression.

I Capuleti e i Montecchi
The Capulets and the Montagues
Tragedia lirica in two acts (four parts) (2h 15m)
Libretto by Felice Romani (a reworking of his libretto, *Giulietta e Romeo*, written for Nicola Vaccai in 1825), after Matteo Bandello's 16th-century novella *Giulietta e Romeo* and a play of the same name by Luigi Sceola (1818)
PREMIERES 11 March 1830, La Fenice, Venice; UK: 20 July 1833, King's Theatre, London; US: 4 April 1837, St Charles Theater, New Orleans
CAST Capellio *b*, Giulietta *s*, Romeo *ms*, Tebaldo *t*, Lorenzo *bar* or *b*; *satb* chorus of Capulets, Montagues, maidens, soldiers, squires

At the end of 1829, while Bellini was in Venice to supervise a revival of *Il pirata*, Giovanni Pacini withdrew from a contract to write an opera for the same 1829–30 Carnival season. The impresario Lanari persuaded Bellini to come to his rescue by composing a new opera in considerable haste – something he was normally most reluctant to do. The task proved possible partly because Romani was able quickly to rework to Bellini's satisfaction a libretto originally set by Nicola Vaccai four years earlier, and partly because Bellini had a store of good music from his unsuccessful previous opera, *Zaira*, waiting to find a more congenial dramatic home. Eight movements are based on material from the ill-fated *Zaira*, and a further one is a revision of 'Dopo l'oscuro nembo' from *Adelson e Salvini*. The opera was ecstatically received: in Bellini's own words, '*Zaira* was revenged in *I Capuleti e i Montecchi*.' At a revival in Paris in 1832, Maria Malibran, apparently at Rossini's suggestion, replaced the final scene of the opera with the corresponding scene from Vaccai's setting, a piece of highhandedness that was long imitated. Despite its theme, Bellini's opera is only tenuously linked to Shakespeare: Romani made some use of Jean-François Ducis's then fashionable French adaptation of Shakespeare, but his primary sources were Bandello's novella and Sceola's play.

SYNOPSIS

Act I   Thirteenth-century Verona. As warfare threatens again between Guelphs and Ghibellines, Capellio, chief of the Capulets, scorns the offer of a pact, to be sealed by the marriage of his daughter Giulietta with Romeo, and agrees that her wedding with Tebaldo should take place without delay. Having failed to persuade Giulietta to elope with him, Romeo and his supporters enter the city in disguise and interrupt the festivities. Romeo reveals himself as Tebaldo's rival.

Act II   Giulietta is persuaded by the family doctor Lorenzo that her only chance of escaping marriage with Tebaldo is to take a sleeping draught so powerful that she will be taken for dead; when she revives in the family burial vault, he and Romeo will be waiting for her. But Lorenzo's plan goes wrong: he himself is arrested, and Romeo, believing Giulietta to be really dead, comes to her tomb and takes poison. She awakes as he is dying, and when Capellio and Lorenzo rush in in a desperate bid to avert catastrophe they find her, broken-hearted and lifeless, lying on Romeo's body.

Though so much of *I Capuleti e i Montecchi* consists of 'parody' (the reworking of pre-existent music to fit a new text and a new dramatic context) – and parody was doubtless a labour-saving device – Bellini took infinite trouble over the procedure, scrupulously reassessing every detail of the original in the light of its new purpose. After the 'philosophical' austerity of *Il pirata* and *La straniera*, Bellini's lyricism begins to relax and smile a little once more: the swaying 9/8 and 12/8 rhythms, the charming ornamental flourishes at cadences, the many dulcet passages where voices and instruments move in parallel thirds, are all characteristic of his full maturity. The orchestration was much admired by contemporary critics: a striking feature is the several instrumental preludes built around a 'song-without-words' type of instrumental solo. The stretto of the Act I finale ('Se ogni speme è a noi rapita'), where the lovers sing a long ecstatic cantabile melody in unison is one of the earliest and most eloquent examples of what was soon to become a hackneyed device; when Berlioz heard a performance of the opera in Florence in 1831 he was, despite his impatience with what he mistakenly took to be a travesty of his beloved Shakespeare, bowled over by the 'wonderful *élan* and intensity' of this passage. Wagner, for whom the performance of Wilhelmine Schröder-Devrient as Romeo had been one of the great artistic experiences of his youth, acknowledged the influence of Bellini's opera on the second act of *Tristan und Isolde*.

La sonnambula
The Sleepwalker
Melodramma in two acts (2h 15m)
Libretto by Felice Romani, after Eugène Scribe's scenario for Jean-Pierre Aumer's ballet *La somnambule, ou L'arrivée d'un nouveau seigneur* (1827) (music by Ferdinand Hérold)
PREMIERES   6 March 1831, Teatro Carcano, Milan; UK: 28 July 1831, King's Theatre, London; US: 13 November 1835, Park Theater, New York
CAST   Count Rodolfo b, Teresa ms, Amina s, Elvino t, Lisa s, Alessio b, Notary t; satb chorus of peasants

At the end of February 1830, while Bellini was preparing the Venetian premiere of *I Capuleti e i Montecchi*, Victor Hugo's *Hernani* had been performed amid clamorous controversy at the Comédie-Française in Paris. Echoes of *Hernani*'s triumph, which signalled the taking over of the French theatre by the representatives of Romanticism and Liberalism, were heard all over Europe, and in the late summer and autumn Bellini and Romani worked on an operatic adaptation. But, in the wake of the series of political insurrections that had occurred during the year, Italian theatre censorship was tightened up, *Ernani* was abandoned, and the two colleagues turned from a revolutionary subject to what was ostensibly the most socially reactionary of all their operas. *La sonnambula* is an Arcadian idyll in which a group of simple Swiss villagers are saved from the consequences of their folly by the benign protection of Count Rodolfo, the 'signor del villaggio'. With its pastoral setting, its Utopian vision of a harmoniously ordered society, and a happy ending reached by way of situations of great poignancy, rather than by the intrigues of comedy, *La sonnambula* is close in spirit to the first classic of the semiseria genre, Paisiello's *Nina* of 1789.

The principal role in *La sonnambula* was composed for Giuditta Pasta, one of the very greatest of the many remarkable sopranos of that era, a consummate artist with whom Bellini established a working relationship as fruitful as that he enjoyed with Rubini (who took the role of Elvino). He once paid tribute to her 'encyclopaedic' artistry, and proved the point by composing for her not only the gracefully tender Amina, but the more austere and powerfully dramatic roles of Norma and Beatrice di Tenda. Thanks to the combination of the exquisite lyricism of Bellini's full maturity and the incomparable vocal arts of Pasta and Rubini the early performances of *La sonnambula* provided some of the most blissful evenings in the annals of Italian opera. The Russian composer Glinka, who witnessed them, left in his *Memoirs* a vivid account of the scenes in the theatre and of the 'tears of emotion and ecstasy' that were continually shed.

SYNOPSIS

Act I The scene is set in a Swiss village. Scene 1: Outside Teresa's mill the village is celebrating the approaching marriage of the orphan Amina to the wealthy farmer Elvino; only the jealous Lisa, hostess of the local inn, finds it difficult to join in ('Tutto è gioia, tutto è festa'). Amina thanks her friends, especially Teresa, who has loved her like a mother ('Come per me sereno . . . Sovra il sen la man mi posa'). Elvino, who has been praying at his mother's tomb, arrives a little late. But now the civil wedding can proceed ('Prendi: l'anel ti dono'); tomorrow it will be solemnized in church. A stranger enters; though the villagers do not know him, he is in fact Rodolfo, their feudal lord, who, on the death of his father, is returning home after a long absence during which he was himself mourned for dead. Learning that the castle is far off, he decides to stay overnight in Lisa's inn. The village scene brings youthful memories flooding back ('Vi ravviso, o luoghi ameni'); and the sight of the young bride reminds him of his own lost love ('Tu non sai con quei begli occhi'). Evening falls; before making their way home, the villagers tell the sceptical Rodolfo of a ghost that has been haunting the vicinity. Elvino is jealous at the attention Rodolfo was paying his bride, but left alone with Amina he is soon reassured ('Son geloso del zefiro errante'). Scene 2: In a room in the inn, Rodolfo is enjoying his homecoming, and when Lisa comes to inquire after his comfort he flirts with her. They are interrupted when the window opens and Amina enters. Lisa hides, dropping a handkerchief; then, believing that Amina has come for an assignation with the count, she hurries out to alert Elvino. Meanwhile Rodolfo realizes that Amina is sleepwalking; tempted as he is to take advantage of her, he is touched by the words she utters in her dream and goes out, leaving her asleep on the sofa. Villagers come to pay homage to the noble guest, and are perplexed to find no one but a sleeping woman. When Lisa returns with Elvino, the sleeper is revealed as Amina; she awakes, to find herself denounced for her shamelessness. Though she protests her innocence ('D'un pensiero a d'un accento'), Elvino declares that there can now be no wedding; only Teresa is moved by Amina's plight.

Act II Scene 1: A wood. The villagers' affection for Amina has revived, and they set out to the castle to ask Rodolfo to clear up the mystery. Amina and Teresa are also going there, but as they pass Elvino's farm Amina's strength fails her. They meet Elvino, who repulses her again and takes back his ring; even the joyful return of the villagers, and their assurances of Amina's innocence, cannot soften his bitterness ('Tutto è sciolto . . . Ah! perchè non posso odiarti?'). Scene 2: The village. The unhappy Alessio, a peasant

who loves Lisa, learns that Elvino has decided to marry her instead of Amina; Lisa exults in her good fortune ('De' lieti auguri a voi son grata'). Rodolfo explains to Elvino the phenomenon of somnambulism; but neither he nor the villagers credit such unlikely tales. When Teresa produces the handkerchief Lisa dropped in Rodolfo's room, Elvino is ready to despair of womankind; but now they are all astonished to see Amina indeed sleepwalking across the roof of the mill. When she reaches the ground she can be heard praying for Elvino and lamenting the loss of his love ('Ah! non credea mirarti'). Rodolfo prompts Elvino to replace the ring he took from Amina's finger. When she wakes, she finds Elvino kneeling at her feet and her friends rejoicing. The lovers are escorted away to church for the wedding ('Ah! non giunge uman pensiero').

La sonnambula is Bellini's first mature masterpiece: the little world of Amina and Elvino is embodied in music of a rare unity of spirit, yet within that unity the melodic invention is of a prodigal richness. Nothing is lost of the expressive directness his music had gained during his 'philosophical' years; but it is now combined with a new elegance and sensibility, heard at its most beguiling in the duet 'Son geloso del zefiro errante'. Aria forms have become more varied, with less dependence on the tight, symmetrical A–A'– B–A' design of the previous years. Bellini's determination to make even the most conventional and formal parts of the opera dramatically meaningful is vividly shown in the introduction to Elvino's 'Tutto è sciolto', where a recitative sung by Amina – a commentary on Elvino's emotional state – is superimposed on the orchestral melody, a device used again with powerful effect in *Norma*. The sense that the leading characters are part of a close-knit community is conveyed musically by the continual interaction of soloists and chorus: in the majority of the arias and ensembles, the solo voices are at some stage or other set in high relief against a background in which colour and harmony are due as much to the chorus as to the orchestra. In writing for Pasta, Bellini was stimulated to extend the expressive range of his lyricism. The magnificent amplitude of Amina's opening cavatina – which embraces ecstatic introspection, tender recitative-like musings and exuberant virtuosity – is new in his work; and in the closing scene her heart-broken 'Ah! non credea mirarti' has good claims to be regarded as the supreme example of those 'long, long, long melodies' that Verdi so much admired.

Norma

Tragedia lirica in two acts (2h 30m)
Libretto by Felice Romani, after Alexandre Soumet's tragedy *Norma* (1831), and drawing on François René, vicomte de Chateaubriand's *Les martyrs* (1809)
PREMIERES 26 December 1831, La Scala, Milan; UK: 20 June 1833, King's Theatre, London; US: 1 April 1836, St Charles Theater, New Orleans
CAST Pollione *t*, Oroveso *b*, Norma *s*, Adalgisa *s*, Clotilde *ms*, Flavio *t*, 2 Children (sons of Norma and Pollione) *silent*; *satb* chorus of druids, bards, eubages, priestesses, virgins, warriors, soldiers

Of all Bellini's operas *Norma* is the one whose reputation has been least affected by changes in fashion. For his librettist, Felice Romani, it was 'the most beautiful rose in the garland'; and this view was shared by Richard Wagner, who, in his Riga years (1837–9), wrote an eloquent essay on what he called 'indisputably Bellini's most successful composition' (as well as an insert aria for Oroveso, 'Norma il predesse'). He went on to praise Romani's libretto, 'which soars to the tragic heights of the ancient Greeks . . . all the passions, so characteristically ennobled by Bellini's melodies, are thereby given a majestic foundation and support, [and] form themselves into grandiose and distinct pictures, that remind us involuntarily of the creations of Gluck and Spontini'. The mastery of Romani's text was not lightly achieved. Bellini, now at the height of his powers and self-confidence, was exacting in his demands, and many sections of the libretto were written over and over again before they satisfied him.

The role of Norma was designed for Giuditta Pasta. It would be ideal, Bellini told her, for a singer with her 'encyclopaedic' range of expression; and he encouraged her, once she had read Romani's text, to let him know if she had any thoughts on the part which he ought to bear in mind when he was composing. A well-authenticated anecdote reports that she at first disliked 'Casta Diva', finding it ill-suited to her voice; that Bellini promised he would rewrite it, if she practised it faithfully every day for a week and still felt the same; that Pasta agreed, was slowly won over by the splendour of the music and, having sent Bellini a charming gift as an expression of contrition, went on to make her performance of it one of the highlights of the score.

Norma enjoyed a less instantaneous success than most of Bellini's operas; the composer blamed hostile factions in the audience for what he felt had been 'a solemn fiasco'. But it rapidly overcame that initial coolness, enjoying 34 performances before the end of the season, and conquering the whole of Europe in the space of a few years. In view of the reputation the opera now enjoys as one of the most demanding in the repertoire, it is astonishing to see the central position it held in popular music-making in the mid 19th century. When Glinka was in Murcia, southern Spain, in 1845, he witnessed a performance given by a local children's theatre; at much the same time Charles Dickens visited Carrara, where he heard an act of the opera performed in the local theatre with a chorus provided by labourers from the marble quarries. On several occasions during the Risorgimento we hear of music from *Norma* serving as the focus for patriotic demonstrations. In 1848, for example, at a service in the cathedral at Palermo to celebrate the liberation of Sicily from the Bourbons, the blessing of the tricolour was accompanied by a performance of 'Guerra, guerra!', the 'war hymn' from Act II of the opera.

SYNOPSIS

Act I Gaul during the Roman occupation, *c.* 50 BC. Scene 1: The sacred forest of the druids; night. Gaulish warriors and druids, led by the chief druid, Oroveso, process to the oak of Irminsul; at moonrise they expect the druidess Norma, Oroveso's daughter, to signal a revolt against the Romans ('Ite sul colle'). Pollione, the Roman pro-consul, and Flavio enter. Pollione's love for Norma has been quenched by a new passion for Adalgisa, an acolyte in the temple of Irminsul; and, despite an ominous dream, he is determined to take her to Rome and marry her ('Meco all'altar di Venere'). Summoned by a gong, the Gauls reassemble. Norma is angered by their impatience, for all will be lost if they strike too soon; then, while priestesses gather the sacred mistletoe, she invokes the moon ('Casta Diva, che inargenti'). But in reality she still longs to win back Pollione's love ('Ah! bello a me ritorna'). Left alone, Adalgisa prays for relief from the emotions that torment her; but when Pollione appears, urging her to abandon the cruel gods of the North, she agrees to elope the following night ('Va crudele . . . Vieni in Roma'). Scene 2: Norma's dwelling. Pollione has been recalled to Rome, and Norma is troubled by the sight of the children she has secretly borne him. Adalgisa comes to confess her love and seek Norma's guidance; Norma, oblivious of the object of Adalgisa's passion, and touched by the story, readily releases her from her vows ('Sola, furtiva, al tempio . . . Ah sì! fa core, abbracciami'). But when Pollione arrives, the truth is clear. Adalgisa is appalled to learn that he is Norma's seducer, and swears she would rather die than let him abandon Norma. As they argue the temple gong sounds; Pollione is warned that for him it signifies death ('Oh! di qual sei tu vittima . . . Vanne, sì, mi lascia, indegno').

Act II Scene 1: The same. Norma watches over her sleeping children, dagger in hand; would it not be better to kill them than to have them carried off to Rome as slaves ('Dormono entrambi')? Since she must die to atone for her guilt, she solemnly entrusts the children to Adalgisa. But in a long, emotional dialogue she is persuaded that all may yet be well: Adalgisa vows to love Pollione no more, but to bring him back to Norma ('Deh! con te, con te li prendi . . . Mira, o Norma . . . Sì, fino all'ore estreme'). Scene 2: A desolate spot close to the druids' forest. The Gauls eagerly await Pollione's departure, but are dismayed to hear from Oroveso that an even harsher pro-consul has been appointed to succeed him; they must be patient a little longer ('Ah! del Tebro al giogo indegno'). Scene 3: The temple of Irminsul. Learning that Adalgisa's mission to Pollione failed, Norma strikes the sacred shield to summon the Gauls. The hour has come for the Romans to be destroyed ('Guerra, guerra!'); all that is wanting is a victim to sacrifice to the god. Pollione is reported captured while sacrilegiously breaking into the virgins' temple enclosure. Norma insists that she be left alone to question him: unafraid of death, he refuses to renounce Adalgisa ('In mia man alfin tu sei'). Norma calls back the Gauls, orders a pyre to be prepared, and reveals that she is herself the sacrificial victim. Her nobility revives Pollione's love; but Oroveso is deeply ashamed, and only Norma's most eloquent prayers can persuade him to accept guardianship of her children. She is stripped of her sacred insignia, veiled in black, anathematized and led off with Pollione to the flames ('Qual cor tradisti . . . Deh! non volerli vittime').

The greatest Bellini is not necessarily the most sophisticated. The noblest pages of *Norma* tend to be sustained by a harmonic vocabulary of no more than three or four basic chords; and it is the dissonant tensions set up between this 'primitive', impassive harmony and the singing voices that soar above that give the music its weight of expressiveness (the arioso 'Teneri figli' encapsulates the style in a few bars). Similarly, Bellini makes no attempt with his orchestra to emulate the verve and wit of Rossini, let alone to explore the new worlds of sound opened up by his French and German contemporaries. There are some beautifully apt orchestral colours in the score – the cool, sacral flute in 'Casta Diva', for example, or the combination of pure string tone and ominously rumbling timpani in 'Qual cor tradisti' – but Bellini's most astonishing achievement in *Norma* is, amid all the more obvious excitements of musical Romanticism, to have asserted his belief that the true magic of opera depended on a kind of incantation in which dramatic poetry and song are perfectly fused.

'In mia man' – a duet without ensemble singing, in which the melody passes dialogue-like from voice to voice – is an ideal place to observe Bellini's art of conjuring poetry, character and drama into song. For 26 bars, as Norma and Pollione are stalemated in a conflict of wills, the music remains virtually motionless, using a vocabulary of three chords, and giving not the slightest hint of a modulation; a glimpse of possible freedom has the music opening up to the relative C major; and when Pollione declines the proffered bargain, it returns inexorably to the home key; the music turns to the minor, and the delivery of the text accelerates nervously as Norma begins to realize that she has no chance of conquering Pollione's will. And all the time, the melody is exquisitely sculpted around the words, highlighting crucial phrases by tessitura, rhetorical word-repetition or 'madrigalisms'. Such perfect fusion of music with dramatic meaning is to be found everywhere in Bellini's mature works.

Norma follows *I Capuleti e i Montecchi* in discarding the popular convention of an aria finale, complete with cabaletta, for the prima donna. In fashioning the closing scene to match the dramatic catastrophe, Bellini apparently had to overcome the resistence of a nervous impresario. But, in his own words, 'these last two pieces ['Qual cor tradisti' and 'Deh! non volerli vittime'] are of so original a type and so effective, that they have silenced any enemies I might have had . . . I think they are the best pieces I have composed so far.'

Beatrice di Tenda

Tragedia lirica (opera seria) in two acts (2h 45m)
Libretto by Felice Romani, after Antonio Monticini's ballet (1832), which was in turn modelled on Carlo Tedaldi-Fores's tragedy (1825)
PREMIERES 16 March 1833, La Fenice, Venice; UK: 22 March 1836, King's Theatre, London; US: 5 March 1842, St Charles Theater, New Orleans
CAST Filippo Maria Visconti, Duke of Milan *bar*, Beatrice di Tenda *s*, Agnese del Maino *ms*, Orombello, Lord of Ventimiglia *t, t, b; satb* chorus of courtiers, ladies-in-waiting, judges, soldiers

The subject of the opera was chosen by the composer in consultation with Giuditta Pasta (they had seen the ballet together in Milan), against the better judgement of Romani and despite the recognized similarities with Donizetti's *Anna Bolena*. After a tormented and protracted gestation, it proved impossible to complete the finale in time for the premiere, and Beatrice's final cabaletta was borrowed from Bellini's *Bianca e Fernando* (1826); Bellini's sketches for the final scene were realized by Vittorio Gui for a series of influential revivals, beginning in the late 1960s. Romani's distaste for the subject and his exasperation with Bellini prompted him to include in the printed libretto a tactless apology for the imperfections of his text. This led to bitter recriminations with the composer and a complete breakdown of their glorious, if often difficult, collaboration. Contemporary reports suggest that Pasta's dignified stage behaviour and magnificent artistry came close to overcoming the audience's hostility; despite a fiasco, Bellini had no doubt that Beatrice was 'not unworthy of her sisters' and it was the only one of his operas to be published in full score during his life.

SYNOPSIS

Act I   The castle of Binasco in 1418. Filippo finds marriage with Beatrice irksome and has fallen in love with Agnese, while Beatrice regrets the blind passion which, after the death of her first husband, has delivered her and her people into Filippo's tyrannical hands. Agnese, jealous of Orombello's adoration of Beatrice, encourages Filippo to believe that his wife is unfaithful. Because of these malicious rumours Beatrice is unwilling to allow Orombello to lead an uprising of her subjects; as they argue, they are surprised by Filippo, who sees in their *tête-à-tête* confirmation of his suspicions, and orders them both to be clapped in prison.

Act II   Under torture, Orombello has compromised Beatrice; but when brought to trial he makes handsome amends, avowing her innocent of all charges. The judges order further torture for him and Beatrice, but by now the consciences of Agnese and Filippo are troubling them, and when it is reported that Beatrice has steadfastly refused to admit to any crime Filippo's rigour wavers. Enraged, however, to find his castle besieged by people clamouring for Beatrice's release, he signs the death warrant. As Beatrice is led to execution, she forgives the now penitent Agnese, and urges her friends to pray for Filippo.

Bellini felt that he had 'corrected' the horror of the story by his music, which would dispel any sense of disgust by exciting fearful and sorrowful emotions. The opera is notable for the part played by the chorus, which, even more than in Bellini's earlier operas, comments on the action, and advises and comforts the protagonists, altogether in the manner of the choruses of classical Greek tragedy. The relationship of chorus and protagonist is sometimes underlined musically, as in the opening scene, where a theme from the first chorus recurs in varied forms during Filippo's 'cavatina', creating a large-scale, thematically unified scene of a kind that is generally associated with Spontini's and Rossini's 'grand operas', but which was becoming increasingly typical of Bellini's work too. Many solo arias return to the formal A–A'–B–A' scheme of pre-*Sonnambula* days, but they are typical of Bellini's ripest style in their fusion of declamatory and coloratura elements, and in the way he draws out their length by the continuous overlapping of phrases.

I puritani
The Puritans

Opera seria (melodramma serio) in three parts (2h 45m)
Libretto by Count Carlo Pepoli, after the historical drama *Têtes rondes et cavaliers* (1833) by Jacques-Arsène Polycarpe François Ancelot and 'Xavier Saintine' (Joseph-Xavier Boniface), in turn derived from Sir Walter Scott's novel *Old Mortality* (1816)
Composed April 1834–January 1835; rev. December 1834–January 1835
PREMIERES 25 January 1835, Théâtre Italien, Paris; UK: 21 May 1835, King's Theatre, London; US: 22 July 1843, Chestnut St Theater, Philadelphia; rev. version: 14 December 1985, Barbican Centre, London (concert); 1 April 1986, Teatro Petruzzelli, Bari
CAST Lord Gualtiero Valton *b*, Sir Giorgio *b*, Lord Arturo Talbo *t*, Sir Riccardo Forth *bar*, Sir Bruno Robertson *t*, Enrichetta di Francia *s*, Elvira *s*; *satb* chorus of soldiers of Cromwell, heralds and armigers of Lords Talbo and Valton, Puritans, lords and ladies, ladies-in-waiting, pages, servants

When Bellini settled in Paris in August 1833, he was besieged by inquiries about possible new operas; the only project that came to fruition, however, was a commission from the Théâtre Italien. Bellini began work on *I puritani* in April 1834, 'after a year of real solid rest'; and he composed it at a more leisurely pace than any of his earlier operas, 'orchestrating it with such indescribable care that I feel very great satisfaction on looking at every piece I complete'. During the composition he consulted Rossini continually; one of Rossini's several services was to persuade the Théâtre Italien to instal an organ for the quartet in part one.

Bellini met Count Carlo Pepoli at the Paris salon of Princess Belgioioso. A political exile from Italy, he was a fluent versifier who had written poems for Rossini's *Soirées musicales*. But Bellini soon found he was no Romani; his exasperation with Pepoli was to lead to a memorable outburst in which he explained his philosophy in drastic terms: 'Carve in your head in letters of adamant: the music drama must draw tears, inspire terror, make people die, through singing.' Even after the unqualified triumph of the opera he continued to deplore the way in which the strong theatrical situations were undermined by the poor dialogue, the 'repetitive, commonplace and sometimes stupid turns of phrase'.

The four principal singers – Giulia Grisi (Elvira), Giovanni Battista Rubini (Arturo), Antonio Tamburini (Riccardo) and Luigi Lablache (Giorgio) – formed as fine an ensemble as has ever been assembled in an opera house; they are remembered to this day as the '*Puritani* Quartet' because none of the other operas they sang together was so beautifully tailored to match their peculiar gifts, or occasioned so delirious a triumph. Such was the enthusiasm at the premiere and so insistent the demand for encores, especially of the

duet 'Suoni la tromba', that immediately afterwards Bellini had to make a number of substantial cuts to prevent the opera over-running. Already at rehearsals the effect of 'Suoni la tromba' had been so great that it was decided to turn it into a finale: the original second act was subdivided into two, and Elvira's 'mad scene', which had followed the duet, was moved to its present position lest it fell flat after the frenzy that 'Suoni la tromba' seemed bound to provoke.

While in Paris, Bellini was asked by the San Carlo in Naples for a new opera for Maria Malibran, who had just enjoyed a spectacular triumph there in *Norma*. Short of time, Bellini agreed to make an alternative version of *I puritani*, in which Elvira became a mezzo-soprano and Riccardo a tenor. He worked on this in December and January of 1834–5; but the revised score arrived in Naples too late to be fitted into the season, and was not performed anywhere until 1985. It includes music cut from the Paris version after the encore-protracted premiere, but not 'Suoni la tromba', on which Bellini was still working in January 1835.

SYNOPSIS

Part I A fortress near Plymouth. Scene 1: A spacious glacis outside the fortress. Day breaks, reveille sounds, the guard is changed and the soldiers look forward to victory over the Stuarts ('Quando la tromba squilla'); a morning hymn is heard from the fortress, and all rejoice at the thought of the forthcoming marriage of Elvira, daughter of the Puritan governor-general Sir Gualtiero Valton. Riccardo, a colonel in the Puritan army, confides his sorrows to Bruno, a fellow officer: Elvira had been promised to him; but, returning to Plymouth after years of soldiering, he finds that she loves Lord Arturo Talbo, a Cavalier, and that her father is unwilling to force his own wishes on her ('Ah! per sempre io ti perdei . . . Bel sogno beato'). Scene 2: Elvira's apartment. Giorgio, Elvira's uncle, turns her melancholy into joy by telling how he has persuaded her father to allow her to marry Arturo ('Sorgea la notte folta'). Cries from the courtyard announce Arturo's arrival. Scene 3: The armoury. The chorus acclaims the bridal pair; Arturo compares his present happiness with the time he had to woo Elvira secretly ('A te, o cara, amor talora'). Valton has been commanded to escort a lady – a suspected Stuart spy – to appear before Parliament. Arturo speaks with her. She proves to be Enrichetta, the widowed queen, and Arturo vows to save her. Elvira now reappears, in part adorned for the wedding, but carrying her veil. Singing of her happiness, she playfully drapes the veil round Enrichetta ('Son vergin vezzosa'). This gives Arturo an idea of how the queen might be rescued, and as soon as Elvira and her companions have left he veils her and hurries her away. When they are challenged by the jealous Riccardo, Enrichetta, fearing bloodshed, reveals herself; Riccardo allows them to make their escape. The wedding party and Elvira reappear and Valton sounds the alarm and organizes the pursuit. Shock and grief at Arturo's disappearance strike Elvira senseless, and in a dreamlike delirium she imagines herself being married to him ('Oh, vieni al tempio, fedele Arturo').

Part II The fortress. A room with an outlook over the English camp. As Giorgio is describing Elvira's ravings ('Cinta di fiori') Riccardo brings news that Parliament has condemned Arturo to the scaffold. The mad Elvira enters, dreaming still of her lost love ('Qui la voce sua soave . . . Vien, diletto, è in ciel la luna'). Giorgio urges Riccardo to save Arturo; otherwise he will have Elvira's death on his conscience ('Il rival salvar tu dei'). Finally Riccardo agrees; but if Arturo is in the Royalist ranks fighting against them on the morrow, he must die ('Suoni la tromba').

Part III Countryside close to the fortress. A loggia in a garden shrubbery; nightfall. Three months have elapsed. While a storm rages and sounds of distant gunfire are heard, Arturo enters and hears Elvira singing. Despite the danger from passing groups of soldiers, he takes up the song ('A una fonte afflitto e solo'). When she appears he falls at her feet, begging forgiveness, and explains why he had to rescue Enrichetta. The lovers embrace ecstatically ('Vieni fra le mie braccia'). But Elvira's mind darkens once more: she imagines that Arturo is again leaving her, and her screams bring Riccardo, Giorgio and the rest hurrying in. Riccardo announces the sentence passed on Arturo, the word 'death' so shocking Elvira that she recovers her senses. In the face of death the lovers stand united, and even Riccardo is moved to compassion ('Credeasi, misera'). The Puritan soldiery are demanding summary execution when a messenger arrives: the Civil War is over; the Stuarts have been defeated, and a general pardon is issued.

Giulia Grisi was a superb singer, but she lacked the 'encyclopaedic' talents of Pasta, and Bellini had no thought of composing for her a tragedy in the grand manner of *Norma*. In *I puritani* all his old sweetness and pathos return; he himself described the opera as 'fundamentally in the style of *La sonnambula* or Paisiello's *Nina*, with a dash of military robustness, and something of Puritan severity'. It derives the robust and severe qualities from the pervasive march rhythm and from the ever-present sound of brass and drums.

The music that Bellini heard in Paris convinced him that, though the French were almost as skilful as the Germans in their use of the orchestra, they had 'little understanding of what real song was'. Certainly a more sumptuous feast of song than *I puritani* can hardly be imagined. It ranges in style from the sparkling coloratura of 'Son vergin vezzosa' (which may well have been inspired more by the idea of Malibran's voice than of Grisi's) to such ecstatically long-drawn cantabiles as 'A te, o cara'; from the plangent nostalgia of 'Ah! per sempre' to the blood-stirring fervour of 'Suoni la tromba'. Rubini's part in particular is one of the truly fabulous tenor roles, demanding a high C♯ at his first appearance on stage, and moving into the vocal stratosphere in the final scene, with a D in his duet with Elvira, and an F in the last finale.

But Bellini also relished showing the Parisians that he too was capable of orchestral and harmonic finesse. French taste encouraged him to go further than before in breaking down the frontiers between lyrical numbers and recitatives and between solos and ensembles.

In the *introduzione*, he seems to attempt to match French rhythmic sophistication: there are as many changes of metre in this single piece as in whole acts of some Bellini operas. All these elements contribute to make *I puritani* the most sophisticated and brilliant of Bellini's operas. No wonder Rossini, who had once found *Il pirata* 'a little bit lacking in brilliance', was impressed, and regarded this last opera as being, along with *Norma*, the most unmistakable proof of Bellini's greatness.

The largo maestoso from the Act III finale ('Credeasi, misera'), adapted by August-Mathieu Panseron to the text of the Lacrymosa, was sung at Bellini's funeral in Les Invalides on 2 October 1835.

Other operas: *Adelson e Salvini*, 1825; *Bianca e Fernando*, 1826, rev. 1828; *Zaira*, 1829

D.K.

ALBAN BERG

Alban Maria Johannes Berg; *b* 9 February 1885, Vienna; *d* 24 December 1935, Vienna

Although Schoenberg also wrote operas, Berg is the only member of the so-called Second Viennese School whose music can regularly be heard in the opera house. True, his personality was warmer and more outgoing and his style more naturally lyrical than Schoenberg's or Webern's. But one might just as well say that he was simply more interested in the theatre and the voice. From the start, he wrote songs. Some 50 survive from before his 20th birthday, and he wrote another 40-odd during and just after his years of study with Schoenberg. Song-writing was displaced by the long-drawn-out composition of his first opera, *Wozzeck* (1914–22); and *Lulu* occupied him from 1928 until his death in 1935, with interruptions for the cantata *Der Wein* (1929) and the Violin Concerto (1935).

Berg came from a cultivated, well-to-do bourgeois Viennese family where reading and plays were part of normal life. He read widely, knew the best writing of his day, and kept up with the theatre. Both his libretti are direct adaptations of successful stage plays: Büchner's *Woyzeck*, whose Vienna premiere Berg attended in May 1914; and Wedekind's 'Lulu' plays, the first of which Berg had read in 1904, while he saw the second performed the following May. This is in marked contrast with Schoenberg, whose stage works are mostly musical enactments of psychological states or abstract concepts. Yet Berg was strongly under Schoenberg's influence from their first meeting in 1905 until his death 30 years later. Schoenberg claimed it was through his teaching that Berg learned how to write extended instrumental movements, and it was certainly under his tutelage that Berg composed his Piano Sonata, Op. 1, and the String Quartet, Op. 3. Schoenberg seems to have opposed *Wozzeck* as an operatic subject, and in general the relationship between master and pupil preserved hidden tensions, which come out in Berg's sycophantic letters that still give little ground on creative matters.

Musically Berg was certainly indebted to Schoenberg's classically based teaching, with its insistence on good formal models and coherent musical argument. But his style owes more to the pluralism of Mahler, with its rich strata of association, than to the tortured intellectualism of Schoenberg. Later, in adopting Schoenberg's serial method (*Lyric Suite*, 1925–6), he adapted it to the point where it loses its strict cohesive function in Schoenberg's music of the time, and takes on a quasi-secret quality that links it with the hidden ciphers in the music of Schumann, as well as with other features of Berg's own music such as the large-scale palindromes and symmetries in the *Chamber Concerto*, *Lyric Suite* and *Lulu*, the Baudelaire subtext of the finale of the *Lyric Suite*, and the cryptic numbers (10 and 23) which play a part in this latter work.

For all the free-sounding Romanticism and natural sweep of his best music, Berg composed slowly and with great effort. Work on *Wozzeck* was constantly interrupted, first by the First World War, in which he served as an officer cadet and later as an official in the War Ministry, then by the heavy demands of Schoenberg's Society for Private Musical Performance (1918–21), as well as administrative duties in connection with the Berg family estate. Later, while at work on *Lulu*, he suffered poor health (he was a severe asthmatic), and like most Viennese had to endure a drastic decline in his living standards as a result of the hyper-inflation of the mid-1920s. Finally, after the accession of the Nazis to power in January 1933, his music was branded as decadent and excluded from performance in Germany, as well as, increasingly, in Austria, which deprived him of any strong practical incentive to finish *Lulu*. The opera was nevertheless virtually complete when, on Christmas Eve 1935, he died of blood poisoning after a short illness resulting from an abscess on his back. It seems certain that, if penicillin had been available (it came into use in 1941), Berg's life could have been saved.

Wozzeck

Opera in three acts (15 scenes) (1h 30m)
Libretto by the composer, from Georg Büchner's play
Woyzeck (1837)
PREMIERES 14 December 1925, Staatsoper, Berlin; US:
19 March 1931, Academy of Music, Philadelphia; UK:
14 March 1934, Queen's Hall, London (concert);
22 January 1952, Covent Garden, London
CAST Wozzeck *bar*, Drum-major *heroic t*, Andres *lyric t*,
Captain *buffo t*, Doctor *buffo b*, 2 Apprentices *deep b, high
bar*, Idiot *high t*, Marie *s*, Margret *c*, Marie's son *treble*,
Soldier *t*; *satb* chorus of girls, wenches, youths and soldiers
and children

The composition of *Wozzeck* took almost eight years, but Berg worked on it for only a fraction of that time. After seeing the play in 1914, he made some musical sketches and set about adapting Büchner's text, but was then interrupted by the war, and returned to the opera only during 1917 and 1918. Act I was finished by summer 1919, Act II in August 1921, and the final act during the following two months (the orchestration took a further six). During this whole period Berg wrote nothing else, except to complete the *Three Or-*

chestral Pieces (1913–15), with whose final movement (Marsch) the opera shares its style and even some material. The first performance was conducted by Erich Kleiber, who programmed it on his own initiative, with no fewer than 34 orchestral and 14 full rehearsals. It was a *succès de scandale*, with disturbances during the performance and a mixed press afterwards, but it led to a stream of productions in Germany and Austria, before the Nazis consigned it to the dustbin of 'decadent art' after 1933.

For its time, *Wozzeck* now seems a highly modern and topical subject. But the play was in fact some 77 years old when Berg saw it in Vienna (its world premiere was in Munich the previous year). Its author, Georg Büchner, had died of typhus in 1837 at the age of 23, leaving *Woyzeck* unfinished and in an unclear and disorganized state. It was first edited into a coherent text by Karl Emil Franzos in 1879, and this edition was further reorganized by Paul Landau for a 1909 publication which formed the basis of the stage premieres and of Berg's libretto. In adapting this text, Berg cut out a few scenes and conflated two or three others, but he retained the essential character of the play, with its many short scenes, its abrupt and sometimes brutal language, and its stark, if haunted, realism – so unusual for its day, but reflecting the fact that Büchner's source was an actual incident (of 1824) in which an ex-soldier had been executed for the murder of his unfaithful mistress.

Büchner, a post-1830 revolutionary thinker, made his Woyzeck a representative of the downtrodden proletariat; a soldier, because soldiers have always been slaves to a cruel and mindless system, but also the helpless victim of modern social experimentation which is more general and insidious in its effects. It is this aspect of the character that Berg portrays most movingly. Wozzeck's fumbling attempts to articulate his thoughts, and to comprehend and control his passions, reverberate in the music, while the social 'machine', with its fads and statistics masking an essential unconcern for the individual, rolls on in the fugues, rhythmic mechanisms and ostinato effects that Berg also loved.

SYNOPSIS

The square-bracketed designations are from a chart drawn up by Berg's pupil Fritz Mahler; they are not included in the score.

Act I [Five Character Pieces] Scene 1 [Suite]: The captain's room: Wozzeck is shaving him. The captain, a high, yapping, grotesque tenor, philosophizes about eternity. Wozzeck acquiesces to everything in a flat monotone, but when the captain impugns his morality Wozzeck quotes the Bible and adds: 'We poor folk . . . I could be virtuous if I were a gentleman with a hat and a watch and an eye-glass and could talk posh.' Scene 2 [Rhapsody]: An open field outside the town. Wozzeck and Andres, another soldier, are cutting sticks. Wozzeck senses mysterious forces around them, and sees in the sunset 'a fire rising from earth to heaven, and an uproar descending like the last trump'. Andres pooh-poohs him, and sings a hunting song. Scene 3 [Military March and Lullaby]: Marie's room. In the street, Margret comments on

Marie's candid admiration for the drum-major. Marie, Wozzeck's mistress, turns angrily back into the house and sings her child a bitter lullaby. Wozzeck looks in through the window and tries to describe his experience in the field, but will not look at his child, and hurries off to barracks. Scene 4 [Passacaglia]: The doctor's study. The doctor, a caricature of scientific positivism, uses Wozzeck as guinea-pig for dietary experiments. When Wozzeck tries to explain his visions, the doctor is delighted with his 'aberratio mentalis partialis, second species' and gives him a rise of one groschen. Scene 5 [Rondo]: The street outside Marie's door. Marie is again admiring the drum-major. After token resistance, she takes him into her house.

Act II [Symphony in Five Movements] Scene 1 [Sonata Movement]: Marie's room. She is admiring a pair of ear-rings given her by the drum-major. When the child wakes up, she sings him a song about a gypsy. Wozzeck comes in and is at once suspicious of the ear-rings, but gives Marie his pay, leaving her guilt-stricken. Scene 2 [Fantasia and Fugue]: A street in the town. The captain and doctor meet and talk, the doctor pretending to see in the captain's florid complexion and bloated physique signs of fatal illness. Wozzeck arrives and they torment him by hinting at Marie's infidelity. Scene 3 [Largo]: The street outside Marie's door. Wozzeck confronts her, obliquely and apocalyptically, with her infidelity. As obliquely, she denies it, defying him to hit her: 'Rather a knife in my body than a hand on me.' Scene 4 [Scherzo]: The garden of an inn. A band plays a ländler to which the customers dance, and two apprentices sing drunkenly. Marie dances with the drum-major, watched jealously by Wozzeck. There is a hunting chorus and a song for Andres with guitar. Finally an idiot, reading the future, smells blood on Wozzeck. Scene 5 [Rondo con Introduzione]: The guardroom in the barracks. Wozzeck, unable to sleep, complains to Andres of inner voices and a vision of a flashing knife blade. The drum-major arrives drunk and boasts of his success with Marie. The two men fight, and Wozzeck is knocked down.

Act III [Six Inventions] Scene 1 [Invention on a Theme]: Marie's room. Marie reads from the Bible about the woman taken in adultery, and Mary Magdalene. In between, the child presses against her, and she tells him a story about a hungry orphan. Scene 2 [Invention on a Note]: A woodland path by a pond. Marie and Wozzeck walk past. Wozzeck kisses her menacingly, then as the moon rises he stabs her in the throat. Scene 3 [Invention on a Rhythm]: A tavern. A frenzied polka on an out-of-tune piano. Wozzeck is drowning his guilt and sings a folksong. Margret draws attention to the blood on his hand, and he rushes out in a panic. Scene 4 [Invention on a Six-note Chord]: The woodland path by the pond. Wozzeck returns for the knife, which he throws into the pond. Then, frightened by the moon, he decides to throw the knife in farther, wades in and drowns. The captain and doctor pass, comment on the eerie scene, and hurry away. [Orchestral Interlude: Invention on a Key.] Scene 5 [Invention on a Regular Quaver Motion]: The street outside Marie's door. Her child is playing with other children. A child announces that

Marie's body has been found, and they all run off, followed by Marie's child.

Though technically 'atonal' (no key signatures and few definite key centres), Wozzeck is really ambivalent in this respect. Its musical world is Viennese Expressionism, with its violently dissonant gestures, dense textures and steep dynamic gradients. Schoenberg's sprechgesang technique figures prominently. But the music also hints at a simpler, more homely tonal language, which stands for normal life, or elusive happiness, or other concepts opposed to the excess, misery and inhumanity we witness on the stage. Marie's lullaby, Andres's hunting song, and above all the great D minor interlude in Act III, all have this quality. Berg also uses conventional music – ländler, march, out-of-tune polka – ironically, in Mahler fashion (the inn scene in Act I is perhaps the most Mahlerian music Berg ever wrote). In the same way he uses background forms for both structure and irony. It is an open question whether the sonata form of Act II Scene 1 or the rondo of Act II, Scene 5, could ever be heard as such, but there is no mistaking the sarcasm of the fugue in Act II, Scene 2, or the obsessiveness of the passacaglia in Act I, Scene 4, with its 21 variations on a ground (a patent influence on Britten's Peter Grimes). Meanwhile the demoniac repeated Bs in the murder scene and the wild ostinato rhythms in the tavern scene following are obviously straight dramatic devices dignified by formal tags.

A unique feature is the cinematic time flow. Not only do the short scenes intercut like a film montage, but this even leads in Act III to an experimental handling of actual clock time. By cutting from the murder to the tavern (where Wozzeck is already drinking) back to the murder scene (where he is just arriving to look for the knife), Berg both speeds up the action and seems to override the physical limitations of the medium (how can Wozzeck already be in the tavern?). This is in fact an adaptation of a real ambiguity of sequence in the play (which admittedly Büchner might have got rid of in due course), and it influenced later operas like B. A. Zimmermann's Die Soldaten, where cinematic devices are used to suggest multiple layers of action.

In other ways Wozzeck is an authentic renewal of the German tradition of symphonic drama. The five scenes in each act play continuously, linked by interludes, and organized by leitmotifs and recurrent harmonies. And while Berg perfected the hyper-modern idea of symbolic characterization ('Captain', 'Doctor', 'Drum-major', etc.), his musical portraiture is as fine and precise as anything in German opera since Mozart. The humanizing of the potentially subhuman Wozzeck and Marie through the music they sing is one of the great miracles of 20th-century theatre.

Lulu

Opera in three acts (2h 45m)
Libretto by the composer from two plays, Erdgeist (1895) and Die Büchse der Pandora (1903; first performed 1918), by Frank Wedekind
Composed 1929–35; Act III ed. and orch. by Friedrich Cerha, 1974

PREMIERES Acts I and II, plus fragments of Act III:
2 June 1937, Zurich; UK: 1 October 1962, Sadler's Wells,
London (Hamburg State Opera); US: 7 August 1963, Santa
Fe; complete version: 24 February 1979, Opéra, Paris;
US: 28 July 1979, Opera Theater, Santa Fe, New Mexico;
UK: 16 February 1981, Covent Garden, London
CAST Lulu *high s*, Countess Geschwitz *dramatic ms*,
Wardrobe Mistress/Schoolboy/Groom *c*, Medical
Specialist/Banker/Professor *high b*, Painter/Negro *lyric t*,
Dr Schön/Jack the Ripper *heroic bar*, Alwa *youthful heroic*
t, Schigolch *high character b*, Animal-tamer/Acrobat *heroic*
b with buffo flavour, Prince/Manservant/Marquis *buffo t*,
Stage Manager *low buffo b*, Clown *silent*, Stagehand *silent*,
Police Commissioner *spoken role*, 15-year-old Girl *opera*
soubrette, Her Mother *c*, Designer *ms*, Journalist *high bar*,
Servant *deep bar*; pianist, attendants to the Prince,
policemen, nurses, wardresses, dancers, party guests,
servants, workers *silent*

After the premiere of *Wozzeck* Berg was soon on the
look-out for another libretto. He made abortive
sketches for an opera called *Und Pippa tanzt* (1928,
based on a play by Gerhart Hauptmann), but then
decided on an adaptation of Wedekind's 'Lulu' plays.
As before, he himself carried out the textual surgery,
which had to be much more extensive than with
Büchner; and this time he adapted as he composed.
The opera was complete in short score by April 1934,
apart from a few passages in Act III (87 bars in all)
where accompanying detail was implicit rather than
explicit. He then started work on the full score, beginning with what was to be the symphonic suite – the
only music from *Lulu* he ever heard performed (11
December 1935; Erich Kleiber had previously conducted it in Berlin, 30 November 1934), and which
included the Variations and Adagio from Act III.
Finally he scored the opera from the start, and had
reached bar 268 of Act III (out of 1,326) at the time
of his final illness.

To complete *Lulu* therefore involved mainly orchestration, plus a small amount of added harmony and
counterpoint, much of it facilitated by the large
amount of musical recapitulation involved. A vocal
score of Act III (by Erwin Stein) was actually ready
for press in 1936, by which time the composer's
widow, Helene, had asked Schoenberg and Webern
(in vain) to finish and edit the full score. Only later
did she adopt the obstructive attitude that kept the
material of Act III virtually unavailable until after her
death in August 1976. Meanwhile *Lulu* was performed
as a torso, normally with only the end of Act III,
mimed to the music of the Adagio from the suite (the
procedure adopted in Zurich in 1937). Cerha's completion was ready by 1974, but not heard until 1979 in
Paris (conducted by Pierre Boulez), since when the
full version has been widely produced.

SYNOPSIS
Prologue The animal-tamer introduces the beasts
in his menagerie (identified by the music as characters
in the opera). Lulu, the snake, 'created to make
trouble', is carried on and presented in person.
Act I Scene 1: The painter's studio. Lulu is having
her portrait painted, watched by Dr Schön (an
'editor-in-chief') and his son Alwa, a composer. The
dialogue makes clear the men's interest in Lulu, or

hers in them. She offers sarcastic respects to Schön's
fiancée. When he and Alwa leave, the painter makes a
heavy pass at Lulu, chasing her round the studio.
There is a bang on the door, which collapses to admit
her husband, the medical specialist. Seeing the two
together, he has a stroke and dies. Lulu, seemingly
detached from events, allows herself to be taken over
by the painter. Scene 2: A very elegant drawing room.
The painter, now married to Lulu, is rich from the
sale of pictures (fixed, it transpires, by Schön). News
of Schön's engagement arrives in the post. The doorbell rings, and the asthmatic old tramp Schigolch
comes in as the painter retires to his studio. Lulu's
father figure, Schigolch, is delighted to see her living
in luxury. He soon leaves, as Schön arrives. Schön
wants to end their affair and live respectably with his
wife-to-be. They are interrupted by the painter, to
whom, as Lulu exits, Schön obliquely explains the
true situation. Shocked, the painter goes out, ostensibly to confront Lulu, in reality to cut his own throat.
Alwa arrives and they break down the door to reach
the body. Seeing his own engagement 'bleeding to
death', Schön calls the police, as Lulu insists, 'You'll
marry me all the same.' Scene 3: A theatre dressing
room. Lulu is dancing in Alwa's latest work. They
drink champagne and discuss Schön, their own first
meeting, and the prince who wants to marry Lulu and
take her to Africa. As she returns to the stage, Alwa
ponders writing an opera about her. Cheering is heard
from the auditorium as the prince enters, soon followed by Lulu, who has seen Schön in the audience
with his fiancée and has shammed a fainting fit. Left
alone with Schön, she threatens to go to Africa with
the prince, and taunts Schön over his engagement. At
last Schön realizes he cannot leave her. She forces him
to write a letter to his fiancée breaking off their
engagement.

Act II Scene 1: A magnificent room (in Schön's
house). Lulu and Schön are now married. The lesbian
Countess Geschwitz has come to invite Lulu to the
lady artists' ball, but quickly leaves in the face of
Schön's disapproval. Schön and Lulu go out together.
The countess returns and hides. Schigolch and two
other admirers, the acrobat and the schoolboy, come
in from the balcony; Lulu also comes back in, and
they talk. Next Alwa is announced and the admirers
hide, as Alwa declares his love for her. Schön overhears and also notices the acrobat, at whom he points
a revolver; he then takes Alwa out, while the acrobat
finds a new hiding-place. Schön returns and gives
Lulu the gun to shoot herself as the acrobat makes
his escape. Schön now discovers the countess and
locks her in the next room. Continuing his argument
with Lulu he again tries to force her to shoot herself,
but as the schoolboy intervenes she shoots Schön
instead. As Lulu implores Alwa to save her, the police
arrive. Interlude: A silent film depicts Lulu's arrest,
trial and imprisonment, her deliberate infection with
cholera, and her escape from the isolation hospital
disguised as the countess. Scene 2: The same room,
shuttered and dusty. Alwa, the countess and the
acrobat await Schigolch, who is to take the countess
to the hospital to change places with Lulu. The acrobat is to marry Lulu and take her to Paris as his

performing partner. Alwa offers the countess money, Schigolch arrives and leaves with the countess, after which the acrobat himself demands money from Alwa. Next the Schoolboy arrives, but is sent packing in the belief that Lulu is dead. Schigolch then returns with Lulu, who is so physically spoilt by illness that the acrobat abandons the plan and goes off to the police. Schigolch departs to collect train tickets. Left alone, Alwa and Lulu declare their love.

Act III Scene 1: A spacious salon (in a Paris casino). A gambling party is in progress. As the company exit to the gaming room, talk is mainly of their booming Jungfrau shares. The marquis threatens to expose Lulu unless she agrees to be sold to a Cairo brothel. The company returns from the gaming room, all having won. The acrobat also tries to blackmail Lulu, who meanwhile abuses Countess Geschwitz as a pervert. A telegram informs the banker of the collapse of the Jungfrau shares. Schigolch now arrives, also asking for money; but he agrees to lure the acrobat to his hotel and murder him. After a brief exchange with the acrobat, the marquis goes for the police. Lulu contrives that the acrobat and the countess go off together to Schigolch's hotel. As the company learns of the share collapse, Lulu changes clothes with the groom and leaves with Alwa just before the police arrive. Scene 2: An attic room (in London). Alwa and Schigolch await the return of Lulu, now a prostitute, with a client. They hide as she comes in with a professor, and while they are in her room Schigolch goes through his pockets. When the professor has gone, Countess Geschwitz arrives with the portrait of Lulu (which has featured in every scene). Alwa nails it up, and Lulu goes back out, followed by the countess. Alwa tells Schigolch that Lulu has infected him with a disease to which she herself is immune. She returns with a second client, a negro. There is an altercation about payment and the negro kills Alwa. Schigolch goes off to the pub, the countess returns, contemplating suicide. Lulu comes in with her third client, Jack the Ripper. They go into her room, where he murders her. On the way out he stabs the countess, who dies as the curtain falls.

Wedekind's ramshackle and contrived narrative was a challenge to Berg that he was partly, but not wholly, successful in meeting. Too many characters have to be accommodated, and at times (Act II, Scene 1; Act III, Scene 1) they get in each other's way. There are too many stock dramatic devices: the doorbell, the telegram, the exchange of garments, not all strictly germane (the Jungfrau shares). And Berg's use of hidden structural process is incredibly elaborate: a treasure trove for analysts but of mixed significance in the theatre. Unlike the abstract forms in *Wozzeck*, those in *Lulu* are deployed sectionally over large spans of music, intercutting with other processes: for instance, Lulu's conversations with Schön about his engagement (Act I, Scenes 2 and 3) form a large sonata movement whose exposition and development are separated by well over 500 bars of music; similarly Alwa's declarations of love in Act II, Scenes 1 and 2, comprise a rondo, and there are two large sets of variations in Act III. In between come shorter, self-contained units

with such titles as 'Chorale', 'English Waltz', 'Cavatina', or vague generic names like 'Chamber Music I', 'Ensemble I'. Some of them employ strict technical devices such as canon, or isorhythm ('Monoritmica', like the 'Invention on a Rhythm' in *Wozzeck*). The somewhat modish film sequence in Act II is a musical palindrome, marking the high point from which Lulu begins her descent to degradation. Embracing everything is a complex scheme of 'leading sections', in which recapitulation serves to remind us of previous incident, while at the same time giving structure. This comes to a head in the final scene, which is substantially built on such reminiscence, reflecting Berg's idea that Lulu's clients should be the avenging spirits of her former husbands.

Berg's serial technique is another aspect of this plurality of formal procedures. Unlike Schoenberg in *Moses und Aron* (1930–32), he uses several 12-note rows, as well as smaller unordered sets, derived from each other by a variety of more or less convoluted operations. They not only bind the music harmonically and thematically, but also act as leitmotifs: each character has his or her own set or series. But the serial treatment itself is extremely free (as in *Der Wein* and the Violin Concerto); and there is a strong tonal emphasis built into the basic ('Lulu') series, brought out in the derivatives, and dwelt on by the music's harmony and texture.

Whatever the importance of this apparatus, *Lulu* works in the end because of its direct musical beauty and richness of portraiture. As a universal morality about the power of sensual experience, it depends on a broad range of characterization: Lulu has to conquer all sorts and conditions of men. And for this Berg, with his emotional breadth and intellectual focus, was brilliantly equipped. As with the best operas of Strauss, there is a cornucopian feeling about the work as a whole, and an endless fascination in its detail (not least orchestral: the *Lulu* sound is unique). Whether Berg would have significantly tightened or revised the score remains an open question. It would surely have remained an essentially diverse experience, with all the virtues and defects of its genre.

S.W.

LUCIANO BERIO
b 24 October 1925, Oneglia, Italy

Born into a family of professional musicians, Berio was trained from an early age by both grandfather and father, and entered the Milan Conservatory in 1945. His strong sense of the potential of the human voice, first instilled in childhood as he listened to his father giving singing lessons, was fortified during his six years of study at the conservatory by work as an accompanist and as a conductor in provincial opera houses, and above all by his marriage, in 1950, to the singer Cathy Berberian, who was to become so notable an interpreter of his works.

Berio began work for Italian Radio and Television (RAI) in 1952, and there developed an electronic studio. The experience, first encountered at this time, of counterpointing dense layers of sound was to have far-reaching consequences in all aspects of his work. He left RAI in 1961 to take up a series of teaching appointments, first on the West then on the East Coast of the United States. A decade later he returned to Italy, but from 1974 to 1980 established a second base in Paris, where he directed the electro-acoustic section of IRCAM. Since 1987 he has directed his own institute, Tempo Reale, in Florence.

It is a reflection of the vivid, gestural nature of Berio's music in the 1950s that his first work for the stage was for mimes. In 1952–3 he had written two pieces, one orchestral, the other electronic, both entitled *Mimusique*. Having received a commission from the 1955 Teatro delle Novità festival in Bergamo he asked Roberto Leydi to devise a scenario around the orchestral *Mimusique*, adding further music where appropriate. The result, *Tre modi per sopportare la vita*, was a rather wooden Brechtian parable. When the 1959 Venice Biennale requested a mime piece, Berio dusted off his composite score, and requested a new scenario from Italo Calvino. This, the final version, was entitled *Allez Hop* – the cry of a travelling showman, one of whose performing fleas escapes and provokes instructive mayhem.

This first series of ventures established a way of working that was to be repeated in most of Berio's future work in the theatre: only once he had established a general musico-dramatic conception – and indeed often composed a good deal of the music for it – would he turn to a collaborator to find specific images that would give it theatrical focus. Although both of the mime pieces mentioned above told stories, they were the last of Berio's theatrical works to do so. Thereafter, a more complex, 'musical' proliferation of visual and verbal materials that found their theoretical counterpart in Umberto Eco's discussions of the 'open work' became the hallmark of his theatre.

The gradual unfolding of Cathy Berberian's extraordinary gifts as a performer had a profound impact on the development of Berio's sense of theatre. The electronic works that he produced with her – *Thema* (*Omaggio a Joyce*) in 1958, and above all *Visage* in 1960–61 – revealed a complex theatre of the voice that was independent of narrative and, in the case of *Visage*, of words. Furthermore the theatricalization of the concert hall in *Circles*, where circular processes proliferate not just within the music but also visually, on stage, pointed directly onwards to his first piece of vocal theatre, *Passaggio*.

Indeed, many of Berio's works of the mid-1960s underline the theatrical aspect of concert-hall performance: notably *Sequenza III* for voice, and *Sequenza V* for trombone. More significant in developing a 'theatre of the mind' was *Laborintus II* (1965). This multi-layered homage to Dante, in which Berio was able to experiment richly with the fragmentation and counterpointing of texts, was in principle 'open' to theatrical realization, but in the main has proved more effective in the concert hall.

Laborintus II and *Sinfonia* (for eight solo voices and orchestra, 1969) were the essential steppingstones from *Passaggio* to Berio's next theatrical work,

Opera (1970). Precisely because of its rich, multilayered nature, *Opera* has also proved a challenge to effective theatrical realization – yet the difficulties that Berio encountered with it enabled him to see his way towards a form of large-scale theatre in which skeletal narrative structures and proliferating imagery are held in fruitful tension. In consequence, between 1977 and 1984 he was able to produce two full-scale operatic works, *La vera storia* and *Un re in ascolto*, which have held the stage with conviction.

Passaggio
Messa in scena (a punning description: both 'something put on stage' and 'Mass on stage') (35m)
Text by Edoardo Sanguineti
PREMIERE 6 May 1963, Piccola Scala, Milan

Berio's initial conception was of the utmost simplicity: a woman slowly tracing a 'passage' from one side of the stage to the other, stopping at various points along the way to sing texts that would reflect the tortuous relationship described in Kafka's *Letters to Milena*. Looking for a congenial collaborator, he approached the radical young poet Edoardo Sanguineti.

Sanguineti brought to the project both an enriching of subject matter, and a poetic style predisposed to musico-theatrical elaboration. The exclamatory, fragmented style of his poems richly evoked the speaking voice; the counterpoint of images (enhanced by using different languages) suggested simultaneous, but interacting, layers that could be literally realized in the theatre. To Berio's Kafkaesque point of departure, he added images inspired by Rosa Luxemburg's prison diaries. The female protagonist, 'She' (the only solo vocal part), now enacts at each of her stopping-points, or 'Stations' (by analogy with those of the Cross), a skeletal story of being hunted down, arrested, brutally interrogated, and finally released into the squalor of an urban bedsit awash with a tangled jumble of possessions. Most of this we infer from visual clues, and from the reactions of two choruses: it is confirmed when, at the end, the singer puts acting behind her, and revisits each site, acknowledging what was represented there. 'She' herself is absorbed in an interior monologue devoted to more intimate memories: of search and sexual arousal, of an idyll in a garden relapsing into nightmare, etc. – the latter in particular echoing Berio's original conception.

But the essence of the drama lies in the tension between what happens on the stage and what happens beyond it. In the pit, alongside the instrumental ensemble, is an eight-part singing chorus that assumes its traditional role as commentator, amplifying the action. More crucial, however, are five speaking groups dispersed around the auditorium giving brutally revealing voice to the reactions of a bourgeois audience. In a counterpoint of Italian, French, English, German and Latin (the latter pointedly reserved for moments of self-confirming gravitas), they invoke social order; abuse, lust after, and cheer on the torture of the protagonist; offer bids for the auction of a 'perfectly domesticated woman'; and chant lists of consumer goods that metamorphose into a catalogue of weapons.

The overtly confrontational element in *Passaggio* was to re-emerge from time to time in Berio's work. But while capitalizing on the technical experiments of *Passaggio*, Berio's theatre was from now on to move into more complex dimensions.

La vera storia
The True Story
Opera in two parts ('a full evening')
Libretto by Italo Calvino
PREMIERES   9 March 1982, La Scala, Milan; UK: 14 May 1994, Royal Festival Hall, London (semi-staged)
CAST   Leonora *s*, Luca *t*, Ada *ms*, Ivo/Commandant *bar*, The Condemned Man *b*, Ugo/Priest *t*, at least 2 Street-singers, Passers-by I, II and IV *actors*, Passer-by III *s*, 3 Voices in the Street; *satb* chorus of at least 60 voices; speakers, mimes, dancers, acrobats

Berio started with his own musico-dramatic conception, and indeed had already begun work on the music before he invited Calvino to fine down the project into a concrete libretto. Part I is built from three interacting but now closely related levels. The first of these concerns the popular feast, or *festa*, embodied in four large choral sections that show collective life in all its ambivalence: anarchic ebullience, sadism in the face of a public execution, rebellion against an oppressive regime, and, when that rebellion is crushed by the authorities, stoic resignation.

Within this framework, Berio and Calvino use individual protagonists to operate what is in effect a structural analysis of the conventions of 19th-century opera. Individual protagonists have names, but little more. They act out a series of stock situations whose emotional urgency is taken entirely seriously, but unembellished by narrative detail. Clearly *Il trovatore* lies in the background: a baby is stolen in an act of revenge, two brothers – one powerful, one not – fight for the love of a passive heroine. The music abets the analytical process: characters wedded to action sing clean, urgent lines, while those to whom circumstance denies the chance of action proliferate into melismatic settings of richly poetic texts. A third level of commentary, some of it decidedly ironic, is provided by a series of six popular ballads, of which the last two, both reflecting Berio's studies of folk music, acquire remarkable intensity.

Part II synthesizes the disjunct verbal and musical material of Part I into a powerful and continuous flow. It reinterprets the framework of Part I in grimly contemporary terms. But in the urban police state of Part II the power of the authorities is omnipresent: the popular solidarity of the Part I *festa* has been silenced; the chorus on stage is almost mute (its powers of articulation being transferred to disembodied voices in the orchestra, as in *Passaggio*), and where individuals dare to raise their voice they are no longer 'characters from an opera' but nameless 'passers-by'. The same story of police brutality and revenge, of revolt and suppression, is enacted, but now under circumstances where, if the voice of stoic resignation that ended Part I is to be heard at all, it behoves the creatures of operatic fiction from Part I to re-enter at the end of Part II and sing on behalf of a silent and utterly crushed chorus. It is one of Berio's bleakest and most powerful conceptions.

Un re in ascolto
A King Listens
'Musical action' in two parts (1h 30m)
Libretto by the composer, after Italo Calvino, W. H. Auden and Friedrich Gotter
PREMIERES   7 August 1984, Kleines Festspielhaus, Salzburg; UK: 9 February 1989, Covent Garden, London
CAST   Prospero *bar*, Producer *t*, Friday *actor*, Female Protagonist *s*, Soprano I (with her Pianist), Soprano II, Mezzo-soprano, 3 Singers *t*, *bar*, *b*, Nurse *s*, Wife *ms*, Doctor *t*, Lawyer *b*, Singing Pianist; Mime (Ariel), Messenger, Stage Designer and Assistants, Seamstress, A Lady to Saw in Half, Acrobats, Clown, 3 Dancers and others, *silent*; *satb* chorus; accordion-player

Un re in ascolto started life as a parable, proposed by Calvino, about a king who deciphers the collapse of his kingdom and the infidelity of his queen from what he hears listening in his palace. Berio transmuted this figure into an elderly theatrical impresario, so closely at one with his latest project – a search for 'another theatre' for which *The Tempest* is to serve as a vehicle – that he himself is called Prospero, and his theatre becomes his island. Prospero listens because he is auditioning a series of three singers in the hope of finding the ideal female protagonist for his production. But his hopes of finding his fantasies made flesh are confounded – indeed each woman addresses to him the same disturbingly personal message. He can never hope to capture the essential 'otherness' of a desired woman within his own world.

Meanwhile his new project is slipping from his control. An ambitious producer is turning it into an extravaganza quite alien to his own aspirations. In desperate revolt he finally starts to tear down some of the producer's scenery, but collapses.

At the start of Part II he is found where he fell (Berio originally intended the whole musical action to be continuous). Realizing that he is dying, those nearest to him react with predictable self-interest, but his players initiate a ragged ceremony of watching with the dying man. Prospero, by now wholly absorbed in his own dreams, takes on the role of the 'listening king' from which Berio and Calvino started – but does so recognizing that his kingdom is not essentially that of lights and scenery, but rather that of 'the sea of music'. Thus fortified, he can now confront one final apparition: the female protagonist for whom he was searching enters to confront him with a summation of all that he has heard during the three auditions: the distance between them is immutable. His players bid him farewell, and, left alone on the island of his theatre, Prospero dies.

Recurrent musical threads run through *Un re in ascolto*. The female protagonist's aria sums up the musical, as well as the verbal materials of Auditions I and II. Three of the four concertati for Prospero's players share common materials. Above all, Prospero's five arias on listening (settings of monologues by Calvino that survived from the original project) all use the same restricted pitch field, and in consequence abound in similar melodic gestures. But it is above all the subtlety of Berio's mature harmonic language, accommodating as it does many echoes from previous generations, that gives *Un re in ascolto* its singular expressive power.

Other operatic work: *Opera*, 1970, rev. 1977

D.O.-S.

IRVING BERLIN
Israel Baline; *b* 11 May 1888, Tyumen', Russia; *d* 22 September 1989, New York

Having moved with his family to New York at the age of five, Irving Berlin worked at an early age as song-plugger, chorister, singing waiter and ultimately song-writer. Despite his lack of formal musical training, he was always able to write songs – both music and lyrics – seemingly effortlessly, in any idiom desired. Whether ragtime ditties, sentimental waltzes, suave 1930s dance tunes, patriotic rousers, blues or up-to-date 1940s show tunes, Berlin's songs always have a persuasive rightness about them, sounding deceptively like the sort of simple songs his listeners imagine they could write themselves – until they try it.

Annie Get Your Gun
Musical comedy in two acts (1h 45m)
Libretto by Herbert and Dorothy Fields; lyrics by Irving Berlin
PREMIERES 16 May 1946, Imperial Theater, New York; UK: 7 June 1947, Coliseum, London; rev. version: 31 May 1966, New York State Theater, New York

A fanciful version of the life of Wild West Show sharp-shooting star Annie Oakley and her love for fellow performer Frank Butler, the show was originally planned for Jerome Kern. Berlin took over the project after Kern's death, and it has held the stage for decades. The score comprises an amazing collection of Broadway classics, the best-known of which include 'You Can't Get a Man with a Gun', 'The Girl That I Marry', 'They Say It's Wonderful', 'Moonshine Lullaby', 'Sun in the Morning', 'Anything You Can Do' and 'There's No Business Like Show Business'. A revision made for a 1966 revival with the original star, Ethel Merman, added one new song and eliminated a sub-plot with its two songs.

Other musicals include: *Watch Your Step*, 1914; *Stop! Look! Listen!*, 1915; *The Cocoanuts*, 1925; *Face the Music*, 1932; *Louisiana Purchase*, 1940; *Miss Liberty*, 1949; *Call Me Madam*, 1950; *Mr President*, 1962

J.A.C.

HECTOR BERLIOZ
Louis-Hector Berlioz; *b* 11 December 1803, La Côte Saint-André, Isère, France; *d* 8 March 1869, Paris

Opera should have been at the centre of Berlioz's composing career, as it was of his life. The musical culture in which he grew to maturity was dominated by it. Once he had decided to be a composer (against the will of his doctor father, who wanted him to take up medicine), opera became his goal. Everything conspired to make him see music – requiem mass, secular cantata, above all opera – as a dramatic, expressive art: his own instincts; the precepts of his teacher Jean-François Le Sueur; the example of Gluck and Spontini and also of Antonio Salieri, Antonio Sacchini, Étienne Méhul and Luigi Cherubini, whose works he immersed himself in from his first arrival in Paris in 1821 and whose cause he defended against the, to him, frivolous, undramatic values of Rossini; and, in the mid-1820s, the discovery of Weber through the performances of *Der Freischütz* at the Odéon. A large part of Berlioz's apprenticeship was practically lived in the opera house (and in the library, where he pored over and analysed the scores he had heard). Even the revelation of Beethoven at the Conservatoire Concerts from 1828 onwards – the crucial event in the evolution of his musical personality and the catalyst that precipitated the *Symphonie fantastique* – did not alter the fundamentally dramatic bias of his outlook. Symphony became a branch of dramatic music, to be developed in the direction opened up by Beethoven's Fifth, Sixth and Ninth. But opera remained a major preoccupation.

Yet it was symphonic and choral, non-operatic music that, in the event, absorbed the greater part of his compositional energies. Though the *Symphonie fantastique* and its successors, *Harold en Italie*, *Roméo et Juliette* and the *Symphonie funèbre et triomphale*, may contain quasi-theatrical elements, as do – even more – the 'dramatic legend' *La damnation de Faust* and the oratorio *L'enfance du Christ*, they were all conceived as concert works. In a career of 40 years Berlioz completed only four operas (five, if we count the lost ballad opera *Estelle et Némorin* of 1823): the first version of *Les francs-juges* (a medieval drama of tyranny and intrigue composed in 1824–6 and musically influenced by Méhul), *Benvenuto Cellini*, *Les troyens* and *Béatrice et Bénédict*.

It was certainly not for want of trying that he did not write more. Throughout his career there was usually some operatic project or other under consideration. Subjects he actively contemplated included *Antony and Cleopatra*, *Romeo and Juliet* (many years after the composition of his symphony on the play) and Scott's *The Talisman*. Undoubtedly Berlioz was more choosy than most of his contemporaries (in the end he became, like Wagner, his own librettist), and also more idealistic and demanding in his attitude to performance. The low standards that his work as music critic brought him daily into contact with may at times have discouraged him from writing operas. But the chief reason was simply the hostility and scepticism of the Paris operatic establishment. In the age of Auber, Meyerbeer and Halévy, Berlioz was not regarded as a good commercial investment: he was an eccentric, and besides – in the pigeonholing way of musical opinion in Paris – he was a 'symphonist' and therefore unfitted for writing opera.

The failure of *Benvenuto Cellini*, which was due to a

combination of factors, among them the extreme technical difficulty of the score and the unfashionably colloquial style of the libretto, effectively ended Berlioz's hopes of establishing himself as an opera composer in Paris. He never had another commission there. As a brilliant and widely read critic, and as protégé of the influential daily newspaper the *Journal des débats*, he could not be entirely ignored; and for a few years, during the 1840s, he was in negotiation with the Opéra to set a libretto by Eugène Scribe, *La nonne sanglante* ('The Bleeding Nun'), based on M. G. Lewis's Gothic novel *The Monk*. The surviving numbers show him making some effort to accommodate his style to the tastes of the Opéra. But neither party had much belief in the collaboration; the project languished, and the libretto was eventually set by Gounod.

In the last 25 years of his career Berlioz's only direct involvement with the Opéra was as musical consultant to productions of operas by Weber and Gluck. In 1841 he composed recitatives for *Der Freischütz* (spoken dialogue being forbidden at the Opéra) and orchestrated Weber's piano rondo *Invitation to the Dance* for the obligatory ballet; and in 1861 he supervised a revival of *Alceste* (repeated in 1866). This followed the Théâtre Lyrique's immensely successful revival, in 1859, of *Orphée*, with Pauline Viardot, in an edition by Berlioz which adapted Gluck's Paris revision of the score to the title role's original alto pitch. It is in this edition that the opera is still usually given.

Berlioz's most regular operatic activity consisted in reviewing the endless succession of mostly ephemeral works that came and went on the Paris stage. The theatrical adaptation of *La damnation de Faust* which he planned to give (under the title *Méphistophélès*) in London in the late 1840s, during his period as musical director of Adolphe Jullien's Grand English Opera at Drury Lane, remained only an idea: Jullien went bankrupt before work could begin on it or on another unspecified opera intended for Jullien. Of Berlioz's last two operas, *Béatrice et Bénédict* was commissioned by a foreign theatre. *Les troyens* he wrote, in the first place, for himself. Then, having completed libretto and score in two years, he spent five years trying to get it put on, and in the end had to settle for performances of Acts III to V only, themselves in truncated form, by an opera house whose resources were inadequate.

Berliozian opera does not lend itself to generalization. In his output as a whole each major work inhabits its own poetic world, with an atmosphere and a style unique to it. The three completed operas of his maturity are quite unlike each other. *Béatrice et Bénédict*, outwardly, is a conventional opéra comique, breaking no new ground. *Benvenuto Cellini* is a most unconventional combination of comedy and grand opera and musically a work of great originality – in terms of rhythm especially, years ahead of its time. *Les troyens* harks back to classical tragédie lyrique and its successor, Spontinian grand opera, but it fuses them with the expressive language of Berliozian musical Romanticism at its most fully developed and highly charged. It has taken the musical world a good hundred years to realize that the work which resulted from this idiosyncratic mixture is among the supreme achievements of the 19th century – in Tovey's words, 'one of the most gigantic and convincing masterpieces of music-drama'.

Benvenuto Cellini

Opera semiseria in two acts (2h 45m)
Libretto by Léon de Wailly and Auguste Barbier, after Cellini's *Memoirs* (1558–66; published 1728)
Composed 1834–8, rev. 1851–3
PREMIERES 10 September 1838, Opéra, Paris; rev. version: 20 March 1852, Hoftheater, Weimar; UK: 25 June 1853, Covent Garden, London; US: 3 May 1975, Boston
CAST Benvenuto Cellini *t*, Giacomo Balducci *b*, Teresa *s*, Ascanio *ms*, Fieramosca *bar*, Pope Clement VII *b*, Francesco *t*, Bernardino *bar*, Pompeo *bar*, Innkeeper *t*; *satb* chorus of metalworkers, foundrymen, maskers, guards, monks, the Pope's retinue, Balducci's female servants and neighbours, people of Rome; dancers

Berlioz apparently did not read the *Memoirs* of Benvenuto Cellini ('that bandit of genius', as he called him) until after his return from Italy in 1832. Yet in an important sense the opera springs from the 15 months he spent there as winner of the Prix de Rome. It celebrates Italy – not the Italy he experienced during his time in Rome (like Mendelssohn, who was there at the same time, he found contemporary Italian culture depressingly decadent and lethargic) but its Renaissance counterpart, an ideal Italy where art is proud and vital and held in high public esteem. The Renaissance artist-hero was a cult among the Romantics (cf. Delacroix's *Michelangelo in his Studio*). The libretto, freely adapted by Barbier and Wailly from Cellini's *Memoirs* (with *commedia dell'arte* additions), showed the triumph of the unorthodox, embattled artist over obstructive officialdom and conventional, academic art – a subject with which Berlioz could identify strongly – in a setting that evoked the colour and energy of 16th-century Rome.

In its original form (1834), that of an opéra comique (i.e. with spoken dialogue), it was turned down by the director of the Opéra-Comique. The following year a revised version, in which Alfred de Vigny had a hand, was accepted by the Opéra, and the work was given there three years later (with Pope Clement VII replaced, at the insistence of the censor, by a cardinal). It had a stormy reception and ran for only four performances (followed by three of Act I only plus a ballet). The opera remained unperformed for 13 years and in 1844 Berlioz used material from it for his concert overture *Le carnaval romain*. On becoming kapellmeister at Weimar, Liszt, a great admirer of the work, chose it as his second major production (the first was Wagner's *Lohengrin*). For the first Weimar performances, in March 1852, Berlioz revised the score, shortening it slightly, simplifying some of its technical difficulties and, with German taste in mind, removing or toning down its more burlesque elements. Before it was given again, in November 1852, Liszt suggested more drastic surgery in the form of a large cut in the final act, removing many scenes so as to achieve a much swifter dénouement. Berlioz concurred; but in order to save a few of the numbers involved he placed them earlier in the action.

This shorter, three-act 'Weimar version' was the one in which the work was generally known and performed for the next hundred years. Recently, however, there has been a return to the fuller two-act form and more logical scene order of the Paris *Cellini* of 1838 (as well as to the pope) and even, beyond that, to spoken dialogue, as in the original opéra-comique conception. (In this connection it is significant that for a production proposed by the Théâtre Lyrique, in 1856, the opera was to have been given with spoken dialogue instead of recitatives.) The Paris version, plus spoken dialogue and the pope, was the form in which Covent Garden presented the opera in 1966; and most subsequent performances, as well as the complete recording based on Covent Garden material, have done the same. So does the following synopsis.

SYNOPSIS
Act I Tableau 1: Shrove Monday, Rome; Balducci's house, evening. Balducci, the papal treasurer, is unhappy because the pope has commissioned the Florentine metalworker Cellini, instead of the official papal sculptor, Balducci's prospective son-in-law Fieramosca, to make a statue of Perseus. Maskers, Cellini among them, annoy Balducci by singing a Carnival song under his window. He goes off angrily. Cellini and Teresa, Balducci's daughter, decide to elope the following night. Fieramosca overhears their plan ('Demain soir, mardi gras'). When Balducci returns, Cellini gets away, but Fieramosca is given a drubbing. Tableau 2: Shrove Tuesday evening; Piazza Colonna, with tavern courtyard and, opposite, Cassandro's open-air theatre. Cellini and his metalworkers sing to the glory of their art ('Honneur aux maîtres ciseleurs'). They plot public revenge on the papal treasurer for the meagre advance payment for Perseus: one of Cassandro's actors will impersonate him in the satirical pantomime about to be performed. Fieramosca and his friend Pompeo plan to foil the abduction of Teresa. Fieramosca brags of his fencing skill ('Ah! qui pourrait me résister'). The revellers have gathered for Cassandro's show, *King Midas with the Ass's Ears*. Among them are Balducci, Teresa, Cellini, Ascanio (Cellini's apprentice), Fieramosca and Pompeo – the last four dressed as monks. Balducci is furious and a fight breaks out between the 'monks'. Cellini kills Pompeo. He is seized and about to be taken away when the Sant'Angelo cannon proclaims the end of Carnival. All lights are extinguished and in the confusion Cellini escapes.

Act II Tableau 3: Ash Wednesday; Cellini's studio, dawn. As a religious procession passes, Teresa and Ascanio pray for Cellini's safety ('Sainte Vierge Marie'). A moment later he appears: they must get away to Florence immediately. Before they can leave, Balducci enters with Fieramosca and denounces Cellini ('Ah! je te trouve enfin'). Their quarrel is interrupted by the arrival of the pope, impatient to see if his Perseus is finished. He grants general absolution ('A tous péchés pleine indulgence') but gives Cellini

an ultimatum: pardon and Teresa if the statue is cast that day. If not, he will hang. Tableau 4: That evening, in Cellini's foundry in the Colosseum, Ascanio looks forward to their 'bronze offspring's baptism of fire' ('Tra la la, mais qu'ai-je donc?'). Cellini gives way to weariness and longs for the simple life ('Seul pour lutter – sur les monts'). Fresh setbacks now threaten him. Fieramosca insists on their fighting a duel. In Cellini's absence the men down tools. But their mood changes when Fieramosca reappears and tries to bribe them to leave Cellini's service; Fieramosca is forced to help in the foundry. The pope arrives and commands the casting to begin. Suddenly Fieramosca announces that they are running out of metal. But Cellini orders his men to throw all his finished works of art into the crucible. The metal fills the waiting mould and the statue is cast. The pope acknowledges divine sanction for Cellini's labours, and all praise the art of the master metalworkers.

Berlioz's own verdict on *Benvenuto Cellini* – 'a variety of ideas, a vitality and zest and a brilliance of musical colour such as I shall perhaps never find again' – hardly seems excessive when the work is performed well. These qualities were, of course, its undoing. The music's rhythmic complexity, its constantly changing pulse and syncopation of orchestral colour, and the sheer pace at which things happen – the means by which the composer evokes the agitated, exuberant life and times of his hero – made it exceptionally difficult to perform. The final section of Fieramosca's fencing aria, to take one example, is metred successively in 7, 6 and 5 – this long before conductors were taught to deal with such irregularities.

Even now it is a virtuoso score, for chorus (male chorus especially) as well as orchestra. The best numbers are also among the most demanding: notably the huge, and hugely vivacious, tumultuous Carnival scene (in which, as Liszt said, 'for the first time in opera the crowd speaks with its great roaring voice') and the swift-moving yet lyrically expansive Act I trio 'Demain soir, mardi gras', music as scintillating as anything by Berlioz. Other striking numbers or passages include the E major prayer sung by Teresa and Ascanio against a background of liturgical chanting, with its softly glowing woodwind scoring; the firecracker finale of the sextet (the whole ensemble shows Berlioz's gift for comic music); the pungent Musorgsky-like recital of the innkeeper's bill for wine; the graphically evocative rhythms and colours of the forging scene; Harlequin's beautiful love song (cor anglais, harp, cello, with comments from the crowd) contrasted with Pasquarello's parody cavatina on ophicleide (tuba) and thumping bass drum, complete with ludicrously prolonged final cadence. The opera's characteristic blend of grandeur and levity is epitomized in the dramatic and musical treatment of the pope – a personage at once awesome and profoundly cynical who, however, places supreme value on art.

La damnation de Faust
The Damnation of Faust
Légende dramatique in four parts (2h 15m)

Text by Gérard de Nerval, Almire Gandonnière and the composer, based on Part 1 of the play *Faust* by Johann Wolfgang von Goethe (1808)

PREMIERES   6 December 1846, Opéra-Comique, Paris (concert); 18 February 1893, Salle Garnier, Monte Carlo; UK: 7 February 1848, Drury Lane, London (Parts I and II; concert); 3 February 1894, Liverpool; US: 12 February 1880, Steinway Hall, New York (concert); 7 December 1906, Metropolitan, New York

Of all Berlioz's dramatic concert works from the *Symphonie fantastique* (1830) to *L'enfance du Christ* (1854), *La damnation de Faust* is closest to the opera house. (For long its popularity eclipsed his actual operas.) Berlioz himself at one time planned to adapt it to the stage; the project, however, came to nothing when the company for which it was intended, Jullien's Grand English Opera at Drury Lane, collapsed in bankruptcy. The appeal of its brilliantly evocative scenes to theatre directors is easy to understand. Yet in its existing form *La damnation* is an opera of the mind's eye, not of the stage. As John Warrack has said, 'The pace is different, the arena impalpable and too varied, the dramatic logic not that of the theatre but of a listener with an imagination able to free itself from physical surroundings and to course with the composer in a flash of thought from scene to scene or dwell upon a held mood of hilarity or tenderness or terror.' If the work suggests any visual medium, it is the cinema that its dramatic technique anticipates.

Berlioz originally composed eight disparate 'Scenes from *Faust*', settings of songs and ballads taken from Nerval's translation of *Faust Part 1*, which he read in 1828. By the time he embarked on a full-scale work, 17 years later, *Part 2* – the redemption of Faust – had been published; but it was *Part 1* (which had ended with the clear implication that the hero will be damned) that he chose to set. The Nerval numbers, revised, were incorporated into a structure which, though episodic, is no more so than Goethe's play. The central idea that governs and binds Berlioz's scenes is Faust's progress towards a deeper and deeper isolation and emptiness of soul – urged on by a Mephistopheles who is the dramatization of his own dark self – as, one by one, all his aspirations turn to dust.

Les troyens

The Trojans
Opera in five acts (3h 45m)
Libretto by the composer, based on Books 1, 2 and 4 of the *Aeneid* by Virgil (*c*. 19 BC)
Composed 1856–8, rev. 1859–60
PREMIERES   Acts III–V, *Les troyens à Carthage*: 4 November 1863, Théâtre Lyrique, Paris; Acts I–II, *La prise de Troie*: 6 December 1890, Grossherzogliches Hoftheater, Karlsruhe; Acts I–V, condensed: 18 May 1913, Königliches Hoftheater, Stuttgart; UK: Acts I–II, *La prise de Troie*: 18 March 1935, Theatre Royal, Glasgow; Acts III–V, *Les troyens à Carthage*: 19 March 1935, Theatre Royal, Glasgow; Acts I–V, with a few cuts: 6 June 1957, Covent Garden, London; complete: 3 May 1969, King's Theatre, Glasgow; US: Acts I–V, condensed: 27 March 1955, New England Opera Theater, Boston; complete: 26 September 1983, Metropolitan, New York
CAST   Cassandre (Cassandra) *ms*, Chorèbe (Corebus) *bar*,

Enée (Aeneas) *t*, Ascagne (Ascanius) *s*, Panthée (Panthous) *b*, Priam *b*, Ghost of Hector *b*, Hécube (Hecuba) *s*, Hélénus (Helenus) *t*, Polyxène (Polyxena) *s*, Andromache *silent*, Astyanax *silent*, Greek captain *b*, Didon (Dido) *ms*, Anna *c*, Iopas *t*, Narbal *b*, Hylas *t*, Mercure (Mercury) *bar* or *b*, 2 Trojan soldiers 2 *b*, Priest of Pluto *b*; *satb* chorus of Trojans, Greeks, Tyrians, Carthaginians, nymphs, satyrs, fauns, sylvans, invisible spirits

The roots of Berlioz's culminating masterpiece lie far back in his boyhood, in the passion for Virgil's *Aeneid* that he conceived while studying Latin under his father's tuition. The characters of the *Aeneid* became familiar inhabitants of his inner world; they were so real to him, he later wrote, that 'I imagine they knew me, so well do I know them.' Though the idea of basing an opera on the fall of Troy and the founding of Rome must have often been in his mind in the intervening years, it was not until the early 1850s that he began to think really seriously of doing so. At first he resisted it, knowing that in the climate of the time the likelihood of the Paris Opéra accepting such a work, by a composer of his dubious reputation, let alone performing it adequately, was practically nil. But in 1856, prompted by the recent unexpected success of his oratorio *L'enfance du Christ* and by the urgings of Princess Carolyne Sayn-Wittgenstein, Liszt's mistress, with whom he had discussed the project on his visits to Weimar (and who made it her mission to get the work written), he changed his mind. Beginning in May 1856, he wrote *Les troyens*, poem and score, in less than two years.

In structure and language the libretto is influenced by the example of Berlioz's beloved Gluck. At the same time it borrows important features (though not its ancient-world subject) from Parisian grand opera: among them the five-act form, the central role of the chorus, the spectacular crowd scenes and the large forces, including stage bands. A further influence is Shakespeare – not only in the Act IV love duet, whose text is inspired by Lorenzo's and Jessica's 'In such a night' in *The Merchant of Venice*, but, generally, in the mixture of genres and juxtaposition of sharply contrasted scenes and in the wide geographical scope of the action. Berlioz described the work as 'Virgil Shakespeareanized'. Reshaped with great skill, the *Aeneid* – chiefly Books 1, 2 and 4, but other parts of the epic as well – provides the material for most of the text, part of which is a direct translation from the Latin.

If the libretto of *Les troyens* contains elements that were old-fashioned by the standards of the day, the music is Berlioz at his most audacious and richly expressive; it is both a summing up – a merging of the two main streams of his compositional life, the operatic and the dramatic-symphonic – and a reaching out into new territory.

Despite its grand scale *Les troyens* is not an exceptionally long opera. But before a note had been heard it had acquired the reputation of being so; and that reputation seemed confirmed when Berlioz subsequently made two operas of it, *La prise de Troie* and *Les troyens à Carthage*. The Théâtre Lyrique, whose offer he had accepted when the Opéra continued to make no serious move to put on *Les troyens*, decided that the work's demands were too great for its resources, and insisted on his dividing it in two; and, so that he could hear it before he died, he reluctantly agreed. In the event only *Les troyens à Carthage* was given and, even then, extensive cuts were made during the run of 21 performances. For nearly a century *Les troyens*, when it was played in the theatre, was given mostly as a two-part work on successive evenings, or, if on one evening, in drastically shortened form. It was not until the near-complete *Troyens* at Covent Garden in 1957 that Berlioz's original conception was vindicated: that of a single epic of the destiny of a people and its tragic consequences in the lives of individual human beings.

SYNOPSIS

Act I   Troy: the abandoned Greek camp outside the walls. The Trojans celebrate their deliverance from ten years of siege. They hurry off to look at the huge wooden horse left by the Greeks, many believe, as an offering to Pallas Athene. Cassandra, the Trojan prophetess and daughter of King Priam, foresees the fate of Troy – the people, led by the king, going blindly to their doom, and with them her betrothed, the young Asian prince Corebus, whom she will not live to marry ('Malheureux roi'). When Corebus appears she rejects his soothing words and, as her vision takes shape, prophesies the destruction of Troy. She urges Corebus to save his life by leaving at once. He dismisses her terrors ('Quitte-nous dès ce soir'). Trojan leaders lay thank offerings at a field altar but their rejoicing breaks off at the arrival of Andromache, widow of Hector, the Trojan hero and son of Priam. Aeneas rushes in and describes the appalling death of the priest Laocoön, devoured by sea serpents as he was inciting the people to burn the wooden horse. The whole assembly is struck with horror ('Châtiment effroyable'). Aeneas interprets the portent as Athene's anger at the sacrilege. Priam orders the horse to be placed beside the temple of the goddess. Cassandra's warning cries are ignored. The torchlit procession draws near, chanting the sacred hymn of Troy ('Du roi des dieux, ô fille aimée'). Suddenly it halts: from within the horse has come a sound like the clash of arms. But the people, possessed, take it as a happy omen. Cassandra hears the procession pass into the city.

Act II   Tableau 1: A room in Aeneas' palace. The ghost of Hector appears to Aeneas and tells him that he must escape and found a new Troy in Italy ('Ah! fuis, fils de Vénus'). Corebus enters at the head of a band of armed men. He reports that the citadel is holding out. They resolve to defend it to the death. Tableau 2: A hall in Priam's palace; at the back a high colonnade. Women pray before an altar to Vesta ('Ha! puissante Cybèle'). Cassandra prophesies that Aeneas will found a new Troy in Italy. But now Corebus is dead, and she would rather take her own life than fall into the hands of the Greeks. Those women too frightened to face death are driven out. The rest, in growing exaltation, vow to die with Cassandra ('Complices de sa gloire'). Cassandra stabs herself. Greek soldiers announce that Aeneas has escaped with the treasure of Troy. With a last cry of 'Italie!',

some of the women throw themselves from the colonnade, others stab or strangle themselves. Fire engulfs the palace.

Act III   Carthage (the city founded by Dido after she fled from Tyre and her brother Pygmalion, murderer of her husband Sychaeus); a hall in Dido's palace, decorated for a festival, on a brilliant day after storms. The people celebrate their city and their queen ('Gloire à Didon') and promise to defend her against the Numidian king, Iarbas. Builders, sailors and farmworkers are presented with symbolic gifts. Alone with her sister Anna, Dido confesses to a mysterious sadness. She denies she is pining for love, and resists her sister's argument that she should marry again. But to herself she admits the appeal of Aeneas's words ('Sa voix fait naître dans mon sein'). Iopas, the court poet, announces the arrival of an unknown fleet, driven ashore by the storm. Dido, recalling her own wanderings ('Errante sur les mers'), gives the strangers audience. Trojan chiefs enter, and Ascanius, Aeneas' son, presents trophies from Troy. Panthous explains Aeneas' mission: to found a new Troy in Italy. Narbal rushes in with the news that Iarbas and his hordes have attacked. Aeneas, till now disguised, offers the dazzled queen an alliance and, after entrusting Ascanius to her care, leads Trojans and Carthaginians to battle.

Act IV   Tableau 1 (*Royal Hunt and Storm*): A forest near Carthage. Naiads bathing in a stream take fright at the sound of hunting horns and vanish as huntsmen enter the clearing. A storm breaks. Dido and Aeneas, separated from the rest, take refuge in a cave and there acknowledge and consummate their love, while satyrs and wood nymphs utter cries of 'Italie!'. The storm passes. Tableau 2: Dido's garden by the sea; night. Narbal and Anna discuss the situation, he full of foreboding, she optimistic: 'Fate calls Aeneas to Italy . . . Love is the greatest of the gods'. Dido, Aeneas and the court watch dances performed to celebrate victory over the Numidians. Iopas, to soothe the queen's restless mood, sings of the fruits of the earth ('O blonde Cérès'). Dido learns from Aeneas that Andromache has married Pyrrhus, son of Achilles the slayer of her husband Hector. She feels absolved ('Tout conspire à vaincre mes remords'). All contemplate the beauty of the night ('Tout n'est que paix et charme'). Alone, Dido and Aeneas pour out their love ('Nuit d'ivresse et d'extase infinie'). As they leave, Mercury appears by a column on which Aeneas' arms are hung and, striking the shield, calls three times 'Italie!'.

Act V   Tableau 1: The harbour of Carthage; night. Hylas, a young Phrygian sailor, sings of his longing for the forests of Mount Ida ('Vallon sonore'). Panthous and the Trojan chiefs agree they must delay their departure for Italy no longer. Two Trojan sentries fail to see why they should go. Aeneas enters, determined to leave but torn by love and remorse ('Inutiles regrets'). The ghosts of dead Trojan heroes appear and urge him to be gone. He rouses the sleeping army. Dido, distraught, confronts him. But her entreaties and her curses are equally vain. Tableau 2: A room in the royal palace. The Trojan fleet is seen setting sail. Dido orders a pyre, on which she will burn all memorials of Aeneas. Alone, she resolves on her death and takes farewell of life, friends and city ('Je vais mourir . . . Adieu, fière cité'). Tableau 3: A terrace overlooking the sea. Narbal and Anna pronounce a ritual curse on Aeneas. Dido ascends the pyre. To the horror of all she stabs herself with Aeneas' sword. Before doing so, she has prophesied the coming of a great conqueror – Hannibal – who will avenge her wrongs. But her final vision is of Eternal Rome.

As a musical epic and a dramatization of Virgil, *Les troyens* necessarily encompasses a wide variety of scenes and atmospheres. It is Berlioz's richest, most eventful score, embracing at one extreme the panoply of the *Royal Hunt and Storm* and the procession of the wooden horse and at the other the chamber-music intimacy of Dido's 'Adieu, fière cité'. But the composer is at great pains to unify its wealth of incident, not only by large-scale tonal design but also by means of innumerable recurring motifs, melodic, harmonic and rhythmic, of which the *Trojan March*, the fateful hymn heard in Acts I, III and V, is only the most obvious. Musically as well as verbally, the central idea of Roman destiny is a constant presence.

At the same time, contrast is a fundamental principle governing the musico-dramatic structure of the work. There is, first and most striking, the contrast between the musical idioms of Acts I and II (Troy) and III and IV (Carthage) – the one harsh, jagged, possessed, rhythmically on a knife edge; the other warm, expansive, sensuous. Then there is the contrast between one act and the next: Act I spacious and, for much of its course, static, followed by the violent, highly compressed Act II – Troy on its final, fatal night – itself giving way to the Arcadian picture of peaceful Carthage in Act III, which, however, like Act I, ends with a fast-moving, highly dramatic and martial finale. Act IV is a sustained lyrical interlude, a time out of war, but ending with a grim reminder of the great questions of fate and war which will come to a head in Act V, the act that draws together and completes the preceding four.

There are also continual smaller-scale contrasts of musical character and dramatic perspective: the Trojans' rejoicing interrupted by the mime scene for the grieving Andromache, with its long clarinet melody, classical as a Grecian frieze, itself followed abruptly by Aeneas' brief, hectic narration of the death of Laocoön and the horror-struck ensemble it provokes; the sudden shift of focus from high romance and affairs of state to the feelings of ordinary people caught up in the tides of history, as Hylas the young sailor sings of his longing for his lost homeland; the Trojan chiefs' earnest discussion of policy giving way to the low-life grumbling of two sentries, for whom 'Italy' means nothing more significant than danger and discomfort, and whose homely dialogue in turn yields to the anguished, exalted mood of Aeneas' monologue, with its extended melodic lines, panting rhythms and heroic orchestration.

The central theme of the work is embodied in music of truly heroic temper. Yet Berlioz has no illusions about great 'causes' and what they can do to the lives of individuals. The juggernaut of Roman destiny rolls across the personal fates of two contrasted but complementary tragic heroines, Cassandra and Dido. Cassandra is virtually Berlioz's own creation, developed from a few glimpses in the *Aeneid* into the fiery protagonist of the opera's first two acts; she is the personification of Troy's doom, which she foresees but is powerless to prevent. The role of Dido is the composer's tribute – a tribute of extraordinary radiance, tenderness and expressive intensity – to the mythical but to him totally real person who had first possessed his imagination 40 years before.

Béatrice et Bénédict

Opéra comique in two acts (1h 30m)
Libretto by the composer, after William Shakespeare's play *Much Ado About Nothing* (1598–9)
Composed 1860–62, rev. 1863
PREMIERES 9 August 1862, Neues Theater, Baden-Baden; 4 June 1890, Opéra-Comique, Paris; UK: 24 March 1936, Glasgow; US: 21 March 1960, Carnegie Hall, New York (concert); 3 June 1964, Lisner Auditorium, George Washington University, Washington, DC
CAST Béatrice (Beatrice) *s*, Bénédict (Benedick) *t*, Héro (Hero) *s*, Claudio *bar*, Don Pedro *b*, Léonato (Leonato) *spoken role*, Ursule (Ursula) *ms*, Somarone *b*; *satb* chorus of people of Sicily, musicians, choristers, lords and ladies at the governor's court; dancers

As early as 1833 Berlioz had contemplated composing an opera on *Much Ado About Nothing*. In the event it was to be his last major work, written nearly 30 years later to inaugurate the new opera house at the fashionable spa town of Baden-Baden in Germany. Since the mid-1850s the manager of the casino, Edouard Bénazet, had engaged Berlioz to give an annual gala concert at the height of the season, with an élite orchestra assembled for the occasion and rehearsed for as long as was necessary. In 1858 Bénazet commissioned an opera from him. The libretto, by Edouard Plouvier, concerned an episode from the Thirty Years War. Berlioz, however, felt little enthusiasm for it, and persuaded Bénazet to release him from his contract (Plouvier's libretto was set by Henry Litolff) and to agree instead to an opera, with spoken dialogue, on *Much Ado*.

Béatrice et Bénédict ('Bénédict' was the standard French form of Shakespeare's 'Benedick') was composed to a text by Berlioz himself, closely based, for the most part, on the play. The Baden-Baden performances of August 1862 were followed by a production, in German, at Weimar in the spring of 1863, with two numbers added to the second act (the women's trio and the distant chorus). In this form the opera was revived at Baden-Baden the following August.

Berlioz had first thought in terms of a one-act opera. Even at its full length *Béatrice* contains only 15 numbers, separated by mostly very short dialogue scenes. The work is a divertissement on one aspect of the play. Composing it, he said, was 'a relaxation after *Les troyens*' – 'I have taken as my text part of Shakespeare's tragi-comedy.' There is no Don John, no sinister sub-plot, no Dogberry and the Watch; and Claudio remains a shadowy figure. The drama consists in 'persuading Beatrice and Benedick that they love each other', and in contrasting with their complex but ultimately more rewarding relationship the conventionally starry-eyed romance of the 'sentimental couple', Hero and Claudio. Somarone, the portrait of a pedantic, fussily conscientious court musician of the old school, is Berlioz's invention, derived from Shakespeare's Balthasar, whose song 'Sigh no more, ladies' comes at the same point in the action as Somarone's *Epithalame grotesque*, and prompts the same comment from Benedick: 'An he had been a dog that should have howled thus, they would have hanged him.'

SYNOPSIS

Act I In the park of the governor, Leonato, the inhabitants of Messina joyfully await the return of the victorious army from the Moorish wars. Hero, Leonato's daughter, learns that Claudio has come back loaded with honours. Beatrice inquires about 'Signor Mountanto' – that is, Benedick, between whom and Beatrice (Leonato explains) 'there is a kind of merry war – they never meet but there's a skirmish of wits'. After a *sicilienne*, the people disperse. Hero reflects on the happiness of being reunited with Claudio ('Je vais le voir'). Beatrice and Benedick mock each other in a duet whose teasing manner does not conceal an exasperated mutual interest ('Comment le dédain'). Don Pedro congratulates. Claudio. Does the example not tempt Benedick? But Benedick is impervious to their jests; he will die a bachelor ('Me marier?'). Don Pedro and Claudio decide to find a way of tricking Beatrice and Benedick into loving one another. Court musicians rehearse the epithalamium which the choirmaster Somarone has written for the bridal couple. Benedick overhears an apparently serious discussion between Don Pedro, Leonato and Claudio about the wonderful behaviour of Beatrice, who has actually fallen in love with him. Benedick, astonished but impressed, resolves to requite her ('Ah! je vais l'aimer'). Hero and Ursula, too, laugh about the deception practised on Beatrice, who has been made to overhear that Benedick has fallen hopelessly in love with her. The two girls sink into a sweetly melancholy reverie on the beauty of the night and the impending wedding ('Nuit paisible et sereine').

Entr'acte: Reprise of the *sicilienne*

Act II A room in the governor's palace. From near by come the shouts of soldiers calling for drink, and Somarone's voice improvising a song in honour of Sicilian wines ('Le vin de Syracuse'). Beatrice enters, in great agitation. She recalls her unexpected sadness when Benedick left for the wars, and her dreams of him during his absence ('Il m'en souvient'). Then, with sudden decision, she faces her feelings: 'Contempt, farewell and maiden pride, adieu: Benedick, love on – I will requite you.' Hero and Ursula affect astonishment to see Beatrice at once agitated and strangely softened. With her they sing of the happiness of a bride about to marry the man she loves ('Je vais d'un coeur aimant'). Alone, Beatrice listens to a distant chorus summoning the bride. Benedick enters, and the two skirmish in a new key. Their embarrassed exchange is cut short by the wedding march. Claudio and Hero sign the contract. The scrivener produces a

second one. 'Who else is marrying?' asks Don Pedro. Beatrice and Benedick confront each other. Each denies loving the other 'more than reason'. Avowals of love in their own hands are produced to confound them. A sign is brought in with the words, 'Here you may see Benedick the married man', which all sing to the music to which Benedick (trio, Act I) swore he'd never marry. Unabashed, Benedick ripostes by acknowledging the power of love and the giddiness of mankind ('L'amour est un flambeau').

Berlioz described *Béatrice et Bénédict* as 'a caprice written with the point of a needle'. It is his most light-fingered score, echoing in a gentler vein the rhythmic high spirits and wit of *Benvenuto Cellini*, and bathed in a kind of late-afternoon glow. The woodwind writing is piquant and luminous. Prominent also are pizzicato strings and finely shaped violin lines of the utmost delicacy. Trombones play only in the latter part of the overture, the middle section of Beatrice's aria, the 13-bar *enseigne* (No. 14) and the final tutti. Tambourines and guitar add a touch of exotic colour. The exuberant overture alludes to half-a-dozen different numbers. Its angular, lilting theme in triplets, full of cross-rhythms, reappears in the final number, in which Benedick and Beatrice, declaring a temporary truce, sing of love as a 'will-o'-the-wisp', a brief but enchanting gleam that 'comes from nowhere and then vanishes, to the distraction of our souls'. The other best numbers include the men's trio 'Me marier?', with its nimble musical repartee; the charming women's trio 'Je vais d'un coeur aimant' in Berlioz's favourite slow 6/8 time; also in 6/8, the nocturne sung by Hero and Ursula, music of great economy used to evoke a mood of deep enchantment; and the noble, long-breathed andante (interrupted by martial sounds reminiscent of *Les troyens*) in which Beatrice recalls her sadness when Benedick left for the wars.

D.A.C.

LEONARD BERNSTEIN

b 25 August 1918, Lawrence, Massachusetts, US;
d 14 October 1990, New York

Bernstein worked with huge success in the fields of both classical music and the Broadway musical theatre. He wrote ballets, musicals and later in life returned to opera. Some of his works, such as *Candide*, have been performed both in theatres and in opera houses. One of his most distinctive contributions was the development of a new direction for popular music-theatre in *West Side Story*.

He first achieved fame as a conductor (studying with Fritz Reiner and serving as assistant to Sergey Koussevitzky and Artur Rodziński). A last-minute substitution for Bruno Walter with the New York Philharmonic in November 1943 led to a huge demand for Bernstein as both conductor and composer. Within months, he had composed the highly successful one-act ballet *Fancy Free*, and he followed it with an impressive series of concert pieces over the following years. His position as principal conductor of the New York Philharmonic from 1956 to 1966 (the first American-born conductor to hold that post), and his television appearances as a commentator on music, made him one of the most familiar faces in American music. In the years following his departure from the Philharmonic, he became one of the most prominent international conductors of his time.

At the same time, Bernstein involved himself with musical theatre on an ever-increasing level of musical complexity and sophistication. He achieved success in many genres, and all but one of his stage works (an unsuccessful collaboration with Alan Jay Lerner) have retained an active stage life. He several times expressed the belief that a living American opera literature can evolve only from its popular musical theatre, and his own efforts contributed to that development. He ranks among the handful of popular composers who had the ability to orchestrate their own musicals (though he in fact delegated part, sometimes all, of this work to others). His first efforts for the Broadway stage aspired to be little more than well-crafted entertainments, but beginning with *Candide* he took pains to unify his theatre scores motivically and to find opportunities for extended musical development. The essay 'Why Don't You Run Upstairs and Write a Nice Gershwin Tune?' from his book *The Joy of Music* (1960) reveals his disappointment that after two musicals he had not produced a truly popular song, but *West Side Story* (in particular, its film version) changed that. Unfortunately, thereafter he composed only sporadically for the musical stage.

On the Town
Musical comedy in two acts (1h 45m)
Libretto by Betty Comden and Adolph Green, based on an idea by Jerome Robbins
PREMIERES   28 December 1944, Adelphi Theater, New York; UK: 30 May 1963, Prince of Wales Theatre, London

Suggested by the ballet *Fancy Free*, this light-hearted show tells of three sailors on 24-hour shore leave in New York City, finding adventure and love. In addition to its tuneful songs (most familiarly 'New York, New York') it features extended dance sequences originally choreographed by Jerome Robbins. The MGM film (1949) omits much of Bernstein's score and adds new songs.

Candide
Comic operetta in two acts (2h 30m: 1988 version)
Libretto by Lillian Hellman (rev. versions, by Hugh Wheeler), based on the novel by Voltaire (1756); lyrics by Richard Wilbur; additional lyrics by John Latouche, Dorothy Parker, Hellman, Bernstein and (in rev. versions) Stephen Sondheim
Composed 1954–6, rev. 1973, 1988–9
PREMIERES   1 December 1956, Martin Beck Theater, New York; UK: 30 April 1959, Saville Theatre, London; US: published rev. version: 18 December 1973, Chelsea Theater Center, Brooklyn, New York

The journey of Voltaire's eponymous hero from naïve optimism to disillusioned knowledge of the world's evil is told in a mock-operetta style. Its music covers a wide range, from allusions to various popular styles (tango, schottische, waltz) through mock operetta, to some passages of fully operatic weight. Its most familiar portions are the pseudo-Rossinian overture (probably Bernstein's most performed concert piece) and the coloratura soprano aria, both sincere and parodistic, 'Glitter and Be Gay'.

Far more popular in revival (sometimes by opera companies) than during its brief Broadway run in 1956, *Candide* has undergone sweeping revisions since its troubled conception. The music used in the Broadway premiere (pre-production manuscripts included many songs and lyrics not used in that production) corresponds to that in the published vocal score and, with some sections omitted, to the original-cast recording. For the first London production, Bernstein supplied a new song ('We are Women'). Then, in a series of US West Coast productions, the libretto was revised and different music was used, culminating in a full-scale revival which began in San Francisco and ended in Washington, DC, closing before its intended Broadway opening.

The 1973 revision, conceived and directed by Harold Prince, moved to Broadway in 1974 and had a successful run there. It became the usual performing version thereafter. Hugh Wheeler supplied a new libretto to replace Hellman's, in one act and with a quite different sequence of events (more faithful to Voltaire in some respects), often more farcical in tone, and with Pangloss and the governor combined into a single role to be played by Voltaire as narrator. Five numbers were omitted and Stephen Sondheim supplied minor lyric revisions as well as words for three new songs.

John Mauceri, who had assembled the music for the 1973 production, performed the same service for New York City Opera when it added *Candide* to its repertoire in 1982. This was closely based on the 1973 version (Prince was still directing), but in two acts and with the five missing songs restored, mostly in new contexts (sometimes with new lyrics, by Wilbur).

A 1988 Scottish Opera production, with yet another reconsidered libretto (still credited to Hugh Wheeler) and additional restorations, established another new text. This adaptation by John Wells and Mauceri aimed to include as much of Bernstein's music as possible, and was able for the first time since 1971 to use the locations, if not the words, of Hellman's libretto. A 1989 concert and a recording by the composer in London used primarily the Scottish Opera version but introduced revisions and restorations of its own.

West Side Story
Musical in two acts (2h)
Libretto by Arthur Laurents, based on a concept by Jerome Robbins after William Shakespeare's *Romeo and Juliet* (1597); lyrics by Stephen Sondheim
PREMIERES   19 August 1957, National Theater, Washington, DC; UK: 12 December 1958, Her Majesty's Theatre, London
CAST   Maria *s*, Tony *t*, Anita *ms/dancer*, Riff *bar/dancer*, Bernardo *bar/dancer*, 4 *adult spoken roles*, dance chorus of

Jets and Sharks (all named roles, with speaking and singing)

West Side Story is now regarded as a classic musical. Among its many important features, it was a landmark in granting dance a central place in the musical, in allowing extended compositional techniques, and in permitting a truly tragic ending. But it was only a moderate success in its first productions. The 1961 film version introduced it to a far wider audience and boosted it to a popularity it has retained ever since. One of the few shows as famous for its dance music (composed by Bernstein rather than relegated to an arranger, and later collected by him in a concert suite) as for its songs, *West Side Story* includes Bernstein's most memorable melodies.

SYNOPSIS
Act I New York's West Side in the 1950s. A dance 'prologue' depicts the growth of the rival gangs, the longer-established Jets (led by Riff) and the Puerto Rican Sharks (led by Bernardo). Tony, a former Jet, meets Maria (Bernardo's sister) at a community dance ('Dance at the Gym'); the two fall in love ('Maria'), not realizing that they are supposed to be enemies. While the two pledge their love ('Tonight'), the Shark women engage in cynical banter about the relative advantages of Puerto Rico and New York ('America') and the Jets prepare for a meeting with the Sharks ('Cool'). Riff and Bernardo arrange a rumble to settle the gang rivalry. Having just exchanged private wedding vows with Maria ('One Hand, One Heart'), Tony interrupts 'The Rumble', trying to make peace, but unintentionally allows Anita his friend Riff to be killed; enraged, he kills Bernardo.

Act II Happily waiting for Tony's return ('I Feel Pretty') Maria instead hears that he has killed her brother. She manages to forgive him ('Somewhere'), and the two determine to flee together; he goes into hiding for the night with the Jets, who are themselves bewildered by the turn of events ('Gee, Officer Krupke'). Anita tries to carry a message from Maria to Tony, but is so abused by the Jets that she instead tells him that Maria is dead. In despair, Tony allows himself to be killed by the Sharks. Only Maria's intervention, pointing out what everyone has lost by the war, stops the bloodshed and provides a hint of some hope for the future.

Other operatic works: *Trouble in Tahiti*, 1952; *Wonderful Town*, 1953; *Mass*, 1971; *1600 Pennsylvania Avenue*, 1976; *A Quiet Place*, 1983, rev. 1984

J.A.C.

HARRISON BIRTWISTLE

(Sir) Harrison Birtwistle; *b* 15 July 1934, Accrington, Lancashire, England

Birtwistle has made a more significant contribution to opera than any other British musician of his generation. He studied at the Royal Northern College of Music (1952–5) and was a member of the New Music Manchester group along with Alexander Goehr, Peter Maxwell Davies, John Ogdon and Elgar Howarth. The Group performed new music, in line with the preoccupation with Webern characteristic of young Continental composers of the time; medieval techniques of composition also formed a strong area of interest. However, the earliest works Birtwistle himself acknowledges date only from 1957, and his first operatic work, *Punch and Judy*, was not written until 1967.

Birtwistle worked as a schoolteacher until a Harkness Fellowship in 1965 enabled him to take up musical studies in America and devote himself to composition. *Punch and Judy* was followed by *Down by the Greenwood Side* in 1969 and in 1973 he embarked on *The Mask of Orpheus*, a project that would not be completed for another ten years. All these works exhibit the interests in mythic narration (whether from classical or English sources), ritualistic patterning and different ways of organizing time that are essential features of Birtwistle's musical thinking. While the subject matter of all these pieces includes murder, violence is tempered by a melody-based style and by dramatic resolutions incorporating the idea of regenerative life force.

In 1975 Birtwistle became the first musical director of the National Theatre, composing incidental music notable for its cohesion with the accompanied dramatic action. *Bow Down* (1977) is a piece that sits midway between theatre and opera in the requirements from its performers. In 1983, Birtwistle took on the more advisory post of associate director, music, and has composed prolifically since then. A television opera, *Yan Tan Tethera*, was written in 1984; *Gawain and the Green Knight* was premiered at Covent Garden in 1991, and *The Second Mrs Kong* was the first new opera to be premiered in the new Glyndebourne opera house.

The somewhat fortuitous appearance of three major scores in 1986 (*The Mask of Orpheus*, *Yan Tan Tethera* and *Earth Dances*) was followed by London festivals of Birtwistle's music in 1987 and 1988; all of which served to establish him at the forefront of modern composition. Official recognition of his standing came with a knighthood in June 1988.

Birtwistle's entire output depends on ideas of musical drama, and the resulting musical language seems ideally suited to the combination of narrative, word, movement and music. Several features are constant throughout Birtwistle's music. One is the technique of creating textures from a single line, embellished with adjacent notes and proliferated via doublings at the octave or fifth. This gives a firm sense of direction even within very complex passages, and enables the violence of many musical gestures to be counterbalanced by an elegiac melodic style which often moves via semitone or tone steps. Alongside this, the consistent use of ostinato patterns enables harmonic, rhythmic and melodic structures to be followed by the ear. Another consistent technique is that of presenting fragments of music again and again, but juxtaposed differently with each other. This is similar to Edgar Varèse's approach to composition, centred on the use of what he called 'musical objects'; blocks of sound appear alongside, above or below each other, as if spatially (rather than harmonically) related. The music is seen from different angles, distances and perspectives, so to speak. This in turn involves a distinctive approach to time: different temporal schemes are explored in order to exhibit the ceaseless interaction of what has passed and what is present. This concern for the 'sanctity of the context', in Birtwistle's phrase, has grown and become ramified in recent years. Thus different versions of narratives (often traditional stories) may be presented in a single operatic work, intercut with each other and with other strands of narrative. This moves the audience away from the sense of being told a story, towards considering the status of the story itself as a lived experience. A literary parallel might be found in the Bergsonian exploration of time and memory in Proust's novel *À la recherche du temps perdu*.

If Stravinsky and Messiaen are two composers for whom Birtwistle acknowledges great respect, they also suggest themselves as the nearest comparisons in this century for a composer who has created a distinctive voice in working and reworking musical concepts with clarity and vision as well as extremism.

Punch and Judy

Comical tragedy or tragical comedy in one act (1h 45m)
Scenario and libretto by Stephen Pruslin
PREMIERES 8 June 1968, Jubilee Hall, Aldeburgh, Suffolk; US: 12 February 1970, Guthrie Theater, Minnesota Opera, Minneapolis
CAST Punch *high bar*, Judy/Fortune-teller *ms*, Pretty Polly/Witch *high s*, Choregos/Jack Ketch *low bar*, Doctor *basso profondo*, Lawyer *high t*, 5 mime dancers

Birtwistle's first operatic work became something of a *cause célèbre* when Benjamin Britten and Peter Pears vacated their box some time before the end of the premiere. One reviewer remembered the performance as seeming 'almost gratuitously offensive'; another described it as 'the baby's tantrum beneath our civilized sociability'. Birtwistle himself has referred to it as a central work in his output, acting as a source for other pieces. The music has the Expressionistic energy of other music-theatre pieces from the 1960s (such as Peter Maxwell Davies's *Eight Songs for a Mad King*), harnessed to a stylized plot that focuses on elemental and violent urges. Punch's desire to destroy leads to four murders (Melodramas), and is linked to the desire to possess by the three Quests for Pretty Polly. These Quests are unsuccessful, and only by escaping from the rules of his own games does Punch eventually win his love.

The work divides into nine sections, plus a prologue and an epilogue. Four sections are Melodramas, and three are Quests. The action opens with Choregos, the Punch-and-Judy man, opening his booth. Melodrama I begins as Punch enters, carrying the baby. He sings a lullaby and then throws the baby into the fire, with the war cry that precedes each of his murders. Judy enters, finds the baby dead, and confronts Punch in a word game. Punch then murders Judy. Punch embarks on his first Quest for Pretty Polly. He journeys east, and serenades her with a gavotte. She rejects his offered sunflower, though, with the words, 'The flaw in this flower is a flicker of flame.'

Melodrama II follows, in which Punch confronts the lawyer and doctor in three riddle games. After this legal and medical disputation, Punch murders the doctor with a hypodermic syringe and the lawyer with a quill pen. He then sets off again on the second Quest for Pretty Polly, travelling west on a hobby-horse. Pretty Polly dances to his allemande. This time she rejects his offer of a gem.

For the third Melodrama, Punch takes on Choregos himself, 'crowning' him by breaking a trumpet, cymbal and drum over his head. He then locks him in his bass-viol case. This time, though, the war cry falters as Punch's creator falls out of the case dead. At this point a Nightmare begins. Punch travels north, where his victims turn on him to exact revenge, Judy appearing as a fortune-teller and Pretty Polly as a witch. He manages to escape from the Nightmare on the hobby-horse; but on the third Quest for Pretty Polly, journeying south, his pavan fails even to make her appear.

In the final Melodrama, Punch again confronts Choregos, who returns in the guise of Jack Ketch, the legendary hangman. After an interview game, Punch is condemned to death; at the last moment, however, he tricks Jack Ketch into trying the noose on himself; as the hangman is hanged, Pretty Polly appears; the final section, 'Punch Triumphans', sees Punch finally united with his love in a maypole dance.

Despite the violence of both subject matter and musical gesture, there are moments of great lyricism and humour in the work. The repeated prayer, 'Let the winds be gentle, let the seas be calm', and the paradox that precedes each death, 'The sweetness of this moment is unendurably bitter', are examples of 'musical signposts' for the audience, along with the use of sequences of colours, dance forms, games and so forth through the different sections. The incessant verbal playing ('Witness, avenging gods, my Choregos in stringent suffering strung on a violent viol vile,' sings Judy) sometimes suffers in the musical turbulence; but by and large, this first theatre piece shows a musical inventiveness that creates great contrasts within a consistent language.

Down by the Greenwood Side

Dramatic pastoral in one act (30m)
Text by Michael Nyman
PREMIERE 8 May 1969, Festival Pavilion, West Pier, Brighton, Sussex

There are strong connections between *Down by the Greenwood Side* and *Punch and Judy*. Emblematic figures and traditional narrative are common to both works.

Two separate sources provide the dramatic material of this piece: the traditional English Mummers' Play, and the Ballad of the Cruel Mother, the refrain of which provides the title. The action of the play concerns the contest between St George and Bold Slasher, the Black Knight (both spoken roles). Twice St George is defeated, revived first by the doubtful medical attentions of a third speaking character, Dr Blood, and then by the 'Green Man', Jack Finney (played by a mime). It is the earth magic of the latter, the reviving power of spring, that vanquishes the evil opponent. The play is presided over by Father Christmas (another spoken role), with all characters dressed in huge, puppet-like costumes. This drama is intercut with the enigmatic figure of Mrs Green – the cruel mother and the only singer in the piece. She sings several different versions of the Ballad, which relates how she murdered her two illegitimate children, 'down by the greenwood side'. Years later, passing near the same place, she meets two naked children. She remarks that were they hers she would give them clothes; to which they reply, 'When we were yours, you drest us in our own hearts' blood.'

The dramatic connections between the two stories become clear in the final section, when Mrs Green is drawn into a dance with Father Christmas and the other characters that is reminiscent of May festivals. The 'green' life force has overcome death at the last.

The scoring is for a chamber ensemble of nine players, and features melodic lines consisting of sustained notes alternating with wide leaps, often in the form of ostinato sections repeated as the accompanied action necessitates.

The Mask of Orpheus

Lyric tragedy in three acts (nine scenes, *parodos* and *exodos*) (3h 30m)
Libretto by Peter Zinovieff
Electronic material realized by Barry Anderson
Composed 1973–5 (Acts I and II), 1981–4 (Act III and electronics)
PREMIERE 21 May 1986, Coliseum, London
CAST Orpheus Man *t*, Orpheus Myth/Hades *t*, Euridice Woman *lyric ms*, Euridice Myth/Persephone *lyric ms*, Aristaeus Man *high bar*, Aristaeus Myth/Charon *high bar*, Oracle of the Dead/Hecate *high s*, The Caller *b-bar*, 3 Furies *s*, *ms*, *c*, 3 Priests *t*, *bar*, *b-bar*; 12-part chorus (in pit); mimes: Orpheus Hero, Euridice Heroine, Aristaeus Hero; troupe of Passing Clouds; 7 mime artists

By far Birtwistle's most ambitious project, *The Mask of Orpheus* brought almost universal acclaim at its premiere, despite reservations concerning the production and major cuts to the final act. The huge forces required to mount the work reflect the scope of the subject matter. The myth of Orpheus, a subject that has fascinated composers since the very birth of opera, is the basis for an exploration of the origins and nature of language, music and myth. The work manages to create its own musical and dramatic form and language, without lapsing into either triviality or pretension. In the words of the librettist, 'The use of the word Mask should suggest a slight connection with Elizabethan English masque, which combined music, dance, poetry, scenic decoration and pageantry to express mythological and allegorical subjects.'

The 13 years between its conception and first performance reflect an interrupted compositional history. Birtwistle halted after completing the first two acts, when the possibility of producing such a complex work seemed to have receded (it was intended originally for Glyndebourne). Six years later, in 1981, he picked up the pieces of the project, a creative feat which he described as 'the worst period of my life'. Not only was the period of composition extended, *The Mask of Orpheus* is also foreshadowed in a number of other vocal pieces, notably *Nenia: The Death of Orpheus* and *On the Sheer Threshold of the Night*.

The work is intricately patterned throughout, dividing its three hours' length into units constituting comprehensible, single gestures. The bulk of the score is made up of 42 'trinities of action': three Magic Formulae, three Orphic Hymns, three Hysterical Arias and so on. These 'trinities' often overlap or occur simultaneously. Although this does entail some exact repetitions of musical material (giving 'reference points' for the audience), recurrent events (such as Orpheus' suicide) are nearly always altered or distorted in some way, often according to whether they are being predicted, observed or remembered. While the musical style is generally more dense and complex than in the other stage works, it ranges from moments of tenderness or pathos to those of sheer horror (as in the oracle of the dead's screams as she attempts to learn singing from Orpheus).

Throughout the action, three different versions of each of the three central characters are present. Each version represents a different aspect of time: the Man self represents the past, the Hero the possible, and the Myth the eternal. Thus the 'reliving' of events explores the interweaving of memory, hope and time. For instance, two different versions of Aristaeus' advances to Euridice are seen simultaneously: she is willingly seduced in one, and raped in the other. Her death is then seen as respectively retribution and deliverance. Later, Orpheus 'remembers' the scene, as Aristaeus' Man self shows him only Euridice's seduction by Orpheus' Hero self. Depths of interpretation are constantly opened up by this sort of treatment of events.

It is difficult to provide a synopsis of the work precisely because of its multi-faceted approach to the Orpheus myth. Different versions of episodes are presented and re-presented in varying perspectives, in a culmination of the techniques familiar from Birtwistle's other works. Each act is built around a different narrative: Euridice's marriage and death in the first, Orpheus' descent to the underworld in the second, and the invention of language and the birth of the cultic myth in the third.

SYNOPSIS

Parodos The sun rises as Apollo gives Orpheus the gifts of speech, poetry and music. His first attempts at words are intercut with his first act of memory, recalling the voyage of Jason's ship the *Argos* (on which Orpheus sailed).

Act I divides into three scenes. In the first, Orpheus falls in love with Euridice and woos her. Their wedding is marred by bad omens, despite Orpheus' love song. The second scene shows the two simultaneous versions of Euridice's death (from a snakebite). The third contains Euridice's funeral, seen from Orpheus' point of view, after which he consults the oracle of the dead in order to pursue her to the underworld.

Act II   Orpheus journeys through 17 arches of the underworld, each with a symbolic name ('Country-side', 'Crowds', 'Evening', and so forth), and leading to his encounter with Hades, Persephone and Hecate, the goddess of witches, (grotesque mythic reincarnations of Orpheus, Euridice and the oracle of the dead) and back. He crosses the Styx by singing to Charon, brings tears to the eyes of the Furies, has his death foretold by the judges of the dead, and passes the dead in torment before standing before the three rulers of the underworld. He escapes them and begins his journey back, believing Euridice to be following him; but it is only her substitutes, Persephone and Euridice's Heroine self, who are there. Orpheus crosses the Styx again, to find Euridice unable to do likewise. Realizing that he has lost her for ever, he hangs himself. (Though the continuous dramatic sweep of this act has led to its being presented as a concert piece, even here the story-telling is not conventional; the act opens with yet another version of Euridice's death, and the narration of the action by Orpheus Man makes it clear that the journey, with its visions and phantoms of Euridice, is all taking place in his sleeping mind, exhausted and traumatized by his bereavement. As Charon carries the last of the three different embodiments of Euridice backwards for ever, Orpheus wakes up.)

Act III consists of nine 'episodes', linked by the image of the tide: in the first three, time flows backwards, so that Orpheus' return from the underworld, then his descent, and then Euridice's death are re-enacted. Then the tide turns; time flows forwards and the journey out of the underworld (with the addition of Orpheus' song to the animals) is followed by Aristaeus' punishment by his own bees; finally Orpheus Hero is killed by Zeus' thunderbolt, and Orpheus Myth is dismembered by the Dionysiac women. Time continues into the future as Orpheus becomes a cultic figure: his head sings as it floats down the river, and Orpheus Myth becomes an oracle, finally silenced by Apollo, Orpheus' spiritual father. In the last episode, time begins to flow backwards once more, as the Dionysiac women again sacrifice Orpheus and eat his flesh. The final *exodos* shows the decay of the myth.

Electronic techniques provide three of the most striking components of the work. In each act, the prevailing seasonal metaphor is indicated by a sound veil (or 'aura') of electronic sounds that acts rather like an aural backdrop to the music. Secondly, there are about 70 points at which Apollo speaks. This vast, deep, voicelike sound was created at the Parisian electronic music institute IRCAM in collaboration with Barry Anderson, and employs an invented language in which the words contain only syllables drawn from the names Orpheus and Euridice (for example, 'RUFÌ AS-RÌ DÌ' means 'Love did it'). Lastly, there are six points at which the action halts in order for a Greek myth to be acted out by the mime troupe, to the accompaniment of short electronic pieces. Three of these mime interludes are entitled 'Allegorical Flowers of Reason' (Adonis, Hyacinth and Lotus representing the Apollonian impulse) and three 'Passing Clouds of Abandon' (Dionysus, Lycurgus and Pentheus representing the Dionysian impulse). The music for these interludes is based on plucked harp notes (recalling Orpheus), resynthesized and greatly altered by computer.

Only the enormous complexity involved in producing this work threatens its recognition as one of the most remarkable pieces of operatic theatre written this century.

Gawain

Opera in two acts (3h, rev. version 2h 30m)
Libretto by David Harsent, after the anonymous 14th-century poem *Sir Gawain and the Green Knight*
Composed 1989–91, rev. 1993–4
PREMIERE ˙ 30 May 1991, Covent Garden, London; rev. version: 14 April 1994, Covent Garden, London
CAST Gawain *bar*, The Green Knight/Sir Bertilak de Hautdesert *b*, Morgan le Fay *s*, Lady de Hautdesert *ms*, Arthur *t*, Guinevere *s*, A Fool *bar*, Agravain *b-bar*, Ywain *t*, Bishop Baldwin *ct*, Bedevere *actor*; *satb* chorus of clerics; offstage: *satb* chorus

The first work by Birtwistle to bear the title 'opera' is a massive work that represents the culmination of his interest in the folklore of the Green Man. The first of his works to be produced at Covent Garden, its premiere was broadcast by radio and recorded for television.

David Harsent's libretto is strikingly faithful to the medievalism of the original poem, though it presents the whole action as controlled by Morgan le Fay, who is on stage but invisible to the other characters for almost the whole opera.

SYNOPSIS

Act I   Arthur's court is celebrating New Year when the Green Knight enters. He issues a challenge for someone to strike a blow at his neck with his axe, and to receive a return blow a year later. Eventually Gawain accepts, and strikes the knight's head from his body. The knight himself picks the head up, tells Gawain to meet him at the Green Chapel, and leaves. During a long representation of the changing seasons, Gawain is prepared for his quest.

Act II   Gawain's journey. He eventually reaches the castle of Sir Bertilak and Lady de Hautdesert, who tell him that the Green Chapel is near by. For three days he is entertained: Bertilak hunts all day while his wife attempts, unsuccessfully, to seduce Gawain. Each evening, fulfilling a pact between them, the two men exchange the day's winnings: a stag, a boar and a fox, for one, two and then three kisses. However, on the third day Gawain also secretly accepts a protective girdle from Lady de Hautdesert. Gawain then goes to the Green Chapel. The Green Knight feints two blows, and cuts Gawain only slightly with the third. The knight is then revealed to be Bertilak, and the cut is retribution for keeping the girdle. Gawain returns to Arthur's court, convinced of his cowardice and refusing to be seen as 'that hero' who was sent out.

There are points of contact between the medieval and contemporary verse. The alliteration of the original is occasionally echoed, as in Gawain's words to the

Green Knight, 'My life is light – easier to lift than the axe', and the overall effect of the libretto derives from the features of the original that must have drawn Birtwistle to it: the mixture of mythic figures (the Green Man; the 'magic site' of the Chapel, a barrow; the Christian symbolism and the repetitions and parallelisms of the text) and the equivocal dénouement, which is preserved without any attempt at more modern didactic point-making.

The half-hour masque that concludes Act I aroused much comment at the premiere, and some found it tedious. Emblematic figures, including Father Time and nature spirits, process carrying symbols of seasonal growth, harvest and death, while the fool and the knights strip, wash and arm Gawain for his journey. Birtwistle indicated then that he might revise this section for future performances, although the difficulties it gave critics seemed to stem from its deliberate adoption of ritually repeated blocks of time rather than a misjudgement of its length. Indeed, for the revival in 1994 Birtwistle cut 30 minutes off the running time of the opera by shortening both the masque, which contained newly written text and music, and the final scene.

The opera is at first sight much more conservative in form than earlier Birtwistle works. There are none of the alternative narratives of The Mask of Orpheus, and no repetition of blocks of action, except for the masque of the seasons and the beheading itself, where the Green Knight enters for a second time to expedite the special effect of the beheading (which was spectacular in the premiere production). The music accompanies the action in a fairly direct manner, with the moments of violence or tenderness set alongside onomatopoeia (the Green Knight's horse's clip-clopping shoes, or, in the hunting scenes, abundant horn calls; these last are used leitmotivically elsewhere, for instance slowed down in the texture of the overture). But if the opera lacks the experimental form of The Mask of Orpheus, it should not be assumed that this is a retrograde stylistic step. Birtwistle's gritty and consistent harmonic language owes much to the techniques of Earth Dances (1986), frequently proliferating melodic lines stratified into separate layers of orchestral texture; this consistency allows great diversity of rhythm and sonority without falling into the bathos that any treatment of myth and metaphor courts. There are moments of parody (Gawain's first kiss is accompanied by a sugary cello phrase), stylistic reference (notably to Stravinsky's Le sacre du printemps), and occasional rhythmic relaxation (for instance in Morgan le Fay's and Lady de Hautdesert's dance). The typical Birtwistle interest in altered repetitions of material follows the parallelisms of the text itself, and melodic repetition is skilfully deployed, for instance for Morgan le Fay's recurring lines 'This is the hour of legacy or loss. / This is the hour of vanity or choice.'

R.J.S.

The Second Mrs Kong

Opera in two acts (nine scenes) (2h 15m)
Libretto by Russell Hoban

PREMIERE 24 October 1994, Glyndebourne, Sussex
CAST Kong t, Pearl s, Anubis/Death of Kong b-bar, Vermeer bar, Mirror/Mirror Echo lyric s, Inanna (Mrs Dollarama) ms, Mr Dollarama bar, Swami Zumzum light t, Orpheus ct, The Sphinx c, Four Models/ Four Temptations 2 s, 2 ms, Euridice lyric s, Monstrous Messenger/Joe Shady b; satb chorus of the dead

Reading the works of Russell Hoban, Birtwistle was attracted by their brevity and structure, and by their up-to-date way of dealing with myth – a recurring characteristic of much of the composer's work – and he approached Hoban for a libretto. They began with the idea of the King Kong of the 1933 film, a subject that intrigued them both, and what emerged after many drafts is a concise, wittily allusive (and elusive) libretto about the impossibility of love, peopled by a weird assortment of characters – familiar, surreal and mythological.

SYNOPSIS

Act I Anubis, the jackal-headed boatman, brings the souls of the dead to the world of shadows. Some of them (the Dollaramas and Zumzum) relive their more bizarre memories; Vermeer recalls his meeting with the woman in his picture, Girl with the Pearl Ear-ring. The film of King Kong arrives, but Kong himself knows he does not belong here as he is merely an idea. Vermeer paints Pearl. A mirror promises to take her into the future; she hears Kong calling out. In the 20th century, Vermeer's picture becomes a popular icon and Pearl, now part of a stockbroker's furniture, searches for Kong with the help of a computer. They fall in love. Kong escapes the world of shadows and sets off, with Orpheus as his pilot, to find Pearl among the living.

Act II Kong and Orpheus are attacked by four temptations (Doubt/Fear/Despair/Terror). Orpheus loses his head, but Kong rescues it. They avoid the pursuing dead and also the sphinx. Orpheus' singing charms a telephone on which Kong speaks to Pearl. Kong fights off the threatening figure of the Death of Kong and realizes that he cannot die. Pearl and Kong meet, but find they cannot reach another. They recall falling in love.

The Second Mrs Kong is less complex and both more lyrical and more immediately accessible than its two operatic predecessors, but its subject matter and sense of humour never obscure the seriousness and compassion behind its quirkily imaginative ideas. The vocal lines are easy on the ear; the ingenious orchestration, omitting trombones, includes an accordion, a cimbalom and two saxophones. According to the composer, the opera 'sits' on the thick texture of the score, which is constructed upon two whole-tone scales. The opera's director/designer Tom Cairns played a vital part in the gestation of the work and the successful premiere of this masterpiece of the 1990s.

A.H.

Other operatic works: Bow Down, 1977; Yan Tan Tethera, 1986

GEORGES BIZET

Alexandre-César-Léopold (Georges) Bizet; *b* 25 October 1838, Paris; *d* 3 June 1875, Le Bougival, nr Paris

Bizet began and ended his career with operas, though he also wrote orchestral music, piano pieces, songs, choral and incidental music. None of his operas was immediately successful in Paris, but from the start his work was original enough to be taken seriously. The faith placed in Bizet by a few contemporaries has been amply justified by the brilliant posthumous triumph of his operatic masterpiece, *Carmen* (1875), an enduring place in the repertoire for *Les pêcheurs de perles* (1863), and a growing appreciation of several of his other operas.

Bizet achieved a vibrant and original amalgam of memorable melody, piquant harmony, vivid orchestration, and on occasion a realistic dramatic power that has rarely been equalled in opera. Though contemporary critics frequently applied the label 'Wagnerian' to Bizet's operas, the composer kept his distance from Wagner's theories and chose to work within the number- and scene-opera tradition; however, his orchestra plays a more active role in presenting melody and countermelody than that of earlier French composers, and its tone colours are essential to the varying of motifs for dramatic ends.

Like most French composers, Bizet formed his skills largely at the Conservatoire (1847–57), where he studied composition with Fromental Halévy; Gounod, perhaps the most potent single influence on his development, came to know Bizet outside that institution. The connection involved not only some composition lessons, but also arrangements of Gounod's works. Bizet's delightful Symphony in C, composed at this time (1855), is clearly modelled on Gounod's Symphony in D.

Bizet's early operas are charming, comic Italianate works, where the models of Rossini and Donizetti show through clearly. As he expanded his range in the 1860s to more dramatic and serious topics, his scores show the influence of others, notably Gounod, Félicien David, Meyerbeer, Halévy, Verdi and Weber. Although their quality is generally uneven, these scores teem with ideas. Abandoned or lost projects from the period 1868–71 obscure the route by which Bizet achieved true artistic maturity. From the 1870s there are just two mature opéras comiques (*Djamileh* and *Carmen*) and an abandoned grand opera *Don Rodrigue*, which remains largely unscored; since rehearsal revisions were normally an essential stage in Bizet's creative process, it is difficult to speculate on the final form this torso might have taken.

Bizet's first two completed operas were written while he was still a student at the Conservatoire. *La maison du docteur* (c. 1855) was probably composed for private performance with his fellow students, but *Le Docteur Miracle* (1856) was given at the Bouffes-Parisiens theatre as one of the prizewinners in a competition conducted by Offenbach to promote opéra comique. A few months later Bizet capped a brilliant student career by winning the Prix de Rome with his cantata *Clovis et Clotilde* (1857). This enabled him to spend nearly three years in Rome, from January 1858 to July 1860. During this time he worked on *Don Procopio*, which he submitted as his first envoi as a Prix de Rome winner (officially this should have been a sacred work). He considered further operatic projects and began some, but completed none until the one-act opéra comique *La guzla de l'émir* (1862, now lost) which, as a Prix de Rome envoi (his last), was due to be performed at the Opéra-Comique, though it was never produced. Instead Bizet turned his attention to *Les pêcheurs de perles*, which in late March or early April 1863 was commissioned by Léon Carvalho, the influential director of the Théâtre Lyrique.

Bizet wrote most of the three-act score in only four months, presumably incorporating large parts of *La guzla de l'émir*. Treated severely by the critics (with the notable exception of Berlioz), *Les pêcheurs de perles* enjoyed little public support. It did not hold the stage for long, and was virtually forgotten until the 1880s; however, Carvalho immediately encouraged Bizet to complete *Ivan IV*. At the outset this grand opera, modelled largely on Meyerbeer, was apparently intended for Baden-Baden (as was, perhaps, the mysterious fragment, *La prêtresse* (?1860), whose florid vocal lines are akin to Leïla's in *Les pêcheurs de perles*). To Bizet's great disappointment and eventual bitterness, *Ivan* was never staged owing both to Carvalho's budget problems and to the Opéra's unwillingness to open its doors to a beginner. Carvalho's substitute project, *La jolie fille de Perth* (1867), took shape while Bizet was crushed by hackwork for publishers. Critics reacted more favourably to it than to *Les pêcheurs de perles*, for here Bizet turned to a style more natural to him, and aimed for charm rather than power.

In 1868 Bizet wrote to a friend that an extraordinary artistic change was taking place in him, but unfortunately no complete original opera score survives from the period 1868–71. The Franco-Prussian War disrupted all artistic activities, but with his marriage to Halévy's daughter, Geneviève, in June 1869, Bizet had new responsibilities that took time and emotional energy away from composition. The responsibility of his beautiful but neurotic wife, and a mother-in-law who suffered at times from attacks of insanity, though it matured and deepened him, was hardly an ideal situation. Furthermore, the considerable financial advantages he anticipated from a generous marriage contract did not materialize. Both to show loyalty to his former teacher and to increase family income, therefore, Bizet completed and orchestrated Halévy's opera *Noé* (1868–9). At this time Bizet also looked at or began work on a half-dozen libretti, but he completed only *La coupe du roi de Thulé* for a competition at the Opéra; there were rumours of corruption as the jury passed over scores by Bizet, Ernest Guiraud, Massenet and others for the effort of an amateur. Bizet soon reused some of the best ideas from his score, much as he had earlier begun to recycle material from *Ivan IV*. In 1870–71 he sketched two opéras comiques, *Grisélidis* and *Clarisse Harlowe*, but abandoned both when the Opéra-Comique and its new co-director, Camille du Locle, withdrew from an earlier commitment to produce a new full-length work.

Bizet's fortunes in the 1870s were tied largely to du Locle and the Opéra-Comique. He was delighted at the prospect of changing a genre he regarded as old-fashioned and insipid. His one-act opéra comique *Djamileh* (1872) is rich in beautiful scoring and dramatic subtlety but was attacked by Parisian critics as 'Wagnerian' and had little success. Du Locle immediately asked Bizet, none the less, to collaborate with the experienced team of Henri Meilhac and Ludovic Halévy on a full-length work; Bizet soon proposed Prosper Mérimée's novella *Carmen*. That summer, however, Bizet turned his attention to providing incidental music and mélodrames for Alphonse Daudet's Provençal tragedy, *L'arlésienne* (1872) at Carvalho's new theatre, the Vaudeville. Though the play failed, Bizet's exquisite suite soon became popular with Parisian concert audiences.

A grand opera, *Don Rodrigue* (1873, based on the Cid legend) was abandoned prior to orchestration, partly because the Opéra was destroyed by a fire (October) and partly because the Opéra administration chose to mount Membrée's *L'esclave* instead. Bizet had continued to work on *Carmen*, and orchestrated it quickly in the summer of 1874. He knew certain critics were prejudiced against him, but had thought this score would finally convert them: 'They make out that I am obscure, complicated, tedious, more fettered by technical skill than lit by inspiration. Well, this time I have written a work that is all clarity and vivacity, full of colour and melody.' After the premiere in March 1875 the more even-handed critics praised individual pieces, but even they often predicted that the work would not attract the public. Bizet fell ill with an attack of quinsy shortly afterwards and never completely regained his health; obsessed by thoughts of death, suffering from rheumatism and an ear infection, he none the less continued planning an oratorio, *Geneviève de Paris*. Three months later, after two heart attacks, he died, aged 36, just before *Carmen* began to conquer the entire operatic world. Its enormous popularity encouraged revival of other Bizet operas in the 1880s and 1890s. *Carmen* remains one of the greatest operas ever written; in an era dominated by Verdi and Wagner, Bizet achieved, within the traditional frame of the number opera, an original and vital solution to the balance of music and drama.

Les pêcheurs de perles
The Pearlfishers

Opera in three acts (four tableaux) (1h 45m)
Libretto by Eugène Cormon and Michel Carré
PREMIERES 30 September 1863, Théâtre Lyrique, Paris; UK: 22 April 1887, Covent Garden, London (as *Leïla*); US: 25 August 1893, Academy of Music, Philadelphia
CAST Zurga *bar*, Nadir *t*, Leïla *s*, Nourabad *b*; *satb* chorus of pearlfishers, Indians and Brahmins

Bizet signed a contract with Carvalho in late March or early April 1863 to complete a three-act opera that would go into rehearsal in August, with an anticipated premiere in mid-September. He responded imaginatively to the setting (originally Mexico, but changed to Ceylon [Sri Lanka]), but to meet the tight schedule had to borrow from several earlier works (including *Ivan IV*) and probably cannibalized most of his last *envoi de Rome*, the one- act opéra comique, *La guzla de l'émir*. Until the rehearsals were under way the opera apparently contained spoken dialogue for several scenes in the first two acts. Other rehearsal revisions centred on the Act II love duet and, in particular, the problematic final scene.

The critical reception of the premiere was largely negative, but Berlioz, writing his last review for the *Journal des débats*, found 'a considerable number of beautiful, expressive pieces filled with fire and rich colouring'. *Les pêcheurs de perles* had 18 performances (respectable for a début work) but was not revived until 1886. At about that time the publisher Benjamin Choudens began tampering with the score. The wonderful Act I tenor–baritone duet lost its triple-metre closing allegro for a dramatically nonsensical return to the more attractive opening andante (some audiences are still loath to give up this posthumous version). To compensate for various cuts Godard wrote a new, but extremely weak, Act III trio, 'O lumière sainte'. Editors also altered both stage action and music in the final scene: first they had Zurga being burned at the stake; later he was stabbed in the back by an Indian. A 1975 edition returns largely to the 1863 vocal score, with orchestration by Arthur Hammond for restored portions (since the autograph manuscript has been missing since the 1890s); however, recent discovery of an 1863 short score has made reconstruction of Bizet's orchestration possible.

SYNOPSIS

Act I On a wild beach in Ceylon the pearlfishers are preparing for the fishing season. Zurga reminds them that it is time to elect a chief. They unanimously choose him and swear absolute obedience. His old friend Nadir the hunter suddenly appears, and Zurga invites him to stay. They recall their last trip, where at the temple in Kandy both had seen and fallen in love with a beautiful young woman leading a religious ceremony ('Au fond du temple saint'); both had sworn to try to forget her so that nothing would trouble their friendship ('Amitié sainte'). A canoe arrives bringing that year's unknown, veiled, virgin priestess (Leïla), who will sing and pray for the safety of the pearlfishers during this season. They all welcome her and attend the initiation ritual where Leïla swears to give up friend, husband and lover, even though at the last minute she has recognized Nadir. Nourabad, the high priest, conducts Leïla to the temple as the sun is setting. Left alone, Nadir admits that despite his oath he had returned to hear Leïla's songs; he remembers the magic of the experience ('Je crois entendre encore') and falls asleep. Leïla now appears on the crag that looks out to sea and begins her prayers ('O Dieu Brahma, O maître souverain'), but her thoughts turn to Nadir, who wakes, comes closer, and recognizes his beloved.

Act II Leïla's forbidden ruined temple. Leïla tells Nourabad how, still a child, she had risked her life to protect a fugitive; this man had given her a necklace as a memento. Left alone, Leïla rejoices that Nadir is again watching over her ('Comme autrefois, dans la nuit sombre'). Nadir arrives and in their happiness the couple forget the danger they risk ('Ton coeur n'a pas compris le mien'). As a storm rumbles in the distance, Nourabad and the guards discover the lovers and catch Nadir as he attempts to flee. Zurga plans to allow the guilty couple to leave – until he recognizes Leïla. Blind with jealousy, he too cries for vengeance. All pray to Brahma, and Nadir and Leïla are led away.

Act III   Scene 1: Zurga, alone in his tent, regrets his rage against his old friend ('O Nadir, tendre ami de mon jeune âge') and recalls Leïla's radiant beauty. Guards bring her to beg for mercy for Nadir ('Je frémis, je chancelle, de son âme cruelle'), but succeeds only in reigniting Zurga's jealous anger when she reveals her love for Nadir. As Leïla is led away she asks a young pearlfisher to give her necklace to her mother; Zurga then recognizes this as the gift he had presented to the brave young girl who saved his life many years earlier. Scene 2: Nadir watches preparations for the execution ('Dès que le soleil'). Leïla and Nadir prepare to face death in each other's arms. Suddenly Zurga enters, hatchet in hand, and announces a fire in the camp. After the Indians have left, he releases Nadir and Leïla and reveals that he started the fire to aid their escape and repay his debt to Leïla. The lovers flee, and Zurga leans against an idol of Brahma while frightened Indians escape through the forest, their children in their arms.

In early 1867 Bizet modestly referred to his début work as 'an opera much discussed, attacked, defended . . . in all, an honourable, brilliant failure . . .' He correctly assessed his first two acts as stronger than the third and his lyric passages and exotic numbers (usually quite imaginatively scored) as more successful than the uneven dramatic portions.

Each of the major soloists has at least one strong solo number, usually indebted to Gounod in style. Among them, Nadir's Act I romance is perhaps the loveliest, not only for its melody but also for its poetic orchestration (cor anglais, muted violins and two solo cellos). The depth of Nadir's obsession is brought out by understatement – high Bs taken pianissimo for his 'mad rapture' much as a high pianissimo B♭ later illustrated Don José's obsession with Carmen.

That Bizet had already developed a fine sense of the grand moment is demonstrated by his preparation for the famous tenor–baritone melody in Act I. He moves from Nadir's eloquent recitative evoking their experience in Kandy to a chromatic descent as Zurga describes that evening, through shimmering muted strings and murmured vocal lines to the tune itself, in flute and harp on the long-delayed tonic. Most wonderfully, however, a chromatic section with shorter phrases maintains tension until the men finally present the marvellous, Gounod-indebted melody, gloriously harmonized. The 'goddess' motif, though rather long for its purpose, recurs frequently, rescored and often

doubled in speed, whenever the two men's friendship is influenced by Leïla.

Portions of the work are indebted to other composers; critics in 1863 cited Gounod, David, Halévy and Verdi, among others. But, despite the score's unevenness, its lyric beauty and unforgettable moments have won Les pêcheurs de perles a place in the standard repertoire.

La jolie fille de Perth
The Fair Maid of Perth
Opera in four acts (five tableaux) (2h)
Libretto by Jules-Henri Vernoy de Saint-Georges and Jules Adenis, freely adapted from Sir Walter Scott's novel *The Fair Maid of Perth* (1828)
PREMIERES 26 December 1867, Théâtre Lyrique, Paris; UK: 4 May 1917, Manchester; US: 10 May 1979, Manhattan Opera Theater, New York
CAST Henri Smith *t*, Mab *s*, Catherine *s*, Ralph *b* or *bar*, Glover *b*, Duke of Rothsay *bar* or *t*, Worker/Major-domo *b*, An Aristocrat *t*; *tb* chorus of armourers, bourgeois Perth residents, the duke of Rothsay's friends, artisans; *satb* chorus of carnival celebrants, young people

Having reconciled his differences with Carvalho over the latter's failure to stage *Ivan IV*, Bizet agreed in July 1866 to write *La jolie fille de Perth*. He completed it by the end of the year, and claimed that he had ignored Saint-Georges's trite verse and forced rhymes. The libretto, perhaps the worst he ever set, consists largely of operatic clichés and unbelievable coincidences and bears very little relation to Scott's novel. When the work finally came to the stage, the press was relatively complimentary, but it nevertheless closed after only 18 performances. Bizet regretted his concession to public taste in the coloratura title role, including a mad scene, originally intended for Christine Nilsson (though not sung by her at the first performance); thereafter he avoided such a florid style.

SYNOPSIS
Act I   As the carnival evening begins, Smith persuades Catherine, a beautiful coquette, to become his valentine, but her subsequent flirtation with the duke of Rothsay angers him. Mab, the gypsy queen, prevents him from striking the duke, and Catherine is in turn jealous, thinking that Smith has a mistress.

Act II   Catherine has spurned the duke, but he turns to Mab (herself a former mistress) for help in getting Catherine to come to the carnival ball. However, Mab disguises herself and she is the 'Catherine' whom Ralph, a rather tipsy apprentice, sees driven away in the duke's litter. He alerts Smith, who has been singing a serenade to Catherine (lifted from Bizet's earlier *Don Procopio*) beneath her window. He hurries off immediately, but Ralph remains long enough to see the real Catherine appear at the window.

Act III   The duke woos the false Catherine (Mab). When the real Catherine and her father arrive to announce her engagement to Smith, Smith denounces her publicly.

Act IV   Ralph, to prove Catherine's innocence,

accepts Smith's challenge to a duel. Smith and Catherine reaffirm their love before he goes off intending to die to restore her honour. Alerted by Mab, the duke stops the duel, but Catherine has already gone mad from the stress. When Mab impersonates Catherine once more while Smith sings his earlier serenade, Catherine's sanity returns and all rejoice.

With *La jolie fille* Bizet returned to a lighter style that has much in common with the opéras comiques of Gounod and Ambroise Thomas (though without spoken dialogue). Filled with delightful scoring and lyric beauty, a surprising number of passages anticipate *Carmen*. The relationship between voice and orchestra has become more supple, the orchestration clearer and subtler. Act II contains Bizet's most sustained inspiration to that date, and Act III includes an offstage minuet, better known, but less effective, in the second suite from *L'arlésienne* (arr. Ernest Guiraud). Unfortunately the improbable action of Act IV did not inspire Bizet, and the work ends lamely. Had Bizet written a final act as strong as the second, the charming score, regardless of the painfully contrived plot, would have qualified *La jolie fille* for a place in the repertoire as a minor masterpiece.

Djamileh

Opéra comique in one act (1h)
Libretto by Louis Gallet, after Alfred de Musset's poem *Namouna* (1833)
Composed summer 1871, orch. winter 1871–2, rev. during rehearsals April–May 1872
PREMIERES 22 May 1872, Opéra-Comique, Paris; UK: 22 September 1892, Manchester; US: 24 February 1913, Boston Opera House
CAST Haroun *t*, Splendiano *t* (or *bar*), Djamileh *ms*, Slave Trader *spoken role*, L'Almée *dancer*, Arakel *silent*; *sa* chorus of slaves and musicians; *tb* chorus of Haroun's friends; offstage: *stb* chorus of boatmen

In 1871 Camille du Locle offered Bizet the book of *Namouna*, renamed *Djamileh* at the director's suggestion. Bizet found the work charming but very difficult to set; however, within two months he had drafted enough of the score to be concerned about eventual casting, which would determine questions of range and key. The effect of a sumptuous production was spoilt by the Djamileh, a beautiful baroness who could not sing. Most critics condemned Bizet's score as bizarre and Wagnerian, and in June 1872 Bizet admitted to a friend that the work was not a success, partly because the poem was untheatrical. He took some comfort in the fact that a one-act opera had been taken so seriously. 'What satisfies me more than the opinions of all these gentlemen is the absolute certainty of having found my way. I know what I am doing.'

SYNOPSIS

Haroun lives in luxury in his Cairo palace, spending his money on gambling and on buying a new slave girl each month. Djamileh's month is coming to an end and Splendiano, Haroun's servant and former tutor, proposes himself as her next protector. However, she has fallen in love with Haroun and persuades Splendiano to let her return as Haroun's 'new' slave on condition that she will become his if Haroun rejects her. Djamileh returns and conceals her identity as Haroun tries to conquer her. A ray of moonlight reveals her, and Haroun is surprised at his feelings. Djamileh swears that she loves Haroun more than her liberty. Haroun at first rejects her, but then capitulates before true love. The pair sing a paean to romantic love.

In this mature and original score Bizet created an atmosphere with greater subtlety and skill than in *Les pêcheurs de perles*, but, more important as a sign of his maturity as an opera composer, in *Djamileh* he drew a sympathetic, multi-dimensional central character. Bizet deliberately contrasts her dramatically intense music with the more diatonic, Gounod-like style of the self-indulgent Haroun and the light opéra-comique couplets of Splendiano (much as he would later use different styles to dramatic effect in *Carmen*). Unfortunately Haroun's last-minute conversion to true love leaves the audience wondering whether this, too, is a whim that will pass with the next full moon.

Bizet had suggested Marguerite Priola or Célestine Galli-Marié (later the first Carmen) for the role of Djamileh. Had one of them sung the part, the work might have had a more successful premiere, for despite magically effective orchestration and a perfumed atmosphere *Djamileh* disappeared after 11 performances and was ignored until the 1890s. The excellent score has never received the attention it merits.

Carmen

Opéra comique in four acts (2h 45m)
Libretto by Henri Meilhac and Ludovic Halévy, after the novella by Prosper Mérimée (1847)
Composed 1873–5; recitatives by Ernest Guiraud, 1875; ballets from *L'arlésienne* (farandole and chorus) and *La jolie fille de Perth* (danse bohémienne) inserted by Guiraud
PREMIERES 3 March 1875, Opéra-Comique, Paris; UK: 22 June 1878, Her Majesty's Theatre, London; US: 23 October 1878, Mapleson Academy of Music, New York
CAST Moralès *bar*, Micaëla *s*, Don José *t*, Zuniga *b*, Carmen *ms*, Frasquita *s*, Mercédès *s* (or *ms*), Lillas Pastia *spoken role*, Escamillo *bar*, Le Remendado *t*, Le Dancaïre *t* (or *bar*), Guide, Soldier *spoken roles*; *satb* chorus of soldiers, men and women of Seville, cigarette-factory girls, gypsies, street vendors; street urchins *trebles*

Bizet himself seems to have proposed Mérimée's *Carmen* as the source for his librettists. The experienced team, Meilhac and L. Halévy, made numerous astute changes to the narrative and provided the necessary opportunities for a variety of musical numbers. They invented the episodic, messenger role of Micaëla (the pure, bourgeois opéra-comique heroine) to serve as a foil to Carmen, the gypsy, an unrepentant sinner who prizes the freedom to control her own life over all else. Escamillo's role was greatly expanded, and Don José, after his gradual descent from dutiful corporal/son to deserter/smuggler, commits only one murder, the final crime of jealous rage (in Mérimée's novella he commits at least three). The extent of Bizet's involvement in shaping the libretto is unknown (though he certainly contributed much of the habanera text and Carmen's death song in the Card Trio). The novella itself was widely admired, but placing such a subject on the Opéra-Comique stage was a bold step in a theatre that depended on a bourgeois clientele. Furthermore, in his quest to renovate the genre, Bizet wrote a score rich in ensembles and choruses, more demanding and complex than his performers and audience were used to. Not surprisingly the chorus (asked to smoke, quarrel, or enter by twos and threes instead of marching in *en masse* to sing simple tunes) threatened to strike after two months of rehearsal; even the orchestra claimed certain passages were unplayable. Some revisions during rehearsals accommodated the performers' limitations; but most of them also refined and sharpened the dramatic impact of each scene. The soloists came to believe strongly in the work, particularly Célestine Galli-Marié (Carmen) and Paul Lhérie (Don José), and with Bizet they resisted the director's and librettists' attempts to tone down their performance.

At the premiere audience response cooled as drama and music moved further away from the traditional opéra comique. Most of the press condemned the plot as too immoral to be staged and, though they praised certain pieces (like the Act II entr'acte and Micaëla's air), they found Bizet's score both overlong and 'scientific'. *Carmen* was not the great success Bizet had hoped for, but there were 35 performances that spring and 13 more the next season, many more than of any of his other operas. *Carmen* had succeeded in 18 other countries before the Opéra-Comique revived the work in 1883; yet by 1905 there had been 1000 performances in that house alone. In most other theatres, *Carmen* was performed with competent recitatives by Bizet's good friend Ernest Guiraud to texts supplied by Halévy; Bizet himself apparently intended to write such recitatives to make the work more widely performable. Ever since the publication of a flawed critical edition in 1964, however, which made a great many passages that Bizet removed during rehearsals more accessible than the final versions themselves and which reinstated the original orchestration for Moralès's couplets in the opening scene and the Act III duel (cuts that date back to 1875), most music directors have opted for a performing version which includes some of the rejected passages alongside Bizet's final text.

SYNOPSIS

Act I   Outside the tobacco factory in Seville soldiers amuse themselves by watching the passers-by ('Sur la place chacun passe'). Micaëla approaches Moralès, looking for Don José; when he tells her José will arrive with the changing of the guard, she flees their assiduous gallantry. The soldiers then return to their initial pastime. Children imitate the guard as they enter ('Avec la garde montante'); this group includes Don José and his new superior officer, Zuniga. The bell sounds and the women factory-workers come outside to take their break, smoking cigarettes ('La cloche a sonné; nous, des ouvrières'); their arrival delights the

men, who apparently wait for them each day. When the gypsy Carmen finally makes her grand entrance, she describes the fickle nature of her love to her many admirers (habanera: 'L'amour est un oiseau rebelle'). She speaks provocatively to Don José, and throws a flower at him before she and the others are summoned inside by the factory bell. José is disturbed by her effrontery, but picks up the flower. Micaëla returns to bring a kiss from José's mother ('Parle-moi de ma mère'), as well as a letter which suggests Micaëla as a suitable wife. José is about to throw away Carmen's flower, but the women suddenly rush out of the factory arguing ('Au secours! n'entendez-vous pas'); Carmen has cut another worker's face. When she refuses to answer Zuniga ('Coupe-moi, brûle-moi, je ne te dirai rien'), he orders José to take her to prison. Left alone with José, she uses all her practised wiles on him. He can no longer resist when she tempts him with the prospect of becoming her next lover (seguidilla: 'Près des remparts de Séville'), and helps her to escape.

Act II   Carmen and her gypsy friends, Frasquita and Mercédès, entertain officers in Lillas Pastia's tavern ('Les tringles des sistres tintaient'). Zuniga tells Carmen that José has been released after a month in prison; she is delighted. The toreador Escamillo enters with his entourage and drinks with the patrons ('Votre toast . . . je peux vous le rendre'). Though Carmen does not encourage Escamillo's attentions, she tells him that it is always pleasant to hope. When all but the three gypsy women and Pastia have left, Le Remendado and Le Dancaïre enter and describe their smuggling agenda for that night (quintet: 'Nous avons en tête une affaire'). They are all astonished when Carmen refuses to participate because she is 'in love'. They urge her to recruit her new lover and leave as they hear José approaching ('Halte-là!'). To celebrate his release Carmen orders a feast and then dances for José ('Je vais danser en votre honneur'), but her joy quickly turns to fury when José announces he must leave because the call to barracks is sounding; she is unmoved when he shows her the flower he has saved ('La fleur que tu m'avais jetée') and claims that if he loved her, he would follow her to the mountains ('Là-bas, là-bas dans la montagne'). José is about to leave when Zuniga returns, hoping to find Carmen alone. When ordered to get out, José, blind with jealousy, attacks his superior officer. He now has no choice but to leave the army and reluctantly throws in his lot with the gypsies.

Act III   The smugglers gather in the mountains ('Écoute, écoute, compagnon, écoute'). Carmen and José argue again. Mercédès and Frasquita pass the time by telling their fortunes with cards ('Mêlons! Coupons!'); when Carmen joins in, she reads death again and again, first for herself, then for José. The smugglers depart to set about their task while the women distract the customs officials ('Quant au douanier, c'est notre affaire'). José stays behind on guard. A guide brings a frightened but determined Micaëla ('Je dis que rien ne m'épouvante'); she hides when José fires a shot and Escamillo enters, calmly examining the bullet hole in his hat. He has heard that Carmen has tired of her latest lover and has come to seek her out ('Je suis Escamillo, toréro de Grenade'). Drawing his knife, the furious José challenges the toreador. Escamillo spares him, but falls in the second round. José is ready to kill him, but Carmen arrives with Le Dancaïre and stops the fight. Escamillo invites her to his next bullfight in Seville and leaves. Micaëla is discovered and tells José that his mother is dying. He leaves with her after threatening Carmen.

Act IV Outside the bullring in Seville merchants hock their wares ('A deux cuartos'). The participants in the bullfight march past ('Les voici! Voici la quadrille!'), and Escamillo arrives with a radiantly happy and beautifully dressed Carmen. Frasquita and Mercédès warn her that José is hiding in the crowd, but Carmen is determined to face him. The crowd follows the procession into the bullring leaving Carmen alone. José confronts Carmen and implores her to leave with him, but she says she no longer loves him; she would rather die than give up her freedom. She is eager to witness Escamillo's triumph, but José blocks her path. When she furiously throws away his ring, José draws his knife and stabs her while Escamillo is fêted in the bullring. As everyone comes out José, confessing his crime, throws himself on the body of his beloved Carmen.

Bizet's ability to create effective local colour is vividly represented in this score. The accelerating gypsy dance that opens Act II is an orchestral *tour de force* in which dissonance and sliding harmonies paint the scene of Lillas Pastia's underworld tavern as surely as any set design. Carmen's mesmerizing entrance piece, the habanera, winds sensually and chromatically above a pedal that provides tonal stability and symbolizes her irresistible sexuality. The seguidilla was Bizet's own invention, but its combination of guitar-like accompaniment, dance rhythm and remarkably ambiguous tonality seem just as 'Spanish' as the borrowed tunes. For Escamillo's entrance aria, Bizet adopted a deliberately popular manner as overstated as the toreador himself. In contrast, the susceptible Don José sings very little in Act I; his first solo is the simple, unaccompanied soldier's march in Act II, sung offstage.

Bizet's orchestration had been quite distinctive in his earlier works, but Richard Strauss regarded *Carmen* as sheer perfection: 'If you want to learn how to orchestrate, don't study Wagner's scores, study the score of *Carmen* . . . What wonderful economy, and how every note and every rest is in its proper place.' Woodwind instruments receive particular attention: the flute is associated with Carmen in the seguidilla and elsewhere and has the famous solo in the lovely entr'acte preceding Act III. The cor anglais makes a rare appearance as José shows Carmen the flower he has kept with him through his month in prison, and flutes and bassoons play a delicate counterpoint to Mercédès's and Frasquita's warning to Carmen just before the final tragedy.

As in earlier operas Bizet imaginatively rescores his motifs for dramatic effect. The flickering 'Carmen' motif (with an augmented second) and its alternate form, the 'fate' motif (with a slower tempo) are used economically. (The 'fate' motif itself appears only at the end of the prelude and in one number of each act.) Unexpected harmonies and modulations advance the drama in virtually every number. The featherlight Act II quintet moves effortlessly from a distant G major back to the tonic refrain in D♭ major. Bizet's contemporaries were shocked by the cadential harmonies of the Flower Song, which are unrelated to the key that surrounds them; after the seamless beauty of the melody itself and Don José's pianissimo high B♭, this harmonic gesture (to the words 'je t'aime') underlines how utterly José is bewitched by Carmen.

Though Bizet's final scenes had often previously fallen short, those in *Carmen* contain his most dramatic and original inspiration (he revised three of the four repeatedly during rehearsals). Certainly the idea for offstage trumpets (duty) playing in counterpoint to Carmen's sensual dance (love) in Act II is a brilliant stroke, but even more powerful is the combination of different styles and recurring motifs in the finale of Act III. Escamillo's suavely popular refrain, Micaëla's Gounod-like message from José's mother, Don José's impassioned threats, and the 'fate' motif build to a climax of great intensity. In the Act IV duet Bizet achieved a dramatic potency that has rarely been equalled in any opera, and in the final section the regular phrasing and diatonic harmonies of the joyful, backstage choruses contrast starkly with the rapid, uncontrolled phrases of the protagonists. The bright F♯ major of the 'Toreador' refrain, celebrating the death of the bull, forms a supremely ironic commentary on the murder outside the bullring. The realism and tragic power that so shocked Bizet's Parisian contemporaries had a profound influence on the verismo composers just a few years later, and has moved countless others ever since. 'I do not know any other instance where tragic humour, which constitutes the essence of love, is expressed . . . in a more shattering phrase than in Don José's last words . . .' (Nietzsche, *Randglossen zu Carmen*).

Other operatic works: *La maison du docteur*, (c. 1855), 1989; *Le Docteur Miracle*, 1857; *Don Procopio*, (1859), 1955; *L'amour peintre* (inc.; lost, 1860); *La prêtresse* (inc., ?1860); *La guzla de l'émir* (lost, 1862); *Ivan IV*, (1865), 1943; *Malbrough s'en va-t-en guerre* (operetta, Act I by Bizet, coll. with Édouard Legouix, Émile Jonas, Delibes; lost), 1867; *La coupe du roi de Thulé* (inc.; manuscript now largely missing, 1869), 1955 (BBC broadcast of fragments); *Noé* (completion of Halévy's opera), (1869); *Clarisse Harlowe*, (sketches, 1871); *Grisélidis*, (sketches, 1871); *Sol-si-re-pif-pan* (operetta; lost), 1872; *Don Rodrigue* (inc., 1873)

L.A.W.

MARC BLITZSTEIN
b 2 March 1905, Philadelphia, US; *d* 22 January 1964, Fort-de-France, Martinique

Marc Blitzstein appeared as a piano soloist with the Philadelphia Orchestra at 15 and went on to study composition with Nadia Boulanger and Arnold Schoenberg. His theatrical sympathies tended strongly toward the confrontational, experimental approach typified by Bertolt Brecht and Kurt Weill; probably his most performed work is the English translation he made of *The Threepenny Opera*. His efforts in musical theatre are each unique experiments, generally to his own texts. His dramatic compositions also include ballets, a great deal of incidental music for the stage, and film and radio music. His music constitutes one of the most successful examples of a meeting of popular and 'serious' idioms in American music. Tuneful, subtle, and sometimes unexpectedly evocative, Blitzstein's music remains individual and important.

The Cradle Will Rock
Play in music in ten scenes (1h 30m)
Libretto by the composer
PREMIERE 16 June 1937, Venice Theater, New York

A musical presenting a plea for industrial unionization in deliberately cartoon-like terms, *The Cradle Will Rock* was further stylized by a catchy score designed to be available to untrained actors' voices. The circumstances of its original production are even more memorable than its intrinsic quality. Originally to be produced by the Federal Theater Project, the controversial nature of the work led both to its being taken on as an independent production by Orson Welles and John Houseman and also to the company being shut out of their theatre and forbidden to perform the play on any other stage. They outwitted the law by buying tickets to an unused theatre, to which the audience was directed, and delivering their roles from their seats while Blitzstein accompanied them onstage at the piano. It was performed exactly the same way for 19 performances before beginning a more regular run elsewhere.

Regina
Opera in three acts (2h 30m)
Libretto by the composer, based on Lillian Hellman's play *The Little Foxes* (1939)
Composed 1946–9, rev. 1953, 1958
PREMIERES 31 October 1949, 46th Street Theater, New York; UK: 16 May 1991, Theatre Royal, Glasgow

The machinations of the greedy Hubbard family, conniving for power in the post-Civil-War South, had made for a highly theatrical and effective play, and provided a solid basis for Blitzstein's only real operatic success. The through-composed score encompasses a variety of vocal textures and frequent period flavourings. Like Weill's *Street Scene* and Menotti's early successes, it was presented in a Broadway theatre, and seemed to herald the arrival of an American operatic literature that could be both popular and sophisticated – an arrival that never quite took place. The revisions Blitzstein made for later productions (to be heard on a 1959 recording) are not reflected in the published score and are not to be taken as definitive. Tommy Krasker and John Mauceri prepared a new edition for Scottish Opera

performances in 1991, based on a re-examination of available materials, even restoring some music cut before the premiere.

Other stage works include: *Triple-Sec*, 1929; *Parabola and Circula*, 1929; *The Harpies*, 1931; *The Condemned*, 1932; *No for an Answer*, 1941; *Reuben, Reuben*, 1955; *Juno*, 1959; *Sacco and Vanzetti* (inc., 1964); *The Magic Barrel* (inc., 1964); *Idiots First* (inc., 1964), completed by Leonard J. Lehman, 1974

J.A.C.

JOHN BLOW
baptized 23 February 1649, Newark, Nottinghamshire, England; *d* 1 October 1708, London

In 1660 Blow was among the first choristers of the restored Chapel Royal, recruited (in effect press-ganged) by Captain Henry Cooke, master of the Children of the Chapel Royal. By the age of 13 he had written three anthems. In 1665 he was given his 'retirement livery' from the chapel, his voice having broken; two years later he was auditioned by Samuel Pepys, on the look-out for a musical servant, who noted his 'extraordinary skill' but thought his inability to keep in tune would 'make a man mad, so bad it was'. His skill brought him through; in 1668 he was appointed organist of Westminster Abbey and was playing the harpsichord in the King's Private Musick. In 1674 he succeeded Pelham Humfrey as master of the Children of the Chapel Royal and composer in ordinary to the king. He was Henry Purcell's teacher, and stepped down from his job at the Abbey to allow Purcell to take over in 1680. After Purcell's death in 1695 he resumed the posts he had passed to his pupil; his book of songs, *Amphion Anglicus* (1700) is a conscious imitation of Purcell's posthumous *Orpheus Britannicus*. The dedication, to the Princess (subsequently Queen) Anne, is a defence of sacred music; however, the contents are wholly secular. Yet by that time, Blow's energies were devoted entirely to sacred music and that is probably what he is most remembered for today. It is remarkable that few of his surviving songs appear to have a theatrical context. *Venus and Adonis* is his one work for the stage, the first surviving through-composed opera in English, and was a decisive influence on Purcell's *Dido and Aeneas* (1689). Besides anthems, songs, and *Venus and Adonis* Blow wrote court and Cecilian odes, harpsichord suites and string sonatas. Since the 18th century there has been a tendency to sweeten the acerbities of his harmonic writing, but there is no doubt that these are deliberate and considered.

Venus and Adonis
A masque for the entertainment of the king in three acts (1h)
Librettist unknown
PREMIERES at court, date unknown; US: 11 March 1941, Cambridge, Massachusetts
CAST Venus *s*, Adonis *b*, Cupid *s*; *sath* chorus of

shepherds, shepherdesses, huntsmen, graces and little cupids

We cannot tell when *Venus and Adonis* was first performed, though we know it was a 'Masque for the Entertainment of the King' and that Venus was played by the actress Mary Davies, once the king's mistress, and Cupid by Lady Mary Tudor, their natural daughter. The little cupids were the boys of the Chapel Royal. The second performance is more substantially documented, since we have an annotated libretto; it took place on 17 April 1684 at Josias Priest's boarding school for young gentlewomen at Chelsea, which is where, in due course, *Dido* was first given. The writer of the libretto is unknown, though it has been attributed to Aphra Behn, and also to James Allestree, a dissolute fellow of Christ Church, Oxford, who wrote the text of Blow's 1682 *New Year Ode*.

The plot follows Shakespeare and Ovid, but the imitation of Lullian tragédie lyrique in miniature demands an allegorical prologue. This wittily satirizes its portentous models; it reflects, ambivalently but accurately, on the morals of Charles's court, where constancy is equated with ugliness.

SYNOPSIS

Act I 'The Curtain opens and discovers Venus and Adonis sitting together upon a Couch, embracing each other.' A hunting party is heard offstage; Venus attempts to persuade a reluctant Adonis to join it since 'Absence kindles new desire, / I would not have my lover tire.' The huntsmen arrive and Adonis leaves with them.

Act II 'Venus and Cupid are seen standing with Little Cupids round about them.' Cupid asks Venus how to 'destroy / All such as scorn your wanton boy'. She answers that he must match the foolish to the foolish, and Cupid amplifies the lesson to the little cupids who repeat after him a list of love's enemies: 'the insolent, the arrogant, the mercenary, the vain and silly'. Then the cupids play at hide-and-seek until Cupid frightens them away. Venus commands Cupid to call the graces, who sing in her praise and in anticipation of 'this joyful night'. The act ends with a sequence of dances; the last is a ground which prefigures the utterly different mood of what is to come.

Act III Venus is standing 'in a melancholy posture'. Cupid, mourning, shakes an arrow at her. She repents that she has let Adonis leave and calls on him to return. Adonis is led in, but fatally wounded, gored by the 'Aedalian boar'. Venus in vain implores the gods to save him, and the scene of love and death culminates in her passionate cries of 'Ah Adonis my love, ah, Adonis'. The mourning cupids lament the 'mighty huntsman', the 'wretched Queen of Love', and their 'forsaken grove'.

The subtlety of Blow's treatment lies in the way in which he negotiates the transition from the public world of the court (in the music of the prologue) to the private world of Venus' ultimate desolation – a move from the social to the tragic and elegiac. The intensity of the opera develops through an increasingly

intense use of chromaticism, notably in Venus' impassioned opening arioso in Act III, and in the duet and lament that follow Adonis' entry; indeed in the best manuscript several of Venus' exclamations of 'Ah' are not notated and demonstrate the way the declamation threatens to break all constraints of musical form.

R.L.

JERRY BOCK
Jerrold Lewis Bock; *b* 23 November 1928, New Haven, Connecticut, US

Jerry Bock discovered his musical ability early, and wrote words and music for shows while in high school and college. With lyricist Larry Holofcener he contributed to a revue and wrote *Mr Wonderful*; shortly after the latter opened, he met Sheldon Harnick, with whom he maintained a collaboration until 1970. Since that date Harnick has continued to write (including opera libretti) but no further work by Bock has been seen on Broadway.

The team's body of work coincides almost exactly with the 1960s and therefore seems to typify the style of that decade, showing great attention to precision of character and locale, as well as a considerable variety of approach.

Fiddler on the Roof
Musical play in two acts (3h)
Libretto by Joseph Stein, based on stories by Sholom Aleichem; lyrics by Sheldon Harnick
PREMIERES 22 September 1964, Imperial Theater, New York; UK: 16 February 1967, Her Majesty's Theatre, London
CAST Tevye *bar*, Golde *c*, Tzeitel *ms*, Hodel *s*, Chava *c*, Yente *ms*, Motel *bar*, Perchik *t*, Lazar Wolf *bar*; other solo parts from *satb* chorus of villagers

With a story whose appeal might have been seen as limited (its authors were constantly worried during its creation that it would become 'too heavy and too Jewish'), Bock and Harnick achieved far and away their biggest success, an international phenomenon that enthralled audiences everywhere it played. In addition to the appeal of the story, whose theme was the response of tradition to changing times, *Fiddler* owed much of its strength to the direction of Jerome Robbins, whose judgement influenced every element of the original production. The score served its purpose perfectly, without providing many detachable excerpts except for the wedding song, 'Sunrise, Sunset'.

SYNOPSIS

Act I The action takes place in the Jewish section of the Russian village Anatevka in the late 19th century. The milkman Tevye chooses a husband for his oldest daughter, Tzeitel, only to find that she and the tailor Motel have already given each other a pledge. At first disturbed by this break with tradition, Tevye finally tricks his wife Golde into agreeing to it. The act ends with the wedding – interrupted by a raid from the Gentile town authorities.

Act II The challenge to tradition continues. Tevye's second daughter, Hodel, wishes to marry a travelling scholar who questions the old ways; Tevye reluctantly gives his blessing. But there can be no blessing when the next daughter, Chava, chooses to marry a Gentile; she is to have no further share in the community – a community which itself is ended when all Jews are ordered to leave Anatevka. The final image is of the circle of tradition joining hands a final time, then dissolving as all the characters (including the symbolically precarious fiddler of the title) go their separate ways.

Other musicals include: *Mr Wonderful*, 1956; *The Body Beautiful*, 1958; *Fiorello!*, 1959; *Tenderloin*, 1960; *She Loves Me*, 1963; *The Apple Tree*, 1966; *The Rothschilds*, 1970

J.A.C.

ARRIGO BOITO

Enrico Arrigo Boito; *b* 24 February 1842, Padua, Italy; *d* 10 June 1918, Milan

Boito's reputation rests on three distinct achievements: first, his contribution as Verdi's librettist for *Otello* and *Falstaff*, as well as for the revised *Simon Boccanegra*; second, his own two operas (*Mefistofele* and *Nerone*); and third, to a lesser extent, his books of poems, *Libro dei versi* and *Re Orso*. Educated at the Milan Conservatory, where he studied composition with Alberto Mazzucato, he and his lifelong friend Franco Faccio, the composer-conductor, won scholarships for study abroad. In Paris, Boito met both Rossini and Verdi, and for the latter he supplied the text for the cantata *Inno delle nazioni*. Returning to Milan, he wrote musical journalism and continued work on his *Faust* opera, a project he had begun as a student in Milan.

It was at a dinner following the premiere of Faccio's first opera, *I profughi fiamminghi* (1863), that the idealistic young Boito made the notorious comment comparing the defiled altars of Italian opera to the splattered walls of a brothel. Verdi assumed Boito included him among the defilers (in fact he was just being over-enthusiastic about Faccio's opera) and took umbrage. That he was deeply offended by it is proved by his allusions to this sentiment, never getting the words quite right, in a number of his letters over the succeeding years. Boito's faith in his friend's skill continued and in 1865 he wrote his first opera libretto, significantly on a Shakespearean subject, *Hamlet*, for Faccio.

Three years later the opportunity arose for Boito himself to demonstrate his hopes for the future of Italian music drama with his *Mefistofele*. The work precipitated a historic fiasco at La Scala, and was withdrawn after two rowdy performances. Proudly hiding his humiliation, Boito spent the next years writing libretti for others (including, as 'Tobia Gorrio', *La Gioconda* for Ponchielli) and supplying a number of translations of songs and operas, including

Wagner's *Rienzi* and *Tristan*. At Bologna in 1875, the drastically revised *Mefistofele* proved successful.

Through Faccio and the music publisher Giulio Ricordi, a *rapprochement* was arranged with Verdi in 1879, with the agreement that Boito would provide a text for *Otello* without any firm commitment on the part of the composer. As a test, Boito was invited to prepare a revision of Francesco Maria Piave's text for *Simon Boccanegra*. That task successfully accomplished, work progressed on *Otello*, but not without some crises. However, by the time *Otello* had its triumphant premiere at La Scala in 1887, Boito had forged a firm friendship with Verdi and their collaboration on *Falstaff* (1893) went much more smoothly. Boito proposed *King Lear* as their next project and began a libretto, but, though he had planned for decades to write an opera on the play (he got as far as sketching a complete scenario in 1850), Verdi finally realized that, at past 80, such an undertaking was beyond him. Boito's relationship with Verdi remained close, and he was present when Verdi died.

As early as 1862, Boito had sketched plans for an opera on the subject of Nero but other commissions had always prevented his working on it consistently. Shortly after Verdi's death, he published his five-act libretto for *Nerone*, which was hailed as a major literary achievement. With the passage of time, Boito suffered from increasing difficulty in concentration, and diminished confidence in his ability to compose this work. When he died, *Nerone* was still incomplete, 56 years after its conception. Although much of the score existed, including sketches for the discarded fifth act, the work required considerable preparation. This was supervised by Arturo Toscanini, who conducted the posthumous premiere at La Scala in 1924.

Mefistofele

Mephistopheles

Opera in a prologue, four acts and an epilogue (originally a prologue and five acts) (2h 15m)
Libretto by the composer, after Johann Wolfgang von Goethe's play *Faust* (1808, 1832)
Composed 1860–67, rev. 1871, 1875, 1881
PREMIERES 5 March 1868, La Scala, Milan; rev. version: 4 October 1875, Bologna; UK: 6 July 1880, Her Majesty's Theatre, London; US: 16 November 1880, Boston; definitive version: 25 May 1881, La Scala, Milan
CAST Mefistofele (Mephistopheles) *b*, Faust *t*, Margherita *s*, Elena *s*, Marta *c*, Pantalis *c*, Wagner *t*, Nereo *t*; *satb* chorus of heavenly host, burghers, witches, sirens; ballet

Boito's revisions, after the failure of the 1868 version of *Mefistofele* (which he conducted himself), included omitting a scene at the emperor's court and an intermezzo sinfonico. Although most of the changes were made for an 1875 production at Bologna, the score did not emerge in its final form until 1881. The opera includes the prologue in heaven and the Helen of Troy scene from the second part of Goethe's *Faust* (both ignored by Gounod in his *Faust*, 1859).

SYNOPSIS

Prologue The Devil, Mephistopheles, wagers with God that he can win the soul of Faust, while the chorus praises the Lord.

Act I   On Easter Sunday, the aged scholar Faust and his disciple Wagner first see Mephistopheles disguised as a grey friar. Later, in his study, Faust contemplates nature, but Mephistopheles appears, introduces himself as the spirit of negation and persuades Faust to exchange his soul for a moment of sublime happiness. Faust signs the fatal pact.

Act II   While Mephistopheles flirts with Marta, Faust woos her friend Margherita and wins the promise of a later assignation. He gives her a narcotic for her mother so that they won't be disturbed. Mephistopheles brings Faust to the Brocken mountains to witness the orgiastic Walpurgis Night.

Act III   Margherita languishes in prison, condemned for the death of her mother, who was poisoned by Faust's sleeping draught, and for drowning the child she bore Faust. Faust comes to her cell, hoping to save her, but the appearance of Mephistopheles fills her with dread. Dying, she remains constant in her Christian faith.

Act IV   In classical Greece, whither Mephistopheles has transported Faust, Elena (Helen of Troy) has a vision of the destruction of Troy. Faust woos her, anticipating a fusion of the classical and Romantic spirits.

The epilogue shows the aged Faust longing for death. Despite Mephistopheles's warnings, he invokes divine forgiveness and dies redeemed.

The projected plan for the work was without equal in Italian opera in the latter half of the 19th century, but, unfortunately, Boito's incapacity as a composer (his frequent inability to develop musical ideas) prevented him from realizing his ambition fully. Boito's revisions, gigantic in scope, brought *Mefistofele* far closer to the conventional operatic forms of the time, emphasizing the romance of Faust and Margherita and the conflict of good and evil. The success the opera enjoyed in its less overtly 'futuristic' version reassured Boito after its initial failure. The music, although at times inspired, on the whole lacks spontaneity – particularly in the rhythm. *Mefistofele* survives today, principally in Italy and the United States, as a vehicle for star basses.

Other opera: *Nerone* (inc., 1918; completed by Vincento Tommasini, Arturo Toscanini and Antonio Smareglia), 1924

W.A.

ALEKSANDR BORODIN
Aleksandr Porfiryevich Borodin; *b* 12 November 1833, St Petersburg; *d* 27 February 1887, St Petersburg

Borodin, whose mere handful of mainly instrumental compositions are regularly performed in the concert hall and whose only opera, *Prince Igor*, is a household name, was an untrained spare-time composer and proud of the fact. Despite the repeated reproaches of his musical friends for not devoting more time to fulfilling his outstanding musical gifts, he resolutely maintained that he was essentially a 'Sunday composer'

and that his professional work obliged him to consider composition simply as a relaxation and indulgence.

Borodin trained as a chemist and at the age of 31 became professor of organic chemistry at the Medico-Surgical Academy in St Petersburg. An exceptionally genial and attractive man, he took his professional duties very seriously and spent most of his time in research, teaching, committee work and looking after the well-being of his students. These biographical details are particularly relevant to *Prince Igor* for they largely explain the otherwise incomprehensible fact that he failed to complete the opera after 17 years of sporadic work on it. At his sudden death, aged 53, the overture had been improvised but not written down, some of the numbers were in a very sketchy form, quite a lot remained unorchestrated and, worst of all, the third act had large chunks missing, including the libretto itself. For this reason *Igor* will always be a problem opera; its extended, diffuse dramatic shape is far from satisfactory and the libretto sometimes lapses into banality. Nevertheless it is packed with magnificent music, wonderful opportunities for solo and choral singing, and the *Polovtsian Dances* that conclude Act II undoubtedly constitute one of the most overwhelming scenes in all opera.

Prince Igor
Knyaz' Igor'
Opera in four acts with a prologue (3h 30m)
Libretto by the composer, based on a scenario by V. V. Stasov
Composed 1869–70, 1874–87
PREMIERES 4 November 1890, Mariinsky Theatre, St Petersburg; UK: 8 June 1914, Drury Lane, London; US: 30 December 1915, Metropolitan, New York
CAST   Prince Igor *bar*, Yaroslavna *s*, Vladimir *t*, Prince Vladimir Galitsky *high b*, Khan Konchak *b*, Khan Gzak *silent*, Konchakovna *c*, Ovlur *t*, Skula *b*, Eroshka *t*, Nurse *s*, Polovtsian Girl *s*; *satb* chorus of Russian princes and princesses, boyars and their wives, elders, Russian warriors, attendant girls, the people, Polovtsian khans, Konchakovna's friends, Konchak's slaves, Russian prisoners-of-war, Polovtsian guards

In 1869 Borodin asked Vladimir Stasov, art historian and literary mentor to the 'Mighty Handful' composers, to suggest a suitable subject for an opera. Stasov recognized Borodin's qualities as an essentially lyrical composer who had inherited Glinka's sympathy with Russia's epic past and astutely prepared a detailed scenario based on the 12th-century national epic *The Lay of Igor's Army*. In this Prince Igor of Seversk (now in the Ukraine) decides to make a show of strength by leading his army against the Polovtsi, a nomadic tribe of Turkish origin which habitually ravaged southern Russia. A battle takes place in which the army is all but annihilated and Igor and his son captured. Eventually he escapes and is reunited with his wife Yaroslavna. The original purpose of the epic was to use the campaign to underline the political and spiritual disunity of the separate principalities of Kiev and to show the need for a united Russia. Borodin was delighted with the idea, but unfortunately decided to write the libretto himself and, instead of finalizing the text before beginning composition, wrote it piecemeal as he went along. In the process the original intention of the epic was watered down and Igor himself, because of his courageous, impulsive but essentially weak character, becomes almost an anti-hero.

SYNOPSIS

Prologue The town square in Putivl, 1185. Igor, with his son Vladimir, prepares to set out with his army, despite the entreaties of his wife Yaroslavna and an ill-omened eclipse of the sun.

Act I Scene 1: Skula and Eroshka, deserters from Igor's army, ingratiate themselves with Yaroslavna's dissolute brother, Prince Galitsky, who boasts of his hedonistic life, 'Greshno tait: ya skuki nye lyublyu' ('I hate a dreary life'). Scene 2: In a touchingly expressive arioso, Yaroslavna describes her loneliness, fear of civil strife and troubled dreams. Boyars enter and solemnly inform her of Igor's defeat and captivity; at the same time the Polovtsi begin to attack Putivl.

Act II Khan Konchak's camp in the eastern steppe. Vladimir has already fallen in love with Konchak's daughter, Konchakovna, and apostrophizes her in a beautifully lyrical aria, 'Medlenno dyen ugasal' ('Slowly the daylight faded'). Igor's thoughts are filled with remorse and longing for Yaroslavna, 'Ni sna, ni otdykha' ('No rest, no sleep'). The barbaric but magnanimous Khan Konchak cannot understand his captive's depression, 'Zdorov li, knyaz?' ('Unhappy, Prince?'), and, in order to entertain him, arranges for his slaves to dance and sing for him (*Polovtsian Dances*).

Act III After hearing of the attack on Putivl, Igor decides to escape, although Vladimir is reluctant to leave Konchakovna and is captured. Konchak admires Igor for his audacity and unites the two lovers.

Act IV Yaroslavna laments Igor's captivity and the devastation of Putivl (vividly described in a hauntingly elegiac unaccompanied chorus), but is overjoyed when he arrives back safely to general rejoicing.

The great strength of *Prince Igor* lies in the distinguished and noble quality of its music rather than its emotional force or sense of dramatic involvement. Act II in particular consists of one outstanding number after another (the arias of Konchakovna, Vladimir, Igor, Konchak), culminating in the barbaric splendour of the *Polovtsian Dances*. The music has a richly lyrical quality that never becomes cloying, and the writing for solo voices, chorus and orchestra is always freshly minted. Although constructed very much as a series of set tableaux, the opera is generally successful in putting over the big-boned, epic quality of the story, and the characters of Yaroslavna and Konchak in particular are finely delineated in their text and music.

After Borodin's death his self-appointed musical executors, Rimsky-Korsakov and Glazunov, were faced with the task of putting the noble torso of *Igor* into performable shape. With Glazunov filling in most of the empty gaps (including writing out the overture from memory), while Rimsky undertook the equally onerous task of editing and orchestrating the rest, they soon produced the only edition of the opera that has ever been published. Although it includes Borodin's Polovtsian March and Trio (featuring the second

subject of the overture), Glazunov's bravely attempted reconstruction of Act III is frequently cut in performance, resulting in the omission of the all-important dramatic episode of Igor's escape.

Other operatic works: *The Valiant Knights* (*Bogatyry*) (pastiche opera farce), 1867; *Mlada* (inc., 1872; coll. with César Cui, Musorgsky and Rimsky-Korsakov)

D.L.-J.

RUTLAND BOUGHTON

b 23 January 1878, Aylesbury, Buckinghamshire, England; *d* 25 January 1960, London

The son of a grocer, Boughton was apprenticed early to a London concert agent. In his teens he published several works and even had a piano concerto performed in London. This early music came to the attention of J. A. Fuller Maitland, who showed it to Charles Villiers Stanford, who in turn found a patron to pay for Boughton to study at the Royal College of Music. This formal study was short-lived, however, and after a few terms poverty forced him to leave to make his living. He became a protégé of Granville Bantock, who employed him on the staff of the Midland Institute of Music (1904–11).

Two influences combined to shape his art: Wagnerian music drama (he went to Bayreuth in 1911) and socialism. Boughton, later a member of the Communist Party, was a musical manifestation of the Arts and Crafts movement of William Morris. His ideas were developed with Reginald Buckley in *Music Drama of the Future* (1911), a book containing Boughton's essay on choral drama, 'Drama of the Future', in the proposed scheme for the Temple Theatre (in which Boughton envisaged a theatre run as part of an agricultural commune, primarily for the local community but with an annual national festival), and finally in the collaborative text of the choral drama *Uther and Igrane*, which became his first opera, *The Birth of Arthur* (1908–9). This was the beginning of a five-part Arthurian cycle which occupied Boughton for almost 40 years.

He established his theatrical base at Glastonbury in an unpropitious year, 1914. But though only a village-hall affair with piano accompaniment, it attracted the support of celebrities such as Bernard Shaw and Edward Elgar. It lasted until 1927 and, while Boughton's own music was featured, many other operas were also produced. The first festival included the premiere of his second opera, *The Immortal Hour*, and this was followed by the second of the Arthurian dramas, *The Round Table* (1916), *Alkestis* (1922), a setting of Euripides in Gilbert Murray's verse translation and Boughton's only opera to be produced at Covent Garden (1924), and finally *The Queen of Cornwall*, which was premiered at the Glastonbury Festival of 1924. In between he set the Coventry Nativity Play in the manner of a folk opera, *Bethlehem*, with choruses based on early English carols (1915). Later he completed the Arthurian cycle with *The Lily Maid* and, during the Second World War, the last two, *Galahad* and *Avalon*, but only the first three of the cycle have ever been produced.

The Immortal Hour

Music drama in two acts (2h)
Libretto by the composer, after the play and poems of 'Fiona Macleod' (William Sharp)
Composed 1910–12
PREMIERES 26 August 1914, Glastonbury (with pf); 7 January 1915, Bournemouth (with orch.); US: 6 April 1926, Grove Street Theater, New York
CAST Dalua *bar*, Etain *s*, Eochaidh *bar*, Manus *b-bar*, Maive *c*, Old Bard *b-bar*, Midir *t*, 2 Spirit Voices *s, c*; *satb* chorus of druids, bards, warriors, maidens, elemental spirits

After its early success in the West Country, *The Immortal Hour* was accepted by the Carnegie publication scheme in 1921, and proceeded to make Boughton a huge reputation in the 1920s. Barry Jackson's production opened at the Repertory Theatre, Birmingham, on 23 June 1921, and moved to London on 13 October 1922 where it ran for a total of 216 consecutive performances, and subsequently for nearly 1000 performances in all. Throughout, Gwen Ffrangçon-Davies was celebrated in the role of Etain. It was one of those interwar excursions into escapism whose magic defied revival. After the Second World War it failed to rekindle the same magic until the BBC broadcast the closing scene in 1978 and received so many letters that it quickly scheduled a Radio 3 revival, which in turn led to a Hyperion recording.

SYNOPSIS
Act I Etain is of the faery folk, but as a mortal becomes Eochaidh's queen, an event manipulated by Dalua, the shadow of whose hand brings forgetfulness, and whose touch is death.

Act II A year later Midir, a prince of faery, comes to the king's court and sings the celebrated 'Faery Song' ('How beautiful they are', which alone kept Boughton's name before the musical public for many years). It reminds Etain of her past, and, as she leaves with the stranger, Dalua touches Eochaidh, who falls dead as the faery chorus fades into the distance.

Boughton maintained music drama to be an expression of a 'living religious experience' which enabled him 'to express the mystery of spiritual drama with conviction. In the music drama the lyric comes as the culmination of passion.' Here atmosphere is all-important, and *The Immortal Hour* succeeds not by virtue of epic qualities, as Boughton had at first envisaged, but through its personal voice, folk-generated melody, somewhat homespun individuality and its memorable choral writing.

Other operas: *The Birth of Arthur*, (1909), 1920; *Bethlehem*, 1915; *The Round Table*, 1916; *Alkestis*, (1922), 1922; *The Queen of Cornwall*, 1924; *The Ever Young*, (1929), 1935; *The Lily Maid*, 1934; *Galahad*, (1944); *Avalon*, (1945)

L.F.

BENJAMIN BRITTEN

Edward Benjamin, Lord Britten of Aldeburgh;
b 22 November 1913, Lowestoft, Suffolk, England;
d 4 December 1976, Aldeburgh, Suffolk

Britten was the first major composer to be born in England for 300 years who was first and foremost an opera composer. The premiere of *Peter Grimes* at Sadler's Wells Theatre on 7 June 1945 is generally accounted a watershed in the history of British music. Although there had been hostility to its production among members of the company, the opera's impact on the public and on most of the critics was likened to a fresh, invigorating storm and it was immediately recognized as the start of a new age for British opera as well as of a brilliant dramatic career for its composer. Within three years it had been produced in the major opera houses of Europe, including Milan, where Tullio Serafin conducted it, and in the United States, where its first conductor was Leonard Bernstein.

There was general astonishment in 1945 that Britten's first opera should be so stageworthy and show such theatrical and dramatic flair. It was then not widely known that during his sojourn in North America from 1939 to 1942 he had composed what he called an 'operetta', *Paul Bunyan*, to a libretto by his friend W. H. Auden. This was performed by university students and was remarkable for its assimilation of the American idiom, so that it both had the zip and immediate melodic appeal of a Broadway musical and also absorbed other elements from spirituals, folk ballads and choral music. *Paul Bunyan* marked out its creator as a 'natural' for stage subjects. With hindsight it can be seen that there was a nascent opera composer in some of the concert works by which his name first became known to British audiences before the Second World War; for example, the symphonic cycle *Our Hunting Fathers* (1936), for voice and orchestra, also to a text compiled and partly written by Auden, is intensely dramatic.

Although *Peter Grimes* was staged at the Royal Opera House, Covent Garden, in 1947, Britten's immediate operatic future was not to be in large opera houses. He was first associated with Glyndebourne, Sussex, where *The Rape of Lucretia* was first performed in July 1946. A second chamber opera, *Albert Herring*, followed a year later, but by then a provincial tour of *The Rape of Lucretia* had been a financial disaster and although John Christie, the owner of Glyndebourne, stood the loss, he stated that this was as far as he would go. Early in 1947, the English Opera Group, with Britten, the writer and producer Eric Crozier and the artist John Piper as artistic directors, was launched as a non-profit-making company.

Touring again proved costly and in 1948 Britten, Peter Pears (Britten's lifelong partner and interpreter) and Crozier founded a festival at Aldeburgh, Suffolk, where Britten and Pears had bought a house. Thereafter many of Britten's works were written specifically for this festival, held in June each year. But, as it happened, Britten's next three major operas were not composed for Aldeburgh. For the 1951 Festival of

Britain he wrote *Billy Budd* for Covent Garden, a return to the large orchestra and chorus of *Peter Grimes*. With its all-male cast and grim story, it was not at first a popular success, but revivals in the 1970s and 1980s established it, in the opinion of many, as Britten's greatest opera. It was followed by *Gloriana*, commissioned by Covent Garden for the coronation of Elizabeth II in 1953. This, too, was a relative failure, the first-night audience being offended by the supposed *lèse-majesté* of the treatment of Queen Elizabeth I and her relationship with the earl of Essex. Wounded, Britten returned to chamber opera, and composed *The Turn of the Screw*, based on Henry James's ghost story, for the Venice Biennale in 1954.

In 1956 Britten visited Bali, where he was profoundly impressed by the sounds of the gamelan. These were not entirely strange to him, since he had been introduced to them in 1939 by Colin McPhee. Henceforward, however, exotic Eastern sounds became a feature of his orchestration, giving rise even to such a homely invention as the 'slung mugs' representing rain in *Noye's Fludde* (1957). Memories of the gamelan lend a supernatural glitter to the score of *A Midsummer Night's Dream* (1960), but find full expression in the three church parables, *Curlew River*, *The Burning Fiery Furnace* and *The Prodigal Son*, composed between 1964 and 1968. Another major influence here was Britten's first encounter with the art of the Noh play in Japan in 1956. In these three works, highly sophisticated as they are musically, Britten achieved his ideal of providing operas that could be performed almost by improvisation in the surroundings of a village church or hall.

Britten's deep pacifist convictions, fuelled by the Vietnam War, led him to select an antimilitaristic short story by Henry James – *Owen Wingrave* – for his next opera, written for television but soon transferred to Covent Garden. His last opera – composed in a grim race against time when his doctors diagnosed a serious heart condition for which surgery was essential – was based on Thomas Mann's *Death in Venice*. This was produced at Snape Maltings, the Aldeburgh Festival's concert hall and opera house, although the composer was too ill to attend the rehearsals and first performance.

Paul Bunyan

Operetta in a prologue and two acts (2h)
Libretto by W. H. Auden
Composed 1939–41; rev., with new instrumental introduction, 1974–5
PREMIERES 5 May 1941, Brander Matthews Hall, Columbia University, New York; rev. version: UK: 1 February 1976, Manchester (BBC radio); 4 June 1976, The Maltings, Snape, Suffolk
CAST in the prologue: *satb* chorus of Old Trees; 4 Young Trees 2 *s*, 2 *t*; 3 Wild Geese 2 *ms*, 1 *s*; Narrator in the Ballad Interludes *bar* or *t*, Voice of Paul Bunyan *spoken role*; Johnny Inkslinger *t*, Tiny *s*; Hot Biscuit Slim *t*, Sam Sharkey *t*, Ben Benny *b*, Hel Helson *bar*, Andy Anderson *t*, Pete Peterson *t*, Jen Jenson *b*, Cross Crosshaulson *b*, John Shears *bar*, Western Union boy *t*, Fido *high s*, Moppet *ms*, Poppet *ms*, Quartet of the Defeated (Blues) *c*, *t*, *bar*, *b*; 4 Cronies of Hel Helson 4 *bar*; Heron, Moon, Wind, Beetle,

Squirrel *spoken roles*; *satb* chorus of lumberjacks, farmers and frontier women

In 1939, when Britten was living in America, his American publisher, Hans Heinsheimer, suggested that he and Auden should write something that could be performed by an American high school. They chose the giant logger of American folklore, Paul Bunyan (who grew as tall as the Empire State Building), and used the subject as the vehicle for Auden's indictment of aspects of modern American society. His libretto follows America from virgin forest to settlement and cultivation, when 'the human task is now a different one, of how to live well in a country that the pioneers have made it possible to live in'.

SYNOPSIS

After a brief prologue and a narrator's ballad describing Paul Bunyan's giant dimensions, Act I shows Bunyan's loggers at work. A Swede, Hel Helson, is their foreman and Johnny Inkslinger, an intellectual, becomes Bunyan's aide-de-camp. When the two male cooks are sacked, a cowboy, Slim, takes over. He is helped in the kitchen by Tiny, Bunyan's daughter. Inkslinger warns Bunyan that Helson could be a bad influence and that some of the loggers want to become farmers.

Act II Bunyan leads some of the men to be farmers at Topsy Turvy mountain, 1000 miles away. In his absence Helson is encouraged to usurp Bunyan's leadership and when Paul returns they fight. Helson loses, admits his folly and is forgiven ('Great day of discovery'). Tiny and Slim have meanwhile declared their love. In the last scene, on Christmas Eve, the camp is breaking up as new jobs are offered to its leaders. Tiny and Slim are to manage a Manhattan hotel, Inkslinger goes to Hollywood, and Helson to Washington. Finally Bunyan bids farewell, telling them that America is what they choose to make it.

The emphasis in *Paul Bunyan* is on ensemble rather than 'star' roles, and Britten's use of the chorus as a dramatic force clearly anticipates *Peter Grimes*. His keen ear for parody and pastiche is here at its most finely tuned, and the score indicates how rapidly he had absorbed the American idiom – though in his cabaret songs of 1937 he had already shown his penchant for composing blues and for writing in the style of George Gershwin and Cole Porter. Some of the 'arias' sound like hit songs from *Oklahoma!*, which *Paul Bunyan* predates by two years, and the ballad interludes are in 'country and western' style. Although Britten himself said he had problems with Auden's self-consciously wordy libretto, the text is in itself a brilliant piece of work and must have stimulated Britten to rival its wit and its extraordinary encapsulation of the spirit of Roosevelt's New Deal. The spirit of Kurt Weill's American musicals also flavours *Paul Bunyan*.

Peter Grimes

Opera in a prologue and three acts (2h 15m)
Libretto by Montagu Slater, after George Crabbe's poem *The Borough* (1810); rev. version published 1961

Composed January 1944–10 February 1945
PREMIERES 7 June 1945, Sadler's Wells, London; US:
6 August 1946, Berkshire Music Center, Lenox,
Massachusetts (Tanglewood)
CAST Peter Grimes *t*, Boy (John) *silent*, Ellen Orford *s*,
Captain Balstrode *bar*, Auntie *c*, Niece 1 *s*, Niece 2 *s*, Bob
Boles *t*, Swallow *b*, Mrs Sedley *ms*, Revd Horace Adams *t*,
Ned Keene *bar*, Hobson *b*, Dr Crabbe *silent*; *satb* chorus of
townspeople and fisherfolk

The plan for an opera on the subject of Peter Grimes
originated when Britten and Pears, staying on the
West Coast of America, read an article by E. M.
Forster about George Crabbe in the *Listener* (29 May
1941). It made them homesick for Aldeburgh, the
subject of Crabbe's poem *The Borough*, and anxious
to read his poetry. Pears found an edition in San
Diego and Britten at once saw the operatic possibilities
of the section dealing with the sadistic fisherman Peter
Grimes, accused of ill-treating and murdering his apprentices. Grimes appealed to Britten as an outsider
in society, the first of several of his operatic heroes (or
anti-heroes) who embody this experience: a reflection
of Britten's own position as a homosexual and conscientious objector.

When Britten was offered a commission of $1000
from the Koussevitzky Music Foundation for a full-
length opera, he and Pears began to sketch a scenario
before they sailed back to Britain in March 1942.
There he approached the playwright Montagu Slater,
with whom he had worked on left-wing plays in the
1930s. This was a prickly collaboration, since Slater
worked slowly and did not always meet Britten's
wishes. Some of the libretto was rewritten during
rehearsals by Eric Crozier (who produced the first
performance), Britten and Pears.

In 1944 Britten played parts of the opera to the
soprano Joan Cross, who was managing Sadler's Wells
Opera during its arduous wartime tours. She became
'possessive' (her own word) about the work and decided it was the ideal opera to reopen Sadler's Wells
Theatre in London when the war ended. But she
encountered fierce hostility from within the company.
Tired and bored by four years of provincial touring of
a limited repertoire, they found this modern score
unattractive and, some of them claimed, unsingable
and unplayable. Nevertheless, Cross had her way.
Pears sang the title role; Cross sang Ellen Orford; the
designs were by Kenneth Green, and Reginald
Goodall conducted. Tension backstage on the first
night was high. However, most of the reviews were
ecstatic, like the public's response, and *Peter Grimes*
was launched on its international career. Pears's
Grimes was one of his strongest characterizations,
never losing sight of Britten's interpretation of the
character as a romantic figure. Another major assumption of the role, rougher and harsher, was that of the
Canadian tenor Jon Vickers. Tyrone Guthrie's Covent
Garden production in 1947 was outstanding for its
handling of the crowd scenes and powerful creation of
the atmosphere of a witch hunt. *Peter Grimes* has
remained the most popular of Britten's operas.

SYNOPSIS

Prologue An inquest is held in the Moot Hall of the
Borough into the death of the young apprentice of the
fisherman Peter Grimes, who explains that on the way
to London to sell a huge catch they were blown off
course and ran out of drinking water. After three days
the boy died. The coroner, Mr Swallow, returns a
verdict of accidental death but advises Grimes not to
get another apprentice. After the court has been
cleared, Ellen Orford, who has befriended Grimes,
pleads with him, in vain, to leave the Borough with
her.

Act I

Interlude I ['Dawn']

Scene 1: Morning by the sea, in a street outside the
Moot Hall and the Boar public house. Women are
mending the nets ('Oh, hang at open doors the nets').
Borough personalities arrive: the Methodist fisherman
Bob Boles, the Boar's landlady Auntie and her two
'nieces' (as they are euphemistically called), Mrs
Sedley, widow of an East India Company employee,
the rector, the Revd. Horace Adams, and Balstrode, a
retired merchant sea captain. When Grimes calls for
help to haul up a boat, only Balstrode and Ned
Keene, the apothecary, go to his aid. Keene tells
Grimes he has found another apprentice at the work-
house. Hobson the carrier will fetch him. Ellen agrees
to accompany Hobson to look after the boy. She
rebukes those who criticize her ('Let her among you
without fault cast the first stone'). The entire cast
sings together of the approaching storm which 'will
eat the land'. Balstrode advises Grimes to join the
merchant fleet, but Grimes says he is rooted in the
Borough. He describes the boy's death ('Picture what
that day was like') and says his ambition is to make
enough money from fishing to buy a shop and marry
Ellen ('They listen to money'). Grimes sings of Ellen
('What harbour shelters peace?').

Interlude II ['Storm']

Scene 2: Inside the Boar, Mrs Sedley awaits Hobson's
return with her consignment of laudanum. Each new
arrival tells of storm damage along the coast. Quarrels
break out, quietened by Balstrode ('We live and let
live, and look, we keep our hands to ourselves').
Grimes enters, wet and dishevelled, and begins a soliloquy ('Now the Great Bear and Pleiades'). Boles,
drunk, tries to attack him, but Balstrode intervenes
and Keene starts up a catch ('Old Joe has gone
fishing'). Hobson, Ellen and the boy (John) arrive and
Grimes immediately takes the boy to his hut on the
cliff.

Act II

Interlude III ['Sunday Morning']

Scene 1: In the street again, on a Sunday morning
some weeks later, Ellen and the boy sit watching the
churchgoers and listening to the hymns ('Glitter of
waves'). Ellen notices a tear in the boy's coat and a
bruise on his neck. Grimes comes to collect the boy –
he has seen a shoal. Ellen pleads for the boy to have a
day's rest and tells Grimes the Borough's gossips will
never be silenced – their own dreams were a mistake.
In anguish, he strikes her and runs after the boy. This
scene has been observed by Keene, Boles and others,
who stir up anger against Grimes ('Grimes is at his
exercise'). Ellen explains her compassion, but is
shouted down. The rector proposes a visit to Grimes's

hut by the men alone, but the crowd follows ('Now is gossip put on trial'). Only Auntie, the nieces and Ellen remain ('From the gutter, why should we trouble at their ribaldries?').

Interlude IV: Passacaglia

Scene 2: In his hut, Grimes dresses the boy to go to sea. He thinks of the life he had planned with Ellen ('In dreams I've built myself some kindlier home'). But he also imagines he can see his dead former apprentice staring at him. He sees the rector's procession coming up the hill and blames the boy and Ellen for gossiping. He opens the cliff door and the boy scrambles out and falls. Grimes goes after him. The rector and his companions find an empty, tidy hut. Looking out of the open door they comment on the landslide. They leave, saying they have misjudged Grimes.

Act III

Interlude V ['Moonlight']

Scene 1: A few days later, on a summer evening in the village street, sounds of a dance are heard. The nieces run from the hall, followed by Swallow ('Assign your prettiness to me'). Mrs Sedley tackles Keene about the missing Grimes and his apprentice ('Murder most foul it is'). He dismisses her but she hides and hears Balstrode tell Ellen that Grimes's boat has returned, although there is no sign of him or the boy. Ellen has found the boy's jersey, on which she had embroidered an anchor ('Embroidery in childhood'). They vow to help Grimes. Mrs Sedley has overheard this conversation and summons Swallow to tell him Grimes's boat is back. Shouting 'Peter Grimes!' the crowd sets off on a manhunt.

Interlude VI

Scene 2: To the distant sounds of a foghorn and the voices of the mob, Grimes enters, weary and demented. Ellen and Balstrode approach him. Balstrode tells him to take his boat out of sight of shore and sink it. Next morning the Borough resumes normal life. Swallow says the coastguard has reported a boat sinking. 'One of these rumours,' Auntie says.

The principal character in *Peter Grimes* is the Borough. Although the opera has a major central figure in Grimes, it repeats the pattern of *Paul Bunyan* in having a number of smaller, vividly drawn parts. Grimes is probably the least well drawn, for, while he is given magnificent music, the romanticizing of Crabbe's brutal fisherman into a misjudged victim of society is at odds with the plot. But such is the power and conviction of Britten's score that this in no way lessens the opera's impact.

In many respects, *Grimes* is less 'original' than *Paul Bunyan*. It is a brilliant synthesis – as is *Bunyan* – of the influences that made Britten the composer he was. It sounds fresh and 'different', but on closer acquaintance one realizes that the novelty is really Britten's ability, also displayed in works such as *Les Illuminations* (1939) and the *Serenade* (1943), to present old forms and musical devices as if they were new. *Peter Grimes* is an opera in the great tradition – with a storm and a mad scene – but it owes something also to Berg's *Wozzeck*.

Britten unified the opera symphonically through six extended orchestral interludes. The pre-act interludes are atmospheric pieces, describing the scene and mood to follow, while those between the scenes are psychological commentaries on the plot and in particular on Grimes himself. The storm (Interlude II), for instance, is not only a wonderful depiction of an east-coast gale, but a penetrating analysis of the conflicts in Grimes's mind as he moves towards madness. The finest interlude is the Passacaglia, a favourite form of Britten's. His word-setting is one of the opera's great features – the prologue, for example, with its naturalistic recitative contrasted with Grimes's arioso.

The Rape of Lucretia

Opera in two acts (1h 45m)
Libretto by Ronald Duncan, based on André Obey's play *Le viol de Lucrèce* (1931)
Composed 1945–6; rev. 1947
PREMIERES 12 July 1946, Glyndebourne, Sussex; US: 1 June 1947, Shubert Theater of Chicago Opera, Chicago
CAST Male Chorus *t*, Female Chorus *s*, Collatinus *b*, Junius *bar*, Tarquinius *bar*, Lucretia *c*, Bianca *ms*, Lucia *s*

In March 1946, when the team that had championed *Peter Grimes* in 1945 resigned from Sadler's Wells – among them the soprano Joan Cross, the producer Eric Crozier, and Britten's partner the tenor Peter Pears – Britten joined them in forming a new company to perform new works at the least possible expense, implying chamber operas. At first the company was called the Glyndebourne English Opera Company, and *The Rape of Lucretia* was premiered at Glyndebourne, which itself had been closed during the war. Its general manager, Rudolf Bing, persuaded its owner, John Christie, that an association with Britten and his colleagues would be worthwhile. Britten agreed to compose an opera for eight singers and twelve musicians for a limited Glyndebourne season in the summer of 1946. Crozier suggested the subject of the rape of Lucretia and Britten chose as his librettist his friend Ronald Duncan, for whose verse play *This Way to the Tomb* he had composed incidental music in 1945. For the first performances at Glyndebourne, the opera was produced by Crozier and the designer was John Piper, who was later to design several other Britten operas. Two casts were assembled, with Kathleen Ferrier and Nancy Evans alternating as Lucretia, and Ernest Ansermet and Reginald Goodall as conductors. The company then took the opera on tour in the provinces and to Holland. For the 1947 Glyndebourne performances of *The Rape of Lucretia*, the libretto was revised and a substitute aria was composed for Collatinus in Act I. After Ferrier's death in 1953, the outstanding Lucretia was Janet Baker, who sang the role on stage and recorded it in 1970. Like *Peter Grimes*, *The Rape of Lucretia* was performed widely in Europe and North America.

SYNOPSIS

Act I Scene 1: The male and female choruses recount how 'the Etruscan upstart' Tarquinius Superbus seized power in Rome and how his son Tarquinius

Sextus has become a warrior leader and 'treats the proud city as if it were his whore'. Their perspective on the action of the opera is in relation to an event still 500 years in the future – Christ's birth and death. The curtain rises to show an army camp outside Rome. In the generals' tent, Collatinus, Junius and Tarquinius are drinking and talking about women. On the previous night, six generals had ridden back to Rome to check on their wives' fidelity. The only wife found virtuously at home was Collatinus' wife, Lucretia. Junius, whose wife was found with a Negro, quarrels violently with the unmarried Tarquinius. Collatinus parts them and proposes a toast to Lucretia. Junius rushes from the tent. He is sick of hearing Lucretia's name because Collatinus will win over political supporters from him on the strength of her chastity. Collatinus joins Junius and rebukes him for his attitude to Lucretia. They shake hands, at which point a drunken Tarquinius leaves the tent and mocks Junius as a cuckold. Collatinus brings them together, leaving the two generals to discuss women and power. Women are whores by nature, Junius says. Not Lucretia, Tarquinius retorts, adding 'I'll prove her chaste' and calling for his horse. In an interlude, the male chorus describes Tarquinius' ride to Rome ('Tarquinius does not wait'). Scene 2: In Lucretia's house in Rome that evening she is sewing while her servants Bianca and Lucia are spinning. She thinks she hears a knock at the gate, but Lucia finds no one there. Before folding the linen, Lucretia sings, 'How cruel men are to teach us love!' The three women prepare to go to bed while the male and female choruses describe Tarquinius' arrival in Rome and his violent knock on Lucretia's door. He asks Lucretia for wine and says his horse is lame. She shows him to a room for the night.

Act II Scene 1: A short introduction by the choruses and offstage voices describes the Etruscan domination of Rome. Then Lucretia is seen asleep in her bedroom with Tarquinius approaching the bed (male chorus: 'When Tarquin desires, then Tarquin will dare'). Tarquinius kisses her and she, dreaming of her husband, draws him to her. She wakes and repulses him ('How could I give, Tarquinius, since I have given to Collatinus?'). They struggle until he draws his sword and rapes her. The choruses, in an interlude, invoke Christ's compassion. Scene 2: In the hall of Lucretia's home, Lucia and Bianca extol the beauty of the morning and arrange flowers ('Oh, Lucia, please help me fill my vase with laughing daffodils'). Bianca has heard Tarquinius gallop away before dawn. Lucretia enters in a trancelike state. She says she hates the flowers and gives an orchid to Lucia for a messenger to take to Collatinus with a message that a Roman harlot has sent it. She makes a wreath from the remaining orchids ('Flowers bring to every year the same perfection'). Bianca tries to stop the messenger, but Collatinus has already arrived with Junius, who alerted him after seeing Tarquinius leave the camp and return at dawn. Lucretia enters in purple mourning ('Now there is no sea deep enough to drown my shame'). She tells Collatinus what has happened. He forgives her, but she stabs herself to death. In an epilogue the choruses ask, 'Is it all?' and conclude that Jesus Christ is all.

Britten unifies the score by two motifs, one for Tarquinius, the other for Lucretia, constructed from a diminished fourth. These dominate the work in various subtle guises. The male and female choruses have a chorale-like motif, which establishes their credentials as Christian commentators. The scoring for the small orchestra is a masterpiece of colour and imaginative sonority, with the harp's contribution a major feature. Like several Britten scores, *The Rape of Lucretia* is full of nocturnal imagery and onomatopoeic sounds – the chirp of crickets, the croaking of bullfrogs. When the female chorus describes the sleeping Lucretia, the evocative instrumentation is alto flute, bass clarinet and muted horn.

The full sound of the chamber orchestra is deployed to brilliant effect in the accompaniment to the male chorus's description of Tarquinius' ride, a remarkable piece of graphic scoring. Lyrical passages abound in the opera: the sensuous trio for the women as they fold the linen and the music, full of summer morning heat, of 'O what a lovely day' at the start of the tragic final scene. Here Britten again employs one of his favourite devices, the passacaglia.

Albert Herring
Comic opera in three acts (2h 15m)
Libretto by Eric Crozier, after Guy de Maupassant's short story *Le rosier de Madame Husson* (1888)
PREMIERES 20 June 1947, Glyndebourne, Sussex; US: 8 August 1949, Berkshire Music Center, Lenox, Massachusetts (Tanglewood)
CAST Albert *t*, Lady Billows *s*, Mrs Herring *ms*, Florence Pike *c*, Vicar (Mr Gedge) *bar*, The Mayor (Mr Upfold) *t*, Miss Wordsworth *s*, Superintendent Budd *b*, Sid *bar*, Nancy *ms*, Emmie *s*, Cis *s*, Harry *treble*

Albert Herring was written as a companion piece to *The Rape of Lucretia* for performance by the same vocal and instrumental forces. It was first performed at Glyndebourne, whose owner, John Christie, disliked it intensely and is said to have greeted members of the first-night audience with the words: 'This isn't our kind of thing, you know.' Nevertheless, nearly 40 years later, in 1985, the Glyndebourne production by Peter Hall was one of the most successful the opera has had. Having shown the tragic aspects of Aldeburgh life in the early years of the 19th century in *Peter Grimes*, Britten now showed its comic side, taking the opportunity to poke fun at a Lady Bountiful, moral hypocrisy, village fêtes, mayors, vicars, schoolmarms and policemen. The gift for parody, which he had exhibited in *Paul Bunyan* and in several of his instrumental compositions, was again to the fore in *Albert Herring* and ranged from the Sullivanesque to self-quotation. In spite of criticism in Britten's own country that the opera was 'cosily provincial' in its treatment of stock characters, *Albert Herring* has proved popular in translation in several European and Scandinavian countries. Like the best comedies, it has a dark side.

SYNOPSIS
Act I Scene 1: The mayor and vicar of Loxford, the schoolmistress Miss Wordsworth and Police Superintendent Budd are meeting Lady Billows in her breakfast room on 10 April 1900 to select a May Queen. Lady Billows announces that she is putting up a prize of 25 sovereigns. Each member of the committee puts forward a candidate, but each name is torpedoed by Florence Pike, Lady Billows's housekeeper, who knows something disreputable about them all. Budd suggests a King of the May and nominates Albert Herring, who works for his mother in her greengrocer's. Encouraged by the vicar and by a general chorus of 'Albert is virtuous', Lady Billows agrees. Scene 2: Mrs Herring's shop. Sid the butcher's assistant taunts Albert for being under his mother's thumb and tells him of delights in store if he breaks the apron strings – 'Courting a girl is the king of all sports'. Nancy from the bakery joins them and Sid makes an assignation with her for that night ('Meet me at quarter past eight'). Left alone, Albert muses that Sid might be right that he misses all the fun. Lady Billows, with the rest of the committee, arrives ('We bring great news to you upon this happy day!'). Albert regards his election as May King as 'daft' and tells his mother he will refuse. But Mrs Herring has heard about the 25-sovereign prize.

Act II Scene 1: Inside the marquee near the vicarage. A trestle table has been set for 11 places. Sid tells Nancy that he plans to put a generous tot of rum into Albert's lemonade ('Just loosen him up and make him feel bright'). The bigwigs now arrive with Albert, who is wearing a straw hat crowned with a wreath of orange blossom. The children sing their welcome to him and present flowers to Lady Billows, Albert and Mrs Herring. Lady Billows orates about the evils of carnal indulgence, gambling and the havoc wrought by gin. After receiving various prizes, Albert calls for three cheers for Lady Billows, drains his glass and promptly has hiccups. Scene 2: The shop. Albert, tipsy rather than drunk, recalls the feast he has just eaten – 'but oh! the taste of that lemonade'. He has been disturbed by Nancy – 'why did she stare each time I looked towards her?' He then hears Sid whistle in the street outside. Nancy joins Sid and Albert overhears them discussing him, saying he'll be all right once he's sown a few wild oats. They kiss and go off to the common. Albert tosses a coin and decides to leave. His mother returns, calls him, and gets no reply. 'Fast asleep, poor kid. Worn out by all this fuss.'

Act III The shop, the following afternoon. Albert is missing and the whole town is searching for him. Nancy, who has a guilty conscience, quarrels with Sid, who doesn't think Albert is dead. Superintendent Budd asks Mrs Herring for a photograph of Albert to send round the police stations. She gives him one in a frame ('It was took on the pier at Felixstowe'). Lady Billows demands that Scotland Yard and Conan Doyle should be called in. The mayor solemnly carries in a tray. Underneath a cloth cover is Albert's orange-blossom wreath, found on a road crushed by a cart. All now assume Albert is dead and sing a threnody 'In the midst of life is death'. As it ends a dishevelled

and mud-stained Albert returns. They turn on him and cross-examine him. He has spent three of his 25 pounds and has been with girls; he got drunk in one pub, until he was ejected, and started a fight in another. He turns on his mother – 'you squashed me down and reined me in'. Lady Billows prophesies he will pay for his sins of the flesh. Albert is left with Sid and Nancy and the village children, who now see him in a new light.

Albert Herring is a brilliantly successful comic opera, almost Rossinian in the speed and dexterity of Britten's treatment of recitatives. Contrapuntal treatment of certain episodes – fugal and canonic – is also extremely adept. The orchestral interludes are as racy, witty and illustrative as anything Britten wrote, and his use of parody and quotation is inspired. The children's street-game song, the hymnlike 'Albert the Good' and the zany patriotism of Lady Billows's speech in the marquee are superb examples of Britten's fertile melodic invention. The committee meeting in Act I is a notable example of Britten's gift for characterization. Each character is given an apposite aria, from the vicar's quasi-ecclesiastical vocalizing to Miss Wordsworth's ballad-like twitterings. When Albert's lemonade is laced with rum and when he drinks it, the love-potion motif from Wagner's *Tristan* coils upwards and when Budd the policeman confides to Sid that he'd find 'a criminal case of rape' preferable to a manhunt, the orchestra quotes Lucretia's motif.

The musical climax is the nine-part threnody in Act III. This begins as a parody of a chant, but it quickly becomes a deeply felt lament, with each of the characters making an individual contribution and, towards the end, joining together in an elaborate piece of polyphonic writing over a pedal B♭. It is at this moment, when the opera turns serious, that one experiences it most strongly as a nostalgic re-creation of a vanished England.

The Little Sweep
A children's opera in three scenes (45m)
Libretto by Eric Crozier
PREMIERES 14 June 1949, Jubilee Hall, Aldeburgh, Suffolk; US: 22 March 1950, Kiel Auditorium, St Louis, Missouri
CAST Black Bob *b*, Clem *t*, Sam *treble*, Miss Baggott *c*, Juliet Brook *s*, Gay Brook *treble*, Sophie Brook *s*, Rowan *s*, Jonny Crome *treble*, Hugh Crome *treble*, Tina Crome *s*, Tom *b*, Alfred *t*

The Little Sweep was the first opera Britten wrote for the Aldeburgh Festival, which he had founded in 1948. It formed part of an entertainment called *Let's Make an Opera!* This was a play (with incidental music) in which adults and children are shown preparing to perform the opera they have written. Part of its purpose was to enable the conductor to rehearse the audience in their contribution. Later the librettist, Eric Crozier, revised the play by enlarging it to two acts. In 1965 he condensed the two acts into one, but he then decided the play did not wear well and it was not reprinted. Ideally, it should be rewritten to suit the circumstances and personalities of any group performing *The Little Sweep*.

SYNOPSIS

Scene 1: Black Bob, the sweepmaster, and his son Clem bring Sam, aged eight, to sweep the nursery chimney at Iken Hall, supervised by Miss Baggott the housekeeper and watched sympathetically by Rowan, the nursery maid, who pleads in vain for Sam not to be sent up the chimney. Sam gets stuck and is rescued by the children of the house and their guests, who hide him and make it appear he has run away. The sweep and Miss Baggott leave to search for him, but Rowan sings, 'Run, poor sweepboy!' The children welcome her as an ally and reveal Sam's hiding-place. Scene 2: The children and Rowan have given Sam a bath. They plan to hide him in the toy cupboard for the night and smuggle him out next day. When Miss Baggott returns and is about to open the cupboard, Juliet 'faints' as a distraction. Scene 3: The next morning. Juliet gives Sam three half-crowns as a gift from her friends who are going home. Sam is packed into a trunk which the coachman and gardener refuse to lift because of its weight. The children help them and wave Sam to freedom.

Britten's skill in writing for children was never better exemplified than in this ingenious little work. As an introduction to opera, it must be unrivalled in its seductive charm. The use of choruses involving the audience, instead of orchestral interludes, is a clever device. Spoken dialogue takes the place of recitative.

Billy Budd

Opera in four acts; rev. as two acts (2h 45m)
Libretto by E. M. Forster and Eric Crozier, adapted from the story *Billy Budd, Foretopman* by Herman Melville (1891)
Composed 1950–51, rev. 1960
PREMIERES four-act version: 1 December 1951, Covent Garden, London; US: 19 October 1952, NBC Television Opera Workshop, New York (excerpts); 7 December 1952, Indiana University Opera Theater, Bloomington, Indiana; two-act version: 13 November 1960 (BBC broadcast); 9 January 1964, Covent Garden; US: 4 January 1966, Carnegie Hall, New York (concert); 6 November 1970, Civic Opera House, Chicago
CAST Captain Vere *t*, Billy Budd *bar*, Claggart *b*, Mr Redburn *bar*, Mr Flint *b-bar*, Lieutenant Ratcliffe *b*, Red Whiskers *t*, Dansker *b*, Donald *bar*, Novice *t*, Squeak *t*, Novice's Friend *bar*, Captain's Cabin Boy *spoken role*, Bosun *bar*, First Mate *bar*, Second Mate *bar*, Maintop *t*, Arthur Jones *bar*, 4 Midshipmen *boys' voices*; *tb* chorus of officers, sailors, powder monkeys, drummers, marines

Britten himself suggested the subject of Billy Budd to Crozier and Forster, who began work on the text in 1949; Crozier was responsible for the technical scenes and the dialogue, Forster for the 'big slabs of narrative'. The libretto is almost wholly in prose, since Forster could not write poetry, though some verses from Melville were interpolated, such as the ballad 'Billy in the Darbies', which is appended to the original story. Melville's first draft (1888) was a short story, *Baby Budd, Sailor*. This was expanded to a novella, *Billy Budd, Foretopman*, and completed in April 1891,

a few months before the author's death. Melville was moved to write the story by events in 1842 aboard the United States brig-of-war *Somers* (and known as the Mackenzie Case), but he transferred the action to the Royal Navy just after the mutinies at Spithead and The Nore in 1797. Britten was attracted by this tale of innocence destroyed, of good crushed by evil and of an 'outsider' against society.

Britten's relationship with both librettists underwent crises during composition of the opera, which is certainly a masterpiece born of creative tensions. The fourth draft of the libretto was finished at the end of 1949. Britten began to compose the music in earnest six months later. The first performance at Covent Garden was to have been conducted by Josef Krips but he withdrew at a late stage and Britten himself took over. Although the opera was fully appreciated by a handful of critics, it was generally received with a cold respect and it was not until nearly 20 years later that it became a real success with the public.

Billy Budd had been planned in two acts, but, for reasons Britten himself could not remember, it was made into four. Three interruptions of the action for intervals weakened the dramatic flow, and in 1960 Britten reverted to the two-act format. In doing so, he deleted a scene at the end of Act I, when Captain Vere addresses his crew with a rousing death-or-glory speech. In the revised version, the crew discuss Vere – 'he cares for us, he wishes us well' – and Billy sings, 'Star of the morning . . . I'd die to save you.'

SYNOPSIS

Act I The action takes place on board the *Indomitable*, a seventy-four, during the French wars of 1797. Prologue: Captain Vere, as an old man, looks back over his life. He has found 'always some flaw' in the good that has come his way, 'some stammer in the divine speech'. Scene 1: The main deck and quarterdeck. A cutter returns to the ship with three press-ganged recruits. One is Billy Budd, a foundling and an able seaman, whose answers reveal that he stammers. But Claggart, the master-at-arms, calls him 'the jewel of great price'. He is placed in the foretop and is exultant ('Billy Budd, king of the birds!'). During this aria he sings farewell to his former merchantman, 'Farewell, old *Rights o' Man*'. This disturbs the officers, who associate the phrase 'Rights of Man' with Thomas Paine's seditious book, a sensitive issue after the mutinies. Claggart calls Squeak, the ship's corporal, and orders him to keep an eye on Billy and to 'tangle up his hammock, mess his kit, spill his grog'. Dansker, an old seaman, warns Billy to beware of Claggart, known as Jemmy Legs. Scene 2: Captain Vere's cabin, a week later. Vere sends for the officers Redburn and Flint to take wine with him. They look forward to being in action ('Don't like the French') and mention Billy's shout of 'Rights o' Man'. Vere dismisses their fears: 'No danger there.' Scene 3: The berth deck. The seamen are singing ('Blow her away'). Billy and Red Whiskers try to persuade Dansker to join in, but he says he's too old. All he misses is tobacco. Billy offers to lend him some and goes to his kitbag. He begins to stammer as he finds Squeak there. Squeak draws a knife. Billy knocks him down just as Claggart appears. Dansker tells him what happened and Claggart has no option but to have Squeak put in irons. Left alone, Claggart sings his evil Credo about Billy: 'Would that I never encountered you . . . I have you in my power and I will destroy you.' The novice joins him and, after some hesitation, agrees to tempt Billy with money to lead a mutiny. Furious, Billy strikes out. The scene has been witnessed by Dansker, who tells him, 'Jemmy Legs is down on you.'

Act II Scene 1: The main deck and quarter-deck some days later. Claggart asks to see Vere, who is visibly irritated by his sycophantic and long-winded manner of presenting his complaint. He still has not reached the point when they are interrupted by a shout of 'Enemy sail on starboard bow'. The crew goes to action stations ('This is the moment'), but the French ship escapes in a mist. Claggart returns to his charge and tells how the Novice was offered gold by Billy to join a mutiny. Vere ridicules him, but agrees to see Billy. Scene 2: Vere's cabin. Vere calls in Claggart, who formally accuses Billy of mutiny. Billy is aghast, stammers, and shoots out his right fist which strikes Claggart's forehead. Claggart falls dead. Vere calls in the three officers to hold a drumhead court martial. Billy pleads with Vere to save him, but Vere stays silent. Scene 3: A bay of the gun deck, shortly before dawn. Billy, in irons, sings his ballad, 'Look! Through the port comes the moonshine astray!' Dansker brings him food. The whole ship is seething, he says, and some of the crew plan to rescue Billy. Billy says they must not or they will hang too. Alone, he sings, 'I've sighted a sail in the storm, the far-shining sail.' Scene 4: The main deck and quarter-deck at 4 a.m. The crew assembles in silence. Billy cries, 'Starry Vere, God bless you!' As he is hanged, an ugly muttering from the crew grows louder. The officers order, 'Down all hands.' Epilogue: Vere as an old man describes the trial of Billy and laments, 'I could have saved him. He knew it. But he has saved me. I was lost in the infinite sea, but I've sighted a sail in the storm, the far-shining sail . . .'

Billy Budd is among Britten's greatest achievements (some are tempted to rank it the greatest). The struggle between good and evil, Billy and Claggart, is symbolized by the opposition of the chords of B♭ major and B minor which is heard in the strings that accompany Vere's musings at the start of the opera. This opposition permeates the whole score. The tonal ambiguity stands, too, for the moral uncertainty that is a feature of the opera, particularly affecting the character of Vere. Yet the music is firmly tonal, with certain keys acting almost as leitmotifs for the characters concerned. Claggart's key is F minor, for example. The opera's harmonic range is extraordinarily wide and its structure is taut and tense, the themes often similar in melodic outline as if to stress the obsessive nature of the piece.

The atmosphere is claustrophobic, but there is no sense of monotony because of the richness and variety of the orchestral score. *Billy Budd* has the largest orchestra of any of Britten's operas; it requires, for example, six percussionists. Claggart's evil is represented by the darker, lower sonorities – trombones, tuba, double bassoon. Billy's stammer is brilliantly depicted by a trill on a muted trumpet and a roll on the block. Potent use is made of the saxophone, while the large wind band is associated with the sea itself and with the harsh life aboard a man-of-war. For deeper human qualities, the strings are used with poignant effect, and Britten's writing for the chorus in the shanties is powerfully moving. Not the least skilful feature of the score is the most obvious – that it is for male voices only, without any sense of limitation or monotony.

The opera is Verdian in its juxtaposition of the public and the private – the external life of the ship and the personal dramas of Vere, Billy and Claggart. Each is given a solo aria of outstanding beauty and memorability. Yet perhaps the most compelling episode in the score is the celebrated passage when Vere tells Billy of his sentence: the stage is empty and the orchestra plays 34 slow chords, each varying in colour and dynamics and eventually reaching an F major that seems to wipe away Claggart's vile influence.

Gloriana

Opera in three acts (2h 30m)
Libretto by William Plomer, based on Lytton Strachey's
Elizabeth and Essex: A Tragic History (1928)
PREMIERES 8 June 1953, Covent Garden, London; US: 8 May 1955, Music Hall, Cincinnati, Ohio (concert); 6 June 1984, Lila Cockrell Theater, San Antonio, Texas
CAST Queen Elizabeth I *s*, Earl of Essex *t*, Countess of Essex *ms*, Lord Mountjoy *bar*, Penelope, Lady Rich *s*, Sir Robert Cecil *bar*, Sir Walter Raleigh *b*, Henry Cuffe *bar*, Lady-in-Waiting *s*, Blind Ballad-singer *b*, Recorder of Norwich *b*, Housewife *ms*, Spirit of the Masque *t*, Master of Ceremonies *t*, City Crier *bar*; *satb* chorus of citizens, maids of honour, ladies and gentlemen of the household, courtiers, masquers, old men, men and boys of Essex's following, councillors; Time *male dancer*, Concord *female dancer*; country girls, rustics, fishermen, morris dancer, *dancers*; pages, ballad-singer's runner, Sir John Harington, French ambassador, Archbishop of Canterbury, phantom kings and queens, *actors*

When Princess Elizabeth became queen in February 1952 her cousin the earl of Harewood, founder editor of *Opera* magazine (and later director of the Edinburgh Festival and managing director of English National Opera), suggested to Britten that he should compose an opera on the subject of Queen Elizabeth I and the earl of Essex to mark the coronation the following year. Royal permission was obtained and Britten laid aside all other creative work in order to complete the opera in time for the premiere on 8 June 1953, when Joan Cross sang the role of Elizabeth I and Peter Pears that of Essex.

Gloriana came at an unfortunate moment in Britten's career. Because of his success and his acceptance by a wide public, there was intense jealousy of him in musical circles (heightened by his appointment as a Companion of Honour at the age of 39) and enmity because of his homosexuality, which was then still a criminal offence. These were undoubtedly factors in the cool reception of *Gloriana*, but the gala audience comprised mainly diplomats and civil servants for many of whom any opera, let alone one by a 20th-century composer, would have been an alien and tedious experience. Because the character of Elizabeth I was not sycophantically treated in the opera, it was said that *Gloriana* was a tasteless choice for the occasion. Later performances were warmly received, but the work had been given a bad name and was soon dropped from the Covent Garden repertoire. When it was revived, in a slightly revised version, by the Sadler's Wells company in 1966 (with Sylvia Fisher in the title role) it enjoyed a popular success. But for many years after its first performance *Gloriana* remained the only Britten opera not to have been recorded in full.

SYNOPSIS

Act I   Scene 1: The earl of Essex and Lord Mountjoy, rivals for the Queen's favour, quarrel at a tournament. The queen rebukes them and they are uneasily reconciled. Scene 2: Sir Robert Cecil warns the queen against Essex's lack of restraint. Essex sings two lute songs to the queen and urges his claim to be made viceroy of Ireland.

Act II   Scene 1: Essex, Mountjoy, Cecil and others attend the queen, who is in Norwich on a royal progress. They watch a rustic masque. Scene 2: At Essex House in the Strand, Mountjoy awaits his lover, Essex's sister Lady Rich. They are joined by Essex and his wife. Essex complains of delay over the Ireland decision and all four agree that when the queen dies they will decide her successor. Scene 3: At a dance in the Palace of Whitehall, the queen humiliates the gorgeously gowned Lady Essex by ordering the ladies to change their linen and herself returning in Lady Essex's dress, which does not fit her. But a moment later she appoints Essex lord deputy of Ireland.

Act III   Scene 1: Essex's Irish campaign has failed. He bursts in on the queen while she is dressing and is without her wig. She orders him to be kept under guard. Scene 2: Essex is proclaimed a traitor after trying to persuade the citizens of London to rebel. Scene 3: Essex has been condemned to death but the queen does not sign the warrant for his execution until she is angered by Lady Rich's haughty demeanour. The opera ends with the queen speaking, not singing, while six brief episodes of her life pass before her.

Gloriana is a succession of tableaux and brilliantly succeeds in giving a dignified and touching portrait of the queen both as a public and as a private individual. All the other characters are subsidiary, even Essex himself. The music is often subtle, as when the first lute song, 'Quick music is best', is undermined in the bass by the motif that stands for the queen's cares of state. The sedition scene (Act II, Scene 2) is Verdian in its dramatic effectiveness, and there is no denying the impact of the queen's spoken epilogue, unorthodox as it may be. In the ceremonial music – the Norwich masque and at the palace ball – Britten evokes the Tudor age without a trace of pastiche.

The Turn of the Screw
Opera in a prologue and two acts (1h 45m)
Libretto by Myfanwy Piper, after the story by Henry James (1898)
PREMIERES   14 September 1954, La Fenice, Venice; UK: 6 October 1954, Sadler's Wells, London; US: 19 March 1958, New York College of Music, New York
CAST   Prologue *t*, Governess *s*, Flora *s*, Mrs Grose *s*, Quint *t*, Miss Jessel *s*, Miles *treble*

The idea for an opera based on Henry James's ghost story was given to Britten by Myfanwy Piper, wife of the artist John Piper, who had been a friend of Britten since 1935 and had provided designs for several of the operas. The theme of *The Turn of the Screw* appealed particularly to Britten – corruption and innocence. It tells of two orphaned Victorian children, brother and sister, living in an Essex country house, who come under the evil influence of the ghosts of their guardian's former valet and the governess he seduced. A new governess discovers what is happening and tries to counteract it, with disastrous consequences. James never states what happens between haunters and haunted. But the story and the opera imply some sexual or erotic relationship, and the impression of evil is all the greater for remaining unspecified. In James the ghosts never speak; Mrs Piper's outstandingly skilful libretto provides words for them to sing and Britten directed that the audience should see them. The reader of the story is left to decide whether the ghosts exist or are figments of the repressed imagination of the distraught governess (Britten's finest soprano role). James himself said he did not know. The dialogue between the ghosts at the beginning of Act II is an invention of Mrs Piper. She quotes a line from W. B. Yeats, 'The ceremony of innocence is drowned.' For Britten this was the heart of the matter.

The opera was written to a commission from the 1954 Venice Biennale. Beginning to write the music in February 1954, Britten had composed the first three scenes when he decided there should be a prologue. Another late insertion was the letter scene, one of the finest in the work. Britten worked on the opera very fast: Imogen Holst, who copied the vocal score several pages at a time and posted them to the publisher, was amazed by Britten's confidence in parting with the start of a scene before he had composed the end of it. He conducted the English Opera Group in the first performance in Venice with a fine cast fortunately preserved in a recording.

SYNOPSIS

Prologue (to be played in front of a drop curtain)   A male narrator relates 'a curious story' written 'long ago' by a woman: it tells how she agreed to become governess to two orphaned children in the country on condition that she would never write to their handsome young guardian because he was so busy.
Act I
Theme
Scene 1: 'The Journey'. The governess is in a coach travelling to Bly ('Nearly there. Very soon I shall know'). How will the old housekeeper welcome her?

Variation I

Scene 2: 'The Welcome'. On the porch at Bly Mrs Grose, the housekeeper, and the excited children, Flora and Miles, await the governess ('Mrs Grose! Mrs Grose! Will she be nice?'). They practise curtseying and bowing. The governess finds them charming and beautiful.

Variation II

Scene 3: 'The Letter'. News comes that Miles has been expelled from school. Mrs Grose tells the governess that she has known him to be wild, but not bad. They watch the children innocently singing 'Lavender's blue' and decide the school has erred. The governess says she will not tell the guardian.

Variation III

Scene 4: 'The Tower', 'evening, sweet summer'. The governess is strolling in the grounds of Bly ('How beautiful it is'). She is enchanted more each day by her 'darling children'. Yet she has heard a cry in the night and a footstep outside her door. Suddenly she sees a man on the tower ('Who is it, who?').

Variation IV

Scene 5: 'The Window'. In the hall Flora and Miles are riding a hobby-horse ('Tom, Tom, the piper's son'). The governess again sees the man, in the window. She describes the apparition to Mrs Grose, whose reaction is 'Quint! Peter Quint! Is there no end to his dreadful ways?' She explains that Quint was the master's former valet. He was 'free with everyone', spent hours with Miles, and 'had his will' with the lovely Miss Jessel, the children's previous governess, who left when pregnant and died. Quint also died when he fell on an icy road. The governess, horrified, vows to protect the children.

Variation V

Scene 6: 'The Lesson'. The governess is giving Miles a Latin lesson in the schoolroom. He sings her a plaintive rhyme ('Malo I would rather be. Malo in an apple tree').

Variation VI

Scene 7: 'The Lake'. On a sunny morning the governess, with a book, and Flora, with a doll, sit by the lake in the park. Flora names the seas she knows, ending with the Dead Sea. She sings to her doll ('Go to sleep, my dolly dear') while the governess reads. The governess sees the ghost of Miss Jessel on the other side of the lake and realizes Flora has seen her too ('They are lost! Lost!').

Variation VII

Scene 8: 'At Night'. Miles, in his nightgown, is in the garden near the tower. Quint's voice calls to him ('I'm all things strange and bold'). Later Miss Jessel, by the lake, calls to Flora. The colloquy between the ghosts and children is interrupted by the governess and Mrs Grose. Miles tells the governess, 'You see, I am bad.'

Act II

Variation VIII

Scene 1: 'Colloquy and Soliloquy' (the setting is 'nowhere'). Quint and Miss Jessel reproach each other and sing that 'The ceremony of innocence is drowned.' They disappear, and the governess sings ('Lost in my labyrinth') of the evil she fears.

Variation IX

Scene 2: 'The Bells'. In the churchyard, Flora and Miles sing a mock-benedicite. Mrs Grose is reassured by 'how sweet they are together', but the governess tells her 'they are not playing, they are talking horrors' and are 'with the others'. Mrs Grose urges her to write to their guardian, but she refuses. As Flora goes into the church, Miles hangs back ('Do you like the bells? I do!'). He asks the governess when he is returning to school. He mentions 'the others' to her. She knows she has been challenged and decides to leave Bly.

Variation X

Scene 3: 'Miss Jessel'. The governess enters the schoolroom to find Miss Jessel sitting at the desk and bemoaning her suffering ('Here my tragedy began'). The governess defies her and she vanishes. The governess decides to stay, but writes to the guardian ('Sir – dear Sir – my dear Sir').

Variation XI

Scene 4: 'The Bedroom'. Miles is singing 'Malo'. The governess tells him she has written to his guardian. Quint's voice calls to the boy, who shrieks and the candle goes out. ''Twas I who blew it,' Miles tells the alarmed governess.

Variation XII, in which Quint is seen hovering ('So! She has written . . . It is there on the desk . . . Easy to take.').

Scene 5: 'Quint'. Quint tempts Miles to steal the letter. Miles creeps into the schoolroom and takes the letter back to his bedroom.

Variation XIII

Scene 6: 'The Piano'. In the schoolroom the governess and Mrs Grose listen admiringly to Miles playing the piano ('O what a clever boy') while Flora makes a cat's cradle. Flora slips away and the two women set off to find her while Miles, his ruse successful, plays triumphantly.

Variation XIV

Scene 7: 'Flora'. Flora is found by the lake. Miss Jessel appears ('Flora! Do not fail me!') and is seen by the governess but not by Mrs Grose and Flora, or so they say ('I can't see anybody'). Flora, shouting abuse at the governess, is led away by Mrs Grose. The governess bewails Mrs Grose's desertion.

Variation XV

Scene 8: 'Miles'. Mrs Grose is taking Flora away from Bly after a night listening to her outpourings of 'things I never knew or hope to know'. She reveals that Miles took the governess's letter. The governess is left behind ('O Miles – I cannot bear to lose you!'). The boy saunters in ('So, my dear, we are alone'). 'I stay as your friend,' she tells him. But he is listening for Quint. As the governess questions Miles, Quint tells him not to betray their secrets. The boy becomes hysterical and admits he took the letter. 'Say the name of him who made you take it,' she says, 'and he will go for ever.' Miles screams, 'Peter Quint, you devil!' Quint disappears. The governess realizes Miles is dead in her arms. She lays him on the ground and sings his 'Malo' tune as a requiem.

The title of James's story gave Britten the clue for the musical plan of the opera. The tension is maintained and heightened by turns of the musical screw, i.e. by the use of variation form. The prologue and 15 scenes are linked by 16 orchestral interludes – the theme and 15 variations – which are as vocal as any words in creating atmosphere. The theme (the 'screw') is 12-note, but it is not a Schoenbergian note row and is not treated as such. The opera's tonal conflict 'turns' between A minor and A♭ major – a conflict similar to that in *Billy Budd*. The first seven scenes are in the white-note keys of the octave. Only in the last scene of Act I, when the two ghosts are heard for the first time, does the first black-note key appear.

Britten's scoring for chamber orchestra in this opera is as beautiful and imaginative as he ever achieved. The use of harp and low woodwind is especially striking, while his obsession with bells contributes powerfully to the opera's potent spell. Britten's employment of children's nursery rhymes, the lyrical writing of the letter by the governess, her ecstatic aria as she strolls through the grounds of Bly, the mock-benedicite, the brilliant pastiche Mozart that Miles (originally performed by David Hemmings, later a film actor) plays at the piano and his poignant 'Malo' song are among the highlights.

Noye's Fludde

Chester miracle play in one act (50m)
Text taken from A. W. Pollard (ed.), *English Miracle Plays, Moralities and Interludes*
PREMIERES 18 June 1958, Orford Church, Suffolk; US: 31 July 1958, New York (radio broadcast); 16 March 1959, School of Sacred Music, Union Theological Seminary, New York
CAST The Voice of God *spoken role*, Noye *b-bar*, Mrs Noye *c*, Sem *treble*, Ham *treble*, Jaffett *treble*, Mrs Sem *girl s*, Mrs Ham *girl s*, Mrs Jaffett *girl s*, Mrs Noye's Gossips *girl s*; children's chorus of animals and birds; *satb* congregation

Britten's written introduction to the full score of *Noye's Fludde* is lengthy and precise. He liked to involve children and amateurs in music-making and was anxious to compose a dramatic work that could be staged in Orford Church during the Aldeburgh Festival. He found the subject of the Flood vividly dealt with in one of the Chester miracle plays which in medieval times were performed by local craftsmen and tradesmen with the church choir. Each guild performed one play from the cycle on a cart that moved around the town. *Noye's Fludde*, Britten wrote, is 'intended for the same style of presentation – though not necessarily on a cart'.

Part of the charm and fun of the work is the devising of costumes and headgear for lions, goats, dogs, wolves, rats, mice, herons, owls, curlews and many more. Britten also stipulated 'as many recorder-players as possible'. He wanted a professional to play the timpani, with at least six amateurs to play the other percussion instruments. 'The slung mugs and sandpaper can be concocted at home.' The mugs were Britten's inspired idea for the depiction of raindrops – 'mugs (or cups) of varying thickness and size – so as to make a kind of scale – slung on string by the handles from a wooden stand and hit with a wooden spoon (by one player)'. As in his cantata *Saint Nicolas* (1948), Britten makes use of familiar hymn tunes in which the audience join. Ideally, the orchestra for

Noye's Fludde numbers a minimum of 67 players, of whom 57 are amateurs. The total cast comprises three adults and 90 children.

SYNOPSIS
While the congregation sings 'Lord Jesus, think on me', Noye has walked through the church to the empty stage, where he kneels. The voice of God, from high up and away from the stage, tells of his intention to flood the earth and destroy all upon it except Noye and his family. He instructs Noye to build a ship. The sons and their wives fall to with a will, but Noye's wife derides the venture and prefers to drink with her gossips (cronies). The Ark is built and God's voice tells Noye to enter it with his family, the beasts and the birds. The rain begins and the animals, heralded by bugle calls, march through the congregation and into the Ark, singing 'Kyrie eleison'. Mrs Noye continues drinking with her cronies. Eventually her three sons pick her up and carry her struggling into the Ark, while the gossips run off screaming. The storm begins in earnest and the inhabitants of the Ark sing 'Eternal Father, strong to save', joined by the congregation for the second and third verses. The storm subsides; the creatures go to sleep, and Noye looks out of the window. Forty days have passed, so he sends a raven to see if there is a dry place anywhere. If it does not return, somewhere is dry. It does not return. He then sends a dove, which returns with an olive branch. God's voice tells Noye to step ashore; the animals leave the Ark, singing 'Alleluia'. God promises that he will never again wreak vengeance on mankind and creates a rainbow as a token of this promise. All the cast, joined in the last verse by the congregation, sing 'The spacious firmament on high', to Tallis's tune, during which the sun, then the moon and stars appear. The animals walk slowly out in procession. Noye is left alone. The voice of God tenderly blesses him.

A Midsummer Night's Dream

Opera in three acts (2h 30m)
Libretto by Benjamin Britten and Peter Pears, adapted from the play by William Shakespeare (c. 1593–4)
Composed October 1959–April 1960
PREMIERES 11 June 1960, Jubilee Hall, Aldeburgh, Suffolk; US: 10 October 1961, War Memorial Opera House, San Francisco
CAST Oberon *ct* or *a*, Tytania *coloratura s*, Puck *boy acrobat, spoken role*, Theseus *b*, Hippolyta *c*, Lysander *t*, Demetrius *bar*, Hermia *ms*, Helena *s*, Bottom *b-bar*, Flute *t*, Snug *b*, Snout *t*, Starveling *bar*, Cobweb *treble*, Peaseblossom *treble*, Mustardseed *treble*, Moth *treble*; *treble* or *s* chorus of fairies

For the 1960 Aldeburgh Festival, the stage and pit of the Jubilee Hall were enlarged and other improvements were made. Britten wanted to compose a new opera as a celebration but in the time left it was impossible to commission a libretto. So he and Pears adapted Shakespeare's *A Midsummer Night's Dream*, cutting the play by about half and simplifying the action. Some of Puck's lines are given to the chorus of fairies and other lines are reallocated among the singers. Britten said he did not feel in the least guilty about the cuts: 'The original Shakespeare will survive.' The whole project was completed in seven months, during part of which Britten was ill, though he conducted the first performance.

SYNOPSIS

Act I The wood, deepening twilight. Oberon, king of the fairies, has quarrelled with his queen, Tytania, because she has 'a lovely boy' as attendant, stolen from an Indian king, and Oberon wants him. Tytania defies him and Oberon plans his revenge, ordering Puck to fetch him a herb of which the juice, sprinkled on a sleeper's eyelids, will make the sleeper 'madly dote upon the next live creature that it sees'. Hermia, in love with Lysander, has been ordered by her father to marry Demetrius, who loves her. She and Lysander plan to flee outside Athens where the ruling will not apply. As they leave, Demetrius and Helena enter. Demetrius tells Helena he does not love her; he is looking for Lysander and Hermia – 'The one I'll slay, the other slayeth me.' Puck returns with the herb. Oberon, who has been eavesdropping, tells of his plan for Tytania ('I know a bank where the wild thyme blows') and orders Puck to find Demetrius – 'Thou shalt know the man by the Athenian garments he hath on' – and to anoint his eyes when he can ensure that 'the next thing he espies' will be Helena. The rustics arrive to rehearse a play, *Pyramus and Thisbe*, to be performed before Duke Theseus of Athens on the occasion of his marriage to Hippolyta. Parts are allotted – Bottom the weaver is to be Pyramus – and they agree to rehearse later. Lysander and Hermia are lost and settle to sleep. Puck sprinkles Lysander's eyelids with juice. When Demetrius and Helena arrive, Helena awakens Lysander who declares his love for her and follows her. Hermia finds herself alone and goes in search of Lysander. Tytania and her retinue arrive. When she is asleep, Oberon squeezes the juice on her eyes.

Act II The wood, dark night. The rustics arrive for their rehearsal. Bottom leaves the clearing (followed by Puck) and returns wearing the head of an ass. Tytania awakes and falls in love with him. When Hermia and Demetrius return, it is obvious that Puck has bewitched the wrong man. Oberon orders him to search for Helena. As Demetrius lies down to sleep, Oberon squeezes juice on his eyes. Lysander is still protesting his sincerity to Helena when Demetrius awakes, declaring passion for Helena, who thinks everyone is playing a joke on her. Hermia returns and the women, formerly close friends, mock and insult each other. Oberon orders Puck to lead the four astray in the wood and to put the juice on Lysander's eyes to restore the status quo.

Act III Scene 1: The wood, early next morning. Oberon, now that he has acquired Tytania's boy attendant, frees her and Bottom from the spell. Bottom rejoins his companions. The four lovers awaken and are reconciled, Lysander with Hermia and Demetrius with Helena. Scene 2: Theseus' palace. The duke tells Hermia he will overrule her father and allow her to marry Lysander. The rustics' play is enacted, after which the couples retire. The fairies and Puck occupy the room ('Now the hungry lion roars'). Oberon and Tytania enter and, with the fairies, sing, 'Now until the break of day, through this house each fairy stray.' They leave the stage to Puck, who addresses the audience: 'Give me your hands, if we be friends, and Robin shall restore amends.'

In *A Midsummer Night's Dream*, Britten found themes congenial to him: night and sleep, the juxtaposition of the natural and the supernatural, marvellous lyric poetry, and the opportunity for a rich display of musical parody. He responded with some of his most inventive, enchanting and evocative music. Each of the three strata of beings in the opera– fairies, lovers and rustics – has its own sound-world, each with distinctive instrumental timbres – harps, celesta, harpsichord and percussion for the fairies, strings and woodwind for the lovers, bassoon and deep brass for the rustics. Two other inspirations contribute to the opera's success: Puck is a spoken role, accompanied by trumpet cadenzas and drums, and Oberon is assigned to a counter-tenor, an other-worldly sound that is both sinister and beguiling. The fairies' music has an acerbic quality. Britten said he had 'always been struck by a kind of sharpness in Shakespeare's fairies'. *A Midsummer Night's Dream* is as melodious a score as he ever wrote. His setting of 'I know a bank' is exquisite, as is the love music for Tytania and Bottom. The rustics' play is a closely organized opera buffa, notable for its witty parodies of Italian opera. And over the whole score lies the magic of the wood, brought before our eyes in the opera's first bars, with its slow portamento sighs depicting the rustling leaves and creaking branches. Although Britten never used serial method as such, the series of major triads, connected by glissandi on the strings, which so vividly depict the wood, covers all 12 notes of the chromatic scale. As they are in false relation to one another, Britten again (as in *Billy Budd*) creates a tonal ambiguity which is continued in the music given to the fairies on their first appearance, Lydian G major spiced with D major and F♯ major. At the end of the opera, in the haunting 'Now until the break of day', a radiant Mahlerian F♯ major is achieved. On the journey to that magical moment, Britten creates a Shakespearian opera to rank with Verdi's masterpieces.

Curlew River

Parable for church performance (1h 15m)
Libretto by William Plomer, based on the medieval Japanese Noh play *Sumidagawa* by Juro Motomasa
Composed February–2 April 1964
PREMIERES 12 June 1964, Orford Church, Suffolk; US: 26 June 1966, Spanish Courtyard, Caramoor Festival, Katonah, New York
CAST Madwoman *t*, Ferryman *bar*, Traveller *bar*, Spirit of the Boy *treble*, Abbot *b*, 3 Assistants (Acolytes); chorus of pilgrims 3 *t*, 3 *bar*, 2 *b*

On a visit to Tokyo early in 1956, Britten saw two performances of the Japanese Noh play *Sumidagawa* (*The Sumida River*). They made an enormous impression on him, haunting him for some years afterwards. Seeking a means of bringing operatic entertainment into the church without involving amateurs and the audience, as *Noye's Fludde* had, he remembered the Japanese play and asked William Plomer to transpose it from a Japanese and Buddhist milieu to the framework of a medieval English religious drama. So the Sumida River became the Curlew River in the East Anglia Britten knew so well. Instead of ancient Japanese music, the opera, or church parable, grew from the plainsong hymn 'Te lucis ante terminum' which is chanted by the abbot and a group of monks and acolytes as they walk to the acting area where the monks who are to play the madwoman, ferryman and traveller are robed for their parts.

Britten had been particularly impressed by the stylized ritual of the play's presentation in Japan: 'the intense slowness of the action . . . the beautiful costumes, the mixture of chanting, speech and singing which, with the three instruments, made up the strange music'. Plomer's adaptation retained some of this stylization. Britten increased the number of percussion instruments in order to achieve the effect of a gamelan and wrote a major part for the flute. He also decided that no conductor was necessary, and, in order to specify which vocal or instrumental part had precedence, he invented a new flexible pause mark, the 'curlew'.

SYNOPSIS
In a church by a Fenland river in medieval times the abbot tells the congregation they will witness a mystery: 'How in sad mischance a sign was given of God's grace, not far away, where, in our reedy Fens, the Curlew River runs.' The ferryman explains it is the day on which people use the ferry to cross to the other bank to pray before a grave where they believe 'some special grace' heals the sick. He hears a strange noise. A traveller says it is a woman who seems to be crazy and is making the people on the road laugh. The madwoman enters ('Let me in! Let me out! Tell me the way!'). She is seeking her child, who was seized as a slave by a foreigner, at her home in the Black Mountains. The ferryman refuses to take her across the river unless she entertains the passengers with her singing. She rebukes him and watches the flight of some birds. 'Common gulls,' says the ferryman, but she calls them 'Curlews of the Fenland'. They sail the river ('Curlew River, smoothly flowing') and he tells the traveller that a year ago to the day a heathen stranger ('a big man arm'd with a sword and cudgel') came aboard the ferry with a 12-year-old Christian boy whom he said he had bought as a slave. The boy looked ill and when they reached the other side he lay on the grass near the chapel. The heathen threatened him, but abandoned him. The river people cared for the boy but he grew weaker. He told them his dead father had been a nobleman and that his mother brought him up near the Black Mountains until the day he was seized while walking alone. He asked to be buried by the path to the chapel so that 'if travellers from my dear country pass this way, their shadows will fall on my grave'. Then he died. The river people believe he was a saint. The boat arrives. The madwoman has been weeping at the story and from her questions everyone realizes that the child was hers. The ferryman leads her to the grave, where she tells of

her search ('Hoping, I wander'd on'). As she prays for the child his voice is heard and finally his spirit appears, freeing her from her madness before returning to the tomb ('Go your way in peace, mother').

In *Curlew River* Britten joins a number of 20th-century composers, from Debussy to Boulez, in inflecting Western music with Eastern procedures. Not far away, too, is the influence of Holst, another composer who was preoccupied with orientalism in his work. The madwoman is one of the finest parts Britten wrote for Pears, the disordered mind poignantly depicted by the use of unequal fourths in the cries of 'You mock me', while 'Hoping, I wander'd on', sung in duet with the flute, is an inspired invention. The score is marked by supremacy of melodic line, derived from the use of plainsong.

The Burning Fiery Furnace
Second parable for church performance, (1h)
Libretto by William Plomer, based on the Old Testament story (Daniel 3)
Composed autumn 1965–5 April 1966
PREMIERES 9 June 1966, Orford Church, Suffolk; US: 25 June 1967, Spanish Courtyard, Caramoor Festival, Katonah, New York
CAST The Abbot, 12 Monks, 5 Acolytes and 8 Lay Brothers *who make up the cast of the parable*: Nebuchadnezzar *t*, Astrologer (Abbot) *bar*, Ananias *bar*, Misael *t*, Azarias *b*, Herald and Leader of the Courtiers *bar*; chorus of courtiers 3 *t*, 2 *bar*, 2 *b*; 5 attendants *trebles*

Encouraged by the success of *Curlew River*, Britten and Plomer devised a second church parable based on a familiar biblical episode, 'something much less sombre, an altogether gayer affair', as Britten said. The idea came to him on holiday in France when he was impressed by the colours of Chartres Cathedral and a sculpture of Nebuchadnezzar and the Fiery Furnace. Plomer intended that Nebuchadnezzar, the cult of the 'god of gold', and the 'resistance movement' of the three Jewish exiles should be relevant 'to our own times'.

SYNOPSIS
The abbot and his company of monks, acolytes and instrumentalists process in, singing. Babylon, the 6th century BC. A herald welcomes Ananias, Misael and Azarias, 'three young men . . . chosen out of all the world for knowledge and skill to take high rank in Babylon' as rulers over three provinces. King Nebuchadnezzar is giving a feast in their honour. He orders the astrologer to tell them their Babylonian names, Shadrach, Meschach and Abednego. The feast begins, entertainers dance and sing ('The waters of Babylon . . . all ran dry. Do you know why?'), but, on religious grounds, the three repeatedly refuse the food handed to them. The astrologer reminds the king that he had warned him against taking on foreigners. Nebuchadnezzar leaves the banquet in panic, declaring that the stars are against him. The three see that they have enemies, but vow to continue as children of Israel. The herald proclaims that a huge golden image of Merodak, the great god of Babylon, is to be erected and that whenever a fanfare is played everyone must

bow down and worship it or be thrown into a burning fiery furnace. When the image arises the three Israelites refuse to kneel and are put into the furnace, heated 'seven times hotter than it ever was before'. They stand unharmed, a fourth figure with them, singing the benedicite. Nebuchadnezzar says the fourth figure is like the Son of God. He approaches the furnace and orders the three out and the fourth figure disappears. Seeing they are unharmed Nebuchadnezzar turns on the astrologer ('Where is your wisdom now?') and dismisses him. The king acknowledges that there is no god except the God of Shadrach, Meshach and Abednego ('Down with the god of gold'). He joins the three in a hymn of peace.

The fount of the opera's thematic material is the plainsong chant with which it opens. The alto trombone supplies the distinctive instrumental timbre of the score, and there is more humour and direct action than in *Curlew River*. This is the most dramatic and perhaps the most appealing of the parables.

The Prodigal Son
Third parable for church performance, (1h 15m)
Libretto by William Plomer, based on the New Testament parable (Luke 15:11–32)
Composed January 1968–22 April 1968
PREMIERES 10 June 1968, Orford Church, Suffolk; US: 29 June 1969, Spanish Courtyard, Caramoor Festival, Katonah, New York
CAST Tempter (Abbot) *t*, Father *b-bar*, Elder Son *bar*, Younger Son *t*; chorus of servants, parasites and beggars 3 *t*, 3 *bar*, 2 *b*; 5 young servants and distant voices *trebles*

To complete their triptych, Britten and Plomer went to the New Testament for what Plomer called a story that 'seems to bring into the clearest possible focus the Christian view of life', the triumph of forgiveness.

SYNOPSIS
Disguised as the Tempter, the abbot mocks the Amen from the opposite end of the church ('What I bring you is evil'). He sets the scene: a country patriarch, a worthy family, a dull life. 'See how I break it up.' After the actors have robed, the chorus gathers round the father, who extols the work ethic. The Tempter waylays the younger son and describes the delights he is missing through keeping himself 'locked up in this desert here of stupid family life'. The younger son confesses his discontent to his father and asks for his portion of the inheritance. The father grants this request, to the disgust of the elder son, and he and the servants bid him farewell. The Tempter accompanies the younger son to the city, where he introduces him to the pleasures of wine, women and gambling. The younger son loses all his money and is deserted by his drinking friends. 'Now you must pay,' the Tempter tells him and advises him to join a band of beggars and to work as a swineherd. The younger son decides to return home and asks his father to let him be one of the servants. But the father welcomes him and orders the killing of the fatted calf to celebrate his return. The elder son objects, but at the father's prompting is reconciled with his brother. The

Tempter disrobes and, as the abbot, points out the moral. He joins the monks and leads them out.

The chorus plays a larger part in this parable than in its predecessors. The trumpet in D and the alto flute are the dominant instruments, with a solo viola representing the younger son's uncorrupted nature. Another striking effect is the use of a conical gourd to suggest trudging through desert sand. Britten fails in his depiction of the temptations of the flesh, but the music for the reconciliation between father and son is both moving and ravishingly scored.

Owen Wingrave
Opera in two acts, (1h 45m)
Libretto by Myfanwy Piper, based on Henry James's short story (1892)
Composed May 1969–August 1970
PREMIERES 16 May 1971, BBC television (recorded at The Maltings, Snape, Suffolk, 22–30 November 1970); 10 May 1973, Covent Garden, London; US: 9 August 1973, Opera Theater, Santa Fe, New Mexico
CAST Owen Wingrave *bar*, Spencer Coyle *b-bar*, Lechmere *t*, Miss Wingrave *dramatic s*, Mrs Coyle *s*, Mrs Julian *s*, Kate *ms*, General Sir Philip Wingrave *t*, Narrator *t*; distant chorus, *trebles*

In November 1967 Britten received a commission from the BBC for a television opera. He had read Henry James's short story *Owen Wingrave* in the 1950s and admired it because it coincided with his own strong pacifist sympathies. He had discussed the possibility of making an opera from it with Myfanwy Piper before 1962. Now the Vietnam War, and in particular the shooting of American students demonstrating against it on the campus of Kent State University, refocused his attention on it. While not particularly interested in television, he accepted the challenge posed by the medium, though there is no doubt that he always intended that *Owen Wingrave* should ultimately be a stage work. Each part was written with a particular singer in mind. The opera was first shown on British television, but within a week it had also been screened in the United States and on 12 European networks. Although its music is admired by many, it has failed to appeal to the public.

SYNOPSIS
Act I Late 19th century. An instrumental prelude describes the ten Wingrave family portraits at their country seat Paramore (the fifth is a double portrait). Each portrait – of a military man – is depicted by a cadenza for a solo instrument. Scene 1: The study at Coyle's military establishment in Bayswater. Coyle is lecturing Owen and his friend Lechmere about battle tactics. Lechmere is anxious to be in the thick of war, but Owen hates it. He tells Coyle he can't go through with becoming a soldier whatever his family may say. Coyle soliloquizes that Owen was his most gifted pupil. Scene 2: Hyde Park/Miss Wingrave's lodgings in Baker Street. Owen, in the park, thinks about death in battle and how its 'glory' is an illusion. Owen's aunt, Miss Wingrave, extols to Coyle the Wingraves' past military feats and says Owen's 'fancy' must be stopped. Scene 3: A room at the Coyles'.

Owen tells Coyle and his wife nothing will change his mind. They drink to Owen's future 'wherever that may lie'. Owen tells Lechmere he dreads going to Paramore: his grandfather knows no life but war, his father was killed in battle, countless other Wingraves had died for their country. Scene 4: At Paramore Owen's aunt is awaiting his arrival, together with Mrs Julian, a widow and dependant, and her daughter Kate, who says, 'He reckons without me . . . he shall not carry out so infamous a plan.' Owen, alone, addresses the portraits, particularly that of his father. His grandfather, Sir Philip, emerges from his study: 'Sirrah! How dare you!' Scene 5: In this abstract scene, spread over a week, the voices of Sir Philip, Miss Wingrave, Kate and Mrs Julian taunt and insult Owen – 'dragging our name in the dirt', 'insulting your Queen and country', 'you are no gentleman', 'I'll court-martial you', 'you're not worthy of Paramore'. Scene 6: The hall at Paramore. The Coyles arrive. Coyle hints at a Paramore ghost and points out the double portrait, Colonel Wingrave and a boy. Owen tells Coyle his encounter with his family has been worse than he thought possible. Scene 7: The dinner table at Paramore. Owen praises Coyle's brilliance as a teacher and this leads to Sir Philip's open attack on Owen. When Mrs Coyle interposes that Owen has his scruples, the others seize on this word for a concerted attack on Owen. He retorts that he would make it a crime to draw a sword for one's country. Sir Philip leaves in a fury.

Act II As a prologue a narrator sings a ballad telling of a young Wingrave who refuses a school friend's challenge to fight after they have quarrelled over boasts about their fathers' property. The Wingrave's father accuses him of cowardice and kills him in an upstairs room at Paramore. On the day of the funeral, the father is found dead 'without a wound' in the same room. Scene 1: The gallery at Paramore. Coyle and Owen are looking at the double portrait of the father and son in the ballad. Owen says the father would not have died from remorse: Sir Philip disinherits Owen. Mrs Julian collapses at this blow to Kate's future. Lechmere immediately begins to flatter Kate, to the Coyles' disgust. Owen bids the portraits farewell. He is joined by Kate and they sing of former days at Paramore ('Why did you spoil it all?'). He rebukes her for flirting with Lechmere and she calls him a coward, challenging him to sleep in the haunted room. He orders her to lock him in it. Scene 2: The Coyles' bedroom, later that evening. Mrs Coyle is still indignant about Kate and Lechmere. Lechmere knocks at their door having overheard Kate's challenge to Owen. They go to the haunted room but at that moment hear Kate crying 'Ah, Owen, Owen, you've gone.' Sir Philip opens the door to find Owen dead.

Britten's use of military music is a feature of the opera. In the *marziale* prelude with which it begins, each Wingrave family portrait is assigned a particular obbligato instrument or instruments, rather as in the linking passages of the *Nocturne* (1958). Trombone and piccolo feature in the double portrait of the father and son in the ballad. Each cadenza passage is in some respect grotesque, for Britten has no admiration for these military ancestors, and they resolve into the memorable horn solo that represents Owen's nobler character.

The three chords forming the basis of a three-bar martial motif in the prelude, which represents the Wingrave army tradition, are evolved from a 12-note series. As in *The Turn of the Screw* and *A Midsummer Night's Dream*, Britten here makes use of note rows, but not in any systematic way. Each row is constructed from diminished triads. There are three different 12-note sets in the prelude – the figure already mentioned, the double portrait (trombone and piccolo) and Owen's father. Owen's portrait, by juxtaposition of perfect and diminished triads, brings out the conflict in Owen's mind through a conflict of major and minor. Subtle references to the material of this prelude honeycomb the rest of the score in the form of diminished triads.

The refining process of the church parables is evident in the orchestral writing, but it may be felt that Britten's invention failed him at climactic moments in the opera, where it suffers alongside comparable episodes in the earlier operas.

Death in Venice

Opera in two acts, (2h 30m)
Libretto by Myfanwy Piper, based on Thomas Mann's novella *Der Tod in Venedig* (1912)
Composed spring 1971–March 1973; rev. 27 August 1973 and early 1974
PREMIERES 16 June 1973, The Maltings, Snape, Suffolk; US: 18 October 1974, Metropolitan, New York
CAST Gustav von Aschenbach *t*, Traveller/Elderly Fop/Old Gondolier/Hotel Manager/Hotel Barber/Leader of the Players/Voice of Dionysus *b-bar*, Voice of Apollo *ct*; *satb* chorus of youths and girls, hotel guests and waiters, gondoliers and boatmen, street vendors, touts and beggars, citizens of Venice, choir in St Mark's, tourists, followers of Dionysus; chorus includes (*s*) Danish lady, Russian mother, English lady, French girl, strawberry-seller, lace-seller, newspaper-seller, strolling player; (*c*) French mother, German mother, Russian nanny, beggar woman; (*t*) hotel porter, 2 Americans, 2 gondoliers, glass-maker, strolling player; (*bar* and *b*) ship's steward, lido boatman, Polish father, German father, Russian father, hotel waiter, guide in Venice, restaurant waiter, gondolier, priest in St Mark's, English clerk in the travel bureau; Polish mother, Tadzio, 2 daughters, governess, Jaschiu, boys and girls, strolling players, beach attendants, *dancers*

The idea of an opera based on Mann's *Death in Venice* had been in Britten's mind for some years. In November 1970 he approached Myfanwy Piper for a libretto, and he began work on the music in the spring of 1971. He completed the short score just before Christmas 1972. For most of the time he was ill, and in the autumn of 1972 his doctors decreed that he needed an operation to replace a deficient heart valve. He made a bargain with them – he would have the operation provided they allowed him to finish *Death in Venice* first. The full score was completed in March 1973. The opera had become an obsession. Not only was it a subject with which he was passionately involved, but he wanted to complete it as a tribute to Peter Pears.

During the operation (in May 1973), Britten had a slight stroke which permanently affected his right hand. He was not well enough to supervise rehearsals of the opera, conducted by Steuart Bedford, nor to attend the first performance at The Maltings. He first saw it at a special, semi-private performance on 12 September and later attended the first London performance at Covent Garden on 18 October. He attended the recording sessions in spring 1974 although very ill, and saw the opera again at the 1975 Aldeburgh Festival and at Covent Garden on 7 July 1975. Thus he heard Pears give the performance of his life in the long, taxing and testing role of Aschenbach and John Shirley-Quirk, equally impressive, in the seven baritone roles.

SYNOPSIS

Act I Scene 1: 'Munich'. Aschenbach, a famous novelist and now a widower, is walking in a Munich suburb and musing on the apparent drying up of his creativity ('My mind beats on and no words come'). He enters a cemetery and reads the texts on the façade of the chapel. He becomes aware of a traveller, who sings of exotic sights in far-off lands ('Marvels unfold! . . . Go, travel to the South'). Aschenbach decides to have a holiday in the sun. Scene 2: 'On the Boat to Venice'. Youths are leaning over the rail shouting to their girls on shore. An elderly fop joins the youths as they sing of 'Serenissima' and starts a popular song, 'We'll meet in the Piazza'. Aschenbach comes on to the deck and is disgusted by the rouged 'young–old horror'. Arrival in Venice is described in an overture based on the Serenissima theme. Scene 3: 'The Journey to the Lido'. Aschenbach is in a gondola and sings his own praise of Serenissima. The old gondolier is not rowing him the way he wants to go. They pass a boatload of boys and girls singing 'Serenissima . . . Bride of the sea'. On arrival at the quayside, Aschenbach is met by a boatman and the hotel porter. The old gondolier has disappeared, without payment. Aschenbach soliloquizes ('Mysterious gondola . . . black, coffin black, a vision of death itself'). Scene 4: 'The First Evening at the Hotel'. The manager shows Aschenbach his room with its superb view of the lagoon. He watches the other guests assemble for dinner – French, American, German, Polish, Danish, English and Russian. The Polish family enters, with the boy Tadzio, whose beauty is immediately noticed by Aschenbach ('Surely the soul of Greece lies in that bright perfection'). Scene 5: 'On the Beach'. Aschenbach watches children playing games and buys some strawberries. Tadzio arrives and joins the games. Scene 6: 'The Foiled Departure'. Aschenbach crosses to Venice from the Lido. The city is hot and crowded and the sirocco is blowing. Back at the hotel, he decides to leave. Just before he goes, Tadzio walks through the hall. Aschenbach learns that his luggage has been sent on to the wrong destination, so he returns to the hotel. The manager has kept his room and reminds him that the wind is now blowing from a healthier quarter. Through the window Aschenbach sees Tadzio playing on the beach ('That's what made it hard to leave. So be it'). Scene 7: 'The Games of Apollo'. On the Lido beach, Aschenbach watches the boys' beach games as if they were in an Olympian world. The voice of Apollo is heard ('He who loves beauty wor-

ships me'). Competing in a variety of games, Tadzio wins each time. Aschenbach, excited, wants but fails to speak to the boy, who passes him and smiles ('Ah, don't smile like that! No one should be smiled at like that'). On an empty stage, Aschenbach exclaims, 'I love you.'

Act II Aschenbach analyses his outburst. Scene 8: 'The Hotel Barber's Shop'. While trimming Aschenbach's hair, the garrulous barber mentions 'the sickness'. Scene 9: 'The Pursuit'. Aschenbach crosses to Venice, where people are reading notices advising precautions against infection. In a newspaper he reads denials of rumours of cholera in Venice. He follows the Polish family into St Mark's and later in a gondola ('They must not leave . . .'). He is in thrall to Tadzio. Scene 10: 'The Strolling Players'. At the hotel, Aschenbach attends an entertainment by strolling players. He taxes their leader about the plague, but is rebuffed. Scene 11: 'The Travel Bureau'. An English clerk is frank with Aschenbach: there is cholera and he should leave. Scene 12: 'The Lady of the Pearls'. Aschenbach decides to warn Tadzio's mother, but he cannot bring himself to speak. Scene 13: 'The Dream'. In his sleep he hears the voices of Apollo and Dionysus, who depict the struggle in his mind. Scene 14: 'The Empty Beach'. Aschenbach watches Tadzio and his friends as they play games desultorily. Scene 15: 'The Hotel Barber's Shop'. Aschenbach has his hair dyed and his face made up. Scene 16: 'The Last Visit to Venice'. Rejuvenated, Aschenbach takes a gondola to Venice, jauntily singing the youths' song from Scene 2. He again trails the Polish family but loses them. Buying strawberries, he finds them musty. In a soliloquy he recalls Socrates ('Does beauty lead to wisdom, Phaedrus?'). Scene 17: 'The Departure'. The guests are leaving the hotel. Aschenbach goes to the empty beach, where Tadzio loses a fight with one of his friends. Aschenbach calls out and Tadzio beckons him, but the writer slumps dead in his chair.

Death in Venice is a *tour de force* of Britten's compositional skill. The long role of Aschenbach combines a Monteverdi-like recitative with Schoenbergian sprechgesang and Mahlerian melody. The atmosphere of decay and decadence is as uncannily evoked as are the sounds of Venice itself. Britten again employs three strata of sound: piano accompaniment for the recitatives, a gamelan percussion for Tadzio and his friends, and the full orchestra for Venice and for the other characters. The silent Polish family are dancers. For the voice of Apollo a counter-tenor is used. Thus the fantasy of *A Midsummer Night's Dream* and the austerity of the parables are tributaries flowing into this rich and compelling elegy.

M.K.

FERRUCCIO BUSONI

Ferruccio Dante Michelangelo Benvenuto Busoni; *b* 1 April 1866, Empoli, Italy; *d* 27 July 1924, Berlin

Busoni enjoyed no regular schooling and matured

young. Although born in Italy, he grew up in a Central European cultural environment and spent most of his adult life in German-speaking countries. He acquired a specialist's knowledge of Bach and Liszt, adored Mozart, and felt a growing antipathy towards Wagner. Schoenberg and many other contemporary composers interested him intensely yet he remained independent of all schools and 'isms', hence acquiring a reputation for aloofness. During his lifetime his worldwide reputation as a virtuoso pianist completely eclipsed his activities as a composer. In recent years a growing familiarity with his works has helped penetrate the barrier of his alleged intellectualism and established him as an important figure in 20th-century music.

His first operatic project, based on Henrik Hertz's *King René's Daughter*, dates from 1883; it came to nothing. In 1884 Busoni negotiated unsuccessfully for a stage adaptation of Gottfried Keller's *A Village Romeo and Juliet* (later set by Delius). During a period of study at Leipzig, he began to compose his first opera, *Sigune, oder Das stille Dorf*. He completed the short score but orchestrated only the prelude before abandoning the work in about 1892. Some of the music was salvaged in the *Konzertstück*, Op. 31a, for piano and orchestra, while an important motif, connected with the building of a cathedral, appears in the *pezzo serioso* of the monumental Piano Concerto (1904). The Piano Concerto closes with a chorus of offstage male voices to a text from Adam Gottlieb Oehlenschläger's play *Aladdin*. This too is the remains of a theatrical plan, a setting of *Aladdin*, 'not as an opera but as a *Gesamtkunstwerk* with drama, music, dance [and] magic'.

During the 1890s Busoni composed relatively little, expending much energy on perfecting his piano technique and widening his repertoire. The world premiere of Verdi's *Falstaff* in 1893 revived his belief in the future of Italian music and influenced his developing style. During this period he worked on the libretto for an opera about the Wandering Jew, *Ahasver*. Although he later abandoned the plan, he was to vary the central theme – the profoundly gifted outsider who strives for immortality – in several subsequent operatic projects, arriving at a definitive version in *Doktor Faust*. Variants of the same idea are to be found in *Der mächtige Zauberer*, *Leonardo da Vinci* and *Dante*. Libretti or sketches for these have survived; several further ideas for opera subjects are mentioned in Busoni's copious correspondence. Although Busoni made sporadic approaches to writers such as Bernard Shaw, Gabriele d'Annunzio and Hugo von Hofmannsthal, he actually wrote all his opera texts himself, in German.

In 1907 Busoni published his controversial *Entwurf einer neuen Ästhetik der Tonkunst* (*Outline of a New Aesthetic of Music*) together with the libretto of *Die Brautwahl*. Although *Die Brautwahl* ultimately failed, Busoni was convinced that opera was the 'universal domain' of contemporary music and that his own musical language was intrinsically theatrical. In the revised edition of the *New Aesthetic* (1916) he elaborates on his idea of opera as a multi-media spectacle which should 'rely on the incredible, untrue

or unlikely'. The opera of the future, he writes, should use music only where it is indispensable, particularly for the portrayal of the supernatural or the unnatural, hence as a magic mirror (opera seria) or a distorting mirror (opera buffa). These theories, coupled with his earliest memories of Italian puppet theatre, form the foundation of his three remaining operas, *Arlecchino*, a one-act 'musical caprice', its companion piece, *Turandot*, and *Doktor Faust*. *Turandot* and *Arlecchino* are grouped together as *la nuova commedia dell'arte*, while *Doktor Faust* is based largely on the early German puppet play of *Faust*.

During the years immediately preceding the First World War Busoni came into contact with progressive artists in various fields – the Viennese Secessionists, the Italian Futurists, d'Annunzio, Rainer Maria Rilke, Schoenberg and Varèse, to name but a few – and himself entered on a period of experiment. The earliest studies for *Doktor Faust*, the *Sonatina seconda* for piano and the *Nocturne symphonique*, for orchestra, date from this time. Apart from their dense, brooding textures, these works are notable for a new harmonic and rhythmic boldness and a distinctive instrumental chiaroscuro. The war effected a gradual change of direction, which finally led Busoni in 1918 to proclaim *Junge Klassizität* ('Young Classicality') as his artistic aim. 'Many experiments have been made in this young century,' he wrote. 'Now . . . it is time to form something durable again.' *Arlecchino* was his first brilliant essay in the new style.

Junge Klassizität is a concept that embraces many possibilities, for Busoni believed that the achievements of past generations could be combined with all new developments, and that a full flowering of Western music would hence lie in the distant future. The libretto of *Doktor Faust* expresses this belief in allegorical form and can be interpreted as the composer's definitive artistic and philosophical statement.

Turandot

Chinesische Fabel in two acts (1h 30m)
Libretto by the composer, after the play by Carlo Gozzi (1762)
PREMIERES 11 May 1917, Stadttheater, Zurich; UK: 12 January 1947, BBC radio; 8 March 1978, Cockpit Theatre London; US: 8 October 1967, Brooklyn Academy of Music (semi-staged)

In 1905 Busoni composed incidental music for Gozzi's *Turandot*; in 1911 Max Reinhardt staged a successful production of the play at the Deutsches Theater, Berlin, using Busoni's complete score. After one further production in London, which was by all accounts a travesty, Busoni resolved to rework his score into an opera. He put this plan into effect in 1917, reducing the orchestration and adding several new sections including arias for Kalaf, Turandot and Altoum, thus devising an apt companion piece for his previous opera, *Arlecchino*. The two works have little in common however, apart from the participation of *commedia dell'arte* characters.

After his father's defeat in battle, Kalaf flees to Peking in search of adventure. He is recognized by his former servant, Barak. The latter tells him of the emperor's daughter Turandot and of the cruel trials imposed on her suitors. Kalaf sees her portrait, is fired with love, and storms off to the imperial palace. Truffaldino, chief eunuch, prepares the great hall for the new trial. Neither the emperor Altoum nor his ministers, Pantalone and Tartaglia, are able to dissuade Kalaf, who steadfastly refuses to reveal his identity and insists on 'death or Turandot'. Turandot's confidante Adelma recognizes him as the man she once vainly loved. The riddle ceremony begins: before the third riddle, Turandot unveils herself, nearly dazzling Kalaf with her beauty. However he triumphs, and, when Turandot refuses to fulfil her pledge of marriage, he counters with the riddle of his name. Nothing can soothe Turandot's rage until Altoum informs her that a messenger has brought him the coveted information; the treacherous Adelma, hoping to win Kalaf for herself, then whispers the name to her mistress. Turandot, dressed in mourning, reveals Kalaf's name to the assembled throng. But she also surprises and delights them by declaring her love for Kalaf and proclaims her wedding. The opera ends with a jubilant choral dance in praise of Buddha.

Much of the thematic material in Busoni's score, based on Chinese, Arabic, Byzantine, Indian and Nubian melodies, is taken from the *Geschichte der Musik* by the Austrian musicologist August Wilhelm Ambros. As the notation of these melodies often implies a superficial similarity to Western music, Busoni detected in them a cultural link which evidently supported his theory of 'the Oneness of music'. In the same spirit, Busoni works the melody of 'Greensleeves' into his score in a delicate, harmonically ambiguous arrangement for female voices.

Doktor Faust

Opera in two preludes, two intermezzi and three scenes (2h 30m)
Libretto by the composer
Composed 1916–24 (inc.); completed by Philipp Jarnach (1925) and Antony Beaumont (1984)
PREMIERES Jarnach version: 21 May 1925, Sächsisches Staatstheater, Dresden; UK: 17 March 1937, Queen's Hall, London (concert); US: 1 December 1964, Carnegie Hall, New York (concert); 25 January 1974, Pioneer Centre for the Performing Arts, Reno, Nevada; Beaumont version: 2 April 1985, Teatro Comunale, Bologna; UK: 25 April 1986, Coliseum, London
CAST Faust *bar*, Mephistopheles *t*, Wagner *b*, Duke of Parma *t*, Duchess of Parma *s*, Master of Ceremonies *b*, Gretchen's Brother *bar*, Lieutenant *t*, 3 Students from Cracow *t*, 2 *bar*, Theology Student *bar*, Law Student *b*, Student of Natural Philosophy *bar*, Beelzebub *t*, Megaeros *t*, Gravis *b*, Levis *bar*, Asmodus *bar*, Student *t*, Poet *spoken role*, Helen of Troy *silent*, Boy *silent*; offstage: 3 *s*; *satb* chorus of churchgoers, soldiers, courtiers, huntsmen, Catholic and Lutheran students, countryfolk; dancers

Busoni consciously conceived *Doktor Faust* as his most significant work and his life's crowning achievement. Before finally deciding on *Faust* he had actively considered several alternatives, including the Wandering Jew, Leonardo da Vinci and Don Juan. He wrote the libretto between 1910 and 1915, the major portion coming to him impulsively during Christmas of 1914. Work on the score was begun in 1916, although the first musical studies for the opera date from 1912. Ill health began to impede Busoni's progress from 1921 onwards and when he died in 1924 two substantial passages were still incomplete, the apparition of Helen of Troy to Faust in Scene 2 and the closing monologue of the final scene. In 1974, hitherto unknown sketches for these missing sections were bequeathed to the Prussian State Library in Berlin by Philipp Jarnach. Antony Beaumont's completion, based on this material, comes closer to Busoni's own concept than Jarnach's hastily written interpretation.

SYNOPSIS
The opera opens with an orchestral introduction (*Symphonia*), in which invisible voices chime out the word 'Pax' like bells, and a spoken prologue in which the poet outlines the genesis of the libretto and stresses its puppet origins. The opening scenes take place in Faust's study at Wittenberg. Wagner, his factotum, admits three students from Cracow, who bring a magic book, *Clavis Astartis Magica*. Following the instructions of the book, Faust summons the servants of Lucifer; they appear to him as six tongues of fire. Mephistopheles, the highest of them, claims to be 'swifter than the thoughts of man'. He draws up a pact which Faust signs with his own blood, against an offstage chorus of Eastertide churchgoers. Faust collapses. The scene changes to a Romanesque chapel (scenic intermezzo), where Gretchen's brother vows to revenge himself on Faust for her seduction and suicide. Mephistopheles engineers his brutal murder.

For the main body of the work the scene changes to the ducal park in Parma. As climax to the duke's wedding celebrations, Faust is presented as a celebrity and astonishes the guests with magic tricks. He conjures up three visions from antiquity (Samson and Delilah, Solomon and the queen of Sheba, Salome and John the Baptist) which express his love for the duchess. With the aid of Mephistopheles he soon succeeds in winning her. The duchess sings of her infatuation for Faust and flees with him. Disguised as court chaplain, Mephistopheles advises the duke to remarry, raising his clawed hand in ghastly benediction. A sombre orchestral sarabande marks the turning-point in the drama (symphonic intermezzo). In a tavern in Wittenberg, Faust mediates in an argument between Catholic and Protestant students, but his words lead only to uproar and dissent. Mephistopheles, disguised as a courier, brings the dead body of the duchess's child. He sets it alight and out of the flames emerges Helen of Troy. Faust tries in vain to grasp the visionary figure. Again he is confronted by the students from Cracow, who tell him that he is to die at midnight. The scene changes to Wittenberg town square; snow is falling. Mephistopheles, as night-watchman, calls the hour: it is ten o'clock. Students skittishly serenade Wagner, who has succeeded Faust as rector of the university. Faust gives alms to a beggarwoman but she is revealed as the ghost of the duchess, who urges him to 'finish the work before midnight'. Faust transfers his soul to the dead child, dying as midnight strikes. The child arises in his place and strides out into the night. Mephistopheles is defeated.

The score is assembled from numerous musical studies, ranging from unfinished fragments (lieder, piano pieces, etc.) to substantial published works. Diverse as the sources are, they are unified by a 'Faustian' musical vocabulary: tonal music of extreme harmonic subtlety, with predominantly polyphonic textures and clear, sophisticated orchestral sonorities.

Busoni distinguished between Wagnerian music drama and his own (epic) theatre, in which words and music are intended to fulfil their own, separate functions. In 1922 he published his essay 'Outline of a Preface to the Score of *Doktor Faust*', in which he stressed that each section of his score is shaped into an organic, if unorthodox, symphonic form: the festivities at Parma are formed into a dance suite, the tavern scene features a scherzo, chorale and fugue. The introspective, Faustian element is countered in each main scene by lighter, extrovert episodes; hence the work can be understood as a mystery play, part folk festival, part Passion. Among those rarefied stage works concerned with artistic creativity and higher philosophical questions (such as Wagner's *Die Meistersinger*, Schoenberg's *Moses und Aron*, Pfitzner's *Palestrina*) it occupies a prominent place.

Other operatic works: *Sigune, oder Das stille Dorf* (not orch., 1892); *Die Brautwahl*, 1912; *Arlecchino, oder Die Fenster*, 1917

A.C.W.B.

C

ALFREDO CATALANI
b 19 June 1854, Lucca, Italy; *d* 7 August 1893, Milan

Catalani is an isolated figure in late-19th-century Italian opera. Eschewing both the Verdian vein of French-influenced international opera and the melodramatic excesses of the emerging verismo school, he pursued a brand of Germanic Romanticism, yet endowed it with an authentic Italian flavour. He was just coming into his own when he died of tuberculosis at 39.

His first musical studies, in Lucca with Puccini's uncle, Fortunato Magi, were followed by further lessons in Paris under François Bazin. Later, he settled in Milan, where he continued his studies in composition at the conservatory with Antonio Bazzini. In 1875 he wrote an eclogue (in effect a one-act opera), *La falce* (to a text by Boito), as his graduation exercise, which won him the support of the publisher Giovannina Lucca, who then underwrote his career for several years.

Encouraged by a modest monthly stipend from Lucca, he embarked on an opera, *Elda*, finishing the first version in 1876, but continuing to revise it until it was premiered in Turin in 1880. Next came *Dejanice* (1883) and *Edmea* (1886); the latter won him favourable critical attention, despite one of Antonio Ghislanzoni's more implausible libretti. *Edmea* is the first of Catalani's scores to hint at his natural inclination towards idiosyncratic Romanticism. The same year he was appointed professor of composition at the Milan Conservatory on the death of Ponchielli, but because of his ill health he was granted the post only on a year's probation.

When Lucca's publishing house was merged with that of Giulio Ricordi in 1888, Catalani failed to find favour with the new regime, and his final works were brought to fruition largely through his own efforts. He embarked on a full-scale revision of *Elda*. Retitled *Loreley*, it was introduced at the Teatro Regio, Turin, early in 1890. It subsequently became the first of Catalani's works to be widely performed outside Italy. His last opera, *La Wally* (1892), to a text by Luigi Illica (commissioned and paid for by Catalani himself), was even more successful. With *La Wally*, he finally earned the goodwill of Ricordi, but by then it was too late.

Catalani struggled to find himself at a time when Italian stages were dominated by the final works of Verdi and by the emergence of the *veristi*. He laboured by trial and error to achieve what came more easily to other opera composers with a stronger instinct for the stage. His ability to create poetically atmospheric orchestral music, as in the 'Dance of the Ondine' in Act III of *Loreley* and the prelude to Act III of *La Wally*, compensates to some extent for his difficulty in projecting clearly individualized personalities for his characters.

La Wally
Dramma musicale in four acts (2h)
Libretto by Luigi Illica, after the novel *Die Geyer-Wally* by Wilhelmine von Hillern (1875)
PREMIERES 20 January 1892, La Scala, Milan; US: 6 January 1909, Metropolitan, New York; UK: 27 March 1919, Manchester
CAST Wally *s*, Stromminger *b*, Afra *ms*, Walter *s*, Giuseppe Hagenbach *t*, Vincenzo Gellner *bar*, Messenger *t* or *b*; *satb* chorus of Tyroleans, shepherds, peasants, hunters, old women, village children

Premiered within months of Verdi's *Falstaff* and Puccini's *Manon Lescaut*, *La Wally* is the clearest example of the 'alternative' direction Italian opera might have taken had not Catalani's death intervened. It is the composer's most successful opera and – initially thanks to the championing of Arturo Toscanini, who conducted its premiere (and named his daughter Wally) – has become an established, if infrequently performed, part of the repertoire.

SYNOPSIS
Act I The setting is the Tyrolean Alps, and the plot turns on the triangle of the independent but vulnerable Wally, Gellner, whom her wealthy father, Stromminger, wants her to marry, and Hagenbach, whom she loves. At Stromminger's 70th birthday party, Wally rejects Gellner and her father turns her out. Wally retreats to the mountains with her friend Walter.

Act II After her father's death, Wally, now rich, comes to a festival at Sölden. There, Gellner urges her to accept him, but Wally is still fascinated by Hagenbach, with whom she dances a *valzer del bacio*. Wally confesses she loves him, but Hagenbach's kiss is derisive, whereupon she orders Gellner to kill him.

Act III That night Wally wishes she could take back her words. Hagenbach comes to ask pardon, but Gellner intercepts him, and hurls him down a ravine. Wally clambers down and saves Hagenbach. Once more she retreats to the heights, leaving her inheritance to Afra, the woman she believes Hagenbach loves.

Act IV High in the Alps, Hagenbach comes to Wally and, their mutual misunderstanding resolved, they rejoice in their love. An ominous storm has gathered and they both perish in an avalanche.

Catalani took advantage of the setting to introduce some local colour into his music, for example, the 'Edelweiss' song sung by Walter, a village boy, in Act I, and the Tyrolean dances in Act II; Wally's 'Ebben? Ne andrò lontana', the best known of all Catalani's arias, is an adaptation of the melody of Catalani's Chanson groënlandaise, but its nordic character is not so pronounced as to make it seem out of place here. While these individual set numbers may be singled out, one of the most significant features of the score is its continuity. Catalani abandoned the number-opera structure of his earlier operas and, no doubt influenced by Wagner and perhaps by Verdi's Otello, created instead an opera where the music flows seamlessly, incorporating and then developing motifs of dramatic significance.

Other operas: La falce, 1875; Elda, 1880; Dejanice, 1883; Edmea, 1886; Loreley (rev. of Elda), 1890

W.A.

FRANCESCO CAVALLI
Pietro (Pier) Francesco Caletti (Caletto, Caletti-Bruni, Caletti di Bruno) detto il Cavalli; b 14 February 1602, Crema, Italy; d 14 January 1676, Venice

One of the major composers of the 17th century, Cavalli played a crucial role in establishing opera as a genre. Although opera had been 'invented' in the 1590s, performances had largely been isolated events mounted for special court occasions. In 1637, however, the concept of public opera, with regular seasons financed by ticket sales, emerged in Venice. This idea stimulated a wave of creativity that quickly won opera a permanent place in the musical world, with Venice as its centre. After the death of Monteverdi (1643), Cavalli became the leading opera composer in Venice; he wrote 32 between 1639 and 1673. Unlike those of his contemporaries, most of his works survive: the Biblioteca Marciana, Venice, preserves 28 manuscript scores from Cavalli's own collection, some autograph, and many bearing his corrections. Moreover, as opera spread throughout Italy in the 1640s and 1650s, Cavalli's works played a vital part in initiating the tradition of opera performance in numerous cities (including Naples). His fame reached beyond Italy to England, Austria and particularly France, and in 1660 he was commissioned to write an opera, Ercole amante, for the wedding of Louis XIV. In an era that constantly demanded new operas, Cavalli's were unusual for their sustained popularity; today many have been revived with considerable success.

Cavalli received his first musical training from his father, Giovanni Battista Caletti, maestro di cappella of Crema Cathedral. In 1616, the boy was brought to Venice by Federico Cavalli, governor of Crema; Francesco later adopted his patron's name. Shortly after his arrival in Venice, Francesco joined the choir at St Mark's, where Monteverdi was the new maestro di cappella. This was the beginning of a lifelong association with St Mark's in which Cavalli rose from soprano to tenor to second organist (1639) to first organist (c. 1645), and finally maestro di cappella (1668).

Cavalli's opera career began in 1639, when he signed a contract with Venice's first opera theatre, S. Cassiano; besides composing, he initially helped finance and manage the company. In 1641 Cavalli teamed up with Giovanni Faustini, librettist and later impresario, with whom he collaborated (on ten operas) until the latter's death in 1651; he subsequently worked for Faustini's brother Marco, who took over as impresario. He composed seven operas to libretti by Nicolò Minato, and three to works by Giovanni Francesco Busenello, author of L'incoronazione di Poppea. Cavalli apparently helped revise Monteverdi's music to Poppea: the Marciana collection includes a score with his annotations.

In 1660 Cavalli accepted Cardinal Mazarin's invitation to Paris. This journey was ill-fated from the start: preparations for the wedding celebrations were over budget and behind schedule, and Mazarin died before they were completed. Ercole amante's premiere was delayed until 1662; in the meantime, a revival of Xerse was staged. Both were adapted to French taste by Lully, who added long ballet entrées. Cavalli's music received little comment, and he departed vowing never to write another opera. He did ultimately finish six more, but two of the last three fell victim to the fickle tastes of the Venetian public. Even so, as maestro of St Mark's, he died in 1676 the most respected musician in Venice. The expressive quality of his music and his gift for dramatic portrayal mark him as a worthy successor to Monteverdi.

L'Ormindo
Favola regia per musica in a prologue and three acts
(2h 15m in abridged Leppard version)
Libretto by Giovanni Faustini
PREMIERES Carnival 1644, Teatro S. Cassiano, Venice; UK: 16 June 1967, Glyndebourne, Sussex (rev. Raymond Leppard); US: 24 April 1968, Juilliard School of Music, New York
CAST Ormindo a, Amida t, Hariadeno b, Erisbe s, Sicle s. Erice t, Osman t, 4 s, 3 ms, a, 3 t; ttb chorus of winds

Since 1967, when Leppard's Glyndebourne revival prompted the rediscovery of Cavalli, Ormindo has been one of the most popular baroque operas. In the 17th century, however, it was just one of many works that entertained audiences for one season, never to be revived. None the less, its libretto and music are typical of the period, and became models for later operas – notably Cavalli's Erismena (1656), which borrowed Ormindo's plot outline, as well as the prison scene.

SYNOPSIS

Act I   Ormindo and his friend Amida discover they both love Erisbe, wife of King Hariadeno. Erisbe declares she loves both equally; she cannot love her husband because he is too old. Amida's jilted lover, Sicle, arrives disguised as a gypsy.

Act II   Sicle reads Amida's palm, revealing to Erisbe his past infidelity. Disenchanted with Amida, Erisbe runs away with Ormindo.

Act III   Sicle's nurse, Erice, lures Amida to a cave, promising a magic spell to reunite him with his beloved. In a fake incantation scene, Erice instead summons the 'ghost' of Sicle, telling Amida that she committed suicide because he left her. When Amida is overcome with remorse, Sicle reveals herself and they are reunited. Hariadeno, furious, orders the arrest of Ormindo and Erisbe, and commands Osman to poison them. They drink the potion, sing a lament, and pass out. On seeing the bodies, however, Hariadeno weeps bitterly, especially after learning from a letter that Ormindo was his own son. Osman finally reveals that he substituted a sleeping potion for the poison. Ormindo and Erisbe awaken and are forgiven by Hariadeno, who bestows on Ormindo both his wife and his kingdom.

Cavalli's music, compared with that of later, more familiar, composers, is distinguished by the rich, varied nature of its recitative, and the high proportion of recitative to arias. During his lifetime, however, arias slowly gained ground, growing in number if not in size. Cavalli's operas also contain frequent short arioso passages that exhibit some features of aria style: for example, Ormindo has several instances where melodious refrains (typical of arias) surround recitative passages.

The arias in *Ormindo* are suave and lyrical, often cast in a lilting triple metre. The expressive details, however, are carefully tailored to the dramatic context: Erisbe's youth is conveyed by sweet thirds and ebullient runs; Ormindo's despair by poignant suspensions and unusual leaps. Arias are short, but tightly constructed; Cavalli uses just enough repetition to give the piece shape without belabouring its message. Many have strophic texts, and individual strophes often repeat the last phrase (ABB') or the first (ABA'); the latter is a prototype of the da-capo aria, the form that eventually dominated opera for a century (e.g. Erisbe's 'Fortunato mio core'). Many of the arias are framed by short instrumental sections; only the most important ones have orchestral accompaniment.

Cavalli is particularly renowned for his treatment of the lament. His favourite scheme involves a descending tetrachord ground bass, usually in the minor with chromatic inflexions; over this is woven a melody whose flexibility contrasts with the rigidity of the bass. A famous example is the prison scene in *Ormindo*.

Giasone

Jason

Dramma musicale in a prologue and three acts (4h)
Libretto by Giacinto Andrea Cicognini

PREMIERES   Carnival 1649, Teatro S. Cassiano, Venice; US: 5 January 1977, Alice Tully Hall, New York (concert); 18 May 1987, Mannes College, New York; UK: 3 August 1984, Opera House, Buxton
CAST   Giasone (Jason) *a*, Medea *ms*, Isifile (Hypsipyle) *s*, Egeo (Aegeus) *t*, Besso *b*, Ercole (Hercules) *b*, 4 *s*, 2 *a*, 2 *t*, 2 *b*; *attb* chorus of spirits, winds

Giasone was the single most popular opera of the 17th century. Along with *Egisto*, *Erismena*, *Xerse*, and Antonio Cesti's *Orontea*, it toured Italy in the repertoire of travelling companies, helping opera take root throughout the peninsula. *Giasone*'s widespread appeal was due partly to Cicognini's complex, fast-moving plot and the profusion of cleverly delineated characters. Particularly noteworthy is Cicognini's blend of comedy and tragedy: the ludicrous escapades and libertine attitudes of the comic characters provide a perfect foil for the tragic predicaments and moral conflicts of their noble counterparts. Ostensibly based on mythology, Cicognini's libretto contains rather more amorous intrigue than myth – in typical mid-17th-century style.

SYNOPSIS

Act I   At Hercules' urging, Jason has abandoned Hypsipyle to continue his search for the Golden Fleece. At the start of the opera, the quest has run aground for a second time in Colchis, where Jason falls in love with Medea. Medea, enchanted with her new lover, scorns her betrothed, Aegeus. In a remarkable incantation scene, she employs her supernatural arts to help the quest.

Act II   Helped by the magic ring supplied by Medea, Jason slays the monsters on guard and carries off the Fleece. To ensure that he marries Hypsipyle, the gods create a storm that shipwrecks Jason and Medea near Hypsipyle's home.

Act III   The suspicious Medea demands that Jason kill Hypsipyle. He agrees, and dispatches Besso to do the deed. But the plan backfires, and Medea is thrown into the sea instead. This mishap brings about the reunion of Medea and Aegeus: Aegeus rescues her, which makes her recognize the value of his constancy. Jason, meanwhile, is tormented by visions of the 'drowned' Hypsipyle on the one hand, and the jealous Medea on the other. When Hypsipyle appears alive, and Medea enters with Aegeus, Jason first refuses to give up Medea. He finally capitulates after Hypsipyle sings a moving lament.

Medea's incantation is one of Cavalli's most celebrated numbers. To create a stark, unnatural mood, he uses four chords, often with bare fifths, repeated incessantly. Medea's forceful arpeggios, compassing the extremes of her range, aptly convey the terrible power she is unleashing. In marked contrast stands Jason's first aria, sung as he staggers from Medea's bed. The mellifluous vocal line and rich, sweet harmonies immediately explain why Jason's heroic quest has stalled: Mars has been vanquished by Venus.

Hypsipyle, like many tragic heroines in Cavalli's early works, sings primarily in passionate recitative and arioso. In her final lament, she explores various emotions as she offers herself to Jason's sword. The central portion is set in aria style over a tetrachord bass; at the climax it erupts into recitative. The lament concludes with a heart-rending farewell, reminiscent of Ottavia's in Monteverdi's *Poppea*.

Cavalli's treatment of comedy is vital to the success of this work. Comic arias tend to be sectional and unpredictable; patter style is common.

La Calisto
Callisto
Dramma per musica in a prologue and three acts (2h 30m)
Libretto by Giovanni Faustini after Ovid's *Metamorphoses*, Book II
PREMIERES 28 November 1651, Teatro S. Apollinare, Venice; UK: 25 May 1970, Glyndebourne, Sussex ; US: 12 April 1972, Cincinnati University, Ohio
CAST Callisto *s*, Giove (Jove) *bar*, Diana *s*, Endimione (Endymion) *a*, Mercurio (Mercury) *t*, Giunone (Juno) *s*, 6 *s*, 2 *a*, *bar*; *satb* chorus of celestial spirits

Calisto is probably Cavalli's best-loved opera today, thanks to Leppard's 1970 revival. In its day, however, it was one of Cavalli's least successful works: attendance at the premiere was meagre, and the opera was shelved after 11 performances. Moreover, Faustini – who was serving as both librettist and impresario – died suddenly in the middle of the run. Whatever the reasons for the opera's initial failure, however, the overall quality of the work is extremely high: as Cavalli's fifteenth opera and his ninth collaboration with Faustini, *Calisto* reveals both men working at the peak of their creative powers.

The libretto fuses together the myth of Jove's seduction of Callisto with that of Diana's affair with Endymion. Although mythological plots were out of fashion at the time, these two stories are laden with potential for love intrigue in the contemporary style: Faustini portrays the gods and goddesses as more or less real humans, with plenty of human flaws.

SYNOPSIS
Act I As a follower of the virgin goddess Diana, the nymph Callisto is sworn to chastity. To win her, Jove cleverly turns himself into Diana (a deceit devised by Mercury); the naïve Callisto is then obedient to his every command, and overwhelmed by the delight of their encounter. Diana, meanwhile, has fallen in love with the shepherd Endymion, despite her own vows of chastity.

Act II Juno, suspecting her errant husband is up to his usual tricks, quickly discovers the truth. Diana's secret affair is discovered by Pan, who has long adored her. Pan and his band of satyrs torment Endymion.

Act III Juno, in revenge, turns Callisto into a bear. In the end, Endymion is rescued by his beloved goddess, and Jove reveals his true identity to Callisto. Although he cannot undo Juno's spell, he elevates Callisto to the stars as the constellation Ursa Major.

Cavalli clearly designed Endymion to be the star of this show: he is awarded some of the most beautiful and substantial numbers (including three out of four accompanied arias) as well as the most moving recitative. Particularly fine is 'Lucidissima face', his salute to the moon goddess Diana. Callisto is another character given to lyricism: as she moves between prim defiance, exultation, despair, confusion, and humble adoration of her great lover, Cavalli captures each moment with a beautifully wrought aria. The final duet between Jove and Callisto is one of many delightful ensembles in this work.

The wood deities Pan, Sylvan, and the Young Satyr provide *Calisto* with an unusual flavour. These are wild, passionate creatures, yet the Satyr is comic as well. Following a tradition for rustic poetry, Faustini concluded each line with a dactyl. Cavalli followed this rhythm, and intensified the strangeness of these 'half-beasts' by eschewing recitative, writing entirely in melodious arioso style.

Other operatic works: *Le nozze di Teti e di Peleo*, 1639; *Gli amori d'Apollo e di Dafne*, 1640; *Didone*, 1641; *La virtù de'strali d'Amore*, 1642; *L'Egisto*, 1643; *Doriclea*, 1645; *Orimonte*, 1650; *Rosinda* (ed. Jane Glover, 1973), 1651; *Eritrea* (ed. Jane Glover, 1975), 1652; *Veremonda l'amazzone di Aragona*, 1652/3; *Orione*, 1653; *Ciro*, 1654 (rev. by Cavalli and Aurelio Aureli of work by Francesco Provenzale and G. C. Sorrentino); *Xerse*, 1655; *Statira principessa di Persia*, 1655/?6; *L'Erismena*, 1656; *Artemisia*, 1656/?7; *Hipermestra*, (1654), 1658; *Elena*, 1659/60; *L'Ercole amante*, 1662; *Scipione Affricano*, 1664; *Mutio Scevola*, 1665; *Pompeo magno*, 1666; *Eliogabalo*, (1667/8); 6 other operas, music lost

J.W.B.

EMMANUEL CHABRIER
Alexis-Emmanuel Chabrier; *b* 18 January 1841, Ambert, Puy-de-Dôme, France; *d* 13 September 1894, Paris

Despite early evidence of his musicality, Chabrier's family insisted on a legal training for him. After graduation he took a civil-service post in Paris but continued to compose. Cultivated and gregarious, his circle was more Bohemian than bureaucratic. As well as musicians, he enjoyed the friendship of painters, including Édouard Manet (Chabrier was the first owner of his painting, *Le Bar aux Folies-Bergère*), and poets, including Paul Verlaine with whom he collaborated in the early 1860s on two uncompleted operettas: *Fisch-Ton-Kan* and *Vaucochard et fils 1er*. A grand opera, *Jean Hunyade*, followed in 1867 and was also left unfinished.

His particular musical character began to focus in the late 1870s with a pair of further comic pieces – *L'étoile* (1877) and *Une éducation manquée* (1879). Their apparent frivolity was compatible with a passion for Wagner: indeed the experience of hearing *Tristan* in Munich (1879) precipitated (as well as the wicked set of piano-duet quadrilles on its principal motifs) the decision to resign his civil-service post and devote himself entirely to composition. A trip to Spain in 1882 seems almost purposely to have realized Nietzsche's call to purge Bayreuth with the Mediterranean. Its most famous result came the following year with the orchestral rhapsody *España*.

Other highlights from his brief maturity include the *Dix pièces pittoresques* (1881) for solo piano and the *Trois valses romantiques* for two pianos (1883); the orchestral *Joyeuse marche* (1888); two ravishing works for women's voices and orchestra, *La Sulamite* (1884) (seminal to Debussy's *Damoiselle élue*) and the *Ode à la musique* (1890), as well as a handful of songs to which Ravel and Poulenc were the appreciative heirs. His later operatic ventures, serious as well as comic, run alongside this small but choice output – *Gwendoline*, *Le roi malgré lui* and the unfinished *Briséïs*. He undoubtedly pinned his most ardent hopes on them and gave them his all – his love was unreciprocated. From the early 1890s his health deteriorated rapidly, and he died aged 53 of general paralysis of the insane.

Chabrier's operatic career shows that, though the comic muse came to him with greater naturalness, there is real substance in his musical make-up to justify his ambition in tackling exalted subjects. And though only *L'étoile* can be called even marginally a repertoire piece, all five add, in different ways, to the range and stature of this mixed-up composer who is so much more significant than he seems.

L'étoile
The Star
Opéra-bouffe in three acts (1h 30m)
Libretto by Eugène Leterrier and Albert Vanloo
PREMIERES 28 November 1877, Théâtre des Bouffes-Parisiens, Paris; US: 18 August 1890, Broadway Theater, New York (arr. John Philip Sousa as *The Merry Monarch*); UK: 7 January 1899, Savoy Theatre, London (arr. Sousa and I. Caryll); 14 April 1970, John Lewis Theatre, London (as *The Lucky Star*)
CAST Ouf *t*, Siroco *b*, Hérisson de Porc-Épic *bar*, Aloès *ms*, Tapioca *t*, Lazuli *s*, Princess Laoula *s*, Maids of Honour (Oasis, Asphodèle, Youca, Adza, Zinnia, Koukouli) 6 *s*, Mayor and Chief of Police *spoken roles*; satb chorus of people, watchmen, courtiers

For all the (to us) charm of Chabrier's first completed opera, it was at first regarded as excessively complicated for an opéra-bouffe. It was accused of Wagnerian orchestration (Henri Duparc, who admired it, later called it 'a French *Meistersinger*'), and both the orchestra and the chorus had difficulty preparing their music. Its original run of 40 performances at the Bouffes-Parisiens was regarded as disappointing, and it was not seen again in Paris until 1941.

SYNOPSIS
Act I Ouf the First roams his city in disguise to find a suitable subject to execute as a 39th birthday treat. Enter, also disguised, Hérisson, his wife Aloès, secretary Tapioca, and Laoula, daughter of the neighbouring monarch. Their mission, of which she is unaware, is to marry Laoula to Ouf. The pedlar Lazuli has already fallen for her. Scolded for flirting with the two ladies (who are disguised as each other), he insults Ouf, who thus finds the desired candidate for death by impalement. Just in time Siroco, the king's astrologer, reveals that Ouf's fate and Lazuli's are inextricably linked. Lazuli is escorted with honour into the palace.

Act II Lazuli longs to escape and join Laoula. Ouf, still unaware of the two women's exchange, furthers the lovers' marriage by having the superfluous husband, Hérisson, imprisoned. Lazuli and Laoula depart happily together, leaving Aloès and Ouf in friendly contact, to the discomposure of Hérisson, who has now escaped. This confusion is resolved and Hérisson orders the pedlar to be shot. Gunfire is heard from the lake. Laoula is brought in, but no Lazuli, so Ouf and Siroco accept that this day will be their last.

Act III Lazuli, who has swum to safety, returns to overhear Ouf and his astrologer drowning their sorrows in green chartreuse and then, when Hérisson enters, an explanation. The men leave; the girls return. Their sadness is dispelled when Lazuli reveals himself, suffering only from a sneeze. A second elopement is planned. But Ouf returns, anxious to implant an heir without delay (an earlier prediction said he would lose his throne if his successor was not sired before he turned 40). Functionaries arrive to perform the marriage. Then when Siroco's latest erratic stargazing tells Ouf that his death is imminent, he releases Laoula and declares the pedlar his heir. His disappointment is lost in the general rejoicing.

The attractions of this charming piece include the tender *romance de l'étoile* where Lazuli first declares his love (its words possibly by Verlaine) and the delicious Tickling Trio which follows. The words for the gruesome punishment which gives the otherwise kindly king such pleasure can surely be attributed in all their salacious innuendo to Verlaine: 'Le Pal / Est de tous les supplices / Le principal / Et le plus fécond en délices.' (The official librettists changed the last line to 'le moins rempli de délices'.) The note of tenderness is struck again in Act III with Laoula's *couplets de la rose* (at the moment when she has lost all hope of finding Lazuli for the second time). Parody of Donizetti / Bellini, lurking everywhere, surfaces in the Green Chartreuse duet a little earlier. But the music's main language is French, the accent unmistakably Chabrier's.

Une éducation manquée
An Unsuccessful Education
Opérette in one act (40m)
Libretto by Eugène Leterrier and Albert Vanloo
PREMIERES 1 May 1879, Cercle de la Presse, Paris (with pf); 9 January 1913, Théâtre des Arts, Paris; US: 3 August 1953, Berkshire Music Center, Lenox, Massachusetts (Tanglewood); UK: 22 May 1955, Fortune Theatre, London
CAST Gontran de Boismassif *s*, Hélène de la Cerisaie *s*, Maître Pausanias *b*

The period is Louis XVI. Gontran and Hélène, newly married, don't know what happens next. The boy's tutor, Pausanias, lives in a world of textbooks; a letter from his grandfather is unspecific; the girl's aunt merely counsels obedience. They kiss, and Hélène departs sadly for bed. Gontran, alone after a blast of useless information from his tutor, gazes moodily out at the rain. It grows thundery. Hélène rushes back in, terrified. They huddle together, and nature takes its course.

This charming miniature is worthy of Bizet both in amorous tenderness and sparkling wit. They combine in its best number, the duet for the lovers when their knowledge is still confined to kissing. And surely the Maître's babbling list of classic authors and off-putting subjects was remembered by Ravel for the fiendish maths problems in *L'enfant et les sortilèges*.

Le roi malgré lui
The Reluctant King

Opéra comique in three acts (2h 15m)
Libretto by Émile de Najac, 'Paul Burani' (Urbain Roucoux) and the composer, after the play by Jacques-Arsène Ancelot (1836)
PREMIERES 18 May 1887, Opéra-Comique, Paris; US: 16 November 1972, Williams College, Williamstown, Massachusetts (concert); 18 November 1976, Juilliard School, New York; UK: 7 November 1992, Queen Elizabeth Hall, London (concert); 1 September 1994, King's Theatre, Edinburgh (new English version by Jeremy Sams and Michael Wilcox)
CAST The French: Henri de Valois *bar*, Comte de Nangis *t*, 5 Seigneurs (Liancourt *t*, Elbeuf *t*, Maugiron *bar*, Caylus *bar*, Villequier *b*); The Poles: Count Laski *b*, Basile (Innkeeper) *t*, soldier *b*, Duc de Fritelli (A Venetian) *bar-bouffe*; The Ladies: Minka (Laski's servant) *s*, Alexina, Duchesse de Fritelli *s*; *satb* chorus of pages, French and Polish lords, Polish ladies, soldiers, populace

The plot of *Le roi malgré lui*, which tells of the events surrounding the election in 1574 of Henri de Valois to the Polish throne, must be among the most complicated ever undertaken by an opera composer. As Harry Halbreich says, 'It is a negative *tour de force* to invent such a confusing story with so few characters in it.'

SYNOPSIS

Act I Henry of Valois has been elected king of Poland. But he and his nobles would rather be in France, while Count Laski is drumming up local support for a rival, the archduke of Austria. Henry – disguised – learns of a plot to kidnap him and escort him out of Poland. He secretly wishes it success, but decides to attend a ball in disguise as his friend Nangis, whom he meanwhile arrests.

Act II At the ball, Henry meets Laski, who lets slip that Alexina (a former love of Henry's) is now the wife of Fritelli, Henry's chamberlain. After a *tête-à-tête* with Alexina (who knows him only as her Venice lover) he takes the conspiracy oath. He summons Nangis and presents him to the conspirators as the king. Nangis grasps Henry's intention, and plays along. But when Laski announces that the 'king' is to die, Henry tries in vain to reveal his true identity. The conspirators draw lots to decide the assassin, and Henry himself is chosen. Nangis escapes with the help of his beloved Minka, a Polish slave.

Act III Henry (still as Nangis) arrives at a wayside inn, proclaiming the archduke of Austria, but hides as Alexina announces that the archduke has fled, believing the plot discovered. Minka arrives looking for the 'king' and, persuaded by Alexina that he is dead, is about to stab herself when the real Nangis appears. Alexina and Henry leave for the frontier, but

are accosted by Nangis and the French guard. Henry decides to be king after all.

Even if the music were as transparent as Offenbach or Sullivan it would be difficult to imagine the complex plot coming over clearly. But Chabrier has lavished upon it enough invention for a lifetime of operetta. The forms are large ('cette opérette colossale' said Reynaldo Hahn) and the richness of detail is extravagant. Size is shown above all in the finales of the first two acts and in the piece's only well-known section, the *Fête polonaise* (in its full form, with voices, the ballroom scene to end all ballroom scenes) that opens Act II. Detail is shown at its most precious in such numbers as the quintet where one heroine, Minka, is rescued from a soldier; the duet she sings in Act III with the other heroine, Alexina (a delectable next step from the duet in Berlioz's *Béatrice et Bénédict*); above all in the Act II barcarolle in which Alexina and the reluctant king recall their former *amour*. These are some of the highlights in a score that contains nothing inferior.

After some initial success in Germany, *Le roi* languished between infrequent attempts at revival. In the 1994 English version, which marked the centenary of the composer's death, the score remains intact, but the obscurity and fustian of the plot are replaced by neat and purposeful absurdity. This matches the musical impulse with such appropriateness as to seem that Chabrier set this book in the first place. It deserves (translated into French) to become an inseparable part of a classic operatic farce that really works.

Other operas: *Fisch-Ton-Kan* (inc., 1864), 1941; *Vaucochard et fils 1er* (inc., 1864), 1941; *Jean Hunyade* (inc., 1867); *Le sabbat* (inc., 1877); *Les muscadins* (inc., 1880); *Gwendoline*, 1886; *Briséïs* (inc., 1891), 1897

R.G.H.

GUSTAVE CHARPENTIER
b 25 June 1860, Dieuze, Meurthe, France; *d* 18 February 1956, Paris

The son of a baker who had moved with his family from his native Lorraine to Tourcoing at the time of the Franco-Prussian War, Charpentier entered the Lille Conservatoire at the age of 15. Success there led to a municipal scholarship to the Paris Conservatoire in 1881. He studied composition with Massenet, and in 1887 won the prestigious Prix de Rome. During his three-year stay in Rome he produced a colourful orchestral suite, *Impressions d'Italie*, which won widespread notice, and a symphonie-drame in four movements, *La vie du poète*, for solo voices, chorus and orchestra, set to his own text. He also began work on the libretto and score for an opera set in working-class Paris and in the village of Montmartre, where he had lived as a student.

After his return to Paris, Charpentier's affinities with the poets gave birth to four Baudelaire settings for voice and piano, and three songs for voice and orchestra on texts by Verlaine. Fashionable interest in the 18th century found expression in a *Sérénade à Watteau*, for solo voices, chorus and orchestra. The manuscript score of a second orchestral suite was accidentally destroyed and the work was lost. His *Fête du couronnement de la muse*, intended for an open-air ceremony in Montmartre organized by the composer himself, was performed in Lille and Paris in 1898. In the meantime Charpentier continued work on his opera, in collaboration with some literary friends, including the writer Saint-Pol-Roux. He incorporated the music of the *Fête du couronnement* as the central scene of the third act. After some delay attributable to the low-life aspects of the libretto, the completed work, now named *Louise*, was accepted by the Opéra-Comique, and at its premiere in February 1900 was an immediate success, attracting enthusiastic audiences from all social classes. It made its way round the opera houses of the world, and was conducted by Mahler, in both Vienna and New York. It also launched the career of the young Scottish singer Mary Garden, who stepped into the leading role in the course of the eighth performance.

In 1902, in accordance with his philosophy and interests, Charpentier founded the Conservatoire Populaire Mimi Pinson, designed to provide a free education in the arts for the working girls of Paris. Thereafter the cultivation of his image as an artist became a substitute for creative production: the only other work of significance that he wrote was *Julien*, a poème lyrique in four acts and a prologue, again to his own libretto. *Julien*, conceived as a sequel to *Louise*, was performed at the Opéra-Comique in June 1913. The score was largely a reworking of the earlier *La vie du poète*, with additional material borrowed from *Louise*. The later work, which substituted fantasy for realism, shared the limitations but lacked the strengths of its predecessor. In 1913 it was already a relic of a bygone age, and it did not survive its initial productions in Paris, Prague and New York. It may have been some consolation for the composer that in the previous year he was elected to succeed his friend and teacher Massenet as a member of the Académie des Beaux-Arts. Other stage projects came to nothing, and the rest of his life was uneventful.

Louise

Roman musical in four acts (five tableaux) (2h 15m)
Libretto by the composer
PREMIERES 2 February 1900, Opéra-Comique, Paris; US: 3 January 1908, Manhattan Opera, New York; UK: 18 June 1909, Covent Garden, London
CAST Louise *s*, Her Mother *ms*, Julien *t*, Louise's Father *bar*, 19 female soloists, 20 male soloists; *satb* chorus of Paris citizens, street sellers, workmen, dressmakers, beggars, street urchins, people of Montmartre, Bohemians, etc.

SYNOPSIS

Act I The action is set in Paris in 1900. Louise, a young dressmaker, is torn between her love for the poet Julien and her attraction to his Bohemian way of life and her loyalty to her devoted but narrow-minded working-class parents.

Act II At first Julien fails to persuade Louise to

abandon her family for freedom and happiness, but she eventually runs away with him.

Act III In a carnival atmosphere Louise is crowned Queen of Bohemia and Muse of Montmartre. But her mother interrupts the celebrations and persuades her to return to see her father, who is dangerously ill.

Act IV Although her father recovers, he is broken by disappointment and bitterness, and her parents use all means to prevent Louise from leaving. But the freedom and pleasures of the life she has tasted are too compelling. After a violent dispute her father orders her from the home. She flees to her lover and his world, and her despairing parent curses the city that has taken her from him.

The attraction of *Louise* lies in its unique amalgam of disparate elements and influences. It owes something to the late-19th-century French school of social realism, as exemplified in the novels of Émile Zola: the portrayal of the bleak existence of the poor and deprived is unadorned. At the same time the pill is sweetened by the romantic portrayal of the Bohemian life of Montmartre, and by the heroine's proclaimed desire, daring in its day, for sensual pleasure. The musical style too is eclectic, with influences ranging from Berlioz and Wagner to Gounod and Massenet, and incorporating a naturalistic treatment of Paris street cries. Some aspects of the work are undoubtedly dated. But at his best, as in the well-known air 'Depuis le jour' and in the crowd scenes, Charpentier displays a genuine melodic gift and a lively theatrical sense which have ensured for *Louise* a distinctive place in the repertoire of French opera.

Other operatic works: *L'amour au faubourg*, (*c.* 1913); *Orphée* (inc., 1913)

B.D.

MARC-ANTOINE CHARPENTIER
b 1643, Paris; *d* 24 February 1704, Paris

Though best known today mainly for his sacred works, Charpentier occupied himself on numerous occasions with music for the stage. Indeed, his first datable compositions after his youthful studies with Giacomo Carissimi in Rome consist of incidental music for Molière's plays: an overture for *La Comtesse d'Escarbagnas* was given on 8 July 1672 together with his brief intermèdes for a revival of *Le mariage forcé*, the latter replacing those provided by Lully for the original in 1664. More ambitious was Charpentier's contribution to Molière's *Le malade imaginaire* (1673), the music of which lasts well over an hour.

Charpentier's association with what was soon to become the Comédie-Française continued for some 12 years after Molière's death in 1673. His scope there, however, was increasingly limited by a series of crippling legal restrictions introduced by Lully to stifle competition with the Académie Royale de Musique, his newly established opera company. These restrictions forced Charpentier to reduce both the quantity of music and the number of performers at the Comédie-Française.

Lully's monopoly also effectively prevented French composers from presenting all-sung dramatic works, at least in public. It was thus not until after Lully's death in 1687 that Charpentier had the chance to compose a full-scale opera. In the meantime he had to content himself, as far as dramatic music was concerned, with short pastorales and similar entertainments for private patrons. Most of those that survive were written for his employer Mlle de Guise, among them *Les arts florissants*, *La descente d'Orphée aux enfers*, *Actéon* and two Christmas pastorales. Two others are courtly works: *La fête de Rueil*, commissioned to mark the unveiling of a statue of Louis XIV in the duc de Richelieu's château at Rueil, and *Les plaisirs de Versailles*, a remarkably unbuttoned comic divertissement said to have been performed in the Sun King's private apartments. Slight though they are, all these works contain fine music and demonstrate Charpentier's gift for capturing a wide range of dramatic moods.

Far grander in scale are *Celse martyr* (1687) and *David et Jonathas* (1688), tragédies that Charpentier wrote for the Jesuit Collège Louis-le-Grand, the most prestigious school in France. Jesuit colleges had quickly latched on to the popular appeal of opera: within little more than a decade of the emergence of Lully's tragédie en musique we find the first adaptations of the genre to the Jesuits' own ends. Why, they would argue, should the Académie Royale de Musique have all the good tunes? Jesuit productions characteristically involved large performing forces and elaborate staging, as *David et Jonathas* amply demonstrates. (Only the libretto of *Celse martyr* survives.)

David et Jonathas

David and Jonathan
Tragédie en musique in a prologue and five acts (2h)
Libretto by Père François de Paule Bretonneau after Kings I (RC Bible)/Samuel I (Hebrew and Protestant Bibles)
PREMIERES 25 February 1688, Collège Louis-le-Grand, Paris; UK: 22 June 1988, Barbican Hall, London (concert)
CAST David *haute-contre*, Jonathas (Jonathan) *s*, Saül (Saul) *b*, Achis (Achish) *b*, Joabel (Joab) *t*, La Pythonisse (The Witch of Endor) *haute-contre*, The Ghost of Samuel *b*, 3 Shepherds 3 *s*, 2 Warriors *t*, *b*, 2 Captives 2 *s*, A Follower of David *haute-contre*, A Follower of Jonathan *b*; *satb* chorus of people, warriors, captives, followers of David and Jonathan, shepherds, Philistines, Israelites, guards

As with other Jesuit opéras de collège, *David et Jonathas* was originally performed in a manner that now seems extraordinary: sandwiched between the prologue and each of the five acts was a Latin spoken tragedy, *Saul*, also in five acts and with its own self-contained but complementary action. (The text of *Saul* is lost, though a detailed synopsis survives.) Since the music alone lasts two hours, the resulting spectacle must have been extremely long.

Like *Saul*, *David et Jonathas* deals with events surrounding the battle between the Israelites and Philis-

tines, during which Saul and his son Jonathan are killed. It is preceded by a prologue in which Saul causes the Witch of Endor to summon up the ghost of Samuel and in so doing learns of Jonathan's and his own impending death.

Because the action of the spoken tragedy anticipates, act by act, that of the opera (albeit from a different perspective), the latter contains far less expository recitative than any contemporary tragédie en musique. It is consequently richer in set pieces, particularly ensembles and choruses. Some of these are remarkably long: the rondo-like sequence of numbers that make up Act I, Scene 1, in which warriors and shepherds welcome the victorious David, lasts almost ten minutes.

While *David et Jonathas* never quite reaches the astonishing power of *Médée*, its musical and dramatic interest is more evenly distributed. Charpentier brings extraordinary poignancy to the scenes involving the parting of David and Jonathan and, later, the deaths of Saul and Jonathan. In depicting the Witch of Endor he establishes an eerie atmosphere, her music unfolding as a manic succession of shifting moods involving keys as remote as G flat major; this prepares especially well for the apparition of the Ghost of Samuel, to the sepulchral accompaniment of four unspecified bass instruments (cf. *Médée*, Act IV, Scene 9). It is indeed fascinating to see how easily the language, both musical and poetic, of the Lullian tragédie could be adapted to the sacred setting. Only the ballet, too lubricious for the Reverend Fathers, is missing, though Charpentier manages to sneak in a few isolated dance movements, just as he does in his histoires sacrées.

Médée

Medea
Tragédie en musique in a prologue and five acts, (3h)
Libretto by Thomas Corneille
PREMIERES 4 December 1693, Paris Opéra (Académie Royale de Musique); UK: 13 February 1953, BBC radio
CAST Médée (Medea) *s*, Créon (Creon) *b*, Créuse (Creusa) *s*, Jason *haute-contre*, Oronte (Orontes) *b*, Nérine (Nerine) *s*; 7 *s*, 2 *haute-contre*, 2 *t*, 2 *b*; *satb* chorus of shepherds and countryfolk, Corinthians, Argians, Cupid's captives, Italians, demons and phantoms

Charpentier's one work for the Académie Royale de Musique, *Médée*, was not particularly successful. There is evidence of 'a cabal of the envious and the ignorant' (Sébastien de Brossard). Too powerful and disturbing for those accustomed to the blandness and optimism of Lully, the opera was taken off after nine or ten performances. Nevertheless, it is arguably the finest French opera of the 17th century, Lully's *Armide* notwithstanding.

SYNOPSIS

Act I With her husband Jason, the sorceress Medea has taken refuge in Corinth, which is now under threat from the Thessalians, who wish to avenge Medea's earlier crimes. In self-defence the Corinthian king Creon has allied himself with Orontes, prince of Argos, by promising him the hand of his daughter

Creusa. Medea, though grateful for the Corinthians' support, begins to suspect that Jason loves Creusa despite his feigned innocence. The citizens celebrate the arrival of Orontes and the Argians.

Act II Creon requests Medea to leave Corinth during the impending battle, since his people are worried that her presence will bring misfortune. For his own ends, Creon encourages the blossoming love between Jason and Creusa, whom Orontes meanwhile vainly tries to woo.

Act III Medea warns Orontes of her suspicions about Jason, and they form an alliance. Her fears are confirmed when she learns that Creon has consented to the marriage of Jason and Creusa. Summoning her demons, Medea poisons a robe that she had promised to Creusa.

Act IV Creusa appears wearing the robe, its poison not yet active. Assuring Orontes that Jason's wedding will not take place, Medea gives Creon an ultimatum: she will not leave Corinth unless Creusa marries Orontes. When the king tries to arrest her, the sorceress uses her powers to force the guards to fight each other, and then drives the king insane.

Act V Reluctantly Medea resolves to kill her children by Jason. Creusa implores her to calm Creon's madness. Medea agrees, on condition that the princess marry Orontes. For her father's sake Creusa reluctantly agrees, but too late: news arrives that the demented king has killed Orontes. Confronted by Creusa, Medea causes the robe's poison to take effect. Jason, finding the princess dying in agony, resolves on vengeance. But the triumphant Medea tells him of the murder of their children. As she disappears on a dragon, her palace collapses.

Although Thomas Corneille borrows lines from his brother Pierre's *Médée* (1635), his libretto differs both from the earlier play and from those of Euripides and Seneca in beginning the action well before Medea has proof of her husband's infidelity. In so doing, he deprives the first two acts of dramatic tension. At the same time he allows scope for his central character to develop with greater psychological depth: Medea's proud, vengeful nature is softened by the compassion she reveals as wife and mother, while her dreadful retribution acquires some justification from Jason's false assurances. To this flawed but psychologically subtle libretto Charpentier responds magnificently. His music, though outwardly following the Lullian model, is shot through with Italian influence and develops with an intensity unparalleled in 17th-century France: its harmonic richness and audacity would remain without equal at the Opéra until the appearance of Rameau 40 years later, while its use of orchestral colour to delineate mood and character is especially imaginative.

Other operatic works: *Le malade imaginaire*, 1673; *Petite pastorale*, ?mid-1670s; *Les plaisirs de Versailles*, early 1680s; *Actéon, c.* 1683–5; *Actéon changé en biche*, 1683–5 (rev. of *Actéon*); *Sur la naissance de N[otre] S[eigneur] J[ésus] C[hrist]*: pastorale, 1683–5; *Pastorale sur la naissance de N[otre] S[eigneur] J[ésus] C[hrist]*, 1683–5; *Il faut rire et chanter: dispute de bergers*, 1684–5; *La fête de Rueil*, 1685; *La couronne de fleurs*: pastorale, 1685; *La descente d'Orphée aux enfers*, ?mid-1680s (inc.); *Les arts florissants, c.* 1685–6; *Idyle sur le retour de la santé du roi*, 1686–7; *Amor vince ogni cosa*, [n.d.]; *Pastoraletta italiana*, [n.d.]

G.S.

LUIGI CHERUBINI
Maria Luigi Carlo Zenobi Salvatore Cherubini;
b 14 September 1760, Florence; *d* 15 March 1842, Paris

Cherubini's background was typical of that of a talented young Italian musician of his time. The son of a harpsichordist at the Teatro della Pergola in Florence, he showed precocious talent. His intermezzo *Il giocatore* (1775) demonstrates a thorough mastery of the idiom made popular by Pergolesi's *La serva padrona*. Cherubini came to the attention of the grand duke of Tuscany, who, in 1778, sent him to study with Giuseppe Sarti, one of the leading composers of the day. In 1780 Cherubini received a commission for a full-length opera seria, *Il Quinto Fabio*, and other operas followed. His early works, generally, show competence without any particular originality or promise of greater things to come. Like many of his contemporaries he sought fortune abroad, and in 1784 he accepted an invitation to London, where an opera buffa, *La finta principessa* (1785), and an opera seria, *Il Giulio Sabino* (1786), were presented at the King's Theatre in the Haymarket. Neither was successful, due, at least in part, to inadequate performances. So in 1787 Cherubini, encouraged by his compatriot the violinist and composer Giovanni Battista Viotti, a leading figure on the French musical scene, took up residence in Paris, which was to become his permanent home.

When Cherubini arrived in the French capital the battle for supremacy at the Opéra between the supporters of Niccolò Piccinni and Gluck, representing traditional and reform opera respectively, was still raging. Cherubini was engaged by Jean-François Marmontel, a leading traditionalist, to set his libretto on the theme of Demophoön, a typically classic theme of love, conflict, and sacrifice and rescue already familiar in a version by Pietro Metastasio. Cherubini's work was weighed against a rival treatment of the same plot by Johann Christoph Vogel, a dedicated follower of Gluck, and was found wanting. Not for the last time Cherubini was saddled with an incompetent libretto, and his imperfect understanding of the French language attracted critical condemnation. But despite its uncertainties *Démophoön* foreshadows Cherubini's mature style in its richly orchestrated accompaniments, its effective choral writing, and the sustained power of the dramatic conclusion.

Cherubini's association with Viotti and the queen's perfumer, Léonard, in forming a new opera company at the Théâtre de Monsieur, intended principally for the promotion of imported Italian opera buffa, established his position as an important influence in the musical life of Paris. The new theatre opened to acclaim in January 1789. With the advent of the Revolution the directors of the company realized that a change of name and of artistic policy was desirable. They commissioned a new building in the rue Feydeau, and the Théâtre Feydeau, as it came to be known, played a prominent role in the theatrical life of Paris throughout the turbulent final decade of the century. The new politically minded audiences rejected traditional opera on classical themes (unless the themes were consonant with the principles of Republicanism), looking instead for subjects of contemporary relevance, with heroic deeds, highly charged action, exotic settings, cataclysmic climaxes. A vehicle for the new style was to hand in opéra comique, whose flexible possibilities had already been explored by André Grétry and his contemporaries in the preceding decades. Cherubini adapted his style at once to this genre. His solidly grounded musical training (not always matched by that of his French contemporaries), a symphonic mode of thinking, and an imaginative command of orchestral colour and texture served him well. His first attempt, Lodoïska, a rescue opera set in Poland, won instant acclaim. First performed in 1791, it remained the longest-running opera of the decade. Its successor, Eliza, written at the height of the Terror in 1794, is a romantic story set in the Swiss Alps. Cherubini's next work, Médée, of 1797, took up in the more liberal post-revolutionary period a central classical legend, in a score of almost unparalleled intensity. In Les deux journées, which opened the new century in January 1800, the composer adopted a simpler idiom to proclaim a message of social and political reconciliation.

This opera, though not his last, marked the apogee of Cherubini's theatrical career. In 1803 his opéra-ballet Anacréon was staged at the Opéra. Its failure was attributed by the composer to a cabal; but it suffers from an inane plot, which was not rescued by some excellent dance music, a dramatic storm, and a sparkling overture much admired by Weber. However, an extended season of his earlier works performed in Vienna the previous year had won him the admiration and applause of the Viennese public, not least among them Beethoven, and Cherubini wrote his next opera, Faniska (1806), to a commission for Vienna. This was a rescue opera in the tradition of Lodoïska on a text by Beethoven's librettist Joseph Sonnleithner. It was initially well received by all, including the aged Haydn, who warmly embraced the composer at the premiere; but the opera did not establish itself. Nor did his next full-length opera, Les abencérages (1813), based on a medieval Spanish theme, despite the colour and opulence of the score.

The anachronistic Ali-Baba, performed 20 years later, was a reworking of much earlier material. It was a total failure, exciting the gleeful derision of Berlioz. Meanwhile the disillusioned Cherubini had turned to church music; the two settings of the Requiem Mass are among his best works. He had been associated with the Conservatoire National de Musique since its creation in 1795, and in 1822 was appointed director. Thereafter administrative and public duties limited his musical output. By the time of his death in 1842 his operas had long since disappeared from the French stage, as the young Wagner, writing from Paris in the previous year, remarked with caustic disapproval.

Cherubini's influence on the course of opera in his adopted country after 1800 was slight. But in the German-speaking countries it was more important. Lodoïska and Les deux journées were widely performed in Europe in the early years of the new century. A season of the four principal operas staged in Vienna in 1802 had a profound effect on Beethoven, who regarded Cherubini as his greatest contemporary – an effect not confined to his obvious indebtedness to Cherubini in Fidelio. Weber, another great admirer, also drew inspiration from Cherubini, notably in Der Freischütz. It is difficult, however, to arrive at an overall assessment of Cherubini's operatic achievement because of the comparative neglect from which his work has suffered.

Médée
Medea
Opera in three acts (2h 15m)
Libretto by François-Benoît Hoffman, after the tragedy by Pierre Corneille (1635)
PREMIERES 13 March 1797, Théâtre Feydeau, Paris; UK: 6 June 1865, Her Majesty's Theatre, London (in Italian, with recitatives by Luigi Arditi); 28 July 1984, Opera House, Buxton; US: 8 November 1955, New York (concert); 12 September 1958, San Francisco
CAST Médée (Medea) s, Dircé (Dirce) s, Néris (Neris) ms, Jason t, Créon (Creon) b, Captain of the Guard bar, 2 Servants s, ms; 2 Children silent; satb chorus of servants of Dirce, Argonauts, priests, warriors, people of Corinth

Médée, by virtue of its dramatic and musical range and intensity, is Cherubini's masterpiece. It is also the only work out of the two thousand or so theatrical productions during the Revolutionary decade in France to maintain a place in the repertoire, albeit until recently in a bowdlerized version. It has links with the pre-Revolutionary classical opera of Gluck and his contemporaries and immediate successors. But in other respects it anticipates the 19th-century conception of tragic opera. The libretto focuses throughout on the personality and situation of the tormented sorceress, torn between her hatred of Jason, who has deserted and betrayed her, and her love for her children, who have been taken from her. The symphonic treatment of the accompaniment heightens the emotional tension, as do the enormous demands on the technique and stamina of the leading singer. The obligatory final catastrophe, the immolation of the children and the destruction of the temple, remains unsurpassed in its dramatic and psychological power. Although coolly received at its premiere, Médée later won the admiration of Beethoven, Weber, Schumann, Wagner and Brahms.

SYNOPSIS
Act I The action takes place at Corinth. Outside the palace of King Creon, preparations are in train for the wedding of the king's daughter Dirce to Jason, who stole the Golden Fleece from Colchis, with the aid of the sorceress Medea. Medea betrayed her family and people to help him, and subsequently bore him two children, before he abandoned her. Dirce is fearful of Medea's wrath. Medea appears, demands that Jason

return to her, and is rebuffed. She curses Jason and swears a terrible vengeance.

Act II Inside the palace Medea is in despair. Her servant Neris urges her to leave. Creon appears and banishes her from the city. Medea, whose schemes of vengeance are taking shape, begs to be allowed to spend a last day with her children. Creon grants her request. Apparently more calm, she asks Neris to take to Dirce two wedding gifts, a cloak and a diadem given to her by Apollo.

Act III Between the palace and a temple. Neris brings the children out of the palace to Medea, who embraces them. Sounds of lamentation come from the palace. The bride is dead, poisoned by Medea's gifts. The enraged populace storms out, seeking revenge. Medea, Neris, and the children take refuge in the temple. Soon a horrified Neris re-emerges, followed by Medea, brandishing the bloodstained knife with which she has slain her sons, and attended by the Furies. Jason dies, to her imprecations. The temple is consumed by fire, and Medea and the Furies disappear in the flames.

The role of Medea was written for a singer of quite exceptional gifts, Julie-Angélique Scio, principal soprano at the Théâtre Feydeau. The range and sustained power necessary to fulfil the requirements of the part ensure that the singer increasingly dominates the action, from her anticipated first appearance in the middle of Act I, to her virtually continuous presence in the final act, in which the interruption of spoken dialogue is reduced to a minimum. The other principals are perceived in relation to the sorceress, and have limited scope; they are none the less clearly delineated in musical terms. The marches in the first two acts are fine examples of their type. The mood of each act is established by the preceding orchestral music. The turbulent one-section overture, in F minor, bears some striking resemblances to the later *Egmont* overture of Beethoven (1810).

Les deux journées, ou Le porteur d'eau

The Watercarrier
Opera in three acts (1h 30m)
Libretto by Jean-Nicolas Bouilly
PREMIERES 16 January 1800, Théâtre Feydeau, Paris; US: 12 March 1811, Théâtre Saint-Phillippe, New Orleans; UK: [an adaptation entitled *The Escapes, or The Water Carrier*, containing some of Cherubini's music, as well as items by other composers, arranged by Thomas Attwood, 14 October 1801, Covent Garden, London]; 27 October 1875, Princess's Theatre, London
CAST Constance *s*, Angelina *s*, Marcellina *s*, Village Girl *s*, Armand *t*, Antonio *t*, Mikeli *bar*, 2 *s*, *t*, 6 *b*; *satb* chorus of inhabitants of Gonesse, guards, soldiers

By the turn of the century, after the years of revolutionary unrest and excess, the taste of the Parisian theatre-going public was moving away from themes of violence towards those of peace and social reconciliation. Bouilly had already distinguished himself as an opera librettist with the rescue text *Léonore*, set by Pierre Gaveaux in 1798 (and destined to be the source of Beethoven's *Fidelio* a few years later). He now produced a new libretto, based (he later imaginatively

claimed) on a real incident which had occurred in the early days of the Revolution. His theme of a rescue transcending class boundaries appealed at once to the public. Bouilly's libretto is, by the standards of the time, of exceptional quality. Concise, well structured, it was cited as a model of excellence by both Goethe and Mendelssohn. Cherubini's score did Bouilly full justice. The composer simplified his usual style (which was regarded by many of his French critics as too complex and learned) and wrote music of sparkling freshness and instant appeal. The opera was immediately successful, and quickly established itself in the German-speaking countries, where it maintained its place in the repertoire into the 20th century. There, and in England, it is known by the original alternative title, *The Watercarrier*.

SYNOPSIS
Act I The action is set in 1647, when Cardinal Mazarin, adviser to the queen regent, was effectively ruler of France. The Parliament of Paris has refused to endorse some new and unjust edicts. It has been dissolved, and its members are fugitives from arrest and imprisonment. A price has been put on the head of their outspoken leader, Count Armand. All the exits from the city are guarded by Mazarin's troops. Armand and his wife, Countess Constance, are offered shelter by Mikeli, a humble but generous and noble-minded watercarrier. Mikeli's son, Antonio, recognizes in Armand the stranger who rescued him from death some years earlier in Switzerland. Mikeli resolves to save the life of his family's benefactor at all costs. He devises a plan to enable the couple to escape from the city. Antonio is to be married the following day at the village of Gonesse outside Paris. Constance will pass through the barriers with him, disguised as his sister, and Mikeli himself will smuggle the count to safety.

Act II At the city barriers the guards are suspicious about the identity of the disguised Constance. Mikeli arrives with his watercart and persuades them to let her through. While he distracts the attention of the guards, Armand, concealed in a compartment of the cart, slips out and escapes. Mikeli goes off down the side streets with his cart. Thus ends the first day.

Act III In the village preparations for the wedding are interrupted by the arrival of soldiers. Armand hides in a tree, but comes out and declares his identity when his wife is arrested. He too is taken prisoner. At this crucial moment Mikeli arrives with news of a free pardon from the queen for all the Parliamentarians. Armand and Constance are reunited. Antonio and his bride are married. Mikeli's courage and devotion are rewarded by the general rejoicing which ends the second day.

The appeal of the opera derives both from its direct and tuneful idiom and from the colourful blending of many different elements: solo numbers and ensembles of varying character, picturesque elements such as a Savoyard *romanza*, a village chorus, soldiers' marches. There are two instances of melodrama (spoken dialogue with orchestral accompaniment), a technique that reached its full potential in *Fidelio*.

Another noteworthy feature is Cherubini's use of two themes as reminiscence motifs in the orchestral accompaniment.

Other surviving operatic works: *Il giocatore* (intermezzo), (1775); untitled intermezzo, 1778; *Il Quinto Fabio* (original lost), 1779, rev. 1783; *Armida abbandonata*, 1782; *Mesenzio re d'Etruria*, 1782; *Lo sposo di tre e marito di nessuna*, 1783; *Olimpiade*, (*c.* 1783); *L'Alessandro nell'Indie*, 1784; *L'Idalide*, 1784; *Demetrio*, 1785; *Il Giulio Sabino*, 1786; *Ifigenia in Aulide*, 1788; *Démophoön*, 1788; *La Molinarella*, 1789; *Lodoïska*, 1791; *Eliza, ou Le voyage aux glaciers de Mont Saint-Bernard*, 1794; *L'hôtellerie portugaise*, 1798; *La punition*, 1799; *La prisonnière*, 1799; *Epicure*, 1800; *Anacréon, ou L'amour fugitif*, 1803; *Achille à Scyros*, 1804; *Faniska*, 1806; *Pimmalione*, 1809; *Il crescendo*, 1810; *Les abencérages, ou L'étendard de Grenade*, 1813; *Ali-Baba, ou Les quarante voleurs*, 1833; 6 others lost

B.D.

FRANCESCO CILEA

b 23 July 1866, Palmi, Italy; *d* 20 November 1950, Varazze, Italy

Cilea is remembered principally for his opera *Adriana Lecouvreur* and certain arias from *L'arlesiana*. Continued success in the opera house eluded him, and he devoted much of his time to teaching, finally becoming the director of the Naples Conservatory, where he had been a student (1881–9). His first opera, *Gina*, was premiered when he was still enrolled there and received enough attention to win him a contract with the publishing house of Sonzogno. His second, *La Tilda* (1892), an over-wrought work seeking to capitalize on the vogue for verismo subjects, was a setback.

Better fortune attended *L'arlesiana* (1897), where Caruso's success with Federico's 'Lament' helped establish Cilea as a relatively prominent member of his generation of Italian composers. Yet, when this opera failed to maintain its initial success, Cilea began to rework it and over the next 40 years he made a number of modifications.

Cilea reached the high point of his career with *Adriana Lecouvreur* (1902), but failed to repeat its success with his remaining operas. Of these *Gloria* was premiered at La Scala under Arturo Toscanini (1907), but survived for only two performances. In 1932 Cilea revised it for Naples, but without happier results. His last opera, *Il matrimonio selvaggio*, was not performed.

Cilea possessed an undeniable melodic gift, as 'Io sono l'umile ancella' from *Adriana Lecouvreur* shows, but his powers of invention were limited. Brief motivic ideas recur, but are rarely developed into a cohesive musical fabric. His operas give the overall impression that the musical materials have been stretched perilously thin.

Adriana Lecouvreur

Opera in four acts (2h 15m)
Libretto by Arturo Colautti, after Eugène Scribe's and Ernest Legouvé's play *Adrienne Lecouvreur* (1849)
PREMIERES 6 November 1902, Teatro Lirico, Milan; UK: 8 November 1904, Covent Garden, London; US: 5 January 1907, French Opera House, New Orleans
CAST Adriana Lecouvreur *s*, Maurizio *t*, Prince de Bouillon *b*, The Abbot of Chazeuil *bar*, Quinault *b*, Poisson *t*, Princess de Bouillon *ms*, Mlle Jouvenot *s*, Mlle Dangeville *ms*, Michonnet *bar*, Major-domo *t*; 4 acted roles; *satb* chorus of ladies, gentlemen, stagehands, servants; ballet

The plot is melodramatic fiction, but the title character (and some of the others) were real people: Adrienne Lecouvreur (1692–1730) was a star actress at the Comédie-Française in Paris. The libretto is quite condensed and rife with unexplained allusions. During the rehearsal period, Cilea had tightened up the score, omitting some episodes that would have rendered the complex plot easier to follow.

SYNOPSIS

Act I In the green room of the Comédie, Adriana tells the stage manager Michonnet, who loves her faithfully, that she is enamoured of Maurizio (who is, unknown to her, comte de Saxe and pretender to the throne of Poland). Adriana and Maurizio meet briefly and, before she leaves to perform onstage, she gives him a bouquet of violets as a memento. Later, the prince de Bouillon intercepts a note asking Maurizio for a meeting; he assumes the note is from Maurizio's mistress, the actress Duclos, but it is in fact written by his own wife. The prince invites the whole company to his house for a post-theatre party.

Act II In a fever of jealous anticipation the princess awaits her rendezvous with Maurizio. When he arrives, she is obsessed with the idea that he loves another woman; to placate her, Maurizio gives her the violets. When the guests are heard arriving, the princess hides in an inner room. Later, Adriana, at Maurizio's request, helps her to leave under cover of darkness, but, while neither is aware of the other's identity, each suspects the other of being her rival.

Act III At a sumptuous party given by the princess, she identifies Adriana's voice as that of her suspected rival and shows her the fading bouquet. In retaliation, the actress recites a scene from Racine's *Phèdre*, thereby making pointed allusions to the princess's promiscuity, an insult the princess vows to avenge.

Act IV It is Adriana's name day, and among the presents she receives is a mysterious box containing violets, which she mistakenly assumes is a token of farewell from Maurizio. He arrives, delighted to see her, but she is dying, killed by the violets that the princess has soaked in poison.

Though not consistently strong musically, *Adriana* continues to maintain itself on the fringes of the repertoire principally because it contains a challenging dramatic soprano role that is not particularly taxing on the upper register.

Other operas: *Gina*, 1889; *La Tilda*, 1892; *L'arlesiana*, 1897, rev. 1898; *Gloria*, 1907; *Il matrimonio selvaggio*, (1909)

W.A.

DOMENICO CIMAROSA

Domenico Nicola Cimarosa (Cimmarosa); *b* 17 December 1749, Aversa, Italy; *d* 11 January 1801, Venice

Cimarosa was, together with Paisiello, the most popular opera composer in the late 18th century. He produced some 60 opere buffe and 20 opere serie, many of which quickly entered the repertoire of opera houses throughout Europe.

Cimarosa studied with Pietro Antonio Gallo in Naples at the Conservatorio di S. Maria di Loreto, and later with the leading opera composer Niccolò Piccinni. His first opera, *Le stravaganze del conte*, was premiered in Naples in Carnival 1772, and he produced a number of comic operas for the Teatro dei Fiorentini, Naples, and (from 1778) for Rome; his first major triumph was *L'italiana in Londra* (1778). He was appointed supernumerary organist of the Neapolitan royal chamber in November 1779, and by the early 1780s he was also a visiting maestro at the Ospedaletto di SS. Giovanni e Paolo, Venice. In 1787, Cimarosa moved to St Petersburg to replace Giuseppe Sarti as maestro di cappella to Empress Catherine II (a post held earlier by Paisiello). His period in Russia was an unhappy one – the court theatre was in severe financial difficulties and Catherine seems to have disliked Cimarosa's music – and when his contract expired in 1791 he moved to Vienna. Emperor Leopold II (whom Cimarosa had known as Grand Duke Leopold of Tuscany) appointed him kapellmeister in place of Antonio Salieri, and Cimarosa's most successful opera, *Il matrimonio segreto*, was staged at the court theatre on 7 February 1792.

The death of Leopold II some three weeks later left Cimarosa unemployed, and he returned to Italy. In 1796, he was appointed first organist to Ferdinand IV, king of Naples, and he continued to write operas for Naples, Rome and Venice. In 1799, the composer came under a political cloud for espousing the libertarian cause of the short-lived 'Parthenopean Republic'. He was arrested and threatened with execution, although after four months in prison the sentence was commuted to exile. Cimarosa moved to Venice, where he died of stomach cancer perhaps contracted during his imprisonment (although some suspected poison). His last opera, *Artemisia*, was left incomplete on his death.

Cimarosa's output includes instrumental works, sacred music, oratorios and cantatas, but operas predominate. His facility as a composer was legendary, but doubtless he also made extensive reuse of material (which has not yet been fully studied) and relied on assistants (for example, to compose recitatives). His first Neapolitan period focused on opera buffa – Cimarosa's first opera seria, *Cajo Mario*, dates from 1780 – and, with some notable exceptions (including *Gli Orazi ed i Curiazi*, 1796), he remained most sympathetic to the comic style. His opere buffe (encompassing intermezzi, farse, commedie per musica and dramme giocose) gradually adopted a standard two-act format, balancing tuneful arias with action ensembles. Their popularity is documented by the large number of performances and adaptations: the resulting spread of

manuscript and printed sources remains a scholarly minefield. Cimarosa's style was much admired by Goethe, Stendhal (who noted his 'glittering array of comic verve, of passion, strength and gaiety'), and the critic Eduard Hanslick; many compared him (often favourably) with Mozart. But the two composers came from very different operatic traditions, and Cimarosa's significance lies in his development of a Neapolitan tradition following on from Piccinni that eventually led, through Paisiello, to Rossini.

Il matrimonio segreto

The Secret Marriage
Dramma giocoso in two acts (3h)
Libretto by Giovanni Bertati, after George Colman's and David Garrick's *The Clandestine Marriage* (1766)
PREMIERES 7 February 1792, Burgtheater, Vienna; UK: 11 January 1794, King's Theatre, Haymarket, London (libretto rev. Lorenzo da Ponte); US: 4 January 1834, Italian Opera House, New York
CAST Geronimo *b*, Elisetta *ms*, Carolina *s*, Fidalma *c*, Count Robinson *b*, Paolino *t*

Cimarosa's best-known opera was so popular that, at its premiere, Emperor Leopold II reputedly ordered that a second performance take place after dinner – the longest encore in operatic history. In the two years after its premiere, the opera was widely performed in Europe and translated into several languages. Cimarosa later claimed that it was not his best work: he preferred *Artemisia regina di Caria*. But Verdi called it a 'true musical comedy, which has everything an opera buffa should', and Hanslick proclaimed it 'full of sunshine'.

SYNOPSIS

Act I Geronimo, a wealthy, albeit deaf, Bolognese merchant, has two daughters, Elisetta and Carolina: their household is run by his sister, Fidalma. Carolina is secretly married to Paolino, who is loved by Fidalma. Count Robinson arrives to wed Elisetta but falls for Carolina, who fails to convince him of her many faults. Geronimo, delighted at the count's supposed interest in Elisetta, organizes a banquet in his honour, but remains confused by the shenanigans.

Act II Geronimo and the count agree a marriage with Carolina; Paolino goes to Fidalma for help but she misinterprets his words as a proposal of marriage, and he faints into her arms. Carolina enters inopportunely and takes some convincing of Paolino's love for her. The count seeks to estrange Elisetta by painting himself as an ogre; she and Fidalma respond by trying to send Carolina to a convent. Paolino and Carolina decide to run away but are caught by Elisetta, who summons the household. The assumption is that the man with Carolina is the count, but he makes a surprise entrance from another room (shades here of the countess in Act IV of *Le nozze di Figaro*), and Paolino and Carolina eventually confess. The count agrees to marry Elisetta, and all ends happily.

While some elements of the opera's music are Mozartian, others anticipate the works of Rossini, for instance the patter of fast words sung on a repeated note, comic nonsense sounds ('ba ba ba') and the overall structure of the work, which, in keeping with the latest developments in Italian opera, contains an extended finale and numerous ensembles. The first performance included Mozart's 'Al desio di chi t'adora' (written for the 1789 revival of *Figaro*) and a *Scena Livornese*, alluding to Cimarosa's meeting with Leopold II as grand duke of Tuscany when the composer was *en route* to St Petersburg. Both are now omitted.

Other operas: *Le stravaganze del conte*, 1772 (Act III also given separately as *Le magie di Merlina e Zoroastro*); *La finta parigina*, 1773; *I sdegni per amore*, 1776; *I matrimoni in ballo*, 1776 (rev. as Act III of *Il credulo*, 1786); *La frascatana nobile* (*La finta frascatana*), 1776; *I tre amanti*, 1777 (rev. as *Le gare degl'amanti*, 1783); *Il fanatico per gli antichi romani*, 1777; *L'Armida immaginaria*, 1777; *Gli amanti comici, o sia La famiglia in scompiglio*, ?1778 (rev. 1796; as *Il matrimonio in commedia*, 1797; as *La famiglia stravagante, ovvero Gli amanti comici*, 1798); *Il ritorno di Don Calandrino*, 1778 (rev. as *Armidoro e Laurina*, 1783); *Le stravaganze d'amore*, 1778; *Il matrimonio per raggiro* (*La donna bizzarra*), ?1779 (rev. 1802), related to *L'apprensivo raggirato*, 1798; *L'infedeltà fedele*, 1779; *L'italiana in Londra*, 1778; *Le donne rivali*, 1780 (rev. as *Le due rivali*, 1791); *Caio Mario*, 1780; *I finti nobili*, 1780; *Il falegname*, 1780 (rev. as *L'artista*, 1789); *Il capriccio drammatico*, ?1781, related to *L'impresario in angustie*, 1786 (rev. 1794); *Il pittor parigino*, 1781 (rev. as *Il barone burlato*, 1784; as *Le brame deluse*, 1787; as *Der Onkel aus Amsterdam*, 1796); *Alessandro nell'Indie*, 1781; *Giannina e Bernadone*, 1781; *L'amante combattuto dalle donne di punto*, 1781 (rev. as *La biondolina*, 1781, as *La giardiniera fortunata*, 1805); *Giunio Bruto*, 1781; *Il convito*, 1782 (rev. as *Der Schmaus*, 1784); *L'amor costante*, 1782 (rev. as *Giulietta ed Armidoro*, 1790); *L'eroe cinese*, 1782; *La ballerina amante*, 1782 (rev. as *L'amante ridicolo*, 1789); *La Circe*, 1783; *I due baroni di Rocca Azzurra*, 1783; *La villana riconosciuta*, 1783 (rev. as *La villanella rapita*, 1793); *Oreste*, 1783; *Chi dell'altrui si veste presto si spoglia*, 1783 (rev. as *Nina e Martuffo*, 1825); *I matrimoni impensati* (*La bella greca*), 1784; *L'apparenza inganna, o sia La villeggiatura*, 1784; *La vanità delusa* (*Il mercato di Malmantile*), 1784; *L'Olimpiade*, 1784; *I due supposti conti, ossia Lo sposo senza moglie*, 1784 (rev. as *Lo sposo ridicolo*, 1786); *Artaserse*, 1784; *Il marito disperato* (*Il marito geloso*), 1785 (rev. as *Die bestrafte Eifersucht*, 1794; as *L'amante disperato*, 1795); *La donna sempre al suo peggior s'appiglia*, 1785; *Il credulo*, 1786 (see *I matrimoni in ballo*, 1776; rev. as *Il credulo deluso*, 1791); *Le trame deluse*, 1786 (rev. as *L'amor contrastato*, 1788; as *Li raggiri scoperti*, 1799); *L'impresario in angustie*, 1786; *Volodimiro*, 1787; *Il fanatico burlato*, 1787 (rev. as *Der adelsüchtige Bürger*, 1791); *La felicità inaspettata*, 1788; *La vergine del sole*, ?1788; *La Cleopatra*, 1789; *Amor rende sagace*, 1793, related to *Le astuzie femminili*, 1794; *I traci amanti*, 1793 (rev. as *Il padre alla moda, ossia Lo sbarco di Mustanzir Bassà*, 1795; as *Gli turchi amanti*, 1796); *Le astuzie femminili*, 1794; *Penelope*, 1795; *Le nozze in garbuglio*, 1795; *L'impegno superato*, 1795; *La finta ammalata*, 1796; *I nemici generosi*, 1796 (rev. as *Il duello per complimento*, 1797); *Gli Orazi ed i Curiazi*, 1796; *Achille all'assedio di Troia*, 1797, related to *Gli Orazi ed i Curiazi*, 1797; *L'imprudente fortunato*, 1797; *Artemisia regina di Caria*, 1797; *L'apprensivo raggirato*, 1798; *Il secreto*, 1798; *L'intrigo della lettera*, 1798; *Artemisia* (inc.), 1801; 26 other undated or doubtful operas

T.C.

AARON COPLAND
b 14 November 1900, Brooklyn, New York; *d* 2 December 1990, Westchester County, New York

Aaron Copland is often regarded as the quintessentially American composer of the mid 20th century. Like Stravinsky, he gained access to a large public through a triptych of ballets – *Billy the Kid* (1938); *Rodeo* (1942); and *Appalachian Spring* (1944) – couched in a national musical idiom. These stage works, and his film scores, show Copland's rare ability to communicate through using the simplest materials in a recognizable and personal way. Copland's more severe side came to the fore in some exploratory works for his own instrument, the piano – the *Variations* (1930), *Sonata* (1941), and *Fantasy* (1957) – as well as some early and late orchestral and chamber works.

Copland's two operas were both written for young performers. When he was a student in Paris, working with Nadia Boulanger, he felt that opera was not part of new music. Composers, for him, fell into two categories: 'those who were "hopelessly" opera composers – such as Rossini, Wagner and Puccini – and those who debate whether and when to write an opera'. Copland, like Debussy, was one of the latter, and it is no surprise that his operas fall into the middle period when he became involved with folk subjects which allowed him to cultivate 'a kind of musical naturalness'. That was Copland's *métier*.

The Tender Land
Opera in three acts (1h 45m)
Libretto by 'Horace Everett' (Erik Johns) inspired by James Agee's book *Let Us Now Praise Famous Men* (1941)
Composed 1952–4 (in two acts), rev. (in three acts) 1955
PREMIERES 1 April 1954, New York City Center; rev. version: 20 May 1955, Oberlin Conservatory Opera Laboratory, Ohio; UK: 26 February 1962, Arts Theatre, Cambridge

In the early 1950s Copland cast around widely for an opera plot and met a number of writers. In 1952 he was commissioned by Richard Rodgers and Oscar Hammerstein II, through the League of Composers, to write an opera for television. NBC foolishly rejected *The Tender Land*, which would film particularly well, and the New York City Center took it on, to be staged by Jerome Robbins and conducted by Thomas Schippers.

Like Copland's ballet *Appalachian Spring*, *The Tender Land* is concerned with rural America: it quotes two folksongs included in Copland's arrangements, *Old American Songs*. The story is set on a Midwest farm in the 1930s at harvest time. The family consists of the grandfather, the mother and her daughter, Laurie, who is about to graduate from high school. Two itinerant workers, Martin and Top, arrive looking for odd jobs and are accepted with some suspicion. Laurie falls for Martin and plans to go away with him to freedom. The grandfather has given the men their notice and Martin, realizing that attachment to Laurie would mean having to settle down, steals off with his companion before she wakes. When Laurie finds that she has been jilted she decides to leave anyway: 'I'm ready for leaving like this harvest is ready to be gathered in.'

Like Copland's first opera, *The Second Hurricane* (1937), *The Tender Land* had an uneasy reception. Both composer and librettist felt they had made mistakes and there was considerable revision – the work became three instead of two acts. In 1965 a concert version of *The Tender Land* was the basis for the recording of excerpts which made it more widely known; it was televised, as originally intended, in 1975; in 1987 a revival in Newhaven using a reduced orchestration ran for over 50 performances. It was revived and recorded by the Plymouth Music Group in 1989, a performance that went to Aldeburgh (1990). The result was again inconclusive; problems with the libretto remain and the ending fails to convince, in spite of some vintage Copland *en route*.

Other opera: *The Second Hurricane*, 1937

P.D.

JOHN CORIGLIANO

John Paul Corigliano; *b* 16 February 1938, New York

Corigliano was born into a musical family – his father was leader of the New York Philharmonic. A pupil of Otto Luening, Vittorio Giannini and Paul Creston, Corigliano worked for radio, record companies and television as writer, producer and arranger and gained valuable experience composing incidental music. Of his series of concertos, the Clarinet Concerto (1977) was acclaimed for its vivid theatrical impact based on a technique of style modulation between and during movements. Corigliano has written fluently for films, and his scores have gained several awards. His first theatre work, *The Naked Carmen* (1970), a mixed-media opera after Bizet, was undertaken for Mercury Records. His first full-scale opera, *The Ghosts of Versailles*, was commissioned by the Metropolitan Opera in 1983.

The Ghosts of Versailles

Grand opera buffa in two acts (3h)
Libretto by William M. Hoffman, after the play *La mère coupable* by Pierre-Augustin Caron de Beaumarchais (1792)
PREMIERE 19 December 1991, Metropolitan, New York

Taking the final part of Beaumarchais's 'Figaro' trilogy, *La mère coupable*, as their starting point, Corigliano and his librettist have created a work in which past meets present. The ghost of Beaumarchais helps the ghost of Marie Antoinette come to terms with her execution and to exorcize the bitterness she feels, by rerunning history with Figaro and the Almaviva family as central characters. Echoes of historical fact are mirrored in the music by pastiche elements including regular quotations from Mozart's and Rossini's 'Figaro' operas and more oblique references to styles ranging from Richard Strauss to Gilbert and Sullivan.

P.D.

PETER CORNELIUS

Carl August Peter Cornelius; *b* 24 December 1824, Mainz, Germany; *d* 26 October 1874, Mainz

Cornelius wrote mainly small-scale vocal compositions; his only large-scale works are his three operas, and it is for the first of these, *Der Barbier von Bagdad*, together with some of his lieder, that he is remembered.

Cornelius's parents were both actors and, though he was given a sound musical education, they initially intended him for a theatrical career. However, after his father's death in 1843 he went to live with his uncle Peter von Cornelius in Berlin, where he studied music with Siegfried Dehn. Through his cousin, a noted painter and sculptor, he also made many contacts in Berlin literary and intellectual circles, and began to develop his skill as a writer and poet. In addition to writing his own libretti, he later translated those of other composers' operas (including four by Gluck) and wrote music criticism, essays and poetry.

In 1852 he was drawn into Liszt's circle in Weimar, and Liszt became, as Cornelius described him in the autograph score of *Der Barbier von Bagdad*, his 'master, friend and benefactor'. Cornelius at first concentrated on lieder, but, encouraged by Liszt, began his opera *Der Barbier von Bagdad* in 1855. Its premiere in 1858 provoked extraordinary opposition, aimed at the artistic creed that Liszt and Cornelius were seen to represent, and it was withdrawn after a single performance, which Liszt conducted. This fiasco precipitated Liszt's resignation as court conductor at Weimar: both he and Cornelius left the city shortly afterwards.

Cornelius spent the next six years in Vienna, where he came under Wagner's direct influence in 1861. There was genuine mutual admiration between the two men; Wagner acknowledged Cornelius as the only one of his adherents 'whom one could rightly call a genius'. Cornelius, though profoundly affected by his connection with Wagner and committed to his cause, did not allow his own artistic personality to be completely overwhelmed. The major work of Cornelius's Vienna years was his second opera, *Der Cid*, which was given a gratifyingly successful premiere in Weimar in 1865.

In the same year he moved to Munich at Wagner's invitation and became reader to King Ludwig II. Two years later he was appointed professor of music theory and rhetoric at the Königliche Musikhochschule. During his time in Munich, though he wrote a number of fine lieder, duets and choruses, he failed to complete any major works. After 1866 he worked sporadically on a third opera, *Gunlöd*, based on the legends of the *Edda*, in which the influence of Wagner's *Ring* is close to the surface. By the time of his death, substantial portions of the opera had been sketched and a few numbers were essentially finished, though none had been orchestrated. The opera was premiered, in a completion by Karl Hoffbauer and Eduard Lassen, in 1891; another version, completed by Waldemar von Bausznern, is included in the complete edition of Cornelius's works, but neither version has entered the repertoire.

Der Barbier von Bagdad

The Barber of Baghdad
Comic opera in two acts (2h)
Libretto by the composer, after *The Tailor's Tale* and *The Barber's Stories of His Six Brothers* from *The Arabian Nights*
PREMIERES 15 December 1858, Hoftheater, Weimar; rev. version: 1 February 1881, Karlsruhe (Mottl version); US: 3 January 1890, New York; UK: 9 December 1891, Savoy Theatre, London
CAST Nureddin *t*, Bostana *ms*, Abdul Hassan Ali Ebn Bekar (the barber) *b*, Margiana *s*, The Cadi, Baba Mustapha *t*, The Caliph *bar*, A Slave *t*, 3 Muezzins 2 *t*, *b*, 4 Armed Men 2 *t*, 2 *b*; *satb* chorus of servants of Nureddin, friends of the Cadi, people of Baghdad, mourning women, followers of the Caliph

Originally planned in one act, the libretto was – on Liszt's advice – expanded to two. Liszt also recommended changes in orchestration, which Cornelius executed. The premiere was a fiasco, and *Der Barbier von Bagdad* was not staged again until after Cornelius's death. Two versions made during the late 19th century – one by Felix Mottl, reworking the opera in one act and orchestrated in highly Wagnerian colours, the other by Hermann Levi, restoring some of Mottl's cuts, but using passages in Cornelius's scoring – have now generally been discredited in favour of the original version.

SYNOPSIS

Act I Nureddin is lovesick for Margiana, daughter of the cadi. Bostana, an old relative of the cadi, tells Nureddin that Margiana is expecting him at midday. She advises him to bath and shave, promising to send him a good barber. When the barber arrives he seems more interested in talking than working, and when he learns about Nureddin's assignation he insists on helping him. With great difficulty Nureddin gets his shave and escapes from the barber.

Act II In the women's quarters of the cadi's house Margiana waits for Nureddin. The delighted cadi comes in, having received an offer for her hand and a chest of gifts from his old rich friend Selim. When the cadi leaves for the mosque Nureddin enters and begins his courtship. The barber, who has arrived outside the house, hears the shrieks of a slave being punished and, thinking they are Nureddin's cries, breaks in. Meanwhile Nureddin has been hidden in the chest. Thinking the chest contains Nureddin's corpse, the servants and the barber are about to carry it off when the cadi returns; he thinks they are stealing his treasure. After much confusion the caliph arrives. The unconscious Nureddin is let out and everything ends happily with his revival and his betrothal to Margiana.

Despite Cornelius's connection with the New German School of Liszt and Wagner, *Der Barbier von Bagdad* is closer in style and in spirit to the earlier German Romantic operas of Weber, Lortzing and Nicolai. Cornelius deviated from previous comic models, however, in writing an opera with continuous music, rather than keeping the traditional structure of individual numbers interspersed with spoken dialogue. Elements such as the use of reminiscence motifs, which might be termed Wagnerian, were already established elements in German Romantic opera. Much of the best music is written for the strongly characterized title role, including a buffo patter song ('Bin Akademiker'), in which the barber lists his many accomplishments.

Other operas: *Der Cid*, 1865, (rev. Hermann Levi, 1891); *Gunlöd* (inc., 1874)

C.A.B.

LUIGI DALLAPICCOLA
b 3 February 1904, Pisino d'Istria, Slovenija; *d* 19 February 1975, Florence, Italy

Dallapiccola was the son of an Istrian schoolmaster, and his teenage education was disrupted when his father's school was closed by the Austrian authorities and the family was interned at Graz. Only at the close of the First World War, when Istria was ceded to Italy, was the family able to return to Pisino. In 1922 Dallapiccola moved to Florence, which was to be his home for the rest of his life. He studied at the conservatory there, where in 1934 he became professor of piano as a second study – a post that he held until his retirement. His compositions of the late 1930s and 1940s showed first a tentative and then an increasingly convinced use of serial techniques, and after the Second World War Dallapiccola emerged as the most authoritative advocate of that tradition in Italy.

In his theatrical work, Dallapiccola was heir to a theatre of philosophical challenge perhaps most strikingly exemplified in Busoni's *Doktor Faust*. He sought to infuse the Italian lyric tradition with a distinctive complexity of musical and dramatic thought and, in so doing, markedly influenced a younger generation of post-war composers, particularly with *Il prigioniero*, whose first performances in 1949 and 1950 were an important index of reviving cultural fortunes in Italy.

Volo di notte
Night Flight
[Opera in] one act (1h)
Libretto by the composer, after Antoine de Saint-Exupéry's short novel *Vol de nuit* (1931)
Composed 1937–9
PREMIERES 18 May 1940, Teatro della Pergola, Florence; US: 1 March 1962, Stanford University, California; UK: 29 May 1963, King's Theatre, Glasgow

Although much of his previous work had shown a strong sense of identity with medieval and renaissance Italian culture, Dallapiccola's first viable theatrical project broke entirely out of this framework to confront a modern subject. Based on the aviator-writer Saint-Exupéry's own experience when working for the Latécoère company, it chronicles the tenacity of purpose of those who pioneered airmail services in South

America. Its protagonist, Rivière, is a portrait of Didier Daurat, the director of those services.

Rivière seeks to maximize the potential of his project through as yet unexplored techniques of night flying: the mail is brought into Buenos Aires, and there transferred to another plane, which will set off for Europe in the middle of the night. The pilot of the flight from Chile, Pellerin, is caught up in a fearful Pacific cyclone while crossing the Andes, yet survives. But that same cyclone engulfs the plane flying up from Patagonia (the route that Saint-Exupéry had himself pioneered). The pilot, Fabien, defying his radio operator's warnings of bad weather, battles on in the darkness. About to run out of petrol, he decides on a crash landing, but, throwing out a flare, discovers that he has been blown out to sea. He glimpses the stars through a gap in the clouds, and, knowing that there is now no hope of safety, directs his plane upwards towards them, and rides above the storm in a new and revelatory realm until his petrol runs out. When it becomes clear that Fabien has been lost, the company staff expect Rivière to abandon his project. But the plane from Paraguay arrives safely: Rivière musters his strength, and orders the pilot for Europe on to the tarmac.

Dallapiccola locates the action entirely within Rivière's office; Fabien's final moment of revelation is relayed through the radio operator. The opera's six scenes are constructed as autonomous musical structures. A good deal of their material derives from the *Tre laudi* that Dallapiccola had composed in 1936–7, the most important instance being the music that opens the opera, and recurs at its climax, as Fabien climbs towards the stars. In its coupling of serial melody with a harmony still rooted in tonal associations, and its rhythmic vitality, *Volo di notte* remains a child of its time – but an interesting and accessible one.

Il prigioniero
The Prisoner
[Opera in] a prologue and one act (55m)
Libretto by the composer, after Count Philippe-Auguste Villiers de l'Isle-Adam's story *La torture par l'espérance* from *Nouveaux contes cruels* (1888), with additions after Charles de Coster's novel *La légende d'Ulenspiegel* (1868), and other sources
Composed 1944–8
PREMIERES 1 December 1949, RAI broadcast; 20 May 1950, Teatro Comunale, Florence; US: 15 March 1951,

Juilliard School of Music, New York; UK: 27 July 1959, Sadler's Wells, London

Dallapiccola first considered the theatrical potential of Villiers de l'Isle-Adam's story in 1939, at the instigation of his Jewish wife, Laura. That story is a more specific study of anti-Semitic persecution than is the libretto that Dallapiccola derived from it, for it centres on a rabbi tortured by the Inquisition in Saragossa. Drawing his imagery from de Coster's extraordinary epic of Flemish defiance to Spanish rule, *La légende d'Ulenspiegel*, Dallapiccola substituted for the rabbi an imprisoned Flemish freedom fighter, simply designated the prisoner. Introducing two new figures, the mother and the gaoler, he fleshed out the spare simplicity of Villiers de l'Isle-Adam's narration so as to emphasize the theme of resistance to tyranny (embodied in the opera in the brooding but unseen presence of Philip II).

Dallapiccola's ground plan is symmetrical. The prisoner's mother enters before the curtain to sing a prologue, recounting her nightly dream of Philip II (derived from de Coster and from Victor Hugo's portrait of Philip in *La légende des siècles*). She is engulfed by the first choral intermezzo, symbolizing the power of the Inquisition. The three main scenes follow: the mother visits the prisoner – as she rightly guesses – for the last time. Next comes the central scene of the prisoner's temptation by the gaoler (Dallapiccola's point of departure when setting to work on the music). The gaoler addresses him as *fratello* ('brother'), urges him to hope, and tells of a Flemish uprising. He departs, leaving the prisoner's door unlocked. The third scene charts the prisoner's fearful progress as, taking advantage of this opportunity, he makes his way along seemingly endless subterranean corridors: miraculously, two passing monks fail to notice him. A second choral intermezzo reasserts the presence of the Inquisition with thunderous force. Finally, in a scene that balances the first of the opera, the prisoner emerges into a nocturnal garden. Ecstatic beneath the night sky, as was Fabien in *Volo di notte*, the prisoner advances to embrace a great cedar tree. Arms shoot out from the tree, and a familiar voice intones 'fratello': it is the grand inquisitor, who, posing as a gaoler, has put the prisoner to the ultimate torture: that of hope. As a fire begins to flicker in the background, he leads the prisoner towards it.

The work is knit together by three different note rows, each used thematically, and by short motifs in part derived from them. The first is associated with the prisoner's prayer, 'Signore, aiutarmi a camminare' ('Lord, help me to walk'), the second with hope, and thus with the 'fratello' motif that announces the insidious presence of the 'gaoler'. The third row, rich in tonal associations, is that of freedom, on which the gaoler's 'aria in three strophes' depicting the revolt in Flanders is based. A further motif depicts Roelandt, the great bell of Ghent (destroyed by Philip II's father, Charles V), which the prisoner is induced to believe may yet ring again. As the prisoner makes his way down the corridor, Dallapiccola summarizes his mental state by three ricercars: one on the prayer note row, one on the 'fratello' motif and one on the 'Roelandt' motif. Such associations and interactions are typical of the opera: in consequence, the score repays repeated listening.

Ulisse
Ulysses
Opera in a prologue and two acts (2h 15m)
Libretto by the composer, after Homer and others
Composed 1960–68
PREMIERES 29 September 1968, Deutsche Oper, Berlin (as *Odysseus*); UK: 20 September 1969, BBC radio

Dallapiccola had already immersed himself in the Ulysses story when he had prepared a new version of Monteverdi's *Il ritorno d'Ulisse* for the Maggio Musicale in Florence in 1942. Intended as a summation of Dallapiccola's work, rather as *Doktor Faust* had been for Busoni, his own *Ulisse*'s combination of a richly worked libretto and a rather austere, unbending musical idiom have denied it as yet any clear-cut place within the operatic repertoire. The figure of Ulysses as conceived by Dallapiccola owes as much to Dante as to Homer: a man plunging into all aspects of human experience in search of a spiritual centre of gravity, which Dallapiccola (but not Homer or Dante) eventually provides not in his homecoming and revenge on Penelope's suitors, but alone at sea in a boat – and needless to say beneath an epiphanic night sky.

Ulisse is structured as a palindrome in 13 sections at whose centre lies his descent to the underworld. At either extreme stand Calypso alone on the seashore meditating on Ulysses' insatiable search, and Ulysses alone in his boat. To section 2, an orchestral representation of Poseidon's rage against Ulysses, corresponds section 12, an orchestral representation of the love of Ulysses and Penelope. To Nausicaa's danced ball game on the beach (3) corresponds the whore Melantho's dance of death (11); to Ulysses' arrival at the palace of King Alcinous (4) corresponds Ulysses' arrival at his own home in Ithaca (10). And so forth. Unity is achieved by grouping together a selection of Ulysses' adventures (up to and including the descent to the underworld) as a narration to King Alcinous and his court (Act I), and the dénouement at Ithaca with Ulysses' solitary epilogue (Act II).

Ulysses is also conceived as a summa of the feminine spirit. As a young man Dallapiccola believed he had found in the *Odyssey* archetypes for five essential aspects of womanhood. Moving from woman to woman through the opera, Ulysses completes a survey of the intractable 'otherness' of femininity. But, tellingly, his own masculine identity is a negative, not a positive, counter-pole. In Dallapiccola's version, the revenge of Poseidon is not the constant threat of annihilation by shipwreck, but a more subtle deliquescence. Ulysses becomes unsure of his own self: he hesitates to use his own name, even the word 'I'. Despite the moment of self-assertion needed to kill Penelope's suitors, it is the fragmented Ulysses who returns to the ocean – unaware until the very last moment of the opera that this scattering of self is the path through which an awareness of God can penetrate.

The sea is an ubiquitous symbol in *Ulisse*. It is therefore appropriate that the basic series from which all else derives is in the form of a wave. An extraordinary range of transformational processes yields all the other series, used motivically in association with specific characters (particularly the various women) or places (Ithaca, the underworld). In view of what was said above, it comes as no surprise that Ulysses does not have a character series as such – but mention of him consistently evokes one of the sea series. It is a solution of which Freud would have approved.

Other operatic work: *Job*, 1950

D.O.-S.

ALEKSANDR DARGOMYZHSKY

Aleksandr Sergeyevich Dargomyzhsky; *b* 14 February 1813, Troitskoye, Tula District, Russia; *d* 17 January 1869, St Petersburg

As a follower of Glinka, Dargomyzhsky helped establish the tradition of national opera that was brought to fruition by the so-called 'Mighty Handful' and Tchaikovsky. He is of great historical importance in the development of Russian music, but is not widely performed in the West.

His father, the illegitimate son of a nobleman, had eloped with Princess Kozlovskaya, a poetess, whose fascination with French culture was passed on to their six children. Dargomyzhsky showed great promise as a pianist and composer from an early age, and became a noted singing teacher in later life, though his own voice was notoriously high-pitched. His first piano teacher, Danilevsky, did not consider composing a suitable occupation for an aristocrat and tried to discourage him. In 1833, Dargomyzhsky met Glinka, who lent him notebooks of counterpoint exercises from his studies in Berlin with Siegfried Dehn; this was Dargomyzhsky's first thorough theoretical training.

Glinka and Dargomyzhsky organized concerts together. Playing piano duets and constant attendance during the preparations of Glinka's *A Life for the Tsar* inspired Dargomyzhsky to write an opera of his own. He toyed with Victor Hugo's *Lucrèce Borgia*, but then discovered a libretto Hugo himself had prepared for *Notre Dame de Paris*, which he translated – by 1841 *Esmeralda* was complete. Its style, that of French grand opera, was unfashionable in the Italian-dominated Russian operatic world, and it was not premiered until 1847. Discouraged by this, and by Glinka's huge success, he went to Paris (1844–5) where he met Auber, Meyerbeer and Halévy, his erstwhile idols. Curiously, like Glinka before him, absence from the homeland made him appreciate the richness of his native folk tradition, which was, as yet, relatively untapped. His songs from the mid-1840s onwards, perhaps his most significant compositions, demonstrate a striving for truth and realism in declamation, favouring dramatic scenes rather than lyric

outpourings of emotion, and often show a racy sense of humour. The opera-ballet *The Triumph of Bacchus* (completed in 1848, but premiered disastrously in 1867) is a retrograde step, favouring French models, though a harmonic quirkiness, which flavours all of his later work, lifts some of the music above the banal. *Rusalka* (1856) shows the most extensive use of folksong in his work, and was the first significant Russian opera to appear after Glinka's *Ruslan and Lyudmila*; but it did not become popular until the late 1860s, and its initial neglect precipitated another trip to Europe. On this trip he was cordially received by Liszt, and scored a great success in Brussels with two orchestral pieces and excerpts from *Rusalka*. By now, his reputation was growing. He had been elected to the Russian Musical Society Committee and was involved with Balakirev's new circle of composers, the Mighty Handful. From this period date two opera fragments, a duet from a setting of Aleksandr Pushkin's *Poltava* and five numbers from a fairy-tale opera *Rogdana* – a hermits' chorus from the latter showing great grandeur and advanced harmonic thinking.

In the last years of his life, beset with chronic illness and even more chronic hypochondria, Dargomyzhsky worked on a setting of Pushkin's *The Stone Guest*, a controversial work that has become a legend but is very rarely heard. His is a curious case, a composer whose ideals and theories were often more fecund than his musical ideas; he lacked the inspiration and ability to carry his conceptions through, but left an indelible mark on the next generation, particularly on Musorgsky.

The Stone Guest

Kamennyi Gost'
Opera in three acts (1h 15m)
Libretto by Aleksandr Pushkin (1830)
Composed 1860–69 (inc.); completed by César Cui and orchestrated by Rimsky-Korsakov
PREMIERES 28 February 1872, Mariinsky Theatre, St Petersburg; US: 25 February 1986, Marymount Manhattan Theater, New York; UK: 23 April 1987, Coliseum, London
CAST Don Juan *t*, Leporello *b*, Donna Anna *s*, Laura *ms*, Don Carlo *bar*, Monk *b*, The Statue *b*, 2 Guests *t*, *b*; *satb* chorus of Laura's guests

In this work, Dargomyzhsky took the unprecedented step of taking one of Pushkin's 'Little Tragedies' and setting it practically word for word, disregarding all operatic conventions and musical closed forms, allowing the words to dictate both structure and musical argument. Thus, there are no arias (except two songs that are called for in the original play) and the opera consists of continuous recitative. It was composed under the eyes of the Mighty Handful, and Dargomyzhsky, when he realized his health was failing, bequeathed its completion to Cui, then the most experienced opera composer in the circle, and its orchestration to Rimsky-Korsakov.

Pushkin kept a detailed list of all the women he had possessed, and his version of the Don Juan legend has an amoral lightness of touch that is ambivalent and disturbing.

SYNOPSIS

Act I Don Juan has returned to Madrid with his servant, Leporello, illegally breaking his exile, which he had incurred for murdering the commander in a duel. He catches sight of Donna Anna, the commander's widow, being escorted to her husband's grave by a monk, and vows to woo her. (Pushkin's version is unique in making Donna Anna the wife of the commander, rather than his daughter.) In Scene 2 Laura, a seductress, is having a supper party. She sings and dismisses her guests, detaining Don Carlo, whose fiery temper reminds her of her old flame, Don Juan. He appears in person, interrupting their love-making, dispatches Don Carlo in a duel, and seduces Laura.

Act II Don Juan, disguised as a monk, waits for Donna Anna by the statue of the commander. He woos her, and eventually she agrees to an assignation. Leporello later appears and is frightened by the statue. Don Juan forces him to invite the statue to Donna Anna's house. They flee.

Act III Don Juan reveals his identity to Donna Anna and swears he loves her. The statue appears and pulls Don Juan into the earth.

The immediate influence of *The Stone Guest* was far-reaching. Cui referred to it as 'the Gospel, which Russian composers will consult on matters of declamation and of faithful word-setting'. Musorgsky completed his own experiment in declamation alongside Dargomyzhsky's in his setting of the first act of Gogol's *The Marriage* (1868) – though these ideas bear greater musical fruit in the inn scene in his *Boris Godunov* – and Rimsky-Korsakov took *The Stone Guest* as a model for parts of his first opera, *The Maid of Pskov*. It may seem that Dargomyzhsky's operatic reforms owe something to Wagner's ideas, well publicized by Aleksandr Serov in the 1860s, but this is not apparent in the light of any musical analysis and, anyway, Dargomyzhsky was unsympathetic to the Wagner he heard (*Lohengrin* and *Tannhäuser*), considering it musically forced and undramatic, the texts overburdened with too much musical significance at the expense of pace.

The Stone Guest goes to the other extreme, containing long expanses of bare recitative with chordal support. One might suppose that the logical end to these reforms would be to omit music altogether. The pace is unvaried, excepting the conclusions of the last two acts; the melodic shapes are often anonymous, with more than a whiff of routine French or Italian recitative about them. Leitmotifs are attached to certain characters, but these are all-purpose labels, expressing neither emotion nor character. Occasional passages are vivid: the irruption of Don Juan and the duel in the first act, as well as the music for the statue. The latter has excited a great deal of comment, being based extensively on the whole-tone scale. Dargomyzhsky uses it with a boldness that suspends tonality for long stretches, quite unlike Glinka's fleeting use to portray supernatural events in *Ruslan and Lyudmila*, though obviously indebted to it: this music does convey genuine unease and terror.

The opera as a whole has many bold harmonic surprises, conceived empirically at the piano, though the wildest of these were ironed out by Rimsky-Korsakov in his well-meant but misguided edition of 1906. It has never been a repertoire piece, even in Russia, though its UK premiere by English National Opera was well received and showed the work, despite its manifold limitations on the page, to have a surprisingly theatrical impact.

Other operatic works: *Esmeralda*, (1841), 1847; *The Triumph of Bacchus (Torzhestvo Vakha)*, (1848), 1867; *Rusalka*, 1856; *Mazepa* (inc., 1860s); *Rogdana* (inc., 1860s)

J.G.

PETER MAXWELL DAVIES
(Sir) Peter Maxwell Davies; *b* 8 September 1934, Manchester, England

Davies has said that he was set on the path to becoming a composer when, at the age of four, he was taken to a Gilbert and Sullivan operetta, and he has written more for the theatre than any other leading composer of his generation: operas, ballets, school operas, and small-scale works of 'music-theatre', a genre he helped establish in the late 1960s. Perhaps the importance to him of the stage springs out of his concern with hypocrisy and betrayal, both intellectual and moral: each of his major dramatic works is concerned with an individual's search for personal authenticity in a mirror world of truth and falsehood, and the theatre – where real people assume roles, where musical thought can be traduced by stage action and vice versa – provides the ideal location for his questioning, ironical imagination.

The musical roots of that imagination lie in the great Austro-German tradition, which Davies absorbed as a boy, and in the alternatives of medieval, Indian and modern music which he encountered as a student in Manchester, where he was part of an extraordinary group of young musicians who interested themselves in the latest music of Boulez, Stockhausen and Nono (other members of the group included Birtwistle and Goehr). In essence his musical world was established by the mid-1950s. It depended on an equivalence between medieval and serial techniques, on a Schoenbergian reverence for developing form, and on a keenness to upset convention by means of complex rhythms, wild sonorities and harmonic double-thought. The idea for the opera *Taverner* came while he was still a student, though he did not begin the score until 1962, meanwhile concerning himself mostly with instrumental pieces and with school music (associated with his time as music master at Cirencester Grammar School, 1959–62).

While working on *Taverner* he found his music becoming more and more extravagant, its ironies exploding into manifest parody: plainsong themes could be converted into Victorian hymns or foxtrots; any and every musical intention could be mocked and guyed. It was out of this deeply unsettled and unsettling time that offshoots from the opera began to appear as pieces of music-theatre, extending the debate about how a man can separate himself (or how a musical idea can separate itself) from masquerades, imitations, forced roles and madness. In order to put on their music-theatre pieces, Davies and Birtwistle founded the Pierrot Players in 1967 (the group continued, after Birtwistle's departure, as The Fires of London, 1970–87), and for that ensemble – consisting of the forces of Schoenberg's *Pierrot lunaire* together with a percussionist – Davies produced a host of dramatic works, chamber pieces and arrangements (or in some cases travesties).

In the early 1970s he settled in an isolated croft on the island of Hoy, and began a new period when the seascapes and tranquillity of Orkney started to wash over the puzzles and hysteria. Then, with his First Symphony (1973–6), he turned his attention more to the orchestra than to chamber groupings, though the operas that have followed *Taverner* have tended to be for reduced forces and have profited from the composer's experience of writing for The Fires.

Taverner

Opera in two acts (eight scenes) (2h 15m)
Libretto by the composer, after 16th-century documents/sources
Composed 1962–8, partly reconstructed 1970
PREMIERES 12 July 1972, Covent Garden, London; US: 12 March 1986, Boston
CAST John Taverner *t*, White Abbot *bar*, King *b*, Cardinal *t*, Jester *bar*, Richard Taverner *bar*, Rose Parrowe *s*, Priest-Confessor *ct*, Boy *treble*, Captain *b*, Antichrist *speaking t*, Archangel Gabriel *high t*, Archangel Michael *low b*, 2 Monks 2 *t*; *satb* and *boy treble* chorus

The opera depends on a misreading of the documents (a misreading that was general at the time the work was begun) which suggested that Taverner, after writing some of the most glorious masses and motets in Henrican England, abandoned his art to become a zealous persecutor of the old faith. But though this may be false history, as fiction it touches important truth: in turning his back on music, the Taverner of the opera rejects what is best in himself, and becomes a vessel of hatred and negation. He becomes a crude caricature, a parody of himself, and the opera discloses this on the largest scale by making its second act a parody of the first: there is a parallel with Liszt's *Faust-Symphonie*, Taverner being a Faust who sells his soul not for power and knowledge but for the security of blind certainty. Like Liszt, Davies deflates and counters his own music's pretensions by means of speed, drastic simplification of melody, and rhythmic crudity, so that the second act is almost a cartoon-strip version of the first. This effect is, however, slightly modified by the fact that parody is at work all through the score: parody in the musicological sense, in that the original Taverner's music provides the basic material for symphonic elaboration, and parody in the more common sense, in that certain scenes (especially Act I, Scene 4) are full of wild musical and dramatic exaggerations. The essential substance of the music, which in depth, inwardness and intensity recalls Schoenberg and Mahler, is thus under a double threat: that of relapse into Renaissance pastiche, and that of hysterical over-emphasis. Taverner's search for the way to save his soul is the music's search for integrity.

SYNOPSIS
Act I The opera opens with a courtroom scene: the composer John Taverner is being tried by the White Abbot for Protestant heresy, but at the last moment he is pardoned by the cardinal, to whom he is too valuable as a musician. Then, in chapel, the composer considers his religious duty while monks seem to be chanting the office, though in fact their words relate the protagonist's past and future. The orchestra then falls silent, to be replaced by a stage band of viols and lute for the first council scene: the king wants a break with Rome; the cardinal temporizes and the jester exposes the self-seeking motives of both parties. The jester remains on stage, reveals himself as Death, and calls up Taverner in order to lead him through a treacherous, nightmare catechism, at the end of which the composer disavows his music and takes up the sword on behalf of a manifestly false Jesus. Death shrieks a salutation.

Act II also opens with a courtroom scene, but at frenetic speed, and this time with the White Abbot at the mercy of Taverner. The abbot is sentenced to the stake, and now when the cardinal appears he has no face. Instead Death is seen controlling a huge wheel of fortune. The second council scene, accompanied like the first by Renaissance instruments, portrays the progress of the Reformation, and the second chapel scene shows a moment in it: the White Abbot and monks are saying Mass when Taverner and soldiers enter to dispossess them. Finally, in a big choral tableau, the townspeople of Boston are gathered to watch the burning of the White Abbot, though the man who is really destroyed is Taverner.

The Martyrdom of St Magnus

Chamber opera in nine scenes (1h 15m)
Libretto by the composer, after the novel *Magnus* by George Mackay Brown (1973)
PREMIERES 18 June 1977, St Magnus's Cathedral, Orkney; US: 29 July 1978, Aspen Music Festival, Colorado
CAST Earl Magnus *t*, Norse Herald/The Keeper of the Loom *bar*, Welsh Herald/The Tempter *bar*, Earl Hakon *b*, Blind Mary *ms*; each singer takes several roles: only the main ones are indicated

Magnus was earl of Orkney in the 12th century, and by repute a Viking unusual for his pacifism. The opera is staged hagiography, devised to be performed in a quite simple, stylized setting, whether in a church or a small theatre (the composer's own preference is for performance in the round). Magnus is to some extent a reincarnation of Taverner, though his path is made easier, and correspondingly there is a musical softening, attributable to the folk-modal flavour that entered Davies's music in the 1970s: only the penultimate scene has the savagery of his immediately pre-Orcadian scores, including *Taverner*. The instrumentation shows Davies's resourcefulness in using the Fires sextet, to which he adds brass for tones of eruption and nobility, and a guitar to bring out the ethnic roots of Blind Mary's songs.

Blind Mary, the opera's chorus figure, introduces the first of the nine scenes, in which Magnus is present at a sea battle between the Norsemen and the Welsh.

He prefers to fight with the words of Psalm 23 rather than with arms, and his side is victorious. In Scene 2 the Keeper of the Loom, the guardian of Magnus's soul, introduces the Tempter, who tries to seduce Magnus with promises of fame, marriage, sovereignty, monastic retirement and the sword. But Magnus refuses them all. Blind Mary then returns to lament the condition of Orkney, torn by civil war between Magnus and Hakon. Heralds of the rival earls meet the bishop to arrange a peace conference on the island of Egilsay (Scene 4); Magnus sings an aria of resolution on his way to the island (Scene 5). The musical style then becomes much fiercer as Hakon orders Magnus's execution, and in Scene 7 both action and music zoom forward to the present, the cast becoming reporters who comment on the developing tension. Scene 8 is fully in the present, or the recent past: Hakon is a hysterical military officer, and Magnus a nameless prisoner who quietly goes to meet his fate. The last scene is Blind Mary's: she prays to Magnus for the return of her sight, and gains it, while the rest of the cast as monks add Magnus's name to the litany of northern saints.

The Lighthouse
Chamber opera in one act with prologue (1h 15m)
Libretto by the composer
PREMIERES 2 September 1980, Moray House Gymnasium, Edinburgh; US: 1 November 1983, Boston
CAST Officer 1/Sandy *t*, Officer 2/Blazes *bar*, Officer 3/ Arthur *b*

The work is scored for very similar forces to those used in *The Martyrdom of St Magnus*, but the pageantry of that work is replaced by atmospheric grimness, by evocations of the cold Northern sea at night, and by parodies that heighten the passions and nightmares of the characters.

The prologue is set at a court of inquiry into the disappearance of three lighthouse keepers from their station. Questions are posed by solo horn, which may sound from the audience, and three officers give answer. Gradually they move from straight testimony into fantastical imaginings of evil during a flashback to the lighthouse; but then we snap back to the courtroom.

In the main act the three singers become the vanished keepers. They have been together for months, long enough to know each other well, and to know how to taunt each other: their relationship is highly unstable. To reduce the tension they sing songs. Blazes begins with a rough ballad of street violence, accompanied by violin and banjo; Sandy, with cello and upright piano, sings of making love; and Arthur, with brass and clarinet, belts out a hymn. But the songs serve only to resurrect in their minds ghosts from the past, and as fog descends each of them becomes convinced that he is being claimed by the Beast. They prepare to meet its dazzling eyes, which become the lights of the relief vessel, and the three men reappear as officers, finding at the lighthouse only an infestation of rats. They leave, and at the end the last hours of the three keepers begin to play over again.

Music-theatre works: *Eight Songs for a Mad King*, 1969; *Vesalii icones*, 1969; *Blind Man's Buff*, 1972; *Miss Donnithorne's Maggot*, 1974; *Le jongleur de Notre Dame*, 1978; *The No. 11 Bus*, 1984; other opera: *Resurrection*, 1988 Children's operas: *The Two Fiddlers*, 1978; *Cinderella*, 1980 Children's music-theatre pieces: *The Rainbow*, 1981; *Jupiter Landing*, 1990; *The Great Bank Robbery*, 1990; *Dinosaur at Large*, 1990; *Dangerous Errand*, 1990; *Computer Chaos*, 1991

P.A.G.

CLAUDE DEBUSSY
Achille-Claude Debussy; *b* 22 August 1862, Saint-Germain-en-Laye, nr Paris; *d* 25 March 1918, Paris

The son of a suburban Parisian shopkeeper who was imprisoned for his part in the Commune of 1871, Debussy studied piano (with Verlaine's mother-in-law, Mme Mauté, and later at the Conservatoire) and turned seriously to composition only when hopes of a virtuoso career receded in the late 1870s. Though to this day best known for his piano and orchestral music, and even though he completed only one opera, he was almost continuously preoccupied with music for the theatre in some form from the early 1880s until shortly before he died. Very few of these projects came to fruition, but they show that Debussy was fascinated by musical theatre and, under favourable conditions, a brilliant exponent of it. His single opera and the one purpose-made ballet of which he composed and orchestrated every note, *Jeux* (1912–13), are both masterpieces. Many other projects, on the other hand, were never even sketched, partly because he perhaps had no real intention of composing them, partly because of his intense self-criticism and partly because other work intervened or circumstances changed. For French composers, the theatre has always been a much stronger presence than for their German or British colleagues, and to some extent Debussy's involvement was an automatic reaction to context. But it was also a genuine creative preoccupation, connected with an early enthusiasm for Wagner, and then with his interest in Symbolist literature and his friendship with some of its best-known exponents (including Mallarmé). It was this literary connection which gave rise to the two abortive Edgar Allan Poe projects of the years following *Pelléas et Mélisande*.

Debussy's earliest proper theatre score is *Rodrigue et Chimène*, which was substantially composed in short score between 1888 and 1892, when it gave way to the first version of the orchestral *Nocturnes*, the *Prélude à l'après-midi d'un faune*, and soon *Pelléas et Mélisande*. Before this, Debussy's most successful works had been songs, including the compact and atmospheric Verlaine settings of the *Ariettes oubliées* (1885–8), and the more elaborate *Cinq poèmes de Baudelaire* (1887–9), with their Wagnerian turn of phrase. *Rodrigue et Chimène* is the sort of first opera one might expect of the composer of the Baudelaire songs. Its conventionally heroic subject suggests many other post-Wagner French operas, and while its harmonic language is that of mature early Debussy, its gesture often lacks the finesse and restraint of the composer at his subtlest. It was in about 1890 that Debussy described to his former composition teacher Ernest Guiraud the sort of operatic text he would like to set: 'The ideal would be two associated dreams. No place, no time. No big scene. No compulsion on the musician, who must complete and give body to the work of the poet. Music in opera is far too predominant. Too much singing and the musical settings are too cumbersome. The blossoming of the voice into true singing should occur only when required . . . My idea is of a short libretto with mobile scenes. No discussion or arguments between the characters, whom I see at the mercy of life or destiny.' This is remarkably prescient of Maurice Maeterlinck's *Pelléas* (as yet neither published nor performed), and a direct rebuttal of the *Rodrigue* kind of opera.

The composition, revision and orchestration of *Pelléas* preoccupied Debussy from 1893 until its first performance in April 1902, and during this period he started no other significant new works except the *Chansons de Bilitis* (1897–8) and *Pour le piano* (1894–1901). But once *Pelléas* reached the stage, he entered a completely new phase of mainly instrumental composition, in which he explored the formal and imaginative possibilities of innovations that had first been prompted, in song or opera, by words. This is the time of the great piano collections, the *Estampes* (1903), *Images* (1905, 1907) and *Préludes* (1910, 1912–13), *L'isle joyeuse* (1904), and the orchestral masterpieces *La mer* (1903–5) and *Images* (1905–12). Yet for much of the same period Debussy tinkered with a one-act opera on Poe's *The Devil in the Belfry*, somewhat later turning to *The Fall of the House of Usher*, sketches for which occupied him, on and off, for the last decade of his life. It is hard to imagine what Debussy could have made of Poe's absurd tale about the devil who makes the midday chimes strike thirteen and thereby brings chaos to the well-ordered life of the Dutch village of Vondervotteimittis. But *Usher*, as a subject, is a direct descendant of Debussy's early Symbolist obsessions. (Poe was a hero of the French Symbolist movement, and was translated by Baudelaire.) It might have made a superbly mysterious successor to *Pelléas*, if Debussy had solved its problems before the rectal cancer that tormented him from 1909 onwards finally made sustained creative concentration impossible.

Pelléas et Mélisande

Drame lyrique in five acts (12 tableaux) (2h 30m)
Libretto by the composer; abridgement of the play by
Maurice Maeterlinck (1892)
Composed ?September 1893–17 August 1895; rev. January
1900 (or earlier)–1902 (orch. ?November 1901–January
1902; interludes composed March–April 1902)
PREMIERES 30 April 1902, Opéra-Comique, Paris; US:
19 February 1908, Manhattan Opera House, New York;
UK: 21 May 1909, Covent Garden, London
CAST Mélisande *s*, Pelléas *t*, Golaud *bar*, Arkel *b*,
Geneviève *ms*, Yniold *s*, Doctor *b*, Shepherd *bar*, 3 Poor Men
silent, Servants *silent*; (offstage) *atb* chorus of sailors

Debussy attended the first performance of Maeterlinck's play at the Théâtre des Bouffes-Parisiens on 17 May 1893. But he had probably already read it (it had been published a year before) and considered setting it to music, having even before that (1891) applied unsuccessfully to Maeterlinck for permission to set his earlier play *La Princesse Maleine*. Over *Pelléas*, the playwright was more accommodating. Debussy set to work initially on the big final scene of Act IV, setting the text as it stood, without cuts. Then, finding his music too Wagnerian, he at once revised the scene, before returning to the start of the drama and composing it through roughly in sequence, omitting four of Maeterlinck's scenes and making extensive cuts to the remainder. At this stage he was seeking a new way of rendering into music Maeterlinck's curious mixture of high-sounding realism and interior symbolism, and finally came up, as he wrote to Ernest Chausson on 2 October 1893, 'with a technique which seems to me quite extraordinary, that is to say, Silence (don't laugh!) as a means of expression!'

Early proposals for performance came to nothing, and even though the new director of the Opéra-Comique, Albert Carré, accepted the work in principle in the spring of 1898, it was another three years before it was firmly scheduled for production. During this time Debussy made substantial revisions, especially to Act IV, and after the work's acceptance he again revised that act, as well as at last carrying out the orchestration. Also, during the rehearsal period, he composed the somewhat Wagnerian orchestral interludes to cover the numerous scene changes (performance is still possible, though unusual, without them). At this stage a row blew up with Maeterlinck over the casting of Mélisande, for whom the Scottish soprano Mary Garden was announced in December 1901. Maeterlinck's determination that his mistress Georgette Leblanc should have the part drove him to the extremes of a formal complaint to the Société des Auteurs, an open letter to *Le Figaro* expressing the hope that the opera would fail, and the printing of a satirical 'synopsis', which was distributed to the audience at the public dress rehearsal on 28 April 1902, which may well have fuelled the near riot at that performance.

Despite these troubles and the work's unusual character, the official premiere passed off well, and *Pelléas* quickly entered the repertoire of the Opéra-Comique. Debussy himself supervised the rehearsals, and even had a hand in the beautiful pre-Raphaelite designs of Lucien Jusseaume and Eugène Ronsin. The first cast was generally strong, and the music sympathetically conducted by André Messager. But casting nevertheless has remained problematic; Pelléas has been sung variously by tenors and baritones (the first Pelléas, Jean Périer, was a 'baryton Martin', a voice like Debussy's own in which the lighter head tone is prominent). But later there was even talk of playing Pelléas as a *travesti* role for soprano. The original Yniold was a boy treble named Blondin, but his performance prompted such hilarity at the public dress rehearsal that a number of cuts were made in his part for the official premiere. (His scene with the sheep in Act IV, however, had probably already been omitted, and was first performed in public only in autumn 1902, when the part was sung by a woman, Suzanne Dumesnil.)

SYNOPSIS

Arkel is king of Allemonde, Geneviève his daughter, and Golaud and Pelléas her sons by different marriages. Yniold is Golaud's son by his first wife, who is now dead.

Act I Scene 1: Golaud, lost in the forest while out hunting, comes upon the frail Mélisande, who is lost too and crying. She recoils from him, evades his questions, and refuses to let him retrieve her crown, which he sees glistening in the pool. Eventually she tells him her name, and he persuades her to go with him. Scene 2: Golaud has written to Pelléas about Mélisande, whom he married six months ago. Golaud fears Arkel (who wished a political remarriage for him). But Arkel, when Geneviève reads him the letter, accepts the will of fate. Pelléas asks to visit a dying friend, but Arkel insists he await Golaud's return. Scene 3: Mélisande is walking in the grounds with Geneviève. They remark on the darkness of the surrounding forests. Pelléas joins them, and they turn their attention to the sea (where the ship that brought Mélisande can be seen and heard departing). Pelléas announces that he is going away the next day.

Act II Scene 1: Pelléas and Mélisande are by a fountain in the park. Mélisande leans over and tries to touch the water, but only her long hair can reach it. Playing with the ring Golaud gave her, she drops it into the water as a harp softly sounds the distant chime of noon. Scene 2: Golaud has been thrown by his horse on the stroke of noon. Nursing him that night, Mélisande complains of being unhappy in the castle, and Golaud tries to find out why. He notices that her ring is missing, and furiously orders her to find it, taking Pelléas with her. Scene 3: Pelléas and Mélisande pretend to look for the ring in a sea cave, but they are scared when they find three starving beggars asleep on the ground.

Act III Scene 1: Mélisande is combing her hair at a tower window. Pelléas appears and persuades her to lean out so far that her hair tumbles down the wall. He makes passionate simulated love to it, winding her hair round himself and then tying it to the branches of a willow. As he does so Mélisande's white doves fly out of the tower. Golaud appears and chides them for their 'childishness'. Scene 2: Golaud takes Pelléas into the vaults. But the air is stifling, and they climb back out – Scene 3 – emerging into the fresh midday air. Golaud lectures Pelléas about his behaviour with Mélisande, who is pregnant. Scene 4: Below Mélisande's window Golaud questions Yniold roughly about her and Pelléas. To each question Yniold replies with a child's elusiveness. A lamp is lit in Mélisande's room and Golaud lifts Yniold to spy on her. Pelléas is with her, but they are merely gazing silently at the lamp.

Act IV Scene 1: Pelléas and Mélisande agree to meet by the fountain. He is going away. His father (who never appears in the opera) has been ill but is now recovering and has ordered him to travel. Scene 2: Arkel expects the recovery of Pelléas's father to revitalize the castle, and he tells Mélisande. But Golaud appears and picks a quarrel with her, accusing her of deception. He takes her by the hair and drags her from side to side, despite Arkel's protests. Scene 3: At the fountain, Yniold is looking for his ball. A shepherd passes with his flock. Yniold asks him why the sheep have stopped bleating. 'Because this isn't the way to the stable.' Scene 4: Pelléas and Mélisande meet for the last time. Passionately they declare their love. But in the distance the castle gates clang shut, and Mélisande realizes that Golaud has followed her in the darkness and is watching them from behind a tree. As they kiss with utter abandon, Golaud runs out and kills Pelléas with his sword.

Act V Mélisande, having given birth to a daughter, lies dying, attended by the doctor and Arkel. Golaud is stricken with remorse, but asks her in desperation if her and Pelléas's love was guilty. It was not, she says; but Golaud accuses her of lying and remains uncertain to the end. The serving women file silently in and, at the moment of Mélisande's death, fall to their knees.

The most celebrated feature of *Pelléas* is its unique vocal declamation, which carries the text on a continuous, fluid cantilena, somewhere between chant and recitative, a note to a syllable. There are no arias or set pieces. Debussy consciously avoided both the broad formal and gestural clichés of French and Italian Romantic opera and the heavy arioso style of Wagner, though he was certainly influenced by the 'endless melody' of *Tristan*. The refinement and subtlety of the word-setting come partly from the French language, with its discreet and flexible accentuation, and are a natural extension of Debussy's Verlaine and Baudelaire songs. But they are also a response to the dreamlike world of Maeterlinck's play, a world of doomed children at the mercy of passions they only dimly apprehend. The play's 'tableau' design, so different from the purposeful symphonic structures of Wagner, must also have appealed to Debussy. His own style was moving towards a kind of suspended-animation harmony in which gentle discords are relished for their sensual beauty rather than their grammar (just as in Proust individual words and phrases take on an almost magical significance while the sentence structure fades into the background). The fact that many of Debussy's favourite chords are Wagnerian in type merely emphasizes the restraint with which he uses them.

In fact *Pelléas* deploys an incredibly small number of harmonic and melodic ideas for such a long work. Leitmotifs are used sparingly. There are motifs for the main characters (some of them distinctly Wagnerian in cut) and for aspects of the drama, like the spirit of remote antiquity conveyed by the solemn modal chords of the prelude; and there are one-off musical ideas for Maeterlinck's symbols, like the crown in Act I or the white doves in Act III. Harmony is used to fix or intensify atmosphere, almost like a kind of musical scenery or lighting. So the menacing scene in the vaults is entirely in whole tones, while the sparkling sunlight and water of the next scene are conveyed throughout in pentatonic harmony which looks forward to piano pieces like *Reflets dans l'eau* or *Cloches à travers les feuilles*. The 'static' character of this kind of writing is tempered by some of the most exquisitely varied orchestration in any opera. The sound is soft and restrained, but the texture mobile and vividly graphic, and the music rises to dramatic climaxes that are all the more effective for their rarity.

Pelléas is a key work for the 20th century. Musically, it established an approach to form, harmony and texture which profoundly influenced composers as various as Stravinsky, Messiaen (who was given the score at the age of nine) and Puccini, who was fascinated by its 'extraordinary harmonic qualities and . . . transparent instrumental texture'. Operatically, it was a shot across the bows of stage realism, as represented by works such as Gustave Charpentier's *Louise* or Massenet's *Werther*. The play's strangeness, admittedly, is a matter more of style than of content, and hidden meanings are less important than the evasive treatment of the commonplace: it is really a bourgeois tragedy slowed down, with a few poetic *non sequiturs* and a strong atmosphere. But these are qualities that lend themselves to musical treatment. It is significant that Maeterlinck's play also attracted avant-garde composers outside France and Belgium: Schoenberg's tone poem was written in 1902–3, and the link with Expressionism comes out in his *Erwartung* (1909). But where Maeterlinck's play has dated, the music it inspired has not, which is only fitting, as Symbolism in France began as an imitation of music, and specifically that of Wagner.

Other operatic works: *Rodrigue et Chimène* (inc., ?1893); *La chute de la maison Usher* (inc., 1917)

S.W.

LÉO DELIBES
Clément Philibert Léo Delibes; *b* 21 February 1836, Saint-Germain du Val, France; *d* 16 January 1891, Paris

Delibes came to Paris from the provinces at the age of 12 after the death of his father. Musical on his mother's side, he studied at the Conservatoire, though his evident melodic gift gained him no outstanding distinctions there. His teachers included the organist-composer François Benoist and the stage composer Adolphe Adam. His own career was divided between church, as chorister and organist, and stage, as ballet and opera composer. Among about 30 stage works his four most important scores are *Le roi l'a dit*, *Lakmé* and the ballets *Coppélia* (1870) and *Sylvia* (1876).

If these four works survive, the remainder testifies more to his industry than to his genius as a composer. Adam's interest in his pupil, a boy chorister at La Madeleine and at the Opéra (he sang in the cathedral scene at the premiere of Meyerbeer's *Le prophète* in 1849), saw Delibes, at the age of 17, appointed organist at Saint-Pierre de Chaillot and accompanist at the Théâtre Lyrique, a modest establishment directed by Hervé, who supplied all its music. These posts brought Delibes into contact with some of the popular composers of the day, notably Victor Massé, who, late with his work on *La Reine-Topaze*, employed the youth as copyist. With the amused blessing of Adam, Delibes also took over from Hervé the setting of *Deux sous*

de charbon, completing it within a few days. Delibes was 19 when this first work was given at the Folies-Nouvelles in 1856. Fourteen other works followed in as many years.

However, between *Le roi l'a dit* (1873) and *Sylvia* (1876), the only notable composition was the song 'Les filles de Cadix'. His music for the theatre was engendered by the need to earn a living and support his widowed mother. His musical ambitions were restricted by these considerations, for after a good start his academic career at the Conservatoire had been disappointing. It seems that he never even thought of competing for the Prix de Rome. Yet the initial success of *Le roi l'a dit* spread his fame abroad, and official honours came his way. Finally, in 1881, he succeeded Henri Reber as a professor at the Conservatoire at the instance of the director, Ambroise Thomas, to whom Delibes disclaimed any knowledge of fugue and counterpoint. Urged to practise those skills, he did, and became an unusually conscientious and dedicated teacher. Essentially ebullient yet shy and unsure, Delibes had a need to be loved that was gratified. The successes of *Jean de Nivelle* (1880) and *Lakmé* (1883) were conclusive; the posthumous performance (1893) of *Kassya* (completed by Massenet) proved an anticlimax.

Lakmé
Opera in three acts (2h 15m)
Libretto by Edmond Gondinet and Philippe Gille, after Pierre Loti's novel *Le mariage de Loti* (1880)
PREMIERES 14 April 1883, Opéra-Comique, Paris; US: 4 October 1883, Grand Opera House, Chicago; UK: 6 June 1885, Gaiety Theatre, London
CAST Lakmé *s*, Mallika *ms* or *c*, Mistress Bentson *ms*, Ellen *s*, Rose *ms*, Gérald *t*, Nilakantha *b*, Frédéric *bar*, Hadji *t*, Gypsy *t*, Chinese Merchant *t*, Pickpocket *bar*; *satb* chorus of Indians, Brahmins, Chinese merchants; ballet

In *Lakmé*, Delibes, already successful as a composer of memorably tuneful ballets, fulfilled his ambition to produce a successful serious opera. Its title role attracted the finest sopranos of the time, such as Adelina Patti, and Luisa Tetrazzini, and its survival is due largely to the vehicle it provides for the coloratura soprano voice.

SYNOPSIS
The plot centres around the fanatical hatred of the Brahmin priests in 19th-century India for the English invaders, who forbid them to practise their religion.

Act I Gérald and Frédéric, two English officers, find themselves in a sacred grove. Catching sight of Lakmé, daughter of the Brahmin priest Nilakantha, Gérald falls in love with her. He is seen by Nilakantha, who swears vengeance on the intruder who has desecrated holy ground.

Act II Gérald and Frédéric meet in a crowded marketplace, whence Gérald has been shadowed by Nilakantha. He commands Lakmé to sing an old Brahmin song ('The Bell Song') so that the intruder will again be drawn to her and Nilakantha will be able to identify him. At the sight of Gérald, Lakmé faints, but she later manages to warn him of her father's plans for vengeance. Nevertheless, during a procession, Gérald is stabbed and slightly injured.

Act III Lakmé is nursing Gérald in a forest hut, where Frédéric finds him and calls him back to duty. Lakmé, realizing that she will lose Gérald, takes poison, and dies just as her father rushes in to find her.

Delibes's desire to please caused him to conform without question to procedures already well worn in the field of opéra comique. *Lakmé* is composed of separate numbers, devoid of musical links between them, with a contrived symmetry of form in each and a subordinate, purely accompanimental role for the orchestra throughout. It has, on the other hand, a melodic fluency that has proved irresistible to singers and listeners alike, a transparency of texture and a French elegance that places it poles apart from the Wagnerian influences of the time to which Delibes's more forward-looking compatriots were prone.

Other operatic works: *Deux sous de charbon, ou Le suicide de Bigorneau*, 1856; *Deux vieilles gardes, ou Double garde, ou Un malade qui se porte bien*, 1856; *Six demoiselles à marier*, 1856; *Maître Griffard, ou Les deux procureurs*, 1857; *La fille du golfe*, (1859); *L'omelette à la Follembuche*, 1859; *Monsieur de Bonne-Étoile*, 1860; *Les musiciens de l'orchestre* (coll. with Offenbach, Camille Erlanger and Aristide Hignard), 1861; *Les eaux d'Ems*, 1861; *Mon ami Pierrot, ou L'enfance de Pierrot*, 1862; *Le jardinier et son seigneur* (*Le lièvre*), 1863; *La tradition*, 1864; *Grande nouvelle*, 1864; *Le serpent à plumes*, 1864; *Le boeuf Apis*, 1865; *Malbrough s'en va-t-en guerre* (Act IV of coll.), 1868; *L'écossais de Chatou, ou Montagnards écossais*, 1869; *La cour du roi Pétaud*, 1869; *Le roi l'a dit*, 1873; *Jean de Nivelle*, 1880; *Kassya* (inc.; orch. by Massenet), 1893; 2 lost *opéras bouffes*

F.A.

FREDERICK DELIUS

Frederick (originally Fritz) Theodor Albert Delius;
b 29 January 1862, Bradford, Yorkshire; *d* 10 June 1934,
Grez-sur-Loing, France

Although Delius's music is regarded by many listeners as quintessentially English, his parents were German and he lived most of his life outside England. His works were appreciated first in Germany, and most of them were inspired by the orange groves of Florida, the mountains and fjords of Norway or his garden in France. His father settled in Bradford from Germany to build up a wool business; although a lover and patron of music, he was implacably opposed to music as a career for his son, who quickly demonstrated that he had no aptitude for commerce.

In 1884 Delius went to Florida to manage an orange plantation at Solana Grove. The oranges were left to manage themselves while Delius studied music with the local organist and taught the violin. The Negro melodies he heard there influenced several of his works, particularly the choral–orchestral *Appalachia* and the opera *Koanga*. By 1886 he had persuaded his father grudgingly to pay for him to enter the Leipzig Conservatory, where he heard concerts and operas conducted by Arthur Nikisch and Gustav Mahler and

formed friendships with the Norwegian composers Christian Sinding and Edvard Grieg as well as with Busoni. In 1888 he settled in Paris. Between 1890 and 1902 he composed five operas. This passion for the stage undoubtedly derived from his admiration for Wagner. He wrote to a friend in 1894: 'I want to tread in Wagner's footsteps . . . For me dramatic art is almost taking the place of religion.'

From 1897, Delius lived at Grez-sur-Loing, near Fontainebleau, with the German artist Jelka Rosen, who became his wife in 1903. A concert of his music was given in London in 1899, but it was in Elberfeld (now Wuppertal) after 1901, where the conductors Hans Haym and Fritz Cassirer became his champions, that his music came to the fore. Thomas Beecham and Henry Wood championed his music, and both conducted works by him in London from 1907 onwards. Of his six operas, Delius saw only three staged during his lifetime.

In the early 1920s Delius developed the first signs of progressive paralysis, the legacy of syphilis contracted in his Bohemian youth in Paris, or perhaps earlier in Florida. By the end of 1925 he was blind and helpless, but in 1928 a young British musician, Eric Fenby, offered his services as amanuensis and during the next few years laboriously took down from Delius's dictation the scores of half a dozen works.

Delius's chromatic harmonies are in the post-Wagnerian idiom of Ernest Chausson and Richard Strauss, spiced with the Nordic flavour of Grieg. He was essentially the poet of regret for the vanished hour and hedonistic delight, epitomized in such orchestral and choral works as *Sea Drift*, *Song of the High Hills*, *In a Summer Garden*, *Brigg Fair*, and the *Songs of Sunset*. It is strange that so ruminative a composer should have been drawn to the operatic stage, but at least in *A Village Romeo and Juliet* he demonstrated that a bucolic *Tristan und Isolde* was feasible and stageworthy, and in all six operas some of his most attractive and characteristic music is enshrined. Curiously, in 1903 Delius negotiated with Oscar Wilde's executors for the rights to make an opera from *Salomé*.

Koanga

Opera in a prologue, three acts and an epilogue (1h 45m)
Libretto by Charles F. Keary from a draft by the composer and Jutta Bell, after George Washington Cable's novel *The Grandissimes: A Story of Creole Life* (1880)
Composed 1895–7, rev. April 1898
PREMIERES 30 March 1904, Stadttheater, Elberfeld (now Wuppertal); UK: 23 September 1935, Covent Garden, London; US: 18 December 1970, Lisner Auditorium, George Washington University, Washington, DC
CAST Uncle Joe *b*, Don José Martinez *b*, Simon Perez *t*, Koanga *bar*, Rangwan *b*, Palmyra *s*, Clotilda *c*, Planters' Daughters 4 *s*, 4 *c*; *satb* chorus of slaves, dancers, servants

Koanga derives from Delius's time in Florida, when he had been entranced by the Negroes' songs. He had hoped for a production in London in 1899, but only concert extracts were performed in St James's Hall on 30 May 1899, under Alfred Hertz. Beecham planned to stage it at Covent Garden in 1910 but it was not until 1935 that he did so. For this Beecham and Edward Agate revised the libretto, which Jelka Delius had translated back into English from her German version. For a 1972 performance in London, a further revision (later published) was made by Douglas Craig (who produced the revival) and Andrew Page.

SYNOPSIS

In a prologue, Uncle Joe, an old slave, tells the planters' eight daughters their favourite story of Koanga and Palmyra.

Act I   On a sugar-cane plantation in Louisiana, a mulatto slave girl, Palmyra, rejects the advances of Simon Perez, foreman of the plantation. The plantation owner, Don José Martinez, tells of a new batch of slaves, which includes Koanga, a West African prince and voodoo priest. Palmyra at once falls in love with the new arrival, who refuses to submit to slavery. Noticing this attraction, Martinez offers Palmyra to Koanga if he will work. But Clotilda, Martinez's wife, protests at losing Palmyra's services as her maid.

Act II   On the wedding day of Koanga and Palmyra, Clotilda tells Perez that Palmyra is her half-sister and promises her to him if he will stop the marriage. Palmyra is abducted by Perez's servants. Koanga strikes Martinez and calls down a voodoo curse on the plantation, which is stricken with plague.

Act III   Koanga returns to rescue Palmyra from Perez, whom he kills. He is pursued into the swamps and brought back mortally wounded. After he dies, Palmyra stabs herself.

The epilogue returns to the planters' daughters listening to Uncle Joe.

Koanga is the most dramatic and powerful of Delius's operas. The score is brilliant and colourful, with Negro spirituals and working songs as background to the start of Act I and an elaborate ensemble for five principals and chorus to end the act. The banjo-accompanied distant voices in the wedding scene are Delius magic, and Act II also contains the well-known Creole choral-dance episode, *La Calinda*, originally a movement in the *Florida* suite and a favourite concert item in the 1931 orchestral arrangement by Eric Fenby. At some stage before the first performance of *Koanga*, Delius substituted the prelude to Act II of *The Magic Fountain* for the music he had written to introduce Act III of *Koanga*. In the 1935 Covent Garden performances, Beecham adapted the original *Florida* suite version of *La Calinda* as the prelude to Act II and included the *Irmelin* prelude as an interlude in Act III (its first performance). Palmyra's lovely Act II aria, 'The hour is near', was composed during the Elberfeld rehearsals, apparently to appease the soprano because she disliked the costume Jelka Delius had designed for her. All the principals have splendid music, Palmyra's final 'Liebestod' being particularly eloquent.

A Village Romeo and Juliet

Opera in six tableaux (1h 45m)
Libretto by the composer, based on the short story *Romeo*

und Julia auf dem Dorfe from the collection *Die Leute von Seldwyla* (1856) by Gottfried Keller
Composed November 1899–1901
PREMIERES   21 February 1907, Komische Oper, Berlin; UK: 22 February 1910, Covent Garden, London; US: 26 April 1972, Opera House, Kennedy Center, Washington, DC
CAST   Manz *bar*, Marti *bar*, Sali (as a boy) *s*, Sali (as a man) *t*, Vreli *s*, Dark Fiddler *bar*, 5 *s*, 2 *ms*, *c*, 3 *t*, 5 *bar*, *b*; *satb* chorus of vagabonds, peasants, bargees

Work on the libretto started in 1897. Delius asked C. F. Keary to write it, but was dissatisfied with the first draft. He then commissioned Karl-August Gerhardi, who produced a German draft in 1898. This still did not please Delius, who turned again to Keary, but finally wrote his own English libretto in 1899. When the opera had its Berlin premiere in 1907, it was sung in a German translation by Jelka Delius. The most famous music in the opera, the entr'acte between Scenes 5 and 6 known as *The Walk to the Paradise Garden*, was expanded in 1906 to cover a scene change.

SYNOPSIS

Scene 1   At Seldwyla, Switzerland, in the mid 19th century, two farmers, Manz and Marti, plough their fields, which are separated by a strip of overgrown land, now up for sale since its owner, the Dark Fiddler, has no legal claim to it because he is a bastard. Their children, Sali and Vreli, play happily together in the woods and there meet the Dark Fiddler, who knows that the farmers are each surreptitiously taking an extra furrow out of his land. When it is all ploughed and no longer a haunt of birds and animals, then beware, he tells them. The farmers quarrel and forbid the children to play together.

Scene 2   Six years later, Sali and Vreli – now grown up – agree to resume their friendship. Both their homes have been impoverished by a lawsuit between their fathers.

Scene 3   They meet in the wild land; the Dark Fiddler appears and invites them to share his vagabond life. Marti comes looking for his daughter and is dragging her away when Sali knocks him down.

Scene 4   Vreli is spending her last night in her old home. Her father has lost his mind as a result of Sali's blow and is in an asylum. Sali joins her and they fall asleep in each other's arms, dreaming that they are being married. On awakening they decide to go to the fair in Berghald.

Scene 5   At the fair they are happy until they are recognized and made to feel uncomfortable. They walk to the Paradise Garden, to a dilapidated riverside inn where they can dance.

Scene 6   The Dark Fiddler is there with four vagabonds. They try to persuade the two lovers to join them, but mock them for their 'respectability'. Sali and Vreli hear bargemen singing on the river. They take a hay barge moored near the inn and decide to 'drift away for ever'. Sali withdraws the plug from the bottom of the barge and the village Romeo and Juliet clasp each other closely as the boat sinks.

The *Village Romeo* contains some of Delius's most

inspired nature music and is on his favourite theme of the world well lost for love. The duets for Sali and Vreli are passionate and lyrical, and the role of the Dark Fiddler is a fine one for a baritone. In Keller's story the Fiddler is a sinister presence; in Delius he represents freedom from conventional family ties and identification with nature – in other words, Delius himself. The fair scene (inspired by *Die Meistersinger*) provides a lively contrast to the ruminative mood of much of the opera. But, as so often in Delius, it is the offstage chorus of distant voices – the vagabonds and bargees – that creates his special brand of theatrical magic.

Fennimore and Gerda

Opera in eleven pictures (1h 15m)
Libretto by the composer, after the novel *Niels Lyhne* (1880) by Jens Peter Jacobsen
Composed 1908–10, rev. 1912–13
PREMIERES 21 October 1919, Opernhaus, Frankfurt; UK: 23 May 1968, Old Town Hall, Hammersmith, London; US: 3 June 1981, Opera Theater of St Louis, St Louis, Missouri
CAST Niels Lyhne *bar*, Fennimore *ms*, Erik *t*, Consul *b*, Gerda *s*, 3 *s*, 3 *ms*, *c*, 2 *t*, 3 *bar*, 2 *b*; *satb* chorus of maidservants, girls, farmhands

In his last opera – which he said was an inappropriate word for what he called 'two episodes . . . in 11 pictures' – Delius returned to the Scandinavian poet and novelist Jens Peter Jacobsen, whose verses he had set in the 1890s. (Jacobsen's *Gurrelieder* were set by Schoenberg.) Originally he set nine scenes from the novel, completing this version in the spring of 1911. Later he added three (eventually two) scenes relating to Gerda. A proposed premiere in Cologne was scuppered by the war, and the successful first performance was given in Frankfurt five years later under Gustav Brecher.

SYNOPSIS
The writer Niels Lyhne and his friend the painter Erik Refstrup are staying with Niels's uncle, the consul, and are both in love with the consul's daughter Fennimore, who marries Erik. After three years the marriage is on the rocks and Erik invites Niels to visit them. Niels discovers that Erik is experiencing a 'creative block' and is drinking heavily. He and Fennimore have a passionate affair. Erik is killed in an accident and the guilt-stricken Fennimore sends Niels away. After wandering abroad for three years, he returns to his childhood home, where he meets and marries his neighbour's teenage daughter Gerda.

Delius regarded *Fennimore and Gerda* as his best and most advanced stage work – a psychological drama in which text and music sprang from the same source. Beecham, on the other hand, disliked it and wrote of 'three rather dreary people who have nothing to sing'. The opera's origins lie somewhere in Delius's friendship with the Norwegian painter Edvard Munch, but it lacks Munch's sense of brooding terror – Delius even substituted a happy ending for the novel's final tragedy. The opera is uncomfortably short, unless it is part of a double-bill, even with Delius's ill-advised afterthought of adding the Gerda episode. Musically, the score is of interest as marking a change of style towards the more astringent harmonies of the *Requiem* (1913–16). He intended to apply a similar approach – i.e. 'pictures' and 'episodes' – to *Wuthering Heights*, but he wrote no more operas.

Other operas: *Irmelin*, (1892), 1953; *The Magic Fountain*, (1895), 1977; *Margot la Rouge*, (1902), 1921

M.K.

GAETANO DONIZETTI

Domenico Gaetano Maria Donizetti; *b* 29 November 1797, Bergamo, Italy; *d* 8 April 1848, Bergamo

Although a handful of Donizetti's 65 operas have always maintained a place in the international repertoire, his reputation has undergone some profound changes. From a position of dominance at the time of his death, when one in every four Italian operas performed in Italy was one of his, his standing declined seriously in the last decades of the 19th century, when his music was often dismissed as facile and imitative. Since the Second World War, however, an extraordinarily widespread re-examination of most of his output has established its importance as a vital link in the development of Italian opera.

To see Donizetti at his true value, it is essential to understand him in terms of his period. Coming from poor parents, he was fortunate to have his talent recognized early, and to acquire as good a musical training (at the hands of Simon Mayr and Padre Mattei) as was then available in Italy. To support himself he had to accept every possible commission offered him. Writing sometimes as many as four operas a year and confronted with the exigencies of an audience that insisted on freshness without eccentricity, he deliberately set out to attain a mastery over the range of operatic types and genres then current in Italy. Not least of Donizetti's attributes as an opera composer was the effectiveness of his writing for every range of voice.

Donizetti first established himself as a potential talent with *Zoraide di Grenata* (Rome, 1822), which was successful enough to win him a contract with the impresario Domenico Barbaja, who brought him to Naples. The next eight years have been described as his 'apprenticeship', a period of experimentation and unflagging productivity. The turning-point of his career was the great success of *Anna Bolena* (Milan, 1830), which won him commissions from all the leading Italian opera houses. Although he never totally renounced comedy (two of his greatest opere buffe, *L'elisir d'amore* (1832) and *Don Pasquale* (1843), were written after *Anna Bolena*), he now chiefly confined himself to tragedy. Some of these works, among them *Lucrezia Borgia* and *Lucia di Lammermoor*, soon made him a household name.

In 1838, Donizetti left Naples for Paris, drawn there not only by the possibility of prestige and larger fees, but also by the greater freedom of subject matter permitted there. In 1842, he was named hofkapellmeister to the Habsburg court in Vienna and for the next three years he divided his time between the French and Austrian capitals, with occasional trips to Italy. In 1846, signs of mental deterioration forced his confinement to a sanatorium at Ivry, but later, paralysed and almost totally bereft of speech, he was brought home to Bergamo, where he was nursed by friends until his death.

As a man, Donizetti was gregarious, good-humoured, and well disposed toward his fellow composers, whom he recognized as working against the obstacles of the censors and the court-controlled theatres. His letters are filled with his spontaneous reactions to his increasingly tragic life. None of his three children lived more than a few days, and his beloved wife, Virginia, died at the age of 29 in 1837 in the midst of a horrifying outbreak of cholera; he never remarried. Thereafter, a morbid streak in his character became more pronounced. His death was ultimately caused by a long-standing syphilitic infection.

It was Donizetti more than anyone else who raised the temperature of drama in Italian opera. Throughout his career, but particularly after 1830, he engaged in as near open warfare with the censors as he dared without losing his livelihood as an opera composer. He protested against the niggling restrictions that long forbade religious topics on the stage. He wanted to show rulers as human beings with human failings and not as mere benign figureheads. His many operas on English subjects, particularly those dealing with the Tudors, were able to pass muster with the Italian censors because they dealt with Protestant, rather than Catholic, kings and queens. *La favorite*, with its scenes of convent life and the delivery of a papal bull, was first given in Italy in mutilated form, as was *Dom Sébastien*, which included a funeral procession with a great catafalque onstage. Parisian authorities were more tolerant; for instance, *Poliuto*, banned in Naples for showing the martyrdom of a Christian saint, was given at the Opéra as *Les martyrs*.

Working within the conventions of his day, Donizetti found a variety of ways to adapt them to his manifold dramatic purposes: as in his fondness for elegiac cabalettas, sometimes slower in tempo than the arias they follow, or in his knack of creating ambiguity between the major and minor modes, and in his way of heightening an emotion by smoothly modulating into an unexpected key (as in Lucia's 'Spargi d'amaro pianto' or Norina's 'È' duretta la lezione' in Act III of *Don Pasquale*). In his late works Donizetti felt freer to foreshorten or even dismember the conventional structures; for instance, in these works he often abandoned the tradition of the aria-finale.

It is difficult to conceive of the phenomenon of Verdi without the foundation stone of Donizetti's works. Verdi's exploitation of the possibilities of the baritone persona finds its antecedents in such powerful roles as Cardenio in *Il furioso*, and in the title roles of *Tasso* and *Belisario*. In such scores as *Lucia*, *La favorite* and *Maria di Rohan* one discovers foreshadowing of the concept of *tinta* that Verdi came to insist on. While not suggesting that there is any conscious imitation, one can scarcely exaggerate the centrality of Donizetti to the tradition of Italian melodramma from which Verdi sprang and which he carried to loftier heights.

Anna Bolena
Anne Boleyn

Tragedia lirica in two acts (3h 15m)
Libretto by Felice Romani, after Ippolito Pindemonte's translation (1816) of Marie-Joseph de Chénier's play *Henri VIII* (1791) and Alessandro Pepoli's play *Anna Bolena* (1788)
PREMIERES 26 December 1830, Teatro Carcano, Milan; UK: 8 July 1831, King's Theatre, Haymarket, London; US: 12 November 1839, Théâtre d'Orléans, New Orleans
CAST Anna Bolena (Anne Boleyn) *s*, Giovanna Seymour (Jane Seymour) *ms*, Smeton *ms*, Percy *t*, Enrico VIII (Henry VIII) *b*, Rochefort *b*, Hervey *t*; *satb* chorus of courtiers

Anna Bolena established Donizetti among the leading composers of his day and introduced him to the audiences of Paris and London. It used to be a critical commonplace that this work marked a watershed in Donizetti's *oeuvre* and that here, in his thirtieth opera, he found at long last his personal style. Today, however, as more and more of his earlier works have been revived, *Anna Bolena* appears, rather, to be the logical culmination of tendencies implicit in his development. The critical factor seems to have been that Donizetti had at his disposal a superior libretto, one that moved him deeply. He also had the incentive of striving to win over the Milanese, till then unimpressed by successes won elsewhere. The element of consistency in Donizetti's development can be demonstrated by his having adapted an aria from his first opera, *Enrico di Borgogna*, as the basis of Anne's famous larghetto in the Tower scene ('Al dolce guidami'). The work retained its currency for nearly 50 years and then lapsed into oblivion, until its successful revival at La Scala with Maria Callas in 1957 provided the incentive for performances elsewhere.

SYNOPSIS
Act I Scene 1: The courtiers suspect that King Henry's fickleness bodes ill for Anne, an impression strengthened by the conscience-stricken Jane Seymour. Anne enters and bids her musician Smeton sing, but he, infatuated with Anne, offers an amorous ditty, reminding her of Percy, her first love ('Come, innocente giovane'). Anne retires, leaving Seymour alone; soon she is joined by the king. She wants this to be their last meeting, declaring that honour forbids the continuation of their relationship. Accused of being more in love with the throne than with him, Seymour begs the king to free her conscience ('Ah! qual sia cercar non oso'). Scene 2: Unknown to Anne, the king has laid her a trap, by arranging a hunting party at which she will unexpectedly encounter Percy, whom he has brought back from exile. Percy questions Anne's brother, Lord Rochefort, about the rumours of Anne's unhappiness ('Da quel dì che lei perduta'). When the hunt appears, Percy approaches to thank the king, but he withdraws his hand; when Percy kisses Anne's hand, she feels his tears of gratitude on it ('Io sentii sulla mia mano'). As the hunt moves on, all hail this auspicious day. The king is happy too; but he has been hunting a different prey. Scene 3: Smeton surreptitiously enters Anne's apartment, carrying her miniature in a locket. Hearing someone approach, Smeton hides. Rochefort asks Anne to grant Percy a

brief interview. When Percy appears, Anne's admission that the king now hates her prompts him to declare his love ('S'ei t'abborre, io t'amo ancora'). Frightened, Anne firmly refuses his request to see her again. Percy draws his sword, and Smeton, misinterpreting Percy's intentions, rushes out, drawing his. Anne faints. The king arrives, enraged, and summons guards. Smeton offers to die as proof of the compromised queen's innocence, and when he tears open his jacket, Anne's miniature falls out at the king's feet. Anne begins an eloquent sextet ('In quegli sguardi impresso'); she wants to explain, but the king declares she must defend herself in court. Anne is shocked ('Anna! ai giudici!') and realizes that her fate is sealed.

Act II   Scene 1: In Anne's apartment in the Tower, her ladies comment on Anne's plight ('Oh! dove mai ne andarono'). Anne appears and prays for consolation. Seymour enters to inform her that the king has promised to spare her life if she will acknowledge her guilt. Anne's astonishment turns to fury when she hears Seymour beg it not only in the king's name but in that of the woman who will succeed her on the throne. Anne calls on heaven to punish her rival. When Seymour tearfully prostrates herself, Anne realizes the identity of her rival and orders her to leave, but Seymour cannot contain her remorse ('Dal mio cor punita io sono'). Scene 2: Hervey announces that Smeton has confessed to adultery with Anne, having been told that such a declaration would spare her life. Anne and Percy are led in. When the king tells her of Smeton's confession, Anne turns the charge of adultery back on him. Percy is willing to die to spare her life, reminding her that she was once married to him. They are led off, leaving the king furious. Seymour comes to beg him to forget her and be merciful. Scene 3: In the Tower, Percy tells Rochefort that he should live to defend Anne's memory ('Vivi tu'). Anne longs for her childhood home and first love ('Al dolce guidami'). Summoned to the scaffold, Anne sings a prayer ('Cielo, a' miei lunghi spasimi'). Cannon announce the king's marriage to Seymour, and Anne calls for heaven's mercy on the guilty couple ('Coppia iniqua!').

Romani clearly outlined the conflicts between the characters, giving Donizetti many opportunities for psychologically apposite expressiveness. This is particularly true in the great duet for Seymour and the king in Act I and in that for Anne and Seymour in the opening scene of Act II. The contrast between the devious menace of the king and the straightforward remorse of Seymour is reinforced by the unusual device of having Seymour repeat one of her melodies from the larghetto section in the cabaletta, a convincing expression of her failure to be convinced by the king's arguments. In the scene between the women, the emotional range is even greater, each shift of feeling being persuasively characterized as this pair, who have every reason to distrust each other, come to a *rapprochement*.

From the start of his career, Donizetti had demonstrated a considerable flair for writing ensembles, more persuasive in the slow movements than in the rapid pendants, where he was as yet restricted by the conventional *settinari* (seven-syllable verses). Especially effec-

tive is the canonic quintet, 'Io sentii sulla mia mano' (adapted from the score of *Otto mesi in due ore*, 1827) near the close of Act I, Scene 2. Even more so is the sextet 'In quegli sguardi impresso' in the next scene on Anne's regaining consciousness, where the interweaving of the parts creates a mood of welling intensity. On almost as high a level is the trio for Anne, Percy and Henry in Act II, Scene 2, 'Fin dall'età più tenera', where the indignation of Anne, the nostalgia of Percy, and the fury of the king are neatly contrasted.

The musical climax of the work comes in the Tower scene, which consists primarily of two full-scale arie-finali. Percy's 'Vivi tu' is full of pathos, but that mood is given even deeper expression in Anne's 'Al dolce guidami', with its purling cor-anglais obbligato and yearning figurations. The *tempo di mezzo* of her scena flowers into a lyrical outpouring at 'Cielo, a' miei lunghi spasimi' (a variant of the melody of 'Home, Sweet Home'), with the solo voice supported by three other voices and a chamber-size accompaniment. The cabaletta, 'Coppia iniqua!', conveys with its driving rhythms and succession of trills the emotional delirium that brings Anne to the point of death.

L'elisir d'amore

The Love Potion
Opera comica in two acts (2h)
Libretto by Felice Romani, after Eugène Scribe's text for Daniel Auber's *Le philtre* (1831), in turn after Silvio Malaperta's *Il filtro*
PREMIERES 12 May 1832, Teatro della Canobbiana, Milan; UK: 10 December 1836, Lyceum, London; US: 18 June 1838, Park Theater, New York
CAST Adina s, Nemorino t, Sergeant Belcore bar, Dr Dulcamara buffo b, Giannetta s; satb chorus of peasants and soldiers

L'elisir d'amore is the earliest of Donizetti's operas never to have left the standard repertoire, and during his lifetime it was the most frequently performed of his works. Although Romani's libretto is at times a literal translation of Scribe's text for Auber's *Le philtre*, it contains a number of significant passages that have no counterpart in the French libretto: the Adina–Nemorino duet 'Chiedi all'aura', the tenor's 'Adina, credimi', and his famous 'Una furtiva lagrima'. All of these additions contribute an element of pathos that Donizetti believed to be a necessary constituent of truly satisfying comedy. Another modification was moving the setting of Scribe's plot from the Basque countryside to rural northern Italy, Donizetti's native soil.

SYNOPSIS

Act I   The gentle Nemorino is hopelessly in love with Adina, who amuses the harvesters by reading to them the story of Queen Iseult and the love potion ('Della crudele Isotta'). Sergeant Belcore and his platoon enter and he gallantly presents Adina with a nosegay ('Come Paride vezzoso'). Nemorino is upset by Adina's apparent susceptibility to Belcore. She tells a disconsolate Nemorino that she will never love him ('Chiedi all'aura'); he protests that he would die for her. The quack Dr Dulcamara arrives to peddle his nostrums

('Udite, udite, o rustici!'). Nemorino, remembering the story of Iseult, buys a bottle of love potion, which he is assured will work in 24 hours ('Obbligato, ah! si obbligato'). Tipsy from the elixir, which in reality is Bordeaux, Nemorino gains in confidence ('Esulti pur la barbara'), but his spirits are crushed when he hears Adina agree to marry Belcore that very evening ('Adina, credimi').

Act II   The wedding feast is under way, and Dulcamara sings a mock barcarolle with the bride-to-be ('Io son ricco, tu sei bella'). Adina forestalls the notary, however, since Nemorino is not present to witness the ceremony. Penniless, Nemorino is desperate to buy more elixir, and on impulse he allows Belcore to enlist him into the army, because an enrollee receives a bounty ('Venti scudi'). Giannetta and the village girls have heard that Nemorino's rich uncle has died, leaving him his heir, and they fawn over him, a response that Nemorino attributes to the elixir. The sight of these attentions astonishes Adina. From Dulcamara she learns the story of Nemorino and the potion, but she assures him her own charms are a more potent weapon in winning a man ('Quanto amore'). Nemorino has observed that Adina has been affected by seeing him with the girls, but he would rather die than live without her ('Una furtiva lagrima'). Adina tells him that she has bought back his enlistment ('Prendi: per me sei libero') and at last confesses that she loves him. The village turns out to celebrate their betrothal, while Dulcamara takes his leave, firmly convinced that his potion has unexpected powers.

Donizetti's score alternates sparkling tunes with emotional melodies. There is not a weak number in the whole opera. The patter song for Dulcamara has an orotund garrulity about it that is irresistible. The scene between Nemorino and the village girls can seem a comic anticipation of that between Parsifal and the Flower Maidens. Donizetti's gift for pungent characterization animates the duet between the smarmy Dulcamara and Adina, confident of her own female wiles. The tenderness of the first Adina–Nemorino duet and their successive arias in Act II, particularly Nemorino's 'Una furtiva lagrima', with its haunting bassoon obbligato and climactic shifts from minor to major mode, are the jewels of this delightful score. Unlike most opere buffe, L'elisir presents us with two characters who develop before our eyes. Nemorino learns to assert himself, and Adina comes to see that a constant heart is preferable to the fickle one of a practised womanizer in uniform.

Lucrezia Borgia
Opera seria in a prologue and two acts (2h 15m)
Libretto by Felice Romani, after Victor Hugo's play *Lucrèce Borgia* (1833)
Composed 1833; ending rev. 1839 and 1841–2
PREMIERES   26 December 1833, La Scala, Milan;
UK: 6 June 1839, Her Majesty's Theatre, Haymarket, London; first rev. version: 11 January 1840, La Scala, Milan; 31 October 1840, Théâtre Italien, Paris (original version trans. as *La rinnegata*); 31 March 1842, Théâtre de Versailles, Paris (rev. as *Nizza di Grenade*); US: 11 May 1843, American Theater, New Orleans

CAST   Lucrezia Borgia *s*, Gennaro *t*, Maffio Orsini *ms*, Alfonso *b*, Astolfo *b*, Rustighello *t*, 2 *t*, 3 *b*; *satb* chorus of maskers, spies, guards, nobles

Because of its sensational plot, *Lucrezia Borgia* made its way slowly in Italy at first, but by 1840 it had established itself as one of Donizetti's most durable scores. After the opera's Paris premiere in October 1840, Hugo sued successfully for plagiarism against the French translation of Romani's libretto. For several seasons, first on 16 January 1843, *Lucrezia* was performed at the Théâtre Italien in a revised version as *La rinnegata*, the action transferred to Turkey.

SYNOPSIS
Prologue   In Venice Gennaro is enjoying Carnival with Maffio and his other friends. Gennaro is attracted by the tender concern of a beautiful woman, but when his friends unmask her he is dismayed to learn that she is the infamous Lucrezia Borgia.

Act I   In Ferrara, Duke Alfonso suspects that his wife, Lucrezia, is having an affair with a young man; he is, in fact, her son by a previous marriage. Gennaro lops off the initial letter of her last name from the crest on the façade of her palazzo, leaving the word 'orgia' – an orgy. Unaware who has so insulted her, Lucrezia insists her honour be avenged. Gennaro, brought in as the culprit, is administered poison by Alfonso, but Lucrezia gives him an antidote and urges him to leave Ferrara.

Act II   Maffio and his friends look forward to a ball at Princess Negroni's. He sings a *brindisi*, but then sinister voices sing of death. The young men seek to escape, but Lucrezia appears, announcing she has poisoned them all for their insults. Horrified to see Gennaro among them, she has the others led away. She swears she never meant her vengeance to extend to him, but he refuses her antidote and dies, horrified in turn when she tells him she is his mother.

Donizetti was unhappy at ending his opera with a cabaletta for Lucrezia, sung over the corpse of the son she has herself poisoned; but Henriette Méric-Lalande, the original Lucrezia, insisted on her prerogatives as a prima donna, which included a complete aria-finale. For La Scala in 1840, he removed the offending cabaletta and supplied a touching arioso for the dying Gennaro. For Giulia Grisi in Paris, he added a cabaletta to her (formerly) one-movement aria in the prologue, and an aria for the tenor in Act II, Scene 1, and cut the concluding cabaletta to a single statement.

There is much fine music in *Lucrezia*. The septet of the unmasking at the close of the prologue works up to a powerful climax. The Act I trio for Lucrezia, Gennaro and Alfonso was to remain in the back of Verdi's memory and the extended dialogue for Astolfo and Rustighello over an orchestral melody is the prototype of the episode between Rigoletto and Sparafucile. The best-known number in the score is Maffio's bumptious *brindisi* in Act II, 'Il segreto per esser felice', but greater intensity is to be found in the anguished figurations of Lucrezia's exquisitely wrought 'M'odi, ah m'odi' in the final scene. With Gennaro's final arioso,

'Madre, se ognor lontano', Donizetti found the idiom to express the tragic persona of the tenor.

Maria Stuarda
Mary Stuart

Opera seria in two acts (2h 30m)
Libretto by Giuseppe Bardari, after Andrea Maffei's translation of the tragedy by Johann Christoph Friedrich von Schiller (1800)
PREMIERES 18 October 1834, Teatro San Carlo, Naples (as *Buondelmonte*; libretto adapted by the composer and Pietro Salatino); original version: 30 December 1835, La Scala, Milan; US: 16 November 1964, Carnegie Hall, New York (concert); 7 March 1972, City Opera, New York; UK: 1 March 1966, St Pancras Town Hall, London;
CAST Maria (Mary) *s*, Elisabetta (Elizabeth) *s*, Leicester *t*, Talbot *bar*, Anna *ms*, Lord Cecil *bar*; *satb* chorus of courtiers, huntsmen, soldiers, servants

After *Maria Stuarda* was banned in Naples by the king while in rehearsal in 1834, Donizetti used most of the score as *Buondelmonte*, but this version has never been revived. Malibran sang the premiere of the original version at La Scala but, as she did not follow the censor's changes, the opera was soon prohibited. In 1865, after Donizetti's death, it was performed in Naples with two substitute numbers taken from Donizetti's lesser works. In contrast to its limited performance history in the 19th century, *Maria Stuarda* has entered the repertoire since its revival at Bergamo in 1958. The discovery of the autograph in a Swedish collection in 1987 has made possible the preparation of an authentic edition.

SYNOPSIS
Act I Scene 1: At Westminster, Queen Elizabeth suspects Leicester's affections are elsewhere engaged. Talbot shows Leicester a portrait and letter from Mary, who is imprisoned at Fotheringay, begging for an interview with the queen. When Leicester asks Elizabeth to grant Mary's request, her jealousy cannot be disguised, but she does not refuse. Scene 2: At Fotheringay, Mary envies the clouds their freedom to sail towards France. Leicester comes to prepare her for the queen's visit. Elizabeth enters and regards her young rival with ill-concealed hostility. When Elizabeth insults Mary, she is stung in turn, declaring that Elizabeth is a 'vile bastard' whose 'foot sullies the English throne'. Furious, Elizabeth orders Mary seized.

Act II Elizabeth debates whether to sign Mary's death warrant, urged on to it by Cecil. When Leicester comes to beg clemency, he is told that he is to witness Mary's execution. Scene 2: At Fotheringay, Mary does not flinch when Cecil delivers the fatal warrant. She turns to Talbot, who wears a cassock beneath his cloak, and confesses her sins. Mary asks her friends to join her in a prayer for all those who have wronged her. Leicester watches helplessly while Mary is led to the block.

Maria Stuarda, which used to have a reputation as an opera that even Maria Malibran could not save, has proved a grateful vehicle for a number of recent singers. Today, it stands as a clear example of Donizetti's eagerness, in the face of the increasingly repressive censors of the 1830s, to expand the range of powerful subject matter for the opera stage. The explosive scene between the two queens, which has no basis in history, is unparalleled in operas of the period for its dramatic immediacy. The hushed, elegiac aria of Mary to the clouds, 'Oh! nube che lieve', is both a masterly piece of tone-painting and a shrewdly low-key anticipation of the fireworks that follow. Donizetti's skill at combining features of the solo aria with a duet, keeping within the conventions but using them in unpredictable ways, is shown in Leicester's aria in the opening scene and in Mary's 'Lascio contento al carcere' as she confesses herself to Talbot. The prayer for Mary with chorus, a magnificent reworking of a musical idea from the early *Il paria*, builds to a fine climax. The whole final scene, including Mary's aria-finale with its unexpected modulations, is one of the composer's major achievements.

Lucia di Lammermoor
Dramma tragico in three acts (2h 30m)
Libretto by Salvatore Cammarano, after Sir Walter Scott's novel *The Bride of Lammermoor* (1819); French version by Alphonse Royer and 'Gustave Vaëz' (Jean-Nicolas Gustave van Nieuwenhuysen)
Composed 1835; rev. (in French) 1839
PREMIERES 26 September 1835, Teatro San Carlo, Naples; UK: 5 April 1838, Her Majesty's Theatre, Haymarket, London; 1839 version: 6 August 1839, Théâtre de la Renaissance, Paris; US: 28 December 1841, Théâtre d'Orléans, New Orleans
CAST Lucia *s*, Edgardo *t*, Enrico *bar*, Raimondo Bide-the-Bent *b*, Arturo *t*, Alisa *ms*, Normanno *t*; *satb* chorus of huntsmen and wedding guests

Lucia has never lost its place in the popular affection, although there has been a change from the days when it was regarded primarily as a vehicle for a coloratura soprano; now, in the wake of the impact of Maria Callas, it has come to be appreciated as a compelling Romantic melodrama. Far from being a conventional score, it is filled with original touches. The prevailing orchestral colour, dominated by horns, and the subtle repetition of brief motivic ideas lend the score its distinctive *tinta*. The psychological and dramatic appositeness of its striking contrasts in situation and melody, now idyllic, now propulsively energetic, add to its richness. Clearly, *Lucia* is one of the scores that Verdi knew during his formative years.

When it was new, *Lucia* was regarded as the last word in Romantic sensibility. And as such it was used by Flaubert in the famous episode in *Madame Bovary* when Emma meets Léon again at the theatre in Rouen; he even wove phrases from the French libretto into the narrative.

SYNOPSIS
Act I Scene 1: Enrico Ashton learns from his huntsmen that his sister Lucia has been meeting his hated rival Edgardo Ravenswood and has fallen in love with him. This disclosure sends Enrico into a murderous rage ('Cruda, funesta smania'). Scene 2: Lucia and her old nurse Alisa are waiting by a fountain, where she has a secret rendezvous with Edgardo. Lucia tells Alisa that she has seen the ghost of her ancestress

who was murdered by a Ravenswood ('Regnava nel silenzio'). When her lover arrives, she sends Alisa off to keep watch. Edgardo wants to ask Enrico to forget their family feud, but Lucia is terrified of her brother's temper. When Edgardo tells her he must go to France (to aid the Stuart cause), she is desolate, but they exchange rings ('Verranno a te sull' aure').

Act II Scene 1: Enrico and his friend Normanno have forged a letter to convince Lucia of Edgardo's infidelity. When Lucia enters, Enrico tells her of his desperate political position and that only her marrying Arturo can save him ('Il pallor funesto'). Weeping, Lucia protests, but she is badly shaken when Edgardo shows her the forged letter. The chaplain, Raimondo, further weakens Lucia's resolution by reminding her of her obligations to her family. Scene 2: The guests greet Arturo on his arrival for the wedding ('Per te l'immenso giubilo'). Half fainting, Lucia has just signed the wedding contract when Edgardo unexpectedly returns to claim her ('Chi mi frena in tal momento'). When Enrico shows him the signed contract, Edgardo curses Lucia, whereupon Enrico demands vengeance.

Act III Scene 1: During a storm, Enrico comes to Edgardo's ruined hall to challenge him to a duel. Scene 2: The wedding festivities are interrupted by Raimondo's disclosure that Lucia has murdered Arturo. Crazed, she appears, blood-stained dagger in hand, believing that she is about to marry Edgardo ('Alfin son tua'), and collapses. Scene 3: Edgardo comes to his family graveyard to meet Enrico. Waiting, he thinks he no longer wants to live since Lucia has proved faithless ('Fra poco a me ricovero'). Learning of her death, he looks forward to their reunion in heaven ('Tu che a Dio spiegasti l'ali') and stabs himself.

Lucia is filled with memorable melodies, but it is easy to overlook their dramatic appositeness and psychological depth. For instance, during the accompanied recitative preceding the famous mad scene, Lucia's mental confusion is underscored by the recurrence of earlier themes in altered form; the one tune she manages to keep straight is that of her Act I duet with Edgardo: 'Verranno a te'. A striking contrast is afforded by the merry chorus at the beginning of Act III, Scene 2, followed by Raimondo's grim narrative, 'Dalle stanze ove Lucia', with its uneasy modulations. It is followed by the elegiac chorus in E major, 'Oh, qual funesto avvenimento', which, like Edgardo's final aria, testifies to Donizetti's unusual skill in expressing grief in the major mode. Although much of the score of Lucia uses conventional compound structures, the dramatic propulsiveness of the plot, combined with Donizetti's melodic inventiveness, endows the work with surprising strength.

L'assedio di Calais

The Siege of Calais
Opera seria in three acts (2h)
Libretto by Salvatore Cammarano, after Luigi Marichionni's Italian adaptation of Philippe-Jacques Laroche's play *Eustache de Saint-Pierre, ou Le siège de Calais* (1822)

PREMIERES 19 November 1836, Teatro San Carlo, Naples; Ireland: 24 October 1991, Theatre Royal, Wexford; UK: 3 March 1993, Guildhall School of Music and Drama, London

This is Donizetti's first explicit attempt to approach the genre of French grand opera; the work includes a ballet divertissement – then an unusual feature in Italy, as operas were characteristically performed in conjunction with a separate full-length ballet. Some details may have been suggested by Luigi Henry's ballet *L'assedio di Calais*, which had been revived at the Teatro San Carlo in 1835. Because of the lack of an adequate leading tenor, Donizetti wrote the important male role of Aurelio for a mezzo-soprano *en travesti*.

The plot deals with the incident of the burghers of Calais, prepared to sacrifice themselves to lift the English siege of their city, their lives being spared through the intercession of the English queen. The score contains a notable and unusually elaborate final ensemble to Act I, but the Act II scene in the council chamber, at which both the mayor, Eustacio de Saint-Pierre, and his son Aurelio volunteer to serve as hostages, must rank among the most powerful pages in all of Donizetti's oeuvre. Probably in 1837, Donizetti added an attractive aria-finale for Aurelio's wife, Eleonora, to strengthen Act III.

Roberto Devereux

Robert Devereux
Opera seria in three acts (2h)
Libretto by Salvatore Cammarano, after François Ancelot's play *Elisabeth d'Angleterre* (1832) and with some indebtedness to Felice Romani's text for Saverio Mercadante's *Il conte d'Essex* (1833), also derived from Ancelot's play
Composed 1837, rev. 1838
PREMIERES 29 October 1837, Teatro San Carlo, Naples; rev. version: 27 December 1838, Théâtre Italien, Paris; UK: 24 June 1841, London; US: 15 January 1849, Astor Place Opera House, New York
CAST Elisabetta (Elizabeth) *s*, Sara (Sarah), Duchess of Nottingham *ms*, Roberto Devereux (Robert Devereux, Earl of Essex) *t*, Nottingham *bar*, Cecil *t*, Gualtiero (Walter Raleigh) *b*, Page *b*, Nottingham's Confidant *b*; *satb* chorus of courtiers

Composed at the time of his wife's death, *Roberto Devereux* reflects Donizetti's effort to assuage his grief by losing himself in a work of great power. Twentieth-century revivals of this opera have proved that its dramatic intensity can still grip audiences. For its demands on a potent singing actress, the role of Elizabeth is worthy of mention alongside Bellini's Norma. The score also shows Donizetti's growing avoidance of lengthy sections of chordally accompanied recitative.

SYNOPSIS

Act I At Westminster, Robert is threatened with arrest for treason for his recent débâcle in Ireland, but Queen Elizabeth loves him and is determined to save him, giving him a ring that will guarantee his freedom. Unknown to the queen, however, Robert is deeply in love with Sarah, who during his absence has been forced into a loveless union with his friend Nottingham. Later, Robert visits Sarah to say farewell, and he entrusts her with Elizabeth's ring, while she gives him a scarf in return.

Act II The ministers of the queen are meeting to decide Robert's fate. They have searched his apartments and bring the queen the scarf. When Nottingham sees it, remembering that he has observed his wife working on it, he bursts into a jealous rage. Deeply offended herself at this apparent evidence of Robert's infidelity, the queen is furious. Robert is sent to the Tower.

Act III Nottingham confronts his wife, ordering her seclusion at home, thereby making it impossible for her to send the ring to Elizabeth. In the Tower, Robert hopes he can restore Sarah's reputation before he is executed. At Westminster, Elizabeth is miserable, wondering why she has not received the ring, wanting Robert to be spared. As a cannon shot announces Robert's execution, Sarah rushes in with the ring, followed by Nottingham, who declares he detained Sarah so that he might have his revenge. The queen orders their arrest and then, haunted by visions of Robert's ghost and her own demise, announces her abdication.

Although the plot plays fast and loose with history, the opera carries its own brand of dramatic conviction. The overture, added for Paris, capitalizes on the tune of 'God Save the Queen'. The terse second act develops considerable tension, exploding at the end into an impulsive trio-finale. Act III opens with a powerful asymmetrical duet for Sarah and Nottingham. Robert's fine aria in the Tower scene, preceded by an almost Beethovenesque prelude, exemplifies Donizetti's canny writing for the tenor voice. Even more wonderful is Elizabeth's aria-finale, 'Vivi, ingrato', which expands in a long arc of restrained emotion, capped by a propulsive cabaletta.

La fille du régiment
The Daughter of the Regiment
Opéra comique (with spoken dialogue) in two acts (1h 30m)
Libretto by Jean-François-Alfred -Bayard and Jules-Henri Vernoy de Saint-Georges
Composed 1839; Italian opera-buffa version (with recitatives) 1840
PREMIERES 11 February 1840, Opéra-Comique, Paris; as an opera buffa: 3 October 1840, La Scala, Milan; US: 2 March 1843, Théâtre d'Orléans, New Orleans; UK: 27 May 1847, Her Majesty's Theatre, Haymarket, London
CAST Marie s, Marquise ms, Tonio t, Sergeant Sulpice b, Hortensius b, Corporal b, Farmer t, spoken roles; Duchesse de Crackentorp, Notary; satb chorus of soldiers, peasants, guests of the Marquise

One of the most popular of Donizetti's comedies, La fille shows no signs of weakening its hold on the public's affections. It is a tribute to the composer's grasp of the Gallic spirit that this opera became a staple of the French repertoire and that Marie's cabaletta in Act II, 'Salut à la France!', attained the status of a patriotic song. Although in the summer of 1840 Donizetti adapted the work as an Italian opera buffa

with sung recitatives, dropping the typically French couplets and inserting some other material, including an aria from Gianni di Calais (1828), this variant has never seriously challenged the appeal of the original opéra-comique version, in which the work is almost always performed today.

SYNOPSIS
Act I Brought up by the soldiers of the 21st Regiment of the French army and adopted by them as their 'daughter', the vivandière Marie confesses to gruff old Sulpice that she is much taken with a strapping Tyrolean, Tonio, who saved her life when she nearly fell off a precipice. The attraction is mutual, for Tonio has been lurking around the encampment hoping to talk to Marie. Seized as a spy, the young fellow is claimed by Marie as her personal prisoner, and in their ensuing duet ('De cet aveu si tendre') their true feelings for one another emerge. Hoping to marry Marie, Tonio is surprised to learn that her husband must be a member of the regiment, tidings that cause him promptly to enlist. The regiment celebrates his decision, calling on Marie to sing the regimental song ('Chacun le sait, chacun le dit'). The aged marquise de Birkenfeld, strangely discomfited by the presence of the campaigning so near her château, learns from Sulpice that a certain Captain Robert had been a member of this very regiment. On the strength of this information, she claims to be Marie's aunt and insists on removing the girl from what in her eyes is a very unsuitable environment. Now in uniform, Tonio has come to claim his bride, but Marie is forced to leave by the marquise's intervention ('Il faut partir, mes bons compagnons d'armes').

Act II At the château, Marie is bored by lessons in dancing and in singing vapid romances, her reluctance strengthened by the presence of Sulpice, whom the marquise has taken in to recover from a wound. Longing for her old freedom and harassed by her aunt's insistence on respectability and that she marry a silly young duke, Marie is overjoyed when the 21st Regiment arrives at the château. Tonio, who has been promoted on the battlefield, pleads with the marquise for Marie's hand. He has been investigating her true parentage and now demands an explanation. During the reception to announce Marie's engagement to the duke, the marquise suffers a change of heart and confesses to the startled company that Marie is in fact her own daughter and consents to her marriage to Tonio. Amid general rejoicing, the opera ends with a patriotic chorus, 'Salut à la France'.

The score is filled with effective numbers. Particularly noteworthy is Marie's regimental song, 'Chacun le sait' (surprisingly adapted from an ensemble in Il diluvio universale, 1830), and her farewell to Tonio, 'Il faut partir', a finely crafted melody with a cor-anglais obbligato that serves as the opening movement of the mid-point finale. A prime moment of comedy is provided by her lesson scene, in which the marquise tries to teach her an old tune by Pierre Garat, while Sulpice cannot resist teasing her into a reprise of 'Chacun le sait'. Tonio has both 'Pour mon âme' in Act I, with its redoubtable series of high Cs, and his tender plea to the marquise in Act II, 'Pour me rapprocher de Marie'. The character of the intrepid Marie stands squarely behind Verdi's portrait of another *vivandière*, Preziosilla in *La forza del destino*. Far from the least attractive aspect of *La fille du régiment* is Donizetti's skill and economy in contrasting military atmosphere with the tone of polite society, established at once by the charming *tyrolienne* that serves as a prelude to Act II.

La favorite
The Favourite
Grand opera in four acts (2h 30m, excluding the ballet)
Libretto by Alphonse Royer, Gustave Vaëz and Eugène Scribe after Baculard d'Arnaud's play *Le comte de Comminge* (1764) among other sources, on to which Scribe grafted the story of Leonora de Guzman
PREMIERES   2 December 1840, Opéra, Paris; US: 9 February 1843, Théâtre d'Orléans, New Orleans; UK: 18 October 1843, Drury Lane, London
CAST   Léonor *ms*, Inès *s*, Fernand *t*, Alphonse *bar*, Balthazar *b*, Don Gaspard *t*; *satb* chorus of monks and courtiers; ballet

In December 1839, Donizetti had completed a four-act semiseria entitled *L'ange de Nisida* for the Théâtre de la Renaissance in Paris, but the management declared bankruptcy before that work could be produced, leaving Donizetti with an unperformed score that, because of the nature of its plot (dealing with a royal mistress of the Bourbons), would offend the Italian censors. In the summer of 1840 when he was in Milan concocting the Italian adaptation of *La fille du régiment*, he was summoned back to Paris to produce a full-length work for the Opéra. Only the existence of *L'ange* and some other unperformed works allowed the resourceful Donizetti to complete *La favorite* and meet his deadline. Most of the major arias were newly composed, being tailored to the vocal characteristics of the cast.

SYNOPSIS
Act I   Castile, 1340. Fernand informs Balthazar, his father and the superior of a monastic order, that he must renounce his novitiate because he has fallen in love with a beautiful woman without being aware of her identity ('Une ange, une femme inconnue'). Balthazar's austere admonitions serve only to strengthen the young man's resolve. Blindfolded, Fernand is taken to the island of Léon, where he is greeted by Inès and other ladies. Léonor appears and tells Fernand that she appreciates his feelings, but she refuses to tell him who she is and asks him to forget her. As a farewell present she hands him a royal commission and leaves. Alone, Fernand determines to win military glory so that he can ask for her hand.
Act II   Alphonse, king of Castile, thinks longingly of his mistress, Léonor, as he walks through the gardens of Alcazar ('Léonor, viens!'). He intends to divorce his wife and make his mistress his queen. Léonor comes to him and sadly begs him to release her from what is an intolerably humiliating position. Alphonse attempts to cheer her up with some dancing (ballet). Balthazar, who is father to the queen as well

as to Fernand, arrives at court with a papal bull of excommunication that will take effect if the king pursues his intention of putting his consort aside. When Alphonse proudly refuses to heed this injunction, Balthazar pronounces an anathema before the horrified courtiers.
Act III   Covered with honour for having defeated the Moors, Fernand comes to make obeisance to the king. Complacently, the king offers to grant any favour that Fernand might request. When the young man asks for Léonor's hand, Alphonse, who cannot believe that Fernand is ignorant of the lady's compromised position, ironically accedes to this happy solution of his dilemma and commands the ceremony be performed at once ('Pour tant d'amour'). Léonor loves the young man's sincerity, but she feels unworthy of him ('O, mon Fernand'). She asks Inès to deliver a note revealing her true position, but one of the courtiers, Don Gaspard, detains Inès so that Fernand goes into the adjacent chapel uninformed. While the ceremony is taking place, the courtiers comment on the dishonourable affair. When Fernand emerges from the chapel, Alphonse confers noble titles on him. The courtiers, however, refuse to acknowledge him as their equal. Balthazar arrives, and from him Fernand learns the truth. Fernand confronts the king; refusing the titles given him, and breaking his sword and casting it at the royal feet, he leaves to resume the cloistered life.
Act IV   Monks dig the grave of the queen, who has just died. Fernand is still haunted by the memory of Léonor ('Ange si pur'). After he leaves to be received into full membership of the order, Léonor, disguised as a novice, appears, ill and conscience-stricken, hoping for a last glimpse of Fernand. When he returns, he starts to order her away, but then, seeing the genuineness of her contrition, he can think only of being with her. For a time, she shares his vain illusion, but her strength fails her and she dies at his feet.

In spite of its diverse sources, the score of *La favorite* is remarkably cohesive. Unlike most grand operas of its period, it has an almost austere and solemn colour, yet it contains much smouldering feeling, particularly in the final act, much admired by the conductor Arturo Toscanini. The sensuous, aristocratic nature of Alphonse is admirably depicted. Once one accepts the odd premiss that Fernand, as the queen's brother, should be ignorant of the identity of his brother-in-law's mistress, the plot is convincing. Although this opera has usually been performed in a not very exact Italian translation and in a version inauthentic in a number of details, the publication of the facsimile edition raises hopes that *La favorite* will regain its former pride of place.

Linda di Chamounix
Opera semiseria in three acts (2h 30m)
Libretto by Gaetano Rossi, after the drama *La grâce de Dieu* by Adolphe d'Ennery and Gustave Lemoine (1841)
PREMIERES   19 May 1842, Kärntnertortheater, Vienna; UK: 1 June 1843, Her Majesty's Theatre, Haymarket, London; US: 4 January 1847, Palmo's Opera House, New York

CAST Linda *s*, Carlo *t*, Marquis de Boisfleury *bar*, Antonio *bar*, Pierotto *ms*, Maddalena *s*, Prefect *b*, Intendant *t*; *satb* chorus of peasants, Savoyards

One of the major successes of Donizetti's career and arguably his finest achievement in the problematic semiseria genre, *Linda* shows well the refinement and melancholic power of the mature Donizetti.

SYNOPSIS

Act I Linda, a tenant farmer's daughter, has fallen in love with Carlo, unaware that he is the vicomte de Sirval, believing him just a poor artist. She, however, has caught the roving eye of the lecherous marquis, Carlo's elderly kinsman, and therefore, to protect his daughter from possible dishonour, her father Antonio decides, with the village prefect's prompting, to send her to France with a party of Savoyard seasonal workers.

Act II Linda is living in high style in Paris, maintained in all innocence by Carlo, who hopes to persuade his difficult mother to allow him to wed the girl of his dreams, but his mother (who does not appear) has different plans for him. Antonio arrives at Linda's luxurious apartment seeking news of his daughter, whom he does not at first recognize; when he does he suspects the worst and curses her. Linda's friend Pierotto appears with the dreadful news that he has heard that Carlo is going to wed an aristocratic girl. Linda promptly loses her reason.

Act III Linda is persuaded to return to her native village by Pierotto playing a familiar tune on his hurdy-gurdy. There she learns that Carlo managed to evade his mother's scheme for his marriage, and he, full of contrition, cannily restores Linda's sanity by the simple device of singing his love theme to her. All ends with a happy ensemble to celebrate the betrothal of Carlo and Linda.

The work has a fine overture (derived from the first movement of one of Donizetti's string quartets) and a number of effective duets; especially notable is the Act I love duet, the principal theme of which, 'A consolarmi affrettisi', serves to restore Linda's reason in time for the happy ending. The best-known aria, Linda's Act I 'O luce di quest'anima', in which she expresses her love for Carlo, was added along with a number of other revisions for the Paris premiere at the Théâtre Italien in November 1842. The true merit of *Linda*, however, lies in Donizetti's rich and apposite musical setting of a drama that sometimes stretches credibility to its limits.

Don Pasquale

Opera buffa in three acts (2h)
Libretto by Giovanni Ruffini and the composer, after Angelo Anelli's libretto for Stefano Pavesi's *Ser Marc'Antonio* (1810)
PREMIERES 3 January 1843, Théâtre Italien, Paris; UK: 29 June 1843, Her Majesty's Theatre, Haymarket, London; US: 7 January 1845, Théâtre d'Orléans, New Orleans
CAST Norina *s*, Ernesto *t*, Dr Malatesta *bar*, Don Pasquale *b*, Notary *b*; *satb* chorus of servants

Donizetti's comic masterpiece is the last product of the golden tradition of opera buffa of the first half of the 19th century to remain in the international repertoire. Designed for the principal quartet of the Théâtre Italien, *Don Pasquale* has a concentration and comic sweep, humanized by touches of Donizettian pathos, that set it in a class by itself. At this point in his busy, occasionally frantic, career Donizetti had accumulated a background of practical theatrical experience unmatched by that of any of his rivals, and this experience in combination with his musical talent produced a work whose freshness has never faltered. In the light of this achievement, it is difficult to realize that before the year was out the illness that would dim his mental capacities would manifest itself.

SYNOPSIS

Act I Scene 1: Don Pasquale impatiently awaits his friend and doctor, determined to disinherit his nephew Ernesto, who to his uncle's displeasure has fallen in love with the widow Norina. Pasquale wishes to consult Dr Malatesta about undertaking a marriage himself and siring some more direct heirs. When Malatesta appears, he informs Pasquale that he knows of the perfect bride for him ('Bella siccome un angelo'), whom he claims to be none other than his own sister, though he intends to employ his cousin Norina as the supposed bride. Pasquale confronts his nephew about his refusal to marry the young woman his uncle has in mind for him, ordering his nephew out of the house and announcing his own impending marriage ('Prender moglie!'). Realizing that his own hopes of marrying Norina are ruined ('Sogno soave e casto'), Ernesto suggests that his uncle should consult Dr Malatesta about this implausible prospect; he is astounded when he learns that the doctor has already given his whole-hearted approval. Scene 2: Norina reads a tale of chivalric love, laughing over its absurdity, and expressing her conviction that real femininity is far more persuasive ('So anch'io la virtù magica'). Dr Malatesta comes to see Norina to enlist her assistance in his plan to bring Pasquale to his senses. She is to pretend to be his sister 'Sofronia', fresh from a convent, and they agree on the details of the impersonation ('Pronta io son').

Act II The disillusioned Ernesto has made his preparations to depart ('Cercherò lontana terra'). In a fever of impatience, Pasquale awaits his bride. The doctor leads in a demure young lady wearing a veil, a spectacle that titillates the susceptible Pasquale ('Sta a vedere'). 'Sofronia' is upset to find herself in a room with a strange man, and, on being questioned, she admits to sewing as her only pastime. Malatesta produces a notary (in reality his nephew Carlino) and a wedding contract is drawn up by which Pasquale endows his bride with half his worldly goods. This arrangement is barely concluded when Ernesto appears to bid his uncle farewell; he is dismayed by Norina's apparent infidelity. No sooner is the contract signed than 'Sofronia' changes character completely, appointing Ernesto her *cavaliere servante*. When Pasquale objects, she insists on having her way. The old man is stunned by this turn of events ('È rimasto là impietrato'). She demands more servants, carriages, and other extravagances, leaving Pasquale close to apoplexy.

Act III Scene 1: Don Pasquale is dismayed at the accumulation of bills run up by his bride. She appears in evening dress, announcing she is going to the theatre. When he objects, she advises him to go to bed. At the height of the altercation, she slaps his face. Now thoroughly disillusioned, Pasquale contemplates the results of his impulsiveness ('È finita, Don Pasquale'). Seeing his discomfiture, Norina feels sorry for him and advises him to get a good night's sleep ('Via, caro sposino'). As she leaves, she drops a note, which Pasquale picks up and reads. Horrified to learn that an assignation in the garden is planned for that very evening, Pasquale summons Malatesta. The servants comment on the turmoil of the household ('Che interminabile andirivieni!'). When Malatesta appears, he and the doctor plot how they will catch 'Sofronia' and unmask her infidelity ('Cheti, cheti, immantinente'). Scene 2: Ernesto serenades his beloved ('Com'è gentil'). Norina steals in, and they sing a tender duet ('Tornami a dir che m'ami'). Pasquale surprises them, but Malatesta resolves the imbroglio by persuading his friend to agree to annul his own marriage and allow Ernesto to marry Norina. Although he feels he has been made a fool of, Pasquale is so relieved to be free of 'Sofronia' that he blesses the young lovers.

Although *Don Pasquale* makes some use of music that had already been used in other contexts, the score seems perfectly homogeneous. Written in a relatively short time, the music was carefully worked out, as the compositional sketches testify. The overture sparkles, and quotes several themes that appear later in the opera: notably Ernesto's Act III serenade and Norina's self-analysing aria from Act I. Malatesta's aria in the opening scene, 'Bella siccome un angelo', in which he describes the charms of his mythical sister, is a fine example of bel-canto irony. The high spirits of the work are neatly epitomized in the duet for Norina and Malatesta that closes Act I, wherein he coaches her in the part she must play to bamboozle Pasquale. Act II, with its unflagging build-up to a hilarious climax, is for many the summit of Donizetti's achievement. Act III contains its own share of riches in three irresistible duets and an apt finale to point the moral of the piece: that December should not tempt fate with May. Instead of the traditional *secco* recitative, the connective passages are string-accompanied. The mid-point finale is a solo quartet without choral reinforcement; indeed, the chorus appears only in the two scenes of Act III.

Maria di Rohan

Opera seria in three acts (2h 15m)
Libretto by Salvatore Cammarano (originally for Giuseppe Lillo, 1839) after the play by Joseph Philippe Lockroy and Edmond Badon, *Un duel sous le cardinal de Richelieu* (1832)
PREMIERES 5 June 1843, Kärntnertortheater, Vienna; rev. version: 14 November 1843, Théâtre Italien, Paris; UK: 8 May 1847, Covent Garden, London; US: 10 December 1849, New York
CAST Maria *s*, Riccardo (Chalais) *t*, Enrico (Chevreuse)

bar, Armando di Gondi *t* (*ms* in rev. version), Visconte di Suze *b*, De Fiesque *b*, Aubry *t*, Servant *b*; *satb* chorus of courtiers, servants

Maria di Rohan is Donizetti's tautest, most melodramatic opera. Beginning slowly, the action accelerates, punctuated by striking clocks, until it erupts in the devastating final scene. It shows the mature Donizetti in complete control of his musico-dramatic goals. The erroneous notion that so-called belcanto operas require only great singing and are devoid of dramatic values is given the emphatic lie by this work.

SYNOPSIS

Act I In Paris during the period of Cardinal Richelieu, Riccardo, le comte de Chalais, has been Maria's lover, and he still loves her. When she comes to him to implore him to use his influence to save her husband Chevreuse, who has killed the cardinal's nephew in a duel, he, unaware of her secret marriage, obliges. When Gondi, a young gallant, insults Maria, Chalais instantly challenges him. Maria's husband, released from prison through Chalais's intercession, volunteers to be his second.

Act II Chalais sends a note of farewell to Maria to be delivered only if he falls in the duel with Gondi. Maria arrives, come to warn him that Richelieu is now his enemy, but she conceals herself when Chevreuse appears to accompany Chalais to the duel. Chevreuse leaves first, and Maria emerges from her hiding-place to insist that Chalais not risk such danger on her account and admits that she still loves him. When he is informed that Chevreuse is about to fight Gondi in his place, he rushes off.

Act III Chevreuse has fought in the place of the tardy Chalais and has sustained a wound in his arm. Learning that Richelieu's men have seized compromising documents in his room, Chalais comes to warn Maria that discovery is imminent and urges her to escape with him. Unaware of these developments, Chevreuse shows Chalais a secret passage, and as Chalais enters it he informs Maria that he will return for her when the clock next strikes if she has not come to him by then. One of the cardinal's men sends Maria off and gives Chevreuse the compromising letter. Consumed by murderous jealousy, he confronts Maria, who refuses to deny that she has been Chalais's mistress. The clock strikes and Chalais returns, whereupon Chevreuse challenges him. They rush off into the secret passage, leaving Maria half fainting as a gunshot is heard. Chevreuse returns to inform her that Chalais has turned his pistol on himself. Maria demands that her husband kill her too, but he condemns her to a life of shame.

There are a number of expressive arias, particularly Maria's larghetto in Act I ('Cupa, fatal mestizia') and Chalais's single-movement air ('Alma soave e cara') at the beginning of Act II. The duet for Maria and Chalais at the end of Act II ('Ecco l'ora') sounds a genuine note of despair. The interchange between Chevreuse and Maria in Act III, when he confronts her with her guilt, has a conciseness and emotional impact that show Donizetti at the height of his powers.

Other operas: *Il Pigmalione*, (1816) 1960; *L'ira d'Achille*, (1817); *Enrico di Borgogna*, 1818; *Una follia*, 1818; *Il falegname di Livonia, o Pietro il grande, czar delle Russie*, 1819; *Le nozze in villa*, 1820/21; *Zoraide di Granata*, 1822; *La zingara*, 1822; *La lettera anonima*, 1822; *Chiara e Serafina*, 1822; *Alfredo il grande*, 1823; *Il fortunato inganno*, 1823; *L'ajo nell'imbarazzo, o Don Gregorio*, 1824, rev. 1826; *Emilia di Liverpool*, 1824, rev. as *L'ermitaggio di Liverpool*, 1828; *Alahor in Granata*, 1826; *Elvida*, 1826; *Gabriella di Vergy*, (1826, rev. 1838), 1869; *Olivo e Pasquale*, 1827; *Otto mesi in due ore*, 1827; *Il borgomastro di Saardam*, 1827; *Le convenienze teatrali*, 1827, rev. as *Le convenienze ed inconvenienze teatrali*, 1831; *L'esule di Roma, ossia Il proscritto*, 1828; *Alina, regina de Golconda*, 1828, rev. 1829; *Gianni di Calais*, 1828; *Il paria*, 1829; *Il giovedì grasso*, 1829; *Elisabetta al castello di Kenilworth*, 1829, rev. as *Il castello di Kenilworth*, 1830; *I pazzi per progetto*, 1830; *Il diluvio universale*, 1830, rev. 1834; *Imelda de'Lambertazzi*, 1830; *Gianni di Parigi*, (1831), 1839; *Francesca di Foix*, 1831; *La romanziera e l'uomo nero*, 1831; *Fausta*, 1832, rev. 1833; *Ugo, conte di Parigi*, 1832; *Sancia di Castiglia*, 1832; *Il furioso all'isola di San Domingo*, 1833; *Parisina*, 1833; *Torquato Tasso*, 1833; *Rosamonda d'Inghilterra*, 1834, rev. as *Eleonara di Gujenna*, 1837; *Gemma di Vergy*, 1834; *Marino Faliero*, 1835; *Belisario*, 1836; *Il campanello di notte*, 1836; *Betly, ossia La capanna svizzera*, 1836, rev. 1837; *Pia de'Tolomei*, 1837; *Maria de Rudenz*, 1838; *Poliuto*, (1838), 1848, rev. as *Les martyrs*, (1839), 1840; *Il duca d'Alba* (inc., 1839; completed by Matteo Salvi), 1882; *L'ange de Nisida*, (1839); *Adelia*, 1841; *Rita, ou Le mari battu*, (1841), 1860; *Maria Padilla*, 1841; *Caterina Cornaro*, (1843), 1844, rev. 1845; *Dom Sébastien*, 1843

W.A.

PAUL DUKAS

Paul Abraham Dukas; *b* 1 October 1865, Paris; *d* 17 May 1935, Paris

Dukas is still best known – even almost exclusively known – for his brilliant orchestral scherzo *L'apprenti sorcier* (1897). But his major works include two distinguished scores for the theatre; the opera *Ariane et Barbe-bleue* and the ballet *La Péri* (1911–12), and he started or planned several other operas.

Dukas studied composition at the Paris Conservatoire with Debussy's teacher Ernest Guiraud (whose own opera, *Frédégonde*, he later helped Saint-Saëns to orchestrate), and he spent much of the 1880s striving without success to emulate Debussy in winning the Prix de Rome, although he was awarded second prize in 1888 for his cantata *Velléda*. Later he published quantities of music criticism (again like Debussy), worked as an editor (of Beethoven, Rameau, Couperin, Domenico Scarlatti) and taught composition: his pupils included Albéniz and Messiaen. But creative work gave him difficulty; he produced only at a very slow pace, and eventually gave up finishing new works altogether, though as with his exact contemporary Sibelius there were always reports of major works in hand. He was a member of the Académie des Beaux-Arts for the last year of his life, and it was to

his chair that Stravinsky failed to secure election in January 1936.

Ariane et Barbe-bleue

Ariadne and Bluebeard
Conte musical in three acts (2h)
Libretto by Maurice Maeterlinck
Composed 1899–1906
PREMIERES 10 May 1907, Opéra-Comique, Paris; US: 29 March 1911, Metropolitan Opera, New York; UK: 20 April 1937, Covent Garden, London (inc.); 17 September 1990, Grand Theatre, Leeds
CAST Barbe-bleue (Bluebeard) *b*, Ariane (Ariadne) *ms*, Nurse *c*, Sélysette *ms*, Ygraine *s*, Mélisande *s*, Bellangère *s*, Alladine *silent*, Old Peasant *b*, 2 Other Peasants *t, b*; *satb* chorus of peasants

Unlike his earlier *Pelléas et Mélisande*, Maeterlinck's text (1899) was always intended as an operatic libretto, which, it seems, he hoped would be set by Grieg. Dukas was thus able to compose it as it stood, apart from minor cuts and a few verbal changes (which tend, in particular, to dilute the eroticism of Ariadne's relationship with Bluebeard's previous wives).

Perhaps because it was meant as an opera, the libretto has more action than usual in Maeterlinck. The chorus of peasants intrudes into Bluebeard's domain almost like the populace breaking into the prison in Verdi's *Don Carlos*, and there is also a good deal of description, by the wives, of vigorous action offstage. The drama is hence much less private than *Pelléas* or than Béla Balázs's later *Bluebeard* libretto set by Bartók, both of which are plays about the communication of inward states or feelings. *Ariane* seems rather to confront the problem of freedom, on the one hand as a social issue (in the feudal and feminist sense), and on the other as a question of what is psychologically consistent with normal human affections. Ariadne, like her Cretan namesake, shows the way out of prison, though this time it is rejected (Maeterlinck subtitled his play 'La délivrance inutile'). The other wives, incidentally, are named after characters in earlier plays by Maeterlinck, and much of the drama's symbolic apparatus is likewise familiar.

SYNOPSIS

Act I   Ariadne, Bluebeard's latest wife, arrives at his castle with her nurse, to the offstage shouts of peasants hostile to Bluebeard but sympathetic to her. She holds the keys to the seven locked doors, but discards the first six (which she is allowed to use) in favour of the forbidden seventh: 'The permitted teaches us nothing.' The nurse nevertheless opens the first six in turn; from each cascade precious stones (respectively amethysts, sapphires, pearls, emeralds, rubies, diamonds). But when Ariadne opens the seventh door it reveals only a shadowy opening, from which surges up the song of the five former wives, based on the folksong 'Les cinq filles d'Orlamonde' (a name that recalls the hidden world of *Pelléas*, Allemonde). Here Bluebeard makes the first of his two brief appearances and tries to prevent Ariadne descending the steps. The crowd breaks into the castle, but she assures them that Bluebeard has not harmed her.

Act II   Ariadne does indeed go down into the subterranean hall to find and free her predecessors.

Though miserable, they are reluctant to escape against Bluebeard's prohibition. All the same, Ariadne leads them joyfully upwards into the light.

Act III   The former wives are regaling themselves in fine clothes and jewellery when Bluebeard returns to the castle. But he is attacked by peasants (offstage) and brought in bound. Believing that the wives will kill him, the peasants withdraw. But in fact the women fuss round him, tending his injuries, and stealing furtive kisses. Finally, Ariadne releases him and, after inviting the other wives, one by one, to accompany her, departs alone with the nurse.

When Dukas started his opera, Debussy's *Pelléas* was substantially composed (though neither completed nor performed until 1902), and Dukas knew much or all of the music, except the interludes, from the private run-throughs Debussy gave for close friends. Dukas's score is more robust than Debussy's (Debussy himself commented, in a letter to Dukas, on 'a certain implacability in the beauty of Ariane . . . [and] the torrent of sound which floods the orchestra'); yet there are many parallels. Dukas even quotes Debussy's opera, at Mélisande's first appearance in Act II, and again when Ariadne unties her hair in Act III. In Act III there are allusions to Debussy's *La mer* (1905).

But Dukas's music seldom actually sounds like Debussy, who indeed later criticized it as un-French. It has a long line which still occasionally recalls Wagner, and which can accommodate lengthy quotations of folksongs such as 'Les cinq filles d'Orlamonde' and 'Au clair de la lune' without incongruity; and there are passages of glittering orchestration, notably in Act III, which suggest a Russian influence. The radical elements in Debussy are lacking. Dukas's recitative is more conventional and rhetorical, and the descriptive music (particularly for the first six doors) may suggest Massenet or Fauré.

Ariane et Barbe-bleue is exceptionally dependent on the female voice. Ariadne herself is onstage almost throughout, and the nurse and the four singing wives all have bigger parts than Bluebeard, who sings for only a few minutes at the end of Act I. The chorus male voices and the small parts for male peasants are a slight counterbalance. But since the male characters are as supine and deferential as the former wives, they between them merely draw attention to the dominating life-force of Ariadne herself and the way she controls the action.

S.W.

ANTONÍN DVOŘÁK

Antonín Leopold Dvořák; *b* 8 September 1841, Nelahozeves, nr Kralupy, Czech Republic; *d* 1 May 1904, Prague

Dvořák's operatic education came largely from playing the viola in the orchestra of the Prague Provisional Theatre from its opening in 1862 until 1871, by which time he had written his first opera, *Alfred*. To say that his operatic career spanned most of his life as a composer is accurate but misleading. *Alfred* was written within five years of his first substantial surviving compositions such as the first two symphonies and the song-cycle *Cypresses* (*Cypřiše*); *Armida* was his last completed composition, premiered only a few weeks before his death. However, the pattern of work that spans these two operas is irregular: between 1882, when he completed *Dimitrij*, and 1897, when he wrote *The Devil and Kate*, Dvořák composed only one new opera. During this 15-year period he was at the height of his powers, writing his three last symphonies, the Cello Concerto, the late chamber music and most of his choral music. His turning away from opera was partly a sign of his frustration with the medium and his lack of success in making any mark abroad with it, and perhaps a recognition that his natural talents lay elsewhere. There were also the practical circumstances that some of this time was spent outside Bohemia – his numerous trips to England (where large-scale choral works were preferred to operas), his three-year stint in America (where he went to the opera only twice and even wrote to a friend that he regretted all the time he had spent writing operas). Nor was there much demand for operas from Prague, which preferred to fill its brand-new National Theatre, at least in the opening decade, with lavishly produced foreign novelties and ballets rather than native operas.

Therefore Dvořák's opera-writing falls into two distinct halves: at the beginning of his life and at the end, bridged by *The Jacobin* in the middle. Dvořák's earlier operatic period epitomizes many of the trends in contemporary Czech opera. His first opera, *Alfred* (1870), was in German, looking back to earlier German-orientated Prague composers. Its subject matter, like that of *Vanda* (1875), was concerned with national conflicts: English against Danes in *Alfred*; Poles against Germans in *Vanda*. This series of large-scale serious operas reaches a climax with *Dimitrij* (1881–2). *Vanda* was written originally in five acts; *Dimitrij* was planned in five acts, though later reduced to four. This, together with their 'political' subject matter, suggests a debt to French grand opera, a model evident in many other aspects of composition, such as the deployment of double choruses and large-scale concerted finales.

Dvořák's three other operas of the 1870s, *King and Charcoal Burner*, *The Stubborn Lovers* and *The Cunning Peasant*, are all instead in the 'village comedy' type of Czech operas of the period. They are all on a smaller scale, the second and third in one and two acts respectively. The musical idiom is lighter and owes more to Lortzing and Nicolai than to Meyerbeer. Uniting both lines of development is an emphasis on instrumental music. All the operas have overtures; most have instrumental dances and recurring motifs to provide unity. It is remarkable that the libretti of these six operas were all by different librettists, in some cases writers completely unknown to Dvořák.

In *Dimitrij* Dvořák had worked closely with the librettist, Marie Červinková-Riegrová, and she provided him with the libretto for his next opera, *The Jacobin* (1887–8). Though Dvořák was not to write another new opera until 1897, the years after *Dimitrij* saw revision of three operas, among them a final version of *King and Charcoal Burner*, and some additions to *The Jacobin*. But the most radical revision was that of *Dimitrij*, rewritten in a sternly 'declamatory' version that jettisoned many of the ensembles. The inspiration behind this was Dvořák's later recognition of Wagnerian music drama: if there are Wagnerian traits in the earlier operas they are a good generation behind the time, the Wagner of *Tannhäuser* and *Lohengrin*.

With this radically changed aesthetic Dvořák approached the three operas written in his final period, which together with a series of tone poems formed the entire output of his final eight years. *The Devil and Kate* avoids duets, though the role of the chorus is undiminished and the piece is studded with recognizable set numbers. Orchestrally there is a great expansion – perhaps too great to accommodate the slender folktale on which it is based. In Dvořák's next opera, *Rusalka*, without doubt his masterpiece, the chorus has less work, but there are a number of real duets, while the final opera, *Armida*, he had slipped back into an aesthetic not noticeably different from that of his first opera over 30 years earlier.

This is symptomatic of the problems with Dvořák's operas. He inherited a conception of opera that was, by current European standards, out of date, and, despite a flirtation with Wagnerian music drama in the 1890s, it did not really change or develop. Though he used recurring themes, they are those of a symphonist attempting to unify a long complex work rather than those of a musical dramatist using leitmotifs to supply extra-musical information. Dvořák's early operas tend to be hit-or-miss affairs, over-dependent on the strength of their libretti. His own compositional personality was not sufficiently developed to override this in the way that it does in later works. With the exception of the flagging *Armida*, his operas from *Dimitrij* onwards all have distinct and forceful musical personalities which have spoken directly to the Czech public, over the heads of the strongly anti-Dvořák lobby that, in the early years of the century, was keen to promote almost any composer other than Dvořák as 'Smetana's successor'. Some of the results of this official disdain are still evident in the niggardly provision of scores and and recordings of the earlier works.

Dimitrij

Dimitri
Grand opera in four acts; 1894–5 version, (3h 15m)
Libretto by Marie Červinková-Riegrová, after Ferdinand Mikovec's *Dimitir Ivanovič*, an adaptation of Johann Christoph Friedrich von Schiller's unfinished *Demetrius*, with material from Aleksandr Ostrovsky's *Dimitrij Samozvanec and Vasilij Šujskij*
Composed 1881–2; rev., 1883, 1885, 1894–5
PREMIERES original version: 8 October 1882, New Czech Theatre, Prague; rev. version: 7 November 1894, National Theatre, Prague; UK: 30 January 1979, University Great Hall, Nottingham; US: April 1984, New York (concert)
CAST Dimitrij Ivanovič *t*, Marfa Ivanovna *s*, Marina Mniškova *s*, Xenie Borisovna *s*, Petr Fedorovič Basmanov *b*, Prince Vasilij Šujský *bar*, Jov, Patriarch of Moscow *b*, 2 *bar*; *satb* chorus of people of Moscow, boyars and their wives, priests, Polish entourage, soldiers, dancers, pages

The plot of *Dimitrij* is a continuation of the story of Boris Godunov, with four characters in common: Dimitrij (assumed son of Ivan the Terrible who, however, genuinely believes in his claim to the throne), the Polish Marina of the princely Sandomír family (now his wife), the Russian Xenie (the daughter of Boris Godunov) and Prince Šujský, now a supporter of Boris, and Dimitrij's chief antagonist.

SYNOPSIS

Act I   After Boris's death the people of Moscow are confused and factionalized. Some (led by the patriarch and Šujský) continue to support the Godunov family; others (led by the army general Basmanov) support the victorious Dimitrij. All depends on whether Marfa, the widow of Ivan the Terrible, will recognize Dimitrij as her son. In the crucial confrontation, Marfa realizes that Dimitrij is not her son, but decides to use him as an instrument of her revenge on her old enemies and publicly acknowledges him.

Act II   shows Dimitrij in a positive light: quelling the fracas that breaks out between Poles and Russians, rescuing Xenie when she is pursued by drunken Poles, breaking up a conspiracy led by Šujský.

Act III   When Šujský is to be executed, Xenie begs Dimitrij for mercy for him, only then realizing the identity of her rescuer. Marina jealously spots the sympathy between Dimitrij and Xenie and in a private scene with Dimitrij plays her most powerful card – revealing that Dimitrij is simply a peasant – only to find that Dimitrij has every intention of remaining tsar. She is crushed by his heroic stance: he repudiates her.

Act IV   Dimitrij urges Xenie to marry him, though his intention is thwarted by (1882 version) Marina's having Xenie murdered or (later versions) Xenie's decision to enter a nunnery. Marina now publicly reveals Dimitrij's origins, which leads to a call for Marfa's renewed identification of Dimitrij. As Marfa hesitates, Dimitrij calls to her not to perjure herself, and is shot by Šujský.

For all its resemblance to Meyerbeer's *Le prophète* (the central figure of an impostor, with a crucial mother–son 'recognition' scene in full public gaze, and the generally French grand-opera conventions), there are vital differences between this opera and an actual French opera on the same subject (Victorin de Joncières's *Dimitri*, 1876). In the French opera, there is no Russian–Polish confrontation (most of the plot takes place before Dimitrij gets to Russia); whereas Dvořák uses his double-chorus confrontations to great effect for opposing nationalities, and with surprisingly convincing imitations of Orthodox chant. Joncières's hero is a philandering weakling, a lyric tenor caught between mistresses; Dvořák's Dimitrij is heroic in voice and action and chooses his consorts politically – the Polish Marina discarded for the Russian Xenie. Dvořák's opera unfolds unevenly, but in its dialectic confrontations, particularly that of Marina and Dimitrij in Act III, and in one of the greatest scenes in all Czech opera, Marfa's hesitation in Act IV, Dvořák shows a handling of dramatic tension that is immensely powerful and unparalleled in his other operas.

The Jacobin

Jakobín
Opera in three acts (2h 45m)
Libretto by Marie Červinková-Riegrová; additions by her
father, František Rieger
Composed 1887–8, rev. 1897
PREMIERES   original version: 12 February 1889, National
Theatre, Prague; rev. version: 19 June 1898, National
Theatre, Prague; UK: 22 July 1947, St George's Hall,
London (concert); 30 October 1968, Aston University,
Birmingham
CAST   Count Vilém z Harasova *b*, Bohuš z Harasova *bar*,
Adolf z Harasova *bar*, Julie *s*, Filip *b*, Jiří *t*, Benda *t*,
Terinka *s*, Lotinka *c*; *satb* chorus of townsfolk, young
people, schoolchildren, musicians, musketeers, country
folk

SYNOPSIS

Act I   Bohuš returns with his wife Julie to his home
town in rural Bohemia. It is 1793; they have been
abroad in Revolutionary France. Bohuš learns that
during his absence his cousin Adolf has contrived to
estrange him from his father, Count Vilém, for his
'Jacobin' tendencies and is due to replace him as the
count's heir.

Act II   Benda, the local teacher, rehearses his choir.
He does not recognize his former pupil Bohuš who
arrives asking for lodging, but, hearing that Bohuš and
Julie are musicians, agrees to take them in. Adolf
meanwhile has heard of the arrival of the 'Jacobin'
and arrests him.

Act III   Julie manages to enter the castle secretly
where she sings to the count a favourite song of his
long-dead wife. The count asks who has been singing,
meets Julie and hears about Bohuš's arrest and
Adolf's machinations. Father and son are reconciled
and at the same time Benda is persuaded to let his
daughter marry her lover Jeník and relinquish the
advantageous match that he had in mind for her.

Dvořák was at first reluctant to take on this libretto,
which had been specially written for him. *The Cunning
Peasant* had failed in Vienna; *Dimitrij*, written with an
eye to foreign markets, had not been taken up abroad
and Červinková-Riegrová's new libretto seemed to
him too local – 'Such a teacher-musician [as Benda]
exists only here and just wouldn't be understood elsewhere.' In many senses he was right: *The Jacobin* can
claim to be one of the most quintessentially Czech
operas. Like many of Smetana's, it is about reconciliation, but this message is less important than the crucial
role of music in the Czech national psyche, a notion
that is stressed three times in the work. It is music –
Julie's lullaby – that effects the reconciliation. Benda's
celebrated choir-rehearsal scene, unlike its model in
Lortzing's *Zar und Zimmermann*, is touching rather
than amusing, and the characterization of Benda himself is an affectionate tribute to generations of Czech
teacher-musicians. The most moving number in the
opera, however, is Bohuš's and Julie's Act II duet
('My cizinou jsme bloudili' – 'We have wandered
through foreign parts') where to poignantly emotional
harmony they tell how in their long exile abroad – the
fate of so many Bohemians – it was only in music that
they found relief.

The Devil and Kate

Čert a Káča
Opera in three acts (2h 45m)
Libretto by Adolf Wenig, after a folktale
PREMIERES   23 November 1899, National Theatre, Prague;
UK: 22 November 1932, Town Hall, Oxford; US: May
1988, Berkeley Opera Company
CAST   Jirka *t*, Káča (Kate) *ms*, Marbuel *b*, Lucifer *b*,
Princess *s*, *s*, *t*, 3 *b*; *satb* chorus of peasants, young people,
musicians, devils, courtiers, offstage populace

SYNOPSIS

Act I   Amid the dancing one summer's evening two
characters stand out: the shepherd Jirka, reluctantly
leaving for work, and the portly and garrulous Káča
(Kate). No one wants to dance with her, and in her
anger she declares that she would dance even 'with
the Devil' – which is the cue for the appearance of the
devil Marbuel, who is making inquiries about the
oppressive local lady of the manor (the princess) and
her steward. Marbuel dances with Káča, who is then
only too pleased to accompany him to his 'red castle'.
The pair promptly vanish through the floor. Jirka,
who has been sacked and told to go to hell by the
steward, volunteers to rescue her.

Act II   When Marbuel arrives in hell with his
burden, he finds he has met his match in Káča. Hell is
eager to be rid of her; she, however, is less eager to
return. A deal is done: Káča will get money if she
leaves; Jirka, who has now arrived in pursuit of her,
will 'save' the princess's steward from Marbuel when
he comes for him and the princess, and claim a
reward from him.

Act III   The princess, now living in fear of her life,
enlists Jirka's services. In return for her abolishing serf-
dom, he frightens Marbuel away by producing Káča.

The Devil and Kate was written at the height of
Dvořák's powers as a symphonist. This shows in the
preponderance of purely instrumental music – partly
justified by the story with its emphasis on dancing in
the Act I pub scene, and in hell. There are also
surprisingly long scene-preludes, including a striking
descent to a Nibelheim-like hell at the beginning of
Act II. Other Wagnerian influences are apparent in
the almost total absence of solo ensemble; though not
of the chorus, which plays a large part. It is one of the
few Czech operas to lack love interest altogether: Act
III ends with Káča's seemingly cynical declaration
that, now she has been richly rewarded for scaring off
the devil, she will be able to afford any bridegroom
she likes. For all its oddness, this is one of Dvořák's
most popular operas in the Czech Republic, largely
perhaps because it reinforces so many popular national assumptions. Musicians open the proceedings
with another of Dvořák's bagpipe imitations, and
continue to provide the fare for the dancing. Most
Czech devils are comically incompetent; Marbuel is
especially so, and is worsted by one of the most
assertive of all the strong women depicted in Czech
opera. And for all the laborious motivic work, it is
the folklike strophic numbers that linger most in the
mind: Jirka, with his touching song about losing his
sheep, or Marbuel with his haunting and magnificently
orchestrated description of his 'red castle'.

Rusalka

Lyric fairy-tale in three acts (3h)
Libretto by Jaroslav Kvapil, after Friedrich Heinrich Carl de la Motte Fouqué's tale *Undine* (1811)
PREMIERES 31 March 1901, National Theatre, Prague; US: 10 November 1935, Sokol Slav Hall, Chicago; UK: 9 May 1950, Peter Jones Theatre, London
CAST Prince *t*, Foreign Princess *s*, Rusalka *s*, Water Goblin *b*, Ježibaba *ms*, 3 *s*, *c*, 2 *t*; *satb* chorus of wood sprites, the Prince's entourage, guests at the castle

SYNOPSIS

Act I Rusalka (a water nymph) wishes to become human to gain the love of the prince. Ježibaba the witch makes two conditions for her magic: that Rusalka be dumb and that her lover be true – otherwise both will be damned. Despite the warnings of the fearful water goblin, Rusalka proceeds on this hazardous path; her prince is captivated by her appearance, and takes her off with him.

Act II At court the dumb Rusalka is no match for the brilliant and evil foreign princess. Rumours circulate about Rusalka's supernatural origins, and the prince rejects her.

Act III Rusalka, a pale shadow of her former self, mourns her state. Her prince, now repentant, returns. She is able to speak to him and explain that he will die if she kisses him. He begs her to do so. At her kiss, he perishes, and Rusalka, released from the curse, disappears into the lake.

Rusalka stands out clearly above all Dvořák's other operas as his most successful and most popular. Unlike the rather thin tale on which *The Devil and Kate* is based, the Undine legend that lies behind *Rusalka* has a haunting resonance which is magically matched by Dvořák's music. The composer found a vein of melodic poignancy that memorably sets off his heroine: for many years Rusalka's 'Hymn to the moon' was all that was known abroad of Dvořák's vast operatic output. The libretto itself cleverly grafted on to its sources (which include Hans Christian Andersen's *Little Mermaid*) a folk periphery that identifies the work as distinctively Czech. Characters such as the doleful water goblin and the malicious witch were by then well known from Erben's ballads and had recently formed the basis of two of Dvořák's tone poems. Kvapil changed the chief characters too, notably Rusalka herself, who is here essentially a suffering Slavonic heroine rather than the skittish Undine in Lortzing's opera of that name. Dvořák responded well to all aspects of the libretto, with the result that the work has an impressive range of characterization, from its poignant heroine and evocative nature scenes to the brilliant court scenes in Act II, and some surprisingly effective comic relief with the mock-serious witch, a kitchen boy and a gamekeeper. For all the Wagnerian ripeness of the harmony and orchestration, Dvořák discarded some of the Wagnerian aesthetic that lay behind *The Devil and Kate* and his revision of *Dimitrij*. The duets he now included were some of his most committed and passionate.

Other operas: *Alfred*, (1870), 1938; *King and Charcoal Burner* (*Král a uhlíř*), (1871), rev. 1874, 1887; *The Stubborn Lovers* (*Tvrdé palice*), (1874), 1881; *Vanda*, 1876, rev. 1880, (1883); *The Cunning Peasant* (*Šelma Sedlák*), 1878; *Armida*, 1904

J.T.

GOTTFRIED VON EINEM

b 24 January 1918, Bern

Of Austrian parentage, von Einem was educated in Germany and England. At the age of 20 he became an apprentice répétiteur at the Staatsoper in Berlin and worked in the same capacity at Bayreuth. He fell foul of the Gestapo and spent the war years, like many of his German colleagues, in 'inner emigration'. His closest allies in the musical world at this time were the composers Carl Orff, Werner Egk and Rudolf Wagner-Régeny. From 1941 to 1944 he studied privately with Boris Blacher, who recalled that von Einem came to him 'already formed' and that his personal style was recognizable even in simple harmony exercises. In 1944 von Einem established his reputation with the world premiere of his ballet *Die Prinzessin Turandot* at the Staatsoper in Dresden. The same institution commissioned his first opera, *Dantons Tod*, but this, by good fortune, was first given in Salzburg and was indeed the first performance of an opera by a living composer ever to be given at the International Festival. Salzburg then commissioned a further work, *Der Prozess*, which was premiered there in 1952. Both operas have since been performed frequently, in Germany and elsewhere, to widespread acclaim.

Von Einem has remained first and foremost a composer of opera and ballet, writing orchestral works almost exclusively to commission. He has occupied a number of high-ranking administrative posts (e.g. director of the Vienna Festival and professor of composition at the Vienna Hochschule für Musik) and sat for some years on the directors' committee of the Salzburg Festival. In 1980 his self-styled mystery play *Jesu Hochzeit* was staged at the Vienna Staatsoper. The libretto, written by von Einem's second wife, Lotte Ingrisch, was denounced by leading members of the Austrian Catholic Church as blasphemous, and the world premiere, which was televised live, provoked a major scandal.

Opinions as to the quality of von Einem's music differ widely. Even his teacher, Blacher (also librettist for four of his operas), later classified him as a 'conservative' and there has been criticism of the discrepancy between his choice of authors (particularly Büchner and Kafka) and his musical style, which is largely straightforward and tonal. His admirers regard him as post-war Germany's leading theatre composer.

Dantons Tod

Danton's Death

Opera in two parts (2h 15m)

Libretto by the composer and Boris Blacher, after the play by Georg Büchner (1835)

PREMIERES 6 August 1947, Festspielhaus, Salzburg; UK: 6 May 1962, BBC radio; US: 9 March 1966, City Opera, New York

Blacher helped his former pupil condense Büchner's original 32 episodes into six scenes, telescoping some of the smaller roles and emphasizing the influence of the chorus – an area where opera offers considerably greater possibilities than spoken drama. Passages from Büchner's letters to his fiancée are also incorporated into the libretto.

Paris, 1794: Danton and Desmoulins criticize Robespierre for his brutality and arrogance. They are arrested and put on trial. Danton defends himself eloquently before the Tribunal but is no match for his devious opponent. Although no verdict is reached, he and his friends are led to the guillotine.

The score consists of 17 separate musical numbers, some linked by orchestral intermezzi, others running continuously. Themes and motifs are not interlinked, although the opening brass chord sequence reappears in the final bars. Diversity of rhythm and form is the vital differentiating feature of the score, while the polyphonic disposition of brief motivic cells invests the chorus writing with a vivacity akin to the *turba* passages of Bach's Passions. Britten's use of the chorus in *Peter Grimes* (which is a close contemporary of *Dantons Tod*) is strikingly similar.

Other operatic works: *Der Prozess*, 1953; *Der Zerrissene*, 1964; *Der Besuch der alten Dame*, 1971; *Kabale und Liebe*, 1975; *Jesu Hochzeit*, 1980; *Tulifant*, 1990

A.C.W.B.

GEORGE ENESCU

George Enescu (Georges Enesco); *b* 19 August 1881, Liveni, Romania; *d* 4 May 1955, Paris

The cellist Pablo Casals once called Enescu 'the greatest musical phenomenon since Mozart'. Sadly, the sheer range of Enescu's gifts – as violinist, conductor, pianist and teacher – helped to obscure his achievements as a composer; most concert-goers in the West know only his two early *Romanian Rhapsodies*, and think of his music (wrongly) as merely 'folkloric'.

After his studies in both Vienna and Paris, Enescu's musical language was deeply influenced by Brahms, Wagner (whose *Ring* he memorized) and Fauré (who taught him). To this mixture he added some Romanian folk characteristics: shifting major/minor modal scales, and heterophony (the superimposition of different versions of the same melodic material). The result was, from the 1920s onwards, a very personal idiom, inhabiting the borderland between richly chromatic late Romanticism and a sparse, elliptical modernism.

Based in both Paris and Romania, Enescu travelled widely as violinist and conductor; time for composing had to be found between concert engagements, and he was a meticulous reviser of his drafts in manuscript. The first sketches of *Oedipe* were written in 1910–14, then lost during the war; a draft of the entire opera was written with great speed during July and August 1921; but it took Enescu another ten years to finish elaborating, revising and orchestrating the work. Though he contemplated another opera in the late 1920s (on the Romanian folk hero Meøterul Manole), *Oedipe* remained his only work in the genre.

Oedipe

Oedipus
Tragédie lyrique in four acts (3h)
Libretto by Edmond Fleg, after Sophocles
Composed 1921–31
PREMIERE   13 March 1936, Opéra, Paris
CAST   Oedipe (Oedipus) *b-bar*, Tirésias (Tiresias) *b*, Créon (Creon) *bar*, Jocaste (Jocasta) *ms*, Sphinx *c*, Antigone *s*, Laïos (Laius) *t*, *c*, *ms*, *bar*, 3 *b*; *satb* chorus of citizens of Thebes, revellers, Eumenides, Athenian elders; dancers

The Swiss Jewish author Edmond Fleg originally wrote a huge two-part libretto, for a diptych opera to be performed on two successive nights. Enescu persuaded him to condense it into a unitary work, which still told the full story of Oedipus' life.

SYNOPSIS

Act I presents the joyful baptism of Oedipus, interrupted by Tiresias' prophecy that he will kill his father (Laius) and marry his mother (Jocasta).

Act II shows Oedipus as a young man, first leaving Corinth (where he has been brought up as a foundling), then at a crossroads where he encounters Laius and kills him, and finally at Thebes, where he kills the Sphinx by answering its riddle and is given Jocasta's hand in marriage.

Act III corresponds to Sophocles' *Oedipus Tyrannus*. Oedipus discovers the truth about his past and blinds himself.

Act IV corresponds to Sophocles' *Oedipus at Colonus*. The old, exiled Oedipus is accompanied by his daughter Antigone; they take refuge in a sacred grove, where he argues defiantly in self-justification and is taken up by the gods.

Though presented (in Acts I, III and IV) as a succession of large-scale, dramatically rather static tableaux, *Oedipe* is musically unified and organic. Enescu uses several (at least 21) inter-related leitmotifs, constantly weaving them into a rich, polyphonic score which he himself once described as a 'symphony'.

N.M.

MANUEL DE FALLA

Manuel María de los Dolores de Falla y Matheu;
b 23 November 1876, Cadiz, Spain; *d* 14 November 1946,
Alta Gracia de Córdoba, Argentina

Falla was the outstanding Spanish composer of the 20th century. His music evolved from the easy outpourings of *La vida breve* to the burning economy of the Harpsichord Concerto (1926) and the pungent austerity of the large-scale 'scenic cantata' *Atlántida*. Meanwhile regionalism made way for a wider view, still intensely Spanish but of supra-national relevance. Falla was born and educated in Cadiz, where, apart from the vital background of Andalusian folksong, there was little but salon music and decent amateur endeavour. When his family moved in 1896 to Madrid, Falla entered the conservatory, completing the seven-year course in two years. The only outlet for an ambitious young composer was the theatre, where light opera in the form of zarzuelas held sway. Unwillingly Falla conformed, writing six zarzuelas, three of them in collaboration with Amadeo Vives. Only *Los amores de la Inés* was performed (1902). Of greater importance was the revelation of the music of Felipe Pedrell (1841–1922), persuaded by Falla to take him as a pupil. In 1904 Falla entered and won two competitions, one a piano contest, the other for one-act operas, for which he submitted *La vida breve*. The authorities' failure to implement the promised Madrid production of the winning piece caused Falla much frustration. His dream of going to Paris was not realized until 1907. Once there he met Dukas, Debussy, Ravel and other French musicians as well as his compatriot Isaac Albéniz. After a long wait *La vida breve* was performed in Nice, Paris and finally, after Falla had returned there in 1914 on the outbreak of war, in Madrid. He completed *Nights in the Gardens of Spain* for piano and orchestra and wrote the two ballets, *El amor brujo* and *The Three-Cornered Hat*.

After his parents' deaths in 1919 Falla moved to Granada, paradoxically ceasing to write overtly Andalusian music. His strange character intensified: he was a devout Catholic, superstitious, a conservative who abhorred violence and militarism. Since he had many friends of liberal tendencies, in the Civil War he suffered mental agony. His health deteriorated. When he left Spain for Argentina in 1939, *Atlántida*, a score

that had already occupied him for more than a decade, was unfinished. Still incomplete at his death, it was eventually realized and completed by Ernesto Halffter. In Granada Falla wrote some incidental music for two autos sacramentales, Calderón's *El gran teatro del mundo* and Lope de Vega's *La vuelta de Egipto*. Many operatic collaborations with friends, including the poet Lorca and the painter Ignacio Zuloaga, were discussed but not started. A curious project towards the end of his second Madrid period was a three-act comic opera *Fuego fatuo* (Will-o'-the-wisp) with a libretto by María Martinez Sierra and music adapted by Falla from Chopin's piano works. Only the outer acts of the three were finished before the scheme was abandoned. In 1976 Antoni Ros-Marbá made an orchestral suite out of the completed acts.

La vida breve

Life is Brief
Lyric drama in two acts (four tableaux) (1h 15m)
Libretto by Carlos Fernández Shaw
Composed 1904
PREMIERES 1 April 1913, Casino Municipal, Nice (in French); US: 6 March 1926, Metropolitan, New York; UK: 9 September 1958, Edinburgh
CAST Salud *s*, La Abuela (Grandmother) *ms* or *c*, Paco *t*, Uncle Sarvaor *bar* or *b*, Manuel *bar*, Carmela *ms*, Cantaor (Singer) *bar*, 3 Street Sellers 2 *s*, *ms*, 2 offstage voices 2 *t*; *satb* chorus of townsfolk (wedding guests)

Falla and the zarzuela writer Fernández Shaw had agreed to collaborate and had started work on their project when a one-act opera competition was announced by the Royal Academy of San Fernando in 1904. Even so, *La vida breve* had to be written quickly. The opera won the prize, but the Madrid production held out as an inducement did not materialize. When Falla showed the score to musicians in Paris they (Dukas especially) were favourably impressed, but not until 1913 was the opera accepted. By then Falla had for practical reasons divided the opera into two acts, touched up the orchestration, expanded the second scene and the second dance, and, on the advice of Debussy, shortened the ending. The success of the Nice premiere induced the Opéra-Comique to perform the work later that year; the further acclaim in Paris caused Madrid to open its doors at last. The success of the first performance in Spanish, on 14 November 1914 in Madrid, was triumphant.

SYNOPSIS

Act I Granada, at the turn of the century. Salud lives with her grandmother in the gypsy quarter above the town. She is anxiously awaiting Paco, a local playboy who has seduced her and promised marriage. The grandmother is reassuring but warns Salud against loving too much. Voices of workmen in a nearby forge are heard, lamenting the miserable poor, born to be anvils, not hammers. Salud enlarges on their words in an aria. Paco arrives, protesting love. Unnoticed by the couple, Sarvaor steals in and confirms to the grandmother the truth of a rumour about Paco's impending marriage to a well-off girl in the town. Paco and Salud arrange to meet next day. The following scene takes place in mime as night falls over Granada. Paco takes leave of Salud. The grandmother restrains Sarvaor from following him.

Act II Scene 1: The front of a house in the town. Night. Through the windows the patio can be seen, illuminated for the wedding of Paco to Carmela. A *cantaor* sings in their honour. During the following dance (familiar in transcriptions as 'Spanish Dance No. 1') Salud appears. She sings of her grief at Paco's betrayal and of her wish to die. Her grandmother and Sarvaor join her. Salud repeats the workmen's hammer-and-anvil comparison. Scene 2: Inside the patio Paco, Carmela and her brother Manuel (the host) are the centre of a throng of wedding guests. There is a second dance, with wordless chorus. Sarvaor appears leading Salud; she holds back, then suddenly denounces Paco. As she advances towards him she falls dead at his feet.

The libretto veers between passionate feelings violently expressed and another form of verismo – a detailed depiction of the sights and sounds of Granada, a remarkable case of empathy (reminiscent of Gustave Charpentier's depiction of Paris in *Louise*) since Falla had not visited the town when he wrote the opera. The music, written in haste when Falla was bursting with invention, is irresistible in spite of stylistic inconsistency. The depiction of Salud, the only character drawn in the round, is highly individual. There is a quality of youthful exuberance in the opera which Falla neither achieved nor sought again.

El retablo de Maese Pedro

Master Peter's Puppet Show
Musical and scenic version of an episode from *El ingenioso caballero Don Quixote de la Mancha* in one act (30m)
Libretto by the composer after Miguel de Cervantes Saavedra's *Don Quixote* (1605, 1615)
PREMIERES 23 March 1923, Teatro San Fernando, Seville (concert); 25 June 1923, Paris (private); UK: 13 October 1924, Victoria Rooms, Clifton, Bristol; US: 29 December 1925, New York
CAST Don Quixote *bar* or *b*, Maese Pedro *t*, El trujamán (The Boy) *boy s*, 5 mime roles, several puppets

In 1919 Princess Edmond de Polignac asked Falla to write a chamber opera for performance in her house in Paris. Falla, who had arranged the music for some private puppet shows in Granada devised by Federico García Lorca, suggested a puppet opera based on an episode in *Don Quixote*. The princess gave permission for a concert performance in Seville (conducted by Falla) a few months before the private Paris premiere. On the latter occasion Hector Dufranne sang Don Quixote, the conductor was Vladimir Golschmann, and Wanda Landowska played the harpsichord.

SYNOPSIS
On a trestle table in the yard of a Spanish inn the travelling showman Master Peter presents a puppet play. The boy, interrupted from time to time by pedantic objections from Don Quixote in the audience, intones the narration. The play is set in the time of Charlemagne. The emperor's daughter Melisendra is a captive of the Moors at Saragossa in Spain. The emperor rebukes her husband, Don Gayferos, for not going to her rescue. From her prison in a tower Melisendra scans the horizon. A Moor steals a kiss and is sentenced by the king, Marsilius, to punishment, which is duly effected. Gayferos sets out on horseback for Spain. The hills resound with horn- and trumpet-calls. Gayferos reaches Saragossa and reveals himself. Melisendra leaps from her tower into his arms. They ride off towards France. When Quixote sees Moors in pursuit of the Christian couple, he rises in fury. Believing the spectacle to be real, he wrecks the puppets with his sword before declaring himself 'knight errant and captive of the most fair Dulcinea' to whom he sings a prayer. Finally he addresses the public on the virtues of knight-errantry.

The opera can be performed by two sets of puppets (large ones for Quixote, Master Peter, his boy and the onlookers, small ones for the players) with the three singers in the orchestra, or by the singers and mimes for the 'real' characters and small puppets for the players. Another possibility is to use singers and mimes with children in the place of puppets – all masked.

El retablo, in every way a more sophisticated work than *La vida breve*, ranks with Stravinsky's *L'histoire du soldat* as a seminal piece of music-theatre. The spontaneity and wide range of expression conceal a carefully prepared synthesis of national, historical and popular elements. Typical are the writing for the boy, whose narrations, delivered in shrill monotone, were based on plainsong and street cries, and the way in which Falla lifts the final scene for Quixote on to a different plane. The scoring, for example in Gayferos's ride through the Pyrenees, shows Falla at his most masterly. So finely calculated are the proportions that the opera feels longer and bigger than it really is.

Other operatic works: *El conde de Villamediana* (lost, 1887); *Fuego fatuo* (Acts I and III; Act II, inc., 1919); *Atlántida* (inc., 1946), 1961
Zarzuelas: *Los amores de la Inés*, 1902; *Prisionero de guerra* (coll. with Amadeo Vives; inc., 1904); lost zarzuelas: *La Juana y la Petra*, or *La casa de Tócame Roque* (1902); *Limosna de amor*, (?1903); *El cornetín de órdenes* (with Amadeo Vives), (1903); *La cruz de Malta* (with Amadeo Vives), (?1903)

R.H.C.

GABRIEL FAURÉ
Gabriel-Urbain Fauré; *b* 12 May 1845, Pamiers, Ariège, France; *d* 4 November 1924, Paris

After a quiet, rather solitary early childhood, Fauré was sent to the École Niedermeyer in Paris at the age of nine. It was a school for budding organists and choirmasters whose founder hoped to propagate a respect for older church music, which he thought grievously neglected. Niedermeyer pupils were therefore instructed thoroughly in the ancient ecclesiastical modes (of which there are traces in Fauré's mature music), and discouraged from investigating modernists such as Schumann and Liszt. When Fauré was 16, however, a new piano teacher was appointed: Saint-Saëns, who introduced him to all that forbidden fruit, and also to the light, polished style of the latest French music. It is not hard to see how the features of the younger composer's style developed from that intensive tuition, at least so far as the songs and the piano and chamber music go. His operatic projects were more unexpected.

Admirers of his songs are often surprised to learn that Fauré wrote an opera at all. In fact he was seeking libretti as early as 1879, and got as far as writing a sextet for *Barnabé*, a one-act *opéra comique*; later he had hopes for a Pushkin project, *Mazeppa*. By the 1890s he was a familiar figure in the artistic salons of Paris, and the princesse de Scey-Montbéliard (later de Polignac) made plans for him: first an opera to be called *La tentation de Bouddha*, for which poor Albert Samain (whose poems Fauré often turned into songs) wrote 750 stanzas in vain, and then a collaboration with Paul Verlaine on *L'hôpital Watteau* – *commedia dell'arte* personages in a hospital ward – which came to nothing because the poet was already a ruined alcoholic. Much earlier, however, Fauré had composed a mythological scene for soloists, chorus and orchestra after Paul Collin, *La naissance de Vénus*, and between 1888 and 1919 he wrote several scores for the theatre: for the *Caligula* of Alexandre Dumas *père*, for a *Merchant of Venice* adaptation called *Shylock* (thriftily recycled later for *Jules César*), and for the London production of Maurice Maeterlinck's *Pelléas et Mélisande*. (The familiar suite from the latter misses out the song composed for Mrs Patrick Campbell's Mélisande; four years later came Debussy's opera.) The year after *Prométhée*, Fauré supplied musical chinoiserie for a mock-oriental morality play by Georges Clemenceau, *Le voile du bonheur*; finally, when he was nearly 75, he brought together one new piece and many old ones – two or three of them 40 years old – for a divertissement conceived by his *Pénélope* librettist, René Fauchois, *Masques et bergamasques*. With the exception of *Le voile du bonheur*, each of these scores included a voice or voices.

It is striking that, though several numbers from those modest theatrical commissions have become staples of the lighter repertoire, not a single extract from the ambitious *Prométhée* or *Pénélope* is familiar to the musical public. That is not evidence that Fauré was unsuccessful on a grander scale – *Prométhée* was designed for particularly lavish resources, and *Pé-*

nélope is too smoothly through-composed to permit excerpts. For deeper reasons, however, both works do stand apart from the rest of Fauré's *oeuvre*. They flank his crucial transition period, from late Romantic to post-Romantic. The outward marks of the change, as shown in his other music of those years, were laconic density and stripped-down textures – whereas the operatic projects required sonorous, rhetorical breadth. To secure that for *Prométhée*, he recalled the church style and the Wagnerian leanings of his earlier years; his *Pénélope*, on the other hand, is something like a magnified, more freely constructed version of a chamber score. Neither has any close parallel.

Just before Fauré began *Pénélope*, he had reviewed the Paris premiere of Richard Strauss's *Salome*; he admired many aspects of the score, but repined at 'so many cruel dissonances which defy all explanation'. Though his own harmonic excursions may strike orthodox Teutonic ears as wayward and elusive, Fauré was rigorously faithful to a Gallic ideal of 'logic' in harmony. No gratuitous surprises: every new chord had to stand in a rational relation to the last, however remote. In Fauré, the result demands more sophisticated attention than the Expressionist shocks in the music of his more famously 'radical' Austrian contemporaries.

Pénélope
Penelope
Drame lyrique in three acts (2h)
Libretto by René Fauchois, after Homer's *Odyssey*
Composed 1907–12
PREMIERES 4 March 1913, Salle Garnier, Monte Carlo; US: 29 November 1945, Cambridge, Massachusetts; UK: 20 November 1970, Royal Academy of Music, London
CAST Ulysse (Ulysses) *t*, Eumée (Eumaeus) *bar*, Antinoüs (Antinous) *t*, Eurymaque (Eurymachus) *bar*, Pénélope (Penelope) *s*, Euryclée (Euryclea) *ms*, Léodès (Laertes) *t*, Ctésippe (Ctesippos) *t* or *bar*, Pisandre (Peisander) *t* or *bar*, A Shepherd *t*, Cléone (Cleone) *ms*, Mélantho (Melantho) *s*, Lydie (Lydia) *s*, Eurynome *s* or *ms*, *ms*, *s*; *satb* chorus of servants and shepherds

Warmly acclaimed at its premiere and still admired by connoisseurs, *Pénélope* is very rarely performed. The libretto that Fauchois made for Fauré keeps the story simple: there are no gods in surveillance, and even Ulysses' son Telemachus is omitted from the action. Though Fauré allows some forceful effect to the climactic slaying of the suitors, the opera is no warrior epic, but at heart a celebration of bourgeois marriage rather as the song-cycle *La bonne chanson* was a celebration of bourgeois engagement – private hopes and doubts resolved at last in secure domestic happiness.

Fauré's own situation was more complicated than that: it is generally accepted that he had discreet arrangements with other ladies during much of his apparently decorous married life. Fauchois's surprising arrangement of his libretto, with a central act that contains no overt action but is given over to an anxious, questioning *rapprochement* between long-neglected wife and still-disguised husband, might have been cunningly devised to capture Fauré's interest –

the libretto was proposed and accepted at a dinner party, and he discovered only later that Fauchois had yet to write it. In any case, the combination of a drama of inner feelings with the composer's refined, temperately intense score seems to have discouraged opera producers; derring-do and mock-Wagner would have gone down better.

SYNOPSIS

Act I After a measured, thoughtful prelude (based on the themes of Penelope and Ulysses), Ulysses' palace on Ithaca is revealed in gloom. While Penelope's serving maids spin, they discuss her unhappy situation: after ten years her husband, Ulysses, has not returned from the Trojan War, and she is beset by rapacious young suitors, who are heard carousing in another room. The maids think her patient waiting has become pointless; by now, she should have settled for one of the suitors. The suitors enter, rudely calling for her and angering her nurse Euryclea. Penelope appears, reiterates her devotion to Ulysses, and reminds the suitors of her promise to choose one of them only when she has finished weaving a shroud for her father-in-law, Laertes. They are dismayed to see how much weaving is still to be done; she has a dance staged to mollify them and meanwhile yearns after her husband ('Ulysse! fier époux!'). He arrives, in the guise of a humble beggar. The suitors abuse him and return to their feast; Penelope welcomes him kindly – for a moment she thinks she recognizes him, but decides not. Euryclea does, but Ulysses enjoins her to silence before going off with her to be fed. Penelope begins to unpick her day's weaving, as she always does; the suitors catch her in the deception, and declare that her choice can be postponed no longer. She and Euryclea prepare to keep their nightly watch for Ulysses' ship. The 'beggar' agrees to join them, and while they fetch a cloak for him he exults in his wife's fidelity.

Act II On a hilltop the old shepherd Eumaeus muses, and greets passing friends. Arriving with Euryclea and Ulysses for their vigil, Penelope recalls how she used to come here with her husband; aside, Euryclea promises to help him rout the suitors. Penelope interrogates the 'beggar', who claims ('O mon hôte, à présent') to be an unlucky Cretan king who recently harboured the storm-tossed Ulysses for 12 days, and assures her that Ulysses is on his way. The wife is overjoyed, and the husband deeply moved. Before the women go home to prepare for the suitors tomorrow, the 'beggar' asks Penelope whether any of them has shown himself worthy of her by managing to draw Ulysses' great bow, and she takes the hint. After they depart he reveals himself to the shepherds, who hail him and swear to assist him.

Act III A surging, angry prelude takes us to the royal hall as day breaks. Alone, Ulysses has prowled the palace all night, and now conceals the sword of Hercules beneath the throne in readiness. Euryclea tells him that Penelope has been sleepless and despairing, and Eumaeus reports that the suitors have ordered up a wedding banquet, which means that the shepherds will be on hand – with their knives. The suitors assemble, Antinous singing the delights of youth and Eurymachus fretting over an ill omen (a crow seen on

his left). There are dances, with flutes. Penelope proclaims that her choice will be fixed by an archery contest with the great bow. As storm clouds gather she describes a foreboding vision, and the jeering suitors become anxious. Servants set up the dozen axes through which the winning arrow must be shot. Not one of the suitors can draw the bow; the 'beggar' steps forward, passes the test and then shoots Eurymachus dead. The shepherds rush forward to assist in the slaughter of all the other suitors. Ulysses and Penelope rejoice in their reunion, and everybody praises Zeus.

Where Fauré had managed to compose his previous opera, Prométhée, in less than six months, Pénélope took him about five years, for in 1905 he had become director of the Paris Conservatoire. Again he adapted the leitmotif method to fix various aspects of the leading roles, as well as the sword, the bow, the shroud. He took great pains to get them right, for each had to be imbued with potent character; there is little room in this score for the picturesque. There is far less 'symphonic' development than in Wagner (once the prelude to Act I is past), but not much straight recitative either, nor any number arias. Only the opening spinning chorus, the little dances and the final eulogy to Zeus are anything like formal set pieces. The vocal writing is eloquent (the principal couple need fairly heroic voices), and all the music follows the sense of the action closely and flexibly. As usual in Fauré's later work, the harmony tends to be 'elliptic': when the music slips into remote tonal areas, as it often does, the intervening steps are implied rather than spelled out. Tonality is stretched hard, without breaking. The conservative Saint-Saëns, who greatly preferred Prométhée, was puzzled and disappointed by Fauré's new style; but modern listeners who have learned to appreciate his later non-operatic music will find no difficulty here.

Other opera: Prométhée, 1900

D.M.

FRIEDRICH VON FLOTOW

Friedrich Adolf Ferdinand (Freiherr von) Flotow; *b* 27 April 1812, Teutendorf, Mecklenburg, Germany; *d* 24 January 1883, Darmstadt, Germany

Remembered today for just two works, *Martha* and *Alessandro Stradella*, Flotow produced a string of Romantic operas in the mid 19th century which, with varying success, combined elements of French opéra comique with the sentimentality and sonorities of German Romanticism and an Italianate melodic style. Born of aristocratic stock, he was originally destined for a diplomatic career. When his musical gifts were recognized, however, he was allowed to study music, and from 1828 to 1830 attended the Paris Conservatoire, where he studied composition with Anton Reicha. In the French capital he experienced at first hand the works of Adam, Donizetti, Halévy, Meyerbeer and Rossini. Among the most important influences were the opéras comiques of Auber, and he later made the acquaintance of Gounod and Offenbach. Work on his first opera was interrupted by the revolution of 1830, and he completed it in Germany. Other early works included a symphony (now lost) and two piano concertos.

Returning to Paris, he wrote a number of operas for private performance before collaboration with the Belgian composer Albert Grisar brought him to prominence. With another collaborator, Auguste Pilati, he wrote *Le naufrage de la Méduse* (1839). When the score was destroyed by fire before a performance in Hamburg, Flotow rewrote the work to a German libretto by 'W. Friedrich' (Friedrich Wilhelm Riese). This was eventually performed in 1845, a year after the composer and librettist won critical acclaim with *Alessandro Stradella*. To this triumph they added *Martha*, performed in Vienna in 1847, which quickly became Flotow's most popular work.

Flotow's later operas failed to live up to these two successes, but he continued to produce work at a prolific rate. In 1852 he wrote the comic opera *Rübezahl* to a text by his friend Gustav Heinrich Gans zu Putlitz, who also provided the libretto for *Indra* (1852), a successful reworking of the earlier *L'esclave de Camoëns*. From 1855 to 1863 Flotow was intendant of the grand-ducal court theatre in Schwerin, for which he wrote *Herzog Johann Albrecht von Mecklenburg*. It was Paris, however, that witnessed three late successes, *Zilda* (1866), *L'ombre* (1870) and, above all, *La veuve Grapin* (1859), a delightful one-act operetta in the mould of Pergolesi's *La serva padrona*. In 1868 Flotow divorced his second wife Anna Theen and married her younger sister, Rose, moving first to Lower Austria, then to Teutendorf (where he wrote his last opera) and finally, in 1880, settling in Darmstadt.

Flotow's output included works in a variety of genres, but was dominated by his operas, of which *Alessandro Stradella* and *Martha* have long eclipsed the others. His music made no pretensions to profundity, and his achievement was to combine various national traditions in a natural, unforced and charming style that pandered unashamedly to popular taste. As such he may be seen as the bridge between opéra comique and the comic operas of later composers such as Sullivan.

Martha, oder Der Markt zu Richmond
Martha, or Richmond Market

Romantic–comic opera in four acts (2h)
Libretto by 'W. Friedrich' (Friedrich Wilhelm Riese), partly after a scenario by Jules-Henri Vernoy de Saint-Georges
PREMIERES 25 November 1847, Kärntnertortheater, Vienna; UK: 4 July 1849, Drury Lane, London; US: 1 November 1852, Niblo's Garden, New York
CAST Lady Harriet Durham *s*, Nancy *ms*, Lord Tristan Mickleford *b*, Plumkett *b*, Lyonel *t*, 3 *s*, *c*, *t*, 4 *b*, silent role; *satb* chorus of maids, servants, huntresses in the queen's retinue, tenants, farmers; silent: pages

Martha had its roots in an earlier project to which Flotow had contributed, Mazilier's ballet-pantomime *Lady Harriette, ou La servante de Greenwich* (1844),

to a scenario by Saint-Georges. Flotow had written Act I (Acts II and III were by Johann Friedrich Burgmüller and Édouard Marie Ernest Deldevez). Much of the music for Act I of *Martha* was taken from the earlier ballet, with Riese providing the text. One of the most celebrated numbers, Lyonel's Act II aria 'Ach so fromm', was actually taken over from Flotow's previous opera *L'âme en peine* (1846).

SYNOPSIS
Act I The setting is England during the reign of Queen Anne, *c.* 1710. Lady Harriet, maid of honour to the queen, is bored with court life and longs to escape from the advances of her elderly foppish cousin Lord Tristan. Her maid, Nancy, vainly suggests diversions until, together with the reluctant Tristan, they decide to join girls on their way to the Richmond hiring fair. There, under the names of Martha and Julia, they are hired by two young farmers, Plumkett and his foster-brother Lyonel.

Act II 'Martha' and 'Julia' find it difficult to adapt to life as working girls. They are rescued by Tristan, but not before Lyonel and Plumkett have fallen in love with them.

Act III On a hunting party with the queen, Lady Harriet and Julia are recognized by their 'employers', but Harriet feigns ignorance.

Act IV Lyonel, it emerges, is the son of the wrongly banished late earl of Derby: now it is his turn to snub Lady Harriet. In order to win him back, Plumkett and Nancy set up another fair in front of the farmhouse, and there, seeing his 'Martha' again, Lyonel takes her into his arms.

Riese's libretto gave Flotow plenty of scope for what he excelled at: lively choruses, enchanting solos and ensembles. With no dialogue to interrupt the flow, the music is one glorious set piece after another. Two favourites quickly established themselves: 'Letzte Rose', sung originally by 'Martha' at the fair, is a version of the Irish melody 'The Grove of Blarney', better known as Thomas Moore's 'The Last Rose of Summer'. The other is Lyonel's 'Ach so fromm', which became hugely popular in its Italian version as 'M'appari'. But there is much more to enjoy, such as the Act II 'spinning' quartet and 'Gute Nacht' quartet, and Plumkett's Act III aria in praise of 'Porterbier'. It is not difficult to account for *Martha*'s astonishing popularity (it was given by Liszt in Weimar in 1848, and was the subject of a number of parodies): the characters are well drawn and Flotow wastes no opportunity to repeat catchy tunes until the audience cannot avoid humming them. He also succeeds in keeping the action moving, thus balancing sentimentality with exuberance. *Martha* may not be great music, but it deserves more attention than it has latterly received in English-speaking countries – not least for its amusing impressions of 'Englishness'.

Other operas: *Pierre et Catherine*, 1835 (in German); *Die Bergknappen*, n.d.; *Alfred der Grosse*, n.d.; *Rob-Roy*, 1836; *Sérafine*, 1836; *Alice*, 1837; *La lettre du préfet*, 1837; *Le comte de Saint-Mégrin*, 1838, rev. as *Le duc de Guise*, 1840; *Lady Melvil* (coll. with Albert Grisar), 1838, rev. as

Le joaillier de Saint-James, 1862; *L'eau merveilleuse* (coll. with Albert Grisar), 1839; *Le naufrage de la Méduse* (Act I by Auguste Pilati, Acts II and III by Flotow), 1839, rewritten as *Die Matrosen,* 1845; *L'esclave de Camoëns,* 1843, rev. as *Indra,* 1852, as *Alma l'incantatrice,* 1878; *Alessandro Stradella,* 1844; *L'âme en peine,* 1846; *Sophie Katharina, oder Die Grossfürstin,* 1850; *Rübezahl,* 1852; *Albin, oder Der Pflegesohn,* 1856, rev. as *Der Müller von Meran,* 1859; *Herzog Johann Albrecht von Mecklenburg, oder Andreas Mylius,* 1857; *Pianella,* 1857; *La veuve Grapin,* 1859; *La châtelaine (Der Märchensucher),* 1865; *Naida (Le vannier),* 1865; *Zilda, ou La nuit des dupes,* 1866; *Am Runenstein,* 1868; *Die Musikanten (La jeunesse de Mozart),* (?1869), 1887; *L'ombre,* 1870; *La fleur de Harlem,* (unperf.); *Rosellana,* 1876; *Sakuntala* (inc.)

M.A.

CARLISLE FLOYD

Carlisle Sessions Floyd Jnr; *b* 11 June 1926, Latta, South Carolina, US

Floyd's opera *Susannah* was a major success when it was staged in New York in 1956. It made him the most highly praised American opera composer of his generation, and the work entered the standard repertoire with astonishing speed.

His early training was in piano as well as composition. Floyd's first opera, the one-act *Slow Dusk,* was to his own libretto – a practice he continued to follow – and was produced at Syracuse University, where Floyd was a student. His second opera was withdrawn after a single performance at Florida State University, but three years later, at the same venue, *Susannah* was launched on its spectacular career.

After this success, Floyd went on to compose *Wuthering Heights* on a commission from Santa Fe Opera. In its original form it was criticized for its cliché-ridden libretto and for the uneven quality of the music. Floyd made some major revisions and this version was more favourably received. One critic found it 'a profound emotional experience . . . one that leaves both performers and audience shaken with the elemental power of the Brontë story'.

Susannah has remained the most frequently performed of Floyd's operas, though *Of Mice and Men,* based on John Steinbeck's novel, has also had numerous productions in the US and in Europe. For the American Bicentennial in 1976 Floyd wrote *Bilby's Doll,* based on Esther Forbes's novel *A Mirror for Witches,* which deals, as does Arthur Miller's play *The Crucible* (and Robert Ward's opera based on it), with the 17th-century witchcraft trials in Massachusetts, a subject Floyd had been considering since the

McCarthy era in the 1950s. He said, 'I believe my opera has a comment to make on our national character and destiny.' He added that the score broke new ground for him in its Romantic lyricism and its use of orchestral colour. The length of the work, however, causes such exuberance to become repetitive and it has not entered the repertoire.

Susannah

A musical drama in two acts (1h 30m)
Libretto by the composer
PREMIERES 24 February 1955, Florida State University, Tallahassee; UK: 27 July 1961, Orpington Civic Hall, Kent

The production of *Susannah* by the New York Opera Company, on 27 September 1956, conducted by Erich Leinsdorf, made history. The opera was given a New York Music Critics' Circle Award after journalists had reached for superlatives. Winthrop Sargeant regarded *Susannah* as 'probably the most moving and impressive opera to have been written in America – or anywhere else, as far as I am aware – since Gershwin's *Porgy and Bess*'.

The story of *Susannah* is based on that in the Apocrypha (on which Handel based his oratorio *Susanna*) but the action is transferred to a modern-day Tennessee mountain valley and the work ends unhappily. Susannah is caught bathing in a creek used for baptisms and is denounced by the elders of the church, who denounce her as being 'of the devil'. At a public revivalist meeting conducted by the Reverend Blitch she is urged to confess and repent. She refuses. Blitch, believing the lies about her, follows her home and attempts to seduce her; in doing so he discovers her innocence. He tries to tell the elders, without incriminating himself, but they are not convinced. Susannah's brother, Sam, finds out what Blitch has done and shoots him at the baptismal creek. The people threaten Susannah and urge her to leave. The experience leaves her embittered and alone.

Much of the force of the opera derives from Floyd's word-setting – a flexible parlando style where pitch and rhythm follow the natural inflexions of speech. Alongside this he presents fully-fledged, lyrical Puccinian arias and – to maintain the American flavour – folk-type tunes, hymns and square-dance melodies.

Other operatic works: *Slow Dusk,* 1949; *The Fugitives,* 1951; *Wuthering Heights,* 1958; *The Passion of Jonathan Wade,* 1962, rev. 1989; *The Sojourner and Mollie Sinclair,* 1963; *Markheim,* 1966; *Of Mice and Men,* 1970; *Bilby's Doll,* 1976; *Willie Stark,* 1981

P.D.

JOHN GAY

b 30 June 1685, Barnstaple, Devon, England;
d 4 December 1732, London

John Gay is unique among the figures treated in this book in that he is not known to have composed a bar of music in his life; but he invented opera's most significant mutant form. Ballad opera, of which Gay's *The Beggar's Opera* is the first and the best, led to German singspiel, French opéra bouffon and the Anglo-American musical. His musical attainments did not extend beyond recorder-playing, but this gave him access to the innumerable songbooks of the day which provided transpositions of the tunes within the compass of that instrument. He went to London as apprentice to a silk mercer; a small legacy enabled him to break the indenture and, in 1708, to embark on a literary career. He became a lifelong friend of Alexander Pope.

From the start Gay's work exploited a deliberate incongruity of form and content; a mordant sense of social reality was given point by being expressed in an effortlessly decorous literary attire. He wrote the libretto for Handel's *Acis and Galatea* (1718), which is notable for its firm and economical construction and for the reanimation of stock material by dint of drastic pruning. At about this time Gay started to explore the possibilities of the broadside ballad: 'Sweet William's Farewell to Black-ey'd Susan' (1720) rapidly acquired tunes by four rival composers. The idea of a 'Newgate Pastoral' had been mooted by Dean Swift, in a letter to Pope, as early as 1715. In 1724 Newgate became especially topical: the highwayman Jack Sheppard was finally captured and hanged, and the informer and receiver Jonathan Wild was knifed in court by one of his victims. Gay celebrated this in 'Newgate's Garland', a ballad to be sung to the tune of 'Packington's Pound', which prefigures the method, setting and substance of *The Beggar's Opera*. But whereas 'Newgate's Garland' is a single song, *The Beggar's Opera* is a three-act drama with spoken dialogue and 69 airs all to existing tunes: English, Irish and Scots traditional melodies, and popular songs by recent composers including Purcell, Handel, Henry Carey and Giovanni Bononcini.

In a sequel, *Polly*, Macheath is transported to the West Indies, marries Jenny Diver, and, disguised as a Negro, turns pirate. He has been followed to the Caribbean by Polly, who, disguised as a man, becomes an honorary member of an Indian tribe which captures him. It is amusing but bland, and Gay seems to have used up his stock of catchy and pointed tunes. It was banned by the lord chamberlain and sold well in consequence; when it was eventually produced it flopped, as did a posthumous ballad opera on a classical theme, *Achilles*.

The Beggar's Opera

Ballad opera in three acts (original version: 3h)
Libretto by John Gay
PREMIERES 29 January 1728, Lincoln's Inn Fields, London; 1733, Jamaica; US: 3 December 1750, New York; UK: Austin arrangement: 5 June 1920, Lyric Theatre, Hammersmith, London; Britten arrangement: 24 May 1948, Cambridge
CAST Peacham *b*, Lockit *b*, Macheath *t*, Filch *t*, Mrs Peacham *ms*, Polly Peacham *s*, Lucy Lockit *s*, Diana Trapes *s, spoken roles*: Beggar, Player; *sa* chorus of women of the town; *tb* chorus of Macheath's gang

There was nothing new about plays with an extensive musical component nor in writing fresh words to existing tunes; Gay's originality lay in seeing how the principle could be extended, making song the predominant element, advancing the action rather than serving merely as its reflection. *The Beggar's Opera* was an immediate success, running for 32 nights consecutively, and 62 in the season altogether. Though there are some contemporary allusions (Lockit as Walpole, the prime minister; Polly and Lucy as Faustina and Cuzzoni, the rival prima donnas from the Italian Opera), Gay did not attempt to make them run consistently through the piece. The satire is general: what distinguishes a military hero from a highwayman in uniform, a woman who marries for money from a prostitute, a politician from a venal gaoler, an operatic aria from a good vernacular song? Many of the original words to the tunes would have been familiar to the audience, and the subversion of the sentiments these express is also part of Gay's design.

It has been claimed, improbably, that Gay originally intended the airs to be unaccompanied. In the event Dr John Christopher Pepusch, harpsichordist at Lincoln's Inn Fields, provided basses for the songs and a lively overture, which has for its allegro an anticipation of Lucy's 'I'm like a ship on the ocean tossed'. The songs would probably have been introduced by the orchestra and doubled as appropriate. Charles

Burney, no great admirer of Pepusch, thought his basses 'so excellent that no sound contrapuntist will ever attempt to alter them'. Nevertheless, in almost every subsquent generation some such effort has been made. Notable 20th-century versions have been those of Frederick Austin (1920, with text edited by Arnold Bennett, décor by Lovat Fraser, and a brilliant production by Nigel Playfair), and Benjamin Britten (1948). It also inspired the completely rewritten Brecht–Weill collaboration *Die Dreigroschenoper* (Berlin, 1928). Weill and Britten radically miscomprehended Gay's intentions by giving acerbic accompaniments to pretty tunes and thus upsetting the whole ironic balance of words and music in the original. Richard Bonynge and Douglas Gamley, in their 1980 travesty, went to the other extreme by sanitizing the text and tinsellizing the music. Austin did not make either mistake. Jeremy Barlow, in 1980, was the first person to attempt a scholarly historical reconstruction.

SYNOPSIS

In a spoken introduction the beggar apologizes for failing to make his opera 'throughout, unnatural, like those in vogue; for I have no Recitative'; otherwise it 'must be allowed an Opera in all its Forms'.

Overture.

Act I takes place in the house of Peachum, an informer and receiver of stolen goods. He is anxious to arrange 'a decent Execution against next sessions', and has his eye on Robin of Bagshot, who proves to be a favourite of his wife's. Mrs Peachum voices her suspicion that their daughter, Polly, is involved with the handsome, free-handed highwayman, Captain Macheath. Taxed with this, Polly confesses her love and her desire to preserve her honour: 'Virgins are like the fair Flower in its Lustre'. Meanwhile Mrs Peachum has discovered the awful truth: Polly has actually married Macheath and, worse, still loves him. Her parents attempt to make Polly see sense, impeach Macheath and have him hanged. She demurs: 'For on the Rope that hangs my Dear/Depends poor Polly's life'. Macheath opportunely calls, and Polly persuades him he must flee.

Act II commences in a tavern near Newgate. Macheath's gang lay their plans and set out singing 'Let us take the Road' to the march from Handel's *Rinaldo*. Macheath, insatiate for women, summons the ladies of the town. Two favourites, while fondling him, take his pistols and signal for Peachum and the constables to enter and seize him. Macheath is removed to Newgate and the custody of Mr Lockit. He is then confronted by Lucy, Lockit's daughter, whom he has seduced and abandoned. Trapped, he agrees to marry her and they go in search of the chaplain. Peachum and Lockit come to blows over the division of the reward for Macheath's capture, but eventually compose their differences, recognizing their 'Mutual Interest'. Lucy and Macheath return, only to encounter a distracted Polly, resolved to stay with her husband 'till Death'. The quarrel between the girls reaches its climax in 'Why how now, Madam Flirt'; finally Peachum has to tear his daughter away, which gives Macheath the chance to persuade Lucy to help him escape.

Act III begins in Newgate. Lockit berates Lucy for her folly and goes to find Peachum. Macheath meets his gang in a gaming house and is recognized by Diana Trapes, who informs Peachum. In Newgate, Lucy, torn by 'Jealousy, Rage, Love and Fear' tries to poison Polly, but when Macheath is brought in, recaptured, Polly drops the laced cordial. Lockit and Peachum hurry him to the Old Bailey. The final scene takes place in the condemned cell, where Macheath laments his fate: 'O cruel, cruel, cruel Case/Must I suffer this disgrace?'. Other wives arrive: 'Four Women more, Captain, with a Child apiece'. 'This is too much,' says Macheath, and the player agrees, imploring the beggar to make the piece end as an opera should, happily. The beggar agrees, a reprieve is granted, and Macheath and Polly lead off the concluding chorus and dance.

Other works: *Polly*, (1728), 1779; *Achilles*, 1733

R.L.

GEORGE GERSHWIN

Jacob Gershvin; *b* 26 September 1898, Brooklyn, New York; *d* 11 July 1937, Hollywood, California

Piano and theory studies at an early age led George Gershwin to work as a pianist at the age of 15. His compositional studies remained haphazard and short-lived throughout his life (his longest period of study with a single teacher was his work with Joseph Schillinger from 1932 to 1936). From working as a song-plugger for a publishing house, he quickly moved to composing songs of his own and getting them interpolated into musicals written by others. He soon had the opportunity to supply whole scores for revues, and for George White's *Scandals of 1922* he provided a 20-minute 'jazz opera', *Blue Monday*.

Gershwin continued to challenge himself by writing instrumental music, and established himself as a leading composer of musicals for the most popular performers of his day; from 1924 onwards he almost always wrote to lyrics by his older brother, Ira. His writing for Gertrude Lawrence and the Astaires conformed to the standard structure of musicals of the period, rarely going beyond the 32-bar form. Noteworthy, however, are his harmonic deftness (often evident at the return to the original theme) and the exceptional care he devoted to verses.

His first venture beyond Broadway conventions, *Strike Up the Band* (1927), was initially a failure, but it was successfully revived three years later, and was followed by two other ventures in similar vein (*Of Thee I Sing* and *Let 'Em Eat Cake*). The libretti satirize (in a broadly entertaining way) certain aspects of American life; Gershwin made the most of this by creating scores with links to the quick-witted style of operetta created by Gilbert and Sullivan, as opposed to the more sentimental Viennese-derived strain that had flourished on Broadway. These operettas, though intended for show, rather than operatic, voices, indulged in such luxuries as passages of recitative and ensemble finales that did not reprise the songs (Leonard Bernstein, in *The Joy of Music*, pointed out the parallels between the Act I finales of *The Mikado* and *Of Thee I Sing*), and a greater variety of musical idioms. The use of marches, waltzes, patter, and other styles meant that these musicals contained fewer hits than Gershwin's more conventional efforts. But they constituted more satisfying overall entities, extending to greater care in the construction of overtures.

Other commercial Broadway enterprises were not totally abandoned during this period: *Girl Crazy* launched an extraordinary number of hit songs. But the real culmination of Gershwin's work for the musical stage was his opera *Porgy and Bess*. In some technical respects it reveals (as had his concert and stage work since 1932) the skills he had learned from Schillinger in terms of handling thematic development, transition, and transformation in an efficient way. From another vantage point it reveals Gershwin reconciling his more ambitious theatrical forms with the abundance of memorable melodies that had characterized his earlier shows: few operas or musicals contain as many famous and unforgettable excerpts as *Porgy*. As he had also achieved success in the film musical during the 1930s, future possibilities seemed limitless for Gershwin, but his life ended tragically early when he died of a brain tumour in 1937.

Gershwin's music retains an indelible place in modern culture. He created songs unsurpassed in the fertility of their melodic invention, the variety of their structures, and the perfection of their craftsmanship. Most of his stage musicals, observing the stage conventions of their time and devised in part as vehicles for distinctive performers, have not borne revival in recent times without extensive alteration – despite the enormous appeal of their music. Perhaps the recent interest in historical performance styles may lead to a revival of Gershwin's musicals on their own terms. Purely on musical grounds, there should always be occasional attempts to bring his earlier shows back to the stage; *Strike Up the Band*, with its merry treatment of an anti-war theme, might well merit first attention. Whether such revivals happen or not, *Porgy and Bess* has secured Gershwin his place as a stage composer of consequence.

Porgy and Bess

Opera in three acts (3h)
Libretto by DuBose Heyward, based on the play *Porgy* by Dorothy and DuBose Heyward (1925); lyrics by DuBose Heyward and Ira Gershwin
PREMIERES 10 October 1935, Alvin Theater, New York; UK: 9 October 1952, Stoll Theatre, London
CAST Porgy *b-bar*, Bess *s*, Crown *bar*, Serena *s*, Clara *s*, Maria *c*, Jake *bar*, Sporting Life *t*, Mingo *t*, Robbins *t*, Peter *t*, Frazier *bar*, Annie *ms*, Lily *ms*, Strawberry Woman *ms*, Jim *bar*, Undertaker *bar*, Nelson *t*, Crab Man *t*; *spoken roles*: Mr Archdale, Detective, Policeman, Coroner, Scipio (boy); Jasbo Brown *pianist*; *satb* chorus of residents of Catfish Row

Having wanted to base an opera on DuBose Heyward's novel *Porgy* since reading it in 1926, Gershwin

had to wait while it enjoyed success as a play. In 1933 a contract was signed and the two men began their collaboration, mostly by correspondence, with Ira brought in later to help with some individual lyrics. During the composition of the score, Gershwin travelled to South Carolina to absorb the milieu at first hand; once back in New York, he tried out passages of the score with cast members as he selected them. The title roles were created by Todd Duncan, a baritone not previously associated with the popular idiom, and Anne Brown, a young Juilliard student; John W. Bubbles, a vaudeville star, played Sporting Life. A private concert performance in Carnegie Hall was followed by a try-out run in Boston during which cuts and alterations were made. The New York production's run was 124 performances – short by Broadway standards, but quite extraordinary for an opera, old or new. Reviews from both music and drama critics expressed mostly condescension, and the general perception was that *Porgy* failed as opera, however appealing its popular excerpts.

As the score had been printed before Gershwin's rehearsals began, it contains music that he cut before the New York opening, but *Porgy*'s operatic identity remained unmistakable. Revivals after Gershwin's death established *Porgy* as a success – and also inaugurated a history of textual meddling. But, now that the stature and quality of *Porgy and Bess* are proven, it should become possible to consider whether some of Gershwin's own cuts might not be considered improvements after all.

SYNOPSIS
The action takes place in the early 20th century, in Charleston, South Carolina. The principal location is the waterfront courtyard called Catfish Row, formerly an elegant mansion, now a Negro tenement.

Act I Scene 1: The sounds of a honky-tonk piano ('Jasbo Brown Blues'), the young mother Clara's lullaby ('Summertime') and a crap game permeate Saturday night in Catfish Row. Clara's husband, Jake, a fisherman, jokingly quiets their baby ('A Woman is a Sometime Thing'), and all greet the crippled beggar Porgy as he arrives in his goat-cart. The mean-tempered stevedore Crown arrives with his woman, Bess, and joins the game. It develops into a fight in which Crown kills Robbins and flees, leaving Bess to fend for herself. Porgy takes her in. Scene 2: All the Catfish Row residents (now including a subdued Bess) come to Robbins's room to mourn with his widow Serena ('Gone, Gone, Gone') and contribute money for the burial ('Overflow'). A policeman investigating Robbins's death takes Peter, a honey salesman, into custody for questioning. Serena mourns her loss ('My Man's Gone Now'), and Bess leads the group in a triumphant spiritual ('Leavin' for the Promised Land').

Act II Scene 1: Several weeks later, Jake and the other fishermen work on their nets ('It Take a Long Pull To Get There'). Bess's love has brought happiness to Porgy's life for the first time ('I Got Plenty o' Nuttin''). Events of the morning include Sporting Life's attempts to peddle 'happy dust' (frustrated by the shopkeeper Maria), the fraudulent lawyer Frazier's offer to divorce Bess from Crown ('Woman to Lady'), and the visit of a sympathetic white man, Mr Archdale, who promises to get Peter out of gaol ('Buzzard Song'). All are preparing for the church picnic, but Bess is content to stay behind with Porgy ('Bess, You is My Woman'). As the picnic parade forms ('Oh, I Can't Sit Down'), Porgy and Maria persuade her to go and enjoy herself. Scene 2: At the picnic on Kittiwah Island ('I Ain't Got No Shame'), Sporting Life presents his cynical philosophy ('It Ain't Necessarily So'). Bess misses the boat back, detained by Crown. He has been hiding on the island and tries to persuade Bess to come back to him. She refuses ('What You Want wid Bess?'), but ultimately is helpless against his insistence. Scene 3: Jake and his men leave for an extended fishing trip. Bess is heard calling out in the delirium in which she has remained for the week since she was found on the island. Peter returns from gaol, and he, Serena, Lily (Peter's wife) and Porgy pray for Bess's recovery ('Oh, Doctor Jesus'). Time passes as the cries of strawberry-, honey- and crab-sellers are heard, and Bess awakes, restored to health. She tells Porgy she wants to stay with him, not Crown, and he assures her that she need fear Crown no longer ('I Loves You, Porgy'). A terrible storm rises. Scene 4: In Clara's room, all are gathered to pray for safety from the hurricane ('Oh, de Lawd Shake de Heavens'). Even Crown shows up, shocking everyone with his irreverence ('A Red-Headed Woman'). When Jake's empty boat is seen outside and Clara runs out to find him, Crown is the only one who will go after her. The others resume their prayers.

Act III   Scene 1: Back in the courtyard, the prayers of everyone for Clara, Jake and Crown are heard as night falls ('Clara, Clara'). Bess is now caring for Clara's baby. Crown crawls back to claim Bess, but in the ensuing fight Porgy manages to kill him. Scene 2: Policemen investigating Crown's death get no help from anyone, and finally take Porgy with them to identify the body. Sporting Life plays on Bess's fear that she is left alone, offering to take her with him to a new life up North ('There's a Boat Dat's Leavin' Soon for New York'). She resists, but finally takes the dope he offers and gives in. Scene 3: Porgy returns, triumphant after his release from gaol. When Bess fails to appear, he becomes desperate ('Oh Bess, Oh Where's My Bess'). The others finally tell him that she has gone to New York with Sporting Life; he resolves to follow her there and get her back. As the curtain falls, he starts on his journey ('Oh, Lawd, I'm on My Way').

With this score, Gershwin proved that the gifts he possessed – a gift for capturing emotion musically, theatrical skill, and the ability to accommodate and accentuate the skills of his chosen performers (in his first try at writing for classically trained voices, he succeeded masterfully) – count for far more in operatic composition than some of the academic techniques he lacked. His song-writing genius had not deserted him, of course; Porgy contains one hit after another. But each is precisely suited to its place in the drama, and hardly any observe the standard 32-bar form. If some of the connecting material sounds more dutiful than inspired, much of it fulfils its purpose effectively;

different textures and rhythms are tellingly contrasted, and a few significant motifs recur effectively at key points (Porgy, Crown, Sporting Life, and the 'happy dust' are among the motivically defined elements). Larger musical recurrences play a role too: Porgy's solos in the first scene contain seeds of music to come in Act II (harmony for 'I Got Plenty o' Nuttin'', a melody for 'Bess, You is My Woman'), and a jazzy strain associated with Catfish Row's social life is turned into a gentle barcarolle for the fishermen's fateful departure. As representative examples of resourcefulness in making the most of the libretto's potential, one might mention the powerful succession of recitative, arioso and duet that comprises the scene between Bess and Crown (written by Heyward as a simple prose dialogue), the six simultaneous unmeasured prayers of the hurricane scene and the rhythmic and vocal contrasts that shape 'My Man's Gone Now'. Indeed, the entire scene containing this impassioned solo shows Gershwin's genius at achieving overall unity through variety: linked choral passages, expressive recitative, one section of spoken dialogue, and two arias (with chorus) combine to create a uniquely varied picture of grief. Even with its minor imperfections and infelicities acknowledged, Porgy stands as the most vital and completely successful of American operas. One of the great might-have-beens of 20th-century music is the thought of the scores Gershwin could have gone on to write if he had lived beyond the age of 38.

Other opera: *Blue Monday*, 1922, as *135th St*, 1925; Musicals: *La-La-Lucille!*, 1919; *A Dangerous Maid*, 1921; *Our Nell* (coll. with William Daly), 1922; *Sweet Little Devil*, 1924; *Primrose*, 1924; *Lady, Be Good*, 1924; *Tell Me More*, 1925; *Tip-Toes*, 1925; *Song of the Flame* (coll. with Herbert Stothart), 1925; *Oh, Kay*, 1926; *Strike Up the Band*, 1927; *Funny Face*, 1927; *Rosalie* (coll. with Sigmund Romberg), 1928; *Treasure Girl*, 1928; *Show Girl*, 1929; *Girl Crazy*, 1930; *Of Thee I Sing*, 1931; *Pardon My English*, 1933; *Let 'Em Eat Cake*, 1933

J.A.C.

UMBERTO GIORDANO
b 28 August 1867, Foggia, Italy; *d* 12 November 1948, Milan

Giordano studied at the Naples Conservatory and became caught up in the verismo movement after the sensational success of Mascagni's *Cavalleria rusticana* (1890). His first opera in this vein, *Mala vita* (1892), which tells of a labourer who vows to reform a prostitute if the Virgin will heal his tuberculosis, created a scandal for its sordidness. It was revised and performed five years later, retitled *Il voto*, but failed to improve Giordano's standing. In the meantime Giordano's next opera, *Regina Diaz* (1894), saw the composer retreat from verismo into the outworn world of romantic melodrama. However, this fared no better than *Mala vita* and it survived for only two performances. The same year Giordano left Naples for Milan with hopes of better fortune.

Success came at last with *Andrea Chénier* (1896). The French Revolutionary subject and Luigi Illica's literate libretto moved Giordano to write music of passionate conviction. It was followed by *Fedora* (1902), based on a play by Victorien Sardou; its ingenious and powerful second act has helped maintain the work on Italian stages. These works represent a plateau of accomplishment that Giordano never attained again. A few of Giordano's later operas have survived on gramophone records or in occasional revivals. *Marcella* is remembered for one aria ('O santa libertà!') for which Italian tenors have a weakness.

Giordano was not without talent, but he lacked the essential resourcefulness and inventiveness to develop beyond his own limitations. He had two veins: one, an emphatic, occasionally strident, emotionalism; and the other, a graceful and predictable nattering that rarely rises above the level of salon music. The shifting of gears between these is all too often crude.

Andrea Chénier

Dramma di ambiente storico in four acts (2h 15m)
Libretto by Luigi Illica
PREMIERES 28 March 1896, La Scala, Milan; US: 13 November 1896, Academy of Music, New York; UK: 16 April 1903, Camden Town Hall, London
CAST Andrea Chénier *t*, Carlo Gérard *bar*, Maddalena di Coigny *s*, Contessa di Coigny *ms*, Bersi *ms*, Madelon *ms*, Roucher *b*, Pietro Fléville *bar*, Fouquier-Tinville *bar*, Mathieu *bar*, The Abbé *t*, An 'Incroyable' *t*, Major-domo *b*, Schmidt *b*; *satb* chorus of courtiers, ladies, soldiers, servants, peasants, prisoners, merchants, etc.

A successful combination of naturalism and historical drama, *Andrea Chénier* has remained a popular repertoire piece since its premiere. Illica's libretto (which, he claimed in a note in the vocal score, did not draw on historical fact but was based on ideas suggested by the editors of the real-life Chénier's poetic works) had originally been written for Alberto Franchetti. Franchetti ceded it to Giordano, who made use of the French Revolutionary background, spicing the opera with quotations of period tunes. The characters are scarcely developed, but the opera is kept alive with effective solos for the three principals and a surging final duet.

SYNOPSIS

Act I The contessa di Coigny is giving a soirée, at which her daughter Maddalena is struck by the ardent libertarianism of the poet Chénier, but the fête is interrupted by peasants in revolt, led by a servant, Gérard, who tears off his livery. The intruders are sent away, and the contessa's guests resume their gavotte.

Act II Five years later, Chénier is disillusioned by the excesses of the Terror, and his friend Roucher, who has procured him a passport, urges him to go abroad. He hesitates because an unknown woman has written to him, asking for an appointment that very evening. It is Maddalena, who seeks out Chénier's protection. Gérard, now Robespierre's agent, appears and tries to abduct Maddalena, but Chénier wounds

him, while Roucher spirits the girl away. When Gérard is asked to identify his assailant, he generously says he cannot.

Act III Chénier has been arrested, and Gérard denounces him as a counter-revolutionary. Maddalena comes to Gérard and begs him to save Chénier, even at the cost of giving herself to him. At his trial, in spite of Chénier's stirring self-defence, Gérard is unable to prevent the sentence of death.

Act IV Chénier awaits execution at the prison of Saint-Lazare. With Gérard's help Maddalena comes, substituting herself for another prisoner, to die with Andrea.

Giordano's quest for veristic naturalism led to the inclusion of the Revolutionary songs 'Ça ira', the 'Carmagnole' and the 'Marseillaise', and contrasting (but historically equally accurate) 18th-century dances and pastoral music. Set against these are the beautiful lyrical melodies for which the opera is famous – Chénier's 'Improvviso', Gérard's 'Nemico della patria', Maddalena's 'La mamma morta', and the final duet 'Vicino a te'. The chorus, representing the 'people' in their many guises, play a larger than usual part, the violence of some of their music (their part is marked *urlando* – 'yelling' – at one point) making a significant contribution to the verismo nature of the work.

Fedora

Melodramma in three acts (1h 45m)
Libretto by Arturo Colautti, after the play by Victorien Sardou (1882)
PREMIERES 17 November 1898, Teatro Lirico, Milan; UK: 5 November 1906, Covent Garden, London; US: 5 December 1906, Metropolitan, New York

Encouraged by the success of *Andrea Chénier*, Giordano soon produced another verismo opera, which was again popular and secured more than a reputation for its composer: word at the time was that '*Fedora* fè d'oro' ('*Fedora* made money'). Like *Chénier* the opera has a revolution as its background, but the action is carried out principally in salons (with the exception of the short final act set in Switzerland), which excludes the 'people', prominent in the earlier opera, and largely eliminates opportunities for choral writing.

In St Petersburg, Princess Fedora comes to visit her fiancé, Count Vladimiro. Shortly thereafter he is brought in, mortally wounded, and his assassin is alleged to be Count Loris Ipanov, who escaped. The suspected motive is a nihilist *coup*. When Vladimiro dies, Fedora vows to avenge him. Fedora and Loris go to Paris, where at a soirée she finds herself drawn to him, but she remembers her oath on Vladimiro's corpse and denounces Loris, along with his family, to a police agent. Fedora asks Loris why he killed Vladimiro. Loris frankly confesses it was a point of honour; he had caught him with his wife, Wanda. Transported by love and pity, Fedora throws herself into his arms. Later, Fedora and Loris are living blissfully in the Swiss Oberland, when word comes from Moscow that Loris's brother has drowned in prison when the Neva overflowed into his cell; his mother has died of grief. Loris guesses that Fedora has been hounding his family and curses her. Fedora has recourse to poison that she carries in a Byzantine cross and, dying, begs Loris's forgiveness, which he grants with a final kiss.

The score of *Fedora* contains routine and trivial music, but Giordano's lyric gift sustains a number of agreeable arias, the most familiar of which is Loris's 'Amor ti vieta' (Act II). A novel effect is obtained when a pianist entertains the guests at the soirée with a Chopinesque nocturne, while Fedora and Loris converse tensely.

Other operatic works: *Marina*, (*c.* 1889); *Mala vita*, 1892; *Regina Diaz*, 1894; *Il voto* (rev. of *Mala vita*), 1897; *Giove a Pompeii* (coll. with Alberto Franchetti), (*c.* 1901), 1921; *Siberia*, 1903, rev. 1927; *Marcella*, 1907; *Mese mariano*, 1910; *Madame Sans-Gêne*, 1915; *La cena delle beffe*, 1924; *Il re*, 1929; *La festa del Nilo* (inc., n.d.)

W.A.

PHILIP GLASS
b 31 January 1937, Baltimore, Maryland, US

Glass is the leading composer of so-called 'minimalist' opera in the late 20th century. He is also one of the most widely performed composers in the world. During 1988, for instance, no fewer than eight of his full-length stage works with more or less continuous music (the simplest way of defining the 'operatic' in an output as varied as it is already alarmingly extensive) were performed. Several works have had more than one production, unusual these days for any composer under 60. Glass's operas are indisputably successful, though their merits are hotly disputed.

Glass's compositions – like those of his fellow Americans La Monte Young, Terry Riley and Steve Reich, who were exploring repetition and often clearly audible structural processes even earlier than he was – have become known as 'minimalist'. Certain similarities to the art of such figures as the sculptor Richard Serra (for whom Glass had acted as an assistant) provide justification for the label, though ironically the term 'minimalism' was not regularly applied to such music until the early 1970s, by which time Glass and others had begun to move away from their early repetitive rigour.

In 1967 Glass returned to the US from lengthy trips to Europe, where he had studied with Nadia Boulanger, and India. Between then and 1978 he wrote most of his compositions for the small amplified ensemble of flutes, saxophones and electric keyboards that still plays his music today, even though much of his energy since has been devoted to writing for the conventional opera house. While the earlier works' high energy level and sheer volume derived in part from rock music, their driving force technically was a rhythmic notion of additive process that came from classical North Indian music.

Glass's reputation prior to the world tour of *Einstein on the Beach* in 1976 was achieved primarily via his contribution to the New York 'downtown' scene which flourished in the 1960s and 1970s, with its crossing of the usual boundaries: between, for instance, the 'cultivated' and 'vernacular' traditions and often between the different media of music, theatre, film and other kinds of performance art, even including the 'fine' arts of painting and sculpture, etc. In fact, much of Glass's early music was written to accompany stage performances. Part of the reason for this was the close involvement of his first wife, JoAnne Akalaitis, with the experimental theatre group Mabou Mines, active first in Paris (the couple's base before 1967) and later in New York. Non-Western theatrical traditions, including those of Indian Kathakali, also encouraged increasingly close collaboration between the writers, designers, directors, actors and musicians involved in the group's experimental productions.

The culmination of this activity came with *Einstein on the Beach*, the brainchild of the American Robert Wilson, who was responsible for the work's basic conception and visual realization (the description of Wilson as 'director-designer' scarcely does justice to his theatrical role). Though sometimes described as an opera, *Einstein* is perhaps more logically regarded as a manifestation of what Wilson himself referred to as the 'theatre of images'.

After *Einstein*, Glass's best-known stage works moved closer to conventional notions of opera. *Satyagraha*, *Akhnaten*, *The Making of the Representative for Planet 8* and *The Voyage*, together with the chamber opera *The Fall of the House of Usher*, all largely eschew the ambiguities of *Einstein*, and substitute aspects more familiar from 18th- and 19th-century operatic practice.

The 'theatre of images' still, however, plays an important part in Glass's work. *The Photographer*, the two contributions to Wilson's *CIVIL WarS* project, *1,000 Airplanes on the Roof* and *Hydrogen Jukebox* all avoid the forces normally found in the opera house; some were written for the composer's own ensemble. Perhaps more importantly, their approach to both dramatic and musical continuity brings them closer to the world of *Einstein* than to opera as conventionally defined. Yet the extent to which they remain disputed territory (even in the composer's own mind) is itself an important dimension of their vitality. Glass also continues to be particularly active as a composer for films and television, as well as for the concert hall.

Einstein on the Beach
Opera in four acts [and five 'kneeplays'] (4h 30m)
Spoken texts by Christopher Knowles, Samuel M. Johnson and Lucinda Childs
PREMIERES 25 July 1976, Avignon Festival, France; US: 21 November 1976, Metropolitan, New York
CAST s, t, Einstein *violinist*, actors, dancers; *satb* chorus (16 voices including second solo s and t), sometimes in the pit, sometimes part of the action

Behind the conception and realization of *Einstein on the Beach* lay Robert Wilson's approach to performance art. Wilson's starting points are usually visual rather than textual: here a set of drawings to which

Glass would respond by writing music, which in turn influenced a reworking of the drawings, which inspired further music and so on.

Einstein, according to its creators, concerns not only the German physicist Albert Einstein but also 'science, technology and ecology'. It eventually became the first part in a trilogy of operas by Glass, each taking a major historical figure and a major human issue for its theme. Since narrative and characterization in the usual sense are absent, it is impossible to give a conventional synopsis. Choreographed movement of various kinds, by no means confined to 'dance', is more important than the text. In addition, the close relationship between dramatic structure and *mise-en-scène* inherent in Wilson's approach presents any other director with unusual problems.

The work is 'about' Einstein, the discoverer of relativity, whose activity as a keen amateur violinist leads to his portrayal not as a singer but (in Wilson's original production at least) as an elderly man who punctuates the action with extended violin solos. A train – which forms the first of three recurring images: the others are a courtroom and a spaceship – also suggests that Einstein's theory of relativity is, however obliquely, being practised on the audience; so also do such things as the slow eclipse of a handless clock by a large black disc in the first trial scene. Yet, at the time of its composition, Glass said that he and Wilson merely 'tried to find out where Einstein was in the piece'. Act I offers the train and a trial scene; Act II the spaceship, hovering above a field of dancers, and then the train again, this time at night. In Act III the courtroom also resembles a prison, and the spaceship moves closer to the dancers. In Act IV all three images are developed more drastically: the train, for example, turning into a building.

While all this can be taken as the main action, the five 'kneeplays', which form the prologue, interludes and epilogue to the four acts, seem of equal significance, even though the first kneeplay is already in progress as the audience enters the auditorium. Their subject matter is, however, related only tenuously to that of the main acts. In the original production, two women sat at tables downstage right; in the fourth kneeplay they lay on glass tables, and for the fifth they became two lovers sitting on a park bench. Other images counterpointed their action (or inaction); all somehow related to experiments in relativity or more directly to Einstein himself.

The recitation of numbers and *solfège* syllables accounts for a significant part of the 'text'. In Wilson's production, eleven other texts were included, the majority provided by Christopher Knowles, an autistic boy whom Wilson had encountered while working with handicapped children. None of their imagery relates in any obvious way to the stage picture; their respect for grammar is somewhat intermittent. The only text – the single one written by Lucinda Childs – even to mention either Einstein or the beach (only the latter, in fact) confines mention of the subject to avoiding the beach. Yet narrative, as well as grammatical, sense is by no means entirely forsaken in these texts, which are all spoken, never sung.

Musically, *Einstein* is crucially 'on the edge'. It retains not only a high degree of repetition but much of the non-developmental, 'non-narrative' approach of true minimalism. But while additive and cyclic rhythmic processes remain its driving forces, the more harmonically and melodically directed approach of Glass's later operas also begins to emerge. The impression that the grammar of a more familiar tonality is under reinvestigation is reinforced, in particular, by the use of chord sequences with clearly defined movement in the bass line.

Satyagraha: M. K. Gandhi in South Africa

Opera in three acts (2h 15m)
Libretto (in Sanskrit) by Constance DeJong and the composer, adapted by DeJong from the *Bhagavadgita*
PREMIERES 5 September 1980, Stadsschouwburg, Rotterdam; US: 29 July 1981, Artpark, Lewiston, New York State
CAST Miss Schlesen *s*, Mrs Naidoo *s*, Kasturbai *ms*, M. K. Gandhi *t*, Mr Kallenbach *bar*, Parsi Rustomji *b*, Mrs Alexander *c*, Arjuna *t*, Krishna *b*; *silent roles*: Count Leo Tolstoy, Rabindranath Tagore, Martin Luther King; *satb* chorus of two hostile armies (Indians and Europeans), an Indian crowd, 8 European men; *silent*: 6 Indian workers, 6 Indian residents, 2 contemporary policemen

Satyagraha became the second opera in Glass's trilogy. Based on Mahatma Gandhi's early years in South Africa, according to the composer it deals with 'politics: violence and non-violence'. *Satyagraha* literally means 'truth-force' but has come to stand for the concept of 'passive resistance'. The *Bhagavadgita*, source of the libretto, is the Sanskrit religious text that was Gandhi's 'dictionary of daily reference'.

SYNOPSIS
Satyagraha covers the period from Gandhi's arrival in South Africa in 1893 to the New Castle March of 1913 (the event that brought the *Satyagraha* movement to an end in that country) as though it were a single day.

Act I introduces turn-of-the-century South Africa via a somewhat ambiguous invocation of the *Bhagavadgita*; Gandhi's workers build Tolstoy Farm and demonstrate against the imposition of identity cards.

Act II White resistance to Gandhi's arrival in Durban is thwarted by the wife of the superintendent of police; the newspaper *Indian Opinion* is set up and distributed; and identity cards are ceremonially burned in retaliation against the government's retraction of its promise to repeal the Black Act.

Act III The striking miners of New Castle and their families march with the *Satyagraha* army in peaceful protest against racial discrimination.

Satyagraha clarifies the crucial differences between Glass's early, minimalist, music and his later, post-minimalist, output. The opera is specifically concerned with the life of Gandhi, who, while hardly subjected to conventional dramatic development, becomes a clearly delineated focus of attention. The structure of the opera is much more conventional than that of *Einstein*, with scenes and acts forming a sequence of tableaux. The use of Sanskrit encourages reflection on the moral lessons of each scene rather than engagement in the dynamic of narrative; the scenes of Gandhi's early life portrayed here do not, in any case, appear chronologically. In addition, the placing of a 'figurative counterpart' above the action of each of the opera's three acts – Count Leo Tolstoy, Rabindranath Tagore and Martin Luther King – suggests the historical continuity of what Gandhi's movement stood for.

Taken as a whole, however, the opera charts a readily comprehensible, conventionally motivated plot. Movement on stage plays a significant role, but the main thrust is conveyed through the conventions of solo aria, duets, trios, etc., and choral singing, in ways closely resembling those adopted by the traditional lyric stage. The more harmonically and melodically directed approach already noted in *Einstein* is here clarified by chaconne-like structures underpinning an often continuous flow of vocal melody.

Akhnaten

Opera in [a prologue,] three acts [and an epilogue] (2h 15m)
Libretto by the composer in association with Shalom Goldman, Robert Israel and Richard Riddell; drawn from Egyptian and Akkadian sources (some in English translation), Psalm 104 (in Hebrew), and sentences from Fodor's and Frommer's guides to Egypt
PREMIERES 24 March 1984, Kleines Haus, Württembergischer Staatstheater, Stuttgart; US: 12 October 1984, Wortham Theater Center, Houston; UK: 17 June 1985, Coliseum, London
CAST Akhnaten *ct*, Nefertiti *c*, Queen Tye *s*, Horemhab *bar*, Aye *b*, High Priest of Amon *t*, Amenhotep *spoken role*, 6 Daughters of Akhnaten and Nefertiti, 3 *s*, 3 *c*, Funeral Party, 4 *t*, 4 *b*; offstage: Tourist Guide (voice-over); *tb* chorus of mourners, priests of Amon, priests of Aten, soldiers, etc.; *satb* chorus of people of Thebes, Akhnaten's entourage, offstage chorus, people of Egypt, soldiers, outlawed priests of Amon; *silent*: funeral cortège; tourists; dancers; onstage musicians

Akhnaten, the final panel in the trilogy of operas beginning with *Einstein on the Beach*, has as its subject the Egyptian pharaoh of the 14th century BC and, more widely, 'religion: orthodoxy and reaction'. Sigmund Freud's *Moses and Monotheism* (1939) and Immanuel Velikovsky's *Oedipus and Akhnaten* (1960) were both crucial influences on the composer and his team of assistant librettists. Shalom Goldman compiled the text from original sources, and the opera is sung in ancient languages – Egyptian, Akkadian and Hebrew – as well as 'the language of the audience', which also serves for narration.

SYNOPSIS
The opera shows the rise and fall of Akhnaten in a series of tableaux. During an orchestral prelude, the narrator reads from ancient Pyramid texts to set the scene.

Act I   The funeral of Amenhotep III, Akhnaten's father. Akhnaten's coronation is followed by a hymn announcing the revolution to come.

Act II   Akhnaten launches an attack on the Amon temple, sings a love duet with his queen, Nefertiti, participates in a dance to mark the inauguration of the city of Akhetaten, and sings his own 'Hymn to the Sun'.

Act III   The progressive withdrawal of Akhnaten and his family from the world and the pharaoh's downfall are represented; the final scene moves to the present, as tourists visit what little remains of Akhnaten's former city.

The epilogue depicts the ghosts of Akhnaten and his entourage amid the ruins.

Akhnaten continues in the tradition of post-minimalist opera established by *Satyagraha*. Dramatically, it is concerned with a central character who – though somewhat distanced by voice type (David Freeman's Houston–London production also drew attention to Akhnaten's reputedly hermaphrodite aspect) – is sympathetically drawn and develops as a real human being. His pivotal 'Hymn to the Sun' in Act II is sung in 'the language of the audience', thus encouraging even greater identification. The sequence of scenes – here chronological, unlike in *Satyagraha* – may still be treated ritualistically (as in Achim Freyer's Stuttgart production); Freeman, however, attempted to demonstrate its propensity for dramatic development in tandem with the evolution of character.

Akhnaten has a wider musical range than its predecessor. The approach to harmony is often much darker and more chromatic. Careful consideration of overall key structure and the use of leitmotifs join the basic techniques already established in *Satyagraha*. Orchestration, too, is more subtle; the lack of violins provoked some original responses to the inevitably darker colouring, as well as an appropriate emphasis at times on somewhat militaristic wind and percussion; Akhnaten himself is frequently accompanied by a solo trumpet. The love duet for Akhnaten and his queen Nefertiti and Akhnaten's 'Hymn to the Sun' are powerfully lyrical utterances.

The Fall of the House of Usher

Chamber opera in a prologue and two acts (1h 30m)
Libretto by Arthur Yorinks, based on the short story by Edgar Allan Poe (1839)
PREMIERES 18 May 1988, American Repertory Theater, Cambridge, Massachusetts; UK: 9 August 1989, St Donat's Castle, Llantwit Major, Wales
CAST William *t*, Roderick Usher *bar*, Madeline Usher *s*, Servant *b*, Physician *t*

Poe's story of demented lust in a crumbling castle is well known; its air of Gothic horror and what Debussy (who never finished his *Usher* opera) called its 'sombre melancholy' are ideally suited to the more chromatic and doom-laden style Glass first developed in *Akhnaten*. The highly charged emotional content and structural compression of Poe's tale seem particularly well suited to the ambiguous ways in which Glass's exploration of familiar-sounding harmonic devices deals with tonal progression. Famously trounced by nearly all British critics, such an idiom perhaps works best when illustrating single emotional and dramatic states, as here, rather than attempting to match the cut and thrust of narrative.

Sunk in the weird introspection of Poe's text, which Glass sets with considerable rhythmic subtlety, *The Fall of the House of Usher* to some extent reclaims the more ambiguous territory between conventional opera and openly modernist notions of music-theatre, while doing full justice to a narrative of cumulative power and terrifying dénouement. As a result, it is one of Glass's best works since *Einstein*.

K.P.

The Voyage

Opera in [a prologue,] three acts [and an epilogue] (3h)
Libretto by David Henry Hwang
PREMIERE 12 October 1992, Metropolitan, New York
CAST The Scientist/First Mate *t*, Commander *s*, Ship's Doctor/Space Twin 1 *s*, Second Mate/Space Twin 2 *lyric b*, Isabella *ms*, Columbus *b-bar*, Earth Twin 1 *ms*, Earth Twin 2 *b*; *satb* chorus of the Music of the Spheres, natives, the Spanish court

The Voyage was commissioned by the Metropolitan, New York, in commemoration of the 500th Anniversary of Columbus's arrival in America. It deals with the idea of voyage and exploration more as an activity of the mind and of the imagination than of geographical heroics.

SYNOPSIS
Prologue The scientist (a character based on Stephen Hawking, the well-known physicist), though confined by illness to a wheelchair, encompasses the stars in his imagination.

Act I A spaceship from outer space crashes on earth in prehistoric times. Each crew member takes one of the ship's directional crystals which will eventually link them again to their home planet. They are asked to imagine the time and place in which they envisage existence on their new planet, and we see them journey towards these goals. The commander in particular anticipates her sensual future among the 'natives', while they likewise await their new encounter with trepidation.

Act II In 15th-century Spain, Columbus is given a triumphant send-off at Isabella's court. But this turns out to be merely his vivid memory as he lies on his becalmed boat. He continues to fantasize that Isabella visits him on the boat; as his obsession with her reaches its climax, land is sighted.

Act III The crystals from Act I have been found coincidentally by the earth twins. When these crystals are brought together, the signals they emit lead the space twins to announce the discovery of a new planet. Another voyage sets off towards this new discovery.

Epilogue Columbus is visited on his deathbed by the ghost of Isabella, unrepentant for her exploitation of his discoveries. He rejects her, and his bed floats up to the stars.

The Voyage develops Glass's powerful choral writing, first shown in *Satyagraha*, to create a large-scale – even spectacular – work appropriate to the venue that commissioned it. In addition, Hwang's poetic and non-realistic text enables the music to remain at a distance from the narrative – as in *Einstein* and *Usher* – which is essential to its functioning in an operatic context.

D.P.

Other operatic works: *Attacca – A Madrigal Opera*, 1980 (as *The Panther*, 1982; as *A Madrigal Opera*, 1985); *The Photographer*, 1982; *The CIVIL WarS* (Rome and Cologne Sections), 1984; *The Juniper Tree* (coll. with Robert Moran), 1985; *A Descent into the Maelstrom*, 1986; *The Making of The Representative for Planet 8*, 1988; *1,000 Airplanes on the Roof*, 1988; *Hydrogen Jukebox*, 1990; *The White Raven*, 1993; *Orphée*, 1993; *La belle et la bête*, 1994

MIKHAIL GLINKA

Mikhail Ivanovich Glinka; *b* 1 June 1804, Novospasskoye (now Glinka), Russia; *d* 15 February 1857, Berlin

Glinka was by no means the first Russian to compose opera, yet he is indisputably the founder of the Russian operatic tradition. Born into a minor landowning family, he was educated in St Petersburg, then settled into the role of a dilettante in the city's salons. Though he had had no proper musical education, he composed a good many undemanding songs and piano pieces, and shared in the current Russian taste for French opera, as well as for Rossini. But by the end of the 1820s Italian opera in general was becoming his central interest, and in 1830 he left for a three-year residence in Italy. He met Bellini, soaked himself in the Italian tradition, but by the end of his stay was turning against it; as he himself put it, 'I could not sincerely be Italian. A longing for my own country led me gradually to the idea of writing in a Russian manner.' On his return journey he delayed five months in Berlin for the only formal composition study of his whole life. The following year he began his first opera, *Ivan Susanin* (better known as *A Life for the Tsar*), and it was a sensation at its first performance in 1836.

Glinka promptly chose Pushkin's *Ruslan and Lyudmila* as the subject of his next opera, but the poet's death in a duel thwarted his hope that Pushkin himself would be its librettist. As it was, the totally unsystematic, even incompetent, way in which the libretto was compiled, coupled with Glinka's equally unsystematic compositional process, could only result in a work hopelessly flawed, and it was a relative failure at its premiere in 1842.

Glinka's two operas are very different pieces. *A Life for the Tsar*, with its grand choruses and formal ballet, depended heavily on the French operatic tradition; but it treated a subject that was thoroughly Russian, and, besides achieving an often remarkable synthesis of Italian and Russian melodic characteristics, Glinka devised a novel arioso-cum-recitative idiom for narrative and dialogue that was to become a fundamental element in many later Russian operas (*A Life for the Tsar* is the first Russian opera not to use spoken dialogue). The opera is very effective on the stage. By contrast, *Ruslan and Lyudmila* is dramatically a disaster. Nevertheless, it represents a very remarkable achievement. Uneven the music may be, but there was abundant stimulus to the imagination in this fantastic tale of the supernatural set in a heroic past, and Glinka's music, at its imaginative best, was not only strikingly original and sometimes very beautiful, but also so new in a specially Russian way that later Russian composers could find in it a richness of stimuli and suggestion for their own creative ventures. *Ruslan and Lyudmila* could indeed claim to be the most seminal work in Russian music.

A Life for the Tsar

(*Ivan Susanin*)
Zhizn' za tsarya
Opera in four acts with an epilogue (3h)
Libretto by Georgy Fyodorovich Rosen; epilogue by Vasily Zhukovsky, rev. Glinka; scene at the monastery (Act IV) by Nestor Kukolnik
Composed 1834–6; scene at the monastery, 1837
PREMIERES 9 December 1836, Bolshoi Theatre, St Petersburg; UK: 12 July 1887, Covent Garden, London; US: 4 February 1936, Schola Cantorum, New York (inc.; concert); 12 December 1936, War Memorial Theater, San Francisco
CAST Ivan Susanin *b*, Antonida *s*, Vanya *c*, Bogdan Sobinin *t*, Polish Commander *b*, Polish Messenger *t*; *satb* chorus of Russian peasants, Poles

In 1613 the first of the Romanov tsars was saved by a peasant, Ivan Susanin, who decoyed a detachment of pursuing Polish troops, perishing at their hands when his deception was uncovered. The subject was suggested to Glinka in 1834, and its Russianness immediately fired him. Having decided that certain incidents were bound to be part of the final work, he worked impulsively as these caught his imagination, sometimes running ahead of his amateur librettist, Georgy Rosen (secretary to the tsarevich), who was thus forced to set words to existing music. Once rehearsals began, the tsar himself showed much interest and, realizing its potential for stirring emotions of patriotic loyalty, approved the suggestion that *Ivan Susanin* should be renamed *A Life for the Tsar*.

The work's premiere was a sensational success, and within Russia it became the most performed of all native operas until the 1917 revolution; indeed, it was then suggested that the melody of the final scene should become the new Soviet national anthem. In 1837 Glinka was persuaded to replace Sobinin's scene at the beginning of Act IV with a new one (Vanya at the gates of the monastery).

A Life for the Tsar had an enormous influence on later Russian music, setting the precedent for a succession of heroic works based on incidents from Russian history. Not surprisingly, it was slower to make its mark abroad; though in Russia it became customary to open the St Petersburg operatic season with it, it seems to have been 30 years before it crossed the frontier (to Prague in 1866).

SYNOPSIS

Act I A chorus of male peasants enters the village of Domnino, to be greeted by their womenfolk; they give thanks that a new tsar has been found. Antonida sadly laments the absence of her betrothed, Sobinin, who has been fighting for the tsar – though today he is to return home. However, her father Susanin brings news: the Poles are threatening Moscow, and there can be no thought of a wedding. Sobinin arrives in a boat along the river (chorus of rowers). He too has news: Moscow is safe. But, without a tsar Russia is

still vulnerable. Sobinin is dismayed that his wedding will be delayed, and in a trio he and Antonida lament, while Susanin promises that Antonida shall finally be Sobinin's bride. However, when Susanin hears from Sobinin that 'their boyar' is to be crowned in Moscow, he agrees to the wedding and all rejoice.

Act II A ball in the fortress of a Polish commander. All are confident Russia will be vanquished. But after the choral polonaise, *krakowiak*, waltz and mazurka, a messenger bursts in with news of defeat; Mikhail Romanov has been elected tsar, though he does not yet know, for he has retired to his estate at Kostroma. After recriminations, a detachment of soldiers leaves to apprehend the new tsar. Those remaining resume dancing.

Act III In Susanin's cottage, Vanya ('the orphan') reflects on how the peasant had adopted him after his mother had been killed. When Susanin enters, Vanya declares he will fight for the tsar when he is grown up. A chorus of men bids farewell to Susanin as they go off for the day's work, and he invites them to the eve-of-wedding celebration. Susanin and Vanya, now joined by Antonida and Sobinin, express in a quartet their happiness, and their hopes for Russia, now that a tsar has been chosen. Sobinin leaves to summon his friends. Suddenly Susanin hears horses, and the Polish detachment appears. Believing Susanin knows the tsar's whereabouts, the Poles demand that he lead them to him. Susanin prevaricates and, as the intruders confer, whispers to Vanya to ride to Kostroma and warn the tsar. Susanin then pretends he will accept the bribe the Poles offer. Antonida enters and is distressed to see her father departing with Russia's enemies but, resisting her embrace, he tells her to celebrate her wedding without him, then leaves with the Poles. Vanya also slips out. A group of girls sings a bridal chorus, and Antonida voices her grief at her father's apparent abduction. Sobinin returns with his friends and they go off to collect others to help in rescuing Susanin. Sobinin lingers to comfort Antonida, then also leaves.

Act IV (1836 version) In a forest glade Sobinin rallies his followers in their search for Susanin, and thinks of Antonida.

Act IV (1837 version) At the gates of the Kostroma monastery Vanya wakens the inhabitants, and convinces them of the danger to the tsar. Susanin and the Poles enter the forest glade. While his captors rest, Susanin reflects on the coming dawn, which will be his last, and recalls the wedding preparations and his family, then quietly sleeps. The Poles rouse him; finally he confesses his deception and is killed.

Epilogue On the square before the Kremlin in Moscow. An offstage chorus praises the new tsar and his warriors (Slavsya chorus). Sobinin, Antonida and Vanya enter and tell of Susanin's heroic death. All praise the new tsar and Susanin.

The fundamental problem for any 19th-century Russian composer was to reconcile indispensable forms and procedures that originated in the West with the kind of music that nature had decreed he should write. Glinka was the first composer to conquer this problem, and *A Life for the Tsar* marked his first victory. His strongest weapon was his outstanding gift for melodies – basically Western, but often fused with characteristics stemming from folksong or church chant. And while the overall organization and structures of the opera remained Western, even these were occasionally shed to allow a passage that could never have occurred except in a Russian opera – the opening chorus of Act I, for instance, or the beautiful bridal chorus in 5/4 in Act III (the most Russian piece in the whole score).

Above all, *A Life for the Tsar* is good drama. True, the story is not very elegantly shaped, and the progress of the music is sometimes correspondingly fitful; the extended dances in Act II are simply the obligatory ballet, and the later use of extracts from these dances as leitmotifs for the Polish soldiers is dramatically disastrous. But when Glinka was faced with a situation of deep emotion or true drama he could respond splendidly. Especially impressive are Susanin's great scena in the 1837 Act IV, which is touchingly filled with recollections of earlier themes, and the corporate rejoicing at the opera's end, the first of those great tableau scenes which were to become one of the glories of the Russian tradition.

Ruslan and Lyudmila
Ruslan i Lyudmila

Opera in five acts (3h 15m)
Libretto by Konstantin Bakhturin (scenario); mostly Valerian Shirkov, but also Nestor Kukolnik, Nikolai Markevich, Mikhail Gedeonov; after the poem by Aleksandr Pushkin (1820)
PREMIERES 9 December 1842, Bolshoi Theatre, St Petersburg; UK: 4 June 1931, Lyceum, London; US: 26 December 1942, Town Hall, New York (concert); 5 March 1977, Boston
CAST Svetozar *b*, Lyudmila *s*, Ruslan *bar*, Ratmir *c*, Farlaf *b*, Gorislava *s*, Finn *t*, Naina *ms*, Bayan *t*, Chernomor *silent role*; *satb* chorus of courtiers, the Gigantic Head, Naina's maidens, Chernomor's followers

Glinka began work on *Ruslan and Lyudmila* in 1837, and had completed several numbers before ever a scenario had been devised. His disorganized life-style ensured that the compositional process was even more disorderly and spasmodic than that of *A Life for the Tsar*, with the libretto provided by a succession of amateur writers (though incorporating some lines of Pushkin), and composition spread over five years. Interest in the work was fanned by public performances of separate numbers, and Liszt was highly approving when Glinka showed him some of the score early in 1842. But, despite radical changes during production, it was tepidly received. Appreciation of the opera seems, however, to have increased fairly steadily. Connoisseurs apparently appreciated its unusual qualities, and it retained an intermittent place in the repertoire. By 1893 it had been performed 300 times in St Petersburg, but there have been few productions outside Russia.

SYNOPSIS
Act I At the court of Svetozar, prince of Kiev, celebrations are in progress before the marriage of his daughter, Lyudmila, to Ruslan, a warrior. The Bayan (a minstrel) sings of the trials in store for Ruslan, though he predicts the victory of true love. Nostalgically, Lyudmila bids farewell to her parents' home, and consoles her unsuccessful suitors, the eastern prince Ratmir and the Varangian warrior Farlaf. Suddenly all darkens; when light is restored, Lyudmila has vanished. Svetozar promises her hand and half his kingdom to the one who rescues her.

Act II In his cave Finn, a good magician, reveals to Ruslan that Lyudmila's abductor is the dwarf Chernomor (whose strength lies in his enormously long beard) and warns Ruslan against the evil enchantress Naina. The scene changes to a deserted place where Naina instructs a very frightened Farlaf to wait at home; she will help him defeat Ruslan and gain Lyudmila. Finally on a deserted battlefield Ruslan reaffirms his resolve, then defeats a gigantic head and draws from beneath it a sword; the head explains he is Chernomor's brother and one of his victims, and that the sword's magic can defeat the dwarf.

Act III In Naina's enchanted palace her maidens are directing their allure at a travel-weary Ratmir, with a Persian song, to the distress of his slave, Gorislava, who loves him. Ruslan appears and is smitten with Gorislava, but Finn intervenes, breaks the seductive spell, and unites Ratmir and Gorislava, and all set out to rescue Lyudmila.

Act IV Confined in Chernomor's enchanted garden, Lyudmila voices her despair and defiance, rejecting her captor's blandishments. On Ruslan's approach, Chernomor casts a spell over her and goes out to fight with Ruslan. Chernomor's followers observe the offstage encounter, in which Ruslan catches hold of Chernomor's beard, then cuts it off. Triumphantly Ruslan returns onstage with it, but is in despair when he finds Lyudmila in an enchanted sleep. He decides to take her back to Kiev.

Act V Ratmir sings of his love for Gorislava. Farlaf steals Lyudmila and speeds to Kiev. Meanwhile Finn gives Ratmir the magic ring that will waken Lyudmila. In Kiev, Farlaf cannot rouse her but when Ruslan arrives with Ratmir he breaks the spell with the aid of the ring. General rejoicing.

The fantasy and romance of Pushkin's *Ruslan and Lyudmila* had a natural appeal to Glinka; the problem was that the subject was totally unsuited to operatic treatment, and the work's fate was sealed when a friend, Konstantin Bakhturin, devised its scenario 'in a quarter of an hour while drunk'. For some four years Glinka worked intermittently on such individual incidents as caught his fancy; by the time he came to knit these together, far too much music of the wrong kind had been composed, and, for all the drastic surgery during rehearsals, nothing could hide the unevenness or remedy the often misshapen structure. Dramatically, *Ruslan and Lyudmila* is an irreparable disaster, and some of the characterization is weak; Farlaf in particular is little more than a conventional opera-buffa figure.

Yet, at its musical best, *Ruslan and Lyudmila* contains some of the most strikingly original invention of 19th-century opera, some separate incidents are brilliantly treated, and some characters transcend the ludicrous situations in which they find themselves. The opera's Russianness is far deeper than that of *A Life for the Tsar*, springing not from the absorption of folk and chant idioms into what was still basically a Western idiom, but from the sometimes novel materials and free structures that Glinka's vivid and totally Russian imagination created. Hence the prodigious seminal importance of the opera. In addition, the clear and bright scoring, which contributes so much colour to the whole opera, established the fundamental style of Russian orchestration.

Though *Ruslan and Lyudmila* is mostly an opera of brilliant moments, Act I does have real consistency, establishing for Russian music its special heroic idiom, which is extended further in Ruslan's great Act II aria. (Act I also contains the famous passage where, to depict the disorientation caused by Chernomor's magic as he abducts Lyudmila, Glinka disrupts the music's tonal course with a descending whole-tone scale.) Earlier in Act II Naina's music introduces something of the special Russian 'magic' idiom, while the oriental idiom appears for the first time in Act III, notably in the voluptuous Persian chorus and the first part of Ratmir's aria. Between these is Gorislava's plangent cavatina, but there is a greater concentration of excellent music in Act IV: in Lyudmila's spirited scena and aria, for instance, and in the languorous delicacy of the choruses for Chernomor's houris – though most immediately arresting, perhaps, are Chernomor's splendidly grotesque march and the fierce oriental *lezginka*. The most memorable movement in Act V is Ratmir's sultry romance.

D.B.

CHRISTOPH WILLIBALD GLUCK

Christoph Willibald Ritter von Gluck; *b* 2 July 1714, Erasbach, nr Berching, Germany; *d* 15 November 1787, Vienna

Gluck came from a family of foresters who worked for the minor nobility. His precocious musical talent led to studies in music (and law) in Prague, probably sponsored by Prince Lobkowitz (father of Beethoven's patron), and travel to Italy, where he studied with Giovanni Battista Sammartini. His first operas were written for Milan and Venice; he then tried his luck in London, producing two operas in 1746. Years later he told the music historian Charles Burney how he admired Handel and English musical taste (this may have been flattery, as Gluck was to say much the same in France about Lully). His search for a permanent position took him to Saxony and Denmark. Recurring visits to Vienna, his wife's home, enabled him to ingratiate himself with the imperial family, some of whom became his pupils. The first of many operas commissioned by the Vienna court was *La Semiramide riconosciuta* (1748); Gluck settled there by about 1750.

His earliest output consisted of conventional opere serie, mainly to libretti by the Caesarean poet Pietro Metastasio. He wrote no opera buffa. Among his earliest surviving music are solidly composed da-capo arias, not without anticipations of his later style; some pieces reappear in his greatest works. Recycling material was common enough at the time not to excite remark, and Gluck, never as fluent as his Italian contemporaries, was certainly justified in searching for better dramatic contexts for his most original conceptions. Some passages display a rugged boldness, as well as a grand melodic span, which were to continue to influence musicians as late as Berlioz.

From Vienna, Gluck made occasional journeys to fulfil commissions in Italy, and at last, most significantly, in Paris. His Viennese work quickly took him away from opera seria, although he continued to produce courtly entertainments. He owed the variety of his experience during the 1750s to the favour of the imperial theatre administrator, Count Durazzo, whose *L'innocenza giustificata* he set (1755), a gesture directed against the virtual monopoly of Metastasio. Durazzo fell in with the fashion for French culture, and gave Gluck the job of adapting and later composing a series of opéras comiques for the court theatre.

Such diverse experiences stood the composer in good stead in the 1760s, when he was drawn towards reform movements in dramatic music. His first significant collaboration was in the ballet *Don Juan* by Gaspero Angiolini (1761), after which came three operas to libretti by Raniero de' Calzabigi: *Orfeo ed Euridice*, *Alceste* and *Paride ed Elena*. Besides his masterpiece of opéra comique, *La rencontre imprévue* (1764), Gluck wrote other occasional works in the 1760s. He has sometimes been accused of backsliding from the radical position adopted in *Orfeo* and *Alceste*. There is, however, no reason to perceive *Orfeo*, an occasional work related to the courtly genres, as an irreversible step. Gluck composed no full-scale opera seria after 1756 (*Antigono*, which won him the papal knighthood of the Golden Spur); even *Telemaco* (1765) can be associated with the spirit of reform.

With the publication of *Alceste*, however, Calzabigi penned a dedicatory preface which Gluck signed, and which is their manifesto of reform. The ideas they had assimilated from French opera and the Parmesan and Viennese reform operas of Tommaso Traetta are justified as a return to the natural and poetic origins of opera, at the expense of mere musicianship, and especially of the virtuoso singer: 'I sought to restrict music to its true purpose of expressing the poetry and reinforcing the dramatic situation, without interrupting the action or hampering it with superfluous embellishments.' Later, in an open letter to the French press, Gluck said that in *Armide* he had striven to be 'more painter and poet than musician'. Consequences of the reform were the greater attention paid to orchestra, chorus and dance; this, however, corresponded with French tragédie lyrique. In *Orfeo* and *Paride*, but not *Alceste* and *Telemaco*, Gluck orchestrated all the recitatives; and in *Alceste* he managed without a castrato. *Alceste* was followed by *Paride ed Elena*, which Gluck must have valued less, since he did not adapt it for Paris; instead he used parts of it (and *Telemaco*) in new operas.

If the architect of reform was Calzabigi, Gluck supported him wholeheartedly. In Paris he took control of his less experienced librettists; yet even when, like Mozart and Verdi, he demanded verses for music already composed, he kept in mind the needs of the drama rather than merely the music. Largely through the influence of his pupil Marie Antoinette (then dauphine, later in 1774 queen of France), he was contracted to present six French operas, including thorough recompositions of *Orfeo* and *Alceste* (he also adapted two opéras comiques). *Armide* completed his *rapprochement* with French tradition by using an old libretto. The threat from the partisans of Italian music, who brought Niccolò Piccinni to Paris, was met by wholesale plunder of Gluck's own Italian music in his last and perhaps greatest masterpiece, *Iphigénie en Tauride*. He had not permanently affected the taste of Vienna, and Italy remained largely indifferent to his reforms. But, as Lully's partisans had feared, he killed off the old French opera; and he withstood the pressure of the Italians who displaced native talents at the Opéra. The failure of *Écho et Narcisse* (1779) sent him home in disgust, but his works continued to dominate the repertoire into the next century.

Gluck's last operatic undertaking was his only one in German, a version of *Iphigénie en Tauride*. He handed *Les Danaïdes* to his protégé Antonio Salieri, and abandoned a setting of Klopstock's *Hermanns Schlacht*, but he wrote some songs and a *De profundis* before his death in 1787. He remained a talisman of dramatic art for several generations. Cherubini, Spontini, Weber and others paid him tribute; Berlioz (his most eloquent partisan), Wagner and Strauss supervised performances. A scholarly edition of his French operas was undertaken by musicians close to Berlioz. Major critical and historical studies have been undertaken this century, and a complete edition of his works is well advanced.

Orfeo ed Euridice/Orphée
Orpheus and Eurydice/Orpheus

Orfeo ed Euridice
First version
Azione teatrale per musica in three acts (1h 45m)
Libretto by Raniero de' Calzabigi
PREMIERES   5 October 1762, Burgtheater, Vienna; UK: 9 March 1773, London; US: 25 May 1863, Winter Gardens, New York
CAST   Orfeo (Orpheus) *a castrato*, Euridice (Eurydice) *s*, Amore (Cupid) *s*; *satb* chorus of shepherds and nymphs, furies and infernal spirits, heroes and heroines from Elysium, followers of Orfeo; ballet of furies and blessed spirits

Orphée
Second version
Tragédie opéra (drame héroïque) in three acts (2h)
Libretto by Pierre Louis Moline, after Calzabigi
PREMIERES   2 August 1774, Opéra (Académie Royale de Musique), Salle des Tuileries, Paris; US: 24 June 1794, Charleston; UK: 17 May 1898, Covent Garden, London
CAST   Orphée (Orpheus) *high t (haute-contre)*, Eurydice *s*, Amour (Cupid) *s*; *satb* chorus of shepherds and

shepherdesses, nymphs, demons and furies, blessed spirits, heroes and heroines; ballet of furies and blessed spirits

The performance of *Orfeo* on the emperor Franz's name day in 1762 involved a rare galaxy of talent and must be accounted one of the major events in 18th-century musical theatre. Calzabigi, with full support from the administrator Durazzo, was the guiding spirit (as Gluck admitted); he manipulated a familiar subject and genre with the intention of restoring naturalness and simplicity to dramatic music. Thus *Orfeo* in no sense proposes the reform of Metastasian opera seria. The choreographer, Angiolini, for whom Gluck had composed a revolutionary action ballet (*Don Juan*) the year before, was also an innovator in his field; the sets were by the ubiquitous Quaglio brothers, and the title role was sung by Gaetano Guadagni, who ten years before had worked with Handel in London and studied acting with David Garrick.

The festa or azione teatrale, like the serenata, an Italian opera on a mythological subject with chorus and dancing, was a feature of courtly celebrations (Gluck had written several already and was to write more). But its musical style was similar to opera seria, particularly in the virtuoso writing for voices. Calzabigi probably designed *Orfeo* to capitalize on Gluck's particular musical strengths, and on his recent dramatic experience. It was preceded by Durazzo's reform gesture (*L'innocenza giustificata*), and by Gluck's French comedies, which trained the composer in directness of utterance. *Don Juan* permitted Gluck to explore extremes of expression, particularly in the final scenes. Calzabigi had been inspired by traditional French opera, notably those of Rameau; Gluck knew the reform operas of Tomasso Traetta, whose *Armida*, based on the French libretto Gluck later used in Paris, was given in Vienna in 1761. From this source came the richly developed tableaux in which chorus, solo singing and dance are alternated and combined. The subject had been used, symbolically, at a critically early stage in the development of opera, and Gluck, unknowingly, revived something of the spirit of those early-17th-century operas by Peri, Giulio Caccini and Monteverdi, particularly in the first two acts, by restoring to recitative its original function as the most expressive and articulate part of the protagonist's role. Yet *Orfeo* feels like a new start rather than the climax of a remarkable tradition. To posterity it has remained, perhaps to an unfair degree, Gluck's masterpiece.

After performances in Italy and England, much abused by additional music, a second authentic version (*Orphée*, 1774) clinched Gluck's reputation in Paris after the disputed success of *Iphigénie en Aulide*. Gluck enlarged his work to occupy a whole evening; he compromised the spirit of the original by adding a bravura air for Orpheus to end the first act, and introduced new ballets, most notably the long *Air de furies* taken from *Don Juan* and the famous *Dance of the Blessed Spirits* for flute and strings, perhaps his most eloquent instrumental solo.

SYNOPSIS (1762 version)
Act I   Scene 1: Orpheus and the traditional pastoral

chorus of nymphs and shepherds are grouped round Eurydice's tomb. A mournful C minor chorus, 'Ah, se intorno a quest'urna funesta', is punctuated by Orpheus' cries: he can only utter Eurydice's name. In a grouping of movements characteristic of reform works, the chorus is used to frame a recitative for Orpheus and a dance-pantomime, during which the tomb is strewn with flowers. Orpheus, alone, sings of his grief, 'Chiamo il mio ben così'. The three verses alternate with powerfully expressive recitatives. He complains that only Echo hears him; her wordless replies are confided to an echo orchestra with chalumeaux. Orpheus shakes off his despair and resolves to recover Eurydice from the dead. Scene 2: Cupid appears to encourage him, for his music can overcome any obstacle. After a short aria Cupid disappears and Orpheus, in recitative, determines to carry the adventure through. (In the 1774 version Cupid has two songs; and Orpheus ends with the aria 'L'espoir renaît dans mon âme', a piece that aroused controversy; its Italian style led to the accusation that Gluck had stolen it from Ferdinando Bertoni. It actually comes from Gluck's *Il Parnaso confuso* and *Le feste d'Apollo*.)

Act II   Scene 1: A hideous landscape near the banks of the river Cocytus. After a fierce sinfonia, Orpheus' lyre (represented by the harp) is heard approaching. It arouses the furies' wrath; they dance frenziedly and sing of the hellish watchdog Cerberus (whose barking is represented by orchestral glissandi). When Orpheus explains his mission they interrupt with cries of 'No!', but as his singing grows in eloquence they display signs of compassion and finally allow him passage. (The 1774 version at this point somewhat incongruously inserts the magnificent *Air de furies* which originally ended the ballet *Don Juan*.) Scene 2: A delectable landscape in Elysium. Ballo. (This was expanded in the 1774 version to became the *Dance of the Blessed Spirits*. The chorus and a soloist, sometimes taken to be Eurydice, sing of their bliss in such a place ('Cet asile aimable').) Orpheus, alone, sings of the beauty around him and its emptiness for him, because he cannot find Eurydice ('Che puro ciel'). Eurydice is brought to him, blindfold; the chorus ('Vieni a' regni del riposo' repeated as 'Torna, o bella, al tuo consorte') exhorts her to return to Orpheus.

Act III   Scene 1: A dark, twisted path in a repellent landscape, leading away from Hades. Eurydice is overjoyed at her release, but Orpheus, in fulfilment of conditions imposed by Cupid (in Act I, Scene 2), has to let go of her hand and must not look at her. She reproaches him for his apparent coldness, and he suffers her unjust suspicions (the first long recitative dialogue of the opera is followed by the duet 'Vieni, appaga il tuo consorte'). Eventually she feels that death was preferable ('Che fiero momento'). Orpheus can bear it no longer; he turns to look at her, and she dies. His grief is embodied in the aria 'Che farò senza Euridice?' Scene 2: Cupid reappears in time to prevent Orpheus' suicide; Eurydice is revived, and the couple are united on earth to the happiness of their friends. Scene 3: All join in praise of Cupid. (In the 1774 version Orpheus joins in the central part of Eurydice's arias and a trio is added from *Paride ed Elena*; many changes were made in the dances, and the work is considerably longer as a result.)

For all the importance of Calzabigi in directing Gluck towards a new type of opera, *Orfeo* owes its perennial freshness to Gluck's musical imagination. When Bertoni set the text, very beautifully but in a conventional idiom (Venice, 1776), the loss of Gluckian directness led to loss of magic and dramatic insight. The aim is truth to nature, in the 18th-century sense of 'imitation' – not only of natural phenomena but of human passions. The new directness of expression appears in the absence of da-capo forms. Instead, Orpheus sings songs: strophic ('Chiamo il mio ben così') or rondo ('Che farò senza Euridice?') in form. 'Che puro ciel', potentially an aria text, is an obbligato recitative; and Orpheus overcomes the furies by short, even fragmentary, outpourings of lyrical intensity. These forms may derive from Renaissance or baroque traditions, particularly 18th-century French ones, but the directness is also from opéra comique, and the gestural exactness of the musical language, not only in the dances, derives from Angiolini's ballet d'action.

The experiment of building scenes out of blocks of interlocked ideas is taken further in *Alceste*, but is never more eloquent than in the dying away of the furies' music. Gluck's other innovations include the abolition of simple recitative (the orchestra plays throughout), an experiment not resumed until *Paride ed Elena*, and a richness of orchestral colouring unprecedented in his work and very unusual anywhere before the 1770s. Cornetti and chalumeaux, in their brief appearances, provide a haunting, antique colour; in 'Che puro ciel' a complex layered sonority includes solo flute, oboe, bassoon, horn and cello over a triplet continuum. The choral sonorities are remarkable, and the dances, in their appositeness to each scene, reveal an exceptional choreographic imagination.

Most prophetic, perhaps, is the continuity. Cadences are only occasionally omitted or elided, but many numbers are too short to be self-contained and in a good performance they flow into each other, forming single, extended complexes. But, in addition to painting unforgettably Eurydice's tomb, Hades, and Elysium, Gluck discovered accents of grief, resignation, pleading, hope and despair that make his conception of the mythological singer the equal of Monteverdi's and raised the possibilities of the musical language of his generation to a level otherwise attained only by his exact contemporary C. P. E. Bach (who wrote no operas).

Orpheus was produced in most European centres, but the original version fell from favour. Berlioz, in 1859, restored the 1762 tessitura to the title role by assigning it to a woman, Pauline Viardot. Tenors still take the role occasionally, in the 1774 keys, but the majority of performances adopt Berlioz's sensible, albeit inauthentic, compromise solution, which involves restoring the 1762 key scheme, while retaining music added in 1774, transposed where necessary. The role is now increasingly sung by male falsettists (counter-tenors).

La rencontre imprévue

The Unexpected Meeting
Comédie mêlée d'ariettes in three acts (2h)
Libretto by L. H. Dancourt, after Alain-René Lesage's and
d'Orneval's *Les pèlerins de la Mecque* (1726)
PREMIERES 7 January 1764, Burgtheater, Vienna;
UK: 21 July 1939, Loughton, Essex; US: 8 June 1951,
Cleveland, Ohio
CAST Ali *t*, Rezia *s*, Dardane *s*, Amine *s*, Balkis *s*, Osmin
t, Sultan of Egypt *t*, Vertigo *bar*, Calender *b*, A Chief of the
Caravan *b*; *spoken roles*: 2 slaves (Banon and Morachin) ;
silent roles: sultan's entourage and guard, Rezia's slave girl,
porters

Among oriental rescue operas, this is the most substantial precursor of Mozart's *Die Entführung*; it makes similar use of 'Turkish' percussion for 'local' colour. It is also Gluck's longest, finest and, in the 18th century, most popular opéra comique. As well as being widely performed in French, it achieved great popularity in German (as *Die Pilgrimme von Mekka*), being played in most centres in the 1770s and 1780s, and it formed part of the repertoire of the German opera company in Vienna itself. In keeping with contemporary French development of the genre (it was performed five days after François-André Danican Philidor's *Le sorcier*), the dialogue is all spoken, in prose, without *timbres*.

SYNOPSIS

Act I The action takes place in Cairo. Osmin, servant of Ali, meets the Calender (leader of an order of mendicant dervishes), who is singing a begging song in a traditional language which he professes not to understand himself. Osmin, being destitute, receives practical advice on begging ('Les hommes pieusement'/'Unser dummer Pöbel meint', well known from Mozart's piano variations, K. 455). He also meets the eccentric French painter Vertigo. Dressed like the Calender, Osmin acts the beggar before Ali, failing to grasp the ancient language ('Castagno' comes out as 'Castrato', etc.); but he is recognized, while the Calender recognizes Ali as prince of Balsora. A serious note is struck by Ali's aria 'Je chérirai, jusqu'au trépas' (with solo violin and cor anglais, an instrument appearing quite frequently in Gluck's opéras comiques). Ali is seeking the Persian princess Rezia, whom he has secretly married, but who was kidnapped by pirates when trying to elope. Balkis, an attendant on the sultan's favourite in the harem, tells them that her mistress has seen Ali and summons him secretly to the palace. Ali is reluctant, but the promise of food decides Osmin and he drags his master inside.

Act II In the palace, Osmin enjoys the good life. Ali is approached in turn by Dardane, seductively, and Amine, provocatively. He spurns their love graciously; nothing will make him unfaithful to Rezia. Amine laughs at him and bets that his constancy will not survive encounter with the real favourite. She is right; it is Rezia herself who has arranged this little test of his fidelity. Their ecstatic reunion is interrupted by Balkis: the sultan is unexpectedly back from hunting. The act ends with a panic-stricken sextet; Osmin saves the day by rushing them off to the Calender.

Act III The Calender assures them of their safety

in his house, and suggests they escape with a caravan on its way to Mecca. However, he seems dangerously interested when Osmin speaks of the huge reward the sultan is offering for Rezia's return. There follows a long episode with Vertigo: after three trios with Balkis and Osmin, the painter sings of scenes of war (a 'rataplan' aria, 'Des combats j'ai peint l'horreur') and pastoral peace. Ali and Rezia have a loving duet; then disaster strikes, for the Calender has betrayed them. An octet is led by the angry sultan in a brisk comic patter which foretells the happy end. When he learns the identity of the suppliants, who are quite prepared to die together, the sultan unites them and offers to execute the Calender instead. The lovers plead for clemency. ¨

Although replete with comedy *La rencontre imprévue* is a full-length opera with serious characters, on the pattern of the contemporary *dramma giocoso* (it is thus designated in Haydn's Italian version, *L'incontro improvviso*, 1775). There is even space for two ballets, near the ends of Acts II and III, but the music does not survive. The arias are longer, some being in a ternary form not unlike the Italian da capo; two are 'parodied' from Gluck's own *Il trionfo di Clelia*, although the extreme virtuosity of Gluck's Italian style is eliminated except from Rezia's Act II ariette 'Ah, qu'il est doux de se revoir'. The musical idiom is thus very close to that of Gluck's reform operas from *Alceste* on, and particularly his French operas.

Alceste

Alcestis

First version
Tragedia per musica in three acts (2h 15m)
Libretto by Raniero de' Calzabigi, after Euripides' play
Alkestis (438 BC)
PREMIERE 26 December 1767, Burgtheater, Vienna
CAST Admeto (Admetus) *t*, Alceste (Alcestis) *s*, Eumelo
(Eumelus) and Aspasia (children of Admeto and Alceste) 2
s, Evandro (Evander) *t*, Ismene *s*, Herald *b*, High Priest of
Apollo *bar*, Oracle *b*, Infernal God *b*; *satb* chorus of
courtiers and citizens, female attendants on Alcestis, priests
of Apollo, infernal deities

Second version
Tragédie lyrique in three acts (2h 45m)
Libretto by Marie François Louis Gand Leblanc du Roullet,
after Calzabigi
PREMIERES 23 April 1776, Opéra, Paris; UK: 30 April
1795, London; US: 11 March 1938, Wellesley College,
Massachusetts
CAST Admète (Admetus) *t*, Alceste (Alcestis) *s*, High Priest
of Apollo *b*, Évandre (Evander) *t* (*haute-contre*), Herald at
Arms *b*, Hercule (Hercules) *b*, 4 Coryphées (chorus leaders)
satb, Apollon (Apollo) *bar*, Oracle *b*, Infernal God *b*; *silent
roles:* 2 children of Admète and Alceste; *satb* chorus of
officers of the palace, female attendants on Alceste,
Thessalians, infernal deities, priests and priestesses in the
temple of Apollo

Euripides' *Alkestis* is a tragi-comedy; but, unlike Philippe Quinault for Lully, Calzabigi omitted the humour and concentrated on the loftiest sentiments whose unrelenting expression makes the original (1767) version both the most radical reforming gesture of

Gluck's career and the most persistently mournful opera ever written. Possibly the subject was intended to convey sympathy to the empress Maria Theresa, widowed in 1765; the libretto is dedicated to her.

Alceste was performed by an opera-buffa troupe rather than singers used to the musical finery of opera seria; for the first time in a full-scale Italian opera, Gluck dispensed with a castrato. A buffo troupe would also be more amenable to being expected to act. Thus it was said of Antonia Bernasconi, who sang Alceste, that 'her gestures followed only the movements of the heart'. The ballets were by Jean-Georges Noverre, who sympathized less with Gluck and Calzabigi than had Angiolini; he presented a final 'grotesque ballet' which some, at least, enjoyed more than the opera. Nevertheless, *Alceste* made a profound impression on the public – which included the 11-year-old Mozart and his father. It is the most challenging gesture of the Viennese reformers, but its severity is such that Gluck should not have been surprised, as he complained in the dedicatory preface to *Paride ed Elena*, that it had found no imitators. As an attempted reform of Italian opera seria, it must be accounted a failure; but in its French form, although preceded by *Iphigénie en Aulide*, it exerted considerable influence. *Alceste* was the second Gluck opera revived with Pauline Viardot in the title role (Paris, 1861). Subsequent revivals have likewise usually used the French version, even if translated back into Italian.

SYNOPSIS

Act I begins with the proclamation that Admetus, the young king of Thebes, is dying; his wife Alcestis is drawn into scenes of communal mourning (1767: 'Io non chiedo, eterni dei'; 1776: 'Grands Dieux! Du destin qui m'accable'). After an imposing religious ceremony, Apollo's oracle pronounces: Admetus can live if someone dies in his place. The people flee (1767: 'Che annunzio funesto./Fuggiamo'; 1776: 'Quel oracle funestre./Fuyons'). Only his wife, Alcestis, has the courage to take this step. 1776: her *secco* recitative ('Popoli di Tessaglia') is replaced by an incisive *accompagnato* and a new aria, which provides a resolution of her dilemma: to die for Admetus is not a sacrifice ('Non, ce n'est point un sacrifice'). She offers herself to the underworld gods ('Ombre, larve, compagne di morte'). 1767: a short scene for Evander and the chorus ends Act I. 1776: the aria (now 'Divinités du Styx') provides a more fitting ending to the act.

Act II 1767: Alcestis, dismissing her confidante Ismene, approaches the gods to beg respite so that she can see Admetus again (this scene is omitted in the French version, much of its music passing to Act III). In both versions, choral singing and dancing celebrate the recovery of Admetus, but nobody knows its price. When Alcestis arrives, her tears seem incomprehensible; in the French version she appears in the midst of the ballet, making explicit the irony behind this rejoicing. Gradually the truth is revealed. In a magnificent tableau she bids farewell to life; the act ends with the aria 'Ah per questo' ('Ah, malgré moi'), embedded in a splendid choral refrain in F minor ('O come rapida' ('Oh, que le songe de la vie')).

Act III 1767: Admetus tries in vain to force Al-

cestis to renounce her sacrifice and let him die ('Misero! E che farò!'). Alcestis bids farewell and dies ('Piangi o Patria', a choral tableau of mourning with solos, reminiscent of the third act of Lully's *Alceste*). But Apollo comes to revoke his dreadful oracle: Alcestis, as well as Admetus, can live after all. 1776: the revised version initially mounted in Paris was threatened with failure, so further revisions were undertaken and the final French version reverts more nearly to Euripides by bringing in Hercules, who owes Admetus a debt of hospitality. The act begins with the mourning tableau ('Pleure, o patrie'), abbreviated. Hercules arrives and learns the truth; he determines to rescue Alcestis (Gluck refurbished an aria from *Ezio*). The scene changes to the underworld. Alcestis, in music from the 1767 Act II, meets the infernal deities; Admetus appears to offer his own life ('Alceste, au nom des dieux'). The infernal deities call on Alcestis; Hercules overpowers them and Alcestis is returned to life with the blessing of Apollo.

Perhaps because *Orfeo* is concerned with a superhuman being, but *Alceste* with human society, the latter did more to set the pattern for tragic opera in years to come. Its elevated tone is reflected in Italian and French tragedies, notably Mozart's *Idomeneo* and Cherubini's *Médée*. The D minor overture and its link with Act I anticipate both *Idomeneo* and *Don Giovanni*. It has been argued that the arpeggio motif that begins the *Alceste* overture is a sort of leitmotif, anticipating the crucial preparation for the speech of the oracle. The thematic connection with the opera is less explicit than in some of Mozart's operas, or in *Iphigénie en Aulide*, but the oracle scene was certainly Mozart's model for the sacrifice scene in *Idomeneo*. One might go further and suggest that the presentation of the nobly suffering heroine is suggestive of the redeeming women of Romanticism, although the music and forms are neo-classical.

Gluck himself was the most constructive critic of the Italian version. Magnificent as it is, its high-flown sentiments and huge static tableaux of repeated choruses surrounding recitative, arias, and dance demand absolute submission: if the tension is lost for a moment, it is bound to appear tedious. The musicologist Donald Tovey observed that Gluck had got rid of the abuses of opera seria by simplifying the drama almost out of existence. Rousseau made an extensive critique of the Italian score: much as he admired it, he deplored the multi-movement arias (which were to arouse opposition from the Piccinnists) and he criticized the cheerful divertissement which greets Admetus' recovery. For Paris, Gluck kept his style of aria, although he eliminated arias for minor characters and the touching intrusion of the children into one of Alcestis' arias. But as well as introducing new dances (some taken from works written in the meantime, *Le feste d'Apollo* and *Paride ed Elena*) he changed the divertissement along lines suggested by Rousseau, omitted much repetition, and added new material including a superb aria for Alcestis in Act I. Like that of *Iphigénie en Aulide*, which intervened between the two versions, the design is fluid; grandeur is lost but theatricality enhanced.

The Italian version follows *Telemaco* rather than *Orfeo* by returning to simple recitative. In proportion to the orchestral (obbligato) recitative it is, however, much reduced from the opera-seria norm. In the French version the recitatives are orchestrated throughout. Gluck's orchestration attains a new depth and richness in the tutti, particularly in the infernal scenes, which are totally different from those in *Orfeo*. The Romantic orchestra, or at least its treatment of the darker colours, begins here, with Gluck's sonorous scoring for full woodwind and trombones, soon taken up in French opera by Piccinni. The orchestra, particularly in 'Ombre, larve, compagne di morte', is made to stand for the voices of the infernal deities, another foretaste of Romantic practice. Yet the orchestration continues the functional, symbolic use of instrumental timbre applied in *Orfeo*. The trombones are used to colour mourning and underworld scenes, while the cors anglais characterize only the former, and chalumeaux the latter. Low flutes colour the ritual march in Act I (which Mozart remembered in *Die Zauberflöte*). Standard orchestration – flutes, oboes, horns, bassoon and strings, with occasional trumpets and timpani – represents normality.

Paride ed Elena

Paris and Helen
Dramma per musica in five acts (1h 45m)
Libretto by Raniero de' Calzabigi
PREMIERES 3 November 1770, Burgtheater, Vienna; US: 15 January 1954, Town Hall, New York; UK: 27 November 1963, Royal Northern College of Music, Manchester

Paride ed Elena was Gluck's last reform opera written with Calzabigi, and the only one not adapted for France. Instead he reused dance movements in *Iphigénie en Aulide* and *Alceste*, a trio in *Orphée*, and an aria in *Écho et Narcisse*. This dismemberment of a score composed with as much care as either of the other Calzabigi operas is the more strange in that it had been published in 1770 with an important dedicatory preface (to the duke of Braganza). Perhaps it has the fault of Calzabigi's *Alceste*, of too leisurely an argument; but the intention of the work is more clearly to entertain, and the extended choral and dance sequences, while they must stand in the way of modern revival except in a period style, are skilfully integrated into the action.

Arriving in Sparta with his Trojan followers, Paris comes to win Helen, the most beautiful woman in the world. The Trojans pay homage to Venus, whom Paris has declared the most beautiful of the goddesses, and request her help. Cupid, disguised as Helen's confidante Erasto, helps Paris. At first, Helen rejects Paris's advances. In Act III, having presented prizes at the games, Paris woos Helen in song, but his ardent desire succeeds only in frightening her. Finally, in Act V, 'Erasto' tells Helen that the Trojans are preparing to depart and succeeds in leading her to betray her true emotions. Cupid reveals himself and the lovers are united. Pallas Athene appears, uttering her terrible prophecy of the devastation Helen's abduction will bring on Troy. The work concludes with celebratory dancing in the Trojan camp.

The orchestration is simpler than in *Alceste*, although the harp is employed rather more freely than in *Orfeo*. The recitatives are orchestrated throughout, however, returning to the advanced position taken up by *Orfeo*, from which Gluck did not retreat again. Paris is a castrato role, the last Gluck wrote; as in many of his court works, there are no low voices.

Whatever Gluck's private opinion, *Paride* is a beautiful opera, some of his finest music clothing a psychological drama in which Helen gradually yields to her ardent lover. The idea that Gluck could not handle love music is given the lie by the title roles: Paris, the ardent wooer who enters with the direct and eloquent 'O del mio court ardor', and Helen, uncertain at first, then gradually overcoming her inhibitions before eloping in the final act. Paris' 'Le bell immagini' and the trio 'Ah lo veggo!' are far more dramatic in their original context than their later incarnations in, respectively, *Écho* and *Orphée*. Gluck was proud of the contrasted national styles (rugged Spartans, effete Trojans) which are presented in the choral and ballet music. Paris is seconded throughout by Cupid in disguise. There are no other characters until Athene appears at the end to music from the overture.

Iphigénie en Aulide

Iphigenia in Aulis
Tragédie opéra in three acts (2h 30m)
Libretto by Marie François Louis Gand Leblanc du Roullet after Jean Racine's tragedy *Iphigénie* (1674)
PREMIERES 19 April 1774, Opéra, Paris; UK: 20 November 1933, Town Hall, Oxford; US: 22 February 1935, Philadelphia
CAST Agamemnon *bar*, Clitemnestre (Clytemnestra) *s*, Iphigénie (Iphigenia) *s*, Achille (Achilles) *t*, Patrocle (Patroclus) *b*, Calchas *b*, Arcas *b*, Diane (Diana) *s*, 3 Greek Women 3 *s*, A Slave from Lesbos *s*; *satb* chorus of Greek soldiers and people, Thessalian soldiers, guards, attendants on the princess, women from Aulis, slaves from Lesbos, priestesses of Diana; dancers

Gluck's first French opera was written speculatively, in the hope of arousing interest in Paris. His campaign bore fruit only four years after the first performance of *Paride*. His objective was to found a new school in the cultural capital of Europe, in the interests of wider diffusion of his reform of serious opera. Insofar as the old French operas rapidly dropped out of the repertoire after 1774, and his new works were widely performed in the original language or in translation, he succeeded. Gluck also created a revolution at the Paris Opéra by insisting that the principals (who included Sophie Arnould in the title role and the most distinguished French tenor and baritone of the time, Joseph Legros and Henri Larrivée), and even the chorus, should act; according to contemporary reports, he had to behave like a sergeant-major to achieve this. He retained elements of French operatic tradition that had been taken over into the Calzabigian reform, notably the integration of choral and dance music, short and freely structured solo vocal numbers, and the serious use of orchestra, and could thus readily adapt *Orpheus* and *Alceste* for Paris; but in the *Iphigénie*s and *Armide* he eschewed the monumentality of the latter, and the slowness of action in all three Calzabigi operas.

The subject of the sacrifice of Iphigenia had been treated in several Italian operas and by Francesco Algarotti in his treatise *Saggio sopra l'opera in musica*. In essence, the story was intended to justify the murder of Agamemnon by his wife Clytemnestra on his return from Troy: Euripides invented the substitution of an animal for the human sacrifice by the offended goddess Artemis (Diana), and the translation of Iphigenia to Tauris. Du Roullet's libretto is adapted from Racine's *Iphigénie*, in which Iphigenia is married to Achilles; Eriphile, whose real name is also Iphigenia, turns out to be the intended sacrifice. Du Roullet's plot is less contrived, although the ending does not prepare for the Tauris drama.

Du Roullet's procedure became standard for the adaptation of neo-classical tragedy into opera. The plot is simplified (two major characters, Eriphile and Ulysses, are omitted); events only described in the play (notably the dénouement) are enacted to satisfy the requirement for choral involvement; danced divertissements are introduced.

Iphigénie en Aulide was never as successful as *Tauride*, but it retained a hold on the repertoire into the 19th century. Its most remarkable revival was organized by Wagner in Dresden (1847); in places this amounted to a recomposition in line with his own development (Mahler revived it in Vienna in 1904). Perhaps the most significant post-war revival was the one using 18th-century sets discovered in the theatre at Drottningholm (1965).

SYNOPSIS

Act I   The Greeks are held up in Aulis by unfavourable winds on their way to attack Troy; a sacrifice is needed to propitiate Diana. Agamemnon agonizes over his dilemma ('Diane impitoyable'); his daughter, Iphigenia, is sent for on the pretext of marrying her to Achilles, but in reality as the sacrifice. Calchas urges Agamemnon to do his duty; the Greek soldiers are heard fiercely demanding the sacrifice, but he is defiant ('Peuvent-ils ordonner'). Agamemnon believes Arcas has forestalled his daughter's coming, but the chorus is heard greeting her and her mother, Clytemnestra. His next ruse is to tell Clytemnestra that Achilles has changed his mind. Iphigenia is devastated at the news, and greets her lover coldly; but his ardour overcomes her resistance.

Act II   Preparations are made for the wedding, but Arcas reveals the truth; Achilles promises to defend Iphigenia, but she is submissive. Achilles confronts Agamemnon (duet, 'De votre audace téméraire'). The infuriated Agamemnon orders the sacrifice, but repents ('O toi, l'objet le plus aimable').

Act III   The first part of the act is punctuated by the angry chorus of Greeks demanding blood. Iphigenia intends to submit to fate, despite Achilles' intention to fight and Clytemnestra's anguish. At the altar, after a solemn hymn, the sacrifice is prepared, but Achilles bursts in with his troops, threatening Calchas' life. Calchas reveals that the gods have relented and the wind is now favourable. Iphigenia, Clytemnestra and Agamemnon rejoice together

For the Paris revival of 1775 minor changes were

made in Act II, and at the end Diana herself appears to bring about the happy ending and urge the Greeks on to the destruction of Troy (this was the version performed at the Paris Opéra into the 19th century, but not published until 1873). The ending, like that of *Tauride*, anticipates the 1790s vogue for operas ending in a rescue.

As the inception of the Gluckist era in France, *Iphigénie en Aulide* has a special place in operatic history. It is also, however, a logical development of his Viennese reform operas; in particular the overture is his finest, its contrasting thematic ideas, arranged in a free form, apparently representing the conflicting demands of authority and human affection that motivate the characters of the opera. In place of the sheer beauty of *Orfeo* and the grandeur of *Alceste*, Gluck concentrates on the variety and development of characterization, particularly of the title role and Agamemnon. To the almost saintly Iphigenia, who, however, is admirably severe when she believes herself jilted in Act I, and the noble, yet devious, Agamemnon are added a one-dimensional but vivid Achilles and a Clytemnestra whose anguish and fury in her arias (Act II, 'Par un père cruel'; Act III, 'Jupiter, lance la foudre') are worthy of the artistic, as well as actual, mother of Electra in Mozart's *Idomeneo*.

Gluck was criticized for surrendering beauty (particularly in the ballets, which are inferior to those in *Orphée*) to the portrayal of strong feeling; it was argued that opera is an art of illusion, and tragedy belongs in the spoken theatre. These qualities, which made *Iphigénie* only a qualified triumph, are precisely those which we value today. Both the orchestration and the recitative (albeit orchestrated throughout) are simpler than in the Calzabigi operas, perhaps because Gluck trusted the Paris orchestra less, and perhaps because he saw no place for trombones in an opera that in its original form had no true supernatural characters. The forms are remarkably fluid, a personal adoption of a French model which was to influence the later revision of *Alceste*. In addition to arias, none long, some very short, there are fine ensembles, and complex scenes built out of arioso and recitative (especially those involving Agamemnon).

Armide

Armida
Drame héroïque in five acts (3h)
Libretto by Philippe Quinault (1686), after an episode from Torquato Tasso's epic poem *Gerusalemme liberata, ovvero Il Goffredo* (1581)
PREMIERES 23 September 1777, Opéra, Paris; UK: 6 July 1906, Covent Garden, London; US: 14 November 1910, New York
CAST Armide (Armida) *s*, Renaud (Rinaldo) *t*, La Haine (Hate) *c*, 9 *s*, 2 *t*, 2 *bar*, *b*; *satb* chorus of coryphées, people of Damascus, nymphs, shepherds and shepherdesses, followers of Hate, demons, blessed spirits

In daring to use virtually unaltered the text of Lully's last completed opera, Gluck presented his strongest challenge both to the supporters of old French opera and to the newly ascendant partisans of Italian music. Usually, reset libretti were considerably altered; Gluck merely omitted the prologue and added a few telling lines for Armida at the end of Act III. In practice *Armide* goes only a little further than *Iphigénie en Aulide* in abandoning the Italian style and form in favour of a highly personal handling of French forms within a language forged for the purpose. It is, however, Gluck's one real success among the reform works that does not use the newly fashionable Greek mythology.

SYNOPSIS

Act I The pagan sorceress Armida has seduced many Crusaders, but she cannot touch the pure Rinaldo, whom she professes to hate. In fact her interest in him is disguised love (a comparison with the first act of Wagner's *Tristan* is not inapposite).

Act II Armida causes Rinaldo to be enticed into a place of beauty. He falls asleep, but she cannot bring herself to kill him. She submits to love and carries him away to an enchanted place.

Act III After the aria that reveals her most intimate feelings, Armida summons Hate for conjurations against love, but then violently rejects them.

Act IV concerns the adventures of two knights coming to rescue the besotted Rinaldo.

Act V After a short love scene – the only time Armida and Rinaldo address one another – the knights shame Rinaldo into departure. Enraged, Armida destroys her magic works.

Gluck's setting matches Lully's in beauty and surpasses it in psychological insight. Gluck had the advantage, too, of the modern orchestra to paint Rinaldo's air 'Plus j'observe ces lieux' (Act II), to underline sentiments (as in the wonderful end to Act III, with the composer's own text, a passage praised by Berlioz), and to end with a symphonic transformation scene, anticipating the orchestral end of Rossini's *Mosè in Egitto*. *Armide* is less likely to return to the repertoire than its contemporaries, because of its leisurely pace; it is surprising that Gluck included the whole of Act IV, in which the essential action is not advanced at all, and in it used less self-borrowing than in the dramatic parts of his work, notably Act III, which is based largely on older music including *Telemaco*, *Don Juan* and various opéras comiques.

Iphigénie en Tauride
Iphigenia in Tauris

First version
Tragédie lyrique in four acts (2h)
Libretto by Nicholas-François Guillard, after Claude Guimond de la Touche's tragedy (1757) and Euripides' play (*c.* 414 BC)
PREMIERES 18 May 1779, Opéra, Paris; UK: 7 April 1796, King's Theatre, Haymarket, London; US: 25 November 1916, Metropolitan, New York

Second version
Tragisches Singspiel in four acts (2h)
Libretto by Johann Baptist von Alxinger, after Guillard
PREMIERE 23 October 1781, Burgtheater, Vienna
CAST Iphigénie (Iphigenia) s, Thoas b, Oreste (Orestes) bar (1781: t), Pylade (Pylades) t (*haute-contre*), 2 Priestesses s, Diane (Diana) s, A Scythian b (1781: t), A Temple Servant b (1781: A Minister b), 1779 only: A Greek Woman

s; *satb* chorus of priestesses, Scythians, Eumenides, Greeks, Thoas' guards

Gluck's last triumph at the Paris Opéra returns to Trojan War material. That Diana should save Iphigenia from sacrifice in Aulis and take her to Scythia (Crimea) as a priestess seems to negate the ending of the earlier opera; but the two themes were separately and incompatibly treated by Euripides, whose light-toned drama lies behind the more serious operas on the subject. The French pair (Niccolò Piccinni's followed in 1781) were directly derived from Guymond de la Touche's play of 1757, still in repertoire at the Comédie-Française in the 1770s. By coincidence Goethe's poetic drama on the subject was written at the same time as Gluck's opera. The second version, in German, is only a little altered. Its designation, 'tragisches singspiel', uses the latter word in its original sense, implying simply 'opera': there is no spoken dialogue.

Iphigénie en Tauride continues to be one of the most often revived of Gluck's operas. In the early 19th century the role was taken by Alexandrine Branchu. The opera was a particular favourite of Berlioz; he wrote enthusiastically to Charles Hallé (who gave a performance in Manchester in 1860) about 'O malheureuse Iphigénie'; this aria was also singled out for praise by Tovey. Richard Strauss rearranged the opera, with additional orchestration and some musical 'modernization', in 1900 (repeated New York, 1916); but his version was considerably less radical than Wagner's of *Aulide*.

SYNOPSIS

Act I Gluck prophetically began this opera without an overture. Instead the orchestra depicts calm at dawn, followed by the storm which (we learn later) brings Orestes, Iphigenia's brother, to Tauris. Through this the voices of Iphigenia and her priestesses are heard imploring the gods' protection. The storm dies away; but Iphigenia declares that it is still raging in her heart. She has dreamed of the death of her father and mother, and then that she herself will raise the sacrificial knife to kill her brother. She turns to Diana, who has brought her to Tauris, in prayer ('O toi, qui prolongeas mes jours'). The savage Thoas, king of Tauris, is afflicted by foreboding ('De noirs pressentiments'); when two strangers appear, driven inland by the storm, he demands their immediate sacrifice in accordance with local custom.

Act II (Guillard originally wrote a five-act drama; it was on Gluck's insistence that two acts were conflated into Act II.) To seek absolution for killing his mother, Clytemnestra, Orestes has been driven by the avenging Furies to recover the statue of Diana, profaned by human sacrifice in Tauris. The other captive is his close friend Pylades. They are separated by guards, and Orestes, after a delusory moment of peace ('Le calme rentre dans mon coeur'), falls into a fit in which the Furies accuse him. At its climax Clytemnestra's ghost appears and seems to merge into the real Iphigenia who comes to question him. Although unaware of Orestes' identity, Iphigenia feels drawn to him; she persuades him to tell her the history of her family, which he ends by announcing his own death. Lamenting his end ('O malheureuse Iphigénie'), she turns for solace to ritual ('Contemplez ces tristes apprêts').

Act III Iphigenia resolves to free one captive, to take a message to her sister, Electra. She hopes Orestes will be saved, but after a magnanimous dispute, in which Orestes cites his own madness as a reason for dying, Pylades agrees to go; he may find help and attempt a rescue ('Divinité des grandes âmes').

Act IV Iphigenia prays for release from her hated duty ('Je t'implore et je tremble'). At the sacrificial altar Iphigenia and Orestes recognize each other; Thoas enters in a rage, singing an air of invective which Gluck required his librettist to supply, and is about to slaughter the victim and priestess together when Pylades appears with the crew of Orestes' ship, kills Thoas, and overcomes the superstitious barbarian guards. Diana descends to confirm that her statue must no longer be profaned by human blood. (A ballet, Les Scythes enchaînés, was added by François-Joseph Gossec, Gluck by this date (1779) apparently regarding such things as 'hors-d'oeuvre'.)

One remarkable aspect of this opera is the absence of sexual love. Gluck concentrates on his heroine, magnificently drawn in four contrasted arias, and on Orestes, whose frenzies, the result of the remorseless grip on his conscience of matricide (symbolized by the Furies) bring the trombones into play. The reminder, by the throbbing violas, that his peace ('Le calme rentre dans mon coeur') is illusory is Gluck's most famous (though by no means unique) piece of psychological instrumentation. When it was criticized for the calm with which Orestes was speaking, Gluck replied: 'He is lying: he killed his mother.'

Iphigénie en Tauride may well be considered the most perfect of Gluck's serious operas. Yet he made even more use than usual of material salvaged from earlier works. The 1765 ballet Semiramis formed the basis for the Furies' music; Iphigenia's longer arias are from La clemenza di Tito and Antigono via Telemaco, which also supplied Orestes' Act II aria 'Dieux! qui me poursuivez' via Le feste d'Apollo; and the opening is derived from L'île de Merlin. The incorporation of Italian arias gives an expansiveness to the characterization which is markedly different from Aulide or Armide, though not unlike Alceste. None of these arias, however, retains its full da-capo form, and they are balanced by shorter pieces. Iphigenia has an aria in each act; those in the first and third are considerably shorter, as are the arias for Thoas and Pylades. The small chorus of priestesses is handled with unprecedented freedom, intervening for single words as well as short choruses, and providing an additional dynamic and emotional resource at the climax of 'O malheureuse Iphigénie'.

Gluck continued to work in massive tableaux, notably in Act II: first Orestes' scene with the Furies, then Iphigenia's mourning, the central part of the original aria being converted into the chorus 'Contemplez ces tristes apprêts' (in the German version this is omitted, being replaced to considerably less effect by a sinfonia). The work also possesses a symphonic dimension

unusual in Gluck, which, however, functions like a ritornello, connecting the opening storm music with the dénouement (the intervention of Thoas to the arrival of Diana), also in D major: the continuity of the music here exceeds even that of the climax of Aulide.

Gluck continued to cultivate flexibility of form, especially in recitatives, where the use of string texture, while prohibiting fast delivery, enabled him to exert an iron control over the tension even in the longest speeches. He makes more use than ever of sustained chordal accompaniment, which permits an immediate response from the orchestra to a crucial word or gesture. The principal formal achievement of this opera is the integration of arias derived from Italian works into a framework that seems entirely French.

Other operas: Artaserse, 1741 (2 arias survive); Demetrio, 1742 (8 arias survive); Demofoonte, 1743; Il Tigrane, 1743 (11 arias and 1 duet survive); La Sofonisba, 1744 (11 arias and 1 duet survive); Ipermestra, 1744; Poro, 1744 (overture, 4 arias and 1 duet survive); Ippolito, 1745 (11 arias and 1 duet survive); La caduta de' giganti, 1746; Artamene, 1746 (6 arias survive); Le nozze d'Ercole e d'Ebe, 1747; La Semiramide riconosciuta, 1748; La contesa de'numi, 1749; Ezio, 1750, rev. 1763; Issipile, 1752 (4 arias survive); La clemenza di Tito, 1752; Le Cinesi, 1754; La Danza, 1755; L'innocenza giustificata, 1755; Antigono, 1756; Il re pastore, 1756; La fausse esclave, 1758; L'île de Merlin, ou Le monde renversé, 1758; La Cythère assiégée, 1759, rev. 1775; Le diable à quatre, ou La double métamorphose, 1759; L'arbre enchanté, ou Le tuteur dupé, 1759, rev. 1775; L'ivrogne corrigé, 1760; Tetide, 1760; Le cadi dupé, 1761; Il trionfo di Clelia, 1763; Il Parnaso confuso, 1765; Telemaco, o sia L'isola di Circe, 1765; La corona, (1765); Il prologo, 1767 (overture and 3 numbers to precede Traetta's Ifigenia in Aulide); Le feste d'Apollo, 1769; Écho et Narcisse, 1779

J.R.

ALEXANDER GOEHR
Peter Alexander Goehr; b 10 August 1932, Berlin

The son of the conductor Walter Goehr, Alexander Goehr went to England with his family in 1933 and has lived there ever since. He studied at the Royal Manchester College of Music (1952–5) with Richard Hall, and formed the so-called New Music Manchester group with, among others, Birtwistle and Maxwell Davies. He later spent a year in Paris studying with Messiaen and Yvonne Loriod. For a few years he was a BBC producer, and he directed the Music Theatre Ensemble (1967–72). Since 1971 he has been a university professor: first at Leeds (till 1976), then at Cambridge, where he has been a strong influence on the teaching, especially of composition, as well as reaching a wider audience through the medium of radio (he gave the BBC Reith Lectures in 1987).

Goehr's father had been a pupil of Schoenberg, and the son has always retained in his own music something of the intellectual rigour and system of that tradition. But he quickly outstripped its orthodoxy, and evolved a more personal and flexible harmonic grammar that also owes something to Messiaen. This harmonic 'feel' has given Goehr's mature work a distinctive flavour and in some ways made it more approachable, though the sort of music he writes is still intensely serious, with a consciousness of 'great traditions'. He has contributed to most of the standard instrumental forms (three symphonies, several concertos and three string quartets), and has written powerful oratorios. But his theatre music has had a chequered career. An early attempt at an opera on Euripides (*The Trojan Women*) was abandoned and its surviving fragments absorbed into the orchestral *Hecuba's Lament* (1959–61). His two subsequent full-length operas both had German premieres in which they fell foul of German theatrical politics, though at least Germany staged them – which, at the time of writing (1995), no established British company has done. As for the triptych of music-theatre pieces, they enjoyed a fashionable career in the early 1970s, when that genre was in vogue and when Goehr's ensemble existed to perform them, but have since fallen into relative neglect.

Arden Must Die

Arden muss sterben
Opera in two acts, (2h)
Libretto by Erich Fried (English version by Geoffrey Skelton), after the anonymous 16th-century play *Arden of Faversham*, and the *Chronicles* of Raphael Holinshed (1577)
PREMIERES 5 March 1967, Staatsoper, Hamburg; UK: 17 April 1974, Sadler's Wells, London
CAST Arden *b*, Franklin *b*, Alice *ms*, Mosbie *t*, Susan *s*, Michael *t*, Greene *bar*, Reede *b*, Mrs Bradshaw *c*, Shakebag *t*, Black Will *b*, *s*, *bar*, *b*, *spoken role*; *satb* chorus of market people and constables

Goehr's first opera was commissioned by Hamburg State Opera, and played there to a noisy reception of the kind so often accorded by post-war German audiences to works with political content, however muted. Fried's adaptation enhances the play's 'morality' or (in Brecht's sense) 'epic' character: individual character is suppressed in favour of a semi-parodistic treatment of human frailty. Authority lines up with the most cynical individual self-interest (in fact is indistinguishable from it), while the majority, represented by the 'neighbour', Mrs Bradshaw (a character invented by Fried), stand by and pretend to be uninvolved.

SYNOPSIS
Act I The characters plot Arden's murder: his wife, Alice, because she wants her lover, Mosbie; others because Arden is supposedly a hard landlord, etc. Arden, who in fact appears a decent man, is called to London to administer lands recently granted him. Alice feigns regret, but at once goes to bed with Mosbie. On the marshes in dense fog, Arden and Franklin cross the river by ferry, while the hired murderers, Shakebag and Black Will, blunder around and Shakebag falls into the river. A shepherd brings Alice and the others news of Arden's murder, but soon afterwards Arden and Franklin themselves return. Arden makes to throw the would-be murderers out; Mosbie draws a dagger but then protests his innocence, and the act ends with a reconciliation.
Act II Shakebag and Will are in London (charac-

terized by quotation from Orlando Gibbons's *Cries of London*) in pursuit of Arden, and observed by Mrs Bradshaw. But again they are thwarted, this time by a window shutter falling on Will's head at the crucial moment. Later they plot to enter Arden's London house at night, but the door is locked against them. Back at Faversham, Arden has dinner guests (the plotters) and this time, despite blunders, the murder is successful. But when the law arrives, in the person of the mayor and constables, the hired killers are appointed hangmen, and hope is offered to the others: 'For those who are contrite the law holds out no terrors. With true deeds they may strive to wipe out ancient errors.' In a spoken epilogue (done in Hamburg but later suppressed) the audience is ironically reassured of its own innocence.

Fried rhymed his text and included set pieces: 'Murderers' Songs', 'Ferryman's Song', etc., in the Brechtian manner. But Goehr's setting only partly respects this formula, and stylistically it owes little or nothing to Brecht–Weill. Like all Goehr's music it has a strong harmonic profile, materializing sometimes into tonal shapes. For a first opera, it is impressively considerate of the voices and as a score it is consistently intriguing. But as drama it perhaps lacks the speed and variety of pace called for by its black-comic subject matter, while the character portraiture is inevitably somewhat one-dimensional. Was Goehr, a self-declared man of the Left, interested in the political message as such? In the Hamburg programme he called *Arden* 'a political opera about the way we act in a crisis', but this remark is absent from the 1974 London programme, even though (in the broadest sense) it is no less than the truth.

Behold the Sun

Opera in three acts (3h)
Libretto by John McGrath and the composer
PREMIERES 19 April 1985, Duisburg (as *Die Wiedertäufer*); UK: 3 October 1987, BBC radio
CAST Berninck *bar*, His Wife *ms*, Christian *coloratura s*, Matthys *bar*, Divara *s*, Bokelson *t*, Blacksmith *b*, Knipperdollinck *bar*, Prince-Bishop *bar*, *s*, 3 *t*, *bar*; *satb* chorus of townspeople; semichorus of Anabaptists

Goehr's earlier study of religious delusion (in *Sonata about Jerusalem*) led him to this full-length treatment of the Anabaptist uprising in Münster in 1534–5. He had considered other more or less messianic subjects, and had sketched a libretto on Shelley's *Prometheus Unbound*. The eventual inspiration for *Behold the Sun* came from Norman Cohn's book *The Pursuit of the Millennium* and from Ernst Bloch's writings on the 'theology of Revolution'. The work uses the mass hysteria in the historical events as a basis for a choral opera with a flavour of the baroque Passion (the chorus is referred to as *turba*), while the big set-piece ensembles are offset by more intimate genre scenes. But the first production, by Deutsche Oper am Rhein, was both brutally cut and partly reorganized at the behest of the producer Bohumil Herlischka, wrecking Goehr's fine balance of the 'real' and the 'possible'.

SYNOPSIS

Act I The merchant Berninck comes home to find his wife reading the Bible and his son, Christian, unfed. In the Cathedral Square in (Lutheran) Münster the Anabaptists arrive from Leyden (Holland), led by Matthys, his wife Divara, and Bokelson. Their prophetic utterances and ecstatic manner infect the townspeople. They kiss, swooningly, to the dismay of the unaffected, including Berninck and the burgomaster Knipperdollinck. Christian embarks on a visionary song with chorus, and the crowd becomes more and more abandoned.

Act II The prince-bishop determines to suppress the Anabaptists. In Münster, Matthys urges the people to be baptized anew and to give up their material wealth. Bokelson threatens a fishwife with a dagger for refusing, but is restrained by Matthys. Berninck, Knipperdollinck and the blacksmith stand up to Bokelson, who kills the blacksmith. Berninck tries to leave with his valuables, but is prevented by the Anabaptists. Matthys walks out on to the town walls and is shot by the besieging troops of the prince-bishop.

Act III Divara comforts the starving townspeople. A lame man utters prophecies. Bokelson, increasingly deranged, presents himself as king; he urges the men to polygamy and takes Divara as his wife. In the Bernincks' house Christian dies of starvation. In the square, the lame prophet works the people into a hysteria; there is an ecstatic dance and a play (Dives and Lazarus) is enacted, at the end of which Lazarus (Bokelson) orders the actual hanging of Dives. Divara intervenes. The episcopal troops arrive, let in by Berninck, to be confronted by the ecstatic crowd led by Divara.

Goehr's score is closely related to a just earlier large-scale choral work, Babylon the Great is Fallen, and its choral scenes are the finest. The music uses refrain forms and recurrent harmonies brilliantly to suggest the gradual growth of mass hysteria. The genre scenes are more conventional and perhaps weaker, and the text, heavily dependent on prophetic utterances, sometimes lacks dramatic direction. But the vocal writing is excellent, and there is a magnificently extravagant soprano part for the visionary boy, Christian, much of which was cut in Duisburg.

Other operatic works: Naboth's Vineyard, 1968; Shadowplay-2, 1970; Sonata about Jerusalem, 1971

S.W.

CHARLES GOUNOD

Charles-François Gounod; b 17 June 1818, Paris; d 18 October 1893, Saint-Cloud, nr Paris

Gounod, widely celebrated for a few years at the height of his career as France's leading composer, could count among his teachers two grand old men of French musical pedagogy in the 1830s, Antonin Reicha and Jean-François Le Sueur. Thorough academic training fertilized his prodigious musical facility and led to the Prix de Rome at the early age of 20. Exposure to Italian cultural treasures on the prize-winner's trip left an indelible mark on Gounod, who was also a gifted painter. Unlike many of his contemporaries, he looked to classical culture in a general way as a model of balance and control for his own work. And, impregnated with classical ideals about the higher role of art in society, he expressed alarm in letters home about the despoliation of music through commercialism. Not surprisingly, Gounod never became comfortable in business matters. His career was also unusual in that, on his return to Paris, he did not seek to achieve success in the world of opera, preferring to devote himself to sacred music and even seriously contemplating the priesthood.

It was entirely characteristic that Gounod was drawn to a classical subject, the death of the poet Sappho, for his first opera. Sapho was composed for the great mezzo Pauline Viardot, who championed the composer after he turned away from the seminary in 1848. Though it was a box-office failure during its first run at the Opéra in 1851, Sapho was enough of a succès d'estime to lead to another commission at the same house, La nonne sanglante (1854), to a libretto by Eugène Scribe. That work was no more enduring, mainly because of a poorly wrought libretto, but Gounod's continuing prominence was assured not only by favourable critical response to his music but also by his appointment in 1852 as director of an important choral society, the Orphéon de la Ville de Paris. He began a number of operatic projects following the demise of La nonne, including an Ivan le terrible which he never completed; that libretto eventually passed into the hands of his young friend Bizet. The planning of Faust (1859), Gounod's first collaboration with Jules Barbier and Michel Carré, began in 1856 with encouragement from the newly appointed director of the Théâtre Lyrique, Léon Carvalho. Before that work was staged, however, Gounod completed a very fine operatic adaptation of Molière's Le médecin malgré lui (1858). Faust itself was well received during its first run, though publishers were slow to take interest. A few weeks after the premiere, Gounod and his librettists struck an agreement with the Choudens firm. By arranging performances in other cities, that publisher set about effectively marketing Faust. Stagings at French provincial theatres followed by productions in Germany, many of them under the title of Margarete to distance the work from Goethe and to reflect more accurately its substance.

Carvalho, eager to follow up the success of Faust with a new work by Gounod, persuaded him to re-route Philémon et Baucis (1860) from its intended destination, the summer theatre at Baden-Baden, to the Théâtre Lyrique. Gounod rather artificially enlarged the scope of Philémon for the Parisian stage and it did not fare well until it was reduced to its original proportions many years later at the Opéra-Comique. In place of Philémon et Baucis, he supplied the Baden stage with La colombe (1860). Demonstrating remarkable productivity for a composer of his generation, Gounod soon completed the five-act La reine de Saba (1862) after a story by Gérard de Nerval, for the Opéra. For the first time in his career (and possibly that of any French composer) several reviewers described the music as *wagnérien*, a term that would be used with similar lack of discrimination in France until the end of the century. In part because of expectations aroused by the success of *Faust*, the opera was Gounod's most resounding failure to date. His subsequent stage work, *Mireille* (1864), did little better at first; nevertheless, on revival and with extensive modifications it eventually did entrench itself in French houses.

Another failure would almost certainly have led precipitously to the end of Gounod's operatic career. In *Roméo et Juliette* he scored a much needed critical triumph that was vigorously sustained at the Théâtre Lyrique box office by an initial run during the Paris World Exhibition of 1867, when the city was well populated by tourists. Personal turmoil brought about by a move to England after the war of 1870 and by a temporary estrangement from his wife produced a lengthy hiatus before his next operatic premiere. Because of a long-distance dispute with the management of the Opéra-Comique, Gounod never completed the setting that he began of Molière's *George Dandin*, a most interesting project since he used Molière's prose text throughout instead of a more conventional verse reworking. Another project during these years was an adaptation of *Polyeucte*, Pierre Corneille's play about Christian martyrdom in Rome. A messy dispute over ownership of the complete autograph full score with Georgina Weldon, a singer of modest accomplishments with whom Gounod had become personally entangled while in England, caused a delay in a staging of that work.

After Gounod's return to France, Léon Carvalho, now hoping to replicate earlier Théâtre Lyrique successes as director of the Opéra-Comique, commissioned *Cinq-Mars* (1877) from him. It disappointed, as did *Polyeucte* when it was finally unveiled on the stage of the Opéra in 1878. The latter failure was a bitter pill since Gounod himself valued the work highly, no doubt largely because of its fusion of classical setting with Christian theme and the difficult personal circumstances surrounding its genesis. With scarcely better luck, he attempted radically different subject matter in his subsequent opera, *Le tribut de Zamora* (1881), a story set in Spain that prominently featured a madwoman's recovery of reason. By this time it was clear that Gounod's operatic career would not be resuscitated; he had not renewed himself musically and was left behind by younger composers such as Massenet. A major overhaul of *Sapho* in 1884, with the addition of much new music, was Gounod's final operatic endeavour. That he could even undertake a recasting of his first opera late in his career is testimony to the short stylistic distance between his first opera and last.

Faust

Opera in five acts (3h 30m)
Libretto by Jules Barbier and Michel Carré, after Michel Carré's *Faust et Marguerite* (1850) and Johann Wolfgang von Goethe's play *Faust*, Part 1 (1808), in the French translation by Gérard de Nerval (1828)
Composed 1856–9; ballet 1868–9

PREMIERES 19 March 1859, Théâtre Lyrique, Paris; UK: 11 June 1863, Her Majesty's Theatre, Haymarket, London; US: 18 November 1863, Academy of Music, Philadelphia; with ballet: 3 March 1869, Opéra, Paris
CAST Faust *t*, Méphistophélès (Mephistopheles) *b*, Wagner *bar*, Valentin *bar*, Siébel *s*, Marguerite *s*, Marthe *ms*; *satb* chorus of young girls, labourers, students, burghers, matrons, invisible demons, church choir, witches, queens and courtesans of antiquity, celestial voices

Gounod's enthusiasm for Goethe's *Faust* was of long standing by the time he set about planning his opera with Barbier and Carré in 1856; he had even composed a setting of the church scene in the late 1840s (the present location of that autograph is unknown). Since Goethe's play offered little character interaction beyond the three principals (Faust, Gretchen – here Marguerite – and Mephistopheles), Michel Carré allowed his own earlier adaptation of Goethe's *Faust* for the Théâtre du Gymnase-Dramatique, with its significantly expanded roles for Valentin and Siébel, to serve as the proximate source for the project. Gounod's opera follows Carré's light boulevard play quite closely, but reintroduces weightier elements from Goethe, such as Valentin's death, the Walpurgis Night (rarely given outside France today), and Marguerite's imprisonment. The return to Goethean elements missing from Carré's play, however, seems to have been motivated in many instances as much, if not more, by purely musical and operatic considerations as by the principle of fidelity to the German playwright. Direct comparison of Gounod's opera with the Goethe play risks obscuring the opera's many qualities.

The work that Gounod originally composed was much longer than the one performed on the opening night. Many numbers, including an Act II duet for Valentin and Marguerite, a more extended Walpurgis Night episode, and a mad scene for Marguerite alone in the last act – doubtless not well suited to the voice of Marie Miolan-Carvalho, creator of the role – were cut in the first rehearsal. At a late rehearsal stage, the 'Soldiers' Chorus' was lifted from Gounod's aborted *Ivan le terrible* to replace a set of couplets composed for Valentin in Act IV. Upheavals to *Faust* continued as its popularity spread. The original spoken dialogue between set pieces was soon replaced on most stages by recitatives supplied by the composer. In some productions, the church scene appeared near the beginning of Act IV instead of in its original position after Valentin's death. For the second set of performances at Her Majesty's Theatre in 1864, the English baritone Charles Santley requested an arrangement of a melody from the orchestral prelude that became 'Avant de quitter ces lieux'; that piece has remained part of the work ever since, despite Gounod's reservations about it. Finally, Gounod composed the well-known ballet music when the work travelled from the Théâtre Lyrique to the Opéra in 1869.

SYNOPSIS

Act I Faust, despondent and alone in his study, resolves to take poison but hesitates when he hears a pastoral chorus. An invocation to Satan conjures up a rather dapper buffo Mephistopheles. Faust yearns above all for sensual gratification and Mephistopheles readily promises to fulfil the philosopher's desires in return for service in the nether regions. When Faust hesitates, Mephistopheles conjures up a vision of Marguerite at her spinning wheel. Faust signs the document and is transformed into a young nobleman, singing of the pleasures that await him ('À moi les plaisirs').

Act II At the fair, townspeople sing a virtuoso chorus ('Vin ou bière'). Valentin appears, clutching a medallion given him by his sister Marguerite; he is about to leave for battle and instructs his friends, including Wagner and Siébel, to look after her ('Avant de quitter ces lieux'). Mephistopheles joins the group and provides blasphemous entertainment with a song about the golden calf ('Le veau d'or'). Valentin is incited to anger when Mephistopheles makes light of his sister, but his sword breaks in mid-air. Alarmed, the men brandish the crossed pommels of their weapons in a gesture of Christian exorcism. Temporarily emasculated, Mephistopheles is left alone on stage, but is soon joined by Faust and a group of waltzing villagers ('Ainsi que la brise légère'). When Marguerite appears among them, Faust offers her his arm; she modestly rejects his advance.

Act III Siébel leaves a bouquet for Marguerite in her garden. Faust, playing well the role of romantic idealist, apostrophizes her home and the protective embrace of nature ('Salut! demeure chaste et pure'). More worldly wise, Mephistopheles positions a jewel box near Siébel's flowers. Marguerite enters and sings a ballad tinged with modal inflexions about the king of Thule. She then discovers both the bouquet and the jewel box and erupts in a buoyant cabaletta (the 'Jewel Song' – 'Je ris de me voir') as she tries on ear-rings and a necklace. Her guardian, Marthe, is not immune to male attentions either, and when Faust and Mephistopheles join the pair she is attracted to the devil. Marguerite allows herself to be embraced by Faust in a duet ('Laisse-moi, laisse-moi contempler ton visage') but is suddenly overcome with shame. Encouraged by Mephistopheles, Faust completes the seduction.

Act IV Marguerite has given birth to Faust's child and is ostracized by girls in the street below. She sits down to spin ('Il ne revient pas'), and Siébel, ever faithful, attempts to encourage her. The scene shifts to a public square for the return of Valentin, bombastic and self-assured ('Soldiers' Chorus'). While Valentin is inside the house, Mephistopheles trenchantly plays a lover delivering a serenade beneath Marguerite's window. Faust declares his responsibility for Marguerite's fall and successfully engages Valentin in a duel. As he dies, Valentin blames Marguerite and damns her for eternity. The next scene shows Marguerite attempting to pray in a church. She eventually succeeds, despite the musical efforts of a chorus of demons, but faints when Mephistopheles unleashes a final imprecation.

Act V It is Walpurgis Night in the Harz Mountains, and Faust is first mesmerized by will-o'-the-wisps and witches and then titillated by legendary courtesans of antiquity. A vision of Marguerite redirects his thoughts to her. She has been imprisoned for infanticide. Through Mephistopheles, Faust obtains the keys to her cell. They sing a love duet about past bliss, and he begs her to flee ('Oui, c'est toi, je t'aime'). With Mephistopheles impatiently goading the two to follow him, Marguerite resists and calls for divine protection ('Anges purs! anges radieux'). Faust looks on with despair and falls to his knees in prayer as her soul rises to heaven.

Faust was considered a difficult work by many during its first run of performances. In part this was due to a full-flowering of Gounod's mature melodic style, one that eschewed mechanistic spinning out of rhythmic motifs and an abundance of coloratura in favour of a tapering of relatively simple surface rhythms around the expressive nuances of the text. Gounod also avoided certain conventions, for example the introductory chorus and the concertato-type finale. It is easy to forget just how unusual the opening scene was in its day, with its long passages of arioso singing by Faust punctuated by offstage music. Marguerite's appearance late in Act II is a refreshingly understated first entry for the prima donna. The magnificent orchestral peroration at the curtain of Act III, a grand statement of a tune previously heard only at softer dynamic levels and fragmented, is another impressive moment, one that proved highly influential on later composers. To conclude with the threefold semitonal rise of 'Anges purs! anges radieux!' was an electrifying, and unprecedented, inspiration.

Marguerite is the most fully developed musical character in *Faust*. Her awakened sensuality is hinted at through recitative interruptions in 'The Ballad of the King of Thule' and is later more fully exposed as she leans out of her window wishing for Faust's return. Her role displays a naturalism uncommon on the French stage at the time, as in her account of her sister's death in the Act III quartet, where, with a brief turn to recitative in the prevailing arioso, she spontaneously recalls rushing to the side of the crib. Her spinning song in Act IV compares favourably with other settings of this text, and she achieves truly heroic musical stature in both the church scene and the final trio. Mephistopheles is something of a demonic Leporello, light-hearted but dangerously cynical, a characteristic given effective musical form (particularly through orchestration) in the Act IV serenade.

Mireille

Opera in five acts (3h)
Libretto by Michel Carré, after Frédéric Mistral's poem *Mirèio* (1859)
Composed 1862–4, rev. and reduced to three acts, 1864
PREMIERES 19 March 1864, Théâtre Lyrique, Paris; rev. version (with recitative): UK: 5 July 1864, Her Majesty's Theatre, Haymarket, London; US: 17 November 1864, Academy of Music, Philadelphia; 15 December 1864, Théâtre Lyrique, Paris
CAST Mireille *s*, Vincent *t*, Ourrias *bar*, Maître Ramon *b*, Taven *ms*, Andreloux *ms*, Maître Ambroise *b*, Clémence *s*; *satb* chorus of mulberry gatherers, townspeople, spirits of the Rhône, farmhands, pilgrims to the chapel of the Saintes-Maries

Mistral's epic Provençal poem was published in 1859, and soon afterwards Gounod was put into personal contact with him through their mutual friend the playwright Ernest Legouvé. Taking up the poet's invitation to visit Provence, he composed most of the score on location and actually visited the site of each tableau in the opera. *Mireille* was not successful in its original five-act form, despite frantic revisions and reorderings during the first run. Consequently, Gounod made important changes to the work within a few months of its premiere, including the addition of a light *valse-ariette*, 'O légère hirondelle', to the title role, a change in dénouement that had Mireille suddenly recover from sunstroke instead of expire, a reduction to three acts, and the conversion of the spoken dialogue into recitative for foreign stages. *Mireille* did not score a real success, however, until a three-act revival in 1889 at the Opéra-Comique, after which it became a staple of the repertoire of that house. Later productions at the Opéra-Comique, most prominently one in 1939 conducted by Henri Büsser, sought to restore Gounod's original intentions, albeit with limited historical accuracy.

Though operas in pastoral settings were not uncommon at the Opéra-Comique in this period, *Mireille* struck a new note by depicting the unsuitability of an amorous relationship because of class entirely within a frame of Provençal peasant society. The choice of a classical five-act layout for such a setting was also unusual – a reflection of the epic nature of the Mistral model. That a farmer's daughter assumes real tragic stature in the opera was found objectionable in some critical circles after the premiere.

SYNOPSIS (original version)
Act I Mireille's friends gently tease her about having fallen in love with Vincent, the son of a mere basketweaver, and the good witch Taven warns her that wealth and poverty are ill-matched. Vincent eloquently voices his love to Mireille, and the two agree to meet at the chapel of the Saintes-Maries should danger befall either of them.

Act II The bull-tamer Ourrias tries to court Mireille but is rebuffed. She goes on to reveal her love for a boy from a lower class to her father, the wealthy farmer Maître Ramon. He vows that Mireille will never see Vincent again.

Act III In a fit of jealousy, Ourrias strikes the unarmed Vincent and for this ignoble act is drowned by a ghostly ferryman on the river Rhône. Taven ministers to Vincent's wounds.

Act IV Despite asssurances given to her of Vincent's safety, Mireille decides to undertake a pilgrimage across the Crau desert to the Saintes-Maries. Exhausted by her journey, she sees a mirage of a city on the edge of a lake. She collapses, but shepherd's pipes in the distance revive her.

Act V At the chapel, Vincent is the first to appear. Stumbling in on the point of death, Mireille is ecstatic at being reunited with him and has a vision of the sky opening to receive her. She dies, but her soul is summoned upward by a celestial voice.

As with Marguerite in *Faust*, Mireille herself is the best-drawn character. Her musical characterization spans the distance from the simple candour of her first appearance – a vocal line with narrow range and simple accompaniment – to music requiring real heroic projection, such as the aria she sings in the Crau desert ('En marche'). The best-known number is the 'Chanson de Magali' sung by Mireille and Vincent in Act II, not based on an actual Provençal folksong but now so popular as to have almost become one. Its strict alternation of two compound metres (6/8 and 9/8) is less interesting than the subtle musical ways in which Gounod paints the text of the metaphorical poem the lovers share. Less successful are the supernatural Rhône scene and the musical portrayal of Ourrias as antagonist.

Roméo et Juliette
Romeo and Juliet
Opera in a prologue and five acts (3h 15m)
Libretto by Jules Barbier and Michel Carré, after William Shakespeare's *Romeo and Juliet* (1597)
PREMIERES 27 April 1867, Théâtre Lyrique, Paris; UK: 11 July 1867, Covent Garden, London; US: 15 November 1867, Academy of Music, New York
CAST Paris *bar*, Tybalt *t*, Capulet *b*, Juliette (Juliet) *s*, Roméo (Romeo) *t*, Mercutio *bar*, Benvolio *t*, Gertrude *ms*, Frère Laurent (Friar Laurence) *b*, Stéphano (Stephano) *s*, The Duke *b*, Frère Jean (Friar John) *b*; *satb* chorus of servants, retainers and kinsfolk to the Capulet and Montague households; maskers

In view of the widely recognized success of the love music in *Faust*, a setting of Shakespeare's *Romeo and Juliet* was a natural project for Gounod. Many episodes that do not centre directly on the relationship of the two protagonists in the play were cut by Gounod and his librettists, with the result that the encounters between the two main characters consume a far greater proportion of the opera than of the play. There is also a glaring discrepancy in the tomb scene: where in Shakespeare Juliet stirs only after Romeo has died, in Gounod (as well as in other 19th-century versions, including Berlioz's dramatic symphony) she awakens in time to sing a final duet with him. In other respects Barbier and Carré followed Shakespeare closely, borrowing directly from existing French translations.

Like so many of Gounod's operas, *Roméo et Juliette* underwent much revision. The celebrated *valse-ariette* 'Je veux vivre' was written at the request of Marie Miolan-Carvalho late in the rehearsal period. Because of her relatively light voice, the dramatic aria originally intended as the centrepiece for the role, 'Amour ranime mon courage' in Act IV, though printed in the first edition, was not performed at the first run, and is still rarely given today. The great confrontation between the Capulets and Montagues at the end of Act III was repeatedly revised: in the first edition, for example, the entry and departure of the duke were accompanied by a pompous stage band that was soon cut. For the revival at the Opéra in 1888 Gounod composed a new musical phrase for Romeo and the chorus to bring down the curtain at the end of that episode, the imposing 'O jour de deuil', and also supplied a ballet for the next act.

SYNOPSIS (following the first edition)
The curtain opens to a declaimed choral prologue summarizing the tragedy about to be enacted.

Act I The assembled guests at a masked ball in the Capulet residence admire the beauty of Juliet when she is escorted into the hall by her father. Romeo Montague and his friends, Mercutio and Benvolio, emerge from hiding. Mercutio makes light of Romeo's dark premonitions with an account of the fantastic realm of the fairy queen Mab ('Mab, la reine des mensonges'). Juliet reappears accompanied by her nurse, Gertrude, and maintains that she is uninterested in marriage ('Je veux vivre'), but after exchanging a few words with Romeo she realizes that their destinies are intertwined. The guests return and Capulet restrains Tybalt from venting his anger at the trespassing Montagues.

Act II Romeo has stealthily made his way into the Capulet garden and apostrophizes Juliet as the morning sun ('Ah! lève-toi soleil'). Shortly after she appears, he reveals his presence. Their tender words are interrupted by Capulet servants, who run through the garden in search of the Montague page Stephano, a comic foil to the elegiac tone of the act. The lovers agree to marry, and reluctantly separate when Juliet is called in by Gertrude.

Act III Friar Laurence sings of nature's wonders, and is soon joined by Romeo and Juliet. As the two kneel, he administers the sacrament of marriage. The scene changes to a street in front of the Capulet house, where Stephano is seen taunting the rival family ('Que fais-tu, blanche tourterelle'). The page's horseplay gives rise to serious consequences: Capulets come out; Montagues appear, and a succession of duels follows during which Romeo mortally wounds Tybalt. Romeo is exiled from Verona by the duke.

Act IV After spending the night with Juliet, Romeo suddenly breaks from her embrace on hearing the morning lark, and Juliet sadly admits that they must separate again. Capulet gives his daughter the news that she is to marry Paris. Friar Laurence explains how she can escape with Romeo by means of a ruse enacted through a potion that will make her appear dead. She summons her courage before drinking the liquid ('Amour ranime mon courage', a dramatic air often omitted). In the next scene Juliet is led into the family ballroom to the strains of a wedding march. She suddenly collapses.

Act V In the underground crypt of the Capulets, Friar Laurence learns from Friar John that Romeo has not received his letter explaining the ruse. After an instrumental interlude, Romeo appears. Believing Juliet to be dead he takes poison. At that moment she awakens, and the two sing of their love – largely through reminiscences of previous music, since a past is all that they now have. As he weakens, Juliet uncovers a sword hidden in her clothes and stabs herself.

The highlights of the score are the four duets for the two protagonists, certainly an unusual (and possibly unprecedented) number of tenor–soprano duets in a single opera: Massenet would follow suit in *Manon* and *Werther*. The passage for *divisi* cellos at the outset of the Act IV duet (surely a model for Verdi in the Act I duet of *Otello*) is a small tone poem about the wedding night; that entire duet exudes an air of sensuousness that was quite new to the French stage in its day. The concluding duet is one of Gounod's least conventional operatic numbers, at least in form: despite its length, it has few passages of ensemble singing or even of voice-dominated music constructed of phrases with regular lengths.

The opera also contains many other fine musical numbers. Romeo's ternary cavatina 'Ah! lève-toi, soleil' is justly renowned; its outer sections feature prominently a chromatic descent against a bass pedal note that illustrates the fading-star metaphor of the text without sacrificing lyric intensity. Mercutio's Queen Mab ballade is brilliantly orchestrated, and in the Act III confrontation between the Montagues and Capulets Gounod achieves a kind of momentum and excitement that are sometimes missing from his work.

Other operas: *Sapho*, 1851; *La nonne sanglante*, 1854; *Ivan le terrible* (inc., 1858); *Le médecin malgré lui*, 1858; *Philémon et Baucis*, 1860; *La colombe*, 1860; *La reine de Saba*, 1862; *George Dandin* (inc., 1874); *Cinq-Mars*, 1877; *Polyeucte*, 1878; *Maître Pierre* (inc., 1878); *Le tribut de Zamora*, 1881

S.H.

FROMENTAL HALÉVY

Jacques-François-Fromental (Fromentin)-Élie (Elias) Halévy (Lévi); *b* 27 May 1799, Paris; *d* 17 March 1862, Nice

The son of Jewish parents, Halévy entered the Paris Conservatoire at the age of nine. There he was a pupil of Cherubini, who was later to assist him considerably in his career. He also studied with Henri-Montan Berton and Étienne Méhul. Before winning the Prix de Rome in 1819 he had already composed a comic opera, *Les bohémiennes*, which was never performed; in Italy he wrote part of an Italian opera, *Marco Curzio*. His first work to be staged was *L'artisan* at the Opéra-Comique in 1827 with a libretto by Saint-Georges; but his greatest successes were *La juive* and *L'éclair* (both 1835), the one grand, the other comic, written in collaboration with respectively Eugène Scribe and Jules-Henri Vernoy de Saint-Georges. Four more grand operas were to follow: *Guido et Ginevra*, *La reine de Chypre*, *Charles VI*, and *Le juif errant*, all set in Renaissance or medieval Europe. There were at least a dozen more comic operas, a genre in which Halévy was equally at home.

Halévy was an intelligent composer and a good writer; he earned a fine reputation also as a choral director (at the Opéra) and as a teacher at the Conservatoire. His pupils included Gounod, Saint-Saëns and Bizet, the latter subsequently becoming his son-in-law. He was an accomplished administrator – indeed, one of the most prominent men of his time. Yet he felt overshadowed by Meyerbeer in the field of grand opera and by Auber and Adam in comic opera. His music is fluent and thoroughly professional; like Meyerbeer he was good at engineering impressive ensembles for a crowded stage, and he was adept at providing local colour and ballet music when required. He ably served the great singers in his vocal writing. His music was admired, though perhaps not wholeheartedly, by both Berlioz and Wagner.

La juive
The Jewess
Opera in five acts (4h; standard cut version 3h)
Libretto by Eugène Scribe
PREMIERES 23 February 1835, Opéra, Paris; US: 13 February 1844, Théâtre d'Orléans, New Orleans; UK: 29 July 1846, Drury Lane, London

CAST Eléazar *t*, Rachel *s*, Princess Eudoxie *s*, Léopold *t*, Cardinal de Brogni *b*, Ruggiero *bar*, Albert *b*; *satb* chorus of the people

The most successful of Halévy's operas, *La juive* remained in the Opéra's repertoire throughout the 19th century and has occasionally been revived, especially as a vehicle for tenors in the role of Eléazar. It was Halévy's first grand opera, staged with unprecedented magnificence in its first production at a cost of 150,000 francs; such splendour in historical costumes, armour and equestrian equipage had never been seen before. The role of Eléazar was derived from Shylock, that of Rachel from Rebecca in Walter Scott's *Ivanhoe*.

SYNOPSIS

Act I The setting is Constance in 1414. Rachel, daughter of Eléazar, a Jewish goldsmith, is in love with 'Samuel', who is working in her father's workshop. The Jews are harassed by the people for working on a Christian holiday.

Act II At the Passover meal Rachel notices that Samuel rejects the unleavened bread, and he confesses that he is a Christian, not a Jew at all. Rachel persuades her father not to kill him for the confession, so long as he marries her. He then admits, to their horror, that he is not free to marry her.

Act III At a sumptuous fête, Eléazar and his daughter deliver a gold chain which Princess Eudoxie has ordered for her husband and find that the husband, Prince Léopold, is none other than Samuel. Rachel, in fury, denounces him for the seduction of a Jewess, namely herself, and Cardinal de Brogni pronounces an anathema on all three: Léopold, Eléazar, and Rachel.

Act IV Léopold is saved from the scaffold by Rachel's declaration of his innocence; the Jews can be saved if they abjure their religion, but they refuse.

Act V Eléazar and Rachel are led to the scaffold. As she is thrown into the boiling cauldron Eléazar reveals his terrible secret to de Brogni: Rachel is in fact de Brogni's long-lost daughter, whom Eléazar saved from the sack of Rome many years before. She is not a Jewess at all.

This sensational dramaturgy with its 'spring-loaded' plot perfectly exemplifies Scribe's theatrical style; each successive revelation causes a horrified reaction, often expressed as a grand static ensemble. Halévy's models were Auber's *La muette de Portici* and Meyerbeer's *Robert le diable*, both of which he surpassed in many respects, earning the admiration of Wagner, Mahler and a faithful public for a whole century. He treated the Jewish scenes as local colour, not suggesting any particular identification as a Jew. The opera's orchestration is advanced for its time; Eléazar's air at the end of Act IV, 'Rachel! Quand du Seigneur', with its plaintive accompaniment by two cors anglais, is the best-known number in the opera.

Other operas: *Les bohémiennes*, (1819); *Marco Curzio*, (1822); *Les deux pavillons, ou Le jaloux et le méfiant*, (1824); *Pygmalion*, (1824); *Erostate*, (1825); *L'artisan*, 1827; *Le roi et le batelier*, 1827; *Clari*, 1828; *Le dilettante d'Avignon*, 1829; *Attendre et courir*, 1830; *La langue musicale*, 1830; *La tentation*, 1832; *Yella*, (1832); *Les souvenirs de Lafleur*, 1833; *Ludovic* (completion of inc. work by Hérold), 1833; *L'éclair*, 1835; *Guido et Ginevra*, 1838; *Les treize*, 1839; *Le shérif*, 1839; *Le drapier*, 1840; *Le guitarrero*, 1841; *La reine de Chypre*, 1841; *Charles VI*, 1843; *Le lazzarone, ou Le bien vient en dormant*, 1844; *Les mousquetaires de la reine*, 1846; *Les premiers pas* (coll. with Adam, Auber and Michele Carafa) 1847; *Le val d'Andorre*, 1848; *La fée aux roses*, 1849; *La tempestà*, 1850; *La dame de pique*, 1850; *Le juif errant*, 1852; *Le nabab*, 1853; *Jaguarita l'indienne*, 1855; *L'inconsolable*, 1855; *Valentine d'Aubigny*, 1856; *La magicienne*, 1858; *Noé* (completed by Bizet, renamed *Le déluge*), 1885; *Vanina d'Ornano* (inc., n.d.)

H.M.

GEORGE FRIDERIC HANDEL

Georg Friedrich Händel; *b* 23 February 1685, Halle an der Saale, Germany; *d* 14 April 1759, London

Although Handel is best known in the English-speaking world for his oratorios and orchestral works, he was primarily an opera composer. Until he was in his mid-fifties, his career centred on the opera house: he took a leading role in the musical management of London's repertoire opera companies and between 1710 and 1740 he composed new operas at a rate averaging more than one major work per year. Working within the musical conventions of Italian opera seria, Handel mainly set libretti that had already been used by other composers in Italy, though he adapted them to the needs of his own performers and, to some extent, to the tastes of his audiences. The well-developed and mature genre of opera seria to which Handel attached himself in his early twenties was already being enriched by elements from French opera (Handel's operas normally begin with a 'French' overture) and influences from French drama. To this form Handel brought formidable composition skills, particularly in the control and extension of melody and harmony, that took the baroque operatic aria to a peak of its development: and, since opera seria relied on the exposition of character and of emotional states through arias, in both of which Handel was supremely skilled, his operas mark the highest point in the genre itself.

In the town of his birth Handel received a firm technical education in music at the hands of Friedrich Wilhelm Zachow, the organist of the Market Church. Just before his 17th birthday he registered as a student at Halle University, and soon after received his first musical appointment as organist of the Calvinist Dom-kirche. However, he apparently nursed musical ambitions that could not be fulfilled in Halle, and two years later he left to join the opera house in Hamburg, initially as a violinist. He had already met one of the opera house's leading young musicians, Johann Mattheson, during a visit to Hamburg and Lübeck in 1703, and may have made preliminary contact with its leading composer, Reinhard Keiser, through his family connections in the area near Halle.

At Hamburg, Handel advanced quickly from second violinist to keyboard accompanist. Early in 1704 he was involved in a duel with Mattheson over the occupancy of the harpsichord at the end of Mattheson's *Cleopatra*. The next year saw the production of Handel's own first operas, *Almira* and *Nero*: the first was a success, but the second ran for only three performances. After this, Handel seems to have withdrawn somewhat from the opera company, though he composed one further opera, apparently so extensive that it was divided over two nights when it was first performed in 1708 (*Florindo* and *Dafne*) – but by then Handel had left Hamburg for Italy. Handel's Hamburg operas have not survived intact: *Almira* is the only one for which a sufficiently complete score survives for modern performance.

Handel's Italian visit lasted from the autumn of 1706 to the early months of 1710. Since he wanted to meet as many contemporary Italian musicians as possible, and to hear their music, he spent periods in a number of different centres. Considerable time was spent in Rome, where Handel enjoyed enlightened patronage and composed many chamber cantatas, developing in them the operatic forms of recitative and aria. But opera itself was absent from Rome, owing to papal opposition. At Florence, on the other hand, opera flourished under the patronage of Ferdinando de' Medici. Handel probably heard works by Alessandro Scarlatti, Giacomo Antonio Perti and Giuseppe Maria Orlandini there, and became acquainted with the libretti of Antonio Salvi, a physician to the Florentine court: it was for Florence that he composed his first all-Italian opera, *Rodrigo*. Venice gave him the opportunity to hear operas by Francesco Gasparini, Antonio Lotti, Tomaso Albinoni, Antonio Caldara and Alessandro Scarlatti, and to produce his own *Agrippina*.

During the Carnival season Venice was a resort for foreign diplomats as well as musicians. There Handel may have made contacts that brought him successively to Hanover and London, among them Agostino Steffani, who had directed the court opera in Hanover during its heyday in the 1690s. When Handel accepted a post at Hanover in June 1710 he must have recognized that the court opera was in abeyance for the foreseeable future, and it was apparently agreed that he would enjoy generous leave of absence to pursue his operatic ambitions elsewhere. Before the year was out, Handel was in London, and early the next year *Rinaldo* was produced at the Queen's Theatre, Haymarket. After a single dutiful return to Hanover, he settled permanently in London in 1712.

Handel's long operatic career in London falls into a number of phases. Although an overall musical continuity is apparent in the type of music presented, the administrations of successive opera companies lurched from one artistic or financial crisis to another. The decade preceding Handel's arrival had seen almost continuous chaos in the management of the London patent theatres: only recently had the idea of all-sung Italian opera become a reality, and the Haymarket Theatre its regular venue. Musical quality, some novel stage effects, and the presence of the leading castrato Nicolini brought success to Handel's first London opera, *Rinaldo*, and contributed to the permanent establishment of Italian opera in London. But managements came and went: sometimes, like Owen Swiney in 1713, they took the money with them. John Jacob Heidegger as manager brought some stability to the situation, but his efforts were temporarily beaten by a political division among the patrons in 1717, which came at the end of a period of gradual financial attrition.

The reunification of the sources of patronage, symbolized by the reconciliation between George I and the Prince of Wales in March 1720, coincided with the most determined attempt to establish Italian opera in London on a permanent footing. The Royal Academy of Music, established by charter in 1719, named Handel as 'Master of the Orchestra', and he was given instructions to undertake a European tour to engage singers, including the castrato Senesino. The Academy presented repertoire seasons whose programmes included operas by several composers and pasticcios assembled from other works. In the first years of the Academy Handel had to share musical authority with other composers, most importantly Giovanni Bononcini, but gradually responsibility devolved to Handel alone. Unfortunately the Academy was eventually overcome by problems of artistic and financial management. By 1728 the commitment of its original patrons had probably run its course, and could not be revived even by the unedifying rivalry between the supporters of the opera company's two leading ladies, Cuzzoni and Faustina Bordoni. After a break during 1728–9, Handel and Heidegger resumed opera seasons under their own management, taking over the Academy's scenery and costume stock. Handel once again visited the Continent to collect singers, including the soprano Anna Strada del Pò and the castrato Antonio Bernacchi; but within the year the latter had been replaced by the return of Senesino.

However, when a rival opera company (The Opera of the Nobility) was established in 1733 Senesino joined the opposition, taking most of the rest of the cast with him. After one season of rivalry, Handel had to cede the premier Haymarket opera house (known as the King's Theatre since the accession of George I in 1714) to the Nobility Opera, taking his own opera company to Covent Garden. The period of the two opera companies, which lasted until 1737, was an uncomfortable one for Handel, but it brought forth some fine operas. In Giovanni Carestini and Francesco Conti he found technically accomplished successors to Senesino, and his programmes were more diverse than those of the Nobility Opera. From 1732

onwards he mixed English oratorios, odes and serenatas with his Italian operas, and in 1734–5 his operas were considerably enhanced by Madame Sallé's dance company.

On the collapse of the Nobility Opera, Handel reoccupied the King's Theatre for two seasons in 1738–9: the emphasis was on opera in the first season and oratorio in the second. Then Handel moved his performances to a less central venue, the theatre in Lincoln's Inn Fields, for two seasons: English works were given in the first season, but the second included new Italian operas, *Imeneo* and *Deidamia*. There Handel gave his last London opera performance, in February 1741: the next year *Imeneo* saw a final revival at his hands as part of his concert season in Dublin. When Handel returned to London, his theatre career centred around English works. He looked back only once, when he inserted five of his Italian opera arias into a revival of *Semele* in December 1744, probably to accommodate Italian singers. It may be significant that this occurred in the one English work that, although performed 'after the manner of an oratorio', was composed to a libretto originally written *c.* 1706 for an English opera and intended for one of London's major theatres.

With the exception of three early German works, Handel wrote all his operas to Italian libretti. None of his English works was given a staged performance in the theatre under the composer: *Acis and Galatea* and *Esther* were probably acted in their earlier versions, at private performances, but when they came to the public theatre Handel presented them as a serenata and an oratorio respectively, without stage action. The genre of theatre oratorio that Handel developed in his later years was differently paced, and differently constructed, from his operas: opinions are divided as to whether staged performances are successful.

Handel revived several of his operas, with consequent changes of cast and musical contents. The versions and voice types listed are those of the first performances; major changes on subsequent revivals are noted in the descriptions. Voices are described according to the clefs used by Handel for the original singer (soprano, alto, tenor, bass), and roles originally composed for castrati are noted as such. The operas generally end with a *coro* sung by all the soloists. The presence of other chorus movements (generally sung by the soloists alone until Handel's operas of the mid-1730s) is noted for the relevant operas. Handel composed his operas to a normal time-span of about three hours' music: the performances must have lasted about four hours with the intervals. *Il pastor fido*, *Flavio*, *Atalanta* and *Imeneo* are rather shorter; *Giulio Cesare*, *Rodelinda* and *Alcina* rather longer.

Agrippina

Drama per musica in three acts (3h)
Libretto by Vincenzo Grimani, based on events *c.* AD 40–50 as related by Tacitus and Suetonius
PREMIERES ?January 1710, Teatro Grimani di San Giovanni Crisostomo, Venice; UK: 27 June 1963, Unicorn Theatre, Abingdon; US: 16 February 1972, Philadelphia (concert); 14 March 1985, Fort Worth

CAST   Agrippina *s*, Poppea (Poppaea) *s*, Nerone (Nero) *s* (castrato), Ottone (Otho) *a*, Claudio (Claudius) *b*, Narciso (Narcissus) *a* (castrato), Pallante (Pallas) *b*, Lesbo *b*, Giunone (Juno) *a*

Agrippina is arguably Handel's first operatic masterpiece. The plot is an anti-heroic satirical comedy. The characters (and their follies) are vividly portrayed with a light touch; yet the seriousness of the motivations and issues that produce the dramatic tensions is never undercut. The libretto is one of the best that Handel ever set and, unusually, was written specially for him. Handel probably composed the score in Venice late in 1709: the Carnival season began on 26 December, and *Agrippina* was apparently the second opera of the season.

SYNOPSIS

Act I   Agrippina, wife of the Roman emperor Claudius, schemes that Nero, her son by a previous marriage, should succeed to the throne. Hearing that Claudius has been drowned, she arranges to have Nero proclaimed, but the ceremony is interrupted by news of the arrival of Claudius, who has been rescued by his lieutenant Otho: in return Claudius has named Otho as his successor. Otho declares his love for Poppaea. Agrippina, knowing that Claudius is also attracted to Poppaea, suggests to Poppaea that Otho has agreed to yield her to Claudius in return for the succession.

Act II   Poppaea sets Claudius against Otho, but subsequently discovers that she has been deceived by Agrippina. Meanwhile, Agrippina plays on Claudius' belief in Otho's treachery and persuades him that he should name Nero as his successor.

Act III   Poppaea receives three admirers, successively hiding Otho and Nero behind curtained doorways, and awaiting Claudius. To him she says that she was mistaken in her previous identification and that his traitorous rival is Nero, not Otho: to prove this, she reveals Nero's presence in the room, and Claudius dismisses him in a fury. Agrippina realizes that Poppaea has denounced Nero, and that her own schemes are in danger of exposure. She responds to Claudius' accusations by saying that she acted for the safety of the city and the throne, and taxes him with being improperly influenced by Poppaea. When she claims that Otho loves Poppaea, Claudius lays the blame for his actions on Nero, and summons all three. He accuses Nero of hiding in Poppaea's room, and orders them to marry, meanwhile naming Otho to the succession. Otho renounces the throne in order to reclaim Poppaea: Claudius approves the exchange of Otho's and Nero's ambitions, and invokes Juno to bless the marriage of Otho and Poppaea. (Juno is not listed in the original printed libretto: the final scene, in which she appears, may have been cut before the first performance.)

Agrippina was a success: according to John Mainwaring, Handel's first biographer, 'The theatre, at almost every pause, resounded with shouts of *Viva il caro Sassone* [an allusion to Handel the Saxon]. They were thunderstruck with the grandeur and sublimity of his

style: for never had they known till then all the powers of harmony and modulation so closely arrayed, and forcibly combined.' The arias in *Agrippina* are shorter and more numerous than in Handel's later operas, but this is appropriate to the nature of the story. The portrayal of Agrippina herself is particularly well managed in the second half of Act II, and Handel's music keeps pace with the succession of comic dénouements in Act III.

Rinaldo

Opera in three acts (3h)
Libretto by Giacomo Rossi, to a scenario by Aaron Hill, after the epic poem *Gerusalemme liberata* by Torquato Tasso (1581)
Composed December 1710–January 1711; rev. 1731
PREMIERES   24 February 1711, Queen's Theatre, Haymarket, London; US: 16 October 1975, Jones Hall, Houston
CAST   Rinaldo *a* (castrato), Goffredo *a*, Eustazio *a* (castrato), Almirena *s*, Armida *s*, Argante *b*, Magician *a* (castrato), Herald *t*, Woman *s*, Mermaids *s*

Handel first arrived in London towards the end of 1710. His music had preceded him: movements from the *Rodrigo* overture had provided incidental music to *The Alchemist* (by Ben Jonson) earlier that year, and an aria from *Agrippina* was introduced into a performance of Alessandro Scarlatti's *Pirro e Demetrio* in December, probably with Handel's co-operation. It can safely be presumed that Handel had received a firm invitation to compose for the Haymarket company before he set out for London. The composer obviously wished to make his mark on London; the opera management for its part welcomed the opportunity for an original work in their programme, which had hitherto been founded on second-hand Italian scores.

In the preface to the printed libretto of *Rinaldo*, Rossi claimed that Handel had composed the opera in a fortnight, and this is possible since he reworked many of his previous Italian arias into the score. No doubt it had been prudent for Handel to leave the composition until he arrived in London and could see his cast in action. The preface by Aaron Hill (manager of the Queen's Theatre) to the libretto indicated his attempt to remedy what he regarded as the defects in the Italian operas hitherto seen in London: 'First, That they had been compos'd for Tastes and Voices, different from those who we're to sing and hear them on the English Stage; And Secondly, That wanting the Machines and Decorations, which bestow so great a Beauty on their Appearance, they have been heard and seen to very considerable Disadvantage.'

As the *Spectator* commented, with only slight exaggeration, on 6 March 1711, 'The opera of *Rinaldo* is filled with Thunder and Lightning, Illuminations, and Fireworks.' Hill exploited the full resources of the stage machinery at the Queen's Theatre. His intention seems to have been to match the virtuosity of the Italian singers with extravagant scenic effects derived from the English masque tradition. In addition to the singers, *Rinaldo* required a full complement of spirits, fairies and armies.

SYNOPSIS

Act I The Christian camp outside the gates of Jerusalem. Rinaldo reminds Goffredo, the captain general of the Crusade force, that he has been promised the hand of Almirena, Goffredo's daughter, if the city is conquered. Armida (an 'Amazonian' enchantress, and queen of Damascus), the mistress of Argante, the Saracen king of Jerusalem, arrives from the air in a fiery chariot and tells him that success in conquering the city depends on detaching Rinaldo from the Christian army. In a delightful grove with singing birds, Almirena and Rinaldo affirm their love. Armida enters and leads Almirena away. When Rinaldo offers resistance, the two ladies are carried away in a black cloud, and Rinaldo is left disconsolate ('Cara sposa, amante cara'). Goffredo and his brother Eustazio enter; Eustazio advises that they consult a hermit in order to defeat Armida. Rinaldo calls on winds and tempests to assist him ('Venti, turbini').

Act II On the seashore, where mermaids are playing, Goffredo and Rinaldo complain about the distance they must travel to find the hermit, but Eustazio assures them that they are close to their destination. A spirit in the shape of a lovely woman lures Rinaldo into a boat, telling him that she has been sent by Almirena. Rinaldo's companions try to prevent him from entering the boat, but he breaks free of them. The boat immediately sails away. In the garden in the enchanted palace of Armida, Almirena complains of her abduction. Argante makes advances, saying that he can prove his affection by breaking Armida's spell, even though this will provoke the enchantress's wrath, but Almirena pleads to be left alone ('Lascia ch'io pianga'). Armida rejoices at Rinaldo's capture but when he is led in, in defiant mood, Armida annoys him further by offering her own love. When this is refused, Armida changes her appearance to that of Almirena: Rinaldo is at first taken in, but when the deception is revealed Rinaldo leaves angrily. Armida is torn between her passion for Rinaldo and her anger that he will not respond to her ('Ah, crudel'). On Argante's arrival, she changes her appearance to that of Almirena again in order to disguise her own distress, only to expose Argante's designs on Almirena. Resuming her own appearance, she upbraids Argante: the alliance between them is at an end and it is now Armida's turn to call for revenge ('Vo' far guerra').

Act III A mountain prospect with the hermit's cave at the bottom and an enchanted palace at the top. The magician-hermit tells Goffredo and Eustazio that Rinaldo and Almirena are prisoners in the palace, but enormous force will be necessary to release them. The Christians' first attempt is repelled by 'ugly spirits', but they escape back to the cave, and the magician gives them 'fatal Wands' that can conquer witchcraft. They climb the mountain and strike the gates of the palace, whereupon the palace, spirits and mountain vanish, and Goffredo and Eustazio are found hanging on to the sides of a vast rock in the middle of the sea. Armida, in her garden, makes to stab Almirena with a dagger; Rinaldo draws his sword to attack Armida, but is restrained by two spirits. Goffredo and Eustazio arrive and Armida invokes the Furies, but with the help of the Christians' wands the

garden vanishes, transformed into the area near the city gate at Jerusalem. Rinaldo is united with his companions and, when Armida again attempts to stab Almirena, he attacks her again: Armida vanishes. Argante and Armida are reconciled. Eustazio announces the approach of the pagan army, and the Christian army gathers (Rinaldo: 'Or la tromba'). In the battle, Rinaldo swings the balance in favour of the Christians. Argante and Armida are captured, Rinaldo and Almirena are united. Armida, deciding that heaven may not intend her destruction, breaks her magic wand: she and Argante profess the Christian faith and are released by Goffredo.

With such an episodic scenario, the strength of *Rinaldo* lies in the power of individual events, their variety and contrast, rather than in dramatic continuity. Handel may have missed a few dramatic tricks, but he matched visual spectacle with its musical equivalent: tuneful hit numbers such as 'Lascia ch'io pianga', the song for the mermaids and the now famous march for the Christian army in Act III. It mattered not that the tunes were second-hand, for the audience had not heard Handel's previous works. Presumably the libretto was adapted, even in places distorted, to accommodate the texts for some of these arias, though from the musical point of view the old tunes were considerably improved. And, where the plot allowed, dramatic characterization was strong: one of the high points is Armida's scene near the end of Act II, beginning with the forceful accompanied recitative 'Dunque i lacci d'un volto' and ending in 'Vo' far guerra', which was a showpiece for Handel too, at the harpsichord in the orchestra pit.

Rinaldo maintained its popularity through several seasons following 1711. Inevitably there were some changes to the score as casts varied: the part of Goffredo was taken over by successive sopranos and that of Argante by an alto castrato, and new arias were added. One of the factors contributing to the initial success of the opera had been the presence of the castrato Nicolini in the title role. When Handel revived *Rinaldo* in April 1731 this part fell to the equally famous Senesino and the rest of the cast was also differently balanced (Goffredo as a tenor, Armida a contralto, and the magician a bass); Handel rewrote virtually the whole score.

Il pastor fido
The Faithful Shepherd
Opera in three acts (2h 30m)
Libretto by Giacomo Rossi, after the play by Giovanni Battista Guarini (c. 1584)
Composed 1712; rev. 1734
PREMIERES 22 November 1712, Queen's Theatre, Haymarket, London; rev. version: 29 May 1734, King's Theatre, Haymarket, London; second rev. version: 9 November 1734, Covent Garden, London; US: 2 March 1952, Town Hall, New York (concert); August 1983, Castle Hill, Ipswich, Massachusetts
CAST Mirtillo *s* (castrato), Silvio *a* (castrato), Amarilli *s*, Eurilla *s*, Dorinda *a*, Tirenio *b*; in 1734 version: *satb* chorus of huntsmen, shepherds and shepherdesses, priests; dancers

Il pastor fido is based on a play that was famous as an

example of the pastoral literary mode: two versions had been performed in London in the early 1700s. While *Rinaldo* is mainly heroic and spectacular, *Il pastor fido* is intimate and charming. No doubt the artistic recipe of *Rinaldo* could not be repeated immediately, but there were also pressing practical reasons for the contrast: the Haymarket opera company began its 1712–13 season without its leading castrato (Nicolini), and was probably unable to finance another grand spectacle immediately. Rossi drastically pruned down the number of characters from Guarini's play for the opera: as in *Rinaldo*, Handel drew on his previous music for some of the arias.

SYNOPSIS
An oracle has told the people of Arcadia that their only escape from the annual sacrifice of a virgin to Diana is by the union of two people of 'Heavenly Race', and a match has been arranged between Silvio and the shepherdess Amarilli. But the shepherd Mirtillo and Amarilli are attracted to each other, and Silvio is more interested in pursuing animal game than young ladies, though Dorinda would like his attentions. Eurilla, in love with Mirtillo and jealous of Amarilli, tricks Mirtillo and Amarilli into an assignation in a cave, in order to expose their relationship. Dorinda hides in a bush and is wounded by Silvio's spear, thrown in the belief that the bush harbours a wild animal. The accident at last produces an affectionate response from Silvio. Amarilli is sentenced to death for being unfaithful to the arranged match with Silvio, and Eurilla rejoices in the elimination of her rival: Mirtillo will now be free to receive her attentions. But Mirtillo offers to substitute himself for Amarilli as the sacrifice, and the lovers assert their fidelity. Tirenio, the high priest, announces that Diana is appeased and that the sacrifice is not to proceed: Mirtillo is of divine descent, and the terms of the oracle ('the exalted Passion of a Faithful Shepherd cancels the ancient Crime of a perfidious Maid') have been fulfilled. The two pairs of lovers are united, and Eurilla is forgiven.

A contemporary diarist commented, 'The Scene represented only ye Country of Arcadia, ye Habits were old. – ye Opera Short.' Certainly *Il pastor fido* is lightweight when compared to *Rinaldo*, and was no doubt inexpensively staged, but the result was an amiable piece of intimate music drama, almost on a chamber scale. Eurilla is a strong character; the development of some of the others was partially controlled by Handel's reuse of previous music, but the audience probably came for good tunes as much as for anything else.

Handel's revivals of *Il pastor fido* in 1734 saw radical changes to the opera. Only eight of the original 32 numbers were retained. New music (much of it borrowed from other works) included some magnificent showy arias appropriate to the talents of the new Mirtillo (Giovanni Carestini), while the part of Eurilla (played by the ageing soprano Margherita Durastanti – Handel's Agrippina in Venice) was reduced. Choruses added some flesh to the structure. Further important changes were made for another revival in Novem-

ber the same year, this time at the Covent Garden theatre. To make good use of a French ballet company under Mme Marie Sallé, dances were introduced into the closing scenes of each act, and the opera was preceded by a one-act opéra-ballet prologue, *Terpsicore*, composed by Handel following a model from Colin de Blamont. Some of the dances gained new popularity in the 20th century through their inclusion in Beecham's suite *The Faithful Shepherd*.

Giulio Cesare
(*Giulio Cesare in Egitto*)
Julius Caesar
(*Julius Caesar in Egypt*)
Opera in three acts (3h 15m)
Libretto by Nicola Francesco Haym, after Giacomo Francesco Bussani's *Giulio Cesare in Egitto* set by Antonio Sartorio (1677) and a 1685 version of the same libretto
PREMIERES 20 February 1724, King's Theatre, Haymarket, London; US: 14 May 1927, Smith College, Northampton, Massachusetts
CAST Giulio Cesare (Julius Caesar) *a* (castrato), Cleopatra *s*, Cornelia *a*, Sesto Pompeo (Sextus Pompey) *s*, Tolomeo Ptolemy *a* (castrato), Achilla (Achillas) *b*, Nireno (Nirenus) *a* (castrato), Curio (Curius) *b*; *satb* chorus of Egyptians, conspirators

Handel probably began the composition of *Giulio Cesare* in the summer of 1723, soon after the last performance of his previous opera, *Flavio*, on 15 June. Compared to the compactness of *Flavio*, *Giulio Cesare* is on an enormous scale: it is one of the longest and most elaborate of Handel's operas. In *Flavio* Senesino received four arias: as *Giulio Cesare* he had eight, as did Cuzzoni playing Cleopatra. During composition Handel subjected the music of Act I to a series of massive revisions, partly to accommodate cast changes but also apparently as a result of alterations to the libretto. Circumstantial evidence suggests that Haym, probably in collaboration with Handel, evolved and revised the libretto with careful thought, drawing ideas from more than one literary source and paying careful attention to dramatic coherence and characterization. The intricate plot and careful organization of the finished libretto make for an elaborate and delicately balanced opera: performances of a shortened version can be a rather bewildering experience.

Giulio Cesare and *Tamerlano* together form the climax of Handel's operas from the Royal Academy period, and indeed are among the greatest operaseria creations by any composer, applying the formal conventions of the genre to superb and sustained dramatic effect. *Giulio Cesare* is also the opera of Handel's that has seen most modern revivals, perhaps because its title gives promise of recognizable historical subject matter.

SYNOPSIS
Caesar has defeated Pompey at Pharsalia in Greece, and pursued him to Egypt: the events forming the historical basis for the action took place in 18–17 BC.

Act I Caesar is welcomed by the Egyptians. He has agreed to an appeal by Pompey's wife and son (Cornelia and Sextus) for a peaceful settlement. When gifts arrive, brought by Achillas on behalf of Ptolemy (who is joint ruler of Egypt with his sister Cleopatra), among them is the severed head of Pompey. Caesar sends Achillas back with a message of contempt and disgust. Cornelia tries to kill herself, then faces an unwelcome proposal of marriage from Curius, the Roman tribune. Sextus swears to avenge his father's murder. Meanwhile Cleopatra, horrified to hear of Pompey's murder, decides to seek an alliance with Caesar against her brother. On Ptolemy's arrival Achillas reports Caesar's reaction to the gifts and promises to kill Caesar, provided he can claim Cornelia as his reward. Caesar reflects on the transitoriness of human greatness. Cleopatra, in the guise of 'Lydia', a noble Egyptian maiden whose fortune has been stolen by Ptolemy, enters and appeals to Caesar for justice. He promises redress, captivated by her beauty. Cornelia pays her last respects to her husband's ashes and snatches his sword from the trophies, crying vengeance on Ptolemy; but Sextus seizes the sword and determines to take the task on himself. Ptolemy invites Caesar to occupy the royal apartments that have been prepared for him; Caesar recognizes that he must be cautious ('Va tacito e nascosto'). Sextus challenges Ptolemy to a duel: Ptolemy orders Sextus' arrest and consigns Cornelia to work in the garden of the seraglio. Achillas offers to secure the release of Cornelia and her son if she will consent to marry him, but she rejects the idea with contempt.

Act II Cleopatra has arranged an elaborate set piece for the seduction of Caesar ('V'adoro, pupille'). It works as planned, and Caesar is promised an assignation with 'Lydia', who will introduce him to Cleopatra. Cornelia, in the seraglio garden, repels advances from Achillas and Ptolemy; she threatens suicide but is restrained by Sextus. Cleopatra's eunuch, Nirenus, brings Ptolemy's order that Cornelia be taken to the harem. Cleopatra waits for Caesar in another garden. After some flirtation, the pair are interrupted by Curius, who tells Caesar that he is betrayed and people are calling for his murder. Cleopatra reveals her true identity, and says that her royal presence will quell the tumult: but she fails, and urges Caesar to leave. He refuses, and goes to face his assailants. Cleopatra asks the gods to preserve him and to have pity on her ('Se pietà di me non senti'). In the seraglio, Ptolemy indicates that Cornelia is his choice. Sextus enters and snatches Ptolemy's sword from the table, but Achillas appears and takes it from him. Achillas tells Ptolemy to prepare for war: Caesar is believed drowned, and Cleopatra has fled to the Romans, who are mustering against Ptolemy. Ptolemy dismisses Achillas as a traitor when the latter reminds him that Cornelia had been promised as his reward for killing Caesar, and then departs expecting a quick victory over the Romans. Sextus attempts to stab himself, but is restrained by his mother: he renews his vengeance against Ptolemy.

Act III Achillas, exasperated by Ptolemy's broken promise, leads his soldiers to join Cleopatra. In the ensuing battle, Ptolemy's forces are victorious, and Cleopatra is taken prisoner. Alone, and mourning for Caesar, she bewails her fate ('Piangerò la sorte mia'): she is led away. But Caesar is not dead: he appears,

having escaped drowning by swimming from the harbour. He has lost contact with his troops and prays for help ('Aure, deh, per pietà'). Achillas, mortally wounded, gives Sextus a seal that will guarantee the loyalty of his troops and tells him of a secret passageway to Ptolemy's palace. Caesar witnesses the scene, takes the seal from Sextus, and hurries off to assemble his forces. As Cleopatra bids her friends farewell Caesar appears with his soldiers to rescue her. Caesar and Cleopatra are reunited. In the 'Royal Hall', Cornelia once again has to repel Ptolemy's attentions: she draws a dagger, and is about to attack him when Sextus enters with drawn sword and claims the right of revenge. In the ensuing duel, Ptolemy is killed. At the port of Alexandria, Caesar and Cleopatra welcome Cornelia and Sextus as friends and proclaim their own undying love: everyone celebrates the return of peace.

In addition to a succession of fine arias, the score contains a remarkable novelty in the set-piece scene at the beginning of Act II. The nine Muses are represented on Mount Parnassus, and Handel provided an onstage band which may have had nine players to consort with Cleopatra/Lydia/Virtue. Another unusual feature was the use of four horns in the opening and closing scenes of the opera. The original (1724) run of *Giulio Cesare* had 13 performances, and it achieved double figures again in Handel's revivals of 1725 and 1730. For the revivals Handel subjected his score to the usual alterations necessitated by changing casts: but mostly these alterations weakened the original conception.

Tamerlano
Tamerlane

Opera in three acts (3h)
Libretto by Nicola Francesco Haym, after Agostino Piovene's *Il Tamerlano* (1711) and *Il Bajazet* (1719) both set by Francesco Gasparini; based on the play by Jacques Pradon, *Tamerlan, ou La mort de Bajazet* (1675)
PREMIERES 31 October 1724, King's Theatre, Haymarket, London; US: 26 January 1985, Indiana University Opera Theater, Bloomington, Indiana
CAST Tamerlano (Tamerlane) *a* (castrato), Andronico (Andronicus) *a* (castrato), Bajazete (Bajazet) *t*, Leone (Leo) *b*, Asteria *s*, Irene *a*

Tamerlano is significant not only as one of Handel's finest Academy operas, but also as one of the few opere serie with a leading role for the tenor voice. Opposite Senesino playing the part of Tamerlane, the self-made ruler of the Tartar empire, Handel cast the tenor Francesco Borosini as Bajazet, the Turkish sultan defeated by Tamerlane in 1402 and who subsequently died while still in captivity to the Tartar. Borosini's contribution to the opera extended beyond that of a soloist. When Handel completed his draft composition score at the end of July 1724, he had been composing to a libretto adapted from Piovene's 1711 libretto for a Venice production with music by Gasparini. In 1719 a much revised version of Gasparini's opera was performed in Reggio, with a significantly changed title: *Il Tamerlano* became *Il Bajazet*, and the strengthened role of Bajazet was played by Borosini. When Borosini arrived in London in September 1724 to take up his place in the opera company, he provided Handel and Haym with the libretto and score of the 1719 version: stimulated by this, Handel revised his own score, in particular incorporating new scenes at the beginning and end of the opera based on the 1719 libretto.

Plays on the subject of Tamerlane already had a niche on the 18th-century London stage: the theatres regularly performed one (most often Nicholas Rowe's) around the beginning of November, to coincide with the triple anniversaries of the foiling of the Gunpowder Plot, the birthday of King William III and his landing in Torbay in 1688. No doubt a political allegory was intended or imposed in these plays, but Handel's opera seems innocent of any such interpretation: nevertheless, the treatment of a familiar subject was no doubt intended as good box office.

SYNOPSIS
Bajazet has been defeated and captured by Tamerlane, who is betrothed to Irene, princess of Trebizond. Tamerlane and Andronicus (a Greek prince in alliance with Tamerlane) have both, unknown to each other, fallen in love with Asteria, Bajazet's daughter. The action takes place in Prusa, the first city that Tamerlane occupied after defeating the Turks.

Act I Bajazet despises his conqueror and attempts suicide, but desists when Andronicus reminds him that this would leave Asteria an orphan ('Forte e lieto'). Rather than return to the throne of Byzantium, Andronicus opts to remain with Tamerlane to learn more about warfare. Tamerlane hopes to use Andronicus to break down Bajazet's resistance to his suit, in return for which Andronicus will receive the hand of Irene. Andronicus is appalled that his action in bringing Asteria to plead for her father's life should have this consequence. Tamerlane agrees to release Bajazet, on condition that he can marry Asteria. Bajazet rejects this proposal, and Asteria accuses Andronicus (who has spoken for Tamerlane) of taking Tamerlane's part in order to gain Irene and a kingdom for himself. She tells Andronicus that she no longer loves him. Irene, arriving at the palace, is surprised when Tamerlane does not come to greet his bride-to-be: she is yet more surprised to learn that Andronicus is to be her husband instead. Alone, Andronicus reflects that he can save Bajazet's life only by concealing his love for Asteria and bearing her anger ('Benchè mi sprezzi').

Act II Tamerlane claims that he now has Asteria's heart: he tells Andronicus to look forward to the double wedding. Andronicus and Asteria each accuse the other of sacrificing their love for a throne. Irene, disguised as a messenger at the suggestion of Andronicus, reproaches Tamerlane for his betrayal, and refuses his offer of the alternative suit. Tamerlane responds that, if Asteria does not prove a satisfactory consort, then he will embrace Irene. Andronicus vows to kill both Tamerlane and himself if Asteria marries Tamerlane. Asteria herself approaches Tamerlane's throne, with murder in her heart. Bajazet enters to prevent the marriage of his daughter: Tamerlane orders Bajazet to prostrate himself – Asteria can

mount the throne over his body. Asteria refuses to do so, nor will Bajazet rise when Tamerlane orders him to. Asteria asks her father's forgiveness, but he refuses and turns his back on the throne as she advances to it. Irene enters, still disguised, and says that Irene will not appear until she has a share in Tamerlane's throne: Tamerlane replies that she will have to force Asteria to leave the throne. Bajazet orders his daughter to descend, or he will renounce her and end his own life, but Asteria at first makes no move. She has to decide between marriage to Tamerlane and renewed imprisonment: she chooses the latter. Tamerlane orders the execution of both father and daughter.

Act III Tamerlane says that he still loves Asteria, and orders Andronicus to tell her that her place at the throne is still vacant. Andronicus reveals his own love for Asteria, which she reciprocates ('Vivo in te'). When Tamerlane orders Bajazet's execution, Asteria pleads for her father's life. Father and daughter are sentenced to the indignity of being dragged forcibly to Tamerlane's table, where Tamerlane orders Asteria to kneel as a slave with his drinking cup. Asteria poisons the cup and offers it to Tamerlane, but Irene, who has seen her place the poison, restrains him from drinking and reveals both Asteria's plan and her own identity. Tamerlane tells Asteria that he will drink if Andronicus and Bajazet will do so first: she decides instead to take the poison herself, but Andronicus dashes the cup from her hands. Tamerlane orders her to be sent to the slaves' seraglio and now promises to marry Irene, who accepts him. Bajazet takes poison; he says farewell to Asteria, and dies breathing fury against Tamerlane. Andronicus offers to kill himself, but Tamerlane restrains him: Bajazet's death has been sufficient bloodshed. He yields Asteria to Andronicus, and will marry Irene himself.

The quality of Handel's music is no less high than in *Giulio Cesare*, but *Tamerlano* has not gained popularity on the strength of individual arias, though Andronicus' 'Bella Asteria' had some circulation in the 18th century. This is perhaps rather surprising, since 'Se non mi vuol amar' (Asteria), 'Par che mi nasca' (Irene), 'A suoi piedi' (Bajazet) and 'Cor di padre' (Asteria) are among Handel's finest arias. The final scenes of Acts II and III are powerful musico-dramatic sequences. At the end of Act II, when Asteria appeals to Bajazet, Andronicus and Irene in turn, reply in short but pointed exit arias. The end of Act III is dominated by Bajazet's last scene: before the opera's first performance Handel cut out a substantial amount of music (including a fine aria, 'Padre amato', for Asteria) so that no concerted numbers remained between Bajazet's death scene and the final minor-key *coro* (sung by the soloists). The scoring of *Tamerlano* is fairly restrained, but there are some novelties. Recorders and flutes double in the duet 'Vivo in te'; the obbligato part in Irene's Act II aria 'Par che mi nasca in seno' was composed for clarinets, misnamed 'cornetti' in Handel's autograph. The unusual prominence of the tenor role limited the opera's appearance in Handel's opera repertoire: he revived *Tamerlano* only once, in 1731.

Rodelinda

(*Rodelinda, Regina de' Longobardi*)
Rodelinda, Queen of Lombardy
Opera in three acts (3h 15m)
Libretto by Nicola Francesco Haym, adapted from Antonio
Salvi's *Rodelinda*, set by Giacomo Antonio Perti (1710)
after Pierre Corneille's *Pertharite* (1652)
PREMIERES 13 February 1725, King's Theatre,
Haymarket, London; US: 9 May 1931, Smith College,
Northampton, Massachusetts
CAST Rodelinda *s*, Bertarido *a* (castrato), Grimoaldo *t*,
Garibaldo *b*, Eduige *a*, Unolfo *a* (castrato), Flavio *silent*

Rodelinda was cast for the same singers as *Tamerlano*,
with a major part for the tenor Borosini as well as
leading roles for Senesino and Cuzzoni. For the subject, Haym turned, not for the first time, to a libretto
dealing with Lombard history. Its action relies on a
complex dynastic background. On the death of Ari-
berto of Lombardy (AD 681) his kingdom was divided
between his sons Bertarido and Gundeberto. A war
developed between the brothers; Gundeberto was mortally wounded, and called on the assistance of Grimoaldo, duke of Benevento, promising him the hand
of his sister Eduige. Faced with an attack from Grimoaldo, Bertarido fled to Hungary, leaving his family
behind: he put out reports of his own death, planning
to return disguised in order to rescue his wife, Rodelinda, and his son, Flavio. Grimoaldo is supported by
Garibaldo, duke of Turin, who has rebelled against
Bertarido.

SYNOPSIS

Act I Rodelinda mourns her supposedly dead husband. Grimoaldo proposes to Rodelinda that he will
restore her to her husband's inheritance if she will
marry him, but she rejects him. Garibaldo professes
his love for Eduige, who has been rejected by Grimoaldo, but his real ambitions are set on her inheritance. Bertarido, in disguise, returns and sees Rodelinda receive a further proposal of marriage from
Grimoaldo, accompanied by a threat that her non-
compliance would lead to the young Flavio's death.
Rodelinda agrees to Grimoaldo's terms, intending to
ask for the traitor Garibaldo's death once she is in a
position of influence. Bertarido is horrified by Rodelinda's acceptance of Grimoaldo.
Act II Eduige is embittered by Grimoaldo's rejection. Rodelinda, saying that she cannot be mother of
the lawful king and wife of a tyrant at the same time,
tells Grimoaldo to murder Flavio before her eyes. In
spite of encouragement from Garibaldo, Grimoaldo
recoils from this. Eduige recognizes Bertarido and
learns that his prime purpose is to regain his family,
not his throne: after Bertarido's death, Eduige has a
claim to Bertarido's kingdom. Unolfo tells his friend
Bertarido that Rodelinda is faithful to him: the reunion between husband and wife ('Io t'abbraccio') is
interrupted by the arrival of Grimoaldo, who puts
Bertarido under arrest and sentences him to death.
Act III Eduige and Unolfo plan Bertarido's
escape. Grimoaldo is encouraged by Garibaldo to
have Bertarido executed, but hesitates because this
would alienate Rodelinda. Bertarido laments his fate
('Chi di voi'). Eduige throws a sword into the dun-

geon. Unolfo goes to release Bertarido, but in the
darkness Bertarido wounds him, mistaking him for a
potential executioner. Unolfo leads Bertarido to freedom by a secret passage. Rodelinda and Flavio, arriving at the dungeon, find blood (Unolfo's) and
Bertarido's cloak: Rodelinda laments her husband's
apparent fate ('Se'l mio duol'). Having bandaged
Unolfo's wound, Bertarido then sets off to find Rodelinda. Grimoaldo approaches, tormented by jealousy,
anger and love: eventually he falls asleep in the garden.
Garibaldo takes the sleeping Grimoaldo's sword and
goes to kill him, but Bertarido, who has been watching
unobserved, intervenes and kills Garibaldo. Returning, Bertarido throws his sword at Grimoaldo's feet.
Rodelinda, entering, is amazed to find her husband
alive. Explanations ensue. Grimoaldo renounces
his claim to Bertarido's inheritance and takes up Gundeberto's former kingdom, with Eduige as his queen.

Rodelinda, though less hot-headed as a heroine than
Asteria in *Tamerlano*, is a strong and faithful wife.
Borosini played Grimoaldo, a tyrant with a softer side
that recoils from murdering the young Flavio: as in
Tamerlano, he received a powerful 'distraction' scene
in Act III. Senesino, as Bertarido, had a no less
remarkable prison scene. Bertarido's aria, 'Dove sei',
familiar as a concert aria to the sentimental text 'Art
thou troubled?', remains as an example of the 'capital
and pleasing airs' that Charles Burney recognized as
one of the strengths of the score. After the initial
season, Handel revived *Rodelinda* twice, in 1725 and
in 1731; as with *Tamerlano*, opportunities for revival
may have been limited by the necessity for a good
tenor.

Alessandro

Alexander
Opera in three acts (3h 30m)
Libretto by Paolo Rolli, after Bartolomeo Ortensio Mauro's
La superbia d'Alessandro (1690) set by Agostino Steffani
PREMIERES 5 May 1726, King's Theatre, Haymarket,
London; US: 21 April 1985, New York (concert)
CAST Alessandro (Alexander) *a* (castrato), Rossane
(Roxana) *s*, Lisaura *s*, Tassile (Taxiles) *a* (castrato), Clito
(Clitus) *b*, Leonato (Leonnatus) *t*, Cleone (Cleon) *a*; *satb*
chorus of soldiers

Alessandro had specific Hanoverian associations, for
Mauro's original libretto had been written for performance at Hanover in 1690, in the heyday of the court
opera there. As electoral prince, Georg Ludwig
almost certainly saw the original production: as King
George I he saw Handel's opera in London. Whether
George was intended to be identified with the Alexander the Great of the opera is unknown, still less
whether the ladies of the story were to be identified
with his supposed mistresses. What is known is that
the attention of the original audiences was focused not
on the royal family but on the 'Rival Queens' on the
stage, the sopranos Cuzzoni and Faustina Bordoni.

SYNOPSIS

Act I At the siege of the Indian city of Ossidraca,
Alexander scales the city walls and eventually tri-

umphs, slaughtering his enemies. He receives the attentions of two ladies, Roxana (a slave) and Lisaura (a Scythian princess): he loves Roxana, but does not want to alienate Lisaura. Taxiles, the Indian king, is in love with Lisaura but, since he owes his throne to Alexander, is unable to intervene when she shows an interest in Alexander. Cleon, one of the Macedonian captains, is also in love with Roxana, but fears the powerful Alexander. Alexander himself claims descent from Jupiter: at a thanksgiving sacrifice in Jupiter's temple Clitus, another Macedonian captain, although a long-standing loyal supporter of Alexander, refuses to take his claims of divine descent seriously.

Act II In a garden scene, Lisaura, while still attracted to Alexander, recognizes his attachment to Roxana. Roxana asks Alexander to demonstrate his love by granting her freedom, which he does after some hesitation. Clitus again refuses to acknowledge Alexander's divine descent. The canopy over Alexander's throne 'is by Conspiracy made to fall': he accuses Clitus of treachery, and has him imprisoned, in spite of Clitus' protestations of loyalty. Taxiles leaves to assemble his army in case Alexander should need support: fears for Alexander's safety lead Roxana to reveal that she returns his love. Leonnatus, a Macedonian captain loyal to Alexander, reports that the Indians, believing Alexander dead, are likely to join his enemies.

Act III Leonnatus, presumably feeling that the situation requires a loyal and experienced general, releases Clitus from prison, substituting another general, the 'fawning Sycophant' Cleon. Cleon calls on his own soldiers, who break down the prison gates, and decides to challenge Alexander. After an uneasy scene between Roxana and Lisaura, the latter asks Alexander outright to return her love, but he replies that to do so would be robbing Taxiles, and Lisaura is moved by his generosity. Supported by Taxiles' troops, Alexander conquers the rebels: Leonnatus and Clitus prove their loyalty in action, and the conspirators are captured. Civil peace and the union of the two pairs of lovers are celebrated in Jupiter's temple.

Handel maintained a high level of invention in the arias, of which Roxana's Act I 'Lusinghe più care' has attained some popularity as a concert item. A nice touch of musical irony occurs in the garden scene of Act II, where the leading ladies in turn hear Alexander in amorous conversation with the other: each lady then quotes back to him the music that he has been singing to her rival. However, the equal weighting of the two sopranos led Handel to a few *longueurs*: of all the late Academy operas, *Alessandro* is the one most inflated by this consideration. But that was what the audience wanted to hear, and it is not surprising that Handel revived the opera in the following season; he also revived a shortened version (with different sopranos) in 1732, and apparently co-operated with the 'Middlesex' opera company in the 1740s in allowing them to revive his opera under the title *Rossane*.

Partenope

Opera in three acts (3h)
Libretto, after Silvio Stampiglia's *La Partenope* set by Luigi Manza, (1699) and (rev. 1707) by Antonio Caldara (1708)

PREMIERES 24 February 1730, King's Theatre, Haymarket, London; US: 15 September 1988, Omaha, Nebraska

CAST Partenope *s*, Emilio *t*, Armindo *a*, Ormonte *b*, Rosmira *a*, Arsace *a* (castrato); *satb* chorus of soldiers

Partenope is a comedy: there is one battle, without any heroics, self-sacrifices or high policies at stake, and this seems to have mainly a symbolic function. For a comparable previous work in Handel's output we have to return to *Agrippina*, and such comparison is appropriate because Handel probably saw a version of *La Partenope* (with music by Antonio Caldara) in Venice the year before he composed *Agrippina*. The libretto of *Partenope* had been considered and rejected by the Royal Academy of Music, so to some extent Handel was in 1730 reviving an old scheme. The result suggests that he found the exercise thoroughly congenial.

SYNOPSIS

Act I Partenope, queen of the city of that name (modern Naples), has three princely suitors: Arsace, Armindo and Emilio. (In Handel's original cast, Armindo was played by a contralto *en travesti*.) Rosmira, princess of Cyprus, formerly betrothed to Arsace, has followed him to Partenope's court, disguised as a soldier, 'Eurimene'. She reveals her identity to Arsace, accusing him of infidelity and, still disguised as 'Eurimene', declares herself to be another suitor for Partenope. This provokes Partenope to assert her devotion to Arsace. Emilio states that he will order his troops to attack the city if Partenope will not promise him her hand. Partenope calls his bluff and after some complications decides to lead her forces herself. Armindo reproaches 'Eurimene' for setting up as his rival for Partenope, but is told that 'his' affections really lie elsewhere.

Act II The armies of Partenope and Emilio join battle: the former win and Emilio is captured. He acknowledges Arsace as his captor, but 'Eurimene' claims the credit for this and challenges Arsace to a duel. Partenope arrests 'Eurimene' and reasserts her love for Arsace. Puzzled by Arsace's defence of 'Eurimene', Partenope nevertheless agrees to his request to release him on condition that he leaves the city. Armindo declares his love to Partenope, who pities him but cannot respond further.

Act III 'Eurimene' explains to Partenope that he challenged Arsace on behalf of a Cypriot princess whom Arsace had betrayed. When Arsace admits the truth of the allegation, Partenope offers her hand to Armindo, rejecting Arsace. The duel between Arsace and 'Eurimene' is arranged. The contestants are allotted weapons and Arsace suddenly declares that he will fight bare-chested. Equity demands that his opponent should do the same. Faced with a choice about what to reveal, Rosmira chooses to declare her real identity, and that her motive had been to test Arsace's fidelity. The pairs of lovers are united and Emilio is consoled with an offer of friendship.

Partenope is a fast-moving story requiring a deft touch and, although there are some extended arias (mainly for the two leading ladies), Handel keeps pace with the drama in his score and there are a number of engaging ensembles: *coro* movements interspersed with sinfonie in the battle sequence, a lively trio for Arsace and his two ladies, and a rare musico-dramatic interaction in a quartet of perplexity near the beginning of Act III. Handel revived the opera in the 1730–31 season and again in 1737, this time in a shortened form with some important voice changes. It must have been a refreshing contribution to the repertoire.

Orlando

Opera in three acts (3h)
Libretto after Carlo Sigismondo Capeci's *L'Orlando, overo La gelosa pazzia* set by Domenico Scarlatti (1711) based on Lodovico Ariosto's epic poem *Orlando furioso* (1516)
PREMIERES 27 January 1733, King's Theatre, Haymarket, London; US: 18 January 1971, Carnegie Hall, New York (concert); 16 December 1981, Cambridge, Massachusetts
CAST Orlando *a* (castrato), Angelica *s*, Medoro *a*, Dorinda *s*, Zoroastro *b*

Orlando returns to the sort of drama that Handel had developed 20 years before, involving a supernatural dimension and transformation scenes: this contrasts with the operas that had been his concern since the start of the Academy, in which the characters, however much fired by jealousy or passion, generally behave rationally. A spectacular element had been creeping back into Handel's opera productions since *Alessandro*: for example, the opera house must have invested in a collapsible city wall, which featured in siege scenes in several operas. At all periods the London opera companies probably employed a fair number of non-singing 'supers', who represented servants or armies as required, and once (in *Admeto*) furies. In *Orlando* they made the significant transition to genii in the service of the magician Zoroastro, a substantial role written for the bass Antonio Montagnana, whose part was enhanced by a contrast in vocal ranges: his was the only low voice.

Orlando had a libretto that had been developed considerably from Capeci's original: the identity of the adapter is not known (this is generally the case with Handel's new libretti after 1729), though it has been suggested that Handel worked from a version that Haym may have prepared before his death in 1729, or even that Handel himself had a hand in the adaptation. One factor in the shaping of the opera may have been the revival, if only temporarily, of English opera by a company in a theatre near to the opera house: perhaps opera was not, for the moment, such a 'foreign' medium. In December 1732 Aaron Hill, the artistic impresario who had promoted *Rinaldo*, wrote a letter to Handel encouraging him to take up opera in English; by then the score of *Orlando* had already been written and, like *Rinaldo*, it embodied spectacular scenes of the type that had been developed by the English masque.

SYNOPSIS

Act I The magician Zoroastro surveys the stars at night and predicts from them that the knight errant

entering, promises that he will follow Glory rather than Love, but after the magician has gone he recants and dedicates himself to the service of Love. In a wood, the lovers Angelica, queen of Catai, and Medoro, an African prince, are seen together; Angelica tells Medoro that he shall share her empire as well as her heart: Medoro has supplanted her former attachment to Orlando. After Angelica has gone, Medoro is detained by the shepherdess Dorinda, to whom he had previously paid court: Dorinda still loves him, but finds his reaction evasive. Zoroastro warns Angelica of Orlando's jealousy. Seeing Medoro approaching, she appeals for help. Zoroastro conjures up a fountain to conceal Medoro, and the scene is transformed, leaving Orlando alone in a garden ('Fammi combattere'). Angelica and Medoro embrace, and are seen by Dorinda: Angelica presents her with a jewel, which Dorinda thinks a poor substitute for Medoro himself.

Act II In a wood, Dorinda laments her situation. Orlando accuses her of linking his name with Isabella, a princess he rescued, but Dorinda says that she believed him attached to Angelica, who is now betrothed to another man. Orlando is horrified by the last piece of news, and falls victim to anger and jealousy ('Cielo! se tu il consenti'). Zoroastro urges Angelica and Medoro to escape ('Tra caligini profonde'); as Medoro leaves, he carves their names on a tree. Orlando sees these names and follows in hot pursuit. He finds Angelica in the wood, and tries to catch her: but a large cloud descends and bears her away. Orlando now crosses the bounds of reason: he imagines himself following the lovers to the underworld, finding Medoro in the arms of Proserpina, who weeps for him. Zoroastro appears in his chariot, scoops up Orlando, and rides off into the air.

Act III Medoro takes refuge in Dorinda's cottage and rather shamefacedly confesses to her that he loves Angelica. Orlando meets Dorinda, but has clearly taken leave of his senses, entering into an imaginary battle with the murderer of Angelica's brother. Dorinda tells Angelica of Orlando's pitiful condition, and reflects on the pains brought about by love ('Amor è qual vento'). Zoroastro changes the scene to a 'horrid Cavern' ('Sorge infausta'). Dorinda, weeping, tells Angelica that Orlando has demolished her cottage, leaving Medoro in the wreckage. Orlando thirsts for revenge. He throws Angelica into the cave, which is transformed into the Temple of Mars, then sinks exhausted to sleep. Zoroastro announces that the time has arrived for Orlando to be released from the power of Love. He waves his wand, and four genii descend with an eagle carrying a golden vessel in its beak. Zoroastro takes the vessel and sprinkles liquor from it over Orlando's face. Orlando revives, restored to his senses, and is told by Dorinda that he has murdered Angelica and Medoro. Filled with remorse, Orlando determines to kill himself; but the lovers appear, having been saved by Zoroastro. Orlando announces that he has triumphed over 'himself and Love', and presents Angelica to Medoro. Dorinda, reconciled to her own situation, invites everyone to celebrate the 'Festival of Love'.

The high point of *Orlando*'s score is the mad scene at the end of Act II, an extended scena in a recognized theatrical tradition, but which may also be related to English musical progenitors such as Purcell's 'Mad Bess' ('From Silent Shades'). The 5/8 passage as Orlando imagines himself reaching Pluto's throne is a novelty, but more telling overall are the obsessive recurrences of a simple gavotte melody ('Vaghe pupille') as Orlando fights for coherence. The opening scenes for Zoroastro and Orlando are hardly less remarkable: in them recitatives and set numbers flow naturally into each other. Although there are some conventional (though dramatically strong) set-piece da-capo arias, the action often breaks anticipated moulds, and there are some particularly effective duets. Act I ends with a remarkable 'romantic triangle' trio ('Consolati, o bella') of great subtlety. All five soloists have strong roles, though Medoro receives fewer musical opportunities than the others. In *Orlando* Handel applied the fast-moving dramatic skills of *Partenope* to a richly symbolic libretto which showed off the powers of Senesino (Medoro), Strada (Angelica) and Montagnana (Zoroastro) to best advantage. It ran for 10 performances in 1733. That Handel never revived it is attributable to the confusion that overcame his opera company at the end of the season, when he lost Senesino and Montagnana to a rival operation.

Ariodante

Opera in three acts (3h)
Libretto after Antonio Salvi's *Ginevra, principessa di Scozia*, set by Giacomo Antonio Perti (1708), itself after Lodovico Ariosto's epic poem *Orlando furioso* (1516)
PREMIERES 8 January 1735, Covent Garden, London; US: 29 March 1971, Carnegie Hall, New York (concert); 14 September 1971, Washington, DC
CAST Ariodante *s* (castrato), Ginevra *s*, Polinesso *a*, Lurcanio *t*, Dalinda *s*, The King *b*, Odoardo *t*; *satb* chorus of shepherds and shepherdesses; dancers

For his 1734–5 season Handel was driven from the Haymarket Theatre by the Opera of the Nobility and set up his company at John Rich's new theatre in Covent Garden, which had opened in December 1732. No doubt Handel had some misgivings about leaving London's premier opera house, which had been his musical home for a quarter of a century. But he took with him an excellent cast, including Carestini and Strada, and the first season was enlivened by the participation of a group of French dancers under the direction of Mme Sallé. Handel made good use of the dancers: ballets were written into Handel's new operas *Ariodante* and *Alcina*, and *Il pastor fido* was revived with a prologue (*Terpsicore*) in which dancing played the major part. At Covent Garden also Handel seems to have regularly employed an independent chorus, which gave a new sound to *coro* movements: these had formerly been rendered by the soloists alone.

Ariodante is set in Edinburgh, with the king of Scotland and Guinevere (Ginevra), his daughter, among the persons represented; but the basis of Salvi's story was Ariosto's *Orlando furioso*. Handel may have seen Perti's opera on Salvi's libretto in Florence in

1708. The outlines of Ariosto's tale provided popular subject matter for dramatists, including Shakespeare in *Much Ado About Nothing*.

SYNOPSIS

Act I In the royal palace Ginevra prepares to meet Ariodante, a vassal prince with whom she is in love. Polinesso, duke of Albany, declares his love for Ginevra. She rejects him, but her lady-in-waiting Dalinda hints he would find a better response from her. Polinesso wonders whether he can use Dalinda's infatuation to take revenge on Ginevra. In the palace garden Ginevra and Ariodante pledge their love. The king interrupts them and, approving of Ariodante, tells Ginevra to prepare for her wedding the next day. Polinesso persuades Dalinda to dress as Ginevra that night and to admit him to the princess's apartments. Dalinda rebuffs Ariodante's brother Lurcanio, who is in love with her. Ariodante and Ginevra share their joy with shepherds and shepherdesses.

Act II At night, Ariodante encounters Polinesso, who suggests that Ginevra is unfaithful to him, and offers to prove it. Ariodante vows to kill himself if the accusation proves true – if false, he will kill Polinesso. Polinesso tells Ariodante to hide and watch. Unknown to them both, Lurcanio is also concealed in the garden. Dalinda, dressed as Ginevra, is seen to admit Polinesso to Ginevra's apartments. Ariodante resolves to end his own life, but Lurcanio urges him to avenge his betrayal. In the palace the king is declaring Ariodante his heir when the courtier Odoardo brings the news that Ariodante has thrown himself into the sea and is dead. On hearing the news Ginevra faints. Lurcanio produces to the king a sworn statement of what he saw that night and accuses Ginevra of unfaithfulness; he offers a challenge to anyone prepared to defend Ginevra. Ginevra herself cannot understand why she is harshly disowned by the king. Furies torment her dreams.

Act III Ariodante, wandering alone, hears cries for help and finds Dalinda, pursued by assassins sent by Polinesso. He drives them off and learns from her the story of Polinesso's deceit: Dalinda herself turns against Polinesso. At the palace, Polinesso offers himself as Ginevra's champion: the king accepts him despite Ginevra's fierce opposition. In the combat, Lurcanio mortally wounds Polinesso: it looks as if the heavens are signalling Ginevra's guilt. A stranger in a helmet with lowered visor comes to her defence. It is Ariodante, who says that he has knowledge of Ginevra's innocence, which he will reveal if the king will pardon Dalinda in advance. Odoardo reports that the dying Polinesso confessed his crime. Dalinda agrees to accept Lurcanio as her lover. The king brings Ariodante to Ginevra, releases her from her confinement, and celebrations begin for the two pairs of lovers, with dances for the 'Knights and Ladies'.

In *Ariodante* Handel managed to combine an intimate atmosphere, in which the cross-currents of personal attractions and conflicts flow strongly, with a platform for Carestini's skill, which reached its apogee in his arias 'Con l'ali di costanza', 'Scherza infida' (at the climax of one of Handel's most powerful scenes, in the garden at the beginning of Act II), 'Cieca notte' and 'Dopo notte'. The recitatives are short and the arias extended, reflecting exactly the balance between the simple actions and the great effects they have on the participants. At the other extremity of scale, there are few more effective scene-setting introductions in opera than the 'moonrise' sinfonia at the beginning of Act II – a mere ten bars. With ravishing arias, some splendid duets (including one in Act I ('Prendi, prendi') in which the king interrupts Ariodante and Ginevra as they are about to embark on their da capo), spectacular dancing integrated with the plot (particularly at the end of Act II) and, incidentally, a good libretto, *Ariodante* is one of the most rewarding of Handel's operas. But it relied to some extent on the individual skills of Carestini: Handel revived the opera only once, in 1736, in a revised form to accommodate another castrato, Conti.

Alcina

Opera in three acts (3h 30m)
Libretto based on ?Antonio Fanzaglia's *L'isola d'Alcina* set by Riccardo Broschi (1728) after Lodovico Ariosto's epic poem *Orlando furioso* (1516)
PREMIERES 16 April 1735, Covent Garden, London; US: 16 November 1960, Fair Park Music Hall, Dallas
CAST Alcina *s*, Ruggiero *s* (castrato), Morgana *s*, Bradamante *a*, Oronte *t*, Melisso *b*, Oberto *s* (*boy treble*); *satb* chorus

Alcina was the last of Handel's operas to be derived from Ariosto's *Orlando furioso*. Handel probably collected the libretto during his visit to the Continent in 1729; as usual, it was considerably rearranged to suit London conditions (recitatives were abbreviated and arias were tailored to the singers' abilities). Of the four Handel operas on libretti derived from Ariosto's epic poem, three (*Rinaldo*, *Orlando* and *Alcina*) include an enchantress and/or enchanter among the leading characters. The nature of the story, set here on Alcina's enchanted island, gave plenty of opportunities for spectacle and scene transformation. As in *Ariodante*, Mme Sallé's ballet troupe was integrated effectively into the opera. Names added by Handel to one of the *coro* movements show that the main cast singers were supplemented by at least one more soprano, an alto (or two), three tenors and two basses in the chorus movements.

Alcina seems to have done well for Handel in the period of rivalry between his company and the Opera of the Nobility: in the original run it had 18 performances. As Burney commented later, *Alcina* was 'an opera with which Handel seems to have vanquished his opponents, and to have kept the field near a month longer than his rival Porpora was able to make head against him'. Burney's further comments are also interesting: 'Upon the whole, if any one of Handel's dramatic works should be brought on the stage, entire, without a change or mixture of airs from his other operas, it seems as if this would well sustain such a revival.' *Alcina* was indeed one of the first operas to re-enter the repertoire and to sustain some place in modern productions of Handel's operas, though it is rarely revived 'entire'.

SYNOPSIS

Alcina has fallen in love with the knight Ruggiero and has detained him on her enchanted island.

Act I Bradamante, Ruggiero's betrothed, arrives at the island in an attempt to rescue him, accompanied by her guardian Melisso: she is disguised as her brother Ricciardo. Bradamante and Melisso are discovered by Morgana, Alcina's sister, who is attracted to 'Ricciardo'. The original scene (a mountain) breaks open to reveal Alcina adorning herself while Ruggiero holds her mirror. The new arrivals introduce themselves and are welcomed by Alcina. 'Ricciardo' asks Ruggiero if he remembers him, the brother of his betrothed: but, under Alcina's spell, Ruggiero has no recollection of any lover but Alcina ('Di te mi rido'). Oronte, Alcina's general, tells Ruggiero that, with the arrival of 'Ricciardo', he may suffer the same fate as the thousands of Alcina's previous lovers who have been turned into streams, beasts, trees and rocks. When challenged, Alcina tells Ruggiero that he still pleases her, for the moment. Ruggiero tries to encourage 'Ricciardo' to return home. Bradamante reveals her true identity, but Ruggiero thinks that this is just one of Alcina's tricks.

Act II In a hall of the palace, Melisso, disguised as Ruggiero's tutor Atlante, gives Ruggiero a magic ring which returns him to his senses. He renews his devotion to Bradamante, but decides to conceal this from Alcina. Before the statue of Circe, Alcina is about to change 'Ricciardo' into a beast, when Morgana, who believes 'Ricciardo' is in love with her, and Ruggiero together persuade her to desist. Oberto, Bradamante's nephew, who has come to the island in search of his lost father, Astolfo, asks Alcina for help, and is told that he shall see Astolfo soon. Bradamante tells Oberto that his father has been changed into a lion. Oronte tells Alcina that he is preparing to leave with the new guests; he taunts Morgana with the faithlessness of her new lover. At first inclined to disbelieve him, Morgana then finds Bradamante and Ruggiero together ('Verdi prati'). In a 'Subterraneous Appartment', Alcina tries to use her powers to detain Ruggiero, but to no avail – he is protected by the ring ('Ombre pallide').

Act III In a courtyard of the palace, Oronte and Morgana, previously lovers, are reconciled. Alcina tries unsuccessfully to dissuade Ruggiero from leaving ('Ma quando tornerai'). A ship awaits Ruggiero and Bradamante, but Bradamante declares that she will not leave until Alcina's enchantments are broken ('Mi restano le lagrime') and life has been restored to her victims. Outside Alcina's palace are the dens of the wild beasts and the urn that contains the 'whole power of the Inchantment'. Ruggiero goes to break the urn with his ring: Alcina and Morgana try to restrain him, but he throws the urn down, whereupon 'the Scene wholly disappears, changing to the Sea, which is seen thro' a vast subterraneous Cavaern where many Stones are chang'd into Men; among them is Astolfo, who embraces Oberto: They form the Chorus and the Dance'.

'Verdi prati' in Act II, which expresses perfectly Ruggiero's regret that the beautiful landscape of the island is about to decay, caught the public's imagination at an early stage: with its sarabande-like rhythm and measured phrases it is reminiscent of Handel's first 'hit' in London, 'Lascia ch'io pianga' from *Rinaldo*. Reputedly, Carestini dismissed the aria when it was first presented to him as being insufficiently brilliant. In the opera its effect is heightened because it is followed immediately by Alcina's attempt to hold Ruggiero by enchantment. Throughout the opera Handel's command of contrast and pacing is masterly, making the most of the interplay between rational and irrational elements in the plot. Remarkably, he makes no attempt to cover a potential weakness in the plot – the fact that Alcina is effectively beaten by the end of Act II – by hurrying over the dénouement. Her developing character, through to her final aria ('Mi restano le lagrime'), is among Handel's most subtly drawn creations. Act III begins with a chain of magnificent and luxuriant da-capo arias, which serve to emphasize the change of pace in the final scenes, when a trio, recitatives, choruses and dances follow in quick succession to complete Alcina's downfall. Although Carestini (Ruggiero) and Strada (Alcina) naturally dominated the score and the stage, the other roles are also quite substantial: even the 15-year-old treble 'Young Mr Savage' as Oberto had a man-size part to sing. Handel revived *Alcina* at the beginning and end of his 1736–7 season, though without the dances at the later perfomances since the arrangement with Mme Sallé's troupe had ended. It may be that the scenic effects of *Alcina* were particularly geared to the facilities of Covent Garden Theatre: Handel never revived the opera after he returned to the King's Theatre in 1738.

Serse

Xerxes
Opera in three acts (3h)
Libretto after Silvio Stampiglia's *Xerse* set by Giovanni Bononcini (1694), itself based on Nicolò Minato's *Serse* set by Francesco Cavalli (1654)
PREMIERES 15 April 1738, King's Theatre, Haymarket, London; US: 12 May 1928, Northampton, Massachusetts
CAST Serse (Xerxes) *s* (castrato), Arsamene *s*, Amastre (Amastris) *c*, Ariodate *b*, Romilda *s*, Atalanta *s*, Elviro *b*; *satb* chorus of soldiers, sailors, politicians, priests

To the 1737–8 opera season at the King's Theatre Handel contributed two new operas, *Faramondo* and *Serse*, and a third work, *Alessandro Severo*, which was musically a 'self-pasticcio' using arias from Handel's previous operas. Otherwise, the programme consisted of revivals of operas by other composers, apparently to the taste of the former Opera of the Nobility patrons. The fact that Handel did not revive any of his own operas probably indicates that he was not in artistic control of the season as a whole. With *Serse* Handel returned to the librettist who had provided *Partenope*, with results in a similar spirit. The dialogue is quite light in tone; there are no great causes or heroics. In addition to dealing in comic situations, the opera includes one unambiguously comic character, the servant Elviro, 'a facetious Fellow'. Even the paragraph 'To the Reader' that takes the place of the conventional 'Argument' in the printed word-book

seems to be a parody of the normal historical and literary justification: 'The contexture of this Drama is so very easy, that it wou'd be troubling the reader to give him a long argument to explain it. Some imbecilities, and the temerity of Xerxes (such as his being deeply enamour'd with a plane tree, and the building of a bridge over the Hellespont to unite Asia to Europe) are the basis of the story, the rest is fiction.'

SYNOPSIS

Act I Xerxes, king of Persia, enjoys the shade provided by the plane tree in a garden ('Ombra mai fu'). His brother Arsamene enters looking for Romilda, with whom he is in love, whose singing is heard coming from elsewhere in the garden: the sound impels Xerxes to love. Arsamene tries to deter his brother by saying that her social station (she is the daughter of a vassal, Ariodate) makes her unworthy of the king's attentions. Undeterred, Xerxes instructs his brother to convey his affectionate intentions to Romilda, much to Arsamene's consternation. Romilda's sister Atalanta, who has her own designs on Arsamene, is present when Arsamene carries out his duty. When Arsamene later interrupts Xerxes' attempt to command Romilda into matrimony, Xerxes banishes him from the court. Romilda rejects Xerxes' love. Amastris, Xerxes' betrothed, arrives disguised as a man and overhears Xerxes reflecting that his plans for a liaison with Romilda will entail deserting Amastris. Arsamene sends his servant Elviro with a love letter to Romilda, asking for a meeting. Atalanta tries to make Romilda doubt Arsamene's constancy. Romilda declares that she will not love Arsamene if he proves unfaithful ('Se l'idol mio'), but warns Atalanta against trying to steal Arsamene from her.

Act II In the city square Elviro, who is masquerading as a flower-seller ('Ah! chi voler fiora'), tells Amastris of the situation between Xerxes, Arsamene and Romilda. Atalanta intercepts Arsamene's letter to Romilda, and then persuades Xerxes that the letter was written to herself. Xerxes determines to force Arsamene to marry Atalanta, and shows the letter to Romilda as proof of Arsamene's infidelity. Romilda is overcome with jealousy, but will still not accept Xerxes as a husband. Xerxes seems convinced that Arsamene loves Atalanta, conveniently leaving Romilda available for himself. But Arsamene protests his continuing devotion to Romilda. Outside the town Xerxes meets Amastris, still dressed as a man. He tries to enlist her into his military service, but the conversation is interrupted by the arrival of Romilda. When Xerxes tries to force his claim on Romilda, Amastris intervenes and says that she will champion Romilda against Xerxes' pressure.

Act III Romilda taxes Arsamene with writing to Atalanta: the deception is revealed. Atalanta claims that Xerxes arrived so suddenly that she had to pretend to be the recipient in order to screen Romilda. Xerxes again makes an approach to Romilda, which she counters by saying that her father's permission is needed. Xerxes tells Ariodate that Romilda is to be given a 'consort of our royal blood': Ariodate gives his consent and agrees to receive the suitor in his apartment soon, assuming that Xerxes has been referring to Arsamene. Romilda claims that she is already committed to Arsamene. Xerxes is not sure whether to believe her, but orders Arsamene's arrest. Arsamene goes to the temple, where he meets Ariodate, who, believing that he is following Xerxes' command, marries Arsamene to Romilda. When Ariodate goes to Xerxes, to thank him for the honour done to his family, Xerxes discovers what has taken place. As he accuses Ariodate of treachery, a page brings Xerxes a letter purporting to come from Romilda: it is from Amastris, who threatens suicide on account of Xerxes' infidelity. Xerxes commands Arsamene to kill his new wife, giving him a sword for the purpose. Amastris takes the sword and turns it on Xerxes himself, at the same time revealing her true identity. Xerxes is reconciled to her and, repenting the violence of his rage, approves the union of Arsamene and Romilda.

The title of *Serse* has remained in public consciousness through one melody – Xerxes' first arietta, 'Ombra mai fu': few of those who recognize 'Handel's *Largo*' (though designated 'larghetto' by the composer) are aware of its origin in Xerxes' paean to a plane tree. The score of *Serse* is indebted in some details to Giovanni Bononcini's setting of the same text, though considerably transformed by Handel. As a whole, *Serse* exhibits more variety in its arias than any other Handel opera: in complete contrast to 'Ombra mai fu' there are some full bravura da-capo arias (e.g. Xerxes' 'Più che penso', 'Se bramate d'amar' and 'Crude furie'). But da-capo arias account for only about half of the score: many arias are through-composed (e.g. Amastris's 'Anima infida' and Atalanta's 'Voi mi dite') and several are curtailed or modified in form by dramatic exigencies (e.g. Romilda's 'O voi che penate!'). Even the duets deviate from the conventional 'lovers' reunion' type: in 'Troppo oltraggi la mia fede' (Act III) Romilda and Arsamene are actually separating emotionally, while in 'Gran pena è gelosia' (Act II) Xerxes and Amastris sing their own separate (but related) thoughts, each unaware that the other is present. Elviro's first scene in Act II is amusingly punctuated by snatches of song as he interrupts his conversations with flower-seller's cries in local dialect.

Perhaps because the plot lacks substantial political overtones, the characters are clearly delineated both individually and in their relationships. The central characters are seriously motivated by love, though Xerxes' behaviour has a touch of exaggeration, which makes it impossible to take him entirely seriously. A lighter touch is provided not only by Elviro but also by Atalanta (who is clearly capricious and likely to get up to fraudulent tricks) and Ariodate. As in *Partenope*, Handel achieved exactly the appropriate musical means to express both the characterization and the plot. That Handel never revived the opera is easily explained: he never again had seven evenly matched soloists for an opera season.

Imeneo

Hymen

Opera in three acts (2h 30m)
Libretto after Silvio Stampiglia's *Imeneo in Atene* set by

Nicola Porpora (1726)
PREMIERES 22 November 1740, Theatre Royal, Lincoln's Inn Fields, London; US: 3 May 1965, Princeton University, Princeton
CAST Imeneo (Hymen) *b*, Tirinto (Tirinthus) *s* (castrato), Rosmene *s*, Clomiri (Clomiris) *s*, Argenio (Argenius) *b*; *satb* chorus

Towards the end of May 1738 Heidegger invited subscriptions for the next opera season, but had to abandon his plans when the response proved to be insufficient. So it is rather surprising that Handel spent time in September drafting a new opera, *Imeneo*: perhaps he was involved with some other scheme that never came to fruition. Handel did give a season at the King's Theatre between January and April 1739, but it was mainly devoted to English works, in particular the new oratorios *Saul* and *Israel in Egypt*. Although this proved quite successful, Handel did not attempt another season of the same type. He changed venues in London, moving to the theatre in Lincoln's Inn Fields for two seasons, apparently at his own choice. His initial plan, which he followed in 1739–40, was to mount a programme of unstaged English oratorios, serenatas and odes, which did not need the resources of a high-profile opera theatre. In 1741, however, he added the castrato Giovanni Batista Andreoni to his basically 'English-speaking' cast, and decided to present operas as well as odes and oratorios. So he returned to his (as yet unperformed) score of *Imeneo*, revising it substantially to suit his present cast and to fill the gaps left by music that he had meanwhile used elsewhere (some in the pasticcio *Giove in Argo*). Thus the opera came to performance more than two years after it was composed – a unique occurrence in the career of a composer who usually wrote to fulfil immediate demand.

SYNOPSIS

Act I   In ancient Athens, Tirinthus laments the absence of Rosmene, to whom he is betrothed, who has gone with other Athenian virgins to take part in the rites in honour of the goddess Ceres. Rumours are heard that the ship carrying the virgins has been captured by pirates. Tirinthus determines to institute a search, but his plans are interrupted by the arrival of Hymen: in order to be near his beloved Rosmene, he was with the virgins, disguised as a woman, and while the pirates were sleeping he killed them. As a reward he claims the hand of Rosmene. The Athenian senator Argenius (whose daughter Clomiris was also on board) agrees to support him, but Tirinthus is horrified at the proposal. Clomiris is upset because she has fallen in love with Hymen herself. Faced with the rival claims of Tirinthus and her rescuer, Hymen, Rosmene gives non-committal answers.

Act II   Argenius tells Rosmene that she should favour Hymen, even at the expense of breaking faith with Tirinthus. Argenius announces that the Athenians support Hymen, but are leaving the decision to Rosmene: both Hymen and Tirinthus urge her to make her choice.

Act III   Rosmene again faces Hymen and Tirinthus, saying that her heart is torn between them. Hymen's declaration that he will marry no one but Rosmene provokes Clomiris to reveal her ill-fated love. Rosmene resolves to announce her choice, but describes, feigning a trancelike state, her descent to Hades, where she dreams she meets the great judge Radamanto carrying a sword in one hand and a balance in the other: he strikes her with the sword and her soul flies from her body. Momentarily overcome, Rosmene asks to be held up, and Tirinthus and Hymen rush to support her. She sends Tirinthus away. Rosmene then reveals that she has chosen Hymen, and she urges Tirinthus to accept the outcome calmly. The Athenians comment that the heart must yield to the dictates of reason.

Imeneo is clearly a 'domestic' drama: it needs no elaborate scenic effects (which indeed might not have been possible at Lincoln's Inn Theatre), nor are any wars or public issues at stake. Although Rosmene's choice is on one level a variant on the familiar love-versus-duty theme, there is little evidence that she feels any overwhelming attraction to either of her suitors. There are ironic aspects to the opera, especially when viewed against the background of Handel's long experience in opera seria. Tirinthus, the part for the castrato, is clearly the leading man, signalled not only by his voice category but by magnificent arias such as 'Sorge nell'alma mia'. The pacing of the plot is extraordinary: instead of the multiplicity of incidents characteristic of opera seria, Rosmene's dilemma is set up quite early in Act I, and little now happens until Rosmene makes her choice in Act III. *Imeneo* works well as a chamber opera: Handel revived it as an unstaged serenata (with the title *Hymen*) at Dublin in 1742. In addition to a delicious mix of arias, there has a number of attractive short choruses: the Athenians cheer for Hymen throughout, their weight counterbalancing the circumstance that Tirinthus' music is more impassioned than Hymen's.

Semele

(The Story of Semele)
Dramatic entertainment in three acts (3h)
Libretto after William Congreve's (c. 1705–6) for John Eccles (unperformed; published 1710)
PREMIERES 10 February 1744, Covent Garden, London; US: January 1959, N.W. University, Evanston, Illinois
CAST Jupiter *t*, Cadmus *b*, Athamas *a*, Somnus *b*, Apollo *t*, Juno *c*, Iris *s*, Semele *s*, Ino *c*; *satb* chorus of priests and augurs, loves and zephyrs, nymphs and swains; (the score also includes one aria for Cupid (*s*), probably cut before the first performance)

Two secular-subject works that Handel performed 'after the manner of an Oratorio' have some claim to attention as near-operas – *Semele* and *Hercules* – and of the two *Semele* has more relevance here because its source libretto was actually written for an opera. (That for *Hercules* was written for a play.) The original text was published in 1710, as 'Semele, an Opera', in a sumptuous edition of Congreve's works. Handel's adapter followed most of Congreve's text fairly faithfully, but cut and adapted sections and added some new material (partly drawn from other works by Alexander Pope and Congreve himself), including a

new scene at the end of Act II. Although Handel performed the work in 'oratorio' style, it is perhaps significant that he ended his first draft of the end of Act II with 'Fine dell' Atto 2do', but a second draft with 'Fine della parte 2da': the uncertainty between 'parts' and 'acts' seems to reveal an equivocation in Handel's view of the work.

SYNOPSIS
Act I   The action begins in Boeotia, at the Temple of Juno, where the marriage of Semele, daughter of Cadmus, king of Thebes, and Athamas, a prince of Boeotia, is about to be solemnized. Semele seems reluctant: she does not want to forgo her present liaison with Jupiter. Suddenly thunder is heard (a sign of Jupiter's activity), and the fire on the altar is extinguished; eventually the altar sinks from sight, and the wedding is abandoned in face of these omens. Ino, Semele's sister, reveals her love for Athamas, and Cadmus reports that, as his party was leaving Juno's temple, an eagle swooped down and carried Semele away; Jupiter now enjoys Semele's favours 'above' ('Endless pleasure, endless Love').

Act II   Juno is incensed by Jupiter's affair with Semele, and she determines to destroy the woman who has displaced her. She decides that she will need help from Somnus, the god of sleep. In her palace, Semele awakes ('O Sleep, why dost thou leave me?'); Jupiter enters and the two renew their affection. But Semele is not entirely happy: she is only a mortal, and feels frightened when Jupiter leaves her. In order to distract Semele from wishing for immortality, Jupiter brings Ino to Semele for company: he transforms the scene to Arcadia ('Where'er you walk') and leaves the sisters together to enjoy the harmony of the spheres.

Act III   Juno and her attendant messenger Iris visit Somnus' cave and (with some difficulty) awaken him. Among Juno's requests to Somnus is one that Ino should be immobilized by sleep so that Juno can impersonate her when she visits Semele; in return, Juno guarantees to Somnus the lady that he desires, Pasithea. Juno, disguised as Ino, goes to Semele; she asks whether Jupiter has consented to Semele's request to join the immortals. Semele replies that she is still mortal, and Juno gives her a mirror in order to admire her own features. Semele gains confidence from what she sees in the mirror, and Juno suggests that Semele should use her attractions to make Jupiter approach her bed 'Not . . . In Likeness of a Mortal, but like himself, the mighty Thunderer': by that means, Juno says, Semele will 'partake of immortality' and be called from the mortal state. Juno leaves as she hears Jupiter approach. Jupiter allows himself to be lured into promising to grant whatever Semele requests. When Semele asks him to appear 'like Jove', Jupiter tries to dissuade her, but to no avail. Jupiter knows that if he appears as he really is, Semele will be consumed by his fire. And thus it turns out: Semele sees Jupiter afar in his true form, and dies. The chorus reflects on ambition that overreaches itself. Ino, returned to the world of mortals, relates that in a dream Hermes told Ino that it was Jupiter's wish that she should now marry Athamas. Athamas enters willingly into the union. A cloud descends on

Mount Citheron, in which Apollo is discovered. He predicts that better times lie ahead, and specifically refers to the creation of Bacchus – 'From Semele's ashes a Phoenix shall rise'.

In terms of the dramatic and musical expectations familiar from Handel's operas, the libretto of *Semele* is entirely coherent. However, allowance must be made for the features that are more effective in unstaged performances and which inevitably affect the dramatic pacing. Semele's aria 'The morning lark', for example, is really a concert-room piece: here Handel effectively invites us to forget the onward pressure of the plot and just listen to the music. Similarly, although the choruses are so arranged that they are sung by participants in the drama (priests, zephyrs, and so on), the chorus movements inevitably delay the action; but no musician would want to be deprived of 'Nature to each allots his proper sphere' in any performance of *Semele*. Perhaps because *Semele* sat uneasily with the general tone of Handel's developing oratorio seasons, the composer revived it only briefly in December 1744 after its original run of four performances earlier that year. Modern circumstances provide more flexibility than Handel himself had for choice between staged and unstaged treatments.

Other operas: *Almira*, 1705; *Rodrigo*, 1707; *Teseo*, 1713; *Silla*, 1713; *Amadigi* 1715; *Radamisto*, 1720, rev. 1720, 1721, 1728; *Muzio Scevola*, 1721; *Floridante*, 1721, rev. 1722, 1727, 1733; *Ottone*, 1723, rev. 1723, 1726, 1727, 1733; *Flavio*, 1723; *Scipione*, 1726; *Admeto*, 1727; *Riccardo Primo*, 1727; *Siroe*, 1728; *Tolomeo*, 1728; *Lotario*, 1729; *Poro*, 1731; *Ezio*, 1732; *Sosarme*, 1732; *Arianna*, 1734; *Parnasso in festa*, 1734 *Atalanta*, 1736; *Arminio*, 1737; *Giustino*, 1737; *Berenice*, 1737; *Faramondo*, 1738; *Deidamia*, 1741
Operas lost or surviving only in fragments: *Nero* [*Die durch Blut und Mord erlangte Liebe*] (music lost), 1705; *Florindo* [*Der beglückte Florindo*], and *Daphne* [*Der verwandelte Dephne*], (1706), music partially lost, performed as two operas, 1708; *Genserico* [*Olibrio*] (inc., 1728); *Titus l'Empereur* (inc., 1731)
London pasticcio operas constructed by Handel from his own music: *Oreste*, 1734; *Alessandro Severo*, 1738: *Giove in Argo*, 1739
London pasticcio operas with music by other composers, arr. (with some new composition of recitatives, etc.) Handel: *Elpidia*, 1725; *Ormisda*, 1730; *Venceslao*, 1731; *Lucio Papirio*, 1732; *Catone*, 1732; *Semiramide riconosciuta*, 1733; *Cajo Fabricio*, 1733; *Arbace*, 1734; *Didone abbandonata*, 1737

D.J.B.

JOSEPH HAYDN
Franz Joseph Haydn; *b* 31 March 1732, Rohrau, Austria; *d* 31 May 1809, Vienna

Although Haydn is best remembered as a composer of symphonies, quartets and oratorios, opera formed a substantial part of his output, and from 1776 to 1790 it dominated his life. Haydn's first operatic music was written in the 1750s, when he was living in Vienna and earning income from a variety of sources. For a singspiel company based at the Kärntnertortheater he wrote *Der krumme Teufel* and *Der neue krumme Teufel*; the music of both operas is lost. A miscellaneous collection of arias in the Austrian National Library suggests that he also composed individual numbers for the company as required. Haydn seems not to have had any contact with the Burgtheater, whose repertoire at the time was dominated by French opéra comique. His first full-time employment (1759–60) was as kapellmeister to Count Morzin, a position that required the composition of instrumental music only.

Haydn's first extant opera dates from the first years of his employment at the Esterházy court, the richest in the Austrian aristocracy; between 1761 and his death he was to serve four successive Esterházy princes, and all but one of Haydn's operas were written for the family. At first they were performed in a theatre in the hall (now Haydnsaal) of Eisenstadt Castle, the main residence, south-east of Vienna, but from 1768 onwards the performances took place in Eszterháza, a new summer palace built in the countryside some 22 miles further south-east by the second and most extravagant of Haydn's masters, Prince Nicolaus. There were two theatres. The larger, for Italian opera and plays, held about 400 people with the prince's seats and retiring rooms on the first floor; the orchestra sat, as was the custom, in a double row in front of the stage; and the stage itself was capable of a deep perspective and was fully equipped with stage machinery. The second, smaller, theatre, opened in 1773, was devoted mainly to marionette performances. Haydn, as Esterházy kapellmeister, was responsible for supervising and directing the music at both these theatres. Until 1775 there were occasional performances, but from then on a full-time opera company was based at Eszterháza, their performances alternating with spoken plays given by visiting troupes of actors. Performances were given of works by most of the leading composers of Italian opera: Pasquale Anfossi, Domenico Cimarosa, Gluck, Pietro Alessandro Guglielmi, Giovanni Paisiello, Niccolò Piccinni, Giuseppe Sarti and others; the busiest year was 1786, when 125 performances of 17 different operas were given, eight of them for the first time at Eszterháza. In September 1790 Prince Nicolaus Esterházy died and the opera season came to an abrupt end just as performances of Mozart's *Le nozze di Figaro* were being prepared; none of Prince Nicolaus's successors was interested in opera, and the theatres at Eszterháza, together with the main house, fell into disuse and later disrepair.

At its zenith, the Esterházy court opera employed some 25 people – singers, designers, administrators, copyists, painters, etc. – plus the regular court orchestra of some 15 to 20 players. As a centre for Italian opera north of the Alps it could fairly be said to have vied in importance with London and St Petersburg. But there were certain characteristics that were peculiar to Eszterháza. The first was its isolation. The nearest large city, Vienna, was 40 miles away and it was on the way to nowhere; consequently, the company could not profit from the more aggressive operatic life of the large European cities. Secondly, the resident composer, Haydns, was unusual in that he was not an Italian, nor did he ever visit Italy; moreover, he had very little knowledge of Italian opera when he started.

Lastly, the Esterházy court did not employ a resident poet, so Haydn did not have the benefit of working in partnership with a librettist in the way that Baldassare Galuppi, Gluck and Mozart did. The libretti of Haydn's operas were sometimes 20 or more years old and had already proved popular in settings by other composers. It is not known who chose the operas that were to be performed at the court (no doubt the prince had the final say), but the two persons who seem to have assisted Haydn in adapting libretti for use at Eszterháza were the tenor Carl Friberth, and the director Nunziato Porta.

Between 1762 and 1783 Haydn composed 16 Italian operas and five German operas. The composer was very proud of his achievement, singling out the operas for special mention in an autobiographical sketch that appeared in 1776 and, apropos La fedeltà premiata, writing as follows in a letter to his publisher, Artaria, in 1781: 'I assure you that no such work has been heard in Paris up to now, nor perhaps in Vienna; my misfortune is that I live in the country.' In assessing these two instances of genuine self-esteem it should be borne in mind that Italian opera was the most international of art forms and Haydn was clearly anxious to claim his rightful place as a figure of more than local significance. Gradually, however, Haydn came to realize that the European public was more interested in his instrumental music – symphonies, quartets, piano sonatas and piano trios – and in the 1780s his output became more and more directed towards meeting this demand, composing symphonies for Paris, quartets for various publishers in Vienna and abroad and Die sieben letzten Worte (the Seven Last Words – an orchestral work) for Cadiz. This courting of international recognition partly explains why Haydn did not compose any operas for the Esterházy court after 1783. In 1787 it was suggested that Haydn might like to compose a new opera for Prague; the composer refused, noting that 'scarcely any man can brook comparison with the great Mozart'.

Haydn's only extant opera for a theatre outside Eisenstadt and Eszterháza was also to be his last, L'animo del filosofo, ossia Orfeo ed Euridice. Written for London in 1791, it was never performed in the composer's lifetime. During Haydn's last years in Vienna, when the composer's reputation was crowned by the oratorios Die Schöpfung (The Creation) and Die Jahreszeiten (The Seasons), there was no hint of an operatic project.

Although opera played an insignificant part in his output in the last 25 years of his life, it should not be thought that Haydn's operas lay forgotten in Eszterháza. Some complete works and many extracts were known and distributed widely. For instance, La fedeltà premiata and Orlando paladino were performed at several venues in Austria and Germany, usually in German translation; La vera costanza formed the basis of an opéra comique called Laurette given at the Théâtre Feydeau, Paris, in 1791; and Armida was performed in Turin in 1805. Some individual arias were published, but the most substantial publication was that of 11 numbers from L'anima del filosofo issued, with the composer's co-operation, by Breitkopf und Härtel in 1806.

The modern revival of the composer's operas began with heavily edited performances in German of La canterina, Lo speziale, L'infedeltà delusa, L'incontro improvviso, Il mondo della luna, L'isola disabitata and Orlando paladino, which took place in Austria and Germany between 1895 and 1939. With the development of Haydn scholarship after the Second World War, performances in the original language and in faithful editions began to be given and are now quite frequently encountered, though Haydn has not yet achieved an indisputable place in the centre of the operatic repertoire. Wider appreciation of the operas has been encouraged by commercial recordings.

Modern evaluation of Haydn as a composer of opera has been conditioned by invidious comparisons with his contemporary Mozart. In general, Haydn's operas certainly lack the psychological insight into human behaviour and the sure-footed pacing of dramatic narrative that characterize Mozart's mature operas. On the other hand, comparison with popular Italian operas of the second half of the 18th century, many of which Haydn himself directed at Eszterháza, yields a more positive appreciation of the composer's talents. As might be expected from a composer whose wider reputation rested – then as now – on instrumental music, the arias frequently have a richness of orchestration, a security of structure and an individuality of melodic and, especially, harmonic content that are rare in operas by his Italian contemporaries. The influence of Gluck's reform operas is sometimes apparent, particularly in the two serious operas, L'isola disabitata and Armida, where extensive use of accompanied recitative coalescing into aria provides a continuity absent from number opera. Equally important for dramatic continuity is Haydn's interest in building his act finales into long sequences (up to ten consecutive sections) linked by their key structure, providing a powerful sense of mounting excitement.

L'infedeltà delusa
Deceit Outwitted

Burletta per musica in two acts (2h 15m)
Libretto by Marco Coltellini, amended by Carl Friberth
PREMIERES 26 July 1773, Eszterháza; UK: 14 October 1960, Royal Festival Hall, London (concert); 18 March 1964, St Pancras Town Hall, London; US: 11 March 1963, Iowa University, Iowa

The opera was written to be performed on the name day of Princess Maria Anna Louise Esterházy, widow of Prince Paul Anton, Haydn's first Esterházy patron. The performance in the Eszterháza theatre was followed by a masked ball and, on the following day, a firework display. A month later the empress Maria Theresa made her first and only visit to the Esterházy court. L'infedeltà delusa was performed on the first night of the visit (31 August) and the marionette opera Philemon und Baucis on the second night. The success of the visit prompted Maria Theresa's later remark, 'If I want to hear good opera, I go to Eszterháza', an indication of the high standards in the Esterházy court in comparison with those in Viennese theatre at the time. After 1774, no further performances of *L'infedeltà delusa* are known in Haydn's lifetime.

Vespina wishes to marry Nencio, and Nanni wishes to marry Sandrina. But Sandrina's father (Filippo) thinks Nencio would make a better match for his daughter. To this end, he persuades Nencio to serenade his daughter. Sandrina spurns him and the spying Vespina strikes him. In Act II Vespina, in a series of disguises (a limping old woman, a German servant, the marquis of Ripafratta and a notary), engineers the action so that Filippo is forced to accept the marriage of Sandrina and Nanni, and Vespina gets her man, Nencio.

The wily, yet sympathetic character of Vespina, a proto-Despina, is well caught in a series of arias in Act II. The innocent victim of the intrigue, Sandrina, is similarly well characterized, especially in the aria sung before the dénouement, 'È la pompa un grand'imbroglio'. The three ensembles, placed at the beginning and end of Act I and the end of Act II, provide a broad framework for a charming narrative that unfolds through recitative (almost entirely *secco*) and aria.

Il mondo della luna
The World on the Moon
Dramma giocoso in three acts (2h 45m)
Libretto by Carlo Goldoni (1750)
PREMIERES 3 August 1777, Eszterháza; US: 7 June 1949, Greenwich Mews Playhouse, New York; UK: 8 November 1951, Scala Theatre, London (inc.); 22 March 1960, St Pancras Town Hall, London
CAST Ecclitico *t*, Ernesto *a*, Buonafede *b*, Clarice *s*, Flamina *s*, Lisetta *c*, Cecco *t*; 4 Students of Ecclitico 4 *b*; *satb* chorus of scholars, knights, pages, servants, soldiers, followers of Ecclitico; dancers

Goldoni's text was one of his most popular, set first by Baldassare Galuppi in 1750 and then by Pedro Antonio Avondano (1765), Paisiello (1774, as *Il credulo deluso*, and 1782) and Gennaro Astarita (1775). The role of Ecclitico in the Astarita version was taken by Guglielmo Jermoli, who from March to July 1777 was a member of the opera company at Eszterháza; he may well have suggested the libretto to Haydn. The opera was first performed as part of the celebrations accompanying the marriage of Count Nicolaus, second son of Prince Nicolaus I, and Countess Maria Anna Weissenwolf. The opera was evidently only a moderate success, for it was not repeated in subsequent seasons at Eszterháza and no contemporary performances outside the court are known.

The libretto is a delightful puncturing of the omniscience of the Age of Reason.

SYNOPSIS

Act I Ecclitico and his students are observing the moon, eager to establish the presence of human life there. The ill-humoured Buonafede ('Good faith') is persuaded by them that a better life exists on the moon. Ernesto, a knight, and his servant Cecco enter, and it emerges that Ernesto and Ecclitico are in love with Buonafede's daughters, Flamina and Clarice, and Cecco with Lisetta, the maid. Ecclitico convinces them

that Buonafede can be tricked into allowing a triple marriage. Buonafede takes a potion which he is told will transport him to the moon. He bids everyone farewell; his daughters imagine that he is dying, but are placated by the reading of a forged will leaving them a handsome dowry.

Act II In Ecclitico's garden, disguised as the moon, Buonafede wakes to the sound and sight of dancing and is prepared for his meeting with the emperor of the moon (Cecco in disguise). Buonafede, now rather a forlorn figure, woos Lisetta, who spurns him; she is about to be crowned the queen of the lunatics. Buonafede is duped into sanctioning the marriage of his two daughters. When he discovers the deceit, everyone asks his forgiveness.

Act III In Ecclitico's house Buonafede agrees to forgive everyone and the triple marriage is sanctioned. Ecclitico announces that he is giving up astrology and everyone commends the good fortune that the world of the moon has brought.

The work is a typical dramma giocoso in that the characters are divided into three groups: the parti buffe are Buonafede, Lisetta and Cecco; the parti serie are Flamina and Ernesto; and the intermediate group, the parti di mezzo carattere, include Clarice and Ecclitico. Haydn's music resourcefully highlights these divisions, particularly in the three Act I arias for the female characters. Buonafede's aria in Act II ('Che mondo amabile') engages the sympathy of the listener as the old man describes his happiness (including whistling in imitation of birds) in the make-believe world of the moon.

Haydn reused many numbers from this opera in later works: the C major overture became the first movement of Symphony No. 63 ('La Roxelane'); Ernesto's aria ('Qualche volte non fa male') the Benedictus of the *Missa Cellensis* (1782), and other movements are included in the six trios for two violins (or flute and violin) and cello.

La vera costanza
True Constancy
Dramma giocoso per musica in three acts (2h)
Libretto by Francesco Puttini, written for Pasquale Anfossi in 1775
Composed 1777–8, rev. 1785
PREMIERES 25 April 1779, Eszterháza; rev. version: April 1785, Eszterháza; UK: 12 February 1976, Curtain Theatre, London; US: July 1980, Katonah, New York

According to Albert Christoph Dies, one of Haydn's first biographers, this opera was commissioned by Joseph II for performance in Vienna. Since there is no documentary evidence to support this statement, many people have doubted its veracity. However, modern scholarship has also suggested that Haydn was indeed commissioned to write an Italian opera by Joseph II, but that he composed only half of it because the emperor became engrossed in the founding of the National Singspiel; Haydn then completed the work for performance in Eszterháza.

The true constancy of the title is that of the fishermaid Rosina, who is secretly married to Count Errico, by whom she has a son. This fidelity is tested by Baroness Irene, by Rosina's intended husband, Villoto, and even by Rosina's husband, all of whom plot at one stage to murder her. She and her son escape, and it is only at the pathetic moment of her rescue from starvation that humanity's better nature triumphs and Rosina and the count are reunited.

Rosina's music in Act II is strongly characterized, and the section in the finale when the boy (a spoken part) leads the rescuers to his mother is 18th-century sensibility at its most affecting. The 'chain' finales to Acts I and II are the most extensive to date in Haydn's operas, accounting for approximately a quarter and a third of their respective acts.

La fedeltà premiata

Fidelity Rewarded
Dramma giocoso in three acts (first version: 3h 15m; second version: 2h 45m)
Libretto adapted by Haydn and an unknown person from Giambattista Lorenzi's text for Domenico Cimarosa's *L'infedeltà fedele* (1779)
Composed 1780; rev. 1782
PREMIERES 25 February 1781, Eszterháza; rev. version: 29 September 1782, Eszterháza; UK: 27 April 1971, Collegiate Theatre, London
CAST Celia *s*, Fileno *t*, Amaranta *s*, Count Perrucchetto *b*, Nerina *s*, Lindoro *t*, Melibeo *b*, Diana *s*; *satb* chorus of nymphs and shepherds, hunters and huntresses, followers of Diana; dancers: shepherds, shepherdesses, satyrs

The opera was written for the reopening of the large opera house in Eszterháza, following its destruction by fire in November 1779, and was revised for the 1782 season. It received 36 performances at Eszterháza in the 1780s and, translated into German, several in the Kärntnertortheater Vienna and in Pressburg.

In the 1782 libretto the genre title was modified to 'dramma pastorale giocoso', an indication of the setting of the opera: woodland, a grotto, rugged rocks and a distant lake, a scene populated by nymphs, shepherds and hunters. The story is of steadfastness eventually rewarded; the fidelity (of Celia and Fileno) is contrasted with more fickle relationships (among Lindoro, Nerina, Amaranta, Melibeo and Perrucchetto).

SYNOPSIS
Act I A loving couple must be sacrificed to placate the sea monster. Amaranta and Melibeo connive to arrange the marriage of Lindoro and Celia; Celia's lover Fileno is comforted by Nerina. Fileno and Celia meet, but, realizing that they risk sacrifice, they part. In the finale, Amaranta, Lindoro and Melibeo persist in bullying Celia to marry Lindoro; Fileno's sadness turns to despair when he hears of these plans; suddenly, satyrs enter and save Celia.

Act II Fileno's despair leads him to contemplate suicide. Celia believes that Fileno is dead. Melibeo has now decided that the sacrificed couple should be Celia and Perrucchetto, and the finale prepares for the fateful moment.

Act III Celia and Fileno are reunited but cannot see a just way of appeasing the sea god. At the moment of sacrifice, Fileno throws himself at the sea monster; it turns into a grotto revealing the goddess

Diana. She resolves the action by sanctioning the marriages of Fileno and Celia, of Lindoro and Nerina, and of Perrucchetto and Amaranta. General rejoicing.

The overture was reused as the finale to Symphony No. 73. Celia's recitative and aria in Act II, 'Ah come il core. . . Ombra del caro bene', was published in Vienna and London as a cantata and was performed in Haydn's benefit concert on 16 May 1791 in the Hanover Square Rooms. This scena and others in Act II for Fileno and Amaranta are some of the highlights of the opera. Even more noteworthy are the 'chain' finales to Acts I and II, both propelled by a sequence of keys featuring a third relationship and forming a sustained drama that shows Haydn at his best in opera.

Orlando paladino

Knight Roland
Dramma eroicomico in three acts (2h 45m)
Libretto by Nunziato Porta, after his own revision of Carlo Francesco Badini's *Le pazzie d'Orlando* written for Pietro Alessandro Guglielmi (1771)
PREMIERES 6 December 1782, Eszterháza; UK: 11 July 1980, Midlands Arts Centre, Birmingham

Porta was engaged from July 1781 as director of the opera at Eszterháza and he proposed the libretto for *Orlando paladino*. The love of Angelica and Medoro is threatened by two errant knights, Orlando and Rodomonte, and protected by the timely interventions of the sorceress Alcina. Orlando is purged of all aggressive behaviour, and the opera ends with the assembled cast declaiming the healing power of love.

As was typical of the dramma-giocoso genre (of which this is a subspecies), the serious-minded action of the higher ranks of society is contrasted with the more comic and human behaviour of Eurilla (a shepherdess) and Pasquale (Orlando's squire). In extravagant boasting the latter outdoes Mozart's Leporello, with two catalogue arias, the first recounting his endless travelling and the second his musical abilities; he also has a robust aria in C major of a type frequently encountered in Haydn's operas. The eponymous figure of Orlando is much talked about but appears too late in the first two acts to make any strong impact; his music, however, is unfailingly attractive, especially the Act III accompanied recitative and aria depicting the awakening of the knight from a long magic sleep. The opera ends with a vaudeville, a rondo-like structure in which the assembled cast declaims the moral for the main theme and the individual characters present their own viewpoint in the episodes. *Orlando paladino*, Haydn's last comic opera, was the composer's most popular opera in his lifetime, with documented performances in 20 towns in central Europe, usually in German translation.

Armida

Dramma eroico in three acts (2h 15m)
Libretto (after Torquato Tasso's epic poem *Gerusalemme liberata* (1581)) taken from Antonio Tozzi's opera *Rinaldo* (1775), slightly amended by Nunziato Porta
PREMIERES 26 February 1784, Eszterháza; US: Spring

1969, YMCA Actors' Studio, New York; UK: 21 July 1988, Opera House, Buxton

This was Haydn's last Eszterháza opera, and it was the most frequently performed in the court theatre (there were 54 performances). It was part of a distinct trend towards featuring more opere serie in the Eszterháza repertoire in the 1780s.

The opera is set at the time of the Crusades, and its theme is the superior call of duty on behalf of Christendom over the sweet voice of love. The person caught in this dilemma is Rinaldo (a former Crusading knight) who is loved by Armida (a sorceress) and reminded of his calling by Ubaldo (a knight). Love seems to triumph, but Armida's affection turns to hatred and the opera ends with the participants pondering their fate against the ironic background of martial music.

In Acts II and III several consecutive numbers run into one another, providing dramatic continuity. The vocal writing is more virtuosic than in Haydn's previous operas, and there are two splendid military arias in C major. In Act III, there is a vivid musical evocation of natural objects and phenomena – a notable foretelling of the composer's oratorios, *The Creation* and *The Seasons*.

Other operas: *Acide* (inc.) 1763, rev. 1773; *La marchesa Nespola*, 1763; *La canterina*, 1766; *Lo speziale*, 1768; *Le pescatrici*, 1770; *Die reisende Ceres* (doubtful), c. 1770; *Der Giötterrath*, 1773; *Philemon und Bancis, oder Jupiters Reise auf die Erde*, 1773, rev. 1780; *L'incontro improvviso*, 1775; *L'isola disabitata*, 1779; *L'anima del filosofo, ossia Orfeo ed Euridice*, (1791), 1951; 9 lost operas

D.W.J.

HANS WERNER HENZE

b 1 July 1926, Gütersloh, Westphalia, Germany

Henze has said of himself that all his music starts out from and returns to the theatre. One of his earliest musical memories was of listening enthralled to a performance on record of the overture to Mozart's *Le nozze di Figaro*. And though it would be an exaggeration to assert that it was this childhood experience that established the pattern of his creative life, he has been at pains to point out on more than one occasion that the theatre is his natural domain. Even in his most seemingly abstract works the instruments often behave in an entirely theatrical way, like personages in a drama.

After a period of military service, during which he was for a short time a British prisoner-of-war, and while continuing his studies with the composer Wolfgang Fortner and the leading Schoenbergian theorist René Leibowitz, he also consolidated his more practical commitment to the theatre as a member of the staffs of the Bielefeld Stadttheater and the Deutsches Theater at Constance, and then as conductor and artistic director of the Wiesbaden ballet. Since then a substantial sequence of operas and music-theatre works has punctuated his prolific output like peaks in a mountain range, each with its own closely related series of orchestral, chamber and other vocal pieces.

Sometimes, indeed, that relationship is particularly intimate – his Fourth Symphony being shaped directly out of part of Act II of the opera *König Hirsch*, and an aria from the *Elegy for Young Lovers* providing the thematic basis of the finale of his Fifth Symphony.

Just when it seemed that he had achieved an impregnable position as one of the most prodigiously gifted and acclaimed of the new post-war generation of German composers, Henze made a sudden, and wholly characteristic, decision in 1953 to break with his German roots and to settle permanently in Italy, first in the Bay of Naples and then in the countryside near Rome. As a composer who has always been responsive to the distinctive qualities of landscape and accent, the impact of his Mediterranean experience was first reflected in his music in its new vein of hedonistic lyricism and fantasy, and later by the slightly harsher inflexions typical of Roman speech.

Then, in the 1960s, the coincidence of his growing sense of disillusionment after the composition of *The Bassarids* and his personal identification with the aims of revolutionary socialism resulted in another radical change of direction, his music abandoning its passive attitude to contemporary reality in favour of a more active and astringently defined participation in its brutal struggles. Yet, even at its most politically explicit, that development can be diagnosed with hindsight as simply a further and logical step in the exploration of the clash between illusion and reality, authority and freedom, social constraints and individual liberty, that has been at the heart of Henze's artistic enterprise since his earliest years.

König Hirsch
King Stag
Opera in three acts (4h)
Libretto by Heinz von Cramer, after Carlo Gozzi's fable *Il re cervo* (1762)
Composed 1952–5; shortened and revised as *Il re cervo, oder Die Irrfahrten der Wahrheit*, 1962
PREMIERES 23 September 1956, Städtische Oper, Berlin (with extensive cuts); rev. version: 10 March 1963, Staatstheater, Kassel; UK: 20 January 1973, BBC radio (in English); rev. version: US: 4 August 1965, Opera Theater, Santa Fe, New Mexico; complete original version: 5 May 1985, Staatsoper, Stuttgart
CAST *Il re cervo*: The King (Leandro) t, The Girl (Costanza) s, The Governor (Tartaglia) b-bar, Scollatella I s, Scollatella II s, Scollatella III ms, Scollatella IV c, Checco buffo t, Coltellino buffo t, 2 Statues 2 s, The Stag silent; satb chorus of voices of forest, courtiers, animals, huntsmen, soldiers, city dwellers, etc.

Although the ideas for Henze's longest and most ambitious opera had begun to crystallize in the minds of its composer and librettist some time before Henze left Germany to settle permanently in Italy, the greater part of *König Hirsch* was written during many months of intense concentration and in almost monastic seclusion at Forio d'Ischia in the Bay of Naples. Over a century earlier the English translator of Carlo Gozzi's memoirs, John Addington Symonds, had suggested that the theatrical fables of the 18th-century Venetian could well furnish excellent libretti for the composers of opera. And, following in the footsteps of the young Wagner of *Die Feen*, of Busoni and Prokofiev, Henze was to discover in Gozzi's miraculous fairy-tale of the king who is metamorphosed into a stag an ideal vehicle for all his most intimate dreams and aspirations, for his first revelatory encounters with Mediterranean culture and landscape and the haunting quality of Italian folksong.

SYNOPSIS
The place is somewhere between sea and forest near Venice, the period some time in antiquity.

Act I Preparations are under way for the coronation of the innocent King Leandro, who has grown up among the forest animals. During a ferocious storm, Scollatella and her doubles argue about who will become queen. The girl Costanza is brought in by her guards and is threatened by the malicious, scheming Tartaglia that to gain her freedom she must kill the new king. Instructed by Tartaglia that he must choose a queen, Leandro spurns the four quarrelsome Scollatellas and finds himself increasingly drawn to the gentle Costanza. When Tartaglia cunningly reveals the dagger hidden in Costanza's clothing, the broken-hearted Leandro's plea for her to be forgiven is rejected and he decides to abdicate and return to the forest. Left alone, the victorious Tartaglia is joined by the hired assassin Coltellino, whom he commands to follow Leandro and murder him.

Act II In the great living, breathing forest Leandro is pursued by Scollatella and her mirror images, and then by Tartaglia, who tries to kill him but fails. A stag is wounded and dies. By means of a magic formula confided to him by a (melancholy) musician Checco, Leandro transforms himself into the stag. But the evil Tartaglia, who has also learned the spell, assumes the appearance of the king and, as another storm breaks over the forest, orders a huge stag hunt that will rid him of Leandro for ever.

Act III The oppressed populace of the decaying city patiently awaits the King Stag which, according to legend, will free it from Tartaglia's tyrannical rule. Leandro in his form as the King Stag duly appears in the deserted streets and is greeted by Costanza. Tartaglia, still disguised as the king, is mistakenly shot and killed by Coltellino. Leandro, using the same transformation spell, is restored to human form and takes Costanza as his bride to general public rejoicing.

So bare an outline of the intricate scenario of *König Hirsch* can give little idea of the variety, richness and prodigality of a work whose music is saturated with the shimmering light, colour and enchanted atmosphere of the Italian landscape. Even before the scandal caused by its savagely cut Berlin premiere, Henze had recycled the evocative and already symphonically shaped music that accompanies the great stag hunt of Act II into his Fourth Symphony. Alerted by the enormous problems created by that first Berlin performance, he and his librettist also produced under the title *Il re cervo* their own official, much shortened and instrumentally reduced version. But, as Henze has insisted, it is only when staged complete that the work can be heard and understood correctly.

Der Prinz von Homburg
The Prince of Homburg
Opera in three acts (2h 15m)
Libretto by Ingeborg Bachmann, after the drama by Heinrich von Kleist (1811)
PREMIERES 22 May 1960, Staatsoper, Hamburg; UK: 26 September 1962, Sadler's Wells, London
CAST Prince Friedrich *high bar*, Princess Natalie *s*, Elector Friedrich Wilhelm *t*, Electress *c*, Dörfling *bar*, Kottwitz *b*, Hohenzollern *t*; *satb* chorus of other officers, ladies-in-waiting, soldiers, servants, etc.

The film director Luchino Visconti first suggested to Henze that the dramatic masterpiece of the 19th-century German playwright Heinrich von Kleist would make ideal operatic material. What both drama and opera are about, in Henze's words, is the glorification of the dreamer, and what clearly appealed to him in Kleist's play was the tension it explores between the poetic individual as hero and the rigidity of his harsh, militaristic background. The libretto fashioned by the Austrian poet Ingeborg Bachmann falls naturally into recitative, aria and ensemble, and the composition of the opera came musically at a time when Henze was steeped, as he puts it, in early-19th-century Italian opera, in the serene melancholy of Bellini, the sparkling brio of Rossini, and Donizetti's passionate intensity, all drawn together and condensed in Verdi's robust rhythms, hard orchestral colours and melodic lines that set the ears tingling.

SYNOPSIS
Act I As his fellow officers while away the time before the coming battle, Prince Friedrich Artur von Homburg sits musing in the moonlit garden of the castle of Fehrbellin. His reverie is interrupted by the arrival of Friedrich Wilhelm, elector of Brandenburg, and his niece Princess Natalie, whose hand the elector promises to the prince in marriage. After their departure, Friedrich remains dreamily fondling the glove left behind by the princess, the symbol of all his hopes and aspirations, of the coming victory and their glorious future together of love and happiness. In a conference room in the castle next morning Field Marshal Dörfling is giving his officers their orders of the day. The prince, however, is still transfixed in his trancelike state. Later, on the battlefield, he checks the orders with his friend Hohenzollern, impetuously commands his cavalry to attack without waiting for the field marshal's signal, and himself rushes into battle. The battle is won, but, angered by the prince's reckless action, the elector orders him to be stripped of his honours and court-martialled.

Act II Prince Friedrich, who has been condemned to death, reflects in his prison cell on the gravity of his situation. In the electress's room he pleads with her to intervene on his behalf, but it is Natalie who goes to the elector to beg for clemency. Pardon will be granted, he tells her, only if Friedrich himself can argue convincingly in his own heart and soul that the sentence is unjust. When the prince rejects the offered compromise, preferring to die rather than betray his self-respect, Natalie decides that she will command her own dragoons to free him by force.

Act III Dörfling warns the elector of Natalie's intentions. What eventually moves him to tear up the death warrant is not, however, the pleading of Natalie or Friedrich's fellow officers, but the prince's adamant refusal to alter his decision that only an honourable death will cleanse his guilt. He is led into the garden prepared for execution, but as his blindfold is removed he realizes that instead of death all he had dreamed of in the opera's opening scene has now become reality.

With its orchestra used predominantly in the spirit of chamber music, each scene has its own specific instrumental grouping and colour, and each is based on a particular form such as fugue, rondo or passacaglia. As was noted at the time of the premiere, this is also in keeping with the opera's themes of understanding and forgiveness, and with the aim of composer and librettist to lift its conflicts out of their strictly Prussian setting and to give them a more universal significance. Thus the elector's words in Kleist's play, 'He will teach you, be assured, what military discipline and obedience are', have been changed in the opera to '. . . what freedom and honour are'. The dedication is to Igor Stravinsky.

Elegy for Young Lovers

Opera in three acts (2h 30m)
Libretto by W. H. Auden and Chester Kallman (German translation by Ludwig Landgraf)
PREMIERES 20 May 1961, Schlosstheater, Schwetzingen (in German); UK: 13 July 1961, Glyndebourne (in English); US: 29 April 1965, Juilliard School, New York
CAST Mittenhofer *bar*, Reischmann *b*, Toni *t*, Elisabeth *s*, Carolina *c*, Hilda *s*, Mauer *spoken role*

An inscription on the title page reads, 'To the memory of Hugo von Hofmannsthal, Austrian, European and Master Librettist, this work is gratefully dedicated by its three makers.' When Henze made his first tentative proposal to Auden and Kallman that they should write a libretto for him, what he had in mind was a chamber opera with a small, subtle orchestra and dominated by beautiful, tender noises. Set in an Alpine chalet in the year 1910, requiring a cast of just six solo voices and with its three acts made up of 34 short scenes each with its own individual title, the opera's true subject matter is the creation of a poem. At its centre is the poet Gregor Mittenhofer, who ruthlessly exploits the personal obsessions of everyone around him to feed his monstrous creative appetites. Every year he returns to his Alpine retreat to write his spring poem, and to renew contact with the coloratura visions of the demented widow Hilda Mack, who, still dressed in the style of the 1870s, has waited in lonely isolation at the inn for the return of her husband who disappeared on the mountain 40 years before.

SYNOPSIS

Act I This year Mittenhofer has brought with him his wealthy patroness and unpaid secretary Carolina, his personal physician Dr Reischmann, and his young companion Elisabeth, who are soon joined by Reischmann's son Toni. Morning life goes on with its everyday bustle as Mittenhofer calls impatiently for his breakfast egg and his daily injection, wheedles money out of Carolina, scolds her for her typing errors, and makes notes of Hilda's hallucinatory visions. But the morning routine is suddenly interrupted when the guide Josef Mauer rushes in to tell them that a body has been found in the ice on the Hammerhorn and that it must be Frau Mack's husband. Elisabeth gently consoles the bewildered Hilda, and the act ends with Hilda's ecstatic realization that her imprisoning crystal has at last been broken and with Toni's ardent recognition of his love for Elisabeth.

Act II Made aware by Carolina of the young couple's clearly expressed love for each other, Mittenhofer first plays on Elisabeth's feelings of guilt but then, in a change of tack, asks Reischmann to bless them, and the lovers to bring him from the mountain a sprig of edelweiss that he needs to complete his poem. However, once they have departed his mood veers abruptly from apparent acceptance to furious rage.

Act III The now completely cured Hilda says her farewells, and Elisabeth and Toni leave for the mountain slope. But though a fine, warm day has been forecast a fierce snowstorm suddenly blows up and, in a switch of scene, the young couple are seen on the Hammerhorn, resigned to a loving death in another's arms. Finally the scene shifts to an auditorium in Vienna where, after acknowledging the applause of his admirers, Mittenhofer silently mouths his newly finished poem, 'Elegy for Young Lovers', against the background of the offstage voices of Elisabeth, Toni, Hilda, Carolina, and the doctor.

With its predominance of silvery sounds and high tuned percussion the instrumental writing breathes an air of sharp, crystalline purity, depicting the sparkling atmosphere and the chill of the Alpine landscape in flashing, translucent colours. Each character is associated with a particular instrument or group of instruments; Mittenhofer, for instance, with horn, trumpet and trombone; Carolina with the plangent, submissive tone of a cor anglais; and Hilda with the flute, whose agile tracery, as it shadows the widely leaping intervals and brilliantly decorative figurations of her hallucinatory coloratura, is directly based on the mad scene from Donizetti's *Lucia di Lammermoor*.

Der junge Lord

The Young Lord
Comic opera in two acts (2h 30m)
Libretto by Ingeborg Bachmann, after the parable *Der Scheik von Alessandria und seine Sklaven* by Wilhelm Hauff (1826)
PREMIERES 7 April 1965, Deutsche Oper, Berlin; US: 17 February 1967, Civic Theatre, San Diego; UK: 14 October 1969, Sadler's Wells, London
CAST Sir Edgar *silent*, His Secretary *bar*, Lord Barrat *t*, Begonia *ms*, Burgomaster *b-bar*, Councillor Hasentreffer *bar*, Councillor Scharf *bar*, Professor von Mucker *t*, Baroness Grünwiesel *ms*, Frau von Hufnagel *ms*, Frau Hasentreffer *s*, Luise *s*, Ida *s*, A Maid *s*, Wilhelm *t*, Amintore La Rocca *t*, A Lamplighter *b*; *silent roles*: Monsieur La Truiare (a dancing master), Meadows (the butler), Jeremy (a Moor); *circus performers*; *satb* chorus of townsfolk

With his fifth full-length opera Henze fulfilled a long-held ambition that can be traced back through *König Hirsch* and the satirical comedy *Das Ende einer Welt* – to write a fully-fledged opera buffa.

SYNOPSIS

Act I In the German town of Hülsdorf-Gotha in 1830, the populace awaits the arrival of the rich English milord Sir Edgar. The grander citizens rehearse their speeches of welcome while the children prepare a celebratory cantata. When Sir Edgar eventually arrives, their curiosity is further aroused by the black valet Jeremy, the Jamaican cook Begonia, and the strange luggage and assorted animals that make up his bizarre retinue. As the confusion mounts, the town's wealthiest and most eligible girl, Luise, and the student Wilhelm take the opportunity to whisper their first secret words together. Later, in the salon of Luise's guardian Baroness Grünwiesel, the society ladies gossip excitedly about the mysterious newcomer, whom they have invited to join them. The baroness does little to conceal her plans for a marriage between Luise and the English aristocrat, but when Jeremy comes in with a note from Sir Edgar declining their invitation she swears in barely contained fury that she will have her revenge for the supposed insult. Only a performance by a travelling circus in the town square can persuade Sir Edgar to leave his house. Incensed by what they believe to be another insult to their self-esteem, the members of the town council attempt to drive the circus away, but Sir Edgar invites the performers inside as his house guests.

Act II As a lamplighter makes his rounds on a dark winter's night he hears blood-curdling screams coming from Sir Edgar's house. While Luise and Wilhelm confess their love, the burgomaster and his colleagues are called in to investigate, but Sir Edgar's secretary explains that what has been heard are no more than the exasperated cries of the milord's nephew Lord Barrat as he tries to learn German. They are put into an even better mood when invited to a grand reception at Sir Edgar's house at which the elegantly dressed Lord Barrat is introduced. Though he says nothing and behaves with unnerving eccentricity, Luise is irresistibly drawn to him, and the dejected Wilhelm leaves in despair. At a party in the great ballroom of the casino, where it is confidently expected that the betrothal of Luise and Lord Barrat will be announced, everyone tries to imitate his bewildering eccentricities. As the dancing becomes increasingly frenzied and Lord Barrat's antics more wildly out of control, he suddenly tears off his clothes to reveal himself as a performing ape, and Luise and Wilhelm are left clutching one another in horror amid the general panic.

It is perhaps no coincidence that the evening before he began work on the score Henze attended a performance in Berlin of Mozart's *Die Entführung*, a snatch of whose Turkish music is quoted early on in the first scene of Henze's opera. But for all the Mozartian economy of instrumentation, it is the brio of Rossini and the elegiac lyricism of Bellini, as filtered through Henze's 20th-century imagination, that cast the longest shadow over his comedy of early-19th-century

bourgeois manners. It is a genuine ensemble opera, with a single aria and duet; its music is witty, elegant and briskly paced. But, unlike the comedies of Rossini, Henze's comedy has an alarming sting in the tail, twisting into tragedy in Act II as music and libretto rip mercilessly away the bourgeois mask of small-town hypocrisy and self-delusion.

The Bassarids

Opera seria with intermezzo in one act (2h 30m)
Libretto by W. H. Auden and Chester Kallman, after Euripides' play *The Bacchae* (407 BC)
PREMIERES 6 August 1966, Grosses Festspielhaus, Salzburg (in German); US: 7 August 1968, Opera Theater, Santa Fe, New Mexico; UK: 22 September 1968, BBC radio; 10 October 1974, Coliseum, London
CAST Pentheus *bar*, Dionysus *t*, Cadmus *b*, Tiresias *t*, Captain *bar*, Agave *ms*, Autonoe *s*, Beroe *ms*, 2 *silent*; intermezzo: Venus *ms*, Proserpina *s*, Kalliope *t*, Adonis *bar*; *satb* chorus of bacchantes, Theban citizens, guards, servants

Before Henze started work on *The Bassarids*, his librettists demanded as a condition of their co-operation that he should go to a performance of *Götterdämmerung* and make his peace with Wagner. Already simmering in his imagination were ideas for a work that would no longer be influenced by the closed, Italianate forms that had mostly dominated his earlier operas, but which would instead be through-composed in a single, broadly designed span. From the great masterpiece of Euripides' old age, Auden and Kallman forged a scenario that falls naturally into four symphonic movements and whose language, Henze has written, is so richly expressive that it immediately suggested musical themes and textures.

SYNOPSIS

After the chorus has described the abdication of Cadmus as king of Thebes in favour of his grandson Pentheus, a distant voice announces the arrival of Dionysus in Boeotia. Ignoring Pentheus' angry denunciation of the dangerous stranger, not only the Theban people, but the blind seer Tiresias, Pentheus' widowed mother Agave and her sister Autonoe are all gradually seduced into the service of the new, erotic god and the religion he embodies.

In the second movement the rash, severely rationalistic Pentheus orders the captain of the guard to round up Dionysus and his disciples. But Pentheus' questioning of the prisoners produces no satisfactory answers.

Playing on the king's youthful voyeurism, Dionysus, in the pivotal third movement, reveals to Pentheus by means of a lascivious charade based on the Judgement of Calliope, and seen through a magic mirror, the true nature of his repressed sexual fantasies and desires. Pentheus is persuaded to dress in women's clothes and go to Mount Cytheron to observe for himself the Dionysian mysteries. The hunter thus becomes the hunted, and his dying screams can be heard in the darkness as the bacchantes, led by his own mother, tear him limb from limb. Slowly Agave is brought back to her senses, and as Henze's Dionysiac passion play reaches its tragic resolution Cadmus and his family are banished by the triumphant god from Thebes, and their palace is ordered to be burnt to the ground.

The first section is a kind of large-scale sonata movement based on the interaction between the more harshly accented music associated with the rigid King Pentheus and the seductively sensuous music identified with the god Dionysus. The second is a scherzo made up of a suite of Bacchic dances, the third an extended adagio whose two parts are separated by a lighter intermezzo, the last a vast passacaglia. And woven into the musical texture at crucial moments are reminiscences of composers from Bach and Rameau to Mahler.

The English Cat
A story for singers and instruments in two acts (2h 45m)
Libretto by Edward Bond, after Honoré de Balzac's tale *Peines de coeur d'une chatte anglaise* (1840)
Composed 1980–83, rev. 1990
PREMIERES 2 June 1983, Schlosstheater, Schwetzingen; US: 13 July 1985, Opera Theater, Santa Fe, New Mexico; UK: 19 August 1987, Leith Theatre, Edinburgh

Henze's second operatic collaboration with playwright Edward Bond (the first was *We Come to the River*, 1976) was also his fourth opera written to an original English text. The basic idea came initially from Henze himself after he had seen a dramatization in Paris of Balzac's feline parable. The cats in Balzac's brief satirical tales encompass all the familiar human types, from the amorous Tom, the demure, empty-headed Minette and her humble, but very pretty, sister Babette, to the aristocratic Lord Puff, his spendthrift nephew Arnold and the money-lender Mr Jones. Bond's version updates the setting from the Directoire to London in the Edwardian period, and he provides a didactic framework for the interwoven stories of marriage and divorce, love and infidelity, vanity, deceit, loyalty and violent death, with the invention of the Royal Society for the Protection of Rats, whose members treat their fellow cats with an adamant, cruelly self-seeking conformity when it suits their own hypocritical ends, but who refrain from eating rats and are kindly to mice in a rather superior way.

In keeping with his aristocratic position, the RSPR's president elect, Lord Puff, is expected to breed and has chosen as his bride the simple country cat Minette. Determined to preserve his inheritance, Puff's insolvent nephew Arnold tries every trick in the book to prevent their marriage, but fails. The wedding goes ahead, but Minette cannot forget the seductive attractions of the basically decent but feckless Tom. When Puff and the entire RSPR burst in to find Tom at Minette's feet, divorce proceedings are instigated. Meanwhile Tom has been discovered to be the long-lost son and heir of the rich Lord Fairport, and when he learns that Puff's owner, Mrs Halifax, has arranged for the pathetic Minette to be drowned he quickly turns his attention to her pretty sister Babette. But just when he is about to claim his inheritance, which he has refused to hand over to the RSPR, Tom is himself murdered. The RSPR gets its money, and one of the mice, Louise, is left bemoaning its treachery.

The libretto is designed in the form of a ballad opera on the pattern established by John Gay's *The Beggar's Opera*, by Brecht and by Auden and Kallman in Stravinsky's *The Rake's Progress*. What Henze has

called his 'sinister, oblique' music also pays its respects to Stravinsky while fleshing out the situations and characters by means of a continuously evolving variation technique modelled on the formal outlines of Beethoven's *Diabelli Variations*. The scoring is for large chamber orchestra with a lavish percussion section, in which various unusual instruments are subtly employed to underpin the distinctive traits of particular characters: Minette by a zither, Lord Puff by chamber organ, and Arnold by a heckelphone or bass oboe.

Other operatic works: *Das Wundertheater*, 1949, rev. 1965; *Ein Landarzt* 1951, rev. 1965; *Boulveard Solitude*, 1952; *Das Ende einer Welt*, 1953, rev. 1965; *Moralities* (three scenic cantatas by W. H. Auden, after Aesop), 1967; *Das Floss der Medusa* (oratorio), 1971; *Der langwierige Weg in die Wohnung der Natascha Ungeheuer* (A Show for 17), 1971; *La Cubana* (vaudeville), 1973; *Pollicino* (children's opera, 1980); *We Come to the River*, 1976; *Don Chisciotte della Mancia*, 1976; *Il ritorno d'Ulisse in patria* (free reconstruction of Monteverdi's opera), 1981 *Das verratene Meer*, 1990; *Venus and Adonis*, 1996

R.L.H.

FERDINAND HÉROLD
Louis-Joseph-Ferdinand Hérold; *b* 28 January 1791, Paris; *d* 19 January 1833, Paris

In a short career Hérold composed much for both opera and ballet stages and achieved, at the end of his life in *Zampa*, one of the most successful of all French opéras comiques. A student at the Paris Conservatoire, he won the Prix de Rome in 1812 and travelled to Rome and Vienna. A collaboration with Adrien Boieldieu in 1816 led to an unbroken succession of works played at the Opéra-Comique, though none scored real success until *Le muletier* in 1823. Hérold belongs to the French tradition of Boieldieu and Nicolas Isouard, although he was also much indebted to Weber.

Zampa, ou La fiancée de marbre
Zampa, or The Marble Bride
Opéra comique in three acts (2h 15m)
Libretto by 'Mélesville' (Anne-Honoré-Joseph Duveyrier)
PREMIERES 3 May 1831, Opéra-Comique, Paris; UK: 19 April 1833, King's Theatre, Haymarket, London; US: 26 July 1833, Boston

Constantly in the repertoire in the 19th century, *Zampa* is still well known for its overture. The title role was written for Jean Baptiste Chollet, the leading light tenor of the day. The opera resembles a parody of *Don Giovanni*, for Zampa, a Sicilian pirate, is constantly threatened and finally consumed by a marble statue of Alice, whom he long ago abandoned. His attempts to snatch his brother's bride Camilla bring about his undoing.

Other operatic works: *La gioventù di Enrico quinto*, 1815; *Charles de France* (coll. with Adrien Boieldieu), 1816; *Les rosières*, 1817; *La clochette, ou Le diable page*, 1817; *Le premier venu, ou Six lieux de chemin*, 1818; *Les troqueurs*, 1819; *L'amour platonique*, 1819; *L'auteur mort et vivant*, 1820; *Le muletier*, 1823; *Lasthénie*, 1823; *Vendôme en Espagne* (coll. with Auber), 1823; *Le roi René, ou La Provence au XVe siècle*, 1824; *Le lapin blanc*, 1825; *Marie*, 1826; *L'illusion*, 1829; *Emmeline*, 1829; *L'auberge d'Auray* (coll. with Carafa), 1830; *La marquise de Brinvilliers* (coll. with eight others), 1831; *La médecine sans médecin*, 1832; *Le pré aux clercs*, 1832; *Ludovic* (completed by Halévy), 1833

H.M.

PAUL HINDEMITH

b 16 November 1895, Hanau, nr Frankfurt, Germany; *d* 28 December 1963, Frankfurt

Hindemith came to prominence in the rebuilding of German musical life after the First World War, by which time he had begun composing and was already working as a professional violinist, violist, clarinettist and pianist. As a violinist in the Frankfurt Opera orchestra he attracted the attention of the conductor Fritz Busch, who was on the look-out for new operas by young composers. In 1921 Busch conducted the Stuttgart premieres of Hindemith's one-act *Mörder, Hoffnung der Frauen* and *Das Nusch-Nuschi* as a double-bill.

Their provocative attitude to sexual matters in a continuing style of German Expressionism attracted public and critical attention. The next year they were supplemented by another one-act opera of a comparable nature, *Sancta Susanna*, first performed at Frankfurt in a triple-bill with the others. Taken in succession they reflect a progress in musical idiom from eclectic late Romanticism to a more disciplined control of structure and expressive character.

During the 1920s, while pursuing an active performing career, Hindemith embraced a style of severe contrapuntal neo-classicism in his music. His first three-act opera, *Cardillac*, premiered in 1926, is the major large-scale example of this (most of the others are chamber works). The following year Hindemith was appointed professor of composition at the Berlin Hochschule für Musik, where the practical application of his teaching was realized in what he termed *Gebrauchsmusik*: 'useful music' for amateurs as well as professionals.

At this time he also took an interest in popular music as exemplified in night-club jazz and the Berlin satirical cabarets, which led to the brief *Hin und zürück* (1927) followed by the three-act *Neues vom Tage* (1929), both with a libretto by Marcellus Schiffer, a leading cabaret writer/artist in Berlin. A concern with the position of the artist in society, partly suggested in *Cardillac* and renewed at a time when the darkening political scene in Germany brought the advent of the Nazi government, led to *Mathis der Maler*, a partly autobiographical allegory, for which he wrote his own libretto and adopted a more expressive musical style.

An outstandingly successful performance of the *Mathis der Maler Symphony*, extracted from the opera in advance of its production and conducted by Wilhelm Furtwängler, brought Hindemith into conflict with the Nazi authorities (Hitler having been offended by a bath scene in *Neues vom Tage*), and his Jewish connections led to a partial boycott of his music from 1934 and a full proscription in 1937. Hindemith left Germany for Switzerland, where *Mathis der Maler* was first staged in 1938, and in 1940 he went to the US, becoming a much admired professor at Yale University and taking US citizenship in 1946.

Mathis der Maler remained unperformed on the German stage until that year. After major revisions to *Cardillac* and *Neues vom Tage* in the early 1950s (published as separate editions), Hindemith turned to another historical subject for *Die Harmonie der Welt* – a commission for the 1957 Munich Opera Festival. By this time he had moved back to Europe and was living at Blonay, by Lake Lucerne. He gave up further teaching at Zurich University to concentrate on composition and conducting and, two years before he died, wrote his remaining opera – on Thornton Wilder's *The Long Christmas Dinner*, his only setting of a libretto in English.

Cardillac

Opera in three acts (four scenes) (1h 30m);
rev. version in four acts (2h 15m)
Libretto by Ferdinand Lion, after E. T. A. Hoffmann's *Das Fräulein von Scuderi* (1819); rev. version by the composer after Lion
Composed 1926; rev. 1952
PREMIERES 9 November 1926, Staatsoper, Dresden; UK: 18 December 1936, BBC radio (in English); 11 March 1970, Sadler's Wells, London; rev. version: 20 June 1952, Stadttheater, Zurich; US: 26 July 1967, Opera Theater, Santa Fe, New Mexico
CAST original version: Cardillac *bar*, His Daughter *s*, Lady *s*, Officer *t*, Cavalier *t*, Gold Merchant *b*, Police Officer high *b*, King *silent role*; *satb* chorus of knights, ladies, police, people; rev. version: Cardillac *bar*, His Daughter *s*, Her Friend *t*, Opera Singer *s*, Officer *b*, Young Cavalier *t*, Singers in Lully's *Phaëton a, t, b*, Rich Marquis *silent role*; *satb* chorus of people, guards, chorus members, theatre staff, dancers

Hindemith was at the height of his concern with a neo-classical baroque aesthetic, exemplified in several works titled *Kammermusik* and in the *Concerto for Orchestra*, when he composed *Cardillac*. It also marked his first expression of a recurring concern with the figure of a creative artist in society, and applied his principles in a strictly musical response to a psychopathic story which might earlier have attracted the Expressionist approach of his one-act operas. Avoiding psychological or illustrative elements, it is laid out in the closed numbers of aria, duet, fugato, passacaglia and the like, intended to symbolize rather than express character and situation, and to generate dramatic impetus by contrast.

SYNOPSIS (original version)
Act I Cardillac is a master goldsmith in late-17th-century Paris, so obsessed by the beauty of his artefacts that he cannot bear to be parted from them. If

persuaded to sell, he regains the treasure by the drastic expedient of murdering the purchaser. Several such crimes have terrorized Paris. A lady is heard promising her favours to a cavalier in return for the finest example of Cardillac's art. When the cavalier brings a golden belt to her bedroom, he is attacked and killed by an intruder, who escapes with the belt.

Act II Cardillac's workshop is visited by a gold merchant, who suspects the goldsmith. Cardillac's daughter and the officer plan to elope. The king and courtiers come to admire Cardillac's handiwork but are rebuffed. Cardillac consents to his daughter's marriage; the officer obtains a gold chain as a wedding present, but Cardillac follows after him.

Act III Cardillac succeeds only in wounding the officer, who recognizes him. The officer refuses to betray Cardillac, who first tries to pin the guilt on the merchant before himself confessing, at which the mob turns on him and puts him to death.

By imposing set polyphonic forms on his text Hindemith felt he was reasserting the music's pre-eminence, but in performance it was found that the two elements moved on separate planes of a listener's perception. For instance, the murder at the end of Act I is accompanied by a two-part flute invention; the daughter's aria is a concerto grosso featuring violin, oboe and horn concertante; the court's visit to the workshop is entirely in wordless mime; the opera's finale is a passacaglia.

Hindemith's 1952 revision involved some rewriting of the text, which he undertook himself, adding an act to incorporate parts of Lully's opera *Phaëton* (1683), and altering the vocal line over a more richly scored orchestral part. Hindemith put an embargo on performing the first version, which was lifted at Wuppertal and the Holland Festival in 1961. The few productions since have preferred the stronger original version.

Mathis der Maler

Mathis the Painter
Opera in seven scenes (3h 15m)
Libretto by the composer
Composed 1934–5
PREMIERES 28 May 1938, Stadttheater, Zurich; UK: 15 March 1939, Queen's Hall, London (concert); 29 August 1952, King's Theatre, Edinburgh; US: 17 February 1956, University Theater, Boston
CAST Cardinal-Archbishop of Mainz *t*, Mathis *bar*, Lorenz von Pommersfelden *b*, Wolfgang Capito *t*, Riedinger *b*, Hans Schwalb *t*, Truchsess (Lord High Steward) von Waldburg *b*, Sylvester von Schaumberg *t*, Graf von Helfenstein *silent role*, Helfenstein's Piper *t*, Ursula *s*, Regina *s*, Gräfin Helfenstein *c*; *satb* chorus of monks, Catholics, Lutherans, women, students, citizens, peasants, farm workers, demons

At a time when the Nazi regime in Germany was beginning to tighten its grip, Hindemith based his second treatment of the creative artist's position in relation to social and political issues on Mathis Grünewald (or Neithardt), court painter in the early 16th century at Mainz, near where Hindemith was born. Grünewald is remembered for the large linked panels of the Isenheim altarpiece (now in the Unterlinden Museum in Colmar), scenes from which are regarded as a metaphor for the peasants' feelings towards their overlords. They prompted ideas for music and a libretto placing the artist at a crucial point in the Peasants' Revolt of 1524.

SYNOPSIS
Prelude: *Engelkonzert*

Scene 1 In the courtyard of St Anthony's monastery at Mainz, Mathis is painting a fresco; he gives his horse to Schwalb, the peasant leader, to help him and his daughter Regina to escape pursuing troops, and promises his support.

Scene 2 Mathis pleads the peasants' cause to the cardinal-archbishop, his patron, and is obliged to leave his service.

Scene 3 Amid preparations for the burning of Lutheran books, Mathis and Ursula pledge their love, though Riedinger, her father, plans she should marry the cardinal.

Scene 4 Mathis protests against the peasants' brutality; Schwalb is killed and Mathis protects Regina.

Scene 5 The Lutheran Ursula is introduced to the cardinal as a prospective bride to help solve his financial problems; her faith wills her to submit to marriage for the sake of her cause, and the cardinal, impressed, chooses to remain celibate while giving permission for Lutherans to declare themselves openly.

Scene 6 Mathis and Regina, in flight, rest in the Odenwald forest; Regina sleeps while Mathis endures visionary temptations as if he were St Anthony, finally redeemed by the cardinal in the guise of St Paul (a subject of the altarpiece).

Scene 7 In Mathis's studio, Regina is dying, tended by Ursula. The cardinal takes a last leave of Mathis, who puts away the tools of his art in humble acceptance of his own impending death.

Into a musical style still predominantly contrapuntal, Hindemith incorporates folksongs such as the medieval 'Es sungen drei Engel' in the prelude, subtitled *Concert of Angels* (another altarpiece subject), which also became the opening movement of the three-movement symphony drawn from the opera in 1934. Use is made of Gregorian chant and of pentatonic melodies modelled on it, while the tonal structure of the opera moves chromatically from C$\sharp$ in Scene 1 to E in the central scene, then reverses the process. The opera is long when given uncut and slow-moving. If the more active scenes lack theatrically effective climaxes, the more reflective passages of exaltation and despair, and the final resignation to the will of God, remain both a metaphor for the circumstances of the composer's experience and a moving expression of artistic principles.

Other operatic works: *Mörder, Hoffnung der Frauen*, 1921; *Das Nusch–Nuschi*, 1921; *Sancta Susanna*, 1922; *Tuttifäntchen*, 1922; *Hin und züruck*, 1927; *Neues vom Tage*, 1929, rev. 1954; *Die Harmonie der Welt*, 1957; *The Long Christmas Dinner*, 1961

N.G.

GUSTAV HOLST

Gustavus Theodore von Holst; *b* 21 September 1874, Cheltenham, England; *d* 25 May 1934, London

Holst's great-grandfather was a Swede who emigrated from Riga to London with his Russian wife in the early 1800s. But Holst himself seems to have been purely English in his preoccupations and intellectual tendencies. He went to Cheltenham Grammar School, then studied with Charles Villiers Stanford at the Royal College of Music from 1893. Much of his working life was spent school-teaching (notably at St Paul's Girls' School, where he became director of music in 1905), or running evening classes (at Morley College from 1907); but he was also deeply involved with amateur music-making, to which he brought a quasi-political conviction of the worth of the common man. All this practical work restricted his time for composition and eventually undermined his health, but it had a significant effect on his music, which is notably free of the conventional academic influences of the day. Like his friend Vaughan Williams, Holst was interested in folk music, as well as in Indian culture (though not specifically Indian music); he taught himself Sanskrit, set a number of Hindu texts in his own translations, and based two operas on Hindu subjects. He was also quick to pick up the sounds of the new Continental music of the years before the First World War. His most famous work, *The Planets* (1914–16), is full of echoes of Debussy, Stravinsky, Skryabin, even Mahler and Schoenberg, worked into a characteristic fusion that is completely radical and individual in its effect.

Despite the pressure on his time, Holst produced a large, if uneven, body of work, dominated by choral and other types of music that reflect his practical bent and his work with amateurs. But he also wrote about a dozen operas, at a time when British opera hardly existed as a serious commodity at all. Not surprisingly, they are a mixed bag, and several of them remain unperformed.

Sāvitri

Chamber opera in one act, (30m)
Libretto by the composer, after an episode from the *Mahabharata*
Composed 1908–9
PREMIERES 5 December 1916, Wellington Hall, London (amateur); 23 June 1921, Lyric Theatre, Hammersmith, London; US: 23 January 1934, Palmer House, Chicago
CAST Sāvitri *s*, Satyavān *t*, Death *b*; offstage *sa* chorus

Holst's interest in Hindu literature seems to have begun while he was on tour with the Carl Rosa Opera Company in Scarborough in 1898, when a friend lent him a book on the subject. Back in London, he learned to decipher the Sanskrit, and began to make his own translations with the help of published cribs. On this basis he wrote the libretti of both *Sita* and *Sāvitri*, as well as the texts for the *Vedic Hymns* (1907–8) and the *Choral Hymns from the Rig Veda* (1903–12).

These works form a very loose grouping, since they spring from a common literary rather than musical impulse. *Sāvitri* is unimaginably different from *Sita* in musical conception, being drastically spare, compact, and having a tiny group of performers. It does away with almost all the normal operatic paraphernalia. It has no overture but opens with a long unaccompanied passage for Death and Sāvitri. In essence it is hardly a theatre piece at all. Holst wanted it played out of doors with 'a long avenue or path through a wood in the centre of the scene'. But his practical instincts warned him to allow 'a small building' as an alternative, and to suggest the 'Hymn of the Travellers' from the third group of *Choral Hymns from the Rig Veda* as an overture for anyone who could not bear to be without one.

SYNOPSIS

A wood at evening. Death announces to Sāvitri that he has come for her husband, the woodsman Satyavān. When Satyavān comes home from his day's work, he sings about the unreality (*Māyā* – 'illusion') of the natural world. But Sāvitri tells him she now sees beyond *Māyā* to 'the heart of every tree'. As Death approaches, Satyavān sinks to the ground lifeless. At first Sāvitri tries to protect her husband. But she then welcomes Death and invites him to stay. He offers her a wish for herself, and she asks for Life. When Death willingly grants her that which she has already, she points out that for her 'the life of woman, of wife, of mother' implies life for Satyavān too. Defeated, Death leaves at once, and Satyavān revives. As husband and wife go off, Death is heard singing of Sāvitri's freedom from illusion, 'for even Death is *Māyā*'. At the very end Sāvitri's voice is heard singing alone.

The score has few exotic elements, and certainly none that is remotely Indian. Its modal character is partly English (from folksong), partly French, with a certain whole-tone colouring as in the recent piano works of Debussy. The music's main individuality lies in its spare but extremely delicate texture, its flexible metre, combining recitative with Holst's favourite seven-beat bars, and its use of a wordless female choir (originally a mixed choir, but changed at the suggestion of Herman Grunebaum, the work's first conductor), a device that obviously anticipates *The Planets*.

Other operatic works: *Lansdown Castle, or The Sorcerer of Tewkesbury*, 1893; *Ianthe*, (*c.* 1894); *The Revoke*, (1895); *The Magic Mirror* (inc., 1896); *The Idea*, (*c.* 1896); *The Youth's Choice*, (1902); *Sita*, (1906); *Cinderella* (lost, 1902); *Opera as She is Wrote* (fragments only, 1918); *The Perfect Fool*, 1923; *At the Boar's Head*, 1925; *The Wandering Scholar*, 1934)

S.W.

ENGELBERT HUMPERDINCK

b 1 September 1854, Siegburg, Germany; *d* 27 September 1921, Neustrelitz

Humperdinck's fame rests on his opera *Hänsel und Gretel*, the success of which has been constant and extraordinary since its first performance. Of his six other operatic works only *Königskinder* is of similar scale and quality, and this enjoyed success in its early years.

Humperdinck studied architecture at the University of Cologne, where he became friendly with the composer Ferdinand Hiller, who recognized his musical talent and persuaded him to become a student of composition, piano and cello. Considered brilliant by his professors, he won the Mozart Scholarship in 1876 which financed further study in Munich with Franz Lachner and Joseph Rheinberger. His first works were published at this time – the *Humoreske* for orchestra (1879) and the choral ballade *Die Wallfahrt nach Kevlaar* (1879). The latter won the Mendelssohn Prize. (Humperdinck was an inveterate prize-winner, and in 1881 he also won the Meyerbeer Prize of 7,600 marks – a huge sum at the time.) This enabled him to visit France and Italy, where, in Naples in 1880, he met Richard Wagner. Wagner invited him to Bayreuth as his assistant, and during 1881–2 Humperdinck helped prepare the score of *Parsifal* for its premiere and publication. He also composed a small fill-in passage, later discarded, for the Act I transition.

After Bayreuth, and short spells in Barcelona and Cologne, in 1888 he joined the music publishers Schott, in Mainz, for whom in 1889 he published an arrangement of Auber's opera *Le cheval de bronze*. He later took three posts in Frankfurt: professor at the Hoch Conservatory, teacher of repertoire at Julius Stockhausen's music school and critic on the *Frankfurter Zeitung*.

In 1896 the kaiser Wilhelm II bestowed on him the title of professor, and in 1897, no doubt with massive royalties from *Hänsel und Gretel*, premiered with overwhelming success four years earlier, Humperdinck retired to Boppard on the Rhine and devoted himself entirely to composition. He wrote spectacles and incidental music as well as orchestral works, songs, a string quartet and operas. In 1900 he was appointed (with only nominal duties) director of the Akademische Meisterschule in Berlin and a fellow of the Royal Academy of Arts there. With the premiere of the final operatic version of *Königskinder* at the Metropolitan in New York in 1910, his success grew abroad, but at the same time he became somewhat pigeonholed at home. His last work to create any significant public impression was his spectacle *The Miracle*, with a scenario by Max Reinhardt, premiered at Olympia in London on 23 December 1911. However, the large London crowds flocking to it appeared to have been drawn solely by the spectacular nature of the production, and the work attracted little attention from musicians.

Hänsel und Gretel

Hansel and Gretel
Märchenoper in three acts (2h)
Libretto by Adelheid Wette, after the tale by the Brothers (Wilhelm and Jacob) Grimm (1812)
Composed 1890–93
PREMIERES 23 December 1893, Hoftheater, Weimar; UK: 26 December 1894, Daly's Theatre, London; US: 8 October 1895, Daly's Theater, New York

CAST Hänsel *ms*, Gretel *s*, Gertrud *ms*, Peter *bar*, Sandman *s*, Dew Fairy *s*, Witch *ms* (sometimes *t*), 6 Echoes 4 *s* 2 *a*; children's chorus, 14 angels *silent*

The early 1890s saw Germany reacting to the bombast of the lesser imitators of Wagner by developing a craze for Italian verismo. But German artists soon grew restive against the lurid plots and the brashness of composers such as Mascagni, and German audiences yearned for a work that was truly German in origin as well as popular. Humperdinck's success with *Hänsel und Gretel* may have been the result of his avoidance of the mainstream German works of Weber, Marschner and Lortzing; his opera inhabits a very different world.

In 1890 Humperdinck's sister, Adelheid Wette, devised a dramatized version of the Grimm story of *Hänsel und Gretel* for her children to perform. In her version the parents are a much less alarming pair than they are in the fairy-tale, where the mother (stepmother in the first version) is actually determined to leave the children out to die in the wood. Wette softened this, perhaps because she knew that her brother's music would supply some of the fear and drama. She also introduced the characters of the father (Peter), the Sandman and the Dew Fairy, as well as the chorus of echoes and the angels, which provided Humperdinck with scope for a ballet.

At first Wette asked her brother to compose four songs for a dramatized family play (1890). Subsequently they decided to make it a full-scale opera. The premiere, conducted by Richard Strauss, was an instant success, and within a year *Hänsel und Gretel* had been produced in over 50 theatres in Germany. It soon joined the repertoire of every lyric theatre in the German-speaking world, and within 20 years had been translated into about 20 languages. Richard Strauss, a constant supporter of Humperdinck (he also conducted the premiere of Humperdinck's *Die Heirat wider Willen* in 1905), described the work as 'a masterpiece of the highest quality . . . all of it original, new and so authentically German', despite his reservation that 'the orchestration is always a little thick'.

Hänsel und Gretel was the first complete opera to be broadcast on radio (from Covent Garden, London, 6 January 1923) and the first to be transmitted live from the Metropolitan, New York (25 December 1931).

SYNOPSIS

The self-contained overture is often performed as a concert piece.

Act I Hänsel and Gretel are at home waiting for their mother, Gertrud, to return. The interior displays the poverty of the family: Hänsel makes brooms for his broom-maker father, Peter, while Gretel knits. Both are bored, restless and hungry. To distract her brother, Gretel shows him a dance game ('Brüderchen, komm tanz' mit mir'), but their playing is harshly interrupted by the arrival of their mother. She is cross at how little work the children have completed, and in her anger she knocks over a jug of milk. She bursts into tears at losing the only food in the house, and sends the children out to pick strawberries in the nearby Ilsenstein forest. Depressed, she falls asleep but is wakened by Peter singing on his way home. She is furious that he is obviously tipsy, but her mood changes at the sight of the food he has bought as the result of a successful day selling brooms. After celebrating with his wife, Peter suddenly becomes aware that the children are not there and their mother admits that they have gone to the Ilsenstein for strawberries. Peter is appalled; he knows this is the home of the witch, who entices children into her cottage and then turns them into gingerbread by baking them alive in her oven ('Eine Hex', steinalt'). Both parents rush out of the house to find their children. Entr'acte: *Hexenritt* – 'Witch's Ride'.

Act II Hänsel and Gretel are in the wood filling their baskets with strawberries ('Ein Männlein steht im Walde ganz still und stumm'). They eat them all, however, and soon Hänsel realizes that they are lost. They become frightened. A mist rises, and a little Sandman appears and throws sand in the children's eyes ('Der kleine Sandmann bin ich'). They kneel down to say their evening prayers ('Abends wenn ich schlafen gehn'). Lying on a bank beneath the trees, they fall asleep in each other's arms. The mist surrounds them and becomes a staircase of clouds as fourteen angels come down from heaven to guard the children through the night. This is accompanied by an extended orchestral postlude ('pantomime').

Act III opens with another orchestral prelude as dawn breaks and the Dew Fairy comes to shake dew drops over the children ('Der kleine Taumann heiss ich'). They cheerfully start to play. The mist clears to reveal a gingerbread cottage with a fence of gingerbread men ('O Himmel, welch Wunder ist hier geschehn'). Intrigued, the children eat little bits of the house, but the witch appears and throws a rope around Hänsel's neck. Hänsel tries to free himself, but the witch immobilizes both children with a spell ('Knusper, knusper Knäuschen'). She puts Hänsel into a cage, intending to fatten him up. She frees Gretel with another spell and makes her help light the oven. Gretel uses the witch's spell to free Hänsel from the cage. The witch, unaware of this, tries to make Gretel look into the oven, but Gretel pretends not to understand. When the witch shows her what to do, the children push her into the oven and slam the door ('Juchhei! Nun ist die Hexe tot'). The oven explodes, and the fence of gingerbread men becomes a row of children; other children who have been baked in the oven rise up from the earth. As they thank Hänsel and Gretel for their deliverance, Gertrud and Peter appear. The witch has been turned into gingerbread, and everybody celebrates her downfall.

The influence of Wagner is evident in the use of leitmotifs (though Humperdinck uses them less strictly than Wagner), as well as in the orchestral and harmonic texture and in the symphonic character of the preludes and interludes. This does not, however, disguise the reliance on the style of traditional German children's songs, and two ('Ein Männlein steht im Walde' and 'Suse, liebe Suse') are taken from the well-known *Knaben Wunderhorn* collection. The work's originality derives from the synthesis of four opposite pairs of concepts – childhood/adulthood, fairy-tale/reality, diatonic/chromatic and through-composition/episodic form. The subtle flexibility with which Humperdinck combined his resources gives the work its unique charm. As an heir to the Wagnerian tradition combined with folksong and realism – a strong influence on the composers of the time – *Hänsel und Gretel* occupies a startlingly individual place in musical history.

An arrangement of *Hänsel und Gretel* by Ludwig Andersen (1927) uses spoken dialogue and a much reduced orchestra. This less vocally demanding version is often used by schools and amateur groups.

Königskinder
Royal Children

Märchenoper in three acts, derived from an earlier melodrama (2h 30m)
Libretto by 'Ernst Rosmer' (Elsa Bernstein-Porges)
Composed 1895–7 (melodrama), 1908–10 (opera)
PREMIERES melodrama: 23 January 1897, Hoftheater, Munich; UK: 13 October 1897, Court Theatre, London; US: 29 April 1898, New York; opera: US: 28 December 1910, Metropolitan, New York; Germany: 14 January 1911, Berlin; UK: 27 November 1911, Covent Garden, London
CAST Goose-girl s, Witch ms, Prince t, Fiddler bar, Broom-maker t, Woodcutter b, 2 ms, 2 t, 2 bar, b; satb chorus of townspeople, children's chorus

Königskinder started out as a melodrama of a type that had no precedent at the time. In this first version the composer anticipated Schoenbergian sprechgesang by devising a speech-notation system that, although not as ambitious as sprechgesang, attempted to set the melodic line of speech without restricting the speaker. Humperdinck wrote, 'The notes for the spoken word generally indicate the relative, not the absolute pitch: the line of the risings and fallings of the voice.' His librettist was Elsa Bernstein-Porges, a distinguished playwright, writing under the name of Ernst Rosmer. She knew Humperdinck from Bayreuth, where her father, Heinrich Porges, had assisted Wagner on the *Ring*.

After the unsuccessful premiere of the melodrama, Humperdinck abandoned the work until a summer holiday in 1908. He then took nearly two years to refashion it into a conventional opera, retaining nearly all the original music. The success of the New York premiere was undiminished by the fact that the same house had seen the first performance of Puccini's *La fanciulla del West* (with Caruso and Toscanini) 18 days earlier. There were 14 curtain calls after the first act, and a 15-minute ovation at the end. American critics hailed *Königskinder* as the crowning work of post-Wagnerian opera, but German critics, although complimentary, felt that Humperdinck had not matched the artistic heights of *Hänsel und Gretel*.

SYNOPSIS

Act I The goose-girl is kept in the forest by the witch's spell. Together they bake a deadly magic loaf. A prince finds her, and gives her his crown as a token of love, but when the spell prevents her leaving with him he abandons her. The fiddler guides the broom-maker and the woodcutter to the witch's hut; the townspeople have sent them to ask her how they can find a king. The witch prophesies that the new king of Hellabrunn will be the first person to enter the town gates on the stroke of twelve. Meanwhile the fiddler has spied the goose-girl and he inspires in her the strength to break the witch's spell. They leave together to find the prince.

Act II   The townspeople, among them the prince (incognito), await the new king's arrival, but it is the goose-girl who enters the gates at noon wearing the crown, with her geese and the fiddler. The people brand her as an impostor, and when the prince defends her they are both driven out.

Act III   Winter. The fiddler now occupies the witch's hut. The woodcutter and broom-maker implore him to return to Hellabrunn, where the town's children are in rebellion; they insist that he help them search for the prince and the goose-girl. The woodcutter and the broom-maker shelter in the hut. Frozen and starving, the prince and goose-girl beg for shelter and finally barter the prince's broken crown for a loaf, unaware of its deadly properties. The fiddler returns to find them dead, and he sings his last song as their requiem.

The elevated and romantic world of the fairy-tale appealed to *fin-de-siècle* German sensibilities, for whom the low-life dramas of naturalism (or, operatically, verismo) were too coarse. Hence the vogue for Symbolist drama, of which Elsa Bernstein-Porges's invented fairy-tale is a typical example. Despite the apparatus of a fairy-tale, the subject is serious – drawing heavily on Nietzsche for its concepts of leadership and 'natural royalty'. There is therefore much less diatonic children's music than in *Hänsel und Gretel*, but instead a complex tonal carpet of Wagnerian development. Above all, Humperdinck found for this work a strain of exquisite elegiac melancholy, of which the fiddler's final song is a poignant example.

Other operas: *Die sieben Geislein*, 1895; *Dornröschen*, 1902; *Die Heirat wider Willen*, 1905; *Die Marketenderin*, 1914; *Gaudeamus*, 1919

P.J.

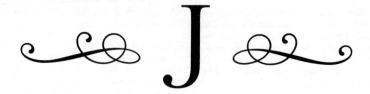

LEOŠ JANÁČEK

Leoš (Leo Eugen) Janáček; *b* 3 July 1854, Hukvaldy, Czech Republic; *d* 12 August 1928, Ostrava, Slovakia

Janáček was almost 62 when his opera *Jenůfa* was finally produced in Prague, bringing him unexpected fame. By then he had written five operas, only two of which had been previously produced (in his adopted town of Brno); the last had been abandoned in sheer despair that it would ever be performed. The success of *Jenůfa* in Prague in 1916, and its espousal by the Viennese publishers. Universal Edition, changed all this. He quickly completed his fifth opera, and in 1919, at the age of 65, embarked on an astonishingly fertile last decade which saw the composition of four major operas and a number of substantial works in other genres, such as the *Sinfonietta*, the *Glagolitic Mass* and the two string quartets. *Jenůfa* soon established his reputation in Czechoslovakia and the German-speaking world, but his later operas made less headway before the Second World War. None of his operas was produced in Britain, and the sole production in the US (*Jenůfa*, in New York, 1924) was not a success. Since the war, and especially from the 1960s and 1970s, Janáček has come to take his place as the best-known Czech operatic composer and one of the handful of the most important opera composers of the 20th century.

Janáček was trained, like his father and grandfather before him, as a schoolteacher, leaving his native Hukvaldy in northern Moravia in 1865 to attend the Augustinian monastery school in Brno, and thereafter a teacher-training course. The musical content in his schooling was substantial and was supplemented by later training at the Prague Organ School (1874–5), by the Leipzig and Vienna conservatories (1879–80), and above all by Janáček's own particularly hard and systematic work. He read widely in literature and philosophy. Other formative influences were a fervent national pride that led to his changing his name 'Leo' to the Czech 'Leoš', and a fascination with the greater Slavonic world. He made a crucial trip to Russia in 1896 and founded a Russian Club in Brno which flourished up to the First World War; two of his completed operas, *Kát'a Kabanová* and *From the House of the Dead*, were based on works by Russian authors, Ostrovsky and Dostoevsky respectively, but he also considered settings of Tolstoy's

Anna Karenina and his play *The Living Corpse*. In 1880, his formal education complete, Janáček returned to Brno, where he married the young Zdenka Schulzová, and taught at the Teacher Training College and elsewhere, notably at the institution he founded, the Brno Organ School. Apart from the Organ School, where he continued to teach until 1919, he retired from all his teaching posts by 1904 in order to devote himself to composition.

Until quite late in life Janáček's contact with opera was minimal. As a young boy he had sung in a performance of Meyerbeer's *Le prophète*. There was no Czech opera in Brno at the time and there is no evidence that he attended (or could have afforded to attend) opera in Prague during his year there as a student. So it is likely that the first operas he saw were in Leipzig in 1880: Weber's *Der Freischütz* and, seven weeks later, Cherubini's *Les deux journées*. 'I wasn't taken by it at all, except for one single place,' he commented on the latter to his future wife. His orientation towards opera came only when, in his thirties, the tiny Brno Provisional Theatre was opened (1884), the first permanent institution in Brno to stage plays and operas in Czech. Janáček's response was characteristically positive. He founded a new musical periodical, *Hudební listy*, one of whose functions was to report on the activities of the Brno theatre. Janáček was the chief music critic, and his knowledge and opinions of the somewhat restricted repertoire (no Wagner, little Mozart, and much Smetana), can be charted in his reviews over the four years that the journal ran (1884–8). In the early 1900s, once he had retired from his schoolteaching, he had more time to travel to Prague, and pick up the novelties there. He was particularly enthusiastic about works such as Puccini's *Madama Butterfly* and Charpentier's *Louise*, and their influence can be detected respectively in his own operas *Fate* and *Kát'a Kabanová*. At a much later date he heard and championed Berg's *Wozzeck* at its controversial Prague premiere.

Although his last operas were written in the 1920s, Janáček was born in the middle of the 19th century and all he wrote was conditioned by a 19th-century training and attitude towards harmony and tonality. If his first opera, *Šárka*, had been a success at the time that he wrote it, Janáček might have been encouraged to remain with its musical idiom – essentially German-centred, though modified by the Czech Romanticism of Dvořák and Smetana. But *Šárka* was not performed at the time, and Janáček turned to other things. His preoccupation from the late 1880s with Moravian folk music, a particularly rich and distinctive resource in terms of mode and rhythm, had the long-term effect of enriching and fertilizing his musical language, though never obliterating its tonal roots. The result was a highly characteristic musical language, fresh and appealing, and one that a wide spectrum of 20th-century audiences have found accessible.

A second factor in Janáček's success arises from his gifts as a musical dramatist. While his mature operas have some of the oddest subject matter of any group of operas, all of them work, in their various ways, as effective stage pieces. They are astonishingly different from one another, inhabiting many distinctive worlds and atmospheres. These range from 19th-century Russian provincial life to Moravian peasant verismo and sophisticated Prague of the 1920s; from the life of animals in the Moravian woods to a Siberian prison camp. What binds them together is their succinctness, Janáček's uncanny ability to suggest and change mood with just a few notes, his terse but passionate lyricism, a compassionate humanity, and an emotional charge as powerful as any in the 20th century.

Jenůfa
Her Stepdaughter
Její pastorkyňa
Opera in three acts (2h)
Libretto by the composer after Gabriela Preissová's play (1890)
Composed 1894–1903, rev. 1907 (rev. and reorch. 1916 by Karel Kovařovic)
PREMIERES 21 January 1904, National Theatre, Brno; Kovařovic version: 26 May 1916, National Theatre, Prague; US: 6 December 1924, Metropolitan, New York; UK: 10 December 1956, Covent Garden, London
CAST Grandmother Buryjovka *c*, Laca Klemeň *t*, Števa Buryja *t*, Kostelnička Buryjovka *s*, Jenůfa *s*, Mill Foreman *bar*, Mayor *b*, Mayor's Wife *ms*, Karolka *ms*, Maid *ms*, Barena *s*, Jano *s*, Aunt *c*; *satb* chorus of recruits, musicians, people from the mill, countryfolk, children

Janáček adapted his own libretto from Gabriela Preissová's controversial play, first produced in Prague in 1890. The genesis of Janáček's opera is hard to document in view of his destruction of sketches and even his autograph score, but in 1894 he began work on the libretto and composed the prelude *Žárlivost* ('Jealousy'), originally planned as the work's overture though never performed as such during Janáček's lifetime. He probably completed Act I in about 1897 and then he seems to have let the project drop for a few years. He took it up again in 1901, and wrote the last two acts quite quickly.

The work was given in Brno, with some success (perhaps out of local patriotism), and was performed there and on local tours about 20 times up to 1913. Partly on the advice of the conductor of the premiere, Janáček's pupil Cyril Metoděj Hrazdira, Janáček revised the work and made several cuts, particularly in ensembles and other set numbers. The vocal score published by a local artistic society in 1908 incorporates these revisions and represents Janáček's definitive version of the piece.

Even before *Jenůfa* was accepted in Brno, Janáček had submitted the opera to the National Theatre in Prague, but the antagonism of its music director, Karel Kovařovic (allegedly hurt by Janáček's dismissive reviews of his opera *The Bridegrooms*) prevented its performance there until 1916. The Prague production under Kovařovic, however, proved a huge success. Two years later *Jenůfa* was given in Vienna in a German version by Max Brod, who subsequently translated most of Janáček's later opera texts. In the decade up to Janáček's death in 1928 *Jenůfa* became a repertoire piece in Czechoslovakia and in German-speaking countries. It remains the composer's most popular opera.

The version heard in Prague in 1916 was one that had been revised, and in particular reorchestrated, by Kovařovic (a condition of its acceptance). It was subsequently published by Universal Edition in this form and, until the 1980s, when Charles Mackerras conducted and subsequently recorded a version nearer to Janáček's original version, this was the only version that could be heard.

SYNOPSIS
Act I   The Buryja mill in a remote village in Moravia. The mill-owner Števa Burjya and his older half-brother Laca are both in love with their cousin Jenůfa. But Jenůfa loves Števa, by whom she is pregnant. She anxiously awaits his return: if he is drafted into the army she will not be able to marry him and her pregnancy will be discovered. Laca watches her jealously, and learns from the mill foreman that Števa has not been conscripted.

The recruits can be heard approaching, singing a conscription song ('Všeci sa ženija') and accompanied by a small village band. At their head is Števa, who demands another song ('Daleko, široko') and then leads the reluctant Jenůfa in a wild dance. At the climax, a stern figure approaches and silences the company. This is Jenůfa's stepmother, known as the 'Kostelnička' (female sacristan). She forbids any marriage between Jenůfa and Števa for a year, during which time Števa must stop his drinking.

Grandmother Buryjovka dismisses the musicians and attempts to comfort Jenůfa, a cue for a slow ensemble ('Každý párek'). The company disperses, leaving a desperate Jenůfa confronting an unrepentant Števa. Laca, who has observed this scene, believes that Števa loves Jenůfa only for her beauty and, after her proud dismissal of him, Laca slashes her cheek in a fit of desperation. He is immediately remorseful, and in a short ensemble he pours out his anguish.

Act II   The Kostelnička's cottage, five months later, winter. Jenůfa, kept in hiding by the Kostelnička, has given birth to a son. The Kostelnička sends her to bed with a sleeping draught. Having summoned Števa to the cottage, she shows him the baby and begs him to marry Jenůfa. But he offers money, not marriage, and hurries out. The next visitor is Laca. He is still anxious to marry Jenůfa, whom he believes, as does the rest of the village, to be in Vienna. The Kostelnička now tells him the truth. He is so dismayed to hear about the baby that the Kostelnička declares that the child died. She sends him away on an errand

and, after a dramatic monologue in which she wrestles with her conscience ('Co chvíla'), runs from the cottage taking with her Jenůfa's baby, to drown it in the icy mill-stream.

Almost immediately, Jenůfa wakes up from her drugged sleep and discovers the baby is missing. Believing that the Kostelnička has taken it to show to the people at the mill, she offers up a prayer to the Virgin ('Zdrávas královno'). The Kostelnička returns frozen from her expedition, and tells Jenůfa that the child died while she was in a fever. Jenůfa accepts the news with tender resignation, and when Laca returns soon after she offers no resistance to his earnest proposal of marriage. As the Kostelnička blesses the union and then curses Števa, the window of the cottage blows open and the Kostelnička, filled with foreboding, cries out in terror.

Act III The Kostelnička's cottage, two months later. Preparations for Jenůfa's wedding to Laca are in progress, though the Kostelnička, broken by her deed, is a shadow of her former self. Guests arrive: the mayor and his wife, Števa and his betrothed (the mayor's daughter, Karolka). Jenůfa adroitly manages a reconciliation between the two half-brothers. Finally girls from the village come to sing a wedding song for Jenůfa ('Ej mamko, mamko'). Grandmother Buryja gives her blessing to the pair. Just as the Kostelnička is about to add hers, a tumult is heard outside. Jano the herdboy runs on with the news that the frozen corpse of a little child has been found in the mill-stream. Jenůfa thinks it is her child, and the gathering crowd accuses her of murder. Laca holds off the mob, but it is the Kostelnička who silences the people with her own confession of guilt. At first appalled, Jenůfa begins to understand the motives that lay behind the Kostelnička's terrible action. She forgives her stepmother, who is then led off to stand trial. Alone with Laca, Jenůfa thinks that he can no longer want her in these circumstances, but, movingly, he pleads for and gains her love.

Janáček took almost a decade over this, his third opera, during which time he changed his whole attitude to the genre. The long pause before beginning Act II seems to have been particularly significant. Even in its final revision, the first act of Jenůfa shows traces of something like a number opera. It opens with what amount to arias for Jenůfa and then Laca; towards the end there is a substantial concertato ensemble and a trio; and the chorus plays a large and fairly conventional part, especially in the folk scenes of Act I.

But even here Janáček had discarded his naïvely propagandist view of Moravian folksong. While his previous opera, The Beginning of a Romance, consists mostly of folksongs, Jenůfa has a number of folksong texts in appropriate places (the recruits scene of Act I; the bridal chorus in Act III), but the tunes are by Janáček (who declared that the opera had not a single folksong in it). A further factor was Janáček's developing preoccupation with 'speech-melody' – his notations of fragments of everyday speech, often documented with details of their emotional context. Speech-melodies were not used to generate melodic material for his operas, but instead helped sharpen Janáček's awareness of the contours of natural speech. This led to a new style of writing whereby musical continuity was concentrated in the still regularly structured orchestra part, with the voice reciting increasingly freely over it. It was inevitable with such an approach that Janáček would set Jenůfa as a prose libretto, the first such in Czech opera.

Osud

Fate or *Destiny*
Three novelistic scenes (1h 15m)
Libretto by the composer and Fedora Bartošová
Composed 1903–5, rev. 1906, 1907
PREMIERES 13 March 1934 (excerpts) and 18 September 1934 (complete), Brno Radio; 30 September 1934, Brno Stadion (concert); 25 October 1958, Brno State Theatre (Vaclav Nosek 'flashback' arrangement); UK: 22 January 1972, BBC radio; 14 August 1983, Queen Elizabeth Hall, London (concert); 8 September 1984, Coliseum, London
CAST Živný *t*, Míla Válková *s*, Doubek (at five) *boy s*, Doubek (as a student) *t*, Míla's Mother *c*, 6 *s*, 4 *c*, 5 *t*, 2 *bar*; *satb* chorus of schoolteachers, students and young girls, visitors at the spa, conservatory students

Even before Jenůfa had been produced, Janáček began a new opera. On holiday in the Moravian spa town of Luhačovice in August 1903 he met a Mrs Urválková, who told him how a malicious portrait of her had been drawn in an opera by Ludvík Čelanský, Kamila (1897). Janáček returned to Brno infatuated with Mrs Urválková and determined to write a new opera which would portray her in a different light. He took early retirement from his teaching post at the Teacher Training College and energetically began sketching a plot that included autobiographical scenes from Luhačovice and a music conservatory (similiar to the Brno Organ School which he had founded), soliciting the services of a young schoolteacher, Fedora Bartošová, to turn his scenario into 'Pushkinesque verse'. As his ardour for Mrs Urválková cooled (at the intervention of her husband), so the plot changed. It was further altered when Janáček began showing Bartošová's efforts to his friends, and by the time Janáček submitted his opera to the Brno National Theatre in October 1906 the work had been substantially revised. Negotiations with a producer and designer were started early in 1907, only to be scuppered by Janáček's wish to see the opera performed at the new Vinohrady Theatre in Prague, where it was immediately accepted by its musical director – ironically the same Ludvík Čelanský who had inspired it. But Janáček got cold feet over the libretto, which prompted another round of advice and further changes, which he completed in November 1907.

Čelanský took his time about the introduction of such an unusual work, and a change of regime at the theatre produced even more delays. When in 1913 the work was eventually and reluctantly put into rehearsal, the singers rebelled, and the management seized on this as a pretext for abandoning the venture. Janáček took legal action, but was persuaded to drop the case on a vague promise of production by the now returned Čelanský. Meanwhile Brno showed further interest and Janáček withdrew the work altogether, submitting it to Brno in the spring of 1914. A production, however, was shelved after the outbreak of the First World War.

After the success of *Jenůfa* in Prague, Janáček began to look at his earlier operas, including *Osud*, but the verdict on the libretto by Max Brod and others was so damning that he gave up all further thoughts about the work. Its first stage production, in Brno in 1958, was in an arrangement by Vaclav Nosek in which Acts I and II were inserted in the middle of Act III as a flashback. Later productions at České Budejovice (1978) and London (1984) restored the original structure.

SYNOPSIS

Act I   A spa. The composer Živný meets up with a former mistress, Míla. Spa life is depicted in all its variety (various artists, fashionable society, women schoolteachers who rehearse a part-song, a noisy group of young people who leave for an 'excursion'). When left alone, the conversation between Živný and Míla reveals that a child had been born of their union, but, submitting to pressure from her family, Míla had married someone else. They decide to go off together, to the consternation of Míla's mother.

Act II   The study in Živný's house, four years later. Živný and Míla are living together with their five-year-old son, Doubek. Míla's mother, now insane and needing constant supervision, also lives with them and can be heard offstage mocking Živný as he plays through his opera to Míla. The opera has Míla's 'shame' depicted in it, and in a fit of remorse Živný begins tearing pages from the score. Míla's mother breaks into the room, accusing Živný of stealing her daughter and her wealth. Míla tries to restrain her mother, and in the struggle both fall to their death.

Act III   The main hall of the conservatory (twelve years later). Students sing through a couple of scenes in Živný's opera, which is to be performed that evening in the theatre. Živný enters, and is persuaded to tell them something about the opera. As he does so a storm breaks out; he imagines that he can see his dead wife and hear her voice, and collapses.

Osud is an important turning-point in Janáček's operatic career. His first three operas belong in different ways to the Czech operatic tradition: with *Osud* he began looking further afield for models, in particular to Gustave Charpentier's opera *Louise*, which had been hugely successful when given in Prague in February 1903, and which Janáček himself saw there in May of that year. He enthusiastically praised aspects of the opera such as its prose libretto and its use of 'speech-melodies', which he had already and independently employed in *Jenůfa*. Other features, not in *Jenůfa*, such as its contemporary subject matter, its more 'urban' style of music, its handling of a large individualized chorus, and its use of offstage 'symbolic' choruses he quietly purloined himself. These are all prominent aspects of *Osud*, and some, for instance the offstage symbolic chorus, persist throughout his later operas.

In the wake of such a major stimulus, *Osud* is a surprisingly independent work. But its experimental character is none the less evident. The libretto was made up more or less as Janáček went along (the middle act in particular went through surprising metamorphoses), and is expressed in an art-nouveau floweriness of diction that makes it sometimes hard to understand. The cinematic succession of scenes has caused problems for staging ever since, though it laid the foundation for Janáček's idiosyncratic dramatic pacing. The opera was, however, written with an overwhelming panache, right from the exuberant opening chorus (there is no overture). The solo sections, the long duet in Act I and Živný's monologue in Act III are particularly fine.

The Excursions of Mr Brouček
Výlety páně Broučkovy

Opera in two parts (four acts) (2h 15m)
Libretto: Part I, the composer with František Gellner, Viktor Dyk, F. S. Procházka and others, after Svatopluk Čech's novel (1888); Part II, F. S. Procházka, after Svatopluk Čech's novel (1889)
Composed 1908–17
PREMIERES 23 April 1920, National Theatre, Prague; UK: 1 May 1960, BBC radio; 3 September 1970, King's Theatre, Edinburgh; 28 December 1978, Coliseum, London: US: 23 January 1981, San Francisco Opera Ensemble (concert); 21 November 1981, Indiana University, Bloomington
CAST Mr Brouček *t*, Mazal/Blankytný/Petřík *t*, Sacristan at St Vitus's Cathedral/Lunobor/Domšík od zvonu *b*, Málinka/Etherea/Kunka *s*, Würfl, Landlord of the Víkarka/Čaroskvoucí/Town Councillor *bar*, Little Waiter/Child Prodigy/Student *ms*, *c*, 3 *t*, *bar*; *satb* chorus of artists, dancers, Etherea's companions, moon artists, armed men, Hussite people, Prague and Taborite soldiers, Taborite boys, Prague girls

With *Osud* successfully accepted (as he thought) by the Vinohrady Theatre, Janáček began a new opera in March 1908. *The Excursion of Mr Brouček to the Moon* was designed as a one-act opera in four scenes based on Svatopluk Čech's satirical novel in which a philistine Prague landlord, Mr Brouček (Mr Beetle) is shown in comic confrontation with the aesthetes on the moon – a barb directed at the precious Art-for-Art's-sake movements of the period. Negotiations with a succession of librettists delayed work and resulted in Janáček's doing much of the adaptation himself (his first helpful librettist, František Gellner, who wrote most of the songs in what is now Act II, was brought in as late as 1912). By 1913, when any hope of staging *Osud* or *Jenůfa* in Prague had been abandoned, Janáček put away the three scenes he had written, but with Prague's change of mind over *Jenůfa* he revised and completed his one-act opera (1916–17) with two more librettists (F. S. Procházka and Viktor Dyk). He finished the troublesome epilogue scene (depicting Brouček back at home), but later abandoned it, and added a second 'excursion' (1917), based on Čech's sequel, in which Mr Brouček is transported to the early 15th century, a heroic period in Czech history when the Czechs fought off armies of crusaders from the rest of Europe. Here Procházka provided the entire libretto, the last time Janáček was to employ a librettist. The complete 'bilogy' was given in Prague under Otakar Ostrčil in 1920, making it Janáček's only opera to be heard first outside Brno.

SYNOPSIS

The Excursion of Mr Brouček to the Moon
Výlet pana Broučka do měsíce
Act I   Outside the Víkarka tavern, Prague. Málinka and Mazal are in the midst of a lovers' tiff. She threatens to marry Mr Brouček, a Prague landlord. Brouček himself, disgruntled by his troubles on earth, dreams of an idyllic life on the moon and, in a drunken stupor, is miraculously transported there. He meets the moon poet Blankytný (who resembles his difficult tenant on earth, Mazal), and Blankytný's betrothed Etherea (Málinka), accompanied by a chorus of singing maidens. Etherea promptly falls in love with Brouček and elopes with him on a winged horse, to the despair of Blankytný and her father Lunobor (Sacristan).

Act II   The moon: the Temple of All Arts. Brouček and Etherea arrive at the court of the 'Maecenas', Čaroskvoucí (Würfl), pursued by Blankytný and Lunobor. Brouček gradually learns that the moon is inhabited by a breed of artistic beings who neither eat nor drink (they live by sniffing nectar) and are devoted entirely to artistic pursuits. He is horrified, and manages to escape back to earth. He is found drunk in a beer barrel, while Mazal and Málinka make up their quarrel.

The Excursion of Mr Brouček to the 15th Century
Výlet pana Broučka do XV. stoleti
Act I   Jewel chamber of Wenceslas IV. Voices are heard (from the nearby Víkarka tavern) discussing the underground passages said to lead from there. Mr Brouček believes firmly in their existence. Soon after, he falls down a hole and finds himself in King Wenceslas's jewel chamber. He eventually makes his way out to the Prague Old Town Square, which is mysteriously transformed into an earlier guise. Mr Brouček stumbles along the ill-lit streets (it is early dawn) and encounters a town councillor, who finds his 19th-century speech hard to understand and arrests him as a spy: Prague is on the eve of the great battle of 1420 in which the Czechs, defending their Hussite faith, win a famous victory. Brouček's cause seems desperate until he is taken in by the kindly Domšík (Sacristan).

Act II   Domšík's house. Brouček wakes up as an honoured guest and accustoms himself to his new surroundings. He is welcomed by Domšík's family and friends as a sturdy warrior who will fight with them in the coming battle. During a meal, Domšík's daughter Kunka enthuses over the sermon given that day, and religious politics of the time are vigorously discussed. The alarm sounds, the men rush off to fight, Brouček reluctantly taking a pikestaff, against the background of prayers and Hussite war hymns. In the ensuing fight Domšík is killed, but the Czechs are victorious. Brouček manages to avoid fighting altogether, though he spins stories of his valour. However, his cowardice has been noticed and he is condemned to be burnt in a barrel. Just as the flames are at the highest, he wakes up in a barrel, and tells the indulgent Würfl about his latest escapade.

Brouček is Janáček's most overtly comic opera, the comedy essentially deriving from the confrontation of Mr Brouček with worlds beyond his limited imagination. The effect, however, is rather different in the two halves. In the first excursion Mr Brouček, in comparison with the rarefied moon artists, offers the voice of sturdy common sense. In the second, Mr Brouček's 'reasonableness' makes a poor showing against the sacrifices of the patriotic Hussites: Janáček's motive for setting this second excursion was a moral appeal to the citizens of the future Czechoslovak Republic.

Despite this moral aim, the more coherent libretto, and the often thrilling use of Hussite chorales (one traditional tune, the rest settings by Janáček of Hussite texts), the 15th-century excursion emerges as the weaker of the two. There are dry passages, especially in the doctrinal disputes among the Hussites, that suggest that Janáček did not completely engage with the material. However, the first excursion, for all its piecemeal production (a virtual scrapbook libretto) and seeming silliness, has music of great charm and liveliness and has proved surprisingly viable on the stage. *Osud* and *Brouček* can together be considered experimental transition pieces, uneven as artistic wholes but of great interest, and which considerably expanded Janáček's range through the impact of new influences (Charpentier, Puccini) and the exploration of new types of subject matter and structure.

Katya Kabanova
Kát'a Kabanová
Opera in three acts (1h 45m)
Libretto by the composer, after Aleksandr Ostrovsky's play *Groza* (*The Thunderstorm*, 1859) trans. Vincenc Červinka (1918)
Composed 1919–21; interludes for Acts I and II 1927
PREMIERES 23 November 1921, National Theatre, Brno;
UK: 28 December 1948, BBC radio; 10 April 1951, Sadler's Wells, London; US: 26 November 1957, Karamu House, Cleveland, Ohio (concert with pf acc.); 2 August 1960, Empire State Music Festival, Bear Mountain
CAST Savël Prokofjevič Dikoj *b*, Boris Grigorjevič *t*, Marfa Ignatěvna Kabanová (Kabanicha) *c*, Tichon Ivanyč Kabanov *t*, Katěrina (Kát'a (Katya)) *s*, Váňa Kudrjáš *t*, Varvara *ms*, Kuligin *bar*, Glaša *ms*, Fekluša *ms*, Drunk Passer-by *silent*, Woman from Crowd *c*, Passer-by *t*; *satb* chorus of townspeople, offstage chorus

With *Kát'a Kabanová* Janáček entered his mature operatic period. His first five operas represent a painfully long operatic apprenticeship with only one clear-cut success (*Jenůfa*), for whose recognition he had to wait until he was almost 62. But what followed is without parallel. Janáček's amazing Indian summer – the last decade of his life – saw the composition of four major operas, on which, together with *Jenůfa*, his reputation rests today.

Kát'a Kabanová is Janáček's own adaptation of Ostrovsky's play *The Thunderstorm*, which he began considering late in 1919. The Russian material was congenial to him, but another strand in its inspiration was his identification of the principal character with a favourite operatic heroine of his, Madama Butterfly, and also with Kamila Stösslová. Janáček had met Mrs Stösslová on holiday in the Moravian spa town of Luhačovice in 1917. This marked the beginning of a passionate, though largely one-sided, relationship which lasted until the end of Janáček's life, documented by the collection of over 700 letters which has only recently been published in full. According to these letters, Kamila Stösslová provided the inspiration for characters in all of Janáček's last four operas, and for the gypsy girl in the song cycle *The Diary of One who Disappeared*. *Kát'a Kabanová* was dedicated to her.

Composition began early in 1920 and proceeded rapidly and unproblematically until the spring of 1921, though Janáček continued to tinker with the score up to its premiere. This took place in Brno in November 1921 under much grander circumstances than that of the Brno premiere of *Jenůfa*. Following the independence of Czechoslovakia the Czechs now had control of the excellent German opera house; *Kát'a Kabanová* was conducted by František Neumann, the new head of opera, who was to preside over all of Janáček's later premieres except for that of *From the House of the Dead*. *Kát'a Kabanová* also set a pattern for the later operas: all were given first in Brno, then in Prague, and published with Max Brod's German translation by Universal Edition. Despite the distinguished conductor of the first German production (Otto Klemperer in Cologne, 1922), and a fine production in Berlin (1926) for which Janáček received the compliments of Schoenberg and Zemlinsky, the work made headway outside Czechoslovakia only after the Second World War. It was Janáček's first opera to be performed in the UK, and has been more frequently produced there than any other of his operas.

After difficulties in early productions with scene changes, Janáček wrote new interludes for Acts I and II which were first given in the Prague German Theatre production in 1928. Its conductor, Hans Wilhelm Steinberg, played the first two acts through without a break, a procedure Janáček enthusiastically endorsed.

SYNOPSIS

Act I Scene 1: Kalinov, Russia, in the 1860s. In a public park on the bank of the Volga, Kudrjáš learns from Boris, his employer Dikoj's nephew, about his passion for a married woman, Kát'a Kabanová, and they watch the Kabanov family come back from church. The family is at loggerheads. Kát'a, a woman of great dignity and sweetness of nature, is married to the weak Tichon, a merchant under the thumb of his domineering mother, known as Kabanicha. He is unable to prevent Kabanicha from tyrannizing his wife, and he meekly complies when she orders him off on a business trip. Scene 2: In a room in the Kabanov household, Kát'a tells Varvara, a foundling girl in the household, about herself. Her narration, at first joyful as she remembers her life at home and her churchgoing, clouds over as she tells Varvara of the dreams that trouble her, and of her guilty love for Boris. Tichon comes in, ready for his departure. Kát'a is anxious because of the temptations that might arise during his absence, and begs him not to go, or to take her with him. But he is helpless against his mother, who furthermore orders him to extract humiliating promises of good behaviour from Kát'a during his absence. Tichon departs.

Act II Scene 1: Towards evening on the same day, in another room in the Kabanov household, Kabanicha reprimands Kát'a for not showing more grief at Tichon's departure. Varvara has already made plans for an assignation between Kát'a and Boris, and gives her the key to the garden gate, which she has stolen from Kabanicha. Kabanicha is visited by Dikoj, Boris's unpleasant uncle, who derives pleasure from confessing his weaknesses to Kabanicha, and receiving her scolding. Scene 2: A hollow overlooked by the Kabanov garden, a summer evening. Kudrjáš sings a song as he waits for Varvara ('Po zahrádce děvucha'), and is surprised by the appearance of Boris, who tells him of the assignation arranged for him. Varvara joins them ('Za vodou, za vodičkou') and runs off with Kudrjáš. Boris is soon joined by Kát'a, terrified by the 'sin' she is committing. Their courtship is interrupted by the other couple, whose more light-hearted relationship takes centre stage, with fragments from the passionate love duet between Boris and Kát'a wafting in from offstage. Then it is time for the lovers to part and Kudrjáš calls Boris and Kát'a. The scene ends with another 'folksong' for Kudrjáš and Varvara ('Chod' si dívka do času').

Act III Scene 1: Two weeks later. People are taking refuge from the afternoon storm in the ruins of an abandoned church overlooking the Volga. Kudrjáš exchanges insults with his employer, Dikoj. The scientifically minded Kudrjáš advises the installation of lightning conductors; Dikoj pooh-poohs this since, as he asserts, storms are a punishment sent by God. Kudrjáš is sought out by Varvara, worried about Kát'a's distraught state at the imminent return of her husband. Kát'a runs on dishevelled and will not be calmed or comforted. Tichon and Kabanicha now enter, and Kát'a, overwrought by the thunderstorm, which she sees as a punishment from God, confesses her adultery with Boris to the assembled company and rushes out into the storm. Scene 2: At twilight Tichon and Glaša, a servant, look in vain for Kát'a in a deserted place on the bank of the Volga. Kudrjáš and Varvara decide to leave for Moscow. Kát'a wanders on in a daze, wanting to see Boris once again and then die. Strange voices call her, but death does not come yet. Eventually Boris joins her. After a brief farewell he leaves (he is being sent off to Siberia by Dikoj), and Kát'a, now at peace with herself, finds death in the Volga. Her body is hauled out and presented to Kabanicha, who thanks the 'good people' for their kindness.

Kát'a Kabanová is Janáček's most lyrical opera. Central to the work is Janáček's conception of the heroine 'of such a soft nature that . . . if the sun shone fully on her she would melt'. Her first vocal utterance is gentle and regular, in sharp contrast to Kabanicha's noisy tirade. Similar 'Kát'a' music reappears in most scenes. Sometimes her music is confined to the orchestra, for instance her radiant appearance in Act I (modelled on the first appearance of Madama Butterfly) or the poignant music for the lovers' silent embrace in the final scene.

While Kát'a's presence is signalled by a type of music, two reminiscence themes are also important.

Varvara's 'Za vodou' tune is heard in the opera even before it is given words in Act II, Scene 2. The eight strokes of the timpani represent a fate theme which is heard softly in the opening bars of the overture, and fortissimo at the end. Speeded up and heard on the oboe against a sleigh-bell accompaniment, it provides the music (first heard in the overture) for Tichon's departure, the event that precipitates the crisis.

Kát'a's gentle nature is contrasted not merely to the despotism of Kabanicha (Janáček's most evil female portrait), but to the light-hearted world of Varvara and Kudrjáš, characterized by their folksongs. The double love scene of Act II, Scene 2, with Kát'a's and Boris's love music heard in the distance against the more practical chatter of Varvara and Kudrjáš on-stage, is one of the glories of the score. Equally fine are Kát'a's two monologues: the first (Act I, Scene 2), in which she travels imperceptibly from religious to sexual ecstasy in her vivid account of her inner life; the second (Act III, Scene 2) where her inner voices are made audible in an offstage chorus.

The Cunning Little Vixen
Příhody Lišky Bystroušky
Opera in three acts (1h 30m)
Libretto by the composer, after the novel *Liška Bystrouška* by Rudolf Těsnohlídek (1921)
PREMIERES 6 November 1924, National Theatre, Brno; UK: 22 March 1961, Sadler's Wells, London; US: 7 May 1964, Mannes College of Music, New York
CAST Gamekeeper *bar*, Gamekeeper's Wife *c*, Schoolmaster *t*, Priest *b*, Harašta *b*, Pásek *t*, Mrs Pásková *s*, Bystrouška the Vixen *s*, Zlatohřbítek the Fox *s*, Young Bystrouška *child s*, Frantík *s*, Pepík *s*, Lapák the Dog *ms*, Cock *s*, Chocholka the Hen *s*, Cricket *child s*, Grasshopper *child s*, Frog *child s*, Midge *child s*, Woodpecker *c*, Mosquito *t*, Badger *b*, Owl *c*, Jay *s*; chorus of hens and creatures of the forest, children's chorus of fox cubs, offstage *satb* chorus; ballet (dragonfly, Vixen as a girl, midges, hedgehog, squirrels)

During the spring of 1920 the Brno newspaper *Lidové noviny* published in daily instalments a tale about a vixen who is captured by a gamekeeper and then escapes back to the woods to find a mate for herself and raise a litter. A particular feature of the serialization was the inclusion of a large number of illustrations. These had in fact come first. *Lidové noviny* acquired Stanislav Lolek's 200 line-drawings (which, in cartoon fashion, told their own story), and then instructed one of its reporters, Rudolf Těsnohlídek, to produce a text. The resulting 'novel', celebrating country life in the forests near Brno, was published in book form in 1921 and has remained popular to this day.

According to Janáček's housekeeper, Marie Stejskalová, it was she who drew the work to Janáček's attention as a possible opera text. But this could have come about through other means. Janáček took the paper and, as a regular contributor himself, had close contacts with its editors. In June 1921 he began dropping hints that *Liška Bystrouška* might be his next opera, but only the next year, with the premiere of *Kát'a Kabanová* out of the way, did he get down seriously to planning the libretto. He began the music

in autumn 1922, and it was essentially finished within a year, with the final act copied up by January 1924. The Brno premiere followed in November, a few months after Janáček's 70th birthday. The piece's foreign success dates from the celebrated Walter Felsenstein production at the Komische Oper, Berlin, in 1956.

Janáček wrote his own libretto. Invited to contribute, Těsnohlídek produced only the gamekeeper's song in Act II – other songs came from folk texts. The first two acts, with many omissions, follow Těsnohlídek closely. But since the vixen's wedding at the end of Act II of the opera closes the novel, the structure of Act III is Janáček's invention, though drawing on various scenes and incidents earlier in the book. The vixen's death, within a context of the cyclical renewal of life, is Janáček's own distinctive contribution.

SYNOPSIS
Act I The forest; summer, a sunny afternoon. The gamekeeper, interrupting the animal life of the forest, lies down and takes a nap. While he sleeps, a young frog tries to catch a mosquito, but lands instead on the gamekeeper's nose and wakes him up. The frog has attracted the attention of Bystrouška ('Sharpears'), the vixen cub. The gamekeeper catches her and takes her home. The farm-yard: autumn, late afternoon sun. Installed at the gamekeeper's, the vixen exchanges stories with the dog and defends herself both against his sexual advances and against the baiting by the two boys, Frantík and Pepík, for which she is tied up. When night falls she appears in her dreams as a young girl. The vixen's plan to entice the hens within her range begins with a harangue about their subservience to the cock; when this fails she threatens to bury herself alive in disgust at their conservatism. The cock is sent to investigate and is soon killed, as are all the hens in turn. Fearing retribution at the hands of the gamekeeper and his wife, the vixen bites through her leash and escapes into the forest.

Act II The forest; late afternoon. Now at large in the forest, the vixen ruthlessly evicts the badger and takes over his comfortable home. The inn. The gamekeeper, the schoolmaster and the priest drink and play cards. The gamekeeper sings a song about the passing of time ('Bývalo, bývalo') and taunts the schoolmaster about his inactivity as a lover; in return the schoolmaster baits him about the escape of the vixen. The forest; moonlight. The schoolmaster, tipsy, has trouble finding his way home, and mistakes the vixen, hiding behind a sunflower, for his distant beloved, Terynka. The priest, separately wending his way home, lets his thoughts wander back to an incident in his youth when he was wrongly accused of seducing a girl. Both men are startled by the gamekeeper, who fires – in vain – at the vixen. The forest; summer, a moonlit night. The vixen meets a handsome fox, Zlatohřbítek ('Goldmane'); she tells him of how she was brought up by the gamekeeper and of her subsequent escapades. They fall in love, observed by gossiping birds, and she is soon obliged to marry. The animals of the forest join in the general merrymaking.

Act III The forest; autumn, midday. Harašta, a

poultry-dealer, is heard approaching ('Déž sem vandroval'); he is accosted by the gamekeeper, who thinks he has been poaching. Harašta tells him he is about to marry Terynka. The gamekeeper leaves a trap for the vixen, but the vixen and her mate and litter make fun of the trap ('Beží liška k Táboru'). The vixen and her fox contemplate their growing family and possible additions. Harašta returns. The vixen, pretending to be lame, lures him into the forest, where he trips over. While he is nursing his injuries, the vixen and her family demolish the chickens. In his anger Harašta shoots and kills the vixen. The inn. The schoolmaster is tearful at the news of Terynka's marriage, and both he and the gamekeeper regret the absence of the priest, who has moved to a new parish. The gamekeeper, feeling his age, sets off home. The forest; as at the beginning. The gamekeeper contemplates the beauty of the scene around him, and remembers the day of his wedding. At peace with nature and with himself, he falls asleep. In his dream, the creatures seen at the opening reappear, including a little vixen, but when the gamekeeper tries to catch her he succeeds only in catching a frog – the 'grandson' of the one in the first scene. His gun falls to the ground.

As always, Janáček was an economical librettist. Where direct or indirect speech was available in the novel he used it, and where there was none he simply wrote music. Thus, in comparison with his previous opera, *Kát'a Kabanová*, based on a play, there is a far greater proportion of purely instrumental music – essential for the short interludes between the many scenes. The music contains some of Janáček's most enchanting orchestral inspirations, for instance the dream sequence of the young vixen in Act I, or at the opening the evocation of the forest with its abundance of life. Janáček's score is articulated in half-act units held together by the recurrence of themes (e.g. the offstage chorus at the beginning of the second half of Act II transformed into the exuberant wedding chorus at the end), or by sets of variations.

Janáček had no inhibitions about the singing of animals. Size is more or less equated with pitch – ranging from the bass badger to the female-voice hens and forest birds, and the inspired use of children's voices for the insects. Children's voices are also used delightfully for the vixen's cubs. Dance is another important element of the score in the evocation of animal life. Apart from the vixen herself, and memorably the little frog at the end of the opera, interactions between the human and animal worlds are sparing, though Janáček reduced his cast slightly by indicating suggestive doublings (e.g. priest/badger, schoolmaster/mosquito).

For such a curious libretto, the work has a surprisingly large emotional range, from the comic episodes with the hens in Act I, to the erotic courtship music in Act II, and the painfully nostalgic inn scene in Act III. Most memorable of all, however, is the gamekeeper's monologue which dominates the end of the opera, and which lifts the original text to an altogether different plane.

The Makropulos Affair
Věc Makropulos
Opera in three acts (1h 30m)
Libretto by the composer, after Karel Čapek's comedy (1922)
PREMIERES 18 December 1926, National Theatre, Brno; UK: 12 February 1964, Sadler's Wells, London; US: 19 November 1966, War Memorial Theater, San Francisco
CAST Emilia Marty (Elina Makropulos) *dramatic s*, Albert Gregor *t*, Vitek *t*, Kristina *s*, Jaroslav Prus *bar*, Janek *t*, Dr Kolenatý *b-bar*, Technician *b*, Cleaning Woman *c*, Hauk-Šendorf *operetta t*, Chamber Maid *c*; offstage male chorus

Janáček saw Karel Čapek's play *The Makropulos Affair* in Prague on 10 December 1922, three weeks after it opened, and was immediately attracted to it as a possible opera text, although he had only just started the composition of *The Cunning Little Vixen*. By February 1923 he was in correspondence with Čapek about it. Čapek himself was accommodating, but there were legal problems to be overcome in securing the rights. On 10 September 1923 the composer heard from Čapek that these had been resolved, and the next day he set to work, even before the score of *The Cunning Little Vixen* was finalized. He worked quickly, with Act I drafted by February 1924 and the whole opera by December that year, though, as was his usual practice, he needed two more drafts before he was satisfied with his work, which he completed a year later, on 3 December 1925. The Brno premiere followed under Václav Neumann in December 1926, and the Prague premiere under Otakar Ostrčil in March 1928 – the last premiere Janáček attended. Though a German production followed under Josef Krips in Frankfurt in 1929, the work took time to establish itself internationally. However, outstanding productions by Sadler's Wells (1964) and Welsh National Opera (1978), both of which were later taken into the English National Opera repertoire, have ensured a regular following in the UK.

Janáček's libretto is a skilful compression keeping the original three-act framework of Čapek's play intact (though not the division of the final act into two scenes). But whereas Čapek wrote his play as a philosophical comedy, which dispassionately explored the merits and drawbacks of a life prolonged to over 300 years, Janáček impatiently cut out much of the speculative banter, and instead concentrated on the emotional state of the extraordinary central character, the 337-year-old Elina Makropulos.

SYNOPSIS
A young Cretan girl, Elina Makropulos, is given an elixir of life devised by her father, physician to Emperor Rudolf II at his court in Prague. She flees with the formula, 'Věc Makropulos' (the Makropulos thing, document), trains as a singer and with literally centuries to perfect her technique becomes one of the greatest singers of all time. Moving from country to country to avert suspicion, she has undergone frequent changes of name, though always retaining the same initials. For the past few years (the date is 1922 – she is now 337), she has been known as Emilia Marty and has returned to Prague, where her extraordinary lease of life began. As it happens, a celebrated lawsuit,

Gregor versus Prus, is reaching the end of its 100-year life. The present claimant, Albert Gregor, maintains that his ancestor Ferdinand Gregor should have inherited a large estate on the death in 1827 of its owner, Baron Josef Ferdinand Prus. The Prus family, however, have successfully contested the claim.

Act I Dr Kolenatý's chambers. Albert Gregor interrupts the historical ruminations of Kolenatý's clerk, Vítek, to find out the latest news of his case. Kristina, Vítek's daughter, returns from rehearsals at the theatre where Emilia Marty is currently appearing, infatuated by her artistry and beauty. She and Vítek leave just as Marty herself enters the office, accompanied by Dr Kolenatý. Marty wants to know about the Gregor–Prus case; her sharp questions and comments indicate an intimate knowledge of the people involved. She reveals that Ferdinand Gregor was Baron Josef Prus's illegitimate son, and that a will in his favour exists somewhere in the house of the present Baron Jaroslav Prus. Gregor makes the disbelieving Dr Kolenatý go and find it. Left alone with the mysterious Marty, Gregor hears more about Ferdinand Gregor's mother, the singer Ellian MacGregor. By then he is completely captivated. She repels his amorous advances and is distraught when he confesses ignorance of the 'Greek papers' she claims he must have. Kolenatý returns with Prus – and with a will. Prus, however, insists that some evidence is still missing. To Kolenatý's amazement, Marty undertakes to provide it.

Act II The empty stage of a large theatre. A cleaning woman and a technician discuss Marty's performance the night before. Prus comes to wait for Marty and, unobserved, witnesses the little scene between Kristina and her boyfriend, his son Janek – to the latter's embarrassment. Marty now appears, upsetting everyone who tries to congratulate her: the tongue-tied Janek, Gregor, and Vítek, who to her great annoyance compares her to a famous past singer. But she is strangely compassionate to her final visitor, the aged and demented Hauk-Šendorf, who sees in her a likeness of his 'gypsy girl', Eugenia Montez, long since dead. After giving Kristina her autograph, she dismisses everyone except Prus. Prus excites her interest by mentioning that together with the will there were letters and 'something else' in a sealed envelope. He adds that his investigations reveal that Ferdinand Gregor's mother is given on the birth register as Elina Makropulos, not Ellian MacGregor, as stated by the document Marty has provided. Consequently no MacGregor (or Gregor) can claim the Prus estates. Marty, however, is more interested in the sealed envelope and offers to buy it. Prus angrily stalks off. Gregor now finds her. She asks him to retrieve the document that she gave to Kolenatý – it needs a different name. When he continues his advances to her, she brutally repulses him and then falls asleep. He tiptoes away, and Marty wakes up to find Janek with her. She urges him to steal the sealed envelope from his father. This scene, however, has been overheard, once again, by Prus, who dismisses his son and who finally agrees to give Marty the envelope in exchange for an assignation that night.

Act III A hotel room. Prus and Marty have spent the night together. She gets her envelope, but Prus feels cheated and is broken by the news that Janek has committed suicide. Prus leaves, meeting Hauk-Šendorf on the way. Hauk-Šendorf proposes to Marty that they elope, but they are forestalled by the arrival of Kolenatý and his party, who accuse her of forgery: the signature on the document she supplied has been written with modern ink. She goes to change while the others rifle her trunk, discovering a variety of historical documents relating to Ellian MacGregor, Eugenia Montez, Elina Makropulos and others. She returns, dressed and a little tipsy. When cross-examined, she insists that her name is Elina Makropulos and she is 337 years old. She tells them about her father and the elixir of life he devised and tried out on her. She had passed this on to the only man she loved, Josef Prus, but with the end of her life approaching she wished to get back the formula. Eventually the company believes her. She collapses and is taken to the bedroom, attended by a doctor. She returns 'as a shadow', at last understanding that death will be a welcome relief – life has become quite meaningless for her. She offers the Makropulos formula to Kristina, who however sets fire to it, as Elina Makropulos dies.

Like the vixen's, Elina's death at the end of the opera was Janáček's addition. This magnificent scene is the best illustration of how completely Janáček transformed Čapek's conversational comedy into a drama conceived on the grandest emotional scale. Here Janáček wrote one of his slow-waltz finales, a haunting, rocking tune played in the extremes of the orchestra with, in the middle, Elina's moving account of how meaningless life has become for her. Its otherworldliness is underlined by the slow pace and by the mysterious offstage male-voice choir repeating her words. This is the only substantial monologue in an opera that otherwise is characterized by its many memorable dialogues. Most striking of these is the verbal duel between Marty and Prus in Act II, complemented by their chilling, almost wordless encounter that brings down the curtain.

The success of the dialogues is due partly to the different atmospheres that Janáček creates in each of them, and partly to his virtuosity in handling the voice parts. Compared with *The Cunning Little Vixen*, or *From the House of the Dead*, this is a wordy libretto – an aspect that has often been criticized. And yet Čapek's elegant prose seems to have offered Janáček a wealth of phrases whose memorable settings realized perhaps more than in any other work Janáček's speech-melody ideal of revealing a character's inner life. This is one reason why all the minor characters come alive in this more than in any other Janáček opera. The vocal writing is accompanied by some of Janáček's most sophisticated and imaginative orchestral developments which, for instance, help to bind the huge span of the long Marty–Gregor dialogue in Act I.

From the House of the Dead

Z mrtvého domu
Opera in three acts (1h 30m)
Libretto by the composer, after Fyodor Dostoevsky's novel

Memoirs from the House of the Dead (1862)
PREMIERES   12 April 1930, National Theatre, Brno
(Chlubna and Bakala arr.); UK: 1 May 1960, BBC radio;
28 August 1964, King's Theatre, Edinburgh; 28 October
1965, Sadler's Wells, London (Janáček's original version);
US: 3 December 1969 (NET Television); 24 March 1983,
New York Philharmonic (concert); 28 August 1990, New
York City Opera, New York
CAST   Alexandr Petrovič Gorjančikov *bar*, Aljeja *ms*, Luka
Kuzmič (alias of Filka Morozov) *t*, Tall Prisoner *t*, Short
Prisoner *bar*, Prison Governor *b*, Old Prisoner *t*, Prisoner
with Eagle *t*, Skuratov *t*, Čekunov *b*, Drunk Prisoner *t*,
Cook *bar*, Smith *bar*, Priest *bar*, Young Prisoner *t*,
Prostitute *ms*, Prisoner playing Don Juan and the Brahmin
b, Kedril *t*, Šapkin *t*, Šiškov *bar*, Čerevin *t*, First Sentry *t*,
Second Sentry *bar*, Voice Offstage *t*, Knight, Elvira,
Cobbler's Wife, Priest's Wife, Miller, Miller's Wife, Clerk,
Devil *silent*; *tb* chorus of prisoners; guests and sentries *silent*

After completing *The Makropulos Affair* in 1925,
Janáček appeared to have no more operatic plans.
The next year, 1926, he wrote the *Sinfonietta*, the
piano *Capriccio* and the *Glagolitic Mass*, and made a
brief visit to England. During this trip he mentioned
to Mrs Rosa Newmarch his idea for a violin concerto
called 'The Journeying of a Soul'. He made sketches,
possibly in late 1926, and in 1927 these were revised
to form the overture to his final opera, *From the
House of the Dead*. Why he chose to set Dostoevsky's novel is not known, apart from his general
sympathy towards Russian literature, but his total
absorption with the appalling world depicted in the
novel, and his feeling of urgency to set it, is vividly
documented in his letters to Kamila Stösslová. By
May 1928 the full score of his opera had been copied
out, though he continued to revise the fair copy. Acts
I and II of this copy contain many additions and
corrections by Janáček; Act III was on his desk when
he died in August 1928. If he had followed the pattern
of previous works, Janáček would have submitted the
score to the Brno Theatre that autumn for performance in 1929. In the event of his death, the premiere
was delayed until 1930 and was complicated by the assumption that the work was incomplete, chiefly because of the sparsity of the verbal text and the thinness
of the musical texture. Accordingly the first producer,
Ota Zítek, filled out the words and stage directions,
and Janáček's pupils Osvald Chlubna and Břetislav
Bakala reorchestrated the work, throwing in for
good measure an apotheosis-like 'optimistic' finale.
In this version the work was published and performed. In 1964 Universal Edition reissued the score
with Janáček's original grim ending (the prisoners
returning to their toils) added as an appendix, and
thereafter productions began to respect this ending.
Janáček's original orchestration has taken longer to
establish itself, despite the efforts of Rafael Kubelik
(who revised the score on the basis of Janáček's autograph), Charles Mackerras and (in Brno) Václav
Nosek. The final state of Janáček's opera was not,
however, the autograph score, but the copyists' score
that Janáček supervised, and to which he made many
additions himself.

SYNOPSIS
Act I   The yard in a Siberian prison camp; winter,

early morning. Prisoners come in from the barracks,
wash and eat. An argument breaks out between two
of them. Alexandr Petrovič, a new prisoner and a
'gentleman', arrives and is interrogated by the prison
governor, who orders him to be flogged. The prisoners
tease an eagle with a broken wing, but admire its
defiance in captivity. The governor's sudden return
puts an end to this; he orders them off to work. Half
the prisoners go off to outdoor work, singing as they
go ('Neuvidí oko již těch krajů'). Others remain, including Skuratov. His singing annoys Luka, who picks a
quarrel with him. Skuratov recalls his life in Moscow,
and his previous trade as a cobbler. He breaks into a
wild dance, then collapses. As he sews, Luka recalls
his previous imprisonment, for vagrancy. He tells how
he incited the other prisoners to rebellion and how he
killed the officer who came to quell the disturbance.
He also describes how he was flogged for this. Petrovič, who has meanwhile been similarly punished, is
brought back by the guards, half dead.
Act II   The bank of the river Irtysh; summer, a
year later. The prisoners are doing outdoor work.
Petrovič asks the Tartar boy Aljeja about his family
and offers to teach him to read and write. With the
day's work over, guests appear, a priest gives his
blessing on this feast day, and the prisoners sit down
to eat. Skuratov tells his story – how he murdered the
man whom his sweetheart Lujza was forced to marry.
The prisoners improvise a stage on which they perform
two plays: *Kedril and Don Juan*, and *The Miller's
Beautiful Wife*. Darkness falls after the plays. The
young prisoner goes off with a prostitute. Against a
nostalgic background of offstage folksongs, Petrovič
and Aljeja drink tea. The short prisoner, resenting
this, picks a quarrel and attacks and wounds Aljeja.
Guards rush on to restore order.
Act III   Scene 1: It is towards evening, and Aljeja,
who is recovering in the prison hospital, cries out in
delirious fever. Čekunov waits on him and Petrovič,
to the anger of the dying Luka. Šapkin describes how
the police superintendent interrogated him and almost
pulled his ears off. Night falls (short orchestral interlude). The silence is broken by the sighs of the old
prisoner. Šiškov, encouraged by Čerevin, tells his
story. He was made to marry Akulka (Akulina), a girl
allegedly dishonoured by Filka Morozov, though in
fact still a virgin. When Šiškov found out that she still
loved Filka he killed her. Luka dies as the story ends;
Šiškov recognizes him as Filka. His body is taken
away by the guards. Petrovič is called for. Scene 2: The
governor, drunk, apologizes to Petrovič before the
other prisoners and tells him that he is to be released.
Aljeja comes in from the hospital to say farewell. As
Petrovič leaves, the prisoners release the eagle and
celebrate its freedom as it flies away. The guards
order them off to work.

This is Janáček's most extraordinary opera. The increasingly extreme musical style of Janáček's last years
is here complemented by a dramaturgy in opera that
was decades ahead of its time. Janáček's sound-vision
of the work is perhaps best characterized by the initial
sketches, which are often conceived in terms of voice

parts, trombones and piccolos – and not very much else. For the first time he adopted his practice, used in other genres, of ruling his own stave lines, and thereby encouraging great economy of texture. The harmonic style is similarly stark. As the curtain opens a motif is heard: a short rocking theme in which each chord is enriched with a dissonant semitone. This motif haunts and characterizes the entire first act (in a more purposeful way than in any other Janáček opera); its most searing version is as a ritornello between the lines of the prisoners going off to work, singing of their exile.

From the House of the Dead has almost no story and, except for one tiny part, its cast is exclusively male and made up of a collective, rather than of interacting soloists – a chorus opera from which individual speakers step out to tell their tales and then merge in with the others again. Janáček's libretto here is more his own work than in any other opera except *Osud*. He composed straight from the original Russian, translating as he went along, and made his own choice and ordering of events. While Dostoevsky's autobiographical account of his time in a Siberian prison is arranged chiefly by topic, Janáček, in order to give some idea of time passing, distributed some of the incidents (such as the account of the eagle or Petrovič's dealings with Aljeja) over the whole opera. He was particularly successful in producing emotional climaxes for the ends of the acts: for instance his having Petrovič return from his flogging to end Act I just after Luka has described a similar event in horrifying detail, or the release and celebration of the eagle's freedom paired off with the release of Petrovič (whose arrival and departure provide the slender narrative frame of the piece). An important element in each act is the monologues in which a prisoner describes his crime (Luka in Act I; Skuratov in Act II; Šiškov in Act III) – all miniature dramas with the virtuosic depiction of a cast of characters, and all strongly contrasting in tone and content with one another. Skuratov's lyrical account of his love for a German washerwoman is appropriately placed in the comparatively relaxed Act II, followed by the rough-and-tumble comedy of the two plays, given mostly in mime. The longest monologue of all, Šiškov's, told in the quietness of the prison hospital at night, is emblematic of the whole work: a harrowing tale held together by the recurrence of a transcendentally gentle theme in the same way that Janáček's warm compassion threads through and transforms his grimmest and yet most uplifting opera.

Other operas: *Šárka*, (1888, rev. 1918, 1924–5), 1925; *The Beginning of a Romance (Počátek románu)*, 1894

J.T.

EMMERICH KÁLMÁN
Imre Kálmán; *b* 24 October 1882, Siófok, Hungary;
d 30 October 1953, Paris

After Lehár, Kálmán remains the most popular
Austro-Hungarian composer of the 20th-century (or
'silver') period of operetta. The recent revival of his
works outside Central Europe (where his operettas
have always been firm favourites), particularly in the
English-speaking world, harks back to the 1920s, when
his works were seen everywhere.

Kálmán had a firm classical background and a
middle-class Jewish upbringing. A hand injury in-
terfered with the boy's desire to become a classical
pianist, but he nevertheless continued his studies at
Budapest's Royal Academy of Music. Fellow students
in his composition class under Hans Koessler included
Bartók, Zoltán Kodály and the future operetta composers Albert Szirmai and Victor Jacobi. Kálmán's
earliest compositions were tone poems and songs, but
his cabaret songs were better received, and this encouraged him to write for the operetta stage. In 1908 at
Budapest's Vígszínhaz (Comedy Theatre), Kálmán
had his first operetta success, *Tatárjárás*. This quickly
attracted attention in Vienna and was presented there
several months later as *Ein Herbstmanöver*. Later, as
Autumn Manoeuvres and *The Gay Hussars*, among
other titles, this military operetta marched happily
through Europe and the US.

Theatrical managers journeyed to Budapest to snap
up the next Kálmán operettas. In the United States,
Kálmán's popularity dated from the 1914 production
of *Sari*, a version of *Der Zigeunerprimas* (1912), the
success of which was due in part to one of Kálmán's
most voluptuous waltzes, 'Du, du, du', or 'Love Has
Wings', as it was christened in New York. Shuttling
between Vienna and Budapest during the First World
War, Kálmán witnessed the disintegration of the old
empire, accompanied by the rise of pro-military comedies and revues and outright operetta escapism.

Berlin, Budapest and Hamburg were among many
European cities charmed by *Die Csárdásfürstin* after
the war. Kálmán scored several hits during the 1920s,
particularly *Das Hollandweibchen* (1920), *Die Bajadere*
(1921), *Gräfin Mariza* (1924) and *Die Zirkusprinzessin*
(1926); the last two are still regularly performed today.
Subsequent stage works were somewhat repetitive and
not quite as popular. In the 1930s Kálmán and his

family went into exile, first to Paris and then to the US,
despite the fascist offer of honorary Aryan
citizenship.

Kálmán's works were banned by the Nazis, though
not until after the great success of the film version of
Die Csárdásfürstin (1934). The composer returned to
Paris after the Second World War, at which time his
works instantly regained their popularity in Berlin,
Vienna, and other cities. Following his death in 1953
he was given a state funeral and burial in Vienna's
Zentralfriedhof.

Kálmán's blend of Viennese whipped cream and
Hungarian paprika recalls Johann Strauss II's *Der
Zigeunerbaron*, though Kálmán's inflexions and instrumentation seem more authentically, moodily Magyar.
It was not a question of introducing cimbaloms and
tambourines into stock operetta depictions of Hungary: songs such as 'Komm, Zigany' (from *Gräfin
Mariza*) and the entrance song of *Die Csárdásfürstin*
are virtual Hungarian folksongs. His waltzes are
easily the equal of Lehár's, and in the supremely vital
comedy duets he surpasses his rival in outright catchiness. The choral and ensemble writing is far ahead of
most of his contemporaries, although, despite some
excellent libretti, he did not often attempt to alter
the standard routine of musical numbers.

Die Csárdásfürstin
The Csárdás Princess
Operetta in three acts (2h 30m)
Libretto by Leo Stein and Béla Jenbach
PREMIERES 17 November 1915, Johann Strauss Theater,
Vienna; US: 24 September 1917, New Amsterdam Theater,
New York (as *The Riviera Girl*; libretto by Guy Bolton and
P. G. Wodehouse, with several numbers by Jerome Kern);
UK: 20 May 1921, Prince of Wales Theatre, London (as
The Gypsy Princess; libretto by Arthur Miller and Arthur
Stanley)

Certain critics found the plot of Kálmán's greatest
operetta decidedly unpatriotic. The story was meant,
however, as an exercise in nostalgia for an age when
titled stage-door johnnies were rampant – the most
famous being Emperor Franz Josef himself, who had
a well-known liaison with an actress from the
Burgtheater.

Prince Edwin Ronald is, much to the disapproval
of his family, greatly attached to a cabaret singer,
Sylva. Despite his parents' plan for him to marry
Countess Anastasia, Edwin persuades Sylva to sign a

marriage contract; she is henceforth known as the Csárdás Princess. After many confusions, and the discovery that Edwin's mother was originally a singer, the wedding takes place.

The work's orchestration was interrupted for a period by the death of Kálmán's brother, and a certain melancholy in the score is said to have resulted from the composer's grief. The first night was a sensation; the critical reaction to the music was very favourable – the *Neue Wiener Tageblatt* admired how the composer kept 'one foot in the Hungarian nightclub and the other in the Viennese dance hall that gave birth to the waltz'. Particularly notable are the cabaret turns, the soubrette–buffo duets, and the succession of pensive and then ebullient waltzes.

Other operettas: *Tatárjárás*, 1908, rev. as *Ein Herbstmanöver*, 1909; *Obsitos* (*The Veteran*), 1910, rev. as *Der gute Kamerad*, 1911, rev. as *Gold gab ich für Eisen*, 1914; *Der Zigeunerprimas*, 1912; *The Blue House*, 1914; *Kiskirály* (*Der kleine König*; *The Little King*), 1914; *Zsuzsi kisasszony* (*Miss Susie*), 1915; *Die Faschingsfee*, 1917; *Das Hollandweibchen*, 1920; *Die Bajadere*, 1921; *Gräfin Mariza*, 1924; *Die Zirkusprinzessin*, 1926; *Golden Dawn*, 1927; *Die Herzogin von Chicago*, 1928; *Das Veilchen von Montmartre*, 1930; *Ronny* (film), 1931; *Der Teufelsreiter*, 1932; *Kaiserin Josephine*, 1936; *Marinka*, 1945; *Arizona Lady*, 1954

R.T.

JEROME KERN
Jerome David Kern; *b* 27 January 1885, New York; *d* 11 November 1945, New York

After musical studies in New York and Europe, Jerome Kern managed to establish himself as a writer of songs for interpolation in operettas by others – with such success that he was asked to write complete scores on his own. From 1915 onwards, he established the ground-breaking Princess Theater series of musicals, novel in their intimacy and their determination to relate all songs and comedy directly to the plot. He continued to write larger-scale shows as well, reaching a climax in the uniquely ambitious *Show Boat*.

After this landmark, Kern continued to experiment with new structures in musicals like *The Cat and the Fiddle* and *Music in the Air*, although the most popular of his later works, *Roberta* (remembered largely because of its film), was thoroughly conventional. From 1934 on, Kern lived and worked primarily in Hollywood. In his lifetime he encompassed, and indeed created, a complete change in attitude about what American musical theatre should and could be; but, however much it evolved with the years, Kern's music always remained recognizable by its deceptively simple melodiousness.

Show Boat
Musical play in two acts (2h 45m)
Libretto by Oscar Hammerstein II, based on the novel by Edna Ferber (1926); lyric for 'Bill' partly by P. G. Wodehouse
PREMIERES 27 December 1927, Ziegfeld Theater, New York; UK: 3 May 1928, Drury Lane, London; authors' rev. version: 5 January 1946, Ziegfeld Theater, New York
CAST Magnolia Hawks/Kim Ravenal *s*, Gaylord Ravenal *t*, Julie Laverne *s*, Joe *b*, Queenie *c*, Ellie May Chipley *dancer/ms*, Frank Schultz *dancer/t*; *spoken roles*: Captain Andy Hawks, Parthy Ann Hawks, Steve Baker; other brief speaking and singing roles (mostly from chorus); *satb* chorus (white) of show-boat patrons, gamblers, World's Fair visitors, Trocadero patrons; *satb* chorus (black) of workers, show-boat patrons, Dahomey villagers

The above voice ranges and orchestration apply to the original version; the authors began to make changes almost immediately after the premiere, and created a major revised version for a 1946 revival. Alterations continue to this day, motivated by changes in vocal style (shifting Ravenal and Julie to lower vocal ranges), in propriety (elimination of offensive racial epithets), and theatrical habits (avoidance of 'front scenes' that exist only to cover scene changes). In all versions, the action remains deliberately episodic, encompassing nearly 40 years to emphasize that time passes, people grow and change, and only nature remains constant.

SYNOPSIS
Act I The action begins in 1890. Captain Andy's show boat *Cotton Blossom* is docked in Natchez, Mississippi. His young daughter, Magnolia, falls in love with the gambler Gaylord Ravenal. When the boat's leading actors, Julie and Steve, are forced to leave because Julie is discovered to be part black, Magnolia and Ravenal take their places. Despite the objections of Magnolia's mother, the pair are married.

Act II The Hawks family visit the 1893 Chicago World's Fair. By 1904, Ravenal's gambling is no longer successfully supporting Magnolia and their daughter Kim, and he leaves them in Chicago. Forced to find a job, Magnolia becomes a singer. In 1927, the newly modernized *Cotton Blossom* welcomes Magnolia and Kim, herself a Broadway star, and Ravenal finally returns.

The original score includes extended musical scenes encompassing solos, ensembles, and speaking over music. The songs themselves will always guarantee revivals, including 'Make Believe', 'Ol' Man River', 'Can't Help Lovin' Dat Man', 'You Are Love', 'Why Do I Love You?' and 'Bill'.

Other musicals: *The Red Petticoat*, 1912; *Oh, I Say!*, 1913; *Ninety in the Shade*, 1915; *Nobody Home*, 1915; *Miss Information*, 1915; *Very Good Eddie*, 1915; *Have a Heart*, 1917; *Love o' Mike*, 1917; *Oh, Boy!*, 1917; *Leave It to Jane*, 1917; *Oh, Lady! Lady!*, 1918; *Toot-Toot*, 1918; *Rock-a-bye Baby*, 1918; *Head over Heels*, 1918; *She's a Good Fellow*, 1919; *Zip, Goes a Million*, 1919; *The Night Boat*, 1920; *Sally*, 1920; *The Cabaret Girl*, 1921; *Good Morning, Dearie*, 1921; *The Bunch and Judy*, 1922; *The Beauty Prize*, 1923; *Stepping Stones*, 1923; *Sitting Pretty*, 1924; *Dear Sir*, 1924; *Sunny*, 1925; *The City Chap*, 1925; *Criss-Cross*, 1926; *Blue Eyes*, 1928; *Sweet Adeline*, 1929; *The Cat and the Fiddle*, 1931; *Music in the Air*, 1932; *Roberta*, 1933; *Three Sisters*, 1934; *Gentlemen Unafraid*, 1938, *Very Warm for May*, 1939

J.A.C.

OLIVER KNUSSEN
Stuart Oliver Knussen; *b* 12 June 1952, Glasgow, Scotland

The precocious son of a leading double-bass player, Knussen burst into prominence when at the age of 15 he conducted a performance of his First Symphony by the London Symphony Orchestra. He took some time to recover from this experience, yet his adult music has fulfilled a lot, if not all, of that early promise. Two further symphonies and several shorter chamber-orchestral works (including some with soprano solo) testify to a brilliant feel for movement and sonority, and a bold sense of the voice as a dramatic instrument, all of which is borne out, within their self-imposed limitations, by his two short operas. A pupil of John Lambert and the American composer-conductor Gunther Schuller, Knussen is a perfectionist who takes a long time to finish a piece. His success as conductor and artistic guru, in the UK and in the US, may therefore be bad news for fans of his music.

Where the Wild Things Are
Fantasy opera in one act (40m)
Libretto by Maurice Sendak and the composer, after the children's book by Sendak (1963)
Composed 1979–83
PREMIERES   28 November 1980, Théâtre de la Monnaie, Brussels (inc.); UK: 22 March 1982, Queen Elizabeth Hall, London (inc.; concert); 9 January 1984, Lyttelton Theatre, London; US: 7 June 1984, Avery Fisher Hall, New York (concert), 27 September 1985, St Paul, Minnesota

Knussen describes the work as 'an attempt to revive and develop the fantasy opera', and he acknowledges the influence of Ravel's *L'enfant et les sortilèges*, Musorgsky's 1872 song-cycle *The Nursery* (and *Boris*), and Debussy's 1913 ballet for children *La boîte à joujoux* (they are quoted). Sendak's picture book supplied both an intense, child's-nightmare atmosphere, and strong scenic ideas, and for the Glyndebourne production Sendak himself made designs based on his original drawings.

Max, a naughty little boy in a white wolf suit, is sent to bed by his mother without any supper. He dreams of revenge. His room turns into a forest, and a boat appears, in which he sails away to an island inhabited by Wild Things (dream monsters of a rather sinister amiability). He quells them with a look. They perform a frenzied, galumphing dance (the 'Wild Rumpus'), after which Max sends the Wild Things to bed without any supper. But he is homesick and hungry, and decides to sail home. The monsters wake up and chase him, but he sets sail safely, the sea and forest dissolve, and he is back in his bedroom. A supper tray is waiting for him, still hot.

With only one main character (Max, a high soprano), assorted monsters (with amplification) and a large mixed chamber orchestra, the stage is set for aural fantasy rather than music drama. Knussen not only quotes his favourite children's composers, but also satirizes the funny-noise school of modern music. But his score is typically discriminating and brilliantly composed, if sometimes too loud for the clear audibility of words.

Other opera: *Higglety Pigglety Pop!, or There Must be More to Life*, 1985, rev. 1990

S.W.

ERICH WOLFGANG KORNGOLD
b 29 May 1897, Brno, Czech Republic; *d* 29 November 1957, Hollywood, California, US

One of the last great Romantic composers, Korngold is today remembered principally for his opera *Die tote Stadt* and for his numerous Hollywood film scores.

At the age of ten (through the influence of his father, Julius Korngold, Vienna's foremost music critic) Korngold was introduced to Mahler, who, declaring the boy a genius, sent him to Zemlinsky for composition lessons. When the 13-year-old Korngold's ballet *Der Schneemann* (orchestrated by Zemlinsky) was given a successful premiere at the Vienna Hofoper in 1910, the young composer was hailed as a wunderkind. And by the time his first two operas, *Der Ring des Polykrates* and *Violanta*, were premiered – as a double-bill – in 1916, he had amassed a distinguished band of supporters, among them Richard Strauss, Arthur Nikisch, Carl Flesch and Artur Schnabel, all of whom championed the young composer's works.

Appointed musical director of his regiment, Korngold was able to keep composing throughout the First World War, producing much-acclaimed incidental music to Shakespeare's *Much Ado About Nothing* (1919) and working on what was to be his most successful opera, *Die tote Stadt*. In the 1920s, much to his own enjoyment but to his father's disapproval, Korngold undertook the arrangement of several operetta scores; these included Johann Strauss II's *Eine Nacht in Venedig*, which consequently became one of the composer's most popular works. In the same year (1923) he began work on *Das Wunder der Heliane*. Korngold always considered the opera his masterpiece, but the combination of hostility between Julius Korngold and supporters of Krenek's opera *Jonny spielt auf* and the disappointment of a public who expected a repeat of *Die tote Stadt* resulted in a less than enthusiastic response to the work.

Korngold was warned by his publisher in 1932 that the increase of anti-Semitism would make future productions of his operas inconceivable. He went to Hollywood in 1934, and in the following year he eagerly accepted an invitation from Warner Brothers to write an original score for the film *Captain Blood*, starring Errol Flynn. Over the next 12 years Korngold wrote 18 full-length film scores, which he referred to as 'opera without singing', winning Oscars for *Robin Hood* and *Anthony Adverse*.

Korngold returned to Vienna in 1949 but found that critical opinion no longer applauded his essentially lyrical, neo-Romantic style, favouring instead the austere atonal idiom of Schoenberg and his followers. When his fifth opera, *Die Kathrin*, received its Viennese premiere in 1950 (its world premiere had taken place in Stockholm in 1939), the critics condemned it as old-fashioned, although it enjoyed considerable success with the public. During his last decade Korngold returned to concert music, making certain moves in the direction of a modern style, notably in his Symphony in F♯ (1950). Although he had plans for a sixth opera, based on a story by Franz Grillparzer, he completed only one more stage work, a musical comedy, *Silent Serenade* (1946). His last works included the arrangement, in 1954, of music by Wagner for *Magic Fire*, a film biography of the composer.

Die tote Stadt
The Dead City

Opera in three scenes ('Bilder') (2h 15m)
Libretto by 'Paul Schott' (Julius and Erich Korngold), after Georges Rodenbach's novel *Bruges-la-morte* (1892)
PREMIERES 4 December 1920, Stadttheater, Hamburg, and Opernhaus, Cologne; US: 19 November 1921, Metropolitan, New York
CAST Paul *t*, Marie/Marietta *s*, Frank *bar*, Brigitta *c*, Juliette *s*, Lucienne *ms*, Victorin *t*, Count Albert *t*, Fritz (A Pierrot) *bar*; Gaston *mime*; *satb* chorus of spirits

With this work Korngold reached his operatic zenith. Its portrayal of the psychological damage of excessive mourning struck a chord in the aftermath of the First World War. At the same time its novel structure – much of it is a dream sequence – and memorable music heightened its impact. Korngold played a piano reduction of the score to Puccini, on a visit to Vienna in 1920, and he considered the work 'the strongest hope of new German music'. Productions were rapidly mounted throughout Europe and it was the first German opera to be performed at the Metropolitan in New York after the war.

SYNOPSIS
Act I Although Paul is gloomily obsessed with the memory of his dead wife Marie (he preserves a room full of her memorabilia), he has met the vivacious Marietta and impetuously asks her to visit him. But Marietta leaves when she sees a portrait of Marie and realizes how much she resembles her. Paul is torn by his devotion to Marie and his feelings for Marietta. In a vision Marie bids him 'see and understand'.

Act II takes place in Paul's imagination: a fantastic sequence of scenes portraying the loss of his friends, Marietta being serenaded, rising from a coffin, arguing with Paul, realizing her rival is a dead woman and deciding to exorcize her predecessor's ghost.

Act III The dream continues, with Marietta eventually desecrating Marie's possessions. Goaded beyond endurance, Paul strangles her with a plait of Marie's hair. When he wakes the plait is intact and, though the memory remains, the mourning is over.

Korngold's Expressionistic opera, with its hallucinatory passages, was adventurous but proved to be a great success; it has remained his most popular opera. The music throughout is intense, with Korngold making full use of the vast forces he had scored for. Rather than relying on full-blown melodies to propel

the action, Korngold organizes his music around a number of short motifs representing various people, places or other aspects of the story. Many of these motifs include the interval of a perfect fourth (or its inversion, the perfect fifth), which consequently takes on a pivotal role in the musical structure of the entire opera. There are, nevertheless, identifiable arias – notably 'Glück, das mir verblieb', sung first by the vision of Marie and later repeated by Paul, and the 'Pierrotlied', which is a serenade to Marietta performed by one of her admirers. Both numbers have enjoyed widespread performance independent of the opera.

Other operas: *Der Ring des Polykrates*, 1916; *Violanta*, 1916; *Das Wunder der Heliane*, 1927; *Die Kathrin*, 1939
Musical comedy: *Silent Serenade* (1946); arrangements of works by Johann Strauss II, Offenbach, Leo Fall and Rossini

C.B.

ERNST KRENEK
b 23 August 1900, Vienna; *d* 23 December 1991, Palm Springs, California, US

Krenek was one of the most prolific creative artists of the 20th century. He responded tirelessly to its major cultural transformations and succeeded in staying in tune with most of its significant musical developments. Fascinated by the potential of the genre through most of his long working life, Krenek completed 21 operas – 11 in Europe before the outbreak of the Second World War, and 10 later in America, his new homeland – as well as other music for the stage.

Krenek's compositional output is remarkable for its stylistic range. The operas make unique use of the colourful harmonic and textural palette established by 20th-century modernists – tonality, atonality, serialism, jazz, dance music and electronic sounds. They also embody his changing attitudes to music itself: the aim of opera – its aesthetic function, its role in society, the relationship of its music to extra-musical ideas – became a dominant concern in the critical and musicological work that Krenek pursued alongside composition.

Brought up by music-loving bourgeois parents in the vicinity of the Viennese Volksoper, Krenek was one of the youngest and most famous of the Imperial Academy composition class tutored by Franz Schreker. Following his teacher to Berlin in 1920, he concentrated initially on instrumental works, rapidly developing an abstract and atonal style seemingly at odds with his training, but in line with the latest avant-garde tendencies influenced by Mahler, Bartók and Schoenberg. His interest in the written word, experience as Paul Bekker's assistant at the opera in Kassel and Wiesbaden (1925–7) and contact with recent artistic developments in Paris (which he visited in 1926) prompted him to write dramatic music relevant to contemporary taste. The tendencies of his first three stage works, in which he explored tragedy and comedy in Expressionist and lighter styles, came to fruition spectacularly in his fourth – the neo-classical jazz opera *Jonny spielt auf* (1926). No other work by

Krenek made such an impact on the public, and his instant fame brought sufficient financial security to enable him to compose full-time.

A trio of appealing one-act works in burlesque operetta and fairy-tale style followed in the afterglow of *Jonny*, and a comic work written in the spirit of Karl Kraus about contemporary Vienna, *Kehraus um St Stephan* (1930), deemed too satirical to be performed. But Krenek had already moved on to more serious subjects and the world of grand opera with *Leben des Orest* (1929), which reflected his childhood affection for the classics, as had his earlier setting of Oskar Kokoschka's Expressionist retelling of the myth *Orpheus und Eurydike* (1923). For Krenek himself the most important work of his European years, if not his entire career, was *Karl V* (1933), a philosophically complex and musically innovative work – the first full-length 12-note opera – which offended the authorities and led to enforced exile.

In America, after an initial period of obscurity, Krenek became increasingly sought after as a university teacher and wrote the chamber operas *Tarquin* (1940), *What Price Confidence?* (1945), *Dark Waters* (1950) and *The Belltower* (1957). Twenty years after *Karl V* he returned to large-scale opera. Prompted by renewed European interest in his music and the political conflicts caused by McCarthyism, Krenek revised *Karl V*, and completed two new works (for performance in Germany) inspired by classical antiquity: *Pallas Athene weint* (1955) and *Der goldene Bock* (1964), the latter for the inauguration of Hamburg's new opera house. Krenek's later operas mark a return to his inimitable comic streak and predilection for special effects: *Ausgerechnet und verspielt* (1962), about gambling with computers, which used serial techniques – one of two works written for television – and the satirical parody *Sardakai* (1969). Thereafter Krenek continued to be fascinated by the possibilities of staged vocal music, working on chamber concert pieces (some using electronics) rather than opera.

Krenek explored the possibilities of opera to the full, experimenting with a variety of artistic intentions and expanding its expressive means. His earliest works were candidly zeitoper, but his subsequent stage works were also intended to have a contemporary application, even when set in the past. According to Krenek, all his operas reveal facets of his philosophical preoccupation with various conceptions of freedom. Most of his works are conspicuously absent from today's operatic repertoire.

Jonny spielt auf
Jonny Strikes Up
Opera in two parts (eleven scenes) (2h)
Libretto by the composer
PREMIERES 10 February 1927, Stadttheater, Leipzig; US: 19 January 1929, Metropolitan, New York; UK: 14 November 1984, Grand Theatre, Leeds
CAST Max *t*, Anita *s*, Jonny *bar*, Daniello *bar*, Yvonne *s*, 4 *t*, *bar*, *b*; *satb* chorus of hotel guests, travellers and audience

One of the greatest hits in 20th-century operatic history, this lively and thought-provoking work is a tribute to Krenek's diverse talents. Its capacity to entertain surprised both the musical establishment and the general public in Germany, where it achieved a record number of performances on more than 30 stages in its first season. Acclaimed for both its musico-dramatic dynamism and its kaleidoscopic impression of Central European culture, which lent itself well to avant-garde staging, the opera also triumphed in more than 20 foreign cities over the next two years, although its New York and Parisian receptions were comparatively cool.

SYNOPSIS
Part I   Max, a brooding intellectual composer (possibly a self-portrait), meets Anita, a sensual prima donna, on top of a glacier. Later, at her house in a Central European city, they begin an affair which results in the composition of a new opera. In Paris for its performance, Anita is unfaithful to Max with Daniello, a virtuoso violinist and womanizer. Meanwhile Jonny, a saxophonist performing at the hotel, steals Daniello's valuable violin. Blamed for the theft, Yvonne, a chambermaid, is sacked and returns with Anita to Germany as her maid. Jonny follows in pursuit, having concealed the violin in Anita's banjo case.

Part II   Max yearns for Anita's return, but on learning of her infidelity he seeks solace back in the Alps, where he communes with a singing glacier. The sound of a loudspeaker transmitting a radio broadcast of Anita singing his aria saves him, however, and he decides to seek a new life with her just as Jonny's jazz band comes on the air. A police car-chase ends up in a railway station, where Daniello is crushed by the locomotive arriving in the nick of time to take all the others, led by Jonny tuning up on the violin, to America.

The music is striking in its juxtaposition of the dissonant chromaticism and traditional forms of the Second Viennese School with lyrically tonal Italianate romanticism and a Teutonic brand of jazz constructed from simple melodies, repetitive rhythms and seventh chords. The label 'jazz opera' is slightly misleading, because Krenek's usage is textural rather than organic. The different styles successfully convey Krenek's idea that only an infusion of Jonny's uninhibited and 'primitive' American jazz can revitalize European music and thus its people, to whom such music appeals more than Max's.

Krenek expressed his commitment to bridging the divide between high art and popular culture in this opera's carnivalesque spirit and symbolic associations. More attention has, however, been paid to the opera's superficial aura of the exotic, and implicitly to Krenek's youthful desire for fame, than to any deeper meaning in the work. Yet Jonny's indulgence in the fashionably escapist fantasies of *Amerikanismus* was no less significant or influential than Kurt Weill's didactic brand of zeitoper, which promoted sociopolitical ideas more explicitly.

Other operatic works: *Die Zwingburg*, 1924; *Der Sprung über den Schatten*, 1924; *Orpheus und Eurydike*, (1923),

1926; *Bluff*, (1925); *Der Diktator*, 1928; *Das geheime Königreich*, 1928; *Schwergewicht, oder Die Ehre der Nation*, 1928; *Leben des Orest*, 1930; *Kehraus um St Stephan*, (1930); *Karl V*, (1933), 1938, rev. (1954) 1958; *Cefalo e Procri*, 1934; *Tarquin*, (1940), 1950; *What Price Confidence?*, (1945), 1962; *Dark Waters*, 1951; *Pallas Athene weint*, 1955; *The*

Belltower, 1957; *Ausgerechnet und verspielt*, 1962; *Der goldene Bock*, 1964; *Der Zauberspiegel*, 1968; *Sardakai, oder Das kommt davon (oder Wenn Sardakai auf Reisen geht)*, 1970

C.I.P.

L

ÉDOUARD LALO

Édouard-Victor-Antoine Lalo; *b* 27 January 1823, Lille,
France; *d* 22 April 1892, Paris

Lalo's principal work was in the field of orchestral and
chamber music. He is now best known for his *Symphonie espagnole* for violin and orchestra (1874), but he
always aspired to success in opera and would probably
have composed more if his work had been staged
earlier. Trained at the conservatories of Lille and
Paris, his career began as a violinist and violist. He
composed piano trios, a quartet and some romances,
but did not venture into opera until 1866, when in
response to an opera competition for the Théâtre
Lyrique, he composed *Fiesque*, to a libretto by Charles
Beauquier based on Johann Christoph Friedrich von
Schiller's *Fiesko*. Despite coming third and being published, it was never staged. Lalo abandoned this lively
and melodious work in the 1880s, when he reused its
material in, for example, the G minor Symphony and
the *Divertissement*. In the mid-1870s, at the height of
his powers, he composed *Le roi d'Ys*, although this
had to wait until 1888 for production. By this time
Lalo's invention had waned and he was unable to
respond to its great success. In 1891 he began a third
opera, *La jacquerie*, concerning a 14th-century revolt,
but finished only the first act – and that was almost
entirely drawn from *Fiesque*. It was completed after
the composer's death by Arthur Coquard and staged
in Monte Carlo in 1895.

Le roi d'Ys

The King of Ys
Opera in three acts (1h 45m)
Libretto by Édouard Blau, after the legend of Ys
Composed 1875, rev. 1886
PREMIERES 7 May 1888, Opéra-Comique, Paris; US:
23 January 1890, French Opera House, New Orleans;
UK: 17 July 1901, Covent Garden, London
CAST Margared *s*, Rozenn *s*, Mylio *t*, Karnac *bar*, Le roi
d'Ys (The King of Ys) *b*, St Corentin *b*, Jahel *bar; satb*
chorus of citizens of Ys, warriors of Karnac

Despite its delayed premiere, *Le roi d'Ys* was a long-
lasting success, owing to its heroic Breton story and
the vigour of its style; it has retained a place in the
repertoire.

SYNOPSIS

Act I The people of Ys are celebrating the peace
brought about by the betrothal of the king's daughter
Margared to Karnac, their former enemy. Margared
tells her sister Rozenn that she loves another man;
she repudiates Karnac, who swears revenge on Ys.
Rozenn is in love with Mylio, who promises to defend
the city and its people.

Act II Margared is jealous of Rozenn; the stranger
she loves is Mylio. The King tells Rozenn she may
marry Mylio if he defeats Karnac. When Mylio is
successful, Margared plots with Karnac to destroy the
city by opening the floodgates that protect it from the
sea.

Act III Mylio and Rozenn are happily married.
Mylio kills Karnac, but it is too late; as the flood
rises, Margared, full of remorse, hurls herself into the
waves. The water subsides.

Planned for the Opéra rather then the Opéra-
Comique, *Le roi d'Ys* contains what Lalo claimed to
be genuine Breton folksongs, reflecting the Wagner-
inspired vogue for subjects drawing on a legendary
Celtic past. Although essentially through-composed,
fine individual arias and duets stand out. The best
known of these is Mylio's aubade 'Vainement, ma
bien aimée' in Act III. The opera requires grand
staging and a strong chorus, whose function is to
emphasize the emotions of the principal characters;
the orchestral and vocal style is impressively fresh and
invigorating.

Other operas: *Fiesque*, (1868); *La jacquerie*, 1895

H.M.

FRANZ LEHÁR

b 30 April 1870, Komáron, Hungary *d* 24 October 1948,
Bad Ischl, Austria

Lehár, the instigator and leading composer of 20th-
century Viennese operetta, was of Czech and Hungarian descent. The son of a military band-master, he
studied at the Prague Conservatory with Josef
Bohuslav Foerster, and briefly with Zdeněk Fibich
and Dvořák, excelling at the violin. He played in his
father's band (alongside the Austrian operetta com-

poser Leo Fall) and later led his own ensembles for infantry regiments stationed in Trieste, Budapest and finally Vienna. During this period his grand 'Russian' opera *Kukuška* (1896) was unsuccessfully produced in Leipzig.

The popularity of his waltz *Gold und Silber* (1902) persuaded Lehár to leave the world of army bands and once again to try the theatre. That same year, two of his operettas were performed at Vienna's two leading operetta theatres, *Wiener Frauen* (Theater an der Wien) and *Der Rastelbinder* (Carltheater), the latter making the more lasting impression with its provincial characters and a sensual, languorous love duet in Act II. After two less successful works, Lehár hit the jackpot in 1905 with one of the most popular operettas ever written, *Die lustige Witwe*.

Several undistinguished works followed *Die lustige Witwe*, until a series of Viennese and international triumphs began with *Der Graf von Luxemburg* (another Parisian romantic frolic, 1909), *Zigeunerliebe* (1910) and *Eva* (again set in Paris, but dealing with industrial relations, 1911). Works written around the First World War period proved less durable, as new rival composers were garnering many more performances.

In the mid-1920s Lehár's fortunes began to rise again, thanks to his association with the Austrian tenor Richard Tauber. The singer had created a sensation taking over a leading part in *Frasquita* (1922) in Vienna, and later appeared in the Berlin premiere of *Paganini* (1925), the first of five new or refashioned romantic operettas written expressly for him. The contemporary charm and cohesive elegance of *Die lustige Witwe* gave way to quasi-historical exoticism. The romantic music instantly brought Puccini to mind, while the subsidiary comic numbers were written in a more vernacular style using modern dance rhythms that nevertheless sounded distinctively Lehárian. Though Tauber looked not remotely like Paganini or Goethe (in *Friederike*, 1928), the force of his voice and persona enraptured Europe. The climax of this partnership was reached with *Das Land des Lächelns* (1929).

The final original work was in fact an operetta transmogrified into an opera, *Guiditta* (1934). During the 1930s the composer wrote several film scores. With a Jewish wife, Lehár remained in retirement in Austria after 1938. His works were still performed (the non-Aryan librettists' names were omitted from the programmes); royalties continued to pour in, and the composer was occasionally feted by the Nazis – Hitler's favourite operetta was reputedly *Die lustige Witwe*.

Die lustige Witwe

The Merry Widow

Operetta in three acts (2h 30m)

Libretto by Viktor Léon and Leo Stein, adapted from the play *L'attaché d'ambassade* by Henri Meilhac (1861) in the German translation (*Der Gesandschafts-Attaché*, 1862) by Alexander Bergen

PREMIERES 30 December 1905, Theater an der Wien, Vienna; UK: 8 June 1907, Daly's Theatre, London; US: 21 October 1907, New Amsterdam Theater, New York

CAST Baron Zeta *t*, Count Danilo Danilowitsch *t*, Camille de Rosillon *t*, Vicomte Cascada *t*, Raoul de Saint-Brioche *t*, Bogdanowitsch *bar*, Kromow *t*, Pritschitsch *bar*, Njegus *bar*, Hanna Glawari *s*, Valencienne *soubrette*, Sylviane *s*, Olga *s*, Praskowia *ms*, 6 *s*; *satb* chorus of Parisians and Pontevedrians, *grisettes*, partygoers, dancers, etc.

No operetta conjures up Habsburg Vienna, turn-of-the-century Paris or the glittering Edwardian era of eternal waltzes quite like *The Merry Widow*. Lehár's rapturous score – which he was never to equal – was his ticket to immortality and enormous profits; it created an international furore the like of which had not been seen since Sullivan's *HMS Pinafore* or *The Mikado* 20 years before.

SYNOPSIS

Act I Baron Zeta, the Pontevedrian ambassador to Paris, anxiously awaits the fabulously wealthy Hanna Glawari, who has recently been widowed. To avoid her millions leaving Pontevedro, she must be prevented from marrying a foreigner. Hanna encounters the playboy Danilo; they once had an affair, but now that she is wealthy he treats her coolly. Baron Zeta, oblivious of his own wife Valencienne's carrying on with Camille, informs Danilo that he must marry Hanna for the sake of his country. In the ballroom, Hanna elects to dance with Danilo, despite his thoroughly obnoxious behaviour.

Act II Hanna gives a party at her home with everyone in their national costumes. She tells her guests a story about a Vilja, a maid of the woods. Danilo and the men remark on the difficulties of handling women, but Danilo is falling in love again. Camille entices Valencienne into a pavilion in the garden. Zeta, looking through the keyhole, is surprised to see not his wife, but Hanna. She has taken Valencienne's place as much to save her friend as to tease Danilo, who angrily leaves.

Act III Hanna explains the incident in the pavilion to Danilo, and they are drawn together by a sensuous waltz. Zeta's marital problems are settled, and, when Hanna announces that she will lose her money on marriage, Danilo asks for her hand. She agrees, and then explains that the millions will pass to her husband.

Possibly the most frequently performed operetta of all time, the work offers a succession of brilliant scenes and superb finales, punctuated by operetta standards such as, in Act I, the entrance songs for both Hanna ('Bitte, meine Herr'n') and Danilo ('Da geh' ich zu Maxim'), in Act II the 'Vilja' song, and the 'Weiber' march, and in the last act the famous waltz ('Lippen schweigen'). Just as glitteringly striking and memorable are the duets for Camille and Valencienne – including his passionate pavilion invitation in Act II, Hanna's description of life 'in the Parisian style' in the Act II finale, and the potent 'Ballsirenen' waltz in the Act I finale.

For the London production Lehár added two new numbers, and, later, a long, formal overture – the original short introduction is infinitely more satisfying in setting the scene. It is generally forgotten today that Lehár's score was considered quite bold and even risqué by some. The silver age of Viennese operetta is said to have begun with *Die lustige Witwe*. Love affairs could become comparatively more realistic, and the orchestra far more lush in support. Lehár had brought operetta into the 20th century.

Das Land des Lächelns
The Land of Smiles
Romantic operetta in three acts (2h 15m)
Libretto by Ludwig Herzer and Fritz Beda-Löhner, after Viktor Léon's libretto to the earlier *Die gelbe Jacke* (1923)
PREMIERES 10 October 1929, Metropoltheater, Berlin; UK: 8 May 1931, Drury Lane, London; US: 5 September 1946, Shubert Theater, New York (as *Yours is My Heart*)

With *Das Land des Lächelns* Tauber's fame and Lehár's commercial success reached their zenith. Herzer and Löhner greatly improved Léon's libretto, their most important changes being the replacement of the original happy ending with a tragic renunciation by the lovers, and the addition of the work's most famous number, 'Dein ist mein ganzes Herz'.

An aristocratic Viennese girl, Lisa, falls in love with the Chinese prince Sou-Chong, but is unable to adapt to the demands made on her in the prince's own country, where all passions are concealed behind enigmatic, disciplined smiles.

In Lehár's opulent score the worlds of Puccini and Richard Strauss meet that of operetta, with *chinoiserie* giving way to melancholy lyricism. Among the other numbers, Sou-Chong's 'Immer nur lächeln' and 'Von Apfelblüten einen Kranz' are particularly vocally demanding, while the duets include 'Bei einem Tee en deux' and the impassioned 'Wer hat die Liebe uns ins Herz gesenkt'. In 1930 alone – the year of the composer's 60th birthday – the work received some 200 productions.

Other operettas: *Fräulein Leutnant*, 1901; *Arabella, die Kubanerin* (inc., 1901); *Das Club-Baby* (inc., 1901); *Wiener Frauen*, 1902; *Der Rastelbinder*, 1902; *Der Göttergatte*, 1904; *Die Juxheirat*, 1904; *Der Schlüssel zum Paradies*, 1906; *Peter und Paul reisen ins Schlaraffenland*, 1906; *Mitislaw der Moderne*, 1907; *Der Mann mit den drei Frauen*, 1908; *Das Fürstenkind*, 1909; *Der Graf von Luxemburg*, 1909; *Zigeunerliebe*, 1910; *Die Spieluhr*, 1911; *Eva*, 1911; *Rosenstock und Edelweiss*, 1912; *Die ideale Gattin* (rev. of *Der Göttergatte*), 1913; *Endlich allein*, 1914; *Der Sterngucker*, 1916; *A pacsirta* (*Wo die Lerche singt*), 1918; *Die blaue Mazur*, 1920; *Die Tangokönigin* (second rev. of *Der Göttergatte*), 1921; *Frühling*, 1922; *La danza delle libellule*, 1922; *Frasquita*, 1922; *Die gelbe Jacke*, 1923; *Cloclo*, 1924; *Paganini*, 1925; *Gigolette* (rev. of *Der Sterngucker* and *La danza delle libellule*), 1926: *Der Zarewitsch*, 1927; *Friederike*, 1928; *Frühlingsmädel* (rev. of *Der Sterngucker* and *Frühling*), 1928; *Schön ist die Welt* (rev. of *Endlich allein*), 1930; *Der Fürst der Berge* (rev. of *Das Fürstenkind*), 1932; *Giuditta*, 1934
Operas: *Der Kürassier* (inc., 1892); *Rodrigo* (inc., 1893); *Kukuška*, 1896, rev. as *Tatjana*, 1905; *Garbonciás diák* (rev. of *Zigeunerliebe*), 1943

R.T.

RUGGERO LEONCAVALLO
b 23 April 1857, Naples; *d* 9 August 1919, Montecatini, Italy

Leoncavallo, the Italian composer and librettist, was admitted to the Naples Conservatory in 1866, where his principal teachers were Beniamino Cesi and Lauro Rossi. Graduating ten years later, he moved to Bologna, where he was much impressed by the poet Giosuè Carducci's lectures. These had a strong influence on his literary interests, and prompted the completion of a libretto entitled *Chatterton*, which he had begun as a student and which he now also set to music. He also fell under the spell of Wagner and planned to write a trilogy – both text and music – on the Italian Renaissance. Unable to interest a publisher in his proposals, he embarked on a journey to Egypt (1882) and later to Paris, supporting himself as an accompanist for *café-concerts*. In the French capital in 1888, he made friends with the baritone Victor Maurel (the original Iago in Verdi's *Otello*), who persuaded the publisher Giulio Ricordi to take on the composer.

Ricordi was more impressed with Leoncavallo's abilities as a theatre poet than with his music, taking a dim view of *I Medici*, the only part of the proposed trilogy Leoncavallo had completed. In 1889 Leoncavallo worked with Puccini on the text for *Manon Lescaut*, but the collaboration lasted only briefly, owing to differences of temperament. When Ricordi definitely refused *I Medici*, Leoncavallo, desperate to establish himself, quickly composed *Pagliacci*, modelling his work on Mascagni's *Cavalleria rusticana*, and exploiting the current trend for verismo opera. The successful premiere of *Pagliacci* in 1892, with Maurel as Tonio and with Arturo Toscanini conducting, made the composer famous overnight. *Pagliacci* became the almost inseparable companion of *Cavalleria* as a double-bill after the Metropolitan Opera House, New York, staged the combination in December 1893.

Fame, however, did not ensure a trouble-free future for the composer. Like *Pagliacci*, *I Medici* was taken up by Ricordi's rival publishing house, Sonzogno, who, hoping to capitalize on *Pagliacci*'s recent success, quickly arranged a performance. But the pretentious panorama of the Renaissance failed to measure up to expectations, despite the composer's unabashed promotion of it, and the opera was deemed a failure. Daunted by this setback, Leoncavallo wisely put aside the remainder of his projected *Crepusculum* trilogy (the title was a distant nod in the direction of *Götterdämmerung*). When Puccini began work on *La bohème*, Leoncavallo simultaneously embarked on the same subject, determined to better his rival with his memories of the Parisian atmosphere he had absorbed in his years of vagabondage. Leoncavallo's score, which was premiered some 15 months after Puccini's, never proved a serious threat, however, despite some beguiling local colour and vocally grateful moments.

Despite earlier failure, *I Medici* was premiered in Berlin in 1894; Kaiser Wilhelm II was greatly impressed and commissioned Leoncavallo to write an opera extolling the Hohenzollerns, placing the Court Opera at his disposal. Leoncavallo worked on the opera for ten years and – he wrote to Caruso – believed it to be his masterpiece. He was sadly mistaken: despite its illustrious patron, *Der Roland von Berlin* (1904) utterly failed to hold its own.

In 1906 Leoncavallo toured the United States and Canada, imitating Mascagni's visit four years earlier, and here he first turned his hand to operetta, a genre that would periodically engage him for the rest of his life.

Leoncavallo's natural aptitude for lighter music, which had already been demonstrated in his song 'Mattinata' (one of the earliest compositions written for the gramophone, it was recorded by Caruso accompanied by Leoncavallo in 1904), was rather at odds with his intense desire to be taken seriously as a composer. Hoping to repeat the now distant success of *Pagliacci*, Leoncavallo set about the composition of *Tormenta*, based on a melodramatic play by Belvederi, set in Sardinia. The First World War led to its abandonment, and Leoncavallo completed no further operas. His final operatic project, a grand opera *Edipo Re* to a libretto by Giovacchino Forzano, was completed by G. Pennacchio and premiered 17 months after Leoncavallo's death. It made only a temporary splash – and that thanks to Titta Ruffo in the title role.

Pagliacci
Clowns

Dramma in two acts and a prologue (1h)
Libretto by the composer
PREMIERES 21 May 1892, Teatro Dal Verme, Milan; UK: 19 May 1893, Covent Garden, London; US: 15 June 1893, Grand Opera House, New York
CAST Canio *t*, Nedda *s*, Tonio *bar*, Silvio *bar*, Beppe *t*; *satb* chorus of villagers

The only one of Leoncavallo's twelve operas and ten operettas to enter the permanent repertoire, *Pagliacci*, along with its almost inseparable sidekick, Mascagni's *Cavalleria rusticana*, best conveys the ethos of verismo, the realistic representation of lower-class characters in the context of 'a bleeding slice of life', to quote Tonio in the prologue of *Pagliacci* – itself a manifesto of the naturalistic aesthetic. Drawing on his memories of a *crime passionel* adjudicated by his magistrate father, Leoncavallo combined the story of a jealous husband and his unfaithful wife with a performance by a *commedia dell'arte* troupe, attaining a climax when real-life emotion supplants the play-acting.

SYNOPSIS
Prologue Tonio alerts the audience that they are to see a drama taken from real life.

Act I On the feast day of the Assumption, Calabrian villagers gather to greet a company of strolling players, and Canio, the troupe's leader, invites them to attend the performance. When one of the bystanders makes a teasing reference to the desirability of Nedda, Canio's wife, he brushes the taunt aside, but not without revealing his jealous nature ('Un tal

gioco'). When the others go off, Nedda stays behind, half afraid that Canio is suspicious of her, but envying the birds their freedom to come and go as they please ('Stridono lassù'). The deformed Tonio, a member of the company, appears and pays clumsy court to Nedda, but she repulses him with a whip, leaving him vengeful. Her lover Silvio appears, and they plan a rendezvous for later that evening ('Decidi il mio destin'). The latter part of their conversation is overheard by Tonio, who fetches Canio. Barely restrained by Beppe from assaulting his wife on the spot, Canio demands to know her lover's name, but Nedda will not tell him. Canio starts to paint his face and put on his clown's costume, although his heart is breaking ('Vesti la giubba').

Act II After a brief prelude (originally intended as an intermezzo), the audience gathers for the performance. First Harlequin (Beppe) serenades his beloved Colombine (Nedda). Next, with heavy irony, Taddeo (Tonio) declares his love for the 'pure' Colombine, but Harlequin arrives and leads him off by the ear. He returns to enjoy a festive supper with Colombine, but soon they are interrupted by Taddeo's announcement that her husband Pagliaccio (Canio) is approaching. Harlequin leaves by the window, but Pagliaccio enters in time to hear Colombine/Nedda repeating the same promise of an assignation that he heard her use in Act I. With difficulty Canio tries to sustain his comic role, but when Colombine refuses to divulge her lover's name he can no longer control himself ('No, Pagliaccio non son!'). When Colombine/Nedda continues to defy him, he stabs her in reality, and with her last breath she utters Silvio's name. Silvio, who has been in the audience, rushes to the stage, but, too late to save Nedda, he becomes Canio's second victim. Hoarsely, Canio announces 'La commedia è finita!' (Originally this line was intended for Tonio, but at least since the time of Fernando De Lucia and Caruso it has usually been spoken by the tenor.)

The score contains a wide variety of music, from Tonio's melodic prologue (which is in effect the mid-section of the Act I prelude), to Nedda's languorous ballatella 'Stridono lassù' (Act I) and her sensuous duet with Silvio, to Canio's two impassioned arias: 'Vesti la giubba' and 'No, Pagliaccio non son!' The dainty music of the harlequinade (the play within the play in Act II) adds a further fillip to the score, which also manifests traces of Leoncavallo's affection for Wagner in the form of a number of symbolic recurring themes. Although each act is cast as a continuous musical entity, the solos and duets usually end in full cadences, allowing for the applause that Leoncavallo knew was a vital ingredient of a success.

La bohème
Commedia lirica in four acts (2h 15m)
Libretto by the composer, after Henri Murger's *Scènes de la vie de bohème* (1845–9) and his play (with Théodore Barrière) *La vie de bohème* (1849)
Composed 1895–6; rev. 1913
PREMIERES 6 May 1897, La Fenice, Venice; 14 April 1913, Teatro Massimo, Palermo (rev. version in three acts, as *Mimì Pinson, scene della vita di bohème*, later discarded);

US: 31 January 1960, Columbia University, New York;
UK: 12 May 1970, Camden Town Hall, London
CAST Mimì *s*, Musetta *ms*, Marcello *t*, Rodolfo *bar*,
Schaunard *bar*, Colline *bar*, Barbemuche *b*, Gaudenzio *t*,
Count Paolo *bar*, Durand *t*, Man on First Floor *t*, Lout *t*,
Eufemia *ms*; *satb* chorus of students, neighbours, café
patrons, waiters, salesmen

Although there are inevitable similarities to Puccini's
better-known treatment of this subject, Leoncavallo's
differs in some significant ways. Instead of, like
Puccini, interweaving scenes of comedy and pathos,
Leoncavallo restricts the comedy to his first two acts,
while the last two are darkly tragic. Furthermore,
he makes Marcello the leading tenor role, assigning
Rodolfo the baritone register and Musetta the
mezzo-soprano.

SYNOPSIS
Act I Christmas Eve. At the Café Momus, the proprietor, Gaudenzio, grumbles at the bohemians' habit
of not paying their bills, but Schaunard assures him
tonight will be different. The friends assemble; Mimì
(already a friend of the group) and Eufemia bring
along Musetta, who is attracted to Marcello. Their
meal complete, they as usual find they cannot pay.
Schaunard challenges Gaudenzio to a game of billiards, wins, and thereby wipes out their debt.
Act II The following April. Musetta has been
evicted from her apartment, her wealthy lover unhappy with the attention she has been paying
Marcello. The friends gather and stage a party,
replete with musical parodies. Tempted by the proposals of Count Paolo, Mimì decides to leave
Rodolfo. The neighbours complain about the brou-
haha below.
Act III October. In their garret, Marcello and
Schaunard decide they must earn money. Musetta,
tired of poverty, decides to leave Marcello and in his
absence writes him a farewell note. Mimì returns to be
reconciled with Rodolfo. He rejects her, and Marcello,
convinced she has turned Musetta away from him, is
furious with her.
Act IV Christmas Eve, the next year. As the
friends are remembering the previous Christmas Eve,
the consumptive Mimì, prematurely turned out of
hospital, returns, her strength failing. When Musetta
appears, she pawns her jewels to get help for Mimì,
but it is too late and Mimì dies.

When Leoncavallo entered the contest with Puccini
for *La bohème* (having once offered him his text,
which was refused), he had no idea how hugely successful his rival's opera would prove. Unfairly
eclipsed, without being the equal of Puccini's score,
Leoncavallo's can boast much attractive light
music in the first two acts and several strong ariosi
in the final two. In a pathetic attempt to compete
with Puccini, Leoncavallo revised his score in 1913,
making Rodolfo a tenor role, but this tinkering failed
to give the work new life and the revision (which was
renamed to distinguish it from its rival) was
discarded.

Other operas: *Chatterton*, (1876), rev. 1896, 1905; *Songe
d'une nuit d'été*, 1889 (private performance); *I Medici* (inc.),
1893; *Zazà*, 1900; *Der Roland von Berlin*, 1904; *Maià*,
(1908), 1910; *Gli zingari*, 1912 ; *Ave Maria*, (abandoned
1915); *Tormenta* (inc.); *Prometeo*, (n.d.)
Operettas: *La jeunesse de Figaro*, 1906; *Malbrouck*, 1910;
La reginetta delle rose, 1912 ; *Are you there?*, 1913; *La
candidata*, 1915; *Goffredo Mameli*, 1916; *Prestami tua moglie*,
1916; *A chi la giarrettiera?*, 1919; *Edipo Re* (inc. 1919;
completed by G. Pennacchio), 1920; *Il primo bacio*, 1923;
La maschera nuda (inc.; completed Salvatore Allegra), 1925

W.A.

GYÖRGY LIGETI

György Sándor Ligeti; *b* 28 May 1923, Tîrnăveni, Romania
(formerly Diciosânmartin [or Dicsöszentmárton],
Transylvania)

Ligeti came late not only to opera but also to the
music he really wanted to write. He began his musical
life in Hungary, where the political climate did not
allow experiment. In 1956 he moved to Vienna and
quickly became involved with Western Europe's most
avant-garde circles, writing electronic music at the
WDR studios in Cologne and producing in the 1960s
a stream of works very different from the total serialism then in vogue. With the orchestral piece *Atmos-
phères* (1961) and the organ composition *Volumina*
(1961–2, rev. 1966) Ligeti created huge swirling clouds
of sound by writing an immensely complex web of
closely packed polyphony. He went on to explore this
further in his celebrated *Requiem* (1963–5, used in the
soundtrack of the film *2001*), *Lontano* (1967, for orchestra), *Melodien* (1971, for chamber orchestra) and
the Double Concerto for flute, oboe and orchestra
(1972).

His operatic music belongs to a different line of
thinking – a joking, perhaps cynical view of the world
that produced the *Poème symphonique* (1962) for 100
metronomes set at different tempi, which lasts as long
as it takes for them all to run down, *Continuum* for
harpsichord (1968), where different metres are superimposed so that the music is in a perpetual rhythmic and
colouristic flux determined by pitch changes, and
Clocks and Clouds for female chorus and orchestra
(1972–3), where the sound of metronomes becomes
gradually less distinct.

His two dramatic entertainments from the early
1960s, *Aventures* and *Nouvelles aventures*, are like late
manifestations of Dadaism, for though the texts are
meaningless phonetics, when allied to the music they
make a disconcerting blend of the playful and the
menacing.

After their success Ligeti wanted to write a larger-
scale 'imaginary opera' to a meaningless text, but
neither that idea nor his next operatic project, a version of the Oedipus myth, came to anything, though
they amalgamated to some extent in the opera he did
eventually write, *Le grand macabre*, a surrealist opera
about death, conceived as a farce.

Le grand macabre

Opera in two acts (four scenes) (2h)
Libretto by the composer and Michael K. J. A. Meschke,
freely adapted from the farce *La balade du grand macabre*
(1934) by Michel de Ghelderode
PREMIERES   12 April 1978, Royal Opera, Stockholm;
UK: 2 December 1982, Coliseum, London
CAST   Piet the Pot *high buffo t*, Miranda (originally
Clitonia) *s*, Armando (originally Spermando) *ms*, Nekrotzar
bar, Astradamors *b*, Mescalina *dramatic ms*, Venus *high s*,
White Minister *spoken role*, Black Minister *spoken role*,
Prince Go-Go *ct*, Chief of the Secret Police *coloratura s*,
Ruffiak, Schabiak and Schabernak 3 *bar*; *satb* chorus of
people of Breughelland; offstage: *satb* chorus of the spirits;
echo of Venus *sa* chorus; boys' chorus; extras: men of the
secret police, executioners, pages and servants at the court
of Prince Go-Go, Nekrotzar's infernal entourage

The opera was commissioned by the Stockholm Royal
Opera in 1965 but took 13 years to be written and
reach the stage. It was an immediate success and was
quickly taken up by European opera houses. The plot
is surreal, though its essence is that the only certainty
of life is that it will end in death and so one might as
well eat, drink and be merry. The setting is also
surreal, a place ruled over by an obese boy prince and
populated by, among others, a transvestite visionary
astronomer with a sadistic and sexually enterprising
wife and a chief of police who is a manic coloratura
soprano. It is called Breughelland, but it could perhaps
be reality.

SYNOPSIS

Act I   Scene 1: After a palindromic prelude for car
horns, one of the citizens of Breughelland, the alcoholic Piet the Pot, sings the praises of his homeland
while Miranda and Armando look for somewhere to
make love; a mysterious figure, Nekrotzar, the figure
of death (the *grand macabre* himself), announces that
the end of the world will occur at midnight. He forces
Piet to help him in his task of world destruction.
Scene 2: The astronomer Astradamors has to feign
death to escape his appalling wife Mescalina's voracious and painfully unorthodox sexual appetites; she
revives him by dropping a spider on him. Through his
telescope he sees a fast-approaching comet and other
signs of Armageddon, while his wife, in a drunken
stupor, implores Venus to send her a man who will
satisfy her desires. Nekrotzar is the man, and, while
Piet and her husband look on, Mescalina dies in ecstasy. A satisfied Nekrotzar takes Piet off to destroy
the palace, leaving a happy Astradamors.

Act II   Scene 3: The boy prince Go-Go tries to chair
a meeting between his two ministers but the absurdities
of politics are beyond him so they play schoolboy
games, understood by everyone, until the secret police
burst in. They are all dressed as birds, and their chief
is a dazzling coloratura soprano. She tells the prince
that the people are in revolt and are marching on the
palace. He pacifies the people but they are all thrown
into a panic when Nekrotzar threatens impending
doom. Though drunk, before he passes out he utters
the words that will bring the world to an end. Scene 4:
No one is really sure whether the end of the world has
actually happened. Nekrotzar seems to think it has

not, or if it has there are too many survivors. He tries
to escape but is chased by the voracious Mescalina,
who emerges from a hearse and remembers him well.
He realizes his mission is a failure and dissolves. The
two lovers emerge from their love nest, oblivious of
the great events that have passed. Everyone realizes
the moral: if death is coming for you, you cannot
escape it, so do not fear it, ignore it.

The music is more in the quick-cutting comic style of
Aventures than the almost static cloudlike sound of
works such as *Lontano*. There are many direct references to other works as well as a feeling that the
frequently tongue-in-cheek characterization is rooted
in the past. The music of the two lovers, Miranda and
Amando, has a Monteverdian richness as entwined as
their bodies, and the opera ends with a baroque conceit, a grand passacaglia. Nekrotzar's entrance in Act
II is preceded by the opera's most obvious quotation
and transformation, the 'Prometheus' theme from the
finale of Beethoven's 'Eroica' Symphony.

Other operatic work: *Aventures/Nouvelles aventures*, 1966

C.B.

ANDREW LLOYD WEBBER
b 22 March 1948, London

Andrew Lloyd Webber was only 23 when *Jesus Christ
Superstar* brought him worldwide acclaim, but his
success was the natural consequence of his life to that
date. Born into a family preoccupied with musical
talent, his childhood grounding was in classical and
church music, and his youth and maturity coincided
with the golden age of pop. By investing the latter
with the authority of the former, he and Tim Rice
created three works, *Joseph and the Amazing Techni-
color Dreamcoat*, *Jesus Christ Superstar* and *Evita*,
that survived the era of popular music in which they
were written.
   Lloyd Webber's work since has generally been enormously successful in commercial terms but has escaped
the full-blooded approbation of the critics. Of these
later works, *Cats* (1981) suffers least from the imbal-
ance of content and spectacle, while *Starlight Express*
(1983) was privately considered extravagant by the
composer. *Aspects of Love* marked a change of direction to the more traditional chamber opera.
   At his worst, Lloyd Webber embodies the subjugation of dramatic and narrative content to marketing
strategies aimed at the 'global' consumer. At his best,
he is an accomplished tunesmith with a genuinely
opportunist ear, and a talent for synthesis that is
often unfairly ignored in assessments of his work.

Joseph and the Amazing Technicolor Dreamcoat

Cantata for children in two parts (original version: 15m;
rev. version: 2h)
Libretto by Tim Rice, after the biblical story (Genesis
30–50)

Composed 1968; expanded and rev. 1972, 1973, 1991
PREMIERES 1 March 1968, Colet Court School, London
(concert); 21 August 1972, Edinburgh (stage); US:
22 December 1976, Brooklyn Academy of Music, New
York; 1991 version: 12 June 1991, Palladium, London

This cantata was originally commissioned for the choir
of Colet Court School, London, to sing at an end-of-
term concert. The Old Testament tale of Joseph and
his envious brothers is given a fresh, witty telling and
is conspicuous for its adroit parodies of popular music.
Although it was subsequently expanded for the
theatre, the main significance of the piece is as an
established part of the school-music repertoire throughout the Christian world.

Jesus Christ Superstar

Rock opera in two acts (1h 30m)
Libretto by Tim Rice
PREMIERES 15 May 1971, Kansas City (concert);
12 October 1971, Mark Hellinger Theater, New York;
UK: 9 August 1972, Palace Theatre, London

Jesus Christ Superstar was composed and recorded
as an oratorio, and its release in America catapulted
the youthful composer and librettist to instant celebrity and considerable wealth. The application of the
profane four-square rhythms of pop to the sacred
subject of the Passion aroused great religious controversy to match the polarized critical responses to the
work.

The early theatre productions of *Jesus Christ Superstar* ranged from the spectacularly vulgar to the
chastely formal, but, like *Joseph*, the piece has now
become an established part of school and church
repertories. The composer's precocious facility for
memorable light melodies and penchant for romantic
orchestration stand out against the rather coarse and
dated hard-rock elements of the piece.

Evita

Opera in two parts (2h 15m)
Libretto by Tim Rice
PREMIERES 21 June 1978, Prince Edward Theatre,
London; US: 8 May 1979, Dorothy Chandler Pavilion,
Los Angeles

Evita, like *Jesus Christ Superstar*, was advertised as an
'opera' but first released as a studio recording in the
popular-music markets. This was followed by numerous successful stage productions.

Like *Jesus Christ Superstar*, *Evita* is a through-
sung work, with the movements of plot linked by the
lyrics and the repetition of motifs by singer and orchestra. The story of Eva Perón and her ascent to power
in Argentina again aroused polarized critical reactions
(including comparison with Monteverdi's *L'incoronazione di Poppea*). All responses start, however, with the
acknowledgement that on its own terms *Evita* is probably the most successful example of the composer's
eclectic talent at work.

Cats

Musical in two acts (2h 15m)
Libretto after T. S. Eliot, with additional material by Trevor
Nunn and Richard Stilgoe
PREMIERES 11 May 1981, New London Theatre, London;
US: 7 October 1982, Winter Garden Theater, New York

Cats began as experimental musical settings of T. S.
Eliot's *Old Possum's Book of Practical Cats* (1939) for
a planned programme along the lines of the Walton–
Sitwell *Façade*. The artfully variegated score none the
less provoked one critic to recall Noël Coward's
remark about the strange potency of cheap music,
while the translation of the original idea into a full-
length piece for singers and dancers made *Cats* the
most commercially successful piece in the history of
musical theatre.

The Phantom of the Opera

Opera in two acts (2h 30m)
Libretto by Charles Hart, with additional lyrics by Richard
Stilgoe, after the novel by Gaston Leroux (1911)
PREMIERES 9 October 1986, Her Majesty's Theatre,
London; US: 26 January 1988, Majestic Theater, New
York

All versions of *The Phantom of the Opera*, including
the three celebrated film versions, have their origins in
Gaston Leroux's 1911 novel about the doomed affair
between a young Swedish soprano and a disfigured
composer who haunts the Paris Opéra. Lloyd
Webber's version was written primarily as a vehicle
for the coloratura soprano of his second wife, Sarah
Brightman. The enormously successful productions in
London and New York leaned heavily on spectacular
staging, while two adept operatic pastiches did not
distract from either the shallowness of the sung characters or the generally wooden nature of the
composition.

Other operatic works: *The Likes of Us*, (1966); *Jeeves*, 1975;
Song and Dance, 1982; *Starlight Express*, 1984; *Aspects of
Love*, 1989; *Sunset Boulevard*, 1993

I.J.M.

FRANK LOESSER

Frank Henry Loesser; *b* 29 June 1910, New York; *d* 28 July
1969, New York

Born into a German immigrant family, steeped in
classical music, Frank Loesser taught himself
popular-style pianism. His first song-writing efforts,
for revues and films, were however as lyricist only.
But, beginning with the Second World War hit 'Praise
the Lord and Pass the Ammunition', he eventually
always wrote both words and music.

Guys and Dolls

Musical fable in two acts (2h 30m)
Libretto by Abe Burrows and Jo Swerling, based on a story
(1932) and characters by Damon Runyon; lyrics by the
composer

PREMIERES 24 November 1950, 46th Street Theater, New York; UK: 28 May 1953, Coliseum, London
CAST Sky Masterson *t*, Sarah Brown *s*, Nathan Detroit *bar*, Adelaide *ms*, Nicely-Nicely Johnson *t*, Benny Southstreet *bar*, Rusty Charlie *b*, Arvide *t*, Harry the Horse *bar*; smaller roles from *satb* chorus of gamblers, dolls, Cubans, frequenters of Times Square

Set in the colourful New York world of gamblers and nightclubs created in Damon Runyon's fiction, *Guys and Dolls* has proved consistently pleasing to audiences since its first performances. It is one of the rare traditional musicals whose interest is distributed equally among four main characters, among whom the male and female starring roles belong to different couples. It has an exceptional score, one equally strong in comedy ('Adelaide's Lament'), romance ('If I Were a Bell', 'I've Never Been in Love Before'), establishment of a milieu ('Fugue for Tinhorns', the title song), and response to a unique situation ('Luck Be a Lady', 'Sit Down, You're Rockin' the Boat').

SYNOPSIS
Act I Nathan Detroit is trying to find a safe home for the 'oldest established permanent floating crap game in New York'; to raise the fee for the only location he can find, he persuades newcomer Sky Masterson to make an unwinnable bet. Sky bets that he can persuade beautiful but icy Sister Sarah of the Salvation Army to go to dinner with him in Havana – and, with a promise of an offering of twelve sinners to the Army, he succeeds. Nathan is also having bad luck with his girlfriend, nightclub chanteuse Adelaide, who is sure that her perpetual cold is caused by Nathan's failure to propose. On her return, Sarah finds the mission full of gamblers; assuming that was the purpose of her trip to Havana, she orders Sky away.
Act II The crap game takes place in the sewer. Sky wins, and orders the losers to the mission as his promised twelve sinners. Sarah and Adelaide confer and decide to marry their men, faults and all, and change them later. The final scene reveals that they have done exactly that.

Other musicals: *Where's Charley?* 1948; *The Most Happy Fella*, 1956; *Greenwillow*, 1960; *How to Succeed in Business Without Really Trying*, 1961; *Pleasures and Palaces*, 1965

J.A.C.

FREDERICK LOEWE
b 10 June 1904, Vienna; *d* 14 February 1988, Palm Springs, California, US

The son of an operetta tenor, Frederick Loewe studied with Busoni, d'Albert, and E. N. von Reznicek. In 1924, already successful as pianist and song-writer, he moved to New York, but he found his compositional skills ill-matched to the current tastes of his new country. A succession of jobs, musical and otherwise, supported him until he eventually found his compositional talents in demand; even after his first Broadway

show he continued to play the piano in restaurants until his meeting with Alan Jay Lerner in 1942.

Lerner's lyrics and libretti proved the perfect complement for Loewe's romantically evocative music. Their first three collaborations revealed a steady growth in artistic assurance, without achieving popular success; but, beginning with *Brigadoon* in 1947, the team established itself as one of the most reliable providers of artistically integrated musical entertainment. They maintained a level that Lerner failed to find with any of his subsequent collaborators (including Richard Rodgers, Burton Lane, André Previn, and Leonard Bernstein), Loewe having essentially retired from active work after *Camelot*.

My Fair Lady
Musical play in two acts (2h 30m)
Libretto by Alan Jay Lerner, based on the play *Pygmalion* by George Bernard Shaw (1913)
PREMIERES 15 March 1956, Mark Hellinger Theater, New York; UK: 30 April 1958, Drury Lane, London
CAST Henry Higgins *bar*, Eliza Doolittle *s*, Alfred P. Doolittle *bar*, Freddy Eynsford-Hill *t*, Colonel Pickering *bar*, Mrs Pearce *c*, Mrs Higgins *spoken role*; other solo roles from *satb* chorus of Londoners

This highly successful musical translation of Shaw's play had record-breaking runs in both New York and London – in both cases with the original stars, Rex Harrison, Julie Andrews and Stanley Holloway. Lerner's libretto followed the film version of *Pygmalion* in suggesting a romantic end for Higgins and Eliza, but otherwise generally maintained Shaw's tone and intent. Such songs as 'I Could Have Danced All Night', 'On the Street Where You Live', and 'I've Grown Accustomed to Her Face' are only the most familiar portions of a score highly attentive to character and situation.

SYNOPSIS
Act I London, 1912. Phonetics professor Henry Higgins, intrigued by the aspirations of Eliza, a young Cockney flower-seller, makes a bet with his friend Colonel Pickering that by changing her speech he can make her pass for a fine lady. She moves into the house where he, Pickering and housekeeper Mrs Pearce live, and begins lessons. Her dustman father, Doolittle, pays a visit, ostensibly to protest about the apparent immorality of the set-up but really to get some money out of it (Higgins, amused by his rhetoric, pays him and recommends him for a speaking engagement). The first attempt at showing Eliza off in society, at the Ascot races, ends in embarrassing failure – though it still wins her an ardent admirer, Freddy Eynsford-Hill. But the final test, an embassy ball with a rival of Higgins looking on, is a success.
Act II After the ball, Eliza, furious with Higgins for his offhand dismissal of her share in the success of the experiment, leaves in the middle of the night and roams the city, followed by Freddy. She encounters her father, made miserably famous and wealthy by Higgins's advocacy, now forced to be respectable and to marry his mistress. Higgins, searching for Eliza the next day, finds her visiting his mother. They argue

once more, and he storms out; on his way home he realizes that he misses her. She returns just as the curtain falls.

Other musicals: *Salute to Spring*, 1937; *Great Lady*, 1938; *Life of the Party*, 1942; *What's Up?*, 1943; *The Day before Spring*, 1945; *Brigadoon*, 1947; *Paint Your Wagon*, 1951; *Camelot*, 1960; *Gigi* (originally film), 1973

J.A.C.

ALBERT LORTZING
Gustav Albert Lortzing; *b* 23 October 1801, Berlin; *d* 21 January 1851, Berlin

Lortzing was the leading German comic-opera composer of the 19th century. Though he lacked the musical sophistication and ambition of such near-contemporaries as Weber and Louis Spohr, his sure sense of theatre and his accomplished and inventive treatment of familiar forms have ensured the lasting popularity of his best works, particularly in Germany.

Lortzing's grasp – and willing acceptance – of the demands of the stage was the product of a lifetime's experience of provincial touring companies. His parents were amateur actors and musicians who turned professional after the failure of the family business. The composer's early experience as a child actor was followed by engagements as both actor and buffo tenor; he also worked as producer, conductor and orchestral cellist. His repertoire as an actor was not restricted to popular comedy but included plays by Schiller, Gotthold Ephraim Lessing and Ferdinand Raimund, as well as the fool in *King Lear*. Several of his operas are based on plays in which he had appeared as an actor.

Lortzing was almost entirely self-taught as a musician, apart from some early theory lessons and piano studies. His earliest compositions included incidental music for several plays. His first opera was a one-act singspiel, *Ali Pascha von Janina*, performed in 1828 by the Detmold Hoftheater company, of which he and his wife were then members. Other works of this period rely to a large extent on arrangements of music by other composers. *Szenen aus Mozarts Leben*, using material from various Mozartian sources, testifies to one of the most important influences on Lortzing's music. He may well have been drawn primarily to Mozart the successful theatrical professional, but the confident handling of ambitious ensembles in his best works suggests that deeper lessons were also learned.

Lortzing suffered acute financial difficulties throughout his career; in the absence of a rational system of royalty payments, the popularity his operas achieved was not enough to secure him an income on which to support his family. The success in 1837 of *Die beiden Schützen*, in which he began to move away from the limitations of singspiel and to develop a more personal operatic language, and the even greater enthusiasm which greeted the first full realization of that language in *Zar und Zimmermann* at its Berlin production two years later, encouraged him to concentrate on composition. But he still needed the financial security only a permanent engagement could provide. In the 1830s he worked in Leipzig at the Altes Theater, finally becoming kapellmeister there in 1844. The following year he was appointed to the same post at the Theater an der Wien, but he failed to find favour with Viennese audiences and was unhappy with his own work there. But he continued to compose, enjoying a repeat of his earlier triumphs with *Der Wildschütz* in 1842. He ventured outside comedy, with the musically ambitious Romantic magic operas *Undine* and *Rolands Knappen*, and, less successfully, with *Regina*, a work on a revolutionary subject, inspired by the events and ideals of 1848. Ultimately unsuccessful in his attempts to secure a contract at another major opera house following the termination of his Vienna engagement, Lortzing was obliged to return to acting. In 1850 he gladly accepted an appointment as kapellmeister at the Friedrich Wilhelm Stadttheater in Berlin, a third-rate house devoted mainly to vaudeville and farce. There he managed to compose a one-act comedy, *Die Opernprobe*, but he was too ill to attend its premiere and died the following day.

Lortzing assimilated the influence of other composers as readily as he did popular forms, turning everything to his own theatrical ends. His works nevertheless display a sound grasp of musical structure, an accomplished – and sometimes original – approach to harmony, a sure sense of melody and orchestration, and, above all, an unfailing ability to match music to character and situation. The attention he devoted to writing and adapting his own libretti enabled him to achieve a successful fusion of music and text that eluded many of his contemporaries.

Zar und Zimmermann, oder Die zwei Peter
Tsar and Carpenter, or The Two Peters
Comic opera in three acts (2h 45m)
Libretto by the composer (with Philipp Düringer and Philipp Reger), after Georg Christian Römer's German translation of *Le bourgmestre de Sardam, ou Les deux Pierres* by Mélesville, Merle and de Boirie (1818)
PREMIERES 22 December 1837, Theater der Stadt, Leipzig; US: 9 December 1851, Astor Place Opera House, New York; UK: 15 April 1871, Gaiety Theatre, London
CAST Peter the Great *bar*, Peter Ivanov *t*, Van Bett *b*, Marie *s*, Marquis de Chateauneuf *t*, Admiral Lefort *b*, Lord Syndham *b*, Widow Browe *c*; *satb* chorus of carpenters, citizens, soldiers, sailors, council officials

Zar [originally *Czaar*] *und Zimmermann* is a comedy of mistaken identity. Lortzing had acted the role of the French ambassador in Römer's translation of Mélesville's comic melodrama, and his opera follows Römer closely until the third act, when the splendid comic set piece of the chorus rehearsal is introduced. At the Leipzig premiere the composer sang Peter Ivanov while his mother played Widow Browe. The popular enthusiasm that greeted the premiere was not matched by critical acclaim until the Berlin production of 1839.

SYNOPSIS
Act I The action takes place in Saardam, Holland, in

1698. Peter the Great is working incognito as a ship-yard carpenter (as he actually did) under the name of Peter Michaelov. A fellow Russian carpenter, an army deserter named Peter Ivanov, is in love with Marie, the niece of Burgomaster Van Bett. Informed by his ambassador, Lefort, of simmering rebellion in Moscow, the tsar resolves to return to Russia. Van Bett arrives, with instructions to locate a foreigner called Peter working in the shipyard. The interest of the English and French ambassadors, Syndham and Chateauneuf, convinces him of the foreign Peter's importance. His suspicions, and Syndham's, centre on Peter Ivanov. Chateauneuf, however, correctly identifies Peter Michaelov as the tsar.

Act II During a wedding celebration for the son of Widow Browe, owner of the shipyard, Chateauneuf (in disguise) concludes an alliance with the tsar, while Syndham (also in disguise) turns his attention on the bewildered Peter Ivanov. The arrival of a party of soldiers with instructions to detain all suspicious foreigners creates a general tumult in which the ambassadors throw off their disguises. Each identifies a different Peter as the tsar. Van Bett, after futile attempts to control the situation, looks on bewildered.

Act III While Van Bett prepares a musical homage to the wrong tsar, Peter Michaelov prepares to escape with the English passport Syndham has given to Ivanov. In return for their assistance in the temporary deception, the tsar gives Ivanov and Marie a letter that licenses their marriage and appoints Ivanov a general inspector of the imperial court. The tsar's ship leaves the harbour to general rejoicing. Van Bett remains confused.

In *Zar und Zimmermann* Lortzing's musical language reaches maturity. A powerful structural coherence underlies his virtuoso treatment of stock characters and situations. Familiar forms and set pieces are firmly integrated into the dramatic whole. Operatic lieder are used in varying contexts to dramatic effect, made to carry psychological as well as atmospheric weight. The musical characterization of the pompous Van Bett, particularly in his buffo aria 'O sancta justitia', with its comic interplay of voice and bassoon and its mixture of nonsensical dog-Latin patter and grandiloquent vocal flourishes, can stand comparison with anything achieved in this vein by Donizetti (whose opera on the same subject, *Il borgomastro di Saardam*, was performed in Berlin in August 1837) or even Rossini. The accomplished construction of the Act II finale reveals a sophisticated – and Mozartian – understanding of comic ensemble, while the chaotic rehearsal of Van Bett's ponderous choral tribute is a masterpiece of self-conscious musical humour. As in several of the mature operas, a colourful and elegant ballet (here a clog dance) shows Lortzing at his most exuberant and unaffected.

Hans Sachs

Comic opera in three acts (2h 15m)
Libretto by Philipp Düringer, Philipp Reger and the composer, after the play by Johann Ludwig Deinhardstein (1827)
Composed 1840, rev. 1845

PREMIERE 23 June 1840, Leipzig; rev. version: 25 May 1845, Mannheim

Hans Sachs, shoemaker and poet, is defeated by Hesse, a member of the Augsburg town council, in a singing competition; the prize is the hand of Kunigunde, daughter of Steffen, the mayor of Nuremberg, with whom Sachs is in love. Emperor Maximilian comes to Nuremberg to discover the author of a poem he admires. Hesse claims authorship but cannot recite the lines convincingly. The emperor recognizes Sachs as the true author and gives him Kunigunde as his bride.

Lortzing's opera, which enjoyed some success at its premiere but has since faded from the repertoire, is chiefly of interest as an earlier treatment of the subject Wagner was to use in *Die Meistersinger*. In *Die Meistersinger* Wagner adopted nearly all of the changes and additions made to Deinhardstein's original by Lortzing and Reger. There are parallels between characters too, and even some curious musical similarities. But the divergences are as significant; Lortzing's Steffen and Kunigunde, for instance, bear little relation to their Wagnerian counterparts, Pogner and Eva.

Der Wildschütz, oder Die Stimme der Natur

The Poacher, or The Voice of Nature
Comic opera in three acts (3h)
Libretto by the composer, freely adapted from August von Kotzebue's comedy *Der Rehbock, oder Die schuldlosen Schuldbewussten* (1815)
PREMIERES 31 December 1842, Altes Theater, Leipzig; US: 23 March 1856, Theater-Lokale des Herrn Flossman, Brooklyn, New York; UK: 3 July 1895, Drury Lane, London
CAST Count Eberbach *bar*, Countess *c*, Baron Kronthal *t*, Baroness Freimann *s*, Nanette *ms*, Baculus *b*, Gretchen *s*, Pancratius *b*; *satb* chorus of huntsmen, servants, villagers, schoolchildren

Lortzing's avowed preference was for literary sources of no great intrinsic merit, which allowed him freedom to create the musical and dramatic effects he required. Here he transforms the coarse impropriety of Kotzebue's original – in which he had acted in Detmold – into well-crafted and good-natured comedy. *Der Wildschütz* is Lortzing's comic masterpiece and proof that in the German spieloper he developed a native theatrical form that was in every way the equal of the French opéra comique or Italian opera buffa whose influences it assimilated.

SYNOPSIS

Act I Celebration of the engagement of Baculus, a schoolmaster, and the much younger Gretchen is interrupted by a letter from Count Eberbach threatening Baculus with dismissal for poaching. Gretchen offers to intercede with the count, but Baculus, knowing his employer's reputation as a womanizer, refuses to let her go. Baroness Freimann, a young widow, sister of the count (whom she has not seen since childhood), arrives with her maid Nanette, both disguised as male students. The count has proposed that his sister remarry; she intends first secretly to observe the suggested groom, Baron Kronthal, a young widower and brother of the count's own wife. The baroness offers to impersonate Gretchen. The count and the baron arrive with a hunting party. Immediately attracted to the supposed Gretchen, they invite her and Nanette (now also 'disguised' as a woman) to the castle.

Act II   In the castle, Countess Eberbach is holding a reading of Sophocles. She attempts to engage the baron in a Greek love scene, unaware that he is the brother she has not seen since childhood, for he too is at the castle in disguise, as a stable lad, his true identity known only to the count. Baculus arrives and succeeds in impressing the countess with his apparent knowledge of the classics. The count, however, is not so easily mollified and Baculus summons 'Gretchen' to assist him. Both the count and the baron are carried away by their passion for her; they react with jealous astonishment to the knowledge that she is engaged to the elderly schoolmaster. A storm offers an excuse to invite the betrothed couple to stay the night. A game of billiards between the count and the baron degenerates into farcical chaos as they vie for the attentions of the disguised baroness, whom the countess finally rescues from beneath the billiard table. Alone with Baculus, the baron offers him 5000 thalers to relinquish his fiancée. Baculus, filled with thoughts of his own magnificent future, agrees.

Act III   The next morning Baculus presents the real Gretchen to the baron, explaining that the woman of the previous night was a male student in disguise. Gradually all involved reveal their true identities, protesting the innocence of their behaviour on the grounds that they had only been following the voice of nature. The tangle of relationships is unravelled and Baculus is pardoned, all the more readily when it emerges he had in fact shot his own donkey rather than one of the count's bucks.

The comic figures of Baculus and the steward Pancratius and the magnificent central billiards scene are among the many inventions and alterations with which Lortzing improved on his source material. The confidence of his musical characterization brings the familiar stock types vividly to life and lends timeless appeal even to his contemporary satire (of educational reformers and of the mania for all things Greek that swept Leipzig after the 1842 performance of Antigone with Mendelssohn's incidental music). Structurally the opera is a model of musical and dramatic refinement and coherence. In contrast to the reliance on operatic lieder in earlier works, Der Wildschütz has only four solo numbers but twelve ensembles. In the comically touching vanity of Baculus's 'Fünf tausend Thaler' Lortzing demonstrates again his mastery of the buffo aria, while in the extended billiard-table quintet ('Ich habe Num'ro eins'), which manages to integrate the cantus firmus of a chorale rehearsed by Baculus into the erotic warfare going on around the disguised baroness, he develops an increasingly complex comedy of musical and dramatic climaxes with Mozartian panache.

Other operatic works: Ali Pascha von Janina, oder Die Franzosen in Albanien, 1828; Der Pole und sein Kind, oder Der Feldwebel vom IV Regiment, 1832; Der Weinachtsabend, 1832; Andreas Hofer, 1832; Szenen aus Mozarts Leben, 1832; Die Schatzkammer des Ynka, 1836; Die beiden Schützen, 1837; Caramo, oder das Fischerstechen, 1839; Casanova, 1841; Undine, 1845, rev. 1847; Der Waffenschmied, 1846; Zum Grossadmiral, 1847; Regina, (1848), 1899 (arr. Adolf L'Arronge); Rolands Knappen, oder Das ersehnte Glück, 1849; Die vornehmen Dilettanten, oder Die Opernprobe, 1851

I.B.

JEAN-BAPTISTE LULLY

Giovanni Battista Lulli; b 28 November 1632, Florence; d 22 March 1687, Paris

Lully's domination of late-17th-century French music was achieved by a combination of good fortune, musical and theatrical talent, skilful management of people and finance, and ruthless pursuit of power.

Lully came to France at the age of 13, to help perfect the Italian of Louis XIV's cousin, the 18-year-old Mlle de Montpensier. He soon became an accomplished violinist, guitarist and dancer, working closely with the composer and singer Michel Lambert. Lully was just 20 when he danced with the 14-year-old Louis XIV in the Ballet royal de la nuit (1653) and when he gained his first court post as compositeur de la musique instrumentale de la chambre. At 23 he was directing the smaller court string orchestra (Les Petits Violons or La Petite Bande) and composing for the ballets de cour, while also drawing on the vocal style of the airs de cour of Lambert. Within weeks of taking charge of the kingdom on the death of Cardinal Mazarin in 1661, Louis XIV appointed Lully as surintendant and maître de la musique de la chambre, the two most powerful posts in the musical establishment. The composer was then 28, and was naturalized later the same year (as Jean-Baptiste Lully). The following year he became maître de la musique de la famille royale, and married Lambert's daughter, Madeleine.

The second decade of Lully's career at court centred on his successful collaborations with Molière: the first was the comédie-ballet Le mariage forcé (1664); the last the tragédie-ballet Psyché (1671, later, in 1678, to be hurriedly transformed into a tragédie en musique). This experience, preceded by Lully's long apprenticeship with the ballet de cour, enabled him to refine the ingredients of the recipe he was to put together so successfully in his operas.

The first operas in 17th-century France were almost wholly imported Italian productions, between 1645 and 1662, concluding with Cavalli's Ercole amante with interludes by Lully. The first French-language operas resulted from initiatives by the poet Pierre Perrin, between 1659 and 1671. Ironically, Lully long opposed the notion, but, nettled by the spectacular success of Robert Cambert's Pomone to a text by Perrin, who had obtained letters patent for Académies d'Opéra, Lully seized the chance to acquire these rights when Perrin was imprisoned for debt in 1672. Establishing the Académie Royale de Musique, Lully ensured his monopoly of staged music performance in France, with privileges obtained from Louis XIV. Until his death 15 years later, he produced a new opera almost every year. Thus, although not its inventor, Lully won acceptance for French-language opera. The form of tragédie en musique evolved by Lully and his librettist Philippe Quinault dominated French opera for the following century.

Lully's development of the 'French' overture widely adopted by Bach, Handel and contemporaries in England and Italy, of dance forms and of a fluid recitative have all long been acknowledged. Also widely admired was the legendary discipline Lully imposed on his performers, ensuring a perfection of ensemble remembered long after his death. Less recognized outside France has been the supremacy of the text itself; yet Lully's clear statement that 'my recitative is meant for speaking' unambiguously underlines the centrality of the dialogue – as important as it is in, say, the works of Gilbert and Sullivan. Contemporary writers emphasized the enormous appeal of the very human text, liberally sprinkled with witty aphorisms (usually emanating from lesser characters, rather than the protagonists). These works were also unashamed propaganda on behalf of Louis XIV, the Sun King, and the plots, loosely based on mythology or fable, were mostly peopled by gods and mortals engaged in improbable confrontation, with the theme of love versus duty rarely absent. Yet there are also many wry observations on the frailty of human nature, even when in godly form. To transmit both plot and commentary unambiguously, Lully uses flowing declamatory recitative (carefully notated in constantly varying time signatures), which frequently evolves from and returns to various forms of air, sometimes based on popular song, as well as comment from the static chorus, which functions much as does that of classical drama. Monologue is a frequently used device at critical moments in the unfolding of the drama. Opera libretti (and candles) were sold to help the public follow the action, and audiences sometimes even sang along with the chorus, as they became familiar with each new work.

Of Lully's operas only *Atys*, *Phaëton* and *Armide* have an 'unhappy' ending. Nor is humour confined to a few early works, as is sometimes suggested, even if it became more subtle later. The overture is heard twice: before and after the prologue, itself usually an allegory of the king's majesty. During the tragedy, audiences are rewarded with substantial divertissements of dances, solos and choruses, for which Lully required his librettists to fit their words to his musical design. Instrumental movements already heard are repeated as entr'actes. From *Bellérophon* (1679) onwards, the score of each opera was published the same year as its premiere (*Isis* had already appeared in separate parts in 1677); the earlier works appeared after Lully's death. Several of Quinault's libretti for Lully were used by later composers, such as André Campra, J.-J. C. de Mondonville, F.-A.-D. Philidor, J. C. Bach, Niccolò Piccinni, François-Joseph Gossec and, most notably, Gluck (*Armide*).

Lully's orchestra was organized as a small continuo group (the petit choeur), usually accompanying the solo singers and comprising solo violins and wind, bass viol(s), bass violin(s), theorbo(es) and harpsichord, and a larger one (the grand choeur) employed in instrumental movements and choruses, and based on a five-part string ensemble (violins, violas in three parts, bass violins), sometimes extended to seven parts. Flutes, recorders and oboes played in both groups; bassoons, trumpets (up to five parts) and timpani were frequently added to the grand choeur. Other instruments occasionally employed included guitar, musette, *taille* (tenor oboe), crumhorn and panpipes.

Alceste, ou Le triomphe d'Alcide

Alcestis, or The Triumph of Hercules
Tragédie in a prologue and five acts (2h 30m)
Libretto by Philippe Quinault after the play *Alkestis* by Euripides (438 BC)
PREMIERES 19 January 1674, Jeu de Paume du Bel-Air, Paris; UK: 4 January 1973, BBC radio; 17 December 1975, London Opera Centre
CAST *prologue*: Nymph of the Seine *s*, La Gloire (Glory) *s*, Nymph of the Tuileries *s*, Nymph of the Marne *s*; *tragédie*: Alceste (Alcestis) *s*, Céphise *s*, Licomède (Lycomedes) *b*, Thétis (Thetis) *s*, Alcide (Alcides or Hercules) *bar*, Admète (Admetus) *t*, Pherès (Pheres) *t*, Charon *b*, Pluton (Pluto) *b*, Proserpine (Proserpina) *s*, Apollo *haute-contre*, Alecton (Alecto) *haute-contre*, Diane (Diana) *s*, 4 *s*, 3 *hautes-contres*, *t*, *bar*, 3 *b*; *satb* chorus of nymphs, naiads, people, soldiers, sea-sprites, spirits, etc.; ballet

Mme de Sévigné, the great letter-writer and thus chronicler of the court of Louis XIV, described *Alceste* as a 'marvel of beauty'; Nevertheless, it did not win immediate acceptance. However, it held a particular place in Louis XIV's affections, and remained in the repertoire for 83 years.

SYNOPSIS
The allegorical prologue is a colourful divertissement in praise of an unnamed hero.

Act I The rejoicings at the marriage of Alcestis and Admetus are shattered when the jealous Lycomedes abducts Alcestis to his island kingdom.

Act II Alcestis laments her fate, but Admetus and Alcides (who also secretly loves Alcestis) lead the expedition to free her. The rescuers are triumphant, but Admetus is mortally wounded. Apollo appears and announces that Admetus can be saved if someone will die in his place; such a person will be immortalized in a monument.

Act III Pheres, Admetus' father, and Céphise plead old age and youth respectively as excuses for not offering themselves for the sacrifice. When Admetus sees the image of Alcestis on the monument, he knows she has made the sacrifice. Alcides offers to rescue Alcestis from the underworld if Admetus will cede to him 'the beauty you have lost'. Admetus agrees, happy that Alcestis may return, even though denied to him. Diana, impressed with such selflessness, assists Alcides' expedition to Hades.

Act IV Pluto and Proserpina are entertaining Alcestis when Alcides arrives, having chained up the three-headed dog, Cerberus, guarding the entrance. Assured that Alcides' father, Jupiter, intends no other intervention in the underworld, Pluto agrees to Alcestis' release.

Act V Alcestis, although touched by Alcides' rescue and his love for her, confesses that it is Admetus she truly loves. Deeply moved by the heart-rending farewells between Alcestis and Admetus, Alcides accepts glory rather than love in renouncing his own passion for her. Apollo descends to join in the concluding divertissement of rejoicing.

The musical proportions of *Alceste* and subsequent operas gained much from Lully's experience with his previous and first true opera, *Cadmus et Hermione*. Most notably, the chorus now sings in all five acts as well as the prologue, and there is less recitative. The musical portrayal of the storm evoked by Lycomedes' sister, Thetis, to prevent pursuit in Act I is matched in Act II by a colourful battle scene for double chorus, onstage wind band, and the full panoply of Lully's orchestra. The hauntingly evocative duo between the grief-stricken Alcestis and her dying husband includes the poignant refrain: 'Alceste, vous pleurez?' 'Admète, vous mourez?' In Act III, a ritournelle, heard earlier when Alcestis declares that only love can save Admetus, heralds the news that he is healed. In an impressive rondeau, the heart-rending refrain 'Alceste est morte' is exchanged between Admetus and Céphise, the intervening recitatives expressing her remorse at failing to prevent Alcestis' death. In complete contrast are the comic rondeau that opens Act IV, 'Il faut passer tôt ou tard', in which Charon sings of his task ferrying the departed across the Styx, and the wordless 'barking' chorus to depict the dog, Cerberus.

Atys

Attis

Tragédie en musique in a prologue and five acts (2h 15m)
Libretto by Philippe Quinault, after Book IV of Ovid's *Fasti*
PREMIERES 10 January 1676, Saint-Germain-en-Laye; US: 17 May 1989, Brooklyn Academy of Music, New York
CAST *prologue*: Le Temps (Time) *bar*, Flore (Flora) *s*, Melpomène (Melpomene) *s*, Iris *s*, A Zephyr *haute-contre*; *satb* chorus; *tragédie*: Atys (Attis) *haute-contre*, Idas *b*, Sangaride *s*, Doris *s*, Cybèle (Cybele) *s*, Mélisse (Melissa) *s*, Celenus (Celaenus) *bar*, Le Sommeil (Sleep) *haute-contre*, Sangar (Sangarius) *b*, 2 *hautes-contres*, *t*, 2 *b*; *satb* chorus of nymphs, zephyrs, heroes, priestesses, spirits, pleasant and bad dreams; ballet

SYNOPSIS

Prologue In a transparent allegory of the might of Louis XIV, Time promises the greatest of heroes eternal fame; Flora, goddess of spring, wishes to pay her tribute before the hero leaves for the wars. But Melpomene intervenes, distracting him with the story of Attis.

Act I At dawn, Attis awakens the Phrygians to prepare a welcome for the goddess Cybele. Idas mocks his enthusiasm and asks if it is Love that keeps him awake? Sangaride enters and feigns delight at the prospect of her marriage to Celaenus, king of Phrygia, especially as Cybele will be present; but, alone, she laments her fate and her unrequited love for Attis. Finding her distressed, Attis confesses his love to the astonished Sangaride.

Act II Both Attis and Celaenus declare their wish to act as high priest for Cybele. Cybele, secretly loving Attis, chooses him, and admits it is for this love she has come, rather than for the nuptials of Celaenus and Sangaride. Attis receives the accolades of his high office.

Act III Cybele causes Attis to fall into a deep sleep. Pleasant dreams sing of love, but bad dreams warn him of the penalties of deceiving the gods. He wakens startled to find Cybele only too ready to console him. Sangaride begs Cybele to save her from marrying Celaenus whom she does not love. Attis, confused, supports her pleas, and Cybele guesses their mutual passion; she laments her fate.

Act IV Sangaride misinterprets Attis' confusion as hidden passion for Cybele, and laments the ungrateful Attis. But he explains, and they swear eternal love. Attis, as high priest, goes to Sangaride's father, Sangarius, commanding him, in the name of Cybele, to cancel the marriage arrangements between Sangaride and Celaenus.

Act V Hearing of this, Celaenus confronts Cybele. Realizing Attis has deceived them, they decide to punish the lovers. Cybele casts a spell on Attis, who, in his blindness, stabs Sangaride. When he sees what he has done, Attis attempts suicide, but Cybele intervenes, transforming him into a tree. She is left to celebrate her hollow victory, and to lament him whom she has lost for ever.

Act I includes the chorus 'Nous devons nous animer d'une ardeur nouvelle', soon to become the source of a Purcell trumpet tune and thus of a score of further parodies. In the same act, Attis confesses his love for Sangaride in one of Lully's most eloquent recitatives. Attis' dreams in Act III are depicted by a memorable orchestral *sommeil* with alternating strings and flutes, but the musical climax of the opera coincides with the tragic dénouement: the chorus attempt to warn Attis of his mistake as he stabs Sangaride – 'Arrête, arrête, malheureux!' they cry – but it is too late, and as Sangaride dies they wail, 'Atys lui-même fait périr ce qu'il aime.'

Armide

Armida

Tragédie en musique in a prologue and five acts (2h 30m)
Libretto by Philippe Quinault, after the epic poem *Gerusalemme liberata* (1581), by Torquato Tasso
PREMIERES 15 February 1686, Palais Royal, Paris; US: 2 February 1953, New York; UK: 6 February 1953, BBC radio; 14 May 1981, Barber Institute, Birmingham
CAST *prologue*: La Gloire (Glory) *s*, La Sagesse (Wisdom) *s*; *satb* chorus; *tragédie*: Armide (Armida) *s*, Phénice (Phoenice) *s*, Sidonie (Sidonia) *s*, Hidraot (Hidraoth) *b*, Arontes *b*, Renaud (Rinaldo) *haute-contre*, Artemidore (Artemidorus) *t*, La Haine (Hate) *t*, Ubalde *b*, Danish Knight *haute-contre*, 4 *s*, *haute-contre*; *satb* chorus of heroes, nymphs, shepherds, demons, furies; ballet

Lully's and Quinault's last tragédie was their most highly developed, both musically and dramatically. A wealth of expressive melody and a spectacular, tragic dénouement helped to ensure its popularity in the Paris repertoire until 1764.

SYNOPSIS

The prologue, eschewing mythology and spectacle, is a moral discourse between Wisdom and Glory, rivals yet both overcoming Love, thus mirroring the new-found piety of the court in the era of Louis XIV's second wife, Mme de Maintenon.

Act I The sorceress Armida's victory over the Christians besieging Jerusalem is incomplete while the most formidable knight, Rinaldo, remains resistant to her. Armida's uncle, Hidraoth, king of Damascus, urges her to turn from war to love, but she will marry only Rinaldo's conqueror. The people's celebrations are interrupted by Arontes, Armida's general, dying after an encounter with Rinaldo. Hidraoth and Armida swear revenge.

Act II Rinaldo, in disgrace because of the defeat, is determined to rehabilitate himself. But Armida and Hidraoth find him and invoke spirits to enchant him. Rinaldo soliloquizes on the beauty of his surroundings. Armida demands to take her vengeance alone, but when she sees Rinaldo she cannot kill him, and she commands her spirits to carry him to her enchanted palace.

Act III Armida and Rinaldo are happy together, but she knows that his love depends on her magic. She summons Hate to exorcize her love for Rinaldo, but relents, and banishes the furies.

Act IV Artemidorus and Ubalde, knights sent to find Rinaldo, are armed with a diamond shield and a golden sceptre to penetrate the enchanted garden. Armida sends spirits to seduce them, but the spirits disappear when touched by the weapons of the knights, who enter the palace.

Act V Armida leaves Rinaldo with spirits to entertain him while she renews her spells. But the knights arrive and bring Rinaldo to his senses. Armida returns and desperately implores Rinaldo to stay, but the knights drag him away. She tries to summon Hate to rekindle her revenge, but she cannot bring herself to harm Rinaldo, and instead destroys the palace and all within it.

Much of Lully's music for *Armide* is on a higher plane than in any earlier work. In Act II, the enchantment of Rinaldo, to the muted-string accompaniment of the composer's most expressive *sommeil*, is followed by Armida's powerfully emotional soliloquy 'Enfin il est en ma puissance', expressing the conflict within her between love and hate. This is Lully's most celebrated monologue, cited by his contemporaries, and later by Rameau, as the model for French recitative, achieving its effect by the skilful use of rests as much as by its melodic and rhythmic vitality.

Other operatic works: *Les fêtes de l'Amour et de Bacchus*, 1672; *Cadmus et Hermione*, 1673; *Thesée*, 1675; *Isis*, 1677; *Psyché*, 1678; *Bellérophon*, 1679; *Proserpine*, 1680; *Persée*, 1682; *Phaëton*, 1683; *Amadis*, 1684; *Roland*, 1685; *Acis et Galathée*, 1686; *Achille et Polixène* (overture and Act I by Lully; remainder by Pascal Collasse), 1687

L.S.

HEINRICH MARSCHNER

Heinrich August Marschner; *b* 16 August 1795, Zittau, Germany; *d* 14 December 1861, Hanover

The most important opera composer in Germany between Weber and Wagner, Marschner made a decisive and distinctive contribution to the development of German Romantic opera. Still obviously rooted in the tradition of singspiel and number opera, his best works nevertheless succeeded in expanding the dramatic range of existing musical forms and in integrating discrete elements into a more ambitious theatrical whole. Adventurous in his use of chromatic harmony and imaginative in the deployment of instrumental effects, Marschner attempted always to subordinate musical sophistication to the demands of the drama. Though he excelled at the depiction of the supernatural and the creation of an atmosphere of horror or suspense, he was more interested in the portrayal of inner conflicts and psychological turmoil than the evocation of setting and local colour.

Marschner's parents were keen amateur musicians, and he showed early talent as a pianist and boy soprano; he is reputed to have sung the role of Julia in Spontini's *La vestale*. He composed his first theatre work, the ballet *Die stolze Bauerin*, when still at school, and soon abandoned law studies in Leipzig in favour of a musical career, taking up employment in 1816 as domestic music teacher and kapellmeister to noble families in Pressburg (now Bratislava). His first attempt at operatic composition, unperformed and apparently intended mainly as a technical exercise, was a setting of Metastasio's *Titus*, using the adaptation Caterino Mazzolà made for Mozart. The breakthrough in Marschner's career came when Weber accepted *Heinrich IV und d'Aubigné* for production in Dresden in 1820. Marschner settled in Dresden the following year, writing incidental music for plays, including Heinrich von Kleist's *Prinz Friedrich von Homburg*. In 1824 he became musikdirektor at the opera. Professional responsibilities to both Italian and German resident companies forced him to steer a diplomatic course between the two national styles, but his personal sympathies lay with the idea of a German national opera, which he attempted to promote with his singspiel *Der Holzdieb*, produced at the Hoftheater in 1825 and published as the first in what was intended to be a series of cheap, easy-to-play piano scores of national operas.

When Weber died in 1826, Marschner, who combined zeal in self-promotion with an inability to make himself agreeable, failed in his attempt to succeed him as royal kapellmeister and left Dresden. During the next year he travelled Germany with his third wife, the singer Marianne Wohlbrück, spending time in Berlin, Danzig, Breslau and Magdeburg before settling in Leipzig in 1827. The premiere of *Der Vampyr*, in Leipzig in March 1828, was his first great success. His reputation was consolidated in December 1829 by *Der Templer und die Jüdin*. In 1831 Marschner was appointed conductor at the Hoftheater in Hanover. Two years later *Hans Heiling* was produced in Berlin. It proved to be the highpoint of Marschner's career. He remained in Hanover for the rest of his life, though his opposition to the Italian tastes of the court made his position there uncomfortable. In the remaining years of his long career he attempted comic opera (*Der Babü*, premiered in Hanover, 1838), historical grand opera in the manner of Spontini (*König Adolph von Nassau*, staged in Dresden, largely thanks to Wagner, in 1845) and a quasi-Wagnerian exercise in through-composition (*Sangeskönig Hiarne*, performed posthumously, Frankfurt, 1863, after Rossini had tried unsuccessfully to secure a Paris production). Songs, male choruses, incidental music and pageants for royal occasions helped maintain his reputation, but changing public taste (and some undoubtedly weak libretti) denied him further major operatic successes. Despite Pfitzner's attempt at revival earlier this century, only *Der Vampyr*, *Der Templer und die Jüdin* and *Hans Heiling* survive on the fringes of today's repertoire.

Der Vampyr

The Vampire

Romantic opera in two acts (2h 45m)

Libretto by Wilhelm August Wohlbrück after the play *Der Vampir oder Die Totenbraut* (1821) by Heinrich Ludwig Ritter, after John Polidori's story (published as *The Vampyre: a Tale by Lord Byron*, 1819)

PREMIERES ·29 March 1828, Sächsisches Hoftheater Leipzig; UK: 25 August 1829, Lyceum, London; US: 9 March 1980, Conservatory of Music, Boston

CAST Malwina Davenaut *s*, Janthe Berkley *s*, Emmy Perth *s*, Edgar Aubry *t*, George Dibdin *t*, Sir Humphrey Davenaut *b*, Lord Ruthven (The Vampire) *bar*, Sir John Berkley *b*, John Perth *spoken role*, The Vampire Master *spoken role*, *ms*, 2 *t*, 3 *b*; *satb* chorus of witches, goblins, ghosts, demons, servants, peasants, priests

Marschner began work on *Der Vampyr* after leaving Dresden in 1826. The choice of subject undoubtedly exploited a contemporary vogue for such themes – Peter Lindpainter's opera of the same title was premiered a few months after Marschner's – but the opera's success was not simply due to fashion. In *Lucretia*, begun in 1820 and staged in Leipzig in 1827, Marschner had attempted to treat a classical subject in a manner that owed something to Spontini, dispensing with spoken dialogue. The work met with a lukewarm response. *Der Vampyr* offered a subject more obviously suited to Marschner's distinctive operatic voice.

SYNOPSIS
Act I The setting is the Scottish Highlands. At a midnight gathering of spirits, the vampire, Ruthven, is granted an extension of his stay on earth, on condition that he sacrifice three brides within the next 24 hours. His first victim is Janthe, whom he kills as Berkley, her father, arrives with a search party and stabs his daughter's assailant. The dying Ruthven asks Aubry, whose life he once saved, to place his body where the moon's rays can revive it, and swears him to secrecy for 24 hours. Aubry flees in horror. His horror is compounded when he discovers his beloved Malwina is to be married to Ruthven before midnight.
    Act II Ruthven's servants are celebrating the marriage of Emmy and George. Ruthven arrives to claim Emmy as his second victim, warning Aubry that he too will become a vampire if he tries to intervene. George is unable to save his bride, but manages to shoot Ruthven. In the moonlight, the vampire revives again and hastens to Davenaut's castle for his own wedding to Malwina, his intended third victim. Aubry succeeds in delaying the marriage ceremony and, after wrestling with his conscience, resolves to break his oath. He denounces Ruthven. As the clock strikes one, the vampire is struck by lightning.

Der Vampyr represents a significant expansion of the dramatic possibilities of number opera. Sustaining tension with reminiscence motif and bold, shifting harmony, vividly underscoring changes of mood with choral and orchestral effects, Marschner combines and contrasts vocal forms of varying emotional range – melodrama, folksong, declamation, arioso, chorus – in a convincing dramatic whole. Pathos and terror are interwoven to create a powerful atmosphere of supernatural horror and suspense. The opera's central figure, victim as well as monster, is a creation of some psychological complexity.

Hans Heiling
Romantic opera in a prelude and three acts (2h 45m)
Libretto by Philipp Eduard Devrient, after a Bohemian legend
PREMIERES 24 May 1833, Hofoper, Berlin; UK: 2 December 1953, Town Hall, Oxford
CAST Queen of the Earth Spirits *s*, Hans Heiling *bar*,

Anna *s*, Gertrude *ms*, Konrad *t*, Stephan *b*; *satb* chorus of spirits, peasants, wedding guests, guards

The libretto of *Hans Heiling* had been rejected by Mendelssohn, for whom it was written in 1827, on the grounds that it was too close in atmosphere to *Der Freischütz*. Devrient, a baritone who had a considerable reputation as an author and producer, sent the text anonymously to Marschner in July 1831 just before he sang Bois Guilbert in the Berlin production of *Der Templer und die Jüdin*. Marschner accepted it with enthusiasm. The success of the premiere, at which Devrient sang Heiling, turned to triumph with the Leipzig production two months later.

SYNOPSIS
Prelude Disregarding all warnings, Hans Heiling, son of the queen of the earth spirits and a mortal man, leaves his mother's underworld realm to live on earth near his beloved Anna.
    Act I Living among men, Heiling is troubled and uncomfortable. Only Anna's love can make him truly mortal. Anna is afraid of him and persuades him to burn the magic book he has brought with him. At a village celebration, she dances with Konrad, reducing Heiling to despair.
    Act II Anna, lost in the forest, is confronted by the queen of the earth spirits, who demands that she give up Heiling. Anna faints and is found by Konrad. They declare their love for each other. Heiling appears with jewels for his bride. Anna says she cannot marry him, because she now knows he is not a mortal. In his rage, Heiling stabs Konrad and flees.
    Act III Heiling appeals to the earth spirits. Scornfully they inform him that Konrad has survived and will soon marry Anna. Determined on revenge, Heiling attends the wedding and calls on the spirits to help him. As he is about to attack Konrad, his mother appears and reminds him of his promise to return to her should his heart be broken. The mortals thank heaven for their salvation.

Devrient's drama of the conflict between two worlds, with its troubled protagonist at home in neither, drew from Marschner a score that blends the traditional with the radical. The rustic world of the mortal characters is depicted within the conventions of singspiel, where dialogue links songlike melodies and cheerful choruses. For the eerie spirit world, and Heiling's inner turmoil – especially in the long, through-composed prelude, a seamless flow of aria, recitative and ensemble that precedes the Romantic tone poem of the overture – Marschner calls on more elaborate resources of harmony and orchestral colour. Within and between the opera's two worlds, contrasting set forms are bridged, their emotional and theatrical range extended by expressive use of melodrama and of flexible, declamatory word-setting, while extensive motivic links and reminiscence ensure musical and dramatic coherence.

Other operas: *Titus*, (1816); *Saidar und Zulima*, 1818; *Heinrich IV und d'Aubigné*, 1820; *Der Kyffhäuserberg*, 1822; *Der Holzdieb*, 1825; *Lucretia*, 1827; *Der Templer und die Jüdin*, 1829; *Des Falkners Braut*, 1832; *Das Schloss am*

Ätna, 1836; *Der Babü* (lost), 1838; *König Adolph von Nassau*, 1845; *Austin*, 1852; *Sangeskönig Hiarne*, 1863

I.B.

BOHUSLAV MARTINŮ

Bohuslav Jan Martinů; *b* 8 December 1890, Polička, Czech Republic; *d* 28 August 1959, Liestal, Switzerland

After Janáček, Martinů is the major representative of Czech opera in the 20th century. Most of Martinů's creative life was spent away from his native Czechoslovakia, but – except during the Second World War – he maintained strong links with his homeland. Following three desultory years (1907–10) at the Prague Conservatory, from which he was expelled, Martinů made a career as a teacher and violinist with the Czech Philharmonic Orchestra, graduating in 1918 to frequent engagements after sporadic appearances beginning in 1913.

After a brief period of study with Josef Suk in 1922, Martinů was awarded a Czech government scholarship to study in Paris in 1923, where he remained for the next 17 years, marrying his French wife, Charlotte Quennehen, in 1931. In 1940, having been blacklisted by the occupying German authorities, Martinů left Paris for the South of France, and in 1941 he travelled to the United States, where he remained, apart from long summer holidays in Europe, until 1953. The last years of Martinů's life were spent in Europe: in Nice, Rome, and Schonenberg in Switzerland.

After the war Martinů had planned to return to Czechoslovakia, but timely warning of the communist takeover of 1948 deterred him. Although his musical output in these late years was deeply affected by his native land, Martinů's unmistakable musical style – with its springy, syncopated melodies, motor rhythms, warm and predominantly diatonic harmonies – crystallized from numerous influences. Early encounters with the English madrigal and the music of Debussy led to a fascination with counterpoint and French-tinted harmony. Jazz and Les Six were important to Martinů in the 1920s, but the signal influence on his music at the start of the 1930s was the baroque concerto grosso. By this stage Martinů's style was fully formed, although he was still to respond positively to musical influences as diverse as Notre Dame polyphony and Haydn.

Music for the theatre occupied Martinů at all stages of his career, some of his earliest works being ballets. Of his fourteen complete operas (*La semaine de bonté*, 1931, and *La plainte contre inconnu*, 1953, are substantial torsos), six, including his first, were full length (*The Soldier and the Dancer*, *The Three Wishes*, *The Plays of Mary*, *Julietta*, *Mirandolina* and *The Greek Passion*). Martinů's operas show that he set his face against Wagnerian music drama and the nationalist subject matter of many of his Czech predecessors, and reveal Martinů's variety of inspiration, based on wide reading, and his propensity for experiment. The latter encompasses contemporary incident and improvisation in *The Soldier and the Dancer*, jazz and surrealism in *Les larmes du couteau* (scored for jazz band), film in *The Three Wishes*, medieval mystery plays in *The Plays of Mary*, commedia dell'arte in *The Suburban Theatre* and *Mirandolina*, and neo-classicism in *Alexandre bis* and *Ariadne*. Martinů was also a pioneer of opera for radio (*The Voice of the Forest* and *Comedy on a Bridge*) and television (*What Men Live By* and *The Wedding*). The more elusive background to the surreal *Julietta* and the political realism of *The Greek Passion* have not prevented these two works from becoming Martinů's most widely performed full-length operas.

Julietta: Snář

Julietta: The Book of Dreams
Lyric opera in three acts (2h 15m)
Libretto by the composer, after the play *Juliette, ou La clé des songes* (*Juliette, or The Key of Dreams*) by Georges Neveux (1930)
PREMIERES 16 March 1938, National Theatre, Prague: UK: 5 April 1978, Coliseum, London
CAST Julietta *s*, Michel *t*, Man in Helmet *bar*, Man at Window *b*, Old Arab *b*, 19 (9) other minor roles (maximum number given first, minimum in brackets), 2 (1) *s*, 5 (2) *ms*, 5 (2) *t*, 2 (1) *bar*, 5 (3) *b*; 6 townsfolk/3 gentlemen, *women's voices*

According to his biographer Miloš Šafránek, Martinů saw Neveux's surrealist play *Juliette* in 1932. Martinů wrote the libretto himself, with the author's permission, deeply impressing Neveux with his understanding of the work's effect on stage. The opera was a radical departure from Martinů's previous operas and remained a favourite with the composer. In his introduction to the published vocal score, Martinů said of *Julietta*, 'The libretto and play are not a philosophical dissertation, but an extraordinarily beautiful and poetic fantasy in the form of a dream.' Martinů responded well to the sharply observed wit and fantasy of his own libretto in what may be described as his operatic masterpiece. The plot, which Martinů himself found difficult to relate, is built up of many apparently disjointed episodes.

SYNOPSIS

Act I Michel, a travelling bookseller from Paris, has returned to a small harbour town to find a girl, Julietta, whose voice has haunted his memory since a previous visit. The strange behaviour of the inhabitants of the town is explained by their lack of memory: they live in a continuous present, seeking to acquire the reminiscences of others for themselves. Michel, with his memory, is understandably, if inevitably somewhat sporadically, an object of fascination. Eventually he finds Julietta. Although it is not clear that she remembers him, he is greeted as a lost lover and the act ends with her asking him to meet her in a wood.

Act II A series of surreal incidents forms a prelude to the meeting of Julietta and Michel. Michel's memories, feeding Julietta's fantasies, form the basis of the exchange. When she eventually runs away from him, he shoots at her, but it is not clear whether the shot has hit her. The act concludes when Michel, uncertain why he came to the town, is preparing to leave by boat when he hears Julietta's voice again.

Act III In the Central Office of Dreams, many come to experience dreams. Michel, wanting to return to his, hears Julietta calling. As the office closes, Michel rushes back into his dream, to find himself once again in the harbour town as at the start of the opera.

Julietta is characterized by subtle orchestral colouring and an acute command of situation. In an opera where large numbers of brief stage appearances form the substance of the action, the composer provides highly effective character studies. Julietta herself, by emerging forcefully as a heroine, does not threaten the dreamlike qualities of the whole. Her exchanges with Michel in Act II are a virtuoso mixture of aspiring lyricism and ironic bathos. Throughout, Martinů preserves the fantasy atmosphere of Neveux's original, although, as he was to recognize in a production at Wiesbaden in 1959, the opera maintains dramatic tension and explores disturbing psychological depths.

The Greek Passion
Řecké pašije

Opera in four acts (1h 45m)
Libretto by the composer and Nikos Kazantzakis, after Kazantzakis's novel *Christ Recrucified* (1948), translated into English by Jonathan Griffin
Composed 1956–7, rev. 1958 and 1959; invariably it is the 1959 revision that is performed
PREMIERES 9 June 1961, Opernhaus, Zurich; UK: 29 April 1981, New Theatre, Cardiff
CAST Manolios *t*, Katerina *s*, Grigoris *b-bar*, Fotis *b-bar*, Kostandis *bar*, Yannakos *t*, Lenio *s*, Panait *t*, 8 minor roles (3 *s*, *c*, 2 *t*, *bar*, *b*), Ladas *spoken role*; *satb* chorus of villagers and refugees; children's chorus

By 1954 Martinů was looking for a libretto with a Czech subject. He was diverted, however, by his discovery of Nikos Kazantzakis's novel *Zorba the Greek*. Since *Zorba* was unsuitable as an opera, Martinů began to write a libretto on another Kazantzakis novel, *Christ Recrucified*, retitling it *The Greek Passion*. Though the basic musical text was complete by early in 1957, Martinů cut and revised it over the next two years. Despite the Greek setting, the musical language is close to the Czech cantatas of the composer's late years. The adaptation of the novel skilfully reduces the Turkish element of the original in order to focus on the drama of the village set against a band of refugees.

SYNOPSIS
Act I A Greek village, Lykovrissi, in the early 20th century. On Easter morning the priest, Grigoris, distributes parts for next year's Passion play. Katerina, a young widow, is chosen as Mary Magdalene, Manolios, a shepherd, as Christ, and Panait, Katerina's lover, as Judas. As the characters dwell on the significance of their roles, night falls and a band of refugees, driven from their homes by Turks, arrives exhausted in the village. Grigoris, suspecting conflict and impov-

erishment for Lykovrissi orders them to leave. The act ends with Katerina offering help and Manolios suggesting that the refugees settle nearby.

Act II It becomes clear that Katerina is obsessed with Manolios. The miser Ladas persuades the pedlar Yannakos, who is to play the apostle Peter, to offer money for the valuables of the needy refugees. Witnessing the simple dignity and hope of the refugees, Yannakos is ashamed of his attempt to cheat them, and presents them instead with Ladas's money.

Act III Manolios's and Katerina's relationship comes to a head when he persuades her that their love can be only spiritual. She learns to accept the fulfilment of the love of Mary Magdalene for Christ. Manolios, becoming still more Christ-like, persuades the villagers to help the refugees as the village elders plot to prevent him.

Act IV As the villagers celebrate a wedding, Grigorios excommunicates Manolios and denounces him. After explaining his actions as the substitute of Christ, Manolios is killed by Panait as the refugees approach. Both parties mourn the death of Manolios, and the refugees prepare to leave the village.

Although built as a series of tableaux, *The Greek Passion* has a powerful sense of dramatic continuity. The characters grow at the same pace as the Passion tragedy, leading to a dénouement of extraordinary power. Much of the force of the work in Acts I and IV is generated through the use of antiphonal choruses. The musical language is warmly diatonic, coloured both by the extensive use of Greek Orthodox chant and by the gentle lyricism associated with many of the works of Martinů's last decade.

Other operas: *The Soldier and the Dancer* (*Voják a tanečnice*), 1928; *Les larmes du couteau* (*Slzy nože*), (1928), 1968; *Trois souhaits, ou Les vicissitudes de la vie* (*Troji přání, aneb vrtkavosti života*), film opera, (1929), 1971; *The Plays of Mary* (*Hry o Marii*), 1935; *La semaine de bonté* (inc.), 1931; *The Voice of the Forest* (*Hlas lesa*), radio opera, 1935; *The Suburban Theatre* (*Divadlo za branou*), 1936; *Comedy on a Bridge* (*Veselohra na mostě*), radio opera, 1937; *Alexander bis* (*Dvakrát Alexandr*), (1937), 1964; *What Men Live By* (*Čím lidé žijí*), television opera, 1953; *The Marriage* (*Ženitba*), television opera, 1953; *La plainte contre inconnu* (inc., 1953); *Mirandolina*, (1954), 1959; *Ariadne* (*Ariane/Ariadna*), 1961

J.A.S.

PIETRO MASCAGNI
b 7 December 1863, Livorno, Italy; *d* 2 August 1945, Rome

Although younger than his contemporaries Puccini and Leoncavallo, Mascagni was the first to taste triumph, and fame came to him in an unlikely way. Against family opposition (his father wanted him to continue the family bakery business), he was determined to follow a musical career, and at the age of 19 he was admitted to the Milan Conservatory to study composition, where his teachers included Ponchielli.

Dismissed during his second year for failure to complete assignments, he supported himself by playing the double-bass at the Teatro Dal Verme in Milan (where he played in the premiere of Puccini's *Le villi*) and conducting opera at Cremona. Unable to interest a publisher in his attempts at writing for the stage, he settled down in Cerignola (Puglia) to give music lessons. In 1889 he saw an advertisement for the publisher Sonzogno's second competition for one-act operas. He was fired with enthusiasm and quickly wrote *Cavalleria rusticana*. Once it was completed, however, he was besieged with doubts and all but decided to submit Act IV of his *Guglielmo Ratcliff* instead. But, unbeknown to him, his wife dispatched the score of *Cavalleria rusticana*, and it was awarded the first prize.

Together with the other two winning works, *Cavalleria rusticana* was performed at the Teatro Costanzi in Rome in May 1890. Mascagni was fortunate to have in the cast two of the most popular singers in Italy: the tenor Roberto Stagno and his fiery wife, Gemma Bellincioni. *Cavalleria* scored an immediate success, and amazingly soon it was heard in theatres all over the world.

Mascagni was instantly famous and was soon acknowledged the harbinger of the group that came to be known as the *veristi* or 'The Young Italian School' (among its leaders would be Leoncavallo, Puccini, Giordano and Cilea). Predictably, anticipation was great for his next work, but, instead of trying to emulate *Cavalleria*, he brought out a naïve idyll set in Alsace, *L'amico Fritz* (1891). In no way an outright failure, this work puzzled and disappointed those who expected Mascagni to exploit the vein of *Cavalleria*.

A string of operas followed over the next decade, ranging in subject from a maritime drama (*Silvano*) to the Japanese *Iris*. But a repeat of the success of *Cavalleria* eluded him, and, restlessly seeking to prove himself as something more than a one-opera composer and to avoid the generally unfavourable attitude of Italian critics, Mascagni decided to give the premieres of his next two operas outside his native country. *Amica*, to a French text by Paul de Choudens, was premiered at Monte Carlo in 1905, but failed to sustain itself. Better fortune greeted *Isabeau* (Buenos Aires, 1911), a sensational variant of the Godiva story, although its success, too, was short-lived. With *Parisina* (1913) Mascagni attempted another premiere in Italy, but, yet again, neither this long-winded score nor that of the sentimental *Lodoletta* (1917) exerted much appeal. The closest Mascagni came to a major success in the later part of his career was *Il piccolo Marat*, based on a French Revolutionary subject, though the opera still failed to enter the repertoire.

In 1929, however, Mascagni's opportunistic nature was confirmed when he succeeded Arturo Toscanini as musical director of La Scala, as he had no scruples about beginning performances with the fascist hymn. In 1932 he reworked the score of an early cantata and brought out *Pinotta* in the unlikely precincts of the San Remo Casino. His last opera, *Nerone*, was introduced at La Scala in 1935 with much preliminary hullabaloo. After the obligatory first round of produc-

tions on Italian stages, it started to gather dust which has scarcely been disturbed since. At Venice, Rome and Milan in 1940, on the occasion of the 50th anniversary of *Cavalleria*, Mascagni conducted his chief claim to fame, filling out the evening with excerpts from its less fortunate sisters. Mascagni did not long survive the collapse of fascism, dying in an obscure Roman hotel.

It is all too easy to dismiss Mascagni as a self-promoting opportunist and a composer of limited achievements. But there is not a score of his that is without some arresting moments, although his creative impetus was short-breathed and lacked continuity. He too readily mistook emotion for the expression of deep feeling. Yet his experiments in setting text and his choice of subjects reveal his responsiveness to the temper of his times. *Cavalleria* will remain his monument, a symbol of his accomplishment as well as his limitations.

Cavalleria rusticana
Rustic Chivalry
Melodrama in one act (1h 15m)
Libretto by Giovanni Targioni-Tozzetti and Guido Menasci, after the play by Giovanni Verga (1883)
PREMIERES 17 May 1890, Teatro Costanzi, Rome; US: 9 September 1891, Academy of Music, Philadelphia; UK: 19 October 1891, Shaftesbury Theatre, London
CAST Santuzza *s* or *ms*, Lola *ms*, Mamma Lucia *c*, Turiddu *t*, Alfio *bar*; *satb* chorus of villagers

The rapidity with which *Cavalleria rusticana* spread throughout the world has been unmatched by any other opera. Within the space of little more than a year it had promulgated operatic verismo and soon spawned a host of imitations, of which only Leoncavallo's *Pagliacci* firmly established itself in the repertoire, supplying the other member of the most performed double-bill of modern times. The idea of writing an opera on Verga's dramatization of his novella was Mascagni's, and he persuaded two of his friends to provide him with the libretto. In terms of influence, the opera's chief significance lies in the fact that it presents ordinary people in credible situations and thus seems to tell a story sufficiently realistic and simple to be true to life.

SYNOPSIS
Some time before Turiddu went off to serve in the army, he had had an affair with Lola. While he was away, Lola married the carter Alfio. On his return Turiddu seduced Santuzza, who is now pregnant by him and has been excommunicated because of her condition. She loves him sincerely, but to her chagrin Lola could not endure seeing Turiddu with another and has resumed her affair with him.

Easter morning in a village in Sicily. Before the curtain rises, Turiddu is heard singing a siciliana ('O, Lola') to his mistress (this forms the final part of the opera's prelude). The villagers comment on the season ('Gli aranci alezzano'). Alfio enters ('Il cavallo scalpita') and soon asks Turiddu's mother, Lucia, about her son's whereabouts. Lucia says he has gone to Francofonte to fetch some wine for the family inn.

When Alfio says he has seen Turiddu near his house, Santuzza hurriedly tells Lucia to keep silent. Further conversation is halted by the Easter Hymn ('Inneggiamo il Signore; non è morto'). When all but Santuzza and Lucia have entered the church, the young woman pours out her heart to Lucia, telling her how Lola has stolen Turiddu and left her desperate. Lucia goes into the church, leaving Santuzza to wait for Turiddu. He soon appears ('Tu qui, Santuzza?') and she implores him to come back to her, informing him that he has been seen at dawn near Lola's house. Turiddu accuses her of jealousy, but then they are interrupted by Lola on her way to church ('Fior di giaggiolo'). After an exchange of barbed remarks between the women, Lola goes to attend the service. Ever more desperately, Santuzza begs Turiddu to return her love, but he rejects her forcibly, throwing her down and running into the church. Now blinded by jealous fury, she sees Alfio and pours out her story of Lola's infidelity ('Oh! Il Signor vi manda, compar Alfio'), while Alfio vows vengeance. After the intermezzo, the congregation throngs out and Turiddu urges them to have a post-ecclesiastical tipple ('Viva il vino spumeggiante'). When Alfio appears, Turiddu offers him a glass of wine, but Alfio refuses, saying it would turn to poison inside him. The villagers draw Lola away. Alfio, in the way of the traditional challenge, bites Turiddu's earlobe. Before they go off to duel behind the church, Turiddu takes leave of his mother, asking that she look out for Santuzza ('Mamma, quel vino è generoso'). The women gather in the piazza, and suddenly a female voice is heard screaming that Turiddu has been killed. Santuzza and Lucia faint.

This concise, passionate tale of Sicilian peasants, ironically occurring on Easter Sunday, elicited from Mascagni crude but effective music that seemed the inevitable mode of expression for his characters. The score, except for Turiddu's serenade in the prologue, begins conventionally enough with an opening chorus and a 'characteristic' song for Alfio, soon followed by the Gounodesque Easter Hymn. It is only with Santuzza's arioso, 'Voi lo sapete, o mamma', that the dramatic temperature begins to rise, reaching a climax with the Santuzza–Alfio duet. The tragic outcome is assured at this point, but then comes the contrast of the serene intermezzo played to an empty stage. This calm before the inevitable storm serves, oddly enough, only to increase the tension.

L'amico Fritz

Friend Fritz

Commedia lirica in three acts (1h 30m)
Libretto by Nicola Diaspuro, based on the novel *L'ami Fritz* by Emile Erckmann and Alexandre Chatrian (1864)
PREMIERES 31 October 1891, Teatro Costanzi, Rome; UK: 23 May 1892, Covent Garden, London; US: 8 June 1892, Academy of Music, Philadelphia

Mascagni's publisher Sonzogno was, understandably, keen that Mascagni should present another opera while the success of *Cavalleria* was still at its height. Aware that some critics were attributing its success

solely to its libretto, Mascagni stated that he wanted 'a simple libretto, with almost a flimsy plot, so the opera could be judged on the music alone'. Sonzogno suggested Erckmann's and Chatrian's play (adapted from the same authors' novel).

Set in Alsace, the plot concerns a wealthy landowner, Fritz Kobus, a bachelor. His friend Rabbi David ignores his protests against marriage, assuring him he will soon wed. When David offers to wager, Fritz offers his vineyard at Clairfontaine. The young daughter of one of his tenants, Suzel, brings him a bouquet. Later, she comes to gather cherries, and Fritz is charmed by her unspoiled innocence. Fritz is unable to come to terms with his new emotions and decides to move to town. Later he returns, realizing that he is in love. In his absence, Suzel's father wants her to marry another, but she must get Fritz's permission to do so. Fritz gradually acknowledges his attachment to her, feelings she readily reciprocates. Rabbi David wins his bet and gives the vineyard to Suzel as a wedding gift.

Although Mascagni was happy with his text, others were less impressed: Verdi considered it 'the worst libretto I've ever seen'. However, the opera's public reception, though nowhere near the level of *Cavalleria*'s, was not unenthusiastic. As in *Cavalleria*, the opera's strength lies in Mascagni's skill as a melodist, most famously demonstrated here in the so-called 'cherry duet' ('Suzel, buon dì') for Fritz and Suzel. Progressing from parlando to arioso before arriving at the duet 'proper', the scene also displays a flexibility of formal structures and a continuity which advance considerably on those of *Cavalleria* and which were to influence other composers.

Other operas: *Pinotta* (adapted from the cantata *In filanda*), (c. 1880), 1932; *I Rantzau*, 1892; *Guglielmo Ratcliff*, 1895; *Silvano*, 1895; *Zanetto*, 1896; *Iris*, 1898; *Le maschere*, 1901; rev. 1905, 1931; *Amica*, 1905; *Isabeau*, 1911; *Parisina*, 1913; *Lodoletta*, 1917; *Il piccolo Marat*, 1921; *Nerone*, 1935; Operetta: *Sì*, 1919

W.A.

JULES MASSENET

Jules-Émile-Frédéric Massenet; *b* 12 May 1842, Montaud, nr Saint Étienne, Loire, France; *d* 13 August 1912, Paris

Massenet was one of the most successful of all French opera composers, for, although his work never equalled the grandeur of Berlioz's *Les troyens*, the genius of Bizet's *Carmen*, or the profundity of Debussy's *Pelléas et Mélisande*, he provided the French operatic stage between 1867 and his death in 1912 with a series of remarkable works of great variety and invention. Two of them, *Manon* and *Werther*, are masterpieces that will always grace the repertoire, and a considerable number of others offer rewarding operatic experience in terms of vocal and orchestral technique, scenic invention, comedy, pathos, sentiment, local colour, and so on. He was a thoroughly professional composer who perfected his craft at an early age and enjoyed the fruits of success. His works fell victim, for the most part, to the very different tastes of the post-1918 generation, and some have not been revived. But he embodies many enduring aspects of the belle époque, one of the richest cultural eras of history.

Massenet was trained at the Paris Conservatoire and he won the Prix de Rome in 1863. He was influenced by Meyerbeer, Berlioz, Gounod and his teacher, Thomas. He was a timpanist at the Opéra for a spell, learning the craft of orchestration from the experience. His grounding in opera came less from his first two operas (both opéras comiques), *La grand' tante* (1867) and *Don César de Bazan* (1872), than from the 'sacred dramas' *Marie-Magdeleine* (1873) and *Eve* (1875), in which human passion is set against a background of religious fervour, a dramatic contrast that was to inform some of his most successful operas, notably *Hérodiade*, *Thaïs* and *Le jongleur de Notre-Dame*. In the field of grand opera with epic scenic effects and abundant local colour, he maintained a long French tradition, although none of the operas of that type (*Le roi de Lahore*, *Hérodiade*, *Le Cid*, *Le mage*, *Ariane*) was able to equal his intimate tragedies (*Manon*, *Werther*), his veristic dramas (*La navarraise*, *Thérèse*) or his comedies (*Cendrillon*, *Don Quichotte*). The variety of his work is indeed astonishing, since there is no ready category for a magical opera such as *Esclarmonde*, nor for the unusual blend of sex and religion found in *Thaïs*, nor for the monastic mystery *Le jongleur de Notre-Dame*.

Massenet was strictly regular in his working habits, a characteristic of many highly fertile composers, and he usually composed with great speed, keeping revision to a minimum. He would sometimes have a vocal score printed before a work went into rehearsal. His full scores are mostly annotated with great precision concerning dates and locations. He worked with a variety of librettists, although the obliging Henri Cain was a regular partner. He liked to find unusual settings for his operas, ranging from classical mythology to the contemporary, and his fondness for the 18th century is manifest. He relished providing special music, such as ballets or set-piece songs within the drama, or 'symphonies' to suggest dramatic action. He had a rare understanding of the human voice, and worked enthusiastically for certain singers – usually sopranos, with whom gossip was wont to link his name. For Sybil Sanderson, for instance, he felt a particular tenderness and wrote some remarkable roles, notably the title roles of *Esclarmonde* and *Thaïs*; for Georgette Wallace (whose stage name was Lucy Arbell) he similarly composed with great sympathy; her chief roles were Dulcinée and the title roles of *Ariane* and *Thérèse*. He always notated vocal parts with extreme precision, a practice he may have learned from studying Verdi's scores.

His affection for his leading ladies has led many to suppose that Massenet depicted only his female characters with real understanding, but this notion is easily refuted. The role of Athanaël in *Thaïs* is hard to project convincingly, but there is no mistaking the depth of des Grieux's agony in *Manon*, or of Werther's, or of Jean's in *Sapho*. *Le jongleur de Notre-Dame* offers a rich variety of male types, and both

Don Quichotte and Sancho Panza evoke the audience's sympathy with a few deft strokes.

Massenet's fondness for religious scenes was derived not from faith but simply from an acute sense of the dramatic in religious ritual and devotions, a striking feature of Catholicism. He loved the 18th-century style, using Handelian mannerisms freely, often for minor characters of the buffo type. He could equally call on medieval pastiche when required. He liked to evoke the world of magic in the manner of Rimsky-Korsakov, or the world of children, as he does in both *Werther* and *Cendrillon*. He could slip easily from tragedy to sentiment to high comedy. His sense of theatrical timing is hard to fault, an operatic instinct he shared with Verdi and Puccini. His structural skill is best observed in the way single scenes are constructed, using tonality and motifs – both vocal and orchestral – to build movements of rounded musical shape and appropriate dramatic pace.

While he aroused the envy of other composers who lacked his success (Saint-Saëns) or his fertility (Debussy), Massenet enjoyed popular acclaim in France and abroad. As a teacher he had a considerable influence on the younger generation, especially on Alfred Bruneau, Gustave Charpentier and Florent Schmitt, all of them sharply individual in their approach to opera. His best work was written in the last two decades of the 19th century, and, although some of his later operas maintained this high level, the lack of any modernity began to disappoint audiences seduced by the shock of Richard Strauss, Dukas and Schmitt, or by the mysterious murmurings of Debussy. His main works survived in the repertoire, though, and will always continue to do so as long as great singing and high operatic craft are held in esteem.

Hérodiade
Herodias
Opera in four acts (3h)
Libretto by Paul Milliet, 'Henri Grémont' (Georges Hartmann) and Angelo Zanardini, after Gustave Flaubert's *Hérodias* (in the *Trois contes*, 1877) (Though Grémont and Zanardini, Ricordi's agent, are credited as co-librettists, their contribution was more impresarial than literary.)
Composed 1878–81; rev. 1883
PREMIERES three-act version: 19 December 1881, Théâtre de la Monnaie, Brussels; final version: 1 February 1884, Théâtre Italien, Paris; US: 13 February 1892, French Opera House, New Orleans; UK: 6 July 1904, Covent Garden, London (as *Salome*)
CAST Jean (John the Baptist) *t*, Hérode (Herod) *bar*, Phanuel *b*, Vitellius *bar*, The High Priest *bar*, A Voice *t*, Salomé (Salome) *s*, Hérodiade (Herodias) *ms*, A Young Babylonian *s*; *satb* chorus of merchants, soldiers, Jews, Roman soldiers, priests, Levites, temple attendants, sailors, Pharisees, Scribes, Galileans, Samaritans, Ethiopians, Nubians, Arabians, Romans; dancers

Four years, an unusually wide gap, separate *Hérodiade* from Massenet's previous opera, *Le roi de Lahore*. Massenet had suggested to Paul Milliet that he write a love poem which mingled Christian mysticism and sensual passion, as if 'a woman's hair became a man's hair-shirt'. The poem was set aside, but it influenced their collaboration on an adaptation of Flaubert's *Hérodias*, encouraged by Massenet's publisher, Georges Hartmann. When the opera was completed, Auguste Vaucourbeil, director of the Paris Opéra, judged the work to be *incendiaire*, owing to its biblical-amorous subject (the same objection that kept Saint-Saëns's *Samson et Dalila* from that stage for many years), so Massenet gladly accepted an offer from the Théâtre de la Monnaie, a much more enterprising stage for young French composers in those years. For the Paris premiere of 1884, Massenet revised his original version, rearranging a number of passages, expanding the opera to four acts, and adding the slaves' chorus and dance (Act II, Scene 1).

SYNOPSIS
To Flaubert's colourful retelling of the biblical Salome story Milliet added the supposition that Salome is in love with John the Baptist.

Act I   Herod the tetrarch is indifferent to the Jews' resentment of the Romans. Salome confesses to Phanuel, an astrologer, that she loves John (the Baptist), who has been prophesying the coming of the Messiah. Herodias, Herod's wife, hates John for his preaching.

Act II   Herod is obsessed with the image of Salome, who, unknown to Herodias, is her long-lost daughter; she sees Salome only as her rival.

Act III   Furious because Salome refuses to yield to him, Herod orders both her and John to be beheaded.

Act IV   Salome and John await their execution and hope that their love may continue in heaven. Salome wants to kill Herodias as the person responsible for John's death sentence, but when she discovers that Herodias is her mother she kills herself instead.

Hérodiade was very successful, at least until the advent of Strauss's *Salome* based on Wilde's much more sensational version of the story. It has occasionally been revived in recent years, although the comparison with Strauss is inevitably unfavourable.

In *Hérodiade*, Massenet is master of his technique, but the work is exuberantly overlong, especially in the last act, when a chorus of Roman soldiers and a set of ballets precede the dénouement. The vocal style, full of boldly shaped phrases, is fully characteristic, and the variety of colour is considerable. Massenet uses a number of recurrent motifs. The opera can succeed only when staged in a grandly sumptuous manner. Salome does not dance.

Manon

Opéra comique in five acts (six tableaux) (2h 30m)
Libretto by Henri Meilhac and Philippe Gille, after the Abbé Prévost's novel *L'histoire du Chevalier des Grieux et de Manon Lescaut* (1731)
Composed May–October 1882, orch. March–August 1883; last scene rev., gavotte inserted in Cours-la-Reine scene, 1884; *fabliau* replaced Act III gavotte (this rev. not generally used), 1898
PREMIERES   19 January 1884, Opéra-Comique, Paris; UK: 17 January 1885, Liverpool; US: 23 December 1885, Academy of Music, New York
CAST   Manon Lescaut *s*, Le Chevalier des Grieux *t*, Lescaut *bar*, Count des Grieux *b*, Guillot de Morfontaine *t*, De Brétigny *bar*, Poussette *s*, Javotte *s*, Rosette *ms*, Innkeeper *b bouffe*, Two Guards *t*; *spoken roles*: maid, seminary porter, sergeant, constable, gambler; *satb* chorus of elegant society, citizens of Amiens and Paris, travellers, porters, postilions, merchants, churchgoers, gamblers, cardsharpers, croupiers

Manon is Massenet's most successful opera and, with *Faust* and *Carmen*, one of the mainstays of the French repertoire to this day. The Abbé Prévost's novel had been set as an opéra comique by Auber in 1856, but had soon faded from the repertoire. The idea for *Manon* came to Massenet in a conversation with Henri Meilhac, who had written numerous libretti for Offenbach and others in collaboration with Ludovic Halévy, but who now collaborated with Philippe Gille, a journalist and dramatist. Despite the claim of Massenet's autobiography that the opera was begun in 1881, his correspondence shows that it was not composed until after *Hérodiade* had been performed. *Manon* was conceived as a quite different opera from his two preceding grandiose works. It was to be an opéra comique, with some speech over music and a more continuous and integrated structure than usual. It called for some 18th-century pastiche and a more intimate manner.

It was completed in October 1882, some of it composed in The Hague, where Massenet occupied the Abbé Prévost's own rooms, at that time a hotel. Part of the gambling scene used music originally intended for *Hérodiade*. In February 1883 a contract was signed with the publisher Georges Hartmann, and the orchestration of the work followed. *Manon* remained a regular item of the Opéra-Comique's repertoire almost without interruption until 1959. It quickly conquered the world's stages. Ten years later Massenet followed up the story of Manon with *Le portrait de Manon*, by which time Puccini had set his version of the novel as *Manon Lescaut* (1893).

SYNOPSIS
Act I   The courtyard of a hostelry at Amiens, *c.* 1720. De Brétigny, a *fermier-général*, and Guillot de Morfontaine, a financier, are calling noisily for food and drink. They are accompanied by three young ladies of doubtful virtue, Poussette, Javotte and Rosette. A bell rings, announcing the forthcoming arrival of the stagecoach from Arras. People crowd into the courtyard to inspect the new arrivals, among them Lescaut, awaiting his young cousin Manon, who is on her way to a convent. Lescaut's interest, it is clear, is in drinking and gambling. Travellers arrive in some confusion, and Manon is greeted by Lescaut. She chatters eagerly about her first experience of travel ('Je suis encore tout étourdie'), then Lescaut goes in search of her luggage. Guillot appears, catches sight of Manon, and makes immediate advances. Lescaut, returning, is offended. He sends Guillot away and gives Manon, who is fascinated by the sophisticated world she sees around her, a few timely words of warning about unwelcome strangers ('Regardez-moi

bien dans les yeux'). Des Grieux appears. He has missed the coach which was to take him to his father ('J'ai manqué l'heure du départ'). Entranced by Manon, he introduces himself. She is captivated too. After only a little hesitation she agrees to leave with des Grieux, taking the coach which Guillot had arranged to abduct her in. Both Lescaut and Guillot are furious when they learn what has happened. Everyone else is amused.

Act II   In the apartment in the Rue Vivienne, Paris, where he and Manon are now living, des Grieux is writing to his father to explain their relationship and to sing Manon's praises ('On l'appelle Manon'). After a noisy disturbance offstage, Lescaut comes in with de Brétigny, disguised as a guardsman. Des Grieux calms Lescaut by assuring him that he plans to marry Manon, and shows him the letter to his father. Meanwhile de Brétigny is tempting Manon to abandon des Grieux for a life of pleasure and riches, a temptation she cannot easily resist. While des Grieux goes out to post the letter, she sings a farewell to their humble life together ('Adieu, notre petite table'). When he returns, he tells her of a daydream he had in which all is paradise, except Manon is not there with him ('En fermant les yeux'). Suddenly a knock is heard. Manon, who knows that des Grieux is to be abducted, fails to stop him answering the door, yet she is overcome by grief as he is taken away.

Act III   Scene 1: The Cours-la-Reine by the Seine. There is much merry-making, with merchants selling their wares and a crowd enjoying a public holiday. Lescaut is spending freely. Manon is arm in arm with de Brétigny, enjoying his attention and wealth. A gavotte is danced ('Profitons bien de la jeunesse'). Des Grieux's father, the count, tells de Brétigny that his son plans to take holy orders and is to preach that evening at Saint-Sulpice. Manon sends de Brétigny away on an errand and then questions the count about des Grieux's feelings. Guillot lays on a divertissement, danced by a troupe from the Opéra, but Manon's thoughts are now elsewhere. Scene 2: The seminary at Saint-Sulpice. The service at which des Grieux was preaching is over. His father congratulates him ('Épouse quelque brave fille'), but he is still full of bitterness. He is determined to take his vows. After the count has left, des Grieux confesses the image of Manon still haunts him ('Ah! fuyez, douce image'). He goes into the church. When he comes back he finds Manon waiting for him. The reunion overcomes all their doubts, and they run off together again.

Act IV   An illicit gaming room in the Hôtel de Transylvanie. Lescaut, Guillot and their friends are at the tables when Manon and des Grieux enter. With Lescaut's support Manon urges an unwilling des Grieux to try his luck. She is again dazzled by the glitter of money and the lure of laughter. Guillot loses to des Grieux, exchanges some sharp words, and goes off to fetch the count and the police. Lescaut escapes, but Guillot has his revenge: des Grieux and Manon are arrested, accused of cheating.

Act V   The road to Le Havre. Des Grieux has been freed, but Manon is to be deported as a prostitute. Lescaut's plan to rescue her has failed. When the guards appear, Lescaut bribes the sergeant to let Manon stay behind for a while, under guard. He then bribes the guard too and leads him away. Des Grieux and Manon are now alone, but she is too weak to flee. She dies in des Grieux's arms.

Manon brought out the best of Massenet's operatic genius. The score shows his great feeling for human passion and also his incomparable skill in scenic management. The principle of dramatic contrast is abundantly used: in the depiction of Manon's character, torn between her devotion to des Grieux and her fatal weakness for a glittering social milieu; in the contrast between adjacent scenes (the solitude of their room in the Rue Vivienne followed by the bustle of the Cours-la-Reine, the devotional atmosphere of Saint-Sulpice followed by the gaming tables of the Hôtel de Transylvanie); and in the contrast of musical styles between the elegant 18th-century pastiche in the Cours-la-Reine scene and the sweeping romantic phrases with which real passion is expressed. The use of speech over music is purposeful (although in a New York performance Massenet allowed these passages to be sung), and the choral scenes are invariably handled with great skill. The opera contains a well-developed set of leitmotifs, two for Lescaut, one each for de Brétigny and Guillot, for example. Manon's earlier motifs pass out of sight as she grows up with great rapidity. Massenet also uses orchestral motifs to identify a scene, for example the gambling motif in Act IV and the soldiers' motif in Act V.

Des Grieux's complex characterization explodes the belief that Massenet could portray only female characters with true feeling, and once Manon has been lured into the social world it is difficult ever quite to believe in her attachment to him as wholly as in his for her. Yet because Manon is the only female character (apart from the puppet-like trio of Poussette, Javotte and Rosette) against five males with various claims on her, she cannot fail to hold our attention when she is on stage. Her plight is no less touching because she appears at times both fickle and shallow. Massenet's sense of her impudence and gaiety makes this image of the eternal feminine perfectly sympathetic.

Le Cid
The Cid

Opera in four acts (ten tableaux) (2h 15m)
Libretto by Adolphe d'Ennery, Louis Gallet and Édouard Blau, after Philippe Corneille's drama *Le Cid* (1637) and Guillen da Castro y Bellvis's play *Las mocedades del Cid* (1618)
PREMIERES   30 November 1885, Opéra, Paris; US: 17 February 1890, French Opera House, New Orleans
CAST   Chimène *s*, The Infanta *s*, Rodrigue (Le Cid) *t*, Don Diègue *b*, The King *bar*, Le Comte de Gormas *b*, St Jacques *bar*, The Envoy Maure *b*, Don Arias *t*, Don Alonzo *b*; *satb* chorus of lords, ladies, bishops, priests, monks, captains, soldiers, people; dancers

Corneille's *Le Cid* had served many earlier composers when Massenet accepted Gallet's libretto, previously offered to Bizet in 1873. Part of the libretto came from a project by d'Ennery, part directly from Corneille, and the vision scene in Act III was taken from Castro's *Cid* and from Flaubert's *S. Julien Hospitalier*. For the music Massenet reused some fanfares written in Venice in 1865 and an unused draft for *Hérodiade*. He collected one motif on a visit to Spain.

SYNOPSIS

Act I The comte de Gormas and his friends talk about Rodrigue, who is to be knighted by the king. Chimène, the comte's daughter, is planning to marry Rodrigue and has her father's approval. At the ceremony in Burgos Cathedral a quarrel breaks out between Gormas and Don Diègue (Rodrigue's father) over the latter's appointment as preceptor for the infanta.

Act II Rodrigue challenges Gormas on his father's behalf and kills him; Chimène learns that Rodrigue has killed her father, and asks the king to serve justice on him. When war with the Moors is announced, the king appoints Rodrigue at the head of the army in place of Gormas.

Act III There is first a love scene for Chimène (despite her loyalties) and Rodrigue, then a vision for Rodrigue in which St Jacques de Compostella promises him victory. The Moors are defeated.

Act IV Rodrigue is reported dead. Chimène at last confesses her love for him. When after all he returns alive, Chimène overcomes her sense of duty and allows herself to be united with him.

Le Cid reverted to the spectacular style of *Hérodiade*, still the prevalent taste at the Paris Opéra, with plenty of Spanish and Moorish colour and many opportunities for lavish settings: the cathedral square at Burgos, for example. The ballets from Act II are still popular in the concert hall, but the popularity of the opera itself scarcely lasted beyond Massenet's lifetime. It has some fine scenes, notably those for Rodrigue and Don Diègue at the end of Act I, Chimène's solo scene at the opening of Act III ('Pleurez, pleurez, mes yeux'), and the duet with Rodrigue that follows.

Werther

Drame lyrique in four acts (five tableaux) (2h 30m)
Libretto by Édouard Blau, Paul Milliet and Georges Hartmann, after Johann Wolfgang von Goethe's novel *Die Leiden des jungen Werthers* (1774)
PREMIERES 16 February 1892, Hofoper, Vienna; France: 16 January 1893, Opéra-Comique, Paris; US: 29 March 1894, Chicago; UK: 11 June 1894, Covent Garden, London
CAST Werther *t*, Albert *bar*, Le Bailli *b*, Schmidt *t*, Johann *bar*, Charlotte *ms*, Sophie *s*, Bruhlmann *t*, Katchen *s*, 6 children 6 *s*

Werther may claim to be Massenet's masterpiece and, next to *Manon*, his best-known opera. In a letter of September 1880 Massenet spoke of his intention to follow *Hérodiade*, then just completed, with *Werther*. The idea had emerged from a conversation in Milan in 1879 with Hartmann, Massenet's publisher, and Milliet, librettist of *Hérodiade*. The plan was shelved

in favour of *Manon* and then *Le Cid*, and Milliet's role as librettist was taken over by Édouard Blau (one of *Le Cid*'s librettists). *Werther* was eventually started in 1885, but evidently it did not go well. Hartmann, knowing Massenet's need for appropriate stimuli, acquired an 18th-century apartment in Versailles for him to work in, and then, on a trip to Bayreuth in August 1886, suggested that they visit Wetzlar, north of Frankfurt, where Goethe had conceived his *Werther*; a similar absorption of the Abbé Prévost's rooms in The Hague had assisted the composition of *Manon* three years earlier.

This visit, though not the original inspiration for *Werther*, as Massenet's autobiography claims, provided a tremendous spur to the completion of the opera. But it was turned down by the Opéra-Comique as too depressing. After that theatre's destruction by fire, its new management preferred the more glamorous *Esclarmonde*. Thus *Werther* did not appear in Paris until 1893; its premiere took place in Vienna in February 1892, following the great success there of *Manon* two years before. It soon conquered every stage and has been a repertoire work ever since.

SYNOPSIS

The action takes place near Frankfurt between July and December 178...

Act I: 'The Bailli's House' July. On the terrace of his house the bailli, a magistrate, is rehearsing his six small children in a Christmas carol. A widower, he is cared for by his elder daughters, Charlotte (20) and Sophie (15). Johann and Schmidt, two of his friends, come in and discuss a ball to be given that evening in Wetzlar, the possibility that Werther (a melancholy young man of 23) may be sent away as an ambassador, and the imminent arrival of Charlotte's fiancé, Albert. They leave, and soon Werther appears, entranced by the beauty of nature and by the children's singing within the house ('O nature, pleine de grâce'). He watches as Charlotte comes out of the house and busies herself with the children. The bailli greets Werther and introduces Charlotte. All, including a number of other guests, go off to the ball, leaving Sophie to care for the children. Albert then arrives, anxious to have news of Charlotte ('Quelle prière de reconnaissance'), and goes into the house. As darkness falls, Charlotte and Werther return, arm in arm. Werther becomes increasingly amorous until the bailli's voice is heard telling Charlotte that Albert is back. When she tells Werther she is to marry Albert since her mother made her promise to, Werther, in despair, tells her to fulfil her promise.

Act II: 'The Lime Trees' September. The church square at Wetzlar. Johann and Schmidt are drinking outside a tavern. Charlotte and Albert, now married, arrive for church, blessing their happiness. Werther appears, cursing the happiness he has missed ('Un autre son époux!'). When Albert comes out of the church, he offers Werther consolation for any regrets he may feel at their marriage and suggests Sophie as an alternative bride. Left alone, Werther realizes he has to leave, and when Charlotte emerges from the church she begs him to go, conceding that they may meet again at Christmas. After she has gone, Werther thinks at once of suicide ('Lorsque l'enfant revient d'un voyage') and leaves, telling Sophie that he will not be back. Charlotte, hearing this from Sophie, is so clearly distraught that Albert realizes that Werther is in love with her.

Act III: 'Charlotte and Werther' Christmas Eve, 5 o'clock. Albert's house. Charlotte confesses that her thoughts are all with Werther and that his letters stir her deeply ('Werther . . . Werther . . .'). Sophie attempts to cheer her up. Charlotte breaks into a passionate prayer for spiritual aid ('Va, laisse couler mes larmes'), then Werther appears at the door. Before long she finds herself in his arms. Overcome with guilt and remorse, she rushes from the room. Werther leaves. Albert enters, calling for Charlotte. She appears, obviously distraught. A servant brings a message for Albert from Werther: since he is leaving for a distant country, would Albert lend him his pistols? Albert orders Charlotte to fetch the pistols. As soon as Albert has gone, she rushes out, praying that she is not too late.

Act IV The same evening. Scene 1: 'Christmas Night', an orchestral tableau leading directly into Scene 2: 'The Death of Werther', in Werther's study. Werther lies mortally wounded, the pistols at his side. Charlotte rushes in, finds him, and attempts to revive him. She confesses she loves him, and they kiss for the first time. As Werther dies, he hears the children singing 'Noël' and imagines he hears angels promising forgiveness.

Goethe's novel was based on the story of a young lawyer, Karl Wilhelm Jerusalem, who shot himself in October 1772 because of his unhappy love for the wife of a diplomat. Jerusalem had borrowed pistols from a friend of Goethe who gave a full account of Jerusalem's death, quoting the text of the note asking for the loan of the pistols. This note was copied by Goethe in his novel and by Massenet in his opera.

The libretto is necessarily a free adaptation of the novel, which consists simply of Werther's letters. Some of Werther's complex pantheistic personality is lost, whereas Charlotte is a more immediate and real figure. Sophie's role is almost entirely the invention of the librettists, and the final act, bringing Charlotte and Werther together for a final death scene, is their creation too: in the novel, Werther dies alone. In Goethe, Werther's malaise may be seen as the hopeless dissatisfaction of a searching, Romantic melancholic, whereas Massenet's Werther is more narrowly the victim of an amorous passion that cannot be satisfied.

Charlotte in the opera presents a wonderfully touching portrait of a girl gradually moved to pull against her mother's wishes and the constraints of her marriage (in Goethe, Charlotte never returns Werther's love with the same ardour). Her solo scene at the beginning of Act III represents one of the greatest moments of self-discovery and self-revelation in opera, and at the same time the reading of the letter in that scene pays tribute to Goethe's epistolary mode. By the end of the opera her diffidence is thrown aside and she can confess, too late, that she returns Werther's love.

As in *Manon*, Massenet finds the intimate style very much to his taste. There are no chorus and no large orchestral effects. He relies particularly on the cor anglais, and there is an unforgettable solo for the saxophone to accompany Charlotte's 'Les larmes qu'on ne pleure pas' in Act III. In contrast to *Manon*, he does not attempt any pastiche musical touches except in the rather exaggerated counterpoint that supports Johann and Schmidt. His melodic invention in creating striking motifs was at its peak, and, although there are some deliberately facile melodies that seem too plain to convey their message, the match of feeling and melody is masterly. Albert's correct *bon ton* is perfectly conveyed, for example, by inner octaves in the texture. Most striking, too, is the wider harmonic palette Massenet draws on in this opera, perhaps a reflection of Wagner's influence (although it never extended to his dramaturgy), and we may detect some darker string textures possibly derived from *Parsifal*. The very opening of the prelude, with its strong melodic dissonances, captures the tone of the opera, followed by a plain diatonic melody that suggests the beauty of nature. Using the children's 'Noël' as contrast and also as ironic accompaniment to Werther's death might have risked banality, but Werther's vision of angels, the idea of rebirth at Christmas, and the straightforward musical coherence of recalling the opera's beginning at its end, plus Massenet's incomparable skill in musical manipulation of such materials, all ensure a deeply tragic, satisfying close.

Thaïs

Comédie lyrique in three acts (seven tableaux) (2h 15m)
Libretto by Louis Gallet, after Anatole France's novel *Thaïs* (1890)
Composed 1892–3, rev. 1897
PREMIERES 16 March 1894, Opéra, Paris; rev. version: 13 April 1898, Opéra, Paris; US: 25 November 1907, Manhattan Opera Company, New York; UK: 18 July 1911, Covent Garden, London
CAST Athanaël *bar*, Nicias *t*, Palémon *b*, Nicias' Servant *bar*, Thaïs *s*, Crobyle *s*, Myrtale *ms*, Albine *ms*, 12 cenobites 6 *t*, 6 *b*, La Charmeuse *dancer*; *satb* chorus of actors, actresses, comedians, philosophers, Nicias' friends, people

Thaïs was written for Sybil Sanderson, Massenet's favourite soprano at the time. Anatole France's novel had caused a sensation in 1890, with its remarkable description of the Thebaïd and its story of Paphnutius the desert monk (Athanaël in the opera), who converts the Egyptian harlot Thaïs to the faith but falls himself a victim to the very carnality he professes to reject. The libretto was written in prose, breaking with a long tradition in French opera; the idea may have come from Gustave Charpentier. The antique setting – Egypt in the early years of the Christian era – appealed greatly to Massenet, and the interlocking claims of religion and love were now established as his special dramatic domain.

SYNOPSIS

Act I Athanaël returns to the Thebaïd from Alexandria to report to his brother cenobites that Thaïs, whom he once knew as a good child, is the leading courtesan in that sinful city. He goes to Alexandria to save her, and contrives to meet her at the house of Nicias. Intrigued by the strange visitor, Thaïs puts on her most lascivious act. Athanaël flees in disgust.

Act II   Athanaël visits Thaïs and attempts to draw her away from the cult of Venus. Her conscience is troubled. Nicias and his friends find her modestly dressed when they expect her to be decked for more conviviality. They threaten Athanaël when they learn that she is destroying her house and her wealth at Athanaël's bidding, but Nicias holds them back.

Act III   Athanaël leads Thaïs to a desert retreat where she is to offer her repentance. But he imposes such duress on her that her strength is failing. Back in the Thebaïd, Athanaël is troubled by impure thoughts and visions of Thaïs as she first appeared to him; he also hears voices that tell him she is dying. He hurries to her side, drawn by her beauty and confessing his carnal passion for her while she expires, full of dreams of divine felicity.

The wide success of *Thaïs* added to Massenet's great celebrity, and the famous 'Meditation' (between Acts II and III), symbolizing Thaïs's awakening conscience, is one of the most famous of all violin solos. Although written for the Opéra, the work lacks large-scale scenes of pageantry and crowd conflict, and concentrates more on the personal predicaments of its two central characters, as in *Werther*. But their simultaneous conversions – Athanaël from self-denial to lust and Thaïs from sin to saintliness – are inherently improbable, for all the passionate intensity of the music, which displays some of the most flexible and lyrical qualities in all Massenet's work. Thaïs's 'Miroir, dis-moi que je suis belle' has enjoyed great celebrity as an operatic extract.

Cendrillon
Cinderella

Fairy-tale in four acts (six tableaux) (2h 15m)
Libretto by Henri Cain, after Charles Perrault's story *Cendrillon*, in *Contes de ma mère l'oye* (1697)
PREMIERES   24 May 1899, Opéra-Comique, Paris; US: 23 December 1902, French Opera House, New Orleans; UK: 24 December 1928, Little Theatre, London (by puppets); 25 February 1939, The Playhouse, Swindon
CAST   Cendrillon (Cinderella) *s*, Mme de la Haltière *ms*, Prince Charming *s*, Fairy *s*, Noémie *s*, Dorothée *ms*, Pandolfe *b* or *bar*, The Dean of the Faculty *t*, The Superintendant of Pleasures *bar*, The Prime Minister *b* or *bar*, The King *bar*, 6 spirits 4 *s*, 2 *a*; *satb* chorus of spirits, servants, courtiers, doctors, ministers, lords, ladies; dancers

While composing *Cendrillon*, Massenet again found inspiration by immersing himself in the appropriate surroundings, in this case a 17th-century house on the Seine in Normandy that had belonged to the celebrated Duchesse de Longueville; he even bought a large antique table on which to spread the pages of his manuscript.

SYNOPSIS

Act I   Mme de la Haltière and her two daughters are

making ready for the royal ball. Her husband, Pandolfe, groaning at his unhappy lot, is sorry to be leaving his daughter Cinderella behind. Cinderella, alone, falls asleep. A fairy appears, provides her with a magnificent dress, and gives her a glass slipper to make her unrecognizable. She must promise to leave the ball at midnight.

Act II   Prince Charming is inconsolable, not even touched by the ballets in his honour. When Cinderella arrives, everyone is captivated by her. She and Prince Charming fall in love. Midnight strikes.

Act III   Scene 1: In her flight Cinderella has lost her slipper. The trio of women upbraid Pandolfe for his bad behaviour at the ball and tell Cinderella that the prince took only a passing interest in the unknown stranger. Scene 2: Cinderella takes refuge in the fairy domain, where the spirits conjure up a meeting with Prince Charming. They join in a fervent embrace.

Act IV   The prince is said to be searching for the owner of the mysterious slipper. Before the whole court Cinderella claims it as hers, and 'all ends happily', in Pandolfe's words.

Cendrillon is one of Massenet's most attractive operas. The characterization of Cinderella's long-suffering father and of her bossy stepmother is deft, and the composer relished the opportunity to write fairy music. There is some pseudo-baroque pastiche (including the use of a viola d'amore) and much witty music in the manner of Verdi's *Falstaff*. There seem to be parodies of Meyerbeer and Wagner's *Parsifal*, too, and occasional hints of Debussy's style. The love music is some of the finest Massenet ever wrote. Cinderella's 'Vous êtes mon Prince Charmant' is one of the opera's best-known extracts. Considering its abundant opportunities for spectacular staging, it has been surprisingly neglected. It should truly be acknowledged as on a par with Humperdinck's *Hänsel und Gretel*. The role of Prince Charming is written for a voice designated *falcon* or *soprano de sentiment*.

Don Quichotte
Don Quixote

Comédie héroïque in five acts (2h 15m)
Libretto by Henri Cain, after Jacques Le Lorrain's play *Le chevalier de la longue figure* (1906), based on Miguel de Cervantes Saavedra's *Don Quixote* (1605, 1615)
PREMIERES   19 February 1910, Salle Garnier, Monte Carlo; US: 27 January 1912, French Opera House, New Orleans; UK: 18 May 1912, London Opera House, London
CAST   Dulcinée *ms*, Don Quichotte *b*, Sancho Panza *bar*, Pedro *s*, Garcias *s*, Rodriguez *t*, Juan *t*, Ténébrun *spoken role*, 2 Valets 2 *bar*, 4 Bandits 2 *t*, 2 *bar*; *satb* chorus of lords, Dulcinée's friends, bandits, crowd

It was appropriate that Massenet's last operatic success should make gentle fun of an elderly man with a fondness for beautiful women. The mockery of Cervantes's masterpiece makes excellent operatic material, and it offered Massenet yet another opportunity for mingling sentiment and comedy, pastiche and contemporary styles. The title role was written for Fyodor Shalyapin, the role of Dulcinée for Lucy Arbell.

SYNOPSIS
Act I   In a crowded square in full fiesta, Dulcinée is courted by four suitors. When Don Quichotte and his faithful servant Sancho Panza arrive, one of the suitors, Juan, mocks Don Quichotte's eccentric ways, while another, Rodriguez, reminds us of the knight's noble ambitions. When all have departed, Don Quichotte serenades Dulcinée, but the jealous Juan interrupts and a duel inevitably follows. Dulcinée intervenes, sends Juan on an errand, and upbraids Quichotte for his hot blood. She asks him to retrieve a necklace stolen from her by the bandit chief Ténébrun. The Don instantly undertakes the heroic task.

Act II   The Don and his servant have set out in the morning mist. Sancho sings a fierce tirade against women. As the mist clears, Quichotte mistakes some windmills for giants and, attacking them, is borne aloft on one of the sails.

Act III   Don Quichotte is close in pursuit of the bandits. While he takes his rest (standing up, like all good knights) he and Sancho are overpowered by the bandits, but the bandits' wicked hearts are quickly won by Quichotte's evocation of his mission as knight errant, and they hand over the stolen necklace.

Act IV   Dulcinée is singing of the caprice of love. Don Quichotte returns with the necklace to everyone's amazement, but his proposal of marriage is turned down on the grounds that since she must be generous in her love she could not bear to deceive him. The old knight is disconsolate, but Sancho protects him from the crowd's mockery.

Act V   Death is near as the Don promises Sancho an 'island of dreams'. He dies, fondly imagining that the planet Jupiter shining in the heavens is a fleeting image of Dulcinée.

Don Quichotte is a highly crafted comedy full of affection and charm. There is some traditional Spanish colour and some folk pastiche, in this case a romanesca antica in Act IV. The scene of Don Quichotte's death mostly presents a quiet pastoral simplicity, but with a touch of harmonic tension as he dies. The boisterous music of Act I recalls both *Cendrillon* and *Falstaff*, with mocking counterpoint for the suitors, a manner used later also for the windmills. The Don himself is characterized with much subtlety and sympathy, an achievement that reflects Massenet's enormous experience and skill.

Other operas: *Esmeralda* (lost or destroyed, c. 1865); *La coupe du roi de Thulé*, 1866; *La grand'tante*, 1867; *Manfred* (inc., c. 1869); *Méduse* (inc., c. 1869); *Don César de Bazan*, 1872; *L'adorable Bel'-Boul'* (destroyed), 1874; *Les templiers* (inc.; lost); *Bérangère et Anatole*, 1876; *Le roi de Lahore*, 1877; *Robert de France* (lost or destroyed, c. 1880); *Les Girondins* (lost or destroyed, 1881); *L'écureuil du déshonneur* (early, lost or destroyed); *Montalte* (lost or destroyed, 1883); *Esclarmonde*, 1889; *Le mage*, 1891; *Le portrait de Manon*, 1894; *La navarraise*, 1894; *Grisélidis*, (1894, rev. 1898), 1901; *Sapho*, 1897; *Le jongleur de Notre-Dame*, 1902; *Chérubin*, 1905; *Ariane*, 1906; *Thérèse*, 1907; *Bacchus*, 1909; *Roma*, 1912; *Panurge*, 1913; *Amadis*, 1922; *Cléopâtre*, 1914

Sacred and profane dramas: *Les erinnyes*, 1873, rev. 1876; *Marie-Magdeleine* (originally performed as oratorio, 1873),

1906; *Eve*, 1875; *Narcisse*, 1877; *La Vierge*, 1880
Orchestration of Delibes's last opera, *Kassya*, 1893

H.M.

NICHOLAS MAW
John Nicholas Maw; *b* 5 November 1935, Grantham, Lincolnshire, England

Maw worked in a bicycle factory before being accepted to study at the Royal Academy of Music with Lennox Berkeley. Later he studied in Paris with Max Deutsch, himself a pupil of Schoenberg. But though serialism affected Maw briefly and superficially, his music has generally avoided system or codifiable method. His first great success, the 1962 BBC Prom commission *Scenes and Arias*, already established the sumptuous idiom, based on expressive line and much extended tonal harmony, which has served him ever since. Its lyric-dramatic treatment of the female voice also looked forward directly to his two operas.

The Rising of the Moon
Opera in three acts (2h 30m)
Libretto by Beverley Cross
PREMIERE   19 July 1970, Glyndebourne, Sussex
CAST   Brother Timothy *high t*, Donal O'Dowd *bar*, Cathleen Sweeney *ms*, Colonel Lord Jowler *b-bar*, Major von Zastrow *high bar*, Captain Lillywhite *t*, Lady Eugenie Jowler *s*, Frau von Zastrow *ms*, Atalanta Lillywhite *s*, Corporal Haywood *bar*, Cornet Beaumont *t*, Widow Sweeney *c*, Lynch *b*; *tb* chorus of Lancers

The Rising of the Moon is a bitter-sweet romantic comedy. While the Irish peasants and the English soldiers are to some extent caricatured, the intended core of the work is a strain of sentiment not unduly disturbed by psychological probability. The genuinely funny if occasionally gauche libretto is based on an original idea, set in Ireland in 1875, the time of the Fenians, and the year in which Charles Parnell entered Parliament (the title is a phrase of one Fenian song, sung in Act II by Lynch to the tune of another, 'The Wearing of the Green').

SYNOPSIS
Act I   The 31st Royal Lancers arrive in the Mayo town of Ballinvourney 'to show the flag . . . and to stop young men from talking revolution'. They include a monocled Prussian 'observer' (Zastrow) and, among their retinue, three ladies (Jowler's and Zastrow's wives, and the captain's daughter Atalanta). When a candidly unmilitary but handsome and self-assured young officer (Beaumont) arrives to join the regiment, Zastrow suggests an initiation test involving the conquest of three women in one night. The locals plan to lead him by a roundabout route to the ladies' hotel.

Act II   Beaumont easily breaks down Lady Eugenie's 'defences', and conquers Frau von Zastrow by reading poetry to her. But his third victory is interrupted by the arrival of Zastrow, with the beautiful Irish girl, Cathleen, in his sights. Zastrow, however, is tricked into Atalanta's room, leaving Cathleen to woo Beaumont for herself.

Act III   The next morning, the fuddled Lancers are rudely awoken by Beaumont's return. His trophies reveal the identity of his conquests, but to save the regiment's honour he offers to resign his commission. As the Lancers leave Ballinvourney in disarray Beaumont also gently detaches himself from Cathleen and departs.

Full of charm and sharp musical observation, the work follows purely traditional models, including Britten and perhaps Strauss. In style it inhabits a middle ground between the atonal and the extendedly tonal, with occasional passages of simple melody, tonally set. There are several big, effective ensembles, and the orchestration is rather full for a comic opera, but individual characterization is precise; for instance, Maw manages to distinguish his four leading female characters without ever lapsing into stereotype.

Other opera: *One Man Show*, 1964

                                                S.W.

GIAN CARLO MENOTTI
b 7 July 1911, Cadegliano, Italy

For at least a generation, in the years following the Second World War, Menotti was the most acclaimed American composer of opera. He has a natural sense of theatre, which stems from his Italian background, and has always shown an intuitive grasp of character and situation.

By the time he was 11, Menotti had written his first opera, *The Death of Pierrot*, and regularly attended theatre and opera in Milan where the family lived. On Toscanini's advice he went to the Curtis Institute in Philadelphia, where, in 1928, Menotti met Samuel Barber, who became his close companion: they both studied composition with Rosario Scalero, who gave a solid grounding based on Brahms rather than on opera.

Menotti and Barber travelled in Italy and Austria, and in Vienna Menotti began composing the one-act opera buffa *Amelia al ballo* (later known as *Amelia goes to the Ball*). The Curtis Institute and New York performances were so successful that the Metropolitan Opera placed it in a double-bill with Richard Strauss's *Elektra* in 1938. The *New York Times* recognized 'something that has not materialized so far from an American-born composer' and admired Menotti's tuneful flexibility and spontaneity. This success brought the composer an NBC radio commission for *The Old Maid and the Thief*, which became a favourite among students and amateurs, and a production at the Metropolitan of an opera seria, *The Island God*, which flopped.

The highly original double-bill of *The Medium* and *The Telephone*, both, as usual, to Menotti's own ingenious texts, was a huge success. These were premiered separately and then united on Broadway. When the backers were losing money, Toscanini again intervened in Menotti's destiny – his three visits to the operas provided enough publicity to boost a long run.

The Consul as a gripping topical tragedy maintained Menotti's high profile as, in a completely different way, did the charm of *Amahl and the Night Visitors*, which gained special fame through being the first opera written expressly for television. After *The Saint of Bleecker Street*, and in the changing climate of the 1960s, Menotti's work began to be received with less enthusiasm and often downright hostility in the press. He changed his focus slightly, writing *Labyrinth* for television; a church opera, *Martin's Lie*; and *Help, Help, the Globolinks!*, a children's opera, for Hamburg. He also wrote the libretti for two of Samuel Barber's operas. Seven more operas, three for children, were premiered during the 1970s; since then he has written four more operas, of which *The Boy Who Grew Too Fast* has been the most successful.

In 1958 Menotti inaugurated the Festival of Two Worlds at Spoleto, and in 1977 he expanded it to Charleston, South Carolina. He enjoyed the entrepreneurial activity involved, although some connected it with a decline in his own work. The power of his earlier operas has never been in question, but in an interview for his 60th birthday in 1971 Menotti tried to disguise his bitterness about the impact of changing fashions on his reputation.

The Medium
Tragedy in two acts (55m)
Libretto by the composer
PREMIERES 8 May 1946, Brander Matthews Theater, Columbia University, New York; UK: 29 April 1948, Aldwych Theatre, London

Menotti had the idea for *The Medium* as early as 1936, when he attended a séance in Austria. In his libretto he created what he called 'a play of ideas [which] describes the tragedy of a woman caught between two worlds, a world of reality which she cannot wholly comprehend and a supernatural world in which she cannot believe'. Along with *The Telephone*, *The Medium* had a run of 211 performances at the Ethel Barrymore Theater on Broadway during 1947–8.

Madame Flora, her daughter Monica and Toby, the mute servant boy, prepare their shabby parlour with tricks to be used during the evening's séance. Mr and Mrs Gobineau arrive, regular clients, and Mrs Nolan, a widow coming for the first time. During the séance Mrs Nolan recognizes her dead daughter, but Madame Flora becomes hysterical when a cold hand seems to touch her throat: she suspects Toby, but he cannot answer their accusations. In the end, Madame Flora, after drinking heavily, shoots Toby in the dark.

The mainstay of the score is a powerfully dramatic recitative-like music, influenced by Puccini. The only aria is Monica's wistful, naïve 'Black Swan' – a gypsy-type tune she sings to calm her mother – which stands in stark contrast to the increasingly dissonant music that reflects Madame Flora's growing alarm. Menotti scored the work for an orchestra of 14 players, including a piano duet, though the original string quintet can be expanded for larger venues.

The Telephone, or L'amour à trois

Comedy in one act (22m)
Libretto by the composer
PREMIERES 18 February 1947, Heckscher Theater, New York; UK: 29 April 1948, Aldwych Theatre, London

The Telephone, subtitled *L'amour à trois*, is a light comedy designed as a curtain-raiser for *The Medium*. Ben wishes to propose to Lucy but is unable to gain her attention for long because of her obsession with her telephone. In desperation, he goes out and telephones with his proposal.

A short typically opera-buffa overture is followed by a light-hearted score which employs a number of recognizable musical styles in a partly satirical fashion. Lucy's telephone conversations (of which we hear only one side) are miniature arias, the first of which, 'Oh Margaret, it's you', is sometimes performed independently.

The Consul

Musical drama in three acts (1h 45m)
Libretto by the composer
PREMIERES 1 March 1950, Philadelphia; UK: 7 February 1951, Cambridge Theatre, London

The New York premiere of *The Consul* on 15 March 1950 established the opera as a classic of its period, and it ran for some eight months. It was awarded the Pulitzer Prize and the Drama Critics' Circle Award and was translated into at least a dozen languages and seen in more than 20 countries.

Somewhere in Europe after the Second World War the secret police are after John Sorel, who has had to leave his wife and baby and go abroad. His wife, Magda, is obstructed by bureaucracy in her efforts to get a visa to follow him. Meanwhile she too is hounded by the secret police and the baby dies. Hearing of this, John braves danger and returns to fetch his wife. But it is too late – he is arrested, and Magda commits suicide.

The subject of Menotti's first full-scale, full-length opera – obtaining a passport to leave a police state – has obvious parallels with Puccini's *Tosca*. The music, too, has Puccinian touches, especially the sentimental 'Now lips, say goodbye' in Scene 1. These echoes are as important to the opera's overall dramatic effect as Menotti's use of a pedantic 5/4 march to represent the secret police and the hallucinatory, naïve 6/8 waltz of the final suicide scene.

Amahl and the Night Visitors

Opera in one act (45m)
Libretto by the composer
PREMIERES 24 December 1951, NBC television; 21 February 1952, Indiana University, Bloomington, Indiana; UK: 6 December 1963, Royal College of Music, London

In this perennial Christmas favourite, Amahl, a boy cripple, sits outside his hut watching the brilliant new star. The three kings, looking for hospitality, arrive with presents for the Holy Child they are seeking. During the night, Amahl's mother tries to steal part of the treasure and there is a struggle. Eventually Amahl offers his crutch as a gift, is miraculously healed, and joins the kings in search of the Christ Child.

Hieronymus Bosch's painting *The Adoration of the Magi* gave Menotti the idea for this opera, which, since its television premiere, has been broadcast annually at Christmas in the US. The opera's appeal to young audiences has made it a popular choice with amateur operatic groups. Menotti composed melodious, short numbers and scored the opera for a small orchestra; he insists that the part of Amahl should always be sung by a boy and not taken by a soprano.

The Saint of Bleecker Street

Musical drama in three acts (2h)
Libretto by the composer ·
PREMIERES 27 December 1954, Broadway Theater, New York; UK: 4 October 1956, BBC television; 27 July 1962, Orpington Civic Hall, Kent

Menotti's tragedy gained the Drama Critics' Circle Award as well as the New York Music Critics' Circle Award and brought the composer his second Pulitzer Prize.

The story is set in Little Italy in New York City. Annina is a deeply religious girl who has been having visions and performing miracles. Her brother, Michele, wants to protect her from public exploitation but is overpowered. Desideria, Michele's mistress, objects to his obsession with his saintly sister; when she accuses him of being in love with Annina, Michele stabs her. Finally Annina dies at the moment of becoming a nun.

Menotti considered *The Saint of Bleecker Street* 'melodically . . . an improvement over *The Consul*'. Certainly the melodic style of the opera – and many of its other features – is more large-scale. Significant use of the chorus (not present in *The Consul*) and a large orchestra give the feeling of 'grand' opera. Critics were loud in their praise, hailing the opera as a technical and dramatic masterpiece. Broadway audiences, however, perhaps put off by its religious subject matter and rather ambiguous message, were not as enthusiastic.

Other operatic works: *Amelia al ballo*, 1937; *The Old Maid and the Thief*, 1939; *The Island God*, 1942; *Maria Golovin*, 1958; *Labyrinth*, 1963; *Le dernier sauvage*, 1963; *Martin's Lie*, 1964; *Help, Help, the Globolinks!*, 1968; *The Most Important Man*, 1971; *Tamu-Tamu*, 1973; *The Egg*, 1976; *The Hero*, 1976; *The Trial of the Gypsy*, 1978; *Chip and his Dog*, 1979; *La Loca*, 1979; *A Bride from Pluto*, 1982; *The Boy Who Grew Too Fast*, 1982; *Goya*, 1986; *Giorno da Nozze*, 1988

P.D.

ANDRÉ MESSAGER

André Charles Prosper Messager; *b* 30 December 1853,
Montluçon, France; *d* 24 February 1929, Paris

Messager, the last true master of classical French
operetta, was trained as an organist at the École
Niedermeycr under Saint-Saëns and Fauré (both of
whom remained lifelong friends). He became organist
at Saint-Sulpice in 1874, and four years later had a
symphony performed at the Concerts Colonne. At the
same time he was writing ballets for the Folies-
Bergère, where he also conducted. In 1883 came his
first attempt at operetta, when he was commissioned
to complete Firmin Bernicat's *François les Bas-Bleus*,
which had a respectable run at the Folies-
Dramatiques.

In 1885, two operettas appeared that showed further
promise; the second, *La béarnaise*, exhibited the delicacy and period flavour for which Messager later
became celebrated. In 1886, Saint-Saëns recommended
Messager's graceful ballet *Les deux pigeons* to the
Opéra; it is still performed. But little else found much
favour in the 1880s, not even the *Souvenirs de Bayreuth*
(*c.* 1886), a quadrille-fantasy for four hands on 'favourite themes from Wagner's *Ring*', written in collaboration with Fauré.

In 1890, Messager's fortunes changed with the successful premiere at the Opéra-Comique of *La basoche*.
The 1891 London production followed Sullivan's *Ivanhoe* as the second and last attraction at D'Oyly Carte's
ill-fated Royal English Opera House. The through-
composed *Madame Chrysanthème* (with an oriental/
occidental theme that predated both Sidney Jones's
The Geisha and Puccini's *Madama Butterfly*) was followed by several operettas and, finally, a sensational
hit, *Les p'tites Michu* (1897), which recalled the tuneful
frivolity of Charles Lecocq's *Giroflé-Girofla* and *La
fille de Madame Angot*, but which was perhaps more
charmingly florid and more tastefully constructed. The
succeeding work, *Véronique*, was even more successful.

In 1898, Messager became musical director of the
Opéra-Comique, and there conducted the premieres
of several new works, notably Debussy's *Pelléas et
Mélisande*, and significant revivals, including Beethoven's *Fidelio*. In 1901, he became manager of the
Grand Opera Syndicate in London until he was appointed to direct the Paris Opéra in 1907, where he
remained until 1914. One operetta from this period,
Les dragons de l'impératrice (1905), deserves re-examination. *Monsieur Beaucaire* (1919), a 'romantic opera'
composed to an English libretto, looks back through
the ragtime craze to the more genteel time of Edward
German. Its centrepiece, a pastoral episode that includes the Arcadian soprano aria 'Philomel', was famously sung by Maggie Teyte.

Messager moved with the times, lightened his
style, and by 1921 was writing for the 'comédie-
musicale' stage. Two years later, he collaborated
with the actor-playwright Sacha Guitry on *L'amour
masqué*, which fortuitously starred the author's
brilliant wife, Yvonne Printemps. The ageing
composer had succumbed to the 1920s taste for tangos
and foxtrots, but gave them a refined touch.

Messager has not enjoyed the revival of interest
shown towards Offenbach, but raucousness was not
his style: elegance, neatness, tripping melodiousness,
orchestral refinement, and a decidedly French grace
were the composer's hallmarks.

Véronique

Opéra comique in three acts (2h 30m)
Libretto by Albert Vanloo and Georges Duval
PREMIERES 10 December 1898, Bouffes-Parisiens, Paris;
UK: 5 May 1903, Coronet Theatre, London; US:
30 October 1905, Broadway Theater, New York

At a Parisian florist's in the 1840s, Hélène de Solanges,
a noblewoman, pretends to be a shop-girl to check up
on her prospective bridegroom, the rakish Vicomte
Florestan de Valaincourt. Florestan gives a picnic for
the employees of the flower shop (purchased with
non-existent funds), and, predictably, falls for the
disguised Hélène (who calls herself Véronique). Instead of reporting to a ball at the Tuileries that
evening to be presented to his so-far unknown bride,
he risks debtor's prison and remains at the picnic
grounds. At the ball, complications are sorted out
between the lovers and, in the presence of the king,
the marriage contract is signed.

Messager's grace and refinement are apparent
throughout this radiant score; even entrance songs are
imbued with a lilting glitter, and more elaborate ensembles (such as the quartet in Act I with the refrain
'Charmant, charmant') are unexpectedly moving. The
finales to Acts I and II are dazzling, the latter with its
'marié ou coffré' tag line. The score's two most popular numbers are the two duets for the lovers in Act II:
the 'donkey' ('De ci, de là') and 'swing' ('Poussez,
poussez, l'escarpolette') songs, which became Edwardian favourites.

Other operatic works: *François les Bas-Bleus* (completion of
operetta by Firmin Bernicat), 1883; *La fauvette du temple*,
1885; *La béarnaise*, 1885; *Le bourgeois de Calais*, 1887;
Isoline, 1888; *Le mari de la reine*, 1889; *La basoche*, 1890;
Miss Dollar, 1893; *Madame Chrysanthème*, 1893; *Mirette*,
1894; *La fiancée en loterie* (coll. with Paul Lacome), 1896;
Le Chevalier d'Harmental, 1896; *Les p'tites Michu*, 1897;
Les dragons de l'impératrice, 1905; *Fortunio*, 1907; *Béatrice*,
1914; *Cyprien, ôte ta main d'là*, 1916; *Monsieur Beaucaire*,
1919; *La petite fonctionnaire*, 1921; *L'amour masqué*, 1923;
Passionnément, 1926; *Coups de roulis*, 1928

R.T.

OLIVIER MESSIAEN

b 10 December 1908, Avignon, France; *d* 28 April 1992,
Paris

Despite a conventional musical training (he was a
pupil of Paul Dukas and Marcel Dupré at the Paris
Conservatoire) Messiaen was a radical from the first.
He rejected German symphonic thought and post-
Wagnerian opulence as well as the mechanical or syn-

thetic neo-classicism of Les Six. In the 1930s, saying he wanted to return mystery to music, he began to write a series of works in which the mysteries of the Roman Catholic Church play a central inspirational role. It was natural, since he was organist at La Trinité in Paris, that his deeply held religious beliefs should find expression in composition for his own instrument (*La nativité du Seigneur, Les corps glorieux*), but they also feature in his instrumental and orchestral music (*L'ascension, Visions de l'amen*) and in his vocal music. Birdsong was a major influence: he went on field trips, wrote down hundreds of individual songs, and integrated these brief snatches of nature into his music.

From quite early on, these aspects of Messiaen's spiritual and physical environment found a response in certain technical procedures. In the search for contemplative depth and richness, he interested himself in elaborate symmetries: in what he called 'non-retrogradable' rhythms (palindromes), and in 'modes of limited transposition', where the traditional major and minor scales are replaced by specially constructed scales with symmetrical interval divisions (the wholetone scale, much used by Musorgsky and Debussy – both profound influences on Messiaen – is his Mode 1). The audible effect of all this on the harmony, melody and rhythm is of a kind of suspension in musical space, or, if the music is quick, of some mystical orbital dance of the spirit. But for a time after the war Messiaen brought these various elements under strict control and laid the foundations for a school of composition led by his pupils and followers (such as Boulez and Stockhausen) which extended the serial organization of pitch formulated by Schoenberg into all the elements of composition.

But the organizational principles were always the means of expressing emotions for Messiaen. His *Turangalîla Symphony* (1946–8), with its sumptuous orchestration, and the extraordinarily erotic sound of that purest of instruments, the electronic Ondes Martenot, is a vast love song related to the myth of Tristan and Isolde, while *Et exspecto resurrectionem mortuorum* (1964) is an immensely personal affirmation of the composer's faith.

After 1964 Messiaen's music became, if not simpler, certainly more accessible. The intricacies of its construction became less apparent and have been replaced by a static, hieratic vision where clock time is less important than the space needed for a musical expression of spiritual contemplation.

It was natural that his only opera, commissioned by Rolf Liebermann for the Paris Opéra in 1975, should fuse these features in portraying the spiritual development of St Francis of Assisi. It is an opera of ritual, not of action, requiring the involvement of the audience's spiritual being rather than its earthy theatrical responses. It has been suggested that it would be better staged in a vast Gothic cathedral than in the decadent interior of our opera houses. It requires enormous forces – a huge orchestra and a chorus of at least 150. The practical problems of rehearsing so long and difficult a work probably mean it will never become a repertoire piece.

Saint François d'Assise

(*Scènes Franciscaines*)
St Francis of Assisi
Opera in three acts (eight tableaux) (4h)
Libretto by the composer, after 14th-century Franciscan writings: the *Fioretti* and *Reflections of the Stigmata*, and St Francis's own *Cantico delle creature*
Composed 1975–83
PREMIERES 28 November 1983, Opéra, Paris; UK: 26 March 1986, Royal Festival Hall, London / BBC radio (concert performance of tableaux 3, 7 and 8); 10 December 1988, Royal Festival Hall, London (semi-staged, complete); US: 10 April 1986, Boston (concert performance of tableaux 3, 7 and 8)
CAST St Francis *bar*, The Angel *s*, The Leper *t*, Frère Léon *bar*, Frère Massée *t*, Frère Élie *t*, Frère Bernard *b*, Frère Sylvestre *b*, Frère Rufin *b*; *satb* offstage chorus

The opera depicts the path of St Francis of Assisi towards a state of spiritual grace.

SYNOPSIS

Act I   Tableau 1: '*La croix*' ('The Cross'). St Francis explains to one of his fellow monks, Frère Léon, that all life's contradictions and sufferings must be endured for the sake of Christ's love, for only through those sufferings will man reach perfect joy. The invisible chorus sings Christ's words 'He who wishes to follow in my footsteps must take up his cross and follow me.'
Tableau 2: '*Les laudses*' ('Lauds'). After the service in a small dark chapel has ended and the brothers have left, St Francis pours out his heart. The God who has created so many simple but wonderful things – time, light, space, the taste of clear water, the song of the wind that changes its note in every tree – has also created ugliness – the poisonous mushroom, the rotting pustulation of leprosy. Francis feels revulsion at the physical presence of the disease and begs that God will help him overcome his nausea and be able to love a sufferer. Tableau 3: '*Le baiser au lépreux*' ('The Embracing of the Leper'). In a colony a leper rejects God and Francis's homilies; he has done nothing to deserve his disfiguring, revolting, painful, ostracizing disease, so why should he listen to the platitudes of monks who can scarcely conceal their disgust for his fetid appearance? An angel, visible only to the audience, sings of God's love and convinces the leper that his own self-disgust is as strong as the disgust others feel for him. Francis is deeply moved and, overcoming his repugnance, embraces the leper, effecting a miraculous cure and, at that moment, becoming a saint. The leper dances ecstatically and the chorus sings that, to those who have truly loved, all is forgiven.

Act II   Tableau 4: '*L'ange voyageur*' ('The Traveller Angel'). The angel is assumed to be another traveller who has come to the monastery to seek advice from Francis; his knock on the door is a terrifying sound that symbolizes the inrush of grace. The vicar, Frère Élie, will not answer the angel's questions about predestination but the angel receives an answer of great wisdom from Bernard, one of the brothers. It is only after the angel equivocates about where he has come from and has left in search of Francis that the brothers wonder if their visitor was in fact an angel. Tableau 5: '*L'ange musicien*' ('The Musician Angel').

In a grotto, Francis recognizes the angel as a messenger from God and is literally entranced by the wonderful music he plays. When the brothers revive him he is ecstatic – had he not fainted, the exquisite pain of the heavenly music would have torn his soul from his body. Tableau 6: '*Le prêche aux oiseaux*' ('Preaching to the Birds'). At the hermitage at the Carceri in Assisi, Francis preaches to and blesses the birds, who answer with a massive chorus – the orchestra alone – divided, as Francis tells one of the brothers, into four groups representing the points of the Cross. He reminds the brother of Christ's words about the birds being looked after by their heavenly father: 'Search for the Kingdom and you will find it through faith.'

Act III Tableau 7: '*Les stigmates*' ('The Stigmata'). Francis prays that before he dies he should be allowed to experience the pain Christ endured on the Cross and feel in his heart the love for mankind which allowed Jesus to die for its salvation. The chorus, symbolizing the voice of Christ, grants him his wish and inflicts the stigmata upon him. Tableau 8: '*La mort et la nouvelle vie*' ('Death and New Life'). Francis, near to death, says goodbye to the brothers and the partly visible chorus. While they sing Psalm 114, the angel and the leper he cured come to comfort his last moments. Francis's final words are, 'Music and poetry have led me to you, by image, by symbol and in default of Truth . . . deliver me, enrapture me, dazzle me for ever by your excess of Truth!' One of the brothers observes that his death is like a golden butterfly which flies from the Cross to go beyond the stars. The chorus praises the mystery of the Resurrection.

Messiaen was adamant that, for all its static drama, his opera is more than a symphonic spectacle. It is an opera in the tradition of the theatre of the fantastic, of the imagination, of the operas which he analysed with his students while he was professor at the Paris Conservatoire – Monteverdi's *Orfeo*, the opéra-ballets of Rameau, *Don Giovanni*, *La damnation de Faust*, *Carmen*, Wagner's *Ring*, *Boris Godunov*, *Wozzeck* and *Pelléas et Mélisande*.

The music too gives an impression of stasis, for each of the characters has his own theme, orchestrated with individual and instantly recognizable timbres, and an associated bird song; the major characters, Francis and the angel, have several. Because Messiaen uses his vast orchestra more as a complex of chamber colours than as an endless stream of loud noise – though the climaxes are overwhelming – only those themes associated with characters who develop emotionally or spiritually are developed equivalently. He also uses two more abstract leitmotifs, one associated with the symbolism of the Cross (a sequence of two highly characteristic chords), the other a little fanfare associated with the concept of 'joy'.

The two purely orchestral episodes are unusual. In the first, the leper's dance in Act I, the music is based on a transformation and expansion of the theme with which he reviled God and Francis before his cure. In the second, the birds' response to Francis's sermon, Messiaen allows the players complete freedom to choose their own tempi, so that the aural and emotional effect is more naturalistic than in his earlier birdsong pieces such as *Réveil des oiseaux* and *Catalogue d'oiseaux*.

C.B.

GIACOMO MEYERBEER

Jakob Liebmann Meyer Beer; *b* 5 September 1791, Vogelsdorf, nr Berlin; *d* 2 May 1864, Paris

The name of Meyerbeer is synonymous with French grand opera, which flourished in Paris in the mid 19th century. With his librettist, Eugène Scribe, he was responsible for the creation of operas more flamboyant than anything seen previously, writing spectacular dramatic works which enjoyed huge public success. Changing fashions and a lack of suitable voices have combined to make performances today a rarity, but Meyerbeer nevertheless retains an important place in operatic history.

Brought up in one of Berlin's wealthiest families, Meyerbeer received the best possible education, including piano lessons from Muzio Clementi. He had a natural aptitude for the instrument, giving public concerts from the age of 11, and for a number of years his performing career took precedence over his composing. Nevertheless, he received training in composition first from Carl Zelter, the lieder composer, and then from Abbé Vogler in Darmstadt from 1810. It was during his two years of study with Vogler that the young Meyerbeer (he had just adopted the one-word form of his name) wrote his first operatic works.

In 1816 Meyerbeer visited Italy for the first time. What started as a short study tour turned into a nine-year sojourn, and was decisive in shaping the composer's subsequent career. At this time Rossini was beginning to dominate the Italian stage, and Meyerbeer no doubt became familiar with his work, while pursuing his own interests in collecting traditional folksongs. His first Italian opera, *Romelda e Costanza*, was staged with some success in 1817. Five more operas followed, received with increasing enthusiasm, and Meyerbeer was seen by many as the great new hope of Italian opera. The premiere of *Il crociato in Egitto* in 1824 was his greatest triumph yet. Years later, the poet Heinrich Heine recalled, 'Never have I seen such frenzy as during the performance of *Il crociato*.' The work was a watershed in more than one respect – not only was it one of the last works written for a castrato, it also established Meyerbeer as a composer of international standing.

Performances of *Il crociato* in London and in Paris were equally successful, and Meyerbeer, fulfilling a long-held ambition, was invited to produce a work for the Opéra. The result was *Robert le diable*, Meyerbeer's first collaboration with Scribe. Paris was to remain the centre of Meyerbeer's operatic activity for the rest of his life, though he never set up home in the city and maintained ties with his native Berlin, composing his only mature German opera, *Ein Feldlager in Schlesien*, for the Prussian court in 1844.

Robert le diable, with its notorious nuns' ballet, was

an even greater success than *Il crociato*. Such was its triumph that it was responsible at least in part for Rossini's decision to write no further works for the Opéra (his last, *Guillaume Tell*, had been premiered in 1829). Over four years elapsed between *Robert le diable* and the premiere of Meyerbeer's next opera, *Les Huguenots*. Work had begun and been abandoned on several projects, including an opéra comique entitled *Les brigands*, which was to have been a collaboration with the author Alexandre Dumas *père*. After overcoming a number of censorship problems *Les Huguenots* was premiered in 1836 to great acclaim. Meyerbeer's ·reputation went from strength to strength.

Throughout his career Meyerbeer tailored the roles in his operas to particular singers – a fact that sometimes caused delays or necessitated rewriting when the singer had to drop out. This happened with *L'africaine*, which Meyerbeer began in 1837, soon after *Les Huguenots*, but which he did not live to see premiered. In this case work was halted when the soprano who was to have sung the title role withdrew, and Meyerbeer turned his attention instead to *Le prophète*. But this, too, ran into difficulties when the principal tenor withdrew, and the opera, completed in 1840, remained unperformed for nine years until, despairing of ever finding a suitable tenor, the composer rewrote the opera giving greater prominence to the mezzo-soprano role Fidès.

In the meantime the man described by the critic François-Joseph Fétis as 'the leader of the German School' had in 1842 been appointed Prussian general-musikdirektor, with responsibilities for composing occasional music for the Prussian court in Berlin. It was in this guise that Meyerbeer composed *Ein Feldlager in Schlesien*, a patriotic Prussian work which was later successfully adapted for Vienna (as *Vielka*). Meyerbeer never attempted to stage the work in Paris but later reused substantial parts of it in his opéra comique *L'étoile du nord*.

Commitments in Berlin were too heavy, and in 1848 Meyerbeer returned to Paris, where he was able to renew work on *Le prophète*. It was ten years since Meyerbeer's last Paris premiere, but any fears the composer may have had about his popularity proved completely unfounded: *Le prophète* was an unprecedented success. It received over 100 performances at the Opéra in little over two years, and Paris was swept by a craze for 'Prophet Skates', the roller-skates used in the opera to simulate a ballet 'on ice'. Two opéras comiques followed before *L'africaine* eventually went into rehearsal in September 1863. Scribe, Meyerbeer's collaborator on all but one of his French works, had died in 1861, and Meyerbeer was anxious about who would be able to make the necessary changes to the text during rehearsals. This worry no doubt contributed to the stress of the rehearsals. On the morning of 2 May 1864, Meyerbeer died, unexpectedly, in his sleep. After an interruption, rehearsals for *L'africaine* continued, Fétis having agreed to sort out a final performing version of the score. (It was Meyerbeer's habit constantly to make revisions as rehearsals progressed.) The work's posthumous premiere in April 1865 was another triumph.

Not everyone was enthusiastic, however. German musicians in particular felt Meyerbeer's success had been achieved by pandering too much to public taste, and they accused him of compromising his artistic integrity. Schumann wrote scathingly of *Les Huguenots*, and Wagner, who early in his career had benefited from Meyerbeer's personal support, did not exclude him from the vitriolic attack in his essay 'Das Judentum in der Musik'.

Although his output was fairly small, Meyerbeer's influence on the development of opera was far-reaching. He retained the spectacle of operas such as Auber's *La muette de Portici*, which had been so popular with the public, and added more exciting – sometimes, as in the case of the dancing nuns in *Robert le diable*, even shocking – elements to the plot. The works made unprecedented demands on the singers, were longer, and increasingly blurred the formal distinctions of recitative, aria and ensemble. And even if the composers who followed did not adopt the dramatic excesses and grand stagings, they made use of the ranges of orchestral colour Meyerbeer had introduced (Adolphe Sax was a friend, and the instruments he invented appear in a number of Meyerbeer's works) and shared his concern that opera be a whole art form – an equal combination of words, music, movement and visual elements.

Robert le diable
Robert the Devil
Grand opéra in five acts (4h)
Libretto by Eugène Scribe, after a sketch by Germain Delavigne
PREMIERES 21 November 1831, Opéra, Paris; UK: 20 February 1832, Drury Lane, London (as *The Fiend-Father*, version by Rophino Lacy); 11 June 1832, London (original version); US: 7 April 1834, Park Theater, New York (Lacy's version)
CAST Alice *s*, Isabelle *s*, Robert, Duke of Normandy *t*, Bertram *b*, Raimbault *t*, Priest *b*, Master of Ceremonies *t*, Alberti *b*, Prince of Granada *silent role*, 10 *t*, 8 *b*, Abbess *dancer*; *satb* chorus of nobles, courtiers, populace, evil spirits, ghostly nuns; dancers

After the success of *Il crociato*, Meyerbeer, taking his cue from Rossini, spent some time revising his Italian operas for the French stage. However, the success of Auber's *La muette de Portici* (1828) and Rossini's *Guillaume Tell* (1829) convinced him that the future lay with grand opera. Meyerbeer persuaded Scribe to change *Robert le diable* from a three-act opéra comique to a five-act grand opera and completed the music in 1831. Its extraordinarily successful premiere transformed Meyerbeer overnight into the most celebrated opera composer of the day. Chopin, who was present, observed: 'If ever magnificence was seen in the theatre, I doubt it reached the level of splendour shown in *Robert le diable* . . . It is a masterpiece . . . Meyerbeer has made himself immortal.' And Fétis wrote: 'It is not only M. Meyerbeer's masterpiece; it is a work remarkable in the history of art.'

SYNOPSIS
Act I The action takes place in the 13th century. Robert, the duke of Normandy, in exile because of

his evil doings, has come to Sicily, where he has fallen in love with the Sicilian princess Isabella. His father, the devil, follows him under the guise of Bertram. Raimbault, a minstrel betrothed to Robert's virtuous half-sister Alice, sings of Robert's misdeeds and is saved from Robert's wrath only by the intercession of Alice. She urges Robert, in vain, to reform and to avoid Bertram. At Bertram's instigation Robert gambles away all his possessions, including his armour, without which he cannot attend the forthcoming tournament where he hopes to win the hand of Isabella.

Act II Isabella and Robert meet in the palace during court celebrations; they pledge their love, and Isabella gives him new armour. However, Bertram prevents him attending the tournament. Robert's honour is compromised, and the prince of Granada wins Isabella's hand in his stead.

Act III After a bantering encounter with Raimbault, Bertram attends an orgy of evil spirits, where he pledges that Robert will soon join their number. Alice, terrified, observes some of Bertram's sinister activities. In a ruined convent Bertram summons from their graves nuns who have broken their vows; they entice Robert to take a magic cypress bough from above the grave of St Rosalie, by means of which his wishes will be granted.

Act IV Now under Bertram's power, Robert uses the bough to gain access to Isabella's rooms. He threatens to carry her off, but she calms him and persuades him to break the bough, thus ending its power.

Act V Bertram attempts to inveigle Robert into making a contract with him, for which his soul is the price; but Alice intervenes, delaying him signing it until eventually, on the stroke of twelve, Bertram disappears. Robert is finally freed from his power. The great doors of the cathedral then open revealing Isabella in her wedding robe.

Robert le diable was the first collaboration between Meyerbeer, Scribe and the director Charles Duponchel and the designer Pierre-Luc-Charles Ciceri, whose spectacular atmospheric sets were an integral part of the opera. The work of this team came to represent the most typical features of grand opera: a plot that wavers between history and the supernatural, an amalgam of musical styles, and tableaux that (as in the Act III finale) used technical resources to achieve the maximum expressive effect.

Meyerbeer's use of extensive orchestral resources achieves bold and powerful effects throughout the opera. However, its success depended to a considerable extent on the effectiveness of the solo vocal parts. Meyerbeer was pre-eminent in giving his singers the opportunity to shine. Robert's *sicilienne* in the first finale, 'Au tournois, Chevaliers', Isabella's solos in Act II and much else are vocally brilliant. Bertram's solo in the Act II finale, 'Nonnes, qui reposez', where he calls the dead nuns from their graves, is splendidly atmospheric with its use of the tam-tam, while the unaccompanied trio 'Fatal moment' for Alice, Robert and Bertram, interrupted after an elaborate three-part cadenza by tremolando strings, is highly effective. One of the finest things in the opera is the extended

dramatic trio 'Que faut-il faire?' for the same three characters, at the end of which Bertram disappears.

Les Huguenots
The Huguenots

Grand opéra in five acts (4h)
Libretto by Eugène Scribe and Émile Deschamps; additions by Gaetano Rossi
Composed 1832–6; original title, *La St Barthélemy*, then *Léonore*, then *Valentine*
PREMIERES 29 February 1836, Opéra, Paris; US: 29 April 1839, Théâtre d'Orléans, New Orleans; UK: 20 June 1842, Covent Garden, London
CAST Marguerite de Valois *s*, Le Comte de Saint-Bris *b*, Valentine *s*, Le Comte de Nevers *bar*, Cossé *t*, Thoré *b*, Tavannes *t*, Méru *b*, Retz *b*, Raoul de Nangis *t*, Marcel *b*, Urbain *s*, Queen's Maid of Honour *s*, Maurevert *b*, Bois-Rosé *t*, 3 monks *t*, 2 *b*, 2 witches 2 *s*, 2 girls *s*, *c*, student *t*, 2 *silent*; *satb* chorus of Huguenots, Catholics, soldiers, pages, citizens, populace, night watch, students, monks, etc.; ballet

After the completion of *Robert le diable*, but before its premiere, Meyerbeer and Scribe began working on an opéra comique, *Le portefaix*. Following the tremendous success of *Robert le diable*, Meyerbeer decided to transform the three-act *Le portefaix* into a five-act grand opera, but he abandoned it when Scribe refused. In October 1832 they signed an agreement for *La St Barthélemy* (later *Les Huguenots*). Meyerbeer promised to complete the music by December 1833, but failed to do so. He could not persuade Scribe to alter Act IV to include more opportunity for female voices, and instead had additions made by his old librettist Rossi. Other changes to the work were made shortly before the premiere to placate the censors, while for Adolphe Nourrit Meyerbeer added the duet 'O ciel! où courez-vous'. In later performances the last act was often omitted.

SYNOPSIS

Act I France, 1572. The Catholic comte de Nevers is holding a banquet in Touraine ('Des beaux jours de la jeunesse'). Because of the king's desire for peace, he has invited a Huguenot nobleman, Raoul. The guests tell tales of amorous adventure: Raoul's story concerns an unknown lady, whom he rescued from a band of riotous students, and with whom he has fallen in love ('Plus blanche que la blanche hermine'). Raoul's servant, Marcel, is horrified to see his master consorting with Catholics and protests ('Seigneur, rempart... 'Piff, paff, piff, paff'). Nevers is summoned to meet a lady in the garden; the guests observe through a window ('L'aventure est singulière'). Raoul recognizes her as the unknown lady. She is Valentine, Nevers's fiancée, and has come to request that she be released from her engagement. Raoul receives a note summoning him to a secret rendezvous.

Act II At the château of Chenonceaux, Marguerite de Valois, sister of the king and fiancée of the Huguenot Henri de Navarre, awaits Raoul's arrival ('O beau pays de la Touraine'). For the sake of peace she plans to promote his marriage to Valentine, daughter of the Catholic leader Saint-Bris. Raoul is brought in blindfold and, once his eyes are uncovered, swears devotion to her ('Beauté divine'). She proposes he marry the daughter of Saint-Bris, and he agrees. She explains her plan to a delegation of Catholic and Huguenot nobles, and all swear eternal friendship ('Par l'honneur'). But when Valentine arrives, Raoul, who does not know of her engagement, mistakenly presumes she is Nevers's mistress and repudiates his promise. Valentine does not understand his reaction; the antagonism between Catholics and Huguenots is renewed.

Act III In Paris a crowd is enjoying the day of rest ('C'est le jour du dimanche'). Huguenot soldiers sing a battle song while a Catholic service is heard from a nearby chapel ('Rataplan'). Nevers is about to be married to Valentine. Marcel delivers a message from Raoul to Saint-Bris challenging him to a duel. Nevers, Saint-Bris and Maurevert plot to ambush Raoul ('Rentrez habitants de Paris'). Valentine, praying in the chapel, has overheard the conversation and, still in love with Raoul, warns Marcel ('Dans la nuit'). The duellers arrive, and a fight between their followers ('Nous voilà') is averted only by the arrival of Marguerite. Valentine emerges from the church, and Saint-Bris is shocked to discover that it is his daughter who had warned Marcel ('Ma fille'). Marguerite clarifies Raoul's misunderstandings about Valentine and Nevers.

Act IV Raoul visits Valentine, now married to Nevers, and resolves to die after seeing her for a last time. She hides him when Saint-Bris and his companions enter, and he overhears their plan for a massacre of Huguenots that night, St Bartholomew's Eve ('Des troubles renaissants'). Nevers refuses to join in. Raoul takes leave of Valentine ('O ciel! où courez-vous') and rushes off to warn the Huguenots.

Act V The Huguenot leaders are celebrating the marriage of Marguerite and Henri de Navarre (entr'-acte and ballet) when Raoul bursts in summoning them to arms ('A la lueur'). Later, sheltering in a churchyard, Raoul and Marcel are joined by Valentine: Nevers has been killed and she wishes to marry Raoul; she renounces her faith. Catholic soldiers challenge them, but they escape to the street with the dying Raoul ('Par le fer'). Saint-Bris orders his men to fire on them, fatally wounding Valentine; he recognizes her too late. Marguerite arrives and helplessly witnesses the continuing savagery of the soldiers.

Les Huguenots is widely regarded as the finest of Meyerbeer's operas; it was the work chosen to open the current opera house at Covent Garden, London, in 1842. It puts immense strains on the resources of an opera house, for seven of its principal roles require singers of the very highest calibre; this has hindered its production during the 20th century, especially since the types of voice and vocal technique that Meyerbeer required are scarcely to be found today. The modern singer's pitch vibrato, so different from the vibrato of intensity in the bel-canto tradition, is not suited to this kind of writing. Marguerite's air 'O beau pays de la Touraine' and her duet with Raoul, 'Beauté divine', are outstanding examples of this style.

The musical style of Les Huguenots is, if anything, even more eclectic than that of Robert le diable, Meyerbeer's choice of style depending on the particular dramatic function of each section. For instance, while choral numbers that progress the action often seek to use local colour to reflect the emotions of specific characters (sometimes through instrumental timbres), solo numbers are frequently written in popular, more conventional, forms. Many numbers show Meyerbeer's keen ear for instrumental effect; for example, Raoul's romance 'Plus blanche que la blanche hermine' with its solo viola accompaniment shows great artistry in the creation of a feeling of simplicity. An incoherent effect is avoided by grouping contrasting numbers into larger units.

One example of this skilful combination of contrasting styles comes at the opening of Act III where the interweaving of the Huguenot soldiers' 'Rataplan' alternates with the song of the Catholic maidens accompanying Valentine's bridal procession and the protests of the Catholic populace against the Huguenot song (perhaps inspired by a similar scene in Louis Spohr's Pietro von Abano, which Meyerbeer greatly admired). Another highlight of the score is the finale of Act III, where a military band is on stage – an excellent example of Meyerbeer's skill in creating an arresting effect with large forces. The septet 'En mon bon droit j'ai confiance' immediately preceding the duel scene in Act III is highly effective on a smaller scale. And Act IV, as a whole, is perhaps Meyerbeer's greatest dramatic achievement. The scene of the 'benediction of the daggers' and the passionate duet for Valentine and Raoul, 'O ciel! où courez-vous', are magnificent theatre.

Le prophète
The Prophet

Grand opéra in five acts (4h)
Libretto by Eugène Scribe
PREMIERES 16 April 1849, Opéra, Paris; UK: 24 July 1849, Covent Garden, London; US: 2 April 1850, Théâtre d'Orléans, New Orleans
CAST Jean de Leyde (John of Leyden) t, Fidès ms, Berthe s, Count d'Oberthal b, Zacharie b, Jonas t, Mathisen b, 2 treble, 2 ms, 6 t, 7 b; satb chorus of peasants, Anabaptists, soldiers, nobles, children; ballet

Within a few weeks of the premiere of Les Huguenots, Meyerbeer and Scribe began consideration of a new grand-opera text. Both Le prophète and L'africaine were discussed. Initially L'africaine was chosen to be Meyerbeer's next opera; he contracted to complete it in 1840, but in 1838 the completion date was extended by two years. Meyerbeer also signed a contract for Le prophète. Two years later Le prophète was substantially finished, but Meyerbeer's appointment as generalmusikdirektor in Berlin in 1842 delayed further progress. When he finally returned to Le prophète it needed thorough revision: the tenor part, originally intended for Gilbert Duprez, who had a remarkable chest-voice range, had to be rewritten for Gustave Roger; the part of Fidès was also rewritten and expanded for Pauline Viardot.

The premiere was again triumphant: leading critics, including Berlioz, regarded it as even surpassing the previous operas. Meyerbeer was promoted to Commandeur de la Légion d'Honneur; the publishing rights were hotly competed for, and the opera was taken up by almost every major theatre in Europe. It held its place in the repertoire throughout the 19th century, and it continued to be performed, though with decreasing frequency, in the 20th. As with Meyerbeer's other grand operas, the difficulty of casting the opera satisfactorily, as well as changing taste, has militated against its production.

SYNOPSIS

Act I The countryside near Dordrecht, Holland. On the eve of the Anabaptist uprising of 1532, people are gathered outside Count Oberthal's castle ('La brise est muette'). Berthe approaches the castle to obtain permission for her marriage to the innkeeper Jean (John of Leyden). Jean's mother, Fidès, accompanies her ('Fidès, ma bonne mère'). Three Anabaptists, Zacharie, Jonas and Mathisen, also arrive to incite the people against their rulers but are driven away by Oberthal's men ('Ad nos ad salutarem undam'). Berthe makes her plea to the count ('Un jour, dans les flots') but he, struck by her beauty, refuses. He has her seized and taken into the castle. The onlooking populace is dismayed and, when the Anabaptists return, is roused to the verge of revolt.

Act II In Jean's inn in Leyden the three Anabaptists, struck by Jean's likeness to a picture of King David in the cathedral, try to persuade him to assume the role of prophet. He, however, is absorbed in his love for Berthe ('Pour Berthe'). Then Berthe rushes in begging to be hidden; she is hotly pursued by Oberthal, who orders Jean to hand her over ('Ils partent'). When Jean refuses, Oberthal threatens to execute Fidès. At this Jean gives way. After Oberthal's departure, Jean agrees to lead the Anabaptists. They leave secretly; Fidès is deceived into thinking that Jean has been murdered by a new prophet and his followers.

Act III The Anabaptists, camped in a forest outside Münster, are making merry. Oberthal is brought into Zacharie's tent as a prisoner. Jean learns that Berthe has escaped and is in Münster. The three Anabaptists wish to execute Oberthal, but Jean decrees that Berthe must decide his fate. When a group of the Anabaptists led by Mathisen is defeated in an attack on the city, Jean, who has been proclaimed a prophet of God, exerts his authority to prevent chaos in the camp. He rallies the people and leads a successful assault.

Act IV In a square in the city, people discuss the situation. Fidès is begging; she meets Berthe and tells her that Jean is dead, murdered by the prophet. Berthe vows revenge ('Un pauvre pèlerin'). In the cathedral, Jean is to be crowned king (Marche du sacre). When he speaks, Fidès recognizes his voice and cries out to him. Jean is then in danger from the people, since they thought him divine, but he escapes the crisis by denying that she is his mother, reasserting his divine parentage.

Act V In the palace at Münster the three Anabaptists plot against Jean; the emperor, who is advancing on the city, has promised them pardon if they will betray the prophet ('Ainsi, vous l'attestez'). Jean and Fides meet secretly. He implores her pardon for denying her, but she refuses it until he agrees to renounce his position and return to Leyden ('Ma mère! ma mère!'). Berthe bursts in with a flaming torch, intending to ignite the building near to the powder magazine, to kill the prophet, his followers and herself. When she recognizes Jean she is happy, but when a soldier enters to report that the emperor is at the gates she realizes that Jean is also the prophet, curses him, and stabs herself to death ('Voici le souterrain'). Jean determines to revenge himself on the Anabaptists. He and Fidès go to the banquet knowing that the powder magazine is about to explode; they, along with the Anabaptists, Oberthal and imperial troops, are all killed in a great explosion.

The music of Le prophète contains all the characteristic features of Meyerbeer's earlier grand operas, but the degree of fusion among these is even greater than before. The strongest characterization is that of Fidès, a role written specifically for Pauline Viardot. Her aria-cabaletta 'O prêtres de Baal' in Act V is an excellent example of the skills employed by Meyerbeer to achieve his dramatic ends. Interesting instrumentation – here, the use of harp and bass clarinet in particular – adds excitement to an otherwise conventional structure, infusing the music with additional emotional depth.

Variety is provided by the grotesque music allotted to the three Anabaptists: for instance, their trio in Act III with its rhythmical striking of a flint to light a lantern. Meyerbeer's remarkable ability to create an effect by bizarre juxtaposition is nowhere better revealed than in the final scene, where a boisterous drinking song ('O versez que tout respire l'ivresse et le délire') is the prelude to the explosion in which everyone perishes. For sheer grandiose magnificence the coronation scene, with its 22-piece stage band, is scarcely to be rivalled; it provided a model for many later opera composers.

Meyerbeer's calculation of effect extended to details of the staging. Le prophète was the first work to be staged at the Opéra with electric lighting. This was put to particularly fine use in the final scene of Act III where, as Jean leads his men to victory, the sun breaks through the mist which had shrouded the earlier part of the scene. Another coup de théâtre in the first production was the use of roller-skates to create the effect of ice-skating on a frozen lake at the beginning of Act III.

L'africaine

The African Girl
Grand opéra in five acts (4h)
Libretto by Eugène Scribe, completed by François-Joseph Fétis
PREMIERES 28 April 1865, Opéra, Paris; UK: 22 July 1865, Covent Garden, London; US: 1 December 1865, Academy of Music, New York
CAST Vasco da Gama t, Don Pédro b, Don Alvar t, Don Diégo b, Inès s, Anna ms, Sélica s, Nélusko b, Grand Inquisitor b, High Priest of Brahma b, Anna s, 4 t, 10 b; satb chorus of priests, inquisitors, councillors, sailors, Indians, attendants, ladies, soldiers; ballet

L'africaine had the longest gestation period of any of Meyerbeer's operas. The idea was first conceived in 1837, shortly after the premiere of Les Huguenots.

When Meyerbeer died it was not fully complete, despite having been put into rehearsal a few weeks earlier (his practice was to make substantial modification to both music and words of his operas during the extensive rehearsal periods he insisted on). After the composer's death it was left to François-Joseph Fétis to supervise the final alterations to the work. The title is curious, for Sélica is actually an Indian queen.

The production of *L'africaine* was one of the most magnificent spectacles in the history of the Opéra. However, despite the fact that Meyerbeer himself thought it his best opera, it was not as successful as his three other grand operas. Though it contains some of Meyerbeer's finest music, its looser structure and somewhat unconvincing characterization undoubtedly make it dramatically weak. These defects might have been minimized to some extent had Meyerbeer lived to make thorough revisions in rehearsal.

SYNOPSIS
Act I   In the Admiralty in Lisbon, Inès longs for news of her beloved Vasco da Gama, who has been away for two years. Her father, Don Diégo, assuming Vasco to be dead, urges her to marry Don Pédro. During a council meeting, Vasco and two captives, the only survivors of the expedition, unexpectedly arrive. When the council refuses to furnish a new expedition Vasco protests and is imprisoned together with his two captives, Sélica and Nélusko.

Act II   Sélica loves Vasco; Nélusko loves Sélica and wants to kill the sleeping Vasco, but Sélica watching over Vasco forbids him. She wakes Vasco and explains that she can guide him to India. Inès enters just as Vasco embraces Sélica in gratitude (she had married Pédro in order to secure Vasco's release). Vasco gives her Sélica as a slave, but is doubly shattered when he learns that Pédro is Inès's husband and is mounting an expedition to the Indies; the jealous Nélusko offers to act as Pédro's guide.

Act III   On board ship a storm is brewing. Nélusko plans to guide the ship on to a reef. Vasco, having mounted his own expedition, comes alongside and boards; he warns them of the reefs. Pédro tries to kill Vasco, but is prevented by Sélica; he orders Nélusko to kill her, but Nélusko refuses. The storm breaks and the ship is wrecked. Indians board and begin to massacre the crew. Recognizing their queen, Sélica, they pay homage to her.

Act IV   Sélica is triumphantly enthroned. Inès has been taken to the mancanilla grove to die by inhaling the poisonous fragrance of the trees. Sélica saves Vasco's life by claiming he is her husband, and they declare their love. Inès has not died, however, and when she and Vasco meet their passion is overwhelming. Sélica nobly renounces Vasco and sends the lovers home.

Act V   From a promontary Sélica watches the departure of Vasco's ship. She inhales the perfume of a mancanilla tree and dies in Nélusko's arms. As the curtain falls he, too, inhales the perfume.

The opera shows Meyerbeer's continuing development towards a more through-composed style, which had been increasingly apparent in his previous operas,

and is mostly constructed in a fluid mixture of recitative, arioso and aria; there are fewer self-contained numbers. Throughout Meyerbeer uses solo wind instruments resourcefully to accompany the solo voices. The scene of Sélica's enthronement at the beginning of Act IV gives him the opportunity to use a large stage band, as in the coronation scene of *Le prophète*, but here he makes the most of the chance to create exotic musical colouring. The final scene is extraordinary and can fairly be described as Meyerbeer's *Liebestod* (he had carefully studied the vocal score of Wagner's *Tristan und Isolde* in 1860): Sélica dies ecstatically to the accompaniment of an offstage chorus.

Other operas: *Abu Hassan* (inc., 1810); *Der Admiral, oder Der verlorene Prozess* (inc., 1811); *Jephtas Gelübde*, 1812; *Wirth und Gast, oder Aus Scherz Ernst*, 1813; *Das Brandenburger Tor*, (1814); *Romilda e Costanza*, 1817; *Semiramide riconosciuta*, 1819; *Emma di Resburgo*, 1819; *Margherita d'Anjou*, 1820; *L'Almanzore*, (1821); *L'esule di Granata*, 1821; *Il crociato in Egitto*, 1824; *Ein Feldlager in Schlesien*, 1844, rev. as *Vielka*, 1847; *L'étoile du nord*, 1854; *Le pardon de Ploërmel (Dinorah)*, 1859

C.A.B.

KARL MILLÖCKER
b 29 April 1842, Vienna; *d* 31 December 1899, Baden, nr Vienna

The son of a Viennese goldsmith, Millöcker studied the flute at the Vienna Conservatory. He played in the orchestra at the Theater in der Josefstadt, then led by Franz von Suppé, and later conducted at the Thalia-Theater, Graz. His initial one-act operettas were produced there in 1865, among them *Der tote Gast*. Another, *Diana*, was produced in Vienna two years later, and a three-act work, *Die Fraueninsel*, in Budapest in 1868.

The following year he became second conductor at Vienna's Theater an der Wien, where he scored a distinct success in 1871 with the songs for a farce, *Drei Paar Schuhe*, which starred Alexander Girardi, a former locksmith from Graz who would become one of the theatre's greatest stars. There were several other farces and musical comedies throughout the 1870s, until *Des verwunschene Schloss* (1878), his first substantial operetta success. In 1879 appeared *Gräfin Dubarry*, which achieved international fame in a heavily revised version by Theo Mackeben in 1931.

Millöcker was meanwhile conducting the first runs of such operettas as Johann Strauss's *Die Fledermaus* (1874). But in 1882 he produced a masterpiece that challenged Strauss's stage works: *Der Bettelstudent*, which made its merry way across Europe and to America and made its composer wealthy. Its successor, *Gasparone*, was a bandit caper in the *Fra Diavolo* mould that remains quite popular in Germany and Austria.

Subsequent operettas – usually starring Girardi – were eagerly sought by German-speaking theatres and American managers as well, the most notable being *Der Feldprediger* (1884), *Der Vize-Admiral* (1866), and

Der arme Jonathan (1890), while works written before *Der Bettelstudent* were performed to capitalize on Millöcker's reputation. His last three operettas were set, respectively, in Scotland, the Black Forest, and Russia, and various pasticcios were concocted after the composer's death.

Der Bettelstudent
The Beggar Student
Operetta in three acts (1h 30m)
Libretto by F. Zell and Richard Genée, after the plays *Fernande* by Victorien Sardou (1870) and *The Lady of Lyons* by Edward Bulwer-Lytton (1838)
PREMIERES 6 December 1882, Theater an der Wien, Vienna; US: 19 October 1883, Thalia Theater, New York; UK: 12 April 1884, Alhambra Theatre, London

This historical romantic comedy is set in Saxon-occupied Poland in 1704 and combines themes of honour, revenge, masquerade, political plotting and romance. Millöcker's score rises to the lively action and is full of incisive musical characterization. It is studded with eminently hummable polkas, krakowiaks, polonaises, marches, and waltzes, and brilliantly constructed and scored. It was one of the most successful Viennese operettas – between 1896 and 1921 there were almost 5000 performances in German; it has been filmed many times in Germany.

Other operettas: *Der tote Gast*, 1865; *Die lustigen Binder*, 1865; *Diana*, 1867; *Die Fraueninsel*, 1868; *Der Regimentstambour*, 1869; *Abenteuer in Wien*, 1873; *Das verwunschene Schloss*, 1878; *Gräfin Dubarry*, 1879; *Apajune der Wassermann*, 1880; *Die Jungfrau von Belleville*, 1881; *Gasparone*, 1884; *Der Feldprediger*, 1884; *Der Dieb*, 1886; *Der Vize-Admiral*, 1886; *Die sieben Schwaben*, 1887; *Der arme Jonathan*, 1890; *Das Sonntagskind*, 1892; *Der Probekuss*, 1894; *Das Nordlicht, oder Der rote Graf*, 1896

R.T.

CLAUDIO MONTEVERDI
Claudio Giovanni Antonio Monteverdi; *b* 15 May 1567, Cremona, Italy; *d* 29 November 1643, Venice

Monteverdi was undoubtedly the most significant composer of opera as it emerged in the first decade of the 17th century. He studied in Cremona with Marc'Antonio Ingegneri, choirmaster of the cathedral, whose solid teaching in the traditional polyphonic style was apparent in Monteverdi's earliest publications.

In 1590 or 1591, Monteverdi moved to Mantua to join the court musicians of Duke Vincenzo Gonzaga. Although employed as a string-player, he continued to publish madrigals and must have become involved in court entertainments. Mantua, then one of the most exciting musical centres in northern Italy, was host to some of the best composers of the period, including, as head of the ducal chapel, Giaches de Wert (1535–96). Wert, perhaps the leading madrigalist of his generation, significantly influenced Monteverdi's maturing style. Moreover, the Gonzaga dukes (Vincenzo and later his two sons, Francesco

and Ferdinando) were keen patrons of music as more than just an essential adjunct of court life. They provided a climate in which all the arts flourished in their city.

Monteverdi participated in the grand performance of Battista Guarini's *Il pastor fido* in Mantua in late 1598. He also accompanied Duke Vincenzo on several trips outside his kingdom, including to Hungary and Flanders, and perhaps to Florence for the wedding celebrations of Maria de' Medici and Henri IV of France in October 1600: the festivities included the first opera to survive complete, *Euridice* by Jacopo Peri. In 1601 Monteverdi finally received a long-sought-for appointment as the head of the duke's musical establishment.

Monteverdi's first opera was *Orfeo*, to a libretto by the court secretary Alessandro Striggio. Although Monteverdi built on the example of the Florentines, by his cautious approach to their revolutionary stance and his own flexibility he removed the element of dilettante experimentation from the new genre of dramma per musica, and established it as a more powerful force in its own right. *Orfeo* was presumably intended to emphasize Mantua's cultural rivalry with Florence. Exchanges between the two cities were hardly surprising: Duke Vincenzo's wife, Eleonora, was a Medici princess, and Prince Ferdinando spent a good deal of his early life in Florentine circles and was closely involved with musicians there, especially Marco da Gagliano.

For the wedding festivities of Prince Francesco Gonzaga and Margherita of Savoy, celebrated in May–June 1608, Monteverdi contributed an opera, *Arianna*, to a libretto by Ottavio Rinuccini (who had collaborated with Peri), plus a dance entertainment, *Il ballo delle ingrate*. But Monteverdi resented what he felt was the shabby treatment accorded him by the Mantuan court, and he disliked the unhealthy climate there. Events were further marred by personal tragedy; after the death first of his wife and then of his favourite pupil, Caterina Martinelli (who was to have sung the title role in *Arianna*), Monteverdi began to look elsewhere for work. His *Sanctissimae Virgini missa . . . ac vespere* (the 'Vespers' of 1610) clearly advertises his availability, and on 19 August 1613 he was appointed director of music at the Basilica of St Mark in Venice.

Monteverdi now enjoyed the fame, responsibility and security of what was possibly the leading musical position in Italy. He was also working for a republic rather than a court. His former employers continued to press him for music for operas, ballets and tournaments, but many of these requests remained unanswered. Monteverdi blamed the pressures of time and his duties at St Mark's, but in fact he now disliked catering for court tastes, where entertainments had to be peopled with mythological, allegorical and (super)natural characters. As he wrote to Striggio in 1616 about one such entertainment, *Le nozze di Tetide*, 'I have noticed that the interlocutors are Winds, Cupids, little Zephyrs and Sirens . . . [but] how can I, by such means, move the passions? Ariadne moved us because she was a woman, and similarly Orpheus because he was a man, and not a wind.' Monteverdi did in fact provide some more entertainment music for Mantua, but in his heart he had left the court behind.

Inevitably, Monteverdi's duties in Venice led him to concentrate on church music. However, as he grew older and relied more on his assistants to provide liturgical music, his thoughts returned to the stage. In the Carnival of 1624 he presented *Il combattimento di Tancredi et Clorinda*, adapting a poet who had been one of his favourite sources for madrigal texts, Torquato Tasso. He was also involved in the entertainments for the wedding of Duke Odoardo Farnese of Parma and Margherita de' Medici, which was celebrated in Parma in 1628, with a prologue, four intermedi and a licenza for the performance of Tasso's *Aminta* as well as music for a tournament. Monteverdi also wrote music for other entertainments in Venice and Vienna.

However, Monteverdi's most striking achievements for the stage came in the last years of his life. In 1637, the first public opera house opened at the Teatro S. Cassiano in Venice, encouraging a new type of opera catering not for a court but for a paying public. This led to inevitable changes both in subject matter and in musical content. Subjects, whether mythological or historical, had to be more accessible and appealing; musical resources, particularly in terms of the chorus and orchestra, had to be pared down to ensure maximum profitability; tuneful arias had to dominate over recitative; and the success or failure of an opera depended ever more on the virtuoso qualities of its lead singers. The resulting changes were striking and far-reaching.

Monteverdi first revised his *Arianna* for the Teatro S. Moisè in Carnival 1640: his choice of a work always close to his heart is significant, but *Arianna* was a court opera and cannot have been entirely appropriate for the new audience. It was far better to begin anew, as he did with *Il ritorno d'Ulisse in patria*, performed in the same season. Here Monteverdi stayed with the mythological world of the court, but now the cast are real-life characters experiencing and conveying immediate, human emotions.

For his second Venetian opera, Monteverdi turned from Homer to Virgil: his *Nozze d'Enea in Lavinia* (now lost) was staged at the Teatro SS. Giovanni e Paolo in Carnival 1641. However, the gradual move towards more concretely historical subject matter was completed only with his last work, *L'incoronazione di Poppea*. With *Orfeo*, Monteverdi had participated in the very birth of opera, marking the genre's first maturity. With *Poppea*, he celebrated a revolution of no less significance that inaugurated a new age in operatic history.

Orfeo
Orpheus

Favola in musica in a prologue and five acts (1h 45m)
Libretto by Alessandro Striggio jnr, after Ottavio Rinuccini's *Euridice* (1600), in turn after Book X of Ovid's *Metamorphoses*
PREMIERES 24 February 1607, Palazzo Ducale, Mantua; US: 14 April 1912, Metropolitan, New York (concert); 11 May 1929, Smith College, Northampton, Massachusetts; UK: 8 March 1924, Institut Français, London (concert); 7 December 1925, Town Hall, Oxford
CAST La Musica (Music) *s*, Orfeo (Orpheus) *t*, Euridice (Eurydice) *s*, Silvia *s*, Speranza (Hope) *s*, Charon *b*, Pluto

b, Proserpina *s*, Apollo *t*; *satb* chorus of nymphs and shepherds, infernal spirits

Orfeo was first performed under the auspices of Prince Francesco Gonzaga and the Accademia degli Invaghiti. The title role was taken by Francesco Rasi, a famous virtuoso from Arezzo who had also sung in Peri's *Euridice* (1600). There was a second performance a week later and a third was planned, though this seems not to have taken place. Unlike the early Florentine operas, the work is clearly divided into acts, although these were probably played without a break. The libretto published for the first performance contains an ending different from the score and closer to the myth: after Orpheus has vowed to renounce women, a crowd of bacchantes enter, berating him for his decision and singing in praise of Bacchus. The two endings may reflect different conditions at different performances, although it is not clear which was used when.

SYNOPSIS

Prologue After three statements of the opening fanfare-like 'toccata' (which reappears in the 1610 'Vespers'), Music enters to a ritornello for strings. This ritornello returns at key points in the opera where music and its power come into play. The prologue consists of five short stanzas sung over the same bass line, each separated by a shortened version of the ritornello. The theme of the opera is the power of music, which can 'soothe each troubled heart and . . . inflame the coldest minds now with noble anger, now with love'.

Act I In the fields of Thrace, Orpheus is to be married to Eurydice. He sings a hymn to his beloved ('Rosa del Ciel'), and nymphs and shepherds rejoice in song and dance.

Act II Eurydice has left with her companions. Orpheus sings to the woods, which once heard his laments but now ring to his joy ('Ecco pur ch'a voi ritorno . . . Vi ricordi, o boschi ombrosi'). But the mood of celebration, so carefully built up over this first part of the opera, is shattered by the sudden entrance of Sylvia, the messenger ('Ahi caso acerbo!'). Her tale slowly emerges ('In un fiorito prato'): Eurydice has died from a snakebite. Orpheus, at first scarcely believing the shattering news, laments his bride ('Tu sei morta') and then resolves to recover her from Hades. The chorus repeats 'Ahi caso acerbo', Sylvia decides to enter solitary exile, and the act ends in lamentation.

Act III A sinfonia of sombre brass instruments marks the change of scene to the Inferno. Orpheus is led by Hope to the gates of Hades, where she must leave him ('Lasciate ogni speranza, voi ch'entrate', 'Abandon all hope, you who enter', quoting Dante). Orpheus reaches the river Styx and the boatman Charon, who, singing to the rough sound of the regal, refuses to let him pass. Orpheus summons up all his musical powers to meet his greatest task, and the ensuing aria, 'Possente spirto', is the literal centrepiece and the climax of the opera. The text is in *terza rima* stanzas (as used by Dante), and each is set as a variation over the same bass, with florid vocal ornamentation reinforcing Orpheus' magical powers. Various instruments (two violins, two cornetts, a double harp) provide ritornelli and echo-like interjections. As Charon remains unmoved, Orpheus changes tack, adopting a much simpler style accompanied by strings. Eventually, the boatman is lulled to sleep by a sinfonia for strings, and Orpheus takes the oars. The chorus comments on the power of man to triumph over all obstacles.

Act IV Pluto, king of the underworld, and his wife Proserpina have heard Orpheus' lament. She pleads on Orpheus' behalf, and Pluto grants that Eurydice return to earth, with the condition that Orpheus leads her from the underworld without looking back. The chorus comments on the mercy to be found even in Hades. Orpheus takes up a joyful song in praise of his lyre ('Qual onor di te sia degno') over a walking bass and two-violin accompaniment. But as he moves earthwards he has doubts: is Eurydice really behind him? He turns to look, only to see her disappearing before his eyes. Orpheus returns to earth alone, and the final chorus comments on the paradox of a man who can conquer Hades, but not his own emotions.

Act V In the fields of Thrace, Orpheus laments his second loss of Eurydice; only an echo responds, and he decides to renounce women. Suddenly the heavens open and Apollo, Orpheus' father, appears in a chariot. He consoles his son, and in a duet ('Saliam cantando al cielo') they both return to heaven, where Orpheus will see Eurydice in the stars. The chorus rejoices in Orpheus' apotheosis and dances a final *moresca*.

Both composer and librettist clearly knew Peri's *Euridice*. Alessandro Striggio was certainly in Florence when it was first performed, and so, probably, was Monteverdi. Striggio's libretto contains many echoes of Rinuccini in both structure and content, although significantly he avoids much of Rinuccini's self-indulgent artistry in favour of a more concise dramatic presentation, as seen in their different narrations of Euridice's death. Monteverdi's recitative, too, owes much to Peri.

However, *Orfeo* also has much broader roots. There are many references to the tradition of the Florentine intermedi: the spectacular stage effects, the mythological subject matter, the allegorical figures, the number and scoring of the instruments, and the extended choruses. The opera also harks back to classical tragedy in the five-part division, the use of a messenger, and the commenting choruses at the ends of acts, and to the pastoral tragi-comedies of Tasso and Giovanni Battista Guarini. Similarly, Monteverdi's music is redolent of 16th-century techniques: the choruses are madrigalian in style, the technique of variation over a repeated bass was typical of earlier improvisatory procedures, and even in his new recitative Monteverdi exploits expressive devices first explored in his polyphonic madrigals, including carefully crafted vocal lines, dissonances and chromaticism.

These backward-looking, Renaissance aspects of the opera are reinforced by its various humanist messages about the power of man and music. But *Orfeo* also looks forward to the baroque. Monteverdi demonstrates his openness to the new styles developed by his Florentine contemporaries, and also to other techniques then being developed, particularly in the duple- and triple-time arias and in the duet textures for voices and/or instruments (as in Monteverdi's *Scherzi musicali* of 1607). Another novel aspect of his score is the detail with which Monteverdi notes his precise intentions in matters of instrumentation and ornamentation (e.g. the ornaments in 'Possente spirto' are written out): here he asserts his control over elements previously left to the performer. As a result, *Orfeo* contains an intriguing mixture of old and new elements. Rather than rejecting previously perfected techniques in an iconoclastic search for novelty, Monteverdi reinterprets the old in the light of the new (and vice versa) to produce a powerful synthesis of undeniable dramatic force. Moreover, and unlike the Florentines, Monteverdi is unquestionably a masterful composer. His attention to the drama, to large-scale structure (witness his symmetrical patterning and tonal planning) and to expressive detail demonstrate his skills to the full, and produced what is arguably the first great opera.

Il ritorno d'Ulisse in patria
The Return of Ulysses
Opera in a prologue and three acts (3h)
Libretto by Giacomo Badoaro, after Books XIII–XXIII of Homer's *Odyssey*
PREMIERES Carnival, February 1640, Teatro S. Cassiano, Venice; UK: 16 January 1928, BBC radio; 16 March 1965, St Pancras Town Hall, London; US: 18 January 1974, Opera House, Kennedy Center, Washington, DC
CAST L'Humana fragilità (Human Frailty) *s*, Tempo (Time) *b*, Fortuna (Fortune) *s*, Amore (Cupid) *s*, Ulisse (Ulysses) *t*, Penelope *s*, Telemaco (Telemachus) *t*, Antinoo (Antinous) *b*, Pisandro (Peisander) *t*, Anfinomo (Amphinomus) *a*, Eurimaco (Eurymachus) *t*, Melanto (Melantho) *s*, Eumete (Eumaeus) *t*, Iro (Irus) *t*, Ericlea (Eurycleia) *ms*, Giove (Jupiter) *t*, Nettuno (Neptune) *b*, Minerva *s*, Giunone (Juno) *s*; *satb* chorus of Phaeacians, celestial spirits, maritime spirits

Ulisse was Monteverdi's first new opera for Venice, and it reveals him coming to terms both with the demands of the new public theatres and with the stylistic developments of his younger contemporaries. Its authenticity, once doubted, now seems clear. The score survives in manuscript in Vienna, but there are significant differences between this score and the surviving manuscript copies of the libretto. The text is a straightforward adaptation of Homer, and Badoaro exploited all the devices now becoming standard in Venetian opera: the moralizing prologue, comic characters (Irus and Eurycleia, Melantho and Eurymachus (cf. Damigella and Valletto in *Poppea*)) and spectacular scenic effects. However, the subject matter of the opera also has a somewhat archaic, courtly feel: witness the prominence of the gods and an almost 'superhuman' hero in the manner of *Orfeo*. The opera seems to have been a success: it was also staged in Bologna in 1640 and again in Venice in 1641.

SYNOPSIS

Prologue Human Frailty acknowledges its submission to Time, Fortune and Cupid, as the following drama will reveal.

Act I In her palace in Ithaca, Penelope awaits the return of her husband Ulysses from the Trojan Wars. She cannot be consoled by her nurse, Eurycleia. Melantho, a maid, and Eurymachus, a shepherd, comment on the pains yet pleasures of their own love ('De' nostri amor concordi'). Neptune, supported by Jupiter, condemns the rescue of Ulysses by the Phaeacians. They have brought him back to Ithaca, leaving him sleeping on the beach. As a punishment, Neptune turns their ship into a rock. Ulysses awakes ('Dormo ancora') and believes himself to have been abandoned. Minerva enters disguised as a shepherd ('Cara e lieta gioventù') and tells Ulysses that the island is his home. She reveals herself to his amazement ('O fortunato Ulisse') and tells him to bathe in a sacred fountain (a chorus of naiads is missing in the score). Here Ulysses will change into an old man so as to enter his palace unrecognized and outwit Antinous, Peisander and Amphinomus, the suitors who have insinuated themselves into the offices of state and are seeking his wife's hand. Meanwhile, Minerva will bring back Ulysses' son Telemachus from Sparta. Ulysses again rejoices ('O fortunato Ulisse'). Melantho urges Penelope to forget Ulysses and love another ('Ama dunque'). Eumaeus, a shepherd faithful to Ulysses, tends his flocks and argues with the social parasite Irus. Ulysses, now disguised, enters and warns Eumaeus of the imminent return of his sovereign ('Ulisse, Ulisse è vivo').

Act II Minerva brings Telemachus on her chariot. Eumaeus welcomes the prince ('O gran figlio d'Ulisse') and presents the old man, who, he says, has news of his father's return. A ray of light descends from heaven to reveal Ulysses in his true form. Father and son are joyfully reunited in a duet ('O padre sospirato/O figlio desiato'), and they plan their return to the palace. Melantho and Eurymachus discuss Penelope's continued devotion to Ulysses. The suitors enter to pursue their advances ('Ama dunque'), but Penelope staunchly resists ('Non voglio amar'). Eumaeus announces the imminent return of Telemachus and Ulysses, and the suitors are disconcerted. They plot to kill Telemachus, but the sight of Jupiter's eagle flying overhead warns them against the plan. They decide instead to redouble their wooing of Penelope ('Amor è un'armonia'). Minerva outlines to Ulysses a plan to remove the suitors, and Eumaeus recounts to Ulysses Penelope's lasting fidelity. Ulysses rejoices ('Godo anch'io'), and they plan to go to the palace. Meanwhile, Telemachus discusses his recent travels with Penelope. Antinous and Irus meet Eumaeus and Ulysses, now disguised as a beggar. Antinous treats them badly, and Ulysses is provoked to fight Irus, thrashing his fat adversary. Penelope orders that the beggar be made welcome. The suitors redouble their efforts to gain her favours with rich gifts. She proclaims that she will marry whoever manages to string Ulysses' great bow. The suitors agree willingly ('Lieta, soave gloria'), but all three fail the test. The beggar asks to enter the competition, while renouncing the prize, and succeeds in stringing the bow. Invoking Minerva's protection, Ulysses looses arrows at the suitors and kills them all.

Act III Irus grieves for his colleagues in a splendid take-off of the typical lament scene (a following scene for Mercury and the ghosts of the suitors is missing). Penelope refuses to believe Eumaeus' claim that the beggar who bent the bow was indeed Ulysses ('Ulisse, Ulisse è vivo'), and even Telemachus cannot convince her. Minerva and Juno decide to plead with Jupiter on Ulysses' behalf ('Ulisse troppo errò'). Neptune is pacified, and choruses of celestial and maritime spirits praise the new accord ('Giove amoroso'). Eurycleia ponders how best to act with Penelope, who still refuses the assurances of Eumaeus and Telemachus ('Troppo incredula'). Even when Ulysses enters in his true form, she fears a trick. Eurycleia claims that it is indeed he ('È questo, è questo Ulisse'): she has seen him in his bath and recognized a scar. But Penelope is finally convinced only when Ulysses correctly describes the embroidered quilt on their nuptial bed ('Hor sì ti riconosco . . . Illustratevi, o cieli'). Husband and wife are rejoined in a blissful love duet ('Sospirato mio sole').

There are clear parallels between *Ulisse* and the styles found in Monteverdi's other later works (e.g. the *stile concitato* first seen extensively in *Il combattimento*). The opera also contains several echoes of *Orfeo*: the recitative laments (e.g. Penelope at the opening of Act I), the virtuosic ornamental writing for Minerva and Juno, the five-part sinfonias, and even the care for large-scale symmetrical structures. But whereas in *Orfeo* it was the recitative that carried the bulk of the action, with arias and duets, etc. interposed only where they could be used realistically (rather as songs in a play), now the style is one of a flexible shifting between recitative, arioso and aria. The duple- and triple-time arias, whether just short phrases or more developed structures, are points of intensification prompted by the drama, by the need to emphasize particular words and by the emotional effect. They also reflect changes in the verse structure of the text. The sensuous triple-time melodies, so much more developed than the simple hemiola patterns of *Orfeo*, are a truly modern characteristic. Indeed, at the age of 73 Monteverdi shows himself to be remarkably *au fait* with the most up-to-date Venetian idioms.

L'incoronazione di Poppea
The Coronation of Poppea
Opera in a prologue and three acts (3h 30m)
Libretto by Giovanni Francesco Busenello, after Tacitus, Suetonius and perhaps Seneca
PREMIERES Carnival 1643, Teatro SS. Giovanni e Paolo, Venice; US: 27 April 1926, Smith College, Northampton, Massachusetts; UK: 6 December 1927, Town Hall, Oxford
CAST Fortuna (Fortune) *s*, Virtù (Virtue) *s*, Amore (Cupid) *s*, Poppea (Poppaea) *s*, Nerone (Nero) *s*, Ottavia (Octavia) *ms*, Seneca *b*, Ottone (Otho) *a*, Drusilla *s*, Arnalta *c*, Nurse *c*, Lucano (Lucan) *t*, Valletto *s*, Damigella *s*, Liberto *t*, A Lictor *b*, Maidservant *s*, 2 Soldiers 2 *t*, Pallade (Pallas Athene) *s*, Mercurio (Mercury) *b*, Venere (Venus) *s*; *atb* chorus of consuls and tribunes, Seneca's companions

Poppea is the first known opera to adopt a factual historical subject: it is set in Rome in AD 64. The earthy, sensuous plot, tempered by Busenello's trenchant view of the world, is typical of new Venetian trends. Certainly there are no high-minded allegories here, and important precedents are established by the oft-remarked 'immorality' of the plot, by the comic interludes, and by the emphasis on virtuoso singers (Octavia was sung by the young Anna Renzi, who later had an outstanding operatic career in Venice).

The surviving sources are complex. We have a scenario associated with the first performances, some manuscript libretti of uncertain date, and Busenello's edition of the libretto in his *Delle hore ociose* (Venice, 1656). The music survives in two manuscripts: one in Naples, perhaps associated with a performance by the travelling Febiarmonici in 1651 (a libretto printed for this performance also survives); the other in Venice, largely copied in the early 1650s by Francesco Cavalli's wife, with performance alterations and annotations by Cavalli himself. These various sources differ, sometimes considerably. The music was first definitely assigned to Monteverdi in 1681 (although the Venice manuscript also bears an attribution of uncertain date), and the extent of his authorship is not entirely clear. Certainly there seems little doubt that *Poppea* as it survives mixes the work of various composers. The text of the final duet between Nero and Poppaea was used in a revival of Benedetto Ferrari's *Il pastor reggio* (Bologna, 1641; now lost), and in an entertainment (1647) by Filiberto Laurenzi. There is also music almost certainly by Cavalli (the opening sinfonia is reworked from his *Doriclea* of 1645) and by Francesco Sacrati (the sinfonias in the consul scene in Act III appear in his *La finta pazza* of 1641). These and other problems pose obvious difficulties for modern productions. The leading exponent of mid-17th-century Venetian opera in the 1960s, Raymond Leppard, viewed these manuscripts as essentially skeletons that were then, and should be now, fleshed out in various ways. He added lavish string accompaniments and made extensive cuts and alterations. One can sympathize with the intent (such pragmatism was clearly characteristic of 17th-century operatic performances), but Leppard's overly romantic 'realizations' have now gone out of favour. More recent productions have followed the surviving scores and contemporary resources more closely, with the result that the dramatic and musical effect, although considerably less opulent, is more stringent and arguably more effective.

SYNOPSIS (Venice manuscript)
Prologue Fortune, Virtue and Cupid dispute their respective powers. Cupid claims to be master of the world, as the story of Nero and Poppea will prove.

Act I Otho arrives at his house and sees Nero's soldiers outside, asleep. He realizes that his betrothed, Poppaea, is with Nero and curses her faithlessness. The soldiers are aroused and complain about their job and the decline of Rome. Nero and Poppaea enter: they take a sensuous farewell as Poppaea emphasizes her love for him ('Signor, sempre mi vedi') and seeks to guarantee their marriage. She is left alone with her nurse, Arnalta, to discuss tactics and ignores Arnalta's common-sense warnings, for Cupid is on her side ('Per me guerreggia Amor e la Fortuna'). Arnalta is left to grumble at her mistress's folly ('Ben sei pazza'). In the emperor's palace Octavia, Nero's wife, acknowledges her humiliation ('Disprezzata regina') while her nurse suggests that she should take a lover. Seneca, shown in by Octavia's secretary, Valletto, urges restraint and appeals to her dignity: Valletto responds by cursing Seneca's pedantry. As Seneca reflects on Octavia's power and the transitory nature of life ('Le porpore regali e le grandezze'), Pallas Athene appears to warn him of his impending death. Seneca welcomes the news. Nero debates his plans about Octavia and Poppaea with Seneca ('Son risoluto al fine'). The philosopher urges reason, but Nero is inflamed to anger. Poppaea enters to calm him down ('Come dolci signor, come soavi'), suggesting that Seneca must be killed. Otho confronts Poppaea over her infidelity, but she dismisses him ('Chi nasce sfortunato di se stesso si dolga e non d'altrui'). He tries to come to his senses ('Otton, torna in te stesso') and vows revenge. Then he turns to Drusilla, who has always loved him, and swears that he will favour her over Poppaea.

Act II Seneca praises Stoic solitude. Mercury appears, warning him again of death, which the philosopher accepts happily ('O me felice'). Liberto, a freedman, enters with Nero's command: Seneca must die by the end of the day. He welcomes his fate, despite the urgings of his companions ('Non morir, Seneca'), and they leave to prepare the bath in which he will open his veins. The tension is broken by a flirtatious scene between Valletto and Damigella. Nero and Lucan celebrate the news of Seneca's death with wine and song ('Son rubini amorosi'). Otho rededicates himself to Poppaea, whom he still loves ('Sprezzami quanto sai'), but Octavia orders him to assume female garb and kill Poppaea. He cannot refuse. Drusilla delights in her love for Otho ('Felice cor mio'), and Octavia's nurse wishes she were in Drusilla's place. Otho enters and explains his plan for Poppaea: Drusilla gives him her clothes. Meanwhile Poppaea rejoices in Seneca's death ('Hor che Seneca è morto') and prays for Cupid to support her. Arnalta lulls her to sleep ('Oblivion soave') as Cupid watches overhead. Otho, dressed as Drusilla, enters and tries to kill Poppaea, but he is prevented by Cupid. She wakes and gives the alarm as Otho escapes. Cupid proclaims his success ('Ho difeso Poppea').

Act III Drusilla joyfully anticipates Poppaea's death, but she finds herself arrested for the attempted murder (Otho was wearing her clothes) and Nero sentences her to death. Otho in turn confesses his guilt, despite Drusilla's persistent attempts to protect her beloved, and Nero banishes them. Nero and Poppaea rejoice now that the way is clear for their marriage ('Non più s'interporrà noia a dimora'). Octavia enters and, in a lament, bids a halting farewell ('Addio Roma'). Arnalta revels in the exaltation of her mistress as empress of Rome (these two scenes are reversed in some sources). Nero crowns Poppaea ('Ascendi, o mia diletta'), and the consuls and tribunes pay homage. Cupid proclaims his triumph to his approving mother, Venus ('Io mi compiaccio, o figlio'). Nero and Poppaea have a final ecstatic duet ('Pur ti miro, pur ti godo').

The uncertain status of *Poppea*, upsetting though it may be for devotees of the single-composer masterpiece, is itself revealing. First, the fact that Monteverdi can be so easily conflated with his contemporaries and successors suggests the similarity of styles exploited in Venetian opera around the middle of the century. Second, it emphasizes the priorities of contemporary opera production, where the librettist and stage designer held sway over such lesser functionaries as musicians. In contrast with *Ulisse*, *Poppea* has a drastically pared-down orchestration and places much more emphasis on the tuneful melodies given to the lead singers. Again the style is one of a flexible shifting between recitative, arioso and aria, although here the arias become more extensive and structurally self-contained. To be sure, Monteverdi, if it is he, can still provide some splendid recitative, such as Octavia's great Act III lament, harking back to *Orfeo* and *Arianna*. But the splendidly lyrical arias now carry the emotional and musical weight of the drama and point the way forward to the prime concerns of later baroque opera.

Other stage works surviving in whole or part: *De la bellezza le dovute lodi*, 1607; *Arianna*, 1608; *Il ballo delle ingrate*, 1608; *Tirsi e Clori*, 1616; 'Su le penne de' venti il ciel varcando' (prologue for Giovanni Battista Andreini's *La Maddalena*), 1617; *Il combattimento di Tancredi e Clorinda*, 1624; *Volgendo il ciel per l'immortal sentiero*, 1638 Lost: *Gli amori di Diana ed Endimione*, 1605; 'Ha cento lustri con etereo giro' (prologue for Battista Guarini's *L'idropica*), 1608; *Le nozze di Tetide* (inc., 1617); *Andromeda*, 1620; *Apollo*, 1620; *La contesa di Amore e Cupido*, etc. (intermedi for E. Marigliani's *Li tre costanti*), 1622; *Armida abbandonata*, (1626); *La finta pazza Licori* (?inc., ?1627); *Gli Argonauti*, 1628; *Teti e Flora*, etc. (intermedi for Torquato Tasso's *Aminta*), 1628; *Mercurio e Marte*, 1628; *Proserpina rapita*, 1630 (one canzonetta survives in Monteverdi's *Madrigali e canzonette*, Venice, 1651); *La vittoria d'Amore*, 1641; *Le nozze d'Enea in Lavinia*, 1641

T.C.

WOLFGANG AMADEUS MOZART
Joannes Chrysostomus Wolfgangus Theophilus Mozart; *b* 27 January 1756, Salzburg; *d* 5 December 1791, Vienna

Mozart is the most famous of all infant prodigies, the little boy who charmed kings and princes as his music continues to charm us today. But far more remarkable than his precocity was his development by the time he was 30 into the composer of works of the greatest beauty, depth and humanity.

After three operas composed by the time he was 12, Mozart had the extraordinary honour of being commissioned to compose the opera seria *Mitridate* for the royal ducal theatre of Milan in 1770 when he was 14, with two more operas for 1771 and 1772. His own personality gradually gained the upper hand over the

Italian models he had assimilated. The next years were frustratingly short of opera commissions. Salzburg had no regular theatre or opera, only occasional touring companies and formal gala occasions, for one of which he wrote the totally undramatic *Il re pastore*. Fortunately the court of the Bavarian elector in Munich gave him the chance of composing *La finta giardiniera* in 1775 and *Idomeneo* – his first truly great opera – in 1781. Soon after, he left the service of the prince archbishop of Salzburg in a stormy scene and settled in Vienna, where his first major task was the composition of *Die Entführung aus dem Serail* (1782), a resounding success. Yet, neither the beautiful music of this singspiel nor the Italian operas begun but soon abandoned because of their hopeless libretti prepare us for his next major opera, *Le nozze di Figaro* (1786). There is no accounting for perfection, but the genius of the librettist Lorenzo da Ponte (to be confirmed in the next two operas, which lacked the benefit of Beaumarchais's brilliant play as a basis), played its part, along with Mozart's greater maturity and deeper experience of life, and the intense application of a unique intelligence. After *Don Giovanni* (1787) and *Così fan tutte* (1790) to da Ponte's libretti, Mozart wrote two totally different operas, both produced within three months of his death in 1791. In *Die Zauberflöte* he miraculously combined a new simplicity with great seriousness and comedy; *La clemenza di Tito* was at the same time a backward glance at opera seria and a work of neo-classical nobility ushering in the new century.

The creation of *Le nozze di Figaro* coincided with two comparable achievements, the series of great piano concertos and the six quartets dedicated to Haydn, but he had a special love for opera: its influence is audible throughout his instrumental music in many a 'vocal' phrase and in the dramatic juxtapositions of mood. The influence of Mozart the instrumental composer on the operas is equally important. Whereas his highly successful contemporary Paisiello regarded modulation as an unsatisfactory substitute for melody, patterns of tonality form the architecture of Mozart's mature operas, both in the total plan and within the individual sections. Could Mozart expect a listener lacking absolute pitch (as most of us do) to take in his schemes of tonality, even when an 18th-century opera-goer was lucky to see a work more than once in a lifetime? The answer must be yes, perhaps subconsciously, since the whole use of sonata form is based on that assumption.

Apart from the formal consideration that operas and finales ended in the key they started in and apart from the traditional keys, C and D for martial occasions, E♭ for solemn ones and so on, Mozart had his own instinct. The most sensual key for him was A major, for most seductions were performed or attempted in it. In *Die Zauberflöte*, C minor always refers to death, while A♭, not the relative major (E♭) but its subdominant, usually brings relief, as in the opening scene. The same key relationship, a tone higher, takes on a structural role in *Don Giovanni*, where D minor, the key of the commendatore and his vengeance, opposes and finally overcomes B♭ major and D major – the Don's principal keys.

The supreme example of Mozart's architecture is perhaps the Act II finale of *Figaro*, which presents a chain of crises appearing and being resolved in turn, each depicted in a 'movement' in sonata form with its rise of tension at the modulation to the dominant and then the reconciliation of the return to the tonic key. The key relationship between the movements is also significant in this finale: from Figaro's entrance in the fourth section it moves to the subdominant every time (G–C–F–B♭–E♭), each move therefore expressing a lowering of tension – but this always proves to be momentary, since a new problem soon appears.

Although Mozart rigorously adheres to the harmonic structure (of sonata, rondo or ternary form), his operas become ever freer about the recapitulation of the melodies. From the time of *Figaro*, Mozart is less liable to repeat words and music for the sake of musical form. New events and emotions arise, requiring new music. By the time of *Die Zauberflöte* the recapitulation of melodies may be vestigial, just a hint to give the listener his bearings.

Not only do keys have a special significance, but melodic phrases or intervals reappear throughout Mozart's vocal music to express similar moods: in *Die Zauberflöte* the exultant rising major sixth that opens Tamino's aria 'Dies Bildnis' is echoed by the equally rapturous 'Tamino mein' sung by Pamina in the Act II finale. These are in different keys, but there is a link of melody and key in the vengeance sworn in Donna Anna's 'Fuggi crudele' in *Don Giovanni* and the Queen of the Night's 'Der Hölle Rache' in *Die Zauberflöte*. Attempts to codify a distinct musical language as used by Mozart go too far, since his thinking was deep and instinctive, but nearly everything in his great opera scores – melody, harmony and orchestration – has a dramatic purpose as well as a purely musical one.

Bastien und Bastienne

Bastien and Bastienne
Singspiel in one act (45m)
Libretto translated from the French parody of Jean-Jacques Rousseau's *Le devin du village* (1752), *Les amours de Bastien et Bastienne* by Harny de Guerville, Charles Simon Favart and Marie Justine Benoite Favart (1753), trans. by Friedrich Wilhelm Weiskern and Johann Heinrich Müller, rev. Johann Andreas Schachtner
Composed ?1767–8
PREMIERES October 1768, the garden of Dr Anton Mesmer's house in Vienna; UK: 26 December 1894, Daly's Theatre, London; US: early 1905, Habelmann's Opera School, New York
CAST Bastienne *s*, Bastien *t*, Colas *b*; shepherds and shepherdesses *silent*

The success of Rousseau's naïve little pastoral opera *Le devin du village* soon gave birth to a parody, in which the Arcadian shepherds were turned into French peasants, while the music consisted of popular melodies. This was performed in Vienna in French, and Mozart set its translation. Georg Nikolaus von Nissen's biography of Mozart states that his 'operetta' was performed in the suburban garden of Dr Mesmer (who gave 'mesmerized' to the language and who was mocked in *Così fan tutte* by Despina with her magnet).

For a later performance Mozart wrote some recitatives with the part of Colas in the alto clef.

SYNOPSIS
The shepherdess Bastienne, regretting the infidelity of her beloved Bastien, consults the magician Colas. He promises that all will be well, but urges her to show some fickleness too. He then warns Bastien that Bastienne no longer loves him but confirms that they can be reunited with the help of his magic. And so they are, after a while. They praise Colas, and he cheerfully joins in.

Mozart's first singspiel finds the right style long before the emergence of the National Singspiel founded by Joseph II to perform works in German: homely texts in a mild Viennese dialect to simple melodies. The bagpipe imitation for the entry of Colas has a rustic colour, and the *intrada*'s single theme (with its oft remarked anticipation of Beethoven's 'Eroica' Symphony) is of the same family. There are several expressive airs in minuet rhythm, but half the pieces are in the two-tempo form learned from opéra comique. Colas has a splendid hocus-pocus aria 'Diggi, daggi, schurry, murry' in C minor, but Mozart is so far from characterizing the young people that he gives them a duet with the same music but sung to different words. Perhaps the fact that they have such similar names and aims made it seem an amusing idea. Their big duet 'Geh! geh! geh, Herz von Flandern' begins with the two at first obstinately refusing a reconciliation, but then, with a hint of the minor, holding out olive branches and, in a short free adagio, turning to happiness, ending with a delicious 3/8 finale. The very simplicity of the 13-year-old's composition is appropriate to this little work.

Mitridate, re di Ponto

Mithridates, King of Pontus
Opera seria in three acts (3h 30m)
Libretto by Vittorio Amedeo Cigna-Santi, originally set by Quirino Gasparini (1767), after Jean Racine's tragedy *Mithridate* (1673) trans. into Italian by Giuseppe Parini (c. 1765)
Composed September–December 1770
PREMIERES 26 December 1770, Teatro Regio Ducal, Milan; UK: 17 March 1979, Logan Hall, London (concert); US: 15 August 1985, Avery Fisher Hall, New York (concert); 30 June 1991, Loretto-Hilton Center, St Louis; Ireland: 27 October 1989, Theatre Royal, Wexford
CAST Mitridate *t*, Aspasia *s*, Sifare *s*, Farnace *a*, Ismene *s*, Marzio *t*, Arbate *s*; guards and Roman soldiers *silent*

In March 1770 the 14-year-old Mozart presented three magnificent arias at a soirée of Count Firmian's in Milan: this led to his first commission, for an opera seria for one of Italy's three principal theatres. It had a powerful orchestra including 28 violins, as opposed to the 12 he would find at the Vienna Burgtheater and the six at the premiere of *Die Zauberflöte*. Mozart duly handed in the recitatives by the end of October, but the arias had to be tailored to the singers. The primo uomo (principal castrato) in the role of Sifare did not arrive until the end of November. The tenor

Guglielmo d'Ettore (Mitridate) was the most trouble-some – Mozart had to rewrite his opening aria three times. The premiere, which lasted six hours (including ballets by another hand), was a great success. The opera was given 22 times, and the composer was re-engaged for the following year.

Mithridates VI Eupator (132–63 BC), king of Pontus (on the Black Sea), was finally defeated by the Romans after a reign of 50 years and many conquests. Like *Figaro*, this libretto has the advantage of being based on a great play. The tension of the drama is maintained throughout in a way that was impossible for tragedies of 18th-century origin with their genteel, rather bloodless behaviour. Unusually for Racine, nobody dies except the fierce old king; the drama thus conforms to the Age of Enlightenment's wish for a happy ending.

SYNOPSIS

Act I King Mitridate has left his empire in the care of his sons Sifare and Farnace while he is away at the wars. Deceived by a rumour of his father's death, Farnace declares his love to Mitridate's betrothed, Aspasia. She seeks the protection of Sifare. Mitridate returns with Ismene as a bride for Farnace. When he hears of Farnace's guilt, he determines to kill him.

Act II Aspasia and Sifare declare their love for each other and mourn that she must marry Mitridate.

Act III When Farnace's treacherous plotting with the Romans is discovered, he reveals in his despair that Sifare is his father's real rival. Mitridate traps Aspasia into confessing her love for Sifare, and con-demns them both to death. Ismene holds off the king's wrath for long enough to let both sons beat off the Roman attack. Mitridate, mortally wounded, re-joices at their loyalty and their coming betrothals.

An Italian composer would have avoided some of Mozart's mistakes, such as setting Aspasia's pleading in the first aria to fierce coloratura, or giving the angry king staccatos in the manner of opera buffa. Gasparini's setting of the same libretto is less attrac-tive, but his version of Mitridate's last aria, 'Vado incontro al fato', with its six top Cs was used in place of Mozart's frankly weaker one. One can always admire Mozart's craftsmanship, for example in Sifare's first aria, 'Soffre il mio cor', the organization of short phrases of the orchestral ritornello, some of which return at the end of the exposition while others are reserved for the end of the aria, or the coloratura subtly varied at its return. He also does his best to characterize – Mitridate's ferocity with great leaps and dynamic contrasts, the gentleness of Sifare op-posed to the far more angular music of his impulsive brother. But when in doubt he turns out a well-made all-purpose piece with a busy orchestra over a drum-ming bass and a good deal of coloratura, his general stand-by until after *Il re pastore* (1775).

The formal patterns of the day demanded long arias, even with the shortened da-capo form. Another type, a succession of slow and fast sections, is used tellingly by Mozart when Mitridate speaks gently to Sifare, then fiercely to Aspasia in 'Tu, che fedel mi sei', but formal convention weakened the drama by demanding a complete repeat (in appropriate keys). The Italian composers generally kept their arias shorter than Mozart did at this stage.

There is, however, more and more music of great beauty as the opera proceeds. There are two agitato pieces in minor keys with no contrasting section to destroy the mood, and some delicious lyrical music, especially in Sifare's 'Lungi da te' with horn obbligato (inspired by contact with the orchestra, for there is an earlier version without the horn) and in the one duet, 'Se viver non degg'io', in which Aspasia and Sifare declare their doomed love. The original version, pre-sumably rejected by the singers, is even more beautiful. The greatest piece is 'Pallid' ombre' with its accompa-nied recitatives, sung by Aspasia when she receives the king's poisoned cup. Her long incantation has the earnestness of Gluck's *Alceste*. When she sings at the lowest range of the voice, it is as a means of intense expression and not to show what the singer could do.

Lucio Silla
Lucius Sulla
Opera seria in three acts (3h 30m)
Libretto by Giovanni de Gamerra
Composed November–December 1772
PREMIERES 26 December 1772, Teatro Regio Ducal, Milan; UK: 7 March 1967, Camden Town Hall, London; US: 19 January 1968, Peabody Concert Hall, Baltimore
CAST Lucio Silla *t*, Giunia *s*, Cecilio *s*, Lucio Cinna *s*, Celia *s*, Aufidio *t*; *satb* chorus of noble Romans, senators, people; guards *silent*

Mozart had to compose *Lucio Silla* more rapidly than *Mitridate*. He could not begin on the arias until the singers were present: the primo uomo, the famous castrato Venanzio Rauzzini (Cecilio), arrived on 21 November, the no-less-famous prima donna, Anna de Amicis (Giunia), on 5 December, but a totally inad-equate tenor in the title role, 'a church singer from Lodi' and a late substitute, turned up only eight days before the first performance! So he was given just two vocally very unambitious arias, which may account for the total lack of motivation for Silla's change of heart at the end. The premiere had only a moderate success, but there were 20 performances. Although the Mozarts stayed on and on in Milan, no further com-missions were forthcoming, and early in March 1773 Wolfgang left Italy, never to return.

The Roman Lucius Cornelius Sulla (138–78 BC) did indeed retire unexpectedly from his tyrannical dictatorship.

SYNOPSIS

Act I Cecilio, a senator banished by the dictator Silla, returns secretly to Rome to hear from his friend Cinna that his bride Giunia has been taken into Silla's household. There we see her wooed by the dictator, who is urged to use gentle ways by his sister Celia but force by his friend the tribune Aufidio. Giunia spurns his advances and goes to pray at her father's tomb, together with other noble Romans who hope to free their country from Silla's yoke. She meets her beloved Cecilio.

Act II Giunia turns down Cinna's suggestion that she marry Silla in order to murder him. Silla confronts her publicly on the Capitol with a demand for her hand as a way to end the civil strife. Cecilio appears with drawn sword and is seized.

Act III　Cecilio is visited in prison by Cinna, who begs his own bride – Celia – to mollify her brother. Giunia is ready to die with Cecilio, but on the Capitol Silla forgives everybody and abdicates.

Nothing in the recent Salzburg works, mostly instrumental, prepares us for the great leap forward Mozart made with *Lucio Silla*. The much stronger emotional engagement must be a sign of the adolescent taking over from the child. The use of the chorus and the dark moods with their *ombra* (shadow) scenes are partly the consequence of the young librettist's leanings towards the reforms of Gluck and the neo-Neapolitans. But Mozart's *recitativi accompagnati* are marvellous compositions, some of which would not be out of place in his later operas. He gives the orchestra a bigger role in them than the Italians did: the harmonic movement is sometimes surprising but always purposeful. At the end of Act I two short orchestral links (added during rehearsals) produce a long stream of continuous music, including the powerful chorus 'Fuor di queste urne' with Giunia's interpolated aria and the happy duet that concludes the act. All these are big steps towards *Idomeneo*, his next opera seria, still eight years away.

Many of the 18 arias still suffer from a rather generalized busy manner, from excessive length, and from long stretches of coloratura. The most awe-inspiring of these are in Giunia's 'Ah se il crudel periglio', of which his father Leopold wrote, 'Wolfgang has put passages in it which are new and quite especially and astonishingly difficult: she [de Amicis] sings them to amaze you and we are on the best of terms with her.' But de Amicis also had the vivid breathless 'Parto, m'affretto' and the solemn 'Fra i pensier più funesti' with its excited middle section. On the other hand, Rauzzini preferred showing his skill in enormous leaps, as from bottom A to the A♭ nearly two octaves higher in 'Ah se a morir mi chiama', rather than in coloratura – surprisingly in view of the motet 'Exsultate, jubilate' with its brilliant and famous concluding 'Alleluia', which Mozart wrote for him soon after. His little minuet in rondo form, 'Pupille amate', is one of those infinitely touching melodies in which the young Mozart excelled his master J. C. Bach. The trio 'Quell'orgoglioso sdegno' prefigures the quartet in *Idomeneo* in some ways, such as the imitative entries: Giunia and Cecilio naturally sing in thirds for much of it, but it is touching to find Silla, moved by the intrepid love of the two, finally joining them. The grand finale is a *ciaconna* with three verses for the chorus alternating with the soloists. Performances usually ended with a danced chaconne, as *Idomeneo* was to do: perhaps there were dancers for this sung chaconne.

Mozart later wrote out Cecilio's 'Ah se a morir mi chiama' with decorations in nearly every bar, both in the first section and then differently in the da capo, as an example to singers, who were always expected to improvise their own version.

La finta giardiniera
The Pretended Gardener
Dramma giocoso in three acts (3h 30m)
Libretto by ?Giuseppe Petrosellini, originally for Pasquale Anfossi (1774)
Composed December 1774; accompanied recitatives rev. by Mozart for German singspiel version, *Die verstellte Gärtnerin* (*Die Gärtnerin aus Liebe*), 1779–80, libretto trans. ?Johann Franz Joseph Stierle the elder
PREMIERES 13 January 1775, Salvatortheater, Munich; US: 18 January 1927, Mayfair Theater, New York; UK: 7 January 1930, Scala Theatre, London; singspiel version: ?1 May 1780, Komödienstadl, Augsburg
CAST Don Anchise (The Podestà) *t*, La Marchesa Violante/'Sandrina' *s*, Belfiore *t*, Arminda *s*, Ramiro *s* or *ms*, Serpetta *s*, Roberto/'Nardo' *b*

Commissioned for the Munich carnival, Mozart's opera was twice postponed and then had only three performances amidst problems with an ailing prima donna and a 'large but rather untidy orchestra'. It was not done again in his lifetime except in the German translation, nor could the Italian version be performed in our own day until the missing recitatives of Act I were found in a copy in Moravia in the 1970s. Niccolò Piccinni's *Buona figliuola* (1760) had started the fashion for opera buffa with a sentimental story, the operatic daughter of Richardson's virtuous maltreated Pamela and, like *La finta giardiniera*, an aristocratic girl working as a gardener's assistant (they all clung to this pastoral activity rather than descend to housework). Petrosellini, the probable author, had written several libretti in this vein. Mad scenes were also popular: Haydn was to write them for *La vera costanza* (1778) with a similar plot and *Orlando paladino* (1782), but the afflicted persons were the tenor heroes (in the tradition of Ariosto's *Orlando furioso*) until Paisiello's *Nina, o sia La pazza per amore* (1789) changed all that. Belfiore and Sandrina proclaim their madness by believing themselves to be all sorts of mythological figures. Auden took up the same idea for the chilling Bedlam finale in Stravinsky's *The Rake's Progress* (1951).

SYNOPSIS

Act I　Don Anchise, the podestà (mayor) of Lagonero, has fallen in love with the new gardener's assistant, 'Sandrina', to the annoyance of the jealous maid, Serpetta. 'Sandrina' is really the disguised Marchesa Violante, who has fled from her violent lover, Count Belfiore. She is accompanied by her servant Roberto under the name of 'Nardo'. The podestà's haughty niece, Arminda, arrives to receive her bridegroom – none other than Count Belfiore. Arminda is recognized by her moping cavalier, Ramiro. Reproaches all round.

Act II　'Sandrina', meaning to test Belfiore, denies that she is Violante, but, when the podestà appears with a warrant for the arrest of Belfiore on the charge of having murdered Violante, she saves him by admitting that she is Violante. Left alone with Belfiore, she denies it again. At this point Belfiore, who has always acted a little strangely, goes completely mad. The jealous Arminda and Serpetta contrive to abandon 'Sandrina' in a wild forest, but 'Nardo', who has been wooing the maid, discovers the plot and goes to the rescue, followed by the entire cast. Unfortunately 'Sandrina' now seems to have gone mad as well.

Act III 'Sandrina' and Belfiore awaken to refound sanity and love. Arminda makes do with Ramiro, and Serpetta accepts 'Nardo'. The podestà decides to wait until another 'Sandrina' turns up.

Serpetta and 'Nardo' are the traditional buffo soubrette and valet; the podestà is a buffo tenor (not bass) with the hoary old cliché of an aria imitating various musical instruments; Arminda and Ramiro are the opera-seria characters; but the heroine wavers between the Marchesa Violante she is and the Sandrina she pretends to be; Belfiore is mainly cast in a buffo light, for his first entry reminds us of Ferrando and Guglielmo taking their tender mock leave in *Così fan tutte*, and the aria 'Da Scirocco a Tramontana', boasting of his good breeding, is certainly comic. Perhaps his mad scenes were meant to be comic too. The idea that the count needs a process of trial and purification to make him worthy of Violante is in the tradition of great comedies. While the librettist hops awkwardly in and out of the comic and serious implications, the score shows the beginning of Mozart's ability to combine these two elements of life – to become the cornerstone of his operatic masterpieces.

Musically, Mozart had taken another gigantic step in the two years since *Lucio Silla*. 'Most of the pieces show the imprint of Mozart's style so clearly,' wrote his biographer Hermann Abert, 'that it would be impossible to think of any other composer.' The arias are mostly in sonata form and mostly of suitable length; there are no da capos. Where there is a change of tempo it is for the sake of the text or to heighten the tension towards the end of an aria. Some of Serpetta's arias would not be out of place among Despina's in *Così fan tutte*. The most striking novelty is in the Act I and II finales, with their rich palette of harmony, instrumentation and rhythm – far beyond anything achieved or indeed even considered by his Italian contemporaries. For the two allegro sections in the Act I finale Mozart employs a loose rondo form, in which the characters impart their own flavour to the main tune by singing it in the minor, or by continuing it in a different way. The excitement mounts as all the voices join in. The finale to Act II, linked by orchestral sections or accompanied recitatives to the three previous arias, provides 26 minutes of continuous music – compared to the great *Figaro* Act II finale of under 20 minutes! It opens in darkness (like the Act IV finale in *Figaro*), though here with an *andante sostenuto* in E♭, the traditional key for an *ombra* scene, as in *Lucio Silla*. The nocturnal sounds of the forest, expressed by the orchestra, are broken by single voices here and there, until Ramiro enters followed by servants with torches. They are accompanied by a busy violin figure until the scene is lit up to the sound of flutes and horns and everybody's identity is revealed. There are so many touches of Mozart's real genius that one cannot help regretting the weaknesses of the libretto.

Il re pastore
The Shepherd King
Serenata in two acts (2h)
Libretto by Pietro Metastasio (1751)
Composed March–April 1775
PREMIERES 23 April 1775, Archbishop's Palace, Salzburg; UK: 8 November 1954, St Pancras Town Hall, London; US: 7 July 1971, Norfolk, Virginia
CAST Alessandro (Alexander) *t*, Aminta *s*, Elisa *s*, Tamiri *s*, Agenore *t*

Two operas on libretti by Metastasio were commissioned by Archbishop Colloredo for the visit of the youngest archduke, Maximilian Franz. The text chosen by (or for) Mozart had been set a dozen times, chiefly for occasions honouring Habsburg princes. (The well-meaning bungler Alexander, as depicted here, foreshadows the career of the archduke's elder brother, the emperor Joseph II.) The opera, or serenata, was performed virtually as a cantata with a minimum of scenery and movement. After this, Mozart was not to see a new opera performed for five years. He began to loathe Salzburg, where musicians were held in no regard and where there was no opera or theatre.

Metastasio cites the ancient historians Curtius and Justinian as his sources for the story that Alexander the Great placed an obscure gardener named Abdolonymus on the throne of Sidon. But this name 'made him sound like a hypochondriac with a stomach ache', so Metastasio changed him into the shepherd Aminta.

SYNOPSIS

Act I Having freed Sidon from the usurper Strato, Alexander determines to put the rightful heir on the throne. With the help of Agenore, he discovers him in Aminta, who was unaware of his origins. Agenore recognizes his own beloved Tamiri, Strato's daughter, disguised as a shepherdess. Aminta, concerned only with his beloved Elisa, is dismayed by Alexander's news. He and Elisa reaffirm their love.

Act II Agenore refuses to admit Elisa to the new king, but Aminta has no desire for the crown. Alexander tells the devastated Agenore that he will arrange for Aminta to marry Tamiri, thus making everybody happy. In the end Tamiri and Elisa pluck up courage to tell him that he is actually making everybody miserable. Aminta hands in his royal robes: let Tamiri reign with another, he says, for he himself prefers Elisa's love to a crown. Alexander appoints Tamiri and Agenore to rule over Sidon, promising Aminta and Elisa the next kingdom he comes upon (another unconsciously ironic reflection on the Habsburgs).

The nature of the occasion and of the libretto precluded anything dramatic in the music, but the melodies are more truly Mozartian than in his earlier opera-seria music. Since his main preoccupation at this time was with instrumental music, it is not surprising to find Mozart using instrumental form for some of the arias, sharing the theme of Aminta's first aria with the G major violin concerto (September 1775) and providing extremely enjoyable scoring, including the virtuoso flutes of Alexander's 'Se vincendo vi rendo felice'. The duet exactly follows the pattern of all his previous opera-seria duets, and the finale is strictly formal in its writing for the 'chorus' of soloists. The most moving music is in Aminta's protestation of love, the famous *rondeaux* 'L'amerò, sarò costante' with solo violin and an accompaniment of flutes, cors anglais, bassoons, horns and muted strings. Almost as touching is Tamiri's simple rondo 'Se tu di me fai dono' that follows it.

Zaide

(Title first used in first edition, 1838)
Fragment of a singspiel in two acts (1h 15m)
Libretto by Johann Andreas Schachtner, after Franz Josef Sebastiani's *Das Serail* (*c.* 1778)
Composed 1779–80
PREMIERES 27 January 1866, Opernhaus, Frankfurt; UK: 10 January 1953, Toynbee Hall, London; US: 8 August 1955, Berkshire Music Center, Lenox, Massachusetts (Tanglewood)
CAST Zaide *s*, Gomatz *t*, Allazim *bar*, Sultan Soliman *t*, Osmin *b*, 4 Slaves 4 *t*, Zaram *spoken role*; guards *silent*

Mozart wrote the 15 pieces of this singspiel (his father described it as 'not quite completed') in the hope of a performance by a touring company in Salzburg or by Joseph II's new National Singspiel.

SYNOPSIS
Act I A group of working slaves tries to remain cheerful, but the new captive, Gomatz, bemoans his fate. As he sleeps, the sultan's favourite, Zaide, falls in love with him and leaves her portrait and a jewel for him to find on awakening. When she reappears, they plan to escape with the help of the overseer Allazim, who has decided to join them.
Act II The sultan is furious at the news, and orders the capture of Gomatz and Zaide. After Osmin's cynical laughing song, he sings a grand aria of revenge. Zaide in prison laments her plight but defies Soliman. Allazim begs him to spare the captives, and a final quartet encompasses all the conflicting emotions.

Zaide contains some striking advances and much music of great beauty. A fascinating innovation is the melodram or melologo, as Mozart called it, in which he interrupts the music for speech. By the time of *Idomeneo* he had forgotten about melodram and wrote sung accompanied recitatives as in Italian opera.

The first aria, Zaide's 'Ruhe sanft', has a melody with an exultant octave leap, which is startlingly beautiful: the muted violins and divided pizzicato violas for Gomatz's slumbers and the oboe for the newly awakened love help to make this one of Mozart's unforgettable pieces. The tiny duet in which Zaide and Gomatz declare their love expresses the heart leaping for joy in five-bar phrases. The trio when the lovers are about to set off with Allazim is one of the ravishing E major 'nature' pieces that recur in the operas. Allazim has strong, virtuoso writing for the baritone voice (Mozart's first), especially in 'Ihr Mächtigen' the best text in the libretto, a noble appeal to the mighty of this world to consider their lower brethren. Soli-

man's arias are in danger of making him a comic figure: in one he compares himself to a roaring lion (complete with sound effects). In a vehement G minor aria, Zaide confuses the picture by calling him a tiger. Mozart made the best of a poor text in 'Ich bin so bös' als gut', Soliman's revenge aria, by loading it with a rich instrumentation. The quartet is the greatest piece in *Zaide*: as in the *Lucio Silla* trio, the lovers bravely facing death are joined by the angry tyrant; Allazim adds his sorrow.

Idomeneo

Dramma per musica in three acts (3h 30m) and ballet (30m)
Libretto by Giambattista Varesco, after Antoine Danchet's five-act tragédie lyrique *Idoménée* set by André Campra (1712)
Composed October 1780–January 1781; rev. 1786
PREMIERES 29 January 1781, Cuvilliés Theater, Munich; UK: 12 March 1934, Glasgow (amateur); 20 June 1951, Glyndebourne, Sussex; US: 4 August 1947, Berkshire Music Center, Lenox, Massachusetts (Tanglewood)
CAST Idomeneo *t*, Idamante *s* (or *t*), Ilia *s*, Elettra (Electra) *s*, Arbace *t*, High Priest *t*, Oracle *b*; *satb* chorus of Trojan captives, Cretan sailors, Cretan people, priests; ballet

The artistic Karl Theodor had succeeded to the Bavarian electorate in 1778 and brought his famous orchestra and opera company with him from Mannheim. Mozart's letters home from his arrival in Munich (on 8 November 1780) until his father joined him (on 25 January 1781) give a fascinating detailed account of the creation of his first operatic masterpiece. His problems with the 67-year-old tenor Anton Raaff and the untalented 'amato castrato del Prato', his Idomeneo and Idamante ('the two worst actors any stage has ever borne'), were not without influence on the music he wrote for them. Mozart's dramatic instinct and common sense are in evidence when he remarks that 'the thunder is presumably not going to cease for Mr Raaff's aria' or 'it seems naïve to think that everybody hurries off (after the oracle has spoken) just to leave Mme Elettra alone'. The music for the oracle was written at least four times, for he believed that it must be short to be credible, adding that the ghost in *Hamlet* would have benefited from greater brevity. In the interests of dramatic tightness he cut three arias from Act III at a late stage (among many smaller cuts). The opera was given only three performances, but Mozart continued to believe in it: nothing came of his hope of making a German opera of it with a bass Idomeneo in Vienna in 1781, but there was one revival by aristocratic amateurs in the Palais Auersperg, Vienna, in March 1786 (when he was completing the score of *Figaro*). For this Mozart made some important changes: Idamante was now apparently a tenor (though the music is mysteriously written in the soprano, not the tenor, clef) and has a new aria with violin obbligato ('Non temer, amato bene'). The Act III duet was almost wholly rewritten to its great advantage ('Spiegarti non poss'io') and small adjustments were made to the trio and quartet.

Gluck's and Piccinni's operas on *Iphigenia in Aulis* and Gluck's *Alceste* were the most famous of the sacrifice operas, but the genre continued into the 19th century. Melchior von Grimm, who had been

Mozart's patron in Paris in 1778–9, remarked that sacrifice operas were 'a very interesting spectacle to behold and offered many situations at once strong and pathetic and suitable for music'. There was certainly more pathos than drama to be got out of them, for all humans can do is submit to the gods. The too pliant and generous Idamante plays the Metastasian role of dying cheerfully for a father he has only just met. Yet the story does contain, at least potentially, the perennial tragedy of the young generation condemned to death by the vows or treaties of their elders.

SYNOPSIS

Act I   The action takes place in Crete after the Trojan War. In the royal palace the captive Trojan princess Ilia laments her fate ('Padre, germani, addio!'), but the Cretan prince Idamante loves her ('Non ho colpa') and sets all the Trojan captives free to prove it. Arbace brings the news that his father, Idomeneo, has been drowned at sea. The fierce Greek princess Electra is jealous of Ilia's power over Idamante ('Tutte nel cor vi sento'). On a stormswept shore the pitiful cries of the sailors ('Pietà! Numi, pietà!') finally give way to the appearance of Neptune himself (in a *pantomima*) calming the storm in answer to Idomeneo's prayer. As King Idomeneo comes ashore he is profoundly unhappy at the vow he has just taken, to sacrifice the first being he meets ('Vedrommi intorno'). His victim, the friendly young man who comes to his aid, turns out to be his son Idamante, saddened that his father seems to reject him ('Il padre adorato ritrovo'). The Cretan people celebrate Idomeneo's safe return.

Act II   In the palace alone with Arbace, Idomeneo resolves to send Idamante to safety in Argos with Electra. Ilia involuntarily reveals her love for his son ('Se il padre perdei'), which increases his despair at the storm in his soul ('Fuor del mar'). Only Electra rejoices at her coming departure with the prince ('Idol mio'), hurrying down to the harbour to join the chorus ('Placido è il mar') and the leave-taking of the king and his son ('Pria di partir'). But suddenly Neptune, infuriated by Idomeneo's attempts to break the vow, sends a monster in a storm ('Qual nuovo terrore!'). Idomeneo begs Neptune to punish him alone, but the tempest continues and the people flee in terror ('Corriamo, fuggiamo').

Act III   In the royal garden Ilia sings to the breeze of her love for Idamante ('Zeffiretti lusinghieri') and, when he promises to kill the monster or die in the attempt, she at last confesses her love. The momentary happiness of their duet ('S'io non moro a questi accenti') is followed by the bleak tragedy of the quartet ('Andrò ramingo e solo'), when Idomeneo once more urges his son's departure with Electra. Arbace now warns him that the people demand action and threaten revolt. Idomeneo goes to meet them in a large square before the palace. Urged by the high priest, he at last reveals that the necessary victim is his own son, to the sorrow of the people ('Oh voto tremendo!'). The scene of the sacrifice is the temple of Neptune near the shore. After Idomeneo's prayer ('Accogli, oh re del mar') there is a momentary ray of hope at the news that Idamante has killed the monster. But he is

brought on as the willing sacrificial victim. Idomeneo's sword is already raised when Ilia rushes in to implore him to kill her, an enemy of Greece, instead. Now the nobility of Ilia and Idamante melts Neptune's anger, and the oracle announces that they shall henceforth reign in Crete. This is followed by universal rejoicing – with the notable exception of Electra, a prey to the Furies who had tormented her brother, Orestes ('D'Oreste, d'Aiace ho in seno i tormenti').

Seen as a whole, *Idomeneo* is a flawed masterpiece without the tension of a great tragedy, but Mozart's score contains some of the greatest operatic music ever written. Traditional elements of opera seria struggle with innovations based on Gluck and the tragédie lyrique, especially in the great dramatic choruses. Infinitely expressive *recitativi accompagnati* link the arias and ensembles to form long stretches of continuous music, leaving few opportunities for the old applauded exit aria: they also bind the music by quoting themes from arias just heard or yet to come and achieve great tension by merging into rhythmic arioso at the approach of an aria or of some important revelation. Ilia has the most beautiful of the arias; her 'Se il padre perdei' early in Act II is one of Mozart's very greatest, accompanied by a concertante wind quartet, not as a virtuoso or merely colourful element but to express every hidden emotion. Mozart avoided giving del Prato coloratura or other problems and made up for this with his orchestration, for example the string runs and chromatic wind to express Idamante's perplexity in 'Non ho colpa'. Idomeneo has the noble prayer 'Accogli, oh re del mar' with the unison chant of the priests and a unique accompaniment of pizzicato strings with a web of interlinking woodwind, but also the return to an earlier style in the coloratura of 'Fuor del mar', ineptly triumphant even if it is meant to represent the storm in his heart. The two other characters have virtually no impact on the story at all. The confidant Arbace sings two very conventional arias, which were heavily cut by Mozart and can easily be omitted. But Electra has the most varied and difficult role in Mozart (along with the equally fierce Vitellia in *La clemenza di Tito*): she can sing of the joys of love as sweetly as any Zaide ('Idol mio') or in her solo in 'Placido è il mar', but her first and last arias express fury beyond the limits of sanity, especially in the manic laugh that concludes the latter. No wonder conductors are reluctant to follow Mozart in cutting 'D'Oreste' at the end of the opera. Unfortunately nobody ever takes the slightest bit of notice of Electra. Perhaps that is why she goes mad.

The duet is little more than a charming pastoral piece: Mozart's 1786 version is the most pertinent criticism of it. The trio ('Pria di partir'), a beautiful piece of conflicting emotions, is, however, overshadowed by the quartet ('Andrò ramingo e solo'), one of Mozart's great tragic utterances – he himself later burst into tears while singing it with friends. The dramatic choruses at the appearance of the monster in Act II and at the revelation of Idamante's fate in Act III are of incomparable eloquence. And there is also the sheer happy lilt of the barcarolle 'Placido è il mar'.

If Mozart tailored each aria to his singer, how

much more he must have fitted the score to his admired Mannheim orchestra. Mozart never created such a rich orchestral part in any other opera. His father wondered how the musicians could survive three hours of it (four hours would be closer if the ballet was done complete) – 'I know your style. Every musician needs astonishing continuous concentration.' Mozart is suddenly freed from the old conventions, the woodwind are wholly independent; he lovingly uses the clarinet for the first time in an opera, as well as the virtuoso oboe of his friend Friedrich Ramm and all the power of four horns, two trumpets and timpani. One must also imagine all the effects of thunder, lightning, crowd movements, swift scene changes and a monster and a god out of the machine, as produced by the experts of the Munich theatre.

For the first time Mozart uses little phrases, not quite leitmotifs but expressions of a particular emotion, such as the anxious trill-like trembling we hear in Electra's first aria and in Idamante's first two arias and throughout the chorus 'Qual nuovo terrore', or the falling phrase associated with Idamante's fate and first heard towards the end of the overture. Lacking Gluck's bold simplicity, Mozart hints at subtler shades of emotion with an orchestral, melodic and harmonic richness far beyond his contemporaries. The premiere took place two days after his 25th birthday.

Die Entführung aus dem Serail
The Abduction from the Harem
Singspiel in three acts (2h 15m)
Libretto by Gottlieb Stephanie the younger, after *Bellmont und Constanze, oder Die Entführung aus dem Serail* by Christoph Friedrich Bretzner set by Johann André (1781)
Composed July 1781–May 1782
PREMIERES 16 July 1782, Burgtheater, Vienna; UK: 24 November 1827, Covent Garden, London; US: 16 February 1860, Brooklyn Athenaeum, New York
CAST Bassa (Pasha) Selim *spoken role*, Konstanze *s*, Blonde *s*, Belmonte *t*, Pedrillo *t*, Osmin *b*, Klaas, a sailor *spoken role*; guards *silent*; *satb* chorus of janissaries and attendants

The composition of *Die Entführung aus dem Serail*. commissioned for Joseph II's singspiel company under Gottlieb Stephanie's direction, took an unusually long time to complete, although Mozart composed three major numbers for it in one day. It had been intended for a visit by Grand Duke Paul Petrovich (later Paul I of Russia) at the end of 1781, which kept being postponed. The opera was Mozart's main preoccupation between May 1781, when he broke with the archbishop of Salzburg and settled in Vienna, and his marriage in August 1782. He wrote three long letters to his father in the autumn of 1781 that give a vivid insight into his creative thinking. He describes how he expressed the emotions, the very heartbeats of Belmonte in 'O wie ängstlich, o wie feurig' and the unbridled fury of Osmin: at the end of 'Solche hergelauf'ne Laffen' he is 'beside himself, so the music must be too, but because passion, however strong, must never be expressed to the extent of disgusting the hearer and music must remain music, I have chosen a key [for 'Erst geköpft, dann gehangen'] that is not a stranger to F [the key of the aria], but a friend, not

the closest one D minor, but A minor'. The actual words of Stephanie's undistinguished text did not really worry him, for Osmin's aria 'was already walking around' in his head before he saw the libretto. He thought that a good composer who understood the stage, helped by the right poet, could steer the drama in the right direction, that words should be the obedient daughters of the music, and that rhyming texts were a waste of time. But there has probably never been a really satisfactory production of *Die Entführung*, and Mozart must bear the main responsibility for this. Stephanie added little to Bretzner's text. He and Mozart even copied the idea of a speaking Selim: a tenor had been planned for the role, but Mozart must have turned against the thought of three tenors and remembered his failure in *Zaide* to give Soliman a serious profile. This means that the only musical opposition comes from the comic Osmin. In the opera that was their model, Bretzner and his composer Johann André had produced a lively ensemble for the elopement scene in Act III; Mozart began a finale for Act II presumably to contain the elopement, with an unfinished duet for Belmonte and Pedrillo ('Welch ängstliches Beben'), but eventually the elopement and recapture of the lovers was allowed to take place in silence. Thus both the main action of the opera and its main character, Selim, in the sense that the plot hangs on his moods and their changes, remain without music. In spite of this, the opera was an instant success and was played in 40 cities during Mozart's lifetime. Goethe, who had himself written libretti for singspiels, said, '*Die Entführung* knocked everything else sideways.' Weber saw that Mozart's artistic experience had reached maturity in *Die Entführung*. The emperor apparently remarked, 'An awful lot of notes, my dear Mozart.'

SYNOPSIS
Act I   The Spanish nobleman Belmonte has arrived on the Barbary or Turkish coast to search for his betrothed Konstanze, who was captured by pirates, together with her maid Blonde and his servant Pedrillo ('Hier soll ich dich denn sehen'). With great difficulty he learns from the grumpy overseer Osmin that he is standing before the palace of Pasha Selim ('Wer ein Liebchen hat gefunden'). When Pedrillo appears, Osmin expresses his lethal loathing for him ('Solche hergelauf'ne Laffen'). When he has gone, Belmonte learns that Konstanze is alive and well: his emotion is boundless ('Konstanze! . . . O wie ängstlich'). The pasha arrives with his retinue ('Singt dem grossen Bassa Lieder') and begins to woo Konstanze once more, but her heart belongs to another from whom she was cruelly parted ('Ach, ich liebte'). Selim gives her one more day to change her mind. She leaves, and Pedrillo introduces Belmonte to the pasha as a talented architect. Selim takes him on, but Belmonte and Pedrillo have the greatest difficulty in getting past Osmin to enter the palace ('Marsch, marsch, marsch!')

Act II   Outside Osmin's house in the palace garden. Blonde has been assigned to Osmin, but soon shows that she has the upper hand. 'I am a free-born Englishwoman,' she tells him, and proceeds to tease him into submission ('Ich gehe, doch rate ich dir'). Konstanze still has nothing to say to Selim except to express her sorrow ('Welcher Wechsel herrscht in meiner Seele . . . Traurigkeit ward mir zum Lose'), but when he threatens her with torture she replies defiantly ('Martern aller Arten'). Blonde is delighted to hear from Pedrillo that they are to escape that very night ('Welche Wonne, welche Lust'). Pedrillo summons up as much courage as he can ('Frisch zum Kampfe!'), then proceeds to get Osmin drunk to get him out of the way ('Vivat Bacchus!'). Belmonte meets his beloved at last ('Wenn der Freude Tränen fliessen'). The women assure their lovers that they have always been faithful to them despite all the hazards of life in a harem ('Ach Belmonte, ach mein Leben!').

Act III Outside the palace Pedrillo sings an old ballad as a signal (romanze: 'Im Mohrenland gefangen war'), and the two men succeed in abducting the women; but a guard discovers the ladder and they are soon brought before Osmin, who is seething with vengeful fury ('O, wie will ich triumphieren'). Condemned to die by Selim, Belmonte reveals that his father is Lostados, governor of Oran. 'He is my greatest enemy,' Selim answers, 'who has robbed me of my beloved, my wealth, my fatherland.' Belmonte and Konstanze await their death, each longing to die for the other ('Welch ein Geschick . . . Meinetwegen sollst du sterben'). But Selim has no wish to emulate the despised Lostados, so he pardons them and sends all four home. The opera ends in the gratitude and rejoicing of everybody except Osmin.

The wonderful freshness of the musical invention more than makes up for the dramatic weakness. Mozart gave the magnificent buffo bass Ludwig Fischer, in the part of Osmin, music of great brilliance and range with frequent descents to evil thoughts and bottom D. The Konstanze, Caterina Cavalieri, was famous for her coloratura and her two-octave leaps: Mozart admitted that he had to sacrifice something to her 'fluent throat' and that he had to express the mood within the limitations of an Italian bravura aria. Her second aria ('Traurigkeit') with its recitative is one of his most moving creations, but when he came to the great showpiece of the opera, 'Martern aller Arten', Mozart abandoned dramatic relevance by adding a virtuoso concertante quartet of flute, oboe, violin and cello. Belmonte opens with a lied, taken from the middle section of the overture, and then Mozart gives him 'O wie ängstlich' – 'everybody's favourite, including mine'. The famous tenor Johann Valentin Adamberger demanded four arias, so he sings one on meeting Konstanze, when a duet would have been far more appropriate, and another in Act III, which is generally omitted. The duet in Act III avoids tragic tones except in the opening recitative, for the lovers are quietly exulting in thoughts of self-sacrifice. Pedrillo's arias are both full of character: in the first a not very courageous little man is trying to wind himself up to the necessary courage for the daring rescue. The romanze, *sotto voce*, with only pizzicato strings, is one of Mozart's strangest compositions: the first three lines pass though the keys of D, A, C, G, F♯ minor and F♯ major. The soubrette Blonde is lyrical and vixenish as the occasion demands.

The quartet, though it does not fit the customary picture of an Act II finale as a crescendo of noise and confusion, is one of Mozart's most enchanting creations. The beginning and end express generalized joy, but the middle part contains its own little drama: the two tenors ask the sopranos, not without due hesitation and embarrassment, if in spite of all the temptations and threats they have remained faithful to them. The women's reactions reassure them. This is not so much a quartet as two simultaneous duets – the two noble lovers with their legato lines, the servants in staccato phrases, the culmination being in Blonde's triplet fireworks (she is still smarting at the insult) against the blissful reconciliation of the others. At the very heart of the quartet there is a serene siciliana in A major of only 15 bars, in which Mozart celebrates the profound happiness of love. He was about to marry his Constanze, despite a father rather less forgiving than the pasha.

One should mention the vivid Turkish music, with its C major, its repeated little phrases and, of course, its percussion, which fills the overture and the choruses. The characters take their leave in a charming vaudeville, the form borrowed from opéra comique.

Der Schauspieldirektor

The Impresario
Comedy with music in one act (music only: 30m)
Text by Gottlieb Stephanie the younger
Composed January–February 1786
PREMIERES 7 February 1786, Orangerie, Schloss Schönbrunn, Vienna; UK: 30 May 1857, St James's Theatre, London; US: 9 November 1870, Stadt Theater, New York
CAST Buff *b*, Monsieur Vogelsang *t*, Mme Herz *s*, Mlle Silberklang *s*; *spoken roles*: Frank, Eiler, Mme Pfeil, Mme Krone, Mme Vogelsang

In the midst of one of the most astonishing creative periods of Mozart's life, which included the composition of *Figaro*, the piano concertos K. 482, K. 488 and K. 491 and a dozen other major works, came the imperial command for a few songs for a comedy to be presented at a court festivity in honour of the governor-general of the Austrian Netherlands, the Archduchess Christine and her husband. The 80 guests were given lunch in the centre of the hall, then this German comedy on a stage at one end followed by an opera buffa, *Prima la musica poi le parole* by Giambattista Casti, with music by Antonio Salieri, at the other end. Mozart wrote an overture and four vocal numbers. Stephanie, director of the National Singspiel, obviously saw himself in the role of the good-natured impresario Frank (though Mozart was one of the few who spoke well of him). The two prima donnas, Caterina Cavalieri (Salieri's mistress and the first Konstanze in *Die Entführung*) as Mlle Silberklang and Aloysia Lange (née Weber, Mozart's sister-in-law and first love) as Mme Herz, must have had a sense of humour to take part in this parody on the vanity of singers.

SYNOPSIS

The impresario Frank, assisted by the buffo singer Buff, is forming a theatrical company to play in Salzburg. Two actresses perform for him and are engaged. Then Mme Herz sings a pathetic arietta ('Da schlägt die Abschiedsstunde') and Mlle Silberklang a rondo ('Bester Jüngling!') to exhibit their strongest points. Each then gives brilliant vocal backing to her claim for the higher fee, but Monsieur Vogelsang manages to effect a truce ('Ich bin die erste Sängerin'). When Frank threatens to abandon the whole plan of forming a company, all unreasonable demands are instantly withdrawn. In a vaudeville ('Jeder Künstler strebt nach Ehre'), everybody, including Buff, recognizes the need for the ambition of artists, provided that it is not at the expense of their colleagues.

Mozart would have preferred to compose the opera buffa (if his work on *Figaro* had permitted it), but he made the very best of his trivial task. The overture is a brilliant, symphonic work with rich orchestration. The pathos of the first aria anticipates the parodies of *Così*: the horn imitating the tolling bell is an especially good touch. A sketch of the vocal line, of which only the first five bars remain in the final version, is a rare surviving example to show us how much Mozart sometimes departed from his initial ideas. Mlle Silberklang has a delicious wind-band accompaniment and the same coloratura figure that is the undoing of many a Donna Anna in 'Non mi dir' in *Don Giovanni*. The trio is a very funny scene in which each lady sings about the nobility of her art while trying to defeat her rival with ever higher notes. The closing song is a simple rondo in gavotte time.

Le nozze di Figaro
Figaro's Wedding
Opera buffa in four acts (3h)
Libretto by Lorenzo da Ponte, after the comedy *La folle journée, ou Le mariage de Figaro* by Pierre-Augustin Caron de Beaumarchais (1784)
Composed October 1785–April 1786; rev. 1789
PREMIERES 1 May 1786, Burgtheater, Vienna; UK: 2 May 1812, Pantheon, London; US: 10 May 1824, Park Theater, New York
CAST Count Almaviva *bar*, Countess Almaviva *s*, Susanna *s*, Figaro *b*, Cherubino *s* (or *ms*), Marcellina *s*, Bartolo *b*, Basilio *t*, Don Curzio *t*, Barbarina *s*, Antonio *b*; *satb* chorus of peasants and the count's tenants

We know very little about the process of composition of *Figaro*, for none of Mozart's letters survives from the months that preceded the first performance on 1 May 1786. When da Ponte came to relate his tale many years later in his autobiography, he was himself the hero of the story: it was he who hurried to the emperor and persuaded him to permit the musical version of a play that had been banned as subversive and he who later foiled the typical Viennese plots. But even da Ponte admitted that the idea of setting *Figaro* came from Mozart. The play had everything to commend it, not least the thrill of having been banned. It used most of the old ingredients of comedy, but in a new way: there was a pair of lovers, but they were a valet and a lady's maid; the comic servant has become his master's successful rival; in the concluding scene of clemency, common to nearly all of Mozart's operas, it is the count, the representative of emperor, pasha

or god, who has to beg for it. We are in the new topsy-turvy world of the French Revolution. Cherubino is a new invention, 'drunk with love' (according to Kierkegaard), the first of the many *travesti* roles which succeeded the youths impersonated by castrati. Beaumarchais, who recognized the potential *frisson*, specified that 'he could be played only by a young and very pretty woman'. The play is brilliantly theatrical, for each act has its *coup de théâtre*: the discovery of the page in Act I, Susanna emerging from the closet in Act II, the revelation of Figaro's parentage in Act III, and the countess as *dea ex machina* in Act IV – and how quietly, almost casually, Mozart brings each one about. The actual plotting does not bear too much scrutiny. How many people in the audience realize that there are actually three mysterious pieces of paper at different points? Unlike *Così fan tutte* with its schematic plot, *Figaro* teems with plots, as life does: all the characters are involved with intrigues of their own, sometimes even against their allies, as when Susanna and Figaro set out to teach each other a lesson in Act IV. But the main plot is clear: although the count is doing everything to cancel or postpone the wedding because of his feelings for Susanna, Figaro and Co. defeat him and bring him back to his wife.

Da Ponte apologized in his preface to the libretto for having had to reduce the number of acts, characters and *bons mots* in the interests of the music. He also had to omit Figaro's more politically subversive remarks, though the tone of 'Se vuol ballare' is defiant enough. The essential difference between the play and the opera was perceptively described by Stendhal in his *Lettre sur Mozart* (1814): 'Mozart, with his overwhelmingly sensitive nature, has transformed into real passions the superficial inclinations which amuse the easy-going inhabitants of Aguas Frescas in Beaumarchais . . . In this sense then it might be said that Mozart could not have distorted the play more. I do not really know if music is capable of depicting French flirtation and frivolity for the course of four acts and in all the characters: I should say it was difficult, for music needs strong emotions, whether of joy or unhappiness . . . the wit remains only in the situations: all the characters have been filled with feeling and passion . . . Mozart's opera is a sublime mixture of wit and melancholy, which has no equal . . .'

The cast included the great actor Francesco Benucci as Figaro (later the first Vienna Leporello and the first Guglielmo), Francesco Bussani as Bartolo and Antonio (later the first Vienna commendatore and Masetto and the first Don Alfonso), his wife, Dorotea, as Cherubino (later the first Vienna Zerlina and the first Despina) and the 12-year-old Anna Gottlieb as Barbarina (later the first Pamina), as well as the English Nancy Storace as Susanna and the Irish Michael Kelly as Basilio and Don Curzio.

On 29 August 1789 began a series of performances of a revival in Vienna with a new cast for which Mozart made a number of revisions, including changes in the count's aria and in the countess's second aria. The new Susanna, Caterina Cavalieri, made him replace her two arias with 'Un moto di gioia' and 'Al desio'.

SYNOPSIS

Act I A half-furnished room in Count Almaviva's castle of Aguas Frescas near Seville. The count's valet, Figaro, and Susanna, the countess's maid, are preparing for their wedding ('Cinque, dieci, venti'). How convenient, thinks Figaro, for their new room to be between those of the count and the countess; and how convenient, Susanna adds, for the count, who has started making advances to her – not that Figaro should doubt her for a moment ('Se a caso madama la notte ti chiama'). Left alone, Figaro is distraught but vengeful ('Se vuol ballare signor Contino'). When he has gone out, Dr Bartolo and his housekeeper, Marcellina, enter: though old enough to be his mother, she is trying to force Figaro into marriage in acquittal of a loan he cannot repay. Bartolo is eager to help her in order to avenge himself on Figaro, who had planned the abduction of his ward Rosina, now the countess ('La vendetta'). Susanna returns, and she and Marcellina soon abandon ironic politeness ('Via resti servita, madama brillante') until Marcellina storms out. The page Cherubino darts in. He is in love with all women ('Non so più cosa son, cosa faccio') but most of all with his godmother, the countess. Hearing the count approach, he hides behind the armchair. The count at once begins to flirt with Susanna, but, hearing the music master Don Basilio outside, he too hides behind the armchair – though not before Cherubino has had time to jump into the armchair and be covered up by Susanna with a dress. Basilio taunts Susanna about Cherubino's passion for the countess. At this the count springs up in a rage ('Cosa sento!'); Basilio enjoys the mischief, and Susanna nearly swoons. The count complacently relates how he has recently discovered Cherubino in the room of the gardener's young daughter, Barbarina, hiding under the tablecloth. Acting out the story, he lifts the dress from the armchair and is stunned to see the page again. There is to be no pardon this time, and Figaro had better know about his bride's relations with the page, thunders the count, a little uneasy that Cherubino has witnessed his scene with Susanna. Figaro leads in the peasants to praise the count for abolishing the wicked old feudal rights over his female tenants. The count, with great presence of mind, postpones the wedding and sends Cherubino off with a commission to his regiment. Figaro warns Cherubino in a rousing finale ('Non più andrai') that a soldier's life is very different from that of an 'amorous great butterfly'.

Act II The grand bedroom of the countess. She is alone, regretting the loss of her husband's love ('Porgi amor'). Figaro unfolds his plan to bring the count back to fidelity: he will send him an anonymous letter claiming that the countess has made a secret assignation with a lover; at the same time Susanna is to make an assignation with him, but they will send Cherubino dressed as a girl in place of her. All this will at least distract the count from averting their marriage. When he has left, Cherubino arrives to perform his latest love song ('Voi che sapete') and to be fitted with his disguise by Susanna ('Venite . . . inginocchiatevi'). The countess is touched to find that he has wrapped a ribbon of hers round his arm. Suddenly the count is heard knocking on the door and demanding entry.

Susanna happens to be out in the dressing room, so the countess quickly shuts Cherubino into a closet and opens the door to the count. She cannot allay his suspicions when a noise is heard from the closet. 'It is only Susanna,' she claims. In a trio ('Susanna, or via sortite') the count orders Susanna to come out, the countess is affronted by his behaviour, and Susanna, who has come into the room unseen by both of them, observes the situation. As soon as the count has gone off with the countess to fetch a hammer to break the closet door down, Susanna releases Cherubino. After a moment of panic ('Aprite presto, aprite'), he jumps out of the window. The count returns, and the countess confesses that he will find not Susanna in the closet but Cherubino. The finale opens with the count ordering Cherubino out and threatening to kill him. When Susanna emerges, all innocence, the count and countess are equally surprised but he asks to be forgiven for his suspicions. Figaro now arrives to remind him that it is time for the wedding ceremony. The count confronts him with the anonymous letter, but Figaro denies any knowledge of it. A new threat appears: Antonio, the drunken gardener, complains that somebody has jumped out of the countess's window on to his geraniums. To allay suspicion, Figaro admits that it was he. 'In that case,' says Antonio, 'you will want these papers you dropped.' The count challenges Figaro to tell him what they are. Prompted by the countess and Susanna, Figaro gradually reveals that they are Cherubino's commission, which needed the official seal. Just as the count fears he has lost the campaign, Marcellina storms in with Bartolo and Basilio to urge her legal claim over Figaro. The count declares that he will hear it at a proper trial in due course, to the noisy despair of Figaro's party.

Act III A grand hall prepared for the wedding feast. The count is puzzled by events but delighted with a surprisingly compliant Susanna, sent in to him by the countess in pursuit of Figaro's plot ('Crudel! perchè finora'). Unfortunately he overhears Susanna whisper to Figaro of her success, and bursts out in jealous fury ('Hai già vinta la causa! . . . Vedrò mentr'io sospiro'). The trial has gone against Figaro, who, confronted by all his enemies, reveals that his parents are unknown: it gradually emerges that he is the bastard son of Bartolo and Marcellina. The rejoicing over this reunion (sextet: 'Riconosci in questo amplesso'), not shared by the baffled count, is interrupted by Susanna with the money to pay off Marcellina. Seeing him in the embrace of her rival, she slaps his face, but the necessary explanations soon bring general contentment. The countess comes in alone to sing of her hope of regaining her husband's love ('E Susanna non vien! . . . Dove sono . . .'). Antonio informs the count that Cherubino is hiding at his house. The countess dictates to Susanna a letter of assignation to the count ('Che soave zeffiretto'). The village girls bring her flowers. Cherubino, who has joined them in disguise, is unmasked by Antonio and the count. Nevertheless the wedding celebrations commence. Figaro is amused to see the count pricking himself on a pin which had sealed a letter of assignation.

Act IV   The garden that night, with various arbours and pavilions. Barbarina is desperately looking for the pin the count had given her to return to Susanna in acknowledgement of their rendezvous. Figaro wheedles this out of the innocent creature and gives way to his despair at being cuckolded on his wedding night. After Marcellina and Basilio each sing a superfluous aria (normally cut), Figaro has his diatribe about women ('Tutto è disposto . . . Aprite un po' quegl'occhi'), then hides to spy on Susanna. She sings of the coming joy of love ('Giunse alfin il momento . . . Deh vieni non tardar') but poor Figaro does not realize that she is thinking of him, not of the count. The moment of the count's assignation is at hand: the plot has been modified in that the countess will herself take Susanna's place, disguised as Susanna, while Susanna is disguised as her mistress. The amorous Cherubino opens the finale, pleased to find Susanna, as he thinks, in the dark: he tries to kiss her, but in the confusion it is the count who gets the kiss and Figaro who receives the count's answering slap. When the count's seduction of the supposed Susanna is getting too close for comfort, Figaro chases them off. He eventually recognizes Susanna's voice beneath her disguise and the injustice of his suspicions. He teases her for a while by pretending to declare his love to the 'countess', and receives another slap for his pains. They make peace and prepare to tease the count, as Figaro flings himself down before Susanna to declare his love for 'Milady'. The count calls the whole establishment to witness this outrageous betrayal by his wife and his servant. He is deaf to universal pleas for mercy, until at last the countess appears, in her disguise as Susanna, and he realizes that it is he who must ask forgiveness. She grants it. There is serene happiness, which explodes into great rejoicing.

Though seven years older than the composer, Lorenzo da Ponte had written only three libretti compared to Mozart's 12 operas. Mozart doubtless played a leading role in their collaboration, but da Ponte was able to understand and satisfy his requirements to a very high degree. The fluidity and freedom of his metres and line lengths, which could blur the transition from recitative to aria, fitted in with Mozart's preference for arias of action rather than contemplation – Susanna's Act II aria ('Venite . . . inginocchiatevi') is sung while dressing Cherubino, her Act IV aria ('Deh vieni non tardar') is designed to tease the eavesdropping Figaro, and Mozart's music follows the words and their meanings, not merely the metre of the verse.

Time and time again Mozart's music humanizes the farce of the libretto. *Figaro* stands out, even in Mozart's work, for having the greatest human warmth and the most natural characters, especially in the central figures. Instead of operatic conventions and vain repetitions we get something like a stream of consciousness. In 'Deh vieni non tardar', for example, the melody winds on rhapsodically, while just enough feeling of formal unity is given by the siciliana rhythm and the recapitulation of the woodwind phrases. Susanna's opening phrase, a sort of quote from 'Che

Susanna ella stessa si fè' in the opening duet, is recapitulated, but in disguise – a third higher. When she changes from teasing the jealous, eavesdropping Figaro to real emotion, the serenade-like pizzicato of the violins changes magically to *coll'arco* sighs, the same accompanying figure Mozart used for the beginning of the Lachrymosa in the *Requiem* six years later, the last notes he ever wrote down. The letter duet, an exquisite piece in which the woodwind illustrate the breezes of the nocturnal tryst, treats the dictating of the letter absolutely realistically, with suitable pauses for Susanna to write, then follows this with the two women reading the letter together and overlapping in their eagerness. Da Ponte once wrote that a finale should be a complete little opera in itself. The sextet in Act III, reputedly a great favourite of Mozart's, could stand alone as the epitome of Mozartean opera buffa. The action is, of course, a parody of the sentimental pieces of the time, in which long-lost parents and children discover each other (and still a subject for parody in Oscar Wilde's *The Importance of Being Earnest*). There is a long calm opening over a pedal for the quiet joy of the reunited family. Susanna arrives with the ransom money, not at all overjoyed at what she sees – the music has moved to the dominant, and agitated violins accompany her. She relieves her feelings by slapping Figaro, but she and the count, whose plans have been spoiled by the discovery, continue to sing in angry dotted rhythms against the serenity of the others. When we arrive at the recapitulation, back in F major, Marcellina has an entirely new text to explain things to Susanna and therefore new music – which Mozart elegantly combines with the original opening melody now played by the woodwind. The next section, in which the incredulous Susanna is introduced over and over again to Figaro's new parents, is the most delicious passage in all comic opera. But the miracle is still to come when the laughter dissolves in tears of happiness, as Susanna's voice lightly runs over the *sotto voce* accompaniment of the others (Mozart crossed out his original idea of doubling her line with flute and bassoon). In the end the count and his henchman, Don Curzio, provide a mildly threatening movement, in case we should lapse into sheer blissful sentimentality.

These are just three examples, briefly described, but every piece in *Figaro* deserves more, from the magic of the overture (with no musical quotation from the opera, but instead an embodiment of its feeling of excitement and tenderness) to the finale of Act IV. Earlier operas had placed the dénouement in an extra act after the second big finale. Mozart and da Ponte accomplish everything within the great Act IV finale – the mounting excitement and gathering of all the characters as well as both reconciliations, Figaro's with Susanna in a playful tone, the count's with the countess in a still moment of the utmost beauty.

Don Giovanni
[Il dissoluto punito, o sia Il Don Giovanni]
The Rake Punished, or Don Giovanni
Dramma giocoso in two acts (2h 45m)
Libretto by Lorenzo da Ponte, after Giovanni Bertati's

opera *Don Giovanni Tenorio, o sia Il convitato di pietra*
(1787)
Composed April–October 1787 rev. 1788
PREMIERES 29 October 1787, Gräflich Nostitzsches
Nationaltheater, Prague; 7 May 1788, Burgtheater, Vienna;
UK: 12 April 1817, His Majesty's Theatre, Haymarket,
London; US: 7 November 1817, Park Theater, New York
CAST Don Giovanni *b* or *bar*, The Commendatore *b*,
Donna Anna *s*, Don Ottavio *t*, Donna Elvira *s*, Leporello
b, Zerlina *s*, Masetto *b*; *satb* chorus of peasants, *tb* chorus
of servants; peasants, servants, musicians and ministers of
justice *silent*; offstage: *b* chorus of demons

The extraordinary number of works of one sort or
another about Don Juan must surely exceed the alleged number of his conquests. Faust and Don Juan
were created by the Counter-Reformation as warnings
against exceeding the bounds set for man – Faust in
seeking metaphysical knowledge and power, Juan for
living in unbounded sensuality without any spiritual
belief. Both are finally overtaken by divine retribution.
Juan first appeared in *El burlador de Sevilla*, a play
written in 1630 by a Spanish monk, Tirso de Molina.
But the play was much more than a pious text. The
story was rewritten many times before (and after)
Mozart's opera, most notably as a play by Molière
and as a ballet by Gluck. By the late 18th century it
had become little more than an effective puppet show:
the two elements that were common to all versions
make for good entertainment – a libertine who seduces
innumerable ladies and a statue that gets up and
comes to dinner. There were at least two new operas
on the subject in 1787 before Mozart's: one was seen
in Rome by Goethe, who noticed the universal delight
in the farcical representation of the story; the other,
by Giuseppe Gazzaniga, performed in Venice in January 1787, became the direct model for da Ponte and,
to some extent, for Mozart. There are some striking
similarities in the text and sometimes even in the
music, such as the use of 'Tafelmusik' for the supper
scene.

The death of the commendatore and his revenge
are the essential parts of the opera. 'The rest is a
parenthesis, the most beautiful and delightful parenthesis in the history of opera but still a parenthesis'
(Luigi Dallapiccola). Gazzaniga's opera was based on
these essentials, but it was only in one act: da Ponte
and Mozart had to fill out the time between the
commendatore's death and his reappearance in the
form of the avenging statue. Apart from a call to
repentance and a supernatural warning, which already
occur in Tirso's play, no events have any real bearing
on the dénouement, since Don Juan is not defeated by
any human revenge or pursuit. The rest of the opera
is therefore filled with the opera-buffa game of
disguises.

Da Ponte later claimed that Mozart had wanted to
write a serious opera and had to be persuaded to add
the comedy. Mozart probably never considered if he
was writing about crime and punishment or divine
vengeance – after all, most of his operas had concluded in the theatrical convention of divine or imperial clemency; this time the divine intervention was
simply of the opposite sort. But he must have seen
this as his first opportunity since *Idomeneo* to write

serious, heroic, tragic operatic music. Mozart is inevitably compared to Shakespeare, not least for the mingling of laughter and tears, but while Shakespeare
used the powerful close juxtaposition of tragedy and
comedy, he surely has no parallel to *Don Giovanni*'s
last scene in which the great heroic duet with the
commendatore is not merely followed, as Duncan's
murder is in *Macbeth*, but actually accompanied by
the patter of the buffoon.

Mozart had enjoyed witnessing the triumph of
Figaro during his first visit to Prague in January 1787.
Only the Bohemian audience seems to have understood what Mozart was, as we believe we do today.
Pasquale Bondini, the manager of the Italian company
there, commissioned *Don Giovanni* and may have even
proposed the subject. *Don Giovanni* proved to be a
triumph, and Mozart was cheered on entering and
leaving the pit. Vienna saw it the following May with
a number of changes demanded by the new cast. The
ever exigent Caterina Cavalieri as Elvira got an extra
scena and aria ('Mi tradì'); Francesco Benucci as
Leporello lost his aria but got a farcical duet with
Zerlina ('Per queste tue manine'), which is now seldom
performed; Ottavio had his aria changed for one with
less coloratura ('Dalla sua pace'). Mozart made some
other changes including cutting the Anna–Ottavio
duet in the final scene, but there is no conclusive
evidence that he authorized the cut of the entire final
scene, which became the rule from the 1790s until the
1920s.

SYNOPSIS

Act I A garden by night. Leporello is complaining
that he has to keep watch in all weathers while his
master is enjoying himself indoors ('Notte e giorno
faticar'), when Don Giovanni rushes out, trying to
escape and hide his face from a furious Donna Anna.
Her father, the commendatore, enters with a sword;
Don Giovanni kills him in a duel and escapes with
Leporello. Anna returns with her betrothed, Don Ottavio; distraught at finding her father dead, she swears
vengeance ('Fuggi, crudele, fuggi!'). A street scene as
dawn breaks. An unknown beauty accosted by Don
Giovanni ('Ah chi mi dice mai') turns out to be
Donna Elvira, whom he had cozened into a pretended
marriage and abandoned. Leporello tells her of his
master's 2065 conquests and of his technique ('Madamina, il catalogo è questo'). Don Giovanni spies a
new prey in the peasant Zerlina, who appears with her
bridegroom, Masetto. Masetto is removed by Leporello, and Don Giovanni has just persuaded Zerlina to
follow him to his pavilion ('Là ci darem la mano')
when Elvira returns to warn her off ('Ah fuggi il
traditor'). She warns Anna and Ottavio too ('Non ti
fidar, o misera') but Giovanni brushes off her accusations as a sign of madness. As he leaves, Donna Anna
recognizes Don Giovanni as her nocturnal assailant:
she describes the attempted rape to the horrified Ottavio and implores him to join in her vengeance ('Or
sai chi l'onore'). (Ottavio then usually sings 'Dalla sua
pace', added for the Vienna revival.) Don Giovanni
gives Leporello instructions about his party for the
peasants ('Fin ch'han dal vino'). In a garden on Don
Giovanni's estate, Zerlina, reproached for her flirta-

tion with the noble stranger, mollifies Masetto ('Batti, batti, o bel Masetto'), but as soon as Giovanni appears she grows weak again (finale, Act I), only being saved by Masetto's presence. Donna Anna, Donna Elvira and Don Ottavio, arriving masked to pursue their vengeance, are invited to join the ball. In Don Giovanni's brightly lit ballroom with servants and peasants, the masked strangers are welcomed and the three orchestras strike up: Anna and Ottavio dance the courtly minuet, Zerlina and Giovanni the middle-class contredanse, and Leporello whisks Masetto off in a rustic German dance. All is confusion when Zerlina's scream is heard offstage. She rushes in distraught, and Giovanni tries to pin the blame on Leporello. The guests now unmask to tell Don Giovanni that he has been found out and that vengeance is nigh.

Act II   A street. Leporello cannot stand his job any longer and tells his master he is leaving him ('Eh via buffone'). Giovanni persuades him with money, but vehemently rejects the notion of giving up his mission to make all women happy. At the moment he is thinking of Elvira's maid, but it is Elvira herself who appears on the balcony. He plans to put on Leporello's clothes and seduce the maid, while Leporello, in his master's clothes, is to keep Elvira out of the way. When he speaks to Elvira of his love, she all too soon falls for his honeyed words again ('Ah taci ingiusto core'), while Leporello is half amused, half pitying. Don Giovanni's plan works, but he has hardly sung his serenade ('Deh vieni alla finestra') when Masetto enters with a band of peasants intending to kill Don Giovanni. The Don, disguised as Leporello, gives Masetto directions on how to find the evil-doer ('Metà di voi qua vadano') and then, getting him on his own, beats him up mercilessly. Zerlina finds Masetto and comforts him ('Vedrai, carino'). In a dark courtyard before Donna Anna's house, Leporello is tired of the amorous Elvira ('Sola, sola in buio loco'), but, just as he tries to escape, Donna Anna and Don Ottavio enter with servants bearing torches, and Zerlina and Masetto come in through another door. They think they have cornered Don Giovanni at last. Ottavio is quite ready to kill him. Elvira pleads for the life of 'her husband', but the others agree that he must die. At this point Leporello reveals himself and whines for mercy. When he escapes, Ottavio decides that it is time to call the police ('Il mio tesoro'). (At this point Elvira's scene and aria ('Mi tradì'), composed for the Vienna revival, is usually inserted.) Meanwhile Don Giovanni has been enjoying himself seducing Leporello's wife. When he laughingly boasts of this to Leporello, whom he meets in the cemetery, it is not only Leporello who is shocked: a mysterious voice tells him that his laughter will be silenced before morning. They find the statue of the commendatore, with the inscription that he waits to be avenged. Don Giovanni orders the terrified Leporello to invite the statue to supper ('O statua gentilissima'). In a room in Donna Anna's house, Donna Anna tells Don Ottavio that she loves him but cannot think of marriage during her sorrow. The finale to Act II takes place in Don Giovanni's dining room. He is eating alone, waited on by Leporello and enjoying a wind band playing an opera pot-pourri, when Elvira bursts in to make one

more attempt to reclaim him from his wicked life. He answers her scornfully; she runs out and is immediately heard screaming frantically. Leporello goes to investigate and screams too; he returns to report breathlessly that the statue is arriving. Don Giovanni himself opens the door to his stone guest, who bids him mend his ways and repent. He refuses, but, in spite of Leporello's terrified entreaties, he accepts the statue's return invitation. As he takes its hand, his strength drains from him. The commendatore leaves, but an invisible chorus of demons warns Don Giovanni of his coming perdition. With a terrible scream he is swallowed up amidst flames. Leporello describes these events to the others. They resolve to get on with their own lives – Don Ottavio to woo Donna Anna once again, Elvira to enter a convent, Leporello to seek a new master, Zerlina and Masetto to have a jolly dinner. The opera ends with the moral that sinners meet with their just reward.

The opening andante of the overture is taken almost entirely from the scene in which the statue confronts Don Giovanni: thus Mozart daringly anticipates the crucial event of the opera, though without the trombones and without the chord of the diminished seventh. Mozart used more ensembles than his contemporaries: *Don Giovanni* in its original form has over 80 minutes of ensemble against less than 40 of arias, and even the arias are ensembles in that each one is sung to somebody or overheard.

Within the vast dramatic range of *Don Giovanni* Mozart still adheres to a semblance of the opera-buffa types. Leporello and the peasants are clearly in the buffa category; Donna Anna and Don Ottavio in the seria, hence her rondo 'Non mi dir' before the Act II finale, suitable to an opera-seria heroine. Donna Elvira has to be *mezzo carattere* (in between): for all her true pathos, she is always being made fun of by Giovanni or Leporello (except in the Vienna addition 'Mi tradì', preceded by the most beautiful of all Mozart's *recitativi accompagnati*, but clearly alien to the original concept).

What of the Don himself? He is everything and nothing. He dominates every moment of the opera, even when not on stage, but he subordinates his own character to that of the others – he adopts Anna's music at his first appearance, then the commendatore's when the challenges are exchanged; he falls into peasant 2/4 and 6/8 rhythms to seduce Zerlina, and into Leporello's buffo terseness when persuading him to stay in his service. Apart from the brief 'Fin ch'han dal vino', the epitome of his energy (he only once draws breath in it), he does not have a real aria of his own. The 21-year-old Luigi Bassi, who created the role, is said to have complained about it. What a Credo he might have sung after Leporello's well-meant suggestion that he should 'lasciar le donne'! But why should he waste time (that could be much better spent) on revealing himself, when his servant can do it for him, as in 'Madamina'? In his last scene he turns into a hero, dramatically and musically, defying heaven and hell as no other operatic hero ever did.

Così fan tutte, ossia La scuola degli amanti

Thus Do All Women, or The School for Lovers
Dramma giocoso in two acts (3h)
Libretto by Lorenzo da Ponte
Composed September–December 1789
PREMIERES   26 January 1790, Burgtheater, Vienna; UK:
9 May 1811, His Majesty's Theatre, London; US:
24 March 1922, Metropolitan, New York
CAST   Fiordiligi *s*, Dorabella *s* or *ms*, Ferrando *t*,
Guglielmo *b*, Despina *s*, Alfonso *b*; *satb* chorus of soldiers,
serenaders; *silent*: servants, musicians

Nothing is known about the creation of *Così* except that the commission is supposed to have followed the successful revival of *Figaro* in Vienna beginning on 29 August 1789. The performances of *Così* were interrupted by the death of the emperor Joseph II on 20 February 1790, but there was a second run from June to August. Mozart entered the Guglielmo aria 'Rivolgete a lui lo sguardo', composed for Francesco Benucci, into his thematic index in advance of the rest, but then replaced it in the opera with the shorter and more apt 'Non siate ritrosi'.

Through most of the 19th century and a good part of the 20th, *Così fan tutte* was regarded as being immoral and frivolous – utterly unworthy of Mozart's genius. Even Bernard Shaw, one of the few people a hundred years ago to have admired Mozart much as we do today, wrote of its libretto, 'The despised book after all has some fun in it, though quite as good plays have often been improvised in ten minutes in a drawing room at charades or dumb crambo.' The story of a lover testing the fidelity of his wife or bride by approaching her in a disguise or magical transformation goes back through Ariosto to Ovid. In our own time *Così* has become as popular as Mozart's other greatest operas, because we believe that the psychological truths beneath the play are revealed by Mozart's music. It just steers clear of the rocky side of 18th-century tales of wagers such as *Les liaisons dangereuses* with its sensual cruelty, but it certainly does not leave the audience with a happy glow. One asks, will any of the four ever feel so deeply again? Mozart, who was responsible for deriving the title from the text (da Ponte referred to the opera as 'The School for Lovers'), might equally well have called it *Così fan tutti* – 'Thus do all men' – but, though he can enter fully into female emotions, his obsessive insistence on repeating the multiplicity of women's deceptions in Guglielmo's 'Donne mie, la fate a tanti, a tanti, a tanti', etc., looks like personal participation.

SYNOPSIS

Act I   In a coffee-house two young officers are boasting about the fidelity of their betrothed. Their sceptical friend, Don Alfonso, wagers 100 zecchini that Dorabella and Fiordiligi would be no more faithful than any other woman, if put to the test. Ferrando and Guglielmo indignantly accept the bet and the condition – to obey Alfonso's orders all day. In a garden by the seashore the daydreams of Dorabella and Fiordiligi ('Ah guarda, sorella') are interrupted by Alfonso's desperate report that Ferrando and

Guglielmo have been ordered to depart at once to the wars. They come to take a tender leave ('Sento, oddio, che questo piede'): everybody is overcome by emotion ('Di scrivermi ogni giorno'). The women and Alfonso wave to the departing ship ('Soave sia il vento'). A room in the house of the sisters. Dorabella's vehement sorrow ('Smanie implacabili') is brushed aside by the maid, Despina: do as soldiers do, she advises the sisters, and find yourselves new lovers ('In uomini, in soldati'). Alfonso bribes her to help him to introduce his two Albanian friends to the sisters. Despina does not recognize them ('Alla bella Despinetta'), but they are, of course, Ferrando and Guglielmo in disguise and under oath to Alfonso to woo the sisters but with new partners – Ferrando, engaged to Dorabella, is to pursue Fiordiligi and Guglielmo Dorabella. They are reassured by the women's indignant reaction to the strangers, especially by Fiordiligi's 'Come scoglio', but their satisfaction in these proofs of constancy is beginning to be mingled with the delights of play-acting and the chase. Ferrando, especially, is intoxicated by love ('Un'aura amorosa'). A more dangerous attack is made in the Act I finale: distraught at the coldness of the strong-hearted maidens, the 'Albanians' gulp poison and drop lifeless at their feet. Despina begs the women to revive them with affection, and then reappears disguised as a doctor to restore the patients to life with an enormous magnet – according to the latest principles of Dr Mesmer. They rise dazedly and beg for a kiss to complete the cure, but the sisters still just manage to resist.

Act II   The women hardly need Despina's encouragement ('Una donna a quindici anni'), for they have already decided that there cannot be much harm in a mild flirtation ('Prenderò quel brunettino'). In the garden by the shore, the 'Albanians' woo them with a serenade ('Secondate, aurette amiche'). Now that Fiordiligi and Dorabella are at last in a romantic mood, the men are overcome by bashfulness. But Alfonso and Despina persuade the two pairs to link hands and to stroll off in different directions ('La mano a me date'). Guglielmo, outrageously overacting the part of the forlorn lover, finds Dorabella succumbing ('Il core vi dono'), and they exchange their lockets as tokens of love. Ferrando, seeing Fiordiligi's agitation, expresses hope of 'success' in an aria ('Ah, lo veggio'), which is normally omitted. When he has left, Fiordiligi admits to herself the tremors of her heart ('Per pietà'). The men compare notes: Guglielmo confesses smugly that he has found Dorabella less pure than the driven snow and adds some cynical observations about women ('Donne mie, la fate a tanti'). Alfonso takes advantage of Ferrando's despair ('Tradito, schernito') to taunt him into making one more supreme attempt on Fiordiligi's honour. Dorabella is altogether happier now that she has given in, and tries to persuade Fiordiligi to follow her example ('È amore un ladroncello'), but her sister is planning to escape temptation by seeking her Guglielmo on the battlefield disguised in one of his own uniforms. There she will be safe in his arms. But Ferrando enters at that moment, and it is into his arms that she falls ('Fra gli amplessi'). Alfonso's bet is won: the two officers have to agree that women are all the same, but the finale is needed for the written proof. A grand room brightly lit, with dinner laid, etc. The wedding celebrations include a chorus and a toast sung in canon. The versatile Despina impersonates a notary to perform the mock marriage. The ink is not dry on the contract before the sound of a familiar military march freezes the ladies' blood. The 'Albanians' flee in terror, and soon Ferrando and Guglielmo return from what was clearly a very short war. But what is a notary doing here, and whose is this contract of marriage? They rush off in pursuit of the 'Albanians', and return to confront the terrified women in the costumes of the 'Albanians' and with the whole truth. Guglielmo taunts Dorabella with the melody that had so idyllically united them. The officers pull Despina's ears to the trill of the magnetic doctor, and pay Alfonso's wager. Fiordiligi and Dorabella beg to be forgiven, and are soon reunited with their original lovers.

As so often in Mozart, the whole opera expresses a comic–serious duality. The division is not always clear, for the sheer beauty of the music hits the listener at a deeper emotional level than the libretto would warrant. The overture provides just the right introduction: after the shortest of andantes (with the five chords to which the men later sing the words 'Così fan tutte') there is a presto entirely constructed of single-bar phrases of the type that usually links more important themes – music of intrigue and laughter behind one's back, with nothing lyrical or sweet about it. Da Ponte's originality was in taking the old plot of the disguised husband or lover testing the fidelity of his own wife or sweetheart and doubling it: providing, as it were, two diagonal seductions. The music of Act I underlines the farcical element of the schematic nature of the plot, for the men and the women tend to move in pairs like puppets – a reminiscence of the popular Casti–Salieri *Grotta di Trofonio* of 1785. The ensemble writing postulated by the double action demanded a taut style based less on melody than on short motifs – for which the overture has prepared us. In 'Alla bella Despinetta', the first piece to bring all six characters onstage, the men and the women move in pairs (singing in thirds); Despina is generally linked to Alfonso, though she sometimes supports the men's pleas. Musically, the whole piece is a pattern of short clichés. The effect is strangely electrifying, and exactly what the situation calls for.

The despair of Dorabella and Fiordiligi explodes in two arias parodying opera seria. Despina predictably propounds the conventional cynicism of the soubrette, though with many a tender musical thought. Mozart cannot resist striking at us with moments of piercing beauty – in the burlesque leave-taking quintet 'Di scrivermi', accompanied by a laughing Don Alfonso, or in the trio 'Soave sia il vento', one of his irresistible E major 'nature' pieces. In the Act I finale the C minor 'death' scene of the poisoned lovers, with a comic bassoon to allay any fears, is followed, after the opera-buffa business of Despina disguised as the doctor, by a reawakening of the men who would be blissful enough to serve for Adam and Eve waking in Paradise.

Mozart's biographer Hermann Abert for once missed the point when he regretted that Mozart had not

continued in Act II with another delicious ensemble to complete both seductions, instead of giving us a string of arias and duets. Mozart and da Ponte realized that the game became serious only in a one-to-one confrontation. So do Ferrando and Guglielmo when first left alone with their victims. Moreover, it is time to see each one as an individual. Guglielmo uses a Don Giovanni touch to get Dorabella at his mercy and still to have time for the aside 'Poor old Ferrando!' In his total confusion, the less cynical Ferrando first gives vent to the rather artificial rondo 'Ah lo veggio' on his hopes about Fiordiligi, then to the more heartfelt 'Tradito, schernito' on his despair about Dorabella. The deepest feelings are expressed by the (relatively) constant Fiordiligi in her rondo 'Per pietà', a wonderful piece with obbligato horns and woodwind, the most moving aria in the opera. The horn, usually the mocker of cuckolds, speaks of fidelity. The duet 'Fra gli amplessi', in which the music convinces us that Fiordiligi's sincerity wins Ferrando from his play-acting to true love, is the climax of the serious side of the opera. But there is one more astonishing moment during the wedding celebration in the Act II finale – 'E nel tuo, nel mio bicchiero', the toast to forgetfulness of the past. The melody is very similar to the moving 'Volgi a me' in which Ferrando had found his true voice in the duet just before, but now (a semitone lower) sung as a canon – the only one in Mozart's operas – to intensify the beauty. When it is Guglielmo's turn to join in he cannot hide his disgust at his recent betrayal by Fiordiligi's capitulation (nor can he manage the higher reaches of the melody), so he merely mutters that he wishes the drink was poison, while Fiordiligi sings his line. An enharmonic change abruptly returns us to the world of farce with the appearance of Despina in the guise of the notary, then of the returning warriors humiliating the women and finally pardoning them. It is a shock to go back to stylized symmetry after all those deeper emotions have been invoked.

Die Zauberflöte
The Magic Flute
Eine Deutsche Oper in two acts, (2h 30m)
Libretto by Emanuel Schikaneder
Composed April–July and September 1791
PREMIERES 30 September 1791, Freihaustheater auf der Wieden, Vienna; UK: 6 June 1811, His Majesty's Theatre, Haymarket, London; US: 17 April 1833, Park Theater, New York
CAST Sarastro *b*, Tamino *t*, An Elderly Priest (The Speaker) *b*, First Priest *b*, Second Priest *t*, Third Priest *spoken role*, Queen of the Night *s*, Pamina *s*, First Lady *s*, Second Lady *s*, Third Lady *s* or *c*, 3 Boys 3 *s*, Old Woman (Papagena *s*), Papageno *b* or *bar*, Monostatos *t*, First Man in Armour *t*, Second Man in Armour *b*, 3 Slaves *spoken roles*; *satb* chorus of priests, slaves, Sarastro's subjects

The premiere of *Die Zauberflöte*, after which Mozart only had another 10 weeks to live, was followed by the most successful run of any of his operas, 197 performances in two years. In his first opera for a popular rather than a court theatre, all the 18th-century irony about the war of the sexes was replaced by an exotic fairy-tale with mystical elements, features of the new German Romanticism. The chivalric quest of the outset turns into a philosophical search for love and virtue. Considering the commonly held view that it is no more than a bungled children's story, the sources of the libretto are surprisingly wide and complex. The opening scene, with the rescue by the three ladies and the appearance of a strange semi-human being, is derived from the 12th-century *Yvain, ou Le chevalier au Lion* by Chrétien de Troyes, then recently translated into German; magic instruments had appeared in Paul Wranitzky's singspiel *Oberon* (1789); the three boys and a model for Monostatos came into *Lulu, oder Die Zauberflöte*, one of the stories in Christoph Martin Wieland's collection *Dschinnistan* (1786); another singspiel, *Der Fagottist, oder Die Zauberzither* (1791) by Wenzel Müller, is also based on one of these stories but with comic additions; Jean Terrasson's recently translated novel *Sethos* (1731), with its ancient Egyptian setting, provided the basis for the trials; the essay on the *Mysteries of the Freemasons* (1784) by one of Austria's most eminent Masons, Ignaz von Born, suggested the words of Sarastro.

Emanuel Schikaneder, since playing Hamlet at 25, had also been singer, playwright, composer, producer and manager. He had first met Mozart in Salzburg in 1780, and they seem to have had a friendly relationship. He wrote later that he and Mozart had thought *Die Zauberflöte* through very busily together. In spite of the naïve versification and some poor jokes, the whole libretto has a natural strength in its very illogicality and a mysterious quality that was perceived by Goethe. Its great superiority over Schikaneder's other works is evidence for Mozart's contribution. Like Mozart, he had been a Freemason. In fact Mozart continued to be one, despite Joseph II's stringent restriction of the order in 1786, and seems to have had a devout belief in the principles of the order as well as obviously enjoying the possibility it offered of mixing with the aristocracy and the intelligentsia on equal terms. The opera made no secret of the fact that the Temple's brotherhood represented the Freemasons, as the libretto had a frontispiece full of Masonic symbols. This glorification of Masonry could not have won the opera any popularity, least of all in official circles. The general public enjoyed the stage tricks, the comedy and the music, but Mozart must have had a purpose in courageously bringing in Freemasonry: it was surely to defend it through allegory. The audience shares Tamino's bewilderment in finding Sarastro no ogre at all but wise and virtuous, while the queen changes from apparently good to clearly evil. It has even been suggested that the plot must have been altered when Schikaneder and Mozart arrived at the Act I finale. The moral he intended is surely this: do not believe what the detractors of the order say, for it is they that turn out to be evil when you look for yourself. Every element in the music of *Die Zauberflöte* – and, indeed, in Mozart's late instrumental music – has been described in terms of Freemasonic symbolism – especially the three chords, the key of E♭ with its three flat signs, bound pairs of notes, counterpoint, clarinets and basset horns – but as all these are present in a great deal of non-Masonic

music it is impossible to assess the precise influence of Freemasonry on his music.

It is notable in the masculine world of the time in general, and of the Freemasons in particular, that Pamina increasingly takes on the central role, both in her suffering and when she leads Tamino through the fire and water. The three boys are a puzzle, since they were recommended as guides by the three ladies and then turn out to be ministers of goodness. They are not servants of the Temple, but rather forces of nature, the constellations that guide our paths, the voice of conscience which keeps us from suicide, the quiet reminder of what we really know. At the start of the finale to Act II they look forward to the end of superstition and the triumph of human wisdom.

Schikaneder gave Papageno – played by himself – the lion's share. The Tamino was another versatile man of the theatre, Benedikt Schack, a composer and a good musician, who could have played the flute on stage (if Mozart had allowed him the tiniest of breaths between singing and playing). The queen was Mozart's sister-in-law, Josepha Hofer.

SYNOPSIS

Act I A rocky region. Prince Tamino is fleeing a huge serpent ('Zu Hilfe! Zu Hilfe!'). As he faints in terror, three ladies appear and kill it. They reluctantly leave the handsome stranger to bring their queen the news. As Tamino comes to, Papageno, a birdcatcher playing pipes and dressed up as a bird, appears ('Der Vogelfänger bin ich ja'). He claims to have throttled the serpent himself, but soon regrets his lie when the three ladies appear and padlock his mouth as punishment. They give Tamino a portrait of the queen's daughter, Pamina, with which he instantly falls in love ('Dies Bildnis ist bezaubernd schön'). The scene changes, for the next aria only, to reveal the Queen of the Night enthroned among transparent stars. She promises Tamino her daughter's hand if he will rescue her from the demon who has kidnapped her ('O zittre nicht, mein lieber Sohn'). The ladies free Papageno but order him to accompany the prince on his dangerous quest (quintet: 'Hm, hm, hm!'). Tamino is given a magic flute and Papageno a magic set of bells. Three mysterious boys are to show them the way. In a splendid Egyptian room, Pamina is being bullied by a lustful Moor, Monostatos. At that moment Papageno wanders in: the feathered man and the black man put the fear of the devil into each other, but Papageno remains to tell Pamina about Tamino's mission and his love for her, whereupon she falls in love with the prince without as much as seeing his picture. She and Papageno sing about love ('Bei Männern, welche Liebe fühlen'). Meanwhile Tamino, guided by the three boys, has come to a grove with three temples (finale Act I). An old priest emerges from the central Temple of Wisdom to dissipate Tamino's hatred for Sarastro, the ruler who has imprisoned Pamina. A distant chorus reveals that she is still alive. Tamino plays his magic flute, and wild beasts come out to enjoy the music. Hearing Papageno's pipes, he rushes out. A moment later Pamina and Papageno run through in their attempt to escape, but Monostatos gleefully captures them. Now it is

Papageno's turn to try his magic instrument: Monostatos and all the slaves are bewitched by the music of the bells and march off singing happily. Sarastro arrives in his chariot drawn by lions. Pamina confesses that she fled because of Monostatos's importunities. Sarastro, too, loves her more than he should, but he recognizes that she loves another. At that moment Monostatos drags in his latest capture, and thus Tamino and Pamina ecstatically behold each other for the first time. Sarastro orders the two strangers to be led to the Temple of Examination. The chorus praises his wisdom.

Act II   A palm grove with pyramids. Sarastro and the assembled priests resolve to let Tamino undergo the trials for admission to the brotherhood. The gods have decided that Pamina is to be his wife. All join in a hymn ('O Isis und Osiris'). Amid thunder, the scene changes to a temple court filled with broken pillars. Two priests lead in the candidates: Tamino, resolved to undergo all the trials, the first of which is to keep silent, and Papageno, caring only about food and drink and his hope of finding Papagena, the woman of his dreams. The three ladies try in vain to rally them back to the queen ('Wie? Wie? Wie?'). In a garden where Pamina is asleep, the lustful Monostatos flees at the approach of the queen, who orders her daughter to murder Sarastro ('Der Hölle Rache kocht in meinem Herzen'). Left alone in despair, Pamina is once more subjected to Monostatos's lewd propositions, but Sarastro drives him off and reassures her ('In diesen heil'gen Hallen'). In another hall Papageno breaks all the rules and chats to an old crone who tells him she is eighteen years and two minutes old and has a sweetheart named . . . Papageno. Before she can reveal her identity, she disappears at a thunderclap. The three boys remind Papageno and Tamino to be steadfast ('Seid uns zum zweitenmal willkommen'). Pamina is heartbroken when Tamino will not speak to her ('Ach, ich fühl's'). In the vault of the pyramids. After another hymn, Sarastro tells Pamina and Tamino that they must part but that they will meet again ('Soll ich dich, Teurer, nicht mehr sehn?'). A glass of wine is all that Papageno really asks of life: it instantly appears, but, having drunk it, he is filled by thoughts of love ('Ein Mädchen oder Weibchen'). The old woman promptly reappears. Only after she reveals that the alternative is eternal incarceration does Papageno promise her his hand. She immediately turns into Papagena, only to be whisked away. The finale to Act II opens in a garden with the three boys, who save Pamina from her attempted suicide. The final trial is set between two large mountains, one a volcano, the other with a waterfall. Two men in black armour lead Tamino in and tell him that whoever walks this difficult path will be purified by fire, water, air and earth and that if he overcomes the fear of death he will be worthy to be consecrated to the mysteries of Isis. He agrees to undergo the tests and is reunited with Pamina, who guides him through fire and water, protected by the magic flute. They are welcomed by the chorus in a brightly lit temple. Back in the garden it is now Papageno who is suicidal for lack of his Papagena. Just in time the three boys remind him of his magic bells, which bring Papagena

to him with the prospect of domestic bliss. The queen and her ladies, abetted by Monostatos, make a secret onslaught on the temple, but they are routed by storms, thunder and lightning. The stage is transformed into a sun. Sarastro receives Tamino and Pamina. Night has been dispersed. The chorus gives praise and thanks.

The overture's only direct quote is in the three chords before the development, which in the opera precede the trials of Act II, but the entire sublime amalgamation of sonata form and fugue is a metaphor for the opera's mingling of narrative with philosophy.

There are traditional ingredients in Die Zauberflöte – five strophic numbers (three of them for Papageno), derived from the singspiel, and opera-seria arias for the queen, but now Mozart completed the revolutionary process begun in Figaro. Away with the vain repetition of words for the sake of the music! The musical form had to fit the text. In 'Dies Bildnis' Tamino is led, through admiration of Pamina's portrait (first subject) and the awakening of love (second subject in the dominant), to the thought of finding her (development ending on a chord of the dominant seventh). The thought is almost too much for him (a whole bar's rest). What would he do then? Well (although he is back in the tonic key), certainly not go back to mere admiration of a portrait, as sonata form would demand. The violins lead him on with a tender phrase, while he expresses with gradually increasing confidence his hopes of embracing Pamina. There is only a vestigial recapitulation of five bars of melody to suggest the musical form. Apart from formal considerations, there is an emotional effect in hearing a melody for the second time, never more so than in those quintessentially Mozartian moments when a melody first heard in the major returns in the minor. In 'Ach, ich fühl's' neither words nor music are recapitulated except Pamina's magical rising phrase 'meinem Herzen' which returns to the words 'so wird Ruhe', but now with the poignant sweetness of the B♭ major phrase turned to the heartbreaking sorrow of G minor. The orchestral coda of this aria seems to echo her cry of 'Sieh, Tamino', with the music fractured as though she were looking at him dazzled by tears. Mozart always maintains the harmonic pattern of sonata form or other forms: the Act I quintet is in rondo form harmonically, but the music is always new for the new events that occur, except for a few short returning phrases that give the hearer at least a suggestion of thematic form. This freedom, which is hinted at in Figaro, has now become universal.

A new freedom is apparent too in the finale to Act I. In this opera the finales are not scenes of mounting numbers of participants and excitement but a free expression of the words and the emotions hidden behind the words. Tamino's dialogue with the old priest goes freely from recitative to arioso, then to the distant chorus: in spite of the stern tone of their conversation, a gentle recurring phrase in the strings indicates that Tamino is drawn to the wisdom of the order. Later in the same finale the duet between Pamina and Sarastro offers another way in which the emotions are painted by the orchestra, which indicates heartbeats of different speed and intensity – Pamina's when she thinks of her mother, Sarastro's when he recognizes that she is not for him, as he had hoped, since she now loves another. The passage from recitative to melody and, later in the next scene, to a chorus interjection is performed with absolute freedom.

The finale to Act II contains the essence of the opera, four pieces so separate that they have even been performed in a different order. Between the scene in which Pamina is held back from suicide by the three boys and the one in which they perform the same service for Papageno is the heart of the opera – in which Tamino and Pamina undergo the ultimate tests. Mozart opens it with six solemn bars in C minor, then an old chorale melody sung by the two men in armour doubled by woodwind and trombones, all in octaves and accompanied by a four-part fugato on the strings, done with the mastery of Bach but with late-18th-century sensibility in the frequent appoggiaturas. It is one of the most overwhelming pieces in any opera, but there is more to come. After a delightfully perky allegretto, in which the two men in armour turn out to be good fellows after all and assure Tamino that Pamina is near and all will be well, comes the final, simple, exultant reunification – 'Tamino mine! What happiness!'/'Pamina mine! What happiness!' There is a very hesitant beginning by sustained horns and strings before the lovers speak again. This is the greatest of many moments which make Die Zauberflöte the most moving of all Mozart's operas.

The scoring is extremely simple, compared with the richness of Idomeneo or Figaro, but each piece has exactly the right orchestration – for example, no double-basses for the airborne three boys. There were various reasons for this simplicity – an orchestra less brilliant than that of the court theatre, the singspiel tradition and a less sophisticated audience – but it is a tendency shared with La clemenza di Tito and the instrumental works of 1791: the concentration on essentials. The music of Die Zauberflöte becomes increasingly concentrated as the opera proceeds: from being quite indulgent about the not very relevant, though absolutely delightful, palaver of the three ladies at the start, Mozart allows Tamino and Pamina a final duet after the completion of the trials of only two bars!

La clemenza di Tito

The Clemency of Titus
Opera seria in two acts (2h 15m)
Libretto by Caterino Tommaso Mazzolà, after Pietro Metastasio (1734)
Composed July–September 1791
PREMIERES 6 September 1791, Gräflich Nostitzsches Nationaltheater, Prague; UK: 27 March 1806, His Majesty's Theatre, London; US: 4 August 1952, Berkshire Music Center, Lenox, Massachusetts (Tanglewood)
CAST Tito (Titus) *t*, Vitellia *s*, Servilia *s*, Sesto (Sextus) *s* or *ms*, Annio (Annius) *s* or *ms*, Publio (Publius) *b*; *satb* chorus of Roman people; guards

La clemenza di Tito was commissioned as part of the celebrations in Prague for the coronation of the new emperor Leopold II as king of Bohemia. Though the Prague public loved Mozart, he was approached only when it became clear that the court composer, Antonio Salieri, was not available. He received the definite commission from Domenico Guardasoni, director of the Italian company, in July 1791 while he was working on *Die Zauberflöte*, but he may have written at least the allegro section of Vitellia's 'Non più di fiori' by April 1791, when it perhaps was performed by Josephine Duschek, and his sketches for a tenor Sextus must have preceded the July contract with the Bohemian Estates which stipulated a castrato Sextus. When Mozart arrived in Prague on 28 August, together with his wife and his pupil Franz Xaver Süssmayr, the score was nearly complete.

The Roman emperor Titus Vespasianus, famous for the noble qualities he had shown in his short reign (AD 79–81), was an ideal subject for a coronation opera: Leopold had been likened to a latterday Titus during his reign as grand duke of Tuscany. If Mozart went back to an opera-seria libretto to please the Italian taste of the new emperor, he had it converted into a 'true opera' (as he noted in his thematic index) to please himself. One third of Metastasio's text was cut; the rest was turned into three duets, three trios, three choruses and two finales for soloists and chorus, leaving just 11 arias. Metastasio's libretto had often been modified in the 40 settings it had inspired, but never so radically as this. That may have been the cause of 'a certain prejudice at court against Mozart's opera', of which Guardasoni complained to the Estates. In spite of all the changes, the libretto for each ensemble concerned a single static situation without any real action or interaction of the characters. For example, in the beautiful trio 'Quello di Tito è il volto', when the guilty Sextus appears before his betrayed emperor and friend, only inner feelings are expressed.

Metastasio's elegant plots and verses are on the whole more suited to the tangled love stories of his famous *L'Olimpiade* and *Demofoonte* than to political subjects. Titus is the only historical character in the drama. The ferocious Vitellia is derived from Hermione in Racine's *Andromaque*, who also sends her doting lover to kill the king who spurned her: she is therefore in marked contrast to the virtuous 18th-century Romans around her, until in her final great scena she turns her back on Racinian passion and becomes another self-sacrificing Metastasian heroine.

When the court left, the public took the opera to its heart. Mozart was delighted to hear of the applause that every number received at the last performance on the day of the equally triumphant first performance of *Die Zauberflöte* in Vienna. For 30 years it remained among Mozart's most popular operas (it was the first to be performed in England), before going underground for the next 150.

SYNOPSIS

Act I *Vitellia's apartments.* Vitellia, daughter of the deposed emperor Vitellius, had hoped to marry the emperor Titus, but he is paying court to the Jewish princess Berenice. The opera opens as Vitellia persuades Sextus, who is in love with her, to join the conspiracy to assassinate Titus ('Come ti piace imponi'). In the forum Titus is praised by the crowd and organizes help for the victims of the eruption of Vesuvius. He tells Sextus that he has decided to send away the foreigner, Berenice, and marry Servilia, Sextus' sister. Sextus' friend Annius, who is himself in love with Servilia, nobly keeps silent, but when he breaks the news to her, they declare their mutual love ('Ah perdona al primo affetto'). Servilia reveals this to Titus, and he praises her candour. Vitellia, hearing that she has been passed over again, promises her hand in marriage to Sextus if he will instantly murder Titus. He departs reluctantly to murder his beloved emperor and friend ('Parto, parto'). No sooner has he left than Annius and the prefect Publius come to pay homage to her as the newly chosen empress. She hysterically tries to call Sextus back, while the others attribute her emotion to excessive joy ('Vengo . . . aspettate . . .'). Below the Capitol. Sextus is torn by conflicting emotions ('Oh Dei, che smania è questa'), but, just as he resolves to save Titus from the conspiracy, he sees that the Capitol is on fire (finale Act I, 'Deh conservate, oh Dei'). The soloists run around in confusion, but Vitellia keeps her head enough to warn Sextus not to blurt out the truth. The Roman people are heard mourning Titus offstage.

Act II   In a garden on the Palatine hill. Annius tells Sextus that Titus has survived, and advises him to seek his mercy. As the identity of the conspirators still seems to be unknown, Vitellia begs Sextus to flee. But Publius approaches to arrest him. Sextus takes a tender leave of her ('Se al volto mai ti senti'). In a great throne room. Thanks are given for Titus' survival ('Ah grazie si rendano'). He cannot believe that his friend is guilty, but Publius warns him not to judge others by his own heart. Annius can only recommend mercy. Titus is torn by inner conflict ('Che orror! che tradimento!'): he envies the happy lot of a simple peasant. Sextus is led in but refuses to reveal Vitellia's complicity ('Quello di Tito è il volto!') and takes his leave of Titus ('Deh per questo istante solo'). Titus eventually tears up the death sentence, for he wishes to be seen by posterity as a clement ruler ('Se all'impero'). Servilia begs Vitellia, the empress-elect, to save Sextus ('S'altro che lacrime'). Vitellia resolves to sacrifice her own happiness and life for the noble Sextus who has not betrayed her ('Ecco il punto, oh Vitellia . . . Non più di fiori'). A crowd has collected by the entrance to the arena, where the wild beasts await the condemned. As Titus is about to pass sentence on the conspirators, Vitellia flings herself at his feet and confesses that she is guiltier than anyone – mistaking his goodness for love, she had hated him for seeming to spurn her. Titus forgives them all. Amidst their praise he resolves to devote himself only to the well-being of Rome ('Tu, è ver, m'assolvi Augusto').

Vitellia is the driving force in the opera: her role contains an amazing range of emotions, from wheedling to hectoring, from feigned love to real despair and hysterical terror, together with a no less amazing vocal range – from bottom A to top D. The most famous piece in the opera, is her rondo 'Non più di fiori' with basset–horn obbligato. The rondo, always reserved for principal singers, had an important place in Italian opera in the 1780s, especially in the works

of Cimarosa and Giuseppe Sarti. It was always in two parts, a slow and a faster, usually a sentimental gavotte. Apart from allowing himself some wild modulations at the start of the allegros, Mozart is true to the Italian model, both in this aria and in Sextus' 'Deh per questo istante'. But Sextus also has his coloratura aria with clarinet obbligato, 'Parto, parto'. (Both obbligati were performed by Mozart's friend Anton Stadler, for whom he also composed the Concerto, the Quintet and the 'Kegelstatt' Trio.) Titus is too predictably merciful ('What will posterity say of us?') and becomes ridiculously obliging when he contemplates marriage to three different women in the course of one day. Antonio Baglioni (also the first Don Ottavio) inspired a gentle lyrical style with long coloraturas. His set-piece aria 'Se all'impero' might have been found in Lucio Silla, but the other arias are in the 1791 pattern of simplicity and brevity, the most beautiful being in the heart of the chorus 'Ah grazie si rendano'. Servilia's tiny gem of an aria and Annius' two affecting pictures of loyalty are surpassed by their delicate duet 'Ah perdona al primo affetto', as irresistible as it is sentimental.

The opera lacks the rich scoring of the previous operas, whether in deference to Italian style or to the 1791 concentration on essentials found in Die Zauberflöte. The recitativo semplice is most probably by Süssmayr; however, Mozart provided highly dramatic recitativi accompagnati at all the decisive moments. The most striking piece is the finale to Act I, in which the people of Rome are heard far away lamenting the assassination of their beloved emperor, at first with exclamations on diminished seventh chords and then antiphonally with the quintet of soloists on stage, in poignant harmonies prophetic of the 19th century. This coronation opera opens with a brilliant overture, its first subject like cheering crowds and pealing bells, and closes with the emperor's almost ecstatic devotion to his people, an exuberant finale which must have inspired the end of Beethoven's Fidelio.

Other operatic works: Apollo et Hyacinthus, 1767; La finta semplice, 1769; Il sogno di Scipione, (1771, rev, 1772), 1772; Ascanio in Alba, 1771; Thamos, König in Ägypten, 1774; L'oca del Cairo (inc.), (1783) 1860; Lo sposo deluso, ossia La rivalità di tre donne per un solo amante (inc.), (? 1783–4), 1953

E.S.

THEA MUSGRAVE
b 27 May 1928, Barnton, nr Edinburgh

Musgrave studied music at Edinburgh University (and composition privately with Hans Gal), then spent four years at the Paris Conservatoire, studying privately with Nadia Boulanger. Returning to the UK, she established a reputation in the early 1960s as the composer of well-wrought, rather subdued instrumental works in an eclectic modernist idiom with its roots in free serialism. But she was also, from early on, much involved with music for the theatre. She wrote a ballet, The Tale of Thieves (1953), based on Chaucer's Pardoner's Tale, and a one-act comic opera, The Abbot of Drimock, based on one of John Mackay Wilson's

Tales of the Border. Later, theatrical motifs began to enter her concert works (as they did the works of leading figures such as Berio, Stockhausen and, in Britain, Maxwell Davies in the early and mid-1960s). She wrote a series of orchestral and chamber concertos in which the inherent drama of the concerto is turned into stylized action, with the soloists as dramatis personae. She also continued to write for the theatre, and six full-length operas (to date) – all but the first commissioned – are solid witness to her aptitude in this field.

In 1970 Musgrave became a guest professor at the Santa Barbara campus of the University of California, and since 1972 she has lived in the US. She now teaches at Queen's University, New York.

Mary, Queen of Scots
Opera in three acts (2h 15m)
Libretto by the composer, after the play *Moray* by Amalia Elguera
PREMIERES 6 September 1977, King's Theatre, Edinburgh; US: 29 March 1978, Norfolk, Virginia
CAST Mary *s*, Moray *bar*, Darnley *t*, Bothwell *t*, Riccio *b-bar*, Gordon *b*, Cardinal Beaton *bar*, Earl of Ruthven *t*, Earl of Morton *bar*, the four Marys 2 *s*; *ms*; *satb* chorus of soldiers, courtiers, lords of the Congregation, monks, people of Edinburgh

A much more direct and conventional opera than its predecessor (*The Voice of Ariadne*), *Mary, Queen of Scots* shows Musgrave's expertise at handling the raw materials of the genre in an effective and approachable way. The Elguera play offered strong dramatic situation and character conflict, with the accent on Mary's bastard half-brother, James Stewart, the earl of Moray. Musgrave accepts the play's flexible view of history, further reduces its burden of marginal characters, but retains its main emphases. It still manages to cover much – perhaps too much – of the essential incident in the period from 1561, when Mary returned to Scotland as queen, and 1568, when she was imprisoned by Queen Elizabeth, appending the murder of Moray (which actually happened 19 months later).

SYNOPSIS
Act I On the eve of Mary's return, the ambitious Moray seizes and imprisons Bothwell's supporter Cardinal Beaton. Mary arrives and is met by Bothwell and Moray, who quarrel. Mary succeeds in holding the balance, but later Gordon tries unsuccessfully to rouse the people against Moray. At a ball in honour of her young English cousin, Darnley, Moray reproves Mary for dancing with Darnley. Bothwell, also jealous, disrupts the French dancing with a wild Scottish reel which Mary joins in. Bothwell physically attacks Darnley and is banished with his men; Moray also leaves.

Act II Despite his unsuitability, Mary has married Darnley and appointed his friend Riccio as secretary. But the lords refuse to accept Darnley as king. Mary summons Moray to appease them, while Moray's agents incite Darnley to demand the crown. Moray expects power, but Mary rejects him. In revenge, Moray incites Darnley to murder Riccio in Mary's presence. Mary flees, pursued by Moray's accusations of complicity in the murder. But, as Moray seems about to seize power, she returns, accuses him publicly, and banishes him.

Act III Weak from the birth of her son, Mary nevertheless refuses Gordon's suggestion that she take refuge from Moray in Stirling Castle. To Gordon's horror, she puts her trust in Bothwell. Bothwell seduces her, but they are discovered by Moray. In the ensuing fight, Bothwell is wounded but escapes. At Moray's urging, the people demand Mary's abdication. She flees to England, but, as she leaves, Gordon kills Moray, leaving her baby son to be proclaimed King James VI.

The score makes fluent and effective use of traditional means, as refracted (perhaps most obviously) through the operas of Britten. As in Britten, drama and text are kept scrupulously clear, and action and reflection are very skilfully balanced. More tonal than before, Musgrave's own music nevertheless retains a muscularity and a technical economy which fit the turbulent subject well. And her use of borrowed material (plainsong, contemporary dances, Scottish pipe music and reels, etc.) is never merely picturesque, but always works to dramatic ends.

Harriet, the Woman called Moses
Opera in two acts (2h 15m)
Libretto by the composer
Composed 1984, rev. in one act 1985
PREMIERES 1 March 1985, Norfolk, Virginia; UK: 3 March 1985, BBC radio

Musgrave's libretto is based on the true story of Harriet Tubman, an escaped Maryland slave who, in the 1850s, helped some 300 other slaves to escape to Canada by way of the so-called 'Underground Railroad'. As before, Musgrave weaves traditional material (Negro spirituals and other types of American folk music) into her own post-tonal style, and it is typical of her that she does not see the politically fashionable aspects of the subject (feminism, human rights) as an excuse for fudging the dramatic issues. *Harriet* is by any standards strong musical theatre.

The opera was commissioned jointly by the Virginia Opera Association and the Royal Opera, Covent Garden, but still awaits its UK stage premiere. After the Norfolk production, Musgrave made a reduced version called *The Story of Harriet Tubman*, designed to make the work accessible to companies with more limited resources. Described as a 'narrated music-drama in one act', it has a smaller cast, a narrator and an orchestra of eight players.

Other operas: *The Abbot of Drimock*, 1959; *The Decision*, 1967; *The Voice of Ariadne*, 1974; *A Christmas Carol*, 1979; *An Occurrence at Owl Creek* (radio opera), 1981 *Simón Bolívar*, 1995

S.W.

MODEST MUSORGSKY
Modest Petrovich Musorgsky; *b* 21 March 1839, Karevo, Pskov District, Russia; *d* 28 March 1881, St Petersburg

Musorgsky and Tchaikovsky (one year his junior) are universally acknowledged as the outstanding masters of 19th-century Russian music. There are, however, two notable factors that distinguish them. Tchaikovsky was the first of a new conservatory-trained generation of professional composers, whereas Musorgsky remained a largely self-taught amateur, albeit one of genius. The scope of their achievements also differs markedly. In contrast to Tchaikovsky's voluminous and masterly output in every genre, Musorgsky's reputation rests essentially on his 65 songs, *Pictures at an Exhibition* for piano (1874, later orchestrated by Ravel), the orchestral *St John's Night on the Bare Mountain* (1867, reworked by Rimsky-Korsakov 1886), and three operas, two of them still unfinished at his early death aged 42. Of these, *Boris Godunov* is in the repertoire of every major opera company and is revered as a music drama of astonishing theatrical power, integrity and trail-blazing originality.

Musorgsky's musical ability was first displayed in his prowess as a gifted pianist and improviser. While still an army cadet in St Petersburg he met Balakirev and from him received vital encouragement and the only form of compositional guidance he ever had. Operatic projects were among his very first attempts at composition (*Oedipus in Athens*, 1858–60; *Salammbô*, 1863–6); but it was as a song-writer – often to his own texts – that he first found his highly individual voice as a composer. For these he chose diverse subjects that were often humorous, satirical or taken from low life. With an astonishing directness of utterance, he displayed an ability to sympathize with and depict in the most uncompromisingly vivid way those whom Dostoevsky classed as 'the humiliated and the injured'. Closely allied to this desire for musical realism was Musorgsky's determination to fashion a vocal line that reflected, with as little recourse as possible to conventional melody, the contours and intonations of human speech. As a result, the songs – especially those written between 1864 and 1870, and the three great cycles, *The Nursery* (1870–72), *Sunless* (1874) and *Songs and Dances of Death* (1875–7) – are unique in their dramatic and realistic power of expression. It is significant that Musorgsky is possibly the only one of the world's supreme song-writers to achieve comparable success in opera.

Musorgsky's artistic credo, then, as displayed in his greatest songs, *Boris Godunov* and, to a lesser extent, *Khovanshchina* (for which broad canvases the songs served as preliminary sketches), resided in his belief in the intimate relationship between the inflexions of the spoken Russian language, the ideas and emotions expressed by it, and the intonation of voice and accompaniment with which it is communicated. This could create a new, fresh form of music that was part of everybody's experience and would serve as an unprecedentedly direct means of communication. At the same time he repudiated the cult of art for art's sake as displayed by the German school of conservatory-trained composers, whose works in sonata form he castigated as 'musical mathematics'.

Having resigned his commission in the Guards to devote himself fully to music, Musorgsky found that the sharp drop in his private income caused by the emancipation of the serfs obliged him to undertake part-time work in the Civil Service. The great turning-point of his career came in 1868 when a friend proposed Pushkin's *Boris Godunov* as a subject that was perfectly suited to his rapidly developing gifts. In order to put his ideas into practice in his first full-length opera, Musorgsky perfected a novel and idiosyncratic musical style which, thanks to his lack of formal training and contempt for conventional musical disciplines, is largely free from formative influences. The voices of Glinka, Aleksandr Serov, Liszt and Berlioz – all highly individual composers in their own right – can be detected at times. For the most part, however, Musorgsky's predominantly chordal language, often presupposing a vocal line and incorporating audacious harmonic procedures, must have been discovered almost empirically at the piano.

The long-delayed production of *Boris* sadly proved to be the watershed of his short life. Though acclaimed by the public and fellow artists, it met with critical incomprehension and hostility, and this, together with the drudgery of his job and more personal, emotional problems, made Musorgsky increasingly introspective and dependent on alcohol. His St Petersburg musical friends tried to help him, but he became disillusioned and listless, and failed to complete, let alone orchestrate, the even larger historical canvas of *Khovanshchina* and his comic Gogol opera *Sorochintsy Fair* which he had unwisely undertaken at the same time. The well-intentioned but excessively distorting editorial work of his friend Rimsky-Korsakov to which most of his output, unfinished or finished, was subjected after his death is now increasingly rejected in favour of a return to the originality of his own texts whenever possible.

Boris Godunov

Opera in four acts with a prologue (3h 15m)
Libretto by the composer, based on Aleksandr Pushkin's historical drama and Nikolai Karamzin's *History of the Russian State* (1824)
Composed 1868–9; rev. 1871–2
PREMIERES definitive version: 8 February 1874, Mariinsky Theatre, St Petersburg; UK: 30 September 1935, Sadler's Wells, London; Rimsky-Korsakov version: 10 December 1896, Great Hall, Conservatoire, St Petersburg; US: 19 March 1913, Metropolitan, New York; UK: 24 June 1913, Drury Lane, London; Shostakovich version: 4 November 1959, Leningrad (St Petersburg)
CAST Boris Godunov *b*, Ksenia *s*, Fyodor *ms*, Nurse *c*, Prince Vasily Ivanovich Shuisky *t*, Andrei Shchelkalov *bar*, Pimen *b*, Grigori (later the Pretender Dmitri) *t*, Marina Mnishek *ms*, Rangoni *bar*, Varlaam *b*, Missail *t*, Hostess of the Inn *ms*, Simpleton *t*, Nikitich *b-bar*, Mitukha *bar*, Boyar in Attendance *t*, Khrushchov *silent*, Lavitzky *b-bar*, Chernikovsky *b-bar* (voice categories not designated by Musorgsky himself); *satb* chorus of boyars and their children, *streltsy* (royal guards), soldiers, police officers, Polish noblemen and ladies, Sandomir girls, blind mendicants, people of Moscow, urchins, vagabonds

Musorgsky broke off work on his experimental setting of Gogol's comedy *The Marriage* when he became fired by the idea of making an operatic version of Pushkin's *Boris Godunov*. Having condensed the Shakespeare-like 25-scene drama down to a mere seven, adding material and rewriting considerably in the process, he began the composition in October 1868, finished it in July 1869, and completed the orchestration in December – an astonishing achievement considering his lack of experience. When the opera in this compact seven-scene initial version was rejected for performance by the Mariinsky Theatre for a complex variety of reasons (novelty, fear of imperial and ecclesiastic censorship, lack of a leading female role, personal intrigues, etc.), Musorgsky set about revising it.

The two most notable features of this revision are the addition of an entirely new act (Act III) set in Poland, thereby providing the leading female role of Princess Marina, and the removal of the scene outside St Basil's Cathedral in order to accommodate a new scene depicting the advance of the pretender's anti-Boris forces and the defection of the Russian people. Musorgsky boldly decided that this wonderful new choral scene should follow and not precede the highly impressive death-of-Boris scene, and thus end the opera with the simpleton singing his solitary lament over the fate of Russia. Act II, in which the character of Boris is most fully revealed, was also substantially revised. Here, in addition to writing new songs for the nurse and Fyodor, Musorgsky largely recast the tsar's great monologue, added a touchingly domestic scene between Boris and his son, and recomposed the Boris–Shuisky confrontation and final hallucination scene, making the whole act incomparably richer in the process. He also rewrote parts of the Pimen cell scene (Act I, Scene 1) and added the hostess's song at the beginning of the following inn scene.

This 'definitive' version was eventually accepted for production largely thanks to the tenacity of the singer Yuliya Platonova, who demanded that the opera be staged as her benefit performance. At the highly successful premiere, with Ivan Melnikov as Boris, Platonova as Marina and Edvard Nápravník conducting, the scene in Chudov monastery (Pimen's cell) was omitted for censorship reasons; it was never staged during the composer's lifetime. It may be safely asserted that no other first opera which has subsequently been acknowledged as a masterpiece has ever been created with such meagre compositional experience and against such a negative cultural and political background.

SYNOPSIS

(The sequence of scenes in the initial version is shown in square brackets.)

Ivan the Terrible died in 1584 leaving two sons: Fyodor, who became tsar, and Dmitri, the tsarevich. Soon the boyar Boris Godunov was appointed regent to the weak-minded Fyodor. In 1591 Dmitri was found dying from a knife wound and it was rumoured that Boris was responsible.

Prologue Scene 1 [i]: The year 1598. Boris is in retreat in the Novodevichy monastery following the death of Tsar Fyodor. The apathetic people are exhorted to beg him to assume the throne by the police and the boyar Shchelkalov. A procession of pilgrims enters the monastery. The people comment cynically on developments. Scene 2 [ii]: A square in the Kremlin. To the famous orchestral evocation of bells, supplemented by real peals on stage, the chorus greets Boris as he emerges from his coronation. In a contemplative monologue Boris acknowledges the people's acclamation, but his soul is filled with foreboding.

Act I Scene 1 [iii]: Six years later. In his cell, the old monk Pimen is completing his chronicle of Russian history ('Yeshcho odno' – 'Still one more tale'). His novice Grigori is tormented with dreams of greatness. Pimen vividly recalls how the child Dmitri was discovered murdered. Grigori realizes that had he lived the tsarevich would have been his own age. Scene 2 [iv]: Grigori has fled from the monastery and is making for Poland to raise an army against Boris. He arrives at an inn on the Lithuanian border with two vagabond monks, Varlaam and Missail. Varlaam sings a racy ballad describing Ivan the Terrible's victory at Kazan. Police arrive with a warrant for Grigori's arrest, but he manages to escape.

Act II [v] The tsar's apartments in the Kremlin. Ksenia mourns the death of her betrothed while Fyodor and the nurse try to comfort and amuse her. Boris enters and speaks affectionately to his children. In his great monologue ('Dostig ya vysshei vlasti' – 'I stand supreme in power') he meditates on his crime and the sufferings of Russia. Prince Shuisky, a rival boyar, brings news that a pretender has appeared calling himself Dmitri, the resurrected tsarevich. Shuisky gives an unbearably graphic account of the murdered child's features, and, aghast, Boris dismisses him. As a mechanical clock with figures begins to chime, the guilt-racked Boris breaks down, haunted by a vision of the murdered child.

Act III Scene 1: A castle in Poland. Princess Marina has fallen in love with the pretender, and her Jesuit confessor, Rangoni, commands her to ensnare him in order to convert Russia to Catholicism. Scene 2: Grigori/Dmitri awaits a rendezvous with Marina in the garden. After a courtly choral polonaise the guests return indoors and Marina taunts Dmitri over his infatuation with her. When she realizes that he is determined to seize the Russian throne, she pours out her love for him in a short but richly melodic love duet that is one of the opera's few concessions to tradition.

[vi, omitted in the definitive version] Outside St Basil's Cathedral, Moscow. As Boris emerges from the cathedral, the starving and disaffected people beg him to give them bread. There is an astonishing confrontation between him and a simpleton, who publicly accuses him of murder. Left alone, the simpleton foretells Russia's troubled future. (Musorgsky himself orchestrated the St Basil scene, although Mikhail Ippolitov-Ivanov reorchestrated it in 1926 so that it could be used as an additional scene to the Rimsky version if required.)

Act IV Scene 1 [vii]: An emergency meeting of the council of boyars is in progress in the Kremlin. Shuisky's description of the overwrought state in which he had recently found the tsar is interrupted by the sudden arrival of the deranged Boris. Pimen enters and describes a miraculous cure performed at the tomb of the tsarevich Dmitri. Boris collapses and then, left alone with Fyodor, begins his simple and intensely moving prayer and death scene ('Proshchai, moi syn, umirayu' – 'Farewell, my son, I am dying') in which he advises his son on the government of Russia and prays for God's protection for his children. Scene 2: In a forest near Kromy an unruly mob taunts a half-lynched boyar. After short scenes between a simpleton and some urchins (transferred from the discarded St Basil scene), Varlaam and Missail and two Jesuit monks, the crowd greets the arrival of the false Dmitri and follows him to Moscow. The simpleton is left alone singing a haunting lament foretelling the troubled times that lie in store for Russia.

The most immediately striking feature of the music of *Boris* is the simplicity and economy of means by which Musorgsky achieves the maximum dramatic and expressive effect. Just as in the first movement of Beethoven's Fifth Symphony, short phrases, harmonized either simply or with audacious originality, etch themselves indelibly on the memory and create an impression of human emotion in the raw. Counterpoint is largely absent, as are colouristic orchestral effects. Instead attention is directed with unprecedented clarity to the vocal line, which graphically communicates the rapidly changing moods of the text. When a character pauses for thought, so, more often than not, does the orchestra; no opera contains more telling silences. In the same way the scenes are all made to fade out at the end, as if in anticipation of cinema technique. The only exception to this is the brilliant coronation scene, in which Musorgsky makes impressive use of the folksong 'Slava' that Beethoven had earlier used in his second Rasumovsky Quartet.

Musorgsky understood the expressive possibilities of the human voice to the full. A more than capable singer and accompanist himself, he extracted the maximum from his singers, and his vocal line is provided with an unusually comprehensive and detailed set of dynamics, expression marks and verbal indications as to how the voice is to be used. Furthermore, in the still modern-sounding Act II 'hallucination' scene his frequent use of the term *glukho* – a word that implies a combination of muffled, toneless and dull – anticipates the technique that Schoenberg and his pupils were to term sprechgesang.

Perhaps Musorgsky's greatest innovation is his promotion of the chorus from its normal subordinate role to that of one of the most important characters in the drama; many would say the chief one. From the very opening pages the people are shown to have unusually lifelike character, and much use is made of individual groups voicing their own thoughts. Given the opera's episodic construction, the treatment of the chorus lends cohesion to the whole more than anything else.

Mention must be made of the notorious editorial problem that besets *Boris*. Although Musorgsky completed and orchestrated two different versions, the second of which was successfully performed during his lifetime, the opera was for many years exclusively performed in the reorchestrated revision of Rimsky-Korsakov. Rimsky believed that the opera's disappearance from the repertoire after Musorgsky's death was largely due to its lacklustre orchestration and 'faulty' compositional technique. It is unfortunate that the appearance of his edition coincided with Fyodor Shalyapin's magisterial assumption of the title role, for the two became synonymous and established a norm. Since 1945 the tendency to return to Musorgsky's own versions has greatly accelerated worldwide, although the Bolshoi Theatre in Moscow still clings to the more sumptuous Rimsky version. Quite frequently the two authentic versions are conflated in performance, for instance by incorporating the St Basil scene from the initial version into the text of the definitive version. Shostakovich made a reorchestration in 1940 which, unlike Rimsky's, at least remained faithful to the text of Musorgsky's vocal score.

Khovanshchina
The Khovansky Affair / Plot
National music drama in five acts (3h)
Libretto by the composer with V. V. Stasov
Composed 1872–80 (inc.)
PREMIERES 21 February 1886, St Petersburg; UK: 1 July 1913, Drury Lane, London; US: 18 April 1928, Philadelphia; Shostakovich version: 25 November 1960, Kirov Theatre, Leningrad (St Petersburg); UK: 18 June 1963, Covent Garden, London
CAST Prince Ivan Khovansky *b*, Prince Andrei Khovansky *t*, Prince Vasily Golitsyn *t*, Shaklovity *b-bar*, Dosifei *b*, Marfa *ms*, Susanna *s*, Scribe *t*, Emma *s*, Lutheran Pastor *bar*, Varsonofev *bar*, Kuzka *t*, Streshnev *t*, 3 *Streltsy* (royal guards) 3 *b* (voice categories not designated by Musorgsky himself); *satb* chorus of *streltsy*, Old Believers, serving girls and Persian slaves, Peter the Great's bodyguards, the people

Musorgsky began work on *Khovanshchina* as soon as he finished revising *Boris*. He avidly collected a vast amount of historical and social detail about the turbulent period of change from 'old' to 'new' Russia in the years following Peter the Great's accession (1682–98), conflating a number of incidents in the interests of concision. Also involved are the religious sect known as Old Believers, who were violently opposed to the new reforms introduced into the ritual of the Orthodox Church. Instead of putting his libretto into a finished state before beginning composition, Musorgsky tried to work on text and music simultaneously, and soon after began a similar process with *Sorochintsy Fair*. As a result the ends of Act II and V (final chorus) had not been composed by the time of his death; neither had he managed to subject the mass of disparate episodes that he had composed to rigorous revision. Nevertheless *Khovanshchina*, though at times opaque and slow-moving, contains some very fine music, and the roles of Marfa, Dosifei, Ivan Khovansky and Golitsyn are particularly rewarding. The haunting prelude to Act I, subtitled 'Dawn over the Moscow River', and the 'Dance of the Persian Slaves' from Act IV are regularly performed in the concert hall.

SYNOPSIS
The complex story of the opera largely concerns the interaction of the chief characters against the political and religious background at the time of the accession of the young Peter the Great. Ivan Khovansky and his son Andrei, in charge of the unruly *streltsy*, are custodians of old, feudal Russia. Prince Golitsyn, wily lover of the regent Sophia, is the representative of the new, Westernized ideas that are being introduced by

Tsar Peter. The reactionary Old Believers are represented by the monk Dosifei and Marfa.

Act I The boyar Shaklovity dictates a letter to a scribe warning the rulers and nobility that Prince Ivan Khovansky and his son Andrei are plotting against the state. Khovansky arrives amid general rejoicing and announces his determination to crush the enemies of the throne. Andrei pursues a young German girl, Emma, but Marfa, a former lover of Andrei, intervenes. A quarrel between father and son over Emma is interrupted by the arrival of Dosifei, who restores peace but foretells times of trouble ahead.

Act II Prince Golitsyn reads a letter from Sophia and decides to be wary of her. In a divination scene, Marfa foretells his disgrace and ruin. After he has dismissed her, a meeting takes place between him, Khovansky and Dosifei. They are interrupted by Shaklovity, who announces that the Khovanskys have been proclaimed traitors.

Act III Marfa sings of her past love for Andrei. She is scolded by Susanna but comforted by Dosifei. The unruly *streltsy* appear singing a drinking song and quarrelling with their wives. The scribe warns them that Tsar Peter's troops are advancing on them. Khovansky advises them to disperse quietly; Tsar Peter has clearly gathered up the reins of power.

Act IV Scene 1: Khovansky is entertained by his serving girls and Persian slaves. Shaklovity arrives, ostensibly to summon him to a council of state, but assassinates him as he prepares to leave. Scene 2: Golitsyn leaves Moscow for exile, and Dosifei reflects on his fall and that of Khovansky. Andrei and Marfa have an altercation and Marfa defies him to summon his *streltsy*. They arrive, but carrying blocks for their own execution. An emissary from Tsar Peter pardons them.

Act V The Old Believers' cause is lost and they prepare for death rather than compromise their faith and yield to the tsar's soldiers. They are joined by Dosifei, Marfa and Andrei, who prepare to immolate themselves in a chapel in a forest clearing. The tsar's soldiers arrive in time to see everyone consumed in flames.

Although very much the work of Musorgsky throughout, *Khovanshchina* can, in a good performance, create an almost Wagnerian cumulative impact which some find more satisfying than the more kaleidoscopic and tersely constructed *Boris*. However, even they would be obliged to concede that here the composer's genius declares itself more fitfully, and that the grandiose concept is handled with less imagination and originality than in *Boris*.

At his death Musorgsky had orchestrated only two short scenes (Marfa's short folklike aria at the start of Act III and the *streltsy* scene in Act IV, Scene 1). In order for the work to be performed, Rimsky-Korsakov undertook the heavy assignment of completing and orchestrating it. In trying to give the material a more manageable shape, he cut some 800 bars while also compressing, transposing and recomposing much else. His most substantial cuts (all restored in the version Shostakovich made for a 1959 film) can be summarized as follows: in Act I the extended scene (over 200 bars) between the people and the scribe immediately preceding Khovansky's arrival; in Act II Golitsyn's reading of his

ex-lover's letter, his scene with a Lutheran pastor, and nearly half of the scene between Golitsyn, Khovansky and Dosifei; in Act III Shaklovity's aria is shortened and Kuzka's song with chorus is lost entirely. Rimsky's version held the stage until 1958, when Shostakovich made his own orchestration, faithfully keeping to Musorgsky's vocal score as reconstructed and published by Pavel Lamm and Boris Asafyev in 1931. Diaghilev commissioned Stravinsky and Ravel to orchestrate additional material for the Paris premiere in 1913. Of this, only Stravinsky's reworking of the final chorus exists in published vocal score (1914).

Sorochintsy Fair
Sorochinskaya Yarmaka

Comic opera in three acts (1h 45m)
Libretto by the composer, after the story *The Fair at Sorochintsy* by Nikolai Gogol (1832)
Composed 1876–81 (inc.)
PREMIERES 13 October 1917, Petrograd (St. Petersburg) (in César Cui's edition); US: 29 November 1930, Metropolitan, New York; UK: 17 February 1934, Fortune Theatre, London

Musorgsky originally decided to start work on this in order to avoid composing two 'heavyweights' one after another, and to provide a good comic role for a friend, the bass Osip Petrov. The opera is set in the Ukraine. Parasya, the daughter of Cherevik, falls in love at the fair with the young peasant Gritsko. There are many humorous and fantastic complications to the plot which involve the popular legend of a 'devil in a red jacket' and Gritsko's rather improbable 'dream' (an excuse to recycle the *Bare Mountain* witches' sabbath music). In the end true love is able to triumph thanks to a crafty gypsy who exposes a love affair between Cherevik's wife Khivrya and the priest's son. All express their joy at this outcome in a gopak.

In keeping with the light-hearted Ukrainian atmosphere as depicted in Gogol, the music is simple, folky and largely devoid of the originality that characterizes the two previous operas. At the time of Musorgsky's death, despite some desperate last-minute borrowing from earlier pieces such as the *Bare Mountain* music, there was much that remained unwritten; even important stretches of the libretto had not been finalized, and only two numbers had been orchestrated: the prelude ('A hot day in little Russia') and Parasya's song (completed by Rimsky-Korsakov); neither has been published. A number of attempts to put the material into performable shape have been made by Anatoly Lyadov (orchestrations of the prelude, Khivra's song, Gritsko's dumka and the final gopak), Vyacheslav Karatygin, Yury Sergeyevich Sakhnovsky, César Cui and Nikolai Cherepnin (Monte Carlo, 1923). Pavel Lamm's 1933 edition in the complete works gave all the Musorgsky material in its original form and included Vissarion Shebalin's completion of the unfinished scenes and orchestration of the whole (1934). This version is probably as authentic as is possible, and the one used almost invariably since then.

Other operatic works: *Salammbô* (inc., 1866); *The Marriage* (*Zhenit'ba*) (inc., 1868), 1909; *Mlada* (inc.; coll. with Borodin, César Cui and Rimsky-Korsakov), (1872)

D. L.-J.

OTTO NICOLAI

Carl Otto Ehrenfried Nicolai; *b* 9 June 1810, Königsberg,
Russia; *d* 11 May 1849, Berlin

Nicolai is considered a significant figure in early
German Romantic opera on the strength of a single
work – *Die lustigen Weiber von Windsor* – which is
still regularly performed in German opera houses. It
comes as something of a surprise, then, to learn that
this was Nicolai's only German opera and that his
remaining four operas, now never performed, were all
Italian works.

Early studies in Berlin with the lieder composer
Carl Friedrich Zelter obviously influenced Nicolai's
early works: his first published compositions, which
appeared in 1830, were solo songs and part-songs. In
1833 he went to Rome as organist at the Prussian
embassy and undertook a study of Italian music,
paying particular attention to the works of Palestrina.
However, Nicolai, like Meyerbeer before him, soon
developed a strong interest in traditional Italian folksong and, again like Meyerbeer, soon felt the pull of
the theatre. The final impetus in Nicolai's case came
as a result of his composing a funeral cantata for the
mezzo-soprano Maria Malibran: 'Even if it's not an
opera,' he wrote, 'at least it's a beginning.' His
longed-for first commission came in 1838, though
Nicolai had already begun work on *Rosamonda d'Inghilterra* two years earlier. The opera was performed,
as *Enrico II*, in Trieste in 1839.

Enrico II and the three other Italian operas that
followed – *Il templario* (based on Sir Walter Scott's
Ivanhoe), *Gildippe ed Odoardo* and *Il proscritto* (to a
text rejected by Verdi) – are all firmly cast in the bel-
canto style, with graceful flowing melodies in the
manner of Bellini, and following conventional Italian
forms and structures. The success of *Enrico II* and *Il
templario* led to Nicolai being hailed as a great Italian
composer. In 1841 he was invited to conduct *Il templario* at the Hofoper in Vienna; its success led to his appointment as kapellmeister there, a post he held for six
years. During this time Nicolai reworked *Il templario*
as *Der Tempelritter* and *Il proscritto* as *Die Heimkehr des Verbannten* and eventually found in Shakespeare's *The Merry Wives of Windsor* the new operatic
subject he had long been seeking. The intendant at the
Opera turned it down, and this probably prompted
Nicolai to leave Vienna, having secured a post as

kapellmeister at the court opera in Berlin. *Die lustigen
Weiber von Windsor* received its premiere there in
March 1849, only two months before Nicolai's un-
timely death after a stroke.

Die lustigen Weiber von Windsor

The Merry Wives of Windsor
Comic-fantastic opera in three acts (2h 30m)
Libretto by Hermann Salomon Mosenthal, after William
Shakespeare's *The Merry Wives of Windsor* (1600–01)
Composed 1845–8
PREMIERES 9 March 1849, Hofoper, Berlin; US: 16 March
1863, Philadelphia; UK: 3 May 1864, Her Majesty's
Theatre, Haymarket, London
CAST Sir John Falstaff *b*, Herr Fluth *bar*, Herr Reich *b*,
Fenton *t*, Junker Spärlich *t*, Dr Caius *b*, Frau Fluth *s*, Frau
Reich *ms*, Jungfer Anna Reich *s*, Citizen *t*, 3 Other Citizens,
Innkeeper *spoken roles*; *satb* chorus of men and women of
Windsor, children, masks of elves and spirits; ballet

Before arriving at Shakespeare's *The Merry Wives of
Windsor*, Nicolai had considered and rejected texts by
Goldoni, Gozzi and Calderón. He had even, in his
desperation, advertised a prize competition to find a
suitable subject, but none of the 30 entries he received
pleased him. *The Merry Wives of Windsor* was suggested by Siegfried Kapper, who had helped Nicolai
make German versions of two of his Italian works. It
proved to be a felicitous choice: the opera has remained in the repertoire in Germany ever since.

SYNOPSIS

Act I Frau Fluth and Frau Reich discover they have
received identical love letters from Sir John Falstaff
and vow to get their revenge. Frau Fluth invites him
to a rendezvous, having made sure that her husband –
whom she considers to be over-possessive – learns of
the arrangement. In mid-assignation, Frau Reich
enters, as planned, to warn of Fluth's imminent arrival. Falstaff is bundled into a laundry basket, to be
thrown into the river.

Act II At the Garter Inn, Falstaff receives a second
invitation from Frau Fluth. Her husband arrives, in
disguise, to try to discover his wife's supposed lover.
Meanwhile Frau Reich's daughter Anna is receiving the
attentions of two unwanted suitors, Dr Caius and
Spärlich, and one wanted one – Fenton. The young
couple pledge their love. Falstaff visits Frau Fluth
again, and is again interrupted by the arrival of her husband; this time he escapes dressed in women's clothes.

Act III The women have explained everything to their husbands, and they discuss how to punish Falstaff further. Anna's father arranges that she shall marry Spärlich, while her mother arranges that she shall marry Caius. In Windsor Park, Fluth, Reich and their neighbours torment the terrified Falstaff. Meanwhile Spärlich and Caius have gone off together, disguised as elves, each thinking the other is Anna, while Anna and Fenton have hurried off to be married. Finally Anna's parents give their blessing, and Falstaff asks forgiveness for his foolish behaviour.

The form of the opera is that of the singspiel. But the Italian influence on much of the music is obvious, and the result is a deep-rooted fusion of the two national styles. Among the most easily identifiable examples of Italian traits are Nicolai's parlando-type handling of the voices in the Act II comic duet between Falstaff and Fluth ('Ja, Sir Bach'), and the melodic construction of Fenton's romance ('Horch, die Lerche') as he courts Anna. Colourful handling of the orchestra – evidence here of the influence of German composers, notably Weber – adds a further dimension to this ebullient score.

Other operas: *Enrico II*, 1839; *Il templario*, 1840, rev. as *Der Tempelritter*, 1845; *Gildippe ed Odoardo* (only a cavatina survives), 1840; *Il proscritto*, 1841, rev. as *Die Heimkehr des Verbannten*, 1846

G.H.

CARL NIELSEN

Carl August Nielsen; *b* 9 June 1865, Sortelung, nr Nørre Lyndelse, on Funen, Denmark; *d* 3 October 1931, Copenhagen

Although Nielsen wrote two successful operas, he is today chiefly considered as a symphonist. He also wrote chamber music (including four fine string quartets), incidental music for more than a dozen plays, many songs and choral works.

Nielsen came from a poor family and was brought up in rural surroundings. Together with his father, he played the violin at local weddings, dances and other celebrations. At the age of 14 he left school and for five years was employed in a military band at Odense, playing the signal horn and trombone. For recreation he played Haydn and Mozart string quartets with his friends. Helped by money supplied by benefactors in Odense, he studied for two years at the Royal Conservatory in Copenhagen. From 1889 until 1905 he played second violin in the orchestra of the Royal Theatre, Copenhagen.

A grant from the Ancker Bequest enabled him to visit Germany in the autumn of 1890. He went to Dresden, where he heard *Der Ring des Nibelungen*, then to Berlin, where he attended a performance of *Die Meistersinger*. But, though overwhelmed by the music of Wagner's operas, he did not succumb to their dramatic theory. In 1894 he went abroad again, to Germany and to Vienna, where he heard *Tristan und Isolde*. He also visited Brahms, who had a greater influence on Nielsen's own compositions than Wagner. Another influence was Johan Svendsen, whom Nielsen succeeded in 1908 as conductor of the Royal Opera, Copenhagen, a post he held until 1914.

The operas date from the period of his early maturity, when he had evolved a personal style of his own. Nielsen had strong views on the nature of opera. In the diary he kept while travelling in 1894 he wrote, 'The plot must be the pole that goes through a dramatic work; the plot is the trunk, words and sentences are fruit and leaves, but if the trunk is not strong and healthy it is no use that the fruits look beautiful.'

For his two operas, Nielsen chose strong poles or trunks: the Books of Samuel in the Old Testament for the first, *Saul og David*, and a comedy by the 18th-century dramatist Ludvig Holberg for the second, *Maskarade*. Given their success and the composer's interest in the genre, the question must be asked, Why did Nielsen stop writing operas at the age of 41? Vilhelm Andersen, the librettist of *Maskarade*, offered him an adaptation of another Holberg comedy, but he thought the subject too similar. Then in 1930, on the 125th aniversary of Hans Andersen's birth, he considered setting the dramatization of one of Andersen's fairy-tales, but instead contributed incidental music and a few songs to a play, *Amor og Digteren* (*Cupid and the Poet*), about Andersen and his love for Jenny Lind.

Nielsen began work on his Second Symphony, 'The Four Temperaments', while still composing *Saul og David*; he began the Third, *Sinfonia espansiva*, four years after finishing *Maskarade*, which is called to mind in the scherzo of the symphony. The Fourth Symphony, 'The Inextinguishable', would follow in another four years. There, perhaps, lies the answer to the question raised above: the symphonist had finally found his true *métier*, and opera, like the string quartet, was abandoned.

Saul og David
Saul and David
Opera in four acts (2h 15m)
Libretto by Einar Christiansen, based on the Books of Samuel
Composed 1898–1901
PREMIERES 28 November 1902, Royal Theatre, Copenhagen; UK: 10 May 1959, BBC radio
CAST Saul *b-bar*, Jonathan *t*, Mikal *s*, David *t*, Samuel *b*, Abner *b*, The Witch of Endor *ms*, Abisay *t*; *satb* chorus of maidservants, priests, soldiers and people

Throughout the composition period of *Saul og David*, Nielsen was a member of the Royal Theatre orchestra. Obsessed by the subject of his opera, he wrote that 'for long periods I could not free myself from it, no matter where I was – even when I was sitting in the orchestra with my second violin, busy with ballets and vaudevilles'. This obsession, apparent in Nielsen's score, lends the opera its particular dramatic strength.

SYNOPSIS
Act I Samuel prophesies that Saul's reign as king of Israel will be over shortly. To comfort his father, Jonathan asks his friend David to sing to the king. David declares his love to Saul's daughter, Mikal.

Act II David defeats the Philistines by slaying the giant Goliath, but Saul is jealous at the people's praise of David and banishes him.

Act III David returns and proves his loyalty by sparing the sleeping king's life. Samuel anoints David as king of Israel and then dies.

Act IV Saul visits the Witch of Endor to consult the spirit of Samuel, who prophesies the deaths of Saul and Jonathan at the hands of the Philistines. The prophecy comes true as Jonathan is mortally wounded and Saul kills himself rather than fall into the hands of the enemy. David is proclaimed king by the Israelites.

Musically and dramatically, the dominant figure of the opera is Saul, who has a fine monologue in the first act as well as an impressive death scene in the fourth. David's music is less original, but the choral music is splendid throughout, while the orchestral preludes and interludes are also highly evocative, in particular those depicting battle scenes.

Maskarade

Masquerade

Opera in three acts (2h 15m)

Libretto by Vilhelm Andersen, after the play by Ludvig Holberg

Composed 1904–6

PREMIERES 11 November 1906, Royal Theatre, Copenhagen; US: 23 June 1972, St Paul, Minnesota; UK: 9 May 1986, Morley College, London

CAST Jeronimus *b*, Magdelone *ms*, Leander *t*, Henrik *b-bar*, Leonard *t-bar*, Leonora *s*, Pernille *s*, *s*, *t*, 3 *bar*, *b-bar*, *b*; *satb* chorus of masqueraders – officers, students, girls; dancers

By the time he had completed composition of two-thirds of *Maskarade*, Nielsen was free, after 16 years, from the nightly grind of playing in the Royal Theatre orchestra and had not yet taken up his post as conductor of the Royal Opera. This unaccustomed freedom is reflected in the exhilaration, high spirits and even frivolity of much of the music.

SYNOPSIS

Act I Copenhagen, early 1723. Jeronimus has arranged a marriage between his son, Leander, and Leonora, daughter of his friend Leonard. Leander, however, has fallen in love with a girl he met the night before at a masquerade and refuses the match. According to Leonard, his daughter is also unwilling – she too has fallen in love with an unknown young man.

Act II In the street outside, Leander and Leonora meet on their way to the masquerade and sing ecstatically of their love, still unaware of each other's identity. Their respective servants, Henrik and Pernille, are also taken with each other.

Act III At the masquerade, Magdelone (wife of Jeronimus) flirts and dances with Leonard, while the two pairs of young lovers express their feelings. At midnight, when everyone unmasks, Leander and Leonora discover that the marriage arranged for them is much to their taste.

Maskarade inevitably invites comparison with Mozart's *Le nozze di Figaro*, especially as regards the characters of Henrik and Mozart's Figaro. But the revolutionary side of Beaumarchais's valet is entirely missing from Holberg's, while the atmosphere of *Maskarade* is light-hearted. Nielsen's music, in particular the dance music of the third act, is sparkling and joyous. The passionate love duet for Leander and Leonora, parodied in the scene between Henrik and Pernille, reveals genuine feeling, while the ensemble pieces are as impressive as those in *Saul og David*, though very different in style. The opera has become a classic in Denmark.

E. F.

JACQUES OFFENBACH
Jacob Offenbach; *b* 20 June, 1819, Cologne, Germany;
d 5 October 1880, Paris

Offenbach, the creator of French operetta, was the second son of a German cantor who had replaced his original surname, Eberst, with that of Offenbach, the town outside Frankfurt where he had once lived. All the Offenbach children were musical, but Jacob was enough of a cello prodigy for his father to have him enrolled at the Paris Conservatoire in 1833. He soaked up Paris's rich musical-theatre attractions; his disposition for the Opéra-Comique and the works of Adam, Auber, Hérold and others was rewarded by a spell as a cellist in the theatre's orchestra.

His experience playing at private salons led to his first compositions, sentimental waltzes such as *Fleurs d'hiver*, or *Rebecca* (using synagogue motifs), and also to public cello recitals. His cello-playing was acclaimed even by the young Queen Victoria. Offenbach's first stage music was for an 1839 Palais-Royal vaudeville, *Pascal et Chambord*, which was unsuccessful. During the political crisis of 1848, after composing further minor stage works, Offenbach returned to Germany. But in 1850 he was back in Paris as chef d'orchestre at the Comédie-Française, a job that entailed conducting a great deal of incidental music and songs, much of which he composed himself. His first notable song, 'La chanson de Fortunio', with its haunting refrain, was written for Alfred de Musset's *Le chandelier*.

Dissatisfied with the Opéra-Comique's reluctance to mount truly comic operas, Offenbach set out to write his own, short operettas much in the style being popularized by Hervé – one-act buffooneries with a few songs sung by two or three characters. The licensing restrictions that deprived Offenbach and his early librettists of more than two or three characters, let alone a chorus, did not seem to dull the success of the first bill at the Bouffes-Parisiens in 1855. Here, at a tiny, rickety magic theatre off the Champs-Élysées, a four-part programme was riotously ended with *Les deux aveugles*, the raffish story of two sham blind beggars. Other one-act works followed, notably *Le violoneux*, and the theatre shifted its operations to winter quarters in the Passage Choiseul.

The permanent theatre opened merrily with a bill that included *Ba-ta-clan*, a musical chinoiserie of considerable cleverness and silliness by Offenbach and Ludovic Halévy (a civil servant and a nephew of Fromental Halévy, the composer of *La juive*). It indulged in musical satire (on Meyerbeer and grand Italian opera), put its contemporary Parisian characters in a fantastic (Chinese) setting, and had them sing and dance an entrancing waltz. Thus, the pattern for many of Offenbach's works was already set. Within a year, the Bouffes was offering not only new Offenbach works but reprises of short comic works by Mozart and Rossini, as well as two winning operettas in a competition for new composers – one by Lecocq and the other by Bizet (both to the same libretto, *Le Docteur Miracle*).

The opéras-bouffes were popular not only in Paris but on tours of the Bouffes company to the French provinces, London, and Vienna. In Britain, as in Austria–Hungary, the frivolity of Offenbach's one-act operettas led to local translations and, later, frank imitations. Suppé's *Das Pensionat* (1860) and Sullivan's *Cox and Box* (1868) were both influenced by Offenbach's style and were instrumental in establishing the national operetta styles of their countries.

By 1858, several characters and a full chorus were permitted at the Bouffes, and on 21 October the first great, full-length, classical French operetta was produced: *Orphée aux enfers*. Its enormous success led to worldwide productions, and the composition of the full-length *Geneviève de Brabant* (1859). Several accomplished short works followed, including *M. Choufleuri restera chez lui le . . .*, *Les bavards*, *Lieschen et Fritzchen*, as well as a ballet, *Le papillon*, and a work for the Opéra-Comique, the three-act *Barkouf*. Neither *Le Pont des Soupirs* (1863) nor *Les Géorgiennes* (1864) was particularly memorable at the Bouffes, nor was Offenbach's romantic opera for the Court Opera in Vienna, *Die Rheinnixen* (1864), although one of its numbers was transformed much later into the barcarolle in *Les contes d'Hoffmann*. But with a new star (Hortense Schneider), a new theatre (the Variétés) and a new team of librettists, there was another triumph, *La belle Hélène*. The fortuitous partnership of librettists Henri Meilhac and Ludovic Halévy ensured almost perfect texts for the great works that followed: *Barbe-bleue*, *La vie parisienne* and *La grande-duchesse de Gérolstein*.

La princesse de Trébizonde (1869), although coming at the very height of Offenbach's powers, also marked the beginning of the end of the public's enchantment with the old opéra-bouffe style. It was tired of the old burlesque methods and operatic parodies, the puns, the travesty, and was beginning to seek a more romantic, heavier weight to its stories, though it did not tire of clever plots and jokes if well written. It also craved spectacle. *Les brigands* (1870) was a compromise between silliness, satire and the romanticism of operas such as Auber's *Fra Diavolo*. The Franco-Prussian War brought to an end the frivolity of the Second Empire with its saucy operettas; Offenbach (still ashamed of his Germanic origins) fled France.

But the composer Charles Lecocq's prediction that operetta would be killed by Prussian shells was wrong: post-war Paris craved either an excess of spectacle or a surfeit of sentimentality. Offenbach, who returned to take over the management of the Théâtre de la Gaîté in 1873, failed, however, to find the perfect recipe for new works. *Le roi Carotte*, although lavish, was too satirical; *Fantasio* was bland, and *Les braconniers* was a weak rehash of *Les brigands*. (Lecocq's *La fille de Madame Angot*, an immense success in Paris in 1873, was exactly what Parisians wanted: a costume romance with reduced silliness and satire.) Offenbach could still write effective short works (*La leçon de chant*, *La permission de 10 heures*) and risqué longer ones with modern settings (*La jolie parfumeuse*), but he increasingly channelled his enormous energies into massive, spectacular versions of older works, and new extravaganzas, at the Théâtre de la Gaîté, which after a profitable start he mismanaged into debt. An aggrandized *Orphée aux enfers* in 1874 was followed much less profitably by an amplified *Geneviève de Brabant*.

In an attempt to recapture his imperial crown, Offenbach worked again with Meilhac and Halévy (*La boulangère a des écus*, *La créole*) and then with Lecocq's writers Henri Charles Chivot and Alfred Duru on *Madame Favart* and, most successfully, *La fille du tambour-major*, a work that harked back to Donizetti and even Méhul, but which displayed Offenbach's late-period charms at their most delightful. But by the end of the 1870s, the triumphs of Robert Planquette and Edmond Audran were foremost in the minds and throats of the Paris operetta public and Offenbach's works fell out of favour. *Les contes d'Hoffmann* was unfinished at the time of the composer's death and was completed at the request of his family by Ernest Guiraud. Standing outside the operetta tradition, it has become, rather ironically, the most frequently performed of Offenbach's works.

Orphée aux enfers
Orpheus in the Underworld
Opéra-bouffon in two acts (1h 45m; rev. version: 2h 45m)
Libretto by Hector Crémieux and Ludovic Halévy
Composed 1858, rev. in four acts 1874
PREMIERES 21 October 1858, Bouffes-Parisiens, Paris; US: March 1861, Stadt Theater, New York; UK: 26 December 1865, Her Majesty's Theatre, Haymarket, London (as · *Orpheus in the Haymarket*); rev. version: 7 February 1874, Théâtre de la Gaîté, Paris
CAST Aristée/Pluton *t*, Jupiter *bar*, Orphée *t*, John Styx *t*, Mercure *t*, Bacchus *silent*, Mars *b*, Eurydice *s*, Diane *s*, Public Opinion *ms*, Vénus *s*, Cupidon *s*, Junon *s*, Minerve *s*, Cybèle *s*, Hébé *s*; *satb* chorus of gods, goddesses; ballet

Orphée aux envers was the first classical (in both senses of the term) full-length operetta, although it was supported by other pieces at its original presentation. What began as a burlesque sketch on the Orpheus legend became something far more substantial, its foolery striking the right, impudent note. The original targets were the posturing excesses of classical performances at the Comédie-Française, still considered sacrosanct during the Second Empire, and the attack was handled by contemporary party-goers in Gustave Doré-style togas. An orgiastic climax was reached during the Act II bacchanal, with a stately minuet of the gods holidaying in hell followed immediately by the *galop infernal* (the can-can).

SYNOPSIS
Act I   Orpheus and Eurydice are bored with each other; the wife particularly loathes her husband's dreadful violin-playing. The shepherd/beekeeper Aristaeus has attracted Eurydice's attentions – in fact he is Pluto, disguised – and he sets a poisonous snake in the fields, which conveniently bites Eurydice. She dies euphorically and is happily transported to hell. Orpheus is delighted at the news, but Public Opinion requires him to journey to Jupiter to demand the return of his wife. On Mount Olympus, the gods are seditious, demanding more excitement and better food. To quell their revolt, Jupiter decides to allow them to accompany him down to the underworld to investigate Orpheus' predicament.

Act II   Once there, Jupiter – disguised as a fly – falls for Eurydice himself. At a rowdy farewell party for the Olympians, Jupiter consents to let the less-than-enthusiastic Orpheus retrieve his wife, providing he does not turn round on his way out. Jupiter then throws a thunderbolt, causing Orpheus to turn. Eurydice is forced to remain down under as a bacchante, to everyone's joy save Public Opinion's.

Because of its irreverent merriment (snatches of Gluck's 'Che farò senza Euridice?' appear), its catchy score, and most of all its can-can – Offenbach's most famous composition (often rather dubiously interpolated into many of his other works) – *Orphée* is constantly performed. Generally, the original two-act version is used, but since the EMI recording of the four-act 1874 aggrandisement, parts of that overblown score have been heard in recent revivals.

La belle Hélène
Beautiful Helen
Opéra-bouffe in three acts (3h)
Libretto by Henri Meilhac and Ludovic Halévy
PREMIERES 17 December 1864, Théâtre des Variétés, Paris; UK: 30 June 1866, Adelphi Theatre, London (as *Helen, or Taken from the Greek*); US: 14 September 1867, Chicago
CAST Pâris (Paris) *t*, Ménélaus (Menelaus) *t*, Agamemnon *bar*, Calchas *b*, Achille (Achilles) *t*, Ajax I *t*, Ajax II *bar*, Hélène (Helen) *s*, Oreste (Orestes) *s* or *t*, Leona *s*, Parthenis *s*, Bacchis *ms*; *satb* chorus of guards, slaves, people, princes, princesses, mourners for Adonis, Helen's entourage

La belle Hélène marked a return to classical antiquity for its creators, who aimed to repeat the triumph of *Orphée aux enfers* – and succeeded. The libretto and characters are far more developed, and its musical pattern subsequently became the basic mould for the classical three-act operetta. There was also a romantic or sentimental streak that Offenbach and his librettists and their followers, and the Viennese, later developed. Meilhac and Halévy turned the events of the rape of Helen of Sparta into a boulevard farce, but a musical farce, and it is the delirious activity of the chorus and principals in their various ensembles that makes *La belle Hélène* so deliciously immortal.

SYNOPSIS
Act I Queen Helen of Sparta is troubled by her marriage to the weak King Menelaus, and feels she is being hounded by the Fates. The shady soothsayer Calchas tells her that he too has heard the rumours of a divine beauty contest involving a golden apple and a handsome shepherd. The shepherd appears and tells Calchas that Venus has promised him the heart of the most beautiful woman in the world. The shepherd wins a wordplay contest and reveals himself as Paris, prince of Troy. Calchas makes sure that Paris and Helen will be alone by manufacturing a divine message that forces Menelaus to journey to Crete.
Act II Paris steals into Helen's boudoir, disguised as a slave. Helen thinks she is dreaming, until Menelaus barges in, discovering the two in bed. She reproaches her husband for having returned without warning. Paris tactfully withdraws, vowing to return.
Act III The royals have gone to the beach at Nauplia for their holidays. A priest arrives on a barge, to proclaim that Helen must now take a trip to Chythera, to atone for the gods' displeasure. As soon as she sails away, the priest reveals himself as Paris, and the Trojan War is set in motion.

While the subject matter of *La belle Hélène* and its disrespectful treatment echoed that of *Orphée*, Offenbach adopted a different musical style, moving away from 18th-century pastiche towards a more modern idiom that involved a greater degree of chromaticism (often in the melodies, for example in Helen's 'Amours divins', where the stepwise falling motion perfectly captures her sadness and longing). There is even an oblique quip at Wagner's *Tannhäuser* during the competition scene, a raucous fanfare which Menelaus passes off as 'German music I commissioned for the ceremony'.

Barbe-bleue
Bluebeard
Opéra-bouffe in three acts (four scenes) (2h)
Libretto by Henri Meilhac and Ludovic Halévy
PREMIERES 5 February 1866, Théâtre des Variétés, Paris; UK: 2 June 1866, Olympic Theatre, London (as *Bluebeard Re-Paired*); US: 13 July 1868, Niblo's Garden, New York

Barbe-bleue took the same group of Variétés comedians that had made *La belle Hélène* such a hit and set them loose in the farcical medieval-legend territory that had previously been evoked in *Geneviève de Brabant* (1859).
Bluebeard, having murdered no fewer than five wives, is determined to find a sixth. He sends his

ministers to the village to crown a Rose Queen, to be chosen by lottery. The winner is the buxom, 'Rubensesque' but uncouth Boulotte, and Bluebeard is delighted. They go off to be married at the castle. But when Bluebeard later fancies Fleurette, daughter of King Bobèche, he must rid himself of Boulotte. The alchemist Popolani is instructed to carry out the execution. But he has a good heart, and offers Boulotte the choice between a vial of poison and one of sugared water. She chooses the latter, and is drugged to sleep. When she awakes, she discovers her five predecessors are also alive, kept by Popolani in his cellar. They seek revenge. Boulotte, dressed as a gypsy palmist, interrupts the nuptials of Bluebeard and Hermia (as Fleurette is now known), and reveals that the gypsy band with her are Bluebeard's five other wives and male victims who similarly avoided the monarch's death sentences. Boulotte rejoins Bluebeard, who not too convincingly pledges to reform himself.
There are moments of horror and suspense, particularly in Act III, where an extended scene of great drama foreshadows *Les contes d'Hoffmann*. The Act II court shenanigans, in which Offenbach satirizes the obsequiousness of courtiers, have little to do with the murderous goings-on of the title character, and have not worn as well. Because of this and other dull libretto patches *Barbe-Bleue* is not played as often today as its delightful score warrants.

La vie parisienne
Parisian Life
Opéra-bouffe in four (originally five) acts (3h)
Libretto by Henri Meilhac and Ludovic Halévy
Composed 1866, rev. 1873
PREMIERES original version: 31 October 1866, Théâtre du Palais-Royal, Paris; US: 29 March 1869, Théâtre Français, New York; UK: 30 March 1872, Holborn Theatre, London; rev. version: 25 September 1873, Théâtre des Variétés, Paris

With *La vie parisienne*, Meilhac, Halévy and Offenbach turned to the troupe of the Théâtre du Palais-Royal and its dizzy farceurs for an unusual contemporary opéra-bouffe planned to capitalize on the forthcoming 1867 Great Exhibition. The work was in fact suggested by a one-act farce the authors had written for the same playhouse two years earlier, which was now craftily embroidered.
A Swedish baron and baroness come to Paris to see the Great Exhibition. At the railway station, a boulevardier, Raoul de Gardefeu, spies the attractive baroness and passes himself off as a tour guide. Raoul takes the couple to his house, which he passes off as an annexe of the Grand Hotel. While Raoul attempts to seduce the baroness, the baron insists that he be introduced to a courtesan, Métella, who was recently Gardefeu's lover. Stalling the baron for a while, Raoul invites him to dine with his glove-maker, his cobbler and their friends, passing themselves off as higher-class hotel guests. At another party at a vacant townhouse – arranged so that Raoul can spend some time alone with the baroness – a group of dressed-up servants carouse drunkenly with the baron. At the Café Anglais, a duel beween the baron and Gardefeu is prevented when Métella and the baroness reveal

that nothing at all happened the previous evening.

Though a thoroughly 'integrated' modern operetta, with gorgeous ensembles and finales, *La vie parisienne* harks back endearingly to the old vaudeville pattern of couplets so familiar to the Palais-Royal audiences. Offenbach was prevented from incorporating many of his usual vocal cadenzas by the fact that the company of the Palais-Royal were essentially actors rather than singers, but he made up with a wealth of memorable dance tunes. The two brilliant party scenes also influenced *Die Fledermaus* (1874), itself based on a Palais-Royal farce by Meilhac and Halévy.

La grande-duchesse de Gérolstein
The Grand Duchess of Gerolstein
Opéra-bouffe in three acts (2h 45m)
Libretto by Henri Meilhac and Ludovic Halévy
PREMIERES 12 April 1867, Théâtre des Variétés, Paris;
US: 24 September 1867, Théâtre Français, New York;
UK: 18 November 1867, Covent Garden, London

La grande-duchesse de Gérolstein, which was the Variétés' contribution to the 1867 Exhibition, was one of the great smash hits of 19th-century operetta. Effectively planned and marketed to coincide with a barrage of royal visitors to Paris, its satire at the expense of militaristic petty states and court intrigue – especially amorous – was directly on target.

Private Fritz of the Gerolstein army is in love with a peasant girl, Wanda. The grand duchess, reviewing her troops, falls for the private. When he explains his military strategy to her, she is so impressed that she makes him a general. In due time, he returns victorious from battle. All of this does not sit well with the displaced General Boum, who with his confederates plots to bring down Fritz. They are eventually joined by the grand duchess herself, exasperated by Fritz's coldness towards her. Fritz's honeymoon with Wanda is disrupted, and he becomes a private once more.

The score is less full of consistently great invention than its predecessors, despite a marvellous first act that is a model of bombastic silliness. More so than la belle Hélène, the grand duchess was a star part for Hortense Schneider, whose offstage reputation remained as loose as possible, perhaps partially for publicity purposes. The operetta was rapturously received around the world, no doubt preceded by whiffs of scandal. The craze for French opéra-bouffe in Britain and the US dates from the *Grande-duchesse*'s initial performances in those countries.

La Périchole
Perichole
Opéra-bouffe in two (later three) acts (2h 30m)
Libretto by Henri Meilhac and Ludovic Halévy, after the play *Le carrosse du Saint-Sacrement* (1830) by Prosper Mérimée
Composed 1868, rev. 1874
PREMIERES 6 October 1868, Théâtre des Variétés, Paris;
US: 4 January 1869, Pike's Opera House, New York; UK: 27 June 1870, Princess's Theatre, London; rev. version: 25 April 1874, Théâtre des Variétés, Paris

La Périchole is set in 18th-century Peru. The usual Meilhac–Halévy silliness is all there, but there is also a more sentimental vein in the leading character, which Offenbach exploited in several numbers, most famously the Act I letter song. The heroine's romantic predicament was still considered quite risqué by British audiences in 1875, when the operetta shared the bill with the first run of Gilbert and Sullivan's *Trial by Jury*.

The street singers La Périchole and Piquillo, much in love, are too poor even for a marriage licence. The viceroy, Don Andrès, is taken by La Périchole's beauty and wants her to move in to his palace as a lady-in-waiting. To do this officially, she must be a married woman, so the viceroy arranges for the lovesick Piquillo – who has just received a despairing farewell letter from his beloved – to marry La Périchole, without knowing her identity. The two are so tipsy by the time of their wedding that they do not recognize one another. Piquillo eventually recognizes her as his wife, and as the viceroy's favourite, and publicly humiliates her. For this, the viceroy has Piquillo dragged down to the dungeon reserved for recalcitrant husbands. Eventually the viceroy pardons them.

Offenbach's score is rich in Spanish (if not Peruvian) suggestions – boleros, seguidillas and fandangos abut galops, waltzes and marches – and is one of his most magical creations; the finales in particular are superb. *La Périchole* was restaged at the Variétés in 1874, in three (rather than two) acts. Since then, the operetta has had a chequered career, but certain productions have been very successful.

Les contes d'Hoffmann
The Tales of Hoffmann
Opéra fantastique in five acts (4h)
Libretto by Jules Barbier, based on the play by Jules Barbier and Michel Carré (1851), in turn based on several tales by E. T. A. Hoffmann, in particular *Der Sandman* (1816), *Rat Krespel* (1818) and *Die Abendteuer der Silvester-Nacht* (1815)
PREMIERES 10 February 1881, Opéra-Comique, Paris (orchestrated, re-arranged and with recitatives by Guiraud); US: 16 October 1882, Fifth Avenue Theater, New York; UK: 17 April 1907, Adelphi Theatre, London
CAST Hoffmann *t*, Nicklausse *ms* (sometimes also sings Muse *ms*, Voice of Antonia's Mother *ms*), Olympia *s* (sometimes also sings Antonia *s*, Giulietta *s*, Stella *s*), Lindorf *b* (also sings Coppélius *bar*, Dr Miracle *bar*, Dappertutto *b* or *bar*), Andrès *t* (also sings Cochenille *t*, Pittichinaccio *t*, Frantz *t*), Spalanzani *t*, Nathanael *t*, Crespel *b* or *bar*, Luther *b*, Hermann *b* or *bar*, Schlemil *b* or *bar*, Wolfram *t*, Wilhelm *b*; *satb* chorus of students, partygoers, Venetians, servants

One of the repertoire favourites, *Les contes d'Hoffmann* has been subjected to many well-intentioned alterations and, more recently, expansions seeking to provide either a satisfying evening at the opera or the format Offenbach perhaps would have wanted had he been alive at the premiere. The celebrated tales of fantasy by E. T. A. Hoffmann inspired many other composers for the stage, including Tchaikovsky, Adam, Audran, Hindemith, and previously Offenbach himself (*Le roi Carotte*, 1872).

The composition of *Les contes d'Hoffmann* (announced for the Gaîté-Lyrique season of 1877–8) taxed Offenbach's powers, especially as he was continually turning out operettas for other theatres to support his family. When bankruptcy hit the Gaîté-Lyrique, Offenbach continued composing. In May 1879, two years after he had begun the work, a *musicale* at his house featuring songs from the opera attracted the attention of Léon Carvalho, manager of the Opéra-Comique. Many of the recitatives were replaced by spoken dialogue, traditionally used at the Opéra-Comique, and vocal assignments were altered. When he died Offenbach had not completed much of Act IV or the end of Act V, nor begun the orchestration.

Shortly after Offenbach's death, Ernest Guiraud was asked to finish the work for production in early 1881. The original Venetian act was dropped entirely, except for the barcarolle, and the role of Nicklausse was shortened because of the star's vocal short-comings. Since it was Offenbach's habit to revise his works in the light of the public reaction to the premiere, we can never know what finished form *Les contes d'Hoffmann* might have taken. The closest we can come to the composer's original intentions is to follow the critical edition made by Fritz Oeser in 1977, which revokes alterations made in other performing versions and, drawing on original vocal parts and on sketches by Offenbach, restores missing passages and probably most nearly approaches the composer's conception.

SYNOPSIS

Act I In a German tavern, adjoining an opera house, the muse of the poet Hoffmann calls on spirits to separate him from his adored Stella, a diva. The muse becomes Nicklausse, Hoffmann's friend. The councillor Lindorf, rival for Stella's affections, plots to undo Hoffmann. During the interval of *Don Giovanni*, the tavern becomes filled with students, who prevail on Hoffmann to sing them a song about the deformed dwarf Kleinzach ('Il était une fois à la cour d'Eisenbach'). In the middle of the song, Hoffmann unexpectedly starts indulging in a reverie about Stella. Brought back to his senses, Hoffmann sees Lindorf, and tells his friends that the councillor has previously thwarted his love affairs. Mellowed by punch, he begins to describe them.

Act II Hoffmann is in love with a woman he thinks is the daughter of an inventor, Spalanzani. The inventor is afraid that Coppélius, who also specializes in gadgets – particularly eyes – will want a share of the profits from his latest invention, and offers to buy him out. The inventor introduces Olympia, the singing doll, to the public; Hoffmann sings of his love for her ('Ah, vivre deux'). While Olympia sings ('Les oiseaux dans la charmille'), Spalanzani winds her clockwork mechanism up whenever it runs down. Despite Nicklausse's warnings, Hoffmann is more and more enchanted by her, though somewhat surprised at her strange behaviour. When Coppélius returns, having been given a bad cheque, he destroys Olympia and Hoffmann finally realizes his error, to the public's delight.

Act III In Munich, Hoffmann has fallen in love with Antonia, seriously ill and hidden away by her father, Crespel, to prevent her from exerting herself. Although forbidden to, she sings ('Elle a fui, la tourterelle!'). Hoffmann finds her, and the two declare their

love ('C'est un chanson d'amour'). The evil Dr Miracle, who attended the death of Crespel's late wife, enters and proceeds to 'examine' Antonia by hypnosis, making her sing. Crespel forces Miracle out, but he returns, takes a violin, and urges Antonia to sing with the voice emanating from her mother's portrait. Antonia collapses as Hoffmann re-enters; the doctor declares her dead.

Act IV In Venice, Hoffmann listens to Nicklausse and the courtesan Giulietta sing a languorous barcarolle ('Belle nuit, o nuit d'amour'). Hoffmann has given up amorous adventures for the pleasures of wine. The shadowy Dappertutto tempts Giulietta with a diamond into obtaining Hoffmann's soul ('Scintille diamant'). Hoffmann falls in love with Giulietta ('O Dieu de quelle ivresse'), and they sing an ecstatic duet ('Si ta présence m'est ravie') during which Giulietta succeeds in obtaining the reflection of Hoffmann Dappertutto demanded. Hoffmann is drawn into a duel with Schlemil, a rival for Giulietta's hand. Hoffmann kills Schlemil, and obtains the key with which Giulietta is locked up at night, only to see his beloved disappearing in a gondola with Pittichinaccio.

Act V Back in the tavern, Nicklausse admits that Hoffmann's loves were different personifications of the same woman – Stella. She appears, but leaves the tavern on Lindorf's arm. Nicklausse reassumes the character of the muse and tells Hoffmann that his poetry will be enriched by his sorrow.

Although, shortly before his death, Offenbach sanctioned the replacement of his planned recitatives with spoken dialogue, *Les contes d'Hoffmann* is far removed from his much essayed operetta tradition. Serious in tone, it eschews the parodistic element of many previous works, instead following closely the combination of reality and fantasy, of the romantic and the grotesque, found in Hoffmann's writings. The removal of the need to ape Meyerbeer or Bellini, for example, allowed Offenbach the opportunity to formulate his own musical style – a style that was not, melodically or harmonically, hugely innovative, but could adapt more readily to a new type of dramatic pacing. Where simple strophic songs were previously presented in the most straightforward manner, here they are often the vehicles of some dramatic development, e.g. Antonia's aria 'Elle a fui, la tourterelle' (Act III) or in Hoffmann's telling of the legend of Kleinzach (Act I). Nevertheless, when appropriate, Offenbach was happy to echo earlier stylistic mannerisms, for instance Olympia's doll song, 'Les oiseaux dans la charmille', which, with its vocal virtuosity, conjures up an effective portrait of a mechanical toy. The famous barcarolle, 'Belle nuit, o nuit d'amour', had originally been composed for *Die Rheinnixen*, Offenbach's ill-fated German Romantic opera, but transferred happily to its Venetian setting; the drinking song that follows was also from that source.

Other operatic works: *L'alcôve*, 1847; *Le trésor à Mathurin*, 1853, rev. as *Le mariage aux lanternes*, 1857; *Pépito*, 1853; *Luc et Lucette*, 1854; *Oyayaie, ou La reine des îles*, 1855; *Entrez messieurs, mesdames*, 1855; *Les deux aveugles*, 1855; *Une nuit blanche*, 1855; *Le rêve d'une nuit d'été*, 1855; *Le violoneux*, 1855; *Madame Papillon*, 1855; *Paimpol et Périnette*, 1855; *Ba-ta-clan*, 1855; *Elodie, ou Le forfait nocturne*, 1856; *Le postillon en gage*, 1856; *Trombalcazar, ou Les criminels dramatiques*, 1856; *La rose de Saint-Flour*, 1856; *Les dragées du baptême*, 1856; *Le '66'*, 1856; *Le savetier et le financier*, 1856; *La bonne d'enfants*, 1856; *Les trois baisers du diable*, 1857; *Croquefer, ou Le dernier des paladins*, 1857; *Dragonette*, 1857; *Vent du soir, ou L'horrible festin*, 1857; *Une demoiselle en lôterie*, 1857; *Les deux pêcheurs*, 1857; *Mesdames de la Halle*, 1858; *La chatte métamorphosée en femme*, 1858; *Un mari à la porte*, 1859; *Les vivandières de la grande armée*, 1859; *Geneviève de Brabant*, 1859, rev. 1867 and 1875; *Le carnaval des revues*, 1860; *Daphnis et Chloé*, 1860; *Barkouf*, 1860 (rev. as *Boule de neige*, 1871); *La chanson de Fortunio*, 1861; *Le Pont des Soupirs*, 1861, rev. 1868; *M. Choufleuri restera chez lui le . . .* (?coll. with Duc de Morny), 1861; *Apothicaire et perruquier*, 1861; *Le roman comique*, 1861; *Monsieur et Madame Denis*, 1862; *Le voyage de MM. Dunanan père et fils*, 1862; *Les bavards*, 1862; *Jacqueline*, 1862; *Il Signor Fagotto*, 1864; *Lischen et Fritzchen*, 1864; *L'amour chanteur*, 1864; *Die Rheinnixen*, 1864; *Les Géorgiennes*, 1864; *Jeanne qui pleure et Jean qui rit*, 1864; *Le fifré enchanté, ou Le soldat magicien*, 1864; *Coscoletto, ou Le lazzarone*, 1865; *Les refrains des bouffes*, 1865; *Les bergers*, 1865; *La permission de dix heures*, 1867; *Robinson Crusoe*, 1867; *Le château à Toto*, 1868; *I'île de Tulipatan*, 1868; *Vert-vert*, 1869; *La diva*, 1869; *La princesse de Trébizonde*, 1869; *Les brigands*, 1869; *La romance de la rose*, 1869; *Mam'zelle Moucheron*, (c. 1870), rev. Delibes, 1881; *Le roi Carotte*, 1872; *Fantasio*, 1872; *Fleurette, oder Naherin und Trompeter*, 1872; *Der schwarze Korsar*, 1872; *La leçon de chant*, 1873; *Les braconniers*, 1873; *Pomme d'api*, 1873; *La jolie parfumeuse*, 1873; *Bagatelle*, 1874; *Madame l'archiduc*, 1874; *Whittington*, 1874; *Les Hannetons*, 1875; *La boulangère a des écus*, 1875; *La créole*, 1875; *Le voyage dans la lune*, 1875; *Tarte à la crème*, 1875; *Pierrette et Jacquot*, 1876; *La boîte au lait*, 1876; *Le docteur Ox*, 1877; *La foire Saint-Laurent*, 1877; *Maître Péronilla*, 1878; *Madame Favart*, 1878; *La marocaine*, 1879; *La fille du tambour-major*, 1879; *Belle Lurette* (completed Delibes), 1880

R. T.

P

GIOVANNI PAISIELLO

Giovanni Gregorio Cataldo Paisiello; *b* 9 May 1740,
Roccaforzata, nr Taranto, Italy; *d* 5 June 1816, Naples

Paisiello was one of the most prolific and successful
opera composers of his generation; his success was
matched only by that of Cimarosa. The exact number
of his operas is unknown but probably reaches 90.
His reputation thoughout Europe was at its highest
during the last two decades of the 18th century. After
about 1800 the popularity of his music declined due
to changes of taste which have never swung back in
his favour.

He received his musical education between 1754
and 1763 at the Conservatorio Sant'Ofronio in Naples,
and then in 1764 began a successful career as a freelance composer of opera. He became a court musician
for the first time in 1776, when he was appointed
music director at the court of the empress Catherine
II in St Petersburg. For the rest of his life he was
always in the employ of a European ruler: Catherine
II of Russia (whom he served from 1776 to 1784);
King Ferdinand IV of Naples (most of the period
1784–1806); Napoleon I (1802–4); King Joseph of
Naples (1806–8); King Joachim Murat of Naples
(1808–15); and finally King Ferdinand again (1815–
16). He did not want to go to Paris in 1802 to become
Napoleon's maître de chapelle, but was forced to as
part of a diplomatic agreement between King Ferdinand and Napoleon. He was not happy in Paris, and
returned to Naples two years later. Napoleon's friendship was, however, invaluable to him between 1806
and 1815, the years of the French occupation of
Naples. Napoleon's brother, Joseph, and Napoleon's
brother-in-law, Joachim Murat, occupied the throne
of Naples in turn, and both retained Paisiello's services
as court composer.

Paisiello produced a constant flow of new operas
for the theatres of Naples and elsewhere until the mid-
1790s. Thereafter his interest in opera gradually declined as his interest in religious music increased. His
late sacred compositions for the chapels of his royal
employers have never, however, acquired the fame of
his earlier works for the secular theatre. He himself
believed that some of his serious operas showed his
art at its best. Nowadays his reputation is based
primarily on his comic operas, for which his brand of
effervescent, melodious music is eminently suitable.

Il barbiere di Siviglia, ovvero La precauzione inutile

The Barber of Seville, or The Useless Precaution
Dramma giocoso per musica in four acts (2h)
Libretto by Giuseppe Petrosellini based on the play *Le
barbier de Seville* (1775) by Pierre-Augustin Caron de
Beaumarchais
PREMIERES 26 September 1782, Imperial Court, St
Petersburg; UK: 11 June 1789, His Majesty's Theatre,
Haymarket, London; US: 10 December 1805, Théâtre
Français, New Orleans
CAST Rosina *s*, Count Almaviva *t*, Figaro *bar*, Bartolo *b*,
Don Basilio *b*, Svegliato *b*, Giovinetto *t*, Notary *b*, Spanish
Sheriff *t*

Il barbiere di Siviglia is Paisiello's most well-known
opera and the best and most original one he composed
during his period in Russia. The subject was selected
in the knowledge that the empress Catherine was an
admirer of Beaumarchais, and the librettist was careful
to retain all the general features of the play (merely
reducing the number of words and translating what
was left into Italian verse). The rather uneven distribu-
tion of the arias and ensembles is a noticeable feature
of this work – Figaro's solos, for instance, all come
near the beginning. This seems the result of a conscious decision by Paisiello and his librettist to make
the music fit the action rather than vice versa.

The success of this opera when it reached Vienna in
1783 spurred Mozart and da Ponte to create a new
opera on Beaumarchais's *Le mariage de Figaro* (the
sequel to *Le barbier*). Many of the musical details of
Mozart's *Le nozze di Figaro* show Paisiello's influence.

For performances in Naples in 1787, Paisiello and
Giovanni Battista Lorenzi revised the opera in a
three-act form, modifying the work to suit local taste.
The original version remained more widely performed,
however.

Il barbiere was one of the few Paisiello works still
popular with the general public in 1816, when Rossini
composed his own *Il barbiere di Siviglia*. The audience
at the Rome premiere that year of the Rossini work
criticized him for having dared to compose an opera
on the same subject as Paisiello. However, opinion
changed once it was perceived that Rossini's was the
stronger setting.

SYNOPSIS
Act I Figaro, an itinerant barber, meets Count Alma-

viva who is courting Rosina, Bartolo's ward, disguised as a student. Bartolo wishes to marry Rosina himself and jealously guards her. Rosina drops the 'student' a message from her balcony. He sings her a serenade, declaring his name is 'Lindoro'.

Act II Figaro tells Rosina of 'Lindoro's' love and obtains from her a letter to give him. The count arrives, now disguised as a soldier billeted on Bartolo. His attempt to hand a written reply to Rosina miscarries, for Bartolo catches him. Rosina saves the situation by exchanging his letter for another.

Act III The count, dressed as 'Alonso', a supposed pupil of Don Basilio, the music master, meets Rosina (who still believes he is 'Lindoro') and gives her a music lesson. Don Basilio, knowing nothing of the count's stratagem, appears and is bribed to leave at once. Figaro shaves Bartolo while the lovers plan their escape. Bartolo breaks up their tête-à-tête.

Act IV At midnight, Bartolo, informed by Don Basilio, tells Rosina that 'Alonso' is an impostor believed to be an agent of Count Almaviva. Disillusioned, she reveals the escape plans. Bartolo goes off triumphantly to find the guard. The count and Figaro climb in at the window and meet Don Basilio and a notary ready with the marriage contract. Once Rosina is told of the count's identity and his love, she signs the contract. Bartolo returns too late, and the sheriff refuses to arrest the supposed housebreaker, recognizing the count.

Other operas: *Il Ciarlone* (*La pupilla*), 1764; *I Francesci brillanti*, 1764; *Madama l'umorista*, 1765; *L'amore in ballo*, 1765; *Le virtuose ridicole*, 1765; *Le nozze disturbate*, 1766; *Le finte contesse*, 1766; *La vedova di bel genio*, 1766; *Le imbroglie de le bajasse*, 1767, rev. as *La serva fatta padrona*, 1769; *L'idolo cinese*, 1767; *Lucio Papirio dittatore*, 1767; *Il furbo malaccorto*, 1767; *Olimpia*, 1768; *La luna abitata*, 1768; *La finta maga per vendetta*, 1768; *L'osteria di Marechiaro*, ?1769; *La Claudia vendicata*, ?1769; *Don Chisciotte della Mancia*, 1769; *L'arabo cortese*, 1769; *La Zelmira*, 1770; *Le trame per amore*, 1770; *Il Demetrio*, 1771; *Annibale in Torino*, 1771; *La somiglianza de' nomi*, 1771; *I scherzi di amore e di fortuna*, 1771; *Artaserse*, 1771; *La Semiramide in villa*, 1772; *Montezuma*, 1772; *La Dardané*, 1772; *Gli amanti comici*, 1772; *L'innocente fortunata*, 1773, rev. as *La semplice fortunata*, 1773; *Sismano nel Mogol*, 1773; *Il tamburo*, 1773, rev. as *Il tamburo notturno*, 1773; *Alessandro nell'Indie*, 1773; *Andromeda*, 1774; *Il duello*, 1774, rev. as *Il duello comico*, 1782; *Il credulo deluso*, 1774; *La frascatana*, 1774; *Il divertimento de' numi*, 1774; *Il Demofoonte*, 1775; *La discordia fortunata*, 1775; *Le astuzie amorose*, 1775; *Socrate immaginario*, 1775; *Il gran Cid*, 1775; *Le due contesse*, 1776; *La disfatta di Dario*, 1776; *Dal finto il vero*, 1776; *Nitteti*, 1777; *Lucinda ed Armidoro*, 1777; *Achille in Sciro*, 1778; *Lo sposo burlato*, 1778; *I filosofi immaginari*, 1779; *Il Demetrio*, 1779 (new setting); *Il matrimonio inaspettato*, 1779; *La finta amante*, 1780; *Alcide al bivio*, 1780; *La serva padrona*, 1781; *Il mondo della luna*, 1783; *Il re Teodoro in Venezia*, 1784; *Antigono*, 1785; *L'amore ingegnoso*, 1785; *La grotta di Trofonio*, 1785; *Olimpiade*, 1786; *Le gare generose* (later as *Gli schiavi per amore*), 1786; *Pirro*, 1787; *Giunone Lucina*, 1787; *La modista raggiratrice*, 1787; *Fedra*, 1788; *L'amor contrastato*, 1788; *Catone in Utica*, 1789; *Nina, o sia La pazza per amore*, 1789; *I zingari in fiera*, 1789; *Le vane gelosie*, 1790; *Zenobia in Palmira*, 1790; *Ipermestra*, 1791; *La locanda*, 1791, rev. as *Il fanatico in Berlina*, 1792; *I giuochi d'Agrigento*, 1792;

Elfrida, 1792; *Elvira*, 1794; *Didone abbandonata*, 1794; *La pace*, 1795; *La Daunia felice*, 1797; *Andromaca*, 1797; *L'inganno felice*, 1798; *Proserpine*, 1803; Epilogue to Simone Mayr's *Elisa*, 1807; *I Pittagorici*, 1808

M.F.R.

KRZYSZTOF PENDERECKI

b 23 November 1933, Dębica, Poland

Penderecki completed his composition studies at Cracow Music Academy in 1958, and thereafter quickly came to prominence. In 1959 he won the first and two second prizes in the composers' competition of the Polish Composers' Union. Soon afterwards, he received his first overseas commission (Donaueschingen Festival); since then his international fame has grown rapidly. His early, mainly instrumental, works are short, modern in musical language, and have a richness of expression which informs all his music. In some vocal works the sound of the words is actually more important than their meaning, and this feature persists in many more recent compositions. Devices such as the cluster and the glissando were also typical from the start.

In about 1964 a change came over Penderecki's music, connected with his growing interest in ritual and archaism. Elements of traditional musical styles from earlier periods (chords based on thirds, quasi-tonal harmony) are combined with modern techniques. He began to write large-scale choral, often religious, works (such as the *St Luke Passion* and *Utrenia*), as well as operas, using Gregorian or Orthodox chant and chorales. This is demonstrated in his operas, particularly the first two – *The Devils of Loudun* and *Paradise Lost*. Penderecki has written orchestral and chamber music, vocal works including oratorios, operas and more than 50 incidental and film scores. He has consistently espoused such universal subjects as evil and expiation, intolerance, fanaticism and death. His international success is due to the fact that his music appeals to a broader audience than most avant-garde music, which in its turn has led to Penderecki being criticized on the grounds that his music is superficial and intended purely for show.

The Devils of Loudun

Diably z Loudun

Opera in three acts (30 scenes) (2h 15m)

Libretto by the composer, based on John Whiting's dramatization (1961) of the novel by Aldous Huxley (1952), in the German translation by Erich Fried

Composed 1968–9, rev. 1972

PREMIERES 20 June 1969, Staatsoper, Hamburg; US: 14 August 1969, Opera Theater, Santa Fe, New Mexico; UK: 1 November 1973, Coliseum, London

CAST Grandier *bar*, Jeanne *dramatic s*, Father Barré *b*, Philippe *high lyric s*, de Laubardemont *t*, Father Mignon *t*, Adam *t*, Mannoury *bar*, Prince Henri de Condé *bar*, d'Armagnac *spoken role*, *s*, *ms*, 2 *c*, *b-bar*, *b*, *basso profondo*, 2 *spoken roles*; *satb* chorus of Ursuline nuns, Carmelites, people, children, guards, soldiers (often offstage)

The story of Father Grandier, who was burned at the stake in Loudun, near Poitiers, in 1634, has exerted a strong fascination for artists and writers. But Penderecki was more interested in the contemporary and universal symbolism of the subject than in its historical aspect. The number of characters and sub-plots in the play is reduced and the dialogues are shortened, the psychological change in Grandier is made less clear, and instead the accent is placed on his fight against fanaticism and evil.

SYNOPSIS

Act I The nuns of the Ursuline convent and their mother superior, Jeanne, have been seized with erotic obsession. Jeanne has had frequent sexual visions of Father Grandier, a handsome parish priest and ladies' man. She tells Father Mignon about them, and her confession is subsequently used against Grandier, as well as influencing the political battle between the town's governor and Cardinal Richelieu over the threatened dismantling of the town's fortifications.

Act II Exorcisms are performed on Jeanne. She tells how she and other nuns have been forced by Grandier to take part in a sexual orgy in the chapel. Further exorcisms (in effect torture) produce nothing of use to Grandier's enemies, but despite this he is arrested by de Laubardemont, the king's special commissioner.

Act III The innocent Grandier refuses to sign a confession. He is tortured and burned at the stake.

The opera's many-layered structure and division into short scenes bring it closer to the form of film, while demanding rapid and frequent change in the music itself, which is characterized by dramatic contrast and great expressive tensions. The characters sing, speak, laugh and scream; the chorus sings in the manner of Gregorian chant, but also shouts and screams. Such devices appeared in earlier works such as the *St Luke Passion*. There is no purely orchestral music; the instruments are mostly used in small groups to produce rapid changes in colour, or for solos.

Other operas: *Paradise Lost*, 1978; *Die schwarze Maske*, 1986; *Ubu Rex*, 1991

Z.C.

GIOVANNI BATTISTA PERGOLESI

b 4 January 1710, Jesi, nr Ancona, Italy; *d* 16 March 1736, Pozzuoli, nr Naples

Pergolesi's stage works include four serious operas, two comic operas, two intermezzi and a sacred drama. These were written during a period of less than six years in Pergolesi's short lifetime and were all first produced in Naples with the exception of his last opera seria, *L'Olimpiade*.

In any discussion of works attributed to Pergolesi, the question of authenticity is an overriding concern. This is particularly true of the many sacred works,

instrumental pieces and independent arias fraudulently inscribed with the celebrated name. This wholesale production of false Pergolesiana by unscrupulous publishers and copyists was a result of the resounding posthumous success of his intermezzo *La serva padrona* in Paris in 1752 and the ensuing battle of words – the so-called *querelle des bouffons* – between the partisans of French and Italian opera.

Nevertheless, with few exceptions, the authenticity of the Pergolesi *oeuvre* for the stage remains not only secure but well documented, even including a partial autograph of his last opera, *Il Flaminio*. Pergolesi also wrote an oratorio, *La morte di San Giuseppe*, a complete autograph of which has recently been authenticated. Among the relatively few Pergolesi misattributions for the stage are the intermezzo *Il maestro di musica* (a pasticcio based on Pietro Auletta's *Orazio*) and the comic opera *Il geloso schernito* (a 1746 work by the Venetian composer Pietro Chiarini, with an overture by Baldassare Galuppi).

Pergolesi was sent at an early age to study at the Conservatorio dei Poveri di Gesù Cristo in Naples. There he had the advantage of studying with such masters as Gaetano Greco, Leonardo Vinci and Francesco Durante. His sacred drama *La conversione e morte di San Guglielmo* was presented, probably as a conservatory exercise, at the monastery of Sant'Agnello in the summer of 1731. Later the same year, Pergolesi was commissioned to write his first opera seria, *La Salustia*, which was received with indifference when it was produced in January 1732. In sharp contrast, his first comic opera, *Lo frate 'nnamorato*, presented later in the same year, was an unqualified success.

Pergolesi's second opera seria, *Il prigionier superbo*, is best known as the conduit for the intermezzo placed between its acts, the immortal *La serva padrona* (1733). The following year saw another intermezzo, *Livietta e Tracollo*, sandwiched between the acts of Pergolesi's third, and perhaps most powerful, opera seria, *Adriano in Siria*. Pergolesi's two final works for the stage were produced in 1735: the opera seria *L'Olimpiade*, in Rome, and the commedia musicale *Il Flaminio*, in Naples.

The diversity of style among these works is remarkable: from the buffo scenes of *La conversione e morte di San Guglielmo* to the virtuosic and extended arias of *Adriano in Siria*; from the folklike canzonas of *Lo frate 'nnamorato* to the delicate and expressive arias of *L'Olimpiade*. They reflect in microcosm the vast stylistic range of much of Pergolesi's non-dramatic work: from the simple textures of his Violin Sonata to the multitudinous sonorities of his Mass in F; from the sensitivity of his *Stabat Mater* to the virtuosity of his Violin Concerto.

Aside from *La serva padrona* and the *Stabat Mater* – which have been performed almost continually since their creation – Pergolesi performances were uncommon until a relatively recent renewal of scholarly interest in the composer.

La serva padrona

The Maid Turned Mistress
Intermezzo in two parts (50m)

Libretto by Gennarantonio Federico
PREMIERES 28 August 1733, Teatro San Bartolomeo, Naples; UK: 27 March 1750, His Majesty's Theatre, Haymarket, London; US: 13 June 1790, Baltimore
CAST Uberto *b*, Serpina *s*, Vespone *silent*

La serva padrona is one of the most universally popular works in the operatic repertoire. Also one of the most influential of stage works, it served as a model for Jean-Jacques Rousseau in his polemic war against French opera and long served as a prototype of the opera-buffa style. The sparkling and witty score is comprised of a brief instrumental introduction and two separate parts, each of which contains both spoken and sung passages and includes an aria for each principal as well as a duet.

SYNOPSIS
Part I Uberto, a bachelor, complains about the incompetence and wilfulness of his maidservant, Serpina, who rules the household with an iron hand and keeps him waiting for his chocolate. He instructs his servant, Vespone, to find him a wife, no matter how ugly, who will bow to his wishes. Overhearing this, Serpina asks her master to take her as his wife, but Uberto refuses.

Part II Serpina conspires with Vespone to trick her master into marrying her. She tells Uberto that she intends to marry a certain Captain Tempest. When her master asks to meet this soldier suitor, she produces Vespone in disguise. Then she informs him that the silent captain requires a dowry or else he will insist that Uberto marry Serpina in his place. Uberto, choosing what he considers to be the lesser of two evils, agrees to marry his servant. When Vespone pulls off his false moustache and reveals his true identity, Uberto realizes that he loves Serpina. Her future as mistress of the house is secured.

Among the outstanding arias in the first part are Uberto's frivolous 'Sempre in contrasti' and Serpina's peevish 'Stizzoso, mio stizzoso'. A highlight of the second part is Serpina's reflective aria 'A Serpina penserete', in which she at first appears to have a softer side. However, later in the same aria, her true nature is revealed. The music of Uberto's aria 'Son imbrogliato io già' is capricious, with alternating buffo and serious elements, thus reflecting his uncertain feelings towards Serpina.

Other operatic works: La conversione e morte di San Guglielmo, 1731; La Salustia, 1732; Lo frate 'nnamorato, 1732; Il prigionier superbo, 1733; Adriano in Siria, 1734; Livietta e Tracollo, ossia La contadina astuta, 1734; L'Olimpiade, 1735; Il Flaminio, 1735;

M.E.P.

JACOPO PERI

b 20 August 1561, ?Rome; *d* on or before 12 August 1633, Florence

Peri is often known as the 'inventor' of opera. He studied in Florence with Cristofano Malvezzi and began his career in various musical positions in churches in the city. In the 1580s he was enrolled among the musicians at the Medici court as a tenor and keyboard-player. He made his début as a composer for court entertainments with music for the first intermedio (entr'acte) of Giovanni Fedini's Le due Persilie (16 February 1583). In 1589 Peri participated in the magnificent festivities for the wedding of Grand Duke Ferdinando I de' Medici and Christine of Lorraine, most prominently in the spectacular intermedi that accompanied the performance of Girolamo Bargagli's comedy La pellegrina (Peri composed and performed an echo madrigal for the fifth intermedio). The 1589 wedding, and indeed the reign of Grand Duke Ferdinando I (reg. 1587–1609), marked a glorious 'Indian summer' in Florence's chequered history. It also initiated a decade of exciting experiment in dramatic entertainments, in part because of the presence of Emilio de' Cavalieri, a Roman now in charge of the court music.

In the 1590s, Peri became associated with the leading patron of music in Florence, Jacopo Corsi. Corsi and the artists under his protection took their lead from the so-called Florentine Camerata headed by Giovanni de' Bardi and active in the 1580s. Both groups speculated on the modern arts and their aesthetic position – some felt inadequacy – compared with classical Greece and Rome. Corsi, perhaps in competition with Cavalieri, encouraged Peri and the poet Ottavio Rinuccini to experiment on a new theatrical genre that would merge drama with music in the manner that many assumed was typical of classical tragedy. Their first collaboration, Dafne, was begun in 1594; it was staged semi-privately in early 1598, 1599 and 1600, and before the court (and the duke of Parma) on 26 December 1604. Only fragments survive.

Rinuccini's and Peri's next collaboration, Euridice, was performed during the festivities celebrating the marriage of Maria de' Medici and Henri IV of France in October 1600. It is the first opera to have survived complete (the score was published in early 1601). The 1600 wedding was a decisive political event for Florence, and clearly the idea was to match the occasion with novel entertainments. As well as Peri's new opera (again sponsored by Corsi) there was a musico-dramatic spectacle by the poet Gabriello Chiabrera, Il rapimento di Cefalo, with music by Giulio Caccini and others. The performance of Euridice was marred by Caccini's insisting that his singers should sing his and not Peri's music, and the work was not a success. Indeed, the Medici seem to have been unenthusiastic about opera, perhaps because it was less suited to providing the blatant propaganda they required of court entertainments. By the time Peri next contributed to Medici wedding festivities, for the marriage of Prince Cosimo de' Medici and Maria Magdalena of Austria in 1608, the court had reverted to the tried-and-tested formula of a comedy with spectacular intermedi that had proved so successful in 1589. Opera took root elsewhere, notably in Mantua in the hands of Claudio Monteverdi.

During the reign of Grand Duke Cosimo II (reg. 1609–1621) Peri continued to write music for court tournaments, ballets, intermedi and other entertainments, particularly as Caccini's star waned. He generally collaborated with other Florentine musicians, especially Marco da Gagliano. Most of this music is lost, apart from a few items scattered in Florentine prints and manuscripts. Peri's chamber songs, published as Le varie musiche in 1609 (reprinted in 1619), also reflect music-making in a courtly environment, while his reputation was emphasized first by a performance of Euridice in Bologna on 27 April 1616 and then by commissions for theatrical performances in Mantua in 1620.

In the 1620s Peri collaborated with Giovanni Battista da Gagliano (Marco's brother) on several sacre rappresentazioni (sacred dramas) performed by the leading confraternity in the city, the Compagnia dell'Arcangelo Raffaello. They matched the new religious climate in Counter-Reformation Florence. However, although Peri continued to provide entertainment and other music for the court, he increasingly retired from official duties, whether because of age and other business interests, or just because of the distaste of a nobleman (as he claimed he was) for practical activity. His last known involvement in court entertainments was for the wedding of Margherita de' Medici and Duke Odoardo Farnese of Parma in 1628. Peri collaborated with the poet Andrea Salvadori (1591–1635) on a new opera, Iole ed Ercole, which was eventually abandoned through the machinations of Francesca Caccini. He then contributed to Marco da Gagliano's opera La Flora, which was performed at the wedding and later published. Peri provided the recitatives for the part of Clori in a style that was becoming rather old-fashioned in the face of newer developments in opera.

Euridice

Favola in musica in a prologue and one act
Libretto by Ottavio Rinuccini, after Book X of Ovid's
Metamorphoses
PREMIERE 6 October 1600, Palazzo Pitti, Florence
CAST La Tragedia (Tragedy) s, Orfeo (Orpheus) t,
Euridice (Eurydice) s, Plutone (Pluto) b, Proserpina s,
Venere (Venus) s, Aminta t, Arcetro a; satb choruses of
nymphs and shepherds, infernal deities

Euridice is based on classical myth, and concerns a demi-god with famed musical powers. The representation of Orpheus' musical magic, an important self-justification for early opera, was to challenge many later composers. Peri himself sang the title role, and another virtuoso tenor, Francesco Rasi, the role of Aminta. (Rasi later sang the title role in Monteverdi's Orfeo.) At the first performance, the continuo group included a harpsichord (played by Jacopo Corsi), a chitarrone, a lirone and a 'liuto grosso'.

There are no scene divisions in the libretto or the score, although the work is in three sections reckoning by setting (earth–Hades–earth), and in five according to the strophic choruses (on classical precedent). Orpheus' bride, Eurydice, dies of a snakebite. He descends to Hades, guided by Venus, to plead with Pluto, king of the underworld, for her return. Now Rinuccini deviates from the myth, as was perhaps inevitable in a wedding entertainment. Pluto, charmed

by Orpheus' singing, releases Eurydice, and the couple return to earth and universal celebration.

Rinuccini and Peri were anxious to connect Euridice with classical tragedy ('Tragedy' sings the prologue). Thus they linked the opera to humanist inquiry in what was perhaps the last flowering of the Florentine Renaissance. But the humanist resonances were intended largely for the sake of academic respectability, as a way of justifying the apparently unrealistic use of music on stage, and Peri eventually admitted (in the preface to his score) that the parallels with Greek and Roman practice were at best tenuous. In fact the opera is entirely typical of its time: it takes over many characteristics of the intermedi, including the mythological subject and particular scenic effects (especially the inferno scene), and belongs generically to the modern pastoral drama recently established by Torquato Tasso's Aminta and Battista Guarini's Il pastor fido.

Euridice contains strophic arias, choruses and instrumental items. But its most distinctive feature, emphasized as such in Peri's preface, is the recitative, a declamatory musical style midway between speech and song. Here Peri developed a free style of writing for the new combination of solo voice and basso continuo that closely followed the form and content of Rinuccini's fine text, matching its emotional and dramatic peaks by intense vocal lines and often exploiting chromaticism and dissonance in a manner reminiscent of contemporary polyphonic madrigals. The reaction of observers was mixed – some felt that the result was too much 'like the chanting of the Passion' – and clearly the opera was on too intimate a scale to impress a court accustomed to spectacular scenic extravaganzas. However, for the first time a musical style for solo voice flexible enough to respond to dramatic effect appeared on stage. The lessons offered by Peri were taken to heart by many early opera composers, not least Monteverdi.

Other stage works: 'Dunque fra torbid'onde' (part of Intermedio 5 for G. Bargagli's La pellegrina, 1589; in Intermedio et concerti . . ., 1591); Dafne, 1598; 'Poichè la notte con l'oscure piume' (final chorus Act III, of Buonarroti's Il giudizio di Paride), 1608; music with new text in Peri's Le varie musiche, 1609; Mascherata di ninfe di Senna (coll. with Marco da Gagliano, Francesca Caccini et al.), 1611; one song in Piero Benedetti, Musiche, 1611; ?untitled tournament (coll. with Marco da Gagliano, Lorenzo Allegri), 1613; La Flora (coll. with Marco da Gagliano), 1628; Iole ed Ercole (one lament survives in manuscript), (1628); c. 18 lost works

T.C.

HANS PFITZNER

Hans Erich Pfitzner; b 5 May 1869, Moscow; d 22 May 1949, Salzburg

Pfitzner was born in Moscow because his father, a Saxon choirmaster, happened to be working there as a violinist. The family soon returned to Frankfurt. Once the young Pfitzner had completed his musical education, he became a teacher and then kapellmeister at the Theater des Westens in Berlin; later he was appointed director of the Strasburg Conservatory and conductor of the symphony orchestra. From 1910 he was director of the opera there, joined in 1914 by Otto Klemperer as his deputy. His first two operas (exactly contemporary with Richard Strauss's *Guntram* and *Feuersnot*) had impressed Humperdinck and Mahler favourably, and for a few years they were performed on many German stages. As with all his stage works, their subjects were consciously Teutonic and Christian.

Pfitzner's interest turned to symphonic music. He had begun as a gentle post-Wagnerian modernist (with a lifelong devotion to the pessimistic philosopher Schopenhauer), but he felt growing dismay at the radicalism of Schoenberg and Busoni, and published angry polemics against their malign influence. His *Palestrina* is plainly a declaration of loyalty to conservative tradition – about which his writings found nothing very articulate to say, beyond reiterating his faith in lyrical spontaneity. Two comparably ambitious imposing works followed later, the huge cantata *Von deutscher Seele* (1921) and the 'choral fantasy' *Das dunkle Reich* (1929).

Notoriously, the first of these came to be venerated within the Nazi movement – which had certainly not inspired it, although until 1936 Pfitzner's career certainly throve with the Nazis. There are conflicting accounts of what his real political sentiments were (as also of his character: sour and waspish; contrariwise, humane and witty). In any case, the end of the Second World War found him bombed out of his Munich house and soon to face a denazification court, his public credit severely devalued. His miserable last years were spent in a Munich old people's home. Shortly before he died, the Vienna Philharmonic Society found him a house in Salzburg, and his 80th birthday was decently celebrated in the Austro-German musical world.

The international musical world has been gingerly about reviving Pfitzner. Among German works from between the wars, Hindemith's are neglected, and only Richard Strauss's have been steadily honoured: one effect of the radical revelations from the Schoenberg–Berg–Webern axis has been the dismissal of lesser conservative composers from hearing. Since Pfitzner counts (by stern recent standards) as unrigorous and sentimentally eclectic, he must survive – or not – by his individual lyrical stamp and his knack for broad, intuitive construction. As the winds of fashion veer this way and that, his music will doubtless enjoy intensive short-term rediscoveries.

Palestrina

Musikalische Legende in three acts (3h 30m)
Libretto by the composer, after historical sources
Composed 1912–15
PREMIERES 12 June 1917, Prinzregententheater, Munich; UK: 10 June 1981, Collegiate Theatre, London; US: 14 May 1982, Berkeley, California (concert)
CAST Pope Pius IV *b*, 2 Cardinal Papal Legates: Giovanni Morone *bar* and Bernardo Novagerio *t*, Cardinal Christoph Madruscht, Prince Bishop of Trent *b*, Carlo Borromeo, Cardinal from Rome *bar*, Cardinal of Lothringen [Lorraine]

b, Abdisu, Patriarch of Assyria *t*, Anton Brus von Müglitz, Archbishop of Prague *b*, Count Luna, Orator to the King of Spain *bar*, Bishop of Budoja *t*, Theophilus, Bishop of Imola *t*, Avosmediano, Bishop of Cadiz *b-bar*, Giovanni Pierluigi Palestrina *t*, Ighino *s*, Silla *ms*, Bishop Ercole Severolus, Master-of-ceremonies at the Council of Trent *b-bar*, Singers of the Chapel of Santa Maria Maggiore 2 *t*, 3 *b*; 9 great dead composers 3 *t*, 3 *bar*, 3 *b*; angelic voices 3 *s*, Lucrezia's spirit *s*; 2 papal nuncios; Lainez and Salmeron, Jesuits; Massarelli, Bishop of Thelesia, Secretary of the Council; Giuseppe, Palestrina's aged servant, *silent*; *satb* chorus of singers from the papal chapel, archbishops, bishops, abbots, heads of religious orders, envoys, ambassadors (procurators) of princes spiritual and temporal, theologians, scholars from all Christendom, servants, soldiers, crowd

Many a work has been designed as a *magnum opus* without attaining any such status, but in its crotchety way *Palestrina* succeeds. Though it deploys awkwardly many performers for a very long time, it justifies its overweening proportions as creditably as it represents Pfitzner's best strengths. The proportions are wilfully odd, with two quite disparate 90-minute acts – visibly linked only by the figure of Cardinal Borromeo – followed by a third which takes a mere half-hour. Preparing his libretto, Pfitzner had immersed himself in the history of the Council of Trent for two years. The 'historical' gist of his operatic conclusions is this: in 1563 the aged Palestrina composed his *Missa Papae Marcelli*, thereby reaffirming the eternal spirit of pure music, and triumphantly persuading the Roman Church not to relinquish it. It is irrelevant that every clause of that proposition is now thought dubious (Palestrina was under 40 in 1563). There is no romantic interest, nor any real note of tragedy – only Palestrina's private despair, and his wry acquiescence in fame. A seasoned opera company is presupposed: the central Council act depends on a ripe team of singing actors who know how to play to one another. The premiere was conducted by Bruno Walter.

SYNOPSIS

Act I Rome, November 1563. Palestrina's pupil Silla has written a new song in the avant-garde Florentine style. His master's son Ighino joins him, and they worry over the ageing composer's gloomy lethargy since the death of his wife, Lucrezia. Palestrina enters with an old friend, Cardinal Borromeo, who warns him that the Council of Trent – nearing its conclusion after 18 years – may resolve to ban polyphonic church music in favour of plainchant, recoiling from fashionably over-ornamented, verbally opaque settings. Borromeo wants Palestrina to compose a Mass that will persuade Pius IV that polyphony can be properly devout. The weary composer declines: nothing has any meaning for him now. Borromeo departs angrily; but, while Palestrina drowses, his great musical ancestors – Josquin, Isaac et al. – appear to urge him on. Angels in glory prompt his *Missa Papae Marcelli* as he begins to write, and his wife's spirit comforts him. After dawn, the boys find him asleep before the completed Mass.

Act II At Trent, the Council is lengthily embroiled in national and personal rivalries. Merely *en passant*, the topic of sacred music is raised; Borromeo reports that he has commanded a Mass from Palestrina, who after steadfastly refusing has been imprisoned. The act ends with a punitive slaughter of embattled hangers-on and rabble.

Act III Back home two weeks later, the dazed composer learns that his secret Mass is being sung in St Peter's: to save him from punishment, his S. Maria Maggiore choristers have handed over the parts to the authorities. The papal singers arrive, full of praise, and then the delighted pope himself comes with Borromeo and an entourage to demand Palestrina's life-long services. Borromeo exults (but Silla has decamped to Florence); the composer resigns himself to his destiny, and begins to muse at the organ.

To the static outer acts, Pfitzner's idiosyncratic art lends subtle musical lines as well as pungent character, and Borromeo's long dramatic monologue in Act I is a *tour de force*. In our 'authenticity'-conscious time the grand close of Act I sounds touchingly dated, with its 'Palestrina' fragments drenched in celestial harps. But Pfitzner never lapses here into plaintive sentiment; and his sardonic sketch of committee futility in Act II is brilliantly calculated for variety and pace. (None of the debate is theological, but any performance must either be sung in the audience's language or enlist surtitles.) A vision is transmitted with considerable power, and it is not a simple one. At the end, Palestrina's tight-lipped reaction to his 'triumph' and the significant absence of young Silla – whose defection to the trendy Florentines is not rebuked – leave an astringent aftertaste. To the extent that *Palestrina* is a grandiose exercise in self-exposure, it eschews self-justification: it is sadder, wiser and more far-sighted than that. The wealth of invention in Pfitzner's score speaks for itself.

Other operatic works: *Der arme Heinrich*, 1895; *Die Rose vom Liebesgarten*, 1901; *Das Christ-Elflein*, 1906, rev. 1917; *Das Herz*, 1931

D.M.

AMILCARE PONCHIELLI

b 31 August 1834, Paderno Fasolaro (now Paderno Ponchielli), nr Cremona, Italy; *d* 17 January 1886, Milan

Ponchielli, of humble origins, received his first musical instruction at home. His talents were recognized early, however, and he was admitted to the Milan Conservatory on a scholarship at the age of nine. He remained there for 11 years (the last three studying composition with Alberto Mazzucato), and graduated in 1854.

He returned to Cremona as a church organist, and for the next 18 years from there and nearby Piacenza he attempted to establish himself as an opera composer. *I promessi sposi* (1856), to a libretto the composer himself probably hacked from Alessandro Manzoni's epic novel, had some local success, but failed to interest directors of important theatres. An extensive revision of this score, to a new text by Emilio Praga, premiered in Milan at the Teatro dal Verme in 1872,

would prove his means of escape from the provinces. Before that lucky event, he composed three more operas, none of which produced the desired impression. The first of them was rejected after being rehearsed in Turin, the second was a turning back to the outworn semiseria genre, and the third received only one performance.

The revised *I promessi sposi* was the pivotal event in Ponchielli's career. It brought him an invitation to compose a ballet for La Scala, *Le due gemelle* (1873), which won him a contract with the publishing house of Ricordi. The prima donna of the refashioned *I promessi sposi*, Teresina Brambilla, married Ponchielli in 1874 (and her relatives harried him for the rest of his life). His reputation, improving with his next work, *I lituani* (1874), was solidified by *La Gioconda* (1876). This work entered the international repertoire. His last two operas were respectfully received but have failed to find a place in the repertoire.

In 1880, Ponchielli became professor of composition at the Milan Conservatory, where he taught Puccini and, briefly, Mascagni. Two years later he assumed the additional duties of maestro di cappella at S. Maria Maggiore in Bergamo. He held both these positions until his death.

As an opera composer, Ponchielli has frequently been dismissed as crude and vulgar, but such snap judgements do not really describe his capacities. Afflicted by torturing self-doubt, he frequently arrived at his ideas by a painful process of trial and error, as the compositional sketches for La Cieca's 'Voce di donna' in Act I of *La Gioconda* and the progressive transmogrifications that four of his operas underwent demonstrate. None the less, he is said to have composed 'The Dance of the Hours' (*La Gioconda*, Act III) at a single sitting. He possessed a gift both for creating atmosphere, as in the prisoners' chorus of *I lituani*, and for powerful dramatic confrontations, witness the final duet for Gioconda and Barnaba. His works show considerable skill in laying out large-scale structures coherently, and many passages are impressive for their adroit orchestration. His influence on Puccini is evident in the concertato in *Edgar* and in des Grieux's impassioned outburst in the embarkation scene of *Manon Lescaut*, which inevitably reminds one of Gioconda's 'Suicidio!' And the intermezzo from *Il figliuol prodigo* set an example that was not lost on Mascagni and the other *veristi*. As an Italian opera composer attempting to launch himself in the mid-1850s, Ponchielli, unlike Verdi, had no firm underpinning in the flourishing tradition of the 1830s, and as a result he laboured and forged a personal idiom, which would later serve Mascagni, Puccini, and other members of the 'Young Italian School' as a point of departure.

La Gioconda

The Ballad Singer (literally, *The Joyful Girl*)
Dramma lirico in four acts (2h 30m)
Libretto by 'Tobia Gorrio' (Arrigo Boito), loosely based on the play *Angelo, tyran de Padoue* by Victor Hugo (1835)
Composed 1874–5; rev. 1876, 1877, 1880
PREMIERES 8 April 1876, La Scala, Milan; first rev. version: 18 October 1876, Teatro Rossini, Venice; second

rev. version: January 1877, Rome; definitive version: 12 February 1880, La Scala, Milan; UK: 31 May 1883, Covent Garden, London; US: 20 December 1883, Metropolitan, New York

CAST La Gioconda *s*, La Cieca *c*, Alvise Badoero *b*, Laura *ms*, Enzo Grimaldo *t*, Barnaba *bar*, Zuàne *bar*, Singer *b*, Isèpo *t*, Pilot *b*; *satb* chorus of monks, senators, sailors, shipwrights, ladies, gentlemen, populace, maskers, guards; ballet

Boito's libretto bears but a slight resemblance to Hugo's play. He transferred the action from Padua to Venice, as the latter afforded more opportunities for spectacle and local colour. He changed the names of the characters and reduced the role of Alvise (Hugo's Angelo) to a subordinate one. During the series of revisions, he telescoped motivation to the point of occasional obscurity, sacrificing credibility for harsh contrasts, laden with irony.

SYNOPSIS

Act I: 'The Lion's Mouth'   The greedy Barnaba wants to possess the street-singer Gioconda, but she rejects him. In revenge, he stirs up the crowd to believe that her blind mother, La Cieca, is a witch. They are about to drag the pious old woman away, when Enzo, a Genoese noble in exile in Venice disguised as a fisherman, attempts to save her. Alvise appears with his wife, Laura, who is masked, and quells the riot. In gratitude, La Cieca gives a rosary to Laura ('Voce di donna'). Enzo recognizes Laura, whom he had loved before her marriage, and Gioconda is filled with passionate gratitude toward Enzo. Barnaba, however, knows Enzo's true identity and offers to arrange for him a rendezvous with Laura on Enzo's brigantine ('Enzo Grimaldo, principe di Santafior'). Alone, Barnaba concocts a letter, denouncing Enzo to the Council of Ten.

Act II: 'The Rosary'   Fishermen gather on the wharf and Barnaba is on hand to watch developments ('Pescator'). Enzo comes on deck to await Laura ('Cielo e mar!'). Laura is rapturously greeted ('Deh, non turbare'), but, when Enzo leaves to attend to their departure, Gioconda appears and faces her rival ('L'amo come il fulgor del creato!'). Suddenly Alvise's ship is seen approaching; Laura prays to the Virgin for help and, recognizing her rosary, Gioconda determines to rescue her mother's saviour. Enzo returns to find not Laura but Gioconda, who alerts him to his danger, whereupon Enzo sets fire to his ship and they escape.

Act III: 'The House of Gold'   Scene 1. Alvise plans revenge on his unfaithful wife. He commands her to drink poison ('Morir! è troppo orribile!'), but Gioconda emerges from hiding and substitutes a sleeping potion for the poison. Scene 2. At Alvise's mansion, the Ca d'Oro, guests are entertained by 'The Dance of the Hours'. Enzo is shocked that these festivities are going on while Laura lies 'dead' in the next room, and tries to stab Alvise. Alvise orders Enzo's arrest, but Gioconda tells Barnaba she will submit to him to save Enzo.

Act IV: 'The Orfano Canal'   Gioconda contemplates suicide ('Suicidio!'). Enzo is furious when he learns she has brought Laura's body to her house.

Soon Laura returns to consciousness, and Gioconda sends the lovers away to safety ('Quest' ultimo bacio'). Awaiting Barnaba, Gioconda tries to pray. He appears, but, as he moves to embrace her, she stabs herself ('Ebbrezza! Delirio!'). Frustrated, Barnaba tells her corpse that he has thrown La Cieca into a canal.

La Gioconda can produce a powerful effect, especially when well sung, though oddly enough its best-known moment, the ballet divertissement 'The Dance of the Hours', is a non-vocal one. There are a number of unconventional arias: La Cieca's 'Voce di donna'; the spy Barnaba's soliloquy 'O monumento' (Act I); Enzo's tenor *romanza* 'Cielo e mar!'; and Gioconda's monologue in Act IV. There are also three dramatic duets: for the rivals, Gioconda and Laura, in Act II; for Alvise and Laura in Act III; and at the end between the desperate Gioconda feigning gaiety and Barnaba as he gloats at the prospect of possessing her. The chorus is treated prominently in *La Gioconda*, and the concertato at the end of Act III develops momentum on a truly grandiose scale. A particular feature of Ponchielli's style is a fortissimo peroration of a prominent tune, as at the close of the concertato or at the end of the trio in Act IV, a practice not lost on the composers of the next generation.

La Gioconda, along with *Aida*, is representative of the absorption during the 1870s of the spectacular effects of French grand opera, including the insertion of ballet into the plot, coupled with overtly emotional Italian vocalism, to produce an amalgamated 'international' style. Apart from its occasional disjointedness, both musically and dramatically, *La Gioconda* exemplifies both the strengths and the weaknesses of a particular aspect of Italian operatic history.

Other operas: *I promessi sposi*, 1856, rev. 1872; *Bertrando dal Bormio*, (1858); *La savoiarda*, 1861, rev. 1870, rev. as *Lina*, 1877; *Roderico, re dei Goti*, 1863; *Il parlatore eterno*, 1873; *I Lituani*, 1874, rev. 1875 and, as *Aldona*, 1884; *I mori di Valenza* (inc., 1874; completed by A. Cadore, 1911), 1914; *Il figliuol prodigo*, 1880; *Marion Delorme*, 1885

W.A.

COLE PORTER

Cole Albert Porter; *b* 9 June 1891, Peru, Indiana, US; *d* 15 October 1964, Santa Monica, California, US

Unlike most of the Broadway song-writers of his time, Cole Porter was born into affluence and avoided the Tin-Pan-Alley, rehearsal-accompanist and amateur-show routes to theatre composition. His interest in music, though it diverted him from the law career his family had planned for him, did not bring him to Broadway on a regular basis until he agreed to write the score for *Paris* in 1928. Thereafter he became a regular contributor to the Broadway scene.

His earlier work tended to feature Parisian locales and naughty lyrics that sometimes provoked trouble with radio censors. His subsequent efforts from the 1930s, with the exception of *Anything Goes*, are never revived, due to libretti deemed hopelessly dated; as with Gershwin and Rodgers and Hart, such a harsh verdict may be undeserved in certain cases. In particular, *Jubilee*, with a libretto by Moss Hart and a workable comic premiss of a royal family taking time off from its duties, might merit investigation; its score would be no problem, boasting as it does 'Why Shouldn't I?', 'A Picture of Me without You', 'Begin the Beguine' and 'Just One of Those Things'. Other shows from this period with well-remembered Porter songs include *Gay Divorce* ('Night and Day'), *Red, Hot and Blue!* ('Ridin' High', 'It's De-Lovely'), *Leave It to Me* ('My Heart Belongs to Daddy', sung and stripteased by Mary Martin in her Broadway début), and *DuBarry Was a Lady* ('Friendship').

Porter's string of successes, only temporarily interrupted in 1937 when a riding accident permanently damaged his legs and left him in pain for the rest of his life, reached a climax with the classic *Kiss Me, Kate*. Though too often stereotyped as a purveyor of either throbbing ballads with a Latin beat or ultrachic 'list' songs, Porter commanded a wide stylistic range, and adapted himself to changing tastes over the years. His music is especially notable for its balance between passion and a chaste coolness, while his lyrics are acknowledged as gems of wit and romance.

Anything Goes

Musical comedy in two acts (1h 45m)
Libretto by Guy Bolton and P. G. Wodehouse, revised by Howard Lindsay and Russell Crouse; lyrics by the composer
PREMIERES 21 November 1934, Alvin Theater, New York; UK: 14 June 1935, Palace Theatre, London

Taking place mostly on board an ocean liner, this farce of flirtation and disguise (originally starring Ethel Merman) remains one of the more revived 1930s musicals because of its wonderful score: 'I Get a Kick out of You', 'All through the Night', 'You're the Top', 'Blow, Gabriel, Blow' and the title song. The New York revivals of 1962 and 1987 (the latter especially well executed) have been recorded; each involved libretto changes, deletion of songs, and interpolation of other Porter songs.

Kiss Me, Kate

Musical play in two acts (1h 45m)
Libretto by Sam and Bella Spewack, based on the play *The Taming of the Shrew* by William Shakespeare (1593–4); lyrics by the composer
PREMIERES 30 December 1948, New Century Theater, New York; UK: 8 March 1951, Coliseum, London
CAST Fred Graham (Petruchio) *bar*, Lilli Vanessi (Kate) *s*, Lois Lane (Bianca) *ms*, Bill Calhoun (Lucentio) *t/dancer*, 2 men *bar*, Hattie *c*, Paul *bar*; other roles from *satb* chorus of actors

The combination of a musicalized *Taming of the Shrew* with the troupe enacting it provided Porter with the context for his richest and most consistently inspired score. It is the only one that has maintained a constant performance history, and was the proof that Porter could provide an integrated score in the new Rodgers and Hammerstein mould. 'Another Op'nin', Another

Show', 'Wunderbar', 'So in Love' and 'Brush Up Your Shakespeare' are especially well known, but nearly every song is familiar to lovers of musicals.

SYNOPSIS
Act I The action takes place in and around a theatre. Actor-manager Fred Graham's floral gift to *ingénue* Lois is delivered by mistake to his leading lady (and ex-wife) Lilli Vanessi, to her pleasure and his embarrassment. Meanwhile Lois's boyfriend Bill has signed Fred's name to a gambling debt to avoid his creditors; Fred cannot understand the threats of the two men who show up to collect the money. The performance of *The Taming of the Shrew* is complicated by the presence of the men (in costume) to prevent Fred's escape, and by Lilli's discovery that the flowers were not meant for her. Fred keeps her from walking out by persuading the men that her departure will close the show, leaving him unable to repay 'his' debt.

Act II The intrigue proceeds offstage and on, with the men finally giving up when they hear that their boss has been bumped off and they now report to a new boss. Lilli is now free to leave the theatre and does so. Fred/Petruchio puts on a brave front onstage, but is sure he has lost Lilli/Kate – until she returns to him at the last moment.

Other musicals: *See America First*, 1916; *Kitchy-Koo*, 1919; *Paris*, 1928; *Wake Up and Dream*, 1929; *Fifty Million Frenchmen*, 1929; *The New Yorkers*, 1930; *Gay Divorce*, 1932; *Nymph Errant*, 1933; *Jubilee*, 1935; *Red, Hot and Blue!*, 1936; *You Never Know* (coll.), 1938; *Leave It to Me*, 1938; *DuBarry Was a Lady*, 1939; *Panama Hattie*, 1940; *Let's Face It*, 1941; *Something for the Boys*, 1943; *Mexican Hayride*, 1944; *Around the World in Eighty Days*, 1946; *Out of This World*, 1950; *Can-Can*, 1953; *Silk Stockings*, 1955

J.A.C.

FRANCIS POULENC

Francis Jean Marcel Poulenc; *b* 7 January 1899, Paris; *d* 30 January 1963, Paris

Poulenc came to opera comparatively late in his composing career: late, that is, for one who started so early. Various historical accidents pushed the young Poulenc into the musical vanguard. His family was rich and well connected, and he soon met all the fashionable composers and artists, who discovered that Poulenc's slender gifts – an infallible ear for melody, an ironic sense of humour – were just what was required by Jean Cocteau, Erik Satie and a whole band of anti-Establishment propagandists. Even his compositional shortcomings, a complete ignorance of structure, orchestration or musical orthography, seemed to suit the post-war fashion for *naïveté* and primitivism.

Fashion was Poulenc's making, and his undoing. It led him to Diaghilev and the Ballets Russes, to worldwide success for his earliest piano pieces and songs. But occasionally it led him to complicate and overembellish his natural style, which was at its most authentic when at its simplest. By the early 1930s

Poulenc the *enfant terrible* was beginning to look a little long in the tooth. His muse faltered and then deserted him completely. The missing ingredient – his rediscovery of his Catholic faith (1935) – unlocked his soul, his psyche and his music. He also rediscovered, via the baritone Pierre Bernac, his love of song, and via Paul Éluard – the most spiritual of the Surrealist poets – a new sensual and lyrical strain.

This can be further heard in the music of the war years. The brittle influence of Stravinsky gives way to that of Ravel and Chabrier: warmer, more French. *Les mamelles de Tirésias* (1944), for all its high jinks, is shot through with this new nostalgia. The final ingredient in the making of an opera composer is to be found in Poulenc's post-war compositions, which can best be described as an acknowledgement of human frailty in music. Poulenc suffered much from depression and hopelessly doomed love affairs (often with younger men). His last two operas, *Les dialogues des Carmélites* and *La voix humaine*, have the courage to depict the blacker moments of human life in terrifying detail. Poulenc ended his career completely out of step with fashion – shamelessly tonal, unembarrassed about emotion, pain, even sentimentality. He had come a long way from the cynical stylist of the early 1920s.

Les mamelles de Tirésias

The Breasts of Tiresias
Opéra-bouffe in a prologue and two acts (1h)
Libretto prepared by the composer, from the play by Guillaume Apollinaire (1903, rev. 1917)
Composed 1944
PREMIERES 3 June 1947, Opéra-Comique, Paris; US: 13 June 1953, Brandeis University, Massachusetts; UK: 16 June 1958, Jubilee Hall, Aldeburgh, Suffolk
CAST Theatre Director *bar*, Thérèse *s*, The Husband *high bar* (later rev. for *t*), The Policeman *bar*, Presto *bar*, Lacouf *t*, Journalist *t*, The Son *b*, Newspaper Vendor *ms*, members of the audience 2 *ms*, *b*; *satb* chorus of the people of Zanzibar

The word 'Surrealist' was coined by Apollinaire in his introduction to the revisions to his play in 1917. The drama's high-spirited topsy-turvydom seems to define the term, but in reality it conceals a deeper and sadder theme – the need to repopulate and rediscover a France ravaged by war. This message, however absurdly stated, must have been at the forefront of Poulenc's mind in 1940, soon after the fall of France, when he began his sketches for the libretto and the prosody of *Les mamelles* – one of many specifically and quintessentially French works written during the dark days of the Occupation.

SYNOPSIS
Prologue Over a long pedal point the theatre director appears before the curtain, exhorting the audience to 'make children'. He disappears, and the curtain rises on the town/city of Zanzibar.

Act I Thérèse is bored with being a woman and decides to change sex; her breasts (two balloons) float away to the sound of a *valse chantée*. Her husband arrives, assumes she has been abducted, and assumes her clothing.

Act II The husband has become a paterfamilias on a grand scale – he has given birth, single-handed, to over 40,000 children in one day. We can hear them yowling in the orchestra pit. He has to find them ration cards which are supplied by the cartomancer, Thérèse – alias Tirésias – in disguise. They are reunited. Around this touching domestic tale mad people pop up and do mad things – always with the conviction that what they are saying and doing makes some semblance of sense. It doesn't.

To set this irresistible nonsense Poulenc deploys the most familiar, almost mundane, of forms – the French operetta from opéra comique to *café-concert*. Thus the music veers from the giddy prestos and polkas of Offenbach and Lecocq to the sentimental waltzes of Messager, even Maurice Chevalier. The harmonies are freely borrowed from Ravel and Stravinsky, the melodies from Chabrier. In other words, it is typical Poulenc. He considered it to be one of his most 'authentic' works, and added much private feeling to it. For example, the setting was, in Poulenc's mind at least, relocated to Monte Carlo in the 1920s, the scene of his earliest triumphs. But the predicament of fallen France is sensible throughout. Whenever Paris is mentioned the music swoons and weeps for a moment before the madness starts up again.

Les dialogues des Carmélites

Dialogues of the Carmelites
Opera in three acts (12 scenes) (2h 45m)
Libretto prepared by the composer, from the drama by Georges Bernanos (1948)
Composed 1953
PREMIERES 26 January 1957, La Scala, Milan; US: 14 July 1957, War Memorial Opera House, San Francisco; UK: 16 January 1958, Covent Garden, London
CAST The Marquis de la Force *bar*, Blanche *lyric s*, The Chevalier de la Force *t*, Mme de Croissy *c*, Mme Lidoine *s*, Mother Marie of the Incarnation *ms*, Sister Constance *light s*, Mother Jeanne *c*, Sister Mathilde *ms*, Mother Gerald/ Sister Claire/Sister Antoine and 5 others *choristers*, Father Confessor *t*, First Officer *t*, Second Officer *bar*, Gaoler *bar*, Thierry *b*, M. Javelinot *bar*; *satb* chorus of nuns, officials of the municipality, officers, police, prisoners, guards, townspeople

Les dialogues des Carmélites has a provenance complicated even by operatic standards. The tale of the martyrdom of the sisters of Compiègne was first told by one of their number, Mother Marie, who survived the French Revolutionary Terror and published her memoirs. The subsequent canonization of the nuns inspired a young German Catholic, Gertrude von le Fort, to tell their story in a novel, *Die Letzte am Schafott* (1931), which described, with grim prescience, the fate of religion under totalitarianism. Le Fort gave life, and indeed her own name, to the heroine Blanche de la Force. There followed various attempts to turn the book into a play, then a film, to which end it arrived in the hands of Georges Bernanos, who was living, or more precisely dying, in South America. He invented further characters and added further personal details, even giving the dying prioress his own age, 59, 'a good age to die'.

By a bizarre coincidence, Poulenc's lover at the time was dying as the composer was writing the music for the same prioress. Indeed, as Poulenc noted in a letter, he breathed his last just as the work was finished. The opera had been commissioned by Ricordi for La Scala, Milan, but the length of time between conception and birth indicates the complications – legal, financial (the rights were a nightmare, as one can see on the title page of the score), and indeed emotional – that the opera brought with it. All this took its toll on Poulenc's health and happiness, both of which, as we can see and hear in the opera, were fragile at the best of times. It is an opera about terror. Personal terror plays against state terror. It opens as it means to go on, in fear.

SYNOPSIS

Act I   Blanche's father and brother, the marquis and chevalier de la Force – French aristocrats – are frightened that Blanche might be frightened. She is not home yet and the streets are unsettled. She is indeed frightened when she arrives, but maintains a great, albeit spurious, calm as she announces her intention to join the Carmelite Order. We then meet the ageing prioress, Mme de Croissy, who explains to Blanche that the Order can protect nobody. She is touched by Blanche's devotion, however, and gives her her blessing. Blanche joins the convent, where she meets Constance, a happy-go-lucky peasant girl who voices one of the opera's themes, that, when we die, perhaps we die in someone else's stead, perhaps we die their deaths. Certainly the prioress is dying a death which she does not deserve: slow, agonizing, undignified and depicted in unflinching detail in both music and words. Mother Marie is in attendance, loyal and solid, keen to avoid involuntary blasphemy. Blanche arrives to watch her new spiritual mother die in torment.

Act II   Blanche's solitary fears begin to be matched by real dangers from the outside world. The first scene opens with the first of the sung prayers that punctuate this act. It is a Requiem for the prioress. Blanche, left alone with the body, panics; she is calmed by Mother Marie, ever watchful. The new prioress, Mme Lidoine, arrives and preaches to the nuns. Blanche's brother is admitted and, in a scene that could almost be described as a love duet, attempts to take Blanche away to safety. The finale is of Verdian proportions. The sisters are led in prayer, then the prioress warns them against the temptation of martyrdom. The noise of the Terror grows; officers arrive and the mob threatens to attack the convent. In the uproar, Blanche drops a statue of the infant Jesus.

Act III   The convent is desecrated, the Order declared illegal. Blanche runs away to her late father's house, where she lives disguised as a servant. She hears that the Carmelites have been arrested. They have been imprisoned in the *conciergerie*, where we see the new prioress inspiring her sisters with strength and courage to face the ordeal ahead. This is depicted with extraordinary realism in the great final scene, consisting of one long prayer, the Salve Regina, sung by the nuns as they go, one by one, to their death by guillotine. The crowd looks on amazed as Blanche steps forward, transfigured and joyful, to join her sisters in martyrdom.

'You must forgive my Carmelites,' wrote Poulenc. 'They can sing only tonal music.' And, indeed, compared to most operas written in the 1950s Poulenc's is astonishingly old-fashioned. His models, indeed the work's dedicatees, were Verdi, Monteverdi, Debussy and Musorgsky. The structure, the alternation of recitative and arioso, is Verdian; the recitative itself owes a huge amount to Monteverdi's *Poppea* and to Debussy's *Pelléas*. From Musorgsky Poulenc learned the sense of menace and nightmare that suffuses the whole work.

The tessituras are meticulously planned, and borrowed from grand opera. Poulenc's models were Verdi's Amneris (Mother Marie) and Desdemona (new prioress), Wagner's Kundry (prioress), Massenet's Thaïs (Blanche) and Mozart's Zerlina (Constance). Each of these characters has leitmotifs that stand not only for her but also for the emotions she embodies, even in other characters. Thus Mother Marie's music (strong, in C major) indicates loyalty and steadfastness not only in Marie but also in Blanche. This is an apt device in an opera in which the sharing of suffering and the universality of grace loom so large. Underpinning everything are two sorts of music: first the prayers, the pulse and counterpoint of Renaissance religious music, which in a cloistered life is at once miraculous and mundane; then the music of fear (typified by a rising minor third which we hear throughout), which always threatens to destroy the age-old structures of the religious world. The Terror versus the Order. It is in the extraordinary final scene that the two are combined: the nuns sing over repeated minor thirds, drowning the mob, conquering fear, moving into posterity.

La voix humaine
The Human Voice
Tragédie lyrique in one act (40m)
Text by Jean Cocteau, after his play (1928)
Composed 1958
PREMIERES   6 February 1959, Opéra-Comique, Paris; US: 23 February 1959, Carnegie Hall, New York; UK: 30 August 1960, King's Theatre, Edinburgh
CAST   'Elle's

The joke at the time was that Poulenc was writing a solo opera for Maria Callas – then notorious for her reluctance to share the stage with anybody. In fact the piece was devised as a showcase for Denise Duval, the leading lady of all of Poulenc's operas and his preferred mouthpiece when trying to describe and depict the nature of fear, depression and nervous exhaustion, which he himself knew so well.

SYNOPSIS
The heroine spends the whole opera on the telephone, talking mostly to her lover but also to various crossed lines and wrong numbers. It becomes evident that her relationship has also been, as it were, 'cut off' – she can no longer get through to him. As she talks, variously, love, lies and self-pitying nonsense, it becomes quite clear that he no longer cares – indeed is probably not even at his home – and she is at the end of her tether, certainly suicidal. In the end she wraps

the telephone cord round her neck and takes the receiver to bed with her, murmuring 'Je t'aime' to an unhearing earpiece.

The opera is scored for a large, sensual orchestra which is then used with extraordinary economy. There is almost more silence than 'music' as the heroine chatters away, listens, responds, chatters again. The overall mood is one of blind panic, punctuated by febrile moments of calm. The only melody is a nostalgic theme, cloying and sickly – purely sentimental and therefore doubly desperate.

This neurotic atmosphere is drawn from life: Poulenc himself was no stranger to obsession and rejection. Indeed *La voix humaine* was written at a time of enforced separation from his then lover, Lucien. The composer described it as 'a sort of musical confession' – 'the protagonist is more or less myself'.

J.C.S.

SERGEI PROKOFIEV
Sergei Sergeyevich Prokofiev; b 27 April 1891, Sontsovka, Ukraine; d 5 March 1953, Moscow

Prokofiev considered himself essentially a man of the theatre. Before graduating from the St Petersburg Conservatory in June 1914 he had already worked on five operas; he completed six more over the next 40 years and left three unfinished. He also wrote nine ballets, including two of this century's most successful (*Romeo and Juliet* and *Cinderella*), incidental music to several dramatic works, and the scores for seven films.

Only one of the operas – the first to be performed, *The Love for Three Oranges* – was a success in his lifetime. All the others had to wait until after his death before their worth could be realistically assessed, divorced from the political considerations that had affected Prokofiev throughout his life.

His first four operas were schoolboy efforts and have not been published or professionally performed. His first mature opera, *Maddalena* (1911), was written when he was still a student at the St Petersburg Conservatory. He orchestrated the first scene but left the other three in piano score when the institution's proposed performance was abandoned because the singers found the music too difficult. A similar fate befell his second opera, *The Gambler*, in 1917, though this time the music was fully orchestrated. The following year, feeling the current state of political turmoil in Russia offered him few opportunities, Prokofiev left for a tour of the US (he had also developed a fearsome reputation as a pianist), and after a successful concert in Chicago the opera house there commissioned an opera from him based on a Russian version of Carlo Gozzi's fairy-tale *The Love for Three Oranges*.

The premiere was beset by delays and, uncommissioned, Prokofiev began work on his next opera, *The Fiery Angel*. With the exception of *War and Peace*, this was to occupy him for longer than any other composition (1919–27) and, although it was never staged during his lifetime, Prokofiev never abandoned his belief that it contained some of his best music.

In 1920 Prokofiev, still unwilling to return to Russia, had moved to Paris, where his ballet *The Tale of the Buffoon* was well received at its premiere the following spring. Over the next few years he built up a successful career in Europe, but, from the mid-1930s, commissions for compositions came increasingly from the USSR rather than from the West. Unlike Stravinsky and Rakhmaninov, Prokofiev had stayed away for practical rather than political reasons and so, with an apparent change in the Soviet musical climate, he moved to Moscow in 1936.

He soon made his name with *Peter and the Wolf* and the patriotic film score *Aleksandr Nevsky*. The latter, written in collaboration with the celebrated film director S. M. Eisenstein, transformed Prokofiev's way of thinking about constructing a dramatic musical work: instead of writing long, musically developing scenes, he chose a format of many short scenes, cut together cinematically. With his imagination fired, he quickly found a suitable story for an opera, heroic and uplifting as the Soviet authorities required, full of incident but easy to follow. This was *Semyon Kotko*, the tale of a young soldier returning from the Great War to the newly founded Soviet Ukraine. Despite all Prokofiev's hopes and efforts the authorities condemned both its musical style and its dramatic content and the work was not a success.

For his next two operas Prokofiev returned to the individual kind of neo-classicism he had earlier demonstrated in the *Classical Symphony* (1916–17) and the film score *Lieutenant Kijé* (1933). In *Betrothal in a Monastery* (1940) and *War and Peace* (1941–52) the music re-creates the period atmosphere through use of musical forms such as minuet and gavotte, using classical-period phrasing and melodic contours familiar in Mozart and Haydn, and simple, but never simplistic, harmonies. In these works Prokofiev adopted rhymed verse and musical set pieces – elements he had eschewed during his early, radical period. He emphasized the romantic elements in the stories, writing lyrical tunes which are a far cry from the brittle style of the early days.

But once again Prokofiev was unlucky with performances. Russia's entry into the Second World War made opera production difficult; and after the war, despite numerous revisions carried out at the suggestion of the authorities, a satisfactory format for *War and Peace* was never arrived at and it was never staged in Prokofiev's lifetime in anything like a form that represented his original concept. Meanwhile the notorious 1948 Moscow Congress of Composers condemned Prokofiev, along with virtually every Soviet composer of any distinction, for writing 'formalist' music (Communist Party leader Andrei Zhdanov's catch-all opposite to socialist realism; Prokofiev himself defined formalism as 'music people don't understand at first hearing'). He sought official rehabilitation with his last opera, *The Story of a Real Man*, based on a patriotic true story of a wartime fighter pilot. The music includes folksongs from the hero's north-Russian homeland linked by uncomplicated and bland arioso passages. As in *Semyon Kotko*, Prokofiev wrote almost cinematically, but added nothing of his own personality to the folksongs and the opera has little dramatic thrust. It was proscribed as 'modernistic, anti-melodic' and was denied a public performance until many years later.

After Prokofiev's death there was a relaxation of the official Russian position and only *The Fiery Angel* remained unknown to Soviet audiences. In the West there has been a different reaction: of the Soviet operas, only *War and Peace* is at all well known, but the early operas are increasingly being performed.

The Gambler

Igrok

Opera in four acts (six scenes) (2h)
Libretto by the composer, after the novella by Fyodor Dostoevsky (1866)
Composed 1915–17 (1st version withdrawn); rev. 1927–8
PREMIERES 29 April 1929, Théâtre de la Monnaie, Brussels; US: 4 April 1957, 85th Street Playhouse, New York; UK: 28 August 1962, King's Theatre, Edinburgh; USSR: March 1963 (concert; radio broadcast); 7 April 1974, Bolshoi Theatre, Moscow
CAST The General *b*, Pauline *s*, Alexei *t*, The Marquis *t*, Mr Astley *bar*, Blanche *c*, Babulenka (Grandmother) *ms*, Prince Nilsky *t*, Potapitsch *bar*, Baroness Würmerhelm *silent*, 21 Gamblers and Croupiers: 2 *s*, 2 *ms*, *c*, 7 *t*, 3 *bar*, 6 *b*; *satb* chorus of gamblers, hotel guests, domestics, porters

This was the first significant opera to be based on a Dostoevsky text. Prokofiev himself adapted the text and kept his own additions to a minimum. His aim was to write a new, conversational kind of opera, free of the influence of acknowledged giants such as Wagner, Tchaikovsky and Rimsky-Korsakov, with their reliance on set pieces. There are virtually no themes but a succession of short, highly characterful and varied motifs, which either exaggerate the natural inflexions of the Russian text or, in the orchestra, serve to amplify the action. The opera had been promised a performance at St Petersburg's Mariinsky Theatre by Albert Coates, the theatre's conductor. But by February 1917 political upheaval added to the problem of a cast and orchestra who would not or could not master the music, and rehearsals stopped. The work's premiere did not take place until 1929 in Brussels, by which time Prokofiev had revised it to include more repetition and development, less motivic complication.

After its premiere the opera was not heard until shortly after Prokofiev's death, when Hermann Scherchen conducted it in Naples in 1953.

SYNOPSIS

Act I In 1865 in Roulettenburg (a mythical German spa) Alexei, tutor of the general's children, obsessively in love with the general's step-daughter Pauline, has lost the money she asked him to gamble with. He is contemptuous of his social superiors, particularly his employer, the general, who is deeply in love with an impoverished opportunist, Blanche, and, because of his gambling, deeply in debt to the marquis. However, all the general's problems will be solved when he inherits the fortune of his elderly relation Babulenka.

Act II The general threatens to dismiss Alexei because of his rudeness to Baroness Würmerhelm (the tutor was carrying out Pauline's orders) but withdraws at the threat of scandal. Alexei realizes that the marquis is a former lover of Pauline's. Babulenka arrives in person, confounding deathbed rumours, and proceeds to gamble away her fortune.

Act III His inheritance gone, the general is abandoned by Blanche. Babulenka returns home to Moscow.

Act IV The marquis too returns to his homeland and releases Pauline from her debt to him (it transpires that this debt was why she asked Alexei to gamble her money in the opening scene). Alexei becomes convinced that with her money he will win and thus win her too. To the astonishment of the other gamblers, Alexei breaks the bank twice and runs to Pauline with the money. She throws it back in his face. He has lost her but fallen for a far more capricious mistress.

The Love for Three Oranges

Lyubov k tryom apel'sinam

Opera in a prologu and four acts (1h 45m)
Libretto by the composer, after Carlo Gozzi's *Fiaba dell'amore delle tre melarancie* (1761)
Composed 1919
PREMIERES 30 December 1921, Auditorium, Chicago; USSR: 18 February 1926, Mariinsky Theatre, Leningrad (St Petersburg); UK: 11 December 1953, BBC radio; 24 August 1962, King's Theatre, Edinburgh
CAST King of Clubs *b*, The Prince *t*, Princess Clarice *c*, Leandro *bar*, Truffaldino *t*, Pantaloon *bar*, Chelio *b*, Fata Morgana *s*, Princess Linetta *c*, Princess Nicoletta *ms*, Princess Ninetta *s*, A Gigantic Cook *b*, Farfarello *b*, Smeraldina *ms*, Master of Ceremonies *t*, Herald *b*, 10 Ridiculous People: 5 *t*, 5 *b*, Advocates of Tragedy *b* chorus, Advocates of Comedy *t* chorus, Advocates of Lyric Drama *st* chorus, Advocates of Farce *ab* chorus, Little Devils *b* chorus; *satb* chorus of courtiers; *silent*: monsters, drunkards, gluttons, guards, servants, 4 soldiers

At the time of this opera's composition, Prokofiev's eclectic style ranged from the aggressiveness of the *Scythian Suite* (which sought to outdo Stravinsky's *The Rite of Spring* in its portrayal of primitive Russian life) to the quasi-18th-century elegance of the *Classical Symphony*. In Gozzi's story Prokofiev saw the chance to synthesize these elements, its fantasy world providing scope for glittering orchestration, brilliant effects and strongly differentiated characterization. Also, he thought his American audience would appreciate a mercurial setting of the type of brittle fairy-story then in operatic vogue; Busoni (and soon Puccini) also selected a Gozzi fairy-tale, *Turandot*, for operatic treatment. Prokofiev wrote his own libretto, in Russian, from a translation by Vsevolod Meyerhold, Konstantin Vogak and Vladimir Solovyov of the play, and created a whimsical opera buffa full of the fantastic and grotesque, the comic and the sad, set within a framework of utmost unreality and maximum theatricality.

The commission, from the Chicago Opera, was signed in January 1919 for production that autumn, but the work was not staged until 1921, when the soprano Mary Garden had become the theatre director. Since its European premiere, on 14 March 1925 in Cologne, it has been the most frequently performed of Prokofiev's operas.

SYNOPSIS

The king believes his son and heir will die unless he can be cured of his melancholia. His enemies, his niece Princess Clarice and the prime minister, Leandro, are determined to prevent a cure, for Leandro plans to marry Clarice and succeed to the throne. The king's magic protector is Chelio; his enemies' is the evil Fata Morgana. The action is played out before the Ridiculous People, who, like a Greek chorus, comment on the events. At crucial moments they intervene to ensure that Good prevails.

In an allegorical prologue, advocates of different kinds of theatre (Tragedy, Comedy, Lyric Drama and Farce) demand to see their favourite entertainment. The Ridiculous People chase them away, and a herald proclaims the beginning.

Act I Doctors tell the king that his son's melancholia is fatal. They say that laughter is the only cure, so the king commands lavish and comic entertainments. Leandro tries unsuccessfully to dissuade him. Chelio loses a symbolic card game to Fata Morgana; Good is endangered. Leandro tells Princess Clarice he has fed the prince a diet of tragic verses to hasten his demise; she wants swifter action. Both are worried that the clown Truffaldino might make the prince laugh. Smeraldina announces that her mistress, Fata Morgana, will be at the entertainment to stop Chelio from intervening.

Act II The prince, in his bedroom, does not laugh at Truffaldino's antics but vomits the tragic verses into a bucket. The prince refuses to attend the king's festivities but, to the strains of the celebrated march, Truffaldino forces him out. The first two divertissements fail to amuse the prince. But when Fata Morgana, disguised as an old woman, slips and falls, legs kicking in the air, the prince laughs hysterically. So does everyone else except Clarice, Leandro and Fata Morgana, who pronounces a spell on the prince: he will fall in love with three oranges and will scour the earth in search of them. It takes effect immediately, and the prince leaves on his quest, accompanied by Truffaldino, blown on their way by the mighty bellows of the devil Farfarello. The king is in despair.

Act III In a desert, Chelio persuades Farfarello to disclose the prince's destination – the castle of Creonte, where the oranges are kept. Chelio's magical powers are too weak to break Fata Morgana's spell, but he warns the prince and Truffaldino to open the oranges only near water, and arms them with a magic ribbon, to distract Creonte's gigantic cook. They are blown into the courtyard and head for the kitchen. While the dreaded cook is distracted by the magic ribbon, the prince steals the oranges and escapes back to the desert, followed by Truffaldino. The oranges have grown very large, and their return is slow. The prince falls asleep exhausted as Truffaldino, forgetting Chelio's warning, cuts into one hoping for a drink. Out steps a beautiful princess, who tells him she must have water otherwise she will die. Truffaldino thinks the second orange might contain some liquid, but when he cuts it out steps another thirsty princess. Both collapse, and Truffaldino flees in panic. When the prince awakes he is angry at Truffaldino's disappearance and puzzled by the two corpses. Realizing

that his future is with the remaining orange and heedless of Chelio's warning, he splits it open and the beautiful Princess Ninetta steps out. They fall in love, and the Ridiculous People intervene with a reviving bucket of water. The prince leaves to arrange for the princess's reception at the palace. Smeraldina appears, changes the princess into a rat, and usurps her place as the entire court arrives. Smeraldina insists that she is the one the prince promised to marry, and the king believes her. The court returns to the city.

Act IV Fata Morgana accuses Chelio of cheating: though he lost the card game, he continues to help his protégés. The Ridiculous People lock Fata Morgana up so that Chelio can return to the palace. The king, the prince and Smeraldina arrive with the rest of court. But the throne is occupied by a giant rat. As the soldiers begin to shoot at it, Chelio, to the prince's joy and the king's confusion, turns it back into Princess Ninetta. The king finally realizes that Smeraldina, Leandro and Clarice are traitors and orders their excecution, but they escape along with Fata Morgana. In the shortest final chorus in all opera, the Ridiculous People drink a toast to the happy couple.

In its subject and its anti-realism *The Love for Three Oranges* is quite different from Prokofiev's previous operas. However, its musical construction bears similarities to his earlier works. As in *The Gambler*, Prokofiev works with short motifs, and their repetition contributes to the ostinato sound of the score. In *The Love for Three Oranges* these motifs function more by association with specific qualities of the *commedia dell'arte*-type characters than with their feelings. Those who are essentially good have music that is essentially diatonic, with smooth, undisturbed rhythms. The music for the evil characters is more chromatic and rhythmically unstable, with brittle orchestration. Prokofiev usually constructed even his symphonic works in this 'patchwork' way, but its success in *The Love for Three Oranges* is to a large extent due to the flamboyance of the motifs themselves and the exuberant manner in which Prokofiev combines them.

The opera's anti-realism was in tune with prevailing post-war artistic attitudes, but it is the strength of the invention and the skill of Prokofiev's handling of his material that have kept the opera in the repertoire. In 1919 Prokofiev composed an orchestral suite on *The Love for Three Oranges*, which enjoyed instant success; this was revised in 1924. It consists of six sections from the opera, including the famous march.

The Fiery Angel

Ognennyi angel
Opera in five acts (2h)
Libretto by the composer, after the historical novel by Valery Bryusov (1908)
Composed 1919–23, rev. 1926–7
PREMIERES 25 November 1954, Théâtre des Champs-Élysées, Paris (concert); 14 September 1955, La Fenice, Venice; UK: 2 February 1959, BBC radio; 27 July 1965, Sadler's Wells, London; US: 22 September 1965, New York City Opera, New York; USSR: 1985, Tashkent; Russia: 28 December 1991, Mariinsky Theatre, St Petersburg
CAST Ruprecht *bar*, Renata *s*, Count Heinrich *silent*,

Jacob Glock *t*, Agrippa of Nettesheim *t*, Mephistopheles *t*, Faust *b- bar*, 10 solo parts: 2 *s*, 2 *ms*, *c*, *t*, 3 *bar*, *b*, 3 Skeletons *s*, *t*, *b*, 3 Neighbours: *bar*, 2 *b*; *sa* chorus of nuns; *tb* chorus of Inquisitor's retinue, *satb* offstage chorus

This study of neurotic female sexuality set in Reformation Germany is far removed from the pantomime world of Gozzi, and the music of *The Fiery Angel* has an Expressionist intensity quite unlike the dispassionate music Prokofiev had previously been writing. He spent some four years composing the short score, but with no performance in view he did not start orchestrating it in detail. In 1926, when Bruno Walter, head of the Berlin State Opera, accepted it for performance the following season, Prokofiev revised it, reorganizing Act II and much of Acts I, III and V and orchestrating the whole opera. The Berlin performance did not materialize, but Prokofiev transferred some of the music into his Third Symphony. In the early 1930s there was talk of the opera being staged by the Metropolitan Opera in New York and Prokofiev began preliminary work on another major revision. This was never finished, the American performance did not take place, and the opera was not staged in Prokofiev's lifetime. Even though it has been widely praised as his strongest and most dramatically intense score, productions (which always use the version prepared for Berlin) have not been frequent.

SYNOPSIS

Act I Since childhood, Renata has been obsessed with her protective angel, Madiel, at first spiritually, then, after puberty, physically. For a year she lived with Count Heinrich, the man she imagined to be Madiel, but he left her. Since then she has been searching for him. She tells all this to Ruprecht after he has found her having hysterical visions; although everyone else agrees that she is a witch, Ruprecht, who has fallen in love with her, agrees to help.

Act II Renata and Ruprecht turn to magic in the quest for Heinrich, acquiring forbidden books and conjuring up dark spirits, though the leading proponent of black philosophy, Agrippa, refuses to assist them.

Act III Renata has seen Heinrich, but he has again rejected her. She demands that Ruprecht avenge her honour. As Ruprecht challenges him to a duel, Renata, seeing Heinrich bathed in light, is again convinced that he is her fiery angel; she commands Ruprecht not to harm him, but when Ruprecht is badly wounded in the duel she is full of remorse. She vows to love him and nurse him back to health. Unseen voices mock her.

Act IV Ruprecht has recovered and Renata leaves him again, determined to punish her own sinfulness by entering a convent. Ruprecht encounters Faust and Mephistopheles; Mephistopheles takes Ruprecht under his wing.

Act V Renata has corrupted the nuns with her visions and obsession with her angel. The Inquisition tries to exorcize the evil to no avail. While Ruprecht looks on, with a triumphant Mephistopheles beside him, Renata is condemned to torture and death.

Prokofiev began *The Fiery Angel* at the only time in his life when religion featured in his intellectual considerations, and it is unique among his theatre works in being written with neither a commission nor a production in view. Its theme of obsession looks back to his pre-Revolution operas *The Gambler* and *Maddalena*. Its form – a set of more or less free-standing tableaux – looks back even further, to Musorgsky. But its musical and dramatic portrayal of ambiguity (the story comes from one of Russia's greatest Symbolist poets) was totally new for him.

Individuals, atmospheres and emotional responses are all given specific themes of characterization – most of them chromatic to some degree. There is only one unambiguously tonal (and therefore stable) character motif in the opera, and this is associated, quite improbably, with the forces of evil. The opera is seen largely through Renata's eyes; consequently, although the text is ambivalent about whether her visions are hallucinatory, the music makes it apparent that for her they are real and terrifying. During the narrative of her life the orchestra abounds in motifs which return when she later experiences similar feelings. Among the most memorable of these are the soaring theme of her love for Madiel, and the theme which recurs whenever Renata's responses to physical masculinity are displayed.

Betrothal in a Monastery (The Duenna)

Obrucheniye v Monastire
Lyric-comic opera in four acts (2h 30m)
Libretto by the composer and Mira Mendelson, after the play *The Duenna* by Richard Brinsley Sheridan (1775)
Composed 1940–41
PREMIERES 5 May 1946, Narodni Divadlo Theatre, Prague; USSR: 3 November 1946, Kirov Opera, Leningrad (St Petersburg); US: 1 June 1948, Greenwich Mews Playhouse, New York; UK: 12 May 1963 (BBC broadcast of performance at Stanislavsky Theatre, Moscow); 15 February 1980, Collegiate Theatre, London
CAST Don Jerome *t*, Ferdinand *bar*, Louisa *s*, Louisa's Duenna *c*, Antonio *t*, Clara *ms*, Mendoza *b*, Don Carlos *bar*, 9 other solo parts: *s*, *c*, 4 *t*, 2 *bar*, *b*; *satb* chorus of servants, maskers, tradespeople, monks, nuns, guests

Prokofiev's first collaboration with the young literary student Mira Mendelson (for whom he was soon to leave his wife) put more emphasis on the romance in Sheridan's sparkling and successful play than on its farce or cynicism. Described by Shostakovich as 'one of Prokofiev's most radiant and buoyant works', it remains – after *Oranges* – his most popular opera.

SYNOPSIS

Act I In 18th-century Seville, Don Jerome arranges to marry his daughter Louisa to Mendoza, an ugly but very rich old fish merchant who has not seen the girl but is enthusiastic. He hears the penniless Antonio serenading Louisa and vows that the wedding must take place soon.

Act II Louisa's duenna hatches a plan that will allow Louisa to marry Antonio and herself to snare Mendoza and his money: Don Jerome must believe that the duenna is acting as a go-between for the lovers; he will then dismiss her, but Louisa will put on the duenna's clothes, escape and elope with Antonio. The duenna, disguised as Louisa, will marry Mendoza instead. Having escaped, Louisa comes across her friend Clara who, feigning distress at her lover's over-ardent behaviour (her lover is Louisa's brother Ferdinand), has decided to take refuge in a monastery. Disguised, this time as Clara, Louisa enlists Mendoza's help in finding Antonio – the merchant is only too pleased to divert his rival's attentions away from Louisa (as he thinks). At Don Jerome's house, Mendoza meets 'Louisa' (the duenna); he is won over by her flattery, and the couple plan to elope.

Act III Antonio meets the real Louisa, and Mendoza, still ignorant of her identity, smiles on young love. Don Jerome, interrupted in his amateur music-making, unwittingly blesses the separate marriages of Louisa and Mendoza. At the convent, Clara pines for Ferdinand.

Act IV A visit from Mendoza and Antonio interrupts the alcoholic revelry of the monks at the monastery. Ferdinand also arrives and, believing that Antonio is about to marry Clara, starts a fight. Confusions are resolved and the monks bless all three marriages. At the wedding ball planned for Louisa, Don Jerome learns of the turn of events and is eventually reconciled to them: his daughter has married a pauper, but Ferdinand has married an heiress.

In *Betrothal*, with its farcical plot, its disguises, mistaken identities and outwitted father, Prokofiev recreated the opera-buffa world of Rossini. The music is diatonic, lucidly harmonized, limpidly orchestrated (with some unexpected tone colours, such as the glass harmonica played by Jerome at the end) and distinctively varied according to the characters on stage. Prokofiev still uses his system of motifs to introduce characters, but they are now the raw material of arias.

War and Peace
Voina i mir

Lyric dramatic scenes – opera in five acts (two parts) – an epigraph and 13 scenes (4h)
Libretto by the composer and Mira Mendelson, after the novel by Tolstoy (1863–9)
Composed 1941–3, rev. 1946–52
PREMIERES 16 October 1944, Moscow (eight scenes, concert with pf); 7 June 1945, Conservatory, Moscow (nine scenes, concert with orch.); two-evening version: 12 June 1946, Maly Theatre, Leningrad (St Petersburg) (Part I); July 1947, Maly Theatre, Leningrad (Part II, private performance); new one-evening version: 26 May 1953, Teatro Comunale, Florence; USSR: June 1953, Moscow (concert, All-Russian Theatrical Association); 1 April 1955, Maly Theatre, Leningrad (11 scenes of 13); 8 November 1957, Stanislavsky Theatre, Moscow (13 scenes, with cuts); another 13-scene version (with epigraph): US: 13 January 1957, NBC television; USSR: 15 December 1959, Bolshoi Theatre, Moscow; UK: 19 April 1967, Town Hall, Leeds (concert); 11 October 1972, Coliseum, London; US: 8 May 1974, Boston
CAST principal characters: Prince Andrei Bolkonsky *bar*, Countess Natasha Rostova *s*, Sonya *ms*, Maria Dmitrievna Akhrosimova *c*, Count Ilya Rostov *b*, Count Pyotr Bezukhov (Pierre) *t*, Hélène Bezukhova *ms*, Prince Anatol Kuragin *t*, Lt Fedya Dolokhov *bar*, Vasska Denisov *bar*,

Field Marshal Prince Kutuzov *b*, Napoleon Bonaparte *bar*, Platon Karataev *bar*; other characters: The Host *t*, Major-domo *t*, Madame Peronskaya *s*, Countess Rostova, Natasha's Mother *ms*, Tsar Alexander I *silent*, Maria Antonovna *silent*, Prince Bolkonsky's Major-domo *b*, An Old Valet *bar*, A Housemaid *s*, Maria Bolkonskaya *ms*, Prince Bolkonsky *b-bar*, Balaga *b*, Matriosha *ms*, Josef *silent*, Dunyasha *s*, Gavrilla *b*, Metivier *bar*, French Abbé *t*, Tikhon *bar*, Fyodor *t*, 2 Prussian Generals *spoken roles*, Andrei's Orderly *t*, 2 Russian Generals *t*, *bar*, Kaizarov *t*, Adjutant to General Compans *t*, Adjutant to Murat, King of Naples *treble*, Prince Berthier, Marshal of France *bar*, Marquis de Caulaincourt, French Ambassador to Russia *silent*, General Belliard *bar*, Adjutant to Prince Eugene *t*, Baron Gourgaud, Aide-de-Camp to Napoleon *b*, Monsieur de Bausset-Roquefort *t*, General Count Bennigsen *b*, Prince Mikhail Barclay de Tolly *t*, General Yermolov *bar*, General Konovnitsin *t*, General Rayevsky *bar*, The Peasant's Daughter *silent*, Captain Ramballe *b*, Lt Bonnet *t*, Mavra *c*, Ivanov *t*, Marshal Davout *b*, A French Officer *bar*, 3 Madmen *t*, *bar*, *silent*, 2 French Actresses *s*, *ms*; *satb* chorus of guests, citizens of Moscow, Russian soldiers, French people, partisans

In choosing to make an opera from selected scenes of one of Russian literature's most revered masterpieces (and also one that was hailed as a cornerstone of socialist realism) Prokofiev was laying himself open to attack. He felt he could infuse the heroic story with his own very popular and characteristic kind of neo-classicism. The work immediately ran into difficulties. In May 1942, with Russia and Germany at war, he was asked to strengthen the patriotic element of the 11-scene piano score he had submitted, so he added heroic marches, arias and choruses to the 'war' sections. This shifted the balance away from the affairs of the individuals to the affairs of the state; it monumentalized the opera's substance. For the first proposed staged performances in 1946 Prokofiev added two more scenes, the glittering ball in Part I and the epic war council at Fili (Scene 10). This 13-scene version was designed to be performed over two evenings but in fact only the first eight scenes were heard in public. After that the political climate made further performances of any of the music impossible, and, although Prokofiev continued revising the work until the end of his life, he never heard the complete opera and was never able to give his approval to a final version. The first Russian performances in the late 1950s were all cut.

SYNOPSIS
Part I: Peace
Epigraph The Russian people affirm their invincibility and the sanctity of their country against all invaders. Scene 1: The young, recently widowed Prince Andrei loses his melancholia when he hears Natasha singing of her happiness at the coming of spring. Scene 2: New Year's Eve 1810. Natasha, at her first society ball, dances with Andrei and the two fall in love. But she has been noticed by the predatory Prince Anatol. Scene 3: February 1812. Natasha and Andrei are engaged, but his father refuses to accept her and insults her. She fears that the year's absence imposed on Andrei will weaken their love. Scene 4: May 1812. At a party, Natasha is swept off her feet by the charming Prince Anatol, even though she realizes that

an affair will sully her love for Andrei. Scene 5: 12 June 1812. Dolokhov, Anatol's friend, tries to persuade him not to elope with Natasha; neither her fiancé nor his wife would acquiesce. Anatol is adamant, summons his troika driver and, after a few more drinks, leaves. Scene 6: The same night. The elopement is foiled by Natasha's hostess's servants, but Anatol escapes. Her aunt, Akhrosimova, rails at her and makes an old family friend, Count Pierre, tell her that Anatol is already married. Pierre also tells her that he has fallen in love with her himself, which confuses her further. Scene 7: The same night. Pierre goes home and finds his wife entertaining friends, including Anatol. He demands that Anatol give up Natasha and leave Moscow immediately. News arrives that Napoleon and his army have crossed the Russian border. Part II: War.

Scene 8: 25 August 1812, before the Battle of Borodino. The Russian volunteer army is assembling, convinced of its invincibility. Andrei joins up hoping to forget Natasha, whom he still loves, and expecting to die. He rejects Field Marshal Kutuzov's offer of a post at a staff headquarters, and as he leaves with his men the first shots of battle are heard. Scene 9: Later that day, behind the French lines, Napoleon cannot believe the extent of the Russian resistance. He feels destiny is turning against him. When a cannonball lands at his feet he calmly pushes it away. Scene 10: Field Marshal Kutuzov, having lost the Battle of Borodino and retreated to Fili, holds a war council to discuss whether or not to defend the ancient and sacred city of Moscow and risk defeat or retreat further so as to regroup and fight again. Against all advice, he decides to abandon Moscow. Alone, Kutuzov meditates on his momentous decision but is confident that the Muscovites will win in the end. Scene 11: French-occupied Moscow is virtually deserted; Count Pierre hears that Natasha's family has fled, taking with them some wounded soldiers, including Andrei (though Natasha has not recognized him). To Napoleon's anger the Muscovites fire their city. Scene 12: Behind the Russian lines. Andrei, wounded and delirious, recalls his love for Natasha. She begs his forgiveness; he longs to live only for her. But it is too late. He dies. Scene 13: November 1812. In the terrible Russian winter the French army, with its prisoners, is in chaotic retreat on the Smolensk road. Those prisoners who cannot keep up are shot. Partisans attack an escort party and free the Russians, among them Pierre. He learns that Andrei is dead and that Natasha is sick, but he dreams that his love for her might now flower. Field Marshal Kutuzov congratulates everyone on a great victory; the people cheer him and reassert their belief in themselves and their country.

In the form and style of *War and Peace* Prokofiev harks back to the historical-tableaux operas of 19th-century Russia, such as Musorgsky's *Khovanshchina* and *Boris Godunov*. The opera's structure is traditional, with set-piece arias and Tchaikovskyan dances. Within each scene there are many short episodes involving different characters, a cinematic technique already encountered in Prokofiev's earlier Soviet operas but here developed more effectively. The composer

brought the characters alive by relaxing his insistence that the music needed to reflect every inflexion of the original words. In fact some of the words were made to fit pre-existing music, for Prokofiev, ever a prolific inventor of ideas and an inveterate hoarder of those not used, pillaged sketchbooks and unperformed scores for *War and Peace*; one of the most pervasive themes, associated with the love of Andrei and Natasha and first heard in Scene 1, was taken over from the incidental music of an unstaged dramatization of Pushkin's *Eugene Onegin* written in 1936, where it also portrayed innocent love destined to be thwarted.

The opera is fundamentally a lyrical work, with expansive melodies, infectious dances and stirring choruses. The good characters (Natasha, Andrei, Pierre) are provided with opulent orchestration; the bad ones (Anatol and his sister Hélène, who together bring about Natasha's fall) have music that matches Tolstoy's description of them as 'false and unnatural' with a spare sound. Napoleon has no melodies, only broken phrases more or less unaccompanied, perhaps symbolizing his distance from the people over whom he rules; the Russian commander, Kutuzov, on the other hand, has finely proportioned themes, strong, slow-moving and full of gravitas. The parallels of these two characters with the contemporary leaders, Hitler (Napoleon) and Stalin (Kutuzov), was played up by Prokofiev on the advice of the authorities.

Other operas: *The Giant* (*Velikan*), 1900; *Desert Islands* (*Na pustinnikh ostrovakh*) (inc., 1902); *A Feast in Time of Plague* (*Pir vo vremya chumi*), (1903; one scene rev. 1909); *Undina*, (1907); *Maddalena* (inc., 1913); (orch. Edward Downes) 1979; *Semyon Kotko*, 1940; *The Story of a Real Man* (*Povest'o nastoyashchem cheloveke*), 1948

C.B.

GIACOMO PUCCINI

Giacomo Antonio Domenico Michele Secondo Maria Puccini; *b* 22 December 1858, Lucca, Italy; *d* 29 November 1924, Brussels

Puccini is generally regarded as the greatest Italian composer of the post-Verdi generation. All but the first two of his operas remain a firm part of the operatic repertoire, and several are among the most popular ever written. During a period in which the Italian operatic tradition was finally coming to an end, he alone among his contemporaries managed to renew himself creatively, to fashion a convincing series of works, repeatedly forging a successful compromise between his native inheritance and the French and German influences that increasingly gained sway in his country.

Puccini was born into a family whose musical tradition extended back five generations. From an early age he received training in Lucca as a church musician, but a performance of Verdi's *Aida* in Pisa in 1876 apparently turned his thoughts to operatic music. In 1880 he went to Milan to study composition at the conservatory with Ponchielli. While still studying there, he achieved some critical acclaim for his final composition exercise, an orchestral *Capriccio sinfonico* (1883); Puccini later borrowed music from this early piece for his operas *Edgar* and *La bohème*. His first opera, the one-act *Le villi*, was written immediately after leaving the conservatory, for a competition sponsored by the publishing house of Sonzogno. Puccini's submission failed to receive even an honourable mention but, undeterred by the lack of success, some influential friends arranged a performance of *Le villi* in a revised, two-act version (1884). This provided the impetus for Puccini's career, as soon afterwards the publisher Ricordi offered him a contract for a new opera. Part of his contract stipulated that the librettist of *Le villi*, Ferdinando Fontana, would write the new libretto; unfortunately, Fontana's melodramatic style was ill-suited to Puccini's expressive powers and, in spite of years of work, *Edgar* (1889) was never a success. The failure nearly cost Puccini Ricordi's support, but the young composer was given a second chance.

With his next work, *Manon Lescaut* (1893), Puccini found a personal voice, and with this and the next three operas, *La bohème* (1896), *Tosca* (1900) and *Madama Butterfly* (1904), all of them written to libretti by Luigi Illica and Giuseppe Giacosa, established himself as the leading Italian composer of his generation. His sense of dramatic pacing was acute, in particular his ability to juxtapose action sections with ones of lyrical repose; and he had a masterly control over balancing the various systems – words, music and staging – that make up an opera, only rarely allowing indulgence of one aspect over the others. On the purely musical level, he managed to assimilate into his personal style such weighty foreign influences as those of Massenet and Wagner; his treatment of recurring motifs, for example, is cavalier on the semantic level precisely because it takes into account the intense dramatic presence of his operatic language.

The relatively long gaps between operas were due to a number of factors. Puccini was eager to taste the fruits of his success, and spent much time indulging his passions for hunting and for the newly invented motor car. On the professional level, work in progress was interrupted by the series of promotional tours that Ricordi arranged in order to launch Puccini's works on the national and international stage. Perhaps most seriously, however, each new creation underwent a tortured genesis. As if in vivid illustration of the fragmented condition of the Italian operatic tradition, the structure of each opera had to be achieved through a painful process of discovery, Puccini's obsession with details of dramatic pacing causing him frequently to change his mind in mid-composition, driving his long-suffering librettists almost to despair.

The three works that secured his international reputation all succeed in part by characterizing a particularly evocative ambience: Bohemian Paris in the 1830s; Rome in 1800, seething with revolutionary and religious tension; early-20th-century Japan. Indeed, one senses that the choice of dramatic setting always had a critical effect on stimulating his desire and ability to find fresh ideas. After *Madama Butterfly*, however, Puccini found it increasingly difficult to locate subjects that were both novel enough to kindle his imagination

and at the same time firmly enough structured to sustain dramatic treatment. Finally, three years after the premiere of *Butterfly*, Puccini discovered a subject set in the California gold rush of 1849. *La fanciulla del West* (1910) had the usual protracted genesis, and was further interrupted by a crisis in Puccini's – frequently stormy – relationship with his wife Elvira. There was an even longer gap before his next work, *La rondine* (1917), which started life as a Viennese operetta and remains (outside a few popular excerpts) the least well known of Puccini's mature operas.

Puccini's next project took up a different dramatic challenge. *Il trittico* (1918) is a group of three sharply contrasting one-act operas that together make up a complete evening: a sinister melodrama (*Il tabarro*); a sentimental religious tragedy, written entirely for women's voices (*Suor Angelica*); and a comic opera (*Gianni Schicchi*). It is clear from the relative speed with which *Il trittico* was produced that the reduced scope of these works allowed Puccini to experiment more freely with dramatic types, to immerse himself in a particular ambience without the necessity of developing a protracted narrative structure. For his final opera, *Turandot*, he returned to exoticism, but this time employed a bold mixture of dramatic types within one work, showing that his creative imagination and dramatic insights remained intact in spite of the increasing self-doubt and pessimism of his later years. Puccini died of throat cancer in 1924, leaving the final scene of *Turandot* unfinished. It was completed by Franco Alfano, a member of the younger Italian generation, and first performed in 1926.

Although Puccini has been cast as a conservative figure in early-20th-century music, he continued to respond to contemporary music when it suited his dramatic purpose. One can, for example, trace through his mature operas a gradual development in complexity of harmonic idiom, and an increasingly sophisticated use of the orchestra. However, Puccini's central innovation lay in his continual attempts to fashion new types of musical drama, to invent for each new work a particular structure, a particular dynamic relationship between its various narrative strands. In spite of these efforts, and in spite of an unprecedented success with the public, Puccini has never been fully accepted by the critical establishment. His operas respond only faintly to the Wagner-influenced analytical and critical techniques that have been in vogue for so long, and this has encouraged some to accuse him of lacking complete artistic seriousness of purpose, of cynically manipulating an easily moved mass audience. But there are signs of a general change in critical attitude. As time passes, and as we gain an increasingly broad perspective on the progress of 20th-century music, Puccini's reputation as a musical dramatist of the highest quality, and as a significant representative of his age, seems bound to grow.

Manon Lescaut

Lyric drama in four acts (2h)
Libretto by Ruggero Leoncavallo, Marco Praga, Domenico Oliva, Luigi Illica and Giuseppe Giacosa (with contributions by Giulio Ricordi and the composer), based on the novel

L'histoire du Chevalier des Grieux et de Manon Lescaut by
the Abbé Prévost (1731)
Composed 1889–October 1892, rev. 1893, 1922
PREMIERES   1 February 1893, Teatro Regio, Turin; UK:
14 May 1894, Covent Garden, London; US: 29 August
1894, Academy of Music, Philadelphia
CAST   Manon Lescaut *s*, Il Cavaliere Renato des Grieux *t*,
Lescaut *bar*, Geronte di Ravoir *b*, Edmondo *t*, A Musician
ms, Dancing Master *t*, Lamplighter *t*, Landlord *b*, Sergeant
of the Archers *b*, Naval Captain *b*, Hairdresser *silent*; *satb*
chorus of girls, townspeople, men and women, students,
musicians, old men and abbés, courtesans, guards, naval
officers, sailors

Soon after the not very successful premiere of his
second opera, *Edgar*, Puccini began searching for a
new libretto. Ruggero Leoncavallo – then better
known as a librettist than as a composer – was the first
to sketch a text, but he soon dropped out of the
project and was succeeded by an alarming succession
of further librettists, each striving to accommodate a
composer who was increasingly difficult to please in
matters of dramatic structure and fine verbal detail.
An added problem was the existence of Massenet's
opera on the same subject: Puccini felt constrained to
make his work sufficiently different from Massenet's
to avoid the charge of plagiarism. The text was eventually completed by Luigi Illica and Giuseppe Giacosa,
who were destined to become the composer's most
faithful – and long-suffering – collaborators. The
opera underwent many subsequent revisions, and even
today several competing versions exist, of Act IV in
particular (at one point Puccini cut the famous aria
'Sola, perduta, abbandonata . . .'). The composer
probably never reached a 'definitive' form for this
opera, his first international success.

SYNOPSIS

Act I   A square in 18th-century Amiens, outside an
inn. A student, Edmondo, and his companions are
interrupted by des Grieux, who mocks love before
joining the others in praise of carefree pleasure. A
coach arrives, and Geronte (a rich, elderly adventurer),
Lescaut and his sister Manon alight. Des Grieux is
captivated by Manon, and soon contrives a personal
encounter in which he discovers that she must go to
join a convent the following day. As Lescaut calls
Manon into the inn, des Grieux persuades her to
meet him again later. Left alone, the young man
muses over Manon's beauty and his awakening love
for her ('Donna non vidi mai'). Geronte admits to
Lescaut that he too is interested in Manon, and plans
to take her off to Paris – with Lescaut's blessing.
Edmondo overhears the plot to abduct Manon and
warns des Grieux, who convinces Manon of his love
and persuades her to run off with him to Paris, taking
advantage of Geronte's waiting carriage. Geronte is
furious that his plan has been foiled, but Lescaut
calms him, assuring him that, when des Grieux's
money runs out, Manon will again be available.

Act II   A luxurious boudoir in Geronte's Parisian
house. Manon has left des Grieux, tempted away by
Geronte's money. Although she relishes her new-
found wealth, she nostalgically recounts to Lescaut
the simple joys of her humble life with des Grieux ('In
quelle trine morbide'). After a dancing lesson, Manon

is left alone. Des Grieux appears – having at last
discovered Manon's whereabouts – and angrily reproaches her for her desertion. In an extended love
duet, she gradually reawakens his love for her, but
they are discovered by Geronte. When Manon taunts
the old man, he retires with a vague threat. Des
Grieux urges her to run away with him, but she
lingers reluctantly over her jewels, causing him to
despair over her foolishness ('Ah Manon, mi tradisce
il tuo folle pensier'). As they at last prepare to depart,
Lescaut appears, warning them that Geronte has denounced Manon and the police are on their way to
arrest her. Manon again delays, attempting to gather
up some of her treasures, and in a hectic climax
Geronte bursts in and triumphantly sends her off in
the hands of the police.

Act III   The port of Le Havre, where Manon is
about to be deported. After an orchestral intermezzo,
Lescaut and des Grieux are seen waiting for dawn in
order to attempt Manon's rescue. Des Grieux locates
the room where she is imprisoned, and tells her
through the window of their plan. But the attempt
quickly fails. The convicted women are brought out
one by one, and the crowd comments on each of them;
Manon and des Grieux sing a bitter farewell. At the
last moment, as the women are led to the convict ship
bound for North America, des Grieux attempts a last
desperate rescue, and then flings himself at the feet of
the captain, pleading to be allowed to accompany his
beloved ('Guardate, pazzo son'). The captain takes
pity on him, lets him come aboard, and gives orders
for the departure.

Act IV   The Louisiana desert, as night is falling.
Manon and des Grieux are again on the run. Manon,
in the last stages of exhaustion, faints, and des Grieux
tries desperately to revive her ('Manon, senti, amor
mio'). He goes off in search of water, and Manon
bemoans her fate ('Sola, perduta, abbandonata . . .').
Soon after des Grieux returns empty-handed, she falls
dead at his feet, singing to the end that her love will
never die.

As befits a youthful work, *Manon Lescaut* still betrays
the influences that formed Puccini's mature style. Passages in the Act II love duet, for example, recall
Wagner's harmonic language (particularly that of *Tristan*), while the close of that act is strongly reminiscent
of middle-period Verdi. On the other hand, in des
Grieux's Act III aria 'Guardate, pazzo son', and
elsewhere, Puccini showed himself adept at the more
'modern' style of Ponchielli. Whatever the influences,
almost all the music bears the stamp of Puccini's
emerging mature style. We can also see the composer's
growing awareness of large-scale structure, of the careful shaping of individual acts. Act I skilfully alternates
hectic action sequences with moments of lyrical repose
(a type of rapid juxtaposition that was much used in
the opening acts of subsequent operas). Act II, on the
other hand, is made up of two sharply contrasting
musical ambiences: first a nostalgic re-creation of
18th-century musical manners; then a sudden plunge
into the torridly expressive world of Manon and her
rejected lover. Act III is perhaps the most perfectly
achieved large structure, the action sequences framing

a magnificently controlled and highly original ensemble movement in which Manon and her fellow prisoners are paraded before the public. Act IV is something of a disappointment, its lack of outward action encouraging Puccini to attempt a 'symphonic' style that interferes with his usually impeccable sense of dramatic pacing. But this final uncertainty does little to shake a general feeling that with this opera Puccini found his authentic voice as a musical dramatist.

La bohème

Opera in four quadri (scenes) (1h 45m)
Libretto by Giuseppe Giacosa and Luigi Illica, based on Henry Murger's *Scènes de la vie de bohème* (1845–9) and his play (with Théodore Barrière) *La vie de bohème* (1849)
Composed 1893–5, rev. 1896
PREMIERES 1 February 1896, Teatro Regio, Turin; UK: 22 April 1897, Comedy Theatre, Manchester; US: 14 October 1897, Los Angeles Theater, Los Angeles
CAST Mimì *s*, Musetta *s*, Rodolfo *t*, Marcello *bar*, Schaunard *bar*, Colline *b*, Parpignol *t*, Benoit *b*, Alcindoro *b*; Act II: *satb* chorus of students, working girls, bourgeois, shopkeepers, street vendors, soldiers, waiters, children; Act III: Customs Officer *b*, tavern drinkers 6 *s*, 3 *a*, scavengers 8 *b*, carters, milkmaids 6 *s*, peasant women 6 *s*

La bohème was, it seems, born in litigation: the first we hear of Puccini's interest in the subject is in March 1893, when he engaged in a public quarrel with Ruggero Leoncavallo over the rights to Murger's source. Around this time, the team of Luigi Illica and Giuseppe Giacosa (who had safely completed Puccini's previous opera, *Manon Lescaut*) were engaged, and work started in earnest. However, and in spite of the continuing 'race' with Leoncavallo (who insisted on continuing work on his own *Bohème*, which was eventually performed in 1897), the opera progressed slowly, in part because the success of *Manon Lescaut* obliged Puccini to undertake a number of extensive promotional tours. The composer overcame a characteristic loss of confidence in the subject (during which he toyed with an opera entitled *La lupa*, based on a short story by Giovanni Verga), and eventually completed the score in late 1895. As would become a regular feature of Puccinian creation, the protracted period of composition saw numerous changes of direction and modification: at one point an entire act (to take place in the courtyard outside Musetta's flat) was discarded; at another the decision was made to divide the original first act into two separate acts. The first performance, given in Turin to delay the inevitable trial by fire at La Scala, Milan, was conducted by the 29-year-old Arturo Toscanini. The Turin audience, fresh from the first Italian performances of *Götterdämmerung*, gave *Bohème* a lukewarm reception, but the opera very soon found its way on to the international circuit, and is today one of the three or four most often performed works in the repertoire. Some time soon after the first performance, Puccini made various adjustments to the score, notably adding the 'bonnet' episode in Act II.

SYNOPSIS

Act I   Christmas Eve (1830) in Paris. Two Bohemian artists, Rodolfo (a poet) and Marcello (a painter), are working in their scantily furnished and unheated garret. They are joined by two friends, Colline (a philosopher) and Schaunard (a musician), and the group decides to visit the Café Momus. Benoit, their landlord, enters to ask for the rent, but they skilfully evade him. As the others leave, Rodolfo stays behind to finish an article, promising to join them soon. A young seamstress, Mimì, shyly knocks at the door to ask for a light for her candle. Rodolfo is charmed and prolongs the encounter; he tells her about himself, and shares with her his dreams of love ('Che gelida manina'). Mimì in turn introduces herself, describing her loneliness and her attic lodgings ('Mi chiamano Mimì'). The shouts of Rodolfo's friends from the courtyard below call him to the window; the moonlight, flooding the room, shines directly on Mimì's face, and Rodolfo is overcome with emotion ('O soave fanciulla'). He and Mimì declare their love, and together go off to join Rodolfo's friends at the Café Momus.

Act II   A bustling, brightly lit street in the Latin quarter. Rodolfo and Mimì meet the other Bohemians outside the Café Momus. The entrance of Marcello's erstwhile mistress, Musetta, causes a sensation: she is on the arm of a rich admirer, Alcindoro. She places herself at a neighbouring table and tries to attract Marcello's attention by singing of the amorous attention her looks inspire ('Quando me'n vo''). Marcello, after initial irritation, capitulates; Musetta creates a scene to get rid of Alcindoro, and throws herself into her former lover's arms. But then, disaster: the bill is presented. Who can pay? As a military band approaches, the Bohemians disappear into the crowd. Alcindoro returns to find Musetta gone and collapses in amazement at the huge bill she has left on his table.

Act III   Outside a tavern on the fringes of Paris. It is a bleak and snowy dawn in February; street-sweepers and peasants pass by on their way to the city. Mimì, weak and afflicted by a terrible cough, enters looking for Marcello, who at that moment comes out of the tavern. She pours out her troubles, telling him how Rodolfo torments her with his constant jealousy. When Rodolfo himself appears, Mimì retreats in confusion, hoping to avoid a confrontation. Rodolfo tells Marcello a different tale: his jealous fits hide despair over Mimì's increasingly serious illness. Mimì's coughing and sobs reveal her presence just as Marcello, hearing Musetta's laugh, rushes back inside. Rodolfo and Mimì agree that they must part, but sing poignantly of their love. Marcello and Musetta come out of the tavern, quarrelling heatedly. In the ensuing quartet, Marcello and Musetta exchange insults while Rodolfo and Mimì agree to stay together until the coming of spring.

Act IV   The Bohemians' garret. Several months have passed. Rodolfo and Marcello are discussing Mimì and Musetta. They feign indifference, but reveal their true feelings in a duet ('O Mimì, tu più non torni'). Colline and Schaunard come in, and the four friends enact a series of charades culminating in a furious mock duel. Musetta's sudden appearance shatters the mood with news that Mimì is outside, very ill.

Mimì is brought in, and her condition spurs the Bohemians to scrape money together for a doctor. Colline decides to pawn his old coat, singing it an aria of mournful farewell ('Vecchia zimarra'). Left alone, Rodolfo and Mimì reminisce about their first meeting. The others return, and Mimì gently drifts into unconsciousness. As Rodolfo busies himself with her comfort, Schaunard discovers that her sleep will be permanent. The curtain falls to anguished cries from Rodolfo as he discovers the truth.

One of the greatest strengths of La bohème is the clarity of its overall structure. Although there are connecting musical links across the score (notably certain recurring themes), each of the four acts projects a characteristic musical atmosphere, and each is placed in telling contrast to its surroundings. Act I (as so often with Puccini, the longest and most musically dense) introduces the hectic energy of the Bohemians but closes with a prolonged period of stasis: the two autobiographical arias and the love duet of Rodolfo and Mimì. Acts II and III might be seen as complementary, the former showing the gaudy exterior of Parisian life, the latter its more sombre side; and each contrasts this evocation of ambience with a central lyrical moment (in Act II the ensemble 'Quando me'n vo'', and in Act III the famous quartet). Act IV returns us to the mood of Act I, but in subtly changed colours: the opening scene for the Bohemians is even more hectic than in Act I, while the conclusion casts a veil of nostalgia over the lovers' first meeting. Certain musical connections heighten this sense of pattern and reprise. The raucous descending triads that open Act II are converted to the fragile descending fifths of Act III; the characteristic bumpy rhythm associated throughout with the Bohemians predominates in the opening scenes of both Acts I and IV, and fragments of the famous Act I arias form the basis of the close of the drama. In the eyes of many perceptive commentators, La bohème is the composer's most perfectly achieved score: the one in which subject matter and musical style are most suited, and in which the overall dramatic effect is most consistently controlled.

Tosca

Opera in three acts (2h)
Libretto by Giuseppe Giacosa and Luigi Illica, based on Victorien Sardou's play La Tosca (1887)
Composed 1896–9
PREMIERES 14 January 1900, Teatro Costanzi, Rome; UK: 12 July 1900, Covent Garden, London; US: 4 February 1901, Metropolitan, New York
CAST Floria Tosca s, Mario Cavaradossi t, Baron Scarpia bar, Cesare Angelotti b, Sacristan bar, Spoletta t, Sciarrone b, Gaoler b, Shepherd Boy treble; silent: A Cardinal, A Judge, Roberti the Executioner, A Scribe, An Officer, A Sergeant; satb chorus of priests, pupils, choir singers, soldiers, police agents, ladies, nobles, bourgeois, populace

The first reference to Tosca in Puccini's correspondence dates from more than ten years before its premiere. The subject had been suggested by Ferdinando Fontana (librettist of Le villi and Edgar), but the subject was given by Ricordi to the by now trusted

Illica and (later) Giacosa. For Puccini, work on Manon and La bohème intervened, and the subject passed to another composer, Alberto Franchetti. But during 1895, with work on Bohème coming to a close, Puccini's interest in Tosca revived and, with Ricordi's help, Franchetti was persuaded to give up his interest in the opera. In spite of continuing reservations on the part of Giacosa about the subject's suitability, work on the opera progressed steadily. As with Bohème, the main interruptions were caused by Puccini's increasingly far-flung visits to supervise revivals of his previous successes. In the later stages of composition, the composer went to considerable trouble to establish a precise sense of local colour: he made a trip to Rome in 1897 to listen to the sound of church bells from the heights of the Castello Sant'Angelo, and he enlisted the help of a priest, Don Pietro Panichelli, to check certain religious details. As the opera neared completion, Ricordi attempted to persuade Puccini to revise part of Act III, in particular a passage in the love duet which Puccini had taken from a discarded passage in Edgar. But the composer managed to defend himself, and the opera moved into rehearsal with few further changes. Puccini had great faith in the premiere cast, which included Ericlea Darclée (Tosca), Emilio de Marchi (Cavaradossi) and Eugenio Giraldoni (Scarpia), but the first performance (conducted by Leopoldo Mugnone) was greeted by a mixed reception. In spite of this, the composer made few alterations to his score, and Tosca fairly soon established itself as a staple of the operatic repertoire.

SYNOPSIS

Act I The church of Sant'Andrea della Valle, Rome, in June 1800. Angelotti, an escaped political prisoner, takes refuge in a side chapel. A sacristan enters, followed shortly afterwards by Cavaradossi, an artist working on a painting of the Madonna. As Cavaradossi prepares to start work, he muses over his painting; although this Madonna is blonde she reminds him of his dark mistress, the singer Tosca ('Recondita armonia'). The sound of the sacristan leaving brings Angelotti from his hiding-place. Angelotti and the painter recognize each other, and Cavaradossi promises to help his friend to escape from Rome. They hear Tosca's voice outside; Angelotti hides again before she enters. The sound of conversation has aroused Tosca's jealousy, but Cavaradossi's assurances calm her, and they join in a passionate duet. When Tosca leaves, Angelotti reappears and he and Cavaradossi plan his flight, but a distant cannon warns them that the prison escape has been discovered; they exit hurriedly together. As a crowd gathers to celebrate the defeat of Bonaparte at Marengo, Scarpia, the chief of police, enters with his henchman Spoletta and orders a search for the escaped prisoner. Tosca returns, and Scarpia, suspicious of Cavaradossi and enamoured of Tosca, tries to trick her into revealing information by inciting her jealousy. When she leaves to seek out her lover, Scarpia has her followed, and, as the crowd intones the Te Deum, Scarpia vows to bring Cavaradossi to the gallows and Tosca into his arms ('Va, Tosca! Nel tuo cuor s'annida Scarpia').

Act II   Scarpia's room in the Farnese Palace. Scarpia muses over his violent desire for Tosca ('Ha più forte sapore'). Spoletta enters to report that Angelotti has not been found, but that he has arrested Cavaradossi for suspicious behaviour. Cavaradossi is brought in and questioned, but he denies all knowledge of Angelotti's escape. Scarpia has sent for Tosca, and she comes in as Cavaradossi is led to the next room to be tortured. Tosca is left alone with Scarpia, and Cavaradossi's cries of pain eventually drive her to reveal Angelotti's hiding-place. Cavaradossi is dragged back onstage just as Napoleon's victory at Marengo is announced. The news elicits a stirring response from Cavaradossi, and the outraged Scarpia has him taken off to prison. Scarpia and Tosca are once again left alone, and Scarpia offers Tosca a hideous choice: she must submit to his lust or cause Cavaradossi's execution. She sings a despairing aria ('Vissi d'arte'), but finally agrees to submit. Scarpia summons Spoletta and pretends to order a faked execution. As Scarpia writes a safe-conduct from Rome for her and Cavaradossi, Tosca surreptitiously takes a knife from the dinner table and, when Scarpia comes forward to claim his prize, plunges it into his chest. She taunts him in his death throes and, when he expires, takes the safe-conduct from his clenched hand and starts to leave. At the last moment she returns to place candles around Scarpia's body and a crucifix on his chest.

Act III   A few hours later, just before dawn on a platform of the Castello Sant'Angelo. Church bells ring, and a shepherd boy sings in the distance. Cavaradossi awaits his final hour, overcome by memories of Tosca and thoughts of his approaching death ('E lucevan le stelle'). Tosca appears and triumphantly displays their safe-conduct. She instructs him on his role in the mock execution, and they sing of their love and hopes for the future. As four o'clock strikes, the firing squad arrives and Cavaradossi is prepared for execution. Tosca watches, hardly managing to restrain herself as the shots ring out and Cavaradossi falls. In an agony of suspense, she waits for the soldiers to depart. At last she tells Cavaradossi to rise, but he does not respond: Scarpia has betrayed her even in death, and her lover lies dead before her. Soldiers rush on to arrest Tosca for Scarpia's murder, but, with a final defiant gesture, she flings herself over the parapet.

The famous opening chords of *Tosca* (associated with Scarpia's evil), which recur during the first two acts of the opera, have been said to herald a new dramatic and musical potential in Puccini's work. In these chords and elsewhere the composer uses 'modernistic' harmonic devices to thrilling dramatic effect. Indeed, the opera as a whole attempts a dramatic level far more grandiose and impressive than *La bohème*, and in some senses it achieves its expanded goals. Act I in particular is a *tour de force*; in spite of a weight of stage action that made his librettists dubious of its operatic viability, Puccini managed to characterize musically all the essential elements of the drama, and even to allow time for the lyrical pauses so necessary to the development of his dramatic intentions. Act II,

scarcely less dense in its activity, though necessarily more sparse in its musical invention, is again magnificently paced, with passages such as the final, orchestrally accompanied mime showing that Puccini was capable of finely calculated dramatic effect even without the stimulus of the voice. As his publisher and friend Giulio Ricordi so acutely observed, Act III is, in spite of many fine moments, hardly on a level with the other two, and tends to flag in its central love duet. However, taken as a whole and with the help of first-class singing actors, *Tosca* can reach an intensity of dramatic effect rarely equalled in Puccini's theatre.

Madama Butterfly
Madam Butterfly

A Japanese tragedy in three acts (2h); second and third versions in two acts/Act II in two parts; fourth version in three acts
Libretto by Giuseppe Giacosa and Luigi Illica, based on David Belasco's play *Madame Butterfly* (1900), itself based on a short story by John Luther Long (1898)
Composed 1901–3 (in two acts); rev. (second version) 1904; further revs 1905; cuts, alterations for Paris, 1906
PREMIERES 17 February 1904, La Scala, Milan; second version: 28 May 1904, Teatro Grande, Brescia; third version: UK: 10 July 1905, Covent Garden, London; US: 15 October 1906, Savage Opera Company, Washington, DC; definitive version (with minor exceptions): 28 December 1906, Opéra-Comique, Paris
CAST   Madama Butterfly (Cio-Cio-San) s, Suzuki ms, Kate Pinkerton ms, B. F. Pinkerton t, Sharpless bar, Goro t, Prince Yamadori t, The Bonze b, Yakuside b, Imperial Commissioner b, Official Registrar b, Butterfly's Mother ms, Aunt s, Cousin s, Sorrow silent; satb chorus of Butterfly's relatives and friends, servants

Puccini's first exposure to *Madama Butterfly* (in June 1900) was at a performance of David Belasco's play in London. It is clear that what initially caught the composer's interest – he knew little English – was a drama intimately tied to a striking new ambience (Japan); and we can guess that this immediately suggested musical possibilities. Very soon afterwards, Puccini expanded his vision. With the help of material from John Luther Long's short story (the source for Belasco's play), he planned to make a two-act opera: the first act set in North America, the second in Japan, thus establishing a dramatic juxtaposition between two distinctive musical ambiences. Once the rights to *Butterfly* had been cleared, Illica set to work on a scenario, and in March 1901 came up with a different plan: Act I would be a kind of prologue, depicting the meeting and marriage of Butterfly and Pinkerton in Japan. Act II was to be in three scenes, with episodes in Butterfly's house framing a scene at the American consulate. Thus, in both parts, the contrast between 'European' and 'Oriental' values could be explored. This plan (elaborated by Illica and Giacosa) held good for over a year, but then, in November 1902, the composer insisted that the consulate scene be discarded. This decision had considerable repercussions. Act II now concentrated single-mindedly on Butterfly: the other principal characters, Pinkerton and Sharpless, were now embarrassingly peripheral, so much so that it later became clear that Pinkerton's part would have to be 'artificially' filled out in the new Act II. The opera's premiere at La Scala, Milan, was a resounding failure, and in the coming years Puccini continued to revise the score, including taking out some of the detailed Japanese local colour in Act I, and adding new material for Pinkerton, notably his aria 'Addio fiorito asil', in Act II, Part II.

SYNOPSIS
The opera takes place near Nagasaki in the early 1900s.
    Act I Outside a little house overlooking the harbour. Pinkerton, an American naval officer, has taken out a 999-year lease. He is making the final arrangements with the Japanese marriage-broker, Goro, for a Japanese wedding. From a discussion with the American consul, Sharpless, we gather that according to Japanese law the marriage will not be binding. Pinkerton revels in his carefree attitude as a 'Yankee vagabondo' who takes his pleasure where he finds it ('Dovunque al mondo'); Sharpless tries in vain to warn him that his 15-year-old bride, Butterfly, is serious about the marriage. Butterfly enters amid a bustle of friends and relatives, singing happily of the love that awaits her. After shyly greeting Pinkerton, she shows him her few belongings – including the ceremonial dagger with which her father killed himself – and the commissioner performs the wedding ceremony. But the festivities are short-lived; her uncle (the bonze) arrives and curses her for converting to Christianity, and her relatives and friends immediately join him in rejecting her. Butterfly is left alone with Pinkerton, who tries to comfort her. Her servant Suzuki prepares her for the wedding night, and she joins Pinkerton in the garden for an extended love duet ('Viene la sera'). He is enchanted with his plaything-wife and, while she speaks tenderly of her love, ardently claims his fluttering, captured butterfly.
    Act II (Part I) The same house, several years later. Butterfly and Suzuki are alone. Pinkerton sailed for America three years ago, but Butterfly remains fiercely loyal and describes to Suzuki her dream of his return ('Un bel dì'). Sharpless, knowing that Pinkerton has taken an American wife and will soon be arriving in Nagasaki with her, attempts to prepare Butterfly for the shock. But Butterfly will not listen and remains stubbornly faithful; she shows Sharpless the child she has borne Pinkerton without his knowledge, convinced that this revelation will ensure her husband's return. Sharpless leaves, unable to face Butterfly with the truth. A cannon shot is heard, and Butterfly and Suzuki see Pinkerton's ship coming into harbour. Butterfly jubilantly prepares for his return, filling the room with flowers and again donning her bridal costume. With preparations complete, the two women and the child sit down to wait for Pinkerton's arrival. Night falls; as Suzuki and the child sleep and Butterfly waits motionless, a humming chorus is heard in the distance.
    Act II (Part II) Dawn. Butterfly has fallen asleep at her post. Suzuki rouses her and she carries the sleeping child into the next room, singing a sad lullaby. Pinkerton and Sharpless arrive and ask Suzuki to talk to Pinkerton's new wife, Kate, who is waiting

outside. Suzuki agrees, but the sight of her distress, together with memories of the past, overcomes Pinkerton. He is filled with remorse ('Addio fiorito asil'), and he leaves rather than face the woman he deserted. Butterfly rushes in, searching desperately for Pinkerton, but she sees only the strange woman waiting in the garden. Suzuki and Sharpless manage to break the news that this is Pinkerton's wife, and that her husband will never return to her. Butterfly seems to accept the blow, and agrees to give up her son, asking only that Pinkerton come in person to fetch him. Kate and Sharpless leave; Suzuki tries to comfort Butterfly, but she asks to be left alone. She takes her father's dagger from the wall and prepares to kill herself. Suzuki pushes the child into the room, and Butterfly drops the dagger, momentarily deterred. After an impassioned farewell ('O a me, sceso dal trono'), she blindfolds the child and, going behind a screen, stabs herself just as Pinkerton rushes in calling her name.

The play of varied 'local colours', always an important feature of Puccini's writing, takes on particular importance in Act I of *Madama Butterfly*, which was structurally conceived along lines very similar to those of *La bohème*. As in the earlier opera, though on a much larger scale, an opening section establishes a musical and dramatic atmosphere of hectic activity, which is then juxtaposed with a lyrical and comparatively static close. However, in *Butterfly* there is a central shift in musical ambience marked by the entrance of the heroine. The final duet in Act I breaks new musical ground and although, as Illica pointed out early on, it superficially resembles that of Rodolfo and Mimì in *La bohème*, it is actually a far more complex musical and dramatic structure. By mediating between contrasting musical ambiences and then gradually blending them, the duet ends with the lovers subsumed in a new musical medium, one that somehow arises from their two quite separately established styles. Act II focuses on the heroine with (for Puccini) unprecedented concentration, and leads inexorably to the tragic dénouement. Whether the music of this final scene is capable of sustaining its weight of dramatic expectation is a matter of debate, but few will deny that *Butterfly* makes an important and brave attempt to break away from established dramatic patterns.

La fanciulla del West
The Girl of the Golden West
Opera in three acts (2h)
Libretto by Guelfo Civinini and Carlo Zangarini, based on the play *The Girl of the Golden West* by David Belasco (1905)
Composed 1908–10
PREMIERES 10 December 1910, Metropolitan, New York; UK: 29 May 1911, Covent Garden, London; Italy: 12 June 1911, Teatro Costanzi, Rome
CAST Minnie *s*, Jack Rance *bar*, Dick Johnson (Ramerrez) *t*, Nick *t*, Ashby *b*, Sonora *b*, Trim *t*, Sid *bar*, Bello (Handsome) *bar*, Harry *t*, Joe *t*, Happy *bar*, Larkens *b*, Billy Jackrabbit *b*, Wowkle *ms*, Jake Wallace *bar*, José Castro *b*, Postilion *t*; *tb* chorus of men of the camp

After considering a variety of subjects – including

Victor Hugo's *The Hunchback of Notre-Dame* – and being constantly distracted by foreign and domestic travels, Puccini finally settled on another 'exotic' subject for his next opera. The composer saw Belasco's *The Girl of the Golden West* in New York in early 1907 (he was there to see the Metropolitan premieres of both *Manon Lescaut* and *Madama Butterfly*), and decided to set it to music after reading an Italian translation. His librettists Zangarini and Civinini were on occasion slow to produce, and a personal tragedy – in which a servant girl of Puccini's was driven to suicide by his wife's unfounded jealousy – forced him to put the work aside for some time. Appropriately enough, the opera received its first performance in America, where it was conducted by Toscanini and greeted with great enthusiasm. The star cast was headed by Emmy Destinn, Enrico Caruso and Pasquale Amato.

SYNOPSIS
At the foot of the Cloudy Mountains (Nubi) in California. A miners' camp at the time of the 1849–50 gold rush.

Act I The Polka Bar. The bandit Ramerrez is at large, and a $5000 reward has been set for him. Sheriff Jack Rance declares his love for Minnie, the chaste darling of the miners ('Minnie, dalla mia casa'), but she rejects him, reminiscing about her parents' love for each other and hoping that she will find true love ('Laggiù nel Soledad'). A man announcing himself as Dick Johnson arrives. He has met Minnie before, and their friendly relationship angers Rance. All the men go out in search of Ramerrez, leaving Minnie alone with Johnson. In their ensuing conversation, Johnson becomes increasingly enamoured, and they agree to meet later in her cabin.

Act II Minnie's cabin, one hour later. Minnie is excitedly preparing for her visitor. Johnson arrives, and as they have supper Minnie tells him how much she loves her life in the mountains ('Oh, se sapeste'). Completely enchanted, Johnson embraces her; she succumbs ecstatically to her 'first kiss'. As he prepares to leave, he discovers that snow is falling heavily outside, and Minnie agrees to let him stay the night. As he goes off to bed, Rance arrives to tell Minnie that 'Johnson' is none other than the bandit Ramerrez. When Rance has left, Minnie angrily confronts Johnson, who pleads for her understanding, telling her how he was fated from birth for the bandit's life ('Una parola sola'), but she orders him to leave. As soon as he has gone, shots ring out and Johnson's body slumps against the door. Minnie drags him in and succeeds in hiding him in her loft. Rance again enters, searching for the bandit, and drops of blood falling on his hand eventually reveal Johnson. In a desperate ploy, Minnie plays Rance at poker: if she wins, Johnson will go free; if she loses, she will agree to marry Rance. She wins by cheating on the last hand, Rance leaves and she collapses, laughing hysterically.

Act III A nearby forest. Rance and friends sit by a fire. News arrives that Johnson has been caught, and the miners prepare to string him up. Johnson is brought in and, after speaking tenderly of Minnie,

begging the miners not to tell her how he died ('Ch'ella mi creda libero'), is led to the makeshift gallows. But Minnie arrives just in time and pleads with the miners to spare him. They eventually agree, unable to refuse her after all she has done for them, and Minnie and Johnson depart for a new life together.

Parts of *Fanciulla* present a musical-dramatic problem even more severe than that in Act I of *Tosca*: the sheer complexity of stage action allows very little time to 'place' events musically, and crowds out the opportunity for those lyrical pauses and developments so necessary to Puccini's art. Clearly the composer willingly embraced this type of drama, but it is at least arguable that by the time of *Fanciulla* his powers of musical invention were less able to sustain such extreme concentration. Like *Tosca* – and perhaps even more so – the opera needs singing actors of the first quality in order to succeed on stage. What is undeniable is that *Fanciulla* is harmonically and orchestrally one of Puccini's most innovative scores, and in these two areas represents a high point in experimentation and musical daring. For this, and for many other reasons, it deserves a better relative placing in the Puccinian canon than it today enjoys.

La rondine
The Swallow
Lyric comedy in three acts (1h 45m)
Libretto by Giuseppe Adami, based on the German libretto by Alfred Maria Willner and Heinz Reichert
Composed 1914–16; rev. 1919; further revs 1920
PREMIERES 27 March 1917, Salle Garnier, Monte Carlo; Italy: 5 June 1917, Bologna; US: 10 March 1928, Metropolitan, New York; UK: 24 June 1929 BBC radio; 9 December 1965, Fulham Town Hall, London
CAST Magda de Civry *s*, Ruggero Lastouc *t*, Rambaldo Fernandez *bar*, Lisette *s*, Prunier *t*, 4 *s*, 2 *ms*, *t*, *bar*, 3 *b*; *satb* chorus of citizens, students, artists, dancers

After *La fanciulla del West* Puccini spent some fruitless years searching for a suitable libretto for his next work. The plan for *La rondine* emerged from a proposal made in 1913 for Puccini to write a Viennese operetta for the Karltheater. Eventually Puccini agreed, though he insisted on writing a comic opera (with no spoken dialogue) and on setting the text in Italian. In due course a German text arrived and was translated by Giuseppe Adami. Puccini finished the score in October 1915, but the outbreak of the First World War had put the whole project in jeopardy, and it was some time before he could secure the rights to arrange a first performance and Italian publication.

SYNOPSIS
Paris and Nice during the Second Empire.

Act I A Parisian salon. Magda (the mistress of Rambaldo, a rich banker) and her maid Lisette playfully discuss the joys of love with Prunier. Ruggero, the son of one of Rambaldo's friends, joins the party, and all decide that, for his first night in Paris, he should go to the popular night spot Bullier. When the guests leave, Prunier and Lisette decide to go out together. Magda, who is feeling wistful and has had adventures there in the past, dons a disguise and decides she too will go to Bullier.

Act II Bullier. Magda and Ruggero meet and dance, becoming strongly attracted to each other. Even though Rambaldo appears and confronts Magda, she will not break off, and eventually she and Ruggero admit their love and leave together.

Act III Some months later. Magda and Ruggero are living together blissfully in Nice. Ruggero tells Magda that he has written to his mother for consent to marry her, but Magda realizes that she will never receive his family's approval. Lisette and Prunier are still together, although Prunier's attempt to put Lisette on the stage in Nice has proved a disaster. Ruggero bursts in with his mother's letter, which blesses his marriage; but Magda tells him she can never become his wife and sadly decides that she must leave him for ever.

La rondine has always been the least performed of Puccini's mature operas, in spite of certain well-known extracts such as Magda's Act I aria 'Che il bel sogno' and the Act II concertato 'Bevo al tuo fresco sorriso'. Various reasons for its comparative lack of success have been suggested, among which the weaknesses of Ruggero's characterization and the shaky motivation of Magda's Traviata-like renunciation are clearly well founded. But perhaps the central problem is with the extensive sub-plot between Lisette and Prunier, which vies with the Magda–Ruggero plot in length and development but in which Puccini found little to stimulate his lyrical fantasy. However, for those who know the opera well, La rondine cannot be easily dismissed; its restraint and lightness of touch suggest a surprising new range in Puccini's musical language – one that many regret he did not explore further.

Il trittico

Triptych of one-act operas
PREMIERES 14 December 1918, Metropolitan, New York; Italy: 11 January 1919, Teatro Costanzi, Rome; UK: 18 June 1920, Covent Garden, London

The idea of combining a collection of one-act operas into a single evening had been on Puccini's mind through most of his career, but had consistently been opposed by his publisher, Ricordi. Puccini first saw Didier Gold's play La houppelande in Paris in 1912, and by 1913 he was in negotiations with Illica about the subject. Eventually, though, a libretto was fashioned by Giuseppe Adami, and work on Il tabarro began in October 1915, immediately after Puccini had completed La rondine. He finished this first panel of the 'triptych' in 1916, with no idea of what the companion pieces were going to be. After considering a host of topics, the answer eventually came from Giovacchino Forzano, who in early 1917 offered Puccini the libretto for a one-act opera set in a convent, Suor Angelica, and (soon afterwards) a second, comic, subject entitled Gianni Schicchi. Puccini accepted both gladly, and finished the remaining two operas by early 1918 – for him, something like record time. The Metro-

politan in New York paid a considerable sum for the rights to the world premiere, which was given that same year, conducted by Roberto Moranzoni. Though Il trittico has occasionally been revived in its complete form, today it is more usual to find two of the three operas performed as a double-bill.

Il tabarro

The Cloak
Opera in one act (55m)
Libretto by Giuseppe Adami, based on the play La houppelande by Didier Gold (1910)
Composed 1915–16
PREMIERES see Il trittico above
CAST Giorgetta (age 25) s, Luigi (20) t, Michele (50) bar, La Frugola (50) ms, Il Tinca (35) t, Il Talpa (55) b, A Song-vendor t, 2 Lovers s, t, An Organ-Grinder silent; satb chorus of stevedores and seamstresses

SYNOPSIS
The opera takes place in contemporary Paris. A barge is tied to a quay beside the Seine, and its owner, Michele, watches the sun set as the stevedores finish the day's work. Michele's wife, Giorgetta, goes about her chores, and as workers come and go and street musicians pass she steals a few moments with her lover, Luigi, who is one of the stevedores. They are interrupted by Michele, who looks at them suspiciously but leaves them alone long enough for them to arrange a rendezvous for later that night. After Luigi has gone, Michele returns and speaks of the past, begging Giorgetta to return to their former love and happiness. But Giorgetta evades his caresses and Michele grimly watches her go inside, convinced of her infidelity. He remains alone in the dark, tormenting himself with thoughts of her betrayal ('Nulla, silenzio'). In silence he lights his pipe, and Luigi, who mistakes the light for Giorgetta's pre-arranged signal, runs aboard the barge. Michele catches Luigi and, after forcing him to confess his love for Giorgetta, chokes him to death. When Giorgetta reappears, Michele conceals the corpse under his cloak; as she approaches, he removes the cloak and triumphantly reveals Luigi's lifeless body.

Il tabarro has many admirers, some even considering it the composer's finest work. The orchestration is highly innovative (as is demonstrated, for example, by the orchestral introduction, in which a texture of Debussy-like clarity and subtlety sets forth the governing ambience of the score); the musical characterization is surprisingly well defined considering the duration of the action, with even minor figures such as Il Tinca (a stevedore) and La Frugola (wife of another stevedore, Talpa) sharply focused. Perhaps most importantly, the timing of the musical drama is impeccable, with lyrical scenes always balancing the action sequences. Realistic touches such as the motor horn in the opening, or the music-seller who offers his clients a snatch of La bohème, are subtly integrated into the generally sombre atmosphere, and, as the major characters all grow out of this ambience, the effect of the drama is all the more compelling.

Suor Angelica
Sister Angelica
Opera in one act (1h)
Libretto by Giovacchino Forzano
Composed 1917
PREMIERES see *Il trittico* above
CAST Suor Angelica *s*, La Zia Principessa (her aunt, the princess) *c*, Suor Genoveva *s*, Suor Osmina *s*, Suor Dolcina *s*, La Badessa (the Abbess) *ms*, La Suora Zelatrice (the monitor) *ms*, La Maestra delle Novizie (the mistress of the novices) *ms*, La Suora Infermiera (the nursing sister) *ms; sa* chorus of alms-collectors, novices, lay sisters

SYNOPSIS
A convent in late-17th-century Italy. As the curtain opens, the nuns are finishing their prayers and joyfully go about their business, while Sister Angelica tries unsuccessfully to hide her unhappiness; in the seven years she has spent in the convent, she has heard no news of her family. But soon the abbess announces that Angelica's aunt, a princess, has come to visit. When the aunt is ushered in, Angelica is checked by the coldness of her aunt's greeting. From their conversation we learn that Angelica has been put in the convent by her family as punishment for having an illegitimate child. As Angelica begs for compassion, her aunt coldly informs her that the child is now dead. The princess leaves Angelica alone to weep despairingly, desiring only to end her sorrows and join her child in heaven ('Senza Mamma'). The other nuns join her in ecstatic praise of the Holy Virgin; when she is again left alone, she drinks poison, singing a joyful farewell to life. Suddenly her calm is shattered: by killing herself she is damned to eternal separation from the child she loves. She prays desperately to the Madonna; angels' voices join in her prayer as the Madonna herself appears, bringing the child to lead his mother into heaven.

As the plot summary indicates, this is an unashamedly sentimental drama, and perhaps gains its full effect only in its original context, framed by the more vivid and immediate *Tabarro* and *Gianni Schicchi*. The religious setting allowed Puccini to indulge in some pastiche of the world of his musical ancestors, and if the resulting pseudo-ecclesiastical vein works well in the less elevated context of the opening section of the opera, it seems strained at the more demanding, miraculous close. But there are moments of considerable effect, in particular the tension-laden meeting between Sister Angelica and her glacial aunt – the latter certainly the most extraordinary of Puccini's female creations; and Angelica's 'Senza Mamma', which follows the princess's exit, remains one of Puccini's greatest soprano arias.

Gianni Schicchi
Opera in one act (55m)
Libretto by Giovacchino Forzano, based on an episode (Canto XXX, l. 32ff.) in Dante's *Inferno* (*c.* 1307–21)
Composed 1917–18
PREMIERES see *Il trittico* above
CAST Gianni Schicchi (age 50) *bar*, Lauretta (21) *s*, Rinuccio (24) *t*, Nella (34) *s*, La Ciesca (38) *ms*, Zita (60) *c*, Gheraldino (7) *c*, Gheraldo (40) *t*, Marco (45) *bar*, Ser

Amantio di Nicolao *bar*, Betto di Signa (indefinable age) *b*, Simone (70) *b*, Maestro Spinelloccio *b*, Pinellino *b*, Guccio *b*

SYNOPSIS
Late-13th-century Florence. The curtain opens on the bedroom of Buoso Donati, a rich old gentleman who has just died. His relatives are gathered round the deathbed, feigning grief to impress each other, until a rumour that Buoso has left all his money to a monastery sends them into a feverish search for his will. The young Rinuccio finds it first, but withholds it from the others until he has extracted a promise from them: when they receive Buoso's money, he will be allowed to marry Lauretta, the daughter of Gianni Schicchi. The relatives hurriedly agree, but are sorely disappointed when they find out that all Buoso's money is indeed left to the Church. Rinuccio suggests turning the problem over to Gianni Schicchi, who is famed for his cunning, even though the relatives scoff at Schicchi's low birth ('Avete torto'). Schicchi himself arrives in answer to a secret summons from Rinuccio, bringing Lauretta with him. The relatives condescend to ask for Schicchi's help, but he refuses; finally Lauretta intercedes, begging her father to make her marriage to Rinuccio possible ('O mio babbino caro'). Schicchi comes up with a plan: they are to hide Buoso's death long enough for him, disguised as Buoso, to make a new will. Delighted, the relatives send for the notary, individually bribing Schicchi to give them the most favourable portion of the inheritance. Schicchi agrees to everything, reminding them that to reveal the trick will mean severe punishment according to Florentine law. When the notary arrives, Schicchi awards the lion's share of Buoso's property to his 'devoted friend, Gianni Schicchi' and the relatives are helpless to intervene. Once the notary has gone, Schicchi drives the relatives from his new home. Rinuccio and Lauretta remain on the terrace, singing of their love for each other. Schicchi returns and, seeing the young lovers, announces to the audience his satisfaction with the way Buoso's money has been used.

It is unfortunate that *Gianni Schicchi* was the only outright comic opera that Puccini wrote. Throughout his career he periodically toyed with comic subjects, but in the end refused to commit himself to anything that strayed so far from the paths in which he had achieved his greatest successes. Again, it is probably thanks to the one-act format, whose more discrete, short-term goals released the composer from his usual doubts, that we have this masterly vignette of medieval Florence. As with *Il tabarro*, the musical characterization is on a very high level, in particular the portraits of Gianni Schicchi and his daughter Lauretta; and the sheer musical invention of the opera, as well as many of its most characteristic idioms, places in the clearest possible context the debt Puccini owed to his great predecessor Giuseppe Verdi, whose final opera, *Falstaff*, paved the way for Puccini's comic masterpiece.

Turandot

Opera in three acts (1h 45m)
Libretto by Giuseppe Adami and Renato Simoni, after the play by Carlo Gozzi (1762)
Composed 1920–24; completed by Franco Alfano 1925–6
PREMIERES 25 April 1926, La Scala, Milan; US: 16 November 1926, Metropolitan, New York; UK: 7 June 1927, Covent Garden, London
CAST Princess Turandot *s*, The Unknown Prince (Calaf) *t*, Liù *s*, Timur *b*, Emperor Altoum *t*, Ping *bar*, Pang *t*, Pong *t*, A Mandarin *bar*, Prince of Persia *t*, Executioner *silent*; *satb* chorus of imperial guards, the executioner's servants, children, priests, mandarins, dignitaries, the eight wise men, Turandot's handmaidens, soldiers, flag-carriers, musicians, ghosts of the dead, the crowd

The idea of setting Gozzi's *Turandot*, and thus of returning to the Far Eastern ambience of *Madama Butterfly*, was first mooted by Giuseppe Adami and Renato Simoni in March 1920, nearly three years after the premiere of Busoni's short opera on the same story. Puccini was enthusiastic, but the opera went through the kind of agonizing genesis that had become the norm in Puccinian creation. Endless prose and verse scenarios were proffered and rejected; and there was a crisis during which Puccini, having completed about half the work, became convinced that its shape should be radically altered: until a fairly late stage, Act I was planned – and, what is more important, musically sketched – to encompass a good deal more of the action than the version we know today, ending where the present Act II now ends, with Calaf's solving of the riddles. When the decision came to split this sequence in two, both halves had to be enlarged: Act I with the finale after Calaf's and Liù's arias, and the new Act II with the addition of an opening scene for Ping, Pang and Pong, and a grand aria for Turandot, 'In questa reggia'.

Everything up to the final scene was finished by the end of March 1924, but the closing duet between Calaf and Turandot was still to be written when the composer died in November. The opera was completed (in part by following sketches left by Puccini) by the young composer Franco Alfano. The first performance (which did not include Alfano's ending) was conducted by Arturo Toscanini.

SYNOPSIS

The action takes place in ancient Peking. Princess Turandot has decreed that she will marry any prince who can solve three riddles, but that if he fails in the attempt he must die. Many have tried; all have failed.

Act I By the walls of Peking. The curtain opens on a crowded scene at sunset amid preparations for the execution of the latest contestant, the prince of Persia. The young Prince Calaf recognizes his father, Timur, who is accompanied by Liù, a slave girl. (Timur's throne has been usurped, and he has escaped penniless from his kingdom.) The execution proceeds; Turandot appears on the palace balcony, luminous in the light of the newly risen moon, to give the signal of death. Calaf is dazzled by her beauty and, as the prince of Persia's death cry rings out, Calaf determines to win Turandot for himself. Emperor Altoum's three ministers, Ping, Pang and Pong, attempt to dissuade

Calaf, and are joined in this by Timur and Liù. Calaf tries to comfort his father, asking Liù to continue to care for Timur ('Non piangere, Liù!'). But his purpose cannot be deflected and, crying out 'Turandot', he strikes three blows on a gong to signal the arrival of a new suitor.

Act II Scene 1: A pavilion of the palace. Ping, Pang and Pong review the endless cycle of executions they have witnessed since Turandot first issued her decree. They dream of a princess transformed by love and restoring peace to China, but a fanfare recalls them to the reality of another trial. Scene 2: The square of the royal palace. Emperor Altoum, weary of the needless deaths, pleads with Calaf to give up the challenge, but Calaf insists on proceeding. Turandot places herself in front of the emperor's throne. She explains that, inspired by an ancient princess who was cruelly betrayed by a man, she has vowed to keep herself pure ('In questa reggia'). The trial begins. One by one, Turandot announces her riddles. To the crowd's gathering excitement, Calaf answers each one correctly. As he solves the third riddle, Turandot collapses in despair, begging her father to release her from her own decree. The emperor is unyielding, but Calaf offers her a chance of release. He gives her a riddle of his own: if she can discover his name by daybreak, he will pay the forfeit and die; if not, she will be his.

Act III Scene 1: The steps of a pavilion in the palace garden that same night. Calaf is lyrically contemplating his coming victory over the princess ('Nessun dorma'). Ping, Pang and Pong arrive, desperate over Turandot's new decree by which all their lives are forfeit if the prince's name is not discovered by dawn. They tempt Calaf with a variety of delights. Calaf remains unmoved until the guards drag in Timur and Liù, who had been seen earlier in the company of Calaf. Turandot herself enters to question Timur, but Liù courageously steps forward, saying that she alone knows the secret of the prince's name. When the soldiers try to force the name from her, her love for Calaf gives her the strength to resist. Finally Liù turns to Turandot and, crying that through her sacrifice, Turandot will learn love ('Tu che di gel sei cinta'), she grabs a soldier's dagger and stabs herself, dying at Calaf's feet. Timur, heartbroken at her death, follows as her body is carried off in mournful procession. Calaf and Turandot are left alone. Their extended duet comes to a first climax as Calaf kisses Turandot passionately. Overcome with a mixture of passion and shame, she begs him to leave for ever, but instead he gives her the answer to his riddle, telling her his name and so placing his life in her hands. Trumpets announce the coming of dawn. Scene 2: In the palace square. Turandot announces triumphantly to the emperor and the crowd that she knows the stranger's name. But then to everyone's surprise she cries out, 'His name is love!' and, to a reprise of 'Nessun dorma', all join in rejoicing.

Turandot has many of the qualities of Puccini's earlier operas – superb dramatic pacing in particular – but what distinguishes it from its predecessors, and is perhaps its most remarkable quality, is its extraordinary richness of musical invention; something all the more surprising from a composer who constantly complained that advancing age was sapping his creative powers. As in many of the best *fin-de-siècle* operas, there is in *Turandot* a riot of competing musical colours, each primarily associated with an element of the drama: the heroic prince, the proud princess, the pathetic slave girl, the bizarre ministers, even the hapless Persian suitor – all create their own musical atmosphere during the course of Act I, and thus discretely dominate sections of the drama. These 'colours' are not restricted to individual characters: there are several distinct sides to the exotic ambience, for example, not merely a blanket characterization of all things 'Eastern'. There is also an unusually large system of recurring motifs and melodies: one thinks immediately of the motif that regularly accompanies Turandot's entrances, or the choruses that welcome the emperor. These are hardly ever used in a developmental way, and almost invariably return in exact repetition and within the same broad musical context. They thus serve to articulate the various contrasting blocks of colour rather than to create connections between them. And all this musical variety is wrapped in an orchestral texture whose richness and invention Puccini had not previously equalled.

Other operas: *Le villi*, 1884; *Edgar*, 1889

E.H./R.P.

HENRY PURCELL
b 1658 or 1659, London; *d* 21 November 1695, London

Purcell is generally regarded as the greatest English opera composer before the 20th century, yet he wrote only one true opera, *Dido and Aeneas*. A pupil of Matthew Locke and John Blow, he had endeavoured to emulate the new French and Italian styles, though his music remained conservative and distinctively English in its predilection for dissonant counterpoint. Purcell is particularly admired for his genius at setting the English language.

Purcell was appointed composer-in-ordinary (that is, with salary) for the King's Violins in 1677 and co-organist of the Chapel Royal in 1682, having already succeeded Blow as organist of Westminster Abbey in 1678, and his early career was naturally centred on the court. He served four monarchs – Charles II (to 1685), James II (1685–88) and William and Mary (1689–95) – during the turbulent years of the Exclusion Crisis and the Glorious Revolution. His earliest public works are anthems for the Chapel Royal and royal welcome songs. During these formative years he also composed much instrumental music, including the fantasias for viol consort – contrapuntal *tours de force* and the last of their kind – and trio sonatas, supposedly in imitation of the new Italian style but in reality continuing to explore the same English vein as the fantasias.

Purcell's first contribution to the professional stage was the incidental music for Nathaniel Lee's tragedy *Theodosius* of 1680. The songs and choruses are modelled on the music of his teacher Locke, who had dominated the London musical theatre until his death in 1677. The *Theodosius* pieces are rather stiff and awkward in comparison to the highly sophisticated instrumental music Purcell was composing at the same time, and give little indication of his later achievement in dramatic song. The political upheavals and management crises of the London theatres during the 1680s afforded him few other opportunities to write for the stage, his output being restricted to anthems, coronation music and festive odes, most notably those associated with the recently established London St Cecilia's Day celebrations.

In the last five years of his life, Purcell's career turned decisively towards the theatre, largely in consequence of William and Mary's drastic curtailment of the Royal Musick, which forced Purcell and many of his colleagues to seek employment outside the court. In 1690 he composed the music for *The Prophetess, or The History of Dioclesian*, adapted by the actor Thomas Betterton from a Jacobean tragi-comedy. *Dioclesian* (as it became known) is a semi-opera, that is, a play with substantial musical episodes or masques which are sung and danced by minor characters – spirits, soldiers, priests, fairies and the like; the main characters do not sing. The choice of Purcell as composer of *Dioclesian*, which proved a great financial and artistic success, was probably influenced by the amateur performance in 1689 of *Dido and Aeneas* at a girls' boarding school in Chelsea. The libretto was written by Nahum Tate, soon to become poet laureate, and the school was run by Josias Priest, a choreographer at the Theatre Royal; both were men of considerable influence in the London theatrical world.

Dioclesian attracted the attention of John Dryden, who offered Purcell the libretto of his semi-opera *King Arthur*, which was produced in 1691, another great success for the Theatre Royal. Because it was conceived as a semi-opera rather than being adapted from an old play, *King Arthur* is much more cohesive than *Dioclesian*, and here Purcell came close to matching the quality of *Dido*; two numbers, the so-called frost scene and the nostalgic song 'Fairest Isle', have achieved immortality.

Purcell's next semi-opera, *The Fairy-Queen* of 1692, was to be the grandest and most lavish of all such works. Adapted anonymously from Shakespeare's *A Midsummer Night's Dream*, it includes Purcell's finest and most sophisticated dramatic music, all of which is collected into four self-contained masques; a fifth was added to a revival in 1693. But *The Fairy-Queen*, which proved as popular as Purcell's previous works, nearly bankrupted the Theatre Royal because of the expense of the scenes, music and dances. No new semi-opera was planned for 1694, and Purcell concentrated instead on writing orchestral incidental music (collected in the posthumous *Ayres for the Theatre* of 1697) and songs for plays. In the latter genre he was eclipsed in popularity by his younger contemporary John Eccles, whose simple and highly dramatic songs were better suited to the actor-singers (such as the celebrated Anne Bracegirdle) than was Purcell's more difficult, highly decorated vocal music.

In early 1695 Purcell's theatrical career suffered another setback when Betterton was given permission to set up a rival theatre in a converted tennis court in Lincoln's Inn Fields. Not only did the old actor persuade most of his colleagues to follow him, but Eccles and virtually all of the professional stage singers also joined the renegades, leaving Purcell with a handful of young and inexperienced singers. He nevertheless composed a great deal of theatre music during the last year of his life, including masques and entertainments for *Timon of Athens*, *The Libertine*, *Bonduca*, a song or two for *The Tempest*, and his last semi-opera, *The Indian Queen*. He did not live to complete this score, and his younger brother, Daniel, was called down from Oxford to compose the final masque.

Purcell's only opera thus came at the beginning of his brief theatre career. Because *Dido and Aeneas* is through-composed and seems to conform to the 19th-century ideal of musical tragedy, it has assumed a central position in Purcell's *oeuvre*. Yet there is no evidence that he was dissatisfied with semi-opera as a genre or frustrated at not having the opportunity to write another all-sung opera. One needs to understand the conventions of semi-opera to appreciate how much better a composer Purcell became after *Dido and Aeneas*.

Dido and Aeneas

Tragic opera in three acts (1h)
Libretto by Nahum Tate, after his tragedy *Brutus of Alba* (1678) and Book IV of Virgil's *Aeneid*
PREMIERES spring 1689, Josias Priest's boarding school for girls, Chelsea; US: 13 January 1924, New York, Town Hall (concert); 18 February 1932, Juilliard School, New York
CAST Dido *s*, Belinda *s*, Second Woman *s*, Sorceress *ms* or *b-bar*, First Witch *s*, Second Witch *s*, Spirit *ms*, Aeneas *t*, Sailor *s*; *satb* chorus of courtiers, witches, sailors and cupids

The circumstances behind the composition and performance of *Dido and Aeneas* are unknown. According to the sole surviving copy of the libretto of the Chelsea production, the opera was performed 'by young gentlewomen', presumably the girls of Priest's boarding school. It was modelled very closely on John Blow's opera *Venus and Adonis*, which had also been performed by an all-female cast at Priest's school in April 1684. That *Dido* was also a spring production is suggested by a couplet of Thomas Durfey's spoken epilogue: 'Like nimble fawns, and birds that bless the spring / Unscarr'd by turning times we dance and sing.' The opera originally included a prologue (music lost) which alludes to William and Mary and welcomes the arrival of spring; so *Dido* may have formed part of the celebrations of their joint coronation on 11 April 1689. Like *Venus and Adonis*, *Dido* is highly unusual for baroque opera in having a tragic ending. Tate based the plot on Virgil's account of Aeneas at Carthage, the main difference being that in the opera the Trojan prince, rather than being prompted by the gods to sail on to Italy, is tricked into leaving Dido by an evil sorceress, Tate's invention.

SYNOPSIS

Act I After escaping from the sack of Troy, Prince Aeneas sets sail for Italy, where he is destined to found Rome. Blown off course to Carthage, he is welcomed by Queen Dido who, being burdened by affairs of state and unspoken grief ('Ah! Belinda'), is reluctant to reveal a growing love for her guest. Urged on by her confidante Belinda and her attendants ('Fear no danger'), Dido tacitly succumbs to Aeneas, and the court rejoices ('To the hills and the vales').

Act II Scene 1: With the playing of a sombre prelude, the scene changes to a cave, where a sorceress and her witches plot Queen Dido's downfall ('Wayward sisters'). Hoping to trick Aeneas into leaving Dido by reminding him of his destiny in Italy, they prepare the charm in an echo chorus ('In our deep vaulted cell'). Scene 2 is set in a grove where Dido and Aeneas, having consummated their love during the previous night, are entertained by Belinda and an attendant ('Thanks to these lonesome vales' . . . 'Oft she visits this lone mountain'). The sorceress (unseen) conjures up a thunderstorm which sends the courtiers running for shelter ('Haste, haste to town'), while Aeneas lags behind to hear a spirit disguised as Mercury order him to leave Carthage ('Stay, Prince, and hear'). He agonizes over his decision to comply with the command.

Act III On the quayside, Aeneas' men are preparing to weigh anchor ('Come away, fellow sailors'). The sorceress and witches reappear to gloat over the impending tragedy ('Destruction's our delight'). The scene shifts back to court, where Dido, having got wind of Aeneas' decision to leave, seeks Belinda's advice ('Your counsel all is urg'd in vain') before bitterly confronting the cowardly Aeneas, who offers to stay but then ignominiously departs. Dido realizes that she cannot live without him. Inconsolable ('Thy hand, Belinda'), she sings her great lament ('When I am laid in earth'), dies, and is mourned by a chorus of cupids ('With drooping wings').

Dido is remarkable for the swift concision of action, its widely contrasting moods (including the comic relief of the sailors' scene) and a deeply tragic ending. For most of these features and a carefully controlled key scheme Purcell was indebted to Blow's *Venus and Adonis*. But *Dido* is much more structured; each scene is built up of units of recitative (or declamatory song), arioso, aria, chorus and dance. Purcell was thus following the formal model offered by Lully's *tragédies en musique*, but his chief innovation, inspired by contemporary Venetian opera, was to concentrate the greatest musical interest in the arias. Dido's are placed at the beginning and end of the opera and both are constructed over ostinato basses: 'Ah! Belinda!' in Act I also displays a da-capo structure, while the famous lament is built over a repeated chromatically descending five-bar bass, also common in Italian opera of the time.

Purcell's recitatives, which have been called the finest in the English language, are regularly measured but with great flexibility of rhythm to reflect the slightest nuance of speech; important words are often decorated with elaborate melismas. The sorceress's part, which Purcell may have conceived for bass-baritone rather than mezzo-soprano as usually heard today, is notable for being set almost entirely in recitative accompanied by four-part strings.

Perhaps because of the involvement of Josias Priest, a professional choreographer, dance dominates the score; key pieces are the triumphing dance (another ground) at the end of Act I, the witches' echo dance (in the style of a French furies' dance) in Act II, Scene 2, and the sailors' dance in Act III, each being radically different in character one from another. And in its brief, sharply contrasting sections, the final witches' dance, which included Jack o' Lantern, resembles a Jacobean antimasque. The opera was even supposed to end with a cupids' dance, which has not survived.

The earliest score of *Dido and Aeneas* dates from nearly a century after the Chelsea performance and differs from Tate's original libretto in several significant ways. Besides the missing prologue mentioned above, the score lacks a dance and chorus of witches at the end of Act II. Many modern producers have therefore felt the need to add music between Aeneas' soliloquy and the beginning of Act III, perhaps the most successful being that arranged by Benjamin Britten from other Purcell works. The original music for this scene, along with the prologue and final cupids' dance, may have been cut from the first public production of *Dido* at Lincoln's Inn Fields Theatre, London, in 1700, when the opera was reordered and inserted into an adaptation of Shakespeare's *Measure for Measure*.

King Arthur, or The British Worthy

Semi-opera in five acts (3h 30m)
Libretto by John Dryden, 1684, rev. 1690–91
PREMIERES May or June 1691, Dorset Garden Theatre, London; US: 24 April 1800, New York
CAST Philadel *s*, Grimbald *b-bar*, Shepherd *t*, Cupid *s*, Cold Genius *b*, Aeolus *b-bar*, Venus *s*; spoken roles

King Arthur was Purcell's second semi-opera (or 'dramatick opera', as Dryden preferred to call it), that is, essentially a tragi-comedy with four or five long musical episodes. As is typical of the genre, the protagonists (King Arthur, Merlin, Oswald, Emmeline et al.) only speak, while most of the music is performed by minor characters; exceptionally, the spirits Philadel and Grimbald both speak and sing. Unlike all of Purcell's other semi-operas, *King Arthur* is not based on an earlier play, and therefore the music is much more closely integrated with the main action. Dryden, who had the year before acknowledged Purcell as an English composer 'equal with the best abroad', conceded that in writing *King Arthur* 'my Art, on this occasion, ought to be subservient to his'. With its spectacular staging, dances and fine music, it was an outstanding success, being frequently revived well into the 18th century.

SYNOPSIS

In a series of set battles with the Saxons, King Arthur and the Britons have regained all the kingdom except Kent. After a heathen sacrifice, Oswald and the

Saxons launch a final assault but are defeated. Urged on by the evil spirit Grimbald, the Saxons resort to treachery, first by trying to lead the Britons on to quicksand and then by kidnapping King Arthur's betrothed, Emmeline, the blind daughter of the duke of Cornwall. Aided by Merlin and Philadel, a good spirit, Arthur attempts to rescue Emmeline from the snares and illusions of an enchanted forest. Meanwhile, the heroine is nearly raped by her gaoler, the Saxon magician Osmond. After breaking the magic spell, Arthur defeats Oswald in single combat, is reunited with Emmeline (her sight now restored), and magnanimously forgives the Saxons. The opera concludes with a masque in praise of Britain – its people, natural resources and institutions.

Apart from the final masque, which lies quite outside the main action, Purcell's music is tightly bound to the drama. The sacrifice scene in Act I ('Woden first to thee') draws somewhat incongruously on the style of the verse anthem, while the scene in Act II in which the Britons pursue the Saxons ('Hither this way') is highly original in the way it advances the plot by rapid alternation between opposing groups of singers. The so-called frost scene in Act III ('What power art thou'), though inspired by a similar episode in Lully's opera *Isis* (1677), is memorable for its quivering string effects and chromatic harmony. Probably the most impressive piece of the score is the long passacaglia in Act IV ('How happy the lover'), a rich tapestry of solos, choruses and dances spun out over a continuously varied four-bar ground bass. The masque in Act V is loosely structured, at times purposefully chaotic, but includes what has been described as Purcell's most perfect song, 'Fairest Isle'.

The Fairy-Queen

Semi-opera in a prologue and five acts (4h)
Libretto, anon., 1692, after the play *A Midsummer Night's Dream* by William Shakespeare (1596)
PREMIERES May 1692, Dorset Garden Theatre, London; rev. version: February 1693, Dorset Garden Theatre, London; US: 30 April 1932, Legion of Honor Palace, San Francisco
CAST Drunken Poet *b-bar*, First and Second Fairies 2 *s*, Night *s*, Mystery *s*, Secresy *ct*, Sleep *b*, Coridon *b-bar*, Mopsa *s* or *c*, Phoebus *t*, Spring *s*, Summer *c*, Autumn *t*, Winter *b-bar*, Juno *s*, Chinese Man *ct*, Chinese Woman (Daphne) *s*, Hymen *b*; spoken roles

The Fairy-Queen, Purcell's third semi-opera, was the most lavish and expensive of all such works. Collaborating with Thomas Betterton as producer (and perhaps the adapter of Shakespeare's play) and Josias Priest as choreographer, Purcell was able for the first time to write exclusively for professional singers, as opposed to actor-singers; the vocal music is correspondingly more elaborate and challenging than any he had written before. The operatic version generally follows the original plot, except that two minor characters are omitted, much of the lyric poetry is modernized or reduced, and the masque of Pyramus and Thisbe, which in Shakespeare is rehearsed by the mechanicals in Act III and performed in Act V, is ingeniously compressed into a single scene in the adaptation. All four masques (a fifth was added to the second version) are self-contained and textually unrelated to *A Midsummer Night's Dream*, but each captures and enhances the atmosphere of the original fairy scenes.

SYNOPSIS

Act I   In accordance with Athenian law, Duke Theseus requires Demetrius to marry Hermia, as her father wishes. But Hermia is beloved of Lysander, while Demetrius is betrothed to Helena. To avoid being mismatched, the pairs of lovers flee the town. In a nearby wood some tradesmen are preparing a play to celebrate the expected weddings. Titania, the fairy queen, has also come into the wood, to escape the rage of her jealous husband, Oberon. The queen's attendants (in the 1693 version) torment a drunken poet (possibly a satire on Thomas Durfey or Thomas Shadwell or both) who has wandered into the wood.

Act II   Puck helps Oberon prepare the love potion while Titania is sung to sleep. The philtre is administered with the familiar confusion.

Act III   Bottom the weaver (with ass's head) entertains the besotted Titania with rustic and highly erotic music.

Act IV   Oberon tries to bring the rightful pairs of lovers back together and releases Titania from the spell. The fairy monarchs' reconciliation is celebrated with a masque of the seasons.

Act V   Oberon presents the disbelieving duke and the other mortals with a Chinese masque (symbolizing enlightenment) in celebration of the state of matrimony.

The music of *The Fairy-Queen* is of the highest quality. The scene added to Act I in 1693 ('Fi– fi– fill up the bowl') is a purposefully disjointed series of ariettas and choruses in which drunkenness and tomfoolery are acutely depicted. In stark contrast the masque of sleep in Act II is an elegant sequence of pieces which grow ever more complex and mysterious. Bottom's masque in Act III juxtaposes the highly dissonant air and chorus 'If love's a sweet passion' and the rollicking dialogue for Coridon and Mopsa 'Now the maids and the men', two of Purcell's best-known vocal pieces. The Act IV masque, framed by a grand chorus in praise of Phoebus ('Hail, great parent'), is rather muted in its differentiation between the seasons. The final masque, which is more loosely organized, includes the counter-tenor air 'Thus, the gloomy world', one of Purcell's finest trumpet songs. *The Fairy-Queen* is remarkable for the way in which all the music, however diverse, complements rather than detracts from the play.

Other semi-operas: *Dioclesian*, 1690; *The Indian Queen*, 1695

C.A.P.

SERGEI RAKHMANINOV

Sergei Vasil'yevich Rakhmaninov; *b* 1 April 1873,
Semyonovo, Russia; *d* 28 March 1943, Beverly Hills,
California, US

Rakhmaninov's operas have never enjoyed a good
press, and productions of them are rare. But while it
is easy to detect the flaws in the libretti of the three
completed works (each in a single act), the scores
contain some of his finest music. As one might expect
from a great song-composer, the writing for the voice
is always grateful, and the instinctive flair for arioso
writing only makes one regret that a suitable libretto
for a full-length opera eluded him. The vocal scores of
all three operas are by Rakhmaninov himself, and are
excellently laid out for the piano.

Rakhmaninov's earliest attempts at opera remain
unfinished: at the age of 15 he sketched parts of
Esmeralda, based on Hugo's *Notre-Dame de Paris*,
and various other early operatic fragments may only
be exercises from his days at the Moscow Conservatory. His last attempts at opera were merely a scenario
for *Salammbô*, after Flaubert (a subject earlier chosen
by Musorgsky), from 1906, and the first act in piano
score of *Monna Vanna*, after Maeterlinck, from 1907.
Monna Vanna has recently been scored by Igor Buketoff, and given in concert performance in America
(Buketoff has also prepared and published an orchestral suite), but the piece remains a tantalizing torso
whose completion was prevented by a contractual
problem. Rakhmaninov achieved great distinction as
an opera conductor in Russia around the turn of the
century, working first with Savva Mamontov's company (where he met Fyodor Shalyapin, whom he
influenced greatly, and who, in turn, inspired some of
his finest vocal writing) and later at the Bolshoi.
Pressure of other compositions and his piano-playing
fought with conducting, and Rakhmaninov's operatic
connections petered out in 1908.

Aleko

Opera in one act (1h)
Libretto by Vladimir Nemirovich-Danchenko, after the
poem *Tsygany* by Aleksandr Pushkin (1824)
PREMIERES 9 May 1893, Bolshoi Theatre, Moscow;
UK: 15 July 1915, London Opera House, London; US:
11 January 1926, Jolson's Theater, New York
CAST Aleko *bar*, Young Gypsy *t*, Old Gypsy *b*, Zemfira *s*,
Old Gypsy Woman *c*; *satb* chorus of gypsies

Although the composition was primarily an examination requirement for the Moscow Conservatory
(which explains why Rakhmaninov was not in a position to alter the libretto), *Aleko* was certainly a successful piece in its day, praised by Tchaikovsky, and often
compared with *Cavalleria rusticana*, with which there
are some structural similarities. Rakhmaninov won
the Great Gold Medal of the Moscow Conservatory
for the work, which he completed and scored in just
17 days, and it has since enjoyed many more productions than its musically superior successors.

SYNOPSIS

Aleko has renounced society to take up with a band
of gypsies, and his former loneliness has been alleviated by the love of Zemfira. Zemfira, however, has
grown tired of Aleko and has taken a young gypsy
as a lover. The old gypsy (Zemfira's father) sings of
his own past tragedy: his mistress deserted him for a
younger man. Aleko impatiently suggests that if he
had been in that position he would not have hesitated
to kill both mistress and lover. Zemfira rocks her
child's cradle, singing an old song about 'my old and
terrible husband', deliberately goading Aleko, who
storms off. He sings of his misery while the camp
sleeps. The young gypsy is heard singing of free love.
Aleko finds Zemfira with the young gypsy and stabs
them to death – Zemfira defiantly affirming her new
love as she dies. The shocked but peaceable gypsies
gather, and punish Aleko with that which he fears
most: exile.

The enthusiasm of the young Rakhmaninov for his
subject crowds the pages of this work, and almost
disguises the rather patchwork nature of the libretto,
which calls for separate numbers, includes dances and
an intermezzo, and allows very little drama to develop
without interruption. The influence of many of the
great Russian opera composers is clear, but, especially
in Aleko's famous cavatina (recorded three times by
Shalyapin), more than a hint of the grand sweep of
Rakhmaninov's mature melodic style is evident. There
are several recurring motifs, which help to hold the
numbers together, and the piece is splendidly orchestrated and gratefully composed for soloists and
chorus, the character of Aleko drawn with much
sympathy. A real burgeoning understanding of musical drama is apparent in the two scenes where the
libretto allows for it: the quarrel between Aleko and

Zemfira, and the discovery *in flagrante delicto* of the lovers.

The Miserly Knight
Skupoi Rytsar'
Opera in three scenes (1h)
Libretto by the composer, an almost word-for-word setting of the 'little tragedy' by Aleksandr Pushkin (1830)
PREMIERES 24 January 1906, Bolshoi Theatre, Moscow; US: 2 December 1910, Boston
CAST The Baron *bar*, Albert *t*, The Duke *bar*, Jewish Moneylender *t*, Servant *b*

Written as a vehicle for Shalyapin, and as the first half of a double-bill with *Francesca da Rimini*, this opera remains a connoisseur's piece whose very story-line precludes much in the way of dramatic opportunity (Pushkin never intended his original playlet to be acted on stage) but allows none the less for very strong musical characterization. The want of female principals or chorus has been unfairly stressed by critics; the drama could not have been treated otherwise, and the second opera provided all possible contrast. Rakhmaninov himself conducted the premiere of both works.

SYNOPSIS
Scene 1 Albert, an impoverished apprentice knight with a miserly father (the baron), has resorted to a moneylender. Asked for collateral, Albert offers his word and his father's reputation. The moneylender refuses, but offers a supply of poison to ensure a speedy inheritance. Albert, appalled, threatens to hang the fellow for his notion, and is immediately offered a loan. But Albert resolves to ask for the duke's help to extract some support from the baron.
Scene 2 The baron gloats over the power his wealth brings, and reflects, unmoved, on the human misery he has caused. He is then seized by fear and mistrust of his son. His desire is to rise from the grave to protect his treasure from inheritance.
Scene 3 The duke agrees to assist Albert. The baron arrives. Albert retires into the next room and overhears the conversation in which the baron accuses his son of robbery and intended patricide. Albert bursts in, calls his father a liar, is challenged to a duel, and accepts the glove as 'the first gift from my father'. The duke takes the glove and turns to calm the apoplectic baron, who collapses and dies.

To a large extent, the shape of the poem determines that of the music: each scene is through-composed and there are leitmotifs for the principals as well as for the various states of mind of the baron. The baron's motifs are outlined in the sombre prelude, which moves straight into the first scene, where a forced levity is an important component in the irony of the conversation between Albert, his servant and the moneylender, showing a side of Rakhmaninov unfamiliar from his orchestral works. More familiar is the unrelieved misery of the baron's monologue, in which Rakhmaninov artfully reflects his judgement on a character intent on self-justification. The short final scene again has more interaction of character,

and the dénouement is skilfully done. Although the amount of stage action in this piece is relatively small, it is compensated for by the depth of the psychological drama.

Francesca da Rimini
Franceska da Rimini
Opera in two tableaux with prologue and epilogue (1h 15m)
Libretto by Modest Tchaikovsky, after Canto V of Dante's *Inferno* (*c*. 1307–21)
Composed 1904–5 (second tableau duet 1900)
PREMIERES 24 January 1906, Bolshoi Theatre, Moscow (conducted by the composer); UK: 28 June 1973, Chester Festival
CAST Ghost of Virgil *bar*, Dante *t*, Lanciotto Malatesta *bar*, Francesca *s*, Paolo *t*, Cardinal *silent*; *satb* chorus of spectres of hell, retinues of Cardinal and Malatesta

Critics have unanimously attacked the many faults in the libretto by Pyotr Tchaikovsky's younger brother, and it is a pity that Rakhmaninov was apparently not in a position to alter it or even to reject it outright, but it came to him in 1898 during his period of great depression after the failure at the premiere of the First Symphony, and the composition of the love duet in 1900 marks the real return of his creative ability. Later conflict with Modest Tchaikovsky produced an unsatisfactory solution of a new revised libretto being printed as an adjunct to the published score with the earlier libretto. Despite the faults of balance – the prologue is larger than either tableau, and the epilogue is very short – the music is full of originality, and the 'infernal' side of Rakhmaninov's musical character was never better expressed.

SYNOPSIS
Prologue The ghost of Virgil reassures a frightened Dante on the steps from the first circle of hell to the abyss. The sounds of tormented spirits are heard, and the ghosts of Paolo and Francesca tell Dante that 'The greatest sadness is the recollection of past happiness amidst present sorrow.'
Tableau 1 At the Malatesta Palace in Rimini, Lanciotto receives the cardinal's blessing before setting off to defend the pope against the Ghibellines. Lanciotto's monologue laments the deceit whereby his brother Paolo wooed Francesca, ostensibly to have her marry Lanciotto. Francesca had then married the lame Lanciotto while loving the handsome Paolo. Lanciotto tells Francesca that he is going away leaving his brother to look after her. He seeks some expression of love from her; she replies only that she will remain dutiful and obedient.
Tableau 2 Paolo reads to Francesca from the story of Lancelot and Guinevere, and they recognize similarities to their own story. Eventually they can suppress their feelings no longer. They are surprised by the planned return of Lanciotto, who stabs them both.
Epilogue Virgil's ghost observes the doomed lovers, who cry Dante's great line 'That day we read no more', and the chorus repeats the lament of 'The greatest sadness . . .'

The dramatic problems are several: the time the music

requires to depict hell – including a doleful fugue which would have delighted Max Reger with its chromatic ingenuity – allows for very little stage action, and Lanciotto's monologue occupies much of the first tableau. The scene where the lovers read together cannot help but be dull, although the love duet is a mighty compensation. The return of Lanciotto and the *crime passionnel* is practically unstageable as it stands – here, as elsewhere, there are simply too few lines of text. The most interesting feature of the work is the use of the chorus, who sing no words at all until the very end of the opera, but act as part of the orchestra, either humming or intoning over a range of sounds that culminates in screaming terror. The demonic power of Rakhmaninov in his 'D minor' mood – comparable with the First Symphony, the First Piano Sonata, the Third Piano Concerto and the *Corelli Variations* (which quotes a passage from the opera) – is sufficient to excuse the faults of the libretto, and this opera, especially with the other half of the double-bill, remains an area of shameful neglect.

Other operatic works: *Esmeralda* (inc., 1888); *Monna Vanna* (inc., 1907), 1984 (concert)

L.H.

JEAN-PHILIPPE RAMEAU
baptized 25 September 1683, Dijon, France; *d* 12 September 1764, Paris

With excusable exaggeration, the *Mercure de France* (1765) concluded its epitaph on Rameau with the words: 'Here lies the God of Harmony.' It was a fitting tribute to the man who, then as now, was seen not only as the outstanding European musical theorist of his era but as France's leading 18th-century composer. To many music-lovers he may nowadays be best known for his keyboard and chamber works. Yet his finest and most ambitious compositions are in the field of dramatic music and include some of the most powerful operas of the period between Monteverdi and Mozart.

Rameau came late to opera. Although his music covers the best part of six decades (1706–c. 1763), all his dramatic works belong to the last three. As he later admitted: 'I have attended the theatre since I was 12, yet I first worked for the [Paris] Opéra only at 50, and even then I did not think myself capable.'

Much of Rameau's early life was spent in the comparative obscurity of the provinces. When he eventually settled in Paris, at the age of 39, it was as a music theorist that he first came to public attention: the epoch-making *Traité de l'harmonie* appeared in 1722, and was followed by some three dozen books and pamphlets on music theory. During his first decade in the capital he published his two best-known keyboard collections, the *Pièces de clavecin* in 1724 and the *Nouvelles suites de pièces de clavecin* and a volume of cantatas in 1729 or 1730; he also tried his hand at incidental music (now lost) for some knockabout comedies at the fair theatres.

For all its undoubted imagination, skill and refinement, there was little in Rameau's previous output to prepare contemporary audiences for the power and complexity of *Hippolyte et Aricie* (1733), his first opera. Never had the French been confronted with a musical style so intensely dramatic. There were those who immediately hailed Rameau as 'the Orpheus of our century'. Others, however, found the music overcomplex, unnatural, misshapen – in a word, baroque. (*Hippolyte* has the dubious distinction of being the first musical work to which that epithet, still pejorative in those days, is known to have been applied.) At the Paris Opéra (the Académie Royale de Musique) two factions soon formed – the *Ramistes*, as his supporters became known, and the *Lullistes*, devotees of the traditional repertoire, who compared the new music unfavourably with that of their revered Lully. The dispute raged around all Rameau's operas of the 1730s; although it gradually subsided during the following decade, echoes could still be heard in the 1750s and beyond.

Increasingly, though, Rameau began to win the acclaim of the French musical public. In 1745 he was adopted as a court composer, with a royal pension and the title Compositeur de la Chambre du Roy. From that time too, he enjoyed the esteem of the intelligentsia, and his works were received at the Opéra and elsewhere with growing enthusiasm. Yet controversy was never far away; during the *querelle des bouffons* (1752–4) – a notorious pamphlet war between supporters of opera buffa and those of serious French opera – this former threat to the musical Establishment was himself attacked as an Establishment figure. And although he was increasingly regarded as the Grand Old Man of French music, criticism that his style seemed outmoded could more often be heard. While a number of Rameau's works remained in the Opéra's repertoire after his death, few survived the radical change in taste brought about by the arrival of Gluck's operas in the mid-1770s.

To his contemporaries, Rameau's operas at first seemed revolutionary. With hindsight, however, they appear securely rooted in French operatic tradition both in their subject matter and overall dramatic structure and in many musical details. Rameau's achievement was to rejuvenate that tradition by bringing to it an astonishingly fertile musical imagination, a harmonic idiom richer and more varied than that of any French predecessor, and a boldness of expression that can still seem almost overpowering. Throughout his operatic career Rameau remained receptive to new musical fashions; consequently the lofty and dignified idiom of his first operas became noticeably influenced during the 1740s and 1750s by the lighter German and Italian styles and softened by a proliferation of ornamental detail.

Even in his late seventies the composer's creative powers remained largely unimpaired, as the amazing quality of his last work, *Les Boréades*, demonstrates. But few would deny that, with the exception of that work and of *Platée* and *Pigmalion*, his most enduring operas almost all belong to the period 1733–44. It is especially sad that in his later years he found few libretti with the dramatic potential of *Hippolyte*, *Castor* or the 1744 version of *Dardanus*.

Hippolyte et Aricie
Hippolytus and Aricia
Tragédie en musique in five acts with prologue (2h 45m)
Libretto by Simon-Joseph Pellegrin
PREMIERES 1 October 1733, Opéra, Paris; 11 September
1742 (with changes); modern revivals: 28 March 1903,
Geneva; US: 11 April 1954, Town Hall, New York
(concert); 4 April 1966, Boston; UK: 13 May 1965,
Birmingham University (in English)
CAST Thésée (Theseus) *b*, Phèdre (Phaedra) *ms*, Hippolyte
(Hippolytus) *t* (*haute-contre*), Aricie (Aricia) *s*, Diane
(Diana) *s*, Pluton (Pluto) *b*, Tisiphone *t* (*taille*), Neptune *b*,
7 *s*, 4 *t* (2 *hautes-contre*; 2 *tailles*), 2 *b*; *satb* chorus of
nymphs, forest-dwellers, priestesses of Diana, citizens of
Troezen, gods of the underworld, sailors, hunters and
huntresses, shepherds and shepherdesses; *ballet*: priestesses
of Diana, gods of the underworld, furies, sailors and citizens
of Troezen, hunters and huntresses, shepherds and
shepherdesses, zephyrs, people of the forest of Aricia

In reworking the story of Phaedra's incestuous love
for her stepson Hippolytus, Pellegrin borrowed elements (including a number of lines) from Racine's
Phèdre (1677); he also returned to features of Racine's
models, Euripides' *Hippolytos* and Seneca's *Phaedra*.
His setting, however, alters the balance beween the
main characters, not so much in its treatment of the
young lovers Hippolytus and Aricia as in that of
Theseus, whose role becomes both more extensive and
more powerful than that of Phaedra, his queen.

SYNOPSIS
Prologue Diana is forced to concede that, one day a
year, her normally chaste forest-dwellers should be
permitted to serve Cupid. She promises to protect
Hippolytus and Aricia.
Act I As the last descendant of Theseus' enemy
Pallas, Aricia is compelled to take vows of chastity in
the Temple of Diana. Before the ceremony, she and
Hippolytus discover their mutual love. When Phaedra
arrives to ensure that Aricia 'takes the veil', she learns
with rage of Diana's pledge to protect the lovers.
Act II Theseus, who is presumed dead, has descended to Hades to rescue a comrade. Eventually
realizing his mission is hopeless, he invokes the help
of his father, Neptune. Before he can escape, the Fates
make their all-important prediction: Theseus may be
leaving Hades, but he will find hell in his own home.
Act III Theseus' wife Phaedra, believing herself a
widow, reveals her love to Hippolytus, her stepson,
but is rebuffed even when she offers him the crown. In
despair, she tries to kill herself with Hippolytus'
sword. As Hippolytus seizes it back, Theseus appears.
Recalling the Fates' prediction and misled by various
insinuations (which his son is too honourable to counter), Theseus jumps to the conclusion that Hippolytus
has attempted rape. Concealing his anguish from the
loyal subjects who celebrate his return, he calls on
Neptune to punish Hippolytus.
Act IV Hippolytus has escaped with Aricia to
Diana's grove. During celebrations in the goddess's
honour, a sea monster carries him off. As the horrified
onlookers react to his apparent death, Phaedra confesses her guilt.
Act V Theseus eventually learns the truth from
the dying Phaedra and is himself about to commit

suicide when Neptune reveals that Hippolytus is alive.
For accepting his son's guilt too readily, Theseus is
condemned never to see him again. The scene shifts to
the forest of Aricia, where Diana causes Hippolytus
to be reunited with his beloved.

Despite some obvious flaws, Pellegrin's libretto comes
nearer to real tragedy than any other that Rameau set
(Voltaire's still-born *Samson* excepted). It provided
the composer with the outlines of two of his most
monumental creations. The magnanimous but fatally
gullible Theseus is given music of consistently elevated
tone, its broad contours and rich harmonies conveying
the king's noble and generous bearing. It reaches its
high points in Theseus' two invocations to Neptune
and in his final dignified acceptance of his punishment,
all of which have a Bach-like harmonic intensity and
(unusual for France) consistently patterned accompaniments. Phaedra, though less subtle or rounded than
her Racinian counterpart, is still a powerful embodiment of passionate jealousy and remorse. Though
initially an unsympathetic character, she gains our
compassion in her anxious prayer to Venus and, above
all, in her final confession of guilt; this last, with its
involvement of the grief-stricken bystanders, is one of
the most powerful moments of pure tragedy in the
entire pre-Romantic operatic repertoire. By comparison, the eponymous young lovers seem pale, though
they project a touching innocence.
The second *Trio des Parques* (Fates) in Act II has
become justly famous for its bold use of enharmonic
progressions – too bold, indeed, for contemporary
performers, so that it had to be cut by about two-
thirds. Scarcely less remarkable are the orchestral
representation of thunder (Act I) and of the boiling
sea (Act III), the latter with the orchestra of strings
and bassoons divided into eight parts. Performance
difficulties and criticism of the work's dramatic structure led to a series of damaging cuts, both before and
during the first run and at successive revivals, so that
in Rameau's day the work was seldom valued as
highly as his other tragedies. It is, however, the most
human of them all, and the most consistently moving.

Les Indes galantes
The Amorous Indies
Opéra-ballet, with prologue and four entrées (2h 30m)
Libretto by Louis Fuzelier
PREMIERES 23 August 1735, Opéra, Paris (prologue and
first two entrées only); third entrée added 28 August 1735;
fourth entrée added 10 March 1736; modern revivals:
18 June 1952, Opéra, Paris (complete); US: 1 March 1961,
New York (concert); UK: 22 May 1974, Banqueting House,
London (concert); 1977, Edinburgh
CAST prologue: Hébé (Hebe) *s*, L'Amour (Cupid) *s*,
Bellone (Bellona) *b*; first entrée: Osman *b*, Emilie *s*, Valère *t*
(*haute-contre*); second entrée: Huascar *b*, Phani *s*, Don
Carlos *t* (*haute-contre*); third entrée: Tacmas *t* (*haute-contre*),
Fatime *s*, Ali *b* (replaced in rev. by Roxane *s*), Zaïre *s*
(replaced in rev. by Atalide *s*); fourth entrée: Damon *t*
(*haute-contre*), Don Alvar *b*, Zima *s*, Adario *t* (*taille*); *satb*
chorus (in prologue and all entrées) of French, Italian,
Spanish and Polish allies, warriors, sailors, Provençal men
and women, Incas, sacrificers, Peruvians, Persian musicians
and slaves, Indian savages; *ballet*: French, Italian, Spanish

and Polish young people, warriors, Hebe's retinue, cupids, sports and pleasures, Osman's African slaves, sailors and sailor girls, Pallas, Incas and Peruvians, Persians, Bostangis, flowers, male and female savages, French women dressed as Amazons, French and Indian soldiers, Indian women, colonial shepherds and shepherdesses

Ignoring the contemporary preference for opéra-ballets based on mythological themes, Fuzelier's libretto reverted to an older type involving believable modern characters, initiated by André Campra's *L'Europe galante* (1697) and briefly in vogue during the first two decades of the 18th century. The prologue retains its allegorical character in order to introduce the work's theme – aspects of love in far-flung lands: the young men of four allied nations (France, Spain, Italy and Poland) forsake the goddess Hebe and, despite Cupid's exhortations, are led off to war by Bellona. The cupids, realizing that Europe is forsaking them, decide to emigrate to the various 'Indies' (then a generic term for any exotic land). These colourful locations become the settings for the ensuing entrées.

The third entrée, added shortly after the premiere, was criticized for what the French regarded as the absurdity of disguising the hero as a woman. Two weeks later, its plot was entirely changed and all but the final divertissement was replaced with new music. The final entrée, added the following year, eventually became one of Rameau's best-loved works of the type.

SYNOPSIS

First entrée: '*Le turc généreux*' ('The Generous Turk') On a Turkish island in the Indian Ocean, Emilie, a young Provençal girl, has been captured and sold as a slave to the pasha Osman. Although the pasha has fallen in love with her, Emilie cannot forget her lover Valère, a French marine officer. During a sudden storm, Valère is shipwrecked on the island and captured. Osman recognizes him as the one who freed him from slavery. After first feigning anger at seeing the couple embracing, Osman shows his gratitude to Valère by releasing them both.

Second entrée: '*Les Incas du Pérou*' ('The Incas of Peru') In the Peruvian desert, the Incas prepare to celebrate the Festival of the Sun in the shadows of a nearby volcano, while Don Carlos, a Spanish officer, and Phani, a young Peruvian princess, declare their love for each other. Phani spurns Huascar, the Inca in charge of the ceremonial. As the sun worship begins, Huascar provokes the eruption of the volcano to convince her that the sun god disapproves of her love for an alien. But Carlos foils his attempt to abduct her, and the jealous Inca, now mad with rage, provokes a further eruption of the volcano and is engulfed by molten rocks.

Third entrée: '*Les fleurs, fête persane*' ('A Persian Flower Festival') (a) Original version: the young Persian prince Tacmas and his confidant, Ali, are each in love with one of the other's slaves: Tacmas loves Zaïre, spurning his own slave Fatime whom Ali loves. On the day of the flower festival, the four meet in a confusing encounter in Ali's garden, where Tacmas is disguised as a woman and Fatime as a Polish slave; but when it emerges that Zaïre and Fatime each love

the other's master, the men exchange slaves and the two satisfied couples take part in the festival. (b) Revised version: Fatime (here the sultana rather than a slave) suspects her husband Tacmas of infidelity with Atalide. Disguised as a Polish slave, she gains Atalide's confidence and thus learns, to her astonishment, of Tacmas's utter fidelity. The happy couple take part in the flower festival.

Fourth [new] entrée: '*Les sauvages*' ('The Savages') In a North American forest near the French and Spanish colonies, a tribe of Indian savages prepares to celebrate peace with its European vanquishers. Two officers – Don Alvar, a jealous Spaniard, and Damon, a fickle Frenchman – are rivals for the hand of Zima, the chief's daughter. But she, declaring that the Spaniard loves too much and the Frenchman too little, follows the instincts of a true child of nature and chooses the honourable Indian brave, Adario. Somewhat shamefacedly the Europeans join with the Indians in the ceremony of the Great Pipe of Peace.

With *Les Indes galantes*, the lightweight genre of opéra-ballet was raised to a new level. Fuzelier's libretto, though widely condemned in Rameau's day, can now be seen to have considerable merits. Each entrée has its own distinct character; each tiny plot holds rather more dramatic interest than is usual in works of this sort. Moreover, apart from the prologue, there are no supernatural interventions. Instead, Fuzelier generates much of the necessary visual and dramatic interest from his cleverly chosen exotic locations and the indigenous ceremonial they provide. (Some of the ethnic detail was culled from published reports of recent events or from first-hand experience.) In the process he manages to portray the interaction of and contrast between European and other cultures – not always to the former's advantage, as the final entrée with its lighthearted but moving tribute to the 'noble savage' demonstrates.

Rameau's response to this unusual material is superb, and the opera is surely among his very finest. He brings to *Les Incas* a dramatic intensity no less than that of the tragedies. The passage from the start of the eruption to the end of the entrée is an almost unbroken sequence of some 350 bars, during which voices and orchestra interact with extraordinary vehemence. The entrée is dominated by Huascar, whose harsh and fanatical but wholly credible character is established with a sureness of touch not found elsewhere outside *Hippolyte et Aricie*. In the other entrées and the prologue it is the grace and variety of the vocal airs and ballet music that impress most. Appropriately, the entrée *Les sauvages* includes a reworking of Rameau's harpsichord piece *Les sauvages*, itself inspired by the dancing of two American Indians in Paris in 1725, which had involved a peace-pipe dance. The movement, as indeed the whole entrée, was to become one of Rameau's most popular in the 18th century.

Castor et Pollux
Castor and Pollux
Tragédie en musique in five acts with prologue (2h 45m)
Libretto by Pierre-Joseph Justin Bernard

PREMIERES   24 October 1737, Opéra, Paris; ?8/?11 June 1754 (rev. version: no prologue, new Act I and other changes), Opéra, Paris; modern revivals: 29 January 1903, Schola Cantorum, Paris (concert); 23 January 1908, Montpellier; UK: 27 April 1929, Glasgow (amateur production in English); 1754 version: US: 6 March 1937, Vassar College, New York (concert); UK: 11 October 1981, Covent Garden, London

CAST   Télaïre (Telaira) s, Phébé (Phoebe) s, Castor t (haute-contre), Pollux b, Jupiter b, High Priest of Jupiter t (taille), Vénus (Venus) s, L'Amour (Cupid) haut-contre or s, Minerve (Minerva) s, Mars b, Mercure (Mercury) dancer (haute contre in 1754), s, t (haute-contre), b (additional soloists, s, t (haute-contre) and b, added in 1754); satb chorus of arts and pleasures, Spartans, athletes, priests, people, celestial pleasures, Hebe's retinue, demons, blessed spirits, stars; ballet: graces, arts, pleasures, cupids, athletes, warriors, Spartan women, Hebe's retinue, celestial pleasures, monsters, demons, blessed spirits, stars, planets and constellations

In its choice of subject matter – the brotherly love of the twins Castor and Pollux, the one mortal and the other immortal – this work is unusual, since contemporary French opera normally gave the central place to romantic love. After an initially cool reception, *Castor* was eventually regarded as Rameau's crowning achievement, especially after the triumphant revivals of 1754 and 1764.

SYNOPSIS
The prologue relates to the Peace of Vienna (1736) which ended the Polish War of Succession: Venus and Cupid, at Minerva's bidding, succeed in subduing Mars with the power of love.

Act I   Castor has been killed in battle. As the Spartans mourn, Pollux is persuaded by Telaira to ask his father Jupiter to restore Castor to life. Pollux agrees for love of Telaira, though he knows that she loves only Castor.

Act II   At first Jupiter tries to dissuade Pollux from his mission. He eventually consents to let Castor return from Hades, but on one condition – that Pollux gives up his immortality and takes his brother's place there. Pollux selflessly agrees.

Act III   At the mouth of Hades, Phoebe, spurned by Pollux, tries to prevent him from entering. Urged on by Telaira, and with Mercury's help, he braves the demons who bar his way and descends to the underworld.

Act IV   In Elysium, Castor has found no happiness, for he still longs for Telaira. He is naturally overjoyed when Pollux arrives. Yet, despite the prospect of seeing Telaira again, he cannot bring himself to accept Pollux's sacrifices. He finally agrees to return to earth, but for one day only.

Act V   Reunited with Telaira, Castor holds to his promise despite her pleas and taunts. Eventually relenting, Jupiter restores Pollux to life. For their selflessness he grants both brothers immortality and a place in the firmament.

At the 1754 revival, the dramatically irrelevant prologue was omitted, and a new expository first act was inserted before the original Act I. To compensate for this, the original Acts III and IV were telescoped into one; at the same time, the libretto was pruned by well over a quarter, the compression being achieved largely by reducing the amount of recitative. The resulting libretto, tauter and better paced, is arguably the best Rameau ever set. Apart from the loss of the prologue (some of it, in any case, incorporated into the revised Act IV divertissement), almost all the most memorable music remains – the mourning chorus 'Que tout gémisse'; Telaira's aria 'Tristes apprêts', grudgingly admired by Berlioz; Castor's ethereal but nostalgic soliloquy 'Séjour de l'éternelle paix', to name only a few. In general, too, the substituted music is scarcely inferior to the original: Pollux's monologue 'Nature, Amour' is replaced by an almost equally moving hymn to friendship, 'Présent des dieux'; moreover, we should scarcely suspect from the liveliness, grace and variety of the new ariettas and dance movements that their composer was by now over 70.

Les fêtes d'Hébé, ou Les talents lyriques
Hebe's Festivities, or The Lyric Talents
Opéra-ballet, with prologue and three entrées
Libretto by Antoine Gautier de Montdorge (with additions by Pierre-Joseph Justin Bernard, Simon-Joseph Pellegrin, Alexandre le Riche de la Pouplinière and possibly others)
PREMIERES   21 May 1739, Opéra, Paris; modern revivals: 21 March 1910 (first entrée only), Brussels; 24 January 1914, Monte Carlo (complete); UK: 29 March 1974, Queen Elizabeth Hall, London (concert); US: 1986, Los Angeles

CAST   prologue: L'Amour (Cupid) s, Hébé (Hebe) s, Momus t (taille); first entrée: Sappho s, Alcée (Alcaeus) b, Hymas b, Thélème (Thelemus) t (haute-contre), s, t (haute-contre), b; second entrée: Iphise s, Tirtée (Tyrtaeus) b, Lycurgue (Lycurgus) t (haute-contre); third entrée: Eglé s (and dancer), Mercure (Mercury) t (haute-contre), Eurilas b, Palémon silent (required to play the oboe); satb chorus of Thessalians, water-dwellers, Lacedemonians, shepherds and shepherdesses; ballet: graces, Thessalians, water-dwellers, warriors, Lacedemonians, Terpsichore's nymphs, fauns, sylvans, shepherds

In Rameau's day this work was generally known by its subtitle, *Les talents lyriques*, which gives a better idea of the content.

SYNOPSIS
The prologue establishes the theme: the gods' cupbearer Hebe, dissatisfied with Olympus, persuades her attendant divinities to journey to the banks of the Seine to celebrate those gifts most cherished on the lyric stage – poetry, music and dance. These lyric talents form the subject matter of the ensuing entrées.

First entrée: '*La poésie*'   On the island of Lesbos, the poet Alcaeus and poetess Sappho are in love. As a result of Thelemus' jealous scheming, Alcaeus has been banished by the Lesbian king, Hymas. But Hymas is greatly touched by an allegorical entertainment mounted by Sappho in his honour, which enables her to reveal Thelemus' treachery. The king rescinds the banishment order and the lovers are reunited.

Second entrée: '*La musique*'   The Spartan princess Iphise is betrothed to Tyrtaeus, famed for the ethical effects of his singing. However, an oracle unexpectedly reveals that she must marry the warrior who vanquishes the Messenians threatening the city. In order to marry Iphise, Tyrtaeus uses the powers of his vocal art to inspire the Spartan army to defeat their attackers.

Third entrée: '*La danse*' The shepherdess Eglé, a favourite of Terpsichore, muse of dancing, must choose a husband. Her choice falls on an unknown stranger, who later reveals himself to be the god Mercury. At his request, Terpsichore receives Eglé into her court as Nymph of the Dance.

Rameau's first opéra-ballet, *Les Indes galantes*, had involved believable modern characters. In returning to stock classical Greek subject matter, its successor may seem retrogressive but it was actually in line with current trends. Montdorge's libretto was initially much criticized, and the second entrée in particular had to be radically revised, probably by the Abbé Pellegrin: the character of Lycurgus was eliminated (it was anachronistic by some two centuries) and scenes involving Tyrtaeus' exhortations of his soldiers and the women's vigil during the battle were substantially reworked; the revision was extensive enough to be described in one libretto as a 'nouvelle entrée', and involved much new music.

For all its lack of distinction, the libretto served Rameau quite well. Each embryo plot provides just enough dramatic momentum to maintain our interest up to the all-important divertissement. Rameau, by now at the height of his powers, contributed a score of astonishing inventiveness. 'C'est une musique enchantée,' wrote one contemporary with little exaggeration. This is specially true of the third entrée, wonderfully rich in that languorous and often deeply nostalgic pastoral music that is one of Rameau's hallmarks. The *loure grave* and two sumptuously scored musettes (the second borrowed from the *Pièces de clavecin* of 1724 along with the dionysiac tambourin and 'L'entretien des muses') must surely be among the century's finest ballet music, yet are only marginally finer than many other movements. Among numerous gems in the earlier entrées, Sappho's water-pastoral entertainment includes an exhilarating mariners' chorus, 'Ciel, O ciel! le fleuve agite son onde', notable for an accompaniment consisting entirely of rapid unison scales.

Dardanus

Tragédie en musique in five acts with prologue (2h)
Libretto by Charles-Antoine Le Clerc de La Bruère
PREMIERES 19 November 1739, Opéra, Paris; 23 April 1744 (as 'nouvelle tragédie', with three acts rewritten); 15 April 1760 (with new alterations); modern revivals: 26 April 1907, Schola Cantorum, Paris (concert); December 1907, Dijon; US: 25 February 1959, Hartford, Connecticut; UK: February 1973, Queen Elizabeth Hall, London (concert)
CAST Dardanus *t* (*haute-contre*), Iphise *s*, Anténor (Antenor) *b*, Teucer *b*, Isménor (Ismenor) *b*, Vénus (Venus) *s*, L'Amour (Cupid) *s*, Arcas *t* (*haute-contre*) added in 1744; 3 *s*, *t* (*haute-contre*), 2 *b*; *satb* chorus of retinue of Jealousy and Cupid, retinue of Jealousy, warriors, people, magicians, Phrygians, dreams, cupids; *ballet*: pleasures, Jealousy and her retinue, troubles, suspicions, mortals, warriors, Phrygians, dreams

Despite its initial run of some 26 performances, *Dardanus* was harshly criticized for its absurd plot and abuse of the supernatural (the latter more or less admitted in the libretto). Rameau and La Bruère subsequently revised the work to the extent of giving Acts III, IV and V an entirely new plot. This version, staged in 1744, at first excited little comment; but when revived in 1760, with further, though less extensive, changes, it was rightly acclaimed as one of Rameau's finest achievements.

SYNOPSIS
In Greek legend, Zeus' son Dardanus was founder of the royal house of Troy. He was assisted in this by the Phrygian king Teucer, whose daughter he then married. La Bruère's libretto invents a stormy prehistory to these events.

Act I   Dardanus is at war with Teucer; at the same time, he has fallen in love with Teucer's daughter Iphise and she with him, though neither knows the other's feelings. Meanwhile Teucer has promised Iphise to a neighbouring prince, Antenor, in return for a military alliance.

Act II   Dardanus obtains from the magician Ismenor a magic ring that disguises him as the magician himself. Iphise comes to beg this pseudo-Ismenor to exorcize her love for her father's enemy; in so doing, she unwittingly reveals to Dardanus the state of her emotions. Overjoyed at the revelation, Dardanus appears in his own form and declares his own love, to Iphise's consternation and dismay.

Act III   Up to this point the 1739 and 1744 versions have virtually identical plots. The former continues with Dardanus' capture. His enemies' celebrations, however, are interrupted by news that Neptune has sent a sea monster to avenge this imprisonment of a son of Jupiter. Antenor resolves to combat the monster.

Act IV   By now, Dardanus has escaped. In his sleep he is visited by Venus and her attendant dreams, who exhort him to slay the monster. When he eventually does so, Dardanus rescues Antenor and takes advantage of the latter's gratitude to extract a promise that Iphise be allowed to refuse Antenor's hand.

Act V   After Teucer reveals Neptune's decree that Iphise should marry whoever vanquishes the monster, Antenor is eventually forced to concede to Dardanus. Venus descends to celebrate the marriage.

The last three acts of the 1744 and later versions involve fewer supernatural interventions.

Act III   The jealous Antenor devises a plan to murder the now-captive Dardanus without appearing to be the perpetrator.

Act IV   Ismenor visits Dardanus' cell and foretells his rescue but warns that his liberator will instead become the victim. Consequently, when Iphise gives Dardanus the chance to escape, he refuses. It is Antenor, remorseful and now mortally wounded, who eventually makes possible Dardanus' escape. In the ensuing battle (represented as an entr'acte between Acts IV and V) Dardanus defeats Teucer.

Act V   Teucer defiantly refuses to give Dardanus Iphise's hand. It is only when the despairing hero asks to be struck down with his own sword that Teucer relents. As in the original, Venus descends to celebrate the union.

In purely musical terms, the first version of *Dardanus* is without doubt one of Rameau's most inspired creations. Two superb ceremonies in Acts I and II – the first where Teucer and Antenor pledge allegiance and prepare for battle, the second where Ismenor displays his occult powers by changing day into night – contain music of astonishing power, at times almost frightening in its intensity. The dream sequence, Iphise's two tortured monologues, her consultation with the pseudo-Ismenor, the scene where Dardanus slays the monster, all are among Rameau's very best creations. The main problem with this version is that the momentum generated by such passages is continually sapped by the plot's ill-motivated twists and turns and by what come to seem increasingly puerile supernatural happenings.

In simplifying the plot and eliminating the supernatural excesses, La Bruère brought to the drama much greater human interest. The action now focuses far more on the conflicting emotions of the principal characters. Musically, it is true, the revision entails the removal of many beauties, among them the dream sequence, the monster scenes and Iphise's second monologue. (Her first monologue is drastically curtailed, too.) But the prologue and Acts I and II, with their two great ceremonies, remain largely intact, while the considerable quantity of new music generally maintains the high quality of the original. Especially notable is Dardanus' F minor prison monologue, with its amazingly bold bassoon obbligato, wonderfully contrasted with the luminous music for Ismenor that immediately follows.

For all its dramatic superiority, the 1744 version has never been revived in modern times, largely because no modern edition exists. Yet it is easily the equal of *Castor et Pollux* and *Les Boréades* if not of *Hippolyte et Aricie*.

Platée
Plataea

Comédie lyrique in three acts with prologue (2h 15m)
Libretto by Adrien-Joseph Le Valois d'Orville, after the play *Platée, ou Junon jalouse* by Jacques Autreau
PREMIERES 31 March 1745, La Grande Écurie, Versailles; 4 February 1749, Opéra, Paris (text altered by Ballot du Sovot); modern revivals: 26 January 1901 Kaim-Saal, Munich; 5 April 1917, Monte Carlo; US: 4 May 1967, Worcester, Massachusetts; UK: 4 October 1983, Sadler's Wells, London
CAST Thespis *t (haute-contre)*, Thalie (Thalia) *s*, L'Amour (Cupid) *s*, Platée (Plataea) *t (haute-contre)*, Cithéron (Cithaeron) *b*, La Folie (Folly) *s*, Momus *t (taille)*, Clarine *s*, Jupiter *b*, Junon (Juno) *s*, Mercure (Mercury) *haute-contre*, 3 *s*, 2 *b*; *satb* chorus of satyrs, maenads, frogs, nymphs, retinue of Momus, Mercury and Cithaeron; *ballet*: satyrs, maenads, harvesting peasants with their wives and children, nymphs, aquilons of the North Wind, retinue of Momus, Mercury and Cithaeron, Folly's retinue, dryads, graces, country-dwellers

Comedy had traditionally played little part in French opera. Lully soon eliminated comic episodes from his tragedies; from then until the appearance of the present work, only a handful of operas had comic themes. That for *Platée* is the mock marriage between the god Jupiter and an ugly marsh nymph. As such, it

seems grotesquely ill-suited to the occasion for which it was commissioned – the wedding of the dauphin and the evidently unattractive Spanish princess Maria Teresa – though it was well enough received at the time. Once transferred in modified form to the Paris Opéra in 1749, it became one of Rameau's best-loved works and was ultimately regarded by many as his masterpiece.

In Le Valois d'Orville's libretto little more than the outline of Autreau's original play remains.

SYNOPSIS
The prologue, entirely the librettist's invention, is subtitled *La naissance de la Comédie* (*The Birth of Comedy*). Thespis, represented here – unusually – as the inventor of comedy, plans with Momus, god of ridicule, Thalia, muse of comedy, and Cupid to teach mortals and gods a moral lesson: they decide to re-enact the episode in which Jupiter cures his wife Juno of jealousy. The comedy itself, the story of which can be traced back to the ancient Greek writer Pausanius, is set throughout in a marsh at the foot of Mount Cithaeron. (It is thus the only multi-act work by Rameau without elaborate scene changes.) Here, with her attendant frogs and cuckoos, lives the marsh nymph Plataea, who, though incredibly ugly, is convinced of her own charms.

Act I In consultation with King Cithaeron, Mercury conceives a plan to cure Juno's tiresome jealousy: Jupiter is to court the ludicrous nymph and go through with a mock marriage. Juno, when she is led to uncover the plan, will be made to look foolishly jealous as the object of her husband's 'affections' is revealed.

Act II In courting Plataea, Jupiter undergoes various metamorphoses – as a cloud, a donkey, an owl – to the nymph's consternation and delight. At last he appears in his own form amid a shower of fire. After making amorous advances, he arranges a divertissement in her honour, led by Momus and Folly, whose followers are dressed respectively as babies and as Greek philosophers.

Act III By now Juno has been alerted and arrives incognito at the mock wedding. Heavily disguised, Plataea is led in on a chariot drawn by two frogs. After an interminable chaconne, danced in *le genre le plus noble*, Momus appears disguised as Cupid with a ridiculously large bow and quiver. Just as Jupiter is about to pronounce his marriage vows, Juno snatches away Plataea's veil . . . and starts to laugh. Mocked by the entire assembly, Plataea retreats to her marsh.

Such a description may well give the impression that the humour of *Platée* is rather sick. On the stage, however, that is not how it seems. While we may laugh at Plataea's plight, our sympathies are with the nymph throughout. Moreover, the cruelty of laughing at an ugly but hopelessly vain woman is kept at a distance by the role of Plataea being sung by a tenor. (This *travesti* role, one of the very few in French operas of the period, was created by the famous *haute-contre* Pierre Jelyotte.) The work's humour comes not just from the extravagant situations but also from wicked parodies of the conventions of serious opera, its descents and transformations, its musical and poetic language. For example, the chaconne that precedes the impatient Plataea's marriage is comic not just because of its absurd length or because it is danced in mock-serious style, but because it is misplaced: chaconnes belong at the culmination of the final divertissement. Musical parody takes many forms – exaggerated vocalises, misaccentuations, vocal acrobatics; imitations of frogs, cuckoos, frightened birds, donkey-Jupiter; elaborate pizzicati for Folly's lyre, double-stoppings for her hurdy-gurdy; even glissandos when Momus presents Plataea with Cupid's gifts (tears, sorrow, cries, languor). The burlesque use of language is seen in Plataea's frequent recourse to a frog-like 'Quoi!', her comic alliterations and her colloquial expressions, including the decidedly unoperatic expletive 'Ouffe!'

Yet there is more to *Platée* than a series of comic effects, genuinely funny though many of them are. Whether mock serious, quirkily descriptive or uninhibitedly gay, Rameau's music is a constant delight. He seems to have relished particularly the chance for elaborate ensembles; those in the prologue and at the ends of Acts II and III have a breadth almost without parallel in his output.

Pigmalion
Pygmalion

Acte de ballet
Libretto by Ballot de Sovot, after Antoine Houdar de La Motte's opéra-ballet *Le triomphe des arts* (1700)
PREMIERES   27 August 1748, Opéra, Paris; modern revivals: 1913, Théâtre des Arts, Paris; UK: 23 May 1985, Hinde Street Church, London
CAST   Pigmalion *t* (*haute-contre*), The Statue *s* (also required to dance), Céphise *s*, L'Amour (Cupid) *s*; *satb* chorus of people, Cupid's retinue; *ballet*: graces, sports, smiles

According to the *Mercure de France*, Rameau wrote *Pigmalion* in less than eight days in an attempt to help the new Opéra management out of financial difficulties. While it never achieved that wellnigh impossible aim, the work proved immensely popular: from its premiere in 1748 until its final 18th-century revival in 1781 it was given more than 200 times at the Opéra and the French court.

SYNOPSIS
The action is simple but effective: the sculptor Pygmalion has fallen passionately in love with one of his statues and rejected the love of Céphise. In desperation, he implores Venus' aid. Suddenly, at a signal from Cupid, the statue comes to life and reveals her love to the ecstatic Pygmalion.

The work borrows its subject matter and some 30 lines from La Motte's libretto for the entrée *La sculpture* in *Le triomphe des arts*, first set by Michel de La Barre in 1700. While such resettings were commonplace elsewhere in Europe, it was not until *Pigmalion* that the practice was adopted in France, 76 years after the emergence of French opera. Even then it was initially criticized, though the work deservedly became one of Rameau's most popular. Prefaced by a viva-cious overture said to depict the sculptor's chisel, the slender but well-paced plot offers a wide variety of moods: the deeply felt yearning of Pygmalion's opening monologues, his bewilderment and elation as the statue comes to life, the uninhibited joy of the final divertissement. It also provides an ingenious pretext for the obligatory ballet, as the statue, once she has come to life, needs to be shown how to move. Cupid duly leads in the Graces and others, who teach her the characteristics of each dance type, each more animated than the last.

Naïs
Neis

Pastorale héroïque in three acts with prologue (2h)
Libretto by Louis de Cahusac
PREMIERES   22 April 1749, Opéra, Paris; 7 August 1764 (with additions by Pierre-Monton Berton); modern revivals: June 1980, Opéra Royal, Versailles; UK: 22 July 1980, The Old Vic, London
CAST   Naïs (Neis) *s*, Neptune *t* (*haute-contre*), Jupiter *b*, Pluton (Pluto) *b*, Astérion (Asterion) *t* (*haute-contre*), Télénus (Telenus) *b*, Tirésie (Tiresias) *b*, 3 *s*, *b*; *satb* chorus of Titans and giants, gods and goddesses, Corinthians, sea divinities, shepherds and shepherdesses, Tiresias' retinue; *ballet*: Titans and giants, retinues of Neptune and Pluto, gods and earth-dwellers, zephyrs, nymphs, Corinthians, athletes, sea divinities, shepherds and shepherdesses, herdsmen

Rameau's *Opéra pour la Paix*, as it was known, celebrated the Treaty of Aix-la-Chapelle which concluded the War of the Austrian Succession (1740–48). Topicality is confined to the prologue, *L'accord des dieux* (*The Gods' Agreement*), an allegory in which the war is represented as the attempt of the Titans to storm the heavens. Magnanimous in victory, Jupiter (Louis XV) shares jurisdiction over the universe with Pluto and Neptune, the latter popularly seen as an inept portrayal of France's former enemy, the English king George II. (No one seems to have noticed the incongruity of making Neptune the hero of the ensuing drama.)

The opera itself is set on the Isthmus of Corinth and concerns Neptune's wooing of the water nymph Neis. Since classical sources mention only her beauty and her entrancing voice, Cahusac supposes Neis to have been daughter of the blind soothsayer Tiresias, who could predict the future by interpreting birdsong.

SYNOPSIS
Act I   After fending off two suitors, Telenus and Asterion, Neis presides over the Isthmian Games; but, as she crowns the *victor ludorum*, her emotions are troubled by the arrival of a handsome stranger – Neptune in disguise.

Act II   In front of Tiresias' grotto, where the shepherds consult the soothsayer, Asterion asks whether the cold-hearted Neis will ever respond to love. From the awakening birds Tiresias divines that a stranger will conquer her heart and that Asterion and Telenus should beware the god of the seas.

Act III   At daybreak over the Corinthian coast, Neis warns the still-disguised Neptune that his rivals are taking up arms against him. But when their ships attack, Neptune causes them to be engulfed. Only then does he reveal his true identity. The lovers find themselves in the god's magnificent underwater palace, surrounded by welcoming sea divinities.

As befits a work in one of the lighter genres, *Naïs* contains little of the serious emotional conflict of the tragédie and little attempt at characterization. It is, however, rich in the spectacle and local colour for which Cahusac was renowned. Moreover, these elements are well integrated, the action continuing to some extent during the colourful divertissements. The disguised Neptune, for example, first pays court to Neis as she presides over the Isthmian Games, involving onstage wrestling, boxing and athletics; a certain dramatic tension arises from the nymph's attempts to conceal her aroused emotions from the other participants. Similarly, Tiresias' interpretation of birdsong (the Act II divertissement) furthers the action in motivating Neptune's rivals to take up arms against him.

The boldest music appears in the prologue. The violent syncopations and pungent dissonances of the overture (representing the Titans' storming of the heavens) continue into the first two choruses to create a long and astoundingly strong opening sequence – and a further anticipation of Gluck. Thereafter the score provides rich contrasts and consistently imaginative music. The pastoral music and birdsong of Act II are particularly fine, as is the music representing the games (a huge chaconne full of gestures suggesting athletic movement), the jaunty arrival of the sea divinities and the final sequence in Neptune's underwater palace.

Zoroastre

Zoroaster or Zarathustra
Tragédie en musique in five acts (2h 30m)
Libretto by Louis de Cahusac
PREMIERES 5 December 1749, Opéra, Paris; 19 January 1756 (three acts largely rewritten); modern revivals: 26 November 1903, Schola Cantorum, Paris (concert); 7 June 1964, Opéra, Paris; UK: 1 May 1979, Queen Elizabeth Hall, London (concert; 1756 version, abridged); US: 24 May 1983, Sanders Theater, Harvard University (1756 version)
CAST Zoroastre (Zoraster) *t* (*haute-contre*), Abramane *b*, Amélite *s*, Erinice *s*, Céphie *s*, Zopire *b*, Vengeance *b*, Oromasès *b* (1756 version only), Narbanor *b* (1756 version only), 5 *s* (2 in 1756), 2 *t* (*haute-contre*) (1 in 1756), *b*; *satb* chorus of Bactrian men and women, Indian savages, magi, elemental beings, idolatrous priests, demons, retinue of Vengeance, shepherds and shepherdesses; *ballet*: Bactrian men and women, Indian savages, elemental beings, priests of Ahriman, cruel spirits of darkness, shepherds and shepherdesses

The subject matter of *Zoroastre* represents a deliberate break with the classical legend and medieval romance of the conventional French tragédie en musique. Inspired by ancient Persian sources, it concerns the conflict between the great religious reformer Zoroaster (Zarathustra) and an ambitious sorcerer Abramane, 'inventor of the cult of idols' (and himself the librettist's invention). The one is portrayed as representative of the Supreme Being, the other as servant of Ahriman, spirit of evil.

SYNOPSIS

Zoroaster, who has been exiled after the death of the king of Bactria, is summoned by a divine voice to deliver the Bactrian people from Abramane's cruel domination. This he does after a series of confrontations with the magician and with much supernatural assistance. In emphasizing the central struggle between the forces of good and evil, the opera pays far less attention than usual to the amorous entanglements of the characters. Indeed, the two main female characters, both Bactrian princesses with claims to the throne, play fairly minor roles: Amélite, Zoroaster's beloved, functions mainly as a pawn in the power struggle; Erinice, whose spurned love for the hero has turned to hate and who has therefore joined forces with Abramane, exists largely to provide the sorcerer with a claim to the Bactrian throne.

In its original form, *Zoroastre* was only a qualified success. Revising it for the 1756 revival, Cahusac and Rameau largely recast Acts II, III and V, giving them an entirely different plot and much new music. Zoroaster is now sent on his mission not by an impersonal divine voice but by Oromasès, king of Genii, whose high priest he has become. The hero is portrayed as a less messianic figure and is motivated at least as much by his love for Amélite as by his sacred mission. Aware that this conventional element diminishes Zoroaster's religious stature, Cahusac elevates the mission itself from the simple liberation of Bactria to the more momentous one of freeing the world from the powers of evil. Greater stress is laid on Zoroaster's preparation for the task, which now includes an impressive initiation scene. In this way the libretto's Masonic symbolism is greatly enhanced (Cahusac was secretary to the comte de Clermont, grand master of the French Grand Lodge). Despite its high ideals, however, the work, even in revised form, involves too many arbitrary reversals of fortune brought about by supernatural agents. While the characters – Abramane in particular – are by no means without interest, the dualistic Persian religion comes to seem a struggle not so much between good and evil as between goodies and baddies.

That said, *Zoroastre*'s most impressive passages involve religious ceremonial. The huge occult sacrifice that occupies virtually the whole of Act IV is superbly handled, working itself gradually into a frenzy and culminating in a series of colossal ensembles and choruses. This is balanced by the hero's devotions to the Supreme Being, represented by the rising sun. Cahusac believed Zoroaster to have initiated a sun cult, and the inclusion of this ritual helps invest him with a mystical quality that effectively counterbalances the love scenes with Amélite. In 1756 a serene 'Hymne au Soleil' was added (a further Masonic element) and the whole ceremony was moved from Act II to Act III, where it forms a better contrast with the occult ceremonial that follows. Impressive, too, are the scenes involving Zoroaster and his religious mentor Oromasès, whose words (like Christ's in Bach's *St Matthew Passion*) are characterized by a halo of sustained double-stopped strings. The passage in which he initiates the hero has something of the same ecstatic character as the sun-worship scenes, the two passages containing some of the most spiritually elevated music in all Rameau.

Zoroastre set an important precedent in abandoning the traditional French prologue. The overture, deliberately intended to replace it, is the first in which Rameau anticipated Gluck by prefiguring not just the opening scene but the entire drama: its three movements depict in turn Abramane's barbarous rule, the renewal of hope, and the rejoicing of the liberated people.

Les Boréades
The Sons of Boreas
Tragédie en musique in five acts (2h 45m)
Libretto attributed to Louis de Cahusac
PREMIERES unperformed in Rameau's lifetime; modern performances: 16 September 1964, Maison de la Radio, Paris (extracts; concert); 21 July 1982, Théâtre de l'Archevêché, Aix-en-Provence; UK: 14 April 1975, Queen Elizabeth Hall, London (concert); 21 November 1985, Royal Academy of Music, London (abridged); 21 April 1993, Mayfair Suite, Bullring Shopping Centre, Birmingham
CAST Alphise *s*, Abaris *t* (*haute-contre*), Sémire *s*, Borilée *bar*, Calisis *t* (*haute-contre*), Adamas *b*, Borée (Boreas) *b*, Polyhymnie (Polyhymnia) *s*, Apollon (Apollo) *bar*, L'Amour (Cupid) *s*, 2 *s*; *satb* chorus of pleasures and graces, Alphise's retinue, Bactrian people, muses, arts, subterranean winds, Boreas' retinue; *ballet*: pleasures and graces, priests, Alphise's retinue, Oritheia and her companions, Boreas' disciples, Bactrian people, north winds, hours, seasons, zephyrs, talents

Until recently, *Les Boréades* was widely believed to have been in rehearsal at the Paris Opéra at the time of Rameau's death but then abandoned for reasons unknown. Archival evidence now reveals that the work was rehearsed more than a year earlier, in April 1763, and that it was probably intended for performance not at the Opéra but before the court at Choisy. Why this remarkable opera should have been put aside can only be guessed at, though it must have to do with changing musical tastes in the 1760s, with the opposition of Mme de Pompadour and others at court, with the fact that the music presents formidable problems, perhaps even with the burning down of the Académie Royale's theatre in the very month of the rehearsals. It has been suggested, too, that since the libretto includes elements that could be construed as Masonic (an initiatory voyage, a magic talisman and various Apollonian symbols) the opera might have been considered politically subversive.

SYNOPSIS
The action, set in the ancient kingdom of Bactria, concerns the love between the queen, Alphise, and a noble foreigner, Abaris, who has been brought up by Adamas, high priest of Apollo, in ignorance of his origins. The obstacle to their love is a tradition that the queen must marry a descendant of Boreas, god of the north wind. Rather than lose Abaris by marrying one of the 'Boréades', Alphise abdicates, much to her subjects' surprise and regret and the god's displeasure.

During a violent tempest, she is carried off to his domain to be tortured among the subterranean winds. The efforts of Abaris to rescue her are assisted by the interventions of the muse Polyhymnia and the god Apollo; Abaris also has the magic arrow which Cupid had given to Alphise. Eventually Apollo reveals that Abaris is his child by a nymph daughter of Boreas, and may therefore marry Alphise with impunity.

While the libretto is ascribed to Cahusac by two independent 18th-century writers, there are problems in accepting the attribution unreservedly. The work takes considerable (and uncharacteristic) liberties with its classical source material, while compared with *Zoroastre* it makes little of the Masonic elements. Moreover, the hymns and ballets figurés, which are such a feature of Cahusac's work, are each represented by a single, undeveloped example; at the same time, the presence of three *simile* arias and other anomalies have no parallel in his other works, though such arias may be found, for example, in Jean-François Marmontel's libretti. It is, however, always possible that the text was among Cahusac's papers at the time of his death (1759) and that the perceived anomalies result from subsequent tinkerings by others.

That said, the libretto is among the more serviceable of those that Rameau set. Despite its overuse of the supernatural and its reduction of hero and heroine to the status of mere agents in a battle between superior forces, it is paced in such a way that successive stages of the plot generate increasing dramatic momentum; this is especially so from the moment of Alphise's unexpected abdication in Act III, through the tempest that dominates the rest of that act and most of the next, to the torture scenes in Act V. Rameau takes full advantage of this to produce a work with greater forward drive than any of his others, exemplified by the way his fearsome tempest continues straight through from the middle of Act III well into Act IV (and, less innovatory, his overture into the first scene). Among musical highlights in a particularly inventive score are the *simile* arias 'Un horizon serein' (Act I), Abaris' despairing monologue 'Lieux désolez', and the descent of Polyhymnia and the muses (Act IV), this last one of the most ravishing single movements in the whole of his output.

Other operatic works: *Samson* (inc., ?1735; lost); *La princesse de Navarre*, 1745; *Les fêtes de Polymnie*, 1745; *Le temple de la Gloire*, 1745; *Les fêtes de Ramire*, 1745; *Les fêtes de l'Hymen et de l'Amour, ou Les dieux d'Égypte*, 1747; *Zaïs*, 1748; *Les surprises de l'Amour*, 1748; *La guirlande, ou Les fleurs enchantées*, 1751; *Acante et Céphise, ou La sympathie*, 1751; *Linus* (inc., ?1752); *Daphnis et Eglé*, 1753; *Lysis et Délie*, (?1753; lost); *Les sibarites*, 1753; *La naissance d'Osiris, ou La fête Pamilie*, 1754; *Anacréon* (i), 1754; *Anacréon* (ii), 1757; *Les Paladins*, 1760; *Io* (inc., n.d.); *Zéphyre*, (n.d.), 1967 (concert); *Nélée et Myrthis*, (n.d.), 1974

G.S.

MAURICE RAVEL
Joseph Maurice Ravel; *b* 7 March 1875, Ciboure, France;
d 28 December 1937, Paris

Ciboure is by the Pyrenees, and though Ravel's family
moved to Paris when he was three months old he kept
a lifelong affection for things Basque (and Spanish)
through his mother. His father was a Swiss civil engineer. It is hard not to see familial traces in the composer's love of polished, ingenious mechanisms, and
the frequent Spanish irruptions in his music. They are
highly characteristic features of his scores – most
obviously of *L'heure espagnole* – and yet they are marginal. Ravel's basic musical language developed from
his revered teacher Fauré, with vital influences from
Chabrier, Debussy (up to *Pelléas*), early Satie and the
New Russian School: Rimsky-Korsakov, Borodin,
Balakirev. The oft-told story of his repeated failures
to win the Prix de Rome at the Paris Conservatoire
(at the fifth and last attempt, in 1905, he was rejected
in the preliminary round, and a great scandal ensued)
is misleading. Ravel was no revolutionary Young Turk
challenging the Establishment, but an inquiring, fastidiously original composer who was neither interested in
the kind of academic exercise prescribed for that competition nor particularly good at it. The piquant
'injustice' of the final rebuff lay in the fact that his
Jeux d'eau, his String Quartet and the *Shéhérezade*
songs were already widely admired; the terms of the
Prix de Rome, however, excluded independent works
from consideration.

That failure cannot have wounded him gravely,
since his most prolific period followed at once. (Of all
petits-maîtres, Ravel was among the least prolific: rigorously self-critical throughout his 40-odd years of composing, he published only a few hours' worth of
music.) Between 1905 and 1911 came the *Introduction
and Allegro* for harp and ensemble, the *Sonatine*,
Miroirs, *Gaspard de la nuit* and the *Valses nobles et
sentimentales* for piano, the suite *Ma mère l'oye* for
piano duet, the *Rapsodie espagnole*, the first sketches
for *Daphnis et Chloé*, many songs, and *L'heure espagnole*. Ravel's name is not popularly associated with
opera, no doubt because the two he completed are
brief and therefore awkward to programme, and they
afford no spectacular vocal or dramatic opportunities
to their leading singers. In fact his thoughts turned
early to the medium. In the late 1890s he had planned
an opera on Maurice Maeterlinck's *Intérieur*, as well
as an E. T. A. Hoffmann operetta *Olympia* (the robot
doll of Offenbach's celebrated piece), and later – like
several other composers of the day – a fairy opera
after Gerhart Hauptmann's *Die versunkene Glocke*
(*La cloche engloutie*, or *The Sunken Bell*). His sketches
were not wasted, for it seems that Dr Coppelius' entry
music from *Olympia* was recycled as the prelude to
L'heure espagnole, and much later some musical ideas
for *La cloche engloutie* were transferred to *L'enfant et
les sortilèges*.

After the successful premieres of *L'heure espagnole*
(though one critic did call it 'a mildly pornographic
vaudeville') and *Daphnis* (with Nijinsky), Diaghilev
asked Ravel to collaborate with Stravinsky in an

unexpected operatic task. They were to produce a
reorchestrated version of *Khovanshchina*, which Musorgsky had left unfinished and Rimsky-Korsakov
had adapted according to his own lights. The new
version was completed and performed by the Ballets
Russes in 1913; unfortunately, the score has never
been retrieved. Then came the First World War, in
which Ravel did non-combatant military service.
During that time the novelist Colette agreed to write a
libretto for the Paris Opéra, and hit upon Ravel as a
suitable composer for the divertissement she conceived. It took him some time to agree; he was profoundly depressed by the war, and by the death of his
mother in 1917, and his glum response to Colette's
original title, *Ballet pour ma fille*, was that he *had* no
daughter. Eventually he warmed to the project, but
his *Tombeau de Couperin* and *La valse* were completed
long before *L'enfant et les sortilèges* was finally
staged, with Victor de Sabata conducting and George
Balanchine as maître de ballet.

Ravel's health was declining. After *L'enfant* he composed, slowly, the newly austere *Chansons madécasses*
and his Violin Sonata, then the *Boléro* for the dancer
Ida Rubinstein and the two concertos for piano. Between the premieres of the latter, he was involved in
the taxi-cab accident that may have triggered his final
collapse. He accepted a film commission to write
three songs for Shalyapin as Don Quixote (he had
actually begun contemplating an opera after Cervantes's novel), but was late in fulfilling it. Those songs
were Ravel's last music; in summer 1933 his muscular co-ordination began to fail, and aphasia set in.
He became unable to compose, and in the sad four
years left to him could manage only some bare
sketches for *Morgiane*, another ballet meant for Ida
Rubinstein.

L'heure espagnole
Spanish Time
Comédie musicale in one act (introduction and 21 scenes)
(50m)
Libretto by Franc-Nohain (Maurice-Étienne Legrand), after
his own comedy
Composed 1907–9
PREMIERES 19 May 1911, Opéra-Comique, Paris; UK:
24 July 1919, Covent Garden, London; US: 5 January
1920, Auditorium, Chicago
CAST Concepción *s*, Gonzalve *t*, Torquemada *t* (*trial*),
Ramiro *bar* (*baryton Martin*), Don Inigo Gomez *b*

Franc-Nohain was surprised when Ravel asked permission to set his highly improper, cod-poetical vaudeville
to music, and when at last Ravel came to play and
sing him the result the playwright's cautious reaction
was that it went on rather long. In fact the composer
set his own Spanish time with expert precision and
crisp habanera rhythms; there are no longueurs, except
in performances that seek to humanize the characters
by letting them moon over their recitatives. Ravel's
score expanded Franc-Nohain's comic analogy between wound-up automata and erotically driven
people much further than the text could do alone, and
yet kept the sung lines natural and colloquial enough
to incur some disapproving sniffs in 1911 (as with his

Jules Renard songs four years earlier, the *Histoires naturelles*). The vocal writing permits the ripe double meanings to be lucid, but they are never crudely underlined. Nor are the characters guyed: besides its poise and verve, the score often glows with the famous Ravel *tendresse*.

SYNOPSIS
Eighteenth-century Toledo. A muscular mule-driver, Ramiro, takes his broken watch to the shop of the clockmaker Torquemada. But it is Thursday, the day when Torquemada regulates all the town clocks; he must leave Ramiro to wait, and his wife Concepción to entertain him. Both are embarrassed: Ramiro because he is shy ('Les muletiers n'ont pas de conversation'), Concepción because she is expecting her poet lover imminently. Her husband has promised her either of two large grandfather clocks, and it occurs to her to beg the muleteer to carry one up to her bedroom. Delighted to have a task, he goes off with it just as Gonzalve drifts in, warbling poetically.

To Concepción's frustration, he is still warbling when Ramiro comes back. She declares a sudden preference for the other clock, and dispatches the muleteer to retrieve the first one; meanwhile she conceals her poet in the second, whereupon the stout banker Don Inigo Gomez arrives unannounced to court her. Ramiro, back again with the first clock, duly carries off the second clock with negligent ease and Concepción as anxious escort. Don Inigo, abandoned, decides that flirtatious whimsy is the card to play, and squeezes himself into the first clock – but prudently shuts the door when Ramiro returns alone, musing on the mysteriousness of woman. Suddenly Concepción reappears in a temper, demanding the instant return of the second clock. While the muleteer obeys, Don Inigo pursues his lascivious strategy with the lady; the upshot is that Ramiro, all unawares, is soon hefting the first clock upstairs once more with Concepción on his heels.

The dismissed poet sings an effusive farewell to his clock dungeon, but hides again as Ramiro comes back, still musing romantically. Concepción descends in a fury – the first clock must go. While Ramiro fetches it, she voices her bitter disappointment ('Oh! la pitoyable aventure!'): Gonzalve would do nothing but rhapsodize, and now Don Inigo is inextricably stuck in his clock. Ramiro returns bearing that clock, ready and eager for the next job. She looks at him with new eyes, and proposes going upstairs again 'sans horloge . . .'. Torquemada comes home to find two gentlemen occupying his clocks and explaining brightly that they are interested customers. By the time his wife reappears, much happier, their reluctant purchases are settled. It takes Ramiro to heave Don Inigo out of his expensive prison, and he also promises to tell Concepción the time each morning when he comes by with his mules. In a final quintet, everybody agrees on a Boccaccian moral: through plain efficiency, the muleteer eventually gets his turn.

The glittering surface of Ravel's score, all Spanish snap with horological icing (continual chimes high and low, a mechanical cuckoo and clock, even three metronomes ticking throughout the prelude), disguises its pure musical invention. Ravel expressly intended to write something more like Italian buffo than French opérette, but what he devised was *sui generis* – an elegantly comic piece for orchestra and singers, through-composed in patterns as intricately and ingeniously connected as those of any watch. The music is aptly laden with displacement jokes: just as the rigorously ticking metronomes in the prelude are all at odds, so the brisk Hispanic dance-rhythms are prone to fractures, the 'popular' harmonies derailed by post-Fauré sophistication, Gonzalve's exquisite little effusions rudely interrupted, and an impossibly low note demanded from Don Inigo by the finale is supplied by a helpful double bassoon. Ravel's Spanishry here surely owes far less to his maternal memories than to Isaac Albéniz, whose music he adored (and who died in the year Ravel completed the opera).

Recent French operas had embraced the Wagnerian leitmotif method to a fault, and Ravel extends it here to absurdity. Don Inigo is identified by a pompous fanfare of short brays, Gonzalve purely by his constant mimicking of effete *fin-de-siècle* art song, Ramiro by a lusty rhythm on timpani – but in his two dreamy fantasies he is also allotted the most richly developed music.

No tag is attached to Concepción, the only character who is both clever and sensible. The music for the gentle Torquemada, to whom perhaps the situation is perfectly clear and the outcome perfectly satisfactory, is of a piece with the tintinnabulating serenity of his shop. That, in turn, is not so very far removed from the magical garden of *L'enfant et les sortilèges*.

L'enfant et les sortilèges
The Child and the Sorceries
Fantaisie lyrique in two parts (45m)
Libretto by Colette (Sidonie-Gabrielle Colette)
Composed 1920–25
PREMIERES 21 March 1925, Salle Garnier, Monte Carlo; 1 February 1926, Opéra-Comique, Paris; US: 19 September 1930, San Francisco; UK: 3 December 1958, Town Hall, Oxford
CAST (The multiple roles are prescribed by the composer) The Child *ms*, Maman (Mother) *c*, Louis XV Chair *s*, Chinese Cup *mc*, Fire/Princess/Nightingale *light s*, Little Old Man (Arithmetic)/Tree Frog *t*, Cat *ms*, Dragonfly *ms*, Bat *s*, Little Owl *s*, Squirrel *ms*, Shepherdess *s*, Shepherd *c*, Armchair *b chantante*, Grandfather Clock *bar*, Teapot *t*, Tom Cat *bar*, Tree *b*; children's chorus of Settle, Sofa, Ottoman, Wicker Chair and Numbers; *satb* chorus of shepherds, frogs, animals and trees

Both Colette and Ravel were cat-lovers, and the feline duet at the centre of *L'enfant et les sortilèges* was conceived *con amore*. Ravel was undoubtedly pleased to have inanimate objects to animate, too, including a much noisier clock than the ones in *L'heure espagnole*, and he must have imagined the garden of the opera on the model of his own at his recently acquired villa, Le Belvédère, in Montfort L'Amaury. It was the composer who tilted Colette's divertissement towards the style of a revue, with her approval: his interest in American popular music had been growing, and would surface again in the 'Blues' of the Violin Sonata and in both the piano concertos. (There is a curious likeness between the cup-and-teapot duet in *L'enfant* and Gershwin's 'Our love is here to stay'.) The challenges the opera presents to a producer's imagination are severe; whimsy would be ruinous in the garden scene, and it would be a rare mezzo-soprano indeed who could make a plausible child of 'six or seven years' as prescribed by the text. After seeing a Disney animated film, Ravel's brother exclaimed that *that* must be the way to do *L'enfant et les sortilèges*.

SYNOPSIS
A naughty child, dawdling over his homework, is reproved by his mother. Left alone, he flies into a tantrum and assaults everything in the room, including the family cat. Then, one after another, all the things he has maltreated come to plaintive life: the long-suffering furniture, the broken clock and the tea service, the offended fire in the grate, the printed shepherds from the slashed wallpaper, the princess from his torn story book. He regrets bitterly the lost ending of the tale ('Toi, le coeur de la rose'), but suddenly his neglected arithmetic pops up to challenge him with impossible exercises. By now quite unstrung, he expects even the cat to speak. Instead, it miaows a mock-Wagnerian erotic duet with its mate in the garden: meanwhile the scene revolves from indoors to outdoors.

At first the garden twitters and murmurs with innocent animal voices; but the trees break in to lament their cruel wounds from the child's pocket knife, and a dragonfly cries after the mate whom the child pinned dead to a wall. A bat grieves for a lost mate too, and a squirrel – reliving its cruel captivity – tries to warn a dim frog of omnipresent danger. A Utopian wildlife ballet ensues, but at the climax the squirrel addresses a poignant rebuke to the child: 'You caged me for the sake of my beautiful blue eyes, but did you know what they reflected? – The free sky and the wind, and my free brothers!' Chastened, the child feels himself rejected from this harmonious animal realm, and he whimpers for his Maman. At once some unforgiving trees and beasts close in upon him; in the commotion, a small squirrel who has been wounded limps towards the child, who binds the squirrel's paw with a ribbon. The other animals reflect on his instinctive kindness and decide to practise calling 'Maman!' on his behalf. Eventually they manage it in chorus, and a light goes on in the house. As Maman comes in answer to the call, they sing, 'Il est bon, l'enfant, il est sage . . .' The child holds out his arms to her, then the opera is suddenly over.

Ravel's score is far more intricately constructed than it pretends to be, with disguised connections between seemingly disparate numbers. There are interesting echoes, too: obviously from the *jardin féerique* of *Ma mère l'oye* in the benedictory final chorus, more subtly from the Violin and Cello Sonata in the princess's opening monologue – and the winding oboe duet that starts the opera and returns reassuringly at the end suggests a delicate shadow of Musorgsky's 'Promenade' in his *Pictures at an Exhibition*. Maman first enters on the same sighing cadence that closes the opera. Two matching modulations, among the most poignantly beautiful in all Ravel's music, adorn the squirrel's plaint (after 'Sais-tu ce qu'ils reflétaient, mes beaux yeux?') and the climax of the farewell chorus.

There are extraordinary and bewitching sounds from the orchestra pit throughout, as well as a prominent piano, which ranges from furious arpeggios to plonking revue-style accompaniments. Ravel wanted it equipped with a *luthéal*, apparently a device for altering and distorting the timbre of the instrument in various ways (he wanted it for his gypsy rhapsody *Tzigane* as well); as far as anyone knows, it is now extinct.

D.M.

ARIBERT REIMANN
b 4 March 1936, Berlin

Reimann's parents were musicians; his father was an organist and Bach specialist, and his mother a concert singer and voice teacher. As a child he experienced the blitz in Berlin at first hand; a brother was killed in a bombing raid, and the family home was subsequently destroyed. In 1945 he fled with his parents before the advancing Soviet troops. Later he experienced the desolation of the first post-war years, alleviated only in 1949 by a period spent in Stockholm. By the age of ten he had composed some first songs and piano pieces; after completing his schooling he studied composition with Boris Blacher and Ernst Pepping in Berlin from 1955 to 1960. There followed periods of study in Vienna and at the Villa Massimo in Rome. An extremely fine pianist, Reimann is in great demand as a soloist and lieder accompanist.

A song-cycle with chorus and orchestra, *Lieder auf der Flucht*, and a piano sonata, both dating from 1957, were Reimann's first published works. An extensive list of subsequent compositions includes a cello concerto, two piano concertos, *Variations* for orchestra, and a substantial string trio. However, Reimann's output is predominantly vocal and displays a catholic taste in poets (Paul Celan, Byron, Shelley, Joyce, Rilke, Louize Labé, e. e. cummings). His choral works include a cantata, *Verrà la morte* (1966), and a *Requiem* (1982). He has also composed two ballets, *Die Vogelscheuchen* (1970, scenario by Günter Grass) for large orchestra (a revision of *Stoffreste*, 1957) and *Chacun sa chimère* for tenor and chamber orchestra (1981). In Germany he has received several major prizes, while the opera *Lear* has brought him worldwide recognition.

Having spent many hours accompanying his mother's voice lessons, Reimann acquired a unique understanding of singing technique. Like earlier opera composers, he rarely creates new roles until the premiere has been cast, tailoring his vocal writing to the specific qualities of the singers chosen. His operatic music is distinguished above all by its intense and brooding qualities, a tendency to sustained hysterical outbursts, complex textures and dark colours. Reimann's childhood experiences have influenced him in his frequent choice of pessimistic or apocalyptic texts. Yet since completing his fifth opera, *Troades*, his touch has lightened appreciably and he has reached a turning-point in his creative development.

Lear

Opera in two parts (2h 15m)
Libretto by Claus H. Henneberg, after *King Lear* by William Shakespeare (1605)
PREMIERES 9 July 1978, Nationaltheater, Munich; US: 12 June 1981, War Memorial Opera House, San Francisco; UK: 24 January 1989, Coliseum, London
CAST King Lear *bar*, King of France *b-bar*, Duke of Albany *bar*, Duke of Cornwall *t*, Kent *t*, Gloucester *b-bar*, Edgar *ct*, Edmund *t*, Goneril *s*, Regan *s*, Cordelia *s*, Fool *spoken role*, Servant *t*, Knight *spoken role*; *tb* chorus of followers of Lear and Gloucester, soldiers, servants

Hearing a performance of his Celan cycle (1971) – 'the dark colour, massive brass agglomerations, concentrated areas in the lower strings' – Reimann became convinced of the possibility of writing another opera, his third. 'From then on all the pieces I wrote . . . were paths towards Lear,' he wrote. It was bold indeed to approach an operatic subject that Berlioz, Debussy and, above all, Verdi had contemplated and abandoned, yet the task was made possible by Claus Henneberg's skilful reduction of Shakespeare's drama to its textual bare bones, making full use of ensembles and scenic simultaneity. The German version also makes some use of the anonymous *Ballad of King Lear and His Three Daughters*, which served Shakespeare himself as source material.

SYNOPSIS

Part I Lear abdicates the throne and divides his kingdom between his daughters, Regan and Goneril. Cordelia, who remains silent out of love for her father, is disinherited and married off to the king of France. Edgar, son of Gloucester, is banished on a false charge of plotting to kill his father. Kent attaches himself to Lear as faithful servant, but Goneril and Regan drive their father away. In a ferocious storm on the heath, Lear becomes demented; Kent and the fool bring him to a hovel where Edgar, feigning madness, has also taken refuge. Gloucester rescues the king and takes him to Dover.

Part II Cornwall (Regan's husband) takes Gloucester captive, blinds him, and is himself stabbed to death. Edgar leads Gloucester to Dover, where he is reunited with Lear. The king is led to Cordelia in the French camp; both are captured by Edmund, Gloucester's bastard son, and Cordelia is strangled. Goneril poisons Regan but, when Edmund is killed by Edgar in single combat, she commits suicide. Lamenting over the corpse of Cordelia, Lear dies of grief.

The strength of *Lear* lies primarily in Reimann's delineation of character. He exploits every musical resource of the voice but strictly avoids extraneous vocal effects, hence his roles are approachable by classically trained opera singers. In the interests of clarity, the vocal lines are set in orchestral frames (a 'window' technique derived from Mozart's operatic scoring), while the fool, a spoken role, is accompanied by

string quartet. The complex and frequently aggressive orchestral textures come close to those of Penderecki. There is, however, a considerable difference in the means employed, for in *Lear* every parameter of the sound picture is notated in minutest detail: the strings are divided into 48 separate parts, rhythmic structures are strictly specified (except, on occasion, in the voice parts), clusters are exactly notated, while quarter-tones are employed to compress the harmony still further.

Dietrich Fischer-Dieskau was the moving force behind *Lear* and the eloquent first interpreter of the title role. Since its highly successful premiere, the work has been widely accepted as a masterpiece of the postwar German operatic repertoire.

Other operatic works: *Ein Traumspiel*, 1965; *Melusine*, 1971; *Die Gespenstersonate*, 1984; *Troades*, 1986; *Das Schloss*, 1992

A. C. W. B.

WOLFGANG RIHM
b 13 March 1952, Karlsruhe, Germany

Rihm studied composition with Eugen Werner Velte, Stockhausen, Huber, Fortner and Searle. A former participant, then tutor, at the Darmstadt summer school, he was appointed to a professorship at the Musikhochschule in Karlsruhe in 1985. One of modern Germany's most prolific composers, he has written numerous orchestral and chamber works, including three symphonies and eight string quartets. Of particular importance in his development were the five *Abgesangsszenen* (1979–81), the *Chiffre* cycle (1982–8) and *Klangbeschreibung I–III* (1982–7). In the mid-1970s Rihm was one of a group of young German composers (they included von Böse, von Schweinitz and Trojahn) who were occasionally termed neo-Romantics. This was a misnomer, for Rihm was primarily concerned to break away from the aridity of doctrinaire post-serialism. His aesthetic position became apparent in *Sub-Kontur* (1974–5), an orchestral work that attempted to plumb the depths of the subconscious. The unfavourable response to the piece at the time of its premiere in Donaueschingen in 1976 did not deter Rihm from pursuing his chosen path. In 1976 he also composed his first work for the stage, the chamber opera *Faust und Yorick*, which revealed a penchant for the theatre of the absurd. A second chamber opera, *Jakob Lenz*, followed a year later. This clearly demonstrated that Rihm's rejection of serialism was linked with an interest in suffering artists on the verge of madness. Psychology tended to be eschewed by the avant-garde in the 1960s, and thus the plight of the schizophrenic historical Lenz, a representative of the *Sturm und Drang* aesthetic who rejected classicism, could be construed in symbolical terms.

Jakob Lenz was followed by *Tutuguri* (Berlin, 1982), a poème dansé based on Antonin Artaud's description of the black rites of the Tarahumara Indians. Artaud's Theatre of Cruelty, which was 'created in order to restore to the theatre a passionate and convulsive conception of life', left its mark on Rihm's next work for the stage, *Die Hamletmaschine*. Based on the play by Heiner Müller, the work dwells on images of horror and despair. This vein is further explored in *Oedipus*. Rihm's latest stage work, *Die Eroberung von Mexico*, is also based on Artaud.

Jakob Lenz

Chamber opera (1h 15m)
Libretto by Michael Fröhling, after the novella *Lenz* by Georg Büchner (1836)
PREMIERES 8 March 1979, Staatsoper, Hamburg; UK: 3 June 1987, Almeida Theatre, London

Büchner's incomplete novella describes with almost clinical accuracy the fate of the schizophrenic 18th-century poet Jakob Lenz. In the opera this psychogram of a personality drifting inexorably to destruction and madness is cast in the form of a kind of multi-layered rondo comprising 15 scenes and five instrumental interludes.

Lenz is seen wandering through the Vosges, pursued by voices. He jumps into the water and is found by Oberlin, a Protestant minister and philanthropist, who takes him home to console him. Unable to sleep, Lenz thinks of Goethe's beloved Friederike Brion. Plagued by voices, he once more jumps into the water. He is permitted to preach to Oberlin's congregation.

His friend Kaufmann incorrectly considers his illness to be eccentricity. The events that follow show that this is not the case. Lenz becomes obsessed with the idea that Friederike will die, and bursts into Oberlin's room at night to ask after her. Later he comes across a dead girl, whom he tries in vain to bring back to life. His condition continues to deteriorate, and Oberlin and Kaufmann are finally forced to put him into a straitjacket. Totally oblivious of his surroundings, he is reduced to uttering the word 'Konsequent!'

One of the opera's principal ideas is a basic chord, B-F-G♭, that, significantly, is a transposed version of Schoenberg's seminal D minor plus G sharp chord. The contrast between the world of normality and Lenz's inner torments is brought out by the evocative use of sarabande, motet, madrigal and chorale on the one hand, and the vocal resources of Expressionist music-theatre on the other. A small and unusual orchestra provides predominantly chamber-music textures.

A.C.

Die Eroberung von Mexico

The Conquest of Mexico
Music-theatre in four acts (1hr 45m)
Libretto by the composer, after Anton Artaud's scenario *The Conquest of Mexico* (1933) and *The Seraphim Theatre* (1937), Octavio Paz's *The Root of Man* (1937) and anonymous 16th-century Native American poems
PREMIERE 9 February 1992, Staatsoper, Hamburg

Die Eroberung von Mexico portrays the impact of the Spanish invasion upon the indigenous Aztec population in the 16th century. Following a scenario by Artaud, the four acts – Omens, Declaration, Upheavals, and Abdication – chart the progression of the invasion from its beginnings in an 'expectant' untroubled land, through the first meeting between Cortez, leader of the conquistadores, and Montezuma, the Aztec king, to the inevitable violent conflict and Montezuma's surrender. Only Cortez and Montezuma (sung by a soprano) are specifically identified in the cast: both are 'shadowed' by speakers or singers in the orchestra pit. A third character, Malinche, Cortez's mistress and translator, is portrayed by a dancer.

The musical range of *Die Eroberung von Mexico* is impressively wide; the use of a large chorus allows Rihm to create spectacular textures recalling his concert work *Dies* (1984). The orchestra is never used descriptively or to accompany the singers, but takes an independent path. Everything in the work, says Rihm, is song, and that becomes most explicit at the end of the final act, when the valedictory duet between Montezuma and Cortez, unaccompanied, develops a Mahlerian intensity.

A.J.C.

Other operatic works: *Faust und Yorick*, 1977; *Die Hamletmaschine*, 1987; *Oedipus*, 1987

NIKOLAI RIMSKY-KORSAKOV

Nikolai Andreievich Rimsky-Korsakov; *b* 18 March 1844, Tikhvin, nr Novgorod, Russia; *d* 21 June 1908, Lyubensk, nr St Petersburg, Russia

By the time Anton Rubinstein founded the St Petersburg Conservatory in 1862, four young men had joined a circle dominated by the pianist-composer Mily Balakirev: César Cui, Musorgsky, Borodin and, the youngest of the group, Nikolai Rimsky-Korsakov. All had originally been destined for careers other than music, but were persuaded to compose by the force of their mentor's magnetic personality. Balakirev's circle was nicknamed *Moguchaya Kuchka* or the Mighty Handful by its ardent supporter the connoisseur and critic Vladimir Stasov.

In the early 1860s, Balakirev started the 17-year-old naval cadet Rimsky on a full-scale symphony, but before it was completed the latter had to interrupt his studies, sailing on a lengthy cruise to the New World. It was not until after his return to St Petersburg in 1865 and the completion of a second symphony, based on the legend of Antar, that he attempted his first opera, *The Maid of Pskov*.

After a change to a more sympathetic conservatory director, Rimsky joined the staff as a professor of practical composition and instrumentation in 1871. (He resigned his naval commission in 1873, and was instead appointed to the part-time civil post of inspector of naval bands.) He studied Tchaikovsky's harmony treatise avidly and immersed himself in academic music, writing a number of fugues and chamber works (of which Balakirev thoroughly disapproved), and getting to know pre-19th-century music. Balakirev's insistence, in 1876, that Rimsky should assist him with the preparation of Glinka's operas for publication helped turn his own thoughts back to opera, though the academic experience he had gained could not be forgotten. His own most lyrical operas, *May Night* and *The Snow Maiden*, soon followed.

After Musorgsky's death in 1881, Rimsky set about arranging and completing the unfinished music for performance and publication. By the time he wrote the three great orchestral pieces of the late 1880s (*Capriccio espagnol*, *Scheherazade* and the *Russian Easter Festival* overture), Rimsky's already assured orchestral technique was matched by his compositional virtuosity. After hearing Wagner's *Ring* in 1889 he determined to concentrate on writing opera. Relations with Balakirev (known for his intransigence) became increasingly strained, and he would have nothing to do with any of Rimsky's later operas; the two men broke off relations in the early 1890s.

Rimsky's influence as a composition teacher was enormous. The most important of his pupils was Stravinsky. More significant than actual technical derivations, however, was the model of the calculating, sensual, pattern-creating world of the later operas. Most of his operas are based on Russian topics and contain folk material or folk intonations. He found fantastic or mythological subjects particularly congenial, but was less successful in treating full-blooded human emotions, achieving this satisfactorily only in *The Maid of Pskov*. The middle-period operas, *May Night* and *The Snow Maiden*, reveal a genuine lyrical gift combined with an ability to depict supernatural and fantastic elements with suitable harmonic piquancy clothed in imaginative and original orchestral colours. But the characterization lacks conviction.

The Maid of Pskov (or Ivan the Terrible)
Pskovityanka
Opera in four acts (first version); prologue and three acts (second version); three acts (third version; 2h 30m)
Libretto by the composer, after the play by Lev Aleksandrovich Mey (1860)
Composed 1868–72; second version 1876–7; third version 1891–2
PREMIERES 13 January 1873, Mariinsky Theatre, St Petersburg; second version: not performed; third version: 18 April 1895, Panayevsky Theatre, St Petersburg; UK: 8 July 1913, Drury Lane, London
CAST Tsar Ivan the Terrible *b*, Prince Yury Tokmakov *b*, Boyar Nikita Matuta *t*, Prince Afanasii Vyazemskii *b*, Mikhail Tucha *t*, Princess Olga Tokmakova *s*, Stefanida Matuta *s*, 2 *ms*, *t*, 2 *b*; *satb* chorus of officers, judges, boyars, burghers' sons, *oprichniki* (the tsar's bodyguards), pages, Muscovite archers, serving maids, boys, people, huntsmen

Although the text is loosely based on Mey's drama, Rimsky wrote most of it himself, and it is in the best tradition of the Mighty Handful. Their realist music dramas, in which the chorus actively participates in the drama and the principal characters are often revealed with psychological intensity, include Cui's *William Ratcliff*, Musorgsky's *Boris Godunov* and Borodin's *Prince Igor*. Tchaikovsky's *The Oprichnik* is of the same type and all these works, except Cui's, were the result of the social and artistic conditions that also inspired Tolstoy's *War and Peace*.

SYNOPSIS (third version)
Act I The action takes place in 1570. Olga loves the young Mikhail Tucha but has been promised to the much older Boyar Matuta by her supposed father Prince Tokmakov, the vice-regent of Tsar Ivan the Terrible in Pskov (her real father is unknown). The lovers meet secretly. In the marketplace, news is brought of the destruction of Novgorod by Ivan, who is marching on the similarly semi-autonomous Pskov. Tokmakov persuades the people to receive him peacefully, but Tucha and his followers resolve to resist.

Act II Ivan's initial wrath disappears when Olga is presented to him, and he decides to forgive Pskov.

Act III During a royal hunt, the young lovers again meet clandestinely, but are discovered by Matuta; he, however, is dismissed angrily by Ivan, who has revealed in a soliloquy that Olga is his daughter. Olga's faith in him, despite his reputation, moves him deeply, but when Tucha appears to rescue her she is killed by a shot intended for him.

This is Rimsky's only opera in which the human characterization is wholly satisfactory. Tsar Ivan's character is very well drawn, both at his most bloodthirsty and, for example, when his heart melts at Olga's trusting and loving nature. Tokmakov is depicted as a kindly, understanding prince, and the young lovers, so often mere ciphers with Rimsky, are exceptionally well portrayed. Tucha is convincing both as a lover and as a young rebel leader. At the close of Act I, Tucha induces a number of men (divided tenors and basses of the chorus) to defend themselves against the tyrannical tsar to the strains of a folksong. Here the chorus propels the action forward in one of the finest scenes in Russian opera, singled out for praise by contemporary critics.

May Night
Maiskaya noch'
Opera in three acts (2h 30m)
Libretto by the composer, after the comic short story in the volume *Evenings on a Farm near Dikanka* by Nikolai Gogol (1832)
PREMIERES 21 January 1880, Mariinsky Theatre, St Petersburg; UK: 26 June 1914, Drury Lane, London
CAST The Mayor *b*, Levko *t*, Hanna *ms*, Pannochka *s*, Mayor's Sister-in-law *ms*, Kalenik *bar*, Distiller *t*, 3 Water Sprites 2 *s*, *ms*; *satb* chorus of villagers

In basing his next opera on Gogol's story, Rimsky abandoned the dramatic realism of *The Maid of Pskov*. With Balakirev, he had been editing the operas of Glinka, and the score is indebted to that composer in many ways, especially to his *Ruslan and Lyudmila*.

SYNOPSIS
Act I The village mayor disapproves of his son Levko's love for Hanna, since he wants her himself. Horrified to learn that his father is his rival, Levko gathers together a band of village lads who sing a mocking song outside the mayor's house.

Act II In the confusion that follows this performance, the mayor's sister-in-law is captured in error and bundled into prison. She chides the mayor, saying his philanderings are common knowledge in the village. He eventually calms her and restores order.

Act III Levko sits on the shores of a nearby lake

singing of his love for Hanna. Suddenly *rusalki* (water sprites) appear. Their leader, Pannochka, asks Levko to identify a witch from among them (this was Pannochka's cruel stepmother in a former mortal life, who drove Pannochka to drown herself). He succeeds and, in gratitude for being released from the evil spell, Pannochka gives Levko a document. The mayor, when he sees it, believes this to be a decree from the commissar sanctioning Levko's marriage to Hanna and reluctantly agrees to the wedding.

There are some excellent comic episodes, including the mayor's ridiculous wooing of Hanna and, later on, his interruption of the reading of the 'commissar's' letter and the bitchy chatter of his sister-in-law, depicted by bustling semiquavers. Excellent folk choruses include the finale of Act I, in which Levko eggs on the villagers to play practical jokes on his father, to a driving accompaniment with (piano and harp) which imitates his vigorous strumming on the bandora. The stylized musical patterns employed for the fantastic episodes are more highly organized than the rest of the material. The opera's main motif, which occurs in its most characteristic form at the opening of Act III, is strikingly similar to the opening of Weber's *Oberon*.

The Snow Maiden

Snegurochka
Opera (spring fairy-tale) in four acts with a prologue (3h 15m)
Libretto by the composer, after the play by Aleksandr Ostrovsky (1873), in turn based on a folktale
Composed 1880–81; second version *c.* 1895
PREMIERES 10 February 1882, Mariinsky Theatre, St Petersburg; US: 5 January 1922, Seattle; UK: 12 April 1933, Sadler's Wells, London
CAST Snegurochka *s*, Lel' *c*, Kupava *s*, Mizgir *bar*, Tsar Berendei *t*, Bobyl' *t*, Bobylikha *ms*, Red Spring *ms*, Father Frost *b*, Woodsprite *t*, *ms*, *t*, 2 *b*; *satb* chorus of peasants, followers of Spring, followers of the tsar, boyars; dancers

SYNOPSIS
Prologue Snegurochka is the daughter of Father Frost and Red (i.e. beautiful) Spring. She seems beautiful and warm, but her heart is ice; she will die if it melts. Fearful for her safety from Yarilo the sun god, her father entrusts her to the care of the woodspite and she is adopted by a peasant couple, Bobyl' and Bobylikha. The true nature of love, controlled by Yarilo, must remain hidden from her.
Act I Snegurochka takes a platonic interest in the warm-hearted shepherd boy Lel', but he prefers Kupava, who is betrothed to Mizgir, who in turn falls in love with Snegurochka.
Act II At a royal feast held to celebrate the end of winter, Snegurochka tells Tsar Berendei that she is incapable of love. He promises a reward to the man who can disprove this.
Act III When Lel' overlooks Snegurochka and kisses Kupava, Snegurochka is distraught. Mizgir tries to comfort her, but she flees from him. Mizgir is prevented from catching her by the woodspite.
Act IV Snegurochka prevails on her mother,

Spring, to warm her heart and soon consents to marry Mizgir, but she is struck by a ray of sun just before the wedding, and melts. Heartbroken, Mizgir throws himself into the lake.

The Snow Maiden was written at one of the happiest times in Rimsky's life and it contains some of his most spontaneously lyrical music. According to his autobiography, it contains six authentic folk melodies, some of them treated modally, as well as many folk intonations. Birds are imitated: for example, the cock in the prologue and the bullfinch in the prologue and in Act IV. Though he knew little of Wagner at the time, Rimsky makes use of leitmotifs, such as the delicate motif for Snegurochka, the rough one for the peasant Bobyl', and the tsar's motif (first heard in the splendid little march to which he enters in Act II, derived from Chernomor's march in Glinka's *Ruslan and Lyudmila*). Rimsky draws particular attention to his invention of a chord of six whole-tone notes of the scale used when the woodsprite embraces Mizgir. The opera abounds in instrumental solos for violin, cello, flute, oboe and, above all, clarinet. Yet the work is ultimately unconvincing, for some of the finest music is thrown away on unimportant scenes, while those which should be dramatically the strongest, such as the final duet of the now warm-hearted Snegurochka and Mizgir, are insipid and ineffective. Nevertheless, because of the fine quality of much of the music, it deserves to be better known.

Sadko

Opera-bylina in seven scenes (three or five acts) (3h 45m)
Libretto by the composer and Vladimir Bel'sky, based on a bylina (epic poem) from the 11th-century 'Novgorod cycle'
Composed 1894–6
PREMIERES 7 January 1898, Solodovnikov Theatre, Moscow; US: 25 January 1930, Metropolitan, New York; UK: 9 June 1931, Lyceum, London

The story of *Sadko*, an opera of which the composer was especially proud, is essentially the same as that behind Rimsky's early orchestral 'musical picture' *Sadko* (1867, rev. 1869 and 1892).
Princess Volkhova, daughter of the king of the sea, helps the poor minstrel Sadko to catch golden fish. Flushed with this success he sets sail, but on his return journey his ship is becalmed; his companions set him adrift as a propitiation to the sea king and he sinks to the bottom of the sea. There he wins Volkhova's hand by the beauty of his singing, but the dancing to his *gusli* (a strummed folk instrument) becomes so frenzied that it causes a terrible storm. Sadko is compelled to return to land, and Princess Volkhova is turned into a river.
The opera's finest moments include the complex folk scene at the quayside (Scene 4), with its songs of the Viking, Venetian and Indian merchants, as well as Sadko's own bardic-style melodies, as adumbrated by Glinka in *Ruslan and Lyudmila* but considerably developed by Rimsky. In the end, however, the earlier, succinct orchestral piece succeeds where the opera fails.

The Tale of Tsar Saltan, of his son the famous and mighty hero Prince Gvidon Saltanovich and of the beautiful Swan Princess

Skazka o Tsare Saltane, o syne evo slavnom i moguchem bogatyre knyaze Gvidone Saltanovich i o prekrasnoi tsarevne lebedi
Opera in a prologue and four acts (3h 15m)
Libretto by Vladimir Bel'sky after the poem by Aleksandr Pushkin (1832)
PREMIERES 3 November 1900, Solodovnikov Theatre, Moscow; UK: 11 October 1933, Sadler's Wells, London; US: 27 December 1937, St James Theater, New York (as *The Bumble-Bee Prince*)
CAST Tsar Saltan *b*, Princess Militrissa *s*, Prince Gvidon *t*, Swan Princess *s*, Povarikha *s*, Tkachikha *ms*, 2 *t*, 2 *bar*, 2 *b*; *satb* chorus of nobles, courtiers, nurses, guards, soldiers, sailors, astrologers, squirrel, bumble-bee, 33 sea-knights, etc.

The recurrent formulaic material employed by Pushkin in his poem was well suited to Rimsky's creative gifts. The opera opens with a fanfare in which are juxtaposed two unrelated harmonies pivoting on a common note. As the composer wrote, it 'has the significance of an invitation to see and hear what will presently be enacted, a novel device eminently suitable for a fantastic tale'.

SYNOPSIS
Act I   Two evil sisters send a false message to Tsar Saltan, who has marched away to the wars, that his wife, their beautiful younger sister Militrissa, has given birth to a monster. He orders that she and her son, Prince Gvidon, be cast into the sea in a barrel.

Act II   They are washed up on an island. Gvidon, now miraculously full-grown, rescues a swan from a pursuing kite. The swan, having turned out to be a maiden, causes a marvellous city with onion-domed churches, gardens and palaces to rise from the ground. Gvidon rules over it.

Act III   Gvidon is anxious to learn of his father, so the swan changes him into a bee and he flies to Tsar Saltan's court (the well-known *Flight of the Bumble-Bee*). The tsar has heard of the magical island, though does not know that his wife and son are there. When Militrissa's sisters try to dissuade the tsar from visiting the island, the bee stings them.

Act IV   The tsar, nevertheless, crosses to the island, where he sees its three wonders: a squirrel that cracks golden nuts containing emerald kernels while whistling a folktune, 33 handsome young warriors cast up on the shore and the swan maiden. She reveals herself to be a princess. Gvidon, whom the tsar has now realized is his son, falls in love with her, and the tsar and his wife are reunited.

Though it bears some resemblance to a folksong, the swan princess's motif is based, probably subconsciously, on a beautiful melody from Tchaikovsky's opera *Vakula the Smith*; the opening is identical, though changed to the major mode. Instead of Tchaikovsky's deeply felt lyricism we have a sharply etched illusion of beauty created by accompanying

washes of sound. Like other material in the opera, it gives an impression of sound for its own sake. It is the logical consistency of Pushkin's fairy-tale world together with its absence of obvious human significance that, as the Russian literary historian D. S. Mirsky has written, makes *Tsar Saltan* paradoxically 'the most universally human of Pushkin's works'. Rimsky's opera, too, has elements of sophisticated beauty and a naïve directness that contribute enormously to its charm. In this context the lack of full-blooded human emotions in the conventional operatic sense does not detract from Rimsky's achievement.

The Legend of the Invisible City of Kitezh and the Maiden Fevroniya

Skazaniye o nevidimom grade Kitezhe i deve Fevronii
Opera in four acts (six scenes) (3h 15m)
Libretto by Vladimir Bel'sky, after a Russian legend
Composed 1903–5
PREMIERES 20 February 1907, Mariinsky Theatre, St Petersburg; UK: 30 March 1926, Covent Garden, London (concert); US: 21 May 1932, Ann Arbor (concert); 4 February 1936, Philadelphia
CAST Prince Yury *b*, Prince Vsevolod Yur'evich *t*, Fevroniya *s*, Grishka Kuterma *t*, *s*, *ms*, *c*, 2 *t*, 4 *b*; *satb* chorus of *streltsy* (royal guards), people, domra-players, Tartars

The story is based on a legend that blends Christianity with nature worship and pantheism, and it may have been this religious element, together with Wagnerian orchestration, that led some contemporary critics to call it a Russian *Parsifal* – rather a fanciful notion. In the decades after its first production it was one of Rimsky's most popular operas, but since the Second World War it has been heard less frequently outside the Soviet Union.

SYNOPSIS
Act I   The maiden Fevroniya lives in the forest and reveres God and Mother Earth. She promises to marry a young man whom she meets when he is injured while hunting. She afterwards learns that he is Prince Vsevolod, son of Prince Yury and joint ruler of the sacred city of Great Kitezh and its domains.

Act II   The bridal procession in Little Kitezh is derided and cursed by the drunken ne'er-do-well Grishka; a horde of Tartars sacks the village and carries off Fevroniya together with Grishka, who is forced to act as the Tartars' guide to Great Kitezh.

Act III   Vsevolod leads the army against the enemy while his father prays; in answer to his prayer, the city is enveloped in a golden mist and disappears into Paradise. Meanwhile Vsevolod and his companions have been slain. The Tartars view with astonishment a flaming cross, all that is left of Kitezh. Grishka and Fevroniya manage to escape but get lost in the forest.

Act IV   The terrified Grishka imagines that he sees the Devil wildly dancing, and sings and whistles to appease him. Soon the birds and flowers spring up around Fevroniya, and the spirit of Vsevolod leads her to Kitezh in Paradise where they are united beyond death.

Kitezh contains some of Rimsky's most beautiful music; the symphonic interlude between Scenes 1 and 2 of Act IV (which forms the finale of the orchestral suite from the opera) is a marvellous instance of the composer's ability to build a fresco of instrumental sounds, including the orchestral sound of church bells, touched on in his *Russian Easter Festival* overture but here taken to unprecedented lengths. Fevroniya's religious, nature-worshipping *naïveté* comes over with great charm – her principal leitmotif is similar to the Snow Maiden's. Grishka's scene in Act IV is masterly, and almost bears comparison with Musorgsky's essays in the same vein, while Prince Yury, in his pious stateliness, is not unlike Pimen in *Boris Godunov.* But other characterization is less satisfactory, and the opera as a whole lacks that crucial dimension of creative inspiration and judgement which would have transformed it into a masterpiece.

The Golden Cockerel

Zolotoi petushok

Opera (dramatized fairy-tale) in three acts with prologue and epilogue (2h 15m)
Libretto by Vladimir Bel'sky, after a poem by Aleksandr Pushkin (1834)
Composed 1906–7
PREMIERES 7 October 1909, Solodovnikov Theatre, Moscow; UK: 15 June 1914, Drury Lane, London; US: 6 March 1918, Metropolitan, New York
CAST Tsar Dodon *b*, Prince Gvidon *t*, Prince Afron *bar*, General Polkan *b*, Amelfa *c*, Astrologer *t altino*, Queen of Shemakha *s*, Golden Cockerel *s*; *satb* chorus of people, boyars, guards, soldiers, cannoniers, female slaves

The designer of the first production of *The Golden Cockerel* was the Russian fairy-tale illustrator Ivan Bilibin, whose cartoon of Tsar Dodon, 'sovereign of the entire earth', contemplating the notion of annexing the moon – a skit on the tsarist expansionism – may well have given Rimsky the idea of using Pushkin's poem as the basis of an opera. Whereas *Tsar Saltan* is Pushkin's longest *skazka*, the ironic *Golden Cockerel*, written three years later, is one of his shortest. This was no disadvantage, since the composer and his librettist Bel'sky (who had also written the libretto for *Tsar Saltan*) were able to expand the original to suit their purpose, adding elements of irony and political satire; for example, the passage in which the astonished tsar asks what the word 'law' means does not occur in Pushkin; new also was the close of Act II, in which the queen's slaves sing of Dodon, a tsar by rank and dress, but a slave in body and soul.

Russia had just lost the Russo-Japanese war, and the resultant unrest caused the temporary closure of the St Petersburg Conservatory and the suspension of Rimsky for his support of the students. As *The Golden Cockerel* is a satire on incompetence in war, it is not surprising that, after completion of the opera on 11 September 1907, there was trouble with the censor. This may have contributed to the recurrence of the composer's angina of which he died, never having heard what many consider to be his greatest work. Perhaps in order to veil the more obvious examples of satire there was obfuscation of the 'meaning' of the tale, but to look for deeper symbolism would be fruitless.

Significantly, the premiere was in Moscow, away from the seat of government, and certain changes were made by the censor. Because some of the parts entail dancing as well as singing, in the Western premiere, on 25 May 1914 in Paris, and in subsequent London performances, Diaghilev's ballet dancers mimed the actions while the singers sat in the theatre boxes, a version originally devised by the choreographer Mikhail Fokine for St Petersburg. However, later interpreters of the roles of the queen and Dodon have been able to cope with the stage business in Act II, and the opera's frequent modern performances are always in Rimsky's authentic version.

SYNOPSIS

Prologue   The astrologer informs the audience that the fantastic tale it is about to witness has a moral.

Act I   The curtain rises on the palace of the aged Tsar Dodon, with a view of the town in the distance which includes people walking about and armed guards soundly asleep. With Dodon are his two sons, Gvidon and Afron, General Polkan and assembled boyars. Dodon asks advice on how to counter a threatened attack. Each prince in turn makes a futile proposal which is greeted with rapturous approval by all but the crusty old general. Not knowing how to solve the problem, they suggest the possibility of consulting an augury, and as they quarrel the astrologer appears. He gives Dodon a golden cockerel which will crow to predict peace, or, as an alarm, point in the direction of the enemy. The delighted Dodon promises the astrologer he may have anything he wishes as a reward. When the astrologer asks that Dodon should put this in writing, according to the law, the astonished tsar exclaims, 'According to the law? What does that word mean? I have never heard of it. In all cases my caprice, my command – that is the law.' The astrologer withdraws, and Dodon dismisses the boyars, climbs into bed, plays with a parrot, and, with the cockerel proclaiming that all is safe, is sung to sleep by his housekeeper, Amelfa. Dodon's dreams of a lovely maiden are twice interrupted by the cockerel crowing to raise the alarm. The first time his none-too-willing sons are sent off at the head of an army, but the second time he dons his rusty armour and, to the cheers of his subjects, himself sets off to war.

Act II   A narrow rocky pass on a misty night. The army has been defeated and among the bodies are those of Gvidon and Afron, who have slain each other in the battle. Dodon and Polkan, with their force, lament but cannot avenge the dead, since they do not know where the enemy is. With the dawn, the mists rise to reveal a magnificent tent. Assuming it to belong to the enemy general, they bombard it with singular lack of success. A beautiful maiden emerges and sings an aria in praise of the sun. She tells Dodon that she is the queen of Shemakha, who can conquer all by her beauty. Polkan, who is getting in the way, is dismissed, and she seduces Dodon, eventually prevailing on him to sing and dance, and laughing at his grotesque endeavours. She accepts his hand in marriage, and they start for home.

Act III   Back in Dodon's capital the procession enters – one of the most spectacular processional marches in the whole of Russian opera. But the rejoicing is interrupted by the appearance of the astrologer, who now claims his reward – the queen of Shemakha herself. Dodon tries to excuse himself and offers alternatives; but the aged eunuch insists, stating that he wishes to take a wife. Dodon, enraged, strikes him fiercely with his sceptre and is disconcerted when he dies as a result, but the queen of Shemakha laughs; when Dodon tries to embrace her, she repulses him. Amid dark clouds and thunder, the cockerel suddenly gives a loud crow, flies down from its perch, and pecks Dodon on the head. He falls down dead, and when the clouds clear the queen and the cockerel have vanished. The people lament, singing of the virtues of their dead tsar.

Epilogue   The astrologer asks the audience not to be alarmed by the tragic outcome, for 'the queen and I were the only living persons in it, the rest – a pale illusion, emptiness . . .'

The many leitmotifs are used as vivid, descriptive recurrent patterns which are treated to various metamorphoses, resulting in an elaborate fresco of sound. Three of the four most important motifs occur in the prologue. First, that of the golden cockerel, a trumpet call initially juxtaposing the triads of D flat and E major. But this is no mere 'invitation to . . . hear what will presently be enacted' as in *Tsar Saltan*, for it is interwoven into the music in many different places; the second phrase becomes the soothing accompaniment to Dodon's slumbers in Act I, and is sung by the frightened chorus after the alarm has been raised. Secondly, the chromatic motif of the queen of Shemakha, redolent of the Orient and depicting her insidious beauty, which accompanies not only the queen herself but also Dodon's dreams in Act I. More importantly, the queen's motif occurs during the astrologer's music in Act I, thus cleverly revealing that there is a subtle connection between him and the queen. And thirdly, the astrologer's own motif of unrelated arpeggiated chords tinkled out by the glockenspiel and the harps in their highest register. Together with the very high tenor register of his voice, this depicts the brittleness of his old age. Finally, the most important of Tsar Dodon's prosaic motifs occurs at the very beginning of Act I and is adroitly incorporated, in inverted form, in the march at the end of that act. There is no important new material in Act III; Rimsky skilfully employs existing material in endless permutations.

Other operatic works: *Mlada* (inc.; coll. with Borodin, César Cui and Musorgsky, 1872); *Mlada*, 1892; *Christmas Eve* (*Noch' pered Rozhdestvom*), 1895; *The Barber of Baghdad* (*Bagdadskii borodobrei*) (inc., 1895); *Mozart and Salieri* (*Mozart i Sal'yeri*), 1898; *The Noblewoman Vera Sheloga* (*Boyaryna Vera Sheloga*), 1898; *The Tsar's Bride* (*Tsarskaya nevesta*), 1899; *Serviliya*, 1902; *Kashchei the Immortal* (*Kashchei bessmertnyi*), 1902, rev. 1906; *The Commander* (*Pan Voyevoda*), 1904; *Sten'ka Razin* (inc., 1906); *Heaven and Earth* (*Zemlya i nebo*) (inc., 1906)

E.G.

RICHARD RODGERS
Richard Charles Rodgers; *b* 28 June 1902, New York; *d* 30 December 1979, New York

Richard Rodgers began writing songs for the stage when aged 14, contributing to summer-camp and club shows. He attended Columbia University, where he wrote for the Varsity Show in collaboration with fellow student Lorenz Hart and, in one song, Oscar Hammerstein II. After a period of intense frustration, a lucky break came with the revue *The Garrick Gaieties* in 1925. The team of Rodgers and Hart thereupon embarked on a remarkable series of collaborations that lasted until 1943, when they revised their *A Connecticut Yankee* for revival. Their work together was characterized by the vivacity and sophistication of Hart's lyrics, for which Rodgers's music provided sometimes a lively support, sometimes a lyrical contrast.

The partnership with Hammerstein that began with *Oklahoma!* in 1943 formed a second career for Rodgers, as illustrious as the one with Hart but today the more familiar of the two: to perform one of their major plays hardly constitutes a revival, for they have remained popular in performance since their premieres. The team's determination that songs should pertain directly to character and situation (reflected in their tendency to write lyrics before music – Hart had worked the other way) justified itself in such popular success that the approach inaugurated a new era and was emulated by most other Broadway writers into the 1960s. The repertoire thus created, by Rodgers and Hammerstein and by others, continues to form the backbone of American musical theatre.

Hammerstein's death in 1960 left Rodgers without a long-term collaborator for the first time in his professional career. He composed one stage score to his own lyrics (*No Strings*), one with Hammerstein's protégé Stephen Sondheim (*Do I Hear a Waltz?*), one with Sheldon Harnick (*Rex*), and two with Martin Charnin. At his death he left behind one of the richest legacies of any Broadway composer: half a dozen musicals that stand up as well as any ever written, and one unforgettable song after another from his other ventures.

Oklahoma!
Musical play in two acts (2h 45m)
Libretto by Oscar Hammerstein II, based on the play *Green Grow the Lilacs* by Lynn Riggs (1931)
PREMIERE   31 March 1943, St James Theater, New York; UK: 29 April 1947, Drury Lane, London
CAST   Laurey *s*, Ado Annie *ms*, Aunt Eller *c*, Curly *bar*, Will Parker *bar*, Jud Fry *bar*, Ali Hakim *t*, Ike Skidmore *bar*, Andrew Carnes *spoken role*; *satb* chorus of farmers and ranchers; dancers

Rodgers's first collaboration with Hammerstein was not necessarily intended to be groundbreaking; nevertheless the tastes of the two writers in adapting this piece of Americana produced the first musical to survive intact as written through several decades. At this distance its old-fashioned aspects are at least equally apparent (strict plot–sub-plot demarcation, conventional handling of the chorus), but its overall rightness, each song suited to the story and the specific situation, remains convincing and satisfying. Besides the title song, the score includes 'Oh, What a Beautiful Morning', 'The Surrey with the Fringe on Top', 'I Cain't Say No' and 'People Will Say We're in Love'.

SYNOPSIS
Indian Territory (present-day Oklahoma), in the early 1900s.

Act I   Laurey and Curly have been carrying on a teasing courtship; she declines to accompany him to a party and finds that the sinister hired hand Jud wants her to go with him. Laurey decides that less harm will ensue if she goes with Jud.

Act II   At the party, Curly saves Laurey from Jud. On the day of his wedding to Laurey, Curly kills Jud in self-defence. At his immediate trial by the assembled community he is declared innocent.

Carousel
Musical play in two acts (2h 45m)
Libretto by Oscar Hammerstein II, based on an adaptation by Benjamin F. Glazer of the play *Liliom* by Ferenc Molnar (1909)
PREMIERES   19 April 1945, Majestic Theater, New York; UK: 7 June 1950, Drury Lane, London
CAST   Julie Jordan *s*, Billy Bigelow *bar*, Carrie Pipperidge *s*, Enoch Snow *t*, Nettie Fowler *a*, Jigger Craigin *b*, Starkeeper *spoken role*, Louise *dancer*; other roles from *satb* chorus of New Englanders, dancers, children

For the successor to *Oklahoma!*, Rodgers and Hammerstein chose similarly to adapt an existing play, but with a more serious outlook and with additional importance given to the music. All the leading roles were written with trained voices in mind, and the 40-piece orchestra was one of the largest ever seen in a Broadway pit.

SYNOPSIS
The coast of New England, 1873.

Act I   Julie, a young millworker, meets Billy, a tough carnival worker who gives Julie a ride on the carousel; the two fall in love and get married. When Billy learns he is going to be a father, he decides to join his old crony Jigger in a robbery.

Act II   Billy is killed attempting the robbery, and in heaven is ordered to do a good deed for his unhappy daughter Louise, now 15 years old. After some unsuccessful attempts, Billy does bring comfort to her, and to Julie as well.

Several songs (including 'Mister Snow', 'If I Loved You', 'June is Bustin' Out All Over' and 'When the Children are Asleep') emerge as the final portions of through-composed musical scenes. With Billy's 'Soliloquy' as an extended piece of character development through song, the 'Carousel Waltz' as the accompaniment for the entirely instrumental first scene, and such additional gems as 'What's the Use of Wondrin'' and 'This Was a Real Nice Clambake', the score may be seen as an exceptionally bountiful one. The final

song, 'You'll Never Walk Alone', was adopted as an unofficial anthem by Liverpool Football Club after Gerry Marsden recorded it in the 1960s. *Carousel* was reportedly Rodgers's own favourite among his works.

South Pacific
Musical play in two acts (2h 45m)
Libretto by Oscar Hammerstein II and Joshua Logan, based on *Tales of the South Pacific* by James A. Michener (1947); lyrics by Oscar Hammerstein II
PREMIERES   7 April 1949, Majestic Theater, New York; UK: 1 November 1951, Drury Lane, London
CAST   Nellie Forbush *ms*, Emile De Becque *b*, Bloody Mary *c*, Joe Cable *t*, Luther Billis *comedy bar*, Liat *spoken role*; other roles from mostly unison *satb* chorus of islanders, sailors, marines, officers

After the artistically ambitious, commercially unsuccessful personal statement of *Allegro* (1947), Rodgers and Hammerstein again adapted an existing source for their next work. Concentrating on two of Michener's stories, for the first time they fashioned a musical for established stars – Ezio Pinza and Mary Martin, appropriately cast as people from different worlds. Nearly every song became a hit; among them 'Dîtes-moi', 'Some Enchanted Evening', 'Nothing Like a Dame', 'Bali Ha'i', 'A Wonderful Guy', 'Younger than Springtime' and 'Happy Talk'.

SYNOPSIS
An island in the South Pacific during the Second World War.

Act I   Nellie, a naïve navy nurse from Arkansas, meets the French émigré planter Emile De Becque. Despite the dissimilarity of their backgrounds, they seem perfect for each other – until she discovers he has two young Eurasian children. Meanwhile Lieutenant Joe Cable, on temporary duty for a secret assignment, is introduced by the trinket-seller Bloody Mary to her daughter Liat.

Act II   Liat wants to marry Cable, who, despite his feelings for her, cannot imagine bringing her home as his wife. Leaving for his mission behind enemy lines, he is joined by De Becque as an expert on local terrain; Cable is killed, but De Becque returns to find Nellie caring for his children and waiting for him.

The King and I
Musical play in two acts (2h 15m)
Libretto by Oscar Hammerstein II, based on the novel *Anna and the King of Siam* by Margaret Landon (1944)
PREMIERES   29 March 1951, St James Theater, New York; UK: 8 October 1953, Drury Lane, London
CAST   Anna *ms*, King *bar*, Tuptim *s*, Lun Tha *t*, Lady Thiang *s*, Louis *boy s*, Prince Chulalongkorn *boy s*, Kralahome *spoken role*, Sir Edward Ramsay *spoken role*; mostly unison *satb* chorus of wives, amazons, priests, slaves; children's chorus of royal princes and princesses; royal dancers

Conceived as a vehicle for Gertrude Lawrence (who died during its initial run), *The King and I* served Yul Brynner equally well, giving him the role with which he remained most associated all his life. The production also provided a showcase for Jerome Robbins's choreography, particularly the ballet based on Harriet

Beecher Stowe, *The Small House of Uncle Thomas*. In this score Rodgers stood by his principle of allowing period and locale to affect his musical language in only minor colouristic ways. His score always sounds recognizably Rodgers, and, as with the previous three Hammerstein collaborations described, nearly all the numbers achieved familiarity outside the theatre. They include 'I Whistle a Happy Tune', 'Hello, Young Lovers', the instrumental 'March of the Siamese Children', 'Getting to Know You' and 'Shall We Dance?'.

SYNOPSIS
Siam in the early 1860s.

Act I Anna, with her son Louis, comes to Bangkok to serve as governess to the royal children. Though not friendly at first, she and the king agree on a plan to receive a visiting English dignitary in a way that will reflect well on Siam.

Act II Despite minor mishaps, all goes well at the reception, and Sir Edward, the visitor, is impressed by what he has seen. Anna and the king congratulate each other afterwards, but their closeness is shattered when the slave Tuptim (captured while trying to escape) is brought in and the king discovers that he cannot beat her with Anna looking on. On the point of leaving Siam, Anna answers a call to the king's sickbed. He passes his authority to his young son Chulalongkorn (who announces policies reflecting Anna's teaching) and dies.

The Sound of Music
Musical play in two acts (1h 45m)
Libretto by Howard Lindsay and Russel Crouse, based on *The Trapp Family Singers* by Maria Augusta Trapp; lyrics by Oscar Hammerstein II
PREMIERES 16 November 1959, Lunt–Fontanne Theater, New York; UK: 18 May 1961, Palace Theatre, London
CAST Maria *ms*, Captain von Trapp *bar*, Abbess *s*, Liesl *ms*, Rolf *t*, Max *bar*, Elsa *s*, 3 Nuns *s*, *ms*, *c*, 6 Children *s* and *a*; other roles from chorus; *sa* (men in unison) chorus of nuns, novices, postulants, friends of Captain von Trapp, concert contestants

For what turned out to be their final collaboration, Rodgers and Hammerstein turned to a true story, with a libretto supplied by others. Though they did not abandon their determination to make songs spring from dramatic necessity, the result resembled older operettas to a greater extent than had their previous musicals. This did not stop *The Sound of Music* from being one of their most popular efforts (even more so in its film version). Rodgers again exhibited considerable versatility within his personal style, successfully evoking church music and folksong in a score that includes the title song, 'My Favourite Things', 'Do-Re-Mi', 'Climb Every Mountain' and 'Edelweiss'.

SYNOPSIS
Austria in 1938.

Act I The novice Maria is told by her abbess that she is not suited for convent life and is given a job as governess to the seven children of the widowed Captain von Trapp. She succeeds in brightening the life of the children and (despite his involvement with his more

sophisticated friends Max and Elsa) of the captain too, as they all find a common love for music. Maria realizes she is falling in love with him.

Act II Maria and the captain are married; their honeymoon interrupted by the *Anschluss*, they find their life threatened by the constant Nazi presence. They finally manage to flee while performing in a concert; as they reach the Swiss border, the curtain falls.

Other musicals: *Poor Little Ritz Girl* (coll. with Sigmund Romberg), 1920; *Dearest Enemy*, 1925; *The Girl Friend*, 1926; *Lido Lady*, 1926; *Peggy-Ann*, 1926; *Betsy*, 1926; *A Connecticut Yankee*, 1927, rev. 1943; *She's My Baby*, 1928; *Present Arms*, 1928; *Chee-Chee*, 1928; *Spring Is Here*, 1929; *Heads Up!*, 1929; *Simple Simon*, 1930; *Ever Green*, 1930; *America's Sweetheart*, 1931; *Jumbo*, 1935; *On Your Toes*, 1936; *Babes in Arms*, 1937; *I'd Rather Be Right*, 1937; *I Married an Angel*, 1938; *The Boys from Syracuse*, 1938; *Too Many Girls*, 1939; *Higher and Higher*, 1940; *Pal Joey*, 1940; *By Jupiter*, 1942; *Allegro*, 1947; *Me and Juliet*, 1953; *Pipe Dream*, 1955; *Cinderella* (from television musical), 1957; *Flower Drum Song*, 1958; *No Strings*, 1962; *Do I Hear a Waltz?*, 1965; *Two by Two*, 1970; *Rex*, 1976; *I Remember Mama*, 1979

J.A.C.

SIGMUND ROMBERG
b 29 July 1887, Nagykanizsa, Hungary; *d* 9 November 1951, New York

Romberg studied in Vienna with Richard Heuberger, though he also studied to be an engineer. In 1909 he moved to the US, where he earned his living as a pianist and later conductor with restaurant orchestras. In 1914 he contributed songs to the revue *The Whirl of the World*, and became a house composer for the Shubert brothers, contributing to the *Passing Show* series from 1914, and the (Franz) Schubert concoction *Blossom Time*, 1921, among several other adaptations and interpolations.

Not until well into the 1920s did Romberg decide to stop interpolating and write his own works. The result was his greatest hit, *The Student Prince* (1924). Two years later came the more enduringly popular *The Desert Song*, and in 1928 Romberg collaborated with Gershwin on *Rosalie*. Later that year came his third great success, *The New Moon*, which, despite an attractive score, was let down by its weak comic elements.

Romberg had a very lean period in the 1930s and early 1940s. He moved to Hollywood, where he wrote some works for the screen, and from 1942 he toured the country with his own orchestra.

A late success was the picture-book musical comedy set in old New York, *Up in Central Park* (1945), which war-weary Broadway audiences supported for over 500 performances.

The Student Prince
Musical play in two acts (1h 45m)
Libretto by Dorothy Donnelly, based on *Old Heidelberg* by

Rudolf Bleichmann (1903), a dramatization of the romantic novella *Alt Heidelberg* by Wilhelm Meyer-Forster (1899) PREMIERES 2 December 1924, Jolsons Theater, New York; UK: 3 February 1926, His Majesty's Theatre, London.

Orchestrated by Emil Gerstenberger, this was the first operetta that Romberg could nevertheless justifiably call his own. Donnelly had already worked with Romberg on *Blossom Time*. The *Student Prince* is thoroughly European in character but recalls in its verve and sentiment the Broadway works of Victor Herbert. The tale – of a young crown prince who falls for a barmaid but has to renounce her for the sake of his royal duty – has a bittersweet flavour and an emotional power that can still move audiences. Romberg's score is correspondingly dashing and sincere, and takes full advantage of the student setting, with rousing marching and drinking choruses, including a version of 'Gaudeamus igitur'. More realistic than many turn-of-the-century Ruritanian operettas, its characters are better developed. It enjoyed the longest run of any of Romberg's operettas – 608 performances.

The Desert Song

Musical play in two acts (1h 45m)
Libretto by Otto Harbach, Oscar Hammerstein II and Frank Mandel
PREMIERES 21 October 1926, Wilmington, Delaware (as *Lady Fair*); 30 November 1926, Casino Theater, New York (as *The Desert Song*); UK: 7 April 1927, Drury Lane, London

The year 1926 saw the box-office hit *Son of the Sheik*, and the death of its star, the matinée idol Rudolph Valentino. With the fashion for Arabiana at its peak, *The Desert Song* was inevitably a success, with a run of 471 performances on Broadway, though first reviews were muted.

The son of the governor of French Morocco feigns foolishness when not leading the Arab rebellion as the masked Red Shadow. At the same time he has a rival in love – a French captain bent on defeating the 'Shadow'. After some improbably speedy changes of costume, the hero wins his girl.

Romberg's first collaboration with Hammerstein resulted in his lushest and most romantic score. With its deathless title love duet, its 'Riff' and 'Sabre' songs, and a spectacular ensemble contrasting 'Eastern and Western Love', *The Desert Song* has remained effective and popular to this day.

Other operettas: *The Blue Paradise* (coll. with L. Edwards), 1915; *Her Soldier Boy*, 1916; *My Lady's Glove*, 1917; *Maytime*, 1917; *The Magic Melody*, 1919; *Love Birds*, 1921; *Blossom Time*, 1921; *The Rose of Stamboul*, 1922; *Springtime of Youth*, 1922; *Caroline*, 1923; *Princess Flavia*, 1925; *Cherry Blossoms*, 1927; *My Maryland*, 1927; *My Princess*, 1927; *The Love Call*, 1927; *The New Moon*, 1928; *Nina Rosa*, 1930; *East Wind*, 1931; *Melody*, 1933; *May Wine*, 1935; *Forbidden Melody*, 1936; *Sunny River*, 1941; *Up in Central Park*, 1945; *My Romance*, 1948; *The Girl in Pink Tights*, 1954

R.T.

GIOACHINO ROSSINI

Gioachino Antonio Rossini; *b* 29 February 1792, Pesaro, Italy; *d* 13 November 1868, Paris

Rossini's theatrical works dominated the repertoire for three decades, from the 1810s through the 1830s. His comic operas were considered supreme examples of the buffo style that had flourished in 18th-century Italy; his Italian serious operas were models for generations of composers; his French operas were fêted and reviled by opposing camps in the contentious Parisian musical world. Although he ceased writing new operas before 1830 and although his serious operas had all but disappeared from public view well before his death in 1868, every operatic composer working in Italy or France during his lifetime had to come to grips with this legacy.

Both Rossini's parents were professional musicians (his mother a singer, his father a horn-player). Even before he entered the Bologna Conservatory in 1806, he had learned to play the piano and cello, performed as a singer, and composed chamber works, overtures, and sacred music. In Bologna he regularly served as maestro al cembalo in the theatre. Early commissions for operas came through the good offices of performers who were family friends and knew the boy's talents. By the end of his 21st year, Rossini had written ten operas for northern Italian theatres. Among them were: a series of five one-act operas (called farse) for the Venetian Teatro San Moisè, which specialized in this genre; an important comic opera, *La pietra del paragone* (1812), for the Teatro alla Scala of Milan, and his first major serious opera, *Tancredi* (February 1813), for the Teatro La Fenice of Venice.

Tancredi and Rossini's next opera, the madcap *L'italiana in Algeri* (May 1813), had an explosive effect: here was a new voice characterized by energy and wit, overflowing with melodic ideas, and sensitive to the most delicate shades of orchestral colour. What is more, Rossini brought to his work a structural clarity that transformed Italian opera: his characteristic forms, which gradually evolved over a period of ten years, were later developed into a system of formal rules as basic for 19th-century Italian composers as the sonata principle was for German ones.

Over the next four years, Rossini composed operas for a wide variety of Italian theatres. During this period, he prepared his major comic and semi-serious operas: *Il turco in Italia* (Milan, 1814), *Il barbiere di Siviglia* (Rome, 1816), *La Cenerentola* (Rome, 1817), and *La gazza ladra* (Milan, 1817), all of which were performed extensively throughout Europe. Working quickly, Rossini sometimes employed collaborators to prepare recitative or even musical numbers (arias for minor characters), but he frequently returned to these works and substituted new pieces of his own composition for those of the collaborators. He also borrowed from himself, usually turning to works unlikely to circulate further and making extensive revisions to suit the new dramatic and musical context.

Naples, where he had made his début in 1815 with *Elisabetta, regina d'Inghilterra*, was the composer's centre of activity from 1817 until 1822. Many modern critics consider Rossini's nine serious operas for Naples, together with his last opera for Italy, *Semiramide* (Venice, 1823), to be his most impressive achievement. Complex works, formally inventive, orchestrally lavish, vocally extravagant, the Neapolitan operas and *Semiramide* defy easy categorization: despite their external similarities, each has its individual character. The range of their sources (from Italian Renaissance verse epic through Shakespearian tragedy, French classical drama, and English Romantic poetry) is noteworthy. Some of these works (*Otello, La donna del lago, Semiramide*) were widely known; others, particularly the more experimental operas (*Armida, Ermione, Maometto II*), did not circulate. Their highly florid vocal style, written to measure for some of the finest singers of Rossini's day (including his future wife, the soprano Isabella Colbran), made them difficult to mount even in Rossini's time and almost impossible after the mid 19th century, when vocal techniques changed radically.

After *Semiramide*, Rossini took up residence in Paris, and became musical director of the Théâtre Italien, where his operas were already the backbone of the repertoire. His reputation as the composer of the political 'Restoration' was enhanced by *Il viaggio a Reims* (1825), written for the coronation of Charles X. Between 1826 and 1829 he prepared four works for the Opéra. Two were revisions of Neapolitan operas; the third (*Le comte Ory*, 1828) borrowed extensively from *Viaggio*. Only with *Guillaume Tell* (1829) did Rossini compose an entirely new opera in French, a work of monumental proportions, mediating between the worlds of Italian melodrama and French tragédie lyrique. The artistic growth Rossini achieved in the period of 20 years between his earliest operas and this final masterpiece is extraordinary.

Guillaume Tell was Rossini's last opera. Many have speculated about the motive behind this retirement, but no single answer is sufficient. The factors were political (the change of government in France), emotional (the death of Rossini's mother, to whom he was deeply attached), economic (a wealthy man, he had no need to continue composing), physical and psychological (his bodily and mental health was deteriorating), and his favoured position at the Opéra was threatened after the 1830 revolution and the 1831 premiere of Meyerbeer's *Robert le diable*; new styles of singing were becoming common, requiring modifications in his compositional technique.

From 1830 to 1836 the composer remained in Paris, overseeing the fortunes of the Théâtre Italien and lending support to his younger Italian colleagues (Bellini, Donizetti and Saverio Mercadante). He then returned to Italy, where despite ill health he served a term as director of the Bologna Conservatory. Only in 1855 did he return to Paris, where he regained his health, resumed active composition (though not in the field of opera), and lived out his final years, an esteemed presence from another era. The musical soirées in Rossini's apartment at the Chaussée d'Antin were attended by *le tout Paris*.

Rossini's reputation for more than a hundred years, that of a composer of comic opera, has changed considerably in the past few decades. Thanks to the efforts of the Fondazione Rossini of Pesaro, many of his operas, particularly the serious ones, have been edited anew. The Rossini Opera Festival of Pesaro has provided models for intelligent stagings of these works, singers have successfully mastered their vocal style, and major theatres around the world have incorporated the operas into their repertoires. Thus the depth and breadth of Rossini's achievement can be experienced anew by modern audiences.

La scala di seta
The Silken Ladder
Farsa comica in one act (1h 30m)
Libretto by Giuseppe Foppa, after François-Antoine-Eugène de Planard's libretto (first set to music by Pierre Gaveaux) *L'échelle de soie* (1808)
PREMIERES 9 May 1812, Teatro San Moisè, Venice; UK: 26 April 1954, Sadler's Wells, London; US: 18 February 1966, War Memorial Opera House, San Francisco
CAST Dormont *t*, Giulia *s*, Lucilla *s*, Dorvil *t*, Blansac *b*, Germano *b*

With *La scala di seta*, the third of the five farse written for the Teatro San Moisè, Rossini produced an operatic jewel. Although its basic situation recalls Cimarosa's *Il matrimonio segreto* (1792), other aspects of the story – its silken ladder to facilitate nocturnal rendezvous, its profusion of characters in various hiding-places, etc. – invoke French comedy, particularly the plays of Beaumarchais. *La scala di seta*, in fact, is the first of many Rossini operas with a libretto derived from the French theatre. The most original character, in both literary and musical terms, is the servant Germano. Little performed in the 19th century, *La scala di seta* has now begun to circulate widely.

SYNOPSIS

Giulia, against her tutor Dormont's wishes but with the approval of an aunt, has secretly married Dorvil. Every night her husband visits by means of a silken ladder, which she lowers from his balcony. Learning that Dormont intends her to marry the vain Blansac, Dorvil's friend, Giulia vows to turn Blansac's affection towards her cousin Lucilla. She enlists Germano's help, without explaining what she wants. The servant imagines himself the object of Giulia's love, but this mistake is soon cleared up. Blansac arrives, bringing along Dorvil (found near the house, from whence he has just departed) as a witness to his triumph. Although Giulia's plan advances, Germano overhears her musing about a nocturnal rendezvous ('Il mio ben sospiro e chiamo'). Thinking Blansac to be the object of Giulia's love, he congratulates the suitor on his good fortune. Blansac is delighted at the prospect of a rendezvous with Giulia. Meanwhile, Germano also informs Lucilla, and each of them decides to hide in Giulia's apartment to learn the ways of love. As midnight strikes, Germano and Lucilla are already present. Dorvil arrives, then hides as Blansac appears, who in turn conceals himself when Dormont, who has heard the racket, climbs up the ladder. After Dormont discovers the concealed characters in their various hiding places, Giulia reveals the secret of her marriage.

Blansac gallantly agrees to marry Lucilla, and the tutor accepts the *fait accompli*.

Long known exclusively for its superb overture, the earliest in the Rossini canon to have survived as a concert piece, *La scala di seta* fulfils the promise of its opening pages. The key characters are Giulia and Germano. Her aria 'Il mio ben sospiro e chiamo' is notable for its rich orchestration and cor-anglais solo. Rossini lavished his most fascinating music on Germano. The role incorporates comic and serious elements, but Germano's ability to pass from lyricism to pure buffoonery is unique. The length, diversity, and complexity of 'Amore dolcemente' justifies comparison with a gran scena. It begins with a splendid melody and coloratura spanning almost two octaves, but concludes with extreme caricature (ingeniously supported by the raucous use of bassoon and horn). All major ensembles involve Germano (a duet with Giulia, a quartet, and the extended finale), and all represent the young Rossini at his finest.

La pietra del paragone
The Touchstone
Melodramma giocoso in two acts (2h)
Libretto by Luigi Romanelli
PREMIERES 26 September 1812, La Scala, Milan; US: 4 May 1955, Hart College of Music, Hartford, Connecticut; UK: 19 March 1963, St Pancras Town Hall, London
CAST Marquise Clarice c, Baroness Aspasia s, Lady Fulvia ms, Count Asdrubale b, Giocondo t, Macrobio b, Pacuvio b, Fabrizio b; tb chorus of gardeners, guests, hunters, soldiers of the count

Through the influence of two singers (Maria Marcolini and Filippo Galli) who already knew his extraordinary gifts, Rossini obtained his first major commission, from the Teatro alla Scala. Romanelli, poet in residence, provided a libretto rich in incident and character. Around the misogynistic Count Asdrubale and the three claimants to his hand, he wove a tapestry of absurd poets, venal journalists, and hangers-on. The poet Pacuvio's ballad 'Ombretta sdegnosa del Missippipi' ('Haughty little ghost of the Mississippi') became so popular that Rossini's authorship was forgotten and the novelist Antonio Fogazzaro, in *Piccolo mondo antico* (1895), considered it a folksong.

SYNOPSIS
A 'touchstone' determines the purity of gold and silver; Romanelli's 'touchstone' tests the sincerity of emotions.
Act I Marquise Clarice (a widow), Baroness Aspasia, and Lady Fulvia all wish to marry the rich Count Asdrubale. Taken with Clarice but dubious about the faithfulness of all women, Asdrubale disguises himself as a Turk. Claiming that the count is indebted to him, the 'Turk' begins to repossess Asdrubale's goods and those of his guests. 'Sequestrara . . . Sigillara' ('Take possession . . . seal them'), he says in pidgin-Italian. False friends (Aspasia, Fulvia, Macrobio, Pacuvio) abandon him; true ones (Clarice and Giocondo) rally to his defence. When Asdrubale's servant, Fabrizio, announces that the debt was previously paid, everyone is thrown into confusion.

Act II The offended Aspasia and Fulvia order Macrobio and Pacuvio to challenge the count and Giocondo to a duel. The action culminates in a reverse masquerade, with 'Lucindo' (Clarice disguised as her soldier brother) seeking to take his unhappy 'sister' home. The thought of losing Clarice is the 'touchstone' that reveals to the count his own feelings. When he admits his love, 'Lucindo' is transformed into Clarice, and the opera concludes with general rejoicing.

The prolix libretto offered Rossini many challenges, and provided situations rich in musical possibilities. From the easy melodiousness of Pacuvio's 'Ombretta sdegnosa' to the extreme caricature of Macrobio's narrative aria 'Chi è colei che avanza', built largely over orchestral themes, Rossini explores diverse aspects of his comic language. But it is the Act I finale, particularly its absurd 'Turkish' scene, that fully reveals his genius. Turks, both comic and serious, appear in several Rossini operas. (Curiously, Filippo Galli, the original Asdrubale, was the protagonist of three of them: *L'italiana in Algeri*, *Il turco in Italia* and *Maometto II*.)

Alongside comic scenes and ensembles, *La pietra del paragone* features music of quite a different cast for Asdrubale and Clarice. Clarice's cavatina 'Quel dirmi oh Dio! non t'amo', to which the count (unseen) provides an echo, is particularly appealing. (Its cabaletta anticipates Tancredi's 'Di tanti palpiti'.) In his final aria, 'Ah! se destarti in seno', Asdrubale's music gains dignity and depth of feeling.

Tancredi
Melodramma eroico in two acts (2h 45m)
Libretto by Gaetano Rossi, with additions by Luigi Lechi, after Voltaire's play *Tancrède* (1760)
PREMIERES 6 February 1813, La Fenice, Venice; rev. with tragic finale, March 1813, Teatro Comunale, Ferrara; UK: 4 May 1820, King's Theatre, Haymarket, London; US: 31 December 1825, Park Theater, New York
CAST Argirio t, Tancredi c, Orbazzano b, Amenaide s, Isaura c, Roggiero s or t; tb chorus of nobles, knights, squires, populace, Saracens (the latter in the original version only); silent: warriors, pages, guards, populace, ladies, Saracens

With *Tancredi*, Rossini both achieved his first maturity as a composer of opera seria and established himself in Italy and abroad as the leading contemporary composer of Italian opera. Although working simultaneously on the two preceding farse, his attention was focused principally on *Tancredi*, for which he composed the *secco* recitatives himself. At the first two performances the indisposition of the Tancredi (Adelaide Malanotte) and the Amenaide (Elisabetta Manfredini) caused the curtain to be brought down during Act II. None the less, enough was heard to enable the reviewer to comment on 'the melodious song, the animated action of the first; the most sweet voice, the ardent and agile coloratura dared by the second'.

After the Venetian season Rossini, Malanotte, and Pietro Todràn took a revised version of the opera to Ferrara. Important changes made for this production were partially due to the suggestions of Luigi Lechi, a Brescian nobleman and the lover of Malanotte, who provided the revised text. The most significant alteration was the introduction of a tragic finale, which brought the plot closer to Voltaire.

The public, however, preferred the happy ending. A production for the Teatro Re of Milan in December 1813, most likely under Rossini's direction, included some of the Ferrarese revisions but restored the Venetian finale. In this production the role of Roggiero was assigned to a tenor, rather than to the original soprano. Both of Argirio's arias were replaced, and the new ones ('Se ostinata ancor non cedi' and 'Al campo mi chiama') were widely performed, even outside Italy. In this form, *Tancredi* continued to be given until the mid 19th century, when it disappeared from the repertoire, although Tancredi's cavatina 'Di tanti palpiti' (actually the text of the cabaletta) remained popular as a concert number. *Tancredi* was revived successfully in 1952 at the Florentine Maggio Musicale. Since the 1974 rediscovery of the tragic finale, which has become the standard ending, the opera has regained a firm place in the repertoire.

SYNOPSIS (original, Venetian version)
Rossini borrowed the overture from *La pietra del paragone*.

Act I   The action takes place in Syracuse, Sicily, in 1005. Faced with an impending attack by the Saracens (led by Solamir), the Syracusans celebrate the newly forged alliance between their ruler, Argirio, and his family's hereditary enemy, Orbazzano. To cement the pact, Argirio promises Orbazzano the hand of his daughter, Amenaide. She joyfully greets her father ('Come dolce all'alma mia') and in an aside expresses her longing for the return of the exiled and outlawed Tancredi, whom she knows to be in Sicily and to whom she has secretly written. (The son of a noble Norman family, Tancredi was forced by factional strife to leave Syracuse with his family when he was a child. He grew up in the court of Byzantium, where he and Amenaide met and fell in love.) Informed of her betrothal to Orbazzano, Amenaide begs Argirio to delay the wedding. In the next scene Tancredi, disguised and accompanied by his squire Roggiero, arrives in Syracuse. He expresses his love for Amenaide in a cavatina ('Tu che accendi . . . Di tanti palpiti'). Because of the Saracen threat, Argirio presses the wedding and informs Amenaide that all enemies of Syracuse, even Tancredi, will be condemned to death by the Senate. In his aria ('Pensa che sei mia figlia'), Argirio demands again that she marry Orbazzano. When Amenaide is left alone, Tancredi re-enters. In a duet ('L'aura che intorno spiri'), she warns him to flee a country where he is in danger of death, while he asks in vain for assurance that she loves him. In anticipation of the wedding, a chorus of nobles and people, joined by Orbazzano's knights, throngs the square in front of the church. Tancredi, incognito, offers to join them in battle against the Saracens. At that moment, Orbazzano arrives bearing Amenaide's letter, which he believes to have been addressed to Solamir. (At the court of Byzantium, Amenaide was also courted by Solamir, but rejected his advances.) In the first finale Amenaide, accused of treachery, is disowned by her father, rejected by Tancredi, and taken prisoner.

Act II   Orbazzano urges Argirio to sign the order for Amenaide's death, while her confidante, Isaura, seeks to stir his paternal pity. Although struggling with the decision ('Ah! segnar invano io tento'), Argirio signs the order. Isaura sorrowfully prays that Amenaide may find consolation ('Tu che i miseri conforti'). Amenaide, in prison, meditates on her fate and resolves to die faithful to Tancredi ('No, che il morir non è'). Since no champion has come forward to defend Amenaide, Orbazzano and a reluctant Argirio arrive with guards to escort her to the execution. Still unidentified, Tancredi appears and challenges Orbazzano. Argirio and Tancredi share their differing sorrows in a duet ('Ah se de' mali miei'), of which the cabaletta is a martial call to battle ('Ecco le trombe'). Amenaide's prayer for Tancredi's victory ('Giusto Dio che umile adoro') is interrupted by joyful music: the chorus proclaims her vindication. Tancredi's triumphal appearance (chorus 'Plaudite, o popoli') is suspended as the unhappy Tancredi, still believing Amenaide unfaithful, prepares to leave Syracuse. Amenaide stops him. In their duet ('Lasciami: non t'ascolto') Tancredi refuses to accept Amenaide's protestation of fidelity, while Amenaide cannot reveal the truth in front of other characters, since to do so would endanger Tancredi's life. Tancredi leaves alone, while Roggiero hopes in a brief *aria di sorbetto* that love and joy will return ('Torni alfin ridente').

In the gran scena ('Dove son io?'), a distracted Tancredi has wandered close to the camp of the Saracens; they appear, vaunting their imminent triumph ('Regna il terror nella Città'). Argirio, Amenaide and the Syracusan forces arrive in search of Tancredi, who accuses the maiden of having come to meet Solamir. The Saracens offer peace in return for Amenaide's marriage to Solamir; Tancredi upbraids Amenaide and defies the Saracens ('Va! palese è troppo omai'). The warriors take the field, while Amenaide and Isaura listen to sounds of battle. Argirio and Tancredi re-enter. Tancredi has killed Solamir, who, dying, has reassured Tancredi of Amenaide's innocence. In the second finale the principal characters express their happiness.

The most important changes in the Ferrara revision occur at the end of the opera. In the new version of the gran scena the Saracens are replaced by Syracusans who already know Tancredi's identity and want him to lead them against the enemy. When Argirio and Amenaide enter, Tancredi orders her to leave for Solamir's camp. Amenaide vainly tries to explain. In his new rondo ('Perché turbar la calma?'), Tancredi asks himself why a traitress has come to disturb him. Though moved against his will by Amenaide's tears, he leaves with the soldiers for the battlefield. The new finale opens with recitative: Argirio returns alone. The Syracusans are victorious, but Tancredi is mortally wounded. The chorus accompanies the entrance of the hero, who invokes Amenaide's name. Argirio informs him that Amenaide's fated letter was directed to Tancredi himself, not to Solamir, and that she has always loved him. As death approaches, the lovers join hands. Their union is blessed by Argirio. After bidding a final farewell to his wife, Tancredi dies to the fading sound of tremolo strings.

Tancredi is Rossini's first great opera seria. Stendhal held it high among the composer's masterworks, referring to its blend of youthful lyricism and rhythmic vitality as 'virginal candour'. The formal procedures Rossini employed in later operas, which so influenced the development of Italian opera, are crystallized in *Tancredi*. Although the division of the opera into closed numbers separated by *secco* recitatives remains, a flexibility of style makes possible extensive dramatic activity within numbers. Lyrical moments, incorporated into larger musical units, are motivated by dramatic events. Rossini's approach is well exemplified in Amenaide's 'Giusto Dio che umile adoro'. Her lyrical prayer is followed by a passage in contrasting tempo and tonality, the chorus describing Tancredi's victory over Orbazzano. The concluding section, or cabaletta, returns to the opening tonality, and Amenaide first expresses her joy lyrically, then exuberantly in florid style.

In the duets Rossini also employs a sectional form. The opening section allows dramatic confrontation between the characters, who express their often differing emotions in parallel stanzas. A more lyrical second section is followed by further dramatic interaction, concluding with a cabaletta in which the changed dramatic configuration is rendered in a new moment of conflict or accord. Although *Tancredi* lacks the larger ensembles which become integral to Rossini's later style, his technique is shown in the Act I finale: it is similar in structure to the duets, balancing musical and dramatic forces. In *Tancredi*, these forms are given life through clear melodies, energetic rhythms, and simple but interesting harmonies. The orchestra is used carefully, with numerous wind solos enhancing the idyllic and heroic moods.

L'italiana in Algeri
The Italian Girl in Algiers
Dramma giocoso per musica in two acts (2h 15m)
Libretto by Angelo Anelli (1808) for Luigi Mosca
PREMIERES 22 May 1813, Teatro San Benedetto, Venice; UK: 26 January 1819, His Majesty's Theatre, London; US: 5 November 1832, Richmond Hill, New York
CAST Mustafà *b*, Elvira *s*, Zulma *ms*, Haly *b*, Lindoro *t*, Isabella *c*, Taddeo *b*; *tb* chorus of eunuchs, corsairs, slaves, Pappataci; *silent*: women, European slaves, sailors

Following *Tancredi* by only a few months, *L'italiana in Algeri* was an equal success for the 21-year-old composer. The subject – the liberation, through a deception and an encounter with a lost lover, of a woman abducted by a tyrant – has roots in Greek and Roman theatre.

Because Rossini was called on to prepare the opera only at the last minute, after another composer failed to respect his contract, it was decided to employ an earlier libretto, by Angelo Anelli, first set by Luigi Mosca for the Teatro alla Scala of Milan in 1808. The few modifications show the dramaturgical hand of Rossini: Anelli's entrance aria for Taddeo (preceding Isabella's appearance) and a duet for Isabella and Lindoro were eliminated, the latter with the effect that the two lovers, like Rosina and the count in *Il barbiere di Siviglia*, never have an intimate scene. The

second-act aria for Isabella was added, as were the zany sections of the large ensembles: 'Nella testa ho un campanello' in the first finale and 'Sento un fremito' in the quintet. Perhaps because of the pressing schedule, *secco* recitatives and probably two short arias (Haly's 'Le femmine d'Italia' and Lindoro's 'Oh come il cor di giubilo') were composed by a collaborator. For a Milanese revival in 1814 Rossini replaced the Lindoro piece with a new aria of his own composition, 'Concedi, amor pietoso'.

The first Isabella was Maria Marcolini, the popular contralto who had participated in the premieres of three previous Rossini operas (*L'equivoco stravagante*, *Ciro in Babilonia* and *La pietra del paragone*). Mustafà was Filippo Galli, perhaps the finest bass of the day. Lindoro was sung by Serafino Gentili, and Taddeo by Paolo Rosich. Rossini participated in and composed music for three later revivals: in Vicenza during the summer of 1813, at Milan's Teatro Re in April 1814, and at the Teatro dei Fiorentini in Naples in the autumn of 1815.

SYNOPSIS
The action takes place in Algiers. The overture, while not melodically related to the opera, captures its spirit delightfully. Rossini never reused it elsewhere.

Act I Elvira, the wife of Mustafà, the bey, grieves that her husband no longer loves her. Her confidante Zulma and a chorus of eunuchs (tenors and basses) advise her to accept this common lot of women. Mustafà enters in a temper: he wants an Italian woman, and gives his captain, Haly, six days in which to produce one. In another part of the palace Lindoro, an Italian recently enslaved by Mustafà's corsairs, languishes for his distant love ('Languir per una bella'). Mustafà informs Lindoro that he must marry Elvira so that Mustafà can be rid of her; Lindoro describes the woman he wants to marry, and Mustafà assures him Elvira is perfect ('Se inclinassi a prender moglie'). Offshore a ship has been wrecked and its passengers taken prisoner. Among them Haly and his men discover an Italian woman, Isabella, and her companion and would-be suitor, Taddeo. Isabella has been seeking her lover, Lindoro, and laments her cruel destiny ('Cruda sorte!'). She determines to conquer the Algerians through womanly wiles. Isabella and Taddeo argue about their relationship ('Ai capricci della sorte'), but they agree to pose as niece and uncle. Back at the palace Mustafà offers to allow Lindoro to leave immediately for Venice if he takes Elvira along. Seeing his opportunity to escape, Lindoro accepts. Haly brings news of the Italian woman, and Mustafà orders his court to assemble. He anticipates his new pleasure ('Già d'insolito ardore'). As the first finale begins, Mustafà is hailed by the eunuchs. Isabella is brought in, and Mustafà and the chorus marvel at her beauty; she flirts with the bey to entrap him. When Taddeo forces his way into the hall, Mustafà threatens to impale him, but then accepts Isabella's 'uncle'. Elvira, Zulma, and Lindoro come to say farewell; Isabella and Lindoro recognize each other and all express stupefaction in a grand ensemble of onomatopoeic nonsense during which Isabella acquires Lindoro as her slave.

Act II Mustafà has fallen in love with Isabella. Haly counsels Elvira to be patient while Isabella's wiles make a fool of the bey. Isabella and Lindoro plan their escape; the latter rejoices at being reunited with Isabella ('Oh come il cor di giubilo'). In order to impress Isabella, Mustafà makes Taddeo his 'Kaimakan' and has him dressed in Turkish costume. Taddeo, not wishing to be a go-between, first declines the title ('Ho un gran peso sulla testa') but accepts with much obsequiousness on seeing Mustafà's anger. Isabella prepares to receive the bey. She orders Lindoro to bring coffee for at least three, and tells Elvira to observe from another room how to handle a man. Mustafà, Taddeo and Lindoro watch from within while Isabella, completing her dressing, invokes Venus to make her more lovely ('Per lui che adoro'). Mustafà arranges to signal by sneezing the moment that the others should leave him alone with Isabella; the subsequent quintet ('Ti presento di mia man') is punctuated by numerous 'atchoos' which are conspicuously ignored. The ensemble is complete when Isabella invites Elvira to take coffee with them, and Mustafà understands that he has been tricked. Haly declares that Italian women excel at making men love them ('Le femmine d'Italia'). Lindoro tells Mustafà that Isabella loves the bey and wants to make him her 'Pappataci', an honourable title given to men who sleep and eat while allowing their women to do just as they please. Isabella has arranged a ceremony involving the other Italian captives and has given the eunuchs and guards much wine. She encourages the Italians with patriotic passion ('Pensa alla patria'). In the second finale the chorus of Pappataci dresses the bey in wig and costume, and Isabella confers the oath in which he swears to be deaf and blind to all her enterprises. Mustafà eats and drinks as the Italians slip away to the waiting ship. Taddeo, realizing that Isabella loves Lindoro, tries to alert the bey, but the latter fulfils his duty as Pappataci; rather than face Mustafà's wrath, Taddeo joins the Italians. Elvira, Zulma, and Haly reveal the deceit to Mustafà; he begs Elvira's forgiveness and renounces Italian women. The entire ensemble proclaims that a woman cannot be kept from having her way.

Within Rossini's bubbling score the scenes range from the sentimental and the patriotic to the farcical and the lunatic. Rossini's treatment of the two genres of opera seria and opera buffa permits considerable overlap and exchange of elements, so we find noble sentiments present within the comic framework. The formal designs seen in *Tancredi* reappear in *L'italiana*, although with greater internal flexibility.

Rossini characterizes well each of Isabella's three lovers. Mustafà's aria 'Già d'insolito ardore' combines buffoonery, elegance, and virtuosity. Lindoro is a sweet, sentimental tenor who describes his sadness in the beautiful cavatina 'Languir per una bella'. Rossini emphasizes its poignancy with solo horn. Taddeo is the stock buffo of the opera and as such can hardly hope to end up with Isabella. His character is displayed in rapid patter and exaggerated leaps, a musical language that mocks its own pretensions.

The Italian girl must assume multiple personalities to triumph over cruel fate. She expresses erotic tenderness in 'Per lui che adoro'. (Rossini in 1814 rewrote the original solo cello obbligato as a flute solo.) Isabella tricks Mustafà and Taddeo time and again, from her initial meeting with the bey in the first finale, to the pretended tête-à-tête which turns into a quintet, to the investiture of Mustafà as Pappataci in the Act II finale. Yet she is also a woman of strength, who encourages her countrymen to escape with profound patriotic sentiments ('Pensa alla patria'). This rondo was considered subversive in an Italy with awakening hopes of nationhood – the words were often changed, or the piece omitted. Despite the censors, Rossini made his point musically: in the chorus preceding 'Pensa alla patria' he embedded a quotation from the 'Marseillaise'.

Il turco in Italia
The Turk in Italy

Dramma buffo per musica in two acts (2h)
Libretto by Felice Romani, after the libretto by Caterino Mazzolà, first set to music by Joseph Seydelman (1788)
PREMIERES 14 August 1814, La Scala, Milan; UK: 19 May 1821, His Majesty's Theatre, London; US: 14 March 1826, Park Theater, New York
CAST Selim *b*, Fiorilla *s*, Geronio *b*, Narciso *t*, Prosdocimo *b*, Zaida *s*, Albazar *t*; *satb* chorus of gypsies, Turks, masqueraders; *silent*: friends of Fiorilla, gypsies, Turks, masqueraders

The Milanese audience, believing *Il turco in Italia* to be a mere inversion of *L'italiana in Algeri*, with numerous self-borrowings, felt cheated by Rossini and did not receive the opera warmly. Except for a few short motifs, however, the work was newly composed, and it is one of Rossini's most carefully constructed comic operas. It is also his most Mozartian work and shows particularly the influence of *Così fan tutte*, which was being produced at the Teatro alla Scala immediately before the premiere of *Il turco*.

Il turco in Italia suffered much from severe alterations during its early career, such as the ravages perpetrated at the Théâtre Italien in Paris for an 1820 revival, in which a dismembered torso of Rossini's score was refitted with numbers lifted from *La Cenerentola*, *L'italiana in Algeri* and *Ciro in Babilonia*, as well as an aria not by Rossini. The composer shared some blame, for he apparently had prepared a one-act reduction for the Théâtre Italien, but no trace of this version survives. The Parisian pastiche was published, thereby confusing critics for a century and a half. After the mid 19th century, *Il turco in Italia* virtually disappeared from the repertoire, returning to the stage in a production with Maria Callas in 1950. The critical edition of the Fondazione Rossini has now made Rossini's original version available.

Several items in the original version are not by Rossini: the *secco* recitatives, the cavatina for Geronio ('Vado in traccia d'una zingara'), the aria for Albazar ('Ah! sarebbe troppo dolce'), and the entire Act II finale. After the premiere Rossini made several changes to this version. Narciso's Act II aria, 'Tu seconda il mio disegno', was added some time during the first season. An alternative cavatina for Fiorilla, 'Presto amiche', and additional pieces for Narciso and

Geronio were prepared in the autumn of 1815 for a revival at Rome, where Rossini also omitted the two arias (for Geronio and Albazar) by his original collaborator.

SYNOPSIS

Act I In their camp on a solitary shore near Naples, gypsies sing about their happy life ('Nostra patria è il mondo intero'), while Zaida, former slave and fiancée of the Turk Selim, mourns her lost love. Prosdocimo the poet thinks gypsies would provide a fine introduction for the dramma buffo he must write. Geronio is searching for a fortune-teller to advise him how to cure his wife, Fiorilla, of her passion for men ('Vado in traccia d'una zingara'). When Zaida and the gypsy girls tell him he was born under the fatal constellation of the ram, he flees. Prosdocimo learns that Zaida's rivals for Selim deceived him into condemning her to death, but the Turk's confidant, Albazar, saved her. Coincidentally, Prosdocimo reports, a Turkish prince is about to visit Italy to observe European customs; perhaps Zaida will find a mediator in him. Fiorilla muses on the folly of loving only a single object ('Non si dà follia maggiore'). Selim's boat appears, and he disembarks, greeting the wonderful country he has so longed to see ('Bella Italia, alfin ti miro'). He is further delighted by the appearance of the Italian ladies, especially Fiorilla. Geronio reveals to Prosdocimo and to Narciso (who also loves Fiorilla) that the Turk is taking coffee with Fiorilla. Geronio and Narciso are both distressed at Fiorilla's inconstancy. The quartet 'Siete Turchi' develops with protestations of anger and love. Fiorilla wants Geronio to allow her complete freedom, but he will have neither Turkish nor Italian men in his house ('Per piacere alla signora'). She threatens to punish him for his cruelty by having a thousand lovers. Selim has prepared his ship to flee with Fiorilla; while the Turk waits on the shore by the gypsy camp, Zaida reveals herself to him and they are reconciled. Narciso enters, complaining of his unrequited love ('Perché mai se son tradito'). Fiorilla and her friends arrive, then Geronio. The interaction of all six characters ('Ah! che il cor non m'ingannava'), particularly the two rival women, concludes the act in what Prosdocimo describes as a *finalone*.

Act II Geronio and Prosdocimo are drinking at an inn. Selim arrives, and Prosdocimo withdraws to observe. The Turk offers to buy Fiorilla from Geronio, according to Turkish custom; Geronio describes the better Italian custom of breaking the would-be buyer's nose ('D'un bell'uso di Turchia'), and the business conversation turns to threats of violence. As the men leave, Fiorilla and her friends arrive ('Non v'è piacer perfetto'). She has come at Selim's invitation and expects to triumph over Zaida, who arrives followed by Selim. The women ask him to choose between them, but he cannot decide. Zaida leaves him to Fiorilla; they muse on the fickleness of the opposite sex, then avow their mutual love ('Credete alle femmine'). Prosdocimo tells Geronio and Narciso that Selim plans to abduct Fiorilla from the masked ball that evening. To thwart him, Zaida will attend, dressed exactly as Fiorilla with Narciso disguised as Selim. At the ball the masked lovers pair off – Fiorilla with

Narciso, Selim with Zaida. Geronio in confusion sees the two couples, and a comic quintet ensues in which Geronio demands his wife, whichever she may be ('Oh! guardate che accidente'). Even the chorus joins in calling Geronio crazy as the lovers leave him breathless and desperate. Prosdocimo suggests that the unhappy husband send Fiorilla away and pretend to sue for divorce. Albazar assures Geronio that Selim is departing with Zaida. Outside Geronio's house Prosdocimo relays this news to Fiorilla and gives her Geronio's letter of dismissal. Chastened, she divests herself of her finery and prepares to return to her parents' home ('Squallida veste, e bruna'). The poet advises Geronio to follow and pardon her. In the Act II finale they are reconciled ('Son la vite'). Selim and Zaida – taking leave of Italy – and Narciso receive Geronio's forgiveness, and Prosdocimo hopes his public will enjoy the happy ending.

Il turco in Italia shows Rossini at his comic best. He responds to the buffoonery of the plot with an inspired and constantly amusing score. *Il turco in Italia* is largely an ensemble opera; only in Fiorilla's role do solo arias play an important part. There is abundant madcap motion, but time and again the composer steps back and, whether for specifically dramatic or more purely musical reasons, creates moments of extraordinary beauty and sensitivity. The Act I finale begins with all the noisy bumptiousness one expects of a Rossini finale. The scene is in turmoil, motivated by the jealous battle of Fiorilla and Zaida, but suddenly the noise stops and the orchestra disappears. The solo voices sing a remarkable unaccompanied phrase, 'Quando sono rivali, rivali in amor'. The effect of the entire *stretta* depends on Rossini's explicit wide-ranging indications of dynamics with phrases developing in unexpected ways.

The quintet in which Geronio tries to find Fiorilla, while the four disguised lovers dance around him, is extraordinarily funny; but, underneath a passage of unaccompanied singing, Geronio declaims his perplexity on a single note, emerging as a genuinely touching character. The little canonic allegro that follows, 'Questo vecchio maledetto', is Rossini's best piece in this genre. Its counterpoints are perfectly placed to set off the tune and help the modulations along.

The trio for Narciso, Geronio and Prosdocimo ('Un marito scimunito!'), in which the last expresses his glee at the developing plot while the other two plan their own revenge on him, is most unusual in design. The ensemble is largely built around a four-bar orchestral phrase in semibreves which appears both as a melody and as an accompanimental figure. Equally delightful is the duet for Fiorilla and Geronio ('Per piacere alla signora'). With wonderful mock realism, Rossini follows husband and wife through their confrontation, showing them in scenes of anger and sentimentality.

Elisabetta, regina d'Inghilterra

Elizabeth, Queen of England
Dramma per musica in two acts (2h 15m)
Libretto by Giovanni Schmidt, after the play by Carlo

Federici (1814) based on the novel *The Recess* by Sophie Lee (1783–5)
PREMIERES 4 October 1815, Teatro San Carlo, Naples; UK: 30 April 1818, King's Theatre, Haymarket, London
CAST Elisabetta (Elizabeth) *s*, Leicester *t*, Matilde (Matilda) *s*, Enrico (Henry) *a*, Norfolk *t*, Guglielmo (William) *t*; *satb* chorus of knights, courtiers, Scottish nobles, royal guards, populace

Elisabetta, regina d'Inghilterra opens Rossini's Neapolitan period. Between 1815 and 1822 he was to write ten operas for Naples (eight for the Teatro San Carlo). In Naples the impresario Domenico Barbaja had assembled a superb orchestra, a large and excellent mixed chorus (only a male chorus had been available for most of Rossini's earlier operas), and some of the greatest singers of the epoch, among them Isabella Colbran, who created the role of Elizabeth and later became Rossini's first wife. Unusually, the Neapolitan company regularly included two first tenors: one of high tessitura and very florid style, usually Giovanni David (but in *Elisabetta* Emanuele Garcia), and one more heroic with a baritonal extension, Andrea Nozzari.

Elisabetta borrows many musical phrases, sections, and entire numbers from earlier works. For the most part, however, these were extensively reworked and fully integrated into the new context. It is as if Rossini wished to present himself to the Neapolitan public by offering a selection of the best music from operas unlikely to be revived in Naples.

SYNOPSIS
Rossini thoroughly reorchestrated the overture from *Aureliano in Palmira* (1813) for *Elisabetta* (he later used it a final time in *Il barbiere di Siviglia*).

Act I At the royal palace, the earl of Leicester is to be honoured by Queen Elizabeth for his victories against the Scots. Elizabeth enters, overjoyed at the prospect of seeing Leicester again, but Leicester is shocked to find among the Scottish hostages his secret wife, Matilda, and her brother, Henry. Torn between love for Matilda and loyalty to Elizabeth, Leicester confides in his friend Norfolk, unaware of the latter's jealousy. Norfolk promptly informs Elizabeth that Leicester has betrayed her. The queen resolves that Leicester and Matilda will pay, and announces to the court that Leicester will become her consort; when Leicester hesitates, she imprisons the traitors.

Act II Elizabeth offers to spare Leicester, Henry and Matilda if the latter will renounce her marriage. Although Matilda (to save her husband) agrees, Leicester proclaims that they prefer to die. Elizabeth, disgusted with Norfolk's betrayal of his friend, exiles the duke, who plays on the people's sympathy for Leicester to raise a revolt. When Norfolk informs the imprisoned Leicester of his plan, Leicester refuses to act dishonourably. Elizabeth comes to the prison (where Norfolk, Matilda, and Henry variously hide themselves) to offer to help Leicester escape; Leicester again refuses dishonour. When Elizabeth implicates Norfolk, the latter, fearing further exposure, attempts to kill the queen, but he is disarmed by Matilda and Henry and arrested. Elizabeth gratefully pardons the three, sanctions the marriage of Leicester and Matilda, and renounces love in her own life.

In his Neapolitan operas Rossini explored the dramatic possibilities of opera seria. His experiments were not always understood or accepted by his audiences. In *Elisabetta* he wrote a conservative bridge between the earlier periods and the mature Neapolitan operas, adapting much of the music from prior works rather than composing a fully original opera, but he invested the older ideas with the rich Neapolitan orchestral palette and surrounded them with new music to suit the context. Notable are the two male solo scenes in Act II: the interaction between chorus and soloist in Norfolk's aria ('Qui sosteniamo . . . Che intesi') anticipates the scene for Assur and chorus in *Semiramide*, and Leicester's prison scene ('Della cieca fortuna') is remarkable for the flexibility of its first sections and its orchestration, with solo writing for two cors anglais.

Il barbiere di Siviglia

(Originally *Almaviva, ossia L'inutile precauzione*)
The Barber of Seville (originally *Almaviva, or The Useless Precaution*)
Commedia in two acts (2h 45m)
Libretto by Cesare Sterbini, after the play by Pierre-Augustin Caron de Beaumarchais (1775) and Giuseppe Petrosellini's libretto for Giovanni Paisiello (1782)
PREMIERES 20 February 1816, Teatro Argentina, Rome; UK: 10 March 1818, King's Theatre, Haymarket, London; US: 3 May 1819, Park Theater, New York
CAST Count Almaviva *t*, Bartolo *b*, Rosina *ms*, Figaro *bar*, Basilio *b*, Berta *s*, Fiorello *bar*, Ambrogio *b*, Officer *b*, Notary *silent*; *tb* chorus of police, soldiers, musicians

During the years of his association with Naples, Rossini wrote several important operas for other Italian cities, including *Il barbiere di Siviglia*, the oldest opera by an Italian composer never to have disappeared from the repertoire and perhaps the greatest of all comic operas. Set to a beautifully constructed libretto and drawing effectively on an important literary source, Rossini's opera achieves melodic elegance, rhythmic exhilaration, superb ensemble writing, and original and delightful orchestration. In it Rossini, with cleverness and irony, adapted the formal models of his art to specific dramatic situations.

In Rome for the premiere of his *Torvaldo e Dorliska* in December of 1815, Rossini signed a contract with the Teatro Argentina to compose an opera for the conclusion of the imminent carnival season. After a subject offered by Jacopo Ferretti had been rejected, Cesare Sterbini, author of *Torvaldo*, was selected to prepare the text. The resulting libretto was *Almaviva, ossia L'inutile precauzione*, a title chosen to distinguish it from Paisiello's well-known *Il barbiere di Siviglia*. In no more than two weeks, Rossini had prepared the score; probably from lack of time he adapted the overture of *Aureliano in Palmira*, which also had formed the basis for the overture to *Elisabetta, regina d'Inghilterra*. The opening-night audience reacted unfavourably to this new and hastily mounted *Barbiere*, but on the second night its brilliance won them over. For the Bologna revival of 1816 there was no necessity to maintain the original title; Rossini's *Il barbiere di Siviglia* had come into its own.

The opera was known in corrupt versions from the

end of the 19th century until the 1960s. Furthermore, its modern performance tradition stressed slapstick gags rather than elegant comedy. The critical edition of the score, edited by Alberto Zedda (1968), and the performances based on it, have allowed the public to hear the work afresh.

SYNOPSIS

Act I   At dawn in Seville Count Almaviva serenades the beautiful Rosina ('Ecco ridente il cielo'). When Rosina fails to appear at her window, he pays off the musicians, who, delighted by his generosity, make an enormous racket before departing. Figaro, the barber, approaches; he loves his profession, which opens every door in the city to him ('Largo al factotum'). He recognizes the count, but the latter wants his identity hidden, for he has followed Rosina secretly. Figaro says she is the ward of old Dr Bartolo, who wishes to marry her himself. Bartolo appears, locks Rosina in, and hurries off to organize the wedding. The count, not wanting Rosina to marry him for his title, pretends to be 'Lindoro', a poor student ('Se il mio nome'). As Rosina starts to respond, the shutters are firmly closed. Promised gold for his assistance, Figaro concocts a plan: the count will enter Bartolo's house disguised as a drunken soldier and claim lodgings ('All'idea di quel metallo'). Inside the house, Rosina has written a letter to 'Lindoro' ('Una voce poco fa'). Figaro appears, promptly followed by Don Basilio, music master and friend of Bartolo, brings word that Count Almaviva, attracted by Rosina's beauty, has arrived in Seville. He suggests they spread malicious rumours about the count ('La calunnia'). Bartolo prefers to marry that day, and they go off to draft the contract. Having overheard the conversation, Figaro warns Rosina. Assuring him she can handle the situation, Rosina inquires about the handsome youth she has just seen with Figaro. He tells her it was his impoverished cousin, madly in love with Rosina. Though feigning surprise when Figaro suggests she write to 'Lindoro', Rosina produces her finished letter ('Dunque io son') and Figaro goes to deliver it. The suspicious Bartolo accuses Rosina of having written to her lover and threatens to lock her up ('A un dottor'). The disguised count arrives noisily ('Ehi, di casa'). He tells Bartolo he seeks lodging. When Rosina appears, the count manages to reveal that he is 'Lindoro'. Bartolo produces an exemption from billeting, but the count dismisses it. In the uproar, he slips Rosina a letter, which she promptly exchanges with a laundry list as the servant Berta and Don Basilio enter. Figaro soon reappears, reporting that their noise can be heard throughout the city. Soldiers knock at the door. All the characters try to explain the situation, creating even more chaos. The officer arrests the count, who shows a document and is promptly set free. Bartolo explodes in anger, and everyone expresses total confusion.

Act II   Another knock at the door announces the count, disguised as a music master, 'Don Alonso' ('Pace e gioia'). He claims to be a student of Don Basilio, sent because his master is ill. To gain Bartolo's confidence, he tells him he has stolen from Almaviva a note written by Rosina. With this evidence, he will

try to convince Rosina that the count merely plays with her affections. Tricked, Bartolo goes to fetch his ward for her lesson. Rosina performs a 'Rondo' from a new opera, The Useless Precaution, and, as Bartolo dozes, she and 'Lindoro' express their mutual affection ('Contro un cor'). Bartolo awakens, bored by this 'contemporary music', and sings some 'music of my time' ('Quando mi sei vicina'). Figaro comes to shave Bartolo, who sends the barber to get shaving materials. Figaro grabs the opportunity to obtain the balcony key, then drops crockery, forcing Bartolo to come after him. Rosina and 'Lindoro' again swear their love. As Figaro begins to shave Bartolo, Don Basilio arrives for Rosina's lesson. The lovers and Figaro provide Basilio with an ample purse, claim he has scarlet fever, and make him withdraw ('Don Basilio! Cosa veggo!'). Figaro continues to shave Bartolo while 'Lindoro' plans with Rosina to elope at midnight. Bartolo overhears the count speak of his disguise and breaks into a rage. Alone, Berta, Dr Bartolo's housekeeper, comments on the foolishness of old men who would marry young women ('Il vecchiotto cerca moglie'). Basilio admits to Bartolo he does not know 'Don Alonso' – perhaps it was the count himself. Bartolo instructs Basilio to fetch the notary immediately. Producing Rosina's letter to 'Lindoro', Bartolo tells her he obtained it from Count Almaviva and persuades her to agree to marry him. A storm rages outside. As Figaro and the count enter through the balcony, Rosina accuses 'Lindoro' of intending to sell her to that vile Count Almaviva. The count throws himself at her feet and admits his true identity. The lovers express their joy, while Figaro urges them to escape ('Ah! qual colpo inaspettato'). By the time they are ready, their ladder has disappeared. Basilio enters with the notary. Figaro has him marry the count and Rosina. Offered the choice between a valuable ring and two bullets in the head, Basilio agrees to be a witness. Bartolo, too late, arrives with soldiers. Count Almaviva reveals his identity and announces that Rosina is his wife ('Cessa di più resistere'). With no choice remaining, Bartolo blesses the marriage. All wish the happy couple love and eternal fidelity ('Di sì felice innesto').

In Il barbiere di Siviglia Rossini most successfully uses his musical style to provide a metaphoric interpretation of, or an ironic commentary on, the unfolding drama. The basic techniques and forms of his musical vocabulary embody in a precise and often delightful way the dramatic situations and characters. For example, the 'Rossini crescendo' (a technique for building musical tension by repeating a short phrase with added instrumental forces, expansions of register, alterations in articulation, and gradual increases in dynamics), though rarely inappropriate for its context, frequently lacks specific links to the drama. In Figaro's cavatina, as the orchestral crescendo gathers force, the barber describes how the demands of his clients become ever more insistent; his words come faster and faster until the momentum reaches its climax and he is left to sing unaccompanied: 'Figaro, Figaro, Figaro, Figaro . . .' In Don Basilio's 'calumny' aria the crescendo becomes the central musical force of the number. As

Basilio describes how the soft voice of rumour gradually spreads until it explodes like a cannon shot, the orchestral crescendo builds to the *colpo di cannone* of the bass drum.

In the trio near the end of Act II Rossini uses another standard musical technique to comment ironically on the action rather than describe the dramatic situation. While the lovers react with ecstasy to their new-found happiness, Figaro urges them to leave. It is standard for Rossini to echo a lyrical vocal melody in the orchestra, giving the singer a chance to breathe at the end of a phrase while maintaining melodic interest. In this trio the echo is both played by the first violins and sung by Figaro, who tries to shake Rosina and the count out of their happy delirium. Although he imitates their very words, the lovers simply do not hear him; it is as if Figaro served as nothing more than the traditional instrumental echo. Furthermore, when the lovers finally realize they must hurry, the three sing 'Presto andiamo via di qua'; as the characters wait for the music to work itself out with standard repeats of the cabaletta theme and cadential phrases, their ladder disappears from under them.

In one number after another, Rossini both captures the essence of the characters and comments ironically, even maliciously, on them. This is an opera that combines the elegance of its literary source with the buffoonery of the Italian *commedia dell'arte* tradition. Even with the recovery of so many of the composer's significant operas over the past 20 years, it remains Rossini's masterpiece.

Otello, ossia Il moro di Venezia

Othello, or The Moor of Venice
Dramma per musica in three acts (2h 15m)
Libretto by Francesco Maria Berio di Salsa, after the play
Othello by William Shakespeare (1604–5)
PREMIERES 4 December 1816, Teatro del Fondo, Naples;
UK: 16 May 1822, King's Theatre, Haymarket, London;
US: 7 February 1826, Park Theater, New York
CAST Otello *t*, Desdemona *s*, Elmiro *b*, Rodrigo *t*, Iago *t*,
Emilia *ms*, Lucio *t*, The Doge *t*, A Gondolier *t*; *satb* chorus
of senators, followers of Otello, ladies-in-waiting to
Desdemona, people

Otello, written for Naples between the Roman operas *Il barbiere di Siviglia* and *La Cenerentola*, was staged at the Teatro del Fondo because the principal theatre, the San Carlo, had been destroyed by fire. Although the title suggests the Shakespearean drama, the libretto actually explores archetypical situations of Italian opera: a secret marriage, a disapproving father, a duel between rivals. Only in Act III, with the scene for Desdemona and Emilia and final confrontation and tragedy, is the literary source apparent.

SYNOPSIS

The overture is distinctly old-fashioned in the context of the opera: it is the last traditional overture Rossini wrote in Naples.

Act I   Otello returns victorious to Venice while the jealous Iago and Rodrigo plot his downfall. Desdemona's father, Elmiro, has intercepted a letter she sent to Otello and believes it was intended for Rodrigo. Desdemona fears that Otello will doubt her love. Elmiro, who has offered his daughter's hand to Rodrigo, tells her only that he has found her a husband. As friends gather for the wedding, Desdemona realizes she is to marry Rodrigo, not Otello, and is torn between filial duty and love. Otello enters and reveals that Desdemona has pledged herself to him.

Act II   Rodrigo pleads his case with Desdemona. Iago gives Desdemona's letter to Otello; not realizing it was meant for him, Otello is consumed by a desire for revenge. Despite Desdemona's efforts to separate them, Rodrigo and Otello fight. Elmiro, furious, curses his daughter.

Act III   Otello has been exiled by the Senate; the grief-stricken Desdemona, hearing a gondolier singing verses of Dante outside her window, intones a doleful song of her own, ending with a prayer for Otello's return. When she is asleep, Otello stealthily enters. Although Desdemona, awakening, protests her innocence, he stabs her. The doge, Elmiro, and Rodrigo arrive. Iago, attempting to murder Rodrigo, has been killed, but before his death he confessed his plotting. The Senate has therefore pardoned Otello; Rodrigo withdraws his claim to Desdemona, and Elmiro is prepared to grant her hand to Otello. Overcome with grief, Otello stabs himself.

Otello lies at a significant juncture in Rossini's compositional development. Although the first two acts are musically and dramatically effective, even inspired, it is the third that elicited Rossini's most original and profound music. Conceived as a whole, the act ranges from the richly scored prelude through Desdemona's magnificent 'Willow Song' to the powerful dénouement. The 'Willow Song' is a masterful demonstration of music's power to enrich a strophic framework with emotional depth. As Desdemona becomes more agitated the vocal line grows more florid; when she attempts to sing the final strophe, the vocal line is stripped of ornament, and she abandons the song without bringing it to completion; finally, she offers her beautiful prayer to the accompaniment of winds alone. Although the first section of the Otello–Desdemona 'duet' is conventional, its ending, which builds in intensity until Otello kills her, is not. Rossini offers no cabaletta, although the text had been fashioned to suggest the typical structure. Throughout this act, the drama is the controlling element; Rossini had come of age as a musical dramatist.

La Cenerentola, ossia La bontà in trionfo

Cinderella, or Goodness Triumphant
Dramma giocoso in two acts (2h 30m)
Libretto by Giacomo (Jacopo) Ferretti, after Charles
Perrault's tale *Cendrillon* (1697), Charles-Guillaume
Étienne's libretto *Cendrillon* (1810), and Francesco Fiorini's
libretto *Agatina* for Stefano Pavesi (1814)
PREMIERES 25 January 1817, Teatro Valle, Rome; UK:
8 January 1820, King's Theatre, Haymarket, London;
US: 27 June 1826, Park Theater, New York
CAST Don Ramiro *t*, Dandini *b*, Don Magnifico *b*,
Clorinda *s*, Tisbe *ms*, Angelina (known as La Cenerentola
(Cinderella)) *ms*, Alidoro *b*; *tb* chorus of courtiers; *silent*:
ladies

Rossini was originally commissioned by the Teatro Valle to set a different libretto, based on a French comedy, but the ecclesiastical censors demanded so many changes that Rossini ultimately rejected it, requesting a new libretto from his friend Ferretti. Because of the shortness of time – Ferretti and Rossini chose the subject on 23 December 1816 – Ferretti did not write a new poem based on the fairy-tale but rather turned to two earlier libretti, written for Paris and Milan respectively. Practically none of the elements familiar from Perrault's fairy-tale figures in Ferretti's libretto. His transformation of the glass slipper into a bracelet was probably to placate the Roman censors, who would not wish to see an unshod feminine foot on stage.

The opera was staged a month later. Rossini borrowed the overture from the Neapolitan *La gazzetta* (September 1816) and employed a Roman musician, Luca Agolini, to assist him in his preparations. Agolini composed all the *secco* recitative and three pieces: an aria for Alidoro ('Vasto teatro è il mondo') in Act I, a chorus ('Ah della bella incognita') to open Act II, and an aria for Clorinda ('Sventurata! me credea') near the end of the opera. For a Roman revival in 1821 Rossini replaced Alidoro's aria with a new composition, 'Là del ciel nell'arcano profondo'.

The nature of the libretto makes *La Cenerentola* significantly different from Rossini's previous comic operas. Although Don Magnifico and Dandini are comic characters in the great Italian tradition, the principal characters, Cinderella herself and Ramiro, are sentimental, not comic. They are heirs of Richardson's Pamela, the virtuous servant girl loved and finally married by a noble patron. From Niccolò Piccinni's setting of Carlo Goldoni's *La buona figliola* (1760) on through the century, Italian opera buffa more and more frequently had sentimental and pathetic heroines, expressing their emotions in a musically simple and popular style.

SYNOPSIS

Act I In a hall of Don Magnifico's castle, his vain daughters Clorinda and Tisbe are primping. Their stepsister, Cinderella, consoles herself with a song about a king who chose a kind-hearted bride ('Una volta c'era un re'). A beggar (actually Prince Ramiro's tutor Alidoro) comes in; Cinderella gives him some breakfast, angering the stepsisters. The prince's knights enter, announcing the imminent arrival of the prince himself, who at a ball will choose the most beautiful woman as his wife. The ensuing excitement generates great confusion. The knights leave; so does the 'beggar', foretelling that Cinderella will be happy by the next day. Quarrelling for the privilege of telling their father the good news, Clorinda and Tisbe awaken him. Don Magnifico interprets a dream he was just having as a prediction of his fortune: the impoverished baron's vision of himself as grandfather of kings is apparently confirmed by his daughters' announcement ('Miei rampolli femminini'). Ramiro, having decided to explore the situation, has exchanged clothing with his attendant, Dandini. When the disguised prince enters the house, he and Cinderella fall in love immediately ('Un soave non so che'). Dandini arrives,

awkwardly playing the prince ('Come un'ape ne' giorni d'aprile'). Clorinda and Tisbe are introduced to him. Cinderella begs her stepfather to take her to the ball ('Signor, una parola'), but Magnifico orders her to stay at home. Alidoro, with a list of the unmarried women of the region, asks Don Magnifico about a third daughter; he says she died. Everyone is confused. Later Alidoro reveals his identity to Cinderella and invites her to the ball, alluding to a change in her fortunes ('Là del ciel'). At the palace Dandini, still disguised as the prince, appoints Magnifico his wine steward; Magnifico proclaims new drinking laws. Clorinda and Tisbe scornfully mistreat Ramiro, believing him to be the squire. All are enchanted by the arrival of a mysterious lady. When she unveils herself they are struck by her uncanny resemblance to Cinderella.

Act II The courtiers laugh at the sisters' distress. Magnifico imagines himself the prince's father-in-law, making money in exchange for his favours ('Sia qualunque delle figlie'). Ramiro overhears Cinderella refusing Dandini's attentions because she loves his 'squire'. Ramiro asks her to be his, but she gives him a bracelet, saying he will find her wearing its twin. If he still likes her, she will marry him. Ramiro reassumes his princely role and determines to look for Cinderella ('Sì, ritrovarla, io giuro'). Dandini encourages Magnifico's fantasies, then reveals his real identity ('Un segreto d'importanza'). Returning home, the sisters find Cinderella by the fire and berate her because she looks like the lady at the ball. Alidoro arranges an accident for the prince's carriage, which overturns in front of the house. Cinderella and Ramiro recognize each other ('Siete voi?'), and everyone expresses amazement ('Questo è un nodo avviluppato'). Ramiro whisks Cinderella away, while Alidoro convinces the sisters to ask forgiveness so as to avoid ruin. At the wedding banquet Cinderella intercedes with the prince for Magnifico and her stepsisters. She reflects on how her fate has changed ('Nacqui all'affanno, al pianto').

La Cenerentola is far from a simple comic opera. Rossini adapts for his purposes not only the popular semiseria genre but even the exalted vocal style of opera seria. When we first meet Cinderella she is a naïve girl singing a little ditty: 'Once upon a time there was a king . . .' The disguised prince begins their duet ('Un soave non so che') with a simple melody that is a transformation of her tune. In the Act II sextet (Siete voi?) Rossini gives Cinderella a coloratura style that none the less remains attached to simple melodic patterns ('Ah signor, s'è ver che in petto'). But in her first appearance at the ball ('Sprezzo quei don') and at the beginning of her rondo ('Nacqui all'affanno, al pianto') she emerges a queen, her florid flights approaching those we normally associate with Rossini's serious operas. Ramiro's Act II aria ('Sì, ritrovarla, io giuro') is a thoroughly elegant piece with spectacular vocal fireworks and a range that ascends repeatedly to exposed and sustained high Cs.

The opening comic aria for Don Magnifico is rather standard, with almost continuous comic patter. Dandini, however, is a more subtle comic character. When he first appears disguised as the prince, Rossini gives him a princely *coro e cavatina* in mock-heroic style, in which extravagant coloratura alternates with patently buffo declamation. The witty duet with Magnifico ('Un segreto d'importanza') is superbly set. Once the secret is out, the tentative opening phrase is transformed into a spirited allegro in which Dandini's buffo style emerges gloriously, with Magnifico babbling in confusion. More revelations lead to the sextet of confusion ('Questo è un nodo avviluppato'), one of the most inspired moments in all Rossini's operas. By using a remarkable palette of musical styles throughout the opera, Rossini leads us through each stage. In the end, Cinderella's transformation is brought about not by supernatural arts, but by the magic of music.

La gazza ladra
The Thieving Magpie
Melodramma in two acts (3h 15m)
Libretto by Giovanni Gherardini, after the play *La pie voleuse* by J.-M.-T. Badouin d'Aubigny and Louis-Charles Caigniez (1815)
PREMIERES 31 May 1817, La Scala, Milan; UK: 10 March 1821, King's Theatre, Haymarket, London; US: October 1827, Chestnut Street Theater, Philadelphia
CAST Fabrizio Vingradito *b*, Lucia *ms*, Giannetto *t*, Ninetta *s*, Fernando Villabella *b*, The Mayor *b*, Pippo *ms*, Isacco *t*, Antonio *t*, Giorgio *b*, Ernesto *b*, Magistrate *b*, Gaoler *silent*, Usher *silent*; *satb* chorus of men at arms, peasants, servants; a magpie

From the second half of 1817 until 1822, Rossini's creative activity was dominated by his artistic ties with Naples, where he concentrated his attention primarily on the production of serious operas. The winter and spring seasons of 1816–17, however, proved to be one of the composer's most intensely prolific periods. Working in a variety of theatres and across a number of genres, Rossini had already affirmed his genius in opera seria (with *Otello* for Naples) and opera buffa (with *La Cenerentola* for Rome). Now he returned to Milan, the scene of his earliest important success, and a city where a large number of works by German and Austrian composers (Mozart, Joseph Weigl and Peter Winter) had been produced since his last visit. Mindful of the lack of enthusiasm generated by his two previous works for La Scala, Rossini devoted considerable attention to his new opera semiseria.

Gherardini, a leading personality in Milanese cultural life, had offered the libretto the preceding year to Ferdinando Paer, but it was not used. The plot is based on a true story: a French servant girl, accused of theft, was tried and executed. When her townspeople later discovered that the thief was a magpie, they instituted an annual mass in her memory, called the 'mass of the magpie'. In a letter to his mother, Rossini proclaimed 'the subject is wonderful'.

La gazza ladra belongs to the 'mixed' genre, born in the mid 18th century. During the Revolutionary period, semiseria operas were frequently rescue operas (the most famous example being Beethoven's *Fidelio*). *La gazza ladra* is a classic example of opera semiseria, but its fusion of comic and dramatic elements is clearly weighted towards the latter.

The opera was an immediate and enormous success. It quickly circulated outside Italy, being heard throughout Europe in the following decade, and remained in the repertoire for over 50 years. Rossini himself directed revivals in Pesaro and Naples, writing some remarkable new arias for the character of Fernando.

SYNOPSIS
The opera begins with one of Rossini's finest overtures, whose opening snare drums and military tone infiltrate much of the drama. Many themes are derived directly from the opera and anticipate its emotional content.

Act I Fabrizio Vingradito, a well-to-do tenant farmer, would like to see his son Giannetto, who is returning from military service, marry Ninetta, their serving girl and the daughter of an honourable soldier, Fernando Villabella: the young couple are in love ('Oh che giorno fortunato!'). Lucia, Fabrizio's wife, complains that the girl is irresponsible and has recently mislaid a silver fork. Ninetta enters ('Di piacer mi balza il cor'); Fabrizio and Lucia go to meet Giannetto. Isacco the pedlar arrives selling his wares ('Stringhe e ferri da calzette'), but is sent on his way by Pippo, a friend of Ninetta in Fabrizio's service. Everyone returns with Giannetto, who embraces Ninetta ('Vieni fra queste braccia'); Pippo sings a drinking song ('Tocchiamo, beviamo'). Alone in the household, Ninetta is joined by a ragged man: it is her father. Having been refused permission to visit his daughter, Fernando fought with his commander, was imprisoned and condemned to death, and now has escaped. He gives Ninetta a silver fork and spoon to sell so that he will have some money ('Come frenar il pianto!'). The mayor, coming to renew his unwelcome amorous overtures to Ninetta ('Il mio piano è preparato'), receives an urgent message; not having his eyeglasses, he asks Ninetta to read it aloud. It is an order to arrest her father, which she falsifies by changing the description of the fugitive ('M'affretto di mandarvi'). Fernando reproaches the mayor for his unwanted attentions to Ninetta ('Respiro. Mia cara!'). Meanwhile, the pet magpie, unobserved, steals a silver spoon. Lucia accuses Ninetta of stealing the missing silver fork and spoon. Pippo inadvertently reveals to the mayor that Ninetta has sold some trinkets to Isacco. The pedlar is summoned and a deposition is taken ('In casa di Messere'); Isacco has already resold the fork and spoon, but he testifies that they had the initials F.V. – those of both Fabrizio and Fernando. Ninetta, unwilling to betray her father, is arrested.

Act II Ninetta, in prison, is visited in turn by Giannetto, to whom she declares her innocence but not the truth about her father ('Forse un dì conoscerete'); by the mayor, whose offer of freedom in return for his love she rejects ('Sì, per voi, pupille amate'); and by Pippo, to whom she gives the money to hide for her father ('E ben, per mia memoria'). Lucia reveals Ninetta's plight to Fernando, who determines to save her at the cost of his own life ('Accusata di furto'). Lucia repents of her accusations ('A questo seno'). At the trial, Ninetta is sentenced to death; all react in pity and horror ('Ahi qual colpo! . . . Tremate o popoli'). Fernando bursts in; too late to help his daughter, he is himself arrested. While Pippo is counting his money in the village square, the magpie steals a coin. The mournful procession to the execution enters the square as the townspeople console Ninetta ('Infelice, sventurata'); it pauses in front of the church while Ninetta prays for her father ('Deh tu reggi'), then leaves the square. Pippo and the prison warder Antonio climb to the magpie's nest in the belltower, where they discover the stolen fork and spoon. However, it seems to be too late; gunfire is heard in the distance. Then a joyful chorus announces it is a signal that Ninetta is safe. A royal pardon arrives for Fernando. All rejoice, except the mayor.

Despite the great wealth of beautiful music in *La gazza ladra*, a modern audience may find its semi-serious tone difficult to grasp. The music moves from a light-hearted, pastoral tone to one of deep tragedy, only to wrest itself back at the last moment. The two most ambiguous characters are Pippo and the mayor. The youthful Pippo announces the return of Giannetto, plays with the magpie, and sings a drinking song; then, in the prison scene, he and Ninetta perform a duet whose beauty and tenderness create a powerful dramatic tension. In the mayor's cavatina ('Il mio piano è preparato') there are elements of opera buffa (in the orchestra, in the comic declamation), but in the following trio he is much more threatening. Showing his 'official' side during the Act I finale, he reveals his fury against Ninetta in a musical language that leaves no doubt about the evil of which he is capable. During the highly charged quintet ('Ahi qual calpo! . . . Tremate o popoli'), he finally expresses remorse but is unable to find a way out. In the finale, when it seems that Ninetta has been executed, it is to the mayor that Rossini gives the weightiest part, while in the face of communal joy he feels intense shame.

The funeral march of the Act II finale is laden with such grief as to set aside the lighter elements. The procession approaches, the orchestra *sotto voce*; it draws nearer, adding chorus (always with the accompanying drums that opened the overture and called the court to session). The prayer, with its introduction for two bassoons and two horns leading to a simple melody, does not end the scene but leads to a reprise of the march, swelling to fortissimo, then dwindling until only bassoon, horn, trombone, and drum remain, fading to nothing. And then the sudden change from clouds to sunlight: Ninetta and Fernando return in triumph, and one of the principal dramaturgical requirements of opera semiseria, a happy ending, is fulfilled, with each character (except the mayor) expressing joy.

Armida

Dramma per musica in three acts (2h 30m)
Libretto by Giovanni Schmidt, after scenes from the epic poem *Gerusalemme liberata* by Torquato Tasso (1581)
PREMIERES 11 November 1817, Teatro San Carlo, Naples; UK: 30 January 1922, Covent Garden, London (concert); US: 29 February 1992, Tulsa Opera, Tulsa
CAST Goffredo *t*, Rinaldo *t*, Idraote *b*, Armida *s*, Gernando *t*, Eustazio *t*, Ubaldo *t*, Carlo *t*, Astarotte *b*; *satb* chorus of paladins, warriors, demons, spirits

With *Armida* Rossini returned to the medieval setting of *Tancredi*, but the opera is far from the pastoral idyll of that youthful work. Rather it indulges the Romantic passion for the exotic and supernatural, while at the same time deeply probing human passion. In Naples Rossini became the lover of the star soprano Isabella Colbran, who created the title role of *Armida*; perhaps the emotion he felt for her poured out in the magnificent love duets of the opera.

SYNOPSIS
Act I Armida, princess of Damascus and a sorceress, comes to the French Crusaders' camp outside Jerusalem, ostensibly to ask their aid against a usurper in Damascus but actually to weaken the Christian forces. She finds there Rinaldo, whom she loves. Gernando boastfully taunts Rinaldo concerning which of them will succeed their recently dead leader, Dudone. Rinaldo angrily kills Gernando and is spirited to safety by Armida.
Act II On Armida's enchanted island the chief spirit Astarotte and a chorus of demons proclaim her magic powers and true intentions. Armida and Rinaldo, arriving in a dragon-borne chariot, declare their love. Nymphs and spirits sing and dance, exalting love's reign.
Act III Carlo and Ubaldo, sent to announce Goffredo's pardon and retrieve Rinaldo, wander in Armida's enchanted garden, where a chorus of nymphs attempts to seduce them. Rinaldo enters with Armida; the knights recall him to his duty. He vacillates; she beseeches; ultimately he goes with them. The desolate Armida, torn between love for Rinaldo and a desire for revenge, calls on her demons to destroy the island. The dragon chariot carries her off amid flame and smoke.

Armida is one of Rossini's most individual operas. In it Rossini presents the differing worlds of manly duty and erotic love through musical contrasts. Act I, set in the 'real world', displays the leadership of Goffredo ('Ardite all'ire') and the bravado of Gernando ('Non soffrirò l'offesa'). Rossini brings us from this into Armida's magical domain of Acts II and III, where the solo violin, solo cello, and colourful combinations of winds predominate. Perhaps the clearest example of Rossini's deliberate 'distortion of reality' is the form the duets for Armida and Rinaldo take in these acts. In Act I they have a standard duet ('Amor, possente nome') with *primo tempo, tempo di mezzo*, and cabaletta. In Act II Rinaldo awakens in Armida's arms and begins a 'duettino' ('Dove son io?') of only 56 bars (nearly half of which is an introduction featuring a cello solo), in which their voices echo at close intervals and entwine with alternating coloratura phrases. In the equally short Act III duet ('Soave catene'), with an introduction for solo violin, the two voices never separate but declaim together.

Mosè in Egitto

Moses in Egypt
Azione tragico-sacra in three acts (1h 30m)
Libretto by Andrea Leone Tottola, after the play *L'Osiride* by Francesco Ringhieri (1760)
PREMIERES 5 March 1818, Teatro San Carlo, Naples;

UK: 30 January 1822, Covent Garden, London (concert); 23 April 1822, King's Theatre, Haymarket, London (as *Pietro l'Eremita*); US: 22 December 1832, Masonic Hall, New York (concert); 2 March 1835, New York
CAST Faraone (Pharaoh) *b*, Amaltea *s*, Osiride (Osiris) *t*, Elcia *s*, Mambre *t*, Mosè (Moses) *b*, Aronne (Aaron) *t*, Amenophis *ms*

Rossini's azione tragico-sacra is an opera in sacred garb, a way to circumvent official sanctions against performing secular works during Lent. The plight of Elcia, the Israelite girl secretly married to the Egyptian crown prince, has little to differentiate it from other depictions of the conflict between love and duty pervading Italian melodramma of the time, and Rossini provides the lovers with music similar to that of his frankly secular opere serie.

At its premiere *Mosè in Egitto* was well received except for the short final act, the crossing of the Red Sea, the staging of which elicited howls of derision. On 7 March 1819 Rossini presented the opera with a revised third act (the version known today), including the prayer, 'Dal tuo stellato soglio', one of Rossini's most popular compositions. In 1827 he presented *Mosè in Egitto* in a revised form, *Moïse et Pharaon*, at the Paris Opéra (see below).

SYNOPSIS
Act I Afflicted by the plague of darkness, Pharaoh agrees to let the Israelites depart from Egypt. In response to the prayers of Moses, the light returns. Osiris, the crown prince, and Elcia lament their resulting separation. Pharaoh, induced by Osiris to revoke his permission, confronts Moses, who brings a new plague of hailstones and fiery rain.

Act II Again Pharaoh agrees to let the Israelites go, after which he will marry his son to the princess of Armenia. Osiris and Elcia hide but are caught by Aaron and Queen Amaltea, who has protected the Israelites during their bondage in Egypt. Pharaoh once more revokes his permission, and Moses threatens the death of Osiris and the other Egyptian first-born at God's hand. Amaltea vainly tries to tell Pharaoh about Osiris and Elcia. Moses and Elcia are brought before Pharaoh and Osiris; revealing that she is Osiris' wife, Elcia offers her life for that of Moses and the Israelites' freedom. When Osiris raises his sword to kill Moses, he is struck dead by a bolt of lightning.

Act III On the shores of the Red Sea, Moses and the Israelites pray for God's help. The waters part. The Egyptian army pursues the Israelites and is overwhelmed by the sea.

What gives the work its particular profile is its treatment of the biblical story. Rossini employs massive ensembles, choral movements, and declamatory solos to relate the story of the exodus from Egypt. The music associated with Moses is in large part declamatory, noble recitative that gives the character weight and dignity. Innovative is the orchestral introduction (the opera has no overture), with a threefold unison C for the entire orchestra, after which the curtain rises on a dark stage, the chorus bewailing in C minor the plague of darkness. Only after the Egyptians vow to free the Israelites does Moses invoke the Lord; the return of light is marked by a radiant change to C major. The interaction of C minor and C major dominates the opera.

Ermione
Hermione
Azione tragica in two acts (2h)
Libretto by Andrea Leone Tottola, after the play *Andromaque* by Jean Racine (1667)
PREMIERES 27 March 1819, Teatro San Carlo, Naples; UK: 10 April 1992, Queen Elizabeth Hall, London (concert); 22 May 1995, Glyndebourne, Sussex; US: 26 June 1992, San Francisco Opera (concert)
CAST Ermione (Hermione) *s*, Andromaca (Andromache) *c*, Pirro (Pyrrhus) *t*, Oreste (Orestes) *t*, Cleone *ms*, Pilade (Pylades) *t*, Fenicio (Phoenicius) *b*, Cefisa *c*, Attalo (Attalus) *t*; *satb* chorus of lords of Epirus, Trojan prisoners, followers of Orestes, Spartan maidens

Of all Rossini's mature operas, *Ermione* made the least impression on his contemporaries; despite a superb cast for its premiere (Colbran, Rosamunda Pisaroni, Nozzari and David), it was soon forgotten and never revived during Rossini's lifetime. Yet Rossini treasured it and spoke of it in later years as his 'little *William Tell*'. In its protagonist he created one of the most fully developed characters in 19th-century Italian opera.

SYNOPSIS
Act I Orestes, already pursued by the Furies for having murdered his mother Clytemnestra and her husband Aegisthus, arrives at the court of Pyrrhus, son of Achilles, leading a Greek delegation. They seek the death of Astyanax, to prevent this child of Hector from ever trying to avenge his father. Using the boy as a pawn, Pyrrhus wrests from his captive mother, Andromache, a promise to marry him.

Act II Pyrrhus' legitimate wife Hermione (daughter of Menelaus and Helen) plays on Orestes' passion for her to persuade him to kill Pyrrhus. Orestes, returning with the bloody dagger, describes the murder of Pyrrhus at the wedding ceremony. Hermione turns on Orestes in fury, berating him for not having understood that she still loves Pyrrhus. Together they acknowledge the Furies that have driven Orestes to this fate. Hermione swoons, and Orestes is dragged off by the fleeing Greeks.

Rossini treats this powerful tale with the utmost artistic integrity. This is focused primarily on the musical realization of the four major characters, as he constantly presses against convention to realize dramatic ends. Each character has a major aria, and there are four intensely dramatic duets: Pyrrhus encounters each woman once, and there are two especially impressive encounters for Orestes and Hermione (one of which opens the first-act finale). Yet the chorus and minor characters participate in most of these numbers, giving them greater dramatic weight.

Rossini's willingness to mix elements from different musical genres is apparent already in the overture, during which a men's chorus of Trojan prisoners sings from behind the curtain. The gran scena for Hermione in Act II is Rossini's finest achievement in a genre that goes back to *Ciro in Babilonia* and recurs in several serious operas. The quality of the recitative is noteworthy. Hermione passes through three lyrical sections of intensely contrasting emotions: grief, love and anger. After Orestes and the chorus enter, the crescendo, already heard in the overture, is transformed to a pianissimo accompaniment. In her cabaletta, Hermione thinks only of revenge. Her melodic line, extremely irregular, flies chromatically from one measure to another and soars in coloratura to its cadence. The final duet for Orestes and Hermione, with its preceding scene of dramatic declamation for Hermione alone, has its roots in French *tragédie lyrique*. Rossini is sensitive to each nuance of the text. Modern revivals of the opera have confirmed that *Ermione* holds a special place among Rossini's works.

La donna del lago
The Lady of the Lake
Melodramma in two acts (2h 15m)
Libretto by Andrea Leone Tottola, after the poem *The Lady of the Lake* by Sir Walter Scott (1810)
PREMIERES 24 October 1819, Teatro San Carlo, Naples; UK: 18 February 1823, King's Theatre, Haymarket, London; US: 26 August 1829, Park Theater, New York
CAST Giacomo (James) V ('Uberto of Snowdon') *t*, Douglas of Angus *b*, Rodrigo of Dhu *t*, Elena *s*, Malcolm Groeme *ms*, Albina *s*, Serano *t*, Bertram *t*; *satb* chorus of Scottish shepherds and shepherdesses, bards, Scottish lords and ladies, Clan Alpine warriors, huntsmen, royal guards

La donna del lago is the most Romantic of Rossini's Italian operas. The source of its libretto is a good clue to its character, being drawn not from the general stock of 17th- or 18th-century French tragedy but rather from a narrative by Sir Walter Scott. Interest in things Scottish was fashionable throughout Europe in this period, and the 'Ossianic' poems of James Macpherson captured a large following, but *La donna del lago* was the first operatic setting in Italy of a libretto based on Scott. The poem was apparently brought to Rossini's attention by a young French composer, Désiré-Alexandre Batton, who was studying in Italy. The spirit and essential story of Scott's poem are respected, and Tottola supplied Rossini with a framework that excited the composer's musical imagination. What makes the opera so unusual is its local colour, derived largely from Scott. In this, *La donna del lago* clearly anticipates *Guillaume Tell*. Although Rossini does not seem to have quoted Scottish tunes, elements such as the so-called Scotch-snap rhythm and the use of hunting horns (six solo horns onstage in the introduction) and bardic harps pervade the score. The atmospheric writing is particularly apparent in the large ensembles opening and closing Act I.

To favour the tenor Giacomo Rubini, Rossini inserted an aria from *Ermione* into the opera at a later revival in Naples; for a Parisian revival he also inserted two numbers from *Bianca e Falliero* into Act II, replacing the difficult trio. Under normal circumstances, however, there can be little doubt that the original version of *La donna del lago* is preferable.

SYNOPSIS
In 16th-century Scotland, King Giacomo V is trying to subdue the Clan Alpine of the Highlands. Among the Highlanders are the chieftain Rodrigo (Roderick) of Dhu, Malcolm Groeme and Douglas of Angus.

Act I At dawn, around Lake Katrine, the shepherds return to work ('Del dì la messagiera'). Elena crosses the lake on a small boat, singing of her love for Malcolm ('Oh mattutini albori!'). She comes across 'Uberto' (King Giacomo in disguise), who claims to have lost his fellow huntsmen. He is struck by her beauty. She offers him hospitality, and they sail to the island in the middle of the lake, the site of her father's cottage. Huntsmen appear, vainly looking for 'Uberto' ('Uberto! ah! dove t'ascondi?'). In the cottage, 'Uberto' learns that Elena's father is Douglas, once a trusted follower of the king – now a rebel against his rule. Douglas, sheltered by the warrior Rodrigo, has agreed to reward him with Elena's hand. Elena's friends sing of her imminent wedding with Rodrigo ('D'Inibaca donzella'). She alludes to her love for another, and the infatuated 'Uberto' mistakenly imagines himself to be the fortunate one ('Le mie barbare vicende'). Everyone leaves, and 'Uberto' is escorted back to shore. Malcolm, returning to the island after a long absence, enters the deserted room and sings of his love for Elena ('Elena! oh tu, che chiamo!'). Serano informs him that Rodrigo's troops are gathering in a valley nearby. Hearing Elena and Douglas enter the room, Malcolm hides. Elena angers her father by resisting the wedding ('Taci, lo voglio'). When Douglas leaves, Elena and Malcolm swear they will die rather than renounce their mutual love ('Vivere io non potrò'). In the valley, Rodrigo is joyously received by his warriors (chorus 'Qual rapido torrente' and cavatina 'Eccomi a voi, miei prodi'). Douglas leads in Elena, and Rodrigo is struck by her lack of enthusiasm (chorus 'Vieni, o stella' and first finale 'Quanto a quest'alma amante'). Malcolm joins them; his reaction on hearing of Elena's engagement leads Rodrigo to suspect Elena's secret love. But the royal troops are approaching, and everyone joins the bards in a warlike chorus ('Già un raggio forier').

Act II 'Uberto' desires to see Elena again, in order to declare his love ('Oh fiamma soave'). Disguised as a shepherd, he reaches the cavern where Elena is taking shelter during the battle. She reveals her love for Malcolm. Respecting her feelings, he gives her a ring that he claims is a gift from the king: should she or her family ever be in danger, she must show the ring to the king in person, and he will protect her. When Rodrigo arrives, 'Uberto' declares himself to be on the king's side ('Alla ragion deh rieda'). The two challenge each other to a duel and leave together. Malcolm is lamenting his loss of Elena ('Ah si pera: ormai la morte') when he hears that the Clan Alpine has been defeated by the royal troops and that Rodrigo is dead. Douglas goes to the royal castle of Stirling and offers his life to the king in exchange for his people's safety. Elena also goes to the castle, to beg mercy for her father by showing the ring. In the final scene in the throne hall, Elena hears 'Uberto' singing ('Aurora! ah sorgerai'); when she sees him before the assembled court, she realizes that 'Uberto' is actually the king. Giacomo forgives Douglas and Malcolm and joins the latter in marriage with Elena, who rejoices in her happiness ('Tanti affetti in tal momento').

Nearing the end of his Neapolitan career, Rossini was fully in control of his expanded musical style, using more and longer ensembles, with a corresponding decrease in the prominence of solo arias, a more dramatic accompanied recitative, and a chorus that has become a participant in the action. The forms of *Tancredi* seem rudimentary in comparison with the complexity and originality of *La donna del lago*. The introduction, for example, encompasses: a chorus of shepherds and hunters; a solo for Elena ('Oh mattutini albori!'), one of the most beautiful melodies Rossini ever wrote; a scene between Elena and the incognito king; their duet based on Elena's solo; and a final chorus of huntsmen that draws on melodic ideas from the opening chorus. In the final tableau of the act, the Scottish warriors sing a martial piece to the accompaniment of trumpets and stage band. Then the Scottish bards sing a hymn to the warriors, to the accompaniment of harp, violas and cellos pizzicato, and a single double-bass – a fine orchestral effect. Finally, in the stretta, Rossini brings all the tunes together contrapuntally, with full orchestra, three separate choruses, soloists, band, trumpets and harp. Throughout the opera Rossini makes unusual use of counterpoint. When Elena and 'Uberto' sing together in the introduction, Elena's original solo tune is treated to imitative counterpoint. In the final return of the cabaletta theme of the long Act I duet, the theme is imitated between the voices.

This tunefulness is an important aspect of *La donna del lago*. There are moments of tender pathos. The 'duettino' for Elena and Malcolm in Act I, 'Vivere io non potrò', is an intimate composition: the orchestra is restricted to strings, clarinets and bassoons. Subtle harmonic effects show Rossini's mastery of detail. When Rodrigo's bluster turns to thoughts of Elena, the music of 'Ma dov'è colei che accende' is of extraordinary sweetness and delicacy, again seconded by an almost chamber orchestration. In contrast are the vocal fireworks of the two arias for Malcolm and the final rondo for Elena: bel canto at its finest.

Maometto II
Mahomet II

Dramma per musica in two acts (3h)
Libretto by Cesare della Valle, after his own play *Anna Erizo* (1820)
PREMIERES 3 December 1820, Teatro San Carlo, Naples; US: 17 September 1988, War Memorial Opera House, San Francisco
CAST Paolo Erisso *t*, Anna *s*, Calbo *c*, Condulmiero *t*, Maometto II (Mahomet II) *b*, Selimo *t*; *satb* chorus of Muslim ladies, Venetian soldiers, Muslim soldiers

Rossini wrote *Maometto II* at the height of his Neapolitan career. Although it was not a popular success, he must have felt great confidence in what was to prove his next-to-last opera for Naples, for he chose this work to open the Venetian Carnival season of 1823 and to revise it for his début at the Paris Opéra in 1826, where it became *Le siège de Corinthe* (see below).

Maometto II sets a love story against the background of historical events, the wars between the Turks and the Venetians, culminating in the fall of Negroponte in 1476. (For Paris the locale was shifted to Corinth, since wars between Greeks and Turks were topical in the 1820s.) In the Naples and Paris versions, the Turks destroy Negroponte/Corinth; in Venice, the Venetians are victorious, and Rossini instructed his copyist to close the resulting happy ending with the final rondo, 'Tanti affetti in tal momento', from *La donna del lago*.

In some ways *Maometto II* is Rossini's most ambitious opera. Here he avoids altogether many 'standard' formal conventions of Italian opera, which he had codified almost single-handedly during the preceding decade, while expanding other forms internally. One can trace stages of the development from *Otello* onwards. But in *Maometto II* Rossini carried his art beyond the capabilities of his Neapolitan audience. That he knew this all too well is seen in the gradual retrenchment after *Maometto II*; in *Semiramide* (1823) Rossini regains a more classical pose, though one that shows the influence of the Neapolitan experiments. To help ensure the success of the opera in Venice and Paris, he smoothed out the more audacious elements of the score. Yet in *Maometto II* we find a work that brings together Rossini's pre-eminent gift for music of immediate appeal and vocal splendour with a considered and profound understanding of musical and dramatic structure. An opera of greater unity than the revised *Le siège de Corinthe*, it is a key work in the history of Italian opera during the early 19th century and gives a clear vision of the directions Rossini might have pursued further had his career as a composer of Italian opera not ended a few years later.

SYNOPSIS (Naples version)
Act I   The local governor, Paolo Erisso, is holding a council: Negroponte is besieged by the Turks, led by Mahomet; Constantinople has fallen. General Condulmiero proposes surrender, but the young general Calbo urges them to resist. Meanwhile Erisso's daughter Anna laments her father's peril ('Ah che invan su questo ciglio'). Erisso arrives with Calbo, and proposes that Anna marry him. She cannot conceal her secret affection for a young man called Uberto, whom she met in Corinth during her father's absence. But the real Uberto had been with Erisso at the time, and Anna is abashed to find she has been duped by an impostor ('Ohimè qual fulmine'). Gunfire interrupts them. As the men leave, Anna hurries to the church, where the women tell her a traitor has opened the gates to the Turks. They join in a prayer ('Giusto Ciel, in tal periglio'). Erisso and Calbo appear with the news that the Turks will not venture further until daylight. Erisso sends forces to the citadel; Anna, together with other women, offers to join the defenders of the city. Refusing, Erisso gives her a dagger with which to kill herself should she be captured (trio: 'Figlia, mi lascia'). Anna and the women seek refuge in the church. At daylight Turkish soldiers appear, threatening fire and slaughter ('Dal ferro, dal foco'). Mahomet acknowledges the obeisance of his followers ('Sorgete!'). With his vizier Selimo he plans the assault on the citadel. Mahomet

reveals that he knows the city, having once travelled in Greece as a spy. Warriors bring news that the Venetian leaders have been seized ('Signor, di liete nuove'). Calbo and Erisso are brought forward in chains. When Erisso discloses his identity, Mahomet is momentarily confused. He asks if Erisso was governor of Corinth and if he is a father. Learning this is so, he offers to spare him and the prisoners if Erisso will persuade his men to open the gates of the citadel. Erisso turns to Calbo in his dilemma ('Giusto Ciel, che strazio è questo!') but remains steadfast. Mahomet orders them tortured ('Guardie, olà'). Anna rushes from the church. Mahomet recognizes her, and she him as the impostor Uberto. She threatens to kill herself if he does not release her father and Calbo, whom she calls her brother. Mahomet yields, promising Anna a life of luxury if she will be his. Calbo is moved by Anna's concern, but her father spurns her in shame.

Act II   Anna grieves in Mahomet's tent. The Muslim girls tell her to enjoy love ('È follia sul fior degli anni'). Anna is protesting indignantly when Mahomet enters. He professes love and repeats his wish to make her queen. Spurning him, Anna begins to weep; Mahomet is moved by her distress ('Anna tu piangi'). He orders his troops to mount another assault on the citadel. Anna, fearing for her safety in his absence, asks for a token of security and receives the ultimate proof of his love – the imperial seal of authority. Mahomet exhorts his forces to new efforts and takes the standard himself ('All'invito generoso'). Anna is inspired to what she calls 'a task of honour'. Erisso and Calbo have hidden in the crypt of the church. Erisso laments Anna's treachery; Calbo defends her ('Non temer'), but to no avail. When Anna appears, Erisso repulses her until she swears fidelity. She gives him Mahomet's seal, which will give them free passage through the city. At her request, Erisso marries her to Calbo before the tomb of her mother; the three express their anguish as father and husband prepare for battle, leaving her to almost certain death ('In questi estremi'). Anna hears the women praying in the church ('Nume, cui 'l sole'). They inform her that the Venetians have put the sultan's army to flight; intent on revenge, the Turks are now seeking her ('Sventurata! fuggir sol ti resta'). Anna prepares to meet her fate ('Alfin compita è la metà'). The Turks enter the crypt and rush upon her, but her calm demeanour in offering herself to their swords stops them. Mahomet enters and demands his seal. Anna reveals that she gave it to her father and Calbo, whom she now names openly as her husband. She stabs herself, and falls dying on her mother's tomb.

There are many striking aspects of the music of *Maometto II*. The richness of the orchestration is immediately apparent. Although Rossini uses a full complement of orchestral resources, in each piece he uses only those instruments he truly needs, and many fine effects are achieved with a reduced palette. Rossini also effectively employs thematic transformation and a series of thematic references across the entire work. The introduction, for example, is bracketed by choral movements for the Venetian warriors. Though the

two choruses are separated by a lengthy ensemble, Rossini transforms the opening, hesitant, triple-time movement into a strong final section in 4/4, giving the entire number dramatic and musical unity.

Of the five independent arias in the opera, only two – Mahomet's cavatina ('Sorgete!' – a show-stopper, timed to unleash a torrent of applause) and Calbo's Act II aria – conclude with regular cabalettas. Anna's cavatina 'Ah che invan su questo ciglio' is a single slow section; the concluding quick section of Mahomet's aria 'All'invito generoso' in Act II never develops into a regular cabaletta. The final aria for Anna, 'Alfin compita è la metà', a multi-sectional piece, also ends without a cabaletta; Rossini gives the dénouement appropriate musical expression without forcing it into a predetermined mould. Thus *Maometto II* concludes with dialogue for Mahomet and Anna over an orchestral crescendo, her suicide, and the horrified reaction of the chorus and Mahomet.

But it is in the Act I 'terzettone' (Rossini's own term) that the flexibility of structure is most apparent. In this ensemble Rossini forces us to perceive musical and dramatic events – passing over even a major change of scene – as a single, coherent composition. He does this by assuming and playing on our knowledge of the way ensembles in Italian opera are conventionally constructed. As a result, the entire first act of *Maometto II* reduces to only five separate numbers – this in one of Rossini's longest operas.

Semiramide

Semiramis
Melodramma tragico in two acts (3h 45m)
Libretto by Gaetano Rossi after the play *Sémiramis* by Voltaire (1748)
PREMIERES 3 February 1823, La Fenice, Venice; UK: 15 July 1824, King's Theatre, Haymarket, London; US: 19 May 1837, St Charles Theater, New Orleans
CAST Semiramide *s*, Arsace *c*, Assur *b*, Idreno *t*, Azema *s*, Oroe *b*, Mitrane *t*, Ghost of Nino *b*, Arbate *silent*; *satb* chorus of magi, Babylonians, foreigners, ladies-in-waiting; *silent*: satraps, wizards, Babylonians, bards, foreign ladies, royal guards, ministers of the temple, Indians, Scythians, Egyptians, slaves

After his definitive departure from Naples in 1822, Rossini composed only one more opera for Italy, *Semiramide*, which had its premiere at the Teatro La Fenice of Venice almost exactly ten years after the premiere of *Tancredi* at the same theatre. Both were written to libretti by Gaetano Rossi, and both were based on dramas by Voltaire, parallels that were not accidental. After the more tormented and experimental Neapolitan works, Rossini sought to recapture a more classical spirit, one that would gain the favour of a wider public. *Semiramide* occupies a unique place in the Rossini canon: a consolidation of past triumphs and a step towards his future French operas. The work captivated the Venetian public, was performed everywhere in Europe, and remained in the repertoire throughout the 19th century.

SYNOPSIS
Act I   In the Babylonian Temple of Baal a throng waits for Queen Semiramide to name the successor to the throne of her husband, Nino, dead for 15 years.

Idreno, king of Indus, pays homage ('Là dal Gange'), and Prince Assur, Semiramide's former lover and her accomplice in the murder of Nino, brings offerings ('Sì, sperate'); both aspire to the throne and to the hand of Princess Azema. Semiramide, awaiting the return of the young commander Arsace, whom she loves, reluctantly begins to name the successor; lightning, thunder and wind extinguish the sacred altar fire, frightening everyone. Arsace, summoned by Semiramide, arrives in Babylon hoping to marry Azema, who loves him ('Ah! quel giorno'). He brings to the high priest, Oroe, tokens of the dead Nino and a scroll that reveals the truth about Nino's murder. Assur reminds Arsace that Azema was betrothed to the missing Prince Ninia, but Arsace's love knows no obstacle ('Bella imago degli dei'). In a separate aria, Idreno professes his love to Azema ('Ah dov'è, dov'è il cimento'). In the Hanging Gardens, Semiramide anticipates Arsace's arrival ('Bel raggio lusinghier'). When Arsace enters he diffidently tries to tell of his love for Azema, but Semiramide believes he loves her ('Serbami ognor'). The queen demands of her subjects an oath of loyalty to the future king, and then names Arsace as king and consort. The ghost of Nino appears and says Arsace must avenge his death with the blood of the murderers ('Qual mesto gemito'). The crowd wonders who is the guilty one ('Ah! Sconvolto nell'ordine eterno').

Act II Assur tries to force Semiramide to make him king; they each threaten to reveal the other's crime ('Se la vita ancor t'è cara'). Oroe reveals to Arsace that Nino was his father and that his mother, Semiramide, conspired with Assur. Arsace accepts the duty of avenging his father ('In sì barbara sciagura'). Idreno entreats Azema to accept him ('La speranza più soave'). Arsace tells Semiramide the marriage cannot take place and shows her the accusing scroll; she offers herself as the sacrificial victim. Arsace pities her, but he will follow his father's instructions and descend into his tomb ('Ebben . . . a te: ferisci'). Assur learns that Oroe has turned the people against him. Shaken by a vision of Nino, he vows to kill Arsace ('Deh . . . ti ferma . . .'). He searches for Arsace in the tomb of Nino; Semiramide follows to protect Arsace; Oroe and the magi are close behind. Groping in the darkness, the three principals are fearful ('L'usato ardir'). When Oroe tells Arsace to strike at Assur, Semiramide steps between them and is killed. Assur is arrested. The horrified Arsace, prevented by Oroe from killing himself, accepts the throne at the behest of the populace.

Continuing Neapolitan developments, *Semiramide* provides attractive vocal opportunities for accomplished singers, and without such singers it makes no sense to perform the work, for Rossini uses this vocalism to project the drama. *Semiramide* is the first of Rossini's non-Neapolitan operas to abandon *secco* recitative: indeed, the accompanied recitative of *Semiramide* is a model of passionate and expressive declamation.

Important differences from its Neapolitan predecessors are the presence of a conventionally constructed overture and a preponderance of arias and duets rather than ensembles. None the less, most of the striking dramatic events in *Semiramide* occur in the three great ensembles, each centred on a supernatural intervention: the expansive introduction, the monumental Act I finale, and the Act II finale.

The arias and duets of *Semiramide* are all constructed according to standard Rossinian design, but in many cases each section is enormously expanded (see, for example, the entries for *Tancredi*, *Armida* and *Maometto II*, where this is already discussed). In duets, the formal confrontation between characters takes place in an opening section, leading to a meditative cantabile. Some of the most stunning music in *Semiramide* is found here, including the famous 'Giorno d'orror! . . . e di contento' in the Act II duet for Semiramide and Arsace, after the queen learns he is her son. A short *tempo di mezzo* leads the characters to a new dramatic stance, expressed in the cabaletta. Rossini often wrote his most memorable melodies in these duet cabalettas: 'Va, superbo, in quella reggia' for Arsace and Assur, and 'Alle più care immagini' in Act I for Semiramide and Arsace. These pieces breathe a majesty and expansiveness that give the opera its sense of monumentality. Even within these numbers, however, there are remarkably original musical and dramatic effects. Most notable is Assur's mad scene preceding the Act II finale, where his tormented mind reels from one emotion to another. Rossini's music leads him graphically through these shifts.

The andantino of the Act I finale, in which all swear to obey Semiramide's command, is particularly beautiful: it uses the theme for four horns that Rossini also employs in the overture. But the centrepiece of the finale is the canonic ensemble in which all the characters react to the appearance of the ghost ('Qual mesto gemito'), a passage accompanied by an ostinato rhythmic figure in the orchestra. One of the musical ideas in this ensemble recurs several times during Act II, recalling the ghost of Nino. In the Act II finale the trio 'L'usato ardir' seems suspended in time.

Semiramide represents the apotheosis of musical neo-classicism in Italy. It is the opera to which the next generation of Italian composers returned almost compulsively, both to imitate and to abjure. Its forms provided models. Its sounds resonated in their hearts. But they rejected its classicism, its unabashed glorification of the power of music.

Il viaggio a Reims, ossia L'albergo del giglio d'oro

The Voyage to Rheims, or The Inn of the Golden Lily
Dramma giocoso in one act (3h)
Libretto by Luigi Balocchi, after the novel *Corinne, ou l'Italie* by Mme de Staël (1807)
PREMIERES 19 June 1825, Théâtre Italien, Paris; Italy: 18 August 1984, Auditorium Pedrotti, Pesaro; US: 12 June 1986, Loretto-Hilton Center, St Louis; UK: 8 June 1987, Guildhall School of Music and Drama, London
CAST Corinna *s*, Marquise Melibea *c*, Countess of Folleville *s*, Mme Cortese *s*, Chevalier Belfiore *t*, Count Libenskof *t*, Lord Sidney *b*, Don Profondo *b*, Baron Trombonok *b*, Don Alvaro *b*, Don Prudenzio *b*, Don Luigino *t*, Maddalena *s*, Delia *ms*, Modestina *ms*, Zefirino *t*, Antonio *b*, Gelsomino *t*; *satb* chorus of musicians, peasants, gardeners, dancers, servants, travellers

Rossini's last Italian opera and the first he wrote in France had its premiere as part of the festivities honouring the coronation of Charles X. Although an occasional piece, *Viaggio* was calculated to establish Rossini's reputation. Conceived for the greatest voices of the time, including Giuditta Pasta as Corinna, the work requires an exceptional cast: three prima-donna sopranos, a contralto and two tenors, and four baritones and basses have leading roles. Lavish costumes, magnificent sets, and a ballet for 40 dancers enhanced the splendour. Contemporary reviews were uniformly ecstatic, but Rossini was jealous of this opera. Aware that a work so tied to a particular historical occasion could not hope to circulate widely, he reused about half the music for *Le comte Ory* in 1828. He was pressed to permit three further performances of *Viaggio*, the proceeds of the last going to charity.

The libretto is inextricably bound to the specific event for which it was written. Hope for a strong Europe at peace, under the leadership of monarchies newly restored after the decisive defeat of Napoleon in 1815, gives symbolic meaning to the international clientele at the inn, and each character during the finale brings his own country's music to the festivities.

The manuscript sources of *Viaggio* were presumed lost until, in the mid-1970s, part of Rossini's autograph was recovered at the library of the Accademia di S. Cecilia in Rome. Other sources were located in Paris and Vienna, permitting a reconstruction of the entire work. (The so-called overture to *Il viaggio a Reims*, a 20th-century invention, is derived from a ballet movement written for one of Rossini's French operas: *Viaggio* never had an overture.)

SYNOPSIS

Travellers on their way to the coronation in Rheims are staying overnight at the Inn of the Golden Lily. The innkeeper, Mme Cortese, and her staff assist them in preparing for the last leg of their journey ('Presto, presto . . . su, coraggio!'). The Parisian countess of Folleville, learning that the carriage bringing her wardrobe has overturned, laments her loss ('Partir, oh ciel! desio'). Baron Trombonok, keeper of the travellers' purse and a lover of music, is responsible for making final arrangements ('Sì, di matti una gran gabbia'). Other travellers arrive: Don Profondo, an antiquarian; the Spanish admiral Alvaro, who escorts the Marquise Melibea, a Polish widow; a jealous Russian general, Count Libenskof, in love with Melibea. When Mme Cortese enters to explain that their departure has been delayed, Alvaro and Libenskof are already about to duel. From behind the scenes, the Roman poetess Corinna improvises an ode to fraternal love ('Arpa gentil'), and momentary peace returns. An English officer in love with Corinna, Lord Sidney, places flowers at her door ('Invan strappar dal core'). The French chevalier Belfiore tries to woo Corinna ('Nel suo divin sembiante'), but she wants nothing to do with him. Don Profondo lists the possessions the travellers are bringing with them ('Medaglie incomparabili'). Trombonok and Zefirino inform the travellers that they cannot go to Rheims after all, because no horses remain to take them there ('Ah! A tal colpo inaspettato'). Mme Cortese suggests an alternative:

her husband has written to describe the festivities being prepared for the king's return to the capital, and the travellers decide to proceed directly to Paris the next morning. In the meantime, they will give a public banquet that evening. Melibea and Libenskof quarrel; he tries once again to win her hand ('D'alma celeste, oh Dio!') and she finally yields. In the garden the banquet is under way. Musicians and dancers provide entertainment. Trombonok proposes a series of musical tributes to the royal family, with each singing in his or her own national style. Corinna offers an improvisation in honour of the new king, and the assembled guests (representing all the nations of Europe) proclaim the glory of Charles X and France.

Because the orchestra of the Théâtre Italien was strengthened with soloists from the Opéra for the first performance of *Viaggio*, instrumental lines could be made particularly demanding (see, for example, the flute solo in the aria of Lord Sidney, 'Invan strappar dal core'). And because each of his singers was a master of Italian vocal style, Rossini could allow his vocal writing to luxuriate in their strengths. Moreover, the musical numbers of *Viaggio* perfectly realize the dramatic situations. The countess of Folleville's aria of misery over the loss of her finery is delectable, precisely because of the contrast between the grandeur of the musical expression and the triviality of the dramatic cause. In Don Profondo's aria ('Medaglie incomparabili'), he is preparing a list of the effects of each traveller so that luggage can be prepared for the journey. He invokes each traveller and writes down what each will be bringing; each strophe characterizes a single person.

The 'Gran Pezzo Concertato a 14 Voci' ('Ah! A tal colpo inaspettato') is one of the glories of *Viaggio*. A slow opening section of astonishment, largely unaccompanied, is motivated by the news that no horses are available. In the second, quick section, the letter from Mme Cortese's husband in Paris alters the dramatic situation. The final section is constructed as a formal cabaletta, in which the characters react to the altered circumstances. The overwhelming effect of the audacious scoring for fourteen solo voices may be seen most clearly in the Rossini crescendo that serves as the concluding section of the cabaletta theme. The first phrase is sung by two voices, the second by nine, and the third by all fourteen.

The national toasts of the finale are either taken from patriotic hymns or based on national musical styles. Among the melodies that flow past are Haydn's 'Gott erhalte Franz den Kaiser', 'God Save the King' and the French 'Charmante Gabrielle'. They are joined by a polonaise, a Russian hymn, a Spanish song, and a tyrolese complete with yodels. The entire company joins in an apotheosis of Charles X to the well-known French song 'Vive Henri Quatre'.

Le siège de Corinthe
The Siege of Corinth
Tragédie lyrique in three acts (2h 30m)
Libretto by Luigi Balocchi and Alexandre Soumet, after Cesare della Valle's libretto (1820) for Rossini's *Maometto II*
PREMIERES 9 October 1826, Théâtre de l'Académie Royale

de Musique, Paris; US: 6 February 1833, Italian Opera
House, New York; UK: 5 June 1834, King's Theatre,
Haymarket, London
CAST   Mahomet II *b*, Cléomène *t*, Pamira *s*, Néoclès *t*,
Hiéros *b*, Adraste *t*, Omar *t*, Ismène *s*; *satb* chorus of
Turks, Greeks, Muslims

For his first encounter with the audience of the
Théâtre de l'Académie Royale de Musique, home of
French opera, Rossini faced the task of developing an
original synthesis, firmly based in the Italian manner
yet appropriate for the French stage, to rouse the
ailing Opéra from its torpor. Having to learn French
and master the intricacies of its declamation, Rossini
approached this task circumspectly. He reserved two
Neapolitan works for adaptation to the French stage,
withholding them from production at the Théâtre
Italien during his tenure as director. Thus *Maometto
II* became *Le siège de Corinthe*, and *Mosè in Egitto*
became *Moïse*.

SYNOPSIS
Following the plan of *Maometto II* with the place,
time, names of characters, and some plot details
changed, the opera relates the victory of the Turks
over the Greeks at Corinth in 1459.

   Act I   Cléomène, governor of Corinth, has promised the hand of his daughter, Pamira, to the young
officer Néoclès, but Pamira is in love with a man
named Almanzor whom she knew in Athens. When
the Turks enter the city, Mahomet confides to his
friend, Omar, that his thoughts still dwell on the
Greek girl he met while travelling under the name of
Almanzor. The remainder of the first act follows the
events of Act I of *Maometto II*.

   Act II   Pamira, in Mahomet's tent awaiting her
wedding, prays to her dead mother for guidance.
Ismène, her confidante, arrives with women who joyfully anticipate the wedding, dancing and singing a
marriage hymn. Néoclès tries to prevent the wedding;
the Greek battle call interrupts, and Pamira, leaving
with Néoclès, swears she will die with her own
people.

   Act III   Néoclès brings Pamira to her father in the
catacombs, where the Greeks have prepared their last
defence. When the victorious Turks burst in, Pamira
stabs herself. Flames engulf the stage, for the Greeks
have set fire to their city, leaving only ruins to the
conquerors.

In *Maometto II* extremely florid vocal lines coexist
with experiments in musical structure. In *Le siège de
Corinthe* both extremes are planed down, resulting in
a more consistent, if less audacious, dramatic continuum and a reduced gulf between declamatory lines
and florid passages. In some reworked passages much
of the original vocal splendour is lost. Similarly modifying the bolder structural experiments, Rossini eliminated internal sections from the 'terzettone' of
Maometto II, leaving a truncated and conventional
residue. In the solo arias for Mahomet, Pamira and
Néoclès he adapted essentially Italian material.
   In the newly composed music Rossini continued to
explore larger units combining solo voices and chorus
more dramatically. The scene in which Hiéros blesses

the soon-to-be-martyred Greek warriors is particularly
impressive. *Le siège de Corinthe* also features much
ceremonial music in the Parisian style: dances, hymns,
choruses, and a brilliantly scored overture.

Moïse et Pharaon, ou Le passage de la Mer Rouge

Moses and Pharaoh, or The Passage through the Red Sea
Opera in four acts (2h 30m)
Libretto by Luigi Balocchi and Étienne de Jouy, after
Andreas Leone Tottola's libretto (1818 and 1819) for *Mosè
in Egitto*
PREMIERES   26 March 1827, Théâtre de l'Académie Royale
de Musique, Paris; UK: 20 April 1850, Covent Garden,
London (as *Zora*); US: 7 May 1860, Academy of Music,
New York
CAST   Moïse (Moses) *b*, Pharaon (Pharaoh) *b*, Aménophis
(Amenophis) *t*, Eliézer (Aaron) *t*, Osiride (Osiris) *b*, Aufide
t, Sinaïde (Sinais) *s*, Elcia *s*, Marie *s*, A Mysterious Voice *b*;
satb chorus of Egyptians and Israelites

Mosè in Egitto was already known in Paris in its
revised version. The original three-act libretto by Tottola, in its 1819 adaptation, was extended to four acts
by the French revisers, who expanded the original
action, placed the Italian pieces (supplied with French
texts) within this grander context, and provided both
appropriate dramatic situations for new musical numbers and connecting recitative. Rossini supervised their
work, suppressing the more old-fashioned numbers of
Mosè in Egitto, while carrying over unchanged the
finest music.

SYNOPSIS
The plot of *Moïse* is similar to that of *Mosè in Egitto*
(see above), but the names of some characters differ
and additional episodes have been inserted.

   Act I   Moses and the Israelites await the return of
his brother, Aaron, who has gone to Pharaoh to
plead the Israelite cause. Pharaoh's son, Amenophis,
is in love with Elcia, daughter of the sister of Moses.

   Act II   This begins with the opening scene of *Mosè
in Egitto*. Pharaoh agrees to permit the Israelite departure, and Queen Sinais persuades Amenophis to marry
the princess of Assyria.

   Act III   An extended ballet divertissement occurs
in the Temple of Isis, where Osiris, the high priest,
demands that the Israelites pay homage to the goddess. Pharaoh orders the Israelites bound and expelled
from Egypt.

   Act IV   In the desert near the Red Sea, Amenophis
tells Elcia he will give up the throne if she will marry
him. Elcia chooses to follow her people; Amenophis
warns that Pharaoh will attack them and goes to join
his father. On the shores of the sea, Moses leads the
anxious people in prayer. The sea divides and the
Israelites cross over. When the pursuing Egyptians
attempt to follow, they are drowned.

Moïse has a more consistent score than its model, but
the addition of so much spectacle for Paris weakens
the dramatic effect of the work. However strong the
new choral opening, transposing the scene of 'darkness' to the beginning of Act II was a strategic error.
But Elcia's Act IV aria ('Quelle horrible destinée') is a

superb addition to the score. One of the most interesting revisions affects Elcia's aria from *Mosè in Egitto*, which is placed in a profoundly different dramatic context in *Moïse*. In *Mosè in Egitto* Elcia pleads with Osiris to marry the Armenian princess and to let her depart with her people. When Osiris threatens to kill Moses, a bolt of lightning strikes him down; Elcia's cabaletta expresses her despair. In *Moïse* the piece is sung by Sinais, the Egyptian queen and mother of Amenophis (Osiris in *Mosè in Egitto*). She makes the same plea as did Elcia, but now the prince acquiesces, so that the final cabaletta, whose music is essentially unchanged, expresses Sinais' joy. That it functions well in both contexts is a measure of Rossini's belief that music is 'ideal' in its expression, not imitative of particular emotions.

Le comte Ory
Count Ory
Opéra [comique] in two acts (2h 15m)
Libretto by Eugène Scribe and Charles Gaspard Delestre-Poirson, after their own play (1816), based on a medieval ballad
PREMIERES 20 August 1828, Théâtre de l'Académie Royale de Musique, Paris; UK: 28 February 1829, King's Theatre, Haymarket, London; US: 22 August 1831, Park Theater, New York
CAST Count Ory *t*, The Tutor *bar*, Isolier *ms*, Raimbaud *bar*, Adèle, Countess of Formoutiers *s*, Ragonde *ms*, Alice *s*, Two Knights *t*, *bar*; *satb* chorus of Ory's men, ladies, Crusaders, peasants

About half of Rossini's music for *Il viaggio a Reims* resurfaced in *Le comte Ory*. How should one think about an opera in which such a large proportion of the music derives, essentially without change, from a work whose substance is entirely different? How should one think about an opera in which the confusion of identity extends so far as to present a tenor disguised as a woman who thinks he is making love to a soprano, when in fact he is making love to a contralto in the role of a man who takes the place of the soprano?

If gender is a problem in the libretto, genre is problematic concerning the opera as a whole. Superficially *Le comte Ory* might seem to be an opéra comique. That it was conceived not for the Théâtre de l'Opéra-Comique but for the Opéra, however, transforms it. Whereas a typical opéra comique consists of relatively short lyrical numbers separated by spoken dialogue, *Le comte Ory* is made up of highly developed, even massive, musical forms, linked by accompanied recitative. Whereas the orchestration of a contemporary typical opéra comique is relatively light, Rossini's forces are large. Despite the Italianate forms of many of its lyrical numbers, the use of accompanied recitative was at odds with the Italian practice of *secco* recitative for comic operas. Furthermore, there is no hint of buffoonish characters, no exaggeratedly rapid declamation. Instead, *Le comte Ory* sparkles with Gallic wit, grace and charm.

In the medieval ballad, Count Ory and his men give siege to nuns in a convent; their notable success became evident nine months later. Scribe and Delestre-Poirson created a one-act vaudeville first performed in Paris in 1816, changing the nuns to ladies whose husbands are away on a Crusade; the Crusaders return before Count Ory and his men achieve their goal. This becomes essentially Act II of the opera. Act I presents events that are described in an air at the beginning of the vaudeville. The librettists grafted a first act to the vaudeville, arranging the action and poetry so that Rossini's music from *Il viaggio a Reims* could be reused. They were also compelled by the enormous differences between the two genres to rewrite the text of their vaudeville, accommodating another two numbers from *Il viaggio a Reims*. Little wonder they originally declined to have their names on the printed libretto! Yet, despite its difficult birth, *Le comte Ory* works splendidly.

SYNOPSIS
The opera takes place *c.* 1200 in and around the castle of the counts of Formoutiers.
Act I The men are on a Crusade, and their wives have taken a vow of chastity and locked themselves in the castle. In order to court the beautiful Countess Adèle, Count Ory disguises himself as a hermit said to specialize in affairs of the heart, and his friend Raimbaud stirs up interest among the local people. Ragonde, stewardess of the castle, announces that her mistress wishes to consult him ('Jouvencelles, venez vite'). The count's tutor, together with his page Isolier, arrives in search of him. Hearing about the hermit, the tutor becomes suspicious ('Veiller sans cesse'). Isolier, not recognizing his master, seeks advice from the 'hermit' about gaining Adèle's love. When he reveals his plan to penetrate the castle disguised as a female pilgrim, Ory decides to adopt the plan himself ('Une dame de haut parage'). Adèle comes to consult the hermit, who advises her to distrust the page of the notorious Count Ory (Isolier), with whom she confesses to be half in love ('En proie à la tristesse'). The tutor recognizes the count and unmasks him ('Ciel! Ô terreur, ô peine extrême'). A letter arrives announcing the successful conclusion of the Crusade: Adèle's brother and the knights will be home the next day. The ladies invite Ory to celebrate with them, but he resolves to use the time remaining to devise another plan to conquer Adèle.
Act II Within the walls of the castle, the women await their men's return, thankful at having escaped Ory's wiles ('Dans ce séjour calme et tranquille'). Outside a storm is raging and cries of distress are heard. Pilgrim women say they are being threatened by Ory. 'Soeur Colette', who turns out to be the count in disguise, thanks Adèle profusely ('Ah! quel respect, Madame'). Left alone, the 'pilgrim women' revel ('Ah! la bonne folie!'); having discovered the wine cellar, Raimbaud provides wine for all ('Dans ce lieu solitaire'), and they sing a lively drinking song ('Buvons, buvons'). Isolier arrives and reveals the hoax to Adèle. Taking advantage of the darkness of her bedroom, Adèle hides behind Isolier; 'Soeur Colette', deceived by her voice, makes advances to the page, whom he mistakes for the countess (trio 'À la faveur de cette nuit obscure'). When trumpets announce the return of the Crusaders, Count Ory and his men are forced to flee ('Écoutez ces chants de victoire').

From *Il viaggio a Reims* Rossini salvaged numbers that could be transferred most easily to other dramatic situations. The introduction is from *Viaggio*, though the short overture is new; part of the air of the tutor is derived from Lord Sidney's aria; the countess's air from the countess of Folleville's aria; the first finale from the 'Gran Pezzo Concertato'; the duet between the count and the countess from that between Corinna and Belfiore; Raimbaud's air from Don Profondo's. Only a single piece in Act I of *Le comte Ory* is entirely new: the duet for Ory and Isolier. In Act II, however, Rossini reused only two compositions from *Viaggio*.

Although the borrowed numbers are artfully adapted to their new surroundings, there are losses. The carefully wrought structure of Don Profondo's aria, where parallel strophes describe different characters, seems arbitrary as the musical setting for Raimbaud's narrative of his discovery of the castle's wine cellar. But most situations, while different in detail, are structurally and emotionally similar. When the drama or characters are markedly different, Rossini intervened: for the tutor, he altered the first section of Lord Sidney's aria, whose sentimentality was ill-suited to the new laments, and made changes in the cabaletta (adding, for example, the canonic obbligato for flute and clarinet in the repetition of the theme).

The jewels of the score are the pieces Rossini prepared directly for *Le comte Ory*. The choral songs for the count and his followers, as pilgrims, are spirited in tone and subtle in their musical realization. The original ballad tune, heard twice before in the opera, becomes the central episode of the drinking chorus. The Act II trio is magical in the nocturnal and insinuating quality of the opening section, its delicate orchestral shading, its erotic chromaticism, the shifting pairings of the voices. Rossini has centred the drama in the sexual and musical shadows, disguises, and illusions of his score.

Guillaume Tell
William Tell

Opera in four acts (3h 45m)
Libretto by Étienne de Jouy and Hippolyte Louis-Florent Bis, with additions by Armand Marrast and Adolph Crémieux, after the play *Wilhelm Tell* by Johann Christoph Friedrich von Schiller (1804)
PREMIERES 3 August 1829, Théâtre de l'Académie Royale de Musique, Paris; UK: 1 May 1830, Drury Lane, London (as *Hofer, or The Tell of the Tyrol*); US: 19 September 1831, Park Theater, New York
CAST Guillaume Tell *bar*, Arnold *t*, Walter *b*, Melchthal *b*, Jemmy *s*, Gesler *b*, Rodolphe *t*, Ruodi *t*, Leuthold *b*, Mathilde *s*, Hedwige *c*, Huntsman *b*; *satb* chorus of Swiss, huntsmen, soldiers

With *Guillaume Tell* Rossini finally offered Parisian audiences an original opera in French. It was intended to initiate his true career as a French composer, after his years at the Théâtre Italien and his earlier arrangements at the Opéra. During the months preceding the premiere he struggled to obtain two long-term commitments from the French government: a lifetime annuity and a ten-year contract.

Rossini wove into the historical panorama of *Guillaume Tell* pastoral elements, patriotic deeds (much in

vogue on the eve of the revolutionary wave soon to sweep Europe), and superbly drawn characters. Yet the development of the libretto, freely derived from Schiller's play, was tormented. The original draft by Étienne de Jouy underwent considerable alteration at various hands. Finally, changes were made during the long rehearsal period and even after the premiere. Some were incorporated into printed editions of the opera (in preparation before the first performance). Others survived in manuscripts of the opera; they have been reconstructed for the critical edition.

What is most fascinating about *Guillaume Tell*, however, is the imaginative way in which its composer responded to the challenge of creating a work for the French Opéra without abandoning his Italian roots. Though certain elements are more 'Italian', others more 'French', it is the combination of these elements that is extraordinary. More than in any other work, Rossini integrates the bel-canto lyricism and formal refinement of Italian opera with the declamatory immediacy and scenic splendour (the latter expressed in extensive choruses and ballet) characteristic of French opera. The grandiose structure, finally, is tied together with a system of musical motifs derived from popular Swiss melodies known as *ranz des vaches*.

SYNOPSIS

Act I The action takes place in medieval Switzerland. The villagers at Bürglen, in the canton of Uri, anticipate a triple wedding, the culmination of their traditional festival ('Quel jour serein le ciel présage!'). A fisherman serenades his beloved, while Guillaume Tell laments the tyrannical rule of the Austrians and their governor, Gesler. Melchthal, patriarch of the village, urges his son Arnold to think of marriage, but Arnold, who serves in the Austrian garrison, loves the Habsburg princess Mathilde. Distant horns announce the governor's hunt. As Arnold seeks to rush off to join Mathilde, Tell reappears. He tries to gain Arnold's support against the increasingly oppressive Austrian rule ('Où vas-tu?'). Arnold swears to join Tell when the moment to strike arrives. Melchthal blesses the couples. The festivities proceed with songs, dances and an archery contest, which Jemmy (Tell's son) wins. His triumph is interrupted by Leuthold, an old herdsman. He has killed an Austrian soldier who was trying to rape his daughter. While Tell ferries Leuthold across the dangerous rapids, Austrian soldiers arrive ('Dieu de bonté'). The Swiss refuse to identify the ferryman; Rodolphe, the commander of the Austrian troops, drags Melchthal away as a hostage and orders the soldiers to loot the village.

Act II In the dusk, huntsmen pass ('Quelle sauvage harmonie'), while villagers return to their homes. Mathilde muses on her feelings for Arnold ('Sombre forêt'). When he approaches, they declare their love ('Oui, vous l'arrachez à mon âme'). As Tell and Walter appear, Mathilde hurries off, having agreed to meet Arnold the next day. The men reveal that Gesler has murdered Melchthal; Arnold swears to avenge his father ('Quand l'Helvétie est un champ de supplices'). Representatives of the three cantons arrive. The patriots vow to throw off the Austrian yoke and gain their liberty ('Des profondeurs du bois immense').

Act III Meeting in a ruined chapel near Gesler's palace, Mathilde and Arnold bid each other farewell ('Pour notre amour, plus d'espérance'). In the main square at Altdorf, the townspeople celebrate Gesler's power ('Gloire au pouvoir suprême'), while the soldiers force the Swiss to sing and dance (*pas de trois*, 'Toi qui l'oiseau', and *pas des soldats*) and to bow before a symbol of Gesler's authority. When Tell refuses to bow, Rodolphe recognizes him as the man who saved Leuthold ('C'est là cet archer redoutable'). Having heard of Tell's skill as an archer, Gesler announces that he can save his life only by shooting an apple from Jemmy's head: otherwise, father and son will die together. Sustained by his son's courage, Tell shoots his arrow through the apple ('Sois immobile'). In the general relief that follows, Tell drops a second arrow, held in reserve for Gesler should his first arrow have killed his son. Tell is thrown into chains, but Mathilde takes Jemmy under her own protection. When Gesler orders that Tell be transported across Lake Lucerne and thrown to the reptiles living in the waters of Küssnacht Castle, the riotous reaction of the Swiss is barely contained by the soldiers.

Act IV Arnold visits his birthplace ('Asile héréditaire'). His companions announce that Tell is a prisoner. Arnold shows them where his father and Tell concealed arms for the day of insurrection. Hedwige is about to beg mercy from Gesler, when Mathilde arrives with Jemmy. The princess offers herself as a hostage in return for Tell. The storm breaks. Leuthold reports that Tell's captors have freed his hands, since he alone can control the boat in the storm. Jemmy gives the signal for the revolt. Tell reaches the shore and, with a bow handed to him by Jemmy, kills Gesler. Arnold and his forces capture the castle of Altdorf. As the storm subsides, the Swiss join in a prayer of thanksgiving for the liberation of their country ('Tout change et grandit en ces lieux').

Carefully written, harmonically daring, melodically purged of ornamentation, orchestrally opulent, *Guillaume Tell* represents a final purification of Rossini's style. Ensembles dominate, and the interests of the drama are well served. The great overture is unabashedly programmatic, and Rossini's orchestral palette is fuller than ever before. The extensive spectacular elements, ballets, and processions, which derive from French operatic tradition, are effectively integrated into the opera.

Many parts of *Guillaume Tell* adhere to Italian structures, most obviously the duet for Mathilde and Arnold in Act II, Mathilde's aria at the opening of Act III, and Arnold's aria in Act IV – all three part of the dramatically ancillary sub-plot. Also frankly Italianate in design is the Act I finale, whose action comes into focus in two major ensemble movements. Within these structures, however, the music remains highly responsive to details of the drama.

Already during his Neapolitan years Rossini had begun integrating French elements into his style: concern with declamation, spectacle, chorus and dance. In *Tell* the recitative is extremely powerful, blending into passionate yet lyrical declamation, enhanced by a consistently rich orchestral texture. This happens especially in complex scenes, such as the Act III finale (including Tell's admonishment to his son) and the concluding scene of the opera. The chorus is central both musically and dramatically, and much of the opera revolves about magnificent choral ensembles such as 'Vierge que les chrétiens adorent' in the Act I finale, or the final ensemble. Some of these choruses are part of large-scale divertissements with ballet.

Act II was particularly appreciated by Rossini's contemporaries, even by hostile critics such as Berlioz. He found 'sublime' the finale, in which the three Swiss cantons, each characterized musically, are called together to plan the revolt. The chorus is the central protagonist of *Guillaume Tell*: the fate of the Swiss people is the subject of the drama. Rossini's quotation and transformation of popular Swiss tunes throughout the melodic fabric of the entire work give it a strong, unified colour. The whole opera is a rich tapestry of Rossini's most inspired music.

Other operatic works: *Demetrio e Polibio*, (before 1809), 1812; *La cambiale di matrimonio*, 1810; *L'equivoco stravagante*, 1811; *L'inganno felice*, 1812; *Ciro in Babilonia, ossia La caduta di Baldassare*, 1812; *L'occasione fa il ladro*, 1812; *Il Signor Bruschino, ossia Il figlio per azzardo*, 1813; *Aureliano in Palmira*, 1813; *Sigismondo*, 1814; *Torvaldo e Dorliska*, 1815; *La gazzetta*, 1816; *Adelaide di Borgogna*, 1817; *Adina, o Il califfo di Bagdad*, 1826; *Ricciardo e Zoraide* 1818; *Eduardo e Cristina*, 1819; *Bianca e Falliero, o sia Il consiglio dei Tre*, 1819; *Matilde (di) Shabran, o sia Bellezza, e cuor di ferro*, 1821; *Zelmira*, 1822

P.G. and P.B.B.

ALBERT ROUSSEL

Albert Charles Paul Marie Roussel; *b* 5 April 1869, Tourcoing, France; *d* 23 August 1937, Royan, France

When Roussel decided to take up music as a profession he was 25, a naval officer with service at home and in the Far East. After leaving the navy, he studied with Eugène Gigout in Paris before joining the Schola Cantorum for a long period of tuition under Vincent d'Indy, during which he himself became a teacher of counterpoint. In 1909 Roussel and his wife made a private journey to India and Indo-China. During the war, prevented by ill health from rejoining the navy, he served in the Red Cross and in the army until he was invalided out in 1918. From 1922 Roussel lived at Varengeville in Normandy, writing a steady stream of music, active as a public figure with 'a strong sense of social responsibility' (Basil Deane). He was president of the music section of the 1937 Paris International Exhibition. His 60th birthday in 1929 was marked by a festival in Paris.

Roussel occupies an independent position between the Schola Cantorum and the Impressionists – the respective worlds of César Franck and d'Indy, Debussy and Ravel. While in his later works the search for clarity and concision led to a form of neo-classicism, he did not lose the hyper-sensitive gift for atmosphere conspicuous in the earlier orchestral works.

Prominent features in his music are astringent, sometimes harsh, harmony and a fondness for motoric rhythms. Sensitivity is balanced by a robust strain possibly deriving from his Franco-Flemish background.

The stage works reveal a strong attraction to mixed genres with a desire to tackle new problems rather than to repeat himself. Of the two hybrids, *Padmâvatî*, though described as an opera-ballet, is less close to Lully and Rameau than the conte lyrique *La naissance de la lyre*. When he died, Roussel was planning a large-scale multi-media spectacle for actors, singers and dancers on the subject of Charles the Bold, duke of Burgundy. The most conventional of his operas is the third, *Le testament de la tante Caroline*, designated opéra bouffe. Roussel wrote three ballets: *Le festin de l'araignée* (*The Spider's Banquet*) (1913), *Bacchus et Ariane* (1931) and the choral *Aenéas* (1935). Nontheatrical music includes four symphonies, several other orchestral works, *Psalm 80* (choral), chamber music and songs.

Padmâvatî

Opera-ballet in two acts (1h 30m)
Libretto by Louis Laloy
Composed 1914–18
PREMIERES 1 June 1923, Opéra, Paris; UK: 6 July 1969, Coliseum, London (concert)
CAST Padmâvatî *c*, Nakamti *ms*, Ratan-Sen *t*, Alaouddin *bar*, The Brahmin *t*, Gora *bar*, Badal *t*, 3 *s*, *c*, 3 *t*, *bar*, *b*; *satb* chorus of warriors, priests, women of the palace, populace

The origins of *Padmâvatî* lie in a visit to the ruins of Chitor in Rajasthan during Roussel's eastern journey of 1909. A few years later the critic and orientalist Laloy devised a libretto out of local legends concerning Chitor. The short score was ready before the outbreak of the First World War; the orchestration was finished after Roussel's demobilization. The work, intended to inaugurate Jacques Rouché's directorship of the Opéra, was not given until 1923. The exotic tradition in French music, present at least from the time of Rameau, erupted towards the end of the 19th century under the stimulus of the Universal Exhibition of 1889. Unlike Debussy and others, Roussel had the advantage of first-hand experience. In *Padmâvatî* his use of Hindu scales suits his harmony, more complex and acrid here than in previous scores.

SYNOPSIS

Act I The 13th-century siege of the Hindu city of Chitor by the Mogul sultan Alaouddin has reached stalemate. Alaouddin comes in person to discuss peace with Chitor's ruler, Ratan-Sen. Their meeting is polite but inconclusive. Alaouddin asks to be shown the city's splendours, adding that he prefers flesh and blood to the marvels of stone. Ratan-Sen shows off his warriors, then his dancing girls. Aware that these are foreign slaves, Alaouddin demands to see the palace women. While he praises their charms, he inquires slyly after Ratan-Sen's queen, Padmâvatî, famed equally for her beauty and her virtue. Unwillingly Ratan-Sen allows the queen to appear on a balcony and, at Alaouddin's insistence, permits her to unveil. Alaouddin departs without concluding a pact. His Brahmin counsellor remains behind. The crowd, recognizing him as a malefactor who had fled the city, kills him. Padmâvatî comes down to the deserted square, sees the body, and is filled with foreboding.

Act II Negotiations have broken down. The Moguls are attacking the city. Padmâvatî and her companions have taken refuge in the Temple of Siva. Ratan-Sen appears, wounded. There is a truce until dawn. Padmâvatî assures him she will die with him. Ratan-Sen has vowed to Siva to save his people: if Padmâvatî will not consent to give herself to the conqueror, the people will be massacred. She indignantly refuses. When Ratan-Sen tries to compel her to obedience she stabs him, preferring the widow's death by burning dictated by their religion to eternal shame. A long ceremony follows during which spirit deities emanating from Siva threaten and coax Padmâvatî. Finally she is allowed to descend to the funeral pyre. When the temple doors are broken down and Alaouddin appears, all he finds is smoke rising from the crypt.

The big dance scenes (the parading of the warriors, dancers and palace women in Act I, and the funeral rites in Act II) arise directly out of the action. The mood is dark, urgent and sinister, relieved only by the lyrical descriptions of Padmâvatî's beauty by the Brahmin and by a girl in the crowd, Nakamti. By French standards of the time the orchestral writing had unusual density. In spite of its high reputation among musicians, *Padmâvatî*, which needs a large company and considerable outlay, has had few stagings. Concert performances, sometimes of Act II only, have been more frequent. The score must be classed among the major achievements of French opera in the present century.

Other operatic works: *La naissance de la lyre*, 1925; *Le testament de la tante Caroline*, 1936

R.H.C.

CAMILLE SAINT-SAËNS
Charles Camille Saint-Saëns; *b* 9 October 1835, Paris;
d 16 December 1921, Algiers

The career of Saint-Saëns, one of the most gifted and
versatile musicians of the 19th century, whose accomplishments were solid as well as brilliant, covered a
momentous span of musical history. Born the year
before the premiere of Meyerbeer's *Les Huguenots*, he
died when Berg had nearly completed *Wozzeck* and
Britten was a schoolboy. At the age of ten Saint-Saëns
made his début as a pianist in Paris playing concertos
by Mozart and Beethoven. His last public appearance
took place in Dieppe 75 years later. His first numbered
symphony was written when he was 18. His last works,
the three woodwind sonatas, were written in the final
year of his life.

In between, Saint-Saëns was unremittingly active as
composer and in other capacities. He was a much
travelled concert pianist, organist (notably at the
Madeleine church in Paris), author, teacher (not at
the Conservatoire where he had studied but at the
École Niedermeyer in Paris) and scholar, who did
much to make Mozart's music known in France and
was general editor of the complete edition of Rameau.
As composer he produced over the years five symphonies, sacred and secular choral works, numerous concertos and concerted works, four orchestral tone
poems, and a quantity of chamber music and songs.
To his regret his operas, with the exception of *Samson
et Dalila*, failed to win the success he achieved in
other, by Parisian standards less important, fields.
Including his part (with Dukas) in the completion of
Ernest Guiraud's unfinished *Frédégonde*, Saint-Saëns
wrote 13 operas, two of them opéras comiques. There
were in addition a ballet, *Javotte*, incidental music for
several plays and a film score. As a widely cultivated
man he understood what was wanted, yet with all his
competence and experience he lacked the 'nose', the
instinct of the theatre animal granted, for example, to
Massenet, who in other forms of music was his inferior. His choice of libretti showed more education than
flair, yet he skilfully adapted the procedures of grand
opera to the needs of the period between the death of
Meyerbeer and the conquest of France by Wagner.
The operatic music of Saint-Saëns by and large has
the same strengths and weaknesses as the rest – lucid-
ity, Mozartian transparency, greater care for form
than for content. His facility, a quality misprized by
those who lack it, tempted him to accept ideas good
or bad, often memorable if rarely profound, as they
came to him. There is a certain emotional dryness;
invention is sometimes thin, but the workmanship is
impeccable.

Samson et Dalila
Samson and Delilah
Opera in three acts (four tableaux) (2h)
Libretto by Ferdinand Lemaire, based on the Old Testament
story (Judges 16)
Composed 1868–77
PREMIERES 2 December 1877, Grand Ducal Theatre,
Weimar; US: 25 March 1892, New York (concert);
4 January 1893, French Opera House, New Orleans;
UK: 25 September 1893, Covent Garden, London (concert);
26 April 1909, Covent Garden
CAST Dalila (Delilah) *ms*, Samson *t*, High Priest of
Dagon *bar*, Abimélech (Abimelech) *b*, An Old Hebrew *b*,
A Philistine Messenger *t*, First Philistine *t*, Second Philistine
b; *satb* chorus of Hebrews and Philistines

Saint-Saëns, who had experience of the English oratorio tradition and shared the national admiration for
Mendelssohn's *Elijah*, intended to use the biblical
story of Samson's betrayal and death for an oratorio.
His librettist, Ferdinand Lemaire, sensing theatrical
possibilities, suggested an opera. Musical friends
showed little enthusiasm for the first passages the
composer tried out on them. On a visit early in 1870
to Liszt in Weimar, Saint-Saëns spoke of his dis-
couragement. Liszt, the champion of the new and
unfamiliar, offered, if Saint-Saëns finished *Samson*, to
produce it in Weimar. Owing to the outbreak of the
Franco-Prussian War and local difficulties, Liszt
could not keep that promise until 1877. Meanwhile
there had been no takers in France. The singer Pauline
Viardot organized a private performance in Paris of
Act II at which she sang Dalila and the composer
played the orchestral part on the piano, but the audience, including the director of the Opéra, remained
unconvinced: the biblical subject would not do.
Rameau and Voltaire had had similar difficulties 150
years earlier with a projected *Samson*. There was a
public concert performance of the first act at the
Châtelet theatre in 1875, but the opera was not performed on the French stage until 3 March 1890, at the
Théâtre des Arts at Rouen. That production was
brought to Paris, not to the Opéra but to the nearby

Théâtre Eden, in October the same year. The Opéra was at last emboldened to accept *Samson*, and it was first seen there on 23 November 1892 with Blanche Deschamps-Jehin, Edmond Vergnet and Jean Lassalle, conductor Édouard Colonne. (Viardot, for whom the role of Dalila was designed, and to whom the opera is dedicated, was now over 70.) Success with the general public in Paris was great and prolonged, but was overshadowed for progressives by the vogue for Wagner. Audiences outside Paris, however, were enthralled: *Samson* became one of the most widely popular of operas.

SYNOPSIS

Act I   A public place at Gaza, before the Temple of Dagon. The Hebrews lament their subjugation by the Philistines. They fear their God has forsaken them. Samson, claiming that God speaks through his mouth ('Arrêtez, ô mes frères!'), attempts to raise their spirits. The satrap Abimelech rebukes the Hebrews for praying to the wrong deity – Dagon would help them. His words incite Samson and the Hebrews to a fervent outburst ('Israël! Romps ta chaîne!'). Abimelech attacks Samson, who slays him. The Hebrews melt away as the temple gates open, revealing the high priest of Dagon, heavily guarded. As he scolds his followers for showing fear, a messenger brings news of an uprising among the Hebrews. The high priest curses Israel. Ready to celebrate the turn of events, Delilah and a group of priestesses advance, ostensibly to crown the victor Samson. Vowing that he reigns in her heart, she beseeches him to visit her again in her lonely dwelling. An old Hebrew warns Samson against the wiles of Delilah. As she dances among her priestesses, the troubled Samson is compelled against his will to follow her voluptuous movements. She sings provocatively ('Printemps qui commence') of her nocturnal vigil, waiting for the hero.

Act II   Outside Delilah's house in the valley of Sorek. Night is falling and a storm is brewing. Delilah, sensing Samson's perplexity, calls on Love to help her ('Amour! Viens aider ma faiblesse!'). Her first visitor is the high priest, to inform her that, since the Israelites have recaptured the city, the downfall of Samson is essential. He offers Delilah money, which she refuses, and reminds her that her previous encounter with the hero had not brought his total submission. She admits that her attempts to prise from him the secret of his strength were unsuccessful. She is their only hope, the high priest assures her; through her, Samson must be enslaved and die. When the coast is clear, Samson steals in, the more shamefully because God has smiled on the Hebrews. This must be the lovers' farewell. Delilah dismisses thoughts of Israel's fate and invokes a more powerful god – Love. Samson dares the lightning to strike him down as he confesses his love. Delilah demands total surrender ('Mon coeur s'ouvre à ta voix') adding that he must entrust her with his secret. Assuming that the thunder is the voice of God, Samson refuses, but finally follows her indoors. Philistine soldiers approach silently. Delilah signals to them to enter the house.

Act III   Tableau 1: The prison in Gaza. Blinded, his hair shorn, Samson turns the treadmill ('Vois ma misère, hélas') while Hebrew voices are heard bemoaning his apparent betrayal of them and their God for a woman's charms. Tableau 2: Interior of the Temple of Dagon, with two marble columns in the centre. A celebration is in progress. The high priest, Delilah and their followers watch a bacchanal. Samson is led in by a small boy. The high priest mocks the hero's weakness. Delilah reminds him of her successful extraction of his secret (the nature of this secret is never revealed in words). At the sacrificial table they invoke their god ('Gloire à Dagon vainqueur!'). A flame appears, signifying the god's presence. The high priest commands Samson to kneel and worship. Samson asks the boy to lead him to the two columns, prays to God to give him back his old strength, and, pushing the columns outwards, brings the temple roof crashing down.

Lemaire's libretto is an intelligent compression of the established five-act formula of Meyerbeerian grand opera. The customary spectacle and ballets form a logical part of the action. The clash between the austere Hebrews and the pleasure-loving Philistines is kept well in the foreground. In Act I the entry of Delilah and her maidens brings refreshment after the Hebrews' lament and Samson's killing of Abimelech. In Act III the pathetic scene of Samson at the treadmill is followed by the appropriately superficial tinklings of Philistine rejoicing. Saint-Saëns made use of his knowledge of the classics: Bach (experienced perhaps through Mendelssohn) goes mainly to the Hebrews, Handel (his light, pagan side) to the Philistines, for instance in the canonic duet for the high priest and Delilah in Act II. In Act II the conflict is left to the protagonists. In the interview between Delilah and her master, Saint-Saëns works short, jagged instrumental phrases in a manner that makes one understand how theatre people in the 1870s were put off by the 'symphonic' nature of the writing in addition to the, to them, unacceptable subject matter. The symphonic aspect blinded them to the attraction of the set numbers. The eventual popularity of these numbers, pulled out of context and ground out by café orchestras, diverted serious musicians from the score's finer qualities. The orchestration is masterly throughout, especially in the second act where the dramatic tension is heightened by the sultry atmosphere – a summer storm circling round and breaking at the climax, the cooing of doves transformed into rushing storm scales.

The character of Delilah is carefully drawn. Each of her three arias adds something. The first is the most purely feminine. The second is an appeal for help and reassurance. In the third, Delilah, who has Samson in her power but still has not discovered his secret, gives him the full works. One may doubt her professions of love. Any tender feelings she may harbour disappear once he is helpless. Her gloating over him at this point and her earlier refusal of the high priest's offer of money imply that patriotism is a motive but, although as an expert she may appreciate Samson's physique, deeper feelings than endangered *amour propre* seem unlikely.

Henry VIII

Opera in four acts (3h)
Libretto by Léonce Détroyat and Armand Silvestre
Composed 1883; rev. as three-act version, 1889; full version restored, 1909
PREMIERES 5 March 1883, Opéra, Paris; UK: 14 July 1889, Covent Garden, London; US: 20 April 1974, New York

A slimmed-down grand historical opera about Henry's defiance of the pope, the annulment of his marriage to Catherine of Aragon, and his subsequent marriage to Anne Boleyn. Catherine, to save her rival Anne from the king's wrath, burns an incriminating love letter to her from the Spanish ambassador, Gomez. The music is of superior quality, the mood predominantly sombre. The portrait of Henry differs from the conventional view of 'bluff King Hal'. The opera can now be seen as a bridge between Meyerbeer and the serious French operas of the early 1890s. *Henry VIII* remained in the Opéra repertoire until 1919. The revival of interest in French opera has recently extended to this work in the US and elsewhere.

Other operas: *La princesse jaune*, 1872; *Le timbre d'argent*, 1877; *Étienne Marcel*, 1879; *Proserpine*, 1887; *Ascanio*, 1890; *Phryné*, 1893; *Frédégonde* (completion, with Dukas, of opera by Ernest Guiraud), 1895; *Les barbares*, 1901; *Hélène*, 1904; *L'ancêtre*, 1906; *Déjanire*, 1911

R.H.C.

AULIS SALLINEN

b 9 April 1935, Salmi, Finland

With four operas under his belt, Sallinen is firmly established as Finland's most successful composer for the stage. He was a leading figure in the national operatic renaissance of the 1970s, when 14 new works were staged in what is a small country with little operatic tradition; to a certain extent this was something of which Finnish composers took advantage, since the absence of tradition presupposed audiences without prejudice.

Sallinen studied in Helsinki with Aarre Merikanto and Joonas Kokkonen. Early preoccupation with atonality and orthodox serialism – in the 1950s still seen as the only true path – gradually gave way to a more personal, lyrical and tonal style. He has composed prolifically in all forms, chamber and symphonic music, oratorio as well as opera, and his music is melodious, colourfully yet fastidiously orchestrated, and notable for a certain sardonic wit that leavens his wholehearted commitment to the subjects he chooses for his operas. His compositional ancestors include Shostakovich and Bartók, as well as the inescapable Sibelius, but their influence is subsumed into a highly personal style. His use of melody is especially individual; his tunes are like coiled springs, full of tension based on small intervals whose latent energy is eventually released, or, as a Finnish commentator has put it,

a current bubbling through the winter ice gradually increasing in force. (Climate and landscape have always been crucial to Finnish composers.) He writes extremely rewardingly for the voice.

Sallinen's music does not always find favour with the sterner critics in his homeland, who see him as conservative if not reactionary, but his operas have all been heard abroad and he is one of his country's most persuasive cultural ambassadors.

The Red Line
Punainen viiva

Opera in two acts (1h 45m)
Libretto by the composer, based on the novel by Ilmari Kianto (1911)
PREMIERES 30 November 1978, Finnish National Opera, Helsinki; UK: 14 June 1979, Sadler's Wells, London; US: 27 April 1983, Metropolitan, New York
CAST Topi *bar*, Riika *s*, Puntarpää *t*, Simana Arhippaini *b*, Young Priest *bar*, Vicar *t*; *satb* chorus of country people

The Red Line is painfully direct in its dramaturgy and musical treatment, yet deeply embedded in the Finnish national experience. It is set at the time of the election of 1907; following the reverses of the Russo-Japanese War, Russification of Finland was relaxed and direct parliamentary elections were allowed – the first in Europe in which women were allowed the vote.

SYNOPSIS
Act I The action centres on a peasant family living at starvation level in a remote northern province. Topi finds the remains of a sheep eaten by a marauding bear, and swears to kill the bear when it awakes from hibernation. The tensions between Topi and his wife Riika caused by their struggle to feed themselves and their three children are painfully explored. Topi dreams of his application to the vicar for poor relief being turned down; the latter offers cheap burial for the children, since the three little corpses can be accommodated in a single coffin. Simana Arhippaini, a pedlar from Russia, passes by, bringing rumours of unrest; Topi returns from the village with news of something called social democracy – words he cannot even pronounce – which will solve all their problems. Husband and wife attend a political meeting, at which Puntarpää, a professional agitator, exhorts the barely literate villagers to draw a red line on their voting slips to usher in the golden age.

Act II Topi and his neighbours ponder how to register their votes: he has never held a pen in his life. They hear dogs barking at what they themselves cannot hear: the bear stirring in its sleep. On election day all proudly go to vote, brushing aside the protests of a young priest, who warns of social strife. While Topi is away earning money at a logging camp, Riika waits in vain for the changes promised by the agitator and looks on helplessly as her children die of malnutrition. Topi returns in time to bury them. News arrives that the election has been won. But the barking of the dogs and the lowing of Topi's one remaining cow indicate that the bear has awoken. Topi rushes out to do battle with it. Riika finds his corpse with his throat slit in a red line.

The greatest single strength of *The Red Line* lies in Sallinen's ability to write about inarticulate and under-privileged human beings without a hint of condescension, indeed with a compassion that suggests burning and furious identification. Despite the doom-laden narrative, this is not a depressing opera: Sallinen has Janáček's secret of using music to turn death and disaster into a celebration of the indomitability of the human spirit. The musical ideas have intense theatricality, from the use of stage brass and chorus to denote the ever-present bear, the catchy quasi-folktune of the Russian pedlar, or the searing funeral march to which Topi displays the corpses of his children to the audience, one by one. The political meeting is a virtuoso piece of operatic composition: the slithery clarinet tune to which the professional agitator insinuates his panaceas into the minds of his victims is gradually transformed into a march of undeniably stirring revolutionary fervour – this is operatic manipulation of audience emotion at its most insidious. *The Red Line* is one of the most immediately theatrical of all post-war operas, silencing through its sheer anger any critical reservations about its generally conservative musical idiom.

Kullervo

Opera in two acts (2h 30m)
Libretto by the composer, based on Runos 31–6 of the *Kalevala* and the play by Aleksis Kivi (1864)
PREMIERES US: 25 February 1992, Dorothy Chandler Pavilion, Los Angeles; Finland: 31 November 1993, Opera House, Helsinki
CAST Kullervo *bar*, Kimmo *t*, Kullervo's Mother *s*, Kalervo *b-bar*, Kullervo's Sister *s*, Unto *bar*, Unto's Wife *ms*, Blind Ballad-singer *bar*, Smith's Wife *ms*; *satb* chorus of observers

Kullervo was commissioned by the Finnish National Opera to open their new opera house in Helsinki; as the completion of the building was delayed, the company instead gave the premiere on tour in Los Angeles, as part of celebrations of the 75th anniversary of Finnish independence.

SYNOPSIS
The choral prologue describes wars between the tribes in which Kullervo's parents are slaughtered by his uncle, Unto.

Act I Kullervo and his friend Kimmo are slaves in his uncle Unto's household and, on discovering the identity of his parents' murderer, Kullervo swears vengeance. Unto resists his wife's urgings to kill the troublesome youth, and instead sells him to the blacksmith Ilmarinen. The smith's wife tries to seduce the inexperienced youth, taunts him for his lack of response, and bakes a stone in his bread on which he breaks the knife he inherited from his father. Kullervo murders her. Kimmo discovers that Kullervo's parents are not dead after all, and reunites the family. This is not a success: when his father, Kalervo, learns that his son is a murderer, he disowns and rejects him, but his mother cannot bear to lose her son a second time and begs him to stay.

Act II The blind ballad-singer describes in his 'Ballad of the Sister's Ravishing' how Kullervo met a beautiful girl and seduced her. When she discovered that they were brother and sister, she committed suicide. This makes it doubly impossible for Kullervo to stay in his parents' house; although his mother is prepared to forgive even this latest crime, he leaves, determined to take revenge on his uncle's tribe. His mother dies of grief, and his father commits suicide. Kullervo teams up with a gang of outlaws, and the slaughter of Unto's tribe is duly accomplished. Kullervo seeks out Kimmo, his last hope of human companionship, only to find that he has gone mad. Kullervo immolates himself.

All myths are interconnected: there are elements of Orestes and Siegmund in the character of Kullervo, a man raised to be alienated from society against a background of unrelenting violence and emotional trauma. 'Am I afraid of death?' he asks before immolating himself. 'It could not be worse than life. This is what the world has made of me.'

To tell this grisly tale Sallinen fined down his musical language to its essentials; it is a score at once sardonic, horror-struck and profoundly compassionate. The deliberately cheap yet insistently catchy pop-song setting of the 'Ballad of the Sister's Ravishing' is alienating in a peculiarly unsettling way, while the mother's song of love for her errant child is one of the most heartfelt passages in all Sallinen's operas. There is a prominent role for chorus, describing and commenting on the continuous acts of violence, at times recoiling in horror, at others – as in *Turandot* – conniving in them. In telling audiences how society creates monsters in its midst, Sallinen cannot possibly have known that within weeks of the premiere the Los Angeles riots would break out; that particular audience could not say that it hadn't been warned.

Other operas: *The Horseman (Ratsumies)*, 1975; *The King Goes Forth to France (Kuningas lahtee Ranskaan)*, 1984; *The Palace (Palatsi)*, 1995

R.M.

ALFRED SCHNITTKE
b 24 November 1934, Engels, Russia

Officially Russian, though of partly German and Jewish descent, Schnittke has, against considerable personal odds, recently become one of the best-known living composers. His relatively late move into opera is a cause of especial interest. Resident in Germany since 1990, he has over the last 30 years evolved a highly original style through a re-evaluation of musical modernism and extensive use of musical quotation. Though he has now seemingly abandoned direct quotation of music of the past, the invocation of popular forms – in particular the tango, which Schnittke usually manages to transform into an emblematic and forcefully personal statement – is crucial to the current work of a composer who represents post-modernism (the composer's own term is 'polystylism') at its most eloquent and serious, as well as often being delightfully entertaining. That Schnittke should feel the lure of opera appears due in part to his long experience of writing music for films, his chief living during the socialist-realist years. Schnittke's musical breakthrough is, happily, mirrored by political and other developments around him, so that what his fellow Russian composer Dimitri Silvestrov has called 'the genetic well of culture' can now be drawn on openly, and yet with increasing subtlety. The Faust cantata *Seid Nüchtern und Wachet* (1982) was a pilot project for what eventually became the opera *Historia von D. Johann Fausten*, premiered at the Hamburg State Opera in 1995.

Life with an Idiot

Zhizn' s idiotom
Opera in two acts (2h 30m)
Libretto by Viktor Yerofeyev, based on his own short story (1980)
Composed 1990–92
PREMIERES 13 April 1992, Het Muziektheater, Amsterdam; UK: 1 April 1995, Coliseum, London

Life with an Idiot tells of a married couple forced, through some unspecified misdemeanour, to share their flat with an idiot who can say only one word, 'Ech', but who, unlike the others, has a name, Vova. Initially, all goes reasonably well in the circumstances. But soon the idiot starts to create havoc around him, and eventually he even has sexual encounters with each of the couple in turn, leading, for the wife (whose increasing derangement is compounded by visions of Marcel Proust), first to an abortion and finally to her murder at Vova's hands, possibly with the approval of her husband, who at the close commits himself to the asylum from which the idiot came.

The premiere production, directed by the 80-year-old Boris Pokrovsky, interpreted this as an allegory of life in the former Soviet Union, with the idiot not merely the dupe but the architect of a situation that renders normal life impossible. The opera is notable for bringing the full panoply of Schnittke's 'polystylism' to the stage for the first time. The ubiquitous tango was performed in the original production by a small pit band led by the conductor, Mstislav Rostropovich, who played the honky-tonk piano.

Other operatic works: *The 11th Commandment* (*Odinnadtsataya zapoved*) (inc., 1962); *Historia von D. Johann Fausten*, (1993), 1995; *Gesualdo*, 1995

K.P.

ARNOLD SCHOENBERG

Arnold Franz Walter Schoenberg [Schönberg]; *b* 13 September 1874, Vienna; *d* 13 July 1951, Los Angeles

The son of a Hungarian-born father and a Czech-born mother (both Jews), Schoenberg was brought up in straitened circumstances and had little academic musical training. He learned the violin and taught himself the cello, and for a time in the mid-1890s he

had composition lessons from Zemlinsky, but he was otherwise self-taught. He played in a string quartet, and his earliest surviving works are mainly for string groups, including the sextet *Verklärte Nacht* (1899). Their style is late Romantic and complicatedly tonal, like contemporary works by Richard Strauss, Max Reger or Zemlinsky. But they also have an extreme melodic and motivic density, and it was in developing this idea to its limits that Schoenberg found himself, within ten years, consciously abandoning tonality. In the D minor String Quartet (1905) and the Chamber Symphony No. 1 (1906) the relentless working of melodic motifs tends to pull the harmony out of focus. So it was logical of Schoenberg, if characteristically intransigent, to ditch tonal harmony altogether and instead, in works such as the song-cycle *Das Buch der hängenden Gärten* and the *Three Piano Pieces*, Op. 11, to allow the chords as well as the melodies to emerge from the motivic process.

In 1906 Schoenberg sketched a first opera, based on Gerhart Hauptmann's play *Und Pippa tanzt*, but abandoned it when Hauptmann held out for a stiff percentage (Alban Berg had a similar experience with this play in 1928). Two unconventional one-act works date from the early atonal period: the so-called 'monodrama' *Erwartung* (1909) and the 'drama with music' *Die glückliche Hand* (1910–13). These are characteristic products of Expressionism, inhabiting a world of neurotic hyper-sensibility. They belong to a group of vocal works, including *Pierrot lunaire* (1912) and the *Four Orchestral Songs*, Op. 22 (1916), in which Schoenberg attempted to resolve certain problems of form, syntax and harmony arising from his rejection of tonality. In the course of writing his next work, the oratorio *Die Jakobsleiter* (never completed), he began to evolve the more systematic processes which led, in a series of instrumental works of the early and mid-1920s to the 12-note, or serial, method that was to have such profound consequences for subsequent 20th-century music.

By this time, Schoenberg was already an established *enfant terrible*, surrounded by a small but fervent group of admiring disciples (including Berg and Anton Webern, who had become his pupils in 1904, and remained attached to him as apostles and assistants until 1933). In Vienna before the First World War performances of his music were greeted with incomprehension and sometimes disruption, and he was the victim of open anti-Semitism. In Berlin, where he settled in 1911, he fared better, and *Pierrot lunaire* had a successful run there in the autumn of 1912. But the outbreak of war curtailed such activities, and in 1915 Schoenberg returned to Vienna and volunteered for military service (within ten months he was invalided out). There in 1919 he founded his Society for Private Musical Performance, which for three seasons gave concerts of new works to member audiences, with the notoriously factious Viennese press specifically excluded. Schoenberg, Berg and Webern themselves did much of the organizing and took part in performances. But the worsening inflation put paid to the venture after 1921. In 1926 Schoenberg returned to Berlin as professor of composition at the Prussian Academy of Arts, and he remained there until driven out by the Nazis in 1933. Among several substantial works composed during these Berlin years were two further operas: the one-act *Von Heute auf Morgen* and, his single attempt at a full-length opera, *Moses und Aron*. In October 1933 he and his family took ship for the US, where he taught briefly at the Malkin Conservatory in Boston before preferring the more benign climate of the West Coast. He spent the last 17 years of his life in Hollywood and Los Angeles.

While there may still be debate about Schoenberg's artistic stature, there is none about his influence, which has been vast. This is partly because of the innate strength of his best music, but it is also because he took procedural decisions that later composers saw as axiomatic, and because he managed to invest these decisions with a sense of moral and historical necessity which has gone on impressing lesser composers faced with similar decisions in their own work. Schoenberg saw the rejection of tonality and the reliance on dense motivic workings as a logical and inevitable consequence of the music of Wagner and Brahms. His serial method was worked out directly from his existing atonal music: the idea of giving equal status to the 12 semitones; the idea of avoiding letting any one note take precedence (as a 'keynote'); the idea of deriving melody and harmony from the same material; the idea of free dissonance; even the idea of a fixed note order, which follows from the concept of an all-pervading motif – all this was already implicit, if unsystematic, in the works he wrote between 1908 and 1915.

This earnest and doctrinaire thinking might not encourage confidence in Schoenberg's potential as a theatre composer. But in fact his theatre music is some of his most brilliant and innovative. This is especially true of *Erwartung* – with its mercurial psychic scenario and spectacular orchestration – and *Pierrot lunaire*, with its witty adaptation of the idea of a cabaret sequence to a cycle of gruesome Symbolist poems accompanied by a small mixed band. During these years, Schoenberg also painted. He exhibited with the Blaue Reiter group and corresponded energetically with its co-founder, Wassily Kandinsky. Though apparently worked out quite independently, Schoenberg's *Die glückliche Hand* is close in concept to Kandinsky's so-called 'stage composition' *Der gelbe Klang*. There is valuable information on both works in their published correspondence, one of the most fascinating exchanges on any aspect of modern music. The later operas perhaps suffer from the streak of academicism in Schoenberg's serial writing, with its tendency towards stereotyping. Even so, *Moses und Aron* has remained his most staged opera, thanks to its vivid crowd scenes, which admirably (and relevantly) offset the somewhat abstract discussions of the issues of language and artistic integrity that form its basic subject matter.

Erwartung
Expectation
Monodrama in one act (30m)
Libretto by Marie Pappenheim
Composed 1909
PREMIERES 6 June 1924, Prague; UK: 9 January 1931 (BBC broadcast conducted by the composer); 25 April 1960, Sadler's Wells, London; US: 15 November 1951, Carnegie Hall, New York (concert); 28 December 1960, Lisner Auditorium, George Washington University, Washington, DC
CAST A Woman *s*

Schoenberg met Marie Pappenheim, a young medical student and poet, in the summer of 1909 and asked her to write an opera text for him. It seems that the choice of subject, and also possibly the idea of limiting the drama to a single character, were hers, though at that time Schoenberg had already sketched *Die glückliche Hand*, which, in its final form, also has only one solo singer. He had recently been setting Expressionist poems by Stefan George (the last two movements of the String Quartet No. 2 and the cycle *Das Buch der hängenden Gärten*). Perhaps Fräulein Pappenheim also knew that the previous year Schoenberg's wife Mathilde (the sister of Zemlinsky) had run off with his and her painting teacher, Richard Gerstl. Mathilde had been persuaded to return, and Gerstl had committed suicide.

Such events may find oblique echoes in the nightmarish dramaturgy of *Erwartung*, with its unfaithful lover slain (possibly) by the 'expectant' protagonist. But the literary apparatus and symbolic imagery (forest, moon, blood) are in fact conventional for the time, as is the Freudian dramatization of guilt. The most striking thing about *Erwartung*, apart from its sheer musical brilliance, is the sense of helpless striving for clarity: for self-knowledge followed by self-communication, in the face of an overwhelmingly alien yet terrifyingly familiar environment. The idea that profound experience is a dream inaccessible to logical explanation or description crops up regularly in the work of the Symbolists and Expressionists of the 1910s (in opera it is the theme of Debussy's *Pelléas*, a subject Schoenberg had used for an early symphonic poem, as well as of Dukas's *Ariane* and Bartók's *Bluebeard*). It would be hard to imagine a better musical analogy than Schoenberg's free-association atonality – all haunted atmosphere and elusive substance.

According to the draft short score, Schoenberg composed this complex work between 27 August and 12 September (the orchestral score took a further three weeks). But it had to wait 15 years for its first performance, at the 1924 ISCM Festival in Prague, conducted by Zemlinsky (with Marie Gutheil-Schoder). Since then stage productions have been rare.

SYNOPSIS
Scene 1 In moonlight, the woman approaches the edge of a dark forest. She is looking for her lover, and knows this means entering the forest, but fears to do so. She plucks up courage and enters.

Scene 2 Groping in the darkness, she feels something crawling, and hears someone weeping. She thinks longingly of the peaceful garden where she had vainly awaited her lover. She hears a rustling and the screech of a night-bird and starts to run, but trips over what she at first thinks is a body but then recognizes as a tree trunk.

Scene 3 She approaches a moonlit clearing. She is startled by her own shadow and imagines it crawling towards her with goggling yellow eyes on stalks. She cries out for help.

Scene 4 On the edge of a forest, by a broad, moonlit road. The woman is exhausted and dishevelled; there is blood on her face and hands. She has not found him, and cannot return home for fear of 'the stranger woman' she thinks her man is with. Then she touches something; it is her lover's bloodstained corpse. She tries to convince herself that it is a figment of the moonlight. Then she tries to rouse him, remembering that they were to have spent the night together. She imagines it is day, and that the moonlight is sunlight. She lies down beside him and kisses him. But in his staring eyes she finds a memory of his suspected infidelity. She tries to banish the memory. Why was he killed? Where is the other woman? She becomes hysterically angry and kicks the body; then again self-pitying, grieving for her love. What is she to do now, since her existence was defined by him? And as she awaits the 'eternal day of waiting', she feels again the darkness, his presence and his kiss.

Erwartung is rare among Schoenberg's early atonal works in being one long continuous movement. There is little doubt that he saw the text as a crucial element in the musical syntax, and that Pappenheim's longdrawn interior monologue was exactly what he needed. Much of the setting is slow, but with rapid instrumental figuration within the texture. But the music moves swiftly from idea to idea, often with little obvious pattern. Linking motifs are hard to detect, though certain harmonies recur. The woman's consciousness – flickering between dream and reality – is reflected in the endlessly varied melodic and rhythmic figures, while her lurking derangement finds a potent metaphor in the tonal instability, incessant tempo changes and general lack of repose of the musical language.

All the same, much of the musical vocabulary is that of late-Romantic German music. The interval of a third is fundamental, just as it is to classical and Romantic harmony, though some chords are based on the fourth, in a way remote from textbooks such as Schoenberg's own *Harmonielehre*, published, curiously enough, a mere two years after he wrote *Erwartung*. Locally, continuity is sometimes achieved by repeated melodic/rhythmic patterns (ostinati). But the main thread is always the voice, with the orchestra providing sympathetic commentary. The vocal writing itself is strenuous, but Schoenberg generally avoids the huge leaps of some of his other Expressionist works for soprano, and there is no sprechgesang. The orchestra is huge, but much of the scoring is of chamber dimensions, with a kaleidoscopic variety of colouring and sudden explosions of full orchestra.

Die glückliche Hand

The Fateful Hand (or *The Knack*)
Drama with music in one act (20m)
Libretto by the composer
Composed 1910–13
PREMIERES 14 October 1924, Volksoper, Vienna; US: 11 April 1930, Academy of Music, Philadelphia; UK: 11 December 1957, BBC radio; 17 October 1962,

Royal Festival Hall, London (concert)
CAST A Man *bar*, A Woman *silent*, A Gentleman *silent*; chorus: 3 *s*, 3 *a*, 3 *t*, 3 *b*

At the time of his first atonal works, Schoenberg was also intrigued by the possibilities of (as he later expressed it) 'music-making with stage media': that is, of using a stage scenario, with its movement and lighting, to act directly on the audience's responses, without the mediation of realistic narrative or characterization in the usual sense. The painter Kandinsky was also fascinated by this possibility, and the published Schoenberg–Kandinsky correspondence is a mine of information on this subject, and reproduces stage designs by Schoenberg for *Die glückliche Hand*, as well as his comments on a proposal (never carried out) to film it.

The text is largely stage directions, with detailed instructions about coloured lighting and a complicated scheme for cueing specific actions and lighting changes to the music. The action itself is rather woodenly symbolic (the man is either the artist torn between following his inner voice and succumbing to the lures of success, or he is the genius who cannot relate to the ordinary world, an interpretation which anticipates *Moses und Aron*).

SYNOPSIS
Scene 1 The man is face down on a darkened stage, with a hyena-like monster crouching on his back. The chorus (mixing sprechgesang with normal singing) urges him not to compromise his inner vision. There is a burst of jollity offstage, and the man leaps to his feet, showing his ragged clothes and bleeding body.

Scene 2 A glaring yellow light suggests the man's visionary longing. A beautiful young woman enters carrying a goblet which (without seeming to move) the man takes and drains. As he does so, her sympathy turns to disdain. An elegantly dressed gentleman appears, and she goes to him and they embrace. As the man shows his dejection, she returns to him; but as he moves his hand towards hers she again rejects him, this time without his noticing: 'Now', he sings, still gazing at his hand, 'I possess you for ever.'

Scene 3 A rocky landscape: the man in a ravine with a bloody sword. Goldsmiths are working at an anvil. Ignoring their hostility, he shows them how to make a diadem out of the gold with a single stroke of the hammer. There is a storm. The woman re-enters, with part of her dress missing. The gentleman holds the missing fragment, but the man cannot reach him. The gentleman throws him the scrap, but the woman recovers it, and, as the man pleads with her, she pushes a large boulder down on to him.

Scene 4 As in Scene 1, there is a burst of jollity, and the man is again face down with the monster on his back. The chorus resumes its expostulations.

Work on *Die glückliche Hand*, begun in 1910, was interrupted by other work, including *Pierrot lunaire* and the pedagogical *Harmonielehre*. The music, nevertheless, is closest in style to *Erwartung*, with which it shares its kaleidoscopic orchestra and bewildering montage of mlodic and rhythmic figures. Being more compact, and with a clear reprise of Scene 1 music in the final scene, it perhaps gives a more structured sense as a whole. Moreover, in a stage performance the score gains an extra dimension from the lighting scheme. The work remains intriguing but elusive and, in the concert performances most often encountered, problematical.

Von Heute auf Morgen
From One Day to the Next
Opera in one act (50m)
Libretto by 'Max Blonda' (Gertrud Schoenberg)
Composed October 1928–January 1929
PREMIERES 1 February 1930, Opernhaus, Frankfurt; UK: 12 November 1963, Royal Festival Hall, London (concert); US: 26 July 1980, Opera Theater, Santa Fe, New Mexico
CAST Husband *bar*, Wife *s*, Singer *t*, Friend *s*, Child *spoken role*

This slice-of-life comedy was the first opera composed with the 12-note method (it was followed by Schoenberg's own *Moses*, Berg's *Lulu* (1928–35) and Krenek's *Karl V* (1931–3)). Schoenberg had devised the method as a purely personal solution to the difficulty he had found with large-scale structure after abandoning tonality in about 1908. The idea was that, by treating the 12 notes to a process of serial ordering, unity and continuity would become semi-automatic, and the composer would once again be free to compose as he liked. But Schoenberg's earliest serial works (1920–28) do nevertheless suggest some residual anxiety on this score; they are instrumental works leaning heavily on classical formal stereotypes. Why Schoenberg turned from such things to a comic opera about marital infidelity is not known. Perhaps he wanted to prove that serial music did not have to be earnest and intellectual. Perhaps he was prompted by some incident in his own marriage or that of a friend (Franz Schreker has been suggested). Or perhaps, above all, he saw in the subject an allegory about the superficiality of modern aesthetic fashion, of which he felt he was himself a victim. 'The merely modern', he told the director Hans Wilhelm Steinberg, 'lives only "from one day to the next" . . . in marriage, but at least as much in art, politics and people's outlooks.'

SYNOPSIS
A husband and wife come home late from a party at which, it transpires, he has flirted with an old friend of hers and she with a well-known tenor. With growing irritation they bicker about their life together, until they both announce their intention of henceforth abandoning propriety and pursuing only their own pleasure. At this point the wife suddenly appears in altered guise, elegantly dressed and freshly made up. Abruptly the husband redirects his passionate attentions to her, but she rejects him with scorn. She is teaching him a lesson. Their child comes in sleepily, but the wife ostentatiously ignores him. There is (oddly) a ring at the door: the gasman demanding payment. But, rather than worry about the gas being turned off, she insists they move into a hotel. The tenor now telephones, and elaborately invites them to join him and the wife's old friend in a nearby bar. Husband and wife continue bickering, then suddenly she is back in a drab housecoat and they are reconciled. The tenor and the friend arrive, and express their disappointment at this sweet accord. They leave, as the reunited family settles down to breakfast.

Von Heute auf Morgen has obvious elements of the 1920s zeitoper, but without the diversity of idiom. Fleeting allusions to modern dance styles, and to Wagner, as quoted by the tenor, are swiftly dispersed by the intensive working of serial motifs. Those who have seen the work staged complain of Schoenberg's lack of real humour, and there certainly are problems of comic pacing (the device of the gasman is an absurdity with no apparently surreal intention; the wife's reversion to type is too abrupt, etc.). The score is nevertheless consistently intriguing, even if its contrapuntal intensity seems ill-suited to a 1920s conversation piece.

Moses und Aron
Moses and Aaron
Opera in three acts (Acts I and II: 1h 45m)
Libretto by the composer
Composed 1930–32
PREMIERES 12 March 1954, Hamburg (concert); 6 June 1957, Zurich; UK: 12 March 1954, BBC radio; 28 June 1965, Covent Garden, London; US: 2 November 1966, Back Bay Theater, Boston
CAST Moses *spoken role*, Aron (Aaron) *t*, Young Girl *s*, Invalid Woman *c*, Young Man *t*, Naked Youth *t*, Another Man *bar*, Ephraimite *bar*, Priest *b*, 4 Naked Virgins 2 *s*, 2 *c*; *satb* chorus of voice(s) from the burning bush, beggars, elderly persons, elders, tribal leaders, bricklayers, priests, tribeswomen, butchers, guardsmen, herdsmen

The first drafts of the libretto were made in October 1928, just as Schoenberg was also starting work on *Von Heute auf Morgen*. He then composed the *Accompaniment to a Film Scene* and the *Six Pieces* for male chorus, before starting serious composition on *Moses und Aron* (so spelt because he was superstitious about a title with 13 letters) in the summer of 1930. We have his own account, in a letter to Berg of 8 August 1931, of progress on the work. With chorus parts to write out and the libretto to revise as he went along, he was finding composition more laborious than usual. Nevertheless Acts I and II were complete by March 1932. Work on Act III did not proceed beyond a few sketches; Schoenberg was suffering from severe asthma, and instead of returning to Berlin he spent the winter of 1931–2 in Barcelona. By the spring of 1933, with the Prussian Academy being purged of Jewish elements, Schoenberg's position in Berlin had become untenable. He left Germany and in October sailed for the US, where he again (in 1934) revised the text of Act III but could not find time to compose the music. In 1944, he applied to the Guggenheim Foundation for a grant to enable him to complete the work, but his application was turned down.

There may also, however, have been internal, creative, reasons why the music for Act III eluded him. In a letter to Walter Eidlitz (15 March 1933) he complained of contradictions in the biblical account of Moses's smiting of the rock, and mentioned that he was engaged on his (at least) fourth revision of the text for Act III. Because this final act consists almost entirely of an extended diatribe by Moses against Aaron's love of graven images, details of the argument were obviously crucial. And yet in sung drama such things cut little ice. If the only meaning of Act III was one the audience would be unlikely to grasp in performance, then it is not surprising that Schoenberg found it hard to compose. Nor would it have escaped him that his difficulty was precisely Moses's: how to put a lofty, abstract vision into words and images without distorting and ultimately destroying it.

SYNOPSIS

Act I   Scene 1: Moses hears the voice in the burning bush, instructing him to free the Israelites and lead them to the Promised Land. Moses objects that he lacks eloquence, but God tells him that three miracles will serve as a sign, aided by Aaron's eloquence. (Moses 'speaks' throughout in sprechgesang, which stands for his lack of articulacy: the voice of God is given to six singers, backed here by a sprechgesang group, standing for the two aspects of God: the word and the hidden meaning.) Scene 2: Moses and Aaron meet in the wilderness. Aware of his role, Aaron (a fluid, lyric tenor) consistently interprets Moses's words in a superficial, concrete sense, while Moses insists on God's unknowability. Scene 3: The Israelites discuss the meeting of Moses and Aaron, expressing various attitudes to the new god: a young girl sees him as the embodiment of love, a young man of spiritual aspiration, and an older man of political hope. Two chorus groups sum up the different reactions, for and against. Moses and Aaron are seen approaching, and the chorus describes their contrasting ways of moving. Scene 4: Aaron interprets Moses's idea of the only, infinite, invisible God, but the people are hostile to an invisible god, even one who, Aaron says, is visible to the righteous. Moses expresses his helplessness in the face of Aaron's simplifications and the people's ridicule. But Aaron wins them over by changing Moses's staff ('the Law') into a writhing snake. Can the power of Moses and the new god force Pharaoh's hand? Aaron now turns Moses's hand leprous, then cures it, as a sign that the sickly, spiritless Israelites must make themselves whole in order to challenge Pharaoh. The people are now on the point of breaking their bonds. But what will they live on in the desert? Pure contemplation, says Moses. But Aaron promises that God will provide for his children by turning 'sand into fruit, fruit into gold, gold into ecstasy, and ecstasy into spirit'; he shows how God has changed the water in his pitcher to blood. God will lead them to a land flowing with milk and honey. The chorus takes up the ideas of the Chosen People and the Promised Land.

Interlude: In the darkness, the people ask after Moses (who has been absent on the Mount of Revelation for 40 days).

Act II   Scene 1: The people are restive, and the rule of law is beginning to break down. The elders tell Aaron that they will not wait for Moses's return from the mountain with the new Law. Scene 2: The people demand their old gods back. Aaron tries to calm them but lets slip that God might have killed Moses. As the people threaten to slaughter their priests, Aaron gives way and promises to build them a visible image of gold. Scene 3: Aaron calls on the people to worship the golden calf. First, animals are brought in for slaughter, and the people devour hunks of raw meat. Then a crippled woman is healed; beggars dedicate their last scraps of food to the calf; old men sacrifice their last moments of life; the Ephraimite and tribal chieftains ride in and bow down to the image. The spiritual young man of Act I, Scene 3, remonstrates with them and is slaughtered. Next comes an orgy of drunkenness, characterized by mutual generosity. Finally four naked virgins are embraced by priests and stabbed at the moment of ecstasy. This leads to an orgy of self-destruction and sexual excess. At the end, lassitude takes over. Scene 4: Moses is seen descending the mountain. He dismisses the calf with a gesture. The people flee. Scene 5: Aaron defends himself against Moses's reproof. Even Moses, he claims, needs images, like the tablets of the Commandments which he holds in his hands. In response, Moses smashes the tablets. Aaron reproaches him for his frailty. The vision, he says, is not so easily falsified. In the background the Israelites are seen following the fiery and cloudy pillars. Aaron follows them, leaving Moses in an agony of frustration at his inarticulacy.

[Act III (uncomposed) late in his life, Schoenberg suggested it might be spoken)   Aaron is brought in in chains. Once more, Moses reproves him for preferring the Image to the Idea. The guards ask if they should kill Aaron, but Moses orders his release, whereupon Aaron instantly falls dead.]

The obvious predecessor of *Moses und Aron* in Schoenberg's work is the unfinished oratorio *Die Jakobsleiter*, and *Moses* itself has attributes of oratorio. The chorus is consistently treated like the *turba* in Bach's Passion settings. Individual characters emerge from it, but in essence it is a symbolic group, reacting collectively to the central dilemma. Much of the choral writing is fugal, as in Bach or Handel. But even in the freer sections the serial method constantly throws up melodic similarities which suggest the imitative vocal styles of earlier times. This 'strictness' of technique is offset by the perhaps surprising vitality of the choral dramaturgy (considering that Schoenberg had never written for a stage chorus before). The final scene of Act I, in particular, is a brilliantly co-ordinated piece of extended ensemble writing. The notorious 'Dance round the Golden Calf' is also skilfully paced, though it contains relatively little vocal writing, while as an orchestral piece it has the vividness of detail and colour, but not the melodic or rhythmic thrust, of the greatest stage dance tableaux, such as the *Danse sacrale* in Stravinsky's *Le sacre du printemps*.

Like all Schoenberg's other serial works, *Moses* is entirely based on a single 12-note row.

Since the 1950s, *Moses* has had several stage productions, without ever quite establishing itself as a repertoire piece. Its dramatic complexities make it difficult to put on, but it also lacks the ingredients for even highbrow popularity. This would not have worried Schoenberg (he expected it), but it is worrying to his admirers. They look, without much hope, for any previous example of great music drama that has not, in the long run, achieved a wide audience. The irony of this is that Schoenberg always saw history as his main justification and support as an artist, yet in his determined unapproachability it gives him no support at all.

S.W.

FRANZ SCHREKER

b 23 March 1878, Monaco; *d* 21 March 1934, Berlin

From 1912 to 1924, Schreker rivalled Richard Strauss as Germany's leading opera composer. He provided musical and dramatic novelty through complicated and advanced harmonies which skilfully delineate characters and illustrate the emotionally charged atmosphere of the text. The brilliantly orchestrated scores, akin to French Impressionism, require grandiose resources to match their spectacularly theatrical music. Schreker largely discarded the traditional German notion of harmony defining structure or musical argument.

Schreker drew his plots more from his own imagination than from pre-existing myths or literature. Their mystical, erotic, post-Freudian themes combine fairytales and realism; the fairy-tales usually required a specific musical illustration or dominating concept (*Der ferne Klang* is about the mystical 'distant sound' sought by the hero), while the realism provided the framework for the drama.

Schreker studied in Vienna and continued living in the city after leaving the conservatory. There, in 1908, he had his first success with the ballet *Der Geburtstag der Infantin* (after Oscar Wilde's *The Birthday of the Infanta*, 1888). The following year the performance of an interlude from an opera he had put aside in 1903 inspired him to complete the score, and this work, *Der ferne Klang* (1912), established his reputation. The music's exhilarating opulence and hedonistic chromaticism, and the fanciful and erotic plot, matched the spirit of the times. Schreker became a sought-after teacher and accepted a post at Vienna's music academy. But his next opera failed, his orchestral music made little impact, and with the First World War intervening Schreker's greatest triumphs, *Die Gezeichneten* (1918) and *Der Schatzgräber* (1920), had to wait. In these works the harmonies are more conventional, post-Debussy, post-Strauss. But in *Irrelohe* (1924) Schreker again assumed the experimental mantle, writing highly chromatic and strongly contrapuntal music which explores the furthest reaches of tonality and polytonality.

In 1920 he had become head of the Berlin Hochschule für Musik and thus a figure of considerable influence, but by 1924 his pupils and the new generation of critics were turning against the luxuriance of his style and his mystical plots. *Irrelohe* was not a critical success. Schreker changed style again and embraced the 'New Objectivity', but none of his later operas found favour. He faced violent anti-Semitic demonstrations at performances in 1932, and never recovered from being swiftly and brutally dismissed from his post after Hitler came to power.

Der ferne Klang
The Distant Sound

Opera in three acts (2h)
Libretto by the composer
Composed *c.* 1901–3 (Acts I and II); completed 1910
PREMIERES 18 August 1912, Frankfurt am Main; UK: 3 February 1957, BBC radio; 14 January 1992, Grand Theatre, Leeds
CAST Grete *s*, Fritz *t*, 2 *s*, 4 *ms*, *c*, 3 *t*, 3 *bar*, 7 *b*, spoken role; *satb* chorus of guest-house clients, waiters and waitresses, guest-house servants, girls, female dancers, men and women, theatre staff, theatre-goers, *Wagenausrufer* (literally: 'coach criers')

Schreker's first operatic success brought him a reputation as a leading modernist along with Schoenberg and Richard Strauss. But Schreker's music, unlike Schoenberg's, found a ready and eager public, charming and exciting them in its novel use of chromaticism and its iridescent colours. Schreker dedicated the work to Bruno Walter, at the time kapellmeister at the Vienna Hofoper alongside Mahler.

SYNOPSIS

Act I A 'distant sound' plays in the imagination of Fritz, a young musician: it sounds like the wind playing with ghostly fingers over a harp. His quest is to find its source, for then he will be famous and return to claim his beloved Grete as his bride. But Grete's family does not share his mysticism. Her father is a drunkard and has gambled Grete away to an innkeeper in a bet. Rather than marry, Grete runs away. She collapses in a wood, where she is overcome by the magical beauty of the light on a lake. A mysterious old woman offers her untold happiness and wealth; Grete accepts.

Act II After ten years as a successful high-class prostitute, Grete is working a sophisticated Venetian nightclub. She recalls the pure beauty of the wood and compares it with her beauty and the lecherousness it provokes in her customers. She suggests a song contest, and offers her love as the prize. The winner is Fritz, led to her after many tribulations by the 'distant sound'. When he learns of her past he angrily rejects her.

Act III Five years later the negative ending of Fritz's new autobiographical play has given great offence. Grete, now a low-class prostitute, hears that Fritz is seriously ill and begs to be taken to him. Their meeting is ecstatic; Fritz realizes the significance of the 'distant sound' – it is enduring love – and now, too late, he has found his Grete again. He realizes that his play's despairing last act is misconceived.

Schreker's score, though suffused with leitmotifs, contains several set pieces, notably Fritz's narration and declaration of love in Act II and the duet at the climax of Act III. There are also significant passages of melodrama, orchestral preludes, and entr'actes of transcendental beauty. The first scene of Act II requires, in addition to the orchestra in the pit, a number of different ensembles playing on different parts of the stage. Alban Berg made the piano reduction of the full score; several commentators have found elements derived from this work's technical and structural innovations in *Wozzeck*.

Other operas: *Flammen*, 1902; *Das Spielwerk und die Prinzessin*, 1913, rev. as *Das Spielwerk*, 1920; *Die Gezeichneten*, 1918; *Der Schatzgräber*, 1920; *Irrelohe*, 1924; *Christophorus, oder Die Vision einer Oper*, (1928), 1978; *Der singende Teufel*, 1928; *Der Schmied von Gent*, 1932

C. B.

FRANZ SCHUBERT
Franz Peter Schubert; *b* 31 January 1797, Vienna; *d* 19 November 1828, Vienna

Though Schubert's songs and instrumental music place him among the greatest composers, none of his operas has joined the standard repertoire. Musically they contain fine moments, but they fail because of their dramatic weaknesses. Whether this is due to an innate inability to construct large-scale dramatic works or to lack of stage experience is impossible to say. Schubert evidently felt constrained by theatrical demands and conventions which hampered the boundless creativity that found a natural and sublime expression in his songs. But there are elements in his last operas which suggest that, had he lived longer, he might have arrived at a highly original conception of opera.

Schubert's exceptional musical talents were already apparent when he became a pupil at the K. K. Stadtkonvikt in 1808, and his composition studies under Antonio Salieri were continued after he left the school in 1813. Salieri impressed on him that a composer should prove himself primarily through his dramatic works: it was certainly expected that composers should write operas. At the Stadtkonvikt Schubert had already made an abortive attempt at a singspiel, *Der Spiegelritter*, but his first substantial operatic work, *Des Teufels Lustschloss*, was composed during the 12 months immediately after he left. In 1815, when he was working as an assistant master in his father's school, he wrote no fewer than four stage works; following the current popular trend, these were all singspiels. The influences of Mozart and of Beethoven's *Fidelio* on these are clear; Schubert was also evidently familiar with the work of contemporary French composers such as Jean-François Le Sueur, Nicolas Dalayrac and Étienne Méhul as well as the popular Viennese singspiels of the day by such composers as Wenzel Müller, Joseph Weigl and Johann Nepomuk Hummel.

From 1816, when he gave up teaching, to 1818 Schubert made only abortive operatic efforts, but in 1819, as a result of the influence of the singer Johann Michael Vogl, he was commissioned to write *Die Zwillingsbrüder*. The 1820 productions of this and the melodrama *Die Zauberharfe*, with its spectacular magic effects, though by no means resounding successes, brought his stage works to public notice.

Schubert wrote four further complete stage works – his last – between 1821 and 1823. Only the incidental music to Helmina von Chezy's *Rosamunde* was performed during his lifetime. His last opera, *Fierrabras*, and sketches for an unfinished work, *Der Graf von Gleichen*, show clearly how far Schubert had progressed since his apprentice days. An individual theatrical style was beginning to emerge which in more than one respect (e.g. stage settings, instrumental accompaniments) anticipates later developments in German Romantic opera.

Alfonso und Estrella
Romantic opera in three acts (3h)
Libretto by Franz von Schober
Composed 1821–2
PREMIERES 24 June 1854, Hoftheater, Weimar (shortened version); 1946, Swiss Radio Beromünster (complete); UK: 7 September 1968, Usher Hall, Edinburgh (concert); 22 February 1977, Reading University; US: 11 November 1978, Ford Auditorium, Detroit (concert)
CAST Froila *bar*, Alfonso *t*, Mauregato *bar*, Estrella *s*, Adolfo *b*; *satb* chorus of hunters, soldiers, people

Much of the opera was composed in the castle of Ochsenburg near St Pölten, where Schubert and Schober were on holiday. Guided by enthusiasm rather than skill, they produced an opera which is rich in variety (Schober happily provided a wide range of situations and settings) but dramatically weak. It is likely that a premiere at the Kärntnertor was offered but later withdrawn after the two intended principal singers expressed unhappiness about the work. Schubert tried in vain to have it staged in Dresden, Berlin and Graz. Its posthumous premiere was conducted by Liszt.

SYNOPSIS
Act I Froila, the deposed king of Leon, has lived peacefully for 20 years in a mountain retreat, with his son Alfonso (who is unaware of his identity) and a few faithful retainers. Meanwhile, in Leon, Estrella, daughter of the usurper Mauregato, spurns the love of the general, Adolfo. When Adolfo asks Mauregato for her hand as a reward for a successful campaign, the king – knowing Estrella's feelings – temporizes, saying that only he who returns the Chain of Eurich to the royal treasury (it is in Froila's possession) can marry his daughter.

Act II Estrella, who has lost her way during a hunt, is discovered by Alfonso. They fall in love, and Alfonso gives her the Chain of Eurich as a token. She returns to Leon, much to the joy of Mauregato, who recognizes the chain. Suddenly a guard brings news of a revolt led by Adolfo: he wants to usurp the throne and win Estrella's hand. The court flees.

Act III The battle between Adolfo's and Mauregato's forces has separated Estrella from her father. Alone with Estrella, Adolfo is trying to force her to submit to him when Alfonso and hunters arrive. Adolfo is captured, and Alfonso defeats the rebels.

Mauregato willingly surrenders the throne to the rightful king, and Froila, in turn, abdicates in favour of Alfonso. The opera ends with general rejoicing.

That Schubert considered this his best stage work demonstrates his lack of dramatic understanding. There is an attempt to build up dramatic tension, but all too often the momentum that has been achieved is dissipated by the insertion of a languorous duet. Taken individually, however, these duets are some of the score's strongest numbers. Schubert had heard Rossini's *Otello* and *Tancredi*, and his aim was probably to write something less frivolous than the average singspiel. The Italian composer's influence can be seen directly in some of the larger ensembles and may have inspired Schubert's decision to abandon spoken dialogue.

Fierrabras

Opera in three acts (2h 30m)
Libretto by Josef Kupelwieser, after the play *La Puente de Mantible* by Pedro Calderón de la Barca and an old German legend, *Eginhard und Emma*
Composed May–October 1823
PREMIERES 7 May 1835, Josefstadt Theatre, Vienna (three numbers; concert); 9 February 1897, Hoftheater, Karlsruhe (shortened version); UK: 6 November 1938, London (excerpts; concert); 10 April 1971, BBC radio; 19 February 1986, Playhouse, Oxford; US: 9 May 1980, Walnut Street Theater, Philadelphia
CAST King Karl *b*, Emma *s*, Eginhard *t*, Roland *bar*, Ogier *t*, Boland *b*, Fierrabras *t*, Florinda *s*, Maragond *ms*, Brutamonte *b*; *satb* chorus of ladies, knights, soldiers

Late in 1821 Domenico Barbaja, director of the Kärntnertortheater, asked Schubert for a German opera for the 1822–3 season. The composer offered both *Alfonso und Estrella* and *Die Verschworenen* (neither of which had yet been performed), but they were rejected and Schubert, anxious to see his stage works performed, set to work on a new full-length opera. Although it was completed in time, *Fierrabras* too was rejected, and its 26-year-old composer did not live to see his last – and most individual – opera performed. *Fierrabras* disappeared until its publication in 1886. It has enjoyed a few revivals since the 1970s (including a significant production at the 1988 Vienna Festival).

SYNOPSIS
Act I Emma, daughter of King Karl, and Eginhard, a young knight, are secretly in love. After a victory against the Moors, Karl sends a mission of peace led by his general, Roland, and including Eginhard. He declares an amnesty for the Moorish prisoners. Among these is Fierrabras, son of the Moorish leader Boland, whose valour has won Roland's admiration. It transpires that Fierrabras has loved Emma since seeing her during a visit to Rome, and that Roland had simultaneously fallen in love with Fierrabras's sister Florinda. That night Fierrabras observes a secret meeting between Eginhard and Emma. Despite his jealousy he does not give them away, even when he is wrongly blamed for trying to abduct Emma and is imprisoned.

Act II Eginhard and the rest of the peace mission are incarcerated by Boland. Florinda, recognizing Roland, determines to save them. She unlocks their prison and provides weapons, but only Eginhard escapes, while the rest of the knights remain barricaded in the tower.

Act III Karl, having discovered the truth about Emma and Eginhard, orders Fierrabras's release. Eginhard, arriving with news of the knights' plight, begs to lead a rescue party. Fierrabras accompanies him. The rescue party arrives just in time to prevent the executions of the knights and Florinda. The opera ends with the couples united and Fierrabras accepted into the chivalric brotherhood of the Frankish knights.

While Schubert employed many of the stock-in-trade devices of contemporary German opera (e.g. the women's spinning chorus, the men's unaccompanied patriotic hymn), *Fierrabras*, undeniably Schubert's strongest stage work, rises above the commonplace and presents a tantalizing example of the composer's fully formed theatrical style. Elements familiar from other composers are here not so much borrowed or copied as assimilated into Schubert's own musical language. Much of the most effective writing is for Florinda (the best-drawn female character in Schubert's dramatic music), whose numbers include an aria accompanied by male-voice chorus ('Des Jammers herbe Qualen') in Act III and a highly dramatic melodrama, as she watches her beloved Roland in battle. Particularly haunting too is the serenade between Eginhard and Emma, 'Der Abend sinkt aus stiller Flor', which begins the Act I finale.

Other operatic works: *Der Spiegelritter* (inc., 1812), 1949; *Des Teufels Lustschloss*, (1814), 1879; *Die vierjährige Posten*, (1815), 1896; *Fernando*, (1815), 1907; *Claudine von Villa Bella* (inc., 1815) 1913; *Die Freunde von Salamanka*, (1815), 1928; *Die Bürgschaft* (inc., 1816), 1908; *Adrast*, (1820), 1985; *Die Zauberharfe*, 1820; *Die Zwillingsbrüder*, 1820; *Sakuntala* (inc., 1820), 1971; *Die Verschworenen*, (1823), 1861; *Rüdiger* (inc., 1823), 1868; *Der Graf von Gleichen* (inc., 1827)

C. A. B.

DMITRI SHOSTAKOVICH
Dmitri Dmitrievich Shostakovich; *b* 25 September 1906, St Petersburg; *d* 9 August 1975, Moscow

Shostakovich's mother was a professional pianist, and he entered the Petrograd (St Petersburg) Conservatory as a pianist at the age of 13. But he also developed rapidly as a composer, under Maximilian Steinberg, a Rimsky-Korsakov pupil. He was still only 19 when his First Symphony was premiered in the again renamed Leningrad in May 1926 (he had already destroyed a student opera based on Pushkin's *The Gypsies*); within two years this brilliant, if derivative, symphony had made him world-famous. A Second and Third Symphony followed – both quite experimental in style – and several theatre works, including the sparkling Gogol opera *The Nose*, two or three ballets, and incidental music to Vladimir Mayakovsky's play *The Bedbug*. By the early 1930s Shostakovich was already moderating his style (as many West European progressives of the 1920s were also doing), and his second opera, *The Lady Macbeth of the Mtsensk District*, mixes modernism and biting satire with revived Romantic- cum-Expressionist elements.

Shostakovich was not yet 30 when this work was violently attacked in *Pravda* in January 1936, and its composer was left shattered and fearful – at a time when even artists were beginning to pay with their lives for deviating from the new ideal of Socialist Realism. Thereafter, he seldom risked serious theatre work. An operetta, *The Silly Little Mouse*, composed early in 1939, is lost, as is the film material of a miniature Pushkin comic opera, *The Tale of a Priest and His Servant Balda*, composed in 1941 but destroyed in the Leningrad bombing that year (a concert suite survives). His setting of Gogol's *The Gamblers* was left unfinished, he tells us in *Testimony*, because he suddenly realized it was morally unacceptable to set to music in wartime Russia (and it would certainly have been so in post-war Russia, when in 1948 Shostakovich was carpeted, along with most of his gifted compatriots, for 'formalism and anti-democratic tendencies'). He seems to have made little progress with an opera based on Tolstoy's *Resurrection* (1940). Later he composed only the operetta *Moscow, Cheryomushki*, though at the time of his death he was planning an opera on Chekhov's *The Black Monk*. The core of his work post-1936 is symphonic, with a parallel stream of chamber works dominated by 15 string quartets. But even while seeking safety in 'abstract' forms, or in film music or cantatas on officially acceptable topics, Shostakovich found it hard to deny his theatrical talent. Both his symphonies and his chamber works are full of essentially graphic writing and barely concealed psychological drama. Though he never wrote an unmistakable operatic masterpiece, it seems quite possible that he would have been one of the great modern opera composers – a worthy successor to Musorgsky and Tchaikovsky – if circumstances had allowed.

The Nose

Nos

Opera in three acts and an epilogue (1h 45m)
Libretto by the composer, after the short story by Nikolai Gogol (1835)
PREMIERES 16 June 1929, Leningrad (St Petersburg) (concert); 18 January 1930, Leningrad; US: 11 August 1965, Opera Theater, Santa Fe, New Mexico; UK: 21 October 1972, BBC radio; 4 April 1973, Sadler's Wells, London
CAST Kovalyov *bar*, Yakovlevich *b-bar*, Police Inspector *very high t*, Ivan *t*, Nose *t*, Mme Podtochina *ms*, Her Daughter *s*, Old Countess *c*, Praskovya Osipovna *s*, Advertising Employee *b-bar*, Doctor *b*, *s*, 7 *t*, 8 *b*; *satb* chorus of worshippers, poor matrons, travellers, passers-by, onlookers, eunuchs, policemen (also spoken roles) – numbers depend on various possibilities of role-doubling

Shostakovich wrote his first opera at the height of the 'anything-goes' period of early Soviet art. For a few years after the end of the civil war the Soviet Union

was in a ferment of artistic experiment, as seemed to befit an emerging revolutionary state. In music, the influence of Western avant-gardists such as Schoenberg, Hindemith and Stravinsky was strong. Berg's *Wozzeck* was staged in Leningrad while Shostakovich was writing *The Nose*, and its influence is apparent, as is that of Prokofiev's *The Love for Three Oranges* (Leningrad, 1926). At the same time the work's absurdism and unremitting grotesquerie suggest a knowledge of Cocteau and Les Six, though its satire against civil servants is purely Russian. In tone and outline it follows Gogol's short story closely, while incorporating material from other books by Gogol, as well as a song from Dostoevsky's *Brothers Karamazov*.

The Nose enjoyed some success in Leningrad, but was not taken up elsewhere. The political climate was already turning against such things, and in any case the piece is forbiddingly hard to stage, with its spiky and difficult orchestral writing and its cast of 70 characters. It returned to favour in the Soviet Union in the 1970s, but has had only occasional productions abroad.

SYNOPSIS

Act I After a brief prologue (Kovalyov being shaved by the barber Yakovlevich), we see Yakovlevich at breakfast. To his (moderate) surprise he finds a nose in his roll, but manages – not without difficulty – to dispose of it in the river Neva. Meanwhile Kovalyov discovers his loss. He tracks the nose down to Kazan Cathedral, where it appears dressed as a state councillor.

Act II Kovalyov tries to report the loss to the police, and to place a newspaper advertisement.

Act III Eventually the nose is apprehended trying to board the Riga coach, and the police inspector returns it to Kovalyov. But the doctor is unable to reattach it. Kovalyov writes to Mme Podtochina, accusing her of masterminding the theft to blackmail him into marrying her daughter. Everyone discusses the rumours about Kovalyov's nose walking the streets.

Epilogue The nose suddenly reappears in its rightful place. The delighted Kovalyov is again able to hold his head up in St Petersburg.

Shostakovich maintained that his music for *The Nose* was not comical. But this may have been to pre-empt the criticism of unseriousness. The work is in fact rich in satire and grotesquerie, and the music is generally graphic rather than symphonic. Its structure is a montage of short scenes with orchestral interludes (cf. *Wozzeck*, whose captain may also have inspired Shostakovich's police inspector, with his ludicrously high-tenor squeak), and there is little sustained dramatic growth or psychological development.

Although he never again wrote music so dependent on parody, many typical Shostakovichisms appear in *The Nose* for the first time. The spiky scherzo ostinati were to become standard in his symphonies, and the jogging minimalism of episodes such as Ivan's balalaika-playing scene (with flexatone), or the final scene on the Nevsky Prospect, was to serve Shostakovich much later in serious or ironic contexts. In general the ability to absorb naïve musical styles into a sophisticated idiom was to prove one of his most individual traits and greatest strengths. *The Nose* may not be a masterpiece, but it is remarkably rich in musical possibilities.

The Lady Macbeth of the Mtsensk District

Ledi Makbet Mtsenskovo uyezda
Opera in four acts (2h 30m)
Libretto by Aleksandr Preis and the composer, after the short story by Nikolai Leskov (1865)
Composed 1930–32; rev. 1935, and (as *Katerina Ismailova*) 1956–63
PREMIERES *Lady Macbeth*: 22 January 1934, Maly Opera House, Leningrad (St Petersburg); US: 31 January 1935, Cleveland, Ohio (semi-staged); UK: 18 March 1936, Queen's Hall, London (concert); 22 May 1987, Coliseum, London; *Katerina Ismailova*: 26 December 1962, Stanislavsky Nemirovich-Danchenko Music Theatre, Moscow; UK: 2 December 1963, Covent Garden, London; US: 23 October 1964, War Memorial Opera House, San Francisco
CAST Katerina Ismailova *s*, Boris Ismailov *high b*, Zinovy Ismailov *t*, Sergei *t*, Mill-hand *bar*, Coachman *t*, Aksinya *s*, Shabby Peasant *t*, Porter *b*, Steward *b*, 3 Foremen 3 *t*, Priest *b*, Chief of Police *bar*, Policeman *b*, Teacher *t*, Drunken Guest *t*, Old Convict *b*, Sentry *b*, Sonyetka *c*, Woman Convict *s*, Sergeant *b*; *satb* chorus of workers, policemen, guests, convicts

Shostakovich first encountered Leskov's brutal tale (published a few years after the emancipation of the serfs) through his artist friend Boris Kustodiev, who illustrated an edition of 1930. But from the start he reacted very differently from Leskov to the tragic heroine. The original Katerina is irredeemably cruel and self-seeking, and is treated by Leskov ironically, whereas Shostakovich saw her as a sympathetic figure driven to crime by intolerable boredom and despair. The social and psychological implications of her predicament struck him as important; it clearly never occurred to him that his graphic treatment of her actions would be taken as signifying approval.

'As a Soviet composer,' he wrote in 1934, 'I determined to preserve the strength of Leskov's novel, and yet, approaching it critically, to interpret its events from our modern point of view.' 'So little was socialist realism understood at first,' Gerald Abraham wrote in *Eight Soviet Composers*, 'that *The Lady Macbeth of Mtsensk* was accepted as an embodiment of it.' In 1934–5 the work was a considerable popular success and was widely performed in and out of the Soviet Union, attracting generally appreciative notices. But on 28 January 1936 there appeared in *Pravda* a lengthy editorial denouncing the opera as 'Muddle instead of Music', attacking its 'deliberately discordant, confused stream of sounds . . . [its] din, grinding and screaming', and its sexual naturalism, in which ' "love" is smeared all over the opera in the most vulgar manner'. 'Is its success abroad not explained', *Pravda* demanded smugly, 'by the fact that it tickles the perverted bourgeois taste with its fidgety, screaming, neurotic music?'

The editorial apparently reflected the opinion of Stalin himself, who had attended a performance in December 1935. In any case, the denunciation was official, and the opera was instantly withdrawn, followed in December by the composer's Fourth Symphony, which had just gone into rehearsal. His Fifth Symphony, which followed in 1937, was subtitled 'the practical reply of a Soviet artist to justified criticism', and is certainly more direct and transparent than either of the withdrawn works, though less of a reaction against their style than is often said. *Lady Macbeth* vanished from the Soviet scene (there was a postwar production in Düsseldorf) until, in the more tolerant early 1960s, Shostakovich produced a major revision under the title *Katerina Ismailova*. This revision is a compromise. It purges textual and scenic details that would still have offended Soviet primness in 1962, but it also makes purely musical changes, especially to vocal lines, as well as somewhat lightening the orchestral texture. However, some of these changes already appear in the published edition of 1935. In particular, the orchestral depiction of Katerina's love-making with Sergei in Act I, Scene 3, is toned down (it completely disappears in 1962). Moreover, the passacaglia interlude after the murder of Boris is reduced for solo organ, and the stage band is cut (both these changes were cancelled in 1962). Since the composer's death, the original (1932) version has returned to favour, both on record and on the stage, and today there seems little reason to prefer the expurgated score.

SYNOPSIS (original version)
Act I Scene 1: Katerina is lying on her bed, bored and frustrated. Boris, her father-in-law, nags her for not giving his son Zinovy a child. Zinovy meanwhile leaves to attend to a burst mill-dam, but before going he presents a new labourer, Sergei, to his father. Boris forces Katerina to swear fidelity in her husband's absence. Aksinya, a cook, tells Katerina that Sergei lost his previous job for carrying on with his master's wife. Boris berates her for not weeping at Zinovy's departure. Scene 2: Sergei and the men are brutally molesting Aksinya when Katerina appears and threatens Sergei with a thrashing. He in turn challenges her to a wrestling match, whose thinly veiled sexual intention takes them both to the ground as Boris comes in. He promises to report her behaviour to Zinovy. Scene 3: Boris orders Katerina to bed and goes out. She undresses, but as she lies down Sergei knocks on the door and asks to borrow a book. He complains of boredom, and she too admits she is bored and would like a child. He makes a pass at her, and they make love. Boris is heard calling Katerina, but Sergei refuses to leave.

Act II Scene 4: A week later Boris is walking about outside, musing on his sexual prowess when young. Seeing a light in Katerina's window, he decides to pay her a visit, and catches Sergei leaving her room. He at once calls in the workers, and personally whips Sergei, watched by Katerina, who slides down the drainpipe and tries to stop him. Sergei is taken away to the store room, while Boris orders Katerina to prepare him some mushrooms and sends the porter for Zinovy. Katerina slips rat poison into the mushrooms, and as Boris collapses she takes the store-room keys from his pocket. A gang of workers arrives, and one of their foremen brings a priest. Boris manages to get out a garbled accusation against Katerina before dying. The priest pronounces a (somewhat light-hearted) requiem. Scene 5: Katerina and Sergei are in bed, but Sergei warns her that when Zinovy returns their love will end. She promises that all will be well. But, as he sleeps, Boris's ghost appears to her and curses her. Suddenly Katerina senses Zinovy's return. Sergei hides and she admits Zinovy, who remonstrates with her for her philandering. Seeing Sergei's belt, he whips her with it, but Katerina and Sergei batter him to death with a candlestick and shove his body into the cellar.

Act III Scene 6: Katerina and Sergei are about to get married, though Zinovy's body is still in the cellar. A shabby peasant sings a drunken song and breaks into the cellar in search of wine. Finding Zinovy's putrid corpse, he rushes off to the police station. Scene 7: At the station, the police sing a jolly hymn to bribery and corruption. They are incensed at not being invited to Katerina's wedding. A 'socialist' teacher is brought in and questioned. When the shabby peasant arrives with news of the corpse, the police see it as 'a gift from God'. Scene 8: At the wedding, the guests are drunk and the priest makes lascivious advances to Katerina. Suddenly Katerina notices that the store-room lock is broken, but, as she suggests to Sergei that they steal the money and run away, the police arrive and the two give themselves up.

Act IV Scene 9: In the convict line by a river on the road to Siberia, Katerina bribes the sentry to let her through to Sergei. But Sergei rejects her, and goes instead to Sonyetka, a convict, who demands that he bring her Katerina's stockings. He tricks Katerina, and takes the stockings to Sonyetka, while the other women convicts, and then Sonyetka herself, taunt Katerina. As the convicts begin to move off, Katerina pushes Sonyetka into the river and jumps in after her. The remaining convicts trudge off.

Technically *Lady Macbeth* is a major advance on *The Nose*. Shostakovich himself drew attention to its symphonic character. The crucial orchestral interludes link the scenes into an unbroken musico-dramatic thread, as well as adding psychological depth and tragic foreboding to the superficially crude narrative. The same expansiveness is apparent in the Fourth Symphony, but it might well be argued that the opera is the more successful work. Its few satirical episodes – the two appearances of the priest, and the scene in the police station – only mildly disrupt the melodramatic texture; indeed, they lighten it usefully. Overall, the pacing is astonishingly assured for a first serious opera.

At the same time, the musical invention is consistently brilliant. Among several superb interludes, the passacaglia (Scenes 4/5) is equal to anything in the symphonies; but so is much else, particularly the bedroom scenes, where Shostakovich shows a rare and astonishing ability to use sustained orchestral counterpoint dramatically. This skill he combines with a strong sense of harmonic architecture and a mastery

of ostinato (in *The Nose* an amusing mannerism) as a device for generating tension. Even more unexpectedly, the vocal writing is grateful and effective, notwithstanding a few passages where screaming takes over. Like Britten, Shostakovich devised a vocal style that adheres to traditional principles without limiting the musical idiom. One of the work's most memorable vocal melodies served him again (in the String Quartet No. 8: Katerina's 'Seryozha, khoroshi moy' in the last scene of the opera). But there are others as good. It is easy to understand why *Lady Macbeth* was popular until Stalin took against it.

Shostakovich had planned a tetralogy of operas about women. That the other three were never written must be accounted one of the major losses of 20th-century opera, even if his choice of heroines (the fourth was to be a Stakhanovite worker at the Dnieper Hydroelectric Works) might seem less than ideally promising. After completing *Lady Macbeth*, late in 1932, he worked instead on a comic opera, *The Big Lightning*, but soon laid it aside (the fragments were glued together by Gennadi Rozhdestvensky, and performed in Leningrad in 1981).

Other operatic works: *The Gamblers (Igroki)*, (1942), 1978; *Moscow, Cheryomushki (Moskva, Cheryomushki)*, 1958

S. W.

BEDŘICH SMETANA
b 2 March 1824, Litomyšl, Bohemia, Czech Republic; *d* 12 May 1884, Prague

Smetana is the outstanding figure in Czech opera of the 19th century. Before him there were only spasmodic and inconsistent attempts to write operas in Czech and together they form no continuous tradition. Smetana bequeathed to the Czech nation a work taken to be the very embodiment of 'Czechness' in opera (*The Bartered Bride*), and explored a variety of contrasting operatic genres as a basis for the future course of Czech opera. These range from large-scale historical and legendary operas to village operas, though his most personal contribution may well be the bittersweet questing dramas of his last years. Smetana's legacy was zealously defended after his death and was turned into a cult that was used to stifle the works of his contemporaries and successors, Dvořák and Janáček in particular.

Smetana's musical education, at the Proksch Institute in Prague (1844–7), allied him to the Liszt–Wagner school, and his earliest mature orchestral works were a series of Lisztian tone poems, striking in their harmonic freedom and their use of thematic transformation. After working abroad in Sweden (1856–61), Smetana returned to Prague at a crucial stage in the city's operatic history: the opening of the Provisional Theatre in 1862, the first theatre built exclusively for Czech use. In 1866, after his first opera, *The Brandenburgers in Bohemia*, was given at the Provisional Theatre and won first prize in the Harrach Competition for new Czech operas, he was quickly taken on at the theatre as chief conductor, ousting Jan Nepomuk Maýr, who had built up the company from scratch. Smetana remained at the Provisional Theatre for eight years (1866–74) in an increasingly embittered tenure, during which musicianship was unchallenged, but conservative factions, unhappy with his Wagnerian orientation, sought to question his ability as a conductor and as music director of an opera company. This period saw more Smetana premieres, though only his second opera, The Bartered Bride, in its final redaction of 1870, achieved real popularity.

What Smetana's critics sought to achieve, however, came about through the sudden onslaught of deafness in 1874. He had to resign his post as conductor, and he courageously set about a career exclusively as a composer. This period saw the composition of his First String Quartet (which depicts the tragic interruption of his working life by the high-pitched tinnitus which was now all he heard), the completion of his cycle of six tone poems, Má vlast, and the composition of three new operas. The first of these, The Kiss, became his most popular opera after The Bartered Bride. But his later years were increasingly unhappy as his illness took its toll, slowing down the rate of composition until he was able to compose only for short stretches at a time. At his death he left incomplete an earlier opera, Viola (after Twelfth Night), which he had returned to in his final years.

For all Smetana's Wagnerian affiliation and inclination, his operas derive from the French and Italian tradition of opera cultivated in the Provisional Theatre. (The German repertoire was the mainstay of the rival German Opera in Prague.) There is evidence of cabaletta technique and concertato in his first opera, and such elements can be found even in his later operas. He never abandoned resources such as the chorus or ensemble singing. With its suitability for genre painting, the chorus was one of the mainstays of Czech national opera and was far too popular to sacrifice; even a serious historical opera such as Dalibor has a popular drinking chorus for the soldiers. The use of solo ensemble is a feature of Smetana's later operas and derives in part from the fervent belief of his last librettist, Eliška Krásnohorská, in this resource. Such ensembles are not found in Dalibor, which has a more austere libretto, though there are important duets even in this work.

Smetana's operas are Italianate also in their use of voice types. He employed tessituras more in keeping with Verdian voices, relying on lighter, brighter voices, rather than the lower, helden- or dramatic voice types of Wagner. In this, he was guided by the voices available in the small pool of solo singers at the Prague Provisional Theatre. No dramatic soprano or heldentenor was a regular or long-lived member of the ensemble. Similarly the absence of low bass parts is related to the early departure of the finest (and lowest) Czech bass, Josef Paleček. Smetana's inactive baritone roles, in contrast to Verdi's villainous baritones or German demonic baritones, are connected with the long-term presence in the company of Josef Lev, a poor actor, but the possessor of a baritone voice of great beauty, heard at its best in slow lyrical music.

The character of Smetana's operas varies noticeably with the different strengths and concerns of his four librettists. The historical operas Dalibor and Libuše, with much emphasis on patriotic sentiments, had libretti from a conservative patriot, Josef Wenzig. Eliška Krásnohorská, the librettist of The Kiss, The Secret and The Devil's Wall, preferred small-scale exploration of character psychology and the evocation of typical Czech milieus. Smetana seemed happy to take over the subjects offered him. He never suggested a libretto topic himself, and seldom went against the conventions implicit in each libretto.

Smetana was emphatically against the direct use of folksong in his operas as a means of conveying 'Czechness', and there are only a handful of documented borrowings in his operas. He had less hesitation in writing imitation folksongs, from Ludiše's 'Byl to krásný sen' in his first opera to Blaženka's 'Což ta voda' in The Secret. Mostly, however, the national character that most Czechs find in his works derives from Czech dance patterns such as the polka (not just in actual dances, but as the basis for other numbers) and from an identification of 'national style' with that of Smetana himself.

The Bartered Bride
Prodaná nevěsta
(*The Sold Bride*)
Comic opera in three acts (2h 15m)
Libretto by Karel Sabina
Composed July 1863–spring 1865; orch. by 15 March 1866; rev. 1869–70
PREMIERES two-act version with spoken dialogue: 30 May 1866, Provisional Theatre, Prague; definitive three-act version, sung throughout: 25 September 1870, Provisional Theatre, Prague; US: 20 August 1893, Haymarket, Chicago; UK: 26 June 1895, Drury Lane, London
CAST Krušina *bar*, Ludmila *s*, Mařenka *s*, Micha *b*, Háta *ms*, Vašek *t*, Jeník *t*, Kecal *b*, Circus-master *t*, Esmeralda *s*, Red Indian *b*, circus artistes, *silent*; *satb* chorus of villagers

The Bartered Bride was not especially popular when it was first given, seeming not to achieve the success of its predecessor, The Brandenburgers in Bohemia. But, while the latter opera dropped out of the repertoire after 1870, The Bartered Bride maintained its place with a steadily increasing number of performances each year. By 1927 it had been performed 1000 times in Prague. From the 1870s it was recognized as the quintessential Czech national opera, setting a standard by which other operas, including those by Smetana himself, were judged.

Especially in its original version, with spoken dialogue and without the dances, it made only modest demands. Unlike the ambitious Brandenburgers in Bohemia (with three tenor parts) or the later Dalibor (which called for a dramatic soprano and a heldentenor), voice parts were written around the fledgling Czech company, which then included an operetta component. The first Esmeralda was a well-known soubrette; the first circus-master was a Czech actor, Jindřich Mošna, who got through his undemanding part in a sort of parlando, playing it altogether 446 times over 30 years.

Smetana tinkered with the opera from the third

performance onwards. The first change was the omission of an ironic couplet for the circus-master and Esmeralda (thought to be too risky to be played before Emperor Franz Josef), and its replacement by the ballet from Act I of *The Brandenburgers in Bohemia*, an unnecessary precaution since the emperor left after the first act. A more drastic revision followed on 29 January 1869, when the first act was divided into two scenes, the first ending with the duet for Mařenka and Vašek, and the second beginning with the newly written drinking chorus. Act II began with a newly composed polka, and Mařenka acquired a new aria ('Ten lásky sen'). The Esmeralda–circus-master couplet was omitted for good.

After four performances, Smetana produced another version (1 June 1869) in which the opera was split into the present three acts, Act I ending with a newly written furiant. The circus scene in Act III was expanded with a march and a *skočná*. It was not until the final version of 25 September 1870, however, that the spoken dialogue was replaced by sung recitatives (written for a performance in St Petersburg) and the furiant received its final position in Act II, after the drinking chorus.

SYNOPSIS

Act I The action takes place at a village fair in Bohemia. During a lull in the opening chorus ('Proč bychom se netěšili'), Mařenka confesses her fears to her lover Jeník. She cannot love anyone but Jeník, but her father is obliged to Mícha, and so she may be forced to marry Mícha's son. Jeník seems strangely unconcerned. Mařenka is also puzzled by Jeník's mysterious past. Why did he leave his home, she asks in the following aria ('Kdybych se co takového')? Jeník explains that after the death of his mother, his father married again and his stepmother soon sent him packing: he went off into the world and worked among foreign people. In a duet, they swear eternal love ('Věrné milování'). The next scene introduces Mařenka's parents, Krušina and Ludmila, and the ebullient marriage-broker Kecal ('Jak vám pravím, pane kmotře'), who gives them a glowing picture of Vašek, the bridegroom proposed for their daughter. Mařenka, who now returns, is less enthusiastic, and to the strains of 'Věrné milování' in the orchestra she declares she loves another. Kecal resolves to seek out Jeník, whom he regards as the chief obstacle. The act ends in a polka with a choral conclusion.

Act II After the opening drinking chorus and furiant, Mařenka's would-be suitor makes his appearance on an empty stage. Vašek is dressed up for the occasion, but is nervous and stammers: his mother has told him that if he does not marry, the whole village will laugh at him ('Má ma-ma-matička'). Mařenka accosts him and, having established that he is her proposed bridegroom (he has no idea who she is), informs him that everyone is sorry for him. Mařenka, she tells him, loves another and will make sure that Vašek meets an early death. She coquettishly woos him in a duet ('Známť já jednu dívčinu'), in which she makes the infatuated Vašek swear that he will not marry 'Mařenka'. Meanwhile Kecal has found Jeník, and in an extended duet attempts to bribe him into

renouncing Mařenka. Jeník agrees to a final figure of 300 gulden on condition that Mařenka marry no one but Mícha's son, and that Krušina's debt to Mícha will be cleared. Afterwards Jeník wonders how Kecal could believe that he would have sold his Mařenka ('Jak možná věřit'). Kecal, however, brings back Krušina and the chorus to witness his negotiating triumph. The chorus is angry about the 'sale' of Jeník's bride.

Act III Vašek's confusion ('To to mi v hlavě leží') is brushed away by the arrival of the circus people, who give a preview of their skill in a lively *skočná*. Disaster has struck, however. The man appearing as the star attraction ('the big American bear') is too drunk to perform. Esmeralda the dancer and the circus-master persuade Vašek to take his place ('Milostné zvířátko'). Vašek's parents are astonished to hear that he does not want to marry Mařenka, but, as soon as Vašek discovers that the girl who charmed him earlier is actually the feared Mařenka, he gladly agrees to marry her. Mařenka, now downcast at Jeník's supposed perfidy, also agrees to think things over. The pathos of her predicament is underlined in a slow sextet ('Rozmysli si, Mařenko') and in the moving aria she sings after it ('Ten lásky sen'). When Jeník joins her to explain, she will not listen ('Tak tvrdošijná divko, jsi'). Kecal calls the company to announce his final success. But Vašek's parents, Háta and Mícha, are amazed to see Jeník, now insisting on his rights as 'Mícha's son' to marry Mařenka. Mařenka realizes how Jeník has outwitted the others and gladly forgives him. Kecal is humiliated, but it is only when Vašek makes his appearance as the 'bear', that Mícha finally concedes that he is too young to marry and gives his blessing to the union of Jeník and Mařenka.

The Bartered Bride is so full of spontaneous charm that it is hard to credit how long it took to reach its final form. The fact that the dances were a late addition is particularly surprising, since dance rhythms underline much of the basic substance of the opera. Many of the numbers are based on polka-type rhythms (fast two-in-a-bar) or *sousedská* rhythms (slow three-in-a-bar). Very few have complex forms, with introductions or changes of tempo and metre: isolated by the spoken dialogue, they must have seemed especially dancelike in the original version. Surprisingly in a 'folk opera', the chorus is given comparatively little to do (the male drinking chorus was another late addition), and instead the heart of the opera is the dazzling succession of duets: a loving duet for hero and heroine at the beginning and an angry one at the end; an immensely skilful one for Mařenka and the stuttering Vašek and, in another contrast of opposites, the brilliant duet for the high-spirited Jeník and the ponderous Kecal. Smetana's character-drawing was especially sharp in this opera, and the self-important Kecal, established in just a few notes of limited range in his opening solo, spawned a whole generation of Czech comic successors. The overture, in Smetana's most brilliant fugal scherzando style, is a frequently performed concert piece in its own right. The opera's successful production by the

Prague National Theatre at the Vienna Music and Theatre Exhibition in June 1892 initiated its popularity abroad, the only Czech opera to achieve this before the advent of Janáček.

Dalibor

Opera in three acts (2h 15m)
Libretto by Josef Wenzig (in German); trans. Ervin Spindler
Composed April 1865–December 1867
PREMIERES 16 May 1868, New Town Theatre, Prague; 2 December 1870, Provisional Theatre, Prague (rev. with cuts and a new ending; US: 13 April 1924, Sokol Hall, Chicago; UK: 17 August 1964, King's Theatre, Edinburgh
CAST Vladislav *bar*, Dalibor *t*, Budivoj *bar*, Beneš *b*, Milada *s*, *s*, *t*; *satb* chorus of judges, royal household, vassals of the king, messengers, servants, people

SYNOPSIS

The action takes place in 15th-century Prague.

Act I The people await the trial of Dalibor, a Czech knight whose crime has been to avenge the death of his friend the musician Zdeněk. Dalibor killed the burgrave of Ploškovice; Milada, the burgrave's sister, demands of King Vladislav that Dalibor forfeit his life. Dalibor's appearance and his brave and defiant defence of his action, however, have an unexpected effect on Milada, who now begs the king to spare Dalibor. But the king declares that the law must take its course, and Milada vows to free him herself.

Act II By disguising herself as a boy musician, Milada enters the service of Beneš, Dalibor's gaoler. Beneš is charmed by his young assistant and allows him down to the cell with a violin that Dalibor has asked for to while away the time. She reveals her identity to Dalibor, who greets her as his liberator. Milada's attempt to buy off Beneš, however, does not succeed.

Act III When the king hears about the plot to rescue Dalibor he takes the advice of his council, and gives instructions for Dalibor to be executed. Milada waits outside with her followers, but instead of Dalibor's signal she hears the death knell. She charges into the prison and, though mortally wounded, she rescues Dalibor before dying in his arms. Dalibor is recaptured and led away to execution.

After the success of Smetana's first two operas, *Dalibor* was received at first politely, then with increasing hostility. It was thought that Smetana had deserted the path of 'Czechness' in search of foreign gods, Wagner in particular. There is some truth in the first part of this accusation. Apart from a soldiers' chorus at the beginning of Act II, *Dalibor* has none of Smetana's usual folk-sounding lighter numbers. The orchestra was used not as a purveyor of Czech dances, but as a powerful scene-setter, for example in the processional music for King Vladislav, a sort of Czech 'Pomp and Circumstance'. Instead of a succession of dancelike numbers, audiences were confronted with long, declamatory sections ingeniously spun out of relatively little material so that the opera is often claimed to be monothematic. The story, for all its claims as a Czech historical opera, bears a striking resemblance to that of *Fidelio* (though with a typically

Czech insistence on the musicianly accomplishments of its main characters). The text was not merely a translation of a German libretto, but one that aped the metrical scheme of the original. It is hardly surprising that the resulting voice parts are frequently misstressed and seldom display typical Czech speech rhythms. It was only in 1886, two years after Smetana's death, that true dramatic voices could be found for the two main parts and a new attempt to stage it was made at the new National Theatre. The result was a triumph that revealed some of Smetana's finest dramatic music and established the work's lasting place in the Czech repertoire.

The Two Widows

Dvě vdovy
Comic opera in two acts (2h 15m)
Libretto by Emanuel Züngel, after the play *Les deux veuves* by Felicien Mallefille
Composed July 1873–January 1874; rev. 10 June–July 1877, 1882
PREMIERES 27 March 1874, Provisional Theatre, Prague (with spoken dialogue); 15 March 1878, Provisional Theatre, Prague (with recitatives and extra numbers); US: 23 October 1949, Sokol Hall, New York; UK: 17 June 1963, Guildhall School of Music and Drama, London
CAST Karolina *s*, Anežka *ms*, Ladislav Podhajský *t*, Mumlal *b*; added in 1877: *s*, *t*; *satb* chorus of young countryfolk

The Two Widows is Smetana's only completed opera based on a non-Czech subject, a light French bourgeois comedy.

SYNOPSIS

Act I The two widows of the title, Karolina and Anežka, are quite different in temperament. Karolina has energetically taken over the running of her estate, where the action is set; her cousin Anežka is mourning guiltily for her unloved husband and is consequently deaf to the pleas of her suitor Ladislav. Ladislav contrives to be arrested as a poacher by Karolina's slow-witted and self-congratulatory gamekeeper, Mumlal. The culprit is duly sentenced and imprisoned within the house.

Act II It takes not only Ladislav's protestations of love but also a little jealousy of an artful Karolina for Anežka to yield. A subsidiary love affair was added in the 1877 revision between Mumlal's daughter Lidka and his assistant Toník which, at first resisted by Mumlal, is also happily resolved.

Richard Strauss is said to have demanded performances of *The Two Widows* on his visits to Prague. One can see why: the appeal of the work, in both the origin of the text and the sophisticated charm of the music, is superficially cosmopolitan and easily accessible. But of all Smetana's operas this is the one most permeated by the rhythm of the polka, which, with its down-beat rhythms, reflects the natural down-beat patterns of Czech speech. Trochaic (i.e. polka-like) verse was provided by the highly experienced librettist and translator Emanuel Züngel, though this is set by Smetana with a virtuosity that avoids monotony. Furthermore, the nub of the plot – the overcoming of internal obstacles that hinder a marriage – foreshadows the concerns of Smetana's later operas set to Krásnohorská libretti. Despite this, the opera was not popular in its original version. As in *The Bartered Bride*, Smetana later replaced original spoken dialogue with through-composed recitatives. At the same time there was an attempt to establish a more identifiably 'Czech' milieu, introducing a comic country couple and a convincing imitation of a folksong for Ladislav at the beginning of Act II. Much later, for a German production in Hamburg in 1882, Smetana reluctantly added a trio in Act I and an alternative ending to Anežka's Act II aria, and consented to a redivision of the opera into three acts.

The Kiss

Hubička

Folk (*prostonárodní*) opera in two acts (1h 45m)
Libretto by Eliška Krásnohorská, after the tale by Karolina Světlá (1871)
PREMIERES 7 November 1876, Provisional Theatre, Prague; US: 17 April 1921, Blackstone Theater, Chicago; UK: 8 December 1938, Liverpool (amateur); 18 October 1948, King's Theatre, Hammersmith, London
CAST Father Paloucký *b*, Vendulka *s*, Lukáš *t*, Tomeš *bar*, Martinka *c*, *s*, *t*, *b*; *satb* chorus of neighbours, girls, musicians, smugglers

Smetana's contacts with Eliška Krásnohorská, the librettist of his final years, began in 1869 with the proposed *Lumír* and were taken further in 1871 with *Viola*, but even this work was soon set aside. *The Kiss* was their first completed collaboration. For all their apparent *naïveté*, Krásnohorská's libretti had the virtue of inspiring the composer – he said he found 'music' in them. He could have found this in her carefully crafted verse, with different metres employed according to character or mood or to differentiate stages in multi-sectioned arias. But equally the subject matter seems to have been congenial for the ageing composer, locked in a loveless marriage. All the Krásnohorská heroes are middle-aged and have difficulty getting together with a suitable partner. It is only through personal learning that success is achieved.

SYNOPSIS
Set in a Czech border village, the opera deals with the relationship of Lukáš, now a widower, and his former sweetheart, Vendulka, who has remained unmarried.
Act I Lukáš is anxious to return to his real love and to give his young baby a mother. The engagement party, however, runs into trouble: out of respect for Lukáš's dead wife, Vendulka refuses to seal the engagement with a kiss. Both stubbornly refuse to budge from their positions, despite a touching scene where they are left together to resolve their differences but where their strong characters increasingly clash. The engagement party is spoilt; Lukáš storms off and gets drunk; Vendulka sings lullabies to the infant.
Act II The quarrel is solved only after both have fled into the borderland forest – Vendulka with her spirited Aunt Martinka on a smuggling expedition, Lukáš in a fit of remorse poured out to his best man, Tomeš. The reconciliation is finally sealed with a kiss.

The Kiss was the first opera Smetana wrote after going deaf. If this left any trace in the work it is in the depth of feeling he brought to the chief characters. Father Paloucký, conceived by the librettist as a comic bore, emerges as a figure of real and touching concern for his daughter. The positions of both Lukáš and Vendulka are made believable, transforming a naïve plot into a work of real depth and tenderness. It was a success from the start, and has remained popular with Czech audiences. Contemporary audiences were particularly taken with what appeared to be the work's 'Czechness'. This was advertised by the work's genre designation and by a rare borrowing by Smetana of a well-known traditional *pastorella* song ('Hajej mů andílku') for Vendulka's first lullaby. But her second lullaby ('Letěla bělounká holubička'), though Smetana's invention, is regarded as no less Czech. As in *The Two Widows*, certain numbers are based on polka rhythms, most prominently in Lukáš's drunken song at the end of Act I.

The Secret

Tajemství

Comic opera in three acts (1h 45m)
Libretto by Eliška Krásnohorská
PREMIERES 18 September 1878, New Czech Theatre, Prague; UK: 7 December 1956, Town Hall, Oxford; US: 7 January 1989, New York
CAST Malina *b*, Kalina *bar*, Panna Roza (Miss Roza) *a*, Blaženka *s*, Vít *t*, Bonifác *b*, Skřivánek *t*, *s*, *t*, *bar*, *b*; *satb* chorus of aldermen, neighbours, boys and girls, threshers, apprentice bricklayers, spirits and apparitions in Kalina's dreams, bagpiper

SYNOPSIS
The setting is a small town beneath the Bezděz mountain in northern Bohemia towards the end of the 18th century.
Act I The plot initially concerns itself with the rivalry of two aldermen, Malina and Kalina. Behind this is the story of bitter love which has left its mark on the main characters. Years ago Kalina had loved Roza, the daughter of Malina, but had been refused by her father, on the grounds of his poverty. Kalina and Roza each misinterpreted this as unfaithfulness on the other's part: he married in a fit of pique (though he is now a widower), and she has remained a spinster. Roza is particularly embittered as Friar Barnabáš told her before his death that he had left a 'secret' with Kalina that would enable him to marry her. This 'secret' comes to light during a fracas between the followers of the two rivals, and knowledge of it is soon passed around the inhabitants of the small town.
Act II Kalina is in debt; he dreams of Barnabáš and a treasure. Inspired by the 'secret', he begins digging a tunnel.
Act III What he finds at the end of the tunnel is human rather than monetary treasure: the secret tunnel leads to Malina's house, and thus to Roza, who accepts her former sweetheart.

The Secret is a development of several aspects of the previous Krásnohorská–Smetana collaboration. Again at its centre is an older couple who missed their chance of happiness earlier on. And again after a symbolic gesture of searching – the dramatic, almost Freudian journey down the tunnel – the internal obstacle is removed. The location of a small town rather than a village provides a different type of genre painting. There is a particularly rich variety of town 'types' – small cameo parts that include a cantankerous foreman, a ballad-singer (accompanying himself on the guitar and attempting to sing a song to flatter both rivals simultaneously), a retired soldier (Bonifác), who tries to woo Roza with his bragging, and a bagpiper, who provides one of the many bagpipe episodes in Czech opera. Most of the cast is assembled for one of Smetana's most appealing late concertati in Act II, which reverses the usual scheme: a gossamer-textured scherzo, followed by a slow ensemble of perplexity ('Ó klamné domnění'). This, rather than the overused portentous 'secret' motif ('Ted' slavně, těžce slibte mi'), provides one of the chief musical delights of the piece, though there are also some of Smetana's finest arias, such as the multi-sectioned 'gold' aria for Kalina at the beginning of Act II and the delightful songs for Malina's daughter Blaženka ('Což ta voda') and the ballad-singer Skřivánek ('Aj k čemu') in Act III.

Other operas: *The Brandenburgers in Bohemia* (*Branibori v Čechách*), 1866; *Libuše*, (1872), 1881; *Viola* (inc., 1884), 1900; *The Devil's Wall* (*Čertova Stěna*), 1882

J. T.

ETHEL SMYTH
(Dame) Ethel Mary Smyth; *b* 22 April 1858, Marylebone, London; *d* 9 May 1944, Woking, Surrey

The daughter of a general, Smyth became a composer against every convention of Victorian life. Not surprisingly, she had little early success in Britain. She studied in Leipzig, and was for a long time better known in Germany than at home. Her first three operas, *Fantasio* (1898), *Der Wald* (1901) and *The Wreckers* (1906), were all premiered there, while her later fame in Britain was more like notoriety, because of her activities as a suffragette (she was imprisoned in 1911 for throwing a brick through the home secretary's window), as a campaigner for women's rights in music, and as an all-round social, sartorial and sexual eccentric, whose association with Bloomsbury included a lesbian affair with Virginia Woolf.

Outside opera, Smyth's most ambitious works (the Mass in D and a late vocal–orchestral piece called *The Prison*) are eclectic in style and uneven in execution. Of her six operas, only *The Wreckers* has been revived since the war, though *The Boatswain's Mate* was popular during her lifetime. She was a prolific and entertaining *mémoiriste*, and a vigorous lobbier of newspaper editors; she never allowed the cause to smother her essential humanity and good humour.

The Wreckers
Opera in three acts (2h 15m)

Libretto by Henry Brewster; an adaptation of a Cornish drama, *Les naufrageurs*
Composed 1903–4
PREMIERES 11 November 1906, Neues Theater, Leipzig (as *Standrecht*); UK: 30 May 1908, Queen's Hall, London (concert); 22 June 1909, His Majesty's Theatre, London

Long famous as a step towards a national British opera (its London stage premiere was conducted by Beecham), *The Wreckers* looks forward in its subject to another tide-mark of British opera, Britten's *Peter Grimes*. *The Wreckers* are almost the entire population of a Cornish fishing village, who, in times of famine, supplement their livelihood by luring storm-bound shipping on to the rocky coast. Even the local Wesleyan preacher, Pascoe, abets them; but his wife, Thirza, helps her lover, Mark, to warn the ships off, and for their pains the two are walled up in a tidal cave and left to drown.

For obvious reasons, Smyth's models are mainly German. Though no Wagnerite, she makes some use of his motivic technique, while the texture, orchestration and even some of the music's dramatic density show knowledge of the works of Richard Strauss. At its best (for instance in the love music of Act II) *The Wreckers* has genuine music-theatrical power. But it also slips too readily into operatic convention, and, as a whole (like other works by Smyth), lacks a strong musical personality of its own.

Other operas: *Fantasio*, 1898; *Der Wald*, 1901; *The Boatswain's Mate*, 1916; *Fête galante*, 1923; *Entente cordiale*, 1925

S.W.

STEPHEN SONDHEIM
Stephen Joshua Sondheim; *b* 22 March 1930, New York

Having studied the writing of musicals in his youth with Oscar Hammerstein II – a neighbour – and composition with Milton Babbitt, Stephen Sondheim earned his living for a time writing television scripts. As early as 1954 he was given the opportunity to write a Broadway score, *Saturday Night*, a project ended by the death of its prospective producer. This exposure secured Sondheim the chance to write lyrics for prestigious shows composed by Leonard Bernstein (*West Side Story*) and Jule Styne (*Gypsy*). Thereafter, with rare exceptions, he has written both lyrics and music for all his projects, and done so on an exceptionally high level.

His recognition as a significant contributor to musical theatre began with *Company* and has grown ever since; each of his new projects is eagerly awaited well in advance of its appearance. His lyrics can exhibit, as the case demands, either a memorable simplicity or a dazzling complexity unmatched even by Lorenz Hart or W. S. Gilbert. His music, supported by reworking of recurring motifs and by textural and rhythmic invention that set new standards for the Broadway score, can encompass extended ensembles and through-composed musical scenes, fragmentary recitative-like passages, or catchy 32-bar show tunes. Though he does not make much use of the classically defined operatic voice categories, his biggest scores are indeed operatic in their scope and integrity.

Follies

Musical in one act (two acts in 1987 version)
Libretto by James Goldman; lyrics by the composer
Composed (intermittently) 1965–71
PREMIERES 4 April 1971, Winter Garden, New York; UK: 26 April 1985, Library Theatre, Manchester; rev. version: 21 July 1987, Shaftesbury Theatre, London

Follies presents a reunion of the Follies girls who used to perform in an annual revue in years gone by. Two of the women in particular, along with the men they married, find themselves dealing with their lifelong problems through reminiscence and a final dreamlike show in which each exposes his or her own 'folly' in song and dance. The show is thus structured as a book musical interspersed with revue songs (the individual reminiscences of Follies veterans) and culminating in a full-scale surrealistic Follies re-creation. In its original form, *Follies* was probably the most affecting of the shows Sondheim has written, and its score may well rank as his richest work.

A Little Night Music

Musical in two acts (2h)
Libretto by Hugh Wheeler, based on the film *Smiles of a Summer Night* by Ingmar Bergman (1955); lyrics by the composer
PREMIERES 25 February 1973, Shubert Theater, New York; UK: 15 April 1975, Adelphi Theatre, London
CAST Desirée Arnfeldt *c*, Fredrik Egerman *bar*, Mme Arnfeldt *c*, Countess Charlotte Malcolm *ms*, Count Carl-Magnus Malcolm *bar*, Anne *s*, Henrik *t*, Petra *c*, Fredrika Arnfeldt *child s*, Liebeslieder Quintet *s*, *ms*, *c*, *t*, *bar*, 4 servants *silent*

Those who had imagined that they understood the direction of Sondheim's work in the 1970s found *A Little Night Music* a surprise: a conventional period story albeit theatrically stylized. It deals with the contemporary themes of suppressed longings, missed connections and sensual fulfilment: it also contains an effervescent waltzing score and Sondheim's best-known song ('Send in the Clowns').

In Sweden at the turn of the century, the lawyer Fredrik Egerman, frustrated with the unwillingness of his young wife Anne to consummate their marriage, turns to his old flame Desirée, an actress. Desirée herself is currently involved with the count, whose wife is a friend of Anne's. Fredrik's son from his first marriage, Henrik, is unhappy with his dedication to religious purity, finding himself attracted to the maid Petra and to his new stepmother. Desirée, in collusion with her mother (Mme Arnfeldt) and daughter (Fredrika), decides to invite everyone to her mother's villa for the weekend. After confrontations, seductions, duels, and disappointments, the pairs are recombined. Anne runs off with Henrik, the count and countess reunite, and Fredrik returns to Desirée.

Sweeney Todd, the Demon Barber of Fleet Street

Musical thriller in two acts (2h 15m)
Libretto by Hugh Wheeler, based on a version of *Sweeney Todd* by Christopher Bond; lyrics by the composer
PREMIERES 1 March 1979, Uris Theater, New York; UK: 3 July 1980, Drury Lane, London
CAST Sweeney Todd *b-bar*, Mrs Lovett *ms*, Anthony Hope *t*, Johanna *s*, Judge Turpin *b*, Beggar Woman *ms*, Beadle *high t*, Tobias Ragg *t*, Pirelli *t*, Jonas Fogg *spoken role*; *satb* chorus of Londoners

The score for this brutal melodrama is Sondheim's most ambitious: rarely interrupted for dialogue, tightly interwoven motivically (several of the motifs derive from the *Dies irae*), with intricate ensembles and a central role for the chorus, which frames the action with 'The Ballad of Sweeney Todd'.

SYNOPSIS
Act I A deported criminal returns to 19th-century London to take revenge on the judge who destroyed his family. With the help of a neighbour, the baker Mrs Lovett, he resumes his trade as a barber under the name Sweeney Todd. He misses his opportunity to cut the judge's throat, and resolves to expand his murderous activities.

Act II A multiple murderer now, with his victims baked into Mrs Lovett's pies, Todd finds his daughter Johanna and uses her as bait to draw the judge back to the barber shop. He finally kills the judge – and also a beggar woman who turns out to be his own wife, whom he had supposed dead. By the time the story ends, he and Mrs Lovett are dead too.

Merrily We Roll Along

Musical in two acts (2h 30m)
Libretto by George Furth, based on the play by George S. Kaufman and Moss Hart (1934); lyrics by the composer
Composed 1980–81; rev. 1985, 1989–90
PREMIERES 16 November 1981, Alvin Theater, New York; UK: 28 March 1983, Guildhall School of Music and Drama, London

The lives of three friends who mostly failed to fulfil their early promise are given poignancy by being shown (as in the source play) in reverse time order, so that their first meeting forms the last scene. The brief New York run has been followed by many amateur productions; the authors have also made some revisions.

Sunday in the Park with George

Musical in two acts (2h 30m)
Libretto by James Lapine; lyrics by the composer
PREMIERES 2 May 1984, Booth Theater, New York; UK: 15 March 1990, National Theatre, London

Act I follows the life and obsessions of Georges Seurat as he neglects his personal life in favour of gathering characters for his Parisian painting *A Sunday Afternoon on the Island of La Grande Jatte* – which is created as a tableau at the close of the act.

Act II shifts to New York and George, the painter's

great-grandson, and contrasts his present-day struggles for artistic expression with those of his ancestor.

This show marked a change in collaborators for Sondheim, and to some extent a stylistic reorientation too, with many songs merging into each other in through-composed recitative-like passages. Despite its seemingly esoteric subject and manner, it had enough popular appeal to run on Broadway for a year and a half, and won a Pulitzer Prize for drama (the sixth to go to a musical).

Into the Woods

Musical in two acts (2h 30m)
Libretto by James Lapine; lyrics by the composer
PREMIERES 5 November 1987, Martin Beck Theater, New York; UK: 25 September 1990, Phoenix Theatre, London

Four familiar fairy-tales interact with a newly invented one: a baker and his wife, in order to remove the curse of barrenness placed by a witch on his family, must obtain Jack's cow, Little Red Riding Hood's cape, Rapunzel's hair and Cinderella's slipper. All five stories are happily resolved at the end of the first act, after which the second act explores the destructive consequences of their actions. *Into the Woods* continued the trend of *Sunday in the Park* towards stretches of near-continuous music combining underscoring, songs (sometimes very short) and gradual transitions. It proved accessible enough to enjoy the second-longest Broadway run of any of Sondheim's shows (after *A Funny Thing Happened on the Way to the Forum*).

Assassins

Musical in one act (1h 45m)
Libretto by John Weidman
PREMIERES 27 January 1991, Playwrights Horizons, New York; UK: 29 October 1992, Donmar Warehouse, London

Seen by fewer theatre-goers during its initial run than any other Sondheim musical (at a limited subscription engagement at a very small off-Broadway theatre), *Assassins* is also the most controversial of Sondheim's shows. Its main characters are the historical figures who have assassinated presidents of the US (or tried to), and its format suggests a revue while utilizing such typical styles of traditional popular music as march, cakewalk, barbershop quartet, guitar ballad and hymn. The score departs from the near-continuous musical texture of Sondheim's previous two creations, instead alternating songs and spoken scenes, sometimes with a framework provided by a folksinging narrator. Some scenes are re-creations of historical events; others allow figures from different eras, such as John Wilkes Booth and Lee Harvey Oswald, to interact.

Passion

Musical in one act (1h 45m)
Libretto by James Lapine, based on the film *Passione d'amore* by Ettore Scola (1981), itself based on the novel *Fosca* by Igino Ugo Tarchetti (1863); lyrics by the composer

PREMIERE 9 May 1994, Plymouth Theater, New York

In 19th-century Italy, the soldier Giorgio is involved in an ardent love affair with Clara, a beautiful married woman. Reassigned to a remote post, he becomes both fascinated and repelled by Fosca, an unattractive and sickly woman. She responds to his politeness with declarations of undying love, and is undeterred by all his attempts to discourage or escape her. Ultimately, Giorgio finds his relationship with Clara lacking in the passion he sees in Fosca, and they part; he returns to Fosca, and is left after her death to reflect on what she taught him about love.

In many ways more a chamber opera than a musical (albeit with substantial spoken scenes, some of which are underscored), *Passion* is as relentless as Fosca herself. It contains little humour, no sub-plot, and no breaks for applause until the very end. Much of the action is conveyed by letters sent by the three main characters, who are indeed the only substantial figures (soldiers and servants comprise a small ensemble). Fosca is one of the more unusual roles in any musical – certainly an opportunity for a skilled singing actress.

Other musicals: *A Funny Thing Happened on the Way to the Forum*, 1962; *Anyone can Whistle*, 1964; *Company*, 1970; *The Frogs*, 1974; *Pacific Overtures*, 1976

J.A.C.

GASPARE SPONTINI

Gaspare Luigi Pacifico Spontini; *b* 14 November 1774, Maiolati, Italy; *d* 24 January 1851, Maiolati

Spontini played a vital part in the formation of early Romantic opera. He enjoyed his greatest success under Napoleon. Like many Italians, he found France a propitious place to work, for although he had composed a dozen operas in Italy, mostly comedies, he made little impression as a composer until he won the patronage of the empress Josephine in Paris. His career there began with three opéras comiques and then blossomed overnight with the appearance of *La vestale* in 1807. This was his masterpiece, and it caught the imagination of the times. Its simple plot and its strongly expressive musical language give it an important place in the development of French opera, leading from the tradition of Gluck and Piccinni towards the styles of Berlioz and Meyerbeer.

Two years later he produced *Fernand Cortez*, in which a tendency towards spectacular staging is evident, perhaps reflecting the grandeur of Napoleonic ambition; and the same emphasis on scenic effect is found in the last of his Parisian operas, *Olimpie* of 1819. His centre of activity then moved to Berlin, as generalmusikdirektor to the king of Prussia, where his work never equalled the standard of his Parisian operas and he found himself embroiled in controversy. Politically conservative and inclined to touchiness, he was a difficult colleague. Yet Berlioz, to whom he was always generous in his support, declared that he loved Spontini; he was a widely respected figure, especially in France. Berlioz's early music owes much to Spontini, and Wagner too drew ideas freely from Spontini's scores.

He was advanced as an orchestrator, often trying new groupings, new effects, especially with mutes, and managing offstage bands with considerable care to create the illusion of distance. He was one of the first to use the metronome. He had an Italian's gift of melody but a Frenchman's care for the expressive projection of words. His operas contributed much to the increasing power required of leading singers, since they not only had to compete with a louder, larger orchestra but were also expected to maintain a high level of intensity. His heroic tenors already belong to the modern type. Spontini exercised a powerful influence over the following generation, but his work did not survive beyond the end of the 19th century; revivals and recordings in modern times have been rare.

La vestale
The Vestal Virgin
Tragédie lyrique in three acts (3h)
Libretto by Étienne de Jouy
PREMIERES 15 December 1807, Opéra, Paris; US: 17 February 1828, Théâtre d'Orléans, New Orleans; UK: 2 December 1826, King's Theater, Haymarket, London
CAST Licinius *t*, Cinna *t*, Julia *s*, High Priestess *ms*, Pontifex Maximus *b*, Chief Soothsayer *b*; *satb* chorus of vestal virgins, priests, matrons, young women, senators, consuls, lictors, warriors, gladiators, children, prisoners

La vestale was Spontini's first work for the Paris Opéra and his greatest success. It was accepted only through the intervention of the empress Josephine. He had composed no opera in Italy or France that gave any foretaste of this modern brand of Gluckian serious opera, and it set a standard that was to be incorporated into French grand opera after the Napoleonic period. It remained in the repertoire during the first half of the 19th century and profoundly influenced both Berlioz and Wagner. The drama presents the classic conflict of love and duty in the person of Julia, the vestal virgin whose vows forbid her to yield to Licinius' passion.

SYNOPSIS
Act I Licinius, the victorious Roman general, confides to his friend Cinna that he cannot enjoy acclamation and honour since Julia, whose hand he has long sought to win, has been forced by her father to become a priestess of Vesta, sworn to chastity. Julia still loves Licinius, despite her vows, and it falls to her to place the crown of victory on Licinius' head. During the ceremony, Licinius learns that Julia has to guard the sacred flame at night.
Act II Licinius visits the temple where Julia is on watch. In the excitement of passion, they allow the flame to go out. With Cinna's help Licinius escapes, but Julia is stripped of her insignia and condemned to death, refusing to name the man who was with her.
Act III Licinius attempts to persuade Pontifex Maximus to exercise his mercy, even admitting his part in Julia's guilt, but is rebuffed. Julia prepares to be entombed alive, when suddenly a storm breaks

and a thunderbolt strikes the altar, relighting the sacred flame and proving Vesta's forgiveness. The lovers are reunited.

The tragédie has a happy ending, but the emotional intensity of the opera, especially in Act II, is on a high dramatic level, worthy of a genuine tragedy. The scenes of solemnity and celebration are inherited from a long tradition in French opera, including Gluck, but the expressive intensity of Julia's music belongs truly to the new century. Its orchestration was considered noisy in its time, but it simply reflects the grandiose tastes of the Empire. In *La vestale* Spontini first revealed his striking gift for dramatic recitative, absorbing elements found in Gluck and Cherubini.

Other operas: *I puntigli delle donne*, 1796; *Adelina Senese, o sia L'amore secreto*, 1797; *L'eroismo ridicolo*, 1798; *Il Teseo riconosciuto*, 1798; *La finta filosofa*, 1799; *La fuga in maschera*, 1800; *Gli Elisi delusi*, 1800; *La petite maison*, 1804; *Milton*, 1804; *Julie, ou Le pot de fleurs*, 1805; *Fernand Cortez, ou La conquête du Méxique*, 1809 (rev. 1817, 1832); *Pélage, ou Le roi et la paix*, 1814; *Les dieux rivaux, ou Les fêtes de Cythère*, 1816; *Olimpie*, 1819 (rev. 1820, 1826); *Nurmahal, oder Das Rosenfest von Caschmir*, 1822; *Alcidor*, 1825; *Agnes von Hohenstaufen*, 1829; 4 lost operas

H.M.

KARLHEINZ STOCKHAUSEN
b 22 August 1928, Mödrath, nr Cologne, Germany

Stockhausen had no professional contact with opera throughout the first quarter-century of his composing life. Many of his works from the 1950s and 1960s have a strong element of spectacle – the concourse of three orchestras in *Gruppen* (1955–7), the response of a pianist and a percussionist to electronic sounds arriving from a tape in *Kontakte* (1959–60), the operation of six performers to extract vibrations from an amplified giant tam-tam in *Mikrophonie I* (1964), the chanting of a circle of six vocalists in *Stimmung* (1968) – but always the dramatic gesture arises from the musical practicality. The only two pieces with a distinct theatrical dimension – *Originale* (1961, a 'happening' with *Kontakte*) and *Oben und Unten* (a 'text composition' of 1968) – are among the few works the composer has not chosen to promote, and were marginal to his main endeavour, which was to conceive and exemplify new systems of composition based on what was known of the nature of sound.

But at the start of the 1970s this changed. Henceforth the rarity is the work that fails to present a dramatic illusion, though Stockhausen's background in instrumental and electronic music, coupled with his experience of Asian theatre as a widely travelling musician in the 1960s, made his approach to the lyric stage unusual. Perhaps his principal innovation was putting instrumentalists on stage as embodiments of dramatic characters, even to the extent that singers are secondary. Also, the lack of a consecutive narrative or of dialogue makes his theatrical works more like ceremonials or dream transcriptions than European plays and operas. Examples include *Trans* (1971) for an orchestra bathed in magenta light, *Harlekin* (1975) for a clarinettist who acts the part of a comic–didactic virtuoso, and *Sirius* (1975–7), where four soloists (trumpeter, soprano, bass clarinettist and bass singer) appear as visitors from another planet to play to the accompaniment of synthesized music. Since this, nearly all his works have been parts of *Licht*, a cycle of seven works with which he is making his operatic début.

Licht: Die sieben Tage der Woche

Light: The Seven Days of the Week
Cycle of seven operas
Libretto by the composer
Composed 1977

The cycle has three principal characters, each of whom may be interpreted by one or more singers, instrumentalists and dancers: Michael, the hero figure, has his avatars in trumpet, tenor and dancer; Eva, the mother and lover, has hers in basset horn, soprano and dancer; and Luzifer, the father and antagonist, has his in trombone, bass and dancer. (The overlap with *Sirius* comes about because since the mid-1970s Stockhausen has worked most regularly with members of his family and entourage, including his trumpeter son Markus and the clarinettist Suzanne Stephens.) Each of the characters is also associated with a melodic formula, and the three formulae function partly as leitmotifs (because they, and different segments and superpositions of them, are linked with characters and events), partly as series (because all the music is notionally extrapolated from them) and partly as ragas (because they provide material for melodic elaboration).

The formulae ensure a certain consistency, and sometimes much more than that: whole sections of the score (e.g. *Luzifers Traum* in *Samstag aus Licht*) echo and re-echo the same harmonies, as if in minute examination of a brief instant of more normal musical time. This extremely static character goes along with the ceremonial nature of the enterprise, and also with the cycle's didactic intentions. Stockhausen works on his audience (and indeed on his performers) as a teacher, come to explain, slowly and steadily, how to listen to this music of melodic extrapolation: the performers, too, are asked to present themselves as instructors, especially in crucial scenes where education through and in music is what happens (*Michaels Reise* in *Donnerstag aus Licht*, *Kathinkas Gesang* in *Samstag aus Licht*, *Evas Lied* in *Montag aus Licht*). However, the general solemnity and slowness are offset by a robust humour and by the great variety of means and forms. Each opera is a sequence of acts, scenes and vignettes which are highly diverse in scoring (drawing on a range of instrumental, vocal and electronic resources) and can be performed separately.

When complete, the cycle will consist of an opera for each day of the week, with different arrangements of the characters dominant in each: *Montag* (Eva: birth), *Dienstag* (Michael–Luzifer: war), *Mittwoch* (Eva–Luzifer: consolidation), *Donnerstag* (Michael: learning), *Freitag* (Michael–Eva: Eva's temptation), *Samstag* (Luzifer: death), *Sonntag* (Michael–Eva–Luzifer: mystic union of Eva and Michael).

Donnerstag aus Licht

Thursday from Light
Opera in a greeting, three acts and a farewell (3h 45m)
Composed 1978–80
PREMIERES 3 April 1981, La Scala, Milan; UK: 16 September 1985, Covent Garden, London

Samstag aus Licht

Saturday from Light
Opera in a greeting and four scenes (3h)
Composed 1981–3
PREMIERE 25 May 1984, Palazzo dello Sport, Milan

Montag aus Licht

Monday from Light
Opera in a greeting, three acts and a farewell (4h 30m)
Composed 1984–8
PREMIERE 7 May 1988, La Scala, Milan

Dienstag aus Licht

Tuesday from Light
Opera in a greeting and two acts (2h 30m)
Composed 1977–91
PREMIERE 10 May 1992, Gulbenkian Foundation, Lisbon

P.A.G.

JOHANN STRAUSS II

Johann Baptist Strauss; *b* 25 October 1825, Vienna; *d* 3 June 1899, Vienna

Johann Strauss II, the celebrated waltz king, was also the composer of the greatest of all Viennese operettas, *Die Fledermaus*, and a few others which still hold the stage. Although he chose his libretti foolishly and often set them mindlessly, the charge that Strauss had no theatrical instinct remains patently false. His music remains for millions the chief embodiment of the last glittering years of the Austro-Hungarian Empire.

Johann Strauss (the first waltz king) discouraged his son from becoming a professional musician. However, after his father left the family in 1842, the younger Strauss took a thorough musical training and his persistence soon paid off among the Viennese music publishers and dance halls, where he conducted his own orchestra. Soon Strauss II was as famous a composer, violinist and conductor as his father, and by the mid-1860s, when the huge success of Offenbach's operettas in Vienna aroused his interest, had also built up an international reputation through concert tours.

Strauss's first wife, Jetty Treffz, took some musical sketches to the director of the Theater an der Wien, Maximilian Steiner, who was able to convince the composer that his music was stageworthy. In 1869 Strauss composed *Die lustigen Weiber von Wien*, which was never produced, but his next operetta, *Indigo und die vierzig Räuber* (1871), was staged at the Theater an der Wien, conducted by the composer. Wags discussing the uncredited, unoriginal libretto referred to the '40 librettists'. But the public went crazy. There were productions abroad. The Paris version included the 'Blue Danube' waltz, whose phenomenal popularity is paralleled in the influence Strauss exerted not only on two generations of Viennese operetta, but on 'serious' composers. Brahms wrote of it, 'Not, unfortunately, by Johannes Brahms.' Wagner was an admirer, and among those who felt the influence of Strauss *fils* were Richard Strauss (no relation) and Maurice Ravel.

In 1873, *Der Karneval in Rom*, the first of Strauss's operettas with an Italian setting, was an even bigger critical and commercial success. Both works were revised and remounted early in the 20th century, but have rarely been seen again. Not so the next work, *Die Fledermaus*. Though not an immediate triumph, it would become the most celebrated operetta of all time, performed not only in the popular theatre but also in the temples of high art, rubbing shoulders with the works of Mozart, Verdi and Wagner.

Thereafter *Cagliostro in Wien* (1875) wedded Italian and Austrian elements, but was distinguished – like its successors – mainly for its principal waltz. For *Prinz Methusalem* (1877), Strauss did not even wait for the German translation of the original French libretto he was setting. This did not prevent the work from doing quite well in Austria and in the US. The next work was even more popular with American audiences: *Das Spitzentuch der Königin* (1880), with a libretto Suppé had declined which had as its principal characters Cervantes and the queen of Portugal. For every operetta Strauss composed, he also wrote various dance arrangements of their tunes, the sales of which were hugely lucrative for him and his publishers, and which served as publicity for the stage productions. Out of motifs from *Das Spitzentuch* came one of Strauss's greatest waltzes, 'Rosen aus dem Süden'. In the mid-1880s Strauss scored two of his greatest triumphs with *Eine Nacht in Venedig* and *Der Zigeunerbaron*; the latter is, after *Die Fledermaus*, the composer's most successful stage work.

None of Strauss's later operettas enjoyed the same acclaim, however, and, despite sporadic attempts to revive them, these works have for the most part passed into theatrical oblivion. In 1892 there were nine performances at the Hofoper of *Ritter Pázmán*, a through-composed work, set once again in Hungary. The *Waldmeister* overture is still occasionally aired, but little if anything is heard today from *Simplicius*, *Fürstin Ninetta*, *Jabuka*, or *Die Göttin der Vernunft*. In recent years, an authoritative edition of Strauss's autograph scores has shed new light on the major operettas, and it is hoped that the minor works will be re-examined on stage as well as in print.

Textual deviations must be tolerated; certainly, all manner of pasticcios using Strauss's tunes appeared after the composer's death. The most famous was *Wiener Blut* (1899), which has been accepted as a genuine Strauss operetta because Strauss authorized its composition and vetted the music chosen before he died. It remains popular as a kitsch paean to early-19th-century Vienna, despite a tiresome book, insipid characters, and lyrics that are often ill-fitted to the music. *Walzer aus Wien* was a barely biographical study of the Strausses, father and son. A worldwide hit from 1931, it has usually been produced with great splendour. In New York it was *The Great Waltz*; in Paris, *Valses de Vienne*; in London, *Waltzes from Vienna*, and it was unimaginatively filmed by Alfred Hitchcock. A Hollywood spin-off entitled *The Great Waltz* (1938) was more popular.

Die Fledermaus
The Bat

Comic operetta in three acts (2h 15m)
Libretto by Carl Haffner and Richard Genée, based on the vaudeville *Le réveillon* by Henri Meilhac and Ludovic Halévy (1872)
PREMIERES 5 April 1874, Theater an der Wien, Vienna; US: 21 November 1874, Stadt Theater, New York; UK: 18 December 1876, Alhambra Theatre, London
CAST Gabriel von Eisenstein *t*, Alfred *t*, Dr Falke *bar*, Frank *bar*, Dr Blind *t*, Frosch *spoken role*, Rosalinde von Eisenstein *s*, Adele *s*, Prince Orlofsky *ms*; *satb* chorus of party guests, servants

Strauss's most brilliant stage work is universally regarded as the Austrian operetta *in excelsis*. Originally planned for the Carltheater in Vienna as a strict translation of the play *Le réveillon*, it was then proposed by a publisher-agent as an operetta with music by Strauss for the rival Theater an der Wien. The play's more *risqué* elements – consorting with a prostitute, for one – were eliminated, and most of the original names were changed. The initial reception was quite favourable, but by 1880 the work had been seen in over 170 German-language theatres and after the Vienna Opera admitted it into its repertoire in the 1890s it was performed all over the world. Curiously, *Die Fledermaus* was not at first as popular in the US as some other Strauss operettas.

SYNOPSIS
Act I In a spa near a large city (Vienna), Eisenstein has been sentenced to prison for a minor offence. Rosalinde, his wife, is serenaded ('Täubchen, das entflattert ist') by a singing teacher, Alfred, who promises to return after Eisenstein has begun his sentence. Adele, Rosalinde's maid, discloses to the audience that she wants to attend a party that evening given by a young Russian prince, Orlofsky. She tells her mistress she wants the night off to visit her sick aunt, but Rosalinde refuses. Eisenstein enters, furious with his inept lawyer, Dr Blind, for extending his gaol sentence ('Nein, mit solchen Advokaten'), but his friend Dr Falke cheers him up by recalling the time Eisenstein left him to walk home from a party in broad daylight in a bat costume. He then mentions the ball to be held at Prince Orlofsky's. If Eisenstein turns up at the prison at six the following morning, after the ball, the governor won't mind. Eisenstein agrees, and dresses for the evening, but tells his wife that he is about to begin his sentence. They bid one another an ironically tearful farewell. Rosalinde, who has dismissed her maid for the night after all, looks forward to her tryst with Alfred. The singing teacher arrives and they settle down to a cosy supper ('Trinke, Liebchen, trinke schnell'), but are interrupted by the arrival of the prison governor, Frank, who, assuming Rosalinde's companion to be her husband, takes Alfred off to prison. Rosalinde, not wishing to be compromised,

encourages this misunderstanding ('Mein Herr, was dachten Sie von mir?'): who else but her husband would be in his dressing-gown?

Act II At Orlofsky's, the prince exhorts his guests to enjoy themselves ('Ich lade gern mir Gäste ein'); Dr Falke explains to the bored prince that he has created 'The bat's revenge' – a scheme to embarrass Eisenstein, who has just arrived in the guise of the Marquis Renard. Eisenstein recognizes Adele, who laughingly denies to the guests that she resembles his chamber-maid ('Mein Herr Marquis'). Eisenstein is introduced first to a 'compatriot', 'Chevalier Chagrin' (Frank), and then to a mysterious, masked Hungarian countess; he flirts with her using his repeater watch, little realizing she is his own wife ('Dieser Anstand, so manierlich'). The 'countess' sings of her Magyar home-land to the party guests ('Klänge der Heimat'), and Eisenstein boasts of his practical joke years before which had had Dr Falke walking home from a ball in a bat costume, to the derision of the townsfolk. Orlof-sky proposes a toast to King Champagne the First ('Im Feuerstrom der Reben'), and, as the guests become more and more mellow, Dr Falke praises the spirit of brotherly (and sisterly) love that has come over them ('Brüderlein und Schwesterlein'). A ballet display (in many productions, a small gala perform-ance with guest stars and interpolated numbers) is followed by a general waltz. As the clock strikes six, Eisenstein and Frank hurriedly depart.

Act III At the gaol, Alfred sings in his cell. The gaoler, Frosch, tries to keep him quiet. In a melodrama, Frank, thoroughly drunk, sits at his desk and falls asleep. Adele and her sister enter in search of the 'Chevalier Chagrin'; Adele is sure he can help her become an actress ('Spiel' ich die Unschuld vom Lande'). Eisenstein arrives to serve his sentence. He is surprised to see his party friend as the prison warden, and more surprised to hear that this man personally arrested Eisenstein the previous evening, and that the prisoner has already begun serving his sentence. Deter-mined to find out who the culprit cavorting with his wife is, Eisenstein disguises himself as Blind, and questions both Alfred and Rosalinde – who has come to the gaol – about their evening together. In a fury, he reveals himself, but is confronted with his own wife's fake Hungarian accent and the watch she clev-erly snatched from him. The other party-goers enter the gaol, and Falke admits the whole set-up. Rather than pursue the evening's indiscretions, the principals decide to blame everything on the champagne ('O Fledermaus, o Fledermaus').

In *Die Fledermaus* Strauss couples the Parisian tend-ency to parody with a Viennese charm that never lapses into sentimentality. The libretto inspired a suc-cession of happy ideas: Adele's high-spirited laughter becomes one of the great soubrette arias, 'Mein Herr Marquis', while the subterfuges of the various charac-ters result, as in Mozart's *Le nozze di Figaro*, in some brilliant ensembles, notably the ironic farewells in Act I ('So muss allein ich bleiben . . . o je, o je, wie rührt mich dies!') and the finales to Acts I and II. Ro-salinde's Hungarian disguise provides the excuse for the spirited csárdás 'Klänge der Heimat', while the

original ballet sequence comprised a sequence of na-tional dances (now usually replaced by a popular Strauss polka). Alfred's transformation from the or-chestra leader of the French original to singing teacher made possible the curtain-raising serenade. Only in Act III do the exuberant pacing and invention seem momentarily to falter; here the antics of the drunken Frosch can form an embarrassing weak link, though a skilled performance can equally provide the icing on the cake, as interpreters such as Franz Muxeneder and Frankie Howerd have proved.

Quite how Strauss himself saw the work within the tradition of great opera is uncertain, though the stutter-ing Dr Blind is a clear descendant of Mozart's Don Curzio, as also is Eisenstein of Count Almaviva; and the Act III melodrama in the gaol recalls comically (and surely unconsciously) *Fidelio*. But ever since Max Reinhardt's Berlin production of 1928, *Die Fledermaus* has been a fully fledged member of the operatic reper-toire, with memorable interpretations from such distin-guished names as Clemens Krauss, Herbert von Kara-jan and Carlos Kleiber.

Eine Nacht in Venedig

A Night in Venice
Operetta in three acts (2h)
Libretto by 'F. Zell' (Camillo Walzel) and Richard Genée, after the comedy *Le Château-trompette*, by Jules Cormon and Michel Carré (1860)
PREMIERES 3 October 1883, Friedrich-Wilhelmstädtisches Theater, Berlin; US: 19 April 1884, Daly's Theater, New York; UK: 25 May 1944, Cambridge Theatre, London

After the Berlin premiere of *Eine Nacht in Venedig* was greeted with howls of derision, the dialogue (which Strauss had not seen prior to the Berlin fiasco) was hastily revised for its Vienna premiere six days later. *Eine Nacht in Venedig* has been a popular favour-ite since those Viennese revisions. Various other revi-sions and new versions have been tried since, the most successful being the one produced in Vienna in 1923, with a new book by Ernst Marschka and a revised score by Korngold.

During Carnival time in 18th-century Venice, the duke of Urbino asks his barber, Caramello, to pro-cure for him the aged Senator Delacqua's comely wife, Barbara. The barber, disguised as a gondolier, delivers his own girlfriend, Annina, who has dis-guised herself as Barbara. Other characters are simi-larly disguised in the incredibly complicated plot.

Though the libretto has never been deemed satisfac-tory, the music is simply, romantically, gorgeous – one of the most opulent of all Viennese operetta scores and the one in which Strauss most artfully melded Italian and Austrian elements. It has been successfully performed at the Vienna Staatsoper and other international opera houses, and lends itself ex-ceedingly well to alfresco presentation.

Der Zigeunerbaron

The Gypsy Baron
Comic opera in three acts (2h)
Libretto by Ignaz Schnitzer, after the novella *Sáffi* by Mor Jokai (1883)

PREMIERES   24 October 1885, Theater an der Wien, Vienna; US: 15 February 1886, Casino Theater, New York; UK: 12 February 1935, Rudolf Steiner Theatre, London (amateur); 9 June 1964, Sadler's Wells, London
CAST   Sándor Barinkay *t*, Kálmán Zsupán *bar*, Ottokar *t*, Count Peter Homonay *bar*, Conte Carnero *bar*, Sáffi *s*, Czipra *ms*, Arsena *s*, Mirabella *a*, Pali *b*; *satb* chorus of gypsies, soldiers, pages, nobles, boatmen, Hungarian peasants, Viennese townspeople

Almost a musical *rapprochement* between the often-feuding dual monarchies of Austria and Hungary, *Der Zigeunerbaron* was received with enormous acclaim in both Vienna and Budapest and probably helped smooth any political friction until the end of the empire.

SYNOPSIS

Act I   In the mid 18th century, the young, exiled Barinkay returns to his estate, accompanied by the royal commissioner, Carnero ('Als flotter Geist'). The old gypsy Czipra reads Barinkay's hand and predicts he will find treasure, as well as a wife. The pig-breeder Zsupán, wealthy but illiterate ('Ja, das Schreiben und das Lesen'), proposes that the young man marry his daughter, Arsena. The girl is produced, but she is already in love with Ottokar, the son of her governess, Mirabella. Arsena proudly informs Barinkay that she cannot marry him, and wouldn't do so in any event unless he had the title of baron. Czipra's daughter Sáffi enters singing a native song ('So elend und so treu') that Barinkay seems to remember from childhood. When the other gypsies proclaim him as their long-lost master, Barinkay, now declaring himself a 'gypsy baron', again asks for Arsena's hand. When she refuses, he asks Sáffi for her hand, and insults Arsena, Zsupán, and Ottokar – who is in love with Arsena.

Act II   Barinkay and Sáffi declare their love for each other ('Mein Aug' bewacht'), and Czipra helps Barinkay locate the site of the buried treasure ('Ha, seht es winkt'). When the injured parties from Act I turn up with a morality commissioner to protest at the Barinkay and Sáffi match, the pair declare ('Wer uns getraut?') that they were married by a bullfinch and serenaded at their nuptials by a nightingale. The provincial governor, Count Homonay, rides in with his hussars to recruit patriots for the war against Spain ('Her die Hand, es muss ja sein'). Zsupán and Ottokar are drafted, and Barinkay joins up when he finds out to his surprise that Sáffi is in fact of noble birth – a Turkish pasha's daughter.

Act III   The war is over, and Homonay's regiment is being fêted in Vienna ('Freuet Euch'). Zsupán, who managed to keep away from the fighting and who has picked the pockets of its victims, is applauded by the crowds. They also cheer Barinkay, whom Homonay creates a real baron. Despite Zsupán's entreaties, Barinkay declares his love for Sáffi and allows Arsena and Ottokar to be wed.

The romantic weight of the libretto drew from Strauss a more intensely emotional score than usual, its impressive Magyar colorations mixed in with his customarily lush and exuberant Viennese style. Outstanding are,

in Act I, Barinkay's entrance song, with its lilting waltz refrain ('Ja, das alles auf Ehr!'), Zsupán's descriptive 'Ja, das Schreiben und das Lesen', and Sáffi's moody gypsy aria, 'So elend und so treu'; in Act II, the ebullient treasure waltz 'Ha! seht es winkt', the natural-marriage duet 'Wer uns getraut?', and Homonay's recruiting song 'Her die Hand, es muss ja sein'.

Other operatic works: *Indigo und die vierzig Räuber*, 1871; *Der Carneval in Rom*, 1873; *Cagliostro in Wien*, 1875; *Prinz Methusalem*, 1877; *Blindekuh*, 1878; *Das Spitzentuch der Königin*, 1880; *Der lustige Krieg*, 1881; *Simplicius*, 1887; *Ritter Pázmán*, 1892; *Fürstin Ninetta*, 1893; *Jabuka*, 1894; *Waldmeister*, 1895; *Die Göttin der Vernunft*, 1897; *Wiener Blut*, 1899

R.T.

RICHARD STRAUSS

Richard Georg Strauss; *b* 11 June 1864, Munich; *d* 8 September 1949, Garmisch-Partenkirchen, Germany

Strauss achieved mastery in three musical genres: opera, of which he composed 15, orchestral tone poems and lieder. He was also one of the great conductors of his day, not only of his own works but also of those by Mozart, Wagner, Beethoven and many others. His father was the principal horn-player in the Bavarian Court Opera orchestra for nearly half a century, and his mother was a member of the wealthy brewing family of Pschorr. His childhood, therefore, was comfortable, and he grew up in a household devoted to music. He composed copiously from the age of six; by the time he was 16 he had heard his first symphony played by his father's orchestra conducted by Hermann Levi. His music attracted the attention of Hans von Bülow, who in 1885 offered Strauss a post as his assistant at Meiningen. There he met Alexander Ritter, a passionate Wagnerian, who persuaded the younger man, brought up on a rigid classical diet, to become a follower of the 'music of the future'. In 1886 Strauss was appointed third conductor at the Munich opera house; he moved to the Weimar Court Opera in 1889, where his adventurous choice of repertoire brought him much publicity. Meanwhile the success of his tone poems *Don Juan* and *Tod und Verklärung* had led Bülow to dub him 'Richard the Third' (since, he said, after Wagner there could be no 'Richard the Second').

While at Weimar, he conducted the world premieres of Humperdinck's *Hänsel und Gretel* (1893) and of his own first opera, *Guntram* (1894). In the latter the principal soprano role was sung by Pauline de Ahna, who had been Strauss's pupil for several years; they were married in September 1894. He portrayed her capricious, tempestuous nature in several of his works, notably *Intermezzo* (Christine) and *Die Frau ohne Schatten* (the dyer's wife). She was a fine interpreter of his lieder, and Strauss's special sympathy for the female voice undoubtedly owes much to her influence and example. Strauss returned to the Munich Opera in 1894, becoming chief conductor there in 1896, and in 1898 he was appointed chief conductor of the

Royal Opera in Berlin, where he remained until 1908, a tenure almost exactly parallel with his friend Mahler's directorship of the Vienna Court Opera. Strauss was chief guest conductor at Berlin until 1919, when he agreed to be co-director at Vienna with Franz Schalk. He also played a leading part in 1920 in establishing the Salzburg Festival. Like many before and after him, Strauss fell foul of Viennese opera politics, and he resigned in 1924. But in his five years there, with some legendary singers, he conducted important new productions of his own and others' operas. Those who heard him conduct *Così fan tutte*, *Fidelio* and *Tristan und Isolde* counted those performances among the great musical experiences of a lifetime.

Guntram, composed during the first rapture of Wagner-worship, was not a success, and seven years passed before Strauss embarked on another opera. It is significant that *Feuersnot*, *Salome* and *Elektra* are one-act operas, stage equivalents of the tone poems with which, between 1888 and 1898, Strauss had established himself among the leaders of contemporary orchestral music. With *Salome* and *Elektra*, emotional blockbusters, he triumphed equally in the opera house, the former encountering resistance in some cities on moral grounds but winning public favour whenever it was performed. *Elektra* is a setting of the version of Sophocles' play by the Austrian poet and playwright Hugo von Hofmannsthal. Thus began the long and fruitful collaboration between composer and librettist which posterity can vicariously share through their absorbingly frank and detailed correspondence – 'We were born for one another,' Strauss wrote.

In *Elektra* Strauss went, in a few passages, as near to the frontier of atonality as he was ever to go in the name of Expressionism. But to interpret the subsequent operas as a retreat from modernism is seriously to misjudge and misunderstand Strauss's achievement. He and Hofmannsthal followed *Elektra* with their biggest popular success, *Der Rosenkavalier*, a Viennese comedy of 18th-century manners. But for all its waltzes and luscious melodies, it also has harmonic progressions as advanced as any in *Elektra*. Strauss's principal operatic ambition, evolved through his experience as a conductor, was for a perfect and democratic fusion of words and music. With this in mind he strove to develop an endless melodic recitative which flowed as naturally as conversation. The beginnings of this style can be detected in *Feuersnot* and throughout much of Act I of *Der Rosenkavalier*.

Indeed Strauss and Hofmannsthal wanted to break fresh ground in the opera house. 'New ideas must search for new forms,' Strauss wrote, and in *Ariadne auf Naxos* they attempted a bold marriage between straight theatre and chamber opera. But, on practical and economic grounds alone, this was doomed to failure and, in a revised version, they substituted a short operatic prologue for the play. In this form, the opera has become firmly established. They followed it with their most ambitious venture, the fairy-tale cum allegory *Die Frau ohne Schatten*, in which Hofmannsthal's verbose flights of fancy were matched by music of outstanding intensity and opulence.

Strauss wrote his own libretto for *Intermezzo*, his dramatization of an episode in his married life, in which the melodic recitative style, developed in the prologue to *Ariadne*, fits the narrative like a glove. The fluidity of this style also ensured the success of *Arabella*, a return to romantic period comedy and the last collaboration with Hofmannsthal (who died before it was complete). Strauss could scarcely envisage the continuation of his operatic career without Hofmannsthal, but by a stroke of luck he met the novelist Stefan Zweig. Their opera buffa *Die schweigsame Frau*, based on Ben Jonson, is one of Strauss's happiest scores, a celebration of his delight in finding a new and congenial partner. But the advent of the Nazis meant the end of Strauss's collaboration with a Jew. On his next three operas he worked, grudgingly, with the Viennese theatre historian Joseph Gregor. In *Friedenstag* and *Daphne* he reverted to the one-act form. For the former, an anti-war opera banned in Germany after 1939, he forged a new and tougher style, while in the pastoral lyricism of *Daphne* can be heard the beginning of his last phase, the so-called 'Indian summer', in which his music combined richness and simplicity. The autumnal splendour continued in *Die Liebe der Danae*, based on a discarded Hofmannsthal sketch, but achieved its operatic apogee in *Capriccio*. Here, in collaboration with the conductor Clemens Krauss, Strauss used the conflict between words and music as the theme of the opera itself. With its aristocratic 18th-century setting, its adorable heroine, its touches of broad comedy and its undercurrent of valediction, *Capriccio* was the perfect vehicle for all the best of Strauss to come together in the last chapter of his important contribution to the development of opera as a vital and progressive form.

Salome

Drama in one act (1h 45m)
Libretto by the composer from Hedwig Lachmann's
German translation of the tragedy *Salomé* by Oscar Wilde
(1893)
Composed November 1904–June 1905
PREMIERES 9 December 1905, Semper Opernhaus,
Dresden; US: 22 January 1907, Metropolitan, New York;
UK: 8 December 1910, Covent Garden, London
CAST   Herod *t*, Herodias *ms*, Salome *s*, Jokanaan (John
the Baptist) *bar*, Narraboth *t*, Page to Herodias *a*, 5 Jews 4
t, *b*, First Nazarene *t*, Second Nazarene *b*, 2 Soldiers 2 *b*,
A Cappadocian *b*, Executioner *silent*

Strauss saw Max Reinhardt's production of Wilde's French play *Salomé* (in a German translation) in Berlin in November 1902, with Gertrud Eysoldt in the title role. He was already sketching themes for an operatic setting, having been sent the play by the Austrian poet Anton Lindner, who offered to fashion a verse libretto for him. But Strauss was not impressed by the first few scenes and decided that he himself would adapt Hedwig Lachmann's translation, which he shortened by about a third.

Strauss offered the first performance to Ernst von Schuch at Dresden. Some of the singers at first read-through wanted to return their parts as too difficult, but the Czech tenor Karel Burian (uncle of the composer Emil Burian), who created Herod, already his by heart. The Salome, Marie Wittich, regarded the opera as improper and refused to perform the Dance of the Seven Veils – 'I won't do it, I'm a respectable woman.' A dancer stood in for her in this scene (a solution sometimes adopted since). In spite of moralistic objections, *Salome* was a sensational success at Dresden (except with the critics) and was performed at 50 other opera houses within two years.

But the Church's and others' objections to the work were still strong. At the Berlin Court Opera, where Strauss was employed as chief conductor, the kaiser would allow it to be performed only if the Star of Bethlehem was shown in the sky (even though Christ's birth took place 30 years before the action of the opera). After its Metropolitan premiere in New York, there was such an outcry, led by the daughter of the financier J. Pierpont Morgan, that further performances were cancelled. Mahler, who regarded it as 'one of the greatest masterpieces of our time', was only dissuaded by Strauss from resigning his directorship of the Vienna Court Opera after the censor refused to allow him to stage it (and it was not performed in Vienna until October 1918). The kaiser said, 'I like this fellow Strauss, but *Salome* will do him a lot of damage.' Strauss's retort was: 'The damage enabled me to build my house in Garmisch.'

After completing the full score of *Salome*, Strauss also worked on a version with Wilde's original French text. In order to adapt his music to this text, he consulted his friend the novelist and poet Romain Rolland. This version (1930) is rarely performed, but was revived at Lyons in 1990 and subsequently recorded.

SYNOPSIS

On the terrace of the palace of the tetrarch Herod Antipas, the Syrian captain of the guard, Narraboth, is looking into the banqueting hall, captivated by the beauty of the 16-year-old Salome, daughter of Herod's second wife Herodias by her first marriage ('Wie schön ist die Prinzessin Salome heute Nacht!'). Herodias's page warns him that something terrible may happen if he looks at Salome too much. The page has been alarmed by how strange the moon seems, 'like a woman rising from a tomb'. Two soldiers are guarding the cistern beneath the terrace where Jokanaan (John the Baptist) is imprisoned for denunciation of Herodias's marriage to her husband's brother. They hear his voice uttering prophecies. Salome leaves the banquet to evade her stepfather's lascivious glances and to escape from the religious arguments among the Jews, and from the Roman soldiers whom she hates. She hears Jokanaan, and wheedles Narraboth into defying Herod's orders and bringing the prophet to meet her.

Jokanaan launches into a tirade against Herod and his wife. When Salome tells him she is the daughter of Herodias, he rails at her ('Zurück, Tochter Babylons!'), but she is fascinated by his voice and longs to touch his body and his hair and to kiss his mouth. At this point, Narraboth, horrified by her conduct, kills himself, but she hardly notices. Jokanaan tells her to seek salvation from the Son of Man and retreats into the cistern, cursing her as he goes.

Herod, Herodias and their attendants come on to the terrace. Herod, too, is disturbed by the strangeness of the moon. He slips in Narraboth's blood, and orders the body to be removed. He feels a cold wind blowing and 'the beating of vast wings', but Herodias tells him he is ill. Herod offers Salome wine and fruit, but she refuses. Jokanaan's voice is heard again. Herodias urges that he be handed over to the Jews, but Herod says, 'He is a holy man who has seen God.' This prompts a heated argument among the five Jews over the question of whether anyone has seen God. After Jokanaan's reference to the 'Saviour of the world' the two Nazarenes tell Herod of the Messiah's miracles, including raising a woman from the dead. This alarms Herod ('I will not allow him to raise the dead') but when Herodias complains that Jokanaan is reviling her, Herod replies, 'He did not speak your name.'

Herod commands Salome to dance for him. She refuses, despite promises of lavish gifts, but agrees when he says she can have whatever she desires. After the dance she claims her reward – Jokanaan's head on a silver charger. Herodias is delighted, but Salome says she wants it for her own pleasure, not to please her mother. Herod tries everything to dissuade her, but she obsessively repeats her demand ('Gib mir den Kopf des Jokanaan!'). Eventually Herod gives in, saying, 'Truly she is her mother's child.' The executioner descends into the cistern and returns with the prophet's head on a silver shield. Salome seizes it and sings a long aria to it, taunting it for being unable to reply to her. 'If you had seen me, you would have loved me. I am hungry for your body.' Herod refuses to stay, and as he climbs the staircase looks back to see Salome lost in ecstasy as she kisses Jokanaan's mouth. Horrified, he orders the soldiers to kill her ('Man töte dieses Weib!'). They crush her beneath their shields.

Salome is a study in obsessions, wrought by a composer whose powers of description in his orchestral tone poems had equipped him to depict in the theatre the strangeness of the happenings on this oriental night, with the moon lighting the scene and inducing an atmosphere of impending violence and madness. There is no overture. A rising arpeggio on the clarinet launches Narraboth into his rapturous vision of Salome and, from then to the end, there is no let-up in the intensity and tension of the score. The 105-strong orchestra is used with an imaginative power that was new to opera in 1905, the exotic tone colours reflecting the action on the stage both graphically and psychologically. The passage of nearly a century has not diminished the startling novelty of the sound as Salome awaits Jokanaan's execution, an effect created by four double-basses 'pinching' the string with thumb and forefinger and striking it with the bow. There are many other equally dramatic moments, with dissonances no less far-reaching in their tendency towards atonality than those that were to follow in *Elektra*.

The role of Salome is a tremendous challenge for a soprano, who ideally should combine a Wagnerian weight of tone with a girlish quality. In 1930 Strauss reduced the orchestration so that a light soprano could sing the part. The 20-minute final aria moves from animal frenzy to a demented erotic yearning. Yet it is not only Salome's obsession that Strauss presents with such calculated vividness. The religious zeal of Jokanaan is equally obsessive and is conveyed in music of lofty and noble quality. The music for Herod also brilliantly delineates the tetrarch's personality: neurotic, superstitious, lascivious – a gift of a part for a character tenor. Whatever the mood in this opera, whether it be sultry, savage, sadistic or sensuous, Strauss finds the orchestral colours to convey it to the listener with overwhelming intensity.

Elektra

Electra
Tragedy in one act (1h 45m)
Libretto by Hugo von Hofmannsthal, based on his own play (1904) after the tragedy by Sophocles (411 or 410 BC)
Composed June 1906–September 1908
PREMIERES 25 January 1909, Semper Opernhaus, Dresden; US: 1 February 1910, Manhattan Opera, New York; UK: 19 February 1910, Covent Garden, London
CAST Elektra (Electra) *s*, Klytemnästra (Clytemnestra) *ms*, Chrysothemis *s*, Aegisth (Aegisthus) *t*, Orest (Orestes) *bar*, Tutor to Orestes *b*, Confidante *s*, Trainbearer *s*, Young Servant *t*, Old Servant *b*, Overseer *s*, First Maid *c*, Second and Third Maids 2 *ms*, Fourth and Fifth Maids 2 *s*; *satb* chorus of servants

Hugo von Hofmannsthal wrote his play *Elektra*, an adaptation of Sophocles, in three weeks in August 1903, when he was 28. It was produced in Berlin the following October by Max Reinhardt and was a major success. Strauss probably saw it then or a few years later and recognized the story's potential as an operatic subject. He and Hofmannsthal met in November 1905, and the poet gave him a free hand to cut the play to make a libretto. Hofmannsthal wrote new lines for two episodes, the recognition scene and the duet between Electra and Chrysothemis after the murders.

Strauss was at first wary of setting *Elektra* immediately after *Salome*, feeling (not unjustifiably) that the emotional contents were similar. But Hofmannsthal pressed him, and the opera was performed at Dresden early in 1909. There and elsewhere it enjoyed a *succès d'estime* rather than a popular success, but its title role was soon to attract a series of superb dramatic sopranos, while the role of Clytemnestra was also to become a favourite. *Elektra* is often spoken of in Freudian terms, but it is by no means certain that Hofmannsthal had read Freud at the time he wrote his play. His main source was Sophocles, and the strength of the work is in its modern adaptation of Greek tragedy, to which Strauss's music added a fearful strength.

SYNOPSIS
The courtyard of the royal palace at Mycenae, where Clytemnestra lives with Aegisthus. Serving women, drawing water from a well, are discussing Electra, daughter of King Agamemnon and Clytemnestra, who lives like a wild, unkempt animal. They all mock her, except one who is whipped for her loyalty. Electra, left alone, laments her loneliness ('Allein! Weh, ganz allein') and recalls the murder of her father Agamemnon by Aegisthus and Clytemnestra. Calling on her father's spirit to help her, Electra dreams of vengeance

after which she will dance for joy. Her reverie is interrupted by her younger sister, Chrysothemis, with news that Clytemnestra and Aegisthus plan to imprison Electra in a tower. She sings of her own longing for a husband and children ('Ich hab's wie Feuer in der Brust').

A procession approaches; Clytemnestra and her entertainers are on their way to the ritual altar. The queen, bedecked with jewels and amulets, decides to consult Electra about how she can stop the horrible nightmares that disrupt her sleep. Electra brings the subject round to her brother Orestes. She does not believe reports that he has gone mad. Electra tells her mother that a sacrificial victim will stop her dreams – Clytemnestra herself. The queen's terror gives way to maniacal laughter when her confidante whispers to her that Orestes is dead.

The same news is given to Electra by Chrysothemis, who refuses to join Electra in killing Aegisthus and their mother. Electra resolves she must act alone ('Nun denn, allein!') and digs frantically for the axe with which Agamemnon was killed and which she has buried in the courtyard. As she digs, a man enters the courtyard. He says he awaits a summons to bring news of Orestes' death. Electra berates him for being alive while a better man is dead. When he discovers who she is, he whispers, 'Orestes lives.' She does not recognize her questioner until servants kiss his garments: 'The dogs in the courtyard know me, but my sister does not.' After the powerful recognition scene that follows, she impresses on him what must be done. He enters the palace, and Electra realizes that she has not given him the axe. But screams from the palace indicate Clytemnestra's death. These bring Aegisthus into the courtyard. Electra, chillingly amiable to him, lights him to the palace door. He shouts for help, to which Electra replies, 'Agamemnon hears you!' Electra begins her dance of joy, dropping dead at its climax. Chrysothemis beats vainly on the doors of the palace for admission, crying, 'Orest.' But Orestes is already being pursued by the Furies.

From the opening onomatopoeic fanfare, 'Agamemnon', it becomes plain that the dead king is the opera's principal leitmotif. *Elektra* is a huge crescendo from start to finish, less lyrical and tonal than *Salome*. The work sounds better organized than its predecessor, probably because the libretto is tauter and less rhapsodic than Wilde's play. It is feasible to regard *Elektra* as a symphonic structure, and it is firmly based on a tonal plan presenting each of the characters and their emotional states in a particular key. Both Electra and Clytemnestra, the most obsessive characters in the opera, are projected bitonally. Clytemnestra relates her dream in near-atonal harmonies as a kind of psychodrama, but it is inaccurate to describe *Elektra* in terms of the Schoenbergian Expressionism of *Erwartung* (1909). *Elektra* is near to being a number opera, with formal introductions to the arias. Although the level of dissonance is higher in *Elektra* than in *Feuersnot* or *Der Rosenkavalier*, it has many points of contact with these works, not least in its use of the waltz in various guises. The music to which Electra leads Aegisthus to his doom might have been written for Baron Ochs in *Der Rosenkavalier*.

If Strauss wrote nothing again like *Elektra*, it was not because he had consciously retreated from avant-garde procedures. He instinctively knew that, with this work and *Salome*, he had gone as far as he could in depicting obsessed heroines of this kind. To have continued would have been to invite the charge of repeating himself which had at first deterred him from setting *Elektra*.

Another important point to note about *Elektra* is that Strauss uses the orchestra to provide the opera with a wordless climax. Not until *Daphne*, nearly 30 years later, was he again to give the orchestra its head so completely. Music here triumphs over words, echoing Electra's opening of her final dance (a waltz) with the words 'Ob ich die Musik nicht höre? Sie kommt doch aus mir' ('You ask if I hear the music? It comes from me.').

Der Rosenkavalier

The Knight of the Rose
Comedy for music in three acts (3h 15m)
Libretto by Hugo von Hofmannsthal
Composed April 1909–September 1910
PREMIERES 26 January 1911, Hofoper, Dresden; UK: 29 January 1913, Covent Garden, London; US: 9 December 1913, Metropolitan, New York
CAST The Feldmarschallin, Princess Werdenberg *s*, Octavian, Count Rofrano *s*, Baron Ochs auf Lerchenau *b*, Herr von Faninal *bar*, Sophie *s*, Marianne Leitmetzerin, Sophie's Duenna *s*, Valzacchi *t*, Annina *c*, Police Commissioner *b*, The Marschallin's Major-domo (Struhan) *t*, Faninal's Major-domo *t*, Notary *b*, Innkeeper *t*, Italian Singer *t*, 3 Noble Orphans *s*, *ms*, *c*, Dressmaker *s*, Pet-seller *t*, 4 Marschallin's Footmen 2 *t*, 3 *b*, 4 Waiters *t*, 3 *b*; *silent*: Leopold, Mahomet, scholar flautist, hairdresser, hairdresser's assistant, widow of noble family; *satb* chorus of footmen, couriers, heyducks, cookboys, guests, musicians, 2 watchmen, 4 little children, various personages of suspicious appearance

The plot of *Der Rosenkavalier* was concocted within a few days in February 1909 by Hofmannsthal and his friend Count Harry Kessler. They borrowed ideas from many literary sources, including Molière, based some of the characters on operatic prototypes (Mozart's countess and Cherubino in *Le nozze di Figaro* and Verdi's *Falstaff*), and also drew inspiration from the graphic arts (Hogarth's *Marriage à la Mode*). Strauss was delighted by the resulting libretto for Act I and set it page by page as he received it. He was highly critical of parts of the plot in Acts II and III, and these were adjusted to accommodate his ideas. Hofmannsthal created a mid-18th-century Vienna in considerable detail, but many of the customs (including the crucial idea of the presentation of a silver rose to the bride-to-be) were his own invention. The sense of class distinction and the subtlety of the language are prime features of the work's 'realism'.

The opera ran into censor trouble in Dresden and Berlin, but the principal threat to the Dresden premiere came from the inadequacy of the producer there. Strauss sent Max Reinhardt to supervise the carrying out of his own ideas, which he did without any credit in the programme. The opera was a huge success, with special trains being run to Dresden from various parts of Germany. The stage designs and production book prepared by Alfred Roller, who had been Mahler's scenic artist in Vienna, played a large part in the success and were used for several decades. London, Vienna, New York, Milan and many other operatic centres were quick to take up a work that remains in the repertoire of every major opera house and shows no sign of losing its popular appeal.

SYNOPSIS
Act I Vienna, during the reign of the empress Maria Theresa. The bedroom of the Princess Werdenberg, wife of the field marshal (hence 'Marschallin'). She has spent the night with her 17-year-old lover Count Octavian. Their breakfast is interrupted by her cousin, Baron Ochs auf Lerchenau, described by Strauss as a 'rural Don Juan'. Octavian disguises himself as a chambermaid ('Mariandel'), with whom Ochs flirts. The baron has come to ask the Marschallin to recommend a young nobleman as bearer of the traditional silver rose – a *Rosenkavalier* – to his fiancée, Sophie von Faninal, daughter of a recently ennobled arms dealer. It is then time for the Marschallin's *levée*. The stage is filled with tradesmen, various petitioners, a widow and her three daughters, a hairdresser, two intriguers (Valzacchi and Annina) and an Italian tenor who sings an aria ('Di rigori armato il seno') which is a pastiche of Mozart's Italian song settings. The song is cut short by an argument over dowry between Ochs and a lawyer. Valzacchi and Annina offer Ochs their services, and Leopold, Ochs's bastard son (a non-speaking part), hands the silver rose to the Marschallin. Left alone, the Marschallin reflects on Ochs's conceit ('Da geht er hin') and compares herself when young with Sophie. At 32 she is acutely conscious of growing old, and when Octavian returns she finds her in a melancholy mood, aware that he will soon leave her for a younger woman. She tells him that time ('Die Zeit, die ist ein sonderbar Ding') slips by so quickly that she often gets up in the night and stops the clocks. When Octavian leaves her, the Marschallin realizes they have not even kissed goodbye. She sends her little black page Mahomet to him with the casket containing the silver rose.

Act II In Herr von Faninal's palatial home, Sophie, Faninal and her duenna are awaiting the rose-bearer's arrival by coach. Octavian ceremoniously presents her with the rose, and they are mutually attracted at first sight. Ochs is ushered in by Faninal and fondles Sophie lecherously. Meanwhile his disreputable bodyguard causes chaos in the household. Sophie is appalled, and Octavian vows to prevent the marriage. Their love duet ('Mit ihren Augen voll Tränen') is abruptly ended when they are apprehended by Valzacchi and Annina, who send for Ochs. Octavian challenges Ochs to a duel and wounds him slightly. Ochs acts as if he has been severely injured, and Sophie tells Faninal she refuses to marry this oaf. Octavian has meanwhile won over Valzacchi and Annina. While Ochs, bandaged, is left alone, Annina brings him a message from the Marschallin's chambermaid 'Mariandel' agreeing to a meeting. Ochs, delighted, sings his favourite waltz ('Ohne mich').

Act III In a private room at an inn, Valzacchi, Annina and others, under Octavian's supervision, rehearse the opening of trapdoors and other devices with which they plan to scare Ochs. Octavian dons his disguise as 'Mariandel' and goes to meet the baron. They sit down to supper, served by Leopold. To the music of an offstage band's waltzes, Ochs tries vainly to seduce the 'girl', who refuses wine and his advances ('Nein, nein! Ich trink kein Wein'). Every time he approaches her, apparitions appear at windows or through trapdoors. Annina, dressed in black as a widow, enters to claim Ochs as her husband and father of her children, who burst in noisily shouting 'Papa!' Ochs calls the police and tells the suspicious commissioner that he is dining with his fiancée, Sophie. Octavian has ordered Valzacchi to send for Faninal and Sophie, who refute Ochs's story. Octavian tells the commissioner the truth, and sheds his female attire. Meanwhile the Marschallin (summoned by Leopold) enters, recognizes the police commissioner as her husband's ex-orderly, and assures him that the affair was 'just a masquerade'. She advises Ochs to leave, which he does, pursued by creditors, children and tavern staff. In the sublime trio for the three soprano voices ('Hab mir's gelobt'), the young lovers sing of their delight and the Marschallin accepts the situation with a good grace. She leaves them together ('Ist ein Traum') while she invites Faninal to ride home with her. The stage is empty, but Mahomet runs in to search for a handkerchief Sophie has dropped. Waving it above his head, he rejoins them and the curtain falls.

Although Hofmannsthal imagined Der Rosenkavalier as a neo-Mozartian opera in the Figaro mould, Strauss's music is post-Wagnerian in its subtle symphonic development of leitmotifs and its use of the orchestra in a richly allusive fashion. The score is both heavy and light, and the vocal writing carries a stage further Strauss's development of a lyrical conversational style that is neither aria nor recitative. The exquisite illustrative detail – whether it be the high polytonal chords for flutes, harps, celesta and three violins which depict the silver rose, the fast movement of the hairdresser's hands as he adjusts the Marschallin's coiffure or the graphic love-making of the prelude to Act I – shows Strauss the tone poet at the height of his creative powers.

All three leading female roles reveal Strauss's extraordinary musical affinity with the soprano voice – the Act III trio is one of the finest ensemble pieces in all opera – while the bass and baritone roles of Ochs and Faninal are also richly rewarding. The role of the Marschallin is one of the greatest of all operatic creations and has attracted a line of distinguished interpreters. Strauss bound the whole work together with a string of memorable waltz tunes (which he later arranged in two sequences for concert performance) and although both he and Hofmannsthal admitted in later years that there were longueurs in Der Rosenkavalier, they never quite recaptured its lyrical élan. With its perennial themes of melancholy at growing old, love at first sight and nostalgia for a vanishing age threatened by social upheaval, Der Rosenkavalier had every ingredient for a lasting popular success. But what has ensured that success is the matchless blend

between a marvellous libretto and the music it called into being.

Ariadne auf Naxos
(Second version)
Ariadne on Naxos
Opera in one act, with prologue (2h)
Libretto by Hugo von Hofmannsthal
Prologue composed 1911–July 1912; second version, May–June 1916
PREMIERES first version: 25 October 1912, Hoftheater, Stuttgart; UK: 27 May 1913, His Majesty's Theatre, Haymarket, London; second version: 4 October 1916, Hofoper, Vienna; UK: 27 May 1924, Covent Garden, London; US: 1 November 1928, Civic Opera, Philadelphia
CAST Composer *s*, Music Master *bar*, Dancing Master *t*, Wig-maker *b*, Lackey *b*, Prima Donna/Ariadne *s*, Tenor/Bacchus *t*, Zerbinetta *s*, Harlequin *bar*, Scaramuccio *t*, Truffaldino *b*, Brighella *t*, Officer *t*, Naiad *s*, Dryad *c*, Echo *s*, Major-domo *spoken role*

Both Hofmannsthal and Strauss were indebted to the producer Max Reinhardt, who, without official credit, had transformed the Dresden production of Der Rosenkavalier. As a thanks-offering, Hofmannsthal devised a novel combination of play and 30-minute opera: the former to be his adaptation of Molière's Le bourgeois gentilhomme, with incidental music for the dances; the latter Ariadne auf Naxos, with Strauss's music, which would interweave elements of opera seria with those of the commedia dell'arte. The opera was conceived as a divertissement after the dinner that concludes the play and was to be performed in the presence of Monsieur Jourdain, the 'bourgeois gentilhomme'. Between the play and opera came a short scene in prose in which those responsible for arranging the entertainments for Jourdain – the composer and the dancing master – were told by Jourdain's footman that the two pieces must be performed simultaneously. This first version was performed in Stuttgart on 25 October 1912, but the evening lasted over six hours (the '30-minute opera' had become a 90-minute opera) and it was obvious to composer and librettist that in this form the work was impracticable, requiring both a drama company and an opera company to perform it.

In 1913 Hofmannsthal hit on a new version, with the opera preceded by a short sung prologue based on the linking scene. He eliminated Monsieur Jourdain and transferred the action of the prologue from 17th-century Paris to the 19th-century house of 'the richest man in Vienna'. Strauss at first was not interested, but in 1916 he composed the prologue. At the Vienna premiere the travesti role of the young composer was sung by Lotte Lehmann, her first outstanding success. Although the original version is occasionally revived, it is the second version that has become part of the international repertoire.

SYNOPSIS (second version)
Prologue In the house of the richest man in Vienna, where a sumptuous banquet is to be held in the evening, two theatrical groups are busy preparing their entertainments. The music master protests to the major-domo about the decision to follow his

pupil's opera seria, *Ariadne auf Naxos*, with 'vulgar buffoonery'. The major-domo makes it plain that he who pays the piper calls the tune and that the fireworks display will begin at nine o'clock. The composer wants a last-minute rehearsal with the violinists, but they are playing during dinner. The soprano who is to sing Ariadne is not available to go through her aria; the tenor cast as Bacchus objects to his wig. There is typical backstage chaos. Seeing the attractive Zerbinetta and inquiring who she is, the composer is told by the music master that she is leader of the *commedia dell'arte* group which is to perform after the opera. Outraged, the composer turns his wrath aside when a new melody occurs to him ('Du, Venus' Sohn'). The major-domo returns to announce that his master now requires both entertainments to be performed simultaneously and still to end at nine o'clock sharp. More uproar, during which the dancing master suggests that the composer should cut his opera to accommodate the harlequinade's dances.

The plot of *Ariadne* is explained to Zerbinetta, who mocks the idea of 'languishing in passionate longing and praying for death'. To her, another lover is the answer. Zerbinetta and the composer find they have something in common when Zerbinetta tells him 'A moment is nothing – a glance is much' ('Ein Augenblick ist wenig – ein Blick ist viel'). 'Who can say that my heart is in the part I play?' Heartened, the composer sings of music's power ('Musik ist eine heilige Kunst'). But when he sees the comedians scampering about, he cries, 'I should not have allowed it.'

Opera The island of Naxos, where Ariadne has been abandoned by Theseus, who took her with him from Crete after she had helped him to kill the Minotaur. Ariadne is asleep, watched over by three nymphs, Naiad, Dryad and Echo. They describe her perpetual, inconsolable weeping. Ariadne wakes. She can think of nothing except her betrayal by Theseus, and she wants death to end her suffering. Zerbinetta and the comedians cannot believe in her desperation, and Harlequin vainly tries to cheer her with a song about the joys of life. She sings of the purity of the kingdom of death ('Es gibt ein Reich') and longs for Hermes to lead her there. The comedians again try to cheer her up with singing and dancing, but to no avail. Zerbinetta sends them away and tries on her own, with her long coloratura aria ('Grossmächtige Prinzessin'), the gist of which is that there are plenty of other men besides Theseus. In the middle of the aria, Ariadne goes into her cave. Zerbinetta and her troupe then enact their entertainment in which the four comedians court her.

The three nymphs excitedly announce the arrival of the young god Bacchus, who has just escaped from the sorceress Circe. At first he mistakes Ariadne for another Circe, while she mistakes him for Theseus and then Hermes. But, in the duet that follows, reality takes over and Ariadne's longing for death becomes a longing for love as Bacchus becomes aware of his divinity. As passion enfolds them, Zerbinetta comments that she was right all along: 'Off with the old, on with the new.'

The second version necessitated considerable revision of the score. Comments on the action by Monsieur Jourdain and others, characters now eliminated, had to be deleted. Zerbinetta's aria was eased by dropping its pitch a whole tone for most of its duration: two major cuts amounting to about 80 bars of music were made, although Strauss replaced the second cut (in the closing section of the aria) by a new coda less than half as long, which contains a duet for voice and flute. A scene just before Bacchus' arrival, in which Zerbinetta interrupts Ariadne's address to her as yet invisible liberator, was deleted.

But the biggest alteration was the ending. In the first version, after the Ariadne–Bacchus love duet, the comedians return and Jourdain's guests depart. Part of Zerbinetta's aria is recapitulated as she points out that what has just occurred supports her view of life and love. The comedians' waltz returns as the four clowns and Zerbinetta sing and dance. Jourdain, who has been asleep, is wakened by a servant who asks if the firework display should begin. Jourdain ignores him and repeats his admiration for the true nobility. His trumpet tune ends the opera.

In *Ariadne auf Naxos*, the two contrasting elements in Strauss's musical personality – the rococo and the heroic – are interwoven much as the opera seria and the harlequinade are intermingled, or, more accurately, juxtaposed, in the plot of the opera itself. It represents a major step forward in Strauss's defence of the musical territory he had mapped out for himself, the antithesis of the Schoenbergian revolution. Yet it is no backward step. The neo-baroque music of the harlequinade belongs as inescapably to the 20th century as does Stravinsky's *Pulcinella*.

A virtuoso feature of the work is Strauss's use of a small orchestra (36 players). So skilful is his scoring that in the passionate final duet for Ariadne and Bacchus it is rich enough to give the impression of a large orchestra. Part of the unique flavour of the second version of *Ariadne auf Naxos* derives from Strauss's brilliant juxtaposition of low comedy and high tragedy. In the prologue, where he made a spectacular advance in his development of a melodic conversational recitative, he is at home depicting the quarrels and chaos of backstage theatrical life. In the opera, he slips easily from the heroic style in which Ariadne's part is composed to the buffoonery of the *commedia dell'arte* characters.

Die Frau ohne Schatten

The Woman Without a Shadow
Opera in three acts (3h 30m)
Libretto by Hugo von Hofmannsthal
Composed July 1914–June 1917
PREMIERES 10 October 1919, Staatsoper, Vienna; US: 18 September 1959, War Memorial Theater, San Francisco; UK: 2 May 1966, Sadler's Wells, London
CAST Emperor *t*, Empress *s*, Nurse *ms*, Spirit Messenger *bar*, Guardian of the Threshold of the Temple *s* or *ct*, Apparition of a Youth *t*, Voice of the Falcon *s*, Voice from Above *c*, Barak the Dyer *bar*, Dyer's Wife *s*, Barak's Brothers: One-eyed *b*, One-armed *b*, Hunchback *t*, Children's Voices 3 *s*, 3 *c*, Voices of the Nightwatchmen 3 *b*; *satb* chorus of imperial servants, children, attendant spirits, spirit voices

Hofmannsthal first outlined his idea for a 'magic fairy-tale' in March 1911. He told Strauss that in it two men would confront two women and 'for one of the women your wife might well, in all discretion, be taken as a model'. Progress on the libretto was slow and was interrupted by the composition of the first version of *Ariadne auf Naxos*. Composer and librettist discussed the project in detail during a trip to Italy in the spring of 1913. Hofmannsthal explained that *Die Frau ohne Schatten* would veer between the world of spirits and the world of humans with an intermediate plane inhabited by the emperor and empress. He described it as standing 'in general terms, to *Zauberflöte* as *Rosenkavalier* does to *Figaro*'. Although the principal subject of the opera is infertility – the 'shadow' is the symbol of parenthood – its main dramatic interest is in the empress's development from a fairy-tale creature into a human being through her realization that other people matter. She is prepared to sacrifice her own and her husband's life rather than allow the humble Barak and his shrewish wife to be forced apart. The libretto is heavy with symbolism and has often been dismissed as pretentious and incomprehensible, but Strauss himself had no difficulty with it and regarded it as Hofmannsthal's masterpiece. The outbreak of the First World War caused further delays, with Hofmannsthal unable to complete the third act until the spring of 1915.

In March 1919 Strauss became joint director of the post-war Vienna State Opera with Franz Schalk. He gave the first performance of the new opera to Vienna, but later admitted that it was a mistake in spite of a cast headed by Maria Jeritza, Lotte Lehmann and Richard Mayr. With the poverty and hunger attendant upon the end of hostilities, this was no time for such a difficult and complicated work to be performed. In addition, Alfred Roller, the director and set designer, surprisingly failed to realize some of the magical effects that were required. Few German theatres were equipped to stage it satisfactorily (the Dresden premiere was a disaster). Consequently the opera made its way slowly and was not staged in New York and London, for example, until 1966. Even in Munich, it is still cut in performance, but it has gradually come to be regarded by many Strauss enthusiasts as his greatest opera.

SYNOPSIS

Before the action of the opera begins, the emperor of the South Eastern Islands was hunting with his falcon and pursued a gazelle. Just as he was about to kill it, it resumed its real form as the daughter of Keikobad, master of the spirit world. The emperor married her, but she has remained neither spirit nor human and has borne no children.

Act I   The nurse is guarding the room where the royal couple are sleeping. Keikobad's messenger appears to tell her that if the empress does not cast a shadow (i.e. become pregnant) within three days the emperor will be turned to stone and the empress be reclaimed by her father. The emperor goes hunting for three days to try to find his falcon, which he has not seen since the day he met his wife. In his absence, the falcon comes to the empress and tells her what Keikobad has threatened. She knows she can obtain a shadow only from a human woman, and forces the nurse to help her find one. They fly down to the earth and go to the impoverished home of the dyer Barak, whose wife is quarrelling with her husband's deformed brothers. She is discontented and knows that Barak wants children. The nurse plans to turn the wife's unhappiness to her advantage. She tries to buy her shadow, promising a life of luxury in return. The wife agrees to refuse her husband's advances for three days, during which time the empress and nurse will be her servants. Barak returns from market to find he has been provided with a single bed.

Act II   While Barak is at work, the nurse continues her temptation of his wife, conjuring up the young man of her dreams. But the dyer's wife pushes the youth away when he tries to touch her. Barak returns with a huge bowl of food for his brothers and the beggar children who have followed him home. His wife refuses to eat. In his falcon-house, the emperor awaits the empress, having been told she will be there. He sees her and the nurse slip secretly into the house, senses they have been in the world of humans, and decides to kill the empress. But he cannot bring himself to do it and flees. Before Barak leaves for work, the nurse gives him a sleeping draught. She again causes the young man to appear. But the wife takes fright and wakens Barak, rebuking him for sleeping in the daytime and leaving her a prey to robbers. The empress, asleep in the falcon-house, is overcome with remorse for Barak. She hears the falcon's cry: 'The woman casts no shadow! The emperor must turn to stone!' She laments: 'Whatever I touch I kill!' Barak's wife taunts him by telling him she was unfaithful while he slept and has sold her shadow. Barak wants to kill her, and the nurse provides a sword. The wife realizes that she loves him and the empress repudiates the shadow bargain. Barak lifts the sword but it is snatched from him. The earth swallows him and his wife while the nurse leads the empress to safety.

Act III   Imprisoned in separate cells, Barak and his wife realize that they belong together. They are freed by servants of the spirit world to seek one another. The empress and the nurse go by boat to Keikobad's temple. The empress recognizes its door from a dream. The nurse tries to dissuade her from entering, warning her that she will be punished. But the empress dismisses the nurse – 'I part from you for ever' – and enters the temple. The voices of Barak and his wife are heard as they search for each other. The nurse says she hates all mankind, and deliberately misleads the couple, sending them in opposite directions. She then tries to enter the temple, but Keikobad's messenger bars her way and throws her into the boat, condemning her to wander henceforth among those she hates. In the temple, the empress wants to face Keikobad. The keeper of the threshold tempts her with a drink from the water of life, after which the dyer's wife's shadow will be hers. She can hear the voices of Barak and his wife. She refuses to drink and is shown the emperor turned to stone, only his terrified eyes remaining alive. She offers to die with him and still refuses to drink. The stage goes dark, and when the light returns the empress is seen to cast a shadow and the emperor is restored to life. Because the empress has learned human feeling, Keikobad has forgiven her. Emperor and empress, Barak and wife are reunited while the voices of their unborn children sing their praises.

Die Frau ohne Schatten is Strauss's largest and most ambitious opera and the one in which the genius he lavished on description and characterization in his tone poems is most liberally applied to the stage. The composer of the opening horn-call of *Till Eulenspiegel* is very obviously the same composer who invented the haunting and unforgettable cry of the falcon in this opera; and there are other striking instrumental effects, such as the use of a glass harmonica to depict the empress's acquisition of a shadow. While some passages are on an opulent, Wagnerian scale, much of the score has the delicacy of chamber music. In this respect it closely resembles the Mahler of the Eighth Symphony and *Das Lied von der Erde* (of all Strauss's scores it comes closest to a homage to his colleague and friend). The exotic, oriental flavour is a further link with *Das Lied von der Erde*.

The score is another refutation of the widespread allegation that Strauss 'went soft' after *Elektra*. While there are such exquisite diatonic episodes as the orchestral interlude in the first scene between Barak and his wife – a simple melodizing around the chord of Db to illustrate the dyer's compassionate and loving nature – there are also any number of examples of rootless harmony and near atonality. The empress's dream, for instance, ends with an orchestral epilogue in which nightmarish harmonies sum up the anguish she has expressed.

Like *Der Rosenkavalier* the opera contains three great roles for women – the empress, Barak's wife and the nurse – and a typically fine Strauss baritone part for Barak. We may wonder if Strauss's supposed hostility to the tenor voice was anything more than a joke on his part when we hear the magnificent music he wrote for the emperor, notably his Act II aria in the falcon-house. Although Strauss told Hofmannsthal that he found it difficult to fill the emperor, empress and nurse with musical red corpuscles as he had the characters in *Der Rosenkavalier*, he nevertheless gave all three characters some of the most powerful and elevated music he ever composed.

Intermezzo

Bourgeois comedy with symphonic interludes in two acts, (2h 15m)
Libretto by the composer
Composed 1919–August 1923
PREMIERES 4 November 1924, Schauspielhaus of Dresden Staatsoper; US: 11 February 1963, Philharmonic Hall, New York (concert); 24 February 1977, Curtis Institute, Philadelphia; UK: 9 September 1965, King's Theatre, Edinburgh
CAST Christine *s*, Robert Storch *bar*, Anna *s*, Baron Lummer *t*, Notary *bar*, Notary's Wife *s*, Conductor *t*, Commissioner *bar*, Lawyer *bar*, Opera Singer *b*, Resi *s*, Business Man *bar*, Franzl (boy) *spoken role*; *silent*: Young Girl, Chambermaid, Housemaid, The Storchs' Cook

After the heady brew of *Die Frau ohne Schatten*, Strauss yearned to write a work in a lighter vein. His ideas were contemptuously rejected by Hofmannsthal, who advised him to approach the Austrian dramatist Hermann Bahr. At a meeting in Salzburg in August 1916, Strauss outlined to Bahr an idea he had for an opera based on an incident in his marriage in May 1902 when Pauline had opened a letter mistakenly addressed to Strauss in which a woman named Mieze Mücke had asked for some opera tickets in Berlin. The actual letter contains no endearments – it begins 'Dear Herr Strauss' and ends 'Yours sincerely' – but Pauline evidently suspected the worst and sent a telegram to Strauss, who was staying in the Isle of Wight after a tour of England, announcing their divorce. The matter was cleared up when it was established that Fräulein Mücke had confused Strauss with Josef Stransky.

After some months, Bahr withdrew, saying that the subject could be satisfactorily handled only by Strauss himself. So Strauss wrote the libretto, a brilliant one, based almost exclusively on real exchanges between Pauline and himself. The opera was first performed at Dresden, the sets being replicas of the Strausses' home at Garmisch. The baritone playing Storch (Josef Correck) wore a mask to make him resemble the composer as closely as possible. Christine was sung (at the first performance only) by Lotte Lehmann. Because the opera was felt to be in dubious taste, it soon dropped out of the repertoire. Pauline herself did not appreciate the joke. But after Strauss's death it was frequently performed in Munich and has gradually become more popular. In Britain, a particularly fine Glyndebourne production, with Elisabeth Söderström, and later Felicity Lott, as Christine, won it many admirers.

SYNOPSIS
Act I At his home on the Grundlsee, the composer Robert Storch is preparing to leave for Vienna, where he is to conduct opera. His wife, Christine, is helping him pack. She'll be glad to have him out of the way for a while – why can't he have a job like other men that takes him out of the house every day? Composing isn't work compared with her household duties. Before he leaves, they have another quarrel, about the publicity attendant upon his career, and she refuses to kiss him goodbye until he says he might be in a train crash for all she knows. Left alone with her maid Anna, Christine bemoans being left to deal with the tax-collector and to look after her little son. She cheers up when a friend telephones to invite her to go tobogganing. On the sledge-run she collides with a young man who introduces himself as Baron Lummer. Her parents knew his family, so she arranges to meet him. They go to a dance in the inn on the Grundlsee. She takes him under her wing and rents a room for him in the house of the local notary, fussing about cleanliness and her protégé's migraines. Christine writes to Robert to tell him about Lummer, who then arrives. Conversation is fitful, and Christine is reduced to reading him extracts from the newspaper. He sounds her out on how far she is prepared to help him in his career as a naturalist. Her husband – whom she now praises to the skies – will help him when he returns, she parries.

After Lummer has left, she meditates on her love for her husband.

In his room, Lummer vents his feelings about the boring Christine. His girlfriend Resi arrives in skiing clothes, but he sends her away for fear his landlady might see her and tell Christine. He writes to Christine, who explodes in anger when she reads his request for 1000 marks. He arrives at the Storch residence, to be given a stern lecture, which is interrupted by the arrival of a letter addressed to Robert. Christine opens it and, horrified, reads: 'Dear Sweetheart, send me two more tickets for the opera tomorrow. Afterwards in the bar as usual. Your Mieze Meier.' Christine at once sends a telegram: 'You know Mieze Meier. Your faithlessness proven, this is goodbye for ever.' She orders Anna to pack all the bags and wakes her child, who says he loves his father and doesn't want to go away.

Act II   In Vienna, the lawyer, the singer, the conductor Stroh and the business man are playing the card-game skat and discussing Christine – 'A frightful woman, how does he put up with her?' When Storch joins them, they continue the banter and tease him about Christine's letter about Lummer. Nothing to worry about, says Storch, we understand one another. Christine's telegram is then delivered. Stroh shows surprise that Storch also knows Mieze Meier. Christine asks the notary to represent her in divorce proceedings, which he assumes, to her annoyance, involve Lummer. She is even more annoyed when he refuses to act without consulting Storch, whom he respects. Storch, pacing agitatedly up and down in the rain in the Prater, is joined by Stroh, who says that Mieze has told him she intended her letter for him (Stroh) but confused the names. Then you must go to Grundlsee and explain it to my wife, Storch replies. At Grundlsee all is chaos as the packing proceeds. Stroh arrives to explain the confusion; later Storch himself returns, to be received coldly because, Christine says, he has not realized how much pain he has caused her. Robert admits he returned because the notary had written to him about Lummer. But he believes in her innocence – and roars with laughter over the 1000 marks. The opera ends with loving reconciliation.

The fact that *Intermezzo* was a slice of Strauss's everyday life for too long obscured its importance, a pioneering opera in which everyday events – e.g. telephone conversations – became operatic fare. Thanks to Strauss's libretto, the action moves swiftly, with a cinematic flowing of one scene into the next. The symphonic interludes, miniature tone poems, sum up and add a dimension to the action. *Intermezzo* is also important as a further and major step in Strauss's lifelong quest for a viable marriage of words and music, in which the words are audible but the music paramount. In a long and fascinating preface to the published score, he warned conductors to pay particular attention to his dynamics, designed to ensure audibility of the text.

The libretto is in everyday conversational prose, which is set to a most subtle melodic recitative, both *secco* and *accompagnato*. The characters' inner feelings are delineated in the orchestral accompaniment, which is witty, allusive and graphic. There is much humour, but also a deep-lying seriousness. Strauss's own agony of mind at the thought of a divorce from his Pauline is starkly evoked in the scene in the Prater; and, although the shrewish side of Pauline/Christine provides the audience with many laughs, her lovable side – and the tenderness her husband felt for her – is very evident. Although he could never have brought himself to treat such a subject, Hofmannsthal went to see *Intermezzo* and perspicaciously wrote to Strauss about its essential seriousness. Schoenberg too, as early as the 1920s, counted it among Strauss's best and most enduring compositions.

Die ägyptische Helena
The Egyptian Helen
Opera in two acts (2h 15m)
Libretto by Hugo von Hofmannsthal
Composed 1923–October 1927, rev. 1932–January 1933
PREMIERES 6 June 1928, Staatsoper, Dresden; rev. version: 14 August 1933, Festspielhaus, Salzburg; US: 6 November 1928, Metropolitan, New York
CAST Helena (Helen) *s*, Menelas (Menelaus) *t*, Hermione *s*, Aithra *s*, Altair *bar*, Da-ud *t*, 2 Servants of Aithra *s, ms*, 3 Elves 2 *s, c*, Omniscient Sea-shell *c*; *satb* chorus of elves, male and female warriors, slaves, eunuchs

Hofmannsthal resumed his collaboration with Strauss in 1922, when they devised a ballet to Beethoven's incidental music for *The Ruins of Athens*. The poet suggested an opera about Helen of Troy. He had for some time been pondering how it was that Menelaus took back Helen as his wife after the Trojan War, which had been caused by her adultery with Paris. Strauss was hoping for a light-hearted piece on the lines of Offenbach's *La belle Hélène*. What he got, as so often from Hofmannsthal, began lightly but gradually acquired all kinds of psychological and symbolical nuances.

Nevertheless he was delighted with the libretto for Act I, and Hofmannsthal, on hearing the music, declared it to be 'light and transparent, for all its high, noble seriousness'. Strauss had realized that the lightness of form at which Hofmannsthal was aiming did not require 'operetta' treatment. *Helena* became a romantic opera. As Strauss said in an interview before the premiere: 'I am afraid this music is melodious, sounds beautiful and unfortunately presents no problems to ears which have developed beyond the 19th century.'

Problems arose over the casting of Helen. The role was conceived for Maria Jeritza, whose physical beauty was a major asset, but Dresden could not afford her enormous fee. When Strauss agreed to the substitution of Elisabeth Rethberg, a good singer but not such a beauty, he was fiercely attacked by Hofmannsthal: 'This will ruin Helena, completely ruin her.' Jeritza sang the role in Vienna. The opera was not a success, nor has it been since, in spite of Strauss's revisions to Act II in 1933 at the request of Clemens Krauss.

SYNOPSIS

Act I In the palace of the sea-god Poseidon, the enchantress Aithra possesses a sea-shell which sees and knows everything and can report it. The sea-shell says that in a ship off the coast Menelaus is about to kill his sleeping wife, Helen of Troy. Aithra wrecks the ship, and Menelaus and Helen take refuge in the palace. Helen now wants to regain Menelaus' love, even though he still plans to kill her for her adultery with Paris. Aithra restores Helen's youthful beauty and gives Menelaus a magic potion to make him believe that Helen was never in Troy with Paris but in an enchanted sleep in the palace of Aithra's father. She promises to build them a magic pavilion on the slopes of the Atlas Mountains, and gives Helen a phial of lotus juice which will make them forget the past.

Act II After a passionate 'second wedding night', Menelaus thinks Helen is a phantom and wants to abandon her. The lotus juice doesn't work. Desert warriors, led by Altair, arrive (at Aithra's command). Menelaus mistakes Altair's son Da-ud for Paris and kills him while out hunting. Aithra discovers that Helen was mistakenly given the antidote to the lotus juice, but Helen offers it to Menelaus because she wants to restore his memory. He accepts her for what she is. Altair tries to seize Helen, but Aithra's warriors defeat him.

Die ägyptische Helena is the least performed and the least highly regarded of the Strauss–Hofmannsthal operas. Yet Hofmannsthal believed it was the best thing he had done, and Strauss described the music as 'Greek Wagner'. Undoubtedly the libretto presents difficulties. The plot is confused and contrived in Act II, and the characters have little life of their own. But the music has much to commend it. The cantabile style of the third act of Die Frau ohne Schatten, which gave rise to Barak's great aria 'Mir anvertraut', is here followed up. Helena is Strauss's bel-canto opera, with arias, ensembles and other set pieces in profusion. Helen herself is a fully developed role, warm and sensuous, with Menelaus a more interesting vocal character than Bacchus in Ariadne auf Naxos. Some of the writing for the voice foreshadows the pure, serene style of Strauss's later works, notably Daphne. The orchestration is rich and bright, with a diamond-like hardness in the harmony.

Arabella

Lyric comedy in three acts (2h 30m)
Libretto by Hugo von Hofmannsthal
Composed 1930–October 1932
PREMIERES 1 July 1933, Staatsoper, Dresden: UK: 17 May 1934, Covent Garden, London; US: 10 February 1955, Metropolitan, New York
CAST Count Waldner b, Adelaide, his wife ms, Arabella s, Zdenka s, Mandryka bar, Matteo t, Count Elemer t, Count Dominik bar, Count Lamoral b, Fiakermilli s, Fortune-teller s, 3 Players 3 b; spoken roles: Welko, Djura, Jankel, Hotel Porter; silent: Arabella's Companion, A Doctor, Groom; satb chorus of cabmen, ball guests, hotel guests, waiters

Hofmannsthal based his last libretto for Strauss on his novel Lucidor (1910), with some elements added from a proposed comedy, Fiaker als Graf ('Cabbie as

Count'). Strauss had been pressing him for some time for 'a second Rosenkavalier without its mistakes and longueurs'. In what became Arabella, Hofmannsthal believed he had found the formula his collaborator required – a Viennese setting with a background of waltzes and a plot based on his favourite theme of love at first sight. He sent the libretto of Act I to Strauss in May 1928. Adjustments were made and the complete libretto was ready by Christmas 1928. Further revisions were delayed by Hofmannsthal's illness. Strauss wanted a substantial monologue for Arabella with which to end Act I, and 'Mein Elemer!' was supplied on 10 July 1929. Strauss telegraphed his thanks and congratulations from Garmisch to Rodaun. But the telegram was not opened. It arrived on 15 July, the day of the funeral of Hofmannsthal's son Franz, who had committed suicide. An hour or so before the service, Hofmannsthal had a stroke and died.

Strauss began to compose Arabella in 1930. He dedicated it to Alfred Reucker and Fritz Busch, intendant and conductor of the Dresden State Opera where it was to be premiered. But in March 1933 the Nazis dismissed both men. Strauss withdrew the score, but Dresden held him to his contract and Clemens Krauss conducted the first performance, with Viorica Ursuleac (who later became his wife) as Arabella. In Vienna Lotte Lehmann sang the title role. The critical response was cool, the general attitude being that it was an attempt to imitate Rosenkavalier, and was not as good. This attitude has gradually given way to admiration for the opera on its own terms, and it has become one of the best loved of Strauss's stage works. It is generally performed in the original three-act version, but Munich favours the producer Rudolf Hartmann's 1939 device of linking Acts II and III by omitting the final waltz and chorus of Act II.

SYNOPSIS

Act I Count Waldner, a retired cavalry officer, and his wife live in a slightly seedy Vienna hotel. They are hard up. Waldner gambles at the card table but rarely wins. They have two daughters, Arabella and Zdenka, but the latter is passed off as a boy because they cannot afford to bring out both girls in Vienna society. It is Carnival Day (Shrove Tuesday) 1860, and Countess Waldner (Adelaide) is consulting a fortune-teller who says that Arabella's successful suitor will be a foreigner, summoned by letter. Left alone, Zdenka admits an army officer, Matteo. He believes Arabella loves him because of the letters he receives from her. But these are written by Zdenka, who adores him. He leaves, threatening suicide or exile. When Arabella enters, Zdenka quarrels with her about her coldness to Matteo. Arabella says she will know the right man when she meets him. In fact she saw a stranger looking at her in the street that morning and wishes he would send her flowers. Count Elemer, one of three suitors, arrives to escort Arabella for a drive. She tells him she must choose a husband before the night is out while she is queen of the Cabbies' Ball. Before they leave, Arabella sees her stranger in the street outside. Waldner tells Adelaide he's been hoping for a letter from a former army comrade, Mandryka, a Croatian. He has sent the rich old man a portrait of Arabella. Sure enough, a waiter says a Mandryka is waiting to see him. But this is a tall, handsome young man, nephew of Waldner's friend, who is now dead. He has inherited his uncle's lands and wealth, and, having seen her portrait, has come to woo Arabella. He shows his bulging wallet to Waldner, and tells him to help himself. After he has left, Arabella sings of the impossibility of marriage with Elemer ('Mein Elemer!').

Act II   At the Cabbies' Ball, Arabella is presented to Mandryka, whom she recognizes as her stranger in the street. They declare their love, and Mandryka tells her of the custom in his village whereby betrothed girls present a cup of clear Danube water to their fiancé as a token of chastity and allegiance. Arabella says she will dance farewell to her girlhood. The cabbies' mascot, the Fiakermilli, hails Arabella as the queen of the ball. Arabella has a final dance with each of her three suitors, Elemer, Dominik and Lamoral. Matteo has been hovering nearby, and is assured by Zdenka of Arabella's love. She gives him a letter, supposedly from Arabella. This exchange is overheard by Mandryka. In the letter, Zdenka says, is the key to Arabella's bedroom (in reality, her own). Mandryka cannot believe this deception, but, when he is given a letter from Arabella excusing herself from the remainder of the evening, he gets drunk, flirts with the Fiakermilli, and insults the Waldners.

Act III   From the main hall of the Waldners' hotel we see Matteo on the landing at the top of the staircase, emerging from what he believes to be Arabella's room. He cannot believe his eyes when he sees Arabella, in her ball gown, in the lobby. He tells her he cannot understand how she can be so distant after what has just passed between them. Arabella is mystified and annoyed. She denies she was upstairs 15 minutes ago. The Waldners and Mandryka arrive. Seeing Matteo, Mandryka is convinced of Arabella's fickleness and orders his servants to pack for departure. Arabella denies that Matteo is her lover. The silence is broken by a cry as Zdenka, in a nightdress, runs downstairs to say farewell to her family before she jumps into the river. She tells Arabella what has happened, and reveals to Matteo that she is a girl and that it was her to whom he has just made love. Mandryka, ashamed, asks Waldner to accept Matteo as a son-in-law. Everyone disperses, leaving Arabella with Mandryka. She asks that his servant should bring her a glass of water to her room to quench her thirst. Mandryka soliloquizes on his stupidity. Then he sees Arabella descending the stairs bringing him the glass of water as in his village custom. 'Take me as I am!' she declares.

Arabella is Strauss's most romantic opera. For their last collaboration, Hofmannsthal eschewed his tendency to overload his libretti with symbols, mysticism and psychological insights. Instead he was content with a tale of love at first sight involving a strange and eccentric but very human group of characters. Just as *Die ägyptische Helena* seemed to reflect the cinema's preoccupation in the 1920s with sheikhs and desert songs, so in *Arabella* there is suggestion of a cinematic plot – awaiting Mr Right. But Strauss's music is of such charm and warmth that the improbabilities of the plot as they involve Matteo and Zdenka in Act III are of no account – one accepts it all. The scoring has a transparency and sweetness rare in 20th-century opera.

In setting the libretto, Strauss continued the parlando style he had been developing so successfully since the *Ariadne* prelude (though it can be found in *Feuersnot* in an embryonic state). *Arabella* created a new kind of music-theatre, combining the finest qualities of opera, operetta and musical.

Too much is made of the fact that Hofmannsthal died before he could revise Acts II and III. Although there are dramatic weaknesses in Act II, they are not fatal – and the Munich habit of running the last two acts together is no improvement in any respect. The comparison with *Der Rosenkavalier* is also overworked. Vienna and waltzes are about the only genuine similarities, both treated in very different ways in *Arabella*.

A feature of the score is Strauss's use of Slavonic folk music to give special flavour to the music for Mandryka. Lyricism is all in *Arabella*, in both the libretto and the music. If it is not Strauss's most profound opera, it is in many ways the most uncomplicatedly enjoyable, which is not to say that it lacks complexities. The heroine herself is a fascinating figure, as Strauss realized when he demanded a big aria for her to end Act I. In 'Mein Elemer!', he and Hofmannsthal provide a character study of Arabella that is the key to the whole opera.

Die schweigsame Frau
The Silent Woman
Comic opera in three acts (3h)
Libretto by Stefan Zweig, freely adapted from Ben Jonson's comedy *Epicoene, or The Silent Woman* (1609)
Composed October 1932–October 1934 (overture, January 1935)
PREMIERES   24 June 1935, Staatsoper, Dresden; US: 7 October 1958, City Center, New York; UK: 20 November 1961, Covent Garden, London
CAST   Sir Morosus *b*, Housekeeper *c*, Barber *bar*, Henry *t*, Aminta *s*, Isotta *s*, Carlotta *ms*, Morbio *bar*, Vanuzzi *b*, Farfallo *b*; *satb* chorus of actors and neighbours

After Hofmannsthal's death, Strauss was introduced to the novelist and playwright Stefan Zweig (1881–1942), who suggested a collaboration. When he received the draft of Act I in the summer of 1932, Strauss was overjoyed: 'The born comic opera – more suited to music than either *Figaro* or *The Barber of Seville*.' The libretto was completed by mid-January 1933. Strauss completed the composition sketch in November 1933 and the full score in October 1934. The Nazis were now in power in Germany and had introduced their anti-Semitic legislation. Zweig, an Austrian, was Jewish, but his libretto for *Die schweigsame Frau* was personally approved by Hitler, who did not wish to attract unfavourable international publicity by acting against Strauss.

While at Dresden for the premiere, Strauss discovered that Zweig's name had been omitted from the programme. He demanded its restoration, threatening to leave if this was not done. He got his way, but meanwhile a letter he had written to Zweig criticizing the regime had been intercepted by the Gestapo and sent to Hitler. After four performances, the opera was banned throughout Germany. Karl Böhm conducted these performances, in which one of the great Strauss sopranos, Maria Cebotari, sang the role of Aminta.

SYNOPSIS

Act I The garrulous housekeeper to Sir Morosus, a retired 17th-century British admiral, tells the barber who comes to shave him every day that the lonely old man needs a wife and she would like this chance. The barber says her constant prattling would drive the old man mad, for an explosion on board ship had damaged the admiral's hearing, leaving him extremely sensitive to noise. However, while shaving Morosus, the barber suggests he should take a young, silent wife. Morosus denies that such a woman exists. Morosus's nephew Henry, whom the old man believed to be lost in Italy, arrives. What need has he now of a wife when he has an heir to leave his treasures? Henry says he has a troupe of friends with him. Morosus thinks he means 'troops' and is horrified to discover that the 'soldiers' are an opera company. Moreover, the prima donna is Henry's wife, Aminta. Morosus disinherits Henry and orders the barber to find him a silent young woman. The barber hatches a plot.

Act II The barber tells Morosus he has found three girls from whom he can choose a wife. They are all impersonated by members of Henry's troupe. Morosus chooses 'Timidia' (in reality Aminta) because she is quiet and meek. A clergyman and lawyer (also disguised actors) perform a wedding ceremony. When Morosus and his 'wife' are left alone, Aminta sees that he is a fine man and wishes she had not become involved. But she plays her part and suddenly turns into a shrieking virago, breaking up his house. Henry promises that he will free Morosus from this dreadful woman next day.

Act III Aminta is supervising a noisy refurbishment of Morosus's living room. Henry, disguised as a music teacher, arrives to give her a singing lesson (Monteverdi and Legrenzi). The noise is driving Morosus mad, until the barber ushers in the lord chief justice and two lawyers (actors, of course). But they cannot find a reason for divorce. However, the barber suggests that 'Lady Morosus' has slept with someone else before marriage. A disguised Henry confirms this. But one of the 'lawyers' rules that it was not stipulated that Timidia should be a virgin. Case dismissed. Morosus is distraught, and at this point Henry and Aminta remove their disguises. Morosus sees the joke, congratulates the actors and calls for wine and music. He reflects on how wonderful a silent wife is when she is married to somebody else.

Strauss's delight in Zweig's libretto undoubtedly arose principally from the fact that at last he had been provided with a light comedy. It offered plenty of opportunities for parody. Like the *Ariadne* prologue, it gave him as characters members of an opera company, a world in which he felt at ease; and, in Aminta, he yet again had a heroine some of whose characteris-

tics resembled those of his wife Pauline and who was also a reincarnation of Zerbinetta.

Several episodes in a work that partially reverts to the format of number opera have a Rossinian sparkle, and there are lyrical interludes of considerable charm. Morosus, another Strauss self-portrait, is vividly drawn, and the opera-company roles – all musical descendants of the comedians in *Ariadne auf Naxos* – are effective in a well-produced staging. Perhaps the finest music comes at the start of Act II, with the touching duet for Aminta and Morosus followed by the bogus wedding ceremony, in which Strauss quotes from the Fitzwilliam Virginal Book.

Somewhere behind it all lurks the shade of Verdi's *Falstaff*. But Strauss does not keep the top spinning as effortlessly as Verdi, mainly because the quality of his melodic invention falls below his best. Even so, *Die schweigsame Frau* does not deserve the neglect into which it has fallen.

Friedenstag
Peace Day
Opera in one act (1h 15m)
Libretto by Joseph Gregor
Composed October 1935–June 1936
PREMIERES 24 July 1938, Nationaltheater, Munich; US: 2 April 1967, University of Southern California, Los Angeles; UK: 29 May 1971, BBC radio; 28 March 1985, Logan Hall, London (concert)
CAST Commandant *bar*, Maria *s*, Sergeant-major *b*, Corporal *bar*, Private Soldier *t*, Musketeer *b*, Bugler *b*, Officer *bar*, Front-line Officer *bar*, Piedmontese *t*, Holsteiner *b*, Mayor *t*, Prelate *bar*, Woman *s*; *satb* chorus of soldiers of the garrison and of the besieging army, elders of the town, women of the deputation to the commandant, townspeople

Among projects suggested to Strauss by Zweig before political considerations ended their collaboration was an opera tentatively called *24 October 1648*, about the end of the Thirty Years War and based partly on Calderón's play *La Redención de Breda* (1625). Strauss proposed that Zweig should supply him secretly with libretti and he would compose the operas and hide them until better times. Zweig realized the impracticability of such a scheme and urged the claims of the Viennese theatrical historian and archivist Joseph Gregor (1888–1960). Strauss grudgingly accepted Gregor but savagely criticized the draft libretto for *Friedenstag*, as the *1648* opera became, and was grateful to Zweig for his amendments and revisions.

Friedenstag seems an unlikely choice of subject for Strauss – 'military matters just do not excite me,' said the composer of the battle scene in *Ein Heldenleben* – so one presumes that its anti-war message appealed to him as topical. It makes Hitler's attendance at the first Vienna performance an act of hypocrisy (or calculated deceit). At the Munich premiere, the part of the commandant was sung by Hans Hotter, with Ludwig Weber as the Holsteiner and Ursuleac as Maria.

SYNOPSIS

It is the last day of the Thirty Years War, 24 October 1648. A besieged city is near to surrender. The inhabitants are starving and the soldiers in the fortress are near to breaking-point. Even the arrival of an

Italian messenger, who sings a love song, does not lift their spirits. A deputation, headed by the mayor, begs the commandant to surrender to save their lives. He refuses; his orders are to fight to the last. But he tells them to await a signal at noon. They leave hopefully, but he tells his soldiers that he intends to blow up the fortress. He gives them the choice of staying or leaving. Those who decide to stay go to the cellars to prepare the gunpowder. The commandant's wife, Maria, senses impending disaster. She knows her husband's inflexible resolve. He tells her of his plan and urges her to go, but she wants to die in his arms. The fuse is about to be lit when shots are heard, followed by bells. Maria realizes that these mean a proclamation of peace. The enemy forces approach the fortress with cannons bedecked with flowers. The commandant believes this is a ruse, and when his Holstein opponent arrives seeking reconciliation he quarrels with him and both men draw their swords. Maria interposes herself between them and, after hesitation, they embrace. The people flood into the fortress and sing jubilantly of peace and brotherhood.

Even if the subject of *Friedenstag* was uncongenial to him, it nevertheless drew from Strauss some of his strongest diatonic music. The chorus has a larger part than in most of his operas. Although the role of Maria enabled him to compose two lyrical soprano arias, male voices predominate. We must be grateful to Gregor for his invention of the Piedmontese messenger whose Italianate song of happiness provides the required contrast during the sombre opening scene.

Strauss's most characteristic music occurs in Maria's second aria and in her impassioned duet with her husband, the commandant. But more impressive, perhaps because rarer in this composer's work, is the stark and despairing music for the starving townspeople's delegation. The role of the commandant, too, with its inflexibility, irony and eventual thaw, gives splendid opportunities to the voice, as might have been expected from some of Strauss's lieder. The final C major hymn to peace perhaps invites comparison with the finale of Beethoven's *Fidelio*; the same ideal and idealism inspired both composers.

Daphne

Bucolic tragedy in one act (1h 45m)
Libretto by Joseph Gregor
Composed summer 1936–December 1937
PREMIERES 15 October 1938, Staatsoper, Dresden;
US: 7 October 1960, Brooklyn, New York (concert);
29 July 1964, Opera Theater, Santa Fe, New Mexico;
UK: 2 May 1987, Grand Theatre, Leeds
CAST Daphne *s*, Peneios *b*, Gaea *c*, Leukippos *t*, Apollo *t*,
4 Shepherds *t*, bar, 2 *b*, 2 Maids 2 *s*; *tb* chorus of shepherds,
maskers; maids *silent*; dancers

The subject of *Daphne* was offered by Gregor to Strauss at their first meeting in 1935. A libretto, revised and approved by Zweig, reached the composer in September of that year. Strauss was severely critical, and two more versions were written before he began to compose any music. Gregor's original idea for the finale – Daphne's metamorphosis into a laurel tree –

was choral. Strauss was dubious about it and discussed it with the conductor Clemens Krauss, with whom he had become increasingly friendly since the *Arabella* premiere in 1933. Krauss suggested that the transformation should be described by the orchestra, with Daphne singing wordlessly from within the tree when the change was completed.

Karl Böhm, to whom the opera was dedicated, conducted the first performance, the ninth premiere of a Strauss opera in Dresden. It was played in tandem with *Friedenstag*, as Gregor had intended, but Strauss then decided that the two one-act operas succeeded better separately. Performances throughout Germany and Austria then followed, but the Second World War held up its introduction elsewhere. However, there was a famous production in 1948 in Buenos Aires conducted by Erich Kleiber.

SYNOPSIS

At sunset on the slopes of Mount Olympus, Peneios summons his shepherds to bring their flocks and herds from the fields so that they can join in the feast of Dionysus. His daughter Daphne sings of her love of nature and of her longing for the daylight, when she feels at one with the trees and birds. Leukippos, her friend since childhood, declares his love for her, but sexual passion has no meaning for her. Daphne's mother, Gaea, tells her to be ready for the feast, but she will not wear the dress provided. Her maids suggest to Leukippos that he should disguise himself as a woman to gain Daphne's love. Peneios senses something divine in the air and tells the shepherds to expect a godly visitation. As a thunderstorm rages, a young cowherd arrives – Apollo in disguise. He is entranced by Daphne and woos her, but she recoils from his passionate kiss, while realizing that this man is no ordinary mortal. The rites of the Dionysian feast begin. Leukippos, in girl's clothes, dances with Daphne, but the jealous Apollo gives the masquerade away and hurls thunderbolts to halt the festivities. Leukippos accuses Apollo of also wooing Daphne in a disguise. The enraged god kills him. Daphne, too late, is heartbroken and refuses to go with Apollo. For his part, Apollo recognizes that he has gone too far. He asks pardon of Dionysus and asks Zeus to grant Daphne her wishes. In the moonlight, Daphne is transformed into a laurel tree, her wordless song calling from its branches.

Daphne is Strauss's pastoral symphony for the stage, chamber music composed for a large orchestra. The music, pentatonic and diatonic, is intensely lyrical, the scoring pure in texture, with a shining transparency which derives from passages in *Die Frau ohne Schatten* and foreshadows the so-called 'Indian summer' in which he composed the Oboe Concerto, the Second Horn Concerto and the sublime *Metamorphosen*.

The title role requires a lyric soprano capable also of intensity in the post-Romantic duet with Apollo. She sings her first long aria, a hymn to nature, 'O bleib, geliebter Tag', to the departing sun in one of the most glorious outbursts for female voice that Strauss ever wrote. The terror that Daphne experiences at the moment when Apollo kisses her is memorably conveyed in music of an unearthly hue. As for Strauss's supposed aversion to tenors, both Leukippos and Apollo are tenors, the first light and boyish, the second heroic. A final feature is Strauss's superb writing for woodwind, from the oboe solo with which the opera magically begins to the final transformation scene.

Die Liebe der Danae

Cheerful mythology in three acts (2h 30m)
Libretto by Joseph Gregor, from a scenario by Hugo von Hofmannsthal
Composed February 1938–28 June 1940
PREMIERES 16 August 1944, Festspielhaus, Salzburg (dress rehearsal only); 14 August 1952, Festspielhaus, Salzburg; UK: 16 September 1953, Covent Garden, London; US: 10 April 1964, University of Southern California, Los Angeles
CAST Jupiter *bar*, Merkur (Mercury) *t*, King Pollux *t*, Danae *s*, Xanthe *s*, Midas *t*, 4 Kings 2 *t*, 2 *b*, 4 Queens: Semele *s*, Europa *s*, Alkmene (Alcmene) *ms*, Leda *c*, Watchmen 4 *b*

In April 1920 Hofmannsthal sent Strauss a scenario in three acts called *Danae, oder die Vernunftheirat* (*Danae, or The Marriage of Convenience*). Perhaps because he was immersed in the affairs of the Vienna Opera and in composing *Intermezzo*, Strauss did not react to it and claimed to have forgotten it when Willi Schuh drew it to his attention in 1936. He was delighted, for it exactly met his wishes for a light, operetta-like piece with which to follow *Friedenstag* and *Daphne*. Coincidentally, Gregor had also sketched a scenario for a *Danae* opera, which he sent to Strauss, who thought it too serious and urged him to adhere to Hofmannsthal's treatment. By the end of June 1940, the opera was finished. Strauss decreed that it should not be performed until at least two years after the end of the war. But Krauss, who became artistic director of the Salzburg Festival in 1941, persuaded him to allow it to be performed at the 1944 Festival in honour of his 80th birthday. Six performances were planned. But the Allied invasion of Europe in June 1944 and the bomb plot against Hitler the following month resulted in a ban on all festivals. Salzburg, by special dispensation, was reduced to one concert and a dress rehearsal of *Die Liebe der Danae*, which Strauss attended. Viorica Ursuleac was Danae, Hans Hotter sang Jupiter and Krauss conducted. The official first performance, with Annelies Kupper as Danae, was at the 1952 Salzburg Festival, three years after Strauss's death. Since then, performances have been intermittent.

SYNOPSIS
Act I On the isle of Eos, King Pollux is warding off his creditors. Wait another day, he pleads: the four kings, his royal nephews by marriage, are seeking a rich husband for his beautiful daughter Danae, and the richest man in the world, King Midas of Lydia, has shown interest. Danae tells her servant Xanthe that she has dreamed she was covered by a shower of gold, which embraced her like a lover. She says she's interested only in a suitor who brings as much gold as she has just dreamed about. Midas, simply dressed, joins her but says he is Chrysopher, who has come to

prepare her for the arrival of his friend Midas. They go to the harbour to await the arrival of 'Midas', who is Jupiter in disguise. Danae recognizes him as the visitor in her dream.

Act II The four queens are decorating Danae's marriage bed. They recognize Jupiter when he walks in. He has been the lover of each of them in different guises, and they grill him about his pursuit of Danae. He confesses to Midas that he finds his four former conquests unattractively middle-aged and is worried that Danae prefers the real Midas to him. He warns Midas that he will return him to his former life as a donkey-driver if he attempts to win Danae's love. The four queens boast to Danae of their previous intimacy with her elderly bridegroom and advise her to stick to his younger companion. Midas/Chrysopher tells her he is Midas and to prove it turns the contents of the room to gold. When they embrace, there is a clap of thunder and Danae turns into a golden statue. Jupiter asks the statue to choose between him and Midas. She chooses Midas. Restored to life, she and Midas disappear.

Act III Midas and Danae are in the desert. Danae realizes that Midas has forfeited his golden touch as the price of loving her. He tells her of his past life and explains how Jupiter had taken his place when the four kings and queens arrived in Lydia with Danae's portrait. Danae, moved, forgets her passion for gold and remembers that she chose a life of poverty with Midas instead of luxury with Jupiter. In a forest landscape, Mercury appears to Jupiter to tell him that everyone on Olympus is laughing at his failure to win Danae. The four queens comfort him, but he bids them farewell. They are followed by Pollux, his creditors and the four kings, all furious with Jupiter for different reasons. Mercury suggests he should placate them with a shower of gold and advises him to pursue Danae. In Midas's hut Danae sings of her new happiness. Jupiter enters and tries to make Danae discontented, but acknowledges defeat.

It is impossible when hearing *Die Liebe der Danae* not to wonder what Strauss and Hofmannsthal might have made of it in 1920. Some of Gregor's libretto is lame, and neither he nor Strauss seems to have been sure whether the opera was to be a 'cheerful mythology', with a touch of operetta, or something more serious. Through self-identification with the role of Jupiter, Strauss – increasingly conscious of his own isolation in Nazi Germany – created a moving character, based on Wotan but with a sense of humour. There are other Wagnerian allusions – one may identify Mercury with Loge and the four queens with the Rhinemaidens – but the music is mainly light in texture. In the last act Strauss regains the warmth and richness of his noontide: in the noble pathos of the orchestral interlude, known as *Jupiter's Renunciation*, and all through the last scene, in which Danae's big aria and her duet with Jupiter point forward to the autumnal profusion of his last works.

In spite of the uneven quality of the first two acts, they contain some of Strauss's wittiest music. The thematic material is on a high level, inventive and strongly characterized, while the orchestration throughout is apt, skilful and glowing with colour. It is unusual among Strauss operas in that, for all the beautiful music given to Danae, it is a male character, Jupiter, who is dominant.

Capriccio

Conversation piece for music in one act (2h 15m)
Libretto by Clemens Krauss and the composer
Composed July 1940–August 1941
PREMIERES   28 October 1942, Nationaltheater, Munich;
UK: 22 September 1953, Covent Garden, London; US:
2 April 1954, Juilliard School of Music, New York
CAST   Countess *s*, Count *bar*, Flamand *t*, Olivier *bar*,
La Roche *b*, Clairon *c*, Monsieur Taupe *t*, Italian Singer *s*,
Italian tenor *t*, Major-domo *b*, 8 servants 4 *t*, 4 *b*, ballet
dancer

Strauss's last opera was on the subject that had exercised him for most of his life: the relationship between words and music in opera. In 1935 Zweig had suggested reshaping Giambattista Casti's comedy *Prima la musica e poi le parole* which had been set by Antonio Salieri (1786). Zweig passed on his idea to Gregor, and together they devised a scenario. Over the next four years Strauss rejected two libretti by Gregor and consulted Clemens Krauss, who wrote a scenario but suggested Strauss should write the text himself. Gregor was dismissed, and together Strauss and Krauss completed *Capriccio*. Although Krauss is credited with the libretto in the printed score, much of it is by Strauss. The first performance was given in Munich with Viorica Ursuleac as the countess, Hans Hotter as Olivier and Georg Hann as La Roche. In spite of the nightly air raids, each performance was fully attended and enthusiastically received. Krauss made several attempts to interest Strauss in writing another opera, but he replied, 'One can only leave one testament.' At Hamburg in 1957, Rudolf Hartmann, the producer of the Munich premiere, divided the opera into two acts, making a break at the point where the countess orders chocolate in the drawing room. This version has been widely adopted elsewhere, including at Glyndebourne.

SYNOPSIS
In a château near Paris *c.* 1775, the young widowed Countess Madeleine, with her brother the count, is listening to a string sextet written in honour of her forthcoming birthday by the composer Flamand. Other members of the house party are the poet Olivier, who has written a play for the occasion, and the theatrical director La Roche, who is to produce it. The count is to act in the play, mainly because he is infatuated with the Parisian actress Clairon, who has recently broken off her affair with Olivier and is expected at any moment. On arrival, she inquires pointedly if Olivier has yet written the love scene. He has that morning written a sonnet as its climax, and this is declaimed from manuscript by the count and Clairon. While a rehearsal of his play begins, from which La Roche excludes him, Olivier reads the sonnet to the countess, for whom it is intended ('Kein Andres, das mir so im Herzen loht'). Flamand, to Olivier's annoyance, promptly sets it to music and sings it to Madeleine and Olivier. Poet and composer quarrel over whose work it now is – the countess says

it is hers, a present from them both. Olivier is summoned by La Roche, and Flamand declares his love to the countess. He demands an answer from her. She says she will meet him next morning at eleven, in the library. Chocolate is now served and La Roche introduces a young ballerina to entertain the company. After the dances (imitations of Couperin), fugal discussion of the relative merits of words and music begins. La Roche then introduces an Italian soprano and tenor, who sing a duet, after which La Roche describes the lavish entertainment he plans for the countess's birthday. This is received with ribald comments which lead to two octets, the first a laughing ensemble, the second a quarrel (during which the Italian soprano eats too many cakes and drinks too much wine). La Roche replies with a long monologue in which he defines the work of a director and asks where the great artists of today are (the text was written by Strauss, and its sentiments are obviously his). The countess suggests Flamand and Olivier should collaborate on an opera for La Roche to direct. Various subjects (*Ariadne* and *Daphne* among them) are rejected. The count suggests it should be 'about all of us and the events of today'. This is agreed, and the company disperses to return to Paris. The servants tidy the salon and discuss what has been happening. The major-domo gives them the evening off after they have prepared the countess's supper. A voice is heard – it is the prompter, Monsieur Taupe, who had fallen asleep and has been left behind. As he is led off to be given a meal, the countess enters, dressed for supper, and stands on the terrace in the moonlight. The major-domo gives her a message from Olivier – he will be in the library at eleven next morning to learn how the opera should end. 'How should it end?' she ponders. Is she more moved by words or music, does she love Olivier or Flamand? Can there be an ending that is not trivial? She curtsies to her reflection in a mirror and goes into supper – humming the melody of the sonnet.

In what he expected to be a dry, academic subject for opera, written for his own amusement – a theatrical fugue, as he described it to Krauss – and unlikely to appeal to a wide audience, Strauss paradoxically found in *Capriccio* a libretto to suit all that he did best. It drew from him a fresh fount of inspiration, and has become one of his most popular works. His technical virtuosity is demonstrated in three vocal octets, the laughing and quarrelling ensembles and the servants' scherzo-like commentary on the day's proceedings. In the music for the Italian singers and the ballerina, his gift for parody is at its keenest and most affectionate. In the strange, half-lit scene for the prompter and the major-domo, with its shifting harmonies and air of mystery, he recaptured something of the poetic fantasy of his *Don Quixote* variations (1897). The instrumental sextet that opens the opera and the scoring throughout the rest of the work are examples of Strauss at his most lyrical and sensitive, but suffused with autumnal melancholy, and in the role of the countess he created one of his most adorable heroines and wrote for her music of intense melodic beauty in which the finest qualities of his lieder and arias are combined to provide the ideal final 20 minutes for a last opera by Strauss.

The Strauss who was able to cut his musical cloth as the dramatic situation dictated is perfectly accommodated in *Capriccio*. Like *Der Rosenkavalier*, the work is gorgeously anachronistic. Although it is set in the late 18th century and a mock-rococo style is sometimes affected, the music belongs inescapably to Strauss's own era, which is one reason why productions updated to the 1920s and 1930s are successful, give or take the resulting ludicrousness of the libretto's references to Goldoni and Gluck as contemporary figures. As in the prologue to *Ariadne auf Naxos* and in *Intermezzo* and *Arabella*, the continuously melodic conversational recitative is here raised to a fine art. All the greatest features of his operas from *Der Rosenkavalier* onwards were filtered through the experience and wisdom gained over 30 years to find their apogee in *Capriccio*. Its resonances and delights increase at each hearing.

Other operatic works: *Guntram*, 1894, rev. 1934; *Feuersnot*, 1901

M.K.

IGOR STRAVINSKY

Igor Fyodorovich Stravinsky; *b* 17 June 1882, Lomonosov (formerly Oranienbaum), Russia; *d* 6 April 1971, New York

Of Stravinsky's twenty or so works for the theatre, perhaps four are definitely operas: *The Nightingale*, *Mavra*, *Oedipus Rex* and *The Rake's Progress*. But many of his best works are hard to categorize, since it was an essential part of his genius to invent genres to suit his subject matter. In 1913 he told a reporter, 'I dislike opera. Music can be married to gesture or to words – not to both without bigamy.' Yet between 'pure' ballet like *Petrushka* and 'pure' opera like *The Rake's Progress* are several works that combine dance with speech and/or singing, with or without narrative in the conventional sense. In such matters Stravinsky was evidently influenced by his compatriot Vsevolod Meyerhold, the theatre director, who rejected the 19th-century notion of stage realism in favour of an open-ended theatre where any resource is legitimate if it serves the central idea of the action. The use of masks (in *Pulcinella*, *Renard* and *Oedipus Rex*), ritualized action (*Le sacre du printemps*, *Les noces*, *Oedipus Rex*), deliberate breaks in style (*Petrushka*, *L'histoire du soldat*, *Persephone*), objectivization in the form of spoken or sung commentaries (*Renard*, *L'histoire du soldat*, *Oedipus Rex*), and other such devices, all originate in the Symbolist techniques of Meyerhold.

The Nightingale (begun 1908 or 1909) already suggests how a magical story can best be presented theatrically by creating a wholly artificial world with its own conventions of time and space. Many of Stravinsky's ballets are enactments of ritual, and some of the late ones tend towards abstraction. But he mostly favoured story works with a ritualistic or symbolic undertone

and a free mixture of genres. Of these *Les Noces* (1914–17, 1921–3) and *Pulcinella* (1919) are ballets enriched by singing, while *Renard* (1915–16) and *L'histoire du soldat* (1918) are fables told through mime, dance and song or speech. Their informal style owes something to the antique Russian travelling theatre of the *skomorokhi* (minstrel buffoons), and they are prototypes of the later genre of music-theatre. Stravinsky returned to this genre in 1961–2 in *The Flood*, a modern miracle play written for television. In the 1920s, however, he reacted against popular theatre and evolved in its place a synthetic ('neo-classical') style based on art models and preferring subjects from classical literature or mythology. The stage works of this period have a certain Homeric grandeur combined with a strong religious symbolism. Nevertheless their treatment is at bottom similar to that of the earlier works, with an essentially simple action gaining depth and complexity through a variety of stage devices and stylistic allusions.

Stravinsky owed his meteoric early success to his association with Diaghilev and the Paris-based Ballets Russes. His upbringing might well have directed him more readily towards opera. His father was leading bass at the Mariinsky Theatre in St Petersburg, and his teacher was Rimsky-Korsakov, at the time when the master was writing his last operas. But Diaghilev wanted a ballet score (for *The Firebird*, 1910) and the result was so brilliant in its vitality of movement and fantastic orchestral colouring that Stravinsky was diverted into a genre that Diaghilev was busy pushing to the forefront of the modern aesthetic movement. Between then and his death in 1929, Diaghilev put on nine further stage works by Stravinsky, six of them ballets. For much of this period Stravinsky was a leading light of the Paris artistic scene (after spending the war years in Switzerland, he settled in France in 1920); and, while often on bad terms with Diaghilev, he numbered many of the prominent artists and thinkers of the day among his friends, including Debussy (until his death in 1918), Picasso, Cocteau, Valéry and Maritain. *Persephone* was the climax of this French stage of Stravinsky's life, completed in the year he became a French citizen (1934). His subsequent theatre works were nearly all written for the US, where he settled in 1940.

In trying to form a picture of Stravinsky's contribution to opera, it is obvious that one cannot wholly isolate his works in that form from his ballets and mixed-media pieces. His whole approach to opera was nourished by the spirit of magic and the intimate artifice he found in the ballets of Tchaikovsky, and *The Nightingale* is much closer in spirit to *The Nutcracker* than to *The Queen of Spades* or even the late magical operas of Rimsky-Korsakov (to which, however, it owes something musically). *Renard* is only a vocal piece in the sense that *Les noces*, on which Stravinsky was stuck at the time, is a vocal piece; and *Les noces* is vocal because the idea for it came from a reading of Kireyevsky's collection of folk verse and is inextricably bound up with the verbal exchanges, the *risqué* jokes and ritual sayings of the traditional peasant wedding. This is Stravinsky at his most drily economical; pithy modal tunes in folk style are given acid, wheezing harmonies and incisive but unpredictable rhythms like those in *Le sacre du printemps* (1913), but without that work's primitive violence.

Later, however, after the end of the war and the Russian Revolution, which cut him off from his home and roots, he turned against this ethnic strain. The songs in *Pulcinella* (1919), a Stravinskyization of music by, or at that time attributed to, Pergolesi, are in a courtly musical and linguistic Italian. *Mavra* (1921–2), though it has a Russian story, studiously avoids peasant types and instead takes as its subject a comic bourgeois tale by Pushkin, and for its musical models Glinka and Tchaikovsky. This is the real start of Stravinsky's neo-classical phase. Now his music is tonal, formal and vocally ornate. *Mavra* is a number opera, like Mozart's or Weber's. The instrumental works of the time allude to Bach, Haydn and Beethoven. In *Oedipus Rex* (1926–7) Handelian choruses and Verdian or Bellinian arias serve to dramatize a bookish and statuesque presentation of Sophocles, with a Latin text (explained somewhat patronizingly by a narrator in evening dress), immobile characters in masks and a two-dimensional set. For some reason this unpromising mixture produces one of the most powerful and moving operas in the history of the genre.

After emigrating to America, Stravinsky fell temporarily into a rut in which his neo-classicism became somewhat routine and predictable. *The Rake's Progress* (1947–51), for all its wit and polished craftsmanship, is conventional in a way no previous Stravinsky theatre piece had been; and, according to his new associate Robert Craft, it was partly out of depression at the lack of newness in his work that Stravinsky let himself be persuaded to study the music of the serial composers Schoenberg and Webern. The vitality of Stravinsky's own serial period (roughly from 1952) is one of the most startling aspects of a career marked by almost continuous renewal. The main thrust of these late works is religious, and it is symptomatic that the one sung drama of the period, *The Flood* – a typically geometric, diamantine piece of writing – should be on a biblical subject.

The Nightingale

Solovyei
Le Rossignol
Conte lyrique in three acts (45m)
Libretto (in Russian) by the composer and Stepan Mitussov, after the story *The Emperor's Nightingale* by Hans Christian Andersen
Composed 1908–9, 1913–14
PREMIERES 26 May 1914, Opéra, Paris; UK: 18 June 1914, Drury Lane, London; US: 6 March 1926, Metropolitan, New York
CAST Nightingale *s*, Cook *s*, Fisherman *t*, Emperor of China *bar*, Chamberlain *b*, Bonze *b*, Death *c*, 2 Japanese Envoys *t*, *b*; *satb* chorus of courtiers and ghosts

In his autobiography, Stravinsky implies that Act I of *The Nightingale* was begun during the winter of 1907–8, and the sketches were shown to Rimsky (died June 1908). Other evidence suggests that only the libretto was drafted by then, and the music was composed between November (or possibly August) 1908 and

November 1909, when the completed act was put aside in favour of *The Firebird*. After the premiere of *Petrushka* (13 June 1911), Stravinsky wrote to Aleksandr Benois (the scenarist and designer of that ballet), proposing a collaboration on *The Nightingale* for 1913, when he envisaged having completed *Le sacre du printemps*. His letter clearly implies that he was already (in July 1911) starting Act II, though he must have shelved it at once to write the Balmont songs and the choral piece *Zvyezdoliki* (*The King of the Stars*), before getting down to *Le Sacre* in September.

In February 1913 Aleksandr Sanine, a chief stage director of the newly founded Moscow Free Theatre, commissioned a three-act work from Stravinsky. Stravinsky responded by offering the existing act of *The Nightingale*, but soon afterwards agreed to Sanine's suggestion that he complete the work for what he later called an 'unrefusable fee' of 10,000 roubles. The final two acts were composed, and the first act revised, by March 1914, and the first performance was given by Diaghilev in Paris two months later (the MFT having meanwhile folded), with production by Sanine, and designs by Benois which Stravinsky later described as 'the most beautiful of all my early Diaghilev works'.

Stravinsky would probably never have written the last two acts but for the MFT fee. Even in 1911 he told Benois he had cooled towards the work, and by early 1913 Act I was about to be published as it stood. His style had changed drastically in three years during which he had written *The Firebird*, *Petrushka* and *Le sacre du printemps*. Act I is in a late-Romantic manner indebted to Rimsky-Korsakov and Debussy, while in March 1913 he was completing *Le sacre*, and already thinking about the austerities of *Les noces*. He partly disguised the problem by revising Act I, sharpening up its orchestration and simplifying its harmony. He was also able to hide behind the chinoiserie of the later scenes, with their artificial and mechanistic detailing which permitted a contrast with the more sumptuous forest music of Act I. Meanwhile this mood could be called up by simple reprises of the Fisherman's Song. In practice, the change of style is unobtrusive.

For the Paris production, Diaghilev adopted the idea of double casting, with dancers onstage and singers in the pit. Stravinsky later extracted from the opera a symphonic poem, *The Song of the Nightingale* (1917) (drawing mainly on the later acts), and this was presented as a ballet by Diaghilev in Paris in February 1920.

SYNOPSIS

Act I The fame of the nightingale has reached the emperor of China, who sends his chamberlain to the forest by the sea to invite her to sing at court. At first the chamberlain and courtiers mistake the bellowing of a forest cow and the croaking of the frogs for the nightingale's song, but with the help of the cook the invitation is at last delivered.

Act II At the emperor's porcelain palace, the nightingale sings to the delight of all; but when envoys arrive from Japan with a mechanical nightingale the real nightingale flies away. The emperor, furious, banishes her and appoints the mechanical nightingale First Singer of the Bedside Table on the Left.

Act III The emperor lies dying and is visited by the ghosts of his past deeds, and by Death herself, wearing the imperial crown. The nightingale sings once more, and Death is so entranced that she agrees to give the emperor back his crown if only the song can continue. At dawn Death departs; the emperor again offers the nightingale a position at court, but she will agree only to come and sing to him each night.

Mavra

Opera in one act (28m)
Libretto (in Russian) by Boris Kochno, after the poem 'The Little House at Kolomna' by Aleksandr Pushkin
PREMIERES 3 June 1922, Opéra, Paris; UK: 27 April 1934, BBC radio; 21 August 1956, King's Theatre, Edinburgh; US: 28 December 1934, Academy of Music, Philadelphia
CAST Parasha s, The Neighbour ms, The Mother c, The Hussar t

Stravinsky's use of Russian folk sources and materials continued spasmodically until the *Symphonies of Wind Instruments* (1920). But in 1921 he made orchestrations for Diaghilev's London revival of Tchaikovsky's *The Sleeping Beauty*, and soon afterwards he composed *Mavra*, an opéra-bouffe, which studiously distances itself from the Russian ethnic tradition and instead argues polemically for the cosmopolitan Russianism of Pushkin, Glinka and Tchaikovsky – to which three artists the score is dedicated.

Mavra is Stravinsky's first important synthetic work, in the sense that its whole style and subject matter are taken over consciously, like 'found objects' which the artist then proceeds to work on in his own way for his own ends. For the first time he published articles defending his aesthetic position. Tchaikovsky and Glinka were now in, Musorgsky and the rest of the Russian nationalists were out. Having come to live in Paris in 1920, Stravinsky may well have been more alert than before to the sharp movement of aesthetic and intellectual fashion in post-war France, and sensed that the most piquant way of shocking the Parisian trendsetters of 1921 was to align himself, intellectually, with a sophisticated Russian art that was unknown in Paris (Pushkin and Glinka) and an equally sophisticated one (Tchaikovsky) that smart Parisians regarded as vulgar. In keeping with this posture, he abandoned his folk-tale sources in favour of a *petit-bourgeois* satire set in suburban 19th-century St Petersburg, and used the heightened and somewhat formal style-types of his models to parody the emotional triviality of that world.

SYNOPSIS

After a short overture, the curtain rises on Parasha at her embroidery, singing a lament for her absent lover, the hussar (Parasha's Song). He appears at the window twirling his moustache, and they sing a duet ending (after the hussar's departure) with a short reprise of Parasha's Song. Enter Parasha's mother, also singing a lament (for her dead cook, Phiocla), after which

comes an elaborate duet with the neighbour, mainly on the subject of the weather and the cost of living. Next Parasha comes back with a new cook, 'Mavra' (the hussar in disguise), and the ensuing dialogue leads to a formal quartet on the virtues of loyal servants. Exeunt the mother and the neighbour, leaving Parasha and 'Mavra' to sing a brilliant love duet. Parasha then leaves with her mother, and 'Mavra', after yet another lament, decides the time has come for a shave, in the middle of which operation the mother comes back, and, mistaking the shaving 'cook' for a burglar, faints away. The hussar escapes through the window.

The flippancy of *Mavra*'s plot conceals a strict and essentially formal musical design. The dialogues and laments are all traceable to models in Glinka or Tchaikovsky and are so written as to remain slightly detached from their trivial context and to retain the dignity and style of the models. *Mavra* marks the re-adoption by Stravinsky of the formulae of tonal music: cadences, definite keys (Parasha's Song is in B flat minor, the ensuing duet in B minor, etc.), and regular periodic barring. On the other hand Stravinsky refracts these techniques through cross-rhythmic patterns, subtle harmonic blurrings, and a highly unorthodox orchestral texture, dominated by wind and with prominent family groupings, as in Glinka.

Mavra flopped in Paris in 1922 and has been staged relatively little since. Certainly its satire is esoteric. But Stravinsky always thought highly of it and resented its failure. It is the only work of his own that he discusses in any detail in the lectures that became *The Poetics of Music* (1939), and recent revivals have shown that his faith in it may not have been misplaced.

Oedipus Rex

King Oedipus
Opera–oratorio in two acts (50m)
Libretto (in French) by Jean Cocteau (Latin sections translated by Jean Daniélou), after the play *Oedipus Tyrannus* by Sophocles (after 468 BC)
Composed 1926–7, rev. 1948
PREMIERES 30 May 1927, Théâtre Sarah-Bernhardt, Paris (concert); 23 February 1928, Staatsoper, Vienna; US: 24 April 1928, Boston (concert); 21 April 1931, Metropolitan, New York; UK: 12 May 1928, BBC radio; 12 February 1936, Queen's Hall, London (concert); 21 August 1956, King's Theatre, Edinburgh
CAST Oedipus t, Jocasta ms, Creon b-bar, Tiresias b, The Shepherd t, The Messenger b-bar, Speaker *spoken role*; tb chorus

The idea for 'an opera in Latin on the subject of a tragedy of the ancient world, with which everyone would be familiar' was Stravinsky's own, as a letter to Cocteau of 11 October 1925 proves. He himself dated the inspiration for *Oedipus Rex* to the chance discovery of Johannes Jörgensen's *Life of St Francis* on a Genoa bookstall in September of that year. On the other hand, the device of a spoken narration in the language of the audience (for which Stravinsky later 'blamed' Cocteau) was probably worked out between them, as was the intended visual handling, with the main characters immobile, like statues, able to gesture only with head and hands, within a monumental, tableau-like two-dimensional setting (a style that goes back to Cocteau's 1922 version of Sophocles' *Antigone*). The conception of a heroic tragedy immured within an antique convention is obviously fundamental, as is the idea of enriching such a conception from various heroic traditions: not only Greek, but Handelian and even Verdian–Bellinian. In one sense, this is no more than the translation into the theatre of the synthetic techniques of early neo-classicism; in another sense it updates the idea of symbolic re-enactment already present in *Renard* and *Les noces*. The argument over whether *Oedipus* is opera or oratorio is thus specious. The subtitle merely refers to the various elements in the work as a whole.

SYNOPSIS

The speaker introduces each scene, describing the events we are about to witness. He 'is in a black suit . . . [and] expresses himself like a lecturer, presenting the story with a detached voice.'

Act I The Thebans implore their king, Oedipus, who vanquished the Sphinx, to rescue them from the plague; Oedipus boastfully promises to do so ('Liberabo, vos liberi'); He reports that Creon, his brother-in-law, has been sent to consult the Delphic oracle; Creon arrives and announces ('Respondit deus') that the murderer of King Laius is hiding in Thebes and must be hunted out before the plague will go. Oedipus undertakes to find the murderer ('Non reperias vetus skelus'). The people implore the blind seer Tiresias to tell what he knows ('Delie, exspectamus'). Tiresias refuses ('Dicere non possum'), but when Oedipus accuses him directly of the murder he retorts that Laius' murderer is another king, now hiding in Thebes. Oedipus angrily accuses both Tiresias and Creon of plotting to seize the throne. At this moment the people hail the arrival of Oedipus' wife, Queen Jocasta.

Act II The final 'Gloria' chorus of Act I is repeated; the score indicates this before the speaker's introduction, but Stravinsky stated in *Dialogues* that he preferred the reprise to follow the introduction and lead straight into Jocasta's aria. Jocasta rebukes the princes for quarrelling ('Non erubescite, reges'). The oracle, she says, is a liar. It prophesied that Laius would be killed by her son, but in fact he was killed at a crossroads by thieves. Suddenly afraid, Oedipus tells Jocasta that once he killed an old man at a crossroads ('Pavesco subito'). He determines to find out the truth. The chorus greets the arrival of the shepherd and the messenger from Corinth ('Adest ominiscius pastor'). The messenger announces the death of King Polybus of Corinth. Oedipus, he reports, was not Polybus' son, but a foundling, discovered on a mountainside and brought up by a shepherd. Jocasta understands and tries to draw Oedipus away. Oedipus accuses her of shame at the discovery that he is not the son of a king ('Nonne monstrum rescituri'), but the shepherd and the messenger spell out the truth: that Oedipus was the son of Laius and Jocasta, abandoned to die. Oedipus acknowledges the truth, that he has killed his father and married his mother ('Natus sum quo nefastum est'). The messenger, helped by the chorus, relates

the death of Jocasta and Oedipus' self-blinding with her golden brooch ('Divum Jocastae caput mortuum'). Oedipus appears, a figure of revulsion. He is firmly but gently expelled from Thebes by the people.

Cocteau's treatment of the story assumes a knowledge of Sophocles, and cannot be properly understood without it. Here is the essential outline. The oracle warned King Laius that, as a punishment for stealing Pelops' son, Chrysippus, he would be killed by his own son; so, when Oedipus was born, Laius and Jocasta exposed him on a mountainside, piercing his feet with leather thongs. There he was found and brought up by a shepherd of the Corinthian King Polybus. Polybus, being childless, adopted (and named) Oedipus; later, Oedipus was taunted about his parentage, and, when he consulted the oracle, was told that he would kill his father and marry his mother. To avoid these crimes, and naturally supposing them to refer to Polybus and his wife, he left Corinth for Thebes, and on the way killed an old man he met at a crossroads, not recognizing him, of course, as King Laius. At Thebes he solved the riddle of the Sphinx, winning the hand of the now-widowed Queen Jocasta. It is crucial that, even when he begins to suspect that he is the murderer of King Laius and thus the cause of the plague in Thebes, Oedipus still does not realize that he is Laius' son. He simply believes his crime to be usurping the marital bed of a man he has killed. One other obscurity is his accusation of Tiresias' complicity with Creon, which is explained by the fact that, in Sophocles, it is Creon who first suggests consulting Tiresias.

Oedipus Rex is one of Stravinsky's greatest works and a climax both of his early synthetic (neo-classical) style and of his lifelong experimentation with theatrical technique. Like *Mavra*, it is a number opera in the classical tradition, though the numbers often evolve into substantial scenes, separated by the narration. The monumental character of each scene goes with the statuesque, sculptural design idea and with the impersonal grandeur of the Latin text. But many details of style break into this monumentality. The most obvious is the spoken narration, which is at first strictly separate from the music, but later intrudes into it to some limited extent. Stravinsky makes rich use of the ironic possibilities of this device. For instance, when (in the narration) Tiresias reveals that 'the murderer of the king is a king', the last four words are set rhythmically to the motif of the chorus's anxious anticipation of the seer's arrival, in which they do not, of course, yet know what he will reveal.

Another obvious 'break' is the mixture of musical styles. Handel seems to have been a conscious influence; but that of Italian opera is more striking, because more surprising. There are clear reminiscences of Verdi, Bellini, and even Puccini, and Stravinsky uses the idea of operatic vocalism itself to a dramatic end. Oedipus' coloratura diminishes with his self-confidence, and his last utterances, when the truth has struck him, are unadorned. These and other associative devices seem to act as a bridge between modern perception and the musically disembodied world of Greek tragedy: through what they sing and what accompanies them, the characters take on an extra dimension of humanity, like statues whose heads turn at the sound of music that is, so to speak, ours rather than theirs.

Both tonally and rhythmically, *Oedipus Rex* contains some of the plainest music Stravinsky ever wrote. The squarely cut choral ostinati (with their persistent minor-third motif) are worlds away from the subtleties of *Mavra*. Much of the score uses fixed tonal centres, contrasted by terracing rather than classical modulation. Moreover the work marks Stravinsky's use of a 'standard' symphony orchestra for the first time since *Le sacre du printemps* and *The Nightingale*.

Stravinsky and Cocteau planned to stage *Oedipus Rex* in 1927 in honour of Diaghilev's 20th season, but the financial arrangements became immersed in Parisian social politics, and in the end the premiere was given in concert form. The first stagings were in February the following year in Vienna and Berlin (Kroll Opera, under Otto Klemperer). In the 1950s Stravinsky came to favour omitting the speaker altogether. But one of the most famous post-war (concert) performances, by Stravinsky in London's Festival Hall in 1959, had Cocteau as the speaker.

The Rake's Progress
Opera in three acts (2h 15m)
Libretto by W. H. Auden and Chester Kallman after the series of prints *A Rake's Progress* by William Hogarth (1735)
PREMIERES 11 September 1951, La Fenice, Venice; UK: 2 January 1953, BBC radio; 25 August 1953, Edinburgh; US: 14 February 1953, Metropolitan, New York
CAST Trulove *b*, Anne Trulove *s*, Tom Rakewell *t*, Nick Shadow *bar*, Mother Goose *ms*, Baba the Turk *ms*, Sellem *t*, Keeper of the Madhouse *b*; *satb* chorus of whores, roaring boys, servants, citizens, madmen

After settling in the US in 1940, Stravinsky went through an uneasy time in which the pressure to fulfil commissions of a 'typically' American, commercial sort went hand in hand with changes in style that were to lead to a completely new direction in his work of the 1950s. One important catalyst of change was his growing interest in pre-classical music. This is the period of the *Mass* (1944–8), and of the ballet *Orpheus* (1947), with its mixture of neo-classical mannerisms and contrapuntal austerities. *The Rake's Progress*, which looks like a summation, is therefore also partly a work of transition.

Stravinsky saw the Hogarth prints at an exhibition in Chicago in May 1947. Later that year, he contacted W. H. Auden and proposed a collaboration (Auden soon brought in Chester Kallman as co-author). Auden was to prove a brilliant collaborator. His gift for investing verse in simple metres with rich meanings perfectly suited Stravinsky's need for variable patterns and a clear ethical thrust, and Auden's virtuosity made him uniquely quick at responding to specific requirements. Beyond question the libretto is one of the best ever written.

Although the work seems at first sight like a straight 18th-century pastiche, complete with *secco* recitative accompanied by harpsichord, it is one of Stravinsky's most complex and many-tiered scores. The influence of Mozart is obvious and well documented. But the actual subject is quite un-Mozartian; it rather suggests the urban world of *The Beggar's Opera*, as do the plain, lilting cut of its melodies, and its preference for strophic or verse-and-refrain forms. But while the dramatic setting of *The Beggar's Opera* clearly has a lot in common with Hogarth, the verse-and-refrain idea also recalls Stravinsky's lifelong interest in ritual forms where repetition and recurrence are more in evidence than organic development in the classical sense. That this was hardly a limitation is shown by the fact that the longest and most serious of the three acts, the third, proceeds almost entirely by interlocking verse forms. Here *The Rake* anticipates the proto-serial works of the 1950s, where the refrain form is ubiquitous.

Auden's view of the subject fitted this aspect of Stravinsky like a glove. Starting with the idea that Tom's downfall comes from his denial of Nature (Anne and ordered country life), he constructed a moving allegory in which the gruesome materialism of the city increasingly usurps the natural virtues – love, marriage, procreation, the ordinary rhythm of life. The opera begins and ends in spring; against Hogarth's London, Auden set up a pastoral idyll in the tradition of Theocritus. Tom is Adonis, who comes to a bad end for disobeying the command of his goddess lover, Venus. Cut off from his moral roots, he falls prey to philosophies of despair – existentialism, moral nihilism – and is about to succumb when the still small voice of love brings him back to his senses, or at least to life (since he does in fact lose his senses). Thus a mixture of antique conventions provides a frame for a strictly modern fable, just as in the music.

SYNOPSIS
'The action takes place in 18th-century England.'

Act I Scene 1: The garden of Trulove's home in the country. A short prelude leads into a duet for Anne and Tom about the joys of spring ('The woods are green'). Later it becomes a trio, with Trulove voicing his fears about the marriage. Trulove suggests that Tom take a job, but Tom has other plans ('Here I stand' and 'Since it is not by merit'). At his words 'I wish I had money', a messenger (Nick Shadow) appears with news that Tom has inherited a fortune (quartet: 'I wished but once'). Tom agrees to go to London to settle his affairs, with Shadow as his servant. In a trio, Tom, Anne and Trulove voice their respective attitudes to easy money ('Laughter and light'). Scene 2: Mother Goose's brothel, London. Roaring boys and whores sing of the joys of debauchery ('With air commanding'). Shadow and Mother Goose rehearse Tom in the catechism of vice. Only when love is mentioned does he falter and beg to be released. Shadow now introduces Tom as a would-be initiate, though Tom's cavatina ('Love, too frequently betrayed', with obbligato clarinet) sustains his regret at betraying true love, to the delight of the sentimental whores. As Mother Goose takes Tom off to her bed, the chorus sings the Lanterloo Chorus. Scene 3: As Scene 1. Anne laments Tom's infidelity but makes up her mind to rescue him ('I go to him').

Act II Scene 1: Rakewell's house in London. Tom, at breakfast, is already bored with fashionable life ('Vary the song'). Shadow enters with a newspaper report about the bearded lady, Baba the Turk, whom he proposes Tom should marry in order to demonstrate his freedom from 'those twin tyrants of appetite and conscience' ('In youth the panting slave pursues'). They sing of appetite and coming notoriety ('My tale shall be told'). Scene 2: The street in front of Rakewell's house. Anne has found Tom's house, but falters in front of the door. Tom enters in a sedan chair, preceded by servants. He presses Anne to leave him to his fate. From the sedan chair Baba demands to be handed down, and, when Tom introduces her as his wife, Anne turns away (trio: 'Could it then have been known'). To the strains of a sarabande, Baba descends from the chair, and briefly gratifies the assembled crowd with a sight of her flowing black beard. Scene 3: As Act II, Scene 1, but the room now cluttered with Baba's possessions. Baba chatters away about her life ('As I was saying'), ending with a lyrical appeal to Tom's finer feelings. Rebuffed, she breaks into a classic rage aria ('Scorned! Abused!'), smashing the china as she sings, until Tom silences her by putting his wig over her face, then himself falls asleep. Enter Shadow with a 'bread-making machine', which he demonstrates to the audience. Tom wakes up, having dreamt of just such a machine, which he imagines will abolish misery in the world (duet: 'Thanks to this excellent device').

Act III Scene 1: The same, but covered with cobwebs and dust; Baba still where she was left. The populace has gathered for the sale of Tom's property. Anne also arrives, looking for Tom. Sellem, the auctioneer, begins ('Who hears me, knows me') with the sale of various curios, culminating in Baba herself, who, as the wig is removed, continues her rage aria where it left off. Offstage, Tom and Shadow are heard in a ballad song ('Old wives for sale!'). The sale grinds to a halt, as Baba advises Anne to go to Tom. Scene 2: A churchyard; night. A short prelude for string quartet (the first music to be composed) leads to the final confrontation between Tom and Shadow. Shadow claims Tom's soul as wages. He proposes suicide on the stroke of twelve, but relents on the ninth stroke, and instead suggests a game of cards to decide Tom's fate. Unexpectedly Tom wins, by trusting the voice of love (that is, Anne, heard offstage). Shadow departs in a fury but condemns Tom to insanity. Scene 3: Bedlam. Tom, now insane, imagines himself as Adonis soon to be visited by Venus ('Prepare yourselves, heroic shades'), but the other inmates refuse to participate ('Leave all love and hope behind'). But Anne does come, sings him to sleep ('Gently, little boat'), and then departs with her father ('Every wearied body must'). Waking to find her gone, Tom seems to die of grief ('Mourn for Adonis'). Like Mozart's *Don Giovanni*, the opera ends with a moralistic epilogue ensemble ('Good people, just a moment').

The Rake's Progress is generally considered the culminating work of Stravinsky's neo-classicism. Its use of a standard 18th-century orchestra and of various operatic formal conventions, of clear tonal schemes and rhythmic periods, perpetuates the tradition of the Symphony in C and the Concerto in D. The formal schemes, and some of its instrumental textures, antici-

pate the *Cantata*, but there is no trace of serialism or any other conscious modernism. *The Rake* was Stravinsky's first setting of an English text (apart from the short cantata *Babel*). Its eccentric prosody has been criticized, but Auden himself pointedly defended it. The fact is that Stravinsky saw words as an element of rhythm, and was always ready to distort natural accentual patterns to enrich the musical movement. His *Rake* technique is essentially no different from his earlier handling of Russian, French or Latin.

Stravinsky worked on the opera for three years, to the exclusion of all else (except negotiations as to where it should be premiered and for how much money). The Venice premiere was fixed up by him over everyone's head and with disastrous consequences in Italian musical politics. (La Scala, Milan, had to be placated by a shared role in the production.) It was a *succès d'estime*, but artistically uneven. Stravinsky conducted effectively, but the cast was variable and Carl Ebert's production pleased neither the composer nor the librettists.

Other operatic works: *Renard* (*Baika*), (1916), 1922; *Persephone*, 1934; The Flood, 1962

S.W.

ARTHUR SULLIVAN

(Sir) Arthur Seymour Sullivan; *b* 13 May 1842, London; *d* 22 November 1900, London

Until the advent of Andrew Lloyd Webber, Arthur Sullivan was by far the most performed and internationally the best-known British composer for the theatre. In his early professional life he was an all-rounder, winning fame before he was 20 with his incidental music to *The Tempest* (1861) and proceeding to a symphony, a cello concerto, etc. But the financial rewards to be reaped from operetta, as well as his own proven mastery of it, led him later to concentrate almost entirely on the theatre and on large-scale choral works. Operetta is the internationally recognized term for the type of work on which William Schwenck Gilbert and Sullivan collaborated under Richard D'Oyly Carte's management (1875–96), but they themselves used the term 'comic opera'.

Carte built the Savoy Theatre in 1882 to house Gilbert and Sullivan's chain of successes, though he himself did not confine the term 'Savoy Opera' to their works. In early days, and later during and after a period of personal estrangement from Gilbert, Sullivan worked with other librettists, notably Francis Cowley Burnand and Basil Hood, later the librettist of Edward German's *Merrie England* (1902). He used the term 'light opera' for *Haddon Hall* (libretto by Sydney Grundy). But his sole venture into what was then called grand opera was *Ivanhoe*, for which Carte built the Royal English Opera House (now the Palace Theatre) in 1891. For Carte, who failed to profit from his investment and had to sell the theatre, *Ivanhoe* spelt failure despite an initial run of 160 consecutive performances – unrivalled for a 'serious' work. The music and libretto received weighty adverse criticism and it has not been successfully revived.

Curiously the operettas, though so often tied to satire on British social life of their own day (the 'aesthetic' craze in *Patience*, parliamentary anomalies in *Iolanthe*), have maintained a perennial life quite unparalleled by any other body of work from the Victorian theatre. They were original works, not adaptations from others. If Gilbert's extraordinary dexterity of language did much for these works, and added not a few proverbial phrases in doing so, Sullivan's scores likewise caught popular taste – and exhibited musical subtleties as well. In every one of the operettas there are numbers that, in contrapuntal wit or harmonic subtlety or musical allusiveness, have continued to make their appeal to sophisticated taste. The contrapuntal yoking of two apparently unrelated tunes became a Sullivan trademark, while his patter songs, extended in *Ruddigore* to a patter trio, are no less effective than their predecessors in Rossini and Donizetti.

Recurrence of a musical motif as a dramatic indicator to the audience is rare; where found, it corresponds more to Bizet's and Gounod's usage than to Wagner's. A deeper level of musical linking has been demonstrated for *The Mikado* and is perhaps waiting to be discovered in others of the operetta scores. The fact that, in the non-English-speaking world, *The Mikado* has been the most widely performed of the operettas (with many translations) is puzzling. The butt of its satire is Britain, not Japan, yet its musical and costumed orientalisms seem to have exerted their own attraction and gained it a place in that special sequence of operatic exotica which ranges from *L'africaine* to *Madama Butterfly*.

NOTE

Voices: voice-types are not specified in the original published scores or libretti of Sullivan's stage works but are here given as usually allotted. A spoken role indicates a chorus performer who has individual speech but no solo singing.

Cox and Box, or The Long-lost Brothers

Triumviretta in one act (original version: 1h; Savoy (1921) version: 30m)
Libretto by Francis Cowley Burnand, after John Maddison Morton's farce *Box and Cox* (1847)
PREMIERES 26 May 1866 (private performance with pf); 11 May 1867, Adelphi Theatre, London; US: 13 August 1875, New York

The farcical interaction of two lodgers, one occupying the accommodation by day and the other by night, provides a framework for the only non-Gilbert operetta of Sullivan's to have survived into the modern repertoire (though *The Zoo* has been broadcast and recorded). The only other character is the landlord, Bouncer (Mrs Bouncer in the original play), whose military posturings allow Sullivan to parody the operatic military manner with a repeated drum figure of 'rat-a-plan, rat-a-plan', best known at that time from Donizetti's *La fille du régiment*. The threesome gives rise to the playful designation of the work as a triumviretta, from *triumviri* (the group of three magistrates governing Ancient Rome) and *operetta*.

Sullivan's 'straight' setting of an absurd lyric ('Hushed is the bacon') was to be a characteristic of his comic style. The composer sanctioned the separate publication of the song with different words as drawing-room fare. Of a similar comic absurdity is the vocalized 'instrumental' accompaniment to the duet serenade 'The buttercup dwells on the lowly mead'. The resolution of the plot when the two lodgers discover they are brothers, though carried out in speech and drawn directly from the play, mocks operatic coincidence (as in *The Marriage of Figaro*, Act III):

BOX   Tell me – in mercy tell me – have you a strawberry mark on your left arm?
COX   No.
BOX   Then it is he!

Originally in ten numbers including the overture, it is now commonly performed in a curtailed 'Savoy' version of nine numbers.

Trial by Jury

Comic opera (originally dramatic cantata) in one act (45m)
Libretto by W. S. Gilbert
PREMIERES 25 March 1875, Royalty Theatre, London; US: 15 November 1875, Eagle Theater, New York
CAST Plaintiff *s*, Defendant *t*, Learned Judge *bar*, Usher *b*, Counsel for the Plaintiff *bar*, Foreman of the Jury *bar*; *satb* chorus of jurymen and bridesmaids

The first time Gilbert and Sullivan collaborated under Richard D'Oyly Carte's management (though Carte had not yet set up his own company) produced an all-sung work, oddly designated in the score as a dramatic cantata. In no subsequent collaboration with Gilbert did Sullivan retain the all-sung form. It is based on the comical extravagance of setting a court action to verse and to music, the action being that of breach of promise of marriage, a type of legal case that was already liable to ridicule. In addition to the impassioned statements of the point at issue, even routine matters such as the swearing in of the (all-male) jury are subjected to full musical treatment. The character of the learned judge (originally taken with much success by Sullivan's brother Fred, who was to die young) is the first of a famous line of comic parts with self-descriptive songs which often reveal moral ambiguities.

SYNOPSIS

The jury is waiting to try the case of 'Edwin, sued by Angelina'. The jurymen are addressed by the usher: he and the jurors are already prejudiced against the defendant, who enters and states his case to guitar accompaniment. The learned judge enters, is greeted, and gives an account of himself ('When I, good friends, was called to the Bar'). The plaintiff enters in bridal dress and attended by bridesmaids. Her counsel tells how she was courted, then jilted for another. The defendant offers, 'I'll marry this lady today, and marry the other tomorrow.' The judge is disposed to agree, until reminded that such a step would constitute 'burglaree' ('A nice dilemma we have here'). No solution emerging to satisfy both sides, the judge (who has taken a fancy to the plaintiff from her first entrance) dismisses the court: 'Put your briefs upon the shelf: I will marry her myself!'

In the choral greeting to the judge before his self-revelatory song, Sullivan parodies Handel's grandest oratorio manner, complete with word-repetition. A more specific parody, not merely of a composer but of an actual operatic number, is the climactic ensemble, 'A nice dilemma': in its imitative vocal entries, in general style, and even in key, it is directly modelled on 'D'un pensiero', the Act I finale to Bellini's *La sonnambula*.

The Sorcerer

Comic opera in two acts (1h 45m)
Libretto by W. S. Gilbert
Composed 1877, rev. 1884
PREMIERES 17 November 1877, Opéra-Comique, London; rev. version: 11 October 1884, Savoy Theatre, London; US: 21 February 1879, Broadway Theater, New York
CAST Sir Marmaduke Poindextre *b*, Alexis *t*, Aline *s*, Constance *s*, John Wellington Wells *bar*, Lady Sangazure *c*, Dr Daly *b-bar*, Mrs Partlet *c*, Notary *b*; *satb* chorus of villagers

Sullivan's first full-length work with Gilbert established what was to be their usual formal pattern – two acts, the first ending with a complex finale in several sections, the second with the reprise of some previous number. The element of the love philtre in the plot took up a motif already familiar in Victorian times from Donizetti's *L'elisir d'amore* (on which Gilbert had written a burlesque, *Dulcamara, or The Little Duck and the Great Quack*). Here, however, the framework is that of the theatrically conventional English village with gentlefolk, vicar, pew-opener (a female verger), and rather cloddish lower-class villagers. The disruptive element is incarnated in the tradesman-sorcerer Mr Wells, who lists his wares in the first of the great Gilbert and Sullivan patter songs ('My name is John Wellington Wells, / I'm a dealer in magic and spells'). He is unique among Gilbert's operatic characters in being allowed to die (supernaturally) in action.

SYNOPSIS
Act I Alexis, a Grenadier Guards officer and the son of Sir Marmaduke Poindextre, is betrothed to Aline, daughter of Lady Sangazure. Constance, however, is unhappy: daughter of the pew-opener Mrs Partlet, she loves the elderly vicar, Dr Daly, unaware that he loves her in return. Sir Marmaduke and Lady Sangazure exchange courtly compliments while (aside) confessing an intense passion for each other. Alexis is so convinced of love as a universal panacea that he has summoned a sorcerer, John Wellington Wells, to devise a philtre that will make everyone fall in love with the first individual to meet the eye. Wells brews his potion, to be administered in tea at a village merry-making: married people will naturally be immune from its effects.

The tea-party begins as Act I ends; at the beginning of Act II the effects of the potion have become visible, but have gone awry. Constance finds herself in love with a notary, Sir Marmaduke with Mrs Partlet, Lady Sangazure with the sorcerer himself (to his consterna-tion) and Aline with Dr Daly. The misplaced magic is expunged when the sorcerer volunteers to die. He descends into the earth, and the merry-making resumes with all lovers rightfully paired.

The military-sounding music appropriate for Alexis as a Guards officer, the 'eerie' orchestral sounds accompanying Mr Wells's incantation, and the amiable sentiments of the Revd Dr Daly (who played the flageolet in the opening production) – all these serve to vary a score of considerable verve, though the ballads allotted to Alexis and Aline now seem too obviously destined to be excerpted for the drawing room. The duet of the two old people, Sir Marmaduke and Lady Sangazure, is particularly resourceful. It is set to one of the old dances to which Sullivan was attracted (a gavotte), and displays both the combination of two dissimilar tunes and the interpolation of asides into normal conversation.

For the 1884 revival Sullivan made changes including a significant shortening of the Act I finale: a formal return to the key of the opening of that finale (adhering to the practice of Mozart's or Rossini's finales) is sacrificed for greater dramatic tautness. He also rewrote the opening of Act II.

HMS Pinafore, or The Lass that Loved a Sailor

Comic opera in two acts (1h 45m)
Libretto by W. S. Gilbert
PREMIERES 25 May 1878, Opéra-Comique, London; US: 25 November 1878, The Boston Museum, Boston
CAST Sir Joseph Porter *bar*, Captain Corcoran *b-bar*, Ralph Rackstraw *t*, Josephine *s*, Dick Deadeye *b*, Mrs Cripps (Little Buttercup) *c*, *ms*, *bar*, *b*, silent role; *satb* chorus of Sir Joseph's relatives, sailors, marines, etc.

Although both of Gilbert and Sullivan's previous collaborations had been given present-day settings, only with *HMS Pinafore* was a pronounced note of political and social satire introduced. Class relations within the navy (and outside it) and the dubious machinations of political appointments are set forth. The character of Sir Joseph Porter was inevitably taken, despite Gilbert's (perhaps ironic) denials, as being aimed at W. H. Smith, the actual First Lord of the Admiralty. All this was set within a highly traditional theatrical frame featuring the upright sailor lad, his faithful sweetheart, and the black-hearted villain (Dick Deadeye: 'It's a beast of a name, ain't it?').

After an initially cautious reception at the box office, *HMS Pinafore* grew into Gilbert and Sullivan's first major success and has remained one of their most popular and frequently revived works, the mock-patriotism of 'For he is an Englishman' becoming proverbial. This work too was the start of Gilbert and Sullivan's North American (and wider) reputation: pirated performances of *HMS Pinafore* were so successful in Boston, New York and elsewhere that Carte decided to take the composer and librettist and their company across the Atlantic to present the work in authentic form (at the same time launching *The Pirates of Penzance*).

SYNOPSIS

Act I A happy regime is maintained aboard HMS *Pinafore*, now anchored at Portsmouth. The bumboat woman Mrs Cripps with her stock of useful and tasty wares is welcomed on board ('I'm called Little Buttercup'). To his sympathetic messmates, Ralph as a humble sailor discloses his audacity in his love for his captain's daughter Josephine. Captain Corcoran, the ship's commander, declares in a self-introductory song that he never uses bad language to his crew ('What, never?' / 'Hardly ever!'). But he is worried that Josephine is disinclined to accept a proposal of marriage from an exalted quarter, the First Lord of the Admiralty, Sir Joseph Porter. Sir Joseph arrives, escorted by sisters, cousins and aunts. An autobiographical song recounts his rise to Cabinet minister ('When I was a lad I served a term / As office boy to an attorney's firm'). He has composed a three-part glee which is performed. Josephine, at first acting her rank, spurns Ralph's love, but after he threatens suicide she joyfully admits she loves him. All his mates, except the malevolent Deadeye, will help the pair get ashore that night to be married.

Act II In the evening, Captain Corcoran sings to the moon of his worry about Josephine. Mrs Cripps tries to warn him of some mystery, but he does not comprehend. Josephine herself is doubtful of the hardships that confront her. But Sir Joseph, thinking to promote his own case in condescending to marry a captain's daughter, tells her that 'Love levels all ranks'. She takes that as arguing Ralph's case and is ready to proceed with the elopement. Warned by Dick Deadeye, her father steps in to prevent it. Ralph speaks up for his rights: 'I am an Englishman' (echoed by the chorus, 'For he himself has said it, / And it's greatly to his credit, / That he is an Englishman'). In reprimanding Ralph, Captain Corcoran says, 'Damme, it's too bad!', a profanity for which Sir Joseph confines him to his cabin while the presumptuous Ralph is taken off to the ship's dungeon.

Mrs Cripps makes a dramatic declaration in song: a former baby-farmer, she had both Ralph and Corcoran in her care as infants and mixed them up. They now re-emerge: Ralph as a captain, Corcoran as an able seaman. All is now serene for the lovers, Corcoran at the same time pairing off with Mrs Cripps and Sir Joseph with Hebe, one of his cousins.

Gilbert's strong characterization is so well fulfilled in Sullivan's music as to override the occasional weakness. The Act I finale, though it gathers a splendid momentum (with a remarkable artifice of rhythmical structure), does not get two opposing sides into dramatic and musical conflict as most of its successors do. The 'Buttercup' waltz is tediously plugged as an entr'acte, and a mere medley of previous tunes serves to end Act II. But Ralph, Captain Corcoran, Sir Joseph and Josephine all live in their interactive music (particularly 'Never mind the why and wherefore') and almost as much musical resource is lavished on two characters parodied from opera or melodrama, Little Buttercup with 'gypsy blood in her veins' and the heavy-treading Dick Deadeye.

The Pirates of Penzance, or The Slave of Duty

Comic opera in two acts (1h 45m)
Libretto by W. S. Gilbert
PREMIERES in skeleton form: 30 December 1879, Royal Bijou Theatre, Paignton; 3 April 1880, Opéra-Comique, London; US: 31 December 1879, New Fifth Avenue Theater, New York
CAST Major-General Stanley *bar*, Pirate King *b*, Frederic *t*, Mabel *s*, Ruth *c*, Sergeant of Police *b-bar*, *s*, *ms*, *b*; *satb* chorus of pirates, police and General Stanley's daughters

Very much in the pattern of its highly successful predecessor, *The Pirates of Penzance* satirized not naval but military anomalies (in the person of the major-general) and the police as well. Mock patriotism is also invoked once again. The mainspring of the plot, however, arises from a recurrent target of Gilbert's satire, the idiocy and sometimes the hypocrisy of a literal-minded devotion to duty: here the knife is artfully twisted, with Frederic rigorously functioning as the 'slave of duty' of the opera's subtitle.

The piece received its formal premiere at the hands of the British company brought by Carte to New York, a mere token staging having been previously given at Paignton, Devon, to establish British copyright. After the American performances Gilbert and Sullivan made several alterations which bore fruit in the London production.

SYNOPSIS

Act I Frederic, apprenticed to the pirate band as a boy, has reached the age of 21 and is congratulated: his apprenticeship over, he can be considered a full member of the band. But, though loyal while he had to be, he has decided to leave and oppose the pirate king and his followers. Ruth, his former nursery-maid, who had led him to the apprenticeship through mishearing 'pilot' as 'pirate' and had herself become a maid-of-all-work to the pirates, hopes to persuade Frederic to marry her. (He has seen no other females to make comparison.) But to his enraptured view a group of young women appears, the daughters of the major-general, on an outing to the beach. To prevent their unknowingly exposing as much as a leg, Frederic announces his presence. He begs any one of them to accept him in marriage – and Mabel, considering it her duty, accepts ('Poor wand'ring one'). Suddenly the pirates appear and are about to abduct the young women when the major-general himself arrives. He persuades them not to rob him, an orphan, of his daughters. Their better nature is touched. Only in an aside does the major-general confess his fib – he is no orphan.

Act II That night, the major-general is not abed as usual; his conscience is tormented by his fib. Under Frederic's command, the police are now to take the vengeance of the law on the pirates. The sergeant of police and his men are disquieted by Mabel's fervent exhortation ('Go, ye heroes, go and die!'). Frederic is confronted by the pirate king and Ruth, who explain 'a most ingenious paradox': having been born on 29 February in leap year, and apprenticed not for 21 years but until his 21st birthday (which will not arrive till 1940), he is still bound to them. Frederic switches his 'duty' and bids a tearful farewell to Mabel. The police re-enter, the sergeant proclaiming that 'A police-man's lot is not a happy one'. The pirates, now informed by Frederic of the major-general's decep-tion, are intent on revenge. The major-general, still conscience-ridden, sings a song ('Softly sighing to the river') accompanied by the police and pirates, of whose presence he is ignorant. The pirates overpower the police but yield when challenged 'in Queen Vic-toria's name'. The pirates themselves are revealed to be all 'noblemen who have gone wrong'; their crimes are forgiven, since 'peers will be peers', and they can marry the major-general's daughters while Frederic and Mabel can get married too.

Musically *The Pirates* is, as Sullivan himself recog-nized, stronger than *Pinafore*. Nowhere in the whole Gilbert and Sullivan canon is anything more deft than the dovetailing of the love duet in waltz time into the chattering 2/4 women's chorus, 'How beautifully blue the sky' in Act I, the whole modulating from B to G and back again. The major-general's song in Act II, with its Schubertian water-rippling accompaniment, is placed as an absolutely straight number within a hilarious comic context – the major-general's una-wareness of the male choruses surely parodying a similar situation in *Il trc vatore*. The process by which, some time after 1900, the melody of 'Come, friends, who plough the sea' was metamorphosed into the American song 'Hail, hail, the gang's all here' has still not been clarified.

Patience, or Bunthorne's Bride

Comic opera in two acts (2h)
Libretto by W. S. Gilbert
PREMIERES 23 April 1881, Opéra-Comique, London;
US: 22 September 1881, Standard Theater, New York
CAST Colonel Calverley *b*, Major Murgatroyd *bar*,
Lieutenant the Duke of Dunstable *t*, Reginald Bunthorne, a fleshly poet *bar*, Archibald Grosvenor, an idyllic poet *b-bar*, Lady Jane *ms*, Lady Angela *s*, Lady Saphir *ms*, Patience *s*, *ms*, Bunthorne's Solicitor *silent*; *satb* chorus of rapturous maidens and officers of Dragoon Guards

One of Gilbert's early *Bab Ballads*, entitled *The Rival Curates* and mocking clerical behaviour, was the origi-nal inspiration for *Patience*. A few clerical references survive ('Your style is much too sanctified, your cut is too canonical'), but, happily for posterity, Gilbert redirected his satire and made a butt of the 'aesthetic movement', associated with various writers and artists but particularly Oscar Wilde (then in his early twen-ties). The innocent dairymaid heroine and the swagger-ing soldiers come from established theatrical conven-tion, but the juxtaposition of different worlds is brilliantly brought off in musical as well as theatrical terms, with the bevy of love-languishing females form-ing a sharply individualized chorus. The puncturing of the pretensions of artistic poseurs, and the triumph of everyday common sense, has continued to make its point long after the fading of once-topical refer-ences ('greenery-yallery, Grosvenor Gallery'). The sub-title is a joke: nobody becomes Bunthorne's bride.

SYNOPSIS

Act I 'Twenty love-sick maidens' of high degree adore the pretentious poet Bunthorne – but the dairy-maid Patience, whom he loves, is indifferent. Fol-lowing an aesthetic ideal the maidens now have no time for their former lovers, the officers of the 35th Dragoon Guards, whose pride is declared by their colonel. Alone, Bunthorne confesses he is 'an aes-thetic sham', posing only to win admiration. Patience is approached by her long-lost childhood playmate, Grosvenor, also a poet; she is attracted to him but for that very reason, having been told that love must be unselfish, she rejects him. Bunthorne, convinced he will never win Patience, puts himself up for raffle. Patience intervenes: since love is unselfish, it becomes her duty to love and wed Bunthorne! The love-sick maidens return to their officers. But the sight of Grosvenor rekindles their aesthetic flame: they cluster round him as they once had round Bunthorne, leaving the officers dismayed.

Act II Stout, elderly Lady Jane laments her pass-ing charms. Grosvenor, who loves Patience, vainly tries to put off the high-born maidens with 'the fable of the magnet and the churn'. Jane encourages Bunthorne, who feels snubbed by the maidens' deser-tion, to challenge Grosvenor directly. To win back their loves, the colonel, major and lieutenant reappear in what they believe to be aesthetic dress and strike poses accordingly. Two of the maidens, Angela and Saphir, are smitten by them. Bunthorne challenges Grosvenor to abandon the aesthetic field: since he can say he did so on compulsion, Grosvenor is delighted to comply and become an ordinary person. Patience can now marry Grosvenor, the lieutenant unexpect-edly proposes to Jane, and everyone is satisfactorily paired except the posing Bunthorne.

Although the once-admired Act I sextet ('I hear the soft note') may now seem over-sentimental, the bounce of the military music and the simple melodiousness of several songs retain their appeal. The quintet with dance in Act II ('If Saphir I choose to marry') has a special exuberance, its 6/8 rhythm pointed by a synco-pated high woodwind counterpoint: this music makes a happy return as the very last number of the operetta. Lady Jane's soliloquy at the beginning of Act II is punctuated by a comically grotesque recitative on the double-bass – an instrument the soloist usually pre-tends to play. But some gifted interpreters actually have played either cello or double-bass on stage.

Iolanthe, or The Peer and the Peri

Comic opera in two acts (2h)
Libretto by W. S. Gilbert
PREMIERES 25 November 1882, Savoy Theatre, London;
US: 25 November 1882, Standard Theater, New York
CAST Lord Chancellor *bar*, Earl of Mountararat *b*, Earl Tolloller *t*, Private Willis *b*, Strephon *bar*, Queen of the Fairies *c*, Iolanthe *ms*, Phyllis *s*, 2 *s*, *ms*; *satb* chorus of dukes, marquises, earls, viscounts, barons and fairies

Iolanthe was the first of the operettas written expressly for the Savoy Theatre (though Carte had moved his company there in the middle of the run of *Patience*), and it is hard to resist the idea that Sullivan found a new musical stimulus in the prospect. Gilbert's dramaturgical scheme is exceptionally strong, especially the counter-marching and conflict of peers and fairies at the end of Act I; an unusual richness of characterization invests the lord chancellor (in other respects the successor of mere patter-song professionals such as Sir Joseph Porter and the major-general) with real pathos at the climax of the plot. The initial staging of the work displayed a helmeted, spear-carrying queen of the fairies as a kind of parodied Brünnhilde, but allegations of Wagnerism in Sullivan's music for the scene of Iolanthe's pardon should be met with scepticism.

SYNOPSIS

Act I   For the chorus of fairies there is little gaiety in life because one of their number, Iolanthe, was banished 25 years ago for marrying a mortal, a crime normally punished by death. The queen of the fairies is persuaded to pardon her, on condition that she does not communicate with her husband. Iolanthe appears, followed by her 24-year-old son, Strephon, who is a fairy only 'down to the waist'. He earns the approval of the queen. His beloved Phyllis, a shepherdess and a ward of Chancery, enters with a solo, followed by a duet with Strephon ('None shall part us from each other'). They leave. Preceded with military pomp by a chorus of peers ('Loudly let the trumpet bray'), the lord chancellor introduces himself ('The law is the true embodiment'). All the peers are smitten with love for Phyllis, and Lords Tolloller and Mountararat in particular lay suit to her. Her declaration that she loves Strephon causes anger: his application to marry a ward in Chancery has already been dismissed. Distraught, Strephon consults his young-looking fairy mother; Phyllis takes Iolanthe for a rival and, thinking Strephon unfaithful, declares her willingness to wed a peer. The queen of the fairies, summoned by Strephon and insulted by the lord chancellor, announces vengeance: Strephon shall go into Parliament and upset its cherished institutions. Fairies and peers exchange defiance.

Act II opens to display the Palace of Westminster: on sentry duty, Private Willis ponders the strange fact of 'ev'ry boy and ev'ry gal' becoming 'either a little Liberal or else a little Conservative' ('When all night long a chap remains'). The fairies are delighted at the legislative havoc being caused now that 'Strephon's a Member of Parliament', but Mountararat points out the dangers of the House of Lords becoming a house of intellectuals ('When Britain really rul'd the waves'). The fairies having begun to love the peers, their queen endeavours to steady them by pointing out ('Oh, foolish fay') how she resists the 'simply godlike' charms of Private Willis. The lord chancellor discloses in a nightmare song ('When you're lying awake with a dismal headache') how his love for Phyllis – a ward of his own court – is upsetting him. Tolloller and Mountararat embolden him, so, although Phyllis and Strephon have removed their mutual misunderstanding, the lord chancellor now decides to claim Phyllis for himself. The only one who can stop him is his former wife, Iolanthe (whom he believes dead). She

declares herself, thus inviting her own death sentence from the queen. The lord chancellor persuades the queen to alter fairy law so that every fairy shall die 'who don't marry a mortal': she engages herself to Private Willis, and all depart for fairyland.

Instead of being a mere medley of tunes (often assembled by one of Sullivan's musical assistants) the overture here is an accomplished sonata-type movement in which the tune of 'Oh, foolish fay' is combined by Sullivan with another tune of Mendelssohnian grace which does not occur in the operetta itself. And so the richness of this score continues, with a romantic pathos for Iolanthe's pardon and her later danger, and with a tiny, changing motif for the lord chancellor. The military strains, though they belong to peers rather than soldiers, are even more imposing than those in *Patience*. The sweetest and subtlest of all Sullivan's love duets (a soprano heroine paired with a baritone rather than a tenor hero) is 'None shall part us', its on-running melody underpinned by delicate harmonic progression.

Princess Ida, or Castle Adamant

Comic opera in three acts (2h)
Libretto by W. S. Gilbert, after the poem *The Princess* by Alfred, Lord Tennyson (1847)
PREMIERES 5 January 1884, Savoy Theatre, London; US: 11 February 1884, Fifth Avenue Theater, New York
CAST King Hildebrand *b-bar*, Hilarion *t*, Cyril *t*, Florian *bar*, King Gama *bar*, Arac *b*, Princess Ida *s*, Lady Blanche *c*, Psyche *s*, Melissa *ms*, *s*, *bar*, *b*, 3 *spoken roles*; *satb*
chorus of soldiers, courtiers, girl graduates, Daughters of the Plough, etc.

Gilbert and Sullivan's only three-act collaboration is also the only one with the dialogue in blank verse, a survival from *The Princess*, Gilbert's spoken play of 1870, itself a burlesque of Tennyson's long narrative poem of that name. Tennyson had prophesied and welcomed the emancipation of women; Gilbert ridiculed it. The satire of the opera ('A women's college? Maddest folly going!') was already out of date when it appeared. Sullivan's score nevertheless has borne regular revival for its mock-military fun and lyrical graces.

SYNOPSIS

Act I   Princess Ida, daughter of King Gama, was betrothed at the age of one to Prince Hilarion, son of King Hildebrand, but 20 years later her father fails to produce her as promised for the marriage. Instead he arrives accompanied only by his three brainless warrior sons. Ida has immured herself at a women's university where men are banned. Hilarion, with his friends Cyril and Florian, decides to go and hunt them out – using only the means of love ('Expressive glances / Shall be our lances').

Act II discloses Castle Adamant, site of the university. Unlike the hypocritical second-in-command, Lady Blanche, Princess Ida voices genuine aspiration in her invocation to Minerva, goddess of wisdom. Cyril and his friends enter, having scaled the walls. Seeing some robes, they put them on and play at being females. The princess fails to detect them, but Florian is recognized by his sister Psyche; she and her friend

Melissa will support the men. Still in female dress, they join the others for lunch, but Cyril gets tipsy and all three men are discovered and seized. Hildebrand's forces arrive outside and begin a siege of the castle.

Act III sees the collapse of Ida's dreams as her female force refuses to fight. She admits her mistakes and lovingly accepts Hilarion.

Gilbert's libretto gave Sullivan the opportunity to recapture the gracefulness of line and harmony to which he had risen in *Iolanthe*, and also to excel in martial patter and in the caricatured portrait of the sharp-tongued King Gama and his three oafish sons. One of the sons, Arac, has a splendid mock-Handelian song when deciding that it would be easier to fight by taking off his armour than keeping it on ('This helmet, I suppose'). It is hardly the composer's fault if the story fails to convince even on its own fable-like terms.

The Mikado, or The Town of Titipu

Comic opera in two acts (2h 15m)
Libretto by W. S. Gilbert
PREMIERES 14 March 1885, Savoy Theatre, London; US: 6 July 1885, Chicago (unauthorized); 19 August 1885, Fifth Avenue Theater, New York
CAST The Mikado *b*, Nanki-Poo *t*, Ko-Ko *bar*, Pooh-Bah *b-bar*, Pish-Tush *bar*, Yum-Yum *s*, Pitti-Sing *ms*, Peep-Bo *ms*, Katisha *c*, (Go-To *b* sometimes added); *satb* chorus of schoolgirls, nobles, guards and coolies

The Mikado was the collaborators' longest-running work (672 performances) and, on its revival in 1896, became the first to achieve 1000 performances at the Savoy. Praised by the Viennese critic Eduard Hanslick, translated into many languages, including Russian (for a performance under Stanislavsky's auspices), it is often considered Sullivan's masterpiece. Perhaps Gilbert's too: characters such as Pooh-Bah and phrases such as 'modified rapture!' and 'let the punishment fit the crime' became proverbial.

It was the first Gilbert and Sullivan piece set in a recognized and strongly identified foreign location, but the 'Japanese' names are all English, obviously in cases such as Ko-Ko, less obviously with Pitti-Sing (baby talk for 'pretty thing'). Through the Japanese mask, Gilbert satirized English abuses or absurdities, the more effectively because Sullivan's music is (typically of him) straight and not grotesque. Seemingly perfect in balance, the score has come down to us in a form not exactly that of the original. Shortly after the opening night the author and composer made two important structural changes, advancing Ko-Ko's 'little list' song within Act I and moving Yum-Yum's 'The sun, whose rays' from Act I to Act II.

SYNOPSIS

Act I Nanki-Poo, a wandering minstrel arriving in the town of Titipu ('A wand'ring minstrel I'), learns from Pish-Tush that Yum-Yum, whom he hoped to marry, is engaged to her guardian, Ko-Ko, a tailor who has become lord high executioner. Ko-Ko expounds his 'little list' of 'society offenders' who could usefully be decapitated. Yum-Yum and her friends

Pitti-Sing and Peep-Bo ('Three little maids from school') are cheeky towards the colossal dignity of Pooh-Bah, 'Lord High Everything Else'. Nanki-Poo reveals to Yum-Yum that he is really the son of the Mikado, fleeing the amorous attentions of the elderly Katisha. After an edict from the Mikado, Ko-Ko nerves himself to begin decapitations. Since Nanki-Poo is about to commit a love-sick suicide, a bargain is drawn: he will be permitted to marry Yum-Yum on condition of consenting to be beheaded in a month's time. Rejoicing is in order, and even the terrifying appearance of Katisha is defied ('For he's going to marry Yum-Yum'). She threatens the Mikado's vengeance.

Act II Yum-Yum, decked for her wedding, sings naïvely of her own beauty ('The sun, whose rays are all ablaze'). Joined in a madrigal by Pitti-Sing and Pish-Tush, the lovers rejoice ('Brightly dawns our wedding day'). But expectations are dampened when Ko-Ko discovers a law by which, when a man is executed, his bride is buried alive. The Mikado's arrival is announced: he identifies himself ('A more humane Mikado never did in Japan exist') and catalogues his own system of justice: 'to let the punishment fit the crime'. Ko-Ko, Pooh-Bah and Pitti-Sing regale him with an account of a supposed recent execution. But the Mikado learns that the 'victim' was Nanki-Poo, his own son: the penalty for encompassing the death of the heir apparent is 'something lingering, with boiling oil in it'. Nanki-Poo refuses to come back to life to exonerate his 'executioners' unless Katisha's amorous attentions can be diverted by Ko-Ko's marrying her, a prospect Ko-Ko views with the utmost distaste (duet: 'The flowers that bloom in the spring, tra-la'). Katisha enters ('Alone, and yet alive!'). By a cunning fable ('Tit-willow') Ko-Ko persuades her to accept him, on the supposition that Nanki-Poo has indeed been executed. When Nanki-Poo appears, now married to Yum-Yum, rejoicing is resumed and even the Mikado is pacified.

The interplay between the supposed Japanese scene and the real England satirized by Gilbert is kept up not merely in words ('The Japanese equivalent for "Hear, hear, hear!"') but in music. The score finds place for a madrigal in Sullivan's 'old English' style, and also for a glee ('See how the Fates their gifts allot'), as well as an authentic Japanese tune for the entrance of the Mikado. Its immediately captivating aspects, from patter to love duet, are underpinned by musical subtleties. In a trio for Pooh-Bah ('I am so proud'), Ko-Ko and Pish-Tush three dissimilar tunes are deftly counterpointed (the suggestion for such treatment came from Gilbert), and later a Bach fugue is cross-rhythmically quoted with the Mikado's reference to 'masses and fugues and ops, / By Bach, interwoven / With Spohr and Beethoven'.

Ruddigore, or The Witch's Curse

originally *Ruddygore*, but re-spelt within two weeks of the opening
Comic opera in two acts (2h 15m)
Libretto by W. S. Gilbert
PREMIERES 22 January 1887, Savoy Theatre, London; US: 21 February 1887, Fifth Avenue Theater, New York

CAST Sir Ruthven Murgatroyd (disguised as Robin Oakapple) *bar*, Richard Dauntless *t*, Sir Despard Murgatroyd *b-bar*, Old Adam Goodheart *b*, Rose Maybud *s*, Mad Margaret *ms*, Dame Hannah *c*, Sir Roderic Murgatroyd *b*, *s*, 4 ghosts *spoken roles*; *satb* chorus of officers, ancestors, villagers and professional bridesmaids

Relying much on the spirit of the old burlesque – with the bold and cheerful sailor, over-modest village maiden, and bad baronet – *Ruddigore* was regarded as out of date in its satire and gained only modest success when first produced. It was not revived until December 1920 (in Glasgow), in a somewhat altered version sacrificing the original finale to Act II. Recent performances, live and recorded, have had recourse to some elements of the original version. The coming to life of an ancestral picture gallery had already been used by Gilbert (in *Ages Ago*, 1870, with music by Frederic Clay); there was originally a second coming to life, at the end of Act II, which was soon wisely replaced. The highly original character of Mad Margaret, probably intended by Gilbert mainly to guy the madness of Shakespeare's Ophelia, gained extra effectiveness from its relevance to the crazed heroines of such operas as *Lucia di Lammermoor*.

SYNOPSIS
Act I In the 18th-century village of Rederring in Cornwall with its corps of professional bridesmaids, Rose remains unwed. She is courted by Robin, but her primness and his shyness stand in the way. Richard, a sailor and Robin's foster-brother, volunteers to commend Robin's suit to Rose. Instead, he successfully proposes to her on his own behalf – only to see her change her mind again and embrace Robin. Mad Margaret enters, her madness induced by love for Sir Despard, the current 'bad baronet of Ruddigore': each successive holder of the title is condemned by a curse to commit a crime a day. The entry of Sir Despard terrifies all, but Despard hates his role and is delighted when Richard (claiming to act from a sense of duty, but really anxious to prise Rose from Robin) reveals that Robin is in fact Sir Ruthven, an elder brother who should have inherited the baronetcy and its curse. Rose returns to Richard and Despard to Margaret.

Act II Robin, now the villainous Sir Ruthven, faces the judgement of his ancestors for failing to commit his daily crime. The ancestors rise from their pictured images. They live a merry life (the resurrected Sir Roderic tells of their festival, 'the ghosts' high noon') but now sternly compel Robin to 'carry off a lady'. Despard and Margaret enter as reformed characters: any reversion to madness on her part can be cured by the word 'Basingstoke'. Robin's servant Adam, dispatched to abduct a lady, brings back Dame Hannah, who draws a dagger and has Robin at her mercy when the ghostly Sir Roderic intervenes. Hannah and he recognize each other as old lovers. Robin argues that to fail to commit a crime is, for a bad baronet, tantamount to suicide; but suicide is a crime, so Sir Roderic should never have died at all! Roderic embraces Hannah, Robin (no longer villainous) embraces Rose, and Richard is content with the principal bridesmaid.

Such powerful music was contributed by Sullivan to the ghost scene that the bounds of comic artificiality are almost burst. There are other features of very strong individuality in the score, notably an unparalleled patter trio for Margaret, Robin and Despard in Act II and a sprightly 'old English' dance in 9/8 time ('Oh, happy the lily that's kissed by the bee') in Act I. Richard's 'nautical' music, sung and danced, freshens an old tradition, while Mad Margaret, whether accompanied by a Lucia-like flute on her first entrance or by comically wooden dance music in her reformed state, is a superb musical as well as dramatic creation.

The Yeomen of the Guard, or The Merryman and his Maid
Comic opera in two acts (2h 15m)
Libretto by W. S. Gilbert
PREMIERES 3 October 1888, Savoy Theatre, London; US: 17 October 1888, Casino Theater, New York
CAST Colonel Fairfax *t*, Sergeant Meryll *bar*, Jack Point *bar*, Wilfred Shadbolt *bar*, Elsie Maynard *s*, Phoebe Meryll *ms*, Dame Carruthers *c*, *s*, 3 *t*, 3 *bar*, 2 *spoken roles*, *silent role*; *satb* chorus of Yeomen of the Guard, gentlemen, citizens, etc.

With *The Yeomen of the Guard* Sullivan came as near as he could to a serious opera within what had been established as the Savoy convention. At the end the jester Jack Point, disappointed in love, falls 'insensible' amid the merry-making of the rest. Gilbert's plot, though originally criticized as uncomfortably close to that of William Vincent Wallace's opera *Maritana* (1845), achieves force as a serious drama in which comic elements are kept subordinate and not allowed to break from the Tudor period to introduce modern satire. None the less the comic juxtaposition of the quick-witted jester and the slow, would-be-funny Shadbolt ('Head Gaoler and Assistant Tormentor' at the Tower of London) gives brilliant contrast to the pathos of the rest. The opening is, for once, not an assertive chorus but a gentle soliloquy in song.

SYNOPSIS
Act I Phoebe, daughter of Sergeant Meryll of the Yeomen of the Guard at the Tower of London, sings at her spinning-wheel ('When maiden loves'). Secretly in love with the unjustly imprisoned Colonel Fairfax, she repulses the clumsy advances of the gaoler Shadbolt. Dame Carruthers, housekeeper of the Tower, sings of its valiant history ('When our gallant Norman foes'). Anxious to rescue Fairfax (who once saved his life) from execution, Meryll plans with Phoebe to release him from his cell and pass him off as Phoebe's brother Leonard, himself due to join the Yeomen. Fairfax appears, reconciled to his fate ('Is life a boon?'), but asks the lieutenant of the Tower to procure him a blindfold bride so that his possessions do not fall into the hands of his persecuting relatives. The arrival of two strolling players, Jack Point and Elsie ('I have a song to sing, O'), is auspicious; Elsie consents to be the blindfold bride. Phoebe wheedles the keys of the cells from Shadbolt ('Were I thy bride'); Fairfax is released and introduced as Leonard. When the time for the execution arrives there is uproar; Fairfax has vanished. Point, loving Elsie, now

cannot court her since her husband Fairfax has not been executed.

Act II   Point persuades Shadbolt to say he saw Fairfax in the river and shot him, in return for which Point will teach Shadbolt the jester's art. A quartet, 'Strange adventure!', for Fairfax, Sergeant Meryll, Dame Carruthers and her niece Kate, discloses that Elsie (who has been heard talking in her sleep) was the mysterious blindfold bride. Elsie herself, still not realizing whom she has married, has fallen in love with the supposed 'Leonard' but may not permit his advances because she must keep her wifely duty to Fairfax. A shot rings out and Shadbolt and Point tell their cooked-up story. Fairfax now being assumed dead, Point courts Elsie – clumsily; Fairfax offers to show him how – but makes the proposal on his own account as 'Leonard' and is accepted. Phoebe, still in love with Fairfax, shows her annoyance – and Shadbolt, realizing that this can be no brother of Phoebe's, sees the extent of the deception. Phoebe is obliged to promise to marry Shadbolt as the price of his silence; similarly Sergeant Meryll buys Dame Carruthers' silence by ending his long resistance to marrying her. A reprieve for Fairfax arrives: he claims his bride, and only after an anguished moment does Elsie realize that her beloved 'Leonard' and her hitherto unseen husband Fairfax are the same. The jester Point, broken-hearted, falls insensible.

A formally unified sonata-type overture (as in the case of *Iolanthe* but not of most of the Savoy pieces) opens with a rising, fanfare-like figure which intermittently serves as a kind of representational theme for the stern Tower of London itself. The strolling players' ballad, 'I have a song to sing, O' is a cumulative structure (like that of the folksong 'Green grow the rushes, O'), a pattern that seems exceptionally to have been suggested by Gilbert himself, though the 'archaic' drone effect of the harmony is a brilliant touch of Sullivan's own. There is not a weak number in *The Yeomen*, and the Act II duet for Dame Carruthers and Sergeant Meryll (omitted in some performances and recordings) is a perfect comic foil to the prevailing seriousness: note the introduction of the lugubrious bassoon when her 'Rapture, rapture!' is replaced by his 'Doleful, doleful!'

The Gondoliers, or The King of Barataria

Comic opera in two acts (2h 15m)
Libretto by W. S. Gilbert
PREMIERES   7 December 1889, Savoy Theatre, London;
US: 7 January 1890, New Park Theater, New York
CAST   Duke of Plaza-Toro *bar*, Luiz *t*, Don Alhambra del Bolero *b-bar*, Marco Palmieri *t*, Giuseppe Palmieri *bar*, Duchess of Plaza-Toro *c*, Casilda *s*, Tessa *ms*, Gianetta *s*, 2 *ms, c, t, bar, b, spoken role; satb* chorus of gondoliers and contadine, men-at-arms, heralds and pages

The Gondoliers marks a reversion, after *The Yeomen of the Guard*, to the fully comic work with topical references introduced into the supposedly 18th-century setting in Venice and the island of Barataria (a location mentioned in *Don Quixote*). The plot treads some old ground, notably in the baby-swapping and the revelation of a secret at the end, but the satire on ultra-democratic sentiments (with the implication of hypocrisy thrown in) marked a subtly fresh turn of the Gilbertian knife. Sullivan rose to the opportunity to impart first an Italian, then a Spanish, flavour. By the design of Gilbert himself, responding to what he knew Sullivan craved in musical autonomy, the piece begins with about 18 minutes of music uninterrupted by speech.

SYNOPSIS

Act I   The gondoliers Marco and Giuseppe choose their brides by a game of blind man's buff; by judicious cheating, Giuseppe catches Tessa and Marco catches Gianetta. The impoverished duke of Plaza-Toro, 'that celebrated, cultivated, underrated nobleman', arrives accompanied by his overweening duchess, his loyal drummer Luiz, and his daughter Casilda, who was married in infancy to the heir to the throne of Barataria. Where is that husband now? Don Alhambra the grand inquisitor knows him well ('no possible doubt whatever') – he is one of two gondoliers. Luiz's mother, who was their nurse, will declare which. This brings consternation to Luiz and Casilda, secretly in love. Marco and Giuseppe return with their new wives: learning that one of them is king of Barataria, they find it easy to drop their republican principles. Reigning jointly as an interim arrangement, they will set sail for Barataria forthwith, leaving their wives behind.

Act II   In Barataria the court is said to display 'a despotism strict, combined with absolute equality': in fact the new monarchs are slaves to their courtiers. They pine for their wives (Marco: 'Take a pair of sparkling eyes'), who unexpectedly arrive from Venice. Celebrations are interrupted by the arrival of the grand inquisitor, who criticizes their egalitarian regime ('When everyone is somebodee, then no one's anybody!'). Only now do Marco and Giuseppe learn to their dismay that one of them had contracted a marriage in infancy (quartet with Tessa and Gianetta: 'In a contemplative fashion'). The duke of Plaza-Toro arrives with his usual entourage; the duchess gives her recipe for duke-taming ('On the day when I was wedded to your admirable sire'). The embarrassment of the three young women (Casilda, Tessa, Gianetta) vis-à-vis the two young gondoliers is evident. At last Luiz's mother is shown in and recounts the deft interchange of babies by which her own son now emerges as the true king. Luiz re-enters, crowned. All is now disentangled, and Venetian music recurs to end the opera.

If 'Take a pair of sparkling eyes' has by sheer lyrical grace become the most famous number of the opera, Sullivan's cleverest contribution was the Act II quartet, where individual voices break out furiously from the artificial calm. Gilbert himself in a letter had modestly suggested some elements of the musical treatment. The Italian and Spanish touches in songs and dances are enhanced by particularly brilliant orchestration, the quick repeated notes on the cornet (at that time used in the theatre in place of trumpets) giving extra excitement to 'Dance a cachucha' (the celebration of the wives' arrival in Barataria).

Other operas: *The Sapphire Necklace* (inc.) (later *The False Heiress*), (1864), overture, 1866 , one further number published 1898 (lost); *The Coutrabandista, or The Law of The Ladrones*, 1867; *Thespis, or The Gods Grown Old*, 1871; *The Zoo*, 1875; *Ivanhoe*, 1891; *Haddon Hall*, 1892; *Utopia Limited, or the Flowers of Progress*, 1893; *The Chieftain*; 1894; *The Grand Duke or The Statutory Duel*, 1896; *The Beauty Stone*, 1898; *The Rose of Persia, or The Story-teller and the Slave*, 1899; *The Emerald Isle, or The Caves of Carrig-Cleena*, (inc.; completed by Edward German), 1901

A.J.

KAROL SZYMANOWSKI

Karol Maciej Szymanowski; *b* 6 October 1882, Tymoszówka, Ukraine; *d* 29 March 1937, Lausanne, Switzerland

Szymanowski was the most important Polish composer to follow Chopin and Stanislaw Moniuszko. He was taught music by his father, then later by Gustav Neuhaus and finally by Zygmunt Noskowski in Warsaw. From 1911 to 1914 he lived mainly in Vienna, where he made contact with Universal Edition, who became his main publishers.

Szymanowski was an energetic traveller. Before the First World War he visited Sicily and North Africa, and these journeys stimulated the interest in ancient and oriental cultures that was to colour works such as the opera *King Roger*, the Third Symphony, *Myths* and *Songs of an Infatuated Muezzin*. Szymanowski also wrote poems, and left sketches and fragments of six novels. The libretto for *King Roger*, written in collaboration with Jarosław Iwaszkiewicz, is derived from his novel *Ephebos*. From 1930 his home was at Zakopane in the Tatra Mountains, and the local folk music influenced his late compositions. At this time, he was also rector of the Warsaw Conservatory (1927–9, 1930–32), and from 1933 to 1936 he worked as a touring musician, playing his own piano music all over Europe. Apart from these episodes, Szymanowski devoted himself wholly to composition and writing.

He wrote music in many genres: four symphonies, two violin concertos, two string quartets, music for violin and for piano, operas, incidental music, a ballet-pantomime, vocal and choral music, and many songs. They display a variety of influences and tendencies easily divisible into three periods. Up to 1914, Chopin and Aleksandr Skryabin are strong influences, but most obviously Richard Strauss – and later Max Reger. With the late-Romantic strain there is also a classical tendency which is manifested in his fascination with counterpoint and the use of dances such as the gavotte and minuet (in the Second Symphony) or the sarabande and minuet (in the Second Piano Sonata). The one-act *Hagith* derives from the spirit of German Expressionism as manifested in Strauss's *Salome*, though Szymanowski's harmony and texture are denser than Strauss's, and his emotional tension even more unrelenting.

In his middle period (1914–20) colour assumed greater importance, and Szymanowski's music became more impressionistic, reflecting his interest in oriental and ancient cultures. His most important opera, *King Roger*, belongs to this period. While working on it, Szymanowski was also composing works, such as the song-cycle *Słopiewnie*, that anticipate his so-called 'national' last period, when his music became simpler in structure and texture, with harmony that uses folk modes and is less chromatic. The major works of this final period are the Fourth Symphony, the Second Violin Concerto and the ballet *Harnasie*, whose Paris performance in 1936 was the composer's last great international success.

Through all his apparent changes of style, Szymanowski's attitude remained Romantic. Emotion is central to his music. As a composer he was prolific, but he was also an influential writer on music, touching on crucial contemporary musical issues and expressing strong views on, for example, the social role of music and on Chopin as a living musical tradition for the 20th century.

King Roger

(*The Shepherd*)
Król Roger
(*Pasterz*)
Opera in three acts (1h 45m)
Libretto by Jarosław Iwaszkiewicz and the composer, after the composer's novel *Ephebos*
Composed 1918–24
PREMIERES 19 June 1926, Wielki Theatre, Warsaw; UK: 14 May 1975, Sadler's Wells, London; US: 24 January 1988, Long Beach, California
CAST King Roger II *bar*, Roxana *s*, Shepherd *t, c, t, b*; children's choir of acolytes; *satb* chorus of priests, monks, nuns, king's guard, Norman knights

In *King Roger* Szymanowski planned an integrated musical spectacle in which music, words and design would form part of a single concept in the manner of the Wagnerian ideal. The composer not only collaborated on the libretto but also gave detailed instructions for the sets. The drama is symbolic: the characters represent ideals, and the dramatic conflict is between the Pagan (personified by the shepherd) and the Christian (personified by Roger).

SYNOPSIS
Act I   Twelfth-century Sicily. In the cathedral at Palermo, the priests ask King Roger to imprison an unknown shepherd, who has proclaimed a philosophy of beauty and pleasure which they see as threatening Christianity. The king is willing to comply, but his beloved wife Roxana begs him to hear the shepherd before deciding. Roger agrees, and invites the shepherd to his castle.

Act II   The shepherd, who comes from India, enters the castle with a group of disciples. They begin to dance. Roxana and the courtiers are won over by the shepherd's charismatic personality and teaching, and when he leaves they follow.

Act III   In the ruins of an ancient theatre Roger searches for Roxana and the shepherd. Soon they appear, and he follows them like a pilgrim. Suddenly the shepherd becomes Dionysus and his disciples bacchantes and maenads. They dance ecstatically, and then depart with Roxana. Roger remains alone, singing a hymn to the rising sun. He has resisted a powerful temptation, and has thereby achieved wholeness.

King Roger combines elements of opera and oratorio. Its statuesque action and important choral part suggest Stravinsky's *Oedipus Rex* or Schoenberg's *Moses und Aron*. But the music itself has little in common with those works. Each act presents a different world – the first Byzantine, the second Arabic–Indian, the third Ancient Greek – and these characteristics determine the musical stylizations, which are not historically or geographically exact, but amount rather to suggestions of old church or oriental music (such as antiphonal psalmody or organum) in Act I; asymmetry of phrase, irregular metre, a narrow melodic range but with much ornamentation and free use of percussion in Act II. There are no quotations and no authentic scales. In Act III the stylization is achieved mainly through the scenery. There is some flavour of Tatra folksong, a symptom of Szymanowski's growing interest in folklore.

The music is extremely varied in texture. Though much of the choral music is archaic in character, the orchestra is sometimes treated as one vast instrument in the late-Romantic manner, offering dense textures and complex modern harmony. It is sometimes divided into smaller chamber ensembles, or there are instrumental solos, in the style of French Impressionism. The dense chromatic harmony is contrasted with the sound of parallel fifths and plain common chords, sometimes in order to differentiate character (King Roger – chromatic; Roxana – modal). This combination of styles produced a work with a unique atmosphere which has no real parallel in either earlier or contemporary music. The best-known number in the opera is Roxana's Act II aria, which is often performed as a violin solo in a transcription by Pawel Kochański.

Other operatic works: *Lottery for a Husband* (*Loteria na mężów* (operetta), (1909); *Hagith*, (1913), 1922; 2 lost operas

Z.C.

PYOTR TCHAIKOVSKY

Pyotr Ilyich Tchaikovsky; *b* 7 May 1840, Kamsko-Votkinsk (Vyatka Province), Russia; *d* 6 November 1893, St Petersburg

Though only two of his operas, *Eugene Onegin* and *The Queen of Spades*, are regularly performed outside Russia, Tchaikovsky occupied himself more with opera than with any other musical genre. He wrote operas at every stage of his career, and they were invariably given productions within a reasonably short time. Much more than ballet, opera charts his development as a composer, even where it does not represent his very best work.

The son of a mining engineer in Votkinsk, some 600 miles east of Moscow, Tchaikovsky moved with his family to St Petersburg when he was eight. As a child, he was almost excessively attached to his mother, and when she died in 1854 he suffered an emotional trauma from which he never completely recovered. Relations with women were a problem for the rest of his life. In 1868 it seems he came close to marrying the Belgian opera singer Désirée Artôt, and in 1877 he allowed himself to be drawn into a disastrous marriage by the desperation of the girl and by his own feelings of guilt. These and his curious epistolary friendship with his patroness Nadezhda von Meck, whom he never met in person, were his only attempts at close relationships with the female sex outside his own family. But, as a homosexual, he suffered still greater agonies of guilt and self-loathing; and eventually the strain was too much and there can be no reasonable doubt that he committed suicide.

There is little sign that Tchaikovsky's student years under Anton Rubinstein at the St Petersburg Conservatory (1862–5) prepared him for operatic composition, and the Russian repertoire in the 1860s offered few models by native composers. Not surprisingly, Tchaikovsky's first experiment with the form, *The Voyevoda* (1867–8), was unsuccessful, while *Undine* (1869) was rejected outright by the Imperial Theatres, and the composer subsequently destroyed it. But he had a good dramatic instinct which could rise to greatness when his personal sympathies were fully engaged, and by the time he tackled his third subject, *The Oprichnik*, he had greatly developed his craft in instrumental music and had magnificently revealed a highly personal style in his fantasy overture *Romeo and Juliet* (1869, revised 1870 and 1880). In fact *The Oprichnik* (1870–72) was not only a great audience success but a notable achievement (though Tchaikovsky's own hostility to it came to exceed even what he felt for its two predecessors). Its individuality was reinforced by its very pronounced Russianness, and in the old boyarina he created the first of those 'suffering women' who were to prove the most memorable characters in his operas.

But already he was being drawn towards his nationalist contemporaries, led by Mily Balakirev, and the Second ('Little Russian') Symphony (1872) especially revealed a radical shift in manner which was confirmed in his fourth opera, *Vakula the Smith* (1874), in which the score's four identified folksongs are supplemented with passages of folksong pastiche. With *Vakula*, however, Tchaikovsky's nationalist phase came to an abrupt end. While the First Piano Concerto (1874–5) signalled a return towards his earlier manner, the heightened turbulence and pathos of the symphonic fantasy *Francesca da Rimini* (1876) seemed almost to foretell the disastrous events of the following year.

Eugene Onegin (1877–8) is inextricably entangled with that traumatic episode: its story had uncanny parallels with Tchaikovsky's own life. It is undoubtedly his greatest opera and also his most characteristic, in both its content and its musico-dramatic technique. Composed under the impression of Bizet's *Carmen*, which Tchaikovsky saw in Paris in 1876 and adored, his handling of Pushkin's ironic verse tale also projects Bizet's concept of happy domesticity and social virtue undermined by inexorable personal tragedy. Especially crucial is the design of its scenario. Three of Tchaikovsky's last six operas are Pushkin-based, and it is in these that the episodic structure to which Russian libretti incline becomes most explicit. It was perhaps because *Eugene Onegin*, *Mazepa* and *The Queen of Spades* were literary classics, known to all educated Russians, that their scenarios could be more selective, relying on the listener's knowledge to fill any gaps in the plots. Be that as it may, all three (like Musorgsky's *Boris Godunov*, also drawn from Pushkin) use a 'strip cartoon' structure, each scene dwelling on a crucial incident in the story, thus giving the composer time to explore in depth the psychological states of his characters. In *Onegin* Tchaikovsky rose to such opportunities magnificently – above all in Tatyana's letter monologue, the finest scene in all his operas. Some consider *Onegin* his masterpiece.

No such claim could be made for *The Maid of Orleans* (1878–9; rev. 1882). *The Maid* suffered from Tchaikovsky's clear determination to compose a grandiose, Meyerbeerish work that would appeal to the taste of Western operatic audiences. But it was not only that 'commercial' considerations seem to have shaped *The Maid*: the traumatic events of 1877 had stunned his creative individuality. He shrank from society as far as possible, to live mostly abroad or with his sister in the Ukraine, and few of the compositions of the next seven years are among his most powerful or characteristic. He attempted no symphony, turning instead to the freer form of the suite and serenade, and only two works are truly outstanding: the Piano Trio (1881–2) and the opera *Mazepa* (1881–3).

In the *Manfred Symphony* of 1885 Tchaikovsky rediscovered his full, most individual powers, and it might have been hoped that his next opera, *The Enchantress* (1885–7), would be a masterpiece matching *Onegin*. But, for all its undeniable fluency and stretches of excellent music, it was crippled by its implausibly melodramatic subject. The Fifth Symphony (1888) and especially the great ballet *The Sleeping Beauty* (1888–9) are on a very different plane, and completely at one stylistically. Yet the most striking feature of *The Queen of Spades* (1890), Tchaikovsky's third Pushkin opera, is the savage stylistic dichotomy between the sombre, sometimes menacing, music prompted by the remorseless obsession of the main character and the bright, cheerful music of the elegant society within which events are set. In several earlier works (most notably the *Rococo Variations* for cello and orchestra (1876)) Tchaikovsky had allowed 'Mozartian' style to mate with his own; now he himself confessed that some music in this opera was no more than 18th-century pastiche. Elsewhere, in the darker scenes and passages, the tragic pessimism of the Sixth Symphony (1893) is anticipated. For the three years after *The Queen of Spades* it seems that Tchaikovsky's creative resources were husbanding themselves for the stupendous achievement of this final symphony. Certainly all the intervening compositions are relatively relaxed, and his last opera, *Iolanta* (1891), is little more than a charming, though at times very affecting, piece.

Vakula the Smith

(rev. as *The Tsarina's Boots*)
Kuznets Vakula (rev. as *Cherevichki*)
Opera in three acts, (rev. in four acts (eight scenes))
(2h 45m)
Libretto by Yakov Polonsky, after *Noch' pered rozhdestvom* (*Christmas Eve*) by Nikolai Gogol (1832); additional libretto in rev. version for Vakula's arioso in Act III by the composer and Nikolai Chayev
Composed June–September 1874; rev. February–April 1885, and late 1886
PREMIERES 6 December 1876, Mariinsky Theatre, St Petersburg; rev. version: 31 January 1887, Bolshoi Theatre, Moscow; US: 26 May 1922, Metropolitan, New York; UK: 17 May 1984, Collegiate Theatre, London
CAST Vakula *t*, Solokha *ms*, The Devil *bar*, Chub *b*, Oxana *s*, Pan Golova, the mayor *b*, Panas *t*, Schoolteacher *t*, Prince *b-bar*, Orderly *t*, Old Peasant *b*, Woodgoblin *bar*; *satb* chorus of peasants, kobza players, *rusalki* (woodsprites), courtiers

Gogol's *Christmas Eve* is a wonderfully vivid, colourful, sometimes very funny tale of Ukrainian village life, blending the real world with that of enchantment and mixing peasant characters with supernatural beings. A libretto based on it, and renamed *Vakula the Smith*, had been intended for Aleksandr Serov, but two years after his death in 1871 it was made the basis of a competition, with performance by the Imperial Opera guaranteed for the winner. Tchaikovsky thought the closing date was in January 1875 (actually it was seven months later), and, since it was June 1874 before he could begin work, he felt under great pressure. Nevertheless, Gogol's tale so fired his imagination that within little more than six weeks the opera was composed; another three, and it was scored. On discovering his error and realizing preparation for production would not begin for over a year, he attempted to withdraw from the competition, being confident his work would be accepted independently by the Imperial Opera. Inevitably he was reprimanded when this manoeuvre came to light. Yet even this could not restrain him, and, though all entries had been submitted under pseudonyms to ensure impartiality, he arranged for the overture to be performed (though withholding its title), then proposed to play the opera through to one of the judges, Rimsky-Korsakov. Despite all these glaring improprieties Tchaikovsky was not disqualified, and his opera was awarded the prize.

Tchaikovsky was delighted with the enthusiasm the performers showed for *Vakula* when rehearsals began, but he felt the audience's response at the premiere was disappointing (in fact, the opera was revived in each of the next three seasons). Perceiving what he felt to be the work's shortcomings, he thoroughly revised it in 1885, cutting about one-eighth but adding about twice as much new music, and simplifying some of the remainder to make it more effective in the theatre. Tchaikovsky himself conducted the five performances of *Cherevichki*, as the revised opera was called, but again success was limited, and it was never revived in his lifetime.

SYNOPSIS (revised version)
Act I Solokha, Vakula's mother and a witch, comes out into the moonlit village street in Dikanka. The Devil is smitten with her and joins in a comic love scene. However, he is furious with her son, who has painted him in the village church to look so ridiculous that all the other devils are laughing at him. Wanting revenge, the Devil plans to steal the moon and raise a snowstorm so that Oxana's father, Chub, will stay at home, and Vakula will not find his beloved alone. However, Chub and his friend, Panas, emerge into the storm, and decide to seek the inn. By now Oxana is admiring herself in front of her mirror. When Vakula creeps in and confesses his love she treats him ungraciously. Chub reappears so covered with snow that Vakula fails to recognize him and throws him back into the street. Oxana upbraids Vakula and pretends she loves someone else. He rushes out distraught before other young villagers arrive to begin celebrating Christmas. When they have left, Oxana privately confesses her love for Vakula.

Act II Back in her cottage Solokha flirts again

with the Devil, until knocking is heard and the Devil jumps into a sack. The mayor enters and flirts with Solokha before there is another knocking and he too hides in a sack. This is repeated after first the schoolteacher then Chub (whom Solokha favours) enter. On Vakula's approach Solokha and her four 'lovers' (whose heads appear from the sacks) join in an alarmed quintet. To leave the cottage free for Christmas festivities, Vakula decides to remove all the sacks. Meanwhile the villagers, young and old, have gathered in the village street. Oxana torments Vakula when he appears with the sacks; then she admires another girl's new shoes and promises that she will marry him if Vakula will get the shoes worn by the empress herself. After a despairing Vakula has left with one of the sacks the villagers notice wriggling in the remaining ones, and they release the mayor, the schoolteacher and Chub. Only Chub can see a joke in what has happened, and the crowd joins in his laughter.

Act III Rusalki disturb a woodgoblin. Vakula sings of his sorrow. The Devil jumps out of the sack, but Vakula tricks him and makes him promise to take him to St Petersburg. On the Devil's back he is borne through the air to a reception room in the imperial palace. With the Devil's aid, he joins a group of Cossacks and reaches the great hall, where a polonaise is in progress. The prince announces a great victory. Vakula's strange request is sympathetically received, a splendid pair of high-heeled leather boots (the *cherevichki* of the title) is given him, and he again jumps on the Devil's back.

Act IV Oxana and Solokha are bewailing Vakula's disappearance. Oxana is now thoroughly contrite, will not join in the festivities, and leaves. Vakula enters, begs Chub's forgiveness for ejecting him, and asks for Oxana's hand. Chub agrees as Oxana reappears. Vakula offers her the boots. 'I don't want them. Without them I'm . . .' she stutters. Chub gives the couple his blessing and the kobza-players lead the general rejoicing.

'I believe unreservedly in *Cherevichki*'s future as a repertoire piece, and I consider it musically wellnigh my best opera,' Tchaikovsky wrote in 1890. His confidence in its quality was well placed. The subject was an excellent one, ideal for that self-consciously Russian idiom which he was currently anxious to exploit, and which is evident especially in the gopak rhythms in which the opera abounds. Yet it is far from just a folky opera; it exploits fully the resources of more traditional operatic lyricism (though the arias are always kept within bounds and the pacing is generally excellent) as well as the descriptive and atmospheric potential of the orchestra. However, it was as much to the rich variety of Gogol's characters as to the tale's pervading Russianness that Tchaikovsky responded, whether it was to the fresh young lovers (Vakula manly and strong, Oxana wilful yet lovable), to the archly spirited Solokha, still capable of tempting the Devil himself, or to the latter – something of a buffoon and capable of being outwitted, but with the forces of nature at his command. Nor in any other opera did Tchaikovsky realize more fully the cameo characters, projecting them mainly by the vivid musical sugges-

tions of their physical demeanour and movements (foretelling the great ballet composer). Solokha's scenes with the Devil and, above all, that in which she receives her succession of suitors reveal Tchaikovsky's formidable comic gift. *Vakula the Smith/Cherevichki* is unique among Tchaikovsky's operas – the most heart-warming, the most unclouded, and still the most sadly neglected.

Eugene Onegin
Yevgenii Onegin
Lyrical scenes in three acts (seven scenes) (2h 30m)
Libretto by the composer, after the verse novel by Aleksandr Pushkin (1831); Triquet's couplets by Konstantin Shilovsky
Composed May 1877–February 1878; *écossaise* added 1885
PREMIERES 29 March 1879, Maly Theatre, Moscow Conservatory; UK: 17 October 1892, Olympic Theatre, London; US: 1 February 1908, Carnegie Hall, New York (concert); 24 March 1920, Metropolitan, New York
CAST Larina *ms*, Tatyana *s*, Olga *c*, Filippevna *ms*, Eugene Onegin *bar*, Lensky *t*, Prince Gremin *b*, Captain *b*, Zaretsky *b*, Triquet *t*, Guillot *silent*; *satb* chorus of peasants, fruit-pickers (female) and ball guests

In May 1877 Tchaikovsky had received a letter from a former Moscow Conservatory student, Antonina Milyukova, who was quite unknown to him, claiming she had been secretly in love with him for some years. Then on 25 May the singer Elizaveta Lavrovskaya suggested to him Pushkin's novel in verse, *Eugene Onegin*, as the subject for an opera. After initial hesitation Tchaikovsky's enthusiasm was aroused, and, working from his own scenario and libretto (using Pushkin's lines as far as possible), he set to work on the scene that he had always found the most compelling: that in which the inexperienced Tatyana writes to Onegin confessing her love (which he rejects). While engaged on this he received a second letter from Antonina. Determined not to play Onegin to her Tatyana, he agreed to meet her, proposed marriage, and on 10 June left for a friend's country estate. When he returned five weeks later for the wedding, he had already composed two-thirds of the opera.

His appalling marital situation drove him to attempt suicide, and in early October he fled from Antonina and was taken abroad by his brother, Anatoly, to recover. At first he was capable only of scoring what he had composed, and in November he proposed to his friend and the head of the Moscow Conservatory, Nikolai Rubinstein, that students should perform the first four scenes. A year later, in December 1878, these scenes were presented at a dress rehearsal, and three months later the entire opera was premiered.

It was Tchaikovsky's express wish that conservatory students should give the first performance, for he feared that the work's special qualities would be smothered by the habits and routine of the professional opera houses. Though a minority immediately perceived the work's rare qualities (Tchaikovsky insisted it should be published as 'lyrical scenes'), and though it received a number of modest productions in Russia during the early 1880s, it was not until the Imperial Opera produced it in St Petersburg in 1884 that it suddenly began to enjoy the success that has made it the most popular of all Russian operas. (In 1885, during this production's run, Tchaikovsky added the *écossaise* in the ballroom scene.) The opera reached Prague in 1888, and in 1892 Tchaikovsky himself was much impressed by a performance in Hamburg conducted by the young Gustav Mahler.

SYNOPSIS

Act I Scene 1: In the garden of her country house Mme Larina gossips with the old nurse, Filippevna, as she listens to her daughters, Tatyana and Olga, singing a sentimental duet inside the house. A group of peasants approaches, bringing in the last of the harvest. They perform a choral dance for Mme Larina, who orders them to be given wine. Meanwhile Tatyana and Olga have entered. Olga draws attention to Tatyana's pallor; she herself, she observes, is always carefree. But Tatyana attributes her own condition to the romantic novel she is reading. Suddenly their neighbour, Lensky, and his friend, Onegin, are seen approaching. Mme Larina receives them, then withdraws. The young people join in a quartet, Onegin comparing Olga unfavourably with Tatyana, Tatyana seeing in Onegin the man fate has chosen for her. Onegin comments patronizingly to Tatyana on the limitations of the world she inhabits; then they retire, leaving Lensky to voice his happiness with Olga. Mme Larina and the nurse return to invite everybody indoors, and notice that Onegin and Tatyana are missing. As the couple re-enter, the nurse sees that Tatyana is under Onegin's spell. Scene 2: That night, as Filippevna helps her prepare for bed, Tatyana asks about the nurse's past, then suddenly confesses she is in love. Requesting writing material and dismissing the nurse, she writes to Onegin declaring her love. By the time she has finished it is morning, and she begs the nurse to send her grandson to deliver the letter. Scene 3: A few days later Onegin returns to give his reply; Tatyana flees into the garden, where he rejects her confession with appalling, if unintended, condescension – telling her, in effect, to grow up. Tatyana is humiliated.

Act II Scene 1: Mme Larina is holding a name-day party for Tatyana. A number of military men are present, as well as Lensky and Onegin. The latter is bored with the occasion, annoyed with Lensky for having brought him, and to get his revenge flirts with Olga by dancing with her. Olga abets him. Triquet, a Frenchman, sings some couplets he has written in Tatyana's honour, to her great embarrassment. During the following mazurka Onegin continues his flirtation with Olga; subsequently the two men exchange words, Lensky becoming increasingly heated until he loses his self-control and denounces Onegin. The guests have to separate them. Lensky rushes out, bidding farewell for ever to Olga, who faints. Scene 2: Next morning on a riverbank Lensky and his second, Zaretsky, are awaiting Onegin. Lensky sings of his love for Olga. Onegin arrives late, bringing his valet, Guillot, as his second. Lensky and Onegin reflect separately on the situation in which they are caught. Preparations for the duel are completed; Onegin fires, and Lensky falls dead. Onegin is horrified at what he has done.

Act III Scene 1: In a splendid St Petersburg mansion Onegin is watching other guests dance a polonaise. After the duel he had left the area and some years have passed, but he remains troubled by what he has done, and bored with the society he finds himself in. An *écossaise* is danced; the arrival of Princess Gremina is announced. When she enters, on her elderly husband's arm, Onegin recognizes Tatyana. Prince Gremin tells Onegin of his love for Tatyana, then introduces his wife to him. Tatyana cuts short the meeting by pleading fatigue, and she and Gremin leave. Onegin confesses his love for Tatyana and leaves as the *écossaise* is resumed. Scene 2: The last encounter between Onegin and Tatyana takes place at her home. She enters distraught, holding the most recent of his letters. Onegin rushes in and falls on his knees. She reminds him how he had rejected her, and asks bitterly whether it is her new status that has induced Onegin to lay siege to her now. She reflects how close happiness had once been for both of them, but says firmly she will remain faithful to her husband. Telling Onegin to go, she confesses she still loves him. He embraces her, but she orders him out. In despair he leaves.

Pushkin's verse novel had concerned itself with the clash between the decadent mores of an opulent St Petersburg society and the simple, wholesome ways of a rural family. However, though the dance scenes (the rural 'hop' of Tatyana's name-day party with its boisterous, unsophisticated dances, and the ballroom scene with its grand polonaise) define this social divide, Tchaikovsky's attention was focused implacably on the pain and suffering endured by individuals whose relationships are twisted or destroyed by the differences of these worlds. The opera's greatest riches lie not in these two tableaux nor in the slightly rambling first scene which establishes both the base for later events and, in the peasant choruses, the thoroughly Russian milieu, but in the intimate encounters of the remaining four scenes, where Tchaikovsky realizes with supreme sensitivity the inner worlds of his characters.

Though Lensky is simply a country squire who has been to university, and his music has at first no more than youthful freshness, when he is about to face Onegin's pistol a depth of pain is revealed that is deeply affecting. Much of Onegin himself remains concealed behind a mask of aloof sophistication until the belated awakening of his love for Tatyana suddenly exposes his helplessness when he becomes the victim of an irrepressible and truthful emotion. Tatyana's transformation, from the ingenuous but deeply serious adolescent of her great letter scene into the mature yet desperately unhappy woman who finally dismisses the man she loves, is disclosed with supreme mastery. The creation of Tatyana is the greatest single achievement of all Tchaikovsky's operas.

Nor should his deft handling of lesser roles be overlooked; the old nurse, Filippevna, the adoring husband, Gremin, and the 'very insipid' (Tchaikovsky's own words) Olga are all very clearly projected.

Mazepa

Mazepa

Opera in three acts (six scenes) (2h 45m)
Libretto by the composer and Viktor Burenin, after the epic
poem *Poltava* by Aleksandr Pushkin (1829)
Composed summer 1881–April 1883, rev. 1885
PREMIERES 15 February 1884, Bolshoi Theatre, Moscow;
UK: 6 August 1888, Liverpool; US: 14 December 1922,
Boston Opera House
CAST Mazepa *bar*, Kochubei *b*, Lyubov Kochubei *ms*,
Mariya *s*, Andrei *t*, Orlik *b*, Iskra *t*, Drunken Cossack *t*;
satb chorus of young girls, Cossacks, guests, Kochubei's
servants, Mazepa's bodyguards, monks, executioners

In 1709 the bid of the Cossack hetman Mazepa to
gain Ukrainian independence from Russia ended in
the defeat of himself and Charles XII of Sweden by
Peter the Great at Poltava. This was one theme of
Pushkin's *Poltava*; the other was the romantic relationship, also based on fact, of the elderly Mazepa with
his own goddaughter, Mariya (Mazepa's apocryphal
ride bound to a wild horse is ignored by Pushkin,
though it conditioned part of Tchaikovsky's orchestral
introduction). Viktor Burenin's libretto, drawn from
Pushkin's epic poem, had been prepared for Karl
Davidov, but he had made little progress and in 1881
Tchaikovsky asked Davidov to assign it to him. Over
the next year he composed a few numbers, but systematic composition did not begin until an enforced
seven-week stay on a friend's country estate in the
summer of 1882. The sketches were completed in late
September, but because of the extra attention Tchaikovsky had been giving to the special problems of scoring
for the opera house this operation was protracted,
and it was April the following year before the opera
was ready. By now Tchaikovsky's reputation in his
native Russia was such that the Imperial Theatres in
both Russia's leading cities competed for the piece,
and it opened in St Petersburg only three days after
its Moscow premiere. In both productions the staging
was excellent, the performance at least adequate, and
the opera enjoyed some success. But, though it was
also produced in Tiflis (Tbilisi) in 1885, *Mazepa* failed
to secure a place in the repertoire.

SYNOPSIS

Act I Scene 1: Mariya, Kochubei's daughter, is in
love with Mazepa and gently rejects the advances of
Andrei. Meanwhile Kochubei is entertaining Mazepa,
who asks for Mariya's hand. Kochubei is horrified
because of their difference in age, but Mazepa protests
his love – and he knows Mariya shares his feelings. A
quarrel grows. Mariya agonizes over the choice she
will have to make between her parents and her beloved. But when finally Mazepa demands she choose,
in terrible agitation she leaves with him. Scene 2:
Lyubov, Mariya's mother, exhorts her husband to
move directly against Mazepa, but Kochubei has a
better plan. Mazepa has confided to him his scheme
to join the Swedish king against Peter the Great in the
cause of Ukrainian independence; now Kochubei will
inform the tsar. Andrei begs to be sent as messenger,
despite all the risks. All join in a chorus of hate
against Mazepa.

Act II Scene 1: In a dungeon beneath Mazepa's
castle, Kochubei is chained to the wall. The tsar has
not believed his accusations against Mazepa, and has
delivered him and his associate, Iskra, into Mazepa's
hands. He is to be executed the next day. Mazepa's
henchman, Orlik, enters to interrogate him further,
for he has not disclosed where his secret treasure is.
Bitterly Kochubei tells Orlik to ask Mariya; she will
show him everything. Orlik summons the torturer.
Scene 2: In the castle, Mazepa is comparing the calm
of the night with the turmoil within his own soul.
Kochubei must die – but how will Mariya react when
she discovers all that has happened? Orlik enters to
tell him Kochubei will not give way, and Mazepa
confirms the execution. Mariya appears and reproaches him for being so preoccupied. Pressed by
her, he reveals his plans for a free Ukraine; soon, he
says, he could occupy a throne. Mariya is excited at
the prospect and vows she will die with him if necessary. He then asks how she would act if required to
choose between her husband and her father. Totally
ignorant of her father's plight, she affirms her choice
would be for Mazepa. Mazepa leaves, deeply troubled.
Lyubov quietly slips in. When she realizes her daughter knows nothing of what has happened, she discloses
the situation. As the appalling truth dawns upon
Mariya a march is heard offstage; the execution is
already beginning. The two women rush out to try to
prevent it. Scene 3: At the place of execution a crowd
has gathered; a drunken Cossack is reproved for untimely merriment. The execution procession enters.
Kochubei and Iskra kneel to pray, then mount the
scaffold. The people crowd round, and the axes fall as
Mariya and Lyubov rush in.
Act III The Battle of Poltava (depicted in a symphonic tableau using the well-known 'Slava' folktune)
has been fought. Andrei enters the ruined garden of
Kochubei's house. He had been searching for Mazepa;
now, painfully, he recognizes where he is. Mazepa and
Orlik enter as fugitives, and Andrei confronts Mazepa,
but is fatally wounded. Mariya, now demented,
emerges into the moonlight. There follows a mad
scene. Finally Orlik persuades Mazepa to leave without her. Mariya perceives the dying Andrei, thinks
he is a child, and, cradling his head in her lap, sings
him to sleep, staring blankly in front of her.

Though uneven and unashamedly melodramatic,
Mazepa is one of Tchaikovsky's best operas. As in the
Pushkin-based *Eugene Onegin*, its finest passages are
those which focus on the predicaments and feelings of
one or two characters; like Tatyana and Onegin in the
earlier opera, Mariya and Mazepa are seen as victims
of fate. Especially impressive is the dungeon scene at
the opening of Act II, virtually a grim monologue for
Kochubei which drew from Tchaikovsky some of the
darkest music he ever wrote. In complete contrast,
Mazepa's musings on the night and his love aria in
the next scene are remarkably beautiful, while the
ensuing love duet is tender, yet reveals much of the
other emotions that affect the spirited Mariya and
tormented Mazepa. The following encounter between
Mariya and her mother is also admirably handled.
Though the first scene sprawls, the full choral sections

in this and the following scene being no more than efficiently conventional, the execution scene is splendidly taut and as fine as any of Tchaikovsky's crowd scenes (its first part, using two folksongs and labelled 'folk scene', is self-consciously national in flavour). The characters of Kochubei and Lyubov are well projected, but, as in *Onegin*, it is the young tragic heroine who most engaged Tchaikovsky's creative sympathies, while Mazepa fades in interest. The final mad scene for Mariya is deeply affecting. The opera had originally concluded with Mariya's suicide and a crowded stage, but for the 1885 revival Tchaikovsky cut this, extending Mariya's lullaby instead. It is an ending whose pathos is absolutely right.

The Queen of Spades

Pikovaya dama

Opera in three acts (seven scenes) (2h 45m)

Libretto by Modest Tchaikovsky and the composer, after the novel by Aleksandr Pushkin (1834); with incorporations from Pyotr Karabanov (the pastoral interlude in Scene 3), Vasily Zhukovsky and Konstantin Batyushkov

Composed January–June 1890

PREMIERES 19 December 1890, Mariinsky Theatre, St Petersburg; US: 5 March 1910, Metropolitan, New York; UK: 29 May 1915, London Opera House, London

CAST Herman *t*, Count Tomsky (also Zlatogor) *bar*, Prince Eletsky *bar*, Chekalinsky *t*, Surin *b*, Chaplitsky *t*, Narumov *b*, Master-of-ceremonies *t*, The Countess *ms*, Liza *s*, Polina (also Milovzor) *c*, Governess *ms*, Masha *s*, Prilepa *s*, Child Commander *spoken role*; *satb* chorus of nurses and governesses, boys, promenaders, girls, guests and gamblers; offstage: church choir

Pushkin's ironic yet chilling short novel *The Queen of Spades* is a masterpiece of clarity and conciseness, and an almost ideal basis for a libretto. In fact, Tchaikovsky had disclaimed any interest in the subject when in 1887 his brother, Modest, had started drawing from it a libretto for Nikolai Klenovsky. But Modest had turned the piece into a romantic melodrama, and in the autumn of 1889, after Klenovsky had made little or no progress, Tchaikovsky himself was attracted to it. Because it was hoped to produce the opera during the following season, in January 1890 he settled in Florence, where he could work undisturbed; the only problem was delays occasioned by Modest, who was completing the libretto back in Russia. The sketches were finished on 15 March and the scoring was begun in Rome on 9 April. So close was Tchaikovsky's identification with his central character, Herman, that he confessed he had wept while composing his death scene, and he was pleased with his friends' enthusiasm when he played the opera through to some of them on his return to Russia. Even more was he delighted with the response of Nikolai Figner, then the darling of the St Petersburg operatic public, who was to create the role of Herman. The premiere was splendidly mounted and performed, and was highly successful, though critical reaction was less approving, and the pregnancy of Medea Figner, Nikolai's wife, who created the part of Liza, meant the opera was suspended from the repertoire two months later.

The Queen of Spades was first produced in Kiev only 12 days after the St Petersburg premiere, and in Moscow on 16 November 1891. By this time critical reaction was becoming more favourable; in 1892 it was mounted in Odessa and Saratov and also in Prague.

SYNOPSIS

The opera is set in St Petersburg in the late 18th century.

Act I Scene 1: In the Summer Garden, while others stroll and children play at soldiers, Chekalinsky, a gambler, and Surin, an officer, discuss Herman; this officer of German extraction obsessively watches others gamble, but will not join in. To a third officer, Tomsky, Herman confesses he is in love, though he does not know the lady's name. Eletsky is congratulated by Chekalinsky and Surin on his engagement. Asked who his fiancée is, the prince points to Liza, who has just entered with her grandmother, the old countess. Herman is in despair, for Liza is his secret beloved. Tomsky tells how in her youth in Paris the old countess had lost heavily at cards. To restore her fortune a count Saint Germain, at the price of a 'rendezvous', had given her the secret of three cards that would always win. She had confided the secret to her husband and one of her lovers, but then a ghost had appeared to her, telling her she would die at the hand of a third man who would come as a lover to wring it from her. Herman rejects the temptation this offers. He vows Eletsky shall never have Liza. Scene 2: In her room, Liza and her friend Polina are entertaining some other girls. Liza, however, is very preoccupied. The others try to raise her spirits, but the governess bustles in to reprove them for unbecoming merriment. Left alone, Liza reflects on her secret obsession. And suddenly that obsession is standing before her: Herman has entered through the balcony's open door. Liza is confused, but Herman begins to plead with her. He is interrupted when the countess is heard outside, and he hides. The old woman wants to know why Liza is still dressed; she orders her to bed, then leaves. Herman emerges muttering the ghost's words, then resumes his declaration of love. Liza finally yields.

Act II Scene 1: In a great hall a masked ball is in progress. After the others have withdrawn while the room is prepared for the interlude, Eletsky asks Liza why she is out of spirits, and reaffirms his love. Herman enters carrying a letter from Liza: he is to meet her after the interlude. The guests are invited to witness the story of Prilepa and her rival lovers, the poor Milovzor and the wealthy Zlatogor. When this pastoral interlude is over, Liza slips Herman a key; next day he is to come to her room, where everything will be settled. But Herman insists he will come that night. The master of ceremonies suddenly announces the empress herself is approaching. All line up to receive her. Scene 2: Herman surveys the countess's empty bedroom. Midnight strikes. On hearing footsteps he hides. The countess's maids lead their mistress through into her dressing room, and Liza passes on to her own room. Prepared for bed, the old woman chooses to sit in a chair, muses to herself, then dismisses her maids. Herman emerges and tries to persuade her to reveal her secret, then draws a pistol and threatens her. She dies of fright. Liza returns from her room, and realizes how Herman has been using her. Desperately hurt and enraged, she dismisses him.

Act III Scene 1: In his room, to the distant sounds of trumpet calls and a church choir, Herman recalls with horror how he had gone to gaze on the countess's body in her open coffin – and how the corpse had winked at him. Suddenly there is a noise outside, and the countess's ghost enters. She has come to give him the secret of the three cards: 'Three . . . seven . . . ace!' Scene 2: Liza, still in love with Herman, has begged him to meet her beside the Winter Canal at midnight. Finally he appears, and they sing of their mutual love. But, when she asks him to leave with her, he wants only to go to the gambling table. She realizes that he no longer recognizes her, and throws herself into the canal. Scene 3: In a gambling house, Eletsky has joined the others. Tomsky entertains the company with a song, and, as play resumes, Herman appears, announcing he wants to play for a very high stake. Choosing three, he wins, then stakes his winnings. Playing on seven, he wins again. When he insists on playing a third time, Eletsky demands to play against him. Herman stakes on ace, but when he picks up his card it is the queen of spades – and the countess's ghost passes across the stage, smiling. Herman stabs himself, and begs Eletsky's forgiveness. The male chorus prays for the peace of his soul.

Tchaikovsky himself invented the sixth (Winter Canal) scene of The Queen of Spades, arguing that the audience would need to know what had happened to Liza. In fact, his decision was also a measure of how completely Modest's libretto had transformed Pushkin's objectively observed characters into hot-blooded mortals. Pushkin had been able to let Liza slip away almost casually, but the opera's audience was bound to identify closely with her and demand to know her destiny. There can be no doubt that it was this 'humanizing' of Pushkin's tale that made it attractive to Tchaikovsky.

The opera uniquely reverses Tchaikovsky's normal preference, for this time it was Herman, a male character, who gripped him. Nor among the female characters was his chief fascination with the young doomed woman, but rather with the aged and totally unsympathetic countess, whose presence, because she is not only a victim but also the agent of fate (for by her own death she achieves fate's purpose), looms over them all. The work is also unique for its extreme stylistic dichotomy, for it incorporates a very large element of rococo pastiche (there are even two substantial quotations from other composers – the aria the countess sings to herself in Act II from André Grétry's Richard Coeur-de-lion (1784), and a polonaise by Jósef Kozlowski (1791) to end the ballroom scene) – which contrasts savagely with the dark, mysterious, sometimes sinister music to which the tragic destinies of the three main characters run their course. Even more, perhaps, than in Eugene Onegin it is the more intimate scenes that make this opera memorable, especially the scene in the countess's bedroom; only the dungeon scene in Mazepa can match this for its harrowing

intensity. But that had had a single dramatic concern – the suffering of Kochubei. This one manifests a complete mastery in projecting a changing dramatic and psychological situation. If Tatyana's letter scene in Eugene Onegin is the most moving scene in all Tchaikovsky's operas, this one is the most totally gripping.

Iolanta

Lyric opera in one act (1h 30m)
Libretto by Modest Tchaikovsky, after the translation by Vladimir Zotov of the play Kong Renés datter (King René's Daughter) by Henrik Hertz (1864)
Composed July–December 1891
PREMIERES 18 December 1892, Mariinsky Theatre, St Petersburg; US: 10 September 1933, Garden Theater, Scarborough-on-Hudson; UK: 20 March 1968, St Pancras Town Hall, London
CAST King René of Provence b, Robert bar, Vaudemont t, Ebn-Hakir bar, Iolanta s, s, ms, c, t, b; satb chorus of Iolanta's friends and attendants, the king's entourage, Robert's followers

Tchaikovsky had first read Hertz's one-act play in 1883, but his decision that he would at some time make an opera out of it seems to date from five years later, when he saw it staged. Then in 1890 the Imperial Theatres commissioned a two-act ballet (Nutcracker) and a one-act opera to make a double-bill. Having first sketched the ballet, he initially felt some ambivalence when he set about Iolanta, though subsequently he warmed to it. As in The Queen of Spades, the Figners were to sing leading roles, and by now it was certain that the premiere would be at least a succès d'estime. But the press bluntly judged the music weak, mauled Modest's libretto, and the double-bill survived only 11 performances. However, the first foreign production of Iolanta by itself (in Hamburg) opened only 16 days after the Russian premiere, and the work has enjoyed some success abroad.

SYNOPSIS

In 15th-century Provence, Iolanta, the daughter of King René, is blind, but does not know she is different from other people. Her attendants are forbidden to mention light, nor is any outsider to enter the garden on pain of death. Iolanta is betrothed to Robert, duke of Burgundy, and by keeping her from the outside world her father has hoped to hide her disability from him until she is cured. A great Moorish physician, Ebn-Hakir, examines her, but tells René a cure is possible only if his daughter longs to see the light – and for this to happen she must be told of her blindness. Robert arrives with his friend Vaudemont, a Burgundian knight. Robert loves another, but when Vaudemont sees Iolanta he is entranced by her. When she is unable to tell red roses from white, he realizes the truth – and Iolanta is now also aware she is not as others are. 'What is light?' she asks. 'The creator's first gift to his world,' Vaudemont replies. When René returns he is appalled, but Ebn-Hakir perceives that the condition for a cure now exists. Suddenly René himself sees how he can rouse his daughter's will to see; Vaudemont has entered the garden without permission, and if Iolanta is not cured he will die, the king declares. At this Iolanta goes off with Ebn-Hakir. When she returns she can see; meanwhile Robert has admitted that his affections really lie elsewhere, and Vaudemont is discovered to be a suitable match for Iolanta. All rejoice.

The refinement and craft displayed in *Iolanta* are very high; its prime weakness lies in the quality of its musical materials. Yet it is not a work that should be lightly rejected. Only one of Tchaikovsky's previous operas (*The Enchantress*, 1887) had been concerned with something more than human drama, and *Iolanta* also has a message. In *The Enchantress* it had been 'love is the redeeming power'; in *Iolanta* it is 'love is the healing power'. Dramatically the fatal flaw of the latter is that Iolanta is not truly driven by an ideal but by the fright her father gives her, while musically Tchaikovsky failed to catch the transcendent tone of this message. He is more successful with the human elements in the story, and his portrayal of the king and Ebn-Hakir is good. But it is Iolanta – yet another of his young, vulnerable heroines – who really captured his creative heart. As in his five previous operas, the scene with which he had started composition drew the best music from him, and the love duet contains the opera's best – sometimes excellent – music.

Other operas: *The Voyevoda* (*Voyevoda*), 1869; *Undine* (*Undina*), (1869); *The Oprichnik* (*Oprichnik*), 1874; *The Maid of Orleans* (*Orleanskaya Dyeva*), 1881, rev. 1882; *The Enchantress* (*Charodeika*), 1887

D.B.

AMBROISE THOMAS

Charles Louis Ambroise Thomas; *b* 5 August 1811, Metz, France; *d* 12 February 1896, Paris

The career of Ambroise Thomas mingled success and failure to a remarkable degree over a long period of time. His fame as an opera composer and his status as an Establishment figure, apparently unassailable, were not proof against reaction, neglect and indifference lasting long after his death. A Conservatoire pupil of Jean-François Le Sueur, Thomas won the Prix de Rome in 1832. A series of mainly comic operas, including notably *Le Caïd*, *Le songe d'une nuit d'été* (not after Shakespeare but about him) and *Psyché*, was followed by a pause before the resounding achievements of *Mignon* and *Hamlet*. Those triumphs were not repeated. After becoming director of the Conservatoire in 1871, Thomas wrote only one major opera, *Françoise de Rimini*. Years later, in honour of the 1000th performance of *Mignon* in 1894, Thomas became the first composer to receive the Grand Cross of the Légion d'Honneur. By then, while the public stayed faithful to *Mignon* and *Hamlet*, his reputation, whether with Wagnerites and Debussyists or the merely fashionable, was extinguished. Chabrier's remark about 'three kinds of music – good, bad and Ambroise Thomas' contains a gleam of truth. He was more follower than originator. There is in

Thomas a deeper vein of lyrical sentiment than can be found in the comic operas of the first half of the century, but he did little to expand the genre. Gounod, Saint-Saëns and Bizet had more personal styles, yet Thomas possessed an amount of skill in writing opera from which they and others after them profited. His melodic gift went with a kind of inspired ordinariness to the heart of the public. For that he was not quickly forgiven.

Mignon

Opéra comique in three acts (five tableaux) (3h)
Libretto by Michel Carré & Jules Barbier after the novel *Wilhelm Meisters Lehrjahre* by Johann Wolfgang von Goethe (1796)
PREMIERES 17 November 1866, Opéra-Comique, Paris; UK: 5 July 1870, Drury Lane, London; US: 9 May 1871, French Opera House, New Orleans
CAST Mignon *ms*, Philine *s*, Wilhelm *t*, Lothario *b* or *bar*, Laërte *t*, Frédérick *t* or *ms*, *b*, *spoken role*; *satb* chorus of gypsies, peasants, comedians, guests

The sequence of events is taken from the parts of Goethe's novel dealing with Wilhelm Meister and the old harper, the girl Mignon and the actress Philine. Except for the title role, characterization is rudimentary, but something remains of the atmosphere of theatrical vagabondage in the 18th century. Thomas, whose early good fortune at the Opéra-Comique had declined, waited some years before producing *Mignon* and was surprised by the warm welcome it received. The popularity of the work, with singers as well as the public, never entirely faded even when the composer's reputation was at a low ebb. From the first interpreter, Célestine Galli-Marié, onwards mezzo-sopranos have been understandably attracted to the role of Mignon.

SYNOPSIS
Act I Wilhelm, a student, and the half-crazy Lothario, searching for his long-lost daughter, rescue a shy young girl called Mignon from a band of gypsies. They are observed by Philine and Laërte, strolling players. Mignon sings of her childhood in a land of golden memories. Philine's interest in Wilhelm arouses Mignon's jealousy. Wilhelm buys Mignon's liberty and offers his protection.

Act II The players are invited to perform in the theatre of Rosenberg Castle. Frédérick, nephew of the owner and in love with Philine, quarrels with Wilhelm. Mignon changes from servant boy's clothes into theatrical costume. Wilhelm is struck by her beauty. Meanwhile, in the palace theatre a play is being given. When it is over, Philine celebrates her triumph in the role of Titania. She asks Mignon to fetch her a bouquet from the theatre. Laërte brings news that the theatre is in flames. Wilhelm rushes out and returns carrying Mignon.

Act III In an Italian country palazzo Lothario prays for Mignon's recovery. A servant tells Wilhelm the family history: the owner, Marquis Cypriani, left Italy after his wife died, believing their small daughter to have drowned. The name Cypriani stirs something in Lothario's mind. Wilhelm, now aware that he loves Mignon, hopes for a word from her. She comes in as if in a dream – she feels she has known the palace and its grounds before. Wilhelm assures her that her past sorrows are over. Their mutual confession of love is interrupted by the distant voice of Philine, reawakening Mignon's fears. Lothario, now richly clad, brings them a casket full of childish mementoes which Mignon recognizes. Lothario explains that he is the Marquis Cypriani and that Mignon is Sperata, his daughter, not drowned but abducted. Philine, volatile but kind-hearted, offers the hand of friendship. She will bestow herself on the delighted Frédérick: Wilhelm is free. General rejoicing.

For London, Thomas made a shorter, alternative conclusion. Philine is heard but not seen, Mignon faints but recovers and is joined in a final trio of thanksgiving by Wilhelm and Lothario. For German audiences who might disapprove of the happy ending, Thomas provided a further alternative in which the reappearance of Philine causes a mortal shock to Mignon. Like *Faust* and *Carmen*, *Mignon* was written as an opéra comique with spoken dialogue. Also for London, Thomas substituted recitatives (in Italian) and made other alterations and additions. Frédérick was promoted from a *trial* tenor to a *travesti* mezzo. The additions, which include a sung version of the Act II gavotte interlude for Frédérick, are a bonus; the recitatives are not.

Hamlet

Opera in five acts (seven tableaux) (2h 45m)
Libretto by Michel Carré and Jules Barbier after the play by William Shakespeare (1600–1601)
PREMIERES 9 March 1868, Opéra, Paris; UK: 19 June 1869, Covent Garden, London; US: 22 March 1872, Academy of Music, New York
CAST Hamlet *bar*, Claudius *b*, Gertrude *ms*, Ophélie (Ophelia) *s*, Laërte (Laertes) *t*, The Ghost *b*, 2 *t*, 3 *b*; *satb* chorus of courtiers, soldiers, players, peasants

Expectations of the poetic and philosophical richness and dramatic scope of Shakespeare must be disappointed by Carré's and Barbier's drastic but ingenious reduction, from which familiar characters and incidents are omitted. Thomas's *Hamlet* obeys the laws not of Elizabethan tragedy but of French 19th-century opera. In many ways it is a model of its kind, combining powerful drama (the scene on the battlements and the confrontation between Hamlet and his mother) with more conventionally conceived episodes. Ophelia's mad scene may be 'floridly inconsequential' by later standards, but it is an effective and affecting example of the genre. The first interpreters of Hamlet and Ophelia, Jean-Baptiste Faure and Christine Nilsson, had many distinguished successors. *Hamlet*, the composer's single great success at the Opéra, remained in the repertoire until 1938: it has recently been revived in Buxton, New York and Sydney.

SYNOPSIS

Act I Elsinore (Denmark). Prince Hamlet is shocked by the unseemly haste of the marriage, just celebrated, of his mother Gertrude, widow of the late king, to his brother and successor, Claudius. Hamlet affirms his love for Ophelia, whom her brother Laërtes, about to leave for Norway, entrusts to Hamlet's care. Hamlet learns that his father's ghost has been seen. On the battlements, the ghost appears to Hamlet and reveals that he was murdered by Claudius. Hamlet swears vengeance.

Act II Hamlet's strange behaviour alarms Ophelia. Gertrude tries to comfort her. Hamlet has invited strolling players to entertain the court. He instructs them to perform a play about the murder of a king. Hamlet and the players carouse together. During the performance Claudius rises in confusion. In a frenzy, Hamlet snatches the crown.

Act III Hamlet broods over his inability to take action. He overhears the prayers of the guilt-stricken Claudius. Gertrude implores Hamlet to marry Ophelia, but he cruelly rejects her. Ophelia returns his ring. Hamlet forces his mother to consider the portraits of her two husbands and reveals that he knows the truth. The ghost materializes, urging Hamlet to slay Claudius but spare Gertrude.

Act IV Peasants dancing by a lake are joined by Ophelia, her reason gone, distributing flowers from a garland. After singing a melancholy ballad, she subsides gently into the water.

Act V Hamlet muses in the cemetery on Ophelia's madness. He is still unaware of her death: the gravediggers do not know whose grave they are preparing. Laertes, returned from his journey, reproaches Hamlet. As they prepare to fight, a procession appears, headed by Claudius and Gertrude, with Ophelia's bier. Hamlet is commanded by the ghost to kill Claudius forthwith and assume the crown. Hamlet does his bidding and is acclaimed king.

For English audiences the original ending, which follows a French version of Shakespeare by Dumas *père* and Paul Maurice, was revised for Covent Garden. The ghost does not return: Hamlet kills Claudius and then kills himself. Richard Bonynge devised a compromise for Sydney (1982) in which Hamlet, mortally wounded by Laertes, is reminded by the ghost of his vow, kills Claudius and dies on Ophelia's body.

Other operas: *La double échelle*, 1837; *Le perruquier de la Régence*, 1838; *Le panier fleuri*, 1839; *Carline*, 1840; *Le comte de Carmagnola*, 1841; *Le guerrillero*, 1842; *Angélique et Médor*, 1843; *Mina*, 1843; *Le caïd*, 1849; *Le songe d'une nuit d'été*, 1850; *Raymond*, 1851; *La Tonelli*, 1853; *La cour de Célimène*, 1855; *Psyché*, 1857; *Le carnaval de Venise*, 1857; *Le roman d'Elvire*, 1860; *Gille et Gillotin*, (1859), 1874; *Françoise de Rimini*, 1882

R.H.C.

VIRGIL THOMSON

Virgil Garnett Thomson; *b* 25 November 1896, Kansas City, US; *d* 30 September 1989, New York

As both composer and critic, Virgil Thomson was one of the most original figures in 20th-century American music. His important contribution to opera resulted from his collaboration with Gertrude Stein (1874–1946), whose techniques of verbal abstraction Thomson was able to translate into music; *Four Saints in Three Acts* and *The Mother of Us All* have become classics of so-called 'non-narrative' opera.

Thomson's childhood gave him roots in an American vernacular – hymns, popular songs and parlour music – which is embedded in his compositions. When, after a period in the US army, he went to Harvard, he found a more cosmopolitan cultural context. One of his teachers, S. Foster Damon, introduced him to the writings of Stein and the music of Erik Satie. He learned about vocal music through assisting Archibald T. Davison at the Harvard Glee Club, and he joined their European tour in 1921. Thomson's link with Paris was inevitable: 'I came in my Harvard years to identify with France virtually all of music's recent glorious past, most of its acceptable present, and a large part of its future.' After 1923 Thomson spent most of his time in Paris until he became critic of the *New York Herald Tribune* in 1940. His voluminous writings have been influential – he had a rare gift for combining spontaneity and provocation; these qualities also inform his music. Though he studied with Nadia Boulanger, he remained independent of both neo-classicism and serialism. The straightforwardness of his music was controversial; as Thomson wrote in *The State of Music* (1939), 'When we made music that was simple, melodic and harmonious, the fury of the vested interests of modernism flared up like a gas-tank . . . I am considered a graceless whelp, a frivolous mountebank, an unfair competitor, and a dangerous character.'

Thomson's first Stein setting was a song with piano, 'Susie Asado' (1926). After he met Stein, in 1926, their collaboration developed, and *Capital Capitals* (1928) for four male voices and piano is confidently written in the style of the first opera, *Four Saints in Three Acts*.

Four Saints in Three Acts

Opera in four (sic) acts with prologue (1h 30m)
Libretto by Gertrude Stein
Composed 1927–8, orch. 1933
PREMIERES   20 May 1933, Ann Arbor (concert);
8 February 1934, Avery Memorial Theater, Hartford,
Connecticut; France: May 1952, Théâtre des Champs-
Élysées, Paris; UK: 27 April 1983, Almeida Theatre,
London (semi-staged)

In his first opera Thomson set out to achieve the 'discipline of spontaneity' which he had recognized in the writings of Stein. His working method was to put the text on the piano and improvise, singing and playing. He did this for several days, and only when he began to repeat himself did he know it was finished. He then wrote it down. Thomson wondered 'whether a piece so drenched in Anglican chant (running from Gilbert and Sullivan to Morning Prayer and back) could rise and sail'. Private performances in Paris convinced him that it could long before he orchestrated *Four Saints* for the Hartford production.

Thomson pointed out that *Four Saints* made theatrical history in several ways: it had an all-black cast (a year before Gershwin's *Porgy and Bess*); it was choreographed by the young Frederick Ashton and John

Houseman, and the Cellophane sets were by Florine Stettheimer; also, it ran for 60 performances on Broadway following the Hartford opening.

Since *Four Saints* is not a conventional narrative opera, there can be no description of the plot. Thomson set everything Stein provided, even the stage directions where the scenes are not even numbered in consecutive order. This all adds to the sense of fun and to the opportunities for production. The scenario, written after the completion of both text and music, is the work of Maurice Grosser, the original producer, who calls *Four Saints* 'both an opera and a choreographic spectacle'. The setting is 16th-century Spain and the principal characters are St Teresa of Avila, St Ignatius Loyola and their confidants, St Settlement and St Chavez (there are 16 named saints in all, again contradicting the title). A compère and a commère comment on the action with studied illogicality. St Teresa is represented by two singers dressed alike. Stein intended St Ignatius' aria 'Pigeons on the Grass Alas' to reflect a vision of the Holy Ghost and specified a procession at the end of Act III, but otherwise, as Grosser put it, 'One should not try to interpret too literally the words of this opera, nor should one fall into the opposite error of thinking that they mean nothing at all.'

Despite its initial reception, *Four Saints* has rarely been professionally staged – it offers few opportunities for vocal display. Thomson set Stein's surrealist text in a manner that defies stylistic categorization: extended monophonic linear passages are juxtaposed with quotations from religious music of all periods and references to nursery rhymes.

The Mother of Us All

Opera in two acts (1h 45m)
Libretto by Gertrude Stein
PREMIERES   7 May 1947, Brander Matthews Hall,
Columbia University, New York; UK: 26 June 1979,
Kensington Town Hall, London

After the Second World War, Thomson returned to Paris to discuss a new opera with Stein. When Thomson suggested a subject from 19th-century American political life she proposed Susan B. Anthony, the pioneer of women's rights, and immediately began research. The libretto was the last thing she wrote.

Thomson's working method was similar to that employed in *Four Saints*, but this time he had to move faster: the premiere took place seven months after he began work. The cast, of students and young professionals, was directed by two composers – Jack Beeson, as répétiteur, and Otto Luening, as conductor. *The Mother of Us All* was well received, although some disadvantages were evident in the student cast and orchestra. However, the work's future lay mostly in such university settings – in the last 30 years *The Mother* has been given over 1000 times in some 200 productions.

The Mother of Us All is based on the winning of votes for women in the US through the activities of Susan B. Anthony (1820–1906). The action, as well as the music, is more continuous than that of *Four Saints*, something Thomson may have learned from his film writing. Thomson once described the score as a 'musical memory' book, referring to his inclusion of 19th-century American ballads, hymns, songs and marches. Stein's licence with time brings together characters who could never have met; the cast also includes the composer and librettist themselves as narrators. A plot is hardly discernible, but in Act I there are political meetings where men in various responsible positions obstruct the progress of Susan B. Anthony's reforming zeal. Sub-plots, such as the relationship between Jo the Loiterer and Indiana Elliot, are used to attack the institution of marriage from the woman's point of view. In Act II the struggle continues – the word 'male' is inserted into the American constitution to hold up women's suffrage. In a moving epilogue a statue of Susan B. Anthony is unveiled in the Halls of Congress some years after her death, when her cause has been achieved. In her final aria, suffused with hymnody, her ghost haunts the scene wondering if the struggle was worth it: 'But do we want what we have got . . . I was a martyr all my life not to what I won but to what was done.'

Other opera: *Lord Byron*, 1972

P.D.

MICHAEL TIPPETT
(Sir) Michael Kemp Tippett; *b* 2 January 1905, London

Tippett was brought up in the Suffolk countryside and educated at first privately and then, from the age of nine, at various boarding schools. His father was a lawyer who became the proprietor of a hotel in the south of France, his mother a nurse who became a novelist and a suffragette. After the First World War his parents lived abroad, and from the age of 14 he had no real home, spending the holidays in those parts of southern Europe where his parents had temporarily settled. From this unusual and stimulating background, coloured not least by his parents' agnosticism, he gained a marked independence of outlook which was to stand him in good stead. He was expected to become a lawyer, but even at preparatory school he had decided to become a composer. Apart from piano lessons he had no formal training until he went to the Royal College of Music in London in 1923. From then on he developed not only a passionate interest in music of all kinds but also the patience to accept that his compositional apprenticeship would take a long time. He was 30 when he completed his first characteristic work, his First String Quartet (1934–5), before which he had returned to the RCM for a second period of study, this time with R. O. Morris.

During the 1930s Tippett experimented with opera composition in four unpublished stage works. While these reveal little evidence of his mature style, they none the less show how he had been testing his ability to apply operatic techniques. His concert music from 1935 until 1946, when he started composing his first opera, *The Midsummer Marriage*, likewise shows him experimenting within the other principal musical genres. He wrote a Second String Quartet, a First Sonata for Piano, his well-known Concerto for Double String Orchestra, his oratorio *A Child of Our Time* and his First Symphony. *The Midsummer Marriage*, completed in 1952, can be seen therefore as the culmination of an extended compositional programme.

This very deliberate approach to composition shows how important the acquisition of technical skill was to him at a time when, in his opinion, English music was suffering from a lack of it. His early works also reveal his attitude towards the force of tradition. In this respect he was greatly influenced by the theoretical writings of T. S. Eliot. In 1937 Tippett met Eliot, who for a while became his 'spiritual and artistic mentor'. It was Eliot who advised him to write his own text for what became *A Child of Our Time*: having seen Tippett's draft he thought it was already a text in embryo, and that any 'poetry' he wrote would be obtrusive and impede the music. Eliot was thus largely responsible for Tippett's subsequent decision to write his own libretti. This has aroused criticism, though Tippett's operatic subject matter, as well as his writing style, is so individual that collaboration could only have resulted in damaging compromises.

Tippett's five operas offer a very distinctive interpretation of the nature of opera, in general proposing that the genre should explore deeper layers of human understanding than can be revealed though the interactions of a conventional plot. His characters may be sharply defined, but they tend towards the representational rather than the individual; while two of his operas, *King Priam* and *The Ice Break*, do have strong 'story lines', these are ultimately no less symbolic than the others. Tippett's prime justification for this approach is that, if dramatic music is poorly equipped to conduct narrative, it is peculiarly well equipped to give perceptible shape to the emotional feelings, forces, intuitions that prompt human behaviour. It follows that opera might also have a socially therapeutic role to play, in enabling its listeners to discover more about their own psychology.

Tippett's commitment to this idea took root in 1938, when, as a result of the break-up of a tumultuous love affair and of problems with his homosexuality, as well as his disillusionment at the menacing political situation in Europe, he undertook a course of Jungian self-analysis. The result of this was not only that he felt better balanced as a person but also that he drew back from his involvement in the left-wing politics of the 1930s (when he had been a Trotskyist sympathizer) and devoted himself to his fundamental vocation as composer. The work in which his new-found attitude is most explicit is *A Child of Our Time*, in which he first showed his readiness to address in music large and seemingly intractable problems – in that case man's inhumanity to man. What gave him the confidence to do so – and also to become a pacifist and a conscientious objector during the Second World War (he was imprisoned in 1943 for refusing to comply with the conditions imposed by a tribunal) – was his Jungian understanding of the 'shadow' and 'light', reflected in the text of the penultimate section of the oratorio: 'I would know my shadow and my light,/so shall I at last be whole./Then courage, brother, dare the grave passage.' These lines enabled him to reach a characteristic affirmative, if in this case restrained, conclusion to the oratorio, even though it was written in wartime (1939–41). They provide the key to much of his subsequent output. *The Midsummer Marriage* is, in effect, a dramatization of them.

From 1940 until 1951 Tippett achieved prominence as director of music at Morley College, where his concert programmes proved to be the most adventurous heard in London during the war and for some years after. He then devoted himself almost entirely to composition.

Not until the 1960s did his music achieve proper recognition, having been frequently dismissed as the product of an impractical, if occasionally inspired, dilettante. This may be ascribed to the originality and complexity of his thought in general (as can also be seen in his published essays and his libretti), as well as to the fact that his musical language seemed to have been overtaken by post-war styles. But from the successful premiere of his second opera, *King Priam*, in 1962, and a BBC broadcast in 1963 of *The Midsummer Marriage*, a reassessment began, and it became apparent that here was a composer of international stature, a judgement reinforced by the inexhaustible invention of those major works that have flowed from his creativity ever since – symphonies, concertos, sonatas, quartets, not to mention operas, which remain at the core of his output.

The Midsummer Marriage

Opera in three acts (2h 30m)
Libretto by the composer
Composed 1946–52
PREMIERES   27 January 1955, Covent Garden, London; US: 15 October 1983, War Memorial Opera House, San Francisco
CAST Mark *t*, Jenifer *s*, King Fisher *bar*, Bella *s*, Jack *t*, Sosostris *c*, The Ancients *b, ms*, Strephon *dancer; satb* chorus of Mark's and Jenifer's friends; dancers

The first performance of *The Midsummer Marriage* has acquired legendary status. Conducted by John Pritchard, produced by Christopher West, with scenery and costumes by Barbara Hepworth and choreography by John Cranko, it also had a strong cast, including Joan Sutherland, Richard Lewis and Otakar Kraus. Yet most press notices were violently hostile, at least to the libretto. This was dismissed variously as meaningless, amateurish or absurdly self-indulgent: Tippett, cripplingly inexperienced as an opera composer, paying the price for an ill-considered pursuit of the vogue for British opera that had followed the success of Britten's *Peter Grimes* in 1945. *The Midsummer Marriage*'s music, however, had not failed to win its admirers, and after a second Covent Garden production in 1968, conducted by Colin Davis, the opera rapidly gained ground and entered the international repertoire.

The opera is closely related to Mozart's *Die Zauberflöte*, having two pairs of lovers, one more elevated than the other but both in quest of enlightenment. Further correspondences are less clear, for in essence

Tippett's libretto comprises a journey into the world of Jungian archetypes, a dreamlike, imaginative realm where a mythological ritual of sacrifice and rebirth can be enacted, and the hero and heroine undergo the experiences that enable them to understand their full selves and embark on a true marriage. As such, it sets out an abiding theme in Tippett's output, which is the power of music to overcome ignorance and illusion about the human psyche and so effect a better understanding of human relationships. In tone the opera is exuberant, lyrical and emphatically affirmative throughout, even though written during the austere post-war years. In this respect it can be seen as Tippett's compensating message of vitality and rejuvenation – against the general character of the period and of much of its music.

SYNOPSIS
Act I   Dawn on Midsummer's Day, the scene a clearing on a wooded hilltop. The chorus is arriving for the runaway marriage of Mark and Jenifer. They notice a strange temple, at the centre of which sounds strange music. They hide, as dancers, led by Strephon (Mark's *alter ego*) and followed by the Ancients, emerge. Mark interrupts their dance, demanding a new one for his wedding day. The Ancients order a repeat of the old dance, during which the He-Ancient trips Strephon, demonstrating that change can be destructive and painful. The dancers and Ancients return to the temple. Mark puts the whole episode aside, settling down to wait for Jenifer. When she arrives, she announces there will be no wedding: 'It isn't love I want, but truth.' Their quarrel is cut short when she notices a spiral staircase by the temple and makes her decision: 'For me, the light! for you, the shadow!' She climbs the staircase and disappears from sight. Distraught, Mark plunges into a hillside cave. As its gates close, King Fisher, a businessman, with Bella his secretary, arrives in pursuit of his absconding daughter, Jenifer. He agrees to Bella's suggestion that Jack, her boyfriend, who is a mechanic, should be asked to help open the gates. King Fisher bribes the men of the chorus to search for Mark. The women are not to be bought off. Jack's first attempt to open the gates fails, and with King Fisher and then with Bella he prepares for a second attempt. As he raises his hammer, a warning voice (Sosostris) tells King Fisher not to interfere. At the height of his frustration, Jenifer is revealed at the top of the staircase, then Mark at the mouth of the cave. The Ancients appear, with the dancers, to announce a contest: the two will sing of their experiences. Jenifer sings of the spiritual purity of hers, Mark of the bodily abandon of his. Jenifer, convinced of her moral superiority, holds up a mirror to Mark so he can see the beast he has become. But his gaze shatters her mirror, and she now enters the cave to seek what has given him such power. In turn Mark decides to share Jenifer's experience, and, while King Fisher is left nonplussed, the chorus happily leaves spiritual journeys to Mark and Jenifer.

Act II   Afternoon. Strephon at the temple, listening. He is frightened by distant voices and hides. Among the voices are Jack and Bella. It being Midsummer's Day, Bella proposes to Jack, and the two sing about their future life together. Three ritual dances follow, in which Strephon in various transformations is pursued by a female dancer similarly transformed. In the first (*The Earth in Autumn*) Strephon is a hare, hunted by a hound; he escapes. In the second (*The Waters in Winter*) he is a fish, is nearly caught by an otter, and is injured. In the third (*The Air in Spring*) he is a bird with a broken wing and cannot escape the swooping hawk. At this point Bella cries out in terror, not knowing whether what she has seen is real or her own dreams. The dancers vanish. Jack comforts her and, her composure regained, she leaves with him, while the chorus is again heard singing behind the hill.

Act III Evening and night. The chorus is enjoying a party. King Fisher sends them away to collect Sosostris, his private clairvoyante, who will outwit the Ancients and restore Jenifer to him. The chorus reappears, not however with Sosostris but with a figure dressed as a jester and carrying a crystal bowl. The impostor turns out to be Jack. In the ensuing confusion the veiled figure of the real Sosostris appears. Jack places the bowl before her. She summons up her oracular powers and describes a vision of Mark and Jenifer making love. King Fisher is incensed, smashes the bowl, and commands Jack to unveil Sosostris. Jack defies him, choosing instead to go off with Bella. King Fisher is left to unveil Sosostris himself. What emerges is not Sosostris but a lotus flower, whose petals unfold to reveal the transfigured Mark and Jenifer in mutual embrace. King Fisher aims a pistol at Mark. Mark and Jenifer turn their gaze towards him and he falls, dead. King Fisher's body is carried into the temple. Strephon and his dancers perform the fourth ritual dance (*Fire in Summer*) before the transfigured couple. Strephon sinks at their feet and is absorbed into the flower, which closes and bursts into flame. The scene becomes dark and cold. Dawn breaks. Mark and Jenifer enter. She accepts the wedding ring and, as they disappear into the distance, the sun rises.

The Midsummer Marriage presents Tippett's 'early', tonal style at its most developed – irrepressibly vital and inventive, lyrical, richly textured and with light-footed rhythmic momentum. The opera's relatively traditional design, separate numbers linked in a continuous flow, disguises a very original dramaturgy, in which the action proceeds to the point of Jenifer's arrival and then shifts into a dream realm, not broken until the lovers reappear a few minutes from the end. Thus the bulk of the opera takes place in a period 'out of time'. This is a context in which Tippett can plausibly delve into the purely imaginative, the mythological and psychological, and in which another individual feature of the work, the integral use of dance, can find its place. The opera is not however entirely set in a fantasy world, for the chorus, as well as some other characters, notably Jack and Bella but including King Fisher, continually relate the action to the everyday.

Among the musical high points are the Act I arias of Jenifer and Mark, in which they sing respectively of their experiences of the Jungian animus and anima, the enchanting Act II duets of Bella and Jack, and the extended Act III aria of Sosostris, a rare instance of an operatic aria for contralto and remarkable evidence of the workings of the creative process. The *Ritual Dances* (the first three linked to the fourth) have become one of Tippett's most frequently performed works as a concert suite, and, if in this guise their operatic function as further projections of the animus and anima is lost, their brilliant narrative imagery and their culminating expression, in the fourth dance, of ecstatic sexual and psychological fulfilment is amply realized, even when the last dance is performed without the voices and chorus.

King Priam

Opera in three acts (2h 15m)
Libretto by the composer
Composed 1958–61
PREMIERE 29 May 1962, Coventry Theatre, Coventry; US: 1 July 1994, Theatre Artaud, San Francisco
CAST Priam *b-bar*, Hecuba *s*, Hector *bar*, Andromache *s*, Paris (as boy) *treble*, Paris (as man) *t*, Helen *ms*, Achilles *t*, Patroclus *bar*, Nurse *ms*, Old Man *b*, Young Guard *t*, Hermes *t*; *satb* chorus of hunters, wedding guests, serving women, etc.

King Priam is exceptional in Tippett's output, not so much because it marked a more radical break with his previous music than at any subsequent stage in his career, or even because its story is traditional, but because it is a tragedy. As such it can be seen as a critique of or a reaction to *The Midsummer Marriage*. Now it is shown that however honourable, human and deeply self-aware someone's actions might be, they may still lead to catastrophe. This is the essential message of an opera that on the surface seems a straightforward, if selective, retelling of Homer's story of how Priam, king of Troy, reversed his decision to have his son Paris killed and thereby set in motion the Trojan War. The death of Priam may be cathartic, in the Aristotelian sense described by Hermes in the opera's last interlude, but it is final: it releases no possibility of life recharged or reborn, as with the endings of Tippett's other operas. This remains a profoundly inspiriting work, however, because Tippett lights up the opera's mounting sequence of violence with moments of human insight and passion. Its accent on violence and brutality can be seen therefore not only as a means by which human values can be dramatized and upheld at times when the gods are at their most capricious, but also as a challenge to the mood of reconciliation that characterized the 1960s. Tippett's attitude in this latter respect was set up in sharp relief at the opera's first performance, which took place just one day before that of Britten's *War Requiem*.

SYNOPSIS

Act I Scene 1: Priam's palace. The birth of Paris. The baby is restless, as is Hecuba, his mother and queen of Troy. The Old Man interprets Hecuba's dream: Paris will cause his father's death. Hecuba's reaction is immediate. The young Priam hesitates, troubled by his conflicting responsibilities as father and king, before commanding that the child be killed. Interlude: The Nurse, Old Man and Young Guard comment on Priam's decision and introduce the course of the opera. Scene 2: Paris was not killed but given to a shepherd. As a young boy, he meets his father and brother Hector while they are on a bull hunt. At the moment of recognition, Priam hesitates again, and then reverses his decision. He takes Paris to Troy. Interlude: Further comment. Wedding guests announce Hector's marriage with Andromache and report of friction between the brothers and of Paris' departure for Greece, where he falls in love with Helen, wife of Menelaus of Sparta. Scene 3: Paris and Helen. The answer to Paris' dilemma – whether to provoke war by abducting Helen – is given in a vision (*The Judgement of Paris*). The god Hermes tells him to give the apple to the most beautiful of three goddesses. Two, Athene and Hera, remind him of his mother and sister-in-law: he gives it to Aphrodite. Despite the curses of Athene and Hera, he takes Helen to Troy.

Act II   Scene 1: Hector taunts his brother for not fighting the Greeks. Priam encourages both his sons and, separately, they rush off to battle. Interlude: Through the agency of Hermes, the Old Man is taken to the Greek camp to gloat over the inertia of Achilles. Scene 2: Achilles, refusing to fight because of a quarrel with Agamemnon, his chief, sings nostalgically of his homeland. His friend Patroclus persuades him of the desperate situation on the battlefield, and Achilles allows Patroclus to fight Hector wearing Achilles' armour. Interlude: The Old Man asks Hermes to tell Priam of the danger. Scene 3: Hector has killed Patroclus and, with his father and brother, sings a hymn of thanksgiving, interrupted by the war cries of Achilles, who has been roused to action.

Act III   Scene 1: The war causes antagonism betweeen Hecuba, Andromeda and Helen, but they are powerless and pray to their tutelary goddesses. Andromache senses the death of Hector. Interlude: Serving-women comment on the impending collapse of Troy, and on the condition of Priam, who has been shielded from news of the war. Scene 2: Paris tells Priam of Hector's death. In torment, Priam relives his decision of the first scene. He begins to accept his own death. Interlude: instrumental. Scene 3: Priam visits the Greek camp to beg the body of Hector from Achilles, who feels pity for him and grants him his wish. They drink to their own deaths at the hands of their respective sons. Interlude: Hermes announces the imminent death of Priam and sings of the power of music to express cathartic experience. Scene 4: Paris tells Priam he has killed Achilles. Priam is unmoved. He dismisses everyone and speaks only to the mysterious Helen. Before he is killed by Neoptolemus, he has a momentary vision of Hermes as a god.

King Priam rejects the burgeoning tonal paragraphs of *The Midsummer Marriage* and is constructed in a series of short scenes and sung interludes (a method owing something to Brecht); in these the orchestra is split up into small ensembles, each character (and many of the concepts) has its own immediately recognizable sound quality, and the musical language is more taut and dissonant. Only once, in the penultimate interlude, does Tippett treat his full orchestra as a unit. So there is little of the carefully modulated textures of *The Midsummer Marriage*, rather a rapid shifting of sound spectrum, between, for example, the horns and piano of Priam and the violins of Hecuba, or between the trumpets and percussion, representing war, and the guitar of Achilles. Some of the characters – Hecuba and Andromache (cellos) for instance – are always represented by the same instruments. But Tippett does not stick rigidly to his methods, and others, notably Priam and the semi-divine Helen and Achilles, also have a rich variety of associated instrumentation.

While there is no lack of lyrical music, Tippett's writing for voices in *King Priam* is typically declamatory in style, especially in the questing monologues which are a feature of the work and which emphasize the characters' individual predicaments and their isolation from one another. The moments of human compassion, between Achilles and Patroclus, or between Priam and Achilles, are correspondingly more poignant, their dramatic impact nicely counterpointed against the stark momentum of the rest of the opera and against its more obviously theatrical (and masterly) moments – such as the ends of Act I and Act II. Tippett's methods in *King Priam* became the source of much, if not all, of his subsequent output, for both the theatre and the concert hall.

The Knot Garden

Opera in three acts (1h 30m)
Libretto by the composer
Composed 1966–9
PREMIERES 2 December 1970, Covent Garden, London; US: 22 February 1974, Northwestern University Opera Theater, Cahn Auditorium, Evanston, Illinois
CAST Faber *bar*, Thea *ms*, Flora *s*, Denise *s*, Mel *b-bar*, Dov *t*, Mangus *t-bar*

Between *King Priam* and *The Knot Garden* Tippett wrote three important concert works, of which the first two, his Second Piano Sonata (1962) and Concerto for Orchestra (1963), explore the style, structural methods and even some of the material of *King Priam*. The third, *The Vision of Saint Augustine* (1965), ventures into realms of mystical experience and the perception of time. With *The Knot Garden* Tippett abruptly returned to earth. It is set in 'the present' and deals with directly contemporary problems – those stemming from a lifeless marriage and touching also on race relations, homosexuality and the torture of political prisoners, while in general exploring the inner as opposed to the public lives of its seven characters. If this bold subject matter was perhaps not unexpected of Tippett, nor the brilliantly faceted musical language, its rapid sequence of short scenes and its gritty style a natural development from *King Priam*, the opera's intimate yet intensely concentrated dramaturgy shows him at his most original. Its speed of movement is a product of his adaptation of television techniques (notably the little 'dissolve' sections which break up one scene in preparation for the next) and of contemporary stage lighting techniques; its essential substance is a product of contemporary psychotherapeutic techniques and of Shakespeare's *The Tempest*, this latter a conspicuous instance of his instinct to draw on cultural tradition while shaping it to his own purposes. Of all Tippett's operas, *The Knot Garden* is the most radical in its rejection of conventional narrative explanation. The whys and wherefores of the 'plot' have therefore to be deduced from what hints the libretto does provide. For all these reasons the opera was immediately recognized as strikingly original in conception and execution.

SYNOPSIS

Thea, a gardener, and Faber, a civil engineer, are a married couple in their mid-thirties. They have a ward, Flora. Thea has asked Mangus, a psychoanalyst, to stay with them so that he can help with Flora's adolescent problems. Mangus realizes, however, that it is the marriage that needs attention, and he plans a therapy in which his charges will be persuaded to project their feelings on to characters from *The Tempest* and act them out in a series of 'charades' he has derived from the play. Faber will be Ferdinand and Flora Miranda. He has asked Thea to invite two friends to be Ariel and Caliban. These are a homosexual couple, Dov, a composer, and Mel, a black writer. Mangus himself will be Prospero, who with his 'magic art' will solve the problems. Thea, tactfully, will not be included. The scene is a high-walled house garden shutting out an industrial city. The garden changes shape metaphorically according to the situations – from a boxed-in knot garden to a tangled labyrinth or to a rose garden.

Act I   The characters are introduced, Mangus testing his ability to summon up a tempest and a magic island, Thea and Faber locked in bitter confrontation, Flora neurotic, Dov and Mel ready to play-act though unsure of themselves. Thea's attempt to attract Mel begins to break open the entrenched positions but what really does so is the unexpected arrival of Denise, Thea's sister and a 'dedicated freedom fighter'. Disfigured from torture, she denounces them all.

Act II   Mangus is understood to be manipulating a nightmarish tempest, in which the characters, in a series of duets, give vent to their suppressed desires and antagonisms. Eventually the two most hurt, Flora and Dov, are left to console each other.

Act III   Before an audience of Thea and Denise, Mangus now masterminds four charades. The characters, including Thea and Denise, are able to some extent to come to terms with themselves – except Dov, who is isolated, and Mangus himself, who suddenly discovers that his behaviour has been grossly presumptuous. He stops the proceedings, all the cast come forward and tentatively sing of the human qualities that, after all, can bind them, and the audience, together. In an epilogue, Thea and Faber are about to embrace.

The emotional drama of *The Knot Garden* is dynamic and fast-moving, but within its pattern of little arias

and ensembles Tippett also leaves room for large set pieces. Act I is geared to lead up to the first of them, a harrowing aria for Denise ('O you may stare in horror'), answered by the second, a septet for the whole cast, which, since it is set in motion by Mel, is a blues, with a boogie-woogie middle section. Although some of Tippett's early music, notably his Concerto for Double String Orchestra, absorbed jazz into his style, this was the first time his interest in popular culture had been shown so directly in one of his operas. Naturally it also affected *The Knot Garden*'s instrumentation, which includes jazz kit and electric guitar. The guitar features prominently in the song Dov sings to Flora at the end of Act II, one of the most conspicuous moments of lyric warmth Tippett places in an otherwise sharp-edged and even astringent score. Flora's song to Dov, immediately before, is another such moment, an exquisitely orchestrated version of Schubert's 'Die liebe Farbe'. Of all the solos in the opera, Thea's Act III aria ('Now I am no longer afraid') is the most beautiful; and of all the ensembles, the concluding quintet the most typical of the opera's intrinsic irony: a humanistic statement ('If for a timid moment we submit to love') punctuated by mocking quotations from some songs for Ariel Tippett had himself written for an earlier Old Vic production of *The Tempest*.

The Ice Break

Opera in three acts (1h 15m)
Libretto by the composer
Composed 1973–6
PREMIERES 7 July 1977, Covent Garden, London; US: 18 May 1979, Savoy Theater, Boston
CAST Lev *b*, Nadia *s*, Yuri *bar*, Gayle *s*, Hannah *ms*, Olympion *t*, Luke *t*, Lieutenant *bar*, Astron *ms* and *t* (or *ct*); *satb* chorus of blacks, whites, hippies

Immediately after *The Knot Garden* Tippett wrote his *Songs for Dov*, a parable explaining what happened to the character, and his Third Symphony, whose vocal second part includes a sequence of blues. By the time he wrote his next major work, *The Ice Break*, he therefore had explored some important resonances of *The Knot Garden* and was ready to confront the broad question set out at the end of the opera, and indeed of the symphony too. Left alone in the universe, can mankind entrust its survival to its own capacity for love and mutual healing? Tippett himself has more starkly described this opera's theme as a question of 'whether or not we can be reborn from the stereotypes we live in'. *The Ice Break* puts this to the test in an uncompromising way. It is more realistic, even surrealistic, than symbolic, and while it does have a moving and encouraging ending, this cannot be regarded as an entirely convincing outcome of the plot. As in most of his work, the opera confronts a very large problem without presuming to offer a tidy solution.

SYNOPSIS

When Lev, a Soviet dissident, was sentenced, his wife Nadia with their baby son Yuri emigrated to the US. After 20 years of prison, labour camps and internal exile, Lev has been released and also allowed to emigrate.

Act I   In an airport lounge Nadia and Yuri await Lev's arrival. They encounter Gayle, Yuri's girlfriend, and Hannah, her black friend, a nurse, who have come to welcome Olympion, Hannah's boyfriend and a 'black champion'. Olympion eventually arrives surrounded by his adoring fans and plays the part expected of him. Nadia suddenly realizes that the soberly dressed man watching her is her husband. In Nadia's apartment they converse. In the airport, Olympion, provoked by the sullen behaviour of Yuri, delivers his creed of black power. Gayle delivers hers of white liberalism, and falls on her knees in front of him. Yuri is incensed. Olympion knocks him down, and the fans divide into hostile factions of black and white. In the apartment, Nadia tells Lev about the disturbing behaviour of Yuri, who now bursts in, dragging Gayle with him. He greets his father venomously.

Act II   Intimate scenes – within the tensions of Lev's family, between Olympion and Hannah, and for Hannah alone – are set against scenes of mounting violence, which eventually reach confrontation and erupt in a race riot. Gayle and Olympion are killed, Yuri terribly injured. As the bodies are taken away, Lev turns to Hannah for comfort.

Act III   Nadia is unable to struggle with life any more. Lev reads to her on her deathbed. They are assured by Luke, a young doctor, and Hannah that Yuri will recover, but Lev asks himself why he has come to this new country just to watch his wife's death and his son's hatred. Nadia lapses into childhood memories. As she dies, Lev cries out for her to wait for him in 'Paradise Garden', where 'seekers of all kinds' await the appearance of Astron, a 'psychedelic messenger'. He enunciates some cryptic messages but, when treated too reverently, evaporates. The scene changes to the hospital, where Yuri's bones have been set and his whole body encased in plaster. The plaster is cut away. As Yuri rejoices in his recovery, the stage is filled with revellers. Hannah wheels Yuri to his father. Father and son embrace.

The opera's title refers to the 'frightening but exhilarating sound of the sound of the ice breaking on the great northern rivers in the spring'. As a musical motif it appears several times, notably when Lev meets his wife and is reconciled with his son. Another striking motif is that associated with Lev's recollections of the poetry that sustained him in Russia and now does so again. It concludes the opera as he completes a passage from Goethe begun while Nadia was on her deathbed. A characteristic sound (rather than motif) is that of the chanting crowds who periodically overwhelm the stage. The chorus sings in a variety of ways, including one akin to rock, and forms a crucial part of the opera's very original dramatic design: anonymous mass behaviour in unpredictable invasions of a continuing domestic narrative. This latter proceeds as best it can, and contains several beautiful numbers which contrast poignantly with the bold and often garish music around them: the Act II duet for

Olympion and Hannah, Nadia's death song and especially the long aria for Hannah placed at the centre of the whole opera.

Unpublished operatic works: *The Village Opera* (realization with additional music of ballad opera by C. Johnson, 1729), 1928; *Robin Hood* (folksong opera), 1934; *Robert of Sicily* (play for children), 1938; *Seven at One Stroke* (play for children), 1939
Other opera: *New Year*, 1989

I.K.

MARK-ANTHONY TURNAGE
b 10 June 1960, Corringham, Essex, England

Turnage came to prominence in the 1980s with a sequence of instrumental and vocal pieces that culminated in his first opera, *Greek*. Its outstanding success earned him international acclaim, and a unique position among composers of his generation for his distinctly lyrical voice, skill at creating complex yet lucid textures, and innate dramatic flair.

Night Dances, winner of the 1982 Guinness Composition Prize, had already presented these qualities in embryonic form. The work's skill and professionalism owed something to a series of distinguished teachers – including Oliver Knussen (at the Royal College of Music), and Hans Werner Henze and Gunther Schuller (at Tanglewood). But its musical essence derived from a personal vision encompassing the work of 20th-century masters from Stravinsky to Miles Davis. Subsequent compositions, including *Lament for a Hanging Man* (1983), *On All Fours* (1985) and *Release* (1987), extended the range and accomplishment of this unusual synthesis.

With the orchestral piece *Three Screaming Popes* (1989), Turnage began a fruitful period as Composer in Association with the City of Birmingham Symphony Orchestra, a collaboration that also resulted in *Momentum* (1991), written for the opening of Birmingham's Symphony Hall. *Killing Time* (1992), a half-hour dramatic piece for BBC Television, contains elements of opera, scena and dramatic song-cycle. In 1995 Turnage was appointed Composer in Association with English National Opera and began work on two major projects for the company: a full-length opera for the 1998–9 season and a chamber opera, jointly commissioned by ENO and the Aldeburgh Festival, for the Festival's 50th anniversary in 1997.

Greek
Opera in two acts (1h 30m)
Libretto by the composer and Jonathan Moore, based on the play by Steven Berkoff (1980)
PREMIERES   17 June 1988, Carl-Orff-Saal, Munich;
UK: 25 August 1988, Leith Theatre, Edinburgh

Though the themes of *Greek* are universal, they acquired a topical status in the charged atmosphere of the late 1980s. Berkoff's play retells the Oedipus story in the context of a contemporary metropolis in which racism, violence and mass unemployment appear as metaphors for the plague blighting the city.

Written for four singers and a large instrumental ensemble (all doubling on percussion), the music matches the fast-moving stage events with a flexible, wide-ranging style, juxtaposing the hard-hitting vernacular of football chants with episodes of passionately lyrical beauty for Eddy (high baritone), the opera's tragic hero.

N.W.

U

VIKTOR ULLMANN
b 1 January 1898, Prague; *d* 18 October 1944, ?Auschwitz

Ullmann studied with Schoenberg in Vienna and later in Prague with Alois Hába in the quarter-tone department of the Prague Musikhochschule. He also worked under Zemlinsky on the music staff of the Deutsches Theater, Prague, and was a member of Schoenberg's Society for Private Musical Performances (two of his song-cycles were performed by the Society in 1924). Like Hába, he was greatly interested in the teachings of Rudolf Steiner. In 1942 he was arrested by the Nazis and interned in Theresienstadt; on 16 October 1944 he was transferred to Auschwitz.

Der Kaiser von Atlantis, oder Die Tod-Verweigerung
The Emperor of Atlantis, or The Refusal to Die
Legend in four scenes (1h)
Libretto by Peter Kien
Composed *c.* 1943
PREMIERES 16 December 1975, Bellevue Centre, Amsterdam; US: 21 April 1977, San Francisco Opera; UK: 7 May 1985, Imperial War Museum, London

The precise circumstances under which *Der Kaiser von Atlantis* was composed are uncertain. In Theresienstadt a fellow prisoner was the poet and painter Peter Kien. He and Ullmann set out to write an opera, drawing on the limited resources available (some distinguished singers and an orchestra of 13 players, including banjo, harpsichord and harmonium). Evidently the work was rehearsed, but the text was interpreted by the authorities as being anti-Hitler and its performance was prohibited. Ullmann and Kien were both subsequently transferred to Auschwitz and met their deaths in the gas chamber. In 1972 an exhibition was devoted to Ullmann in Prague. Documents came to light which suggested that autograph material had by some miracle survived the Holocaust. Two years later, while working on Theresienstadt documentation, H. G. Adler discovered the performing materials, the manuscript score as well as a handwritten and a typed copy of the libretto in London. Kerry Woodward collated the diverse sources, completing sketchy or illegible passages to produce a performing edition of the score which he himself conducted at the world premiere.

The kaiser of Atlantis has proclaimed a 'holy war'. Death abdicates his duties in protest, and the kaiser's authority is further undermined by a rebellion. A girl and a soldier from opposing sides fall in love. Finally Death agrees to return to work, but only on condition that the kaiser should be his first victim. During the course of the action the kaiser loses touch with reality and becomes an almost sympathetic figure. The supposed analogy to contemporary events is shown to be superficial: anyway, it is Death who dominates the entire action.

The dramatic circumstances under which *Der Kaiser von Atlantis* was composed were an obvious bonus for the work's posthumous promoters. However, the powerful libretto needs no special pleading and, despite stylistic allegiances to Eisler and Weill, moments of Straussian harmony and jazz influence, Ullmann's score has sufficient individuality to stand on its own. Since its rediscovery it has been widely performed, recorded and televised.

Other works: *Peer Gynt*, (1928); *Der Sturz des Antichrist*, (1936); *Der zerbrochene Krug*, 1942

A.C.W.B.

RALPH VAUGHAN WILLIAMS

b 12 October 1872, Down Ampney, Gloucestershire,
England; *d* 26 August 1958, London

With his friend Gustav Holst, Vaughan Williams was
one of the architects of the so-called English musical
renaissance at the start of the 20th century. They
deliberately turned away from Continental influences
– as far as that was ever possible – to become 'English'
composers. The son of a clergyman and descended on
his mother's side from Darwins and Wedgwoods,
Vaughan Williams was educated at Charterhouse, the
Royal College of Music and Trinity College, Cambridge. At the RCM he was a composition pupil of
both Hubert Parry and Charles Villiers Stanford. His
earliest compositions were chamber music and songs,
the latter including the popular *Linden Lea* (1901) and
Songs of Travel (1904). At this time he became deeply
involved in collecting folksongs, following the example
of Cecil Sharp. From 1904 to 1906 he also edited the
music of a new hymn book, *The English Hymnal*.

Although his choral setting of Walt Whitman,
Toward the Unknown Region, was a success at the
1907 Leeds Festival, he was dissatisfied with his
progress and in 1908 went to Paris for a period of
intensive study with Ravel. Ironically, it was this
foreign influence, rather than folksong, that released
his creative originality. In the three years after his
return from France he composed his First String
Quartet, a song-cycle (*On Wenlock Edge*) based on
A. E. Housman's *A Shropshire Lad* poems and the
Fantasia on a Theme by Thomas Tallis for strings, and
completed his large-scale *Sea Symphony* (Whitman
again), which was the outstanding success at the 1910
Leeds Festival and placed him in the vanguard of his
generation of British composers.

Primarily associated with choral and orchestral
works (nine symphonies), Vaughan Williams wanted
to succeed as an opera composer. In 1913, he was
director of music to Sir Frank Benson's Shakespeare
company at Stratford-upon-Avon. At this time he was
completing his first opera, *Hugh the Drover*. After
four years' active war service in 1914–18, he revised it
for its first performance in 1924. Five operas followed,
but, apart from the short *Riders to the Sea*, none has
won a regular place in the repertoire. On the day he
died he was working on a seventh opera, *Thomas the
Rhymer*.

Riders to the Sea

Opera in one act (40m)
Libretto: an almost verbatim setting of the play *Riders to
the Sea* by John Millington Synge (1902)
Composed 1925–32
PREMIERES 1 December 1937, Parry Opera Theatre, Royal
College of Music, London; US: 26 February 1950, Western
Reserve University, Cleveland, Ohio
CAST Maurya *c*, Bartley *bar*, Cathleen *s*, Nora *s*, Woman
ms; women's chorus; men and women, *non-singing*

The play and opera deal with the lives of fisherfolk on
the Isle of Arran.

SYNOPSIS

After a short prelude, Nora asks her sister Cathleen
to help her identify clothes taken off a drowned
corpse. She believes they belonged to their brother
Michael, lost at sea like his father and four of his
brothers. They hide the clothes in the loft so that their
mother, Maurya, will not see them. She enters, worried
that her last living son, Bartley, is to take horses to
Galway Fair, which involves a sea crossing. Bartley
arrives to fetch a rope. Rejecting their pleas to him to
stay, he says he will ride the red mare, with the grey
pony following. The sisters reproach Maurya for not
giving Bartley her blessing and force her to take him
some food for the journey. While she is away, they
identify the clothes as Michael's. Maurya returns,
distressed. She has seen Bartley riding to the sea on
the mare, with Michael, wearing new clothes, on the
pony. Cathleen tells her Michael is dead, and Maurya
realizes her vision means Bartley will die. As she sings
of the deaths of her menfolk, Bartley's dripping body
is carried in. Maurya, almost relieved, sings that the
sea can hurt her no more. 'No man at all can be living
for ever, and we must be satisfied.'

This is Vaughan Williams's most successful opera and
in every respect a key work in his output. Notwithstanding the depressing story, the subject of man
against nature was one that always inspired strong
music from him. The score is organized almost symphonically, much of the thematic material being derived from the short prelude. Also, the character of
Maurya is fully developed, her final aria being Purcel-
lian in its elegiac simplicity. The orchestration is subtle
and evocative, with foreshadowings of the bleak and

ghostly finale of the Sixth Symphony (1944–7). The keening of the women's voices as Bartley's body is taken into the house and the constant sound of the sea also anticipate the *Sinfonia Antartica* of 1952.

The Pilgrim's Progress

Morality in a prologue, four acts and an epilogue (2h)
Libretto by the composer founded on *The Pilgrim's Progress* (Part I, 1674–9; Part II, 1684) by John Bunyan, with interpolations from the Bible and verse by Ursula Vaughan Williams
Composed 1925–36; rev. 1942, 1944–9, 1951–2 (*The Shepherds of the Delectable Mountains* episode was composed in 1921; first sketches for a *Pilgrim* opera date from 1906.)
PREMIERES 26 April 1951, Covent Garden, London; US: 28 April 1968, Brigham Young University, Provo, Utah
CAST Bunyan *b-bar*, Pilgrim *bar*, Evangelist *b*, Watchful *high bar*, Herald *bar*, Apollyon *b*, Lord Lechery *t buffo*, Lord Hate-Good *b*, Woodcutter's Boy *s* or *boy s*, Mr By-Ends *t buffo*, Mrs By-Ends *c*, 3 Shepherds *t*, *bar*, *b*, Voice of a Bird *s*, 4 *s*, 2 *ms*, 3 *c*, 6 *t*, 4 *bar*, 4 *b* (many parts are doubled, and 11 singers are sufficient); *satb* chorus of men and women of the House Beautiful, 'certain persons clothed in gold', Doleful Creatures, Traders in Vanity Fair, chorus in the Celestial City, chorus on Earth; dancers

This ambitious work was the culmination of Vaughan Williams's lifelong belief that Bunyan's allegory could form the basis of an opera. It preoccupied him for over forty years. In 1906 he wrote incidental music for a semi-amateur stage adaptation in Reigate, Surrey. In 1921 he composed the one-act episode *The Shepherds of the Delectable Mountains*, now incorporated into the larger work as Act IV, Scene 2, with an altered ending. He worked sporadically on Acts I and II from 1925 to 1936, when he abandoned the project and used some of the themes in his Fifth Symphony, begun in 1938 and first performed in 1943. His enthusiasm was rekindled in 1942 when he composed 38 sections of incidental music for a BBC dramatization by Edward Sackville-West. Some of this was incorporated into the final operatic version, on which he worked from 1944 to 1949.

SYNOPSIS
In a prologue, Bunyan is seen in Bedford Gaol writing the last words of his book.

Act I begins as he reads, and Pilgrim is seen with a burden on his back. He is directed by the Evangelist to the Wicket Gate, where his neighbours fail to persuade him to turn back. He kneels in front of the Cross. Three Shining Ones take his burden and lead him to the gate of the House Beautiful, where he is robed.

Act II Pilgrim takes to the King's Highway. He is given armour. In the Valley of Humiliation he hears the howling of the Doleful Creatures and defeats Apollyon in a fight but is wounded. Two Heavenly Beings revive him, and the Evangelist invests him with the Staff of Salvation, the Roll of the Word and the Key of Promise.

Act III At Vanity Fair, Pilgrim rejects the seductive pleasures on offer. He is taken before Lord Hate-Good and condemned to death. In prison he bewails his fate until he remembers the Key of Promise. He unlocks the gates and walks to freedom.

Act IV A Woodcutter's Boy directs Pilgrim to the Delectable Mountains. On the way he encounters Mr and Mrs By-Ends, who decline to accompany him. Then follows the scene with the Shepherds. A Celestial Messenger summons him to the Celestial City and pierces his heart with an arrow. A trumpet sounds as Pilgrim passes through the River of Death and ascends to the gates of the city. In an epilogue, Bunyan offers his book to the audience.

Although criticized for its lack of dramatic action and for the leisurely tempo of much of the music, *The Pilgrim's Progress* can be a most affecting and impressive theatrical experience. The howling of the Doleful Creatures and the bustle of Vanity Fair are effectively represented; and the music for Pilgrim's arming, much of it familiar from the Fifth Symphony, and for his sojourn in prison is Vaughan Williams at the height of his powers, as is the uplifting penultimate scene when the Celestial City is reached. Having been composed over so long a period, the opera forms a synthesis of Vaughan Williams's stylistic progress over the years, from the pastoral meditation of the 1920s to the angry music of the middle symphonies and eventually the more experimental phase of the *Sinfonia Antartica* in his last decade. The composer's summing-up of its failure in 1951 was: 'It's not like the operas they are used to, but it's the sort of opera I wanted to write, and there it is.'

Other operatic works: *Hugh the Drover, or Love in the Stocks*, (1914), 1924, *The Shepherds of the Delectable Mountains*, 1922; *Sir John in Love*, 1929, rev. 1933; *The Poisoned Kiss, or The Empress and the Necromancer*, 1936

M.K.

GIUSEPPE VERDI

Giuseppe Fortunino Francesco Verdi; *b* 9/10 October 1813, Roncole, nr Busseto, Italy; *d* 27 January 1901, Milan

Giuseppe Verdi is one of a tiny group of composers who set the supreme standards by which the art of opera is judged; of his 28 operas – several of which exist in more than one version – about a dozen form the backbone of the standard operatic repertoire. He was the dominant figure in Italian opera for 50 years, and was largely responsible for a radical transformation of its character. But in many ways his revolution was a deeply conservative one, and he carried popular audiences with him almost to the end.

Born in a village in the rural depths of what is now the province of Parma, Verdi received his earliest musical education from church organists in Roncole and Busseto. His gifts made a deep impression on local music-lovers, and in 1832 one of them, a merchant named Antonio Barezzi, undertook to finance a year of study for him at the Milan Conservatory. Though Verdi did sit an entrance examination, he was in fact too old to be admitted and had to study privately instead, working under Vincenzo Lavigna. Lavigna was, Verdi recounted many years later, 'very good at counterpoint, a little pedantic, and didn't care for any music but Paisiello'.

Having completed his studies, Verdi returned to Busseto to take up a position as director of music in the commune and marry Barezzi's daughter Margherita. Three years later he was back in Milan with his family, for he had been able to arrange for his first opera, *Oberto*, to be staged at La Scala. The premiere, in November 1839, was successful enough for the publisher Giovanni Ricordi to want to purchase it, and for Bartolomeo Merelli, impresario of La Scala, to offer Verdi a contract for three further operas. Between August 1838 and June 1840, however, both his two children and his wife died; in September 1840, his second opera, *Un giorno di regno*, was an inglorious fiasco, and Verdi's life, personal and professional, lay in ruins. Merelli's confidence in him did not falter, and his faith was rewarded when *Nabucco* triumphed in March 1842. This third opera established Verdi as a national figure; it also marked the beginning of what he was to call his *anni di galera* (years in the galleys), for impresarios from all over Italy were now eager to engage the rising star, and he was inescapably drawn into a life of grinding routine, composing, rehearsing and staging operas all over Italy and sometimes further afield. In the 17 years from *Nabucco* to *Un ballo in maschera* he composed 20 operas.

With its central theme of a chosen nation dreaming of deliverance from foreign bondage, *Nabucco* had a certain topicality in Risorgimento Italy; and the eloquence with which Verdi's music expressed moods of religious and national fervour played no small part in its success. Such Risorgimento overtones recur again and again during the *anni di galera*. Fastidious music-lovers of an older generation were sometimes repelled by the violence and noisiness of the young Verdi, but the majority of his operas enjoyed huge popular success, and made an important contribution to Italian national self-awareness. It was a providential coincidence that the name Verdi formed an acronym for 'Vittorio Emanuele, Re D'Italia'; and during the 1850s, as the Savoy monarchy became the focus for Italian national aspirations, the commonplace acclamation 'Viva Verdi' acquired a thrilling patriotic resonance.

This nationalist dimension contributed little, however, to the deepening of his art that took place between *Nabucco* and the so-called 'popular trilogy' – *Rigoletto*, *Il trovatore* and *La traviata* – of the early 1850s. *Nabucco* had given Verdi entrée to the best social and artistic circles: among the friends he made were Andrea Maffei, whose wife Clara was hostess of Milan's most cultivated salon, and Giulio Carcano, Italian translators of, respectively, Schiller and Shakespeare. During the 1840s Verdi developed into something of a literary connoisseur, an avid reader of dramatic literature from all over Europe. Inspired by this reading, his dramatic vision deepened; he acquired a sense of the potentialities of poetic drama, and hence of musical drama, that extended far beyond the conventions of Romantic opera. In his Hugo operas – *Ernani* (1844) and *Rigoletto* (1851) – his Schiller operas – particularly *Luisa Miller* (1850) – and his Shakespeare opera – *Macbeth* (1847) – we find Verdi stretch-

ing and bending the conventions inherited from his predecessors to give his operas an expressive range and a uniqueness of characterization and atmosphere that matched that of the greatest dramatists. Another Shakespearean project, *Re Lear* (*King Lear*), had first attracted Verdi as early as 1843. A libretto was written (by Antonio Somma, based on preliminary work by Salvatore Cammarano); but, though Verdi returned to the subject frequently and sketched much music for it, the scheme remained unrealized.

The repertoire of opera on which Verdi had been brought up as a student in the 1830s had been almost exclusively Italian. It was, however, infiltrated by French elements, mediated primarily through the operas written by Rossini in the late 1820s. It was Verdi's emulation of such models that gave both *Nabucco* and *I lombardi* something of the cut of French grand operas. As his reputation spread and invitations took him to London and Paris, he had the opportunity to experience grand opera at first hand, and made his first attempt at composing it himself – significantly, *Jérusalem* (1847) is a revised version of *I lombardi*. His attitude to Parisian grand opera proved to be ambivalent; but the genre, and its greatest exponent, Giacomo Meyerbeer, certainly exerted a profound influence on his music in the 1850s and 1860s. After *Jérusalem* he composed two more French grand operas, *Les vêpres siciliennes* (1855) and *Don Carlos* (1867), and two of his Italian operas are based either on grand-opera libretti (*Un ballo in maschera*, 1859) or on French scenarios in the grand opera manner (*Aida*, 1871). It was while he was in Paris in 1847 that he met up again with Giuseppina Strepponi, who had sung in the first performances of *Nabucco*, and who in due course (1859) was to become his second wife.

With *Un ballo in maschera* the *anni di galera* came to an end. Verdi was world famous and very wealthy, and had begun to enjoy the life of a country gentleman. In 1848 he had bought, in an 'unimproved' state, a property (Sant'Agata) near Busseto; he moved there in 1851, and worked for decades developing and beautifying it. Since he had by now earned an outstandingly honourable place in the life of his resurgent nation, Count Cavour – prime minister of the united Italy that finally materialized in 1860 – persuaded him to become a deputy in the Turin parliament: he represented his local district, Borgo San Donnino (now Fidenza), from 1861 to 1865. Verdi was now less productive as a composer, accepting new commissions only when they really interested him. Between 1860 and 1870 he wrote three operas; their performance venues – St Petersburg, Paris, Cairo – vividly express the reach of his reputation. Each opera is on a huge scale, and the last of them, *Aida*, achieves to perfection that fusion of the Italian and French traditions of opera that Verdi had long pursued. He was by now nearly 60, and many assumed that *Aida* marked the end of his operatic career. In 1874 he produced the *Messa da Requiem* in memory of Alessandro Manzoni.

Unlike Wagner, Verdi left no theoretical writings. But from his vast correspondence, particularly from his letters to his librettists and his publishers, it is not difficult to extract a Verdian 'aesthetics of opera' that rivals Wagner's in comprehensiveness and perhaps surpasses it in clarity. He never wavered in his loyalty to values inherited in his youth: a good opera was an opera that was acclaimed all over Italy by enthusiastic audiences in packed theatres; its object was the exploration of human passions and human behaviour in situations of extreme dramatic tension, and its principal means of expression was the fusion of poetry and music in dramatic song. He sought out subjects bolder than anything an earlier generation would have dared, and characters became more idiosyncratic, but his sense of values was in the classical Italian tradition. In rehearsal he was a rigorous disciplinarian, demanding absolute compliance with his demands; and these extended beyond the music to virtually every element of the staging. From *Les vêpres siciliennes* onward, his publisher Ricordi issued production books – *disposizioni sceniche* – which record how most of his operas were staged.

The 1870s were, for the most part, years of disillusion. The reality of the new Italian state did not match up to the dreams of those who had come to maturity in the heroic decades of the Risorgimento; its chronic financial difficulties had plunged opera houses into crisis, and many were closing. Worst of all for Verdi was his feeling that a younger generation was abandoning the traditions of Italian civilization to pursue fashions or ideals emanating from France and Germany. Wagner had become a major force among the avant garde, and, though there was much in Wagner that Verdi admired, he did not see him as a good model for Italian composers. The primacy of song, the clarity of form and luminosity of sound to which Italian art had always aspired, a firm basis in humanist ethics – all seemed under threat.

His friendship with two remarkable men a generation younger than himself – the publisher Giulio Ricordi and the poet and composer Arrigo Boito – did much to draw Verdi out of this unhappy phase and make possible the glorious 'Indian summer' of the 1880s and 1890s. He composed three operas in collaboration with Boito, to each of which Ricordi served as a kind of midwife – a second version of *Simon Boccanegra* (1881), and the two operas that stand as the most eloquent testimony to his lifelong veneration of Shakespeare, *Otello* (1887) and *Falstaff* (1893). None was to rival *Rigoletto, Il trovatore* or *La traviata* in popularity. But the very sophistication (especially in matters of harmony and instrumentation) that popular audiences sometimes found a little taxing appealed deeply to those educated in the German musical tradition, and many musicians came to love and admire *Ernani* and *Nabucco* via an enthusiasm for the late Verdi.

By the 1890s Verdi had, in the words of Giuseppe Depanis, a Turin journalist, come to be seen as 'the patriarch, the guardian deity of the fatherland'. His rare public appearances were occasions of astonishing demonstrations of affection and veneration; at his funeral, close on 30,000 people are reported to have lined the streets of Milan and to have joined spontaneously in singing 'Va, pensiero' from *Nabucco*.

Oberto, conte di San Bonifacio

Oberto, Count of San Bonifacio
Opera (dramma) in two acts (2h)
Libretto by Temistocle Solera, rev. from a libretto by Antonio Piazza, probably called *Rocester*
Composed summer 1835–summer 1839, rev. October 1840 and January 1841
PREMIERES 17 November 1839, La Scala, Milan; UK: 8 April 1965, St Pancras Town Hall, London (concert); 17 February 1982, Collegiate Theatre, London; US: 18 February 1978, Amato Theater, New York
CAST Cuniza *ms*, Riccardo, Conte di Salinguerra *t*, Oberto, Conte di San Bonifacio *b*, Leonora *s*, Imelda *ms*; *satb* chorus of knights, ladies, vassals

Verdi's first opera emerged from a complicated process of composing and rewriting that stretched over four years. During this time, the opera went under two, perhaps three, different names – (?*Lord Hamilton*), *Rocester* and *Oberto* – at least two librettists worked on the text, and the action was moved from, presumably, 17th-century Britain to 13th-century Italy. However frustrating for the composer, this long gestation did give him time to impress influential friends with his music, notably the impresario Bartolomeo Merelli, who accepted the work for La Scala – a remarkable theatre in which to make an operatic début – and whose advice affected the opera's final form. *Oberto* enjoyed a fair success, prompting Merelli to commission more operas from the young composer, and encouraging Giovanni Ricordi, Milan's leading music publisher, to enter into a business relationship with him that was to prove uniquely advantageous to both parties.

SYNOPSIS
The scene is set in Bassano, in Ezzelino's castle and the vicinity in 1228. Defeated in battle by Ezzelino da Romano, Oberto has taken refuge in Mantua, leaving his daughter Leonora in the care of an aunt. She has been seduced by Riccardo and then abandoned, for he is to marry Cuniza, Ezzelino's sister.

Act I   While Riccardo is escorted into Bassano by a welcoming party of courtiers, Leonora and Oberto make their way thither secretly, bent on revenge. Cuniza's reputation for magnanimity encourages Leonora to confide in her, and the noble lady does indeed take the wronged girl's part against the man who was about to become her own husband.

Act II   Cuniza insists that Riccardo should keep faith with Leonora, and under her sponsorship their vows of love are renewed. But Oberto, believing that a duel to the death is the only way of satisfying family honour, will have no part in any reconciliation. He is fatally wounded; a remorseful Riccardo flees into exile, and Leonora looks forward to an early death in a cloister.

Verdi made his début at a time when the leading composers of Italian opera, Donizetti and Saverio Mercadante, were becoming rather self-conscious about their native traditions, and attempting various types of 'reform', often French or German in inspiration. But Verdi seems quite at ease in the world of

Italian Romantic melodrama. The sensation-packed, pseudo-historical libretto is typical of the earlier Donizetti; the musical architecture, formalized and often symmetrical, is modelled on Bellini; there is no questioning the primacy of the singing voice and the purely secondary role that refinements of instrumentation or harmony played in the young composer's scheme of things. Nevertheless a distinct musical personality is already emerging. There is a vehement and propulsive energy in the score, and a keen sense of what matters dramatically. Recitatives are carefully and expressively composed; characters are vividly brought to life, particularly in the ensembles, where Verdi is already adept at a kind of psychological counterpoint (cf. the Leonora–Oberto duet 'Del tuo favor' in Act I); and the austerity and formal freedom of Leonora's rondo finale shows the young composer unafraid to discard convention in the cause of dramatic verisimilitude.

Un giorno di regno/Il finto Stanislao

King for a Day/The False Stanislas
Melodramma giocoso in two acts (2h)
Libretto by Felice Romani, a revision of his earlier libretto for Adalbert Gyrowetz, *Il finto Stanislao* (1818), in turn based on the comedy *Le faux Stanislas* by Alexandre Vincent Pineu-Duval (1808)
Composed spring–summer 1840
PREMIERES 5 September 1840, La Scala, Milan; 11 October 1845, Teatro San Benedetto, Venice (as *Il finto Stanislao*); US: 18 June 1960, Town Hall, New York; UK: 21 March 1961, St Pancras Town Hall, London
CAST Cavaliere di Belfiore *bar*, Barone di Kelbar *b buffo*, Marchesa del Poggio *s*, Giulietta di Kelbar *s*, Edoardo di Sanval *t*, La Rocca *b buffo*, Ivrea *t*, Delmonte *b*; *satb* chorus of the baron's servants and vassals

The premiere of *Un giorno di regno*, the first of the three operas commissioned by the impresario Merelli after the success of *Oberto*, marked the lowest ebb of Verdi's career. Composed to an old-fashioned libretto, during a period of great personal distress – Verdi's wife Margherita died in June 1840 – and feebly performed by artists most of whom were ill at ease in the comic style, *Un giorno di regno* was hissed ignominiously from the stage and very rarely revived. At the first of the few revivals (Venice, 1845), Romani's original title, *Il finto Stanislao*, was restored.

SYNOPSIS
During the political crisis of 1733, the Cavaliere di Belfiore has, to distract attention from the genuine monarch, assumed the identity of King Stanislas of Poland, and arrived with much pomp at the castle of Baron Kelbar near Brest. There he finds himself in the middle of preparations for two weddings: the baron's daughter Giulietta is, most unwillingly, to marry the elderly La Rocca, while a local military official is hoping for the hand of the Marchesa del Poggio. This news astonishes Belfiore and makes his task more complicated, because he himself is the marchesa's lover. 'Stanislas' resourcefully uses his supposed regal authority to rescue Giulietta from marriage to La Rocca. Eventually a messenger arrives with news that

the Polish crisis is resolved; Belfiore casts off his disguise, and claims the marchesa's hand.

Opera buffa in the Rossinian manner was in terminal decline by 1840, and it needed a composer with a lighter touch than Verdi's to derive much fun from its ageing mannerisms. *Un giorno di regno* demands exceptional tact from its performers; for, instead of sparkle, the orchestral colouring has a monochrome stridency, and rhythms that might have danced are merely galumphing. But composing it did give Verdi the chance to practise his hand at a more flexible and conversational style of ensemble, an experience that was to pay off magnificently in *Nabucco* and the operas that followed.

Nabucodonosor (Nabucco)

Nebuchadnezzar
Dramma lirico in four parts (2h 15m)
Libretto by Temistocle Solera, after the play *Nabucodonosor* (1836) by Anicet-Bourgeois and Francis Cornue, and the scenario of the ballet *Nabucodonosor* by Antonio Cortesi (1838)
Composed 1841; rev. August and December 1842
PREMIERES 9 March 1842, La Scala, Milan; UK: 3 March 1846, Her Majesty's Theatre, London (as *Nino*); US: 4 April 1848, Astor Opera House, New York
CAST Nabucodonosor (Nabucco), King of Babylon *bar*, Ismaele *t*, Zaccaria *b*, Abigaille *s*, Fenena *s*, High Priest of Baal *b*, Abdallo *t*, Anna *s*; *satb* chorus of Babylonian and Hebrew soldiers, Levites, Hebrew virgins, Babylonian women, magi, grandees of the kingdom of Babylon, populace, etc.

Nabucco occupies in Verdi's career very much the position that *Der fliegende Holländer* occupies in Wagner's: 'With this opera', he remarked, in the *Autobiographical Sketch* dictated to Giulio Ricordi in 1879, 'it is fair to say my career began.' After the humiliation of *Un giorno di regno* Verdi seriously considered giving up all ambitions for a career in opera. But Merelli, the impresario of La Scala, did not lose faith in his talent. Early in 1841 he brought off a psychological masterstroke by suddenly thrusting a new libretto into the unsuspecting composer's hand, and bundling him out of his office. Verdi later insisted that he read Solera's libretto very reluctantly; but its biblical grandeur and pathos moved him deeply, haunted and finally obsessed him. By the autumn the opera was finished.

After the premiere, Milan's leading newspaper acclaimed a 'clamorous and total success'; *Nabucco* revealed Verdi as a major new force in the Italian theatre, and gave the rather gauche young provincial entrée into the best social and artistic circles in the city. By the end of the year it had enjoyed 65 performances at La Scala, and within two years had been sung all over north and central Italy, and as far afield as Vienna, Cagliari, Barcelona and Lisbon. More than any other Verdi opera, *Nabucco* – by virtue of its great central theme of national humiliation and renewal – was to prove a major spiritual experience for Italians during the Risorgimento era; in later decades it became an indispensable element of Risorgimento mythology.

SYNOPSIS

The scene is set in Jerusalem (Part I) and Babylon (Parts II, III and IV) in 587 BC.

Part I: 'Jerusalem' Inside Solomon's Temple. As Nabucco's Assyrian hordes press upon Jerusalem, the Hebrews take refuge in the temple. Zaccaria, the high priest, has taken hostage Nabucco's daughter, Fenena; he urges the Hebrews to trust God and fight bravely ('D'Egitto là sui lidi . . . Come notte a sol fulgente'). Fenena is left in the care of Ismaele; they have been lovers since he once led an embassage to Babylon, and she has become sympathetic to the Hebrew god. A group of soldiers bursts into the temple, led by the warlike Abigaille, Nabucco's elder daughter. She too loves Ismaele, and tries to woo him away from Fenena, promising to spare the otherwise doomed Jewish people. These now stream back into the temple, and Nabucco rides triumphantly in on horseback. Zaccaria threatens to kill Fenena ('Tremin gl'insani'), but Ismaele saves her from the high priest's sword, and she flees to the arms of her father. Nabucco and Abigaille shout for plunder and slaughter, while Zaccaria and the Hebrews anathematize Ismaele ('Mio furor, non più costretto . . . Dalle genti sii reietto').

Part II: 'The Wicked Man' Scene 1: Apartments in the palace. It has emerged that Abigaille is the offspring of slaves, and in the king's absence it is Fenena who is invested with his authority. But Abigaille has stolen the document that betrays her secret; moreover she has an ally in the high priest of Baal, who circulates a rumour that Nabucco has died in battle and leads demands for Abigaille to become queen ('Anch'io dischiuso un giorno . . . Salgo già del trono aurato'). Scene 2: Another room in the palace. Zaccaria reads holy scripture and prays for the gift of prophecy ('Tu sul labbro dei reggenti'). He reveals that Fenena has embraced the faith, and is now a fellow Jew. Rumour of Nabucco's death reaches them, but when Abigaille and her priests arrive and dispute Fenena's authority they are confounded by the return of the king himself ('S'appressan gl'istanti'). Nabucco orders Babylonians and Jews alike to worship him as god, and is struck mad by a thunderbolt. He querulously calls for help ('Chi mi toglie il regio scettro?'), but Abigaille snatches up his fallen crown and reaffirms the glory of Baal.

Part III: 'The Prophecy' Scene 1: The Hanging Gardens. Babylonians acclaim Abigaille; the high priest demands that all Jews be killed, beginning with the traitorous Fenena. Nabucco appears, unkempt and still out of his wits, and attempts to reimpose his authority. But, alone with Abigaille ('Donna, chi sei?'), he is tricked into putting his seal to the death warrant; when he realizes what he has done, and then sees Abigaille destroy the proof of her lowly birth, he pathetically, but fruitlessly, appeals for compassion ('O di qual'onta aggravasi . . . Deh perdona, deh perdona'). Scene 2: The banks of the Euphrates. The Hebrews dream nostalgically of their distant homeland ('Va, pensiero, sull'ali dorate'). Zaccaria prophesies the downfall of Babylon.

Part IV: 'The Broken Idol' Scene 1: An apartment in the palace. Nabucco awakes from his deranged slumbers (portrayed in an extended orchestral prelude)

to hear the sounds of the procession conducting Fenena to her death. In a flash of inspiration he recognizes that Jehovah is the one omnipotent god, and kneels in prayer ('Dio di Giuda!'); then, his reason restored, he summons his warriors ('O prodi miei, seguitemi'). Scene 2: The Hanging Gardens. Fenena and the condemned Hebrews seek strength in prayer ('Oh, dischiuso è il firmamento!'). When Nabucco arrives, the statue of Baal crumbles to dust. All join in worship of Jehovah ('Immenso Jehova'). Meanwhile Abigaille has taken poison; she begs forgiveness from Fenena, and dies in the fear of the Lord ('Su me . . . morente . . . esanime . . .'). (After the first two performances the closing scene was regularly cut, presumably with Verdi's authorization, to finish with 'Immenso Jehova'.)

Nabucco is a thrilling opera, but it has little of the urgent theatrical *élan* that was soon to become a hallmark of Verdi's style; its musical structure is altogether more massive than that of most of the operas he wrote in the 1840s, owing something to French grand opera, especially Rossini's *Moïse*. Each act contains at least one substantial tableau, and it is in these that the typical Risorgimento intermingling of religion and nationhood is clearest. Part I, for example, begins with a huge choral movement in which the Jews bewail the desecration of their land by Nabucco, and are exhorted by their high priest to remain true to the faith. The preoccupation with nationhood in Solera's text is matched in Verdi's music by the emphasis laid on the chorus, which, whether in lament, denunciation or worship, represents the whole national and religious community. Early Milanese audiences were so enthusiastic about the choral music in *Nabucco* and its successor *I lombardi* that they styled Verdi '*il padre del coro*'. Much of it, including the greater part of 'Va, pensiero', is in unison and, in view of its dramatic and expressive function, might appropriately be described as community singing.

Contemporaries were also struck – sometimes disconcerted – by the brassiness of Verdi's orchestral palette. A stage band appears for no fewer than four formal marches, and choral melodies and even solo arias are often doubled on trumpet and/or trombone; like those of Moses in Rossini's opera, many of Zaccaria's recitatives are accompanied by brass. At the same time, *Nabucco* is the first of Verdi's operas in which certain scenes – Abigaille's death scene for example – are given a more intimate intensity by being accompanied by a small ensemble of instruments. Verdi's genius for musical characterization comes to a first climax in the turbulent rhythms and the vaulting and plunging melodies of Abigaille's music, and in its radical contrast with the bland cantabiles of Fenena.

I lombardi alla prima crociata
The Lombards at the First Crusade
Dramma lirico in four acts (2h 15m)
Libretto by Temistocle Solera, after the epic poem *I lombardi alla prima crociata* by Tommaso Grossi (1826)

Composed 1842–3, rev. July 1843; rev., as *Jérusalem*, 1847, see below
PREMIERES   11 February 1843, La Scala, Milan; UK: 12 May 1846, Her Majesty's Theatre, Haymarket, London; US: 3 March 1847, Palmo's Opera House, New York
CAST   Arvino *t*, Pagano *b*, Giselda *s*, Oronte *t*, 2 *s*, *t*, 2 *b*; *satb* chorus of nuns, city fathers, hired ruffians, armed retainers in Folco's palace, ambassadors from Persia, Media, Damascus and Chaldea, knights and soldiers of the Crusade, pilgrims, Lombard women, women of the harem, celestial virgins

When Bartolomeo Merelli, impresario of La Scala, saw the effect of *Nabucco* on his customers, he boldly presented Verdi with a blank cheque for the third of the commissions he was to write for the theatre. After consulting Giuseppina Strepponi, his prima donna and later his second wife, the composer demanded, and received, the same fee that Bellini earned for *Norma*. Solera, who this time chose to model his text on one of the most admired works of Milanese literary Romanticism, designed *I lombardi* as a kind of companion piece to *Nabucco*, providing ample scope for marches, hymns and grandiose tableaux. With its baptism scene and an 'Ave Maria' aria – which had to be altered to 'Salve Maria' – *I lombardi* brought Verdi his first brush with the censors. The opera's premiere was as triumphant as that of *Nabucco*, and for many years *I lombardi* rivalled its predecessor in popularity; it was the first Verdi opera to be performed in America.

SYNOPSIS

The action takes place in 1096–7; Act I is set in Milan, Act II in and around Antioch, Acts III and IV near to Jerusalem.

Act I: 'Vengeance'   Pagano, one of the sons of Folco, lord of Ro, returns from a pilgrimage undertaken to atone for his attempt on the life of his brother Arvino, whose wife he loves. But his passion is unassuaged, and at the very ceremony of reconciliation he is again plotting Arvino's death with a servant he has suborned. In error, Pagano kills not his brother but his aged father, Folco, and is overcome with remorse.

Act II: 'The Man in the Cavern'   Arvino is leading the Lombard forces on the Crusade, and at Antioch his daughter Giselda is captured by the Muslims. In despair, he consults a local hermit, who proves to be – though Arvino does not recognize him – the penitent Pagano. The two brothers lead an assault on the city, and Giselda is freed. But she denounces them for the un-Christian slaughter they have encouraged, and mourns the supposed death of the Muslim prince, Oronte, whom she loves.

Act III: 'The Conversion'   As the Crusaders advance on Jerusalem they are overtaken by Oronte, who has recovered from his wounds; Giselda flees with him from the camp. They are pursued by Arvino's soldiers, and Oronte is wounded again, this time fatally. Before dying, he is baptized in the Jordan by the hermit (Pagano).

Act IV: 'The Holy Sepulchre'   The Crusaders are tormented by weariness and thirst; but a vision, vouchsafed to Giselda, leads them to the brook of Siloam,

where they refresh themselves for the final, victorious assault on Jerusalem. In the battle the hermit is mortally wounded; at last he reveals his identity, and the brothers are reconciled.

Episodic, even ramshackle in structure, *I lombardi* lacks the spiritual unity of *Nabucco*. But in certain respects it is the bolder work: the studied effects of harmonic and instrumental colour, for example in Giselda's 'Salve Maria!', the bold refashioning of conventions, as in her cabaletta 'No! . . . giusta causa', and many other passages testify to Verdi's unwillingness simply to repeat himself. For the first time he abandons the full-length overture in favour of a brief preludio, whose solemn strains are surely designed to set the keynote for the whole opera. The Act IV chorus 'O Signore, dal tetto natio' – one of the movements that do seem to aim at replicating a *Nabucco* model ('Va, pensiero') – became one of Verdi's best-loved pieces; its citation in Giuseppe Giusti's poem 'Sant'Ambrogio' is the most notable reference to Verdi's music in contemporary Italian literature.

Ernani

Dramma lirico in four acts (parts) (2h 15m)
Libretto by Francesco Maria Piave, after the tragedy *Hernani* by Victor Hugo (1830)
Composed November 1843–February 1844, rev. September and December 1844
PREMIERES   9 March 1844, La Fenice, Venice; UK: 8 March 1845, Her Majesty's Theatre, Haymarket, London; US: 13 April 1847, Park Theater, New York
CAST   Ernani *t*, Don Carlo, King of Spain *bar*, Don Ruy Gomez de Silva *b*, Elvira *s*, Giovanna *s*, Don Riccardo *t*, Jago *b*; *satb* chorus of rebel highlanders and bandits, knights and members of Silva's household, maids in attendance on Elvira, knights in attendance on Don Carlo, Spanish and German noblemen and their ladies; extras: highlanders and bandits, electors and grandees of the imperial court, pages of the imperial court, German soldiers, ladies, male and female followers

By now theatres all over Italy were keen to engage Verdi. Having seen his first four operas staged at La Scala, he decided the time had come to accept an invitation from La Fenice, Venice, next to La Scala the leading opera house in northern Italy. And, since much of the correspondence that now began to flow between Milan and Venice survives, *Ernani* provides us with a vivid picture of how the young Verdi went about his work. It is not surprising to find that he expects to be well paid; he insists on selecting his own singers, and on having time to rehearse thoroughly; he explains – and this was rare in Italy at the time – that he began to compose only when the libretto was completed to his satisfaction, because 'when I have a general conception of the whole poem the music always comes of its own accord'.

After the grandiosities of *Nabucco* and *I lombardi* Verdi was looking for a different kind of drama, faster moving and more fiery in its passions. And he embarked on what was to become a typical procedure, reading widely in Byron and Dumas and other heroes of Romanticism, until he came across something – in this case one of the landmarks of French Romantic theatre – in which, in a flash of intuition, he sensed an opera was latent. The librettist for *Ernani*, the Venetian poetaster Francesco Maria Piave, whom Verdi did not yet know personally, was soon to become his most trusted collaborator; not because he had more talent than Solera, but because he was so compliant. Already Verdi had very precise ideas about what he wanted from his librettist; and in his letters about *Ernani* we find him emphasizing two issues that were to remain obsessions for the rest of his life: the poet must be as concise as possible, and he must remain as faithful as possible to the situations and the words of the original play. Despite *Hernani*'s notoriety, it was possible, thanks to the comparatively liberal censorship in Venice, to get the libretto approved without too much trouble. The censors were exercised by a few passages, notably the conspiracy scene. They insisted that this should be as brief as possible, that the conspirators should not draw their swords, that the king's words of pardon should be 'liberal and impressive'; and they drew something of the republican sting from Piave's text 'Si ridesti il Leon di Castiglia', which, however, was still able to inspire one of the most spine-tingling of the hymns to liberty that stud Verdi's early operas.

Verdi arrived in Venice at the start of December, allowing himself three months to compose, orchestrate and rehearse the opera, as well as supervising a revival of *I lombardi*. It was a trying winter: there were acute difficulties over assembling a suitable cast; *I lombardi* flopped, and Verdi became increasingly apprehensive as the Venetians hissed two more operas off the stage; last-minute hitches meant that neither sets nor costumes were quite ready for the premiere.

Nevertheless, *Ernani* was an immediate and lasting triumph. The first Verdi opera to be performed in Britain, it did more than any other to spread his reputation internationally during the 1840s, and remained a repertoire work for half a century. In the post-war Verdi renaissance it has proved to be, with *Nabucco*, the most resilient of his pre-*Macbeth* scores.

SYNOPSIS

The action takes place in 1519.

Act I (Part I: 'The Bandit') Scene 1: The mountains of Aragon; Don Ruy Gomez de Silva's Moorish castle is visible in the distance. Ernani joins his roistering company of outlaws. He loves Elvira, and has just heard that her guardian, Silva, is to marry her himself on the morrow; the outlaws plan to abduct her ('Come rugiada al cespite ... O tu, che l'alma adora'). Scene 2: Elvira's richly appointed room in Silva's castle. Night. Elvira fears and detests Silva; his gifts serve only to sharpen her longing for Ernani ('Ernani! ... Ernani, involami ... Tutto sprezzo che d'Ernani'). Don Carlo also loves Elvira, and in Silva's absence makes one last attempt to persuade her to elope with him ('Da quel dì che t'ho veduta ... Fiero sangue d'Aragona'). They are interrupted by Ernani, the king's deadly enemy in politics as in love. As Elvira struggles to keep them from one another's throats

('Tu se' Ernani!'), Silva returns. Finding his bride-to-be in the company of two strange men, he bewails his shame and prepares to avenge himself ('Infelice! e tu credevi': the cabaletta 'Infin che un brando vindice' is a later addition). When the king's identity is revealed, however, Silva changes his tone ('Oh cielo! è desso il re!!!'). Quixotically moved to help Ernani escape, Carlo describes him as one of his own servants; then in an ensemble, as Ernani and Elvira plan their elopement, and Ernani vows to avenge his father's death (for which Carlo was responsible), the king and Silva discuss political affairs.

Act II (Part II: 'The Guest') A magnificent hall in Don Ruy Gomez de Silva's castle. Rumours of Ernani's death are rife; Elvira has despaired of delaying her marriage any longer, and Silva's household is celebrating the wedding day. Ernani has, however, escaped; disguised as a pilgrim, he gains admission to the castle, where he hears that Silva and Elvira are about to be married. Once alone with him, Elvira persuades him of her undying love, and Silva returns to find them embracing passionately; the arrival of the king delays the execution of his vengeance ('Ah morir potessi adesso ... No ... vendetta più tremenda'). Carlo has come in pursuit of Ernani, but Silva, ever punctilious in the laws of hospitality, refuses to surrender him. The king orders his men to search the castle; as they find nothing, he takes Elvira hostage ('Lo vedremo, o veglio audace ... Vieni meco, sol di rose'). Silva releases Ernani from his hiding-place, presents him with a sword, and demands the instant satisfaction of honour. Ernani refuses to fight an old man, and points out what Silva had not previously realized: that the king is their rival for Elvira's love. Silva agrees to let Ernani help him rescue Elvira, but only on the grimmest condition: Ernani gives him a hunting horn, and pledges that if he wishes him dead he need only sound it; they ride off in pursuit ('Ecco il pegno: nel momento ... In arcione, in arcion, cavalieri').

Act III (Part III: 'Clemency') Subterranean vaults enclosing the tomb of Charlemagne at Aquisgrana (Aachen). The new Holy Roman Emperor is about to be named. Carlo, knowing that a group of conspirators is to meet in the vaults by Charlemagne's tomb, hides himself. Ambitious now for eternal glory, he bids farewell to the follies of youth ('Oh de' verd'anni miei'). The conspirators assemble – Ernani and Silva among them. Ernani is chosen to kill Carlo, and refuses, even when offered his own life in exchange, to yield the privilege to Silva; all conspirators join in a hymn to freedom ('Si ridesti il Leon di Castiglia'). Then, as three cannon shots announce Carlo's election, he steps from Charlemagne's tomb and denounces the conspirators. Electors, nobles and soldiers stream into the vaults; Carlo condemns the rebels to condign punishment, but in response to Elvira's entry he emulates the clemency of Charlemagne ('Oh sommo Carlo').

Act IV (Part IV: 'The Mask') The terrace of Don Giovanni d'Aragona's (Ernani's) palace in Saragossa. A crowd of guests, momentarily troubled by a masked figure in black, celebrates the wedding of Ernani and Elvira. Hardly are the lovers left alone before a horn is heard in the distance; the masked man approaches and reveals himself as Silva, come to demand the honouring of the pledge; unable to soften his obduracy, Ernani stabs himself and Elvira swoons ('Cessaro i suoni, disparì ogni face . . . Solingo, errante e misero . . . Ferma . . . crudele, estinguere').

With *Ernani* Verdi moved from the high-minded communal concerns of *Nabucco* and *I lombardi* to a world of passionate individualism. His attention focuses on the possibilities of musical characterization, and in particular – given a dramatic situation in which three men pay court to one woman – the expressive qualities of the three types of male voice. *Ernani* provides the archetypal pattern for a whole tradition of opera: the tenor, a youthful, suffering lover; the bass, an elderly ruthless egotist; and, most distinctively, the baritone, a psychologically more complex type, torn between tenderness and violence, self-indulgence and idealism.

Ernani is not a sophisticated work, but in scene after scene it shows the young Verdi at his most effective. The magnificent breadth of conception of the conspiracy scene (despite the censors), and its evocative orchestral colouring; the lyrical fervour of the arias ('Ernani! . . . Ernani involami', 'Vieni meco, sol di rose', etc.), and the enthralling expressive details of the recitatives (especially in Act IV) set standards that he was not to surpass for some years. And if the prelude that henceforth generally takes the place of the overture is intended to act as a microcosm of the drama, no later example does it more effectively than *Ernani*'s, with its juxtaposition of tender lyricism and tragic solemnity (the motif associated with Ernani's oath).

I due Foscari

The Two Foscari
Tragedia lirica in three acts (1h 45m)
Libretto by Francesco Maria Piave, after the historical tragedy *The Two Foscari* by Lord Byron (1821)
Composed May–October 1844; rev. March 1845; additional aria: December 1846
PREMIERES 3 November 1844, Teatro Argentina, Rome; UK: 10 April 1847, Her Majesty's Theatre, Haymarket, London; US: 10 May 1847, Howard Athenaeum, Boston
CAST Francesco Foscari *bar*, Jacopo Foscari *t*, Lucrezia Contarini *s*, Jacopo Loredano *b*, *s*, 2 *t*, *b*; *satb* chorus of members of the Council of Ten and the Giunta, maidservants of Lucrezia, Venetian ladies, crowd, masked men and women; extras: Il Messer Grande (Chief of Police), 2 small sons of Jacopo Foscari, Comandadori, prison warders, gondoliers, sailors, crowd, maskers, pages of the doge

I due Foscari was a subject for which Verdi had already sketched out a synopsis in the summer of 1843, when he was pondering his Venice commission. Unacceptable to the authorities there because of its unflattering portraits of some distinguished Venetian families, *I due Foscari* was temporarily shelved, only to be taken up a year later for Verdi's first Roman commission. It soon became clear that Byron's play was lacking in 'theatrical grandeur' (letter to Piave), and in making the operatic adaptation much of Verdi's care was devoted to the question of how best to

enliven the spectacle and to make the hero, Jacopo Foscari, a more energetic figure. The premiere, by all accounts abysmally sung, was felt by the composer to have been a 'mezzo-fiasco'; as the singers settled into their roles audiences enjoyed the opera much more, but it never shared the popularity of its three predecessors.

SYNOPSIS
Act I   Venice, 1457. The Foscari family is implacably hated by Loredano. Jacopo Foscari, exiled and homesick, is discovered to have been engaged in forbidden correspondence with another state; charged also with complicity in a murder, he is brought back to Venice for interrogation; his octogenarian father, Francesco, though doge, is powerless to intervene on his behalf.

Act II   Jacopo's wife, Lucrezia, and the doge visit Jacopo in prison, to warn him that he will again be exiled. Swayed by Loredano, the Council of Ten confirms the sentence, despite the sensational appearance at their deliberations of Lucrezia and her children, whose appeal for clemency comes close to moving many of them.

Act III   Amid scenes of popular revelry, Jacopo is brought to the ship and bids Lucrezia farewell. Meanwhile, in the doge's palace, the charge of murder has been proved false. The doge's joy is short-lived, however, for Lucrezia returns to tell him that, weakened by torture and broken-hearted, Jacopo died as he boarded the ship. The Council of Ten, led by Loredano, now comes to demand Foscari's resignation; he resists them indignantly for a while, but finally succumbs, falling dead as the great bell of San Marco acclaims his successor.

In *I due Foscari*, Verdi's growing interest in musical characterization takes an unexpected form: each of the principals – the doge, Jacopo and Lucrezia – is given a distinctive orchestral theme, which accompanies them at each of their more important appearances on stage. A fourth recurring theme, this time vocal in origin ('Silenzio, mistero'), is associated with the Council of Ten. Despite the attempts of Verdi and Piave to enliven the drama, this opera remains one of the composer's most intimate and introspective scores; in 1848 he was to describe it as 'a funeral [with] too uniform an atmosphere and colour from beginning to end'. But that is to overlook many admirable qualities, among which one may mention a new refinement of craftsmanship, and a real attempt to match the 'delicacy and pathos' Verdi had admired in Byron's poem.

Giovanna d'Arco

Joan of Arc
Dramma lirico in a prologue and three acts (2h)
Libretto by Temistocle Solera, in part after the 'Romantic tragedy' *Die Jungfrau von Orleans* by Johann Christoph Friedrich von Schiller (1801)
Composed November 1844–January 1845, rev. December 1845
PREMIERES 15 February 1845, La Scala, Milan; US: 1 March 1966, Carnegie Hall, New York (concert); UK: 4 November 1963, Kensington Town Hall, London; 14 May 1976, Brooklyn Academy, New York

CAST   Carlo (Charles VII of France) *t*, Giovanna (Joan) *s*,
Giacomo *bar*, *t*, *b*; *satb* chorus of officers of the king,
villagers, people of Rheims, French and English soldiers,
blessed spirits, evil spirits, grandees of the realm, heralds,
pages, children, marshals, deputies, knights and ladies,
magistrates, halberdiers, guards of honour

After *I lombardi*, the impresario Merelli tried, but
failed, to persuade Verdi to write yet another opera
for La Scala; before the composer went to Venice to
produce *Ernani*, however, he did agree to come back
to La Scala the following year with a new work.
Sadly, during the 1844–5 season, the deteriorating
standards of Merelli's productions soured relationships between impresario and composer, and after
Giovanna d'Arco it was 36 years before another Verdi
premiere was staged at La Scala. Despite frictions in
the company, between Verdi and Merelli and among
the singers, *Giovanna* was well performed and ecstatically received; for a time its popularity rivalled that
of Verdi's earlier collaborations with Solera. In Rome
and southern Italy, for reasons of religious susceptibili-
ity, it was for many years supplied with an amended
text entitled *Orietta di Lesbo*.

SYNOPSIS
The action takes place in France, in Dom-Rémy,
Rheims and near Rouen in 1429.
    Prologue On the point of surrendering to the Eng-
lish, the dauphin Charles is inspired by a dream to
visit a sanctuary in the forest near Dom-Rémy. There
he meets Joan, the very incarnation of his dream, who
prophesies that France's travail will soon be at an
end.
    Act I   Joan's appearance in the French ranks has
transformed the course of the war, and the English
are close to defeat. But Joan's father, Giacomo, a
clergyman who fears that she is in the grip of demonic
powers, believes it his duty to deliver her into the
hands of the English. The inner voices that have
always troubled Joan become more insistent as she
acknowledges that she loves Charles.
    Act II   As Charles, Joan and the people stream
out of the cathedral after the coronation, they are
accosted by Giacomo, who challenges his daughter to
deny that she is possessed by devils. She remains
speechless, and he leads her away, hoping to save her
immortal soul by having her burned at the stake.
    Act III   Giacomo realizes the terrible mistake he
has made when he finds Joan, now a prisoner in the
English camp, at prayer. He releases her, and watches
as she leads the French forces to victory on the
battlefield. Mortally wounded, Joan is reverently
borne back to camp, where she dies.

For modern ears, no opera illustrates more disconcertingly than *Giovanna d'Arco* the chasm between Verdi's
best and worst music. While some of the solo and
ensemble writing, particularly that for Joan and
Charles, is as fine as anything the young composer
did, his mystic choruses – variously accompanied by
harmonium and triangle (demons) and harp and fisarmonica (angels) – are likely to be felt to embody 19th-
century taste at its most abysmal. But, as Verdi's
young composition pupil, Emanuele Muzio, enthusi-

astically declared, they are certainly 'popular, truly
Italian . . . full of seductive ideas that can be sung
straight away after a couple of hearings'; and when
we read that within a few weeks of the premiere the
favourite melodies of *Giovanna* were being ground out
on the barrel organs on the streets of Milan we may
be confident that the choruses were among them. An
oft-noted curiosity in the score is the resemblance to
'Hearts of Oak' of the chorus 'O duce, noi sempre
mirasti' sung in Act I by the English soldiers.

Alzira

Tragedia lirica in a prologue and two acts (1h 30m)
Libretto by Salvatore Cammarano, after the tragedy *Alzire,
ou Les Américains* by Voltaire (1736)
Composed May–July 1845
PREMIERES 12 August 1845, Teatro San Carlo, Naples;
US: 17 January 1968, Carnegie Hall, New York (concert);
UK: 10 February 1970, Collegiate Theatre, London

In the earlier part of Verdi's career La Scala and La
Fenice in the north of Italy and the San Carlo, Naples,
in the south were the leading opera houses in the
peninsula; and when the opportunity of composing
for Naples arose Verdi seized it eagerly. Why *Alzira*
turned out so poorly – 'a really ugly one' was the
composer's own final assessment – is not easy to
explain. One factor was certainly that, because of an
exaggerated respect for his librettist's long stage experience, he took a less active role than usual in fashioning
the libretto to his own needs. An inability to identify
himself with the subject and an ominous dependence
on routine is suggested in a remark made to a Milan
friend, that he wrote the opera 'almost without noticing and with no trouble at all'. In only a handful of
scenes – notably the Act I finale, where memories of
the Act II finale of *Lucia di Lammermoor* are in the
air – did Verdi's imagination really catch fire. A
full-length sinfonia was commissioned separately,
during rehearsals, when the theatre management
found the opera too short. Enthusiastically received at
the dress rehearsal, *Alzira* was already on the wane by
the second night; it has only occasionally been
revived.

SYNOPSIS
Gusmano, Spanish governor of Peru, and Zamoro, an
Indian chieftain, are rivals for the love of the Inca
princess Alzira. For most of the drama the Spaniard's
ruthlessness is ironically contrasted with the magnanimity of the 'savages'. But, when Zamoro stabs him
as he is about to marry Alzira, he undergoes a deathbed enlightenment, pardons his rival, and restores
Alzira to his arms.

Attila

Dramma lirico in a prologue and three acts (1h 45m)
Libretto by Temistocle Solera with alterations by Francesco
Maria Piave, after the tragedy *Attila, König der Hunnen* by
Zacharias Werner (1808)
Composed September 1845–March 1846; substitute arias
(both to replace 'Chi non avrebbe il misero') for later
revivals composed September and December 1846
PREMIERES 17 March 1846, La Fenice, Venice;

UK: 14 March 1848, Her Majesty's Theatre, Haymarket, London; US: 15 April 1850, New York
CAST Attila, King of the Huns *b*, Ezio *bar*, Odabella *s*, Foresto *t*, Leone (Leo) *b*, *t*; *satb* chorus of chieftains, kings and soldiers, Huns, Gepids, Ostrogoths, Heruls, Thuringians, Quadi, Druids, priestesses, populace, men and women of Aquileia, maidens of Aquileia in martial dress, Roman officers and soldiers, Roman virgins and children, hermits, slaves

The composition of *Attila* was bedevilled by problems. The original plan was for the Venetian librettist Piave to write the libretto, on the basis of a synopsis provided by Andrea Maffei – poet, translator and connoisseur of German literature – a close friend of Verdi, who was probably responsible for interesting him in Werner's play in the first instance. Having offered Piave a great deal of advice on the treatment of the subject, Verdi – for reasons unknown, but perhaps because he was beginning to think of *Attila* as a potential grand opera in the French style – decided that it would be preferable to entrust the text to the flamboyant Solera. But Solera disappeared to Spain just when he was most needed, and it was Piave who came to the rescue – if that is the apt phrase – by completing and revising Solera's unfinished text to Verdi's specifications. Verdi was ill for virtually the whole of the time he was composing the opera and, after the equivocally successful premiere, was ordered to take a six-month rest cure.

SYNOPSIS
Aquileia and the Adriatic lagoons, and near Rome, about the middle of the fifth century.
Prologue As Attila and his hordes advance into Italy, Odabella and a group of women who have escaped the slaughter impress him by their courage; he presents her with his sword and takes her into his entourage. Ezio, a Roman general, comes to parley, but Attila rejects his proposal that they share out the world between them. Meanwhile Foresto, Odabella's betrothed, arrives at Rio-Alto and urges the other Aquileian refugees to build a new city there – the future Venice.
Act I Meeting Foresto, Odabella denies betraying the Italian cause; rather she awaits an opportunity to kill the tyrant. Meanwhile Attila is trying to shake off the memory of an awe-inspiring dream. But his courage fails when the vision becomes a reality: Pope Leo (disguised for reasons of censorship as an 'aged Roman') and attendants process into his camp to bar his way to Rome.
Act II Foresto and Ezio (who has been invited to one of Attila's banquets) lay plans for the defeat of the Huns. Sinister omens darken the atmosphere at the feast, and the king is saved from poisoning only by the intervention of Odabella. As her reward, Attila declares that she shall be his bride.
Act III During the wedding, the Romans surround the Huns' camp; as they attack, Odabella stabs Attila.

Perhaps from force of circumstance, *Attila* was to emerge as one of the crasser products of Verdi's 'galley years', which is sad, for he began the opera

determined that he would not relapse into routine. There was to be no onstage band, he declared, because that was a piece of nonsensical provincialism that Italian theatres should be growing out of; nor was he going to compose lots of marches that might make the opera sound like a pale imitation of *Nabucco* or *Giovanna d'Arco*; as for the finale, that would be unlike anything anyone had ever written before. The positive fruit of these aspirations is not much in evidence, and the sheer noisiness of *Attila* made it a *bête noire* of fastidious critics. Verdi's interpretation of the subject was coloured by Mme de Staël's celebrated book *De l'Allemagne* (1810), which he urged Piave to read: in the rabid tones of Odabella's cavatina (prologue), for example, we may surely sense Verdi's desire to portray his heroine as, in Mme de Staël's words, 'a goddess of war'.

Macbeth
Opera (melodramma) in four acts (2h 30m)
Original version: libretto by Francesco Maria Piave (with additions by Andrea Maffei), after the tragedy by William Shakespeare (1605–6)
Revised version: French text translated from Piave (who revised the 1847 text himself) and Maffei by Charles Nuittier Alexandre Beaumont
Composed September 1846–February 1847, rev. November 1864–February 1865
PREMIERES 14 March 1847, Teatro della Pergola, Florence; US: 24 April 1850, Niblo's Garden, New York; Ireland: 30 March 1859, Theatre Royal, Dublin; UK: 2 October 1860, Theatre Royal, Manchester; revised version: 21 April 1865, Théâtre-Lyrique, Paris; UK: 21 May 1938, Glyndebourne, Sussex; US: 24 October 1941, 44th Street Theater, New York
CAST Duncano (Duncan), King of Scotland *silent*, Macbeth *bar*, Banco (Banquo) *b*, Lady Macbeth *s*, Lady Macbeth's Lady-in-Waiting *ms*, Macduff *t*, Malcolm *t*, Fleanzio (Fleance) *silent*, Doctor *b*, Macbeth's Servant *b*, Assassin *b*, 3 Apparitions 2 *s*, *b*, (rev. version: Herald *b*, Hecate, Goddess of the Night *silent*); *satb* chorus of witches, king's messengers, Scottish noblemen and exiles, assassins, English soldiers, bards, aerial spirits; (rev. version: ballet)

The breakdown of Verdi's health at the time of *Attila* was a blessing in disguise: during the six-month convalescence that followed he was able to recover an artistic idealism he had been in danger of losing in the relentless routine of the previous two years. *Macbeth*, conceived at this time, was the boldest, the most consistently inventive and the most idealistic opera he had yet written. Verdi was already an ardent Shakespearian and was determined to do all he could to make his opera worthy of its model; sending Piave a first synopsis, he described *Macbeth* as 'one of mankind's grandest creations', and demanded from the librettist 'extravagance and originality . . . brevity and sublimity'.
Macbeth is the first of Verdi's operas in which we find him taking as minute an interest in the staging as in the text and music. He would not commit himself to writing it until he knew he could have Felice Varesi – a supremely intelligent singer and actor – for the title role; he warned the Florence impresario, Alessandro Lanari, that no production expenses could be spared, since chorus and stage machinery were so

important; he paid scrupulous attention to such details as lighting, the historical accuracy of the settings, the gestures and movements of the singers. In her memoirs, Marianna Barbieri-Nini, the first Lady Macbeth, described the unprecedented demands Verdi made on his performers: working on the sleep-walking scene, she found herself 'for three months, morning and evening, attempting to impersonate someone who speaks in her sleep, who (as the maestro put it) utters words . . . almost without moving her lips, the rest of the face motionless, the eyes shut'.

At the Florence premiere *Macbeth* was very warmly received. There was some critical unease that an Italian artist should have invested such enthusiasm in a subject in the genere fantastico – a transalpine aberration of taste, to the minds of many Italians – but the extraordinary quality of Verdi's dramatic vision was recognized and admired on all sides. The special place the opera held in his own affections is shown, first, in his dedication of it to Antonio Barezzi, the father-in-law to whom he owed so much, and, second, in the fact that it was the first opera for which he refused to provide *puntature* (adaptations of the arias for singers with different types of voice).

In 1863 Léon Carvalho, director of the Théâtre Lyrique in Paris, asked Verdi to compose a ballet and a new choral finale for *Macbeth*. Returning to the score, Verdi found himself being drawn into a more radical revision than either he or Carvalho had anticipated. Despite the fine quality of this new music, the Paris *Macbeth* was relatively unsuccessful and has established itself as a repertoire work only during the last half-century.

SYNOPSIS
The scene is Scotland, principally Macbeth's castle.

Act I   Scene 1: A wood. As Macbeth and Banquo, two generals in Duncan's army, make their way home from battle, they come across a coven of witches. The witches foretell, among other prophecies, that Macbeth will be king of Scotland and Banquo the father of future kings – prophecies that chime strangely with Macbeth's own secret ambitions ('Due vaticini compiuti or sono . . . Oh, come s'empie costui d'orgoglio'). The witches disperse ('S'allontanarono!'). Scene 2: A hall in Macbeth's castle. Lady Macbeth reads a letter telling of her husband's military successes and of the witches' prophecy. She doubts if, without her prompting, he is ruthless enough to attain his ambitions. When a messenger announces that Duncan is accompanying Macbeth to the castle that night, she realizes that the time has come to act ('Vieni! t'affretta! . . . Or tutti sorgete, ministri infernali'); and on Macbeth's return he is soon persuaded that Duncan must be killed. After nightfall, the vision of a bloody dagger leads him on to the murder ('Mi si affaccia un pugnal?!'). He returns, already racked by conscience; his wife chides him for his faint-heartedness and goes to Duncan's chamber to incriminate the guards ('Fatal mia donna! un murmure'). Macduff, a Scottish nobleman, and Banquo come to attend on the king; the murder is discovered ('Schiudi, inferno, la bocca ed inghiotti').

Act II   Scene 1: A room in the castle. Macbeth is now king of Scotland, and Duncan's son Malcolm has taken refuge in England. Since the witches have prophesied that Banquo's sons will succeed to the throne, Macbeth and his wife resolve that they too must be killed (1847: 'Trionfai! securi alfine'; 1865: 'La luce langue, il faro spegnesi'). Scene 2: A park. Banquo and his son, Fleance, make their way towards Macbeth's castle ('Come dal ciel precipita'); they are attacked by assassins, but Fleance escapes. Scene 3: A magnificent hall. Macbeth and his queen welcome their guests, and the wine is soon flowing ('Si colmi il calice'). An assassin enters to tell Macbeth what happened in the park. As the king rejoins the banquet, he is appalled to see the figure of Banquo sitting in his appointed place. Lady Macbeth tries to dispel the gathering shadows, but the ghost of Banquo returns. By now Macbeth's behaviour is filling his guests with suspicion ('Sangue a me quell'ombra chiede'); Macduff decides to join the exiles.

Act III   A gloomy cavern. The witches are brewing potions and casting spells. (In the 1865 version there follows a ballet of spirits, devils and witches, in honour of Hecate.) Macbeth enters, and in response to his questioning the witches conjure up a series of visions. These warn him to beware Macduff, but assure him that he need fear no man born of woman, and that he will be invincible until Birnam Wood (*sic*) moves against him. But then, terrified by the apparition of eight kings, followed by Banquo carrying a mirror ('Fuggi, regal fantasima'), Macbeth swoons, and the witches dance around him. When he recovers, he determines to exterminate Macduff and his family (1847: 'Vada in fiamme, e in polve cada'; 1865: 'Ora di morte e di vendetta').

Act IV   Scene 1: A deserted place on the borders of Scotland and England; in the distance, Birnam Wood. Scottish refugees bewail the plight of their country under Macbeth's rule ('Patria oppressa! il dolce nome'). Macduff, heartbroken to hear of the deaths of his wife and children, is urged by Malcolm to seek comfort in revenge ('Ah, la paterna mano . . . La patria tradita'). Plucking branches from the trees, they advance towards Macbeth's castle. Scene 2: A room in Macbeth's castle. A doctor and lady-in-waiting watch in horror as the sleepwalking Lady Macbeth muses over the murders she and her husband have committed ('Una macchia è qui tuttora'). Scene 3: A room in the castle. Macbeth is already so overwhelmed with melancholy ('Pietà, rispetto, amore') that the news of his wife's death leaves him unaffected. When his men report the moving of Birnam Wood, however, and when later, on the battlefield, Macduff tells how he was 'from his mother's womb untimely ripp'd', Macbeth realizes that he is doomed. 1847: he dies at Macduff's hands, cursing the ambition that had delivered his soul to the powers of Hell ('Mal per me che m'affidai'); 1865: Macbeth and Macduff exeunt fighting; a few minutes later Malcolm's victorious troops enter, rejoicing in the liberation of their country ('Macbeth, Macbeth ov'è?').

Verdi's insistence that as much as possible of the quality of Shakespeare's tragedy should be preserved in the libretto had a transfiguring effect on his music, most clearly in what he called 'the two most important pieces in the opera'. In the great duet that follows the murder of Duncan in Act I, a densely packed sequence of poetic images taken from the play inspires a matching sequence of musical images, creating an exceptionally flexible operatic design, whose dramatic intensity never flags. And in the sleepwalking scene, where Shakespeare writes a highly charged prose, periodically lit up with phrases of shocking expressive power, Verdi contrives to match him by composing an orchestral backcloth packed with mysterious patterings and sighs, against which Lady Macbeth sings broken declamatory phrases, periodically opening up into great arches of cantabile melody. Both scenes are landmarks in Verdi's development as a master of dramatic orchestration, the broad daubs of his early style giving way to a more scrupulous selection and blending of colours.

A criticism sometimes directed at the 1865 revision is that the greater sophistication of the new music makes it impossible for the climactic scenes of the original to stand out as the dramatic peaks they were obviously intended to be. The greatest gains from a musical point of view are, first, Lady Macbeth's 'La luce langue', an aria of gloomy magnificence replacing an icily virtuosic cabaletta, and, second, the rewritten scene of the apparitions (Act III) where, with subtler phrasing, harmony and instrumentation, the strangeness of atmosphere is sustained with fewer lapses into the commonplace. The magnificent choral music in the last act is also largely a result of the Paris revision.

I masnadieri

The Brigands
Melodramma in four parts (2h 15m)
Libretto by Andrea Maffei after the drama *Die Räuber* by Johann Christoph Friedrich von Schiller (1781)
Composed (?)September–November 1846, March–July 1847
PREMIERES 22 July 1847, Her Majesty's Theatre, Haymarket, London; Italy: 12 February 1848, Teatro Apollo, Rome; US: 31 May 1860, Winter Gardens, New York
CAST Massimiliano, Count Moor *b*, Carlo *t*, Francesco *bar*, Amalia *s*, 2 *t*, *b*; *satb* chorus of erring youths (later brigands), women, children, servants

Like *Macbeth*, *I masnadieri* was conceived during Verdi's convalescence in the summer of 1846, when Maffei was a constant companion; if his imagination was less challenged in this opera, it was probably because of the old-fashioned cut of his friend's libretto. For a composer with so keen a business sense as Verdi, the prospect of a London commission was enticing. But, though he earned considerably more for *I masnadieri* than for any earlier opera, his hopes of further lucrative commissions foundered with the failure of the opera. Arbiters of taste in London still found Verdi's music disagreeably violent, and in making the tenor the focus of dramatic interest he failed to exploit the unique popularity enjoyed in the city by Jenny Lind, the original Amalia. *I masnadieri* was performed only four times and is rarely revived even in Italy.

SYNOPSIS
The action is set in Germany, at the beginning of the 18th century, and covers a period of about three years.

Part I Francesco Moor, having sown bitter dissension between his brother Carlo and their father Massimiliano, employs the vilest machinations to prevent reconciliation. In the meantime Carlo, driven to despair by what he believes to be his father's rejection, becomes the leader of a gang of brigands. When Massimiliano is told, falsely, that Carlo is dead, he apparently dies of shock.

Part II Francesco has installed himself as the new Count Moor. But his attempts to win the orphaned Amalia, Massimiliano's ward and Carlo's beloved, are vain.

Part III A chance encounter with Amalia brings Carlo a momentary and illusive glimpse of happiness. But he relapses into despair and later, when he learns that Massimiliano is imprisoned in a nearby ruin, violence. The old man is released, and the outlaws vow to wreak terrible vengeance on Francesco.

Part IV After the brigands have destroyed Francesco's castle, Amalia is carried off to their camp. Despite Amalia's love for him, Carlo relapses into blasphemous despair, stabs her, and goes off to deliver himself into the hands of the law.

One wonders how far it was the circumstance of composing for an unfamiliar audience that prompted Verdi to fashion his music as much to match the talents of his performers as the requirements of his dramatic theme: a prelude consisting largely of an eloquent solo for the principal cellist of the theatre orchestra, Alfredo Piatti; choruses of unusual length and sophistication of texture; above all, music for Amalia, the rather cool elegance and floridity of which were clearly inspired by the peculiar and, as Verdi felt, slightly anachronistic gifts of Jenny Lind. *I masnadieri* contains much more fine music than is commonly supposed; but it has an unusually high proportion of solo arias, and a correspondingly small number of the dramatic ensembles and confrontational duets that commonly generate so much of the theatrical voltage in Verdi; and he seems ill at ease with the Teutonic metaphysics with which Maffei occasionally (as in the Part III finale) loads the libretto.

Jérusalem

Jerusalem
Opera in four acts (2h 30m)
Libretto by Alphonse Royer and 'Gustave Vaëz' (Jean Nicolas Gustave van Nieuwenhuysen), a translation and adaptation of *I lombardi alla prima crociata*
Composed August–October 1847
PREMIERES 26 November 1847, Opéra, Paris; US: 24 January 1850, Théâtre d'Orléans, New Orleans; Italy: 26 December 1850, La Scala, Milan; UK: 31 March 1990, Grand Theatre, Leeds
CAST Gaston *t*, Le Comte de Toulouse *bar*, Roger *b*, Hélène *s*, *s*, 2 *t*, 3 *b*; *satb* chorus of knights, ladies, pages, soldiers, pilgrims, penitents, Arabs, sheiks, women of the harem, people of Ramla; ballet

There is something of the flavour of French grand opera in all the works Verdi composed in collaboration with Solera, and since 1845 he had from time to time considered adapting one of them for production at the Paris Opéra. When he arrived in Paris on his way back from London after the production of *I masnadieri* he was offered an attractive contract which provided the opportunity to try his hand at grand opera without the risk involved in composing an entirely new work (cf. Rossini's *Le siège de Corinth* and *Moïse et Pharaon*): *I lombardi* was to be radically revised and supplied with the obligatory ballet, and Verdi would be paid as for a new opera. Typically for an Italian, his attitude to the Opéra was equivocal: astonishment at the magnificence of the spectacle failed to alleviate a certain boredom with the total musico-dramatic experience; and by the time he had rehearsed *Jérusalem* for twice as long as even *Macbeth* had needed in Italy he was rather bored with his 'new' opera too. For Paris, it proved a useful rather than indispensable addition to the repertoire; feebly translated by Calisto Bassi as *Gerusalemme*, it failed to supersede *I lombardi* in the affections of Italian audiences.

SYNOPSIS
The scene is set in Toulouse and Palestine; the period is 1095–9.

Act I On the eve of their departure for the Crusade, the betrothal of Gaston, Vicomte de Béarne, and Hélène, daughter of the Comte de Toulouse, seals the reconciliation between the two families. But Roger, the comte's brother, also loves Hélène and engages an assassin to kill Gaston. In error it is the comte who is attacked, and Gaston on whom the blame for the murder attempt – which is bungled – is laid.

Act II The Crusaders pass the Saracen city of Ramla, near which the penitent Roger lives as a hermit; he begs to be allowed to join them in their battle against the infidel. Meanwhile Hélène has learned that Gaston, who has been driven into exile, is a prisoner in Ramla; she too is captured as she searches for him.

Act III Hélène is immured in the harem, where the ballet takes place (no scenario for it has survived). Ramla is captured by the Crusaders and Hélène is rescued; but Gaston is dragged away to the public square and stripped of his accoutrements of nobility in readiness for execution on the morrow.

Act IV While the Crusaders advance on Jerusalem, the hermit (Roger) is asked to administer the last rites to the condemned Gaston. Recognizing him, he absolves him and gives him a sword. In the battle for Jerusalem, Gaston covers himself in glory, while Roger is mortally wounded; on his deathbed he reveals his identity, confesses his guilt, and is reconciled with his brother.

Royer's and Vaëz's radical rewriting of the libretto of *I lombardi* clarifies the dramatic action considerably, reducing the number of scenes and eliminating otiose characters, while at the same time providing full scope for stage spectacle in the Parisian manner. In reworking his opera Verdi availed himself of the more ample choral and instrumental resources in Paris (several moments feature the cornets); but for the most part it

is in the new fastidiousness of the craftsmanship – notably the carefully wrought linking passages between one movement and another – rather than in the inherent musical inventiveness that *Jérusalem* scores over *I lombardi*. Of the newly composed music, the Act III finale – the scene of Gaston's public humiliation – is outstanding; magnificently performed at the premiere by Gilbert Duprez, it occasioned, according to Théophile Gautier, 'shudders of admiration' in the audience.

Il corsaro
The Corsair
Melodramma tragico in three acts (1h 30m)
Libretto by Francesco Maria Piave, after the poem *The Corsair* by Lord Byron (1814)
Composed November 1847–February 1848 (partly sketched in 1846)
PREMIERES 25 October 1848, Teatro Grande, Trieste; UK: 15 March 1966, Camden Town Hall, London; US: 12 December 1981, Main Theater, Stony Brook, New York
CAST Corrado *t*, Medora *s*, Gulnara *s*, Pasha Seid *bar*, 3 *t*, *b*, Anselmo (a corsair) *silent*; *satb* chorus of corsairs, guards, Turks, slaves, odalisques, Medora's handmaidens,

The origins of *Il corsaro* go back to 1843–4, a period of Byronic enthusiasm which produced *I due Foscari* and plans for operas on *The Bride of Abydos* and *Cain*; by the summer of 1846 the libretto was written and several scenes were fully sketched. There is no reason to doubt that Verdi composed the opera with as much conscientiousness as anything else he wrote, but the dislike he came to feel for Lucca, the publisher who commissioned it, soured his attitude to it. And as he was in Paris at the time of the premiere he made, most exceptionally, no attempt to take an active part in its production. He did, however, send a long letter to Marianna Barbieri-Nini, the original Gulnara, in which he offered much advice on the interpretation of her role; at the same time he suggested that the opera should be performed as if it had only two acts, the first two acts of the published score being run together without interval: 'The whole opera will thus gain in brevity and interest.'

SYNOPSIS
The scene is set on an island in the Aegean Sea and in the city of Coron. The period is the beginning of the 19th century.

Act I Despite the forebodings of his beloved, Medora, Corrado prepares to embark with his corsairs on a mysterious mission against the Turks.

Act II While his men set fire to Pasha Seid's fleet, Corrado gains admission to his palace disguised as a dervish. The fire threatens to engulf the seraglio, and, as Corrado organizes the rescue of the women, he is captured. Gulnara, the pasha's favourite, but a reluctant inmate of his harem, leads the women's appeals for mercy for the prisoner.

Act III Having failed to save Corrado, Gulnara resolves to release him from prison herself, even though she has first to kill Seid. Corrado and Gulnara return to the corsairs' island only to find Medora on the point of death, for, believing Corrado dead, she has taken poison; in despair, Corrado hurls himself into the sea.

What to Verdi seemed the most interesting scenes in *Il corsaro*, the prison scene and the final trio, were sketched as early as 1846, and when he returned to the opera nothing else stirred him quite so much. After the comparative weightiness of the previous three operas (each in its different way), *Il corsaro* seems a slight, even sketchy, piece, the interest of the choral music is negligible, and there are few signs of Verdi's new-found orchestral sophistication. The attentive listener will, however, often be rewarded: there is, for example, no doubt that, even in something less than his best form, the composer is designing his arias more imaginatively (cf. the treatment of the reprises in 'Tutto parea sorridere' in Act I and 'Cento leggiadre vergini' in Act III); and both the andante and allegro movements in the Act II finale are as finely crafted and as imaginatively sustained as any comparable movements in Verdi's earlier works.

La battaglia di Legnano
The Battle of Legnano
Tragedia lirica in four acts (1h 45m)
Libretto by Salvatore Cammarano, after the play *La bataille de Toulouse* by Joseph Méry (1828)
Composed November 1848–January 1849
PREMIERES 27 January 1849, Teatro Argentina, Rome; UK: 31 October 1960, Cardiff; US: 28 February 1976, Cooper Union Great Hall, New York
CAST Rolando *bar*, Lida *s*, Arrigo *t*, *ms*, 2 *t*, *bar*, 4 *b*; *satb* chorus of Cavaliers of Death, magistrates and leaders of the people of Como, Lida's serving maids, people of Milan, senators of Milan, soldiers from Verona, Novara, Piacenza and Milan, German army

By 1848, the year of revolutions, virtually the whole of the Italian peninsula was simmering with liberal and patriotic enthusiasms. It was the librettist Cammarano who suggested the subject of *La battaglia di Legnano* to Verdi, because he supposed that at such a time 'there burns in you as in me the desire to evoke the most glorious episode of Italian history, that of the Lombard League'. He was right: Verdi, now resident primarily in Paris, was eager to make some artistic contribution to the pan-Italian cause in which he believed so fervently – it was during a lull in work on the opera that he composed the patriotic song 'Suona la tromba', and sent it to the republican leader Mazzini, expressing the hope that 'it might soon be sung amid the music of the cannon on the Lombardy plain'. The performance of so flagrantly political an opera in Rome was possible only because, the pope having fled the city late in 1848, it was temporarily governed by a republican triumvirate. Once the revolutionary upheavals of 1848–9 were quelled *La battaglia di Legnano* was doomed; it was occasionally revived in sober Flemish disguise as *L'assedio di Arlem*.

SYNOPSIS
Acts I, III and IV take place in Milan; Act II in Como. The period is 1176.
Act I: 'He is Alive!' During the wars between the Italian communes and the German emperor Frederick Barbarossa, Arrigo, a warrior from Verona, is gravely wounded and reported dead. Returning to Milan after a long convalescence, he finds his fiancée,

Lida, married to his own closest friend, Rolando, a Milanese duke.
Act II: 'Barbarossa!' Rolando and Arrigo try to persuade the citizens of Como to ally themselves with the Lombard League, but their conference is interrupted by the arrival of Barbarossa and his army.
Act III: 'Infamy' Arrigo is sworn in as one of the 'Cavaliers of Death'. The hour of the decisive battle with Barbarossa approaches, and Rolando bids his wife and child farewell. When the secret of Lida's and Arrigo's love is betrayed to him, he takes the cruellest revenge he can conceive: he locks up Arrigo, so that, unable to fight with the Cavaliers of Death, he will be an object of eternal infamy; but Arrigo manages to escape.
Act IV: 'To Die for the Fatherland' Barbarossa's army has been routed; but, as Milan celebrates the Lombard victory, Arrigo is borne in mortally wounded. He solemnly testifies to Lida's innocence, is reconciled with Rolando, and dies embracing the Italian banner.

Verdi's most explicitly patriotic opera is, as far as its musical style is concerned, one of his most Parisian: alongside movements in the traditional Italian forms, one finds a three-part (ABA) 'romanza' in the French manner ('Ah! m'abbraccia d'esultanza'), and a duet ('È ver? . . . Sei d'altri?') in something resembling a classical sonata form; instrumental marches and grandiose choruses, generally more hymnic now than in *Nabucco*, provide much of the musical colouring. It is pageant as much as it is drama, a cunningly ordered sequence of processions and tableaux. The opening chorus, 'Viva Italia', is conceived as a kind of hypothetical national anthem, and recurs at strategic moments throughout the opera as the musical emblem of the Italian patriots. This opera closes a phase of Verdi's career: as an ideological testament it is unequivocal, and once it had been composed he felt no further need to burden his works with the Risorgimento overtones that are periodically to be detected in the operas of the 1840s.

Luisa Miller
Melodramma tragico in three acts (2h 15m)
Libretto by Salvatore Cammarano, after the 'bourgeois tragedy' *Kabale und Liebe* by Johann Christoph Friedrich von Schiller (1784)
Composed August–October 1849
PREMIERES 8 December 1849, Teatro San Carlo, Naples; US: 27 October 1852, Academy of Music, Philadelphia; UK: 3 June 1858, Her Majesty's Theatre, Haymarket, London
CAST Count Walter *b*, Rodolfo *t*, Federica, Duchess of Ostheim *a*, Wurm *b*, Miller *bar*, Luisa *s*, Laura *ms*, peasant *t*; *satb* chorus of maids-in-waiting to Federica, pages, members of the household, bowmen (bodyguards), villagers

The idea of composing an opera based on *Kabale und Liebe* originated in the summer of 1846, when Verdi was convalescing at Recoaro and much in the company of Andrea Maffei, Schiller's Italian translator. As usual when he found a subject that excited him, he at first imagined an opera that would follow closely in the steps of its literary model. But the opera was intended for Naples, the most old-fashioned of the major operatic centres of Italy, and Cammarano recognized at once that they would never get it past the censors without eliminating some episodes and raising some of the characters 'to a nobler plane'. There is no doubt the composer would have been more completely happy about *Luisa Miller* had it proved possible to keep closer to Schiller: he particularly regretted the sacrifice of Lady Milford, the prince's mistress (replaced by Federica, a 'respectable' widow), but Cammarano explained that, quite apart from the problem of censorship, no leading singer in Naples would be prepared to undertake such a role.

The opera was warmly received at its premiere, and has always been admired without ever quite gaining for itself the central place in the repertoire that most Verdians feel it deserves.

SYNOPSIS

The action takes place in the Tyrol, in the first half of the 17th century.

Act I: 'Love' Scene 1: A pleasant village. Luisa Miller, daughter of a retired and widowed soldier, is touched by the birthday greetings of the villagers, but no longer feels truly happy when separated from her beloved 'Carlo'. She assures Miller that there never was a more honourable young man ('Lo vidi, e'l primo palpito'); and when 'Carlo' joins the celebrations her happiness is complete ('T'amo d'amor ch'-esprimere'). In conversation with Wurm, castellan to Count Walter, and another admirer of Luisa, Miller insists that his daughter must choose for herself whom she will marry; but he is dismayed to learn that 'Carlo' is in fact Rodolfo, Walter's son ('Sacra la scelta è d'un consorte . . . Ah! fu giusto il mio sospetto!'). Scene 2: A room in Count Walter's castle. Walter, musing over his tormented relationship with Rodolfo ('Il mio sangue, la vita darei'), hears of his love for Luisa, and insists that the wedding planned for him with Federica, a young widow, must go ahead without delay. Left alone with Federica, a friend since childhood, Rodolfo decides to confess the truth; but she loves him too much to react with anything but indignation ('Dall'aule raggianti di vano splendor . . . Deh! la parola amara . . . Arma, se vuoi, la mano'). Scene 3: Inside Miller's house. As Miller is telling Luisa what he has learned from Wurm, Rodolfo enters, and swears that he will keep faith with her. Walter himself now appears; his insults prompt Miller to draw his sword on him, and Walter's bodyguard takes both Miller and Luisa prisoner. Rodolfo tries every means to persuade his father to release them; finally, vowing that he will make known to all the world how Walter came to his title, he hurries away; the count orders the Millers to be freed.

Act II: 'Intrigue' Scene 1: Inside Miller's house. The villagers tell Luisa that her father is imprisoned in Walter's castle. Wurm tells Luisa that her father will die unless she does exactly what she is told. At his dictation she writes a letter, professing that she has always known who Rodolfo was, and that ambition prompted her association with him. Initially she recoils from the task ('Tu puniscimi, o Signore'); but when Wurm reminds her of the conse-

quences she completes and signs the letter ('A brani, a brani, o perfido'). She is then made to swear that, when necessary, she will publicly proclaim her love for Wurm. Scene 2: The castle – Walter's apartment. Walter promises Wurm that he has nothing to fear, even though Rodolfo has found out about the murder they plotted together to seize the title ('L'alto retaggio non ho bramato'). Federica enters, and Luisa is brought in to confirm that there are no longer any ties between herself and Rodolfo. Finally, she professes to love Wurm ('Come celar le smanie'). Scene 3: Hanging gardens in the castle. Luisa's letter has destroyed all Rodolfo's hopes of happiness ('Quando le sere al placido'). Wurm is challenged to a duel, but by discharging his pistol into the air he brings Walter and attendants rushing to the scene. Rodolfo is persuaded that the fittest way to be revenged is to marry Federica ('L'ara o l'avello apprestami').

Act III: 'Poison' Inside Miller's house. The villagers express their sorrow at Luisa's distress. Resolved to take her life, Luisa is writing a last letter to Rodolfo when her father enters, released from prison. She confesses what she intends to do; but such is the old man's despair that she relents, and agrees to join him in a life of exile from their old home ('La tomba è un letto . . . Andrem, raminghi e poveri'). Music sounds from the church where Rodolfo and Federica are about to be married; but a moment later Rodolfo appears, brandishing Luisa's letter. As he questions her, he contrives for both of them to drink poison. Via accusations, tears and solemn warnings the ghastly truth emerges ('Piangi, piangi il tuo dolore . . . Maledetto, maledetto il dì ch'io nacqui'). Miller returns to the scene only to receive the embraces of his dying daughter, and Rodolfo's prayers for forgiveness ('Padre ricevi l'estremo addio'). By now all have assembled; Rodolfo, with one last effort, runs Wurm through with his sword, then falls dead beside Luisa.

After the stylistic adventures of *Macbeth* and the French-inspired operas of the late 1840s, Verdi returned to the mainstream of Italian melodrama, but at a higher level of sophistication and expressiveness. The music is more consistently inventive, such purely conventional elements as formal introductions and cadences are pared away or given expressive meaning, and the structures of aria and ensemble become more various and flexible. The wonderful duets in Act III best illustrate Verdi's habit of fashioning the musical forms to match the dramatic purpose: in the final section of 'Andrem, raminghi e poveri', Luisa does not, in the customary fashion, sing on equal terms with Miller; instead, in an ethereal, 'barely perceptible' descant, she hovers over him, guardian-angel-like; in 'Piangi, piangi il tuo dolore' no musical reconciliation is brought about between the pure-heartedness of Luisa and the blasphemous despair of Rodolfo: to the bitter end, the music of each remains distinct in melodic style, in colour and texture.

The opera owes much of its distinctive ethos to the simple eloquence of its choruses, notably those that open each of the three acts. In using the chorus so charmingly to evoke a vision of an idyllic and harmonious community Verdi was surely remembering Bellini's *La sonnambula*.

The full-length overture, one of Verdi's finest, is a monothematic sonata movement, based on a theme that recurs in various guises throughout the opera – but especially in Act III – as a symbol of the malign fate that destroys the lovers' happiness.

Stiffelio

Stiffelius
Dramma lirico in three acts (1h 45m)
Libretto by Francesco Maria Piave, after the play *Le pasteur, ou L'évangile et le foyer* (1849), by Émile Souvestre and Eugène Bourgeois
Composed July–November 1850
PREMIERES 16 November 1850, Teatro Grande, Trieste; 26 December 1968, Teatro Regio, Parma (uncensored); UK: 19 October 1969, BBC radio; 14 February 1973, Collegiate Theatre, London; US: 4 June 1976, Brooklyn Academy, New York
CAST Stiffelio *t*, Lina *s*, Stankar *bar*, Raffaele *t*, Jorg *b profondo*, *ms*, *t*, *spoken role*; *satb* chorus of members of Stankar's household, friends and followers of Stiffelio

Of all Verdi's many bold choices of subject, that of *Stiffelio*, a tale of treachery and adultery, revenge and forgiveness among the members of an extreme Protestant sect, is surely the most unusual. The opera's viability was utterly destroyed when, at the last moment, the ecclesiastical censor in Trieste inflicted a series of bowdlerizations – notably in the final church scene – that made it dramatically pointless and in large measure unintelligible. Not surprisingly, it was coolly received, and it fared little better with a rewritten libretto (which incurred the composer's grave displeasure) in which the problematic central character became a German politician, Guglielmo Wellingrode. Fond of *Stiffelio* as Verdi was, it soon became clear that it had no future in the censor-ridden Italy of the 1850s, and by 1854 he had decided that the only way to salvage its remarkable music was by adapting it to a new libretto (see *Aroldo*, below). As a consequence of this rewriting, *Stiffelio* disappeared from view entirely; a full score was discovered only in the 1960s, and the opera received its belated uncensored Italian premiere in 1968.

SYNOPSIS
The scene is set in and near to Count Stankar's castle in Germany on the banks of the river Salzbach (*sic*) at the beginning of the 19th century.
Act I While Stiffelio is away on a preaching mission, his wife Lina is lured into an adulterous liaison with Raffaele. On Stiffelio's return, Lina's father, Stankar, prevents her from confessing her wrongdoing; he does, however, challenge Raffaele to a duel.
Act II The duel is interrupted by Stiffelio; but when he hears what is at issue he insists on fighting Raffaele himself. Psalm-singing from the nearby church, and the solemn words of Jorg, an elderly minister, recall him to his duty as a man of God.
Act III Stiffelio offers Lina the chance of a divorce; she persuades him that she has always loved him, but has been treacherously seduced. When he goes to administer condign punishment to Raffaele, Stiffelio finds that Stankar has already killed him. Joining his flock in church, he tries to recover his

serenity of mind by reading from the Bible. It falls open at the story of the woman taken in adultery.

Verdi's music, in keeping with the dramatic theme, is as boldly unconventional as anything he had yet composed. Typical of the opera are movements in which the overall musical effect seems less important than a profusion of expressive detail designed to heighten the tensions of the moment. Stiffelio's Act I aria 'Vidi dovunque gemere' is so sensitive to the changing moods of the troubled Lina, to whom it is addressed, that it has the effect of a whole series of sharply contrasting ariosi. The finale, the Bible-reading scene so mauled by the censor, marks the most radical break with the stylistic conventions of the day: its single lyrical phrase, the climactic 'Perdonata! Iddio lo pronunziò', stands out electrifyingly from an austere context of recitative intonation and quietly reiterated instrumental ostinati. Such textural bleakness marks only one extreme of a wide spectrum of colours, some of which – the elaborately subdivided string patterns in Lina's Act II aria 'Ah, dagli scanni eterei', for example – are exceptionally rich.

Rigoletto

Melodramma in three acts (2h)
Libretto by Francesco Maria Piave, after the tragedy *Le roi s'amuse* by Victor Hugo (1832)
Composed November 1850–March 1851
PREMIERES 11 March 1851, La Fenice, Venice; UK: 14 May 1853, Covent Garden, London; US: 19 February 1855, Academy of Music, New York
CAST Duke of Mantua *t*, Rigoletto *bar*, Gilda *s*, Sparafucile *b*, Maddalena *c*, Giovanna *ms*, Count Monterone *bar*, Marullo *bar*, Matteo Borsa *t*, Count Ceprano *b*, Countess Ceprano *ms*, Court Usher *t*, Duchess's Page *ms*; *tb* chorus of gentlemen of the court; extras: ladies, pages, halberdiers

If the ruination of *Stiffelio* was the most crushing blow Verdi ever received at the hands of the censors, the triumph of *Rigoletto* marked his most famous victory over them. In this instance problems were anticipated from the start – even in liberal Paris *Le roi s'amuse* had been banned after a single performance – and Verdi's determination to produce a worthy operatic version of Hugo's notorious play was resourcefully abetted by the Venetian theatre management. *Le roi s'amuse* thrilled him as no other subject since *Macbeth* had done; he found it 'the greatest subject and perhaps the greatest drama of modern times', and deemed Triboulet (who became Rigoletto) 'a creation worthy of Shakespeare'. Recognizing that the motif of the curse was both the seed and the moral of the drama, Verdi proposed to call the opera *La maledizione*, and probably during November 1850 it was fully sketched under that title, using the setting and the names of Hugo's play. Despite earlier assurances that the subject was acceptable, when the censors read Piave's libretto they were appalled, expressed their regrets that he and the 'celebrated maestro' had squandered their talents on a subject of 'such repellent immorality and obscene triviality', and forbade absolutely the performance of such an opera in Venice. Only after two rewritings was Piave able to produce a libretto that satisfied both Verdi and the censors: the first, *Il duca di Vendome*, though acceptable to the censors, was dismissed out of hand by the composer because it eliminated everything that was original and powerful; the second, however – *Rigoletto* – satisfied both parties. By such ruses as shifting the action from the French court of François I to the court of an anonymous duke, and by eliminating some of the more flagrantly libertine passages, Piave soothed the political and moral sensibilities of the censors; but in all essentials Hugo's grotesque and macabre drama emerged unscathed. After his experience with *Stiffelio*, Verdi would have accepted nothing less.

The premiere was a brilliant popular success, and within ten years *Rigoletto* had been staged in some 250 opera houses all over the world. But its early history was more problematic than that might suggest. Not all censors were as accommodating as those in Venice, and for a decade and more a number of alternative versions of the opera – *Viscardello*, *Lionello*, *Clara di Perth* – were all that could be seen in many theatres. Sometimes the ending had to be altered, and Gilda emerged from her sack in good health to join Rigoletto in giving thanks for the 'clemenza del cielo'. Nor was censorship always the problem. In Bergamo, in September 1851, the opera was withdrawn from the repertoire after only one and a half performances, because of audience protests. Nevertheless, *Rigoletto* is the earliest of Verdi's operas whose popularity has survived essentially unimpaired from its first performance to the present.

SYNOPSIS

The scene is set in and near Mantua during the 16th century.

Act I   Scene 1: A magnificent hall in the ducal palace. A party is in progress. The libertine duke proclaims his philosophy of taking his pleasure where he finds it ('Questa o quella per me pari sono'); he flirts with the Countess Ceprano, a sardonic commentary being provided by his jester, the hunchback Rigoletto. Enraged by Rigoletto's insults, Ceprano arranges for a group of courtiers to meet at his palace that night. The revelry is interrupted by Monterone, a political opponent whose daughter has been ravished by the duke; mocked by Rigoletto, he lays a solemn curse on the duke and his jester. Scene 2: The end of a blind alley. Rigoletto, haunted by Monterone's curse ('Quel vecchio maledivami!'), is accosted by Sparafucile, a professional assassin; he converses long with him, then compares his own way of life with that of his new acquaintance ('Pari siamo! io la lingua, egli ha il pugnale'). Unknown to the world at large, Rigoletto is a widower, who, all too familiar with the vices of the court, keeps his daughter, Gilda, in the strictest seclusion. He tells her of her mother, and solemnly enjoins the duenna Giovanna to guard her vigilantly ('Deh, non parlare al misero . . . Veglia, o donna, questo fiore'). As they are speaking, the duke (in disguise – he later introduces himself as a poor student, Gualtier Maldè) creeps into the courtyard, and is astonished to learn that his new flame is Rigoletto's daughter. When Rigoletto has gone indoors, he steps forward with a passionate avowal of love ('È il sol dell'anima'). Sounds of footsteps in the street disturb them, and the duke bids a hasty farewell, leaving Gilda in ecstatic reverie ('Caro nome'). The footsteps were those of the courtiers gathering at Ceprano's house. They trick Rigoletto into allowing himself to be blindfolded; then he unwittingly helps them ransack his own house ('Zitti, zitti, moviamo a vendetta'), carrying off Gilda; Rigoletto hears her cries in the distance, tears off his blindfold, and recognizes in what has happened the force of Monterone's curse.

Act II   A reception room in the ducal palace. The duke fears he has lost Gilda: returning to her house shortly after their parting he had found it deserted ('Ella mi fu rapita! . . . Parmi veder le lagrime'). But when the courtiers tell him of their night's exploits he realizes that she is in his power, and hastens away to take his pleasure ('Possente amor mi chiama'). Rigoletto enters, searching anxiously for Gilda. Overhearing the courtiers' evasive replies when a page asks for the duke, he realizes that she must be with him; he turns on them, denouncing them as contemptible hirelings ('Cortigiani, vil razza dannata'). Gilda appears, burning with shame; Rigoletto drives out the courtiers, and weeps as he hears her story ('Tutte le feste al tempio'). Monterone is escorted through the room on his way to prison; to Gilda's horror, Rigoletto assures the departing figure that he will soon be avenged ('Sì, vendetta, tremenda vendetta').

Act III   The right bank of the Mincio. Having engaged the services of Sparafucile, Rigoletto brings Gilda to a half-ruined tavern where they observe the duke settling down for an evening's drinking and whoring ('La donna è mobile'). He has been lured there by Maddalena, Sparafucile's sister, and now begins to make love to her; Gilda despairs, while Rigoletto meditates revenge ('Bella figlia dell'amore'). Rigoletto sends his daughter home, then arranges with Sparafucile to return at midnight for the duke's body. A storm rises. Gilda returns in disguise, and hears Sparafucile and Maddalena arguing: Maddalena has fallen for the young man, now asleep upstairs, and wants to spare him. Sparafucile agrees that if someone else calls at the inn before Rigoletto's return, he can be murdered instead. With a short prayer, Gilda resolves to sacrifice herself; as the storm reaches its height, she enters the tavern ('Se pria ch'abbia il mezzo la notte toccato'). Rigoletto returns for the body, which is handed over in a sack. The sound of the duke's singing in the distance rouses him from his meditations; he tears open the sack and discovers Gilda, still just alive. As she dies, she tries to comfort her distraught father ('V'ho ingannato! colpevole fui'); Monterone's curse is fulfilled.

Rigoletto marks Verdi's most radical break yet with the conventions of *ottocento* opera: there are no formal entrance arias (*sortite*) for the principal characters and no ensemble finales; for long stretches there is no conventional recitative; and – part of its unique colouring – female voices are excluded from the chorus. Perhaps the most Verdian touch of all is that this revolutionary opera is, on the surface, simpler, more tuneful and popular than anything he had written before.

The key to *Rigoletto* is to be found in the characterization in Hugo's play, and Verdi's attempt to re-create it in musical terms. The split personality of the central character – 'grossly deformed and absurd but inwardly passionate and full of love', as Verdi put it – is the source of those veerings of tone, from darkness to light, from comedy to tragedy, which give *Rigoletto* an almost Shakespearian expressive range and a breadth of sympathy typical of all Verdi's greatest operas from this time forward. The hedonistic duke makes his entry, not with the customary formal aria, but with a *ballata* (dance song) that falls naturally into place as part of the festivities of the opening scene, and follows this with a duet, accompanied by an instrumental minuet whose echoes of *Don Giovanni* are unlikely to be accidental. Gilda, a girl wholly lacking in prima-donna-ish egotism, finds her proper medium of expression in a series of duets with the two men she loves. Her only aria, 'Caro nome', is a single movement in a unique form: a series of delicately musing variations on a theme, first played by the flutes, that serves as an emblem of her lover's (pretended) name. The Act III quartet, 'Bella figlia dell'amore', is one of Verdi's greatest and most characteristic achievements, resolving a situation of excruciating emotional complexity into a torrent of passionate but exquisitely shaped song.

The impression of some early critics that the vocal writing in *Rigoletto* was 'less splendid' than the orchestration seems largely unintelligible today. But it does highlight the remarkable originality of Verdi's score, and the freedom with which he availed himself of colouristic and harmonic resources rarely accorded high priority in the Italian tradition. The Rigoletto–Sparafucile dialogue in Act I, probably inspired by the duettino 'Qui che fai?' from Donizetti's *Lucrezia Borgia*, demonstrates his art of conjuring atmospheric colours from the orchestra and underlining certain phrases ('Sparafucil mi nomino') with harmonic progressions of rare audacity.

Il trovatore
The Troubadour
Dramma in four parts (2h 15m)
Libretto by Salvatore Cammarano and Leone Emanuele Bardare, after the play *El trovador* by Antonio García Gutiérrez (1836)
Composed ?September 1851–January 1853; rev. for Paris 1856
PREMIERES 19 January 1853, Teatro Apollo, Rome; US: 2 May 1855, Academy of Music, New York; UK: 10 May 1855, Covent Garden, London
CAST Il Conte di Luna *bar*, Leonora *s*, Azucena *ms*, Manrico *t*, Ferrando *b profondo*, Ines *s*, Ruiz *t*, Old Gypsy *b*, Messenger *t*; *satb* chorus of companions of Leonora, nuns, members of Luna's household, men-at-arms, gypsies

When Verdi first read García Gutiérrez's play it was, as usual, the strong situations and the characters, especially the gypsy Azucena, that fired his imagination: he saw in the bizarre plot and the insane passions of the protagonists a pretext for more operatic boldness along the lines of *Rigoletto*. He wrote to a friend, 'The more Cammarano provides me with originality and freedom of form, the better I shall be able to do.'

And he went on to speculate about an operatic ideal 'in which there were neither cavatinas, nor duets, nor trios, nor choruses . . . and the whole opera was (if I might express it this way) one single piece'. Cammarano had his usual sobering effect on Verdi's revolutionary impulses, but the collaboration on *Il trovatore* was singularly harmonious, and it was tragic that the librettist died in July 1852, when composition was still at an early stage. He had completed a first version of the libretto virtually on his deathbed, but all revisions and additions that Verdi later found necessary were made by a young friend of Cammarano, Leone Emanuele Bardare: they include several of the best-loved numbers, including 'Stride la vampa!', 'Il balen del suo sorriso' and 'D'amor sull'ali rosee'.

The success of the premiere surpassed even that of *Rigoletto*, and the speed with which *Il trovatore* swept the world, literally from Scotland to the South Pacific, was even more sensational: street-theatre parodies were widely enjoyed (by Verdi as much as anyone) for decades. Despite, indeed in part because of, its demotic tone, *Il trovatore* has come to be seen as one of the composer's supreme achievements, and the Verdian critic – especially if he is Italian – is likely to extol its sublime vulgarity with an enthusiasm that soars to mystic heights: 'the definitive melodrama . . . the Via Crucis of Italian song . . . this is where Verdi's art, which is all in subversion, deformation, sublime caricature, sets the four corners of the world on fire' (Bruno Barilli). The opera's irrational magical power is encapsulated in a familiar anecdote told of the first Italian prime minister, the utterly unmusical Count Cavour, who, on receiving the Austrian ultimatum that was to bring France into alliance with Piedmont in the War of Italian Unity, could find no more effective way of expressing his excitement than throwing open the window and singing 'Di quella pira' at the top of his voice.

In 1856 Verdi was commissioned to adapt *Il trovatore* for the Paris Opéra by adding an extended ballet to the third act; this version, *Le trouvère*, which included a number of other revisions, was staged under the composer's direction in January 1857.

SYNOPSIS
The action takes place partly in Biscay, partly in Aragon, during the early 15th century.
Part I: 'The Duel' Scene 1: A hall in the palace of Aliaferia. Ferrando tells the story of Azucena, daughter of a woman who, 20 years before, had been burned for witchcraft because she cast the 'evil eye' on Luna's infant brother; to avenge her, Azucena allegedly threw the infant on the embers of the pyre ('Di due figli vivea padre beato'). Scene 2: The gardens of the palace. In the days before the civil war began, an unknown knight won Leonora's love by his bravery at a tournament. Since then he has sometimes returned in the guise of a troubadour to serenade her ('Tacea la notte placida . . . Di tale amor che dirsi'). Through the garden her two admirers approach: Luna (quietly) and Manrico (in full-throated song – 'Deserta sulla terra'). Hastening to greet Manrico, Leonora blunders into the arms of Luna. The count is enraged to discover that his rival is Manrico, a rebel in the civil

war; the men rush away to duel ('Di geloso amor sprezzato').

Part II: 'The Gypsy'   Scene 1: A ruined hovel at the foot of a mountain in Biscay. Manrico has defeated Luna in the duel, but spared his life; in turn wounded by Luna in the wars, he has been nursed back to health by Azucena, supposedly his mother. She sings a ballad about a woman – it proves to be her mother – who was burned at the stake ('Stride la vampa!') and goes on to tell the ghastly story of how, seeking to avenge her, she had thrown into the flames not the infant Luna but her own baby son ('Condotta ell'era in ceppi'). Then, confused, she tries to reassure Manrico: of course he is her son. A messenger brings news that Leonora, believing her beloved dead, is about to take the veil; Manrico hastens away ('Perigliarti ancor languente'). Scene 2: The porch of a place of retreat near Castellor. Luna has also heard of Leonora's intention and plans to abduct her ('Il balen del suo sorriso . . . Per me, ora fatale'). As Leonora bids farewell to her companions, Luna steps from the shadows; but he is confounded by the appearance of Manrico ('E deggio . . . e posso crederlo?'), who with his own followers hurries Leonora away.

Part III: 'The Gypsy's Son'   Scene 1: An encampment. Luna's troops prepare to assault Manrico's stronghold ('Squilli, echeggi la tromba guerriera'). Some soldiers have arrested a gypsy on suspicion of spying, and Ferrando recognizes her as Azucena; in terror she calls out for Manrico, so revealing that he is her son ('Giorni poveri vivea'). Luna is exultant: by burning her before the walls of Manrico's fortress, he can torment his rival and at the same time avenge his brother's death ('Deh, rallentate, o barbari'). Scene 2: A room adjacent to the chapel at Castellor. In the beleaguered castle Manrico and Leonora are about to be married ('Ah! sì, ben mio'). Ruiz reports that a pyre has been erected outside the walls, and that Azucena is being dragged towards it in chains. Manrico leads off his men to the rescue ('Di quella pira').

Part IV: 'The Execution'   Scene 1: A wing of the palace of Aliaferia. Leonora comes, armed with a phial of poison, to rescue Manrico, who is now imprisoned with Azucena; from the castle she hears monkish chants of death and Manrico's own singing (the so-called 'Miserere' scene: 'D'amor sull'ali rosee . . . Miserere d'un alma già vicina . . . Ah, che la morte ognora . . . Tu vedrai che amore in terra'). She accosts Luna. At first deaf to her appeal, he assents when she offers herself as the price for Manrico's freedom; she takes the poison ('Mira, di acerbe lagrime . . . Vivrà! . . . contende il giubilo'). Scene 2: A horrid dungeon. Manrico comforts the fearful Azucena, and she sleeps ('Sì, la stanchezza m'opprime, o figlio . . . Ai nostri monti . . . ritorneremo'). Leonora comes to free Manrico; refusing to leave without her, he begins to suspect the bargain she may have made with Luna and, since she makes no denial, denounces her ('Parlar non vuoi? . . . Balen tremenda!'). When she sinks dying at his feet, he is overcome with remorse; Luna enters ('Prima che d'altri vivere') and consigns Manrico to immediate execution, forcing Azucena to watch from her prison window. As Manrico dies, she reveals to Luna that he has killed his own brother; her mother is avenged!

Despite Verdi's first thoughts on the subject, *Il trovatore* is an opera that rejoices unashamedly in the peculiar strengths of traditional Romantic melodrama, and generally makes fewer demands of the singers' acting skills or intelligence than does *Rigoletto*: Caruso once famously, if discouragingly, remarked that all one needed for a good performance were the four greatest singers in the world. In most scenes the traditional forms are clearly audible, contributing much to the sense of concentrated emotional intensity so characteristic of the score. Many numbers owe much of their expressive force to a style of melody that the composer had been developing from his earliest years, and which in *Il trovatore* reaches full maturity: typically the arias start from quiet, sometimes even unremarkable, openings, gradually unfolding in mounting waves of melody to culminate in grand engulfing phrases employing the full extension of the voice. The opera's extraordinary range of scenic, psychological and musical expression is best seen in the so-called 'Miserere' scene, where the customary ingredients of scena, cantabile and cabaletta are enriched by episodes of ecclesiastical chanting, by a declamatory soliloquy for Leonora accompanied by shuddering ostinato rhythms for the full orchestra, and by the heart-broken ecstasy of Manrico's offstage troubadour song. The masterly juxtaposition and combination of these elements make the 'Miserere' scene a supreme moment not only of Italian Romantic melodrama but of the whole art of opera.

For some years the rebel, the non-conformist and the outcast had been favourite figures in Verdi's operas: in *Il trovatore* a matching sense of alienation is vividly expressed in the music. The finely nuanced cantabiles of Leonora and Luna leave no doubt of their aristocratic breeding; but the music of Azucena and (more equivocally) Manrico is popular and balladesque in manner – particularly distinctive are the pervasive strumming rhythms in 3/8 metre.

La traviata
The Fallen Woman
Melodramma in three acts (2h)
Libretto by Francesco Maria Piave, after the play *La dame aux camélias* by Alexandre Dumas *fils* (1852)
Composed January–February 1853, rev. March–April 1854
PREMIERES 6 March 1853, La Fenice, Venice; rev. version: 6 May 1854, Teatro Gallo di San Benedetto, Venice; UK: 24 May 1856, Her Majesty's Theatre, Haymarket, London; US: 3 December 1856, Academy of Music, New York
CAST Violetta Valéry *s*, Flora Bervoix *ms*, Annina *s*, Alfredo Germont *t*, Giorgio Germont *bar*, Gastone, Viscomte de Letorières *t*, Baron Douphol *bar*, Marquis d'Obigny *b*, Dr Grenvil *b*, Giuseppe *t*, Flora's Servant *b*, Messenger *b*; *satb* chorus of ladies and gentlemen, friends of Violetta and Flora, matadors, picadors, gypsies, servants of Violetta and Flora, masquers; dancers

For extended periods between August 1847 and March 1852, Verdi lived in Paris; it was the time when the new artistic vogue of realism was emerging, and *La traviata* is the most eloquent witness to the movement's influence on him. He may well have seen Dumas's *La dame aux camélias* when it was first staged in February 1852; but it was not until October, when he eventually acquired a copy of the play, that he decided to make an opera of it.

Warm memories of the *Rigoletto* premiere made it easy for the management of the Fenice theatre in Venice to engage Verdi for another opera. In addition to its high musical standards, Venice had the advantage of an unusually liberal censorship, without which *La traviata* would hardly have been possible at all. Nevertheless, despite the fact that this opera is one of his most intimate and personal creations, Verdi, having heard bad reports of the singers, approached its premiere with less eagerness than might have been expected.

There is no truth in the oft-repeated tale that the opera's initial failure was due to its contemporary setting; in fact, despite Verdi's wish to have it performed in modern dress, it was set '*c*. 1700', and it was not until the 1880s – by which time, of course, the 1850s were a generation distant – that 'realistic' productions were attempted. Nor is there anything to support the claim that the plump Fanny Salvini-Donatelli made a laughably inept consumptive heroine: her performance in the role of Violetta was one of the few things at the premiere that met with general approval. The root of the problem, according to Felice Varesi, the distinguished baritone for whom Verdi had already composed the roles of Macbeth and Rigoletto, and who now appeared as the first Giorgio Germont, was that Verdi had composed the opera with sublime disregard for the vocal capabilities of his principals, and that 'this caused much strong feeling among the Venetian public'. After the premiere, Verdi withdrew the opera until the opportunity arose to stage it with an ideal cast and/or to revise it.

Antonio Gallo, impresario of the Teatro San Benedetto, had meanwhile been impressed with *La traviata*, and bombarded the publisher, Ricordi, with requests to stage the work in his own theatre. Eventually Verdi consented, and took back five movements of his autograph score for revision (all from Acts II and III: the Violetta–Germont duet, the cabaletta of Germont's aria, the largo of the Act II finale, the Violetta–Alfredo duet, and the Act III finale). In this revised form *La traviata* was enthusiastically received; it soon rivalled *Il trovatore* in popularity, even in Victorian England, where its premiere had been greeted by a denunciatory leading article in *The Times* and where early Covent Garden productions refrained from supplying translations, out of consideration – it was implied – for patrons' moral well-being.

SYNOPSIS

The scene is set in Paris and its vicinity in about 1850.

Act I A salon in Violetta's house: August. At a party given by the notorious courtesan Violetta Valéry, Alfredo Germont is introduced as an admirer. After a *brindisi* ('Libiam ne' lieti calici'), the guests move to an adjoining room for dancing. Violetta, afflicted by a fit of consumptive coughing, remains behind, and finds herself attended by a solicitous Alfredo. He urges her to abandon a way of life that can lead only to an early grave ('Un dì felice'). The party guests leave, and Violetta muses: could Alfredo really be the redeemer of whom she has dreamed ('È

strano! . . . è strano! . . . Ah, fors'è lui')? She shrugs off her foolish fancy ('Sempre libera degg'io').

Act II Scene 1: A country house near Paris: January. For three months Alfredo and Violetta have lived together in the country. But Alfredo's happiness turns to shame when by chance he learns that Violetta has been selling her possessions to maintain them ('De' miei bollenti spiriti . . . O mio rimorso! o infamia!'), and he hastens away to Paris to rearrange his affairs. Violetta is visited by an elderly gentleman, who proves to be Germont senior. He begs her to leave Alfredo for the sake of a younger daughter, whose prospects are threatened by her brother's liaison ('Pura siccome un angelo'); he dismisses all Violetta's hopes of happiness as delusions, transient as youth and beauty ('Non sapete quale affetto . . . Un dì, quando le veneri'); finally he extracts from her a promise to renounce Alfredo for ever ('Dite alla giovine . . . Morrò! . . . la mia memoria'). When Alfredo returns, Violetta bids him a passionate farewell, pretending that she is absenting herself only for a few hours. A little later he is brought a letter telling the truth: she is returning to a former protector, Baron Douphol. While Germont tries to comfort him ('Di Provenza il mar, il suol . . . No, non udrai rimproveri'), Alfredo broods on vengeance. Scene 2: A gallery in Flora's palace. Flora's guests are entertained with masquerades of gypsies and bullfighters. Alfredo arrives, followed by Violetta and Douphol, and wins large sums of money at cards. The guests are summoned to dinner, but a moment later Violetta and Alfredo return alone: fearing for his life, she urges him to leave the party. Instead, he summons the revellers, and, announcing that he is paying off Violetta for services rendered, hurls the money he has just won at her feet. At that moment his father arrives. In the finale the multitude of different passions provoked by Alfredo's insult are expressed.

Act III Violetta's bedroom: February. Despite Dr Grenvil's encouraging words, Violetta knows that she has only a few hours to live. She reads over a letter from Germont: Alfredo, who fled abroad after wounding Douphol in a duel, has been told of her sacrifice, and is hurrying back to Paris for her forgiveness. But, alone and dying, Violetta has, realistically, only God's mercy to depend upon ('Addio, del passato'). The sound of Shrove Tuesday revels in the street contrasts ironically with the desolation within. Alfredo does return, however, and the lovers dream of escape from Paris, of health and happiness; but, as Violetta tries to dress she collapses, and both realize she is on the point of death ('Parigi, o cara, noi lasceremo . . . Gran Dio! morir sì giovane'). Grenvil returns, and Germont too arrives, anxious to make amends for the suffering he has caused. Giving Alfredo a medallion to remember her by, and praying that he will find a wife more worthy of him, Violetta dies ('Prendi; quest'è l'immagine').

La traviata shares with *Rigoletto* and *Il trovatore* a magnificent directness of utterance: the three operas embody the principles of *ottocento* opera with sovereign mastery and freedom, and an unerring sense of dramatic purpose, and popular opinion is not deceived in seeing in them the ripest harvest of Italian Romantic melodrama. *La traviata* is the most elegant and refined of the three: typically its profusion of 3/8 rhythms – as common here as in *Il trovatore* – are evocative less of the primitive strummings of popular music than of the sensual swaying of the waltz. Its scoring is also the most delicate, its translucence serving in part (in the prelude and in much of Act III) as a musical symbol of the consumptive Violetta.

The clarity of the plot and the overwhelming presence of a single moral idea – that of an ideal of love which survives all man's attempts to exploit and corrupt it – prompted Verdi to make fuller use than in any earlier opera of a single recurring theme. In the cantabile of the Act I duet, Alfredo and Violetta are characteristically contrasted, the hesitant phrases of the shy idealist being juxtaposed and later counterpointed with the fickle brilliance of the 'woman of pleasure'. Alfredo's solo rises to a magnificent climactic hymn to love ('Di quell'amor'), and in Violetta's great solo scena at the close of Act I she takes up the same theme at the climax to the cantabile ('Ah, fors'è lui'), where she dreams of the true love that might one day redeem her. Between the two statements of her cabaletta ('Sempre libera'), it returns again, sung by Alfredo from the street below her window; and this is a masterstroke of dramatic psychology as well as a *coup de théâtre*, for to remind Violetta of Alfredo's love as she is in the midst of reasserting her philosophy of pleasure is to turn what might have been merely a brilliant cabaletta into a conflict of hedonism and idealism. In Act III the same theme recurs twice more, now in purely orchestral form; for all illusory hope has vanished, and Violetta cherishes only the memory of what might have been.

Germont is as vividly characterized as the two lovers, his music made up in part of nostalgic Bellinian memories ('Pura siccome un angelo', 'Di Provenza il mar, il suol'), in part of songs in which his didactic manner is suggested by downbeats heavy with flurries of short notes ('Un dì, quando le veneri', 'No, non udrai rimproveri'). His Act II duet with Violetta is as magnificent a musico-dramatic achievement as anything Verdi ever wrote: the inexorable tragic thrust of the argument is embodied with rare finesse in a seemingly kaleidoscopic, but in fact masterfully controlled, sequence of short movements.

Les vêpres siciliennes

The Sicilian Vespers
Dramma in five acts (3h, including Act III ballet of *c.* 25m)
Libretto by Eugène Scribe and Charles Duveyrier,
adapted from their earlier libretto *Le duc d'Albe* (1838)
Composed January 1854 – ?April 1855; one substitute aria,
'O toi que j'ai chéri', ?summer 1863
PREMIERES 13 June 1855, Opéra, Paris; UK: 27 July 1859, Drury Lane, London; US: 7 November 1859, Academy of Music, New York
CAST Guy de Montfort *bar*, Henri *t*, Jean Procida *b*, La Duchesse Hélène *s*, *c*, 3 *t*, *bar*, 2 *b*; *satb* chorus of Sicilian men and women, French soldiers, monks, etc.; extras and corps de ballet: French soldiers, betrothed couples, pages, nobles, officials, penitents, executioner, Sicilians, zephyrs, naiads, fauns, bacchantes

Since his Parisian début with *Jérusalem*, Verdi's international reputation had continued to grow; on his return to the Opéra he was able to insist that the great Scribe himself should be the librettist, and that he should be allowed a three-month rehearsal period and be guaranteed 40 performances within ten months of the premiere. The libretto was adapted from a text on which both Halévy (briefly in 1838) and Donizetti (intermittently, but at length, from 1839) had laboured in vain; and it was transformed into *Les vêpres siciliennes* by the fashionable device of 'anatopism', transferring the action from Flanders to 'a climate full of warmth and music' (Scribe). Warmly received at first – Berlioz found in it 'a grandeur, a sovereign mastery more marked than in the composer's previous creations' – *Les vêpres siciliennes* soon lost its hold on the repertoire and was not revived at the Opéra after 1865.

In Italy it was quite impossible to stage it under its original title until the relaxation of censorship that followed the Unification of 1861. In the Italian translation the action was shifted to 17th-century Portugal, and the opera became *Giovanna da Guzman*. Its vogue was restricted by the Act III ballet (which had been much admired in Paris, but was beyond the resources of most Italian theatres) and, probably in 1856, Verdi authorized removal of the ballet in Italian productions.

Les vêpres siciliennes is the earliest of Verdi's operas for which there survives a production book (a *mise-en-scène*, or detailed account of the original production). Verdi's Italian publisher, Ricordi, had this translated for *Giovanna da Guzman* and issued similar *disposizioni sceniche* for most of Verdi's later operas; they afford fascinating insights into the style of 19th-century opera production.

SYNOPSIS
The scene is set in and around Palermo; 1282.

Act I Sicilian resentment against the occupying French is fanned by Hélène, sister of the late Duke Frederick of Austria; the appearance of the hated viceroy Guy de Montfort rapidly disperses the crowd. Henri, a loyal follower of Frederick, refuses Montfort's offer of employment, and defies his warning to keep away from Hélène.

Act II Procida tells Henri and Hélène that he has failed to win foreign support for the Sicilians. Their cause receives a further setback when Henri is arrested for declining an invitation to a viceregal ball. At the festival of Santa Rosalia, Procida deliberately inflames anti-French feeling by encouraging French soldiers to carry off a group of peasant girls.

Act III Henri, whom Montfort has discovered to be his own illegitimate son, spurns his father's affection. But at the ball, where guests are entertained by a ballet, he frustrates an assassination attempt by Procida and Hélène. As they are dragged away to prison, the Sicilian conspirators curse Henri as a traitor.

Act IV Learning why Henri saved Montfort, Hélène readily forgives him: and he, having paid his father the debt of life, is ready to die with the conspirators if he cannot obtain a pardon for them. On condition that Henri will acknowledge him as his father, Montfort does issue a pardon; he further decrees that his son and Hélène shall marry without delay, to seal the new Franco-Sicilian amity.

Act V As the approaching marriage is celebrated, Hélène is appalled to learn from Procida that the wedding bells are to serve as a signal for a massacre. Her despairing attempts to stop the marriage are vain; bells ring out, and the Sicilians fall murderously upon the unsuspecting French.

What to Berlioz seemed 'grandeur and sovereign mastery' has sounded to many modern critics more like self-conscious and contrived artifice. *Les vêpres siciliennes* conspicuously lacks the seemingly effortless flow of invention, and the perfect matching of musical means to dramatic ends that distinguished its three predecessors. But Verdi was now looking to enlarge his range, and in that sense the opera was enormously fruitful. At this period Meyerbeer, the master of Parisian grand opera, was the contemporary Verdi most admired, and much of the music seems an attempt to lay hold on the resources of Meyerbeer's style for Verdi's own purposes: grandiose 'stereophonic' effects, the bold exploration of new vocal and instrumental textures in new lyrical designs, and everywhere an unprecedented flexibility in the handling of rhythm. But Verdi was not slavish in his emulation. It is typical of his more urgent sense of theatre that, after the intimate scenes of Act IV (traditional in grand opera), he refused to allow Scribe to dissipate the dramatic tension by the usual return to grandiosity in Act V; instead the spectators' attention is held firmly focused on the plight of his central characters.

Simon Boccanegra (I)

Opera in a prologue and three acts
Libretto by Francesco Maria Piave, with additions by
Giuseppe Montanelli, after Antonio García Gutiérrez's drama
Simón Bocanegra (1843)
Composed autumn 1856–early 1857
PREMIERE 12 March 1857, La Fenice, Venice

As work on *Les vêpres siciliennes* drew to a close, Verdi was planning to go on to revise *La battaglia di Legnano* and *Stiffelio* so that they would get past the censors; and he still longed to create a *King Lear*. It was not until the summer of 1856, when he signed another contract for Venice, that he started to think about quite new projects. He chose as a subject García Gutiérrez's *Simón Bocanegra*, perhaps hoping it would capture the public imagination as *Il trovatore* had done. Piave was nominally the librettist, but with Verdi now so much in Paris close collaboration was difficult, and much of the revising and polishing was done by Giuseppe Montanelli, an Italian poet in exile in Paris. García Gutiérrez's play is a rambling historical chronicle set at a period of political turmoil in 14th-century Genoa; Piave found it beyond his powers to make a lucid reduction of it, and the libretto was generally condemned as one of the most unintelligible ever to have reached the stage. Verdi's music was admired by some connoisseurs for its expressive and dramatic 'conscientiousness'; but the overriding impression it made on contemporaries was of gloomy and sometimes recondite experimentation, in which

declamation had very much the upper hand over song: 'Not even Wagner would have ventured so far along this road,' declared one bemused critic. Revivals were few and rarely successful. In due course Verdi came to feel that the opera, quite apart from the incoherence of its plot, was 'too sad, too desolate', and in 1880 he agreed to make a radical revision in collaboration with Arrigo Boito. (See *Simon Boccanegra (II)*, below)

Aroldo

Harold
Melodramma in four acts (2h)
Libretto by Francesco Maria Piave, adapted from his and Verdi's 1850 opera *Stiffelio*, borrowing names from Bulwer-Lytton's novel *Harold, the Last of the Saxon Kings* (1843), and with hints from Sir Walter Scott's *The Betrothed* (1825) and *The Lady of the Lake* (1810)
Composed spring 1856–summer 1857
PREMIERES 16 August 1857, Teatro Nuovo, Rimini; US: 4 May 1863, Academy of Music, New York; Ireland: 1959, Theatre Royal, Wexford; UK: 25 February 1964, St Pancras Town Hall, London
CAST Aroldo (Harold) *t*, Mina *s*, Egberto (Egbert) *bar*, Briano (Brian) *b profondo*, Godvino (Godwin) *t, ms, t, silent role; satb* chorus of Crusader knights, gentlemen and ladies of Kent, esquires, pages, heralds, huntsmen, Saxons, Scottish peasants

Having given up all hope of seeing *Stiffelio* performed as he conceived it, Verdi transformed it into *Aroldo* during 1856–7, and the opera was staged to mark the opening of a new theatre in Rimini. It was the first collaboration between Verdi and one of the rising stars of Italian music, Angelo Mariani, the outstanding conductor of his generation, and the first Italian – unless one counts Spontini – to abandon the traditional manner of directing performances from the first violin desk and to conduct with a baton. The premiere caused enormous excitement in Rimini, but in the greater operatic centres audiences were less easily persuaded of *Aroldo*'s merits: the opera was widely performed for a few years, but never established itself as a repertoire item.

SYNOPSIS

The scene is set, for the first three acts, in Egbert's castle near Kent (*sic*); for Act IV on the shores of Loch Lomond in Scotland; *c.* 1200.

Act I While Harold, a Saxon knight, is away at the Crusades, his wife Mina enters into an adulterous liaison with Godwin, a soldier of fortune. When Harold returns, accompanied by Brian, a hermit he has met in Palestine, she is prevented from confessing her wrong-doing by her father Egbert, who, however, challenges Godwin to a duel to avenge the family honour.

Act II The duel is interrupted by Harold. When he realizes the matter at issue, he insists on fighting Godwin himself; but sacred songs from a nearby church remind him of his religious oaths as a Crusader, and dissolve his sanguinary mood.

Act III Having concealed Godwin in an adjoining room to overhear the conversation, Harold offers Mina the chance of a divorce. She persuades him that she has always loved him, but has been treacherously seduced. Harold goes to avenge himself on Godwin, but finds that Egbert has already killed him.

Act IV Still tormented by jealousy, Harold has withdrawn from the world in company with Brian. Mina and her father, outlaws from England because of Egbert's killing of Godwin, are providentially led to Harold's hut; and there the estranged husband and wife are reconciled.

Most of the new music in *Aroldo* is found in the first and last acts; the comparative sophistication of the newly composed choruses – the drinking song in Act I, the pastoral introductory scene and the prayer in Act IV – and the orchestral virtuosity of the storm in Act IV show Verdi taking advantage of the new discipline that Mariani was instilling into Italian singers and players. Everywhere in the opera one may admire the mellowing sensibility and the shrewder craftsmanship of Verdi's middle years. The rewriting gives *Aroldo* an appropriate, warrior-like vigour, and Mina is a more fully realized figure than her Stiffelian prototype. But *Stiffelio* had been one of the most ethically 'advanced' dramas Verdi ever set; shifting its subject matter backwards from the 19th century to the Middle Ages undermined its psychological plausibility entirely.

Un ballo in maschera
A Masked Ball
Melodramma in three acts (2h 15m)
Libretto by Antonio Somma, after the libretto *Gustave III, ou Le bal masqué* by Eugène Scribe, originally set by Daniel Auber (1833)
Composed autumn 1857–early 1858
PREMIERES 17 February 1859, Teatro Apollo, Rome; US: 11 February 1861, Academy of Music, New York; UK: 15 June 1861, Lyceum, London
CAST 'American' version: Riccardo, Count of Warwick *t*, Renato *bar*, Amelia *s*, Ulrica *c*, Oscar *s*, Silvano *b*, Samuel *b*, Tom *b*, Judge *t*, Amelia's Servant *t*; 'Swedish' version: Gustavus III *t*, Count Anckarstroem *bar*, Amelia *s*, Mademoiselle Arvidson *c*, Oscar *s*, Christian *b*, Count Ribbing *b*, Count Horn *b*, Judge *t*, Amelia's Servant *t*; *satb* chorus of deputies, officers, sailors, guards, men, women and children of the populace, gentlemen, followers of Samuel/Ribbing and Tom/Horn, servants, masquers and dancing couples

While in Venice in 1853 for the production of *La traviata*, Verdi became friendly with the lawyer and playwright Antonio Somma; and he was delighted when Somma, a poet of some distinction in his day, volunteered to write a libretto for him. But the subject proposed did not, Verdi explained, have 'the variety my crazy brain would like'. And therefore, though the poet knew next to nothing about the technicalities of libretto-writing and needed a great deal of detailed advice, Verdi put him to work on *King Lear*, the libretto of which he managed to complete to the composer's satisfaction. Having signed a contract with the San Carlo at Naples early in 1857, Verdi spent several months negotiating with the theatre with a view to producing an opera on this theme; the plan eventually foundered, ostensibly because of his lack of confidence in the cast. With time running out, he now resorted to desperate measures, abandoning the search for a new subject and taking up an old libretto by Scribe, *Gustave III, ou Le bal masqué*.

First approaches to the Neapolitan censors resulted in a crop of irritating demands: the king must become a duke, resident anywhere in the north 'except Norway or Sweden'; the action must be set in an age that believed in witchcraft; the hero must be tormented by remorse, etc. So when Verdi arrived in Naples early in 1858 to start rehearsals, the libretto, now called *Una vendetta in domino*, was set in 17th-century Pomerania; but the prospects of even this version being permitted vanished on 13 January, when an assassination attempt was made on the life of Napoleon III. The censors now demanded more fundamental alterations, and engaged a Neapolitan poet to rewrite the libretto (*Adelia degli Adimari*, set in 14th-century Florence). When the composer refused to have anything to do with a text that was quite alien to the spirit of his music, he was sued for breach of contract. The case was eventually settled out of court, but meanwhile Verdi had been in touch with the impresario Vincenzo Jacovacci about the possibility of staging the opera in Rome. Here, after some preliminary skirmishing, the censors agreed to let the subject stand, provided only that the hero be downgraded to a count, and the action removed from Europe altogether. It was Somma who, from the alternatives offered, chose colonial Boston; but he remained piqued with the indignities to which his libretto had been subjected, and refused to let his name appear on it.

Despite some shortcomings in the casting, *Un ballo in maschera* was an immediate triumph; though it was too sophisticated a score to find ready acceptance in smaller or provincial theatres, it is the only Verdi opera between *La traviata* and *Aida* to have been regularly performed and consistently admired through all changes of taste and fashion. Among the more 'interesting' revivals may be mentioned the opera's Boston premiere, when patrons were invited to join in the masked ball, extended for the occasion by a specially composed galop by the conductor, Verdi's pupil and friend, Emanuele Muzio. Verdi was quite happy with the Americanization of his opera, and never expressed any desire to transfer it back to Sweden; but, since a Danish production in Copenhagen in 1935, there has been an increasing tendency to restore the opera to its original setting.

SYNOPSIS ('American' version)
The action takes place in Boston and its vicinity at the end of the 17th century.

Act I Scene 1: A hall in the governor's residence. Officials attend on Riccardo, the easy-going governor of Boston; most are devoted to him, but there are among them some conspirators, led by Samuel and Tom. Riccardo's chief concern is the guest list for a forthcoming ball; the name of Amelia plunges him into romantic reverie ('La rivedrà nell'estasi'), and he is embarrassed to be interrupted by her husband Renato his friend and secretary. Renato brings news of a conspiracy, and reminds him that his people's destiny depends upon him ('Alla vita che t'arride'). A judge demands an order of banishment on the enchantress Ulrica, but Riccardo heeds rather the pleas for clemency voiced by the page-boy Oscar ('Volta la terrea'). He proposes that he and his officials disguise themselves and visit Ulrica to discover what she really does ('Ogni cura si doni al diletto'). Scene 2: The enchantress's dwelling. Disguised as a fisherman, Riccardo enters Ulrica's hovel and finds her at her conjuring watched by a throng of women and children ('Re dell'abisso, affrettati'). She prophesies wealth for Silvano, a sailor, and Riccardo drops a commission into his pocket. One of Amelia's servants requests a private audience for his mistress: she seeks a cure for a guilty love that torments her; Ulrica's remedy involves picking herbs at midnight at the foot of the gallows; Amelia is determined to do what duty demands ('Segreta, acerba cura . . . Della città all'occaso . . . Consentimi, o Signore'), and the eavesdropping Riccardo resolves to join her; Amelia departs. Court officials now crowd into the cave, and Riccardo asks to be told his fortune ('Dì tu se fedele'). When Ulrica warns of imminent death at the hands of the man who first shakes his hand, Riccardo laughs it off ('È scherzo od è follia'); Renato joins them, and is greeted by a handshake. Riccardo's identity is revealed, and Silvano leads an anthem in his praise ('O figlio d'Inghilterra').

Act II   A solitary field on the outskirts of Boston. Amelia is terrified by spectral imaginings, and tormented by the conflict of love and duty ('Ecco l'orrido campo . . . Ma dall'arido stelo divulsa'). When Riccardo appears, she repulses him: let him spare her good name and keep faith with his friend, but he presses her to confess her love ('Non sai tu che se l'anima mia . . . Oh, qual soave brivido'). Renato arrives to warn Riccardo that conspirators are closing an ambush round him. Seconded by Amelia, who has veiled herself at her husband's approach, he persuades Riccardo to take an indirect route to the city; meanwhile, he will escort the veiled lady back without speaking to her ('Odi tu come fremono cupi'). But they are waylaid by the conspirators, and in the ensuing argument Amelia lets fall her veil. Renato's humiliation is a source of ribald mirth ('Ve', se di notte qui colla sposa'); determined to avenge himself, he invites Samuel and Tom to his house on the morrow; then he leads his wife home.

Act III   Scene 1: A study in Renato's house. Finding Renato determined to kill her, Amelia begs to be allowed to bid their son farewell ('Morrò, ma prima in grazia'). Left alone, Renato reflects that death is too severe a fate for her; but not for Riccardo, who has poisoned every source of his friend's happiness ('Eri tu'). When Samuel and Tom arrive, he demands to join in their conspiracy ('Dunque l'onta di tutti sol una'); an argument about who should kill Riccardo is resolved in Renato's favour by the drawing of lots. Oscar brings an invitation to a masked ball at the governor's residence, and Amelia is filled with foreboding ('Di che fulgor, che musiche'). The conspirators agree on costumes and a password. Scene 2: A sumptuous small apartment in Riccardo's residence. Riccardo is resolved to send Amelia and Renato back to England ('Ma se m'è forza perderti'). Oscar brings a letter warning him that an assassination attempt will be made during the evening; but, as this will be his last farewell to Amelia, he hastens recklessly to the ball. Scene 3: A huge and richly decorated ballroom, splendidly illuminated and adorned for the ball. The conspirators despair of finding Riccardo; but Renato detects Oscar who, after some teasing ('Saper vorreste'), unwittingly betrays Riccardo's disguise. Amelia urges Riccardo to escape; he tells her his plans, and is bidding farewell when Renato stabs him. In the finale, the dying Riccardo swears that Amelia is chaste; Renato is overcome with remorse, and all mourn the death of their beloved governor.

The central moment in any Italian Romantic opera is the ensemble – the *pezzo concertato* – at the heart of its Act I or Act II finale: some revelation or confrontation freezes the action, and the tension is discharged in ecstatic song. What is extraordinary in *Un ballo in maschera* is that in both *pezzi concertati* – that in Act I prompted by Ulrica's prophecy that Riccardo is soon to die; and that in Act II occurring when the veiled lady escorted by Renato proves to be his own wife – the tension is resolved not merely in song, but in laughter too: nervous in Act I, mocking in Act II. This is Verdi's most successful essay in the blending of tragedy and comedy in Shakespeare's manner; the sombre tale of guilty passion and murderous jealousy is lit up by flashes of 'brilliance and chivalry', and by an all-pervasive 'aura of gaiety' (Verdi).

This distinctive chiaroscuro is already unmistakable in the prelude and introduction; in both movements a darkly muttering theme, associated throughout the opera with the conspirators, casts its shadow over the otherwise serene harmonies and impulsive lyricism. The opera's ambivalent tone owes much to the blending of Verdi's native style with traits borrowed from French opera, such as the rhythmic *élan* of the galop-like Act I ensemble 'Ogni cura si doni al diletto'. French influence is particularly clear in the music of the page-boy, Oscar – a projection of the insouciant gaiety of Riccardo's own character – whose arias are in the French couplet form (strophes with refrain); both numbers, like several others in the opera, seem to borrow hints from Auber's setting of the text.

If the opera has nevertheless sometimes been described as Verdi's *Tristan* it is because no other of his mature operas places the love duet so centrally, or makes of it the dramatic fulcrum of the score, or invests it with such flaming incandescence. The transfiguring of the link between cantabile and cabaletta ('La mia vita . . . l'universo' etc.) into an ecstatic lyrical climax, and the subtly transformed recurrence of this before the duet verse of the cabaletta help ensure that the emotional exaltation achieved in the early part of the scene is sustained to the close, without interruption or anticlimax.

La forza del destino
The Force of Destiny
Opera in four acts (3h 15m)
Libretto by Francesco Maria Piave, based on the drama *Don Alvaro, o La fuerza del sino* (1835) by Angel de Saavedra, Duke of Rivas, and incorporating material

adapted from *Wallensteins Lager* (1799) by Johann Christoph Friedrich von Schiller, translated by Andrea Maffei (1869 revisions by Antonio Ghislanzoni) Composed, but not fully orchestrated, August–November 1861; rev. autumn 1868–early 1869
PREMIERES 22 November 1862, Bolshoi Theatre, St Petersburg; US: 24 February 1865, Academy of Music, New York; UK: 22 June 1867, Her Majesty's Theatre, Haymarket, London; rev. version: 27 February 1869, La Scala, Milan
CAST Il Marchese di Calatrava *b*, Leonora *s*, Don Carlo di Vargas *bar*, Don Alvaro *t*, Preziosilla *ms*, Father Superior (Padre Guardiano) *b*, Fra Melitone *bar*, Curra *s*, The Alcalde *b*, Mastro Trabuco *t*, Spanish Military Surgeon *t*; *satb* chorus of muleteers, Spanish and Italian peasants, Spanish and Italian soldiers of various ranks and their orderlies, Italian recruits, Franciscan friars, peasant girls, *vivandières*; ballet: Spanish and Italian peasant women and *vivandières*, Spanish and Italian soldiers; extras: host, hostess, inn servants, muleteers, Italian and Spanish soldiers of all ranks, drummers, buglers, peasants, peasant women and girls of both nations, tumbler, various pedlars

The 17 'years in the galleys' had ended with *Un ballo in maschera*; by the close of the 1850s Verdi was leading the life of a country gentleman, prosperous, world famous, with no obligation to compose operas except on his own terms, when a commission really interested him. *La forza del destino* resulted from the first such commission: an invitation from the Bolshoi Theatre of St Petersburg for the 1861–2 season. Verdi was in theory given a free hand over the choice of subject, though in fact his first proposal, Victor Hugo's *Ruy Blas*, was unceremoniously rejected by the censor. His choice eventually alighted on *Don Alvaro* by one of Hugo's Spanish imitators, the duke of Rivas – an already rambling play, which Verdi elaborated further by incorporating into the encampment scene episodes from Schiller's *Wallensteins Lager*. The premiere was delayed by almost a year; for when Verdi arrived in Russia late in 1861 he found the prima donna unsatisfactory and refused to proceed if she could not be replaced.

The opera stands alone in the Verdi canon in having an abstract idea for its title. By now, Verdi was more insistent than ever that the age of 'operas of cavatinas, duets, etc.' was past, and that the future belonged to 'operas of ideas'. *La forza del destino*, inspired by what he called a 'powerful, singular, and truly vast' play, is one of the clearest demonstrations of this conviction. And because the 'idea' concerns chance – the sheer random fortuitousness with which fate chooses its victims – the normal cut of a Verdian opera, which is concentrated, concise and thrusting, is replaced by a vast, shambling panorama of loosely related episodes during which the principals disappear from the scene for whole acts at a time.

Staged at a period when Russian musical life was in ferment, *La forza del destino* met with a confused reception. It earned the composer the Order of St Stanislas, but most critics found it wearisomely long, and it did not escape a hostile demonstration – apparently from a nationalist faction – at the third performance. Nevertheless, it is tempting to see in its chronicle-like panorama of life in time of war one of the prototypes of *Boris Godunov*, and thus of a whole

tradition of Russian opera. Early performances in Italy were also only equivocally successful, largely because of dissatisfaction with the carnage at the opera's blasphemous and nihilistic close. After much thought, Verdi and the librettist Ghislanzoni (Piave had been incapacitated by a stroke in 1867) arrived at a visually more discreet and spiritually more resigned dénouement, in which the influence of Alessandro Manzoni, the revered grand old man of Italian literature, has plausibly been detected. At the same time the events in Act III were reordered; many scenes were revised in detail, and the familiar full-length overture was composed to replace the original prelude. Even in revised form, the opera established itself slowly, probably because it needed a first-rate conductor to co-ordinate it successfully. A famous production at Dresden in 1926 under Fritz Busch was a milestone in the 20th-century Verdi renaissance. By the early 1990s some interest was being shown in reintroducing the original St Petersburg version.

SYNOPSIS
The scene is set in Spain and Italy towards the middle of the 18th century.

Act I Seville. Leonora, daughter of the marchese di Calatrava, has agreed to elope with Alvaro, a South American half-caste prince. The thought of abandoning her home fills her with remorse ('Me pellegrina ed orfana'), but when Alvaro arrives she soon declares herself ready to follow him to the ends of the earth ('Seguirti fino agli ultimi . . . Sospiro, luce ed anima'). They are interrupted by her father. Alvaro throws his pistol at the marchese's feet as a gesture of surrender; the gun goes off, fatally wounding the old man, who dies cursing his daughter.

Act II The village of Hornachuelos and vicinity. Scene 1: A large kitchen in the inn. The muleteer Trabuco arrives with an unknown youth (Leonora in disguise). Among the crowd is her brother Carlo, who is pursuing Leonora and Alvaro, intent on avenging his father's death; he too is disguised, as a student. The gypsy girl Preziosilla tells of the wars in Italy, singing the praises of military life ('Al suon del tamburo'). Pilgrims pass by, and those in the inn join in their prayer ('Su noi prostrati e supplici'). The alcalde now suggests that the student tell them who he is; posing as one Pereda, Carlo claims to have left university to help a friend hunt down his sister and her seducer; the villain has however escaped across the seas ('Son Pereda, son ricco d'onore'). Scene 2: The monastery of Our Lady of the Angels, outside Hornachuelos. Having overheard her brother's story Leonora feels betrayed by Alvaro's flight; she prays for forgiveness and a quiet mind ('Madre, pietosa Vergine'). The father superior (Padre Guardiano) has been forewarned of her visit, and after questioning her ('Più tranquilla l'alma sento') agrees to help her live as an anchoress in a nearby cave ('Sull'alba il piede all'eremo . . . Tua grazia, o Dio'). The friars vow to respect the young penitent's solitude; the father superior leads them in prayer ('La Vergine degli Angeli') and Leonora hastens to her hiding place.

Act III In Italy, near Velletri. Scene 1: A wood; night. Alvaro, now in the Spanish army, muses on the harshness of destiny and, believing her to be dead, prays to Leonora ('O tu che in seno agl'angeli'). Cries for help send him hurrying to the rescue; he returns with Carlo; they introduce themselves (using false names), and vow eternal comradeship. A surgeon and some orderlies watch the battle: the Italian–Spanish forces carry the day, but they are dismayed to see 'Don Federico Herreros' (Alvaro) fall injured. He is borne in, attended by Carlo, who is astonished by his violent reaction to the name Calatrava. Before Alvaro receives medical attention, he entrusts to Carlo some papers, to be destroyed in the event of his death ('Solenne in quest'ora'). The suspicion dawns on Carlo that his new friend is the long-pursued Alvaro; he resists the temptation to read the papers ('Urna fatale del mio destino'), but looking through Alvaro's other belongings finds a portrait of his sister, Leonora. When the surgeon pronounces Alvaro safe, Carlo exults: now for revenge! ('Egli è salvo! oh gioia immensa'). Scene 2: A military encampment near Velletri. Carlo challenges Alvaro to a duel. Reminding Carlo of their oath of friendship, Alvaro protests his innocence; he learns that Leonora is alive, and joyfully imagines that all may yet be well. But Carlo is adamant: both Alvaro and Leonora must die to satisfy family honour; the two men are soon fighting furiously ('No, d'un imene il vincolo . . . Stolto! fra noi dischiudesi'). They are separated by a patrol, and Alvaro decides to retreat to a monastery. As reveille sounds, the camp comes to life: Preziosilla is telling fortunes ('Venite all'indovina'), and Trabuco bargaining with some soldiers; peasants are begging for food, and new recruits are consoled by the *vivandières* (Tarantella). The merry-making is interrupted by Melitone's 'sermon' ('Toh, toh! . . . Poffare il mondo!'), which incenses the soldiers. Preziosilla beats the drum to turn their thoughts to serious business ('Rataplan, rataplan, della gloria'). [1862: the scene between Alvaro and Carlo follows the encampment scene and ends differently. They fight their duel to the bitter end, Alvaro, as he imagines, killing his adversary; in despair he returns to the battlefield to seek death ('S'affronti la morte').]

Act IV In the vicinity of Hornachuelos. Scene 1: A courtyard inside the monastery of Our Lady of the Angels. Five years have elapsed. Melitone is serving soup to the poor; as he and the father superior talk of one 'Padre Rafaello', we realize that this mysterious friar must be Alvaro ('Del mondo i disinganni'). The bell rings and Carlo enters. He demands to see 'Rafaello', and brusquely announces his intention of killing him. Alvaro's saintly behaviour provokes only insult; finally he snatches the sword Carlo offers and they hasten away to duel. Scene 2: A gorge between precipitous rocks. Leonora has found no peace of mind ('Pace, pace, mio Dio!'). She hears the sound of fighting, and Alvaro rushes in, entreating the hermit to give absolution to a dying man. As Leonora rings the bell to summon the father superior, she and Alvaro recognize one another; he speeds her away to comfort her brother. A moment later a scream is heard: Carlo, even as he died, could not forgive Leonora, and stabbed her as she bent over him. Alvaro's blasphemous despair is softened by her prayers and the grave words of the father superior ('Non imprecare; umiliati'); and as Leonora dies Alvaro too glimpses some hope of redemption. [1862: the duel and the stabbing of Leonora take place on stage; the opera ends with Alvaro throwing himself into a ravine as the father superior and monks approach.]

The nature of the subject means that in *La forza del destino* episodic genre scenes and 'character songs' play a more conspicuous part than in any other Verdi opera. At the same time the overriding dramatic idea of a malevolent destiny is embodied in a theme – often described as the leitmotif of destiny – that pervades much of the opera: it launches the overture, is heard at the tragic climax of Act I when Calatrava disturbs the eloping lovers and is accidentally killed, and recurs in several later scenes, particularly those in which Leonora is haunted by a pursuing nemesis. No other theme is used as extensively; but the long clarinet concertino that prefaces Act III and punctuates its opening scene – it was composed for St Petersburg's star clarinettist, Ernesto Cavallini, an old acquaintance from Verdi's student days – is a remarkable example of a thematic reminiscence (from the Act I duet, where Alvaro dreams of a happy future with Leonora) developed into an independent movement (in a context of heart-broken memories).

For all the novelty of the overall design, the familiar Verdi is present in every scene, and his musical language is developing in the most idiosyncratic ways. Act I, one of the fastest-moving and most densely packed acts in all Verdi, is full of such individual touches. Its opening scene, pitching the spectator into the middle of the dramatic action, is a casual dialogue set against a quietly sustained orchestral backcloth, and marks the composer's final rejection of the formal, decorative introductions of operatic tradition. Even when he does use traditional forms, his fast-developing musical language transfigures them; this is especially the case with the cabalettas: where once they derived their energy from pounding rhythmic repetitions, most of them now acquire their urgency from the fleetly moving basses and rapidly changing harmonies. Leonora's Act I aria 'Me pellegrina ed orfana' is one of the few pieces that have tangible links with the long-pondered *King Lear*; the text is taken directly from Somma's *Lear* libretto, though obviously that does not prove that the music was intended for *Lear*. In the improvisatory freedom of form, the chromatic nuances of the harmony and the flexibility of the instrumentation, it encapsulates much of Verdi's mature lyrical style.

Don Carlos/Don Carlo

Grand opera in five acts (3h 30m)/Opera in four acts (3h)
French libretto by Joseph Méry and Camille du Locle, based on the dramatic poem *Don Carlos, Infant von Spanien* by Johann Christoph Friedrich von Schiller (1787) and on the play *Philippe II, roi d'Espagne* by Eugène Cormon (1846); libretto of four-act version rev. du Locle; Italian translation by Angelo Zanardini, based on Achille de Lauzières's translation of the original five-act opera
Composed early 1866–February 1867, rev. November–December 1872; rev. (four-act) version June 1882–March 1883

PREMIERES   11 March 1867, Opéra, Paris; UK: 4 June 1867, Covent Garden, London (in Italian); US: 12 April 1877, Academy of Music, New York; four-act version: 10 January 1884, La Scala, Milan; hybrid five-act version: 29 December 1886, Modena
CAST   Philippe II (Philip II) *b*, Don Carlo (Don Carlos) *t*, Rodrigue (Rodrigo), Marquis of Posa *bar*, Grand Inquisitor *b*, Monk *b*, Elisabeth de Valois *s*, Princess Eboli *ms*, Thibault *s*, Voice from Heaven *s*, Countess d'Aremberg *silent role*, Woman in Mourning *silent role*, Count de Lerma *t*, Royal Herald *t*, 6 Flemish Deputies 6 *b*, 6 Inquisitors 6 *b*; *satb* chorus of lords and ladies of the French and Spanish courts, woodcutters, populace, pages, guards of Henri II and Philip II, monks, officers of the Inquisition, soldiers

Together with Shakespeare and Hugo, Schiller was the playwright Verdi most revered. But the size and ideological complexity of his plays made operatic adaptation difficult and, *I masnadieri* and *Luisa Miller* notwithstanding, it is not until *Don Carlos* that we find Verdi getting to grips with the great German dramatist in all his rambling magnificence. The death of Meyerbeer in 1864 prompted the management of the Opéra to approach Verdi with a libretto found among Meyerbeer's papers, in the hope of persuading him to make a return to Paris. He dismissed the libretto out of hand, but when they returned to the charge the following year and offered him a scenario for *Don Carlos* it 'really thrilled him'. He went to Paris in November 1865, signed a contract, and spent some four months there, hammering out a libretto with Méry and du Locle, before returning to Busseto in the spring to complete the composition. The Fontainebleau scene and the *auto-da-fé* were the most substantial of several incidents borrowed from a contemporary play on Philip II by Eugène Cormon.

In its stirring depiction of the conflict between libertarianism and dogmatism Schiller's play appealed to some of Verdi's deepest convictions. Every scene of the opera breathes a passionate high-mindedness that makes it, for many listeners, the most inspiring of all his works. Sadly, as in the past, the Paris Opéra disappointed the composer's hopes: the endless tedium of the rehearsals, the lack of spontaneity and enthusiasm in the performance, the multitude of opinionated busybodies who hung about the place, were to provide him with material for satirical reflection for many a year.

No other Verdi opera has so complicated a stage history, and none survives in so many different forms: the *edizione integrale* distinguishes eight 'authentic' versions of the score. For all practical purposes these may be reduced to three, all of which now have a place in the repertoire: the five-act French grand opera (1867), the four-act Italian *Don Carlo* (1884), and the hybrid 'Modena version' (1886) which, broadly speaking, reinstates the original Act I while leaving the remaining acts in their revised 1884 form. What exactly constitutes the 1867 score is a complicated question. The immense length of the opera led to cuts being made during rehearsals, and when at the first dress rehearsal it was found to be still well over three and a half hours long (excluding intervals) it was cut more drastically (it had to finish before midnight, as the last trains to the Paris suburbs left at 12.35). The most ruthless excisions involved the opening chorus

of Act I, and the duet in Act IV in which Philip and Carlos mourn the dead Posa. (Some of the deleted material from this served as the seed for the 'Lachrymosa' in the *Requiem*; and all the abandoned material was recovered and reconstructed by Verdi scholars in the 1960s and 1970s.) Cuts continued to be made, especially when the opera began to appear in Italy, and for a Naples production in 1872–3 Verdi himself revised and abbreviated several scenes. But *Don Carlos* stubbornly resisted popular success, and in 1882 the composer embarked on a more drastic rewriting. Only Carlos's romance 'Je l'ai vu' (revised) survives from the original Act I, and much else – notably the Philip–Posa duet in Act II and the closing scene of the opera – was radically revised; in the process the opera draws closer to its Schiller model. This 1884 version is certainly 'more concise and vigorous' (Verdi); but the desire to reinstate the Fontainebleau act, which led to the hybrid 'Modena version' of 1886, is understandable: it restores much superb music (some of it drawn on in episodes of reminiscence later in the opera) and it makes plot and motivation much clearer.

Perhaps not surprisingly, despite the passionate admiration of some connoisseurs, *Don Carlos* was for long regarded as a 'problem opera'. In Paris it disappeared completely from the repertoire after 1869; even during the Verdi renaissance between the wars – indeed as late as the 1950s and 1960s – many opera houses felt it necessary to stage adaptations that 'improved' it in some way or another. It was not until well into the second half of the 20th century that *Don Carlos* came to be recognized not only as Verdi's most ambitious opera but as one of his supreme achievements.

SYNOPSIS

Act I takes place in France, Acts II–V in Spain; the period is *c.* 1560.

Act I   The forest of Fontainebleau. France and Spain have long been at war. Carlos has come to France, impatient to be with Elisabeth, to whom he is betrothed ('Je l'ai vu et dans son sourire'). Elisabeth has lost her way in the forest during a hunt, and Carlos, introducing himself as a member of the Spanish diplomatic mission – for Elisabeth does not yet know him – undertakes to protect her while Thibault goes for help. He produces a portrait that shows that he is the man she is to marry; when the sound of cannon from the palace confirms that a peace has been concluded, their joy is complete ('De quels transports poignants et doux'). Thibault returns, followed by courtiers and people: as a pledge of the peace, Elisabeth is to marry Carlos's widowed father, the great King Philip himself. Recognizing that the well-being of her people depends upon her, Elisabeth assents ('L'heure fatale est sonnée . . . O chants de fête').

Act II   Scene 1: The cloisters at the monastery of Yuste. Monks meditate by the tomb of the emperor Charles V ('Charles-Quint, l'auguste Empereur'); Carlos is startled by the resemblance of one of the monks to his late grandfather; he is joined by his dearest friend, Rodrigo, marquis de Posa. Just returned from the Netherlands, Posa paints a grim picture of the oppression it suffers. And, when he hears of Carlos's hopeless passion for Elisabeth, he urges him to go to Flanders and learn there to be a king: they renew their vows of fellowship in the service of liberty ('Mon compagnon, mon ami . . . Dieu, tu semas dans nos âmes'). Scene 2: A pleasant spot by the gates of the monastery of Yuste. Thibault, Eboli and the ladies of the court shelter from the heat ('Sous ces bois au feuillage immense') and pass the time with song ('Au palais des fées' – the so-called 'Song of the Veil'). The queen joins them, then Posa, who delivers two letters: one from her father, the other, which she reads while Posa engages Eboli in gallantries, from Carlos. Posa requests an audience for Carlos ('L'Infant Carlos, notre espérance'), for Philip is unsympathetic to his troubles; Eboli imagines Carlos may be in love with her. Carlos appears and, dismissing her attendants, Elisabeth struggles to remain calm; she agrees to help persuade Philip to send him to Flanders, but, to her distress, he swoons and raves ('O bien perdu . . . Trésor sans prix') then hurries away. Philip is angry to find his queen unattended and orders the guilty lady-in-waiting, Countess d'Aremberg, back to France; Elisabeth bids her farewell ('O ma chère compagne'). Posa is detained by the king and seizes the opportunity to protest about the plight of Flanders ('O Roi! j'arrive de Flandre'); he urges him to give his people freedom. Impressed by Posa's integrity, Philip warns him to beware the grand inquisitor and confides his worries about Carlos and Elisabeth, and asks him to keep a watch on them. (The Philip–Posa scene is always performed in the 1884 form.)

Act III Scene 1: The queen's gardens; an enclosed grove. Festivities have been arranged for the eve of Philip's coronation. But Elisabeth wishes to spend the night in prayer, and, entrusting her with her mantilla, necklace and mask, asks Eboli to stand in for her. Eboli, seeing the chance to make sure of Carlos's love ('Pour une nuit me voilà reine'), writes him a hasty note. A sumptuous ballet ('La Peregrina') is staged. (This opening scene is commonly omitted in favour of the Act II prelude of the 1884 version.) Mistaking Eboli for Elisabeth, Carlos declares his love ('C'est vous, c'est vous! ma bien-aimée'). When she unmasks, his confusion perplexes her: she warns him that Posa is now a confidant of the king, and that only she can protect him ('Hélas! votre jeunesse ignore'). Suddenly it dawns on her that Carlos and Elisabeth are lovers; at the same moment Posa appears. Despite his threats, she is determined to exact revenge by exposing the queen's liaison with her stepson ('Malheur sur toi, fils adultère'). Scene 2: A large piazza in front of the cathedral at Valladolid. A throng of people, gathered for an *auto-da-fé*, sings the king's praises ('Ce jour heureux'); Philip's coronation oath requires him to act as God's avenger with sword and fire. Carlos presents a group of deputies from Flanders and Brabant: they beg Philip to show clemency, a prayer in which the queen, Posa and most of the crowd join; but Philip's persecuting obduracy is encouraged by the monks ('Sire, la dernière heure'). Carlos now demands that his father entrust to him the regency of Flanders; when Philip dismisses the request, Carlos draws his sword and vows to be the saviour of

that unhappy land. All are scandalized by this breach of etiquette; Posa disarms Carlos, and is elevated to a dukedom by Philip. The *auto-da-fé* continues: an angelic voice is heard comforting the dying.

Act IV Scene 1: The king's cabinet at Valladolid. Philip muses wretchedly over his failure to win Elisabeth's love ('Elle ne m'aime pas! . . . Je dormirais dans mon manteau royal'). The grand inquisitor is led in; he assures Philip that, if it is for the good of the faith, there can be no objection to having Carlos killed. But Posa represents a greater danger; and if Philip persists in protecting a heretic he will have to answer for it to the Holy Office ('Dans ce beau pays'). Elisabeth is indignant to find her jewel box stolen; Philip has it on his table and, when she refuses to open it, forces it himself; a portrait of Carlos is found among her treasures. When he denounces her as an adulteress, she faints. At the king's summons, Eboli and Posa enter; Posa realizes that immediate action must be taken to save Carlos ('Maudit soit le soupçon infame'). Left alone with the queen, Eboli begs forgiveness: she stole the casket; what is worse, she is herself guilty of the adultery of which Elisabeth stands suspected. (The original French version makes no mention of the fact that Eboli is the king's mistress.) The queen banishes her from the court: she must choose exile or the cloister. Eboli curses her own beauty; before taking leave of the world she resolves to save Carlos ('O don fatal et détesté'). Scene 2: Carlos's prison. Posa comes to bid Carlos farewell and encourage him in his great libertarian mission. Two men appear at the cell door and Posa is shot. As he dies, he tells Carlos that Elisabeth will be at Yuste the next day ('Ah! je meurs, l'âme joyeuse'). The king enters and returns Carlos's sword; but his son repulses him. (Omitted before the Paris premiere: Philip and Carlos mourn Posa ('Qui me rendra ce mort').) The clanging of the tocsin signals a popular uprising; for a moment Philip seems in danger, but the appearance of the grand inquisitor reduces the mob to submission. Meanwhile Eboli enables Carlos to make his escape. (The whole scene following the death of Posa is normally performed in the shorter 1884 form.)

Act V The monastery of Yuste. Elisabeth recognizes that her earthly task will soon be done ('Toi qui sus le néant'). Carlos comes to bid farewell: Elisabeth blesses his Flanders mission, and they look forward to meeting again in a better world ('Oui, voilà l'héroïsme . . . Au revoir dans un monde'). The king appears, attended by the grand inquisitor and his officers; Carlos is anathematized. As he tries to evade the inquisitors he retreats towards Charles V's tomb, which suddenly opens; the monk from Act II reappears and is recognized as Charles V himself; Carlos is hurried away into the monastery. (The whole scene from Carlos's arrival is normally performed in the revised 1884 version, which does not include the anathematizing of Carlos by the inquisitors.)

'Severe and terrible like the savage monarch who built it,' wrote Verdi of the Escorial on a visit to Spain in 1863. As a dramatic character Philip enthralled Verdi, and it was at his insistence that *Don Carlos* included two of the king's great scenes of confrontation – with

Posa in Act II, with the grand inquisitor in Act IV – that offered negligible scope for the conventionally operatic. The confidence that he could hold an audience spellbound with a scene of ideological debate was amply justified in the latter case: the fearsome clash of private sorrow and ruthless dogmatism, the whole expressed in vocal and orchestral colours of a chilling blackness, is one of the things in opera that, once heard, are never likely to be forgotten. The Philip–Posa scene, on the other hand, cost Verdi endless trouble (its alternative forms occupy almost 90 pages of vocal score in the *edizione integrale*); but every revision had the effect of eliminating relics of traditional lyricism, and bringing the scene closer to Schiller's thrilling dialectic.

Not only in the grand-inquisitor scene but throughout *Don Carlos* Verdi's genius for the dramatic exploitation of colour, which had appeared fitfully as early as *Macbeth*, even *Ernani*, is revealed in full splendour: colours of garish magnificence in the *auto-da-fé*, other-worldly colours like the mysterious chords (high woodwind and deep horn pedal note) set against male voices in the prayer at the start of Act II, colours of desolating melancholy in Philip's incomparable 'Elle ne m'aime pas'. Nothing, however, contributes more to the dramatic colouring than the fact that the opera is, or should be, sung in French (even the 1884 version was conceived with a French text, then translated into Italian). Of course it is not Verdi's first French opera, but never before has it seemed so to matter that French imposes certain constraints on the manner of singing which in turn make possible an inwardness and a type of sensibility new to Italian opera. The consequences are particularly remarkable in Carlos's music – far less extrovert, far more delicate in nuance than that of any earlier Verdi tenor.

All of which is not to imply any lack of lyrical abundance: on the contrary, what has been called Verdi's '*Aida* manner' might with equal justice be called his '*Don Carlos* manner'. The nervous sensibility of the principal characters is expressed in a lyrical style of exceptional richness; for in arias and ensembles alike every nuance of every experience calls forth its own melody.

Aida

Opera (melodramma) in four acts (2h 15m)
Libretto by Antonio Ghislanzoni, after a scenario by Auguste Mariette and a French prose version by Camille du Locle
Composed July 1870–after November 1870 (rev. continued until December 1871)
PREMIERES 24 December 1871, Opera House, Cairo; Italy: 8 February 1872, La Scala, Milan; US: 26 November 1873, Academy of Music, New York; UK: 22 June 1876, Covent Garden, London
CAST The King *b*, Amneris *ms*, Aida *s*, Radamès *t*, Ramfis *b*, Amonasro *bar*, High Priestess *s*, Messenger *t*; *satb* chorus of priests, priestesses, ministers, captains, soldiers, functionaries, slaves and Ethiopian prisoners, Egyptian people

In November 1869, during celebrations to mark the completion of the Suez canal, a new opera house was opened in Cairo with a performance of *Rigoletto*. But the khedive of Egypt, abetted by the distinguished French Egyptologist Auguste Mariette, was also determined to commission a specially composed opera for his theatre; since Mariette was a friend of Camille du Locle, one of the *Don Carlos* librettists, it was through him that Verdi was approached. In April 1870 Mariette sent du Locle a scenario he had written; though conventional in plot, it was rich in local colour and scenic detail, and Verdi liked it. In fact he was to show an almost Puccinian curiosity about the ambience of this drama, seeking advice on Egyptian religion, music, history and geography, and experimenting with flutes and trumpets specially constructed in a spurious ancient Egyptian style, for the scenes of ritual and celebration. Du Locle, working under Verdi's supervision, elaborated Mariette's synopsis into a French prose libretto, which in turn was rendered into Italian verse by Ghislanzoni. Dozens of letters between composer and librettist show Verdi taking as full a part as ever in planning the text: conceiving certain scenes himself (Amneris and her attendants and slaves in Act II, Scene 1); urging Ghislanzoni boldly to cast away convention when it did not serve the dramatic purpose (the Aida–Amonasro duet in Act III); dictating the metrical details in arias and ensembles (the Act IV finale: 'You can't imagine what a beautiful melody can be written in so strange a form.').

Originally scheduled for January 1871, the premiere had to be delayed until the following season, for Mariette – who had gone to Paris in July 1870 to advise du Locle and the designers, so that the opera would be 'composed and executed in a strictly Egyptian style' – found himself immured in the city when the Franco-Prussian War broke out a few days later. The Prussian victory at Sedan (Verdi contributed part of his fee for *Aida* for the benefit of the French wounded) formed a suggestive background for the composition of the 'Triumph' scene (Act II, Scene 2): with some distaste, Verdi referred Ghislanzoni to Kaiser Wilhelm's victory telegram as a suitable model for the priests' chorus!

Both in Cairo, where it was conducted by the double-bass virtuoso Giovanni Bottesini, and in Milan, where it was in the trusty hands of Franco Faccio, *Aida* was enthusiastically received. It has remained one of Verdi's most popular operas, and in particular a natural first choice for open-air festival performances such as those that began at Verona in the early 20th century. For the Paris Opéra premiere (in French) in 1880, the Act II ballet was extended by some 90 bars; this expanded version of the scene at once became the standard form. On the other hand, the full-length overture written at Ricordi's suggestion for the Milan premiere was discarded before the performance even took place, and was first heard under Toscanini in 1940. Another abandoned movement was a chorus 'alla Palestrina', placed at the start of Act III; the definitive Act III *introduzione* was composed only in August 1871.

SYNOPSIS

The action takes place in Memphis and Thebes, in the time of the pharaohs.

Act I Scene 1: A hall in the royal palace at

Memphis. In the wars with Ethiopia, Aida has been captured and brought to Memphis as a slave for Amneris, daughter of the Egyptian king: her father, the Ethiopian king Amonasro, has launched an invasion to rescue her. The young captain Radamès dreams of being chosen to lead the Egyptian forces; ironically, his longing for glory is inspired by Aida, whom he loves ('Celeste Aida'). Radamès in turn is loved by Amneris, who suspects that Aida may be her rival. The Egyptian king receives a report on the invasion; he announces that Isis has declared Radamès commander of the army, and leads the assembly in patriotic song ('Su! del Nilo al sacro lido'). Aida is torn between love of Radamès and love of her homeland ('Ritorna vincitor!'). Scene 2: The interior of the Temple of Vulcan at Memphis. The divinity is invoked with mystic song and dance, and the high priest Ramfis consecrates Radamès for his mission.

Act II Scene 1: A room in Amneris's apartments. Amneris is arrayed for the triumphal return of the Egyptian army ('Chi mai fra gl'inni e i plausi'). In a long dialogue ('Fu la sorte dell'armi a' tuoi funesta') she poses as Aida's friend, tricks her into admitting her love for Radamès, and finally exults arrogantly over her. Scene 2: One of the gateways into the city of Thebes. The victorious host passes before the king ('Gloria all'Egitto, ad Iside'); Radamès is crowned with the victor's wreath, and offered any gift he chooses. The Ethiopian prisoners are led in, and though Amonasro is disguised as a common soldier Aida at once recognizes him. He tells the Egyptian king a false tale about his own death, and begs him to show magnanimity and release the prisoners ('Ma tu, Re, tu signore possente'). Despite the warnings of the priests, the crowd takes up his plea, and the issue is settled when Radamès adds his voice. The king bestows Amneris's hand on the young warrior, and the scene ends with a resumption of the triumphal anthems with which it commenced.

Act III The banks of the Nile. Ramfis escorts Amneris to the temple where she is to spend the night before her marriage in prayer. Aida comes down to the river to meet Radamès; she fears she will never see her homeland again ('O patria mia'). To her astonishment, Amonasro suddenly appears. Once more he has invaded Egypt; this time, with Aida's help, the Ethiopians can win; and with a relentless barrage of moral blackmail he forces her to agree to get Radamès to reveal the Egyptians' military plans ('Rivedrai le foreste imbalsamate'). Amonasro hides, and Aida sets about persuading her lover to elope with her. Reluctantly, he accepts her argument ('Pur ti riveggo, mia dolce Aida . . . Fuggiam gli arbori inospiti . . . Sì, fuggiam da queste mura'): if they make their getaway tonight, they will be able to pass the Napata gorges before the army moves into them. When he realizes that Amonasro has overheard him, Radamès is overcome with shame. Amneris and Ramfis re-emerge from the temple; Radamès saves Amneris from a murderous attack by Amonasro, then surrenders himself as Aida and her father escape.

Act IV Scene 1: A hall in the royal palace. The Ethiopians have been routed again and Amonasro killed; Aida has disappeared. Amneris halts the procession escorting Radamès to his trial: if only he will make some effort to explain himself, she will plead for mercy; but Radamès has lost all he values in life, and is resolved to die ('Già i sacerdoti adunansi . . . Chi ti salva, sciagurato'). Amneris listens in mounting anguish to the progress of the trial; Radamès is sentenced to be buried alive under the altar of the god he has offended. Scene 2: The Temple of Vulcan. Anticipating Radamès's fate, Aida has hidden herself in the vault, and as he is entombed there she emerges from the shadows. She consoles him with her vision of a paradise where love will be unalloyed ('Morir! sì pura e bella . . . Vedi? di morte l'angelo'), and, as priestesses perform a sacred dance in the temple above and Amneris prays for Radamès, they die in one another's arms ('O terra addio, addio o valle di pianti').

Aida is a summation of all that Verdi had hitherto achieved, brilliantly combining the strengths of Italian Romantic melodramma with those of French grand opera. No work epitomizes more splendidly the qualities the world admires in grand opera. But its dramatic pace belongs to Verdi's native tradition; so does its sense of priorities, for in Acts III and IV the external splendours recede, and we have to concern ourselves solely with the tormented humanity of the protagonists. Contemporaries saw signs of Wagner's influence too, probably in the comparatively superficial fact that recurring themes play a large part in the score. Both Aida and Amneris have their identifying themes – each in its own way sensuous and alluring – and another theme, severe and contrapuntal in character, is associated with Ramfis and the priests. A more distinctive feature of the opera is its uniquely powerful sense of time and place: the prominence of flutes, trumpets and harps helps evoke a world of bardic antiquity, while modal inflexions (most evident in the scene of Radamès's consecration) often colour the harmony.

The interaction of tradition and innovation that perplexed some early critics is best seen in the magnificent series of duets that runs through the opera, in all of which the starting point was a text in basically conventional form. It is fascinating to see how Verdi elaborated and varied this, sometimes playing up to, sometimes frustrating the audience's expectations. In the Aida–Amneris duet, for example (Act II, Scene 1), the 'cabaletta' is in large part a kind of descant set against an offstage reprise of the chorus 'Su! del Nilo'; while in the duet finale of Act IV the (slow) cabaletta is provided with a supremely ironic commentary from Amneris. This closing scene occasioned Verdi some anxiety: he questioned Bottesini closely about the effect of what he described as an experiment in the 'ethereal genre'. Thomas Mann, using Hans Castorp in *The Magic Mountain* as his mouthpiece, saw it as a supreme instance of music's idealizing tendency, its power to transfigure and beautify even the harshest realities.

Simon Boccanegra (II)

Melodramma in a prologue and three acts (2h 15m)
Libretto by Francesco Maria Piave and Arrigo Boito (a rewriting by Boito of Piave's 1857 libretto of the same name)

Composed December 1880–February 1881
PREMIERES   24 March 1881, La Scala, Milan; US:
28 January 1932, Metropolitan, New York; UK:
27 October 1948, Sadler's Wells, London
CAST   Simon Boccanegra *bar*, Jacopo Fiesco *b*, Paolo
Albiani *b*, Pietro *bar*, Maria Boccanegra (under the name of
Amelia Grimaldi) *s*, Gabriele Adorno *t*, Captain of the
Crossbowmen *t*, Amelia's Maidservant *ms*; *satb* chorus of
soldiers, sailors, people, Fiesco's servants, senators, the
doge's court

In November 1880 Verdi's publisher Giulio Ricordi
raised the question of reviving *Simon Boccanegra*.
Verdi was interested, but the opera would need revision – it was 'too sad, too desolate' as it stood – and he
went on to mention, as a means of lightening the
gloom, 'two stupendous letters' by the 14th-century
poet Petrarch. Addressing himself to the doges of
Genoa and Venice, Petrarch had rebuked them for
embarking on a fratricidal war when they were 'both
born of the same mother, Italy . . . how wonderful' –
remarked Verdi – 'this feeling for an Italian fatherland
at that time!' Verdi's friend the composer/librettist
Arrigo Boito, already well advanced on a libretto for
Otello, was at first reluctant to undertake the revision;
but Verdi had not yet committed himself to *Otello*,
and almost certainly the shrewd Ricordi encouraged
the *Simon Boccanegra* collaboration so that the two
men could have the experience of working together on
something slightly less momentous than a new opera.
Verdi was not prepared to contemplate rewriting on
the scale Boito suggested; so, apart from a number of
comparatively minor revisions, the librettist had to
limit himself to creating a new second scene for Act I
– the great council-chamber scene. But the admiration
Verdi felt for the way he did that – the general
conception, the distinction of the verses, the ingenuity
in solving niggling little problems of detail – was a
major factor in persuading the composer that Boito
was an ideal colleague. Boito himself 'attributed no
artistic or literary merit to the patchwork I have made
from poor Piave's libretto', and refused to allow his
name to be publicly linked with the revised *Simon
Boccanegra*.

Except for Act II, the least revised and therefore
the most old-fashioned in style, the new *Simon Boccanegra* was warmly received. But for all Boito's ingenuity, and for all the magnificence of the 'late Verdi'
style that here emerges for the first time, it remains a
perplexing and sombre drama – an opera for connoisseurs rather than a popular favourite. Brahms, who
saw it in Vienna in 1882, spoke for many: he found
'something talented and gripping everywhere, but after
a while . . . ceased all investigations into the meaning
of the libretto'.

SYNOPSIS

The action takes place in Genoa and its vicinity,
about the middle of the 14th century. Twenty-five
years elapse between the prologue and the drama.

Prologue   A piazza in Genoa. A new doge is about
to be elected; the goldsmith Paolo persuades Pietro,
leader of the plebeian party, to vote for Simon Boccanegra, a corsair in the service of the republic. The
sight of the darkened Fiesco palace prompts specula-

tion on the fate of the unhappy Maria ('L'atra magion
vedete?'), incarcerated there because her father disapproves of her love for Simon. Fiesco emerges from the
palace: Maria has died ('Il lacerato spirito'); but his
pride is unbroken, and he scorns Simon's offer of
reconciliation. Only if he entrusts to Fiesco the daughter Maria has borne to him Simon will be forgiven; but
the young Maria has disappeared without trace ('Del
mar sul lido'). Simon enters the palace determined to
see Maria once more; he discovers her corpse just as a
throng of plebeians proclaims him doge.

Act I   Scene 1: The garden of the Grimaldi palace
outside Genoa. Amelia impatiently awaits her beloved, Gabriele Adorno ('Come in quest'ora bruna . . .
Cielo di stelle orbato'). She is worried at the risks
he and her guardian Andrea – in fact Fiesco – are
running by conspiring against Boccanegra. Learning
that the doge (Simon), whose visit is now announced,
is likely to seek her hand for Paolo, Gabriele agrees to
ask 'Andrea' to bless them as man and wife ('Vieni a
mirar la cerula . . . Sì, sì, dell'ara il giubilo'). His love
is unshaken when the supposed Amelia Grimaldi
proves to be an orphan girl, and 'Andrea' blesses him
('Vieni a me, ti benedico'). Greeting the doge, Amelia
tells him her heart is already engaged; as Simon questions her, he recognizes her as his long-lost daughter
Maria ('Orfanella il tetto umile . . . Figlia! a tal nome
io palpito'). The spurned Paolo plots to abduct
Amelia. Scene 2: The council chamber in the Palazzo
degli Abati. A council meeting is interrupted by the
sound of a brawl; a mob of plebeians drags in Gabriele
and Fiesco. Gabriele tells the doge that Amelia has
been abducted; he has killed the man who did it, but
believes the abductor was acting on Simon's instructions. He now tries to kill Simon, but is prevented by
the appearance of Amelia. Simmering hostility between patricians and plebeians threatens to break out
into open fighting; appealing to ideals of brotherhood
and patriotism, Simon re-establishes his authority
('Plebe! Patrizi! Popolo'); then he compels Paolo to
anathematize the traitor in their midst.

Act II   The doge's room in the ducal palace in
Genoa. Paolo puts poison in Simon's water jug; he
fails to enlist Fiesco in his plan to murder Simon, but
enrages Gabriele by claiming that Amelia is the play-
thing of the doge's lust. Meeting Amelia, Gabriele
denounces her bitterly; but she cannot yet explain her
feelings for Simon ('Parla, in tuo cor virgineo'). As
Simon approaches, Gabriele hides. Despite new evidence of Gabriele's plots, Amelia persuades her father
to forgive him; he insists on being left alone, drinks
from the poisoned water, and falls asleep. Amelia,
fearful of what might happen, has only pretended to
leave, and when her lover emerges, bent on murder,
she intervenes. Their argument wakens the doge; his
relationship to Amelia can be concealed no longer,
and Gabriele is appalled by what he has tried to do
('Perdon, perdon, Amelia'). Again insurrection is
heard in the streets, and Simon is determined to seek
reconciliation. If Gabriele can negotiate a peace,
Amelia shall be his reward.

Act III   Within the doge's palace. The Guelphs
have been routed, and Paolo captured. As he is led to
execution he meets Fiesco, who expresses his loathing

of the poisoner and abductor. The sounds of the wedding of Amelia and Gabriele are heard from a distant part of the palace. Simon enters, the effects of the poison already far advanced; as he gazes out to sea, Fiesco emerges from the shadows. When Simon recognizes the old man, he surprises him by claiming the reconciliation that had been offered 25 years before; now he can fulfil the conditions: Amelia Grimaldi is Fiesco's long-lost granddaughter, and he gladly restores her to him. Fiesco's pride is broken at last, and, weeping, he embraces the dying Simon ('Piango, perchè mi parla'). The doge blesses the newly married couple and nominates Gabriele his successor ('Gran Dio, ti benedici').

Once Verdi had Boito's revised text, he composed/revised 'everything in sequence, just as if it were a matter of a new opera'. The more mechanical conventions of the 1850s now seemed intolerable to him, and there were few scenes – even where the libretto remained unaltered – that he did not scrutinize rigorously and, where necessary, rewrite. In the broadest terms the musical continuity is more skilfully sustained (thanks particularly to a more sophisticated use of the orchestra); the new material is of course in a riper and richer style, and the dramatic characterization is more interesting. Fiesco, through his Act I duet with Gabriele, acquires a warmer humanity, and Paolo becomes one of Boito's mephistophelean villains. Good examples of Verdi's musical transformation of an unaltered text are to be found in the first scene of the prologue, where the dialogue, instead of being punctuated by the customary figurations of accompanied recitative, is set against a gravely flowing orchestral theme made much of in Liszt's *Réminiscences de Boccanegra*, 1882); and in the duet 'Orfanella il tetto umile', where the conventional cadenza is replaced by an exquisitely tender and poetic coda. Nevertheless, discrepancies between Verdi's 1857 manner and his 1880 manner are an inescapable feature of the opera and have a singular effect; for Verdi, we must suppose, was moved to revise most radically those scenes he felt most deeply. At such critical moments the characters might be said to rise to the occasion, and express themselves with a subtlety and power unknown in the 1857 score.

The most substantial new number is the Act I finale – the council-chamber scene. Inspired by those Petrarch letters, Verdi, who as a young composer had had a positive genius for music in the most demotic manner, finds a voice worthy of his by now patriarchal status in Italian society. The magnificent declamatory fervour of Simon's solo, the radiance of Amelia's lyricism, the searching harmonies, the consummate craftsmanship of the whole ensemble combine to make the scene one of the noblest visions of social idealism in music.

Otello

Othello

Dramma lirico in four acts (2h 15m)
Libretto by Arrigo Boito, after the tragedy *Othello* by William Shakespeare (1604–5)
Composed December 1884–November 1886; rev. April 1887

PREMIERES 5 February 1887, La Scala, Milan; US: 16 April 1888, Academy of Music, New York; UK: 5 July 1889, Lyceum, London
CAST Otello *t*, Iago *bar*, Cassio *t*, Roderigo *t*, Lodovico *b*, Montano *b*, Herald *b*, Desdemona *s*, Emilia *ms*; *satb* chorus of soldiers and sailors of the Venetian Republic, Venetian ladies and gentlemen, Cypriot people, Greek men-at-arms, Dalmatians, Albanians, children of the island *trebles*; an innkeeper, 4 inn servants, ship's crew

During the last 20 years of Verdi's life, Arrigo Boito was to become one of his closest friends, and their working relationship was one of the most remarkable in the history of opera. It was a position he did not win easily: almost 30 years Verdi's junior, he had deeply offended him with a foolish poem published in the 1860s, and it took all his generosity of spirit and all Ricordi's diplomacy to bring about a reconciliation. Their two Shakespearian operas, *Otello* and *Falstaff*, are widely regarded as the twin peaks of the whole Italian tradition of opera; a few critics, however, judge the collaboration more captiously, and deplore what they see as the artificiality and self-conscious intellectualism of Verdi's last operas.

In adapting *Othello*, Boito omitted the first, Venetian, act – save for a number of hints that are ingeniously recapitulated later, notably in the love duet in Act I; otherwise he followed the play closely. But his understanding of Shakespeare's characters had its roots in Continental sources – in the writings of August Wilhelm von Schlegel and Jean-François-Victor Hugo (whose French translation was his primary source), and in the style of Shakespeare performance growing up in Italy around the actors Ernesto Rossi and Tommaso Salvini. With Otello, Boito's emphasis lies on the 'Ethiopian' core of savage passion only fragilely contained beneath a veneer of Mediterranean civility; Desdemona, on the other hand, is a saintly idealization, 'a type of goodness, of resignation, of self-sacrifice' (Verdi). For Iago too, Boito and Verdi drew on this interpretative tradition; but, equally, his diabolical cynicism makes him one with a whole family of mephistophelean villains conceived by Boito for his opera libretti. The peculiar fascination Iago exerted over both men is seen from one of Boito's additions to Shakespeare's play, the 'Credo' in Act II – which Verdi found 'most beautiful and wholly Shakespearian' – and from the fact that for years they were disposed to call the opera *Jago*. They finally resolved to challenge comparison with Shakespeare by using his title only in January 1886, not much more than a year before the premiere.

No other opera, if one excepts *King Lear*, occupied Verdi so long. The possibility of composing *Otello* had first been put to him in earnest during a visit to Milan in June 1879, and a first draft of Boito's libretto was written during the summer and autumn; but it was not until November 1886 that Verdi was ready to declare the opera finished, and he continued to tinker with details even during the rehearsals. Franco Faccio, who conducted the premiere, rehearsed his cast with exemplary zeal, and no detail of casting, *mise-en-scène* or general organization was too tiny for Ricordi's attention; even so, to the last moment Verdi reserved the right to withdraw the opera if anything failed to satisfy him. In the event he was not pleased with the premiere, but it was recognized internationally as an artistic occasion of the first importance, and prompted scenes of wild enthusiasm: the *Times* critic reported that at one o'clock in the morning the streets outside Verdi's hotel were still full of 'an eager multitude . . . shouting and yelling'.

For the first performance at the Paris Opéra in October 1894, Verdi composed a short ballet; it forms part of the ceremony of welcome for the Venetian ambassadors in the Act III finale.

SYNOPSIS

The scene is set in a maritime city on the island of Cyprus at the end of the 15th century.

Act I Outside the castle. A crowd watches as the ship bearing Otello, the new governor, battles into harbour through a hurricane; the Venetians have routed the Turks, and a celebratory bonfire is prepared. Otello's ensign, Iago, who hates both Otello and the young officer Cassio, promises to help Roderigo enjoy the love of Otello's wife, Desdemona; and, as the bonfire dies down ('Fuoco di gioia!'), sets his plan in motion. Wine flows freely in honour of the nuptials of Otello and Desdemona ('Inaffia l'ugola!'), Cassio is soon drunk; when Montano, the retiring governor, orders him to the ramparts, Roderigo and Iago easily provoke a brawl. Roderigo goes to raise havoc through the city, alarm bells clang, and Otello reappears, roused from his bed. Furious to find Montano wounded, and believing what 'honest Iago' tells him, he dismisses Cassio, appoints Iago in his stead, and sends him to re-establish order in the streets. Desdemona has also been roused by the pandemonium; the lovers are left alone, to recall the strange chances of fortune that brought them together ('Già nella notte densa').

Act II A hall on the ground floor of the castle. Having advised Cassio to ask Desdemona to intercede for him with Otello, Iago confesses his nihilistic creed ('Credo in un Dio crudel'). He urges Otello to watch Desdemona's behaviour with Cassio: it may be less innocent than he supposes. Otello is disturbed, but, when he sees the islanders paying homage to his wife in the garden ('Dove guardi splendono'), his suspicions are disarmed. When Desdemona pleads with him for Cassio, he is reminded of Iago's warning, becomes irritable, and throws down the handkerchief she offers him; Emilia picks it up. In the quartet ('Dammi la dolce e lieta parola del perdono'), Desdemona beseeches Otello to forgive her for any offence given; he muses gloomily; Iago snatches Desdemona's handkerchief from Emilia. Otello's dreams of love and glory are fast evaporating ('Nell'ore arcane della sua lussuria . . . Ora è per sempre addio'), and he demands proof of his wife's guilt. Iago recounts how he has recently slept beside Cassio, who, in his dreams, was unmistakably making love to Desdemona ('Era la notte'); what is more, only the day before, he was carrying the handkerchief Otello had once given her. Otello swears to exact bloody vengeance ('Sì, pel ciel marmoreo giuro!').

Act III The great hall of the castle. Iago outlines a plan to make Cassio chatter about Desdemona while

Otello eavesdrops. Otello greets Desdemona with elaborate courtesy ('Dio ti giocondi, o sposo'); but as soon as she mentions Cassio he becomes agitated and, after an argument about her missing handkerchief, drives her away; the grief occasioned by her falseness is unendurable ('Dio! mi potevi scagliar'). Iago re-enters, followed by Cassio, who is soon talking about his mistress, Bianca ('Essa t'avvince coi vaghi rai'). Otello, unable to catch Bianca's name, imagines the ribald laughter to be about Desdemona; when Cassio produces the handkerchief, no further proof is required. While a distant chorus is heard greeting ambassadors from Venice, Otello and Iago plan how to kill the guilty pair. The ambassadors have come to recall Otello; Cassio is appointed his successor. But affairs of state are overshadowed by Otello's behaviour ('A terra! . . . sì . . .'); soon he is delirious; he drives everyone but Iago from the scene, curses Desdemona, and swoons. Cries of 'Viva Otello!' resound in the distance, while Iago spurns the prostrate figure with his heel.

Act IV Desdemona's bedroom. While she prepares for bed, Desdemona sings the 'Willow Song' ('Piangea cantando nell'erma landa') she once learned from her mother's maid. She bids Emilia goodnight and, having said her prayers ('Ave Maria'), lies down to sleep. Otello enters, extinguishes the lamp, and kisses Desdemona; she realizes that he has come to kill her. Her entreaties are in vain, and he smothers her just as Emilia comes hammering at the door to announce that Cassio has killed Roderigo. Aghast to find Desdemona dying, she raises the alarm: Cassio, Iago, Lodovico and later Montano enter. As the truth emerges, Iago makes his escape, and Otello is disarmed. But he has a dagger hidden in his robes, and, having bidden a solemn farewell to his comrades and a heart-broken one to the dead Desdemona, he stabs himself, and falls dying beside her.

As so often in Verdi, the musical characterization is the key to the opera's individuality. Otello, he remarked, 'now the warrior, now the passionate lover, now crushed to the point of baseness, now ferocious like a savage, must sing and shout'; Desdemona 'must always, always sing'; but Iago 'has only to declaim and mock'. Again and again in *Otello*, Desdemona's pure-hearted and passionate lyricism, an expression of all the love and idealism that the art of opera had been invented to express, is juxtaposed with, counterpointed against and undermined by Iago's nonchalant parlando, which is graced only with a few slithering and trilling touches of arioso, and which could, Verdi noted, 'with the exception of a few outbursts, be sung *mezza voce* throughout' – an unforgettable musical image of the mephistophelean 'spirit of denial'.

In 1882, when work on the opera was still at a very early stage, Verdi predicted that *Otello* would be 'Italian in scale and Italian in who knows how many other ways . . . Perhaps a few melodies . . . (if I can find any) . . . and melody is always Italian . . .'. A few critics were deluded by the opera's seamless continuity, the sumptuousness of the orchestral writing and the sophistication of the harmony into imagining that he was at last coming round to a Wagnerian ideal of music drama. But the essence of his art remained the wedding of poetry and song in balanced lyrical forms; what is different in the later Verdi is that these forms are not confined to arias and ensembles, but blossom wherever poetry and the spirit of the drama suggest. In the opening scene, for example, two distinct musical shapes – one a prayer ('Dio, fulgor della bufera'), one an exclamation of joy ('Vittoria! vittoria!') – materialize out of the orchestral turmoil of the hurricane. Conversely, it is out of the songs and celebrations marking Otello's safe arrival that the dramatic action re-emerges: Iago's *brindisi* is the source of the musical figures that propel the brawl, just as the wine he sings of is the source of the drunkenness that causes it.

Many sections of the score draw inspiration directly from Shakespeare's poetry: for example, Otello's two great solos, 'Nell'ore arcane' in Act II ('What sense had I of her stol'n hours of lust?') and 'Dio! mi potevi scagliar' in Act III ('Had it pleas'd heaven to try me with affliction'). No Shakespeare-inspired detail is more telling than the threefold recurrence – at the close of the Act I love duet; when Otello enters Desdemona's bedchamber to kill her; and at the end of the opera – of the so-called 'kiss' motif: 'I kiss'd thee ere I kill'd thee; no way but this, killing myself to die upon a kiss.'

Falstaff

Commedia lirica in three acts (2h)
Libretto by Arrigo Boito, after the comedy *The Merry Wives of Windsor* by William Shakespeare (1600–1601) and incorporating material from his histories *Henry IV, Parts I and II* (1597–8)
Composed ?August 1889; March 1890–December 1892; major revs March 1893 and January 1894
PREMIERES 9 February 1893, La Scala, Milan; UK: 19 May 1894, Covent Garden, London; US: 4 February 1895, Metropolitan, New York
CAST Sir John Falstaff *bar*, Ford *bar*, Fenton *t*, Dr Caius *t*, Bardolph *t*, Pistol *b*, Alice Ford *s*, Nannetta *s*, Mistress Quickly *ms*, Meg Page *ms*, Host of the Garter Inn *silent role*; Robin, Falstaff's Page *silent role*; Ford's Little Pageboy *silent role*; *satb* chorus of burghers and commoners, Ford's servants, masquerade of elves, fairies, witches, etc.

Falstaff was Verdi's first comic opera since *Un giorno di regno*. There were those who felt, as Rossini did, that he was 'too melancholy and serious' to compose a successful one; but since *Luisa Miller* he had used elements of comedy to set off the prevailing tragic mood in his operas, and at various times since the 1860s he had considered making another attempt at comedy, if a suitable subject could be found. He was not interested in buffoonery: for all its Latin spirit, *Falstaff* was not an opera buffa, Verdi insisted, but a depiction of character.

As a result of their collaboration on *Otello*, Verdi now had complete trust in Boito, and embarked on this new enterprise – at first a secret between the two of them – with much zest. Shortly after receiving a first draft of the plot (summer 1889) he was experimenting with 'comic fugues' (it is likely that the opera's finale was conceived at this time), and when he received the complete libretto (March 1890) he drafted the whole of Act I in little more than a week. Such bursts of intense activity were to recur throughout the

three and a half years he worked on *Falstaff*; but there were distractions and sorrows too (particularly the deaths of several of his closest friends) that drove music out of his head for months on end. It is obvious from the manuscripts and early printed sources that Verdi worked over every scene again and again, refining the craftsmanship, enriching the musical fabric, sharpening the wit. The process of revision continued while the score was being printed, throughout the period of rehearsals, and even during the first run of performances. Further rewriting, sometimes quite substantial, took place before the Rome performances in April 1893, and before the French premiere the following year.

Falstaff had long been one of Verdi's favourite characters – a supreme embodiment of Shakespeare's genius for 'inventing truth' – and Boito's libretto is the most brilliant of all operatic adaptations of Shakespeare. He adroitly condenses and clarifies the plot of *The Merry Wives*, while drawing freely on the two parts of *Henry IV* to give us a Falstaff in all his prodigious abundance of personality; at the same time Shakespeare's quintessential Englishness is translated to 'the gardens of the *Decameron*', the verse given an antique tang and raciness with vocabulary drawn from Boccaccio and the satirists of the Italian Renaissance. The libretto is beautifully formed: each act is subdivided into one scene of character depiction for a small group of soloists and one of teeming action and elaborate ensembles.

No production book for *Falstaff* survives, but there is plenty of evidence that Verdi, who supervised a huge number of rehearsals in January and February 1893, insisted on a more naturalistic style of performance than in his tragic operas (a newspaper account survives of him demonstrating to Fenton how to kiss Nannetta with suitable ardour); and the designer Adolph Hohenstein was sent off to London and Windsor to ensure that sets and costumes were as authentic as possible. The premiere was a brilliant occasion, and aroused worldwide excitement. But a high proportion of opera-lovers, especially perhaps in Italy, were frankly bewildered, and the admiration of connoisseurs was not matched by the kind of popular enthusiasm that had attended the greater part of Verdi's career. It was in large part due to Toscanini, who made his superlatively drilled performances cornerstones of the repertoire in every opera house he directed, that *Falstaff* came to be regarded as a national classic rather than an object of bewildered admiration.

SYNOPSIS

The scene is set in Windsor, in the reign of Henry IV of England.

Act I Part 1: Inside the Garter Inn. Falstaff's carousing is interrupted by Dr Caius, who threatens to report him to the Star Chamber. Unable to ruffle Falstaff's bibulous calm, Caius turns on Bardolph and Pistol, who the previous night had made him drunk and emptied his purse; the charges are denied, and Caius storms out. Finding they have no money to pay the bill, Falstaff blames his companions. Bardolph's glowing nose means they can economize on lanterns, but the savings are more than consumed in wine bills. He outlines a new enterprise: two wealthy citizens, Ford and Page, have beautiful wives; he will lay siege to their virtue as a means of getting at their husbands' money ('V'è noto un tal'). Bardolph and Pistol refuse to assist so dishonourable an enterprise; Falstaff harangues them on the subject of honour ('L'Onore! Ladri! . . . Può l'onore riempirvi la pancia?'), before kicking them out. Part 2: The garden by Ford's house. Alice and Meg have received identical love letters from Falstaff ('Fulgida Alice! amor t'offro'), and decide he must be taught a lesson. Ford enters with Fenton and Caius (rivals for Nannetta's hand) and Bardolph and Pistol, from whom he learns that Falstaff is bent on seducing his wife and emptying his money bags. While the women engage Mistress Quickly to lure Falstaff to an assignation, Ford plans to visit the Garter Inn in disguise to investigate these tales. Twice Nannetta and Fenton break away from their companions to kiss in the shadow of the trees ('Labbra di foco!').

Act II Part 1: Inside the Garter Inn. Mistress Quickly arrives with the answer to Falstaff's letters ('Reverenza!'): both wives love him, but only Alice is able to receive him – any day between two and three, when her husband is always out. Bardolph announces 'Mastro Fontana' ('Master Brook'): 'Fontana' introduces himself as a wealthy man accustomed to want for nothing; but he has fallen in love with Ford's wife, and all his wooing has been in vain ('C'è a Windsor una dama'). The gold he has brought with him is Falstaff's if he can seduce her; for once she has fallen to a man of the world like Sir John she is more likely to listen to his own suit. Falstaff accepts the challenge; indeed it is almost won already, for he has an assignation with the lady in half an hour. He excuses himself a moment, and Ford is left alone, a prey to jealousy ('È sogno? o realtà? . . . L'ora è fissata'). Falstaff returns, dressed to kill, and they go out together. Part 2: A room in Ford's house. Mistress Quickly reports on the success of her mission ('Giunta all'Albergo della Giarrettiera'). A screen is set up, a lute laid ready, and servants carry in a laundry basket; they all look forward to the adventure ('Gaie comari di Windsor'). Falstaff arrives, woos Alice ardently, and recalls the days of his slender youth ('Quand'ero paggio'). But Ford is heard approaching; Falstaff hides behind the screen, while Ford, assisted by Caius, Bardolph and Pistol, seeks high and low for the intruder. Ford soon rushes off to another part of the house, Falstaff is bundled into the laundry basket, and Fenton and Nannetta retreat behind the screen. While Ford closes in on – as he supposes – his wife and Falstaff, Nannetta and Fenton continue their romantic tête-à-tête. The screen is snatched away, to reveal only the young lovers, and a new hunt for Falstaff begins on a false scent laid by Bardolph. The laundry basket is hauled to the window, and as soon as Ford returns Falstaff is tipped into the river.

Act III Part 1: A courtyard outside the Garter Inn. Falstaff broods over his humiliation ('Mondo ladro'); but the consolations of steaming wine are infallible. Mistress Quickly brings a letter inviting him to a midnight assignation in Windsor Park; but he must come disguised as the 'Black Huntsman' who haunts the forest. The conversation is overheard by Meg, Alice, Ford, Caius and Fenton; and while Falstaff accompanies Mistress Quickly into the inn they plan the details of the midnight masquerade. Mistress Quickly reappears to hear Ford plotting Nannetta's marriage with Caius. Part 2: Windsor Great Park. Fenton's musings ('Dal labbro il canto estasiato vola') are interrupted by the wives: to outwit Ford and Caius, last-minute changes of mask and costume are necessary. As midnight strikes, Falstaff enters; but his wooing of Alice is interrupted by the approach of a horde of spirits. With Falstaff prostrate on the ground in terror, Nannetta, disguised as the queen of the fairies, and her attendants weave a spell in solemn song and dance ('Sul fil d'un soffio etesio'). Then, while she and Fenton are hurried away, fantastically garbed figures torment Falstaff and conduct him through a litany of repentance. In the excitement Bardolph loses his hood; further unmaskings follow, and Falstaff realizes he has been made an ass of. Ford proposes that the betrothal of the queen of the fairies be celebrated: Caius's bride proves, when unveiled, to be Bardolph, while another masked couple brought forward for blessing are revealed as Nannetta and Fenton. Ford accepts the situation philosophically, and Falstaff leads the company in a fugal chorus celebrating the absurdity of the human condition ('Tutto nel mondo è burla').

It is not difficult to see why early audiences were sometimes bemused. By far the greater part of Falstaff moves at such a giddy pace that only the most fleeting glimpses of musical forms are perceived: the choicest melodies are come and gone with teasing rapidity, giving an effect that is at once virtuosic and tender, and beautifully suggestive of the spirit of Shakespearian comedy. Only in the final scene, as order returns and reconciliation is achieved, does the musical pace broaden out into a sequence of almost ceremonial movements: serenade, dance, litany, fugue. In many passages musical continuity is achieved by the orchestral development of short melodic and rhythmic figures, a procedure more 'symphonic' than anything heard in Verdi's operas hitherto. Some of these symphonic passages are based on trenchant vocal phrases – 'dalle due alle tre' and 'te lo cornifico' in Act II, Part 1, for example – in which Verdi shows that his vaunted parola scenica – the 'theatrical word' that 'carves out a situation or a character' – can be as brilliantly apt in the comic vein as in the heroic or tragic.

With a passage for muted double-basses in the final scene of Otello, Verdi had become the first Italian since Spontini to earn a place in Berlioz's Treatise on Orchestration, as revised by Richard Strauss. Many an episode in Falstaff – Falstaff's self-portraits in the opening scene; his ruminations on his ducking in the river, culminating in the celebrated trill cum tremolo for virtually every instrument in the orchestra; the fairy music in the last act – demonstrates that for sheer virtuosity in tone-painting the elderly Verdi rivalled Strauss himself. But it is orchestration of exquisite translucency: instruments are virtually never used simply to reinforce the voices. To sing unsupported by the orchestra was only one of the unfamiliar demands Verdi made on his performers; he knew that Italian singers in particular would be severely tested, for there was, he declared, no room in *Falstaff* for 'artists who want to sing too much . . . and fall asleep on the notes'; above all they would need to 'loosen up their tongues and clarify their pronunciation'.

D.K.

RICHARD WAGNER
Wilhelm Richard Wagner; *b* 22 May 1813, Leipzig,
Germany; *d* 13 February 1883, Venice

Wagner is a major figure in the history of opera and
one of the most controversial (and written about)
figures of the 19th century. Late photographs of him
show an expensively dressed man wearing a velvet
beret: his calm and stately expression those of a
prince among artists. The carefully nurtured image of
the distinguished 'reformer', however, disguises his
mercurial nature and nervous disposition (though they
were noticed by Renoir in a startling portrait sketched
as late as 1882) and above all belies a turbulent career
marked almost from the start by radical ideas and
actions.

No detail of Wagner's life was too sordid to be
aired in public in the 19th century (his liking for silk
underwear and supposedly homosexual relations with
his patron Ludwig II of Bavaria were two favourites).
Yet this lurid fascination would have been unthinkable
without the two things that will always be most important about him: the power of his music and the
ambitious artistic claim he made for opera. In a sense,
he marks a return to the noble spirit of court opera in
the 17th century – opera, that is, as a festive, unique
and spectacular event. Seen in this light, his sheer
good luck in finding in Ludwig II a modern royal
patron prepared to sponsor him on a reasonably lavish
scale seems only logical given the nature of the Wagnerian enterprise. Through the agency of history and
myth and the universal humanity he saw in them, the
'extraordinary' operatic occasion, as opposed to the
day-to-day opera routinely organized in the public
sphere according to market demands, was to be a
celebration not so much of royal dynasties as of a
notion of art as redemption and catharsis addressed
to the entire human race. Drama on the highest level
and music aspiring to the condition of the symphony
were combined with a passion for allegory in a bid to
reconcile the modern age of science with some highly
ambivalent feelings about it. In other words, a performance of a Wagner 'drama' (posterity is still oblivious of the fact that he rejected the term 'music drama')
was not just a special occasion transcending the everyday commercial success of 'modern' opera by, for
example, Rossini or Meyerbeer: it was also intended
as a drastic form of cultural therapy.

Wagner's worldly polemics (which he set down in
16 substantial volumes of prose works) look clumsy
now next to the unshakeable distinction of his art. His
defence of the *Gesamtkunstwerk* – a utopian idea
adapted from Johann Gottfried Herder and the early
Romantics proposing the inherent unity of all the arts
– and his crusade against opera-as-a-business and the
decline of German culture pale before the intoxicating
effects of his music and his daring modernity. That he
discovered the world of dreams and the unconscious
long before Freud, and that he is 'indisputably the
father of the structural analysis of myth' (Claude
Lévi-Strauss), are claims that have long since been
inscribed in tablets of stone in some areas of modernist
lore. The German philosopher Theodor Adorno even
spoke of 'the birth of film out of the spirit of [Wag-
ner's] music', though the remark was intended more as
a polemical paradox than as a compliment. (Adorno
meant that the seamless musical continuity of
Wagner's works, each seductively flaunting its unique
identity and the artistic individuality of its creator,
had actually anticipated a technological art and subtle
means of persuasion that is essentially anonymous
and mass-produced.)

Wagner's influence both on the development of
opera and on purely instrumental music is immense.
He began writing operas in the early 1830s. The
bloated dimensions of his early efforts, *Die Feen* and
Das Liebesverbot (which are often explained away as
youthful inexperience), are already a sign of an attempt
to push opera to its limits. The decisive breakthrough
came with the huge local success of *Rienzi* in Dresden in
1842 (in a heavily cut version), though it was Wagner's
fourth opera, *Der fliegende Holländer*, first performed
to less enthusiastic audiences a few months later in the
same city, that marked his break with provincialism
and the real beginning of his distinctive style.

Wagner's greatest musical hero was unquestionably
Beethoven, and especially the Beethoven of the symphonies. Wagner emulated him in parts of his operas
up to *Lohengrin* (and in many early instrumental
works now mercifully forgotten), but developed a
large-scale quasi-symphonic style of his own only by
the time he began work on the music of the *Ring*. The
symphonic element in Wagner's operas is said to have
ensured their international success because it was 'the
essence of what had been expected of German music
since the time of Haydn and Beethoven' (Carl Dahlhaus). But arguably the much vaunted symphonic

'unity' of Wagner's famous system of leitmotifs was less crucial than the way his leitmotifs imprinted themselves on the memory (Adorno likened them to advertising jingles). Indeed, his uncanny sense of musical metaphor, which he refined through an intense study of early Romantic lieder and then applied on a much larger and hence more public scale in his stage works, probably did more than anything else to establish his enormous fame by attracting ears previously deaf to opera and the classical style.

One of Wagner's principal aims was to make music come of age, so to speak, by proceeding from the notion of the sublime (as opposed to the beautiful) and by fusing music in an unprecedented way with literary and philosophical ideas. For Wagner this meant nothing less than the end of opera with its schematic sequence of set pieces (during the first stages of writing the *Ring* he declared publicly that he was going to write 'no more operas') and a widening of tonality and thematic continuity. To put it another way, Wagner found a cogent justification for taking music beyond its perceived limits of expression by cutting opera loose from its traditional moorings. Whatever the validity of his rationale now, the historical impact of the music that resulted from it is undeniable. He was able to organize vast tracts of continuously flowing music in which swift changes in stylistic level and syntax were possible – a bold adventure in harmony and large-scale structure that left an indelible mark on the late-19th-century symphony. On a subjective level, his musical innovations led to new extremes of sensibility, and for many a dangerous feeling of disorientation that Nietzsche likened to the sense of losing one's depth in a large ocean. Others have simply compared his music to a drug.

In almost every respect Wagner's most radical work is *Tristan und Isolde*. Based on a medieval source noted for its vivid depiction of existential love and 'eternal death', and overlaid with a provocative interpretation of Arthur Schopenhauer's 'Metaphysics of Sexual Love', it was a *cause célèbre* by the end of the 19th century mainly on account of the explicit eroticism of its music. It is still Wagner's most incandescent work, standing on the threshold of musical modernity with its daring harmonies and open-ended musical syntax. At the same time its stubborn individuality and hot-house aestheticism – the sensual yearning for death and nothingness that has prompted its critics to accuse Wagner of cultural exhaustion and a pernicious nihilism – are at odds with Wagner's ideal of opera as a unique and revitalizing communal experience. Not surprisingly, Wagner retreated from the extreme position of *Tristan*. Schopenhauer's negation of the will and denial of life (or rather Wagner's version of them) are transformed in subsequent works into a more conciliatory and beguiling form of world-sorrow by the inclusion of more obviously humanistic themes such as the popularity of art and the principle of nation (*Die Meistersinger*) and the conquering of sensuality by a divine moral code (*Parsifal*). Wagner's music became more accessible after *Tristan* too, but paradoxically also much richer and more refined than before.

Wagner was an outstanding performer and producer of his own works as well as those of others, including Gluck, Mozart and Beethoven. He influenced a whole generation in the art of conducting. But perhaps the most significant thing he did, apart from composing several masterpieces, was to organize the building of the Bayreuth Festival Theatre. It was constructed according to his specifications with an auditorium in the form of an amphitheatre (the opposite of the hierarchical seating arrangement in the court theatres with their tiers of boxes), a sunken and invisible orchestra, and a double proscenium which creates an illusion of perspective concentrating attention on to the stage image. It was an experiment in what Wagner called 'public art' that attempted to evade the then prevailing social and commercial conditions of opera in order to turn each performance of his works into something 'special' and available to all. From the first it could never be entirely independent of the conditions it sought to escape, as Wagner himself came to realize. But it still stands as a monument to that ideal.

Wagner's description of vocal parts is sometimes confusing and frequently inconsistent. Wotan in *Die Walküre* is a 'high bass', for instance, although now he would be called a 'bass-baritone' or even a 'heroic baritone'. Alberich, Fasolt and Gunther in the *Ring* are also each described as a 'high bass'. This does not mean of course that they are to be cast with the same kind of voice. Wagner's descriptions usually refer to the vocal range, as opposed to the character, of a role. In *Siegfried* the Wanderer (Wotan) is thus a straightforward bass, as the tessitura of the part is lower than the Wotan in *Die Walküre*. In the following entries the voice specifications used by Wagner in his manuscript scores and first printed editions have been retained without further comment.

Rienzi, der Letzte der Tribunen
Rienzi, the Last of the Tribunes

Grosse tragische Oper in five acts (4h 45m)
Libretto by the composer, after the novel *Rienzi, the Last of the Roman Tribunes* by Edward Bulwer-Lytton (1834)
Composed: libretto 1837–8, French translation 1839–40; music 1838–40
PREMIERES 20 October 1842, Königlich Sächsisches Hoftheater, Dresden; US: 4 March 1878, Academy of Music, New York; UK: 27 January 1879, Her Majesty's Theatre, Haymarket, London
CAST Cola Rienzi *t*, Irene *s*, Steffano Colonna *b*, Adriano *s*, Paolo Orsini *b*, Raimondo *b*, Baroncelli *t*, Cecco del Vecchio *b*, Messenger of Peace *s*, Herald *t*, Ambassador of Milan *b*, Ambassadors of the Lombard Cities *t*, *b*, Ambassador of Naples *t*, Ambassadors of Bohemia and Bavaria 2 *b*; *satb* chorus of Roman nobles and guardsmen, followers of the Colonna and Orsini families, priests and monks of all religious orders, senators, Roman men and women, messengers of peace; pantomime (Act II): Collatinus, Lucretia, Virginia, Lucretia's virgins, Tarquinius, Tarquinius' warriors, Brutus, friends of Collatinus, young Romans, knights, the goddess of peace

According to Wagner's autobiography (written in 1865 80), he first had the idea for *Rienzi* in the summer of 1837 when, at an almost disastrously low point in his relations with his first wife, Minna, he read Bulwer-Lytton's novel *Rienzi, the Last of the Roman Tribunes* (1834; German translation, 1836). In contemporary letters and an account of his life written in the early 1840s, however, he refers to a 'favourite idea' he had 'already been considering'. Before he read the novel, therefore, he could already have been acquainted with the subject from a different source. The version Wagner is most likely to have known is Mary Mitford's successful 'tragedy' *Rienzi* (1828). Unlike Bulwer, Mitford condensed Rienzi's two careers as tribune and senator into one, just as Wagner was to do in his opera. Other similarities, too, suggest that Wagner may have been acquainted with the play, though there is no doubt that Bulwer's more epic account was his main source.

The earliest known document for the opera (which in its complete form turned out to be Wagner's longest work) is a short prose sketch written in the summer of 1837 in Blasewitz or Travemünde outlining the entire action in just thirteen lines. Serious work on the project did not begin until June 1838 in Riga. By April 1839 the full score of Act I and a draft of Act II were finished. Now reunited with his wife, Wagner undertook with her a perilous and illegal journey without passports to escape from creditors via Norway to England, and eventually to Paris. He finished the full score of Act II on 12 September 1839 in Boulogne-sur-Mer, where he also met Meyerbeer for the first time. After a break of a few months, during which he tried unsuccessfully to gain a foothold in Paris with a number of works (including an aria for the high priest to be inserted in Bellini's *Norma* and the first version of his *Faust* overture), he began composing Act III in February 1840. By November of the same year the full score of the entire opera was complete.

Contrary to a widely held belief, Wagner did not conceive *Rienzi* solely with a Paris production in mind. A letter of November 1838 to August Lewald, the editor of the literary monthly *Europa*, clearly states his intention of producing the opera 'in German', preferably at the Court Opera in Berlin. Paris was not excluded as a possibility from the start; but only after Wagner's decision to flee Riga in 1839 did it become his principal goal. He translated the libretto into French himself. During 1840, however, as the prospect of a Paris premiere grew increasingly dim, he quickly reverted to his original idea of a performance in Germany, not even bothering to adjust the French translation to changes in the libretto made during the composition of the last three acts. With the help of a recommendation from Meyerbeer and the active support of friends in Saxony, the opera was accepted for performance by the Dresden Royal Court Opera in June 1841. The premiere was conducted by Wagner in Gottfried Semper's new opera house on 20 October 1842 with Joseph Tichatschek as Rienzi and Wilhelmine Schröder-Devrient in the *travesti* role of Adriano. Despite the length of the performance (it lasted until past midnight), the occasion was one of the greatest public triumphs of Wagner's entire career, surpassed not even by the success of *Die Meistersinger* in 1868.

SYNOPSIS

Act I Rome in the mid 14th century. The pope has fled to Avignon. His departure has fanned the flames of a feud between the noble houses of Orsini and Colonna. Anarchy prevails. It is night. Paolo Orsini and his followers try to abduct Irene, the sister of Rienzi. They are interrupted by the Colonnas. Adriano, the son of Steffano Colonna, frees Irene, but without managing to separate the warring factions. Only at the entrance of Rienzi is order restored. The nobles, intimidated by Rienzi's charisma, unwillingly agree to retire to continue their fight outside the city gates. Baroncelli and Cecco, representing the people, urge Rienzi to seize power. Assured of the support of Raimondo, the papal legate, Rienzi promises to act, urging the populace to gather at dawn when they hear the signal of revolution (already heard at the beginning of the overture): a long-held note played on a single trumpet. Adriano sharply criticizes Rienzi's political methods. But his heart has been softened by his love for Irene, and Rienzi has little trouble in winning him over. In full armour in front of the Lateran Church, Rienzi proclaims the freedom of Rome ('Erstehe, hohe Roma, neu!'), but refuses to be made king. Shrewdly, he accepts the more modest, and in the long run more popular, title of tribune.

Act II A large hall in the Capitol. Rienzi has defeated the nobles, who appear to submit to his command. In reality they are secretly planning to kill him. Adriano overhears the plot and threatens to betray them. Betrayal would be tantamount to patricide, Steffano Colonna retorts, since he, as leader of the conspiracy, would certainly be executed if it failed. After an inner struggle, Adriano decides to warn Rienzi. Peace celebrations are in progress. Towards the end of a pantomime presenting the rape of Lucretia (an allegorical mirror of the 'rape' of Rome by the nobles) Orsini tries to stab Rienzi, but his dagger cannot penetrate the chain-mail vest Rienzi is wearing under his robe for protection. The conspirators are condemned to death. Adriano and Irene beseech Rienzi to pardon them. To everyone's surprise, he yields to their demands on condition that the nobles swear a new oath of allegiance to the law of Rome. Rienzi manages to convince his bewildered followers of his magnanimity. In a jubilant chorus ('Rienzi, dir sei Preis'), they praise him once more as a hero of peace.

Act III A square in the old Forum. The nobles have broken their oath and are gathering forces outside the city for a march against Rienzi. The people are outraged. Rienzi inspires them to rise up without mercy against the traitors. Adriano is torn between his allegiance to Rienzi and loyalty to his father, and expresses the hope that the two will be reconciled ('Gerechter Gott, so ist's entschieden schon'). Rienzi enters on horseback to intone the battle hymn 'Santo spirito cavaliere'. Adriano tries to intercept him, but in vain. The warriors march out accompanied by the priests, while the women, Irene and Adriano remain behind, calling on the Holy Virgin to protect the sons of Rome. The warriors, sadly depleted, return victorious. Among the enemy dead carried in is Steffano Colonna. Adriano throws himself on to his father's body swearing revenge against Rienzi. The people uneasily acclaim Rienzi victor and liberator.

Act IV The square in front of the Lateran Church. In disguise, Adriano has called Baroncelli, Cecco and their followers to a secret council. Baroncelli accuses Rienzi of complicity with the nobles. When the others demand proof, Adriano reveals his true identity and offers himself as a witness. All resolve to kill Rienzi. Intimidated by the power of the Church, the new conspirators have to be goaded on by Adriano to stand in front of the Lateran to await the arrival of their victim. Rienzi arrives at the head of a procession. The conspirators try to block his way. Noticing their uncertainty, he chides them for their lack of idealism. Crushed with embarrassment (to the annoyance of Adriano), they are about to give way to Rienzi when Raimondo and the priests come forward to announce that he has been excommunicated. Rienzi is abandoned by everyone except Irene, who remains in a long embrace with her brother.

Act V A hall in the Capitol. Rienzi fervently implores God not to jeopardize his mission ('Allmächt'ger Vater, blick' herab'). Irene is ready to stand by her brother to the death; not even Adriano can shake her resolve. A square in front of the Capitol. The people are setting the Capitol on fire. Rienzi delivers a terrible curse on Rome and its citizens, declaring them to be degenerate (*entartet*) and unworthy of his ideals. He remains in an embrace with Irene on the balcony. As Adriano enters the burning Capitol, the tower with the balcony collapses, burying all three. The nobles are seen returning to begin a violent attack on the people.

Charles Rosen has called *Rienzi* 'Meyerbeer's worst opera'. The clever reversal of Hans von Bülow's *bon mot* (he sardonically referred to the opera as Meyerbeer's best) is wide of the mark, in terms of both the quality of *Rienzi* and its historical significance. For one thing, the opera owes more to Spontini and the Auber of *La muette de Portici* than it does to Meyerbeer. Wagner's revolutionary hero is also not unrelated to Rossini's *Guillaume Tell* – a grand opera that continued to exert an influence on Wagner (which he never properly acknowledged) long after he had repudiated the genre. For another thing, Wagner's declared ambition to 'outdo' grand opera included such a reckless appropriation of other styles ranging from the operas of Bellini and Weber to Beethoven's symphonies that to call *Rienzi* a grand opera at all is to ignore its peculiarities and unique historical position. Not only is Rienzi the first of a notable line of Wagnerian heroes portraying the lonely idealist and would-be saviour of humanity, the utopian dimensions and diverse style of the opera also clearly point to (even if they do not match) the daring large-scale vision and wide-ranging musical ambition of Wagner's mature dramas.

Despite the overwhelming success of the Dresden premiere, *Rienzi* was taken up only slowly by other theatres. Wagner began to make cuts before the premiere, and with the five following performances (until the end of November 1842) he continued to experiment with further excisions and alternative versions of certain passages. At the beginning of 1843 he tried to avoid cuts by allowing the opera to be performed in two halves on successive evenings. The public complained bitterly (among other things because they were in effect paying twice for one opera) and Wagner was forced to revert to another one-evening version on 19 November 1843. With further cuts it was this version that was produced in Hamburg in March 1844 and again in Berlin in October 1847 (the latter with a new, more euphoric, version of Rienzi's last words, written with the volatile political climate that eventually led to the revolution of 1848/9 in mind). After Wagner's death, Cosima Wagner instigated a version supposedly 'according to the wishes of the Master' with drastic cuts and distortions that tried to obliterate all 'operatic' features from the work. It was published in 1899 and frequently performed, despite the protests of Richard Strauss and the prominent music scholar Guido Adler. Apart from the critical edition begun in 1974, the most complete published scores are based on the much shortened Dresden version of 1843. However, as the original manuscript score is missing (it was in the possession of Adolf Hitler until the end of the Second World War), even the critical edition is incomplete. Performances since the Second World War have all been heavily cut. A studio performance broadcast by the BBC on 27 June 1976 was a notional reconstruction of the work as Wagner originally conceived it, part of which had to be orchestrated from sketches and other supplementary sources published in the critical edition.

Der fliegende Holländer

The Flying Dutchman

Romantische Oper in three acts (2h 15m)

Libretto by the composer

Composed: libretto 1840, 1841; music 1840, 1841, rev. 1842, 1846, 1852, 1860

PREMIERES 2 January 1843, Königlich Sächsisches Hoftheater, Dresden; UK: 23 July 1870, Drury Lane, London; US: 8 November 1876, Academy of Music, Philadelphia

CAST Daland *b*, Senta *s*, Erik *t*, Mary *c*, Daland's Steersman *t*, The Dutchman high *b*; *tb* choruses of sailors from the Norwegian ship, the Flying Dutchman's crew, *sa* chorus of young women

It is not certain when Wagner decided to turn the subject of the Flying Dutchman into an opera. However, there is no doubt that his chief model was Heinrich Heine's *Memoirs of Herr von Schnabelewopski*, though he could have been acquainted with other sources such as Wilhelm Hauff's fairy-tale *Geschichte vom Gespensterschiff* (1825). The first surviving document is a prose scenario in French written during May 1840. Wagner's intention was to offer it to Meyerbeer's librettist Eugène Scribe, who would turn it into a libretto for a one-act curtain-raiser to a larger ballet (a practice then in vogue in Paris) which he, Wagner, would then be commissioned by the Opéra to compose. The plan was not new. Indeed, with a similar goal in mind Wagner had already sent Scribe a detailed scenario for a projected opera, *Die hohe Braut*, from Königsberg as early as 1836. But, like practically all Wagner's Paris plans, this one fell on stony ground.

Wagner received promises from the Opéra for an audition of three numbers (Senta's ballad and the two sailors' songs in what is now Act III), which he composed between May and July 1840. The audition, however, never took place.

In 1841 Wagner sold the original scenario to the Paris Opéra for 500 francs. The Opéra then commissioned two librettists and the composer Pierre-Louis-Philippe Dietsch, later the conductor of the ill-fated Paris *Tannhäuser* performances in 1861, to turn Wagner's draft into *Le vaisseau fantôme*, which after only 11 performances disappeared, like the ship of its title, into eternal oblivion. According to Wagner's biography, he was forced to sell the scenario in order to rent the piano he needed to compose the opera himself. Much has been made of Wagner's 'humiliation' at having to do this. But the French prose scenario and the opera he eventually made out of it are actually very different. Wagner not only expanded the scale of the work, he also altered its 'tone' in order to introduce, or to elaborate on, several literary motifs in a way that went far beyond the scope of the first version, not to say notions of opera current at the time. The Dutchman's nihilism and yearning for death; the quasi-Christian idea of redemption; Senta's preoccupation with dreams and folly or illusion (*Wahn*); the transformation of Senta's suitor into a hunter whose humble profession and clumsy demeanour serve as a foil to her utopian release (in effect a *Liebestod à la Tristan*) from the narrow world he represents: all these elements meant that by the time Wagner had finished the libretto of *Holländer* in May 1841 he had included, at least in embryo, many of the major themes that were to dominate his later works.

The new version was so much more ambitious than the first that Wagner had no hesitation in offering it to the Court Opera in Berlin as a fully fledged opera that could fill an entire evening. With Meyerbeer's help, it was accepted in March 1842. But delays, and a counter-offer from Dresden, following the huge success of *Rienzi* there in October 1842, prompted Wagner to withdraw it. The opera was eventually given four performances in Dresden under Wagner's direction, with Johann Michael Wächter as the Dutchman and Wilhelmine Schröder-Devrient in the role of Senta. It was only a moderate success. A few performances followed in 1843 in Riga and Kassel (where it was conducted by Spohr), and then in Berlin in 1844. The opera quickly disappeared from the repertoire until Wagner himself revived it in Zurich in April and May 1852.

SYNOPSIS

Act I   The Norwegian coast. A steep cliff. Forced by fierce weather to cast anchor, Daland has gone ashore to reconnoitre. He recognizes Sandwike, a bay just seven miles from his home. He curses the wind – 'blowing out of the devil's crevice' – that prevents him from seeing Senta, his daughter. He returns on board and retires to his cabin, assuring his crew that all is well. The steersman is left on watch. He too sings of a loved one tantalizingly close. As he falls asleep, the storm revives and the Flying Dutchman's ship appears. The Dutchman, dressed in black Spanish cos-tume, comes ashore. He is condemned to travel the seas for ever, returning to land every seven years in a hopeless search for salvation ('Die Frist ist um'). Only the Day of Judgement can save him, when the world will shatter and eternal oblivion will be his. Daland returns on deck and shakes his steersman awake. He catches sight of the Dutchman, who asks him for hospitality and the hand of his daughter in return for unimaginable riches. Daland readily agrees. The steersman announces a favourable wind from the south, and the rest of the Norwegian crew join in a jubilant final verse of his song.

Act II   A large room in Daland's house. A picture of a pale, bearded man wearing a black Spanish costume hangs on the wall. Senta is transfixed by it. Her governess Mary and the other women sit round a fire, spinning. The women sing of their spinning-wheels creating enough wind to bring their lovers home. They mock Senta for falling in love with the old picture. She retorts by singing the ballad of the legendary Dutchman ('Traft ihr das Schiff im Meere an'). Salvation awaits him only if he can find a woman faithful unto death. 'I am that woman,' Senta declares, to the consternation of all. Only Erik's announcement of Daland's return brings her to her senses. Erik and Senta are alone. Erik is convinced that his hunter's livelihood will not qualify him in Daland's eyes as Senta's suitor and begs her to persuade her father otherwise. She feels more for the picture than for him, he complains. When she leads him close to the portrait to convey her feelings, he is certain that the Devil has taken possession of her. He tells her of his dream ('Auf hohem Felsen lag ich träumend'). Senta listens enraptured: a strange ship; two men, one Senta's father, the other pale, wearing a black cloak; she kisses the stranger wildly; they both flee out to sea. Senta knows the dream is true. Daland and the stranger arrive. As Senta now gazes on the real Dutchman, Daland formally introduces them ('Mögst du, mein Kind'), but they ignore his banal speech about marriage and wealth. After Daland has discreetly withdrawn in amazement, the Dutchman expresses his mixed feelings about Senta ('Wie aus der Ferne'). Is she a long-lost dream come true? Or one of Satan's tricks? Senta asks if this is folly, an illusion ('ist's ein Wahn?'). She is deeply moved by the Dutchman's suffering. In turn, the Dutchman is touched by her compassion. She is an angel. He warns her of the terrible sacrifices she must make if she promises eternal faithfulness ('Ach! könntest das Geschick du ahnen'). But Senta is overcome by a powerful magic and does not flinch from her resolve to save him. Daland returns with a curious crowd. They are delighted at what they think is going to be a successful marriage.

Act III   A bay on a rocky shore. In the foreground to one side is Daland's house. The Norwegian ship, light and festive, is in the background, with the Dutchman's vessel, shrouded in darkness, anchored nearby. The sailors celebrate ('Steuermann, lass' die Wacht!') and joke that the crew of the other ship are either all dead or like dragons guarding their hoard. Despite the Norwegian sailors' taunts, the strange vessel stays silent. Suddenly a fierce storm flares up around the Dutchman's ship and its crew sing that Satan has charmed it so that it will sail until eternity. The Norwegians flee in terror. Erik is horrified that Senta has agreed to marry the Dutchman. Does she not remember embracing him, as if to confess her love? ('Willst jenes Tag's du nicht dich mehr entsinnen'). The Dutchman overhears the conversation and misinterprets it. As he suspected, Senta is unfaithful: he will never find salvation. Senta frantically tries to convince him that he is wrong. Erik calls for help. The Dutchman reveals who he is, and in ecstasy Senta cries out to him as he departs ('Preis deinen Engel'). She leaps into the ocean, and immediately the Dutchman's ship sinks. Against the rising sun, Senta and the Dutchman appear transfigured, soaring upwards hand in hand above the wreck of the vessel.

Wagner always insisted that *Der fliegende Holländer* was the opera that marked the real beginning of his career. From a critical point of view he was undoubtedly right. Historians have protested that *Rienzi* (in which the sublime and the unspeakably banal are disconcertingly entwined) has been seriously misjudged largely because of Wagner's over-negative and highly influential critique of it. Yet, despite the magnificent moments in *Rienzi* and the fact that it is close to *Holländer* chronologically (at one point Wagner was working on both operas simultaneously), there is no denying that *Holländer* is in almost every respect a superior work.

Exactly how Wagner turned virtually overnight into a composer of genius is not an easy question to answer. The change from the historical subject matter of *Rienzi* to the more suggestive, and for Wagner always more sympathetic, world of myth and legend in *Holländer* clearly made a difference. So, too, did the dire circumstances of his life. An exile in Paris suffering endless setbacks in the fight for recognition, Wagner was arguably more deeply touched by the image of 'the Wandering Jew of the ocean' (Heine) than he ever had been by *Rienzi*'s grandiose idealism. To see experiences in life as sources of artistic inspiration may no longer be fashionable, but it would be a cold critic who ignored a possible connection between Wagner's serious existential doubts in his early Paris years and the bleak intensity of some of the best music in *Holländer*. The words 'in need and care' (*in Noth und Sorgen*) written at the end of the composition draft on 22 August 1841 meant exactly what they said.

Wagner was preoccupied at regular intervals with the Dutchman throughout a major period of his life. For the first performances he transposed Senta's ballad from A minor into G minor and relinquished his original idea of playing the three acts as one without an interval. (The current fashion for producing the opera in its original, supposedly 'authentic', one-act version should be weighed against the fact that Wagner never conducted, or encouraged, a performance of the opera in this form.) He undertook major revisions of the orchestration in 1846, and again in 1852 when he retouched the instrumentation of the ending of the overture. For a performance in

Weimar in 1853 he expressly asked Liszt, who was to conduct the opera, to change the orchestration of a single chord: the accompaniment of Senta's cry at the start of the Act II finale. For his Paris concerts in 1860 he made two major additions to the ending of the overture and added a trumpet and two harps to its orchestration. He even began a completely new version of Senta's ballad (a sketch of which has survived) for a model performance of *Holländer* in Munich commissioned in 1864 by King Ludwig. Cosima von Bülow (later Wagner) reported to Ludwig in 1866 that Wagner was intending to revise *Holländer* so that it would be 'worthy to stand alongside *Tannhäuser* and *Lohengrin*'. During Wagner's last years, she noted in her diary (9 April 1880) that he 'wants to postpone the dictation of the autobiography until after the performance of *Parsifal* when he also wants to revise *Der fliegende Holländer*'. Not long afterwards, Cosima recorded one of his most famous remarks: 'He says that he still owes the world *Tannhäuser*' (23 January 1883). Wagner might have added that he still owed the world *Der fliegende Holländer* as well.

Tannhäuser und der Sängerkrieg auf Wartburg
Tannhäuser and the Song Contest on the Wartburg
Grosse romantische Oper in three acts; from 1859/60 onwards, *Handlung* in three acts (*c.* 3h; so-called Paris version: 3h 15m)
Libretto by the composer
The genesis and revisions of the work (libretto and music) have been divided into four stages as follows: Stage 1 (June 1842–premiere (19 October 1845): libretto June 1842–April 1843; music July 1843–October 1845. Stage 2 (the preparations for the second performance (27 October 1845)– the first engraved f.s. (June 1860)): libretto spring 1847; music October 1845–May 1847, September 1851. Stage 3 (the preparations for staging the work in Paris (from autumn 1859)–the Paris performances (13, 18, 24 March 1861)): Wagner translates libretto into French September 1859–March 1861; music August/September 1860–March 1861. Stage 4 (August 1861–the Vienna premiere (22 November 1875)): Wagner reworks libretto into German August/September 1861–spring 1865; music from summer/autumn 1861 (the so-called Paris version played today is actually this version)
PREMIERES 19 October 1845, Königlich Sächsiches Hoftheater, Dresden; US: 4 April 1859, Stadt Theater, New York; UK: 6 May 1876, Covent Garden, London
CAST Hermann *deep b*, Tannhäuser *t*, Wolfram von Eschenbach *high b*, Walther von der Vogelweide *t*, Biterolf *b*, Heinrich der Schreiber *t*, Reinmar von Zweter *b*, Elisabeth *s*, Venus *s*, A Young Shepherd *s*, 4 Pages 2 *s*, 2 *a*; *satb* chorus of Thuringian knights, counts and nobles, noblewomen, older and younger pilgrims, sirens, naiads, nymphs, maenads; in stages 3 and 4 also: the three Graces, young men, cupids, satyrs, fauns

According to Wagner's autobiography he was already making plans for *Tannhäuser* in 1841–2 during his first sojourn in Paris. The earliest surviving document is a prose scenario begun on 28 June 1842 after he had returned to Dresden. Here, and in the first libretto (completed in April 1843), the opera is called *Der Venusberg*. Wagner appears to have changed the title soon after finishing the libretto. In a letter to Schumann of 13 June 1843 he referred to the project as *Tannhäuser und der Wartburgkrieg*, and in a letter written to his brother the next day simply as *Tannhäuser*.

The word 'and' (as opposed to the conventional 'or') in the opera's final title reflects its derivation from two separate legends: the theme of Tannhäuser and Venus on the one hand and Heinrich von Ofterdingen's defeat in the Wartburg song contest on the other. Wagner was less interested in the epic accounts of the two stories he found in his sources (of which there are more for *Tannhäuser* than any of his previous works) than in bringing them into dramatic conflict with one another. Two key texts were Heinrich Heine's 'Tannhäuser': in *Der Salon* (1837) – the same collection in which Wagner found the tale of *Der fliegende Holländer* – and Johann Ludwig Tieck's story 'Der getreue Eckart und der Tannenhäuser' from the *Phantasus* collection (1812–17). Wagner never acknowledged his debt to Heine, though he does mention Tieck and E. T. A. Hoffmann's 'Der Kampf der Sänger' from *Die Serapionsbrüder* of 1819. But he is disparaging about them – and silent, too, about another source he must have known: Ludwig Bechstein's *Sagenschatz des Thüringerlandes* (a 'treasury of tales from Thuringia') of 1835, in which the song contest on the Wartburg and its hero Heinrich von Ofterdingen and the legend of Tannhäuser and the Venusberg are loosely connected. In his Paris years Wagner came across an obscure monograph, *Der Krieg von Wartburg* by C. T. L. Lucas (1838), which boldly claimed that Ofterdingen and Tannhäuser were one and the same person. The bizarre notion was immediately pilloried by the academic establishment. But for Wagner (as he more or less admitted in his autobiography) it was the key to a brilliant idea: the antithesis of two worlds dividing the hero against himself in a tragic conflict between sensuality and asceticism.

Tannhäuser has been described as Wagner's 'most medieval work' (Volker Mertens). This may be true in the sense that Wagner returned via German Romanticism to the spirit of the medieval tale of penance with (for instance) the idea of redemption through love in an afterlife that is deemed to be real, and with the image of the burgeoning staff as a symbol of God's grace for all mankind (including the worst of sinners). Yet Wagner's synthesis of his materials is so strikingly original and modern (the fear that it would be perceived otherwise may have been one reason why he was so coy in acknowledging some of his sources) that to see the opera as medieval at all is to miss its point. The pre-modern world of miracles and burning Christian faith becomes in Wagner's hands an allegory of a modern society impoverished by precisely those Christian values it claims to represent. The dialectical strategy (which Wagner later perfected in *Parsifal*) embraced other modernist issues, including the alienated artist who yearns for the world of the imagination, yet is fatally attracted to the real world as well. For the first time, the opera also betrays Wagner's uninhibited (and masochistic) attitude to sex, especially in his portrayal of Venus, whom he made even more explicit by contrasting her with Elisabeth, her exact opposite. Elisabeth is remotely related to a real historical charac-

ter, the wife of Landgrave Ludwig IV (1200–1227). But as a virgin and quasi-Christian antithesis to Venus, the pagan goddess of love, she is entirely Wagner's invention.

SYNOPSIS

The action takes place in Thuringia and the Wartburg at the beginning of the 13th century.

Act I A subterranean grotto inside the Venusberg (Hörselberg, near Eisenach). Sirens, naiads, nymphs and bacchantes dance ecstatically. The song of the sirens ('Naht euch dem Strande') interrupts the wild movement at its orgiastic climax, and exhaustion and calm ensue. (In the Paris–Vienna versions, stages 3 and 4, Wagner added satyrs, fauns, young men, and an allegory in which the three Graces, with the help of cupids, quell the orgy. An image of the 'rape of Europe', riding on a white bull drawn through a blue sea by tritons and nereids, emerges through the mist at the end.) Tannhäuser, half kneeling before Venus, his harp at his side, yearns for release from the endlessly pleasurable, artificial world of the Venusberg. Human society and death, measured by real time and marked by pain and freedom, are drawing him away. Full of burning admiration for Venus and her charms ('Dir töne Lob!'), he begs her to let him leave. In despair, she curses him and the cold humans tempting him to abscond. Death will rebuff him, she warns; but he may return when it does. Invoking the Virgin Mary, Tannhäuser breaks away from the magic of the Venusberg. He finds himself at the foot of the Wartburg. A shepherd is singing and playing a pipe in praise of spring. A chorale sung by passing pilgrims moves Tannhäuser to kneel in prayer, as if to atone for his sins. Hunting horns are heard and Hermann, the landgrave of Thuringia, appears with a large retinue. Astonished, the knights recognize Tannhäuser, who long ago parted from their company. He refuses their invitation to rejoin them. Only when Wolfram mentions the name of Elisabeth and tells of how much she misses him does he change his mind.

Act II Elisabeth greets the hall in the Wartburg where at last she is to see Tannhäuser again ('Dich, teure Halle, grüss' ich wieder'). Tannhäuser is led by Wolfram to Elisabeth. They rejoice at their reunion while Wolfram remains in the background, convinced that he has lost Elisabeth's love. The landgrave sees that Elisabeth is perturbed. He tells her to keep her feelings to herself, at the same time announcing the forthcoming song contest in which Tannhäuser will once again participate. The power of song, he suggests, may offer a solution. The local nobles with their wives arrive at the Wartburg for the contest. The landgrave gives the competing singers the task of defining the essence of love in song. Elisabeth will give the winner as his prize whatever he is bold enough to demand. The contest begins. Wolfram, Walther and Biterolf conceive love as something abstract and moral, while Tannhäuser, with increasing vehemence, opposes them with an image of love as a joyous, sensual experience. A fight nearly ensues, prevented only by a pious and conciliatory song from Wolfram ('O Himmel, lass dich jetzt erflehen'). But this merely goads Tannhäuser into singing a fourth verse of the song he sang to Venus at the beginning of the opera, this time with words praising the lusts of the flesh, and culminating in the demand that all should hasten to the Venusberg to learn the real meaning of love. The assembled company is scandalized. In the ensuing tumult, Elisabeth shields Tannhäuser from the knights rushing forward to kill him ('Zurück von ihm! Nicht ihr seid seine Richter'). She implores the landgrave to pardon the sinner, for whose salvation she is prepared to offer her life. Tannhäuser is expelled and ordered to go to Rome to seek forgiveness. As the hymn of the young pilgrims on their way to Rome sounds in the distance, Tannhäuser kisses the hem of Elisabeth's robe, and rushes out to join them.

Act III   The Wartburg valley. It is autumn; evening is approaching. Elisabeth looks in vain for Tannhäuser among the pilgrims returning from Rome. She prays to the Virgin to take her from this earth ('Allmächt'ge Jungfrau, hör mein Flehen'), insisting to Wolfram that she must go her way alone. Wolfram is distraught at Elisabeth's decision to sacrifice her life. To calm himself, he begs the evening star to greet Elisabeth as she ascends to heaven ('O du, mein holder Abendstern'). Night has fallen. Tannhäuser, his pilgrim's garb torn, enters with faltering steps. He tells Wolfram of his journey to Rome ('Inbrunst im Herzen') and in particular the pope's harsh words to him: 'Just as this staff in my hand can never blossom, so can you never be redeemed from the flames of hell.' Tannhäuser is convinced he is damned, and seeks to return to the Venusberg. In the first Dresden version (stage 1) his 'Rome narration' gradually turns into a delirious vision of the Venusberg. In desperation, Wolfram invokes the name of Elisabeth, at which point a chorus behind the scenes announces her blessed martyrdom. Tannhäuser has found salvation through her death, and expires in Wolfram's arms. In the revised Dresden version and all later versions (stages 2, 3 and 4) Venus appears in person and calls Tannhäuser to her. At Wolfram's naming of Elisabeth, a funeral procession with chorus appears from the direction of the Wartburg carrying her body on an open bier. Tannhäuser is transfixed at the sound of her name, whereupon Venus vanishes, lamenting that she has lost him. No longer spurned by death and redeemed at last, Tannhäuser sinks down dying over Elisabeth's body. The younger pilgrims enter with a staff that has put forth leaves, celebrating God's miracle with hallelujahs as the rising sun bathes the scene in the morning light.

Wagner did not break entirely with operatic convention in Tannhäuser; but by building the opera out of complex scenic units (which often resemble jumbled baroque allegories) he did move several steps beyond it. The richly suggestive dramaturgy, however, was not easy to translate into music. Already in 1843 Wagner hinted to friends that he was having difficulties with the composition of the opera. Considering the musical demands placed on him by the dialectical structure of the action this was hardly surprising. (Tannhäuser's song to Venus, for instance, had to sound not only noble and earnest as he longs for the real world in Act I, but also deliriously sensual when he yearns again for Venus in Act II.) The full score was completed in April 1845 and the first performance took place in Dresden in the following October under Wagner's baton, with Joseph Tichatschek in the title role and Wilhelmine Schröder-Devrient as Venus. Audience reaction to the premiere was lukewarm, and Wagner immediately began to revise the score with cuts in the finales of Acts I and II and a new orchestral introduction to Act III. Other alterations followed with the revival in Dresden on 1 August 1847, including a radical recomposition of the ending. Following Liszt's lead in Weimar in 1849, the opera was taken up in the 1850s by nearly every theatre in Germany, which prompted an unceasing flow of instructions and interpretations from Wagner's pen, and still more changes to the score. Wagner reserved his most drastic revisions for the three disrupted Paris performances of 1861 in French (which were all different from each other), and still persisted in tinkering with the opera for the productions he supervised in Munich (1 August 1867) and Vienna (22 November 1875). The Paris revisions included the expansion and recomposition of the opening bacchanal and the second scene, as well as extensive modifications to the song contest. Unlike in the Vienna production, the overture was played in full by popular demand in the Paris and Munich performances, even though Wagner had insisted on cutting it and merging it without a break into the bacchanal (ironically a practice now familiar from the so-called Paris version). The version known today as the Paris version is in fact the Vienna version of 1875.

To the end of Wagner's life the preoccupation with the music of Tannhäuser never left him, as numerous remarks in Cosima's diaries prove. With the possible exception of Der fliegende Holländer, it is his only major score that, in a sense, he never finished composing.

Lohengrin

Romantische Oper in three acts (3h 30m)
Libretto by the composer
Composed: libretto 1845; music 1846–8
PREMIERES 28 August 1850, Grossherzogliches Hoftheater, Weimar; US: 3 April 1871, Stadt Theater, New York; UK: 8 May 1875, Covent Garden, London
CAST Heinrich der Vogler, deutscher König (Henry the Fowler, King of Germany) b, Lohengrin t, Elsa von Brabant s, Duke Gottfried silent, Friedrich von Telramund bar, Ortrud s, King's Herald b, 4 Brabantine Nobles 2 t, 2 b, 4 Pages 2 s, 2 a; satb chorus of Saxon and Thuringian counts and nobles, Brabantine counts and nobles, noblewomen, pages, vassals, women, servants

Written between summer 1845 and April 1848, Lohengrin was intended originally for Dresden. To prepare the way for the premiere, Wagner conducted a concert performance of the finale of Act I at the Royal Saxon Court Theatre on 22 September 1848. The scenery was duly commissioned and a full-scale production was announced to the press in January 1849. Wagner's involvement in the events leading to the ill-fated Dresden revolution of May 1849 prevented the project from going ahead. The eventual first performance, in

Weimar, was conducted by Liszt, the opera's dedicatee, on the 101st anniversary of Goethe's birth. The place and date were symbolic. After the failed revolutions of 1848/9, increasing nostalgia for Weimar's former cultural glory and Wagner's burgeoning reputation as the radically new hope of German art both focused critical attention on the event. The authorities inadvertently played their part by refusing to grant Wagner clemency. He was in political exile in Switzerland, and in the eyes of Germany's cultural vanguard his conspicuous absence only made the premiere yet more significant. (According to Wagner's autobiography, he spent the evening in Lucerne in a tavern called the Swan 'watching the clock and closely following the hour of the opera's beginning and its presumed end'.) Though Wagner conducted excerpts in concerts in Zurich (1853), London (1855), Paris (1860) and Brussels (1860), nearly 11 years elapsed before a partial amnesty enabled him to hear the whole opera for the first time in a dress rehearsal in Vienna in May 1861.

In contrast to the idealism symbolized by the place and date of the premiere of *Lohengrin*, Wagner found its subsequent popularity irksome, especially the fame of its most celebrated item, the Bridal Chorus. Wagner introduced it to English audiences in his London concerts in 1855. Three years later, at the marriage of Queen Victoria's daughter Princess Victoria to Frederick Wilhelm of Prussia it earned a permanent place in the history of popular culture when it was coupled for the first time with the Wedding March from Mendelssohn's *A Midsummer Night's Dream*. In its original context the Bridal Chorus is a masterpiece of sweet foreboding and a prelude to marital disaster; the irony of its transformation into a much-loved public symbol of faith in the institution of marriage was not lost on Wagner, who sensed almost from the start that undue focus of attention on the best-known 'numbers' in *Lohengrin* left it open to serious misinterpretation. In 1853, when the opera was taken up by several German houses (and not long after by several foreign companies as well), he persuaded Breitkopf und Härtel to publish a brochure with production details and illustrations of scenery and costumes, which he described as 'according to my wishes'. Perhaps rightly resisting this somewhat peremptory authorial vigilance, hardly a single producer responded. Wagner continued to complain of inadequate performances and publicly expressed his dissatisfaction in an open letter of 7 November 1871 to Arrigo Boito. Though Wagner conducted the opera several times, he personally supervised only two productions of it. The first (conducted by Hans von Bülow) was given on 16 June 1867 in Munich; the second (conducted by Hans Richter) took place in Vienna on 15 December 1875. The Munich production, Wagner told Boito, was the first time the work had been rehearsed according to its 'rhythmic–architectonic structure'.

SYNOPSIS

Act I   The first half of the tenth century. A meadow on the bank of the river Scheldt near Antwerp. After a nine-year truce, the Hungarians are again threatening to attack Germany. King Heinrich I of Saxony (Heinrich der Vogler) has come to Brabant to recruit men to help fend off an attack from the east. He finds the country in disarray, and demands to know what is wrong. Friedrich von Telramund explains that he was granted the right to care for Elsa and her younger brother Gottfried, the children of the deceased duke of Brabant. Gottfried has disappeared, and Friedrich now formally accuses Elsa of murdering him at the instigation of a secret lover. Friedrich is so convinced that Elsa has lost her heart to another man that he has renounced his right to her and married Ortrud instead, the daughter of Radbod, prince of Friesland. Elsa is guilty of fratricide, Friedrich argues, and, as he is himself next of kin to the dead duke, he has a legitimate claim to be ruler of Brabant in her stead. Elsa is summoned and declares with a powerful radiance that she has dreamed of a knight who will come to protect her. Friedrich, certain that the knight is Elsa's secret lover, agrees to a trial by combat. In the distance a swan is seen drawing a boat carrying a knight in shining armour. The swan appears, accompanied by the growing excitement of the onlookers. Lohengrin steps on to the shore, and Elsa, at first spellbound by his presence, throws herself enraptured at his feet. He asks her whether she will marry him if he wins on her behalf, and lays down his conditions: never is she to ask about, or brood upon, his origin, his lineage or his name. Heinrich leads a prayer ('Mein Herr und Gott'): may God weaken the strength of the liar and give power to the true hero. Lohengrin wins the fight and magnanimously spares Friedrich's life. All rejoice, while Ortrud broods ominously on the mysterious knight who is thwarting her plans to rule with Friedrich.

Act II   The citadel of Antwerp. Night. Friedrich and Ortrud, both shabbily dressed, are sitting on the steps of the minster in the foreground. The windows of the knights' dwelling at the back are brightly lit as the celebrations continue. Friedrich accuses Ortrud of lying to him about Elsa's supposed murder of Gottfried. Ortrud retaliates by calling Friedrich a coward. To regain his honour he must sow doubts in Elsa's mind by accusing Lohengrin of sorcery. If that fails, force must be used: those made strong by magic lose their strength merely by losing the smallest limb. Elsa appears on a balcony and tells the breezes of her happiness ('Euch, Lüften, die mein Klagen'). Her pity is cunningly aroused by Ortrud. As Elsa retires for a moment to let Ortrud inside, Ortrud's false pathos rapidly disappears in an abrupt and violent passage during which she invokes the pagan gods to help her regain power ('Entweihte Götter'). Elsa returns, and Ortrud begins to insinuate doubt into her mind with the almost casual warning that her nameless protector could one day leave her just as mysteriously as he came. As day breaks, the herald makes four announcements: Friedrich is banished; Brabant is given to Lohengrin, who has relinquished the title of duke for that of 'protector'; the wedding between Lohengrin and Elsa is to take place that day; on the next, Lohengrin will lead the men of Brabant into battle. A small group of four nobles dissents. As Elsa approaches the minster where she is to marry her protector, Ortrud interrupts the procession to demand the revelation of

Lohengrin's identity. No sooner has Lohengrin tried to comfort Elsa than Friedrich steps forward as well to accuse him of sorcery. Elsa manages to suppress her darkening dismay, but not before she receives unwelcome attention from Friedrich. He whispers to her that he can enter the bridal chamber that night to remove a fingertip from Lohengrin, which would break his magic strength. Lohengrin intervenes: he leads his bride solemnly into the minster and, as they reach the highest step, Elsa turns to him in deep emotion, only to catch a glimpse of Ortrud, her arm raised, as if certain of victory.

Act III The bridal chamber. An exuberant orchestral introduction leads into the gentle Bridal Chorus ('Treulich geführt'). It reflects the transition from highly public events to an intimate space where, after the wedding trains have left, the sense of claustrophobia increases as Elsa's doubts gain control. Nuptial bliss gradually turns insidiously into marital trauma. Elsa finally asks Lohengrin his name and origin, at which point Friedrich and the four disaffected nobles burst in to attack him. Lohengrin kills Friedrich and orders the four nobles to carry the body before Heinrich, where, in front of the people of Brabant, Elsa's questions will be answered. Day breaks as the scene changes to the meadow as in Act I. Lohengrin announces that he cannot now lead the Brabantines into battle. He justifies the slaying of Friedrich and announces that Elsa, poisoned by treachery, has broken her vow. He reveals that in a wondrous castle in a faraway place is the holy cup carried to earth by an angel host ('In fernem Land'). Once a year a dove is sent to renew its strength: it is the Grail, and it imparts supernatural power to the knights it selects. The Grail sends the knights to distant lands on errands of chivalry, but only on condition that they depart once their identity is known. Lohengrin announces that he is the son of Parsifal, king of the Grail, and utters his own name. The swan is seen returning. Lohengrin tells Elsa that had he been able to stay for only one year at her side the power of the Grail would have returned her brother to her. Lohengrin gives Elsa three objects to pass on to her brother if he ever does return: a horn to assist him in danger, a sword to make him victorious in battle and a ring to remind him of his sister's protector. Ortrud gloats on her apparent triumph ('Fahr' heim, du stolzer Helde!'), bragging that it was she who made Gottfried disappear by using a magic chain to turn him into a swan. Lohengrin answers her with a prayer. The white dove of the Grail hovers over the boat and the swan is miraculously transformed into Gottfried, a beautiful youth in gleaming silver apparel. As Lohengrin proclaims him leader of Brabant, Ortrud sinks powerless to the ground. Gottfried bows to Heinrich and rushes into the arms of his sister, while Lohengrin, standing with head bowed in the boat now being drawn by the dove, recedes into the distance. Elsa's soul leaves her body as she gradually collapses in her brother's arms.

The music of Lohengrin is hard to describe as forward-looking, yet equally difficult to dismiss as reactionary. In the first editions of the libretto and full score Wagner called Lohengrin a romantic opera,

though he later withdrew the designation. The aura of chivalrous romance in Lohengrin notwithstanding, the opera also has an oddly 'classical' air about it. The polyphonic orchestral writing much admired by Richard Strauss, the close motivic relationships, and above all the neat, often uncomfortably schematic dramatic and musical symmetries (the recapitulation of the Grail music in Act III for instance) are all evidence of Wagner's ambition to inject into the medium of opera something of the spirit of the great classical symphonists.

The musical details of Lohengrin, however, are rarely judged properly, mainly because Wagner's progressive tendencies, usually traced by historians with depressing regularity exclusively to Tristan and Parsifal, are said to consist of near-atonal chromaticism and irregular phrase structure. In fact, the antichromatic moments of Lohengrin are often the most striking (the opening of the prelude for instance), and even the regular phrases of the Bridal Chorus can seem daring and ambivalent in context. In a sense, Lohengrin is a contradiction in terms: it mixes genres that do not mix (fairy-tale opera and grand historical drama), and its music can still sound original precisely where, according to the conventional view of musical progress, it is least avant-garde.

With the exception of the prelude, which was written last, Lohengrin is the first work Wagner composed systematically from beginning to end with almost polemical disregard for clear demarcations between operatic set pieces. (Ernest Newman's statement that the last act was composed first and the second act last is contradicted by the sketches.) The new method added irony to the initial success of the opera as a series of popular concert pieces, though it must be pointed out that Wagner's indulgence in allowing its large-scale formal rhythm (more akin to a symphony than an opera) to co-exist with more short-winded 'numbers' that could satisfy the most conservative of operatic tastes was part and parcel of his aesthetic strategy from the start. Wagner always rightly insisted, however, that Lohengrin is closer to the grand designs and seamless continuity of his later music dramas than it is usually thought to be. This may account for the fact that, in contrast to his other early operas, he was never tempted to revise it. The only substantial change he made was a cut in Lohengrin's Grail narration in Act III which he communicated to Liszt shortly before the first performance.

Der Ring des Nibelungen

Ein Bühnenfestspiel für drei Tage und einen Vorabend
The Ring of the Nibelung
A stage festival play for three days and a preliminary evening
Libretto by the composer
PREMIERES as a cycle: 13–17 August 1876, Festspielhaus, Bayreuth; UK: 5–9 May 1882, Her Majesty's Theatre, London; US: 4–11 March 1889, Metropolitan, New York

Der Ring des Nibelungen is the biggest work in the history of Western music. It took 28 years to write, rewrite, rehearse, and finally to perform in its entirety at the first Bayreuth Festival in 1876. Wagner conceived it initially as an allegory of the social unrest in Europe that began with the Paris uprisings in February 1848. (The first documented reference to the project is 1 April of that year.) It soon turned into a parable of riddles and emotional conflict that dissolved politics into philosophical poetry, as it were, and reached far beyond the political upheavals that first inspired it. Even before the revolutions of 1848/9 Wagner's political views had been part of a utopian quest for a new kind of theatre that could reflect different truths about society that were less acute and yet – clouded by paradox and contradiction as they often were – more suggestive than politics or philosophy ever could be. Wagner saw the *Ring* as his *summum opus* that represented this ideal in its most radical form.

The *Ring* began relatively simply as the libretto of a single work, *Siegfrieds Tod* (later revised and retitled *Götterdämmerung*), which was first sketched in October 1848. Wagner's main source was the Middle High German *Nibelungenlied*, though he was by no means the first to consider its operatic possibilities. The philosopher F. T. Vischer had already published an essay in 1844 suggesting that the epic poem – regarded since its discovery in the mid-1700s as a kind of German *Iliad* – could be used as the subject of a new kind of musical drama which he called 'a grand heroic opera'. Probably following Vischer's example, Wagner designated *Siegfrieds Tod* in the same way and based the opera mainly on the first half of the *Nibelungenlied*, amplifying it with details from the second and from other versions of the legend.

In 1851 Wagner made the momentous decision to expand *Siegfrieds Tod* into a cycle of four dramas, which he called collectively *Der Ring des Nibelungen*. By this time he had undertaken a much more thorough study of the older oral tradition of the Nibelung myth. Among the works he examined and re-examined were the Old Norse Eddic poems, the so-called *Poetic Edda*, Snorri Sturluson's 13th-century explanatory account of Scandinavian myth known as the *Prose Edda*, and the ancient narrative accounts in the *Völsunga Saga* and *Thidreks Saga*. From the *Poetic Edda* Wagner adapted the technique of *Stabreim* (the linking of words and lines by alliteration instead of end rhyme) as a new way of writing the texts for the additional dramas *Das Rheingold*, *Die Walküre* and *Der junge Siegfried* (as *Siegfried* was then called). The wealth of mythical·situations that Wagner found in the older sources – the trials, contracts, riddles, prophecies, to name only a few – were also bound to tempt him to try something more than just another series of operas in the German Romantic tradition. His utopian journey from 'grand heroic opera' to a complex world myth or 'drama of the future', as he liked to refer to the new project, was inseparable from his discovery of the Nibelung myth in what he believed to be its most archaic form.

Another reason for Wagner's decision to write a four-part cycle (or more precisely a trilogy with a preliminary evening) was his conception of the project as a festival event. Here his model was the ancient Greek festival of Dionysus at Athens. His intention was not to imitate the awesome Athenian spectacles, but rather to revive their sense of communal celebration (as opposed to art as mere entertainment) which in his view the modern theatre totally lacked. Certain dramatic techniques, however, and even the idea of a thematically related cycle of festival dramas itself, were borrowed directly from Aeschylus. The blending of politics and myth; the interplay of gods and humans; the curse that drives the action forward with the oppressive memories of past events; the rule of law and the resolution of guilt; the cosmic mythical presentation of nature: the shaping of the *Ring* drama clearly owed a good deal to the *Oresteia* and to *Prometheus Bound*.

Almost from the start, the idea of the *Ring* project as a festival occasion went hand in hand with the notion of a theatre built specially for its performance. Two years after writing the libretto of *Siegfrieds Tod*, Wagner was already seriously thinking of designing and building a temporary theatre for it outside Zurich to which he would 'invite the most suitable singers, and organize everything necessary for a special event' (letter to E. B. Kietz, 14 September 1850). The idea was not carried out; nor did a later, far more ambitious, project fare much better when Ludwig II placed Wagner under contract in the mid-1860s to complete the *Ring* and ordered plans to proceed for a festival theatre to be built on the Gasteig in Munich, only to see the scheme aborted through political intrigue. The realization of this, for its creator, extremely important aspect of the *Ring* had to wait until the building of the Bayreuth Festival Theatre in the 1870s, which Wagner managed to bring about largely through private initiative and the co-operation of the Bayreuth authorities. Ludwig II, irritated that Wagner had relinquished Munich as a festival site, was eventually persuaded to support the project.

In many other respects, however, the *Ring* is not at all like Greek drama. Nor in the course of its history has it ever really been dependent on Wagner's original festival concept. In a sense it is a return to the detailed scenic images of nature and mythological symbolism characteristic of 17th-century opera, and also to what Walter Benjamin has called the 'allegorical drapery' of the baroque trauerspiele (literally 'sorrow-plays') to which the *Ring* text, richly embroidered as it is with powerfully suggestive icons, is by no means unrelated. (Wagner was a great admirer, for instance, of the allegorical plays of the Spanish dramatist Calderón.) The *Ring* is also a strange amalgam of poetic and musical imagery borrowed from early Romantic lieder, techniques indebted to Beethoven's monumental symphonic style, modernist ideas about politics and myth inherited mainly from the philosopher Friedrich Hegel's critics (the so-called Young Hegelians), the world of fairy-tale and, last but not least, a wonderfully inventive harmonic language indebted in part to the works of Franz Liszt.

Wagner published the *Ring* libretto in a private edition early in 1853, several months before he began composing the music for it. He read the entire text several times to groups of friends and acquaintances (many of whom later reported on the riveting power of his delivery), and published it again in revised form in 1863, this time with a preface containing an appeal to a 'princely patron' who might be found to help finance the project. It was this first public edition of the *Ring* text that drew the attention of the young Ludwig II and led to the famous association between the two men that changed the course of Wagner's life. Repercussions from the earlier private edition, however, had not been so positive. Without music, the words of the *Ring* on their own either seemed gratuitously artificial and inept (even to some of Wagner's friends) or gave the impression of an arcane, neogothic disinterment of medieval legend that was merely of academic interest. Indeed, a not insignificant detail in the history of the *Ring* is the fact that the first book about it to appear (by Franz Müller) was not so much about the cycle and its wider implications but was rather an introduction to its medieval sources – and moreover was published as early as 1862, before a note of the music had been performed in public. It is true that not long afterwards Wagner conducted excerpts from the music he had composed so far in two concerts in Vienna. But misunderstanding – and ridicule – of the *Ring* libretto persisted and was certainly a factor in Wagner's negative reaction to the premieres of *Das Rheingold* and *Die Walküre* ordered to take place by Ludwig II and conducted by Franz Wüllner in Munich in 1869 and 1870. Wagner did not attend the performances (though a large portion of Europe's musical intelligentsia did), partly on the reasonable grounds that an incomplete production of the cycle, which he had not even finished composing, could only lead to further misapprehension. He refused access to the full score of the third act of *Siegfried*, without which the premiere of the third drama in the cycle planned by the king for 1871 could not take place. And, in blatant breach of his 1864 contract with the king, he undermined all attempts by Munich to procure *Götterdämmerung*, the full score of which was finally finished on 21 November 1874.

Eventually, after superhuman efforts on Wagner's part, the first performance of all four dramas as a cycle took place under his direction in the newly built Festival Theatre in Bayreuth in August 1876 with a cast that included Amalie Materna as Brünnhilde, Franz Betz as Wotan and Albert Niemann as Siegmund. Wagner entrusted the conducting to his protégé Hans Richter, among other reasons because of Richter's immense knowledge of instruments that proved invaluable in helping the orchestral musicians to solve some formidable technical problems in a score that at the time counted as one of the most modern and sophisticated in existence. Financially, the event was so disastrous that Wagner had to close the Festival Theatre for the next six years. The performances themselves were a different matter. Uneven as they were, they convinced many critics and observers that, far from simply resurrecting an archaic legend that for years had been the preserve of university professors, Wagner had successfully created, largely through the power of his music, a completely new myth that could provide a key to an interpretation and deeper understanding of the contemporary world for a wider audience.

Preliminary Evening: Das Rheingold
The Rhinegold
In one act (2h 30m)
Composed: libretto 1851–2; music 1853–4
PREMIERES 26 December 1862, Theater an der Wien, Vienna (excerpts from Scenes 1, 2 and 4; concert); 22 September 1869, Königliches Hof und Nationaltheater, Munich; 13 August 1876, Festspielhaus, Bayreuth (as part of the *Ring* cycle); UK: 5 May 1882, Her Majesty's Theatre, Haymarket, London; US: 4 January 1889, Metropolitan, New York
CAST Gods: Wotan *high b*, Donner *high b*, Froh *t*, Loge *t*; Goddesses: Fricka *low s*, Freia *high s*, Erda *low s*; Nibelungs: Alberich *high b*, Mime *t*; Giants: Fasolt *high b*, Fafner *low b*; Rhinedaughters: Woglinde *high s*, Wellgunde *high s*, Flosshilde *low s*; *tb* chorus of Nibelungs

SYNOPSIS
Scene 1 At the bottom of the Rhine. In greenish twilight steep rocks are visible. Water swirls around them at the top, while the waves dissolve into a damp mist lower down. The Rhinedaughters circle round the central reef which points upward to the brighter light above. Alberich comes out of a cleft in the rocks and makes advances to the Rhinedaughters, who cruelly lead him on. Alberich eventually realizes that he is being ridiculed. Silenced by anger, he catches sight of the gleaming Rhinegold high on the central reef. Wellgunde imprudently reveals that whoever can fashion an all-powerful ring from the gold will inherit the world ('Der Welt Erbe gewänne zu eigen'). To the accompaniment of the famous Wagner tubas (sounding here for the first time), Woglinde adds that the required magic can be attained only by renouncing love ('Nur wer der Minne Macht entsagt'). Alberich curses love with hideous passion and snatches the gold before vanishing into the depths.

Scene 2 An open space high in the mountains. The light of dawn reflects off the battlements of a magnificent castle. Wotan dreams of eternal power and a fortress for the gods. His wife, Fricka, rudely awakens him. While Wotan gazes enraptured at the magnificent edifice he has just been dreaming about, Fricka bluntly reminds him of its price. Built by the giant brothers Fasolt and Fafner, the fortress is to be paid for by giving them Freia, keeper of the golden apples of eternal youth. Freia rushes in, complaining that she has been threatened by Fasolt. The giants enter, and Fasolt proceeds to lecture Wotan on the significance of contracts. The more pragmatic Fafner, however, knowing that Freia is indispensable to the gods, proposes to abduct her by force. Donner and Froh, Freia's brothers, hurry in to protect their sister, but the giants invoke their contract. The long-awaited god of fire, Loge, on whom Wotan is relying to find a way out of the dilemma, joins the gods at last and tells of many things ('So weit Leben und Weben'), including Alberich's theft of the gold and the mighty ring he has fashioned from it. The giants agree to take Freia away as a provisional hostage until evening, and then to hand her over in exchange for the gold. A pallid mist fills the stage. The gods begin to age, fearfully looking to Wotan for a way out of their plight. Wotan decides to travel with Loge to Nibelheim to take possession of the gold.

Scene 3 A subterranean cavern. Tormented in the first scene, Alberich is now the tormenter. With great skill, his brother Mime has created the Tarnhelm, a magic helmet which enables its wearer to assume any form at will. Alberich takes it from him by force, and vanishes in a column of mist. Mime writhes in agony from Alberich's invisible whiplashes. Alberich takes off the Tarnhelm and drives a pack of Nibelung dwarfs laden with treasure before him. Eventually he notices Wotan and Loge. Unable to resist a demonstration of his power, he kisses the ring on his finger, causing the screaming Nibelungs to scatter, and dons the Tarnhelm again to turn himself into a monstrous dragon. Loge cunningly suggests to Alberich that a small creature would better escape danger, but that the transformation would probably be too hard to accomplish. Alberich rises to the challenge and turns himself into a toad. Loge and Wotan easily capture him and drag him away.

Scene 4 An open space high in the mountains. Alberich is forced to give up the hoard, which is dragged up through a cleft by the Nibelungs. Already humiliated in front of his own slaves, Alberich is completely ruined when Wotan violently takes the ring from him. Driven to confront Wotan, among other things with the telling argument that his own theft of the gold was a peccadillo compared with Wotan's present betrayal of the laws he supposedly upholds, Alberich curses the ring just as he cursed love in order to create it ('Wie durch Fluch er mir geriet, verflucht sei dieser Ring'). Henceforth no one who possesses the ring will escape death. The giants enter with Freia and plant two stakes in the ground on either side of her. They demand that the hoard be piled up until her shape is concealed. Now it is Wotan's turn to be humiliated: to fill the final crack the giants demand the ring. Wotan refuses until Erda, the goddess of earth, intervenes to deliver a sphinx-like warning about the end of the gods ('Ein düstrer Tag dämmert den Göttern'), advising him to discard the prize. With sudden resolve he throws the ring on to the pile. Freia is free and the gods return to their immortal state, at least for the moment. But to their horror they witness the first effects of the curse as Fafner kills Fasolt in the ensuing struggle for the ring. Donner conjures up a storm to clear the sultry air. The fortress, Valhalla, lies gleaming in the evening sun at the end of a rainbow bridge which the gods begin to cross in triumph. Diffidently joining the procession, Loge remarks that the gods are really hastening to their end ('Ihrem Ende eilen sie zu'). Their refurbished glory is also dimmed momentarily by the Rhinedaughters, who lament from the depths that their demand that the gold be returned to its original purity has gone unheeded.

First Day: Die Walküre
The Valkyrie
In three acts (3h 45m)
Composed: libretto 1851–2; music 1854–6
PREMIERES 26 December 1862, Theater an der Wien, Vienna (excerpts from Acts I and III; concert); 26 June 1870, Königliches Hof und Nationaltheater, Munich; 14 August 1876, Festspielhaus, Bayreuth (as part of the Ring cycle); US: 2 April 1877, Academy of Music, New York, UK: 6 May 1882, Her Majesty's Theatre, Haymarket, London
CAST Siegmund *t*, Hunding *b*, Wotan *high b*, Sieglinde *s*, Brünnhilde *s*, Fricka *s*, Valkyries: Gerhilde, Ortlinde, Waltraute, Schwertleite, Helmwige, Siegrune, Grimgerde, Rossweisse *s* and *c*

SYNOPSIS

Act I The interior of a house at the centre of which stands the trunk of a huge ash tree. A man is being pursued. He enters the house and staggers towards the hearth. The wife of Hunding, the absent master of the house, gives him water. The stranger explains that a storm has driven him there and prepares to leave. But the woman begs him to stay. A secret bond begins to grow between them. Hunding returns from combat. He is instinctively distrustful of the stranger, but reluctantly grants him hospitality for the night. Hunding insists on knowing his guest's name. The stranger says he calls himself 'Woeful' (*Wehwalt*) and explains by telling the story of his childhood. He and his father, Wolf, returned one day from the hunt to find his mother murdered and his twin sister abducted. He eventually lost track of his father and has been cursed with bad luck ever since, hence his name. A woman forced to marry someone she did not love had asked him for help, whereupon he killed her brothers whose kinsmen are now hunting him. Hunding, realizing that 'Woeful' is the killer, reveals that he is one of the hunters and challenges the stranger to combat the next day. Only the laws of hospitality protect him for the moment. Hunding's wife has tried to intervene, but Hunding orders her to leave to prepare his nightly drink. Alone, the stranger recalls his father's promise to provide him with a sword when in direst need ('Ein Schwert verhiess mir der Vater'). The woman returns. She has put a sleeping draught in Hunding's drink and proceeds to show the stranger a sword thrust into the tree. It was put there by a one-eyed man during her wedding to Hunding. None of the guests, nor anyone since, has had the strength to draw it out. She believes that the hero who can will more than make up for the shame she has had to endure since robbers forced her to marry Hunding. She embraces the stranger passionately as the great door opens to let in a beautiful spring night. The stranger sings in praise of spring which, like a brother, has freed love, its sister, from the storms of winter ('Winterstürme wichen dem Wonnemond'). The metaphor soon turns into a reality. The woman knew from the single eye of the old man who planted the sword that she was his daughter. Seeing the same look in the stranger's eyes, she suspects that she is related to him too. The stranger asks her to give him a name she loves. When he tells her that his father's name was not Wolf, but Wälse, she knows for certain that he is the Wälsung for whom the sword is intended. She calls him Siegmund. Revelling in his name ('Siegmund heiss ich und Siegmund bin ich') Siegmund pulls the sword, Notung, from the tree with a mighty wrench. Rapt with wonder and delight, the woman tells him that she is his twin sister Sieglinde. They embrace in ecstasy as Siegmund calls for the blossoming of the Wälsung race.

Act II A wild and rocky mountainside. Wotan knows that Siegmund and Sieglinde are fleeing from Hunding and that Hunding will eventually overtake them. He charges his favourite daughter, Brünnhilde (borne to him by the earth goddess Erda), with the task of ensuring Siegmund's victory in his forthcoming duel with Hunding. Brünnhilde warns Wotan of the 'violent storm' in store for him from his wife, Fricka, the guardian of marriage, who is approaching in a chariot drawn by a pair of rams. Fricka insists that Hunding has a right to vengeance. She upholds the law in the face of Wotan's advocacy of nature. The power of spring may have brought the twins together, but their incestuous union is a monstrous affront to reason. As for Wotan's grand idea of a free hero who would allow the gods to escape their guilty complicity in the theft of the Rhinegold, this is just false: Siegmund is not free, but merely a pawn in a game invented by Wotan, who is himself severely compromised by his promiscuity. Humbled by the sheer force of Fricka's reasoning, Wotan agrees to forbid Brünnhilde to let Siegmund win the battle against Hunding. The hero must be sacrificed to preserve the divine law. Alone with Brünnhilde, Wotan confesses that all along he has been deceiving himself. Master of the laws of the universe, he is also their victim. Only the end of everything he has built will cleanse the guilt of the gods ('Auf geb' ich mein Werk: nur eines will ich noch: das Ende!'). And for that end Alberich is working. He has created a son whom Wotan now blesses: may the hate of Alberich's child feed on the empty glory of the gods' divinity. Brünnhilde cannot accept Wotan's bleak nihilism and argues to protect Siegmund. Wotan threatens her with the direst consequences if she rebels. Siegmund and Sieglinde enter. Sieglinde is haunted by nightmarish visions of Hunding and his dogs in pursuit of them. She faints in Siegmund's arms. Brünnhilde appears to Siegmund and announces his impending death ('Siegmund! Sieh auf mich!'). But he refuses to go to Valhalla if Sieglinde cannot join him. Rather than put her and their unborn child at the mercy of a hostile world, he threatens to kill them. Brünnhilde is overcome by this display of human emotion and promises to defy her father's command. Hunding's horn is heard summoning Siegmund to battle. Sieglinde's nightmare is now a reality. Brünnhilde protects Siegmund with her shield. But Wotan intervenes and forces Siegmund's sword to shatter on his spear. Hunding drives his spear into the breast of the unarmed Siegmund. Wotan looks in anguish at Siegmund's body, and with a dismissive wave of the hand causes Hunding to fall down dead. Meanwhile Brünnhilde has fled with Sieglinde on horseback after gathering up the pieces of the broken sword. In a thunderous rage, Wotan storms off in pursuit of them.

Act III On the summit of a rocky mountain. The Valkyries gather together with warlike exuberance, each with a slain hero destined for Valhalla on the saddle of her horse. To their astonishment, Brünnhilde arrives with a woman. The Valkyrie sisters, fearful of Wotan's wrath, refuse to protect them. Brünnhilde tells Sieglinde to flee to a forest in the east where she will be safe. There she will give birth to the noblest hero of the world ('den hehrsten Helden der Welt'). Brünnhilde gives her the shattered pieces of the sword and names the hero Siegfried, 'one joyous in victory', predicting that he will one day forge the fragments anew. Sieglinde sings a striking motif in reply ('O hehrstes Wunder! Herrlichste Maid!') which Wagner called the 'Glorification of Brünnhilde'. Brünnhilde faces Wotan without the protection of her sisters. To their horror, he condemns her to lie defenceless in a magic sleep, vulnerable to the first man who finds her. The Valkyries gallop away wildly. Left alone with Wotan, Brünnhilde justifies her actions. Although she is not wise, she knew in her heart that Wotan loved Siegmund ('Nicht weise bin ich, doch wusst'ich das eine, dass den Wälsung du liebst'), which is why she disobeyed his order. Wotan is moved against his better judgement by her courage. Reluctantly he grants her only request. She is to be surrounded by a magic fire which only the freest hero who knows no fear can penetrate. With great emotion, Wotan bids farewell to his daughter and summons Loge to encircle her with fire: only one freer than himself will be able to win her.

Second Day: Siegfried

In three acts (4h 15m)
Composed: libretto 1851–2; music 1856–7 (–end Act II in second draft), 1864–5 (orchestration of Act II), 1869–71 (Act III)
PREMIERES 1 January 1863, Theater an der Wien, Vienna (excerpts from Act I; concert); 16 August 1876, Festspielhaus, Bayreuth (as part of the *Ring* cycle); UK: 8 May 1882, Her Majesty's Theatre, Haymarket, London; US: 9 November 1887, Metropolitan, New York
CAST Siegfried *t*, Mime *t*, The Wanderer (Wotan) *b*, Fafner *b*, Erda *c*, Brünnhilde *s*, Woodbird *boy s*

SYNOPSIS
Act I The opening of a cave in the forest. Mime is frustrated that he can neither forge a sword strong enough for Siegfried nor piece together the shattered fragments of Notung ('Zwangvolle Plage'). Notung is the only weapon adequate for the task Mime has in mind for his powerful charge: the killing of the dragon – previously a giant – Fafner in order to win back the ring. Siegfried enters boisterously from the forest. He has no respect for the puny dwarf who pretends to be his father. Siegfried forces him to confess the truth. A dying woman emerged from the forest to give birth in the cave. She entrusted the child to Mime, insisting that he should be called Siegfried, and gave him the fragments of Notung which had been shattered when the child's father was slain. Siegfried is thrilled by the story and, before racing back into the forest from which he senses freedom at last ('Aus dem Wald fort in die Welt ziehn'), orders Mime to mend the sword. The Wanderer, dressed in a dark blue-grey cloak, appears uninvited at Mime's hearth. Mime can be rid of him only by agreeing to a game of riddles. The Wanderer stakes his head on three questions from his unwilling host, who, over-confident in his own cunning, agrees to ask them ('Drei der Fragen stell' ich mir frei'). The unwanted guest answers correctly, and insists that Mime stake his own head on three questions in turn. But Mime, panic-stricken, cannot solve

the third riddle: who will weld Notung together again? The Wanderer solves it for him: 'only one who has never felt fear' – and the one to whom, he adds casually, Mime's head is now forfeit. Mime promises to take Siegfried to Fafner's lair to teach him fear. Disconcertingly for Mime, Siegfried is only too willing to co-operate. Siegfried starts to forge Notung himself, deliberately ignoring Mime's expertise. Dimly aware of Siegfried's destiny, Mime brews a poison to kill him once he has slain the dragon. Siegfried sings lustily of Notung as he forges ('Notung! Notung! Neidliches Schwert'), and Mime skips around the cave in delight at the secret plan he has concocted to save his head. With the finished sword, Siegfried cuts the anvil in two and exultantly lifts Notung high in the air as Mime falls to the ground in fright.

Act II Deep in the forest at night. Alberich is on watch outside Fafner's cave. The Wanderer enters and stops to face Alberich, who, as a shaft of moonlight illuminates the scene, quickly recognizes his adversary. Alberich, suspicious of the Wanderer's nonchalance, confronts him with his main weakness: his inability to steal the hoard yet again – an act that would shatter the rule of law once and for all. As if to prove his indifference, the Wanderer generously tells Alberich of Mime's plans to get the hoard for himself, and suggests warning Fafner, who, to avoid being murdered, might relinquish the ring to Alberich before Mime arrives. The Wanderer even offers to waken the dragon himself. He knows full well, however, that everything is set on a course that no one, not even Alberich, can alter ('Alles ist nach seiner Art, an ihr wirst du nichts ändern'). Predictably, the dragon refuses to listen and goes back to sleep. Siegfried and Mime arrive as day breaks. Mime conjures up threatening images of Fafner. But Siegfried is more intent on ridding himself of his guardian, whom he finds increasingly repulsive. Mime leaves Siegfried beneath a linden tree to muse on his origins. Siegfried cuts a reed pipe and tries to play it in order to converse with the birds. He loses patience and instead uses his silver horn. As the sounds of the horn grow faster and louder, Fafner begins to stir. Spewing venom out of its nostrils, the dragon heaves itself up to crush the interloper, only to expose its heart, into which Siegfried swiftly plunges his sword. Realizing that his killer is only a naïve boy being used by someone more sinister, the dying Fafner warns Siegfried of Mime's true plans. Some of the dragon's blood spills on to Siegfried's hand. After involuntarily licking it, Siegfried can at last understand the song of one of the birds, who tells him that the hoard is now his ('Hei! Siegfried gehört nun der Niblungen Hort!'). After Siegfried has gone into the cave to look for the treasure, Mime and Alberich scuttle into sight, quarrelling about their right to the hoard. Siegfried emerges from the cave looking thoughtfully at the ring and the Tarnhelm he is carrying. Alberich withdraws as Mime persuades Siegfried to take the poisonous drink. But the dragon's blood also enables Siegfried to hear the murderous intent beneath Mime's ingratiating phrases. In a moment of disgust, Siegfried kills Mime with a single stroke of his sword. Alberich's mocking laughter echoes in the background, but Siegfried, oblivious, simply asks the Woodbird for a new

and preferably more congenial companion. The Woodbird obliges by telling him of Brünnhilde, who, asleep on a high rock and imprisoned by a magic fire, awaits a fearless hero to set her free. The Woodbird flies off to show Siegfried the way.

Act III A wild region at the foot of a rocky mountain. The Wanderer arouses Erda from a deep sleep. Bleakly observing that nothing can change the destiny of the world, he still wants her advice on 'how to slow down a rolling wheel' ('wie zu hemmen ein rollendes Rad?'). She replies that her mind is growing 'misty with the deeds of men' ('Männertaten umdämmern mir den Mut'). She was raped by Wotan and bore him Brünnhilde. She is confused and not even clear who her rude awakener is. Irritated but not surprised, the Wanderer announces the coming end of her wisdom, and the triumph of his will: the fall of the gods. The Wanderer awaits Siegfried, who enters in high spirits. Their banter is good-humoured until the old man asks the young hero who it was who created Notung. The Wanderer laughs at Siegfried's ignorance, and Siegfried, hurt by the condescension, in turn pours scorn on the Wanderer. With a single blow Siegfried cuts the Wanderer's spear in two. The Wanderer picks up the pieces and disappears in total darkness. Siegfried puts his horn to his lips and plunges into the billowing fire spreading down from the mountain. On the tip of Brünnhilde's rock, Siegfried reaches the sleeping Brünnhilde, whom he mistakes at first for a male warrior. He cuts away the armour to discover a feminine form that fills him with a strange emotion that he knows is fear. He sinks down, as if he were about to die ('wie ersterbend'), and with closed eyes places a kiss on Brünnhilde's lips. She awakens slowly from the darkness of sleep, sitting up gradually to praise the sun and the earth. Siegfried and Brünnhilde are lost in delight, until she realizes that his love for her (not to mention his destruction of her armour) will impede the fierce independence she knew as a Valkyrie. Miraculously regaining his fearlessness, Siegfried overcomes Brünnhilde's qualms. Together they become ecstatically blind to the world, welcoming its destruction and the death of the gods with the delirium of 'radiant love, laughing death' ('leuchtende Liebe, lachender Tod').

Third Day: Götterdämmerung
Twilight of the Gods
Prologue and three acts (4h 15m)
Composed: libretto 1848–52; music (sketches for *Siegfrieds Tod* 1850) 1869–74
PREMIERES 1 March and 6 May 1876, Musikvereinssaal, Vienna (excerpts from prologue and Acts I and III; concerts); 17 August 1876, Festspielhaus, Bayreuth (as part of the *Ring* cycle); UK: 9 May 1882, Her Majesty's Theatre, Haymarket, London; US: 25 January 1888, Metropolitan, New York
CAST Siegfried *t*, Gunther *high b*, Alberich *high b*, Hagen *low b*, Brünnhilde *s*, Gutrune *s*, Waltraute *low s*, First Norn *c*, Second Norn *s*, Third Norn *s*; Rhinedaughters: Woglinde *s*, Wellgunde *s*, Flosshilde *c*; *tb* chorus of vassals, *s* chorus of women

SYNOPSIS
Prologue On the Valkyries' rock. The three Norns,

daughters of Erda, spin the golden rope of world knowledge that binds past, present and future. The rope was once tied to the World Ash Tree, until Wotan desecrated the tree to create his spear and establish his rule of order over the universe. The Norns try to keep the rope taut. But the threads tangle and it snaps. The continuum between past and future is broken: the Norns' primeval wisdom is at an end. Outside a cave, Brünnhilde and Siegfried emerge with the rising of the sun, he in full armour, she leading her horse, Grane. Brünnhilde sings that her love for Siegfried would not be true if she refused to let him go forth into the world to perform new deeds ('Zu neuen Taten'). Siegfried leaves Brünnhilde the ring as a token, and she in turn gives him Grane. Carrying his sword, he begins his descent from the rock and vanishes with the horse. His horn is heard from below as Brünnhilde bids him farewell.

Act I   The hall of Gunther's court on the Rhine. Hagen, the illegitimate son of Alberich and Grimhild, is plotting to regain the ring for his father. His legitimate half-siblings Gunther and Gutrune, who have inherited their kingdom from their dead parents Gibich and Grimhild, sit on a throne to one side. Hagen gives them some (seemingly) sensible advice. If they are to retain the respect of their subjects, they must marry without delay. Hagen suggests Siegfried for Gutrune and Brünnhilde for Gunther. The lacklustre Gibichungs are overwhelmed with the thought, but sceptical until Hagen suggests a way of attracting their powerful partners-to-be. Gutrune is to give Siegfried a potion that will erase his memory of all other women. Once Gutrune has captured his heart, it will be easy for her brother to persuade him to woo Brünnhilde on his behalf. Siegfried's horn sounds from his boat on the Rhine. Hagen calls out to him to come ashore. Siegfried steps on to land with his sword and Grane. He tells Gunther of the Tarnhelm and the ring. As planned, Gutrune offers him the potion of forgetfulness, which he unwittingly accepts, dedicating his first drink to Brünnhilde and faithful love. Its effect is immediate: spellbound by Gutrune, he hears Gunther talk of the woman Gunther desires but cannot win because she lives on a high mountain surrounded by a fire. Siegfried shows no sign of recognition. Knowing that he can penetrate the fire, he offers to woo the woman, using the Tarnhelm to disguise himself as his host. After sealing his promise with an oath of blood brotherhood, he sets off with Gunther for Brünnhilde's rock, leaving Hagen to guard the hall. Hagen savours the plot he has set in motion ('Hier sitz' ich zur Wacht'). On the Valkyries' rock, Brünnhilde sits in front of the cave gazing rapturously at the ring. Dark storm clouds appear as Waltraute, one of the Valkyries, arrives to tell her of Wotan seated morosely amidst the gods and heroes in Valhalla, waiting passively for the end ('Höre mit Sinn, was ich dir sage'). Despite Waltraute's pleading, Brünnhilde refuses Wotan's only remaining wish: to free the gods from the curse by returning the ring to the Rhinedaughters. Brünnhilde vows never to renounce the ring, or the love it supposedly symbolizes ('Die Liebe liesse ich nie'). Waltraute hastens away, distraught. The brightening flames and the sound of a horn herald the arrival of Siegfried. But to Brünnhilde's horror a different figure steps out of the fire. In Gunther's shape, Siegfried wrestles with her and wrenches the ring from her finger. He forces her into the cave and lays his sword between them as witness that his wooing of Gunther's bride is chaste.

Act II   In front of the hall of Gunther's court, Hagen is asleep. As the moon suddenly appears, Alberich can be seen in front of him, resting his arms on his son's knees. He exhorts Hagen to keep faith with their plan to ruin Siegfried and win back the ring ('Sei treu, Hagen, mein Sohn! Trauter Helde!'). With the help of the Tarnhelm, Siegfried arrives at the Gibichungs' court ahead of Gunther and Brünnhilde. In a detailed dialogue with Hagen and Gutrune, he describes his successful wooing of Brünnhilde for Gunther and announces their imminent arrival. As if calling the Gibichung vassals to battle, Hagen summons them to greet Gunther and his bride. The vassals do not understand Hagen's warlike tone, or the need for the sharp weapons and bellowing horns. Hagen explains by proposing a barbaric feast, including the slaughter of animals for the gods, and uninhibited drunkenness. Solemnly, the vassals greet Gunther and Brünnhilde as they disembark. Brünnhilde appears crushed and humiliated, until she sees the ring on Siegfried's finger. Roused to furious anger, she declares that Siegfried is her husband and flings desperate charges at him. To clear his name, Siegfried swears an oath on Hagen's spear that its point may pierce his body if he is lying about who he is. Brünnhilde dedicates the sharp blade to Siegfried's downfall. After Siegfried has left to prepare for his marriage, Brünnhilde tells Hagen that she did not protect Siegfried's back with her magic, as he would never have turned it towards an enemy. Now his enemy, she reveals that his back is the only place where he can be mortally wounded. Gunther, the deceived deceiver, is convinced of Siegfried's treachery by Hagen, but worried about the effect Siegfried's death will have on Gutrune. Hagen decides to make it look like a hunting accident. All are now dedicated to Siegfried's death. Calling on Wotan, guardian of vows, Brünnhilde and Gunther swear an oath of vengeance. Hagen in turn invokes the spirit of his father, Alberich, lord of the ring ('des Ringes Herrn'). Siegfried returns with Gutrune and the bridal procession, while Hagen forces Brünnhilde to join Gunther to prepare for a double wedding they know will never take place.

Act III   A forest area on the banks of the Rhine. An elf has lured Siegfried away from his hunting companions to the riverbank where the Rhinedaughters are playing. They tell him he will die later that day if he keeps the ring. Laughing, he ignores them. They lament his blindness and swim away to 'a proud woman' ('ein stolzes Weib') who will soon inherit his treasure and give them a better hearing. Siegfried rejoins his hunting companions, who sit down to rest and drink. At Hagen's prompting he regales them with stories of Mime and Notung, of Fafner and the Woodbird. But Hagen has a servant slip an antidote into Siegfried's drink that enables him to tell the true story of Brünnhilde as well. Siegfried gives a rapturous account of how he learned about her from the Woodbird and how passionately she embraced him after his bold kiss. Wotan's two ravens fly up out of a bush. Hagen asks Siegfried if he can understand them too. Siegfried turns, and immediately Hagen thrusts his spear into Siegfried's back. Perjury is avenged, Hagen gloats to the horrified onlookers. The vassals take up Siegfried's body to form a solemn cortège as the magnificent funeral march recollects and reflects on the hero's life. In the hall of Gunther's court, Gutrune has been plagued by disturbing dreams and the sight of Brünnhilde walking to the banks of the Rhine. When she discovers Siegfried's body, brought back by the hunters, she nearly faints with shock. Hagen freely admits the murder and kills Gunther in a fight over the ring. But when Hagen reaches for the ring the dead Siegfried's hand rises menacingly to prevent him from taking it. Brünnhilde comes forward to silence Gutrune's lament and to contemplate the dead Siegfried. She orders his body to be placed on a funeral pyre ('Starke Scheite schichtet mir dort am Rande des Rheines zuhauf'). Now, after talking to the Rhinedaughters, she understands Wotan's will to end the gods, to rid them of the curse that also ensnared her innocent lover. She takes the ring, puts it on her finger, and casts a torch on the pyre. To cleanse the ring from the curse with fire before it is returned to the Rhinedaughters, she leaps with her horse into the burning pyre, united with Siegfried in death. The Rhine overflows its banks and pours over the flames. As the Rhinedaughters appear on the waves, Hagen rushes headlong into the flood to demand the return of the ring. Woglinde and Wellgunde draw him into the depths, while Flosshilde holds up the ring in triumph. The hall has collapsed, and in its ruins the men and women watch apprehensively as an increasingly bright glow appears in the sky. Gradually the hall of Valhalla becomes visible, filled with gods and heroes just as Waltraute described it in Act I. As the orchestra recalls Erda's prophecy in *Das Rheingold* of the end of the gods ('Ein düstrer Tag dämmert den Göttern'), the hall of the gods appears to be completely consumed by bright flames.

Wagner's *Ring* has been interpreted in so many wildly contradictory ways that it probably counts as the most ingratiating work ever written for the operatic stage. Yet the fact that it has far transcended its original destiny as a 'stage festival play' and German national epic is testimony not only to the potency of Wagner's self-made myth, but also to the consistently superior quality of his music. The search for archetypal images and mythical heroes in the forging of the *Ring* libretto would have been unthinkable without the assistance of pioneering works such as Jacob Grimm's *German Mythology* (1835) and Karl Simrock's *Lay of the Amelungs* (1843–9), which provided the building blocks of, and methods of linking, the various stories and legends Wagner needed to create his own myth. But for the composition of the music there was no such help. Wagner's five-and-a-half-year musical silence between the completion of *Lohengrin* in April 1848 and the start of work on the music of the *Ring* in November 1853 suggests that the difficulties were formidable: at no other point

in his life was Wagner musically silent for so long.

Once a start had been made on the music, however, the composition proceeded so rapidly that it is hard to believe that Wagner had no premeditated strategy in mind. Astonishingly, he finished the first drafts of *Das Rheingold* and *Die Walküre* in (respectively) only two and a half and six months. Wagner himself, and most of his biographers since, have related this rush of invention to certain events in his (usually turbulent) private life. Seventeen coded messages to Mathilde Wesendonck, for instance, the wife of a rich friend and benefactor, with whom he fell in love in 1854, were inserted into the first draft of Act I of *Die Walküre*. But Wagner surely must have used some of his long musical silence to think out, at least in broad terms, strategies that were determined to a large extent by the interaction of the different levels of his myth. The network of leitmotifs, the highly original use of keys and form that usurps all sense of traditional operatic set numbers, not to mention the mirroring of the drama through extremely differentiated orchestration, are worked out too carefully and consistently (at least in the first half of the cycle) for anything else to seem possible.

Alone the sheer quantity of motifs (there are over a hundred) Wagner needed to fill out about 15 hours of music suggests an important difference between the leitmotif system he invented specifically for the *Ring* and the well-tried operatic device of the so-called reminiscence motif he had used, albeit with great originality, in his earlier operas. (In *Lohengrin*, for instance, there are only six main motifs in the entire opera, fewer than in the first scene of *Das Rheingold* alone.) In short, the necessity of another kind of motivic network arose because of Wagner's decision in the *Ring* finally to abolish the contrast between unstructured recitative and musically highly organized 'set pieces' typical of conventional opera. Usually for reasons of dramatic irony, Wagner reinvented the contrast at certain places in the *Ring* (the start of Loge's laconic narration to the gods in the second scene of *Das Rheingold* for instance), but basically he set out to create a continuous musical–dramatic dialogue that relies for its coherence not on predictable stylistic changes but on a steady interchange of related motifs that can be joined, combined and varied in countless ways without loss of identity. The technique is fundamentally an extension of Berlioz's *idée fixe* (a resilient theme symbolizing a central figure in a story that returns in different shapes and sizes during the course of the narrative). This is not to deny the originality of Wagner's daring concept of motifs in series that not only represent significant aspects of the unfolding drama but also relate to each other to provide the narrative with a semblance of logic and a scaffold for its monumental structure on a musical level.

Contrary to a widely held belief, Wagner named a few of the leitmotifs in the *Ring* in his sketches and occasionally to friends. The practice, usually thought to be the invention of Hans von Wolzogen, the compiler of the first leitmotif guides, has often been misused and misunderstood. Wagner called the motif sung by Alberich when he renounces love to steal the gold in the opening scene of *Das Rheingold* the 'curse on love' (*Liebesfluch*). But he did not intend to suggest (and arguably neither did Wolzogen) that the meaning of the motif stays literally the same later in the cycle. Avid leitmotif-watchers have all noticed Wagner's 'inconsistency' and apparently lamentable lack of rigour in Act I of *Die Walküre* when he allows Siegmund to sing the motif in its original key of C minor as he pulls the sword out of the ash tree – a moment leading to a triumphant announcement of the so-called 'sword' motif in C major when Siegmund, far from having cursed love, seems to have discovered it for the first time. Few have considered the reverse parallel (of which there are many in the *Ring*) with the opening scene of *Das Rheingold*, when, after the dazzling presentation of the gold in C major by the Rhinedaughters, the music shifts gradually to C minor and Alberich's snatching of the treasure. By moving emphatically in the opposite direction, Siegmund's music in *Die Walküre* promises to negate the consequences of Alberich's primal crime – a possible reading that suggests that Siegmund's singing of the motif is not a 'mistake', but an attempt to exorcize its original meaning. That Siegmund turns out to be the wrong hero for the task and the promise a false one only adds irony to the moment in retrospect. Indeed, after Siegmund is killed, the memory of the past weighs so oppressively on the motif that Wagner can use it again to great ironic effect in Act I of *Götterdämmerung* when Brünnhilde tells Waltraute in all sincerity that she will never renounce her love for Siegfried, only to do just that at the end of Act II. Nearly all the motifs in the *Ring* resonate similarly with memories of past events which, though the actual notes of the motifs may stay exactly the same, never cease to accumulate and hence to be gradually transformed as the tragedy unfolds.

Wagner deliberately used one motif so sparingly that there could be no mistake about it. Bernard Shaw was puzzled by it (as many later commentators have been), calling it 'the most trumpery phrase in the entire tetralogy', the sole valuable quality of which was its 'gushing effect'. He was referring to the motif that, 'since it undoubtedly does gush very emphatically', dominates the concluding moments of the cycle. In effect the ending of the *Ring* is a vast musical recapitulation. Salient motifs, cadences, keys, fragments of form and even details of orchestration return from earlier parts of the tetralogy to sum up a great parable of human existence. The feeling of circular movement, of going back over the whole cycle to the beginning, could be seen as a metaphor for Wotan's pessimism – a static, spatial image that is filled with what Walter Benjamin called 'the disconsolate chronicle of world history'. At the same time the motif Wagner chose to end the *Ring* has been heard only once before, when Sieglinde sings it to Brünnhilde in Act III of *Die Walküre* after Brünnhilde has alluded to Siegfried's future destiny. The last-minute development of it in the final moments of the *Ring* is so unexpected that it appears to cut across the feeling of endless return, as if to break the circle of history, by celebrating instead Siegfried's victory in reconciling, through his death, the conflict between nature and society at the root of the myth. The motif is certainly triumphant, as Wagner stressed when, in contrast to the leitmotif guides, he called it not the 'redemption through love' but the 'glorification of Brünnhilde' – a perfectly logical description since it is Brünnhilde who successfully brings the story to an end by announcing that its true hero has completed his task.

Tristan und Isolde

Handlung in three acts (3h 45m)
Libretto by the composer
Composed: libretto 1857; music 1856–9
PREMIERES 12 March 1859, Prague (prelude with concert ending by Hans von Bülow; concert); 25 January 1860, Théâtre Italien, Paris (prelude with concert ending by Wagner; concert); 10 March 1863, St Petersburg (prelude and Transfiguration; concert); 10 June 1865, Königliches Hof und Nationaltheater, Munich; UK: 20 June 1882, Drury Lane London; US: 1 December 1886, Metropolitan, New York
CAST Tristan *t*, King Marke *b*, Isolde *s*, Kurwenal *bar*, Melot *t*, Brangäne *s*, Shepherd *t*, Steersman *bar*, Voice of Young Sailor *t*; *tb* chorus of ship's crew, knights and pages

Inspired by his reading of the philosopher Arthur Schopenhauer, Wagner first conceived *Tristan und Isolde* in the autumn of 1854. Another immediate stimulus was a dramatization of the story by his friend Karl Ritter, of which he was extremely critical, calling it too elaborate and packed with adventurous incidents'. One of two operatic foretastes of Wagner's masterpiece is the famous light-hearted account of Tristan and Isolde in Donizetti's opera *L'elisir d'amore*, the title of which is itself an allusion to the tale. (Wagner probably knew the opera, as it was in the repertoire of the Dresden Court Opera when he was conductor there in the 1840s.) The other is a scenario of an opera *Tristan und Isolde* in five acts written in 1846 by the poet Robert Reinick for Schumann, who eventually decided not to compose it. (In all likelihood Wagner knew this too, since he conversed regularly with Schumann in 1845 and 1846 at the Engelklub in Dresden about their respective artistic plans.) As an operatic venture and in terms of its sheer rigour and boldness, however, Wagner's *Tristan* is without precedent, even when compared with his previous works.

Wagner's main source was Gottfried von Strassburg's medieval epic *Tristan* (*c.* 1215) – in the 19th century a work admired for its style and pilloried for its suspect morality in about equal measure. There were several reasons for Wagner's sudden decision to adapt it, including its (for medieval texts) unusual subject of fated and enchanted, as opposed to courtly, love that leads to physical destruction and 'eternal death' (êweclîchez sterben). The idea was in tune not only with Wagner's newly awakened interest in Schopenhauer, who believed that the preconscious Will was an expression of the sexual drive and the road to salvation its negation, but also with his increasing love for Mathilde Wesendonck, the wife of his long-suffering patron Otto Wesendonck – a love that Wagner knew, because of his dependency on the latter, would be unlikely to become a reality. This interpretation is at least not hard to read into a famous letter about *Tristan* he wrote to Liszt in December 1854: 'Since I have never enjoyed the real happiness of love in my life, I want to erect another monument to this most beautiful of dreams in which love will be properly sated from beginning to end.'

Wagner called *Tristan* 'the most full-blooded musical conception'. In the end the musical challenge was perhaps his most important reason for writing it. (His wife Cosima later wrote in her diaries on 11 December 1878 – carefully omitting to mention the role of Mathilde Wesendonck – that 'he had felt the urge to express himself symphonically for once, and that led to *Tristan*'.) In 1857 Wagner interrupted work on the *Ring* at the end of *Siegfried* Act II and finished *Tristan* two years later, often working at breakneck speed to deliver each act to the printer on time before moving on to the next. Indeed, half the score was already in print before he finished composing it – an odd situation that had to do with the comical fact that he was desperate for cash from the publisher, who would pay him only an act at a time. After its publication in 1860 the work was widely regarded as unperformable. The first performance was planned for the Vienna Court Opera in 1861, but abandoned after 77 rehearsals. The premiere eventually took place in Munich in 1865, conducted by Hans von Bülow with Ludwig Schnorr von Carolsfeld and his wife Malwina in the leading roles. Nine years elapsed before a second production was attempted in Weimar.

SYNOPSIS

Act I An awning on board Tristan's ship during a crossing from Ireland to Cornwall. Isolde is being taken to Cornwall against her will to marry King Marke. Resolved to die, she tells her confidante Brangäne to call Tristan to speak to her. Tristan is politely evasive and, when Brangäne insists, his trusted companion Kurwenal leaps up to sing a mocking song about Morald, a knight of Ireland who came to Cornwall to collect its tribute, only to be killed by Tristan. Now Morald's head hangs in Ireland as payment. The knights and the ship's crew join lustily in the refrain. A furious Isolde confides to Brangäne her version of the story ('Wie lachend sie mir Lieder singen'). Morald was her fiancé and in his fatal battle with Tristan seriously wounded him. Sick and dying, Tristan returned to Ireland in a small boat, where he was found by Isolde and nursed back to health. Disguised as 'Tantris', he went unrecognized by her until she noticed a notch in his sword that perfectly matched a splinter extracted from Morald's body. She raised a sword to kill him, but as he looked longingly into her eyes she let it fall. Now he has repaid her kindness by returning to claim her as a bride in a loveless marriage. Brangäne tries to calm her by reminding her of her mother's elixir of love. But Isolde will hear of only one of her mother's magic potions: the elixir of death. Kurwenal enters to announce their imminent landing and the approach of Tristan. Isolde demands vengeance for the death of Morald and offers Tristan a drink of atonement. Recognizing the elixir of death, Tristan drinks to Isolde. She wrenches the cup from his hand and drains it herself. Grimly expecting to die, they are overcome by passionate love instead, oblivious to the cries of the knights and the sailors as the ship prepares to land. Brangäne confesses in despair that she has substituted the elixir of love. Isolde, dismayed that she is now condemned to live, falls unconscious on to Tristan's breast.

Act II A garden with tall trees in front of Isolde's apartment in King Marke's royal fortress in Cornwall. It is a summer night, and the king's hunting party can be heard setting out. Isolde is impatiently waiting for Brangäne to extinguish the torch burning by the door as a signal to Tristan that he can come to her safely. But Brangäne is hesitant, believing that Tristan's best friend Melot, who has arranged the hunt so that the lovers can meet, has actually set a trap. Isolde is scornful, impatiently putting out the torch herself and ordering Brangäne to stand watch in the tower. Tristan enters, and the lovers fall passionately into each other's arms. Both deliver a curse on 'the spiteful day' ('dem tückischen Tage') that has bedazzled them, and a hymn to the night, a symbol of death that will ensure the eternal existence of their love ('O sink hernieder, Nacht der Liebe'). They ignore Brangäne's warnings about the imminent break of day, and enter into an ecstatic duet which is brutally interrupted at its climax by the sudden entrance of Kurwenal, who warns of King Marke's approach. Marke enters with Melot and the hunting party. In an extended monologue, the bewildered king asks in vain how his faithful nephew could betray him ('Dies, Tristan, mir?'). Tristan yearns for the night. As he bends down to kiss Isolde, Melot draws his sword. Instead of defending himself, Tristan lets his guard fall and sinks wounded into the arms of Kurwenal.

Act III Tristan's fortress in Brittany. The sound of a melancholy tune played by an old shepherd awakes Tristan from a deep coma. Overjoyed, Kurwenal tells how he brought Tristan back to his homeland to recover. Kurwenal is hourly awaiting Isolde's ship, and the shepherd will play a joyful melody when it is sighted. In demented excitement Tristan curses the terrible elixir of love ('verflucht sei, furchtbarer Trank!') and imagines he sees the ship approaching with Isolde on it transfigured and full of grace. Suddenly the shepherd sounds his joyful melody. Tristan rips the bandages off his wound and leaps from the sickbed to struggle forward to meet Isolde as she enters, only to die in her arms with her name on his lips. A second ship arrives, and King Marke, Melot and their retinue pour into the castle. In a rage, Kurwenal kills Melot, but collapses seriously wounded, dying at the feet of the dead Tristan. Brangäne tells Isolde that she has explained everything about the fatal elixir of love to the king, who has come to Brittany to forgive Tristan. But Isolde is deaf to her words. She sees Tristan awakened to new life in eternal death ('Mild und leise, wie er lächelt') and falls, as if transfigured, into Brangäne's arms.

Bernard Shaw once admitted that Wagner had retraced 'poetic love' to its 'alleged origin in sexual passion, the emotional phenomena of which he has expressed in music with a frankness and forcible naturalism which would possibly have scandalized Shelley'. Shaw was thinking especially of *Tristan und Isolde*, which from the first, with its graphic 'translation into music of the emotions which accompany the union of a pair of lovers', posed a moral as well as a musical challenge to 19th-century audiences. That Duchess Sophie of Bavaria was not allowed to attend the first performance of *Tristan* in 1865 out of moral considerations, despite the fact that she was a mature 20-year-old woman married to Duke Carl Theodor of Bavaria, is only one historical detail illustrating the point. Wagner's need to present unquenchable yearning and sexual passion in a convincing way, however, led him to widen the scope of his musical resources so drastically that *Tristan* almost inevitably soon became one of the most important musical works of the 19th century. In 1878 he explained to Cosima his need at the time of *Tristan* 'to push himself to the limit musically'. And indeed the unprecedented expansion of harmonic possibilities audible in the very first chord of the work (the so-called 'Tristan chord' is by far the most widely analysed collection of four notes in Western music) and the sheer freedom and invention in the handling of individual chromatic lines mean that it is quite justifiable to speak of the music of *Tristan* as a harbinger of the new music of the 20th century. (The music of *Tristan* is never actually atonal, though it energizes the tonal system from within to near breaking-point.) Composers have frequently acknowledged and parodied the modernist ambition of *Tristan* by using its opening phrase in their own works, including Wagner himself, who, in Act III of *Die Meistersinger*, was the first to cite it. Perhaps the subtlest use of it is in the final movement of Alban Berg's *Lyric Suite*, where it recalls not only the avant-garde aspect of *Tristan* but also its erotic *raison d'être*. Berg blended Wagner's music into a 12-note movement in such a way that it can be explained, as Berg himself pointed out, in terms of the working of the 12-note row. At the same time it was intended as part of a secret programme referring to his affair with Hanna Fuchs-Robettin, the sister of Franz Werfel and wife of a rich industrialist. The parallel with Wagner's infatuation with Mathilde Wesendonck, one of the inspirations behind *Tristan* and also the wife of a wealthy businessman, was obviously not a coincidence.

Die Meistersinger von Nürnberg

The Mastersingers of Nuremberg
In three acts (4h 15m)
Libretto by the composer
Composed: libretto 1845, 1861–2, 1866–7; music 1862–4, 1866–7
PREMIERES 1 November 1862, Gewandhaus, Leipzig (prelude; concert); 26 December 1862, Theater an der Wien, Vienna (excerpts from Act I, Scene 3, Assembly of the Mastersingers' Guild, for orchestra alone and Pogner's address; concert); 5 November 1863, Prague (Sachs's Shoemaker Song from Act II; concert); 12 July 1865, Residenztheater, Munich (excerpts from Act I, Scene 3, including Walther's Trial Song; concert); 4 April 1868, Liedertafel Frohsinn, Linz (Sachs's closing address and final chorus from Act III; concert, conducted Anton Bruckner); 21 June 1868, Königliches Hof und Nationaltheater, Munich; UK: 30 May 1882, Drury Lane, London; US: 4 January 1886, Metropolitan, New York
CAST Mastersingers: Hans Sachs (shoemaker) *b*, Veit Pogner (goldsmith) *b*, Kunz Vogelgesang (furrier) *t*, Konrad Nachtigall (tinsmith) *b*, Sixtus Beckmesser (town clerk) *b*, Fritz Kothner (baker) *b*, Balthasar Zorn (pewterer) *t*, Ulrich Eisslinger (grocer) *t*, Augustin Moser (tailor) *t*, Hermann Ortel (soap-boiler) *b*, Hans Schwarz (stocking-weaver) *b*, Hans Foltz (coppersmith) *b*; Walther von Stolzing *t*, David *t*, Eva *s*, Magdalene *s*, Night-watchman *b*; *satb* chorus of men and women from every guild, journeymen, apprentices, young women, populace

Die Meistersinger is an exception among Wagner's works in that it is not substantially based on any narrative source, though no end of literary and historical detail was lavished on it. Characterizations of its main figure, Hans Sachs, and other background material were provided by Goethe's poem 'An Account of an Old Woodcut Showing Hans Sachs's Poetic Calling' and Georg Gottfried Gervinus's influential *History of German Literature*, as well as Lortzing's 1840 opera *Hans Sachs* (an adaptation of a play written in 1827 by the Viennese court dramatist J. L. F. Deinhardstein). Ironically, Wagner had no hesitation in resorting to the well-known methods of his arch-rival Meyerbeer with some painstaking research into local colour, including details of medieval Nuremberg, various folk traditions, and the doctrine and practices of the historical mastersingers, which he gleaned mostly from J. C. Wagenseil's *Buch von der Meister-Singer holdseligen Kunst* (1687). But, apart from some ideas taken from E. T. A. Hoffmann's *Meister Martin der Küfner und seine Gesellen* (1819) and a few other sources, the story of the opera is largely Wagner's own invention.

Wagner first sketched out a scenario for *Die Meistersinger* in 1845. He wrote later that he conceived it then as a work that stood in relation to the song contest on the Wartburg in *Tannhäuser* 'like a richly textured satyr play', just as in ancient Athens 'a comic satyr play would follow a tragedy'. Not long after the fiasco of the revised Paris *Tannhäuser* in 1861 the idea reasserted itself, but with the key difference that it took its bearings this time from *Tristan* and the philosophy of Schopenhauer. The passion of the young nobleman for the woman he wins in the singing competition in the first version became a blind urge driven by fate in the second (at one point Eva explains to Sachs that she did not choose to love Walther, rather her love 'chose' her and became an 'unheard-of torment'), and Sachs was transformed into a far more substantial figure who beneath his jovial appearance is himself distracted by irrational feelings for the same woman. But Wagner also deliberately turned the tables on *Tristan* and Schopenhauer's pessimism by (among other things) fleshing out the conclusion of *Die Meistersinger* until it glowed with robust health and life. Sachs announces warmly that Walther's prize song has 'strength to live', resigning himself cheerfully to his loss of Eva with noble thoughts on the 'folly' (*Wahn*) of the world at the mercy of the blind Will. Despite their compulsive attraction to one another, Walther and Eva are prevented from renouncing society (that is – in the language of *Tristan* – from experiencing an inevitable love-death) and live happily ever after. The 'richly textured satyr play' to *Tannhäuser*, in other words, became a richly ironic counterpart to *Tristan* instead.

The premiere in Munich of *Die Meistersinger*, conducted by Hans von Bülow, was a resounding triumph comparable only to the first performance of *Rienzi* in Dresden in 1842. Over the years the mellow irony of the 'internal' drama of *Die Meistersinger* has proved to be its most enduring quality. But its immediate success was due more to its extrovert nationalism, which found enormous resonance in the years leading up to the 1870 Franco-Prussian War. There is a world of difference between this and Hitler's misappropriation of *Die Meistersinger* as the official opera of the Nuremberg party congresses during the Nazi period. Even though the sheer genius of the work transcends that part of it that has its origins in the growing nationalist fervour in Germany in the 1860s, its concluding propaganda on behalf of the hegemony of German art is for some still hard to accept, despite efforts to see it in historical perspective.

SYNOPSIS

Act I   Nuremberg; the mid 16th century. St Catherine's Church. Walther von Stolzing, a young Franconian knight who has sold his estate with the help of the goldsmith Veit Pogner, has made his home in Nuremberg and fallen in love with Pogner's daughter, Eva. After the afternoon service on the eve of Midsummer's Day, Eva and her nurse Magdalene tell Walther that Pogner has promised the hand of his daughter to the mastersinger who wins the singing competition due to take place on the morrow. Walther has no alternative but to join the mastersingers' guild. An examination for membership is about to take place, and Magdalene persuades her sweetheart David to initiate Walther into the mastersingers' rules and regulations without delay. Pogner is flattered that a nobleman wishes to join the guild and lends Walther his support. Walther tells the assembled masters that his singing teacher was an ancient book by Walther von der Vogelweide and his school the depths of the forest ('Am stillen Herd in Winterszeit'). But the reaction is sceptical: only Hans Sachs senses something out of the ordinary. Walther is allowed to proceed to a formal trial song, and the town clerk Sixtus Beckmesser, a mastersinger who is just as determined to win Eva's hand, acts as marker to note each fault. Out of Beckmesser's formal invitation to begin ('Fanget an') Walther improvises a dithyramb in praise of nature and love. But Beckmesser soon chalks up enough mistakes to exceed the statutory limit. Sachs's admiration for the boldness and originality of the candidate falls on deaf ears. Walther is declared by the majority to have failed the test.

Act II   A street with the houses of Pogner and Sachs. Eva hears the bad news about Walther from Magdalene. Snatches of Walther's trial song continue to haunt Sachs, who cannot grasp how the song could sound old, yet at the same time so new ('Es klang so alt, und war doch so neu'). Walther and Eva decide to flee, only to find their escape thwarted by Sachs. Beckmesser appears with his lute, ready to try out his prize song on Eva, who, forewarned, has asked Magdalene to take her place at her window. Sachs constantly interrupts Beckmesser with a deliberately coarse shoemaker's song (a delicious parody of Siegfried's forging song in the *Ring*) and finally agrees to listen only if Beckmesser lets him act as marker. Sachs strikes the soles of the shoes he is making every time Beckmesser makes a mistake. Beckmesser tries to drown the blows by singing louder, only to wake the neighbours, including David, who, at the sight of Beckmesser apparently serenading Magdalene, becomes furiously jealous. David attacks Beckmesser, and their fight quickly escalates into a violent free-for-all during which Walther and Eva again try to escape. Sachs intervenes to separate them, giving the half-swooning Eva into the protection of her father, while he quickly leads Walther into his workshop. At the sound of the approaching night-watchman's horn, the tumult ends almost as suddenly as it began.

Act III   Sachs's workshop the next morning. David comes to offer his apologies for the night before. Left alone, Sachs continues reading a large folio, musing on the folly he sees everywhere beneath the self-torment of the human race ('Wahn, Wahn! Überall Wahn!'). Walther enters and sings Sachs a song that has just come to him in a dream. Sachs helps him to shape the first two verses, sensing something new at last that can be reconciled with the mastersingers' rules. After they have left, Beckmesser limps into the workshop and discovers a sheet of paper on which Sachs has written the song. He immediately takes it to be a prize song by Sachs, who suddenly looks like yet another dangerous rival. On his return Sachs calms Beckmesser's fears and generously gives him the manuscript, though cannily forgetting to mention its real author. Eva enters, and Walther, transfixed by the sight of her, improvises the third verse of his song. Sachs knows he himself will never realize his love for Eva, but prefers to be nobly cheerful about it. The woes of King Marke in the sad story of Tristan and Isolde, he tells Eva, are not for him (at which point Wagner cites his own *Tristan*). After a moving quintet in celebration of the 'baptism' of Walther's prize song by Sachs ('Selig, wie die Sonne'), the scene changes to the festival meadow outside Nuremberg where the singing competition is to take place. The first candidate is Beckmesser, who proceeds to bowdlerize the words of the song given to him by Sachs ('Morgen ich leuchte in rosigem Schein'). He is ridiculed by the townspeople and in a rage declares that Sachs is the author of the poem. But this only gives Sachs an ideal opportunity to call on the true author. Walther delivers an impassioned rendering of his song ('Morgenlich leuchtend im rosigen Schein') which wins unanimous approval from populace and mastersingers alike. The prize and Eva's hand are Walther's, though he instinctively recoils from accepting the guild's chain of honour. After Sachs voices his opinion about the importance of the masters and their art for Germany ('Verachtet mir die Meister nicht'), Walther changes his mind and joins in the celebration of Sachs as the embodiment of 'holy German art'.

Wagner's original intention in 1861 after the famous *Tannhäuser* débâcle in Paris was to complete the *Ring*, which he had abandoned four years before to write *Tristan*. Suddenly in October he wrote to his publisher that he had decided instead to cheer himself up with 'something lighter' that would be finished much faster, in a year. That year turned into six – the last note of the score of *Die Meistersinger* was written on 24 October 1867 at eight o'clock in the evening – and probably no other single fact about the opera is more eloquent than this about the difficulties Wagner had in composing it. Finding a musical style for *Die Meistersinger* that stood in the same relation to *Tristan* as its libretto – a style, that is, which would turn the earlier work on its head without letting the ironic reversal descend into emptiness or banality – proved to be a trickier task than Wagner had anticipated.

Simplicity was hard for Wagner. The overture and Act I of *Die Meistersinger* took four and a half years to complete, which, even accounting for interruptions, was for him a surprisingly long time. If he found it difficult at first to write music that concealed its highly advanced technique so well that the most distinctive thing about it would be its apparent lack of sophistication, once he had discovered the right stylistic balance for the work (or – in the language of the mastersingers – its correct 'tone') it took him only another year and a half to finish it. One of the results of this hard thinking is that large sections of *Die Meistersinger* are written in inverted commas, so to speak, yet retain a powerful semblance of immediacy in spite of – or perhaps even because of – the fact that they are historical stylizations. The music of *Tristan* is placed inside the robust diatonicism of Lutheran chorales and quasi-baroque counterpoint which become richly tinged with chromatic harmony as a result. The new is passed through the filter of the old, just as Walther's prize song in the last act is subjected by Sachs to the rules of the mastersingers' guild. Though he took longer than usual to do it, Wagner had once more discovered an ingenious musical metaphor that mirrored a central concern of the drama: the widening divide between high art and popular culture and the fracturing of tradition by the radically new.

Parsifal

Bühnenweihfestspiel ('stage dedication play') in three acts (4h– 4h 30m)
Libretto by the composer
Composed: libretto 1865, 1877; music 1877–82
PREMIERES 25 December 1878, Haus Wahnfried, Bayreuth (prelude; concert); 12 November 1880, Königliches Hof und Nationaltheater, Munich (prelude; concert); 26 July 1882, Festspielhaus, Bayreuth; UK: 10 November 1884, London (concert); 2 February 1914, Covent Garden, London; US: 3 March 1886, New York (concert); 24 December 1903, Metropolitan, New York
CAST Amfortas *bar*, Titurel *b*, Gurnemanz *b*, Parsifal *t*, Klingsor *b*, Kundry *s*, First and Second Knights of the Grail *t, b*, First and Second Squires 2 *s*, Third and Fourth Squires 2 *t*, A Voice *c*, Klingsor's Flower Maidens: 6 *s*, 2 *sa* choruses; *tb* brotherhood of the knights of the Grail, *at* young men, *sa* boys

Parsifal has never been a work to attract moderate comment. Variously described as sublime, vicious or merely decadent, it has always fascinated critics, who have seen it as a 'superior magic opera' which 'revels in the wondrous' (Eduard Hanslick) or as a 'profoundly inhuman spectacle, glorifying a barren mascu-line world whose ideals are a combination of milita-rism and monasticism' (Peter Wapnewski). Given the suggestive allegory Wagner designed for what he called his 'last card' and 'farewell to the world', the controversy is hardly surprising. However, whether *Parsifal* is a sinister millenarianist fantasy about the redemption of an Aryan Jesus from Judaism (as Ger-many's most vociferous post-war anti-Wagnerite Hartmut Zelinsky seems to think) or just a feeble Armageddon cocktail with large twists of Schopen-hauer, critics of its supposed inhumanity will always find it hard to account for the fascinating beauty of its score and the inconvenient fact that militancy and aggression could not be further removed from its central idea.

Parsifal is based on the notion of compassion (*Mitleid*) borrowed from the philosophy of Schopen-hauer and subjected to some characteristically Wag-nerian variations. Schopenhauer and Wagner saw compassion as a specific moral response to the violent chaos of the world – a beatific annihilation of the Will, so to speak, achieved through a denial of Eros and (in Wagner's personal version of the doctrine) a deep sympathy with the suffering in others caused by the torment of sexual desire. *Parsifal* has been called anti-*Tristan* (where salvation depends on the opposite notion of consummated sexual longing), though it is probably best understood as a dialectical counterpart offering a different solution to the same, and for Wagner always extremely important, problem of blind carnality and the pain it inflicts. In fact, Wagner's first idea in 1856 had been to introduce Parsifal into Act III of *Tristan*: during his wanderings in search of the Grail, Parsifal would visit Tristan on his sickbed. But Parsifal's compassionate response to Tristan's suf-fering had so many implications of its own (at one point in the early *Tristan* sketches he asks whether the whole world is not just 'unquenchable longing' and how it can ever be 'stilled') that Wagner decided to drop the plan and to make Parsifal the subject of a separate work.

The idea of compassion also influenced Wagner's radical treatment of his main literary source, Wol-fram von Eschenbach's early-13th-century romance *Parzival*. Wagner discussed Wolfram and sexual asceti-cism at length in his letters to Mathilde Wesendonck in the late 1850s (in view of his rapidly cooling feelings towards her after finishing *Tristan* this was perhaps to be expected) and came to the conclusion that he would have to compress Wolfram's enormous 24,810-line poem into just 'three climactic situations'. In the final work these have been turned in effect into three successive stages of compassion (a concept foreign to Wolfram's poem, incidentally, at least as Schopen-hauer and Wagner understood it), which begins as a vague and unformed feeling in Parsifal's response to the Grail ceremony in Act I, progresses to a burning insight into Amfortas's suffering at the moment of Kundry's kiss in Act II, and with the baptism of Kundry and the healing of Amfortas's wound in Act III is finally and miraculously transformed into an act of redemption. *Parsifal* is fundamentally a cathartic ritual that unfolds in three cycles, each more intense than the last. The melancholy history of the Grail community, however, which has taken place before the action begins, slowly asserts itself too as the work progresses. *Parsifal* is by no means just a comforting vision of a possible future state of grace. The gradual fulfilment of the prophecy announced at the start – the coming of the redeemer made wise through compassion – is also precariously balanced against irrevocably painful memories of the past. It is therefore important first to explain the past events weighing on the action of the drama.

The action takes place in Spain in two contrasting worlds on the same mountain range. To the north on the Christian side lies Monsalvat, the castle of the knights of the Grail. It was built by Titurel as a shrine for the chalice used at the Last Supper and in which Joseph of Arimathea caught the blood of Christ on the Cross, and for the spear that pierced Christ's side. Only those who are chaste through spiritual self-examination may take part in the life-giving ritual of the unveiling of the Grail (i.e. the chalice) by Titurel's son Amfortas, the present king. On the southern slope facing Moorish (i.e. heathen) Spain is Klingsor's castle. Klingsor, once a pious hermit unable to suppress sinful desire through reflection, castrated himself and was spurned by the Grail community. Determined to possess the chalice and the spear for himself, he turned to paganism and magic in order to lure the Grail knights into his magic garden, where his seductive flower maidens trap them with the very power the knights have learned to repress.

Linking the two worlds is Kundry, who once laughed at Christ on the Cross and is condemned to live for eternity, both as a decoy and prostitute in Klingsor's castle, and as a repentant slave in the kingdom of the Grail. Klingsor has absolute power over her, as only he knows of her history and her tormented double existence, from which she seeks in vain to be delivered through death. On his orders she once seduced Amfortas, who had set out with the holy spear to put an end to Klingsor's threat. Klingsor stole the spear, with which he seriously wounded Amfortas in the side. Amfortas was led home by his trusty knight Gurnemanz to administer the unveiling of the Grail. But his wound refuses to heal, with the consequence that the ritual has become a torture and his kingdom increasingly desolate.

SYNOPSIS

Act I A shady forest in the region of the Grail castle. After recounting the oppressive past weighing on the Grail community to some of its younger members, Gurnemanz tells of a prophetic saying that came to Amfortas in a vision: a blameless fool made wise through compassion ('durch Mitleid wissend, der reine Tor') will one day redeem him and become king of the Grail. The young knights are disturbed by the arrival of a youth who has killed a swan. Gurnemanz questions him, but the intruder is aware of nothing, not even his name: only Kundry knows he is an orphan. Gurnemanz thinks he may have found the innocent fool who will redeem Amfortas. During a long transformation scene he leads him into the castle of the Grail. They witness Amfortas's torment as, under pressure from his father Titurel,

he unwillingly unveils the Grail. The stranger is moved by the event, but cannot grasp its deeper meaning.

Act II Klingsor's magic castle. Klingsor wakes Kundry and commands her to trap the simple youth approaching his domain, against whom he will again wield the holy spear. After easily resisting the flower maidens, the youth is transfixed when Kundry calls out 'Parsifal' – the name his mother once gave him in a dream. Kundry inveigles him with her charm, cleverly exploiting his deep feelings of guilt about his mother's death. She gives him a long kiss on the mouth. He jumps up in shock: now he senses the terrible consequences of sinful longing, the torment of Amfortas's wound that burns in his own heart ('Amfortas! – Die Wunde!'). Furious that he continues to reject her sensual allure, Kundry summons Klingsor. But Parsifal regains the spear and Klingsor's castle crumbles to dust.

Act III In the region of the Grail castle. Years have passed. Amfortas has refused to unveil the Grail, and the knights, debilitated and distressed, await their deliverer. Gurnemanz is an old man living as a hermit on the edge of the forest. He discovers Kundry again, almost dead. Parsifal enters in black armour with the holy spear sunken at his side. Gurnemanz knows that the moment of salvation has come: he anoints Parsifal as the new king of the Grail while Kundry washes the feet of the new king and receives from him the baptism of absolution. It is the magic of Good Friday: nature has regained its lost innocence. Kundry's tears of repentance are tears of benediction, Parsifal tells her gently, and the meadow smiles ('du weinest – sieh! es lacht die Aue'). The scene changes gradually into the castle of the Grail, as in Act I. The knights urge Amfortas to unveil the Grail; but he refuses and demands that they kill him. This time Parsifal understands: he takes the spear and places its tip on Amfortas's side. The wound heals, and the power of the holy spear is restored (the spear was deconsecrated the moment it pierced Amfortas, who had sullied the purity of Christ through his transgression in Kundry's arms). Now the taint of sin has been removed from the spear, the symbol of Christ's sacrifice. Parsifal orders the unveiling of the Grail. Kundry dies, and the chorus quietly intones a new saying: 'Redemption to the Redeemer' ('Erlösung dem Erlöser').

Although the first performance of *Parsifal*, conducted by Hermann Levi, made a profound impression, Wagner insisted, as he had already agreed with Ludwig II in 1880, that the work be performed only in Bayreuth. Ironically, the first to ignore the stipulation was Ludwig himself, who ordered three performances of the Bayreuth production to take place at the Munich Court Opera in 1884 and 1885. The whole work was occasionally given in concert in countries that were not signatories to the Bern Convention (London 1884, New York 1886, Boston 1891, Amsterdam 1896) and there were unauthorized productions at the New York Metropolitan on 24 December 1903 and in Amsterdam on 20 June 1905 respectively. (The New York production was also taken on tour throughout the United States, when it was performed no fewer than 130 times.) As the full score of *Parsifal* had been widely available since 1883, however, it is actually more surprising that the 'rape of the Grail' (as the New York production became known to the Bayreuth faithful) had not already happened much sooner. Cosima Wagner petitioned the Reichstag twice to extend the copyright beyond the statutory 30 years after the composer's death, first in 1901 and again in 1912, this time armed with 18,000 signatures. But her efforts were unsuccessful. When the copyright lapsed in 1914 nearly every major opera house rushed to mount its own production: *Parsifal* was deconsecrated, and its secular existence began.

Before 1914 modern composers who wanted to hear *Parsifal* (and most of them did) had to make the pilgrimage to the Bayreuth shrine to witness its yearly unveiling. Debussy went in 1888, Berg in 1909, and Stravinsky was easily tempted by Diaghilev to go with him in 1912, even though it meant interrupting work on *Le sacre du printemps*. Berg complained of the 'empty-headed folly' (*leerer Wahn*) of Bayreuth, and Stravinsky noted in dismay that the inside of the theatre was like a crematorium (and a very old one at that). Indeed, the fading iconic world of the German Empire that the Festival Theatre represented seems to have been repellent to many of Europe's visiting intelligentsia. For Berg, however, the sophisticated refinement and sheer loveliness of the music of *Parsifal* was worth the trip. Stravinsky, who is wrongly supposed to have rejected *Parsifal* out of hand during his visit, deliberately stayed silent about the music, preferring to lambast the audience and the cult-like atmosphere of the performance. Debussy saw the gulf between Wagner's musical genius and the rest of his Bayreuth legacy in the work itself. The score is 'one of the most beautiful monuments ever raised to music', he wrote a few years after his visit, while the 'moral and religious ideas' represented by the allegory 'are completely false'. The startling volte-face is a suspect critical strategy, though it has been used by other prominent critics, including Nietzsche and Adorno, and tends to reflect modern opinion. The baroque-like rhetorical figures and highly intricate musical textures in *Parsifal*, however, are metaphorical reflections on its supposedly creaky allegory which are arguably still only imperfectly understood.

Other operas: *Die Feen*, (1834), 1888; *Das Liebesverbot, oder Die Novizie von Palermo*, 1836

J. W. D.

WILLIAM WALTON

(Sir) William Turner Walton; *b* 29 March 1902, Oldham, Lancashire, England; *d* 8 March 1983, Ischia, Italy

The son of an organist and choirmaster in industrial Lancashire, Walton won a choral scholarship to Christ Church Cathedral School, Oxford, in 1912. His early compositions (songs and anthems) date from about 1916 and won the interest of Hubert Parry. In 1919, while an undergraduate, he was 'adopted' by the Sitwells, the extraordinary trio of literary siblings – Edith, Osbert and Sacherevell – and first attracted attention in 1922 with his collaboration with Edith

Sitwell on the entertainment *Façade*. From 1925, when he composed *Portsmouth Point*, until the outbreak of war in 1939, he was in the forefront of his generation with a succession of works – the Viola Concerto (1929), the cantata *Belshazzar's Feast* (1931), the First Symphony (1935) and the Violin Concerto written for Jascha Heifetz (1939).

In 1941 Walton and Cecil Gray pondered the possibility of an opera about the Italian composer Gesualdo. Gray completed a libretto, but no music was forthcoming. Six years later, the BBC commissioned an opera from Walton. He chose the subject Troilus and Cressida, with Christopher Hassall as librettist. The opera was not completed until 1954, by which time Walton had settled permanently on the island of Ischia in the Bay of Naples. A Covent Garden premiere was only moderately successful, but productions followed in Milan and San Francisco. Deeply wounded by failure, Walton for the next twenty years searched for singers and producers who would do justice to his opera and, with the promise of a Covent Garden revival in 1976, recast the role of Cressida for the mezzo-soprano Janet Baker.

Meanwhile in 1967 he had completed a short one-act opera, *The Bear*, based on a vaudeville by Chekhov. This had been commissioned by the Aldeburgh Festival at the suggestion of Peter Pears and was from the first a success. Walton's light touch and his gift for parody, evident as early as *Façade*, were admirably deployed in this sparkling piece and make it all the more regrettable that he never proceeded with a suggestion to base an opera on Oscar Wilde's *The Importance of Being Earnest*, a subject that would surely have suited him ideally. Walton undoubtedly had dramatic talents, as *Belshazzar's Feast* indicated early in his career, but they led him to the film studio more frequently than to the opera house.

He composed the music for Laurence Olivier's three Shakespeare films, *Henry V* (1944), *Hamlet* (1947) and *Richard III* (1955), and among the best known of his other film scores are those from *The First of the Few* (1942), about R. J. Mitchell, who designed the Spitfire fighter aircraft, and Bernard Shaw's *Major Barbara* (1941). Orchestral suites have been extracted from several of his film scores. The *Henry V* music, on a large and ambitious scale, is one of the finest examples of music inspired by the cinema.

Troilus and Cressida

Opera in three acts (2h 15m)
Libretto by Christopher Hassall, after *Troilus and Criseyde* by Geoffrey Chaucer (*c.* 1380–82) and other sources
Composed 1948–54; rev. 1963, 1972–6
PREMIERES 3 December 1954, Covent Garden, London; US: 7 October 1955, War Memorial Opera House, San Francisco; rev. version: 12 November 1976, Covent Garden, London
CAST Troilus *t*, Cressida *ms* (originally *s*), Pandarus *t buffo*, Evadne *ms*, Calkas *b*, Antenor *bar*, Horaste *bar*, Diomede *bar*; *satb* chorus of priests and priestesses of Pallas, Trojans and Greeks

Walton was spurred to compose *Troilus and Cressida* by the success of Britten's *Peter Grimes* in 1945. Rivalry had always encouraged his creativity. 'I thought it was not a good thing', he said, 'for British opera to have only one opera by one composer', a statement that took no account of Delius and Vaughan Williams. His intention was to write an English bel-canto opera.

SYNOPSIS

Act I The Trojan War has lasted ten years. The high priest of Troy, Calkas, father of Cressida, says that the Delphic oracle advises surrender to the Greeks. When the crowd turns on him he is defended by Prince Troilus, who is in love with Cressida. She is a war widow and tends the altar in the temple because she knows her father is preparing to desert, as he later does. Her dandyish uncle, Pandarus, encourages the relationship with Troilus and persuades Cressida to leave her crimson scarf as a love token.

Act II After a night of love in Pandarus' house, where they are marooned by a thunderstorm, the lovers are interrupted by the arrival of the Greek prince Diomede, who announces that Cressida must join Calkas as the price of her father's services in exchange for a Trojan prisoner. Diomede is attracted by Cressida's beauty. Troilus promises to send her daily messages and to bribe the Greek sentries to allow them to meet. He returns the scarf as a symbol of their love.

Act III Ten weeks later, Cressida has not heard from Troilus and agrees to marry Diomede, to whom she gives her scarf. Her servant Evadne has been intercepting and burning Troilus' messages on the orders of Calkas. Troilus, meanwhile, has arranged her ransom, and visits the Greek camp during a truce. He sees the scarf on Diomede's helmet and claims Cressida as his own. He attacks Diomede, but is stabbed in the back by Calkas. Diomede, aghast, orders Calkas to be returned to the Trojans but insists that Cressida remain as a soldier's whore. She picks up Troilus' sword and stabs herself.

In spite of much beautiful and compelling music – such as the 'scarf' motif and several of Cressida's arias – *Troilus and Cressida* fails to fulfil its composer's ambitions for it. The libretto, too flowery and diffuse, is partly to blame, but the music is uneven in quality and does not achieve the heroic style that was needed to make *Troilus and Cressida* credible. The finest characterization in the opera is the tenor buffo role of Pandarus, sung originally by Peter Pears. It comes near to parody of Britten, but it has its own elegant wit. The orchestral score, too, is consistently splendid. But the parts somehow do not add up to a whole, and it is arguable whether Walton improved matters by transposing the heroine's part for a mezzo.

A newly revised version, which restores the role of Cressida to the original soprano tessitura but keeps the composer's later cuts, was prepared by Stuart Hutchinson for the 1995 revival by Opera North.

The Bear

Extravaganza in one act (50m)
Libretto by Paul Dehn and the composer, based on the vaudeville *Medved* by Anton Chekhov (1888)

PREMIERES 3 June 1967, Jubilee Hall, Aldeburgh, Suffolk; US: 15 August 1968, Aspen Music Festival, Colorado CAST Yeliena Ivanova Popova *ms*, Grigory Stepanovitch Smirnov *bar*, Luka *b*

Walton received a commission for an opera from the Koussevitzky Music Foundation in 1958, but did not undertake it until 1965, when the Aldeburgh Festival wanted a work from him for the English Opera Group. He had met and liked the writer Paul Dehn in Ischia, and together they adapted the short Chekhov play.

SYNOPSIS

Mme Popova is an attractive young widow. She claims she will mourn for the rest of her life, but her manservant Luka urges her to start life again: her husband had been unfaithful and did not deserve her loyalty to his memory. They are interrupted by Smirnov, a huge bear of a man, who forces his way in to demand immediate payment of a debt incurred by her husband for oats for the horse Toby. Smirnov, too, urges her to put off her widow's weeds and unveil like Salome. They argue over whether men or women are more faithful in love. She calls him a boor, and asks Luka to show him out. Smirnov challenges her to a duel – he is now attracted by her spirit. She fetches her husband's pistol, but Smirnov has to show her how to use it. She has fallen for him. There is no duel.

In *The Bear*, Walton at 65 recaptured something of the insouciance that marked *Façade* when he was 19. The score is full of affectionate and subtle parodies of, among others, Puccini, Richard Strauss, Britten and Offenbach – for instance, Smirnov's parody of the Russian aristocrat's use of French in 'Madame, je vous prie' and Popova's catalogue of her husband's infidelities in 'I was a constant, faithful wife'. The opera is a thoroughly effective caricature.

M.K.

CARL MARIA VON WEBER

Carl Maria Friedrich Ernst (von) Weber; *b* ?18 November 1786, Eutin, Germany; *d* 5 June 1826, London

Weber played a key role in the development of German Romantic opera. His most enduringly successful work, *Der Freischütz*, combines national characteristics in both plot and music with dramatic vitality, vivid musical imagery and appealing directness of style. These qualities ensured not only that it enjoyed extraordinary popularity in its own day, but also that, alone of early-Romantic German operas, it still retains a firm place in the standard operatic repertoire. Weber's later operas, *Euryanthe* and *Oberon*, though they contain some of his finest music, are, for very different reasons, flawed masterpieces.

Weber's childhood was spent in a theatrical environment, accompanying his father's touring theatre company as it travelled around Bavaria performing fashionable plays and singspiels. His education was haphazard; he received some instruction in music from his half-brother Fridolin and sporadic lessons from teachers in the various towns where the troupe performed. In Hildburghausen, J. P. Heuschkel laid the foundations of his later pianistic virtuosity; in Salzburg he took lessons from Michael Haydn, and in Munich he took singing and composition lessons. With the help of the Munich court organist, Johann Nepomuk Kalcher, the 13-year-old Weber composed his first opera, a singspiel, *Die Macht der Liebe und des Weins*, in 1798. The score was destroyed in a fire at Kalcher's house shortly after its composition. His second opera, *Das Waldmädchen*, was composed shortly afterwards in Freiberg, to a libretto by Carl von Steinsberg, by whose travelling company it was performed.

By 1801 Weber was back in Salzburg, continuing his studies with Michael Haydn, where he wrote his third opera, *Peter Schmoll und seine Nachbarn*. Early in 1803 it was staged in Augsburg, where his half-brother Edmund was conducting at the theatre. Later that year Weber moved to Vienna, intending to study with Joseph Haydn, but he came instead under the influence of the Abbé Vogler, whose impact on Weber's musical development was profound and lasting.

At Vogler's recommendation, the 17-year-old Weber was offered the post of kapellmeister at the Breslau theatre in 1804. During his two years in Breslau he attempted to reform the repertoire, but encountered considerable opposition. He began another opera, on a libretto based on Johann Karl August Musäus's 'Rübezahl' story, but only three numbers, which show no perceptible advance in his creative power, survive. Weber's departure from Breslau was precipitated when he accidentally drank engraving acid. Returning to work after a two-month convalescence, he found that most of his reforms had been undone, and he resigned.

After a sojourn in Karlsruhe, where he composed his two symphonies, Weber moved in 1807 to Stuttgart as secretary to Duke Ludwig of Württemberg. Encouraged by the hofkapellmeister there, Franz Danzi, Weber continued to compose for the theatre, writing incidental music for Schiller's *Turandot* (1809) and working on the opera *Silvana*, which he completed after he had moved to Stuttgart in 1810. The first ideas for *Der Freischütz* came later that year in Darmstadt when, on a visit to Stift Neuberg, he and Alexander von Dusch got as far as sketching a scenario. But Dusch, an amateur cellist, had insufficient time to prepare a libretto and the project was postponed. Apart from the singspiel *Abu Hassan*, Weber composed no stage works during this period, turning his attention instead to instrumental works and to his own tours as a concert pianist. Early in 1813, however, he was persuaded to accept the post of kapellmeister at the Prague opera. Here, as earlier in Breslau, he immersed himself in his work of reforming the running of the opera house and its repertoire (basing it on the works of Mozart and on French opera), a task that left him little time to pursue his own compositions and which took its toll on his health. Disagreements with the opera's directors were constant, and in October 1816 he handed in his resignation and left for Berlin.

Within a few months he had secured himself a position as royal Saxon kapellmeister in Dresden. While this gave him authority over the city's German opera, local taste favoured Italian opera so the challenge set Weber in fostering an indigenous opera was substantial. He set about the task with his customary diligence and enthusiasm, once again leaving himself little time for composition. But, meeting Friedrich Kind, the idea of an opera on the *Freischütz* story was rekindled. Work proceeded fitfully – interruptions included a royal commission for an opera, *Alcidor* (later cancelled) – but by May 1820 *Der Freischütz*, Weber's first opera for nine years, was complete (except for one aria, added the following year). The premiere was a triumph, and the opera was rapidly taken up throughout Europe, making Weber an international celebrity.

The success of *Der Freischütz* led to a commission for a new opera for the 1822–3 season at the Kärntnertortheater in Vienna. Weber embraced the project with enthusiasm and, laying aside his work on *Die drei Pintos* (a comic work he had begun in the summer of 1820), began seeking a suitable subject. Unfortunately, both his choice of Helmina von Chezy as librettist and *Euryanthe* as subject proved disastrous. Despite a respectfully received Vienna premiere, *Euryanthe*'s weaknesses soon became apparent, and it was withdrawn after 20 performances.

For more than a year after the premiere of *Euryanthe*, Weber composed almost nothing. But, in August 1824, he was invited by Charles Kemble to write a new opera for London and, persuaded that by this means he would be able to provide for his family's financial security after his death, he accepted the commission. Against his doctor's advice, he travelled to London in February 1826 for the production of *Oberon*; he died the day before he had planned to travel home.

Der Freischütz

The Free-shooter
Romantic opera in three acts (2h 30m)
Libretto by Johann Friedrich Kind, after *Gespensterbuch* by Johann August Apel and Friedrich Laun (1811)
PREMIERES 18 June 1821, Schauspielhaus, Berlin; UK: 22 July 1824, Lyceum, London; US: 2 March 1825, New York
CAST Max *t*, Kilian *bar*, Cuno *b*, Caspar *b*, Ännchen *s*, Agathe *s*, Hermit *b*, Samiel *spoken role*, 4 Bridesmaids 4 *s*, Prince Ottokar *bar*; *satb* chorus of hunters, peasants, spirits, bridesmaids, followers of the prince

Weber considered writing an opera on the *Freischütz* story in 1811, after reading the tale in Apel and Laun's newly published *Gespensterbuch*. When he became kapellmeister in Dresden in 1817, he revived the idea and discussed it with Friedrich Kind, who rapidly produced the draft of a libretto. At this stage it was entitled *Der Probeschuss* ('The Test Shot'). The story had already been used as the basis of a number of other theatrical pieces: by Franz Xaver von Caspar with music by Carl Neuner (1812); by Ferdinand Rosenau (1816); by Aloys Gleich with music by Franz Roser (1816). In 1818 Louis Spohr, with the collaboration of Georg Döring, also began to compose an opera based on Apel's tale but, on hearing that Weber was working on the same subject, abandoned it in favour of *Zemire und Azor*.

Weber's poor health, his efforts on behalf of the German opera in Dresden, and the pressure of other commissions slowed down the composition of *Der Freischütz*. In 1819 he began to work more intensively on the score (by then known as *Die Jägersbraut* ('The Hunter's Bride')) after he had reached an agreement that it should open the newly rebuilt Schauspielhaus in Berlin. (In fact, the Schauspielhaus was opened with a Goethe play, but *Der Freischütz* was the first musical piece to be performed there.) The premiere was a triumph, and the opera was soon being performed throughout Europe.

Der Freischütz was by far the most popular German opera of the first half of the 19th century. But its tremendous popularity is only partly explained by its musical and dramatic characteristics. It came at an opportune moment in German history, when the upsurge of patriotic feeling, following the defeat of Napoleon, was at its height. With its powerfully German character, in both drama and music, *Der Freischütz* seized the German imagination and remained a significant symbol of national identity throughout the difficult times that followed.

By 1830 *Der Freischütz* had been translated into Danish, Swedish, Czech, Russian, English, French, Hungarian, Polish and Dutch. It was also produced in many severely mutilated versions, and its success led to a number of parodies. In 1824 a piece was published under the title *Samiel, oder Die Wunderpille*, and in England 'Septimus Globus' issued '*Der Freischütz*, a new muse-sick-all and see-nick performance from the new German uproar. By the celebrated Funnybear'. In the same year Castil-Blaze also produced his French version as *Robin des Bois*, which infuriated the young Berlioz. But Berlioz was later persuaded, albeit reluctantly, to supply recitatives and a ballet for a Paris production of *Der Freischütz* in 1841.

SYNOPSIS

Act I In front of an inn in the Bohemian forest, peasants are congratulating Kilian on his victory over Max, a forester, in a shooting competition ('Victoria, victoria'). They taunt Max, and only the arrival of Cuno, the head forester, prevents a fight. Caspar, another forester (who has made a compact with Samiel, the Black Huntsman), mockingly suggests that Max should call on the dark powers for assistance. Cuno rebukes Caspar, but warns Max that if he fails in the shooting test he will not be allowed to marry Cuno's daughter Agathe. The peasants exit to a waltz; Max, alone, ponders his lack of success ('Durch die Wälder') while Samiel observes him. Caspar joins Max and insists on drinking several toasts with him; his coarse drinking song ('Hier im ird'schen Jammerthal') enrages Max. Caspar offers to help Max pass the test, and proves the point by giving him his gun, with which Max miraculously shoots an almost invisible eagle. Caspar explains that it was loaded with a magic bullet, and that seven more can be cast if he will come to the Wolf's Glen at midnight. Caspar plans to offer Max as a victim to Samiel in place of himself, and exults in Max's impending damnation ('Schweig, schweig').

Act II In Cuno's house, Ännchen is rehanging a portrait which had fallen down, hitting Agathe. She cheers her cousin in a lively arietta ('Kommt ein schlanker Bursch gegangen') and Agathe relates how, that morning, the hermit, warning her of impending danger, gave her holy roses for her protection. Agathe's uneasiness gives way to joy when she hears Max approaching ('Leise, leise'). Her uneasiness returns, however, when Max explains that he must collect a stag which he has shot near the Wolf's Glen ('Wie? Was? Entsetzen!'). In the Wolf's Glen, as midnight strikes, Caspar summons Samiel, who accepts the substitute victim. Max arrives and, together, they cast seven bullets. Between each of the castings there are increasingly horrific supernatural manifestations; finally Samiel himself appears. Caspar and Max fall unconscious and calm returns.

Act III The following day Max, out hunting, has made three magnificent shots and has only one magic bullet left; Caspar has used all his three. Agathe is praying ('Und ob die Wolke'). She dreamt that she was a white dove; when Max fired his gun she fell, but the dove vanished and she was Agathe again, while a black bird lay bleeding at her feet. Ännchen tries to dispel Agathe's anxiety with a merry tale ('Einst träumte'). The bridesmaids arrive and sing a folksong ('Wir winden dir den Jungfernkranz'). Ännchen arrives with a box containing flowers, but a funeral wreath instead of a wedding wreath. They decide to make a new wreath from the hermit's roses. The shooting test is about to begin. Prince Ottokar chooses a white dove as target. As Max takes aim, Agathe enters and cries to him to hold fire since she is the dove. The hermit causes the dove to fly off to another tree, behind which Caspar is hiding. Max shoots, and both Agathe and Caspar fall. Everyone thinks Max has shot Agathe ('Schaut, o schaut'), but the bullet has hit Caspar; he dies cursing. Max makes a full confession and, after the intervention of the hermit, the prince pardons him.

The overture sets the scene for the opera; its two principal tonalities – C major and C minor – represent the opposing forces of good and evil. The appearance of the diminished-seventh chord, associated with Samiel (F$\sharp$, A, C, E$\flat$), foreshadows the dark side of the drama. The molto-vivace section is based on passages to come later in the opera: Max's 'Doch mich umgarnen finstre Mächte' (from 'Durch die Wälder'), full of foreboding, and Agathe's exultant 'Süss entzückt entgegen ihm' (from 'Leise, leise').

Throughout the opera, keys play an important part in underlining the conflict between good and evil. The major keys, particularly the sharp keys, are associated with simplicity and goodness, while the minor keys, especially C minor, characterize the dark powers. Samiel's diminished-seventh chord appears periodically and acts as a leitmotif, warning of approaching evil. The whole of the Wolf's Glen scene is built round tonalities based on the individual notes of this chord: the music begins in F$\sharp$ minor; at Samiel's appearance it moves to C minor; as Max arrives it modulates to E$\flat$; it returns to C minor and they begin casting the bullets; then, as the bullets are cast, the music alternates between C minor and A minor with copious use of diminished sevenths; at the end, when Caspar and Max fall unconscious, the tonality returns to F♯ minor.

Weber's brilliant orchestration creates dramatic atmospheric effects. In the opening section of the overture horns conjure up a vision of forests and hunting, while low clarinets and timpani create a sense of foreboding. The shrill piccolo is used to give a devilish quality to the end of Caspar's aria, and masterly orchestration plays a significant part in creating the powerful atmosphere of the Wolf's Glen scene, which was regarded as a *locus classicus* of German Romantic imagery and imagination during the 19th century. Perhaps the most important musical contribution to the enduring success of the opera, however, is the vigour of Weber's melodic invention. His handling of both the folksong-like choruses and solos and the weightier arias and ensembles is equally successful.

Euryanthe

Grand heroic-romantic opera in three acts (2h 45m)
Libretto by Helmina von Chezy, after the 13th-century French romance *L'histoire du très-noble et chevalereux prince Gérard, comte de Nevers, et de la très-virtueuse et très chaste princesse Euriant de Savoye, sa mye*
PREMIERES 25 October 1823, Kärntnertortheater, Vienna; UK: 29 June 1833, Covent Garden, London; US: 23 December 1887, Metropolitan, New York
CAST King Louis VI *b*, Adolar *t*, Lysiart *b*, Euryanthe *s*, Eglantine *s*, Rudolf *t*, Bertha *s*; *satb* chorus of ladies, noblemen, knights, hunters, peasants

As a direct result of the success of *Der Freischütz* Weber was invited to compose an opera in the same style for Vienna. He decided, however, to write a very different kind of work. Like Spohr and Schubert, who were each working on through-composed operas (respectively *Jessonda* and *Alfonso und Estrella*) at about the same time, Weber decided to dispense with spoken dialogue in favour of continuous music.

The premiere, conducted by Weber, achieved a *succès d'estime*, but many found the plot confusing and the whole opera too long. Weber himself sanctioned cuts totalling 172 bars, and after his departure from Vienna a further 352 bars were excised. *Euryanthe* was subsequently staged in many theatres, but it has retained only a tenuous place in the repertoire. Attempts to make it more viable through the production of new performing versions have not succeeded.

SYNOPSIS
Act I In King Louis VI's hall Adolar praises the virtue of his absent bride, Euryanthe. Lysiart wagers his lands against Adolar's that he can prove Euryanthe unfaithful. Meanwhile, in Adolar's castle, Eglantine, who is also in love with Adolar and who covertly hates Euryanthe, persuades her to reveal the secret of the ghost of Adolar's sister, Emma, who committed suicide with poison contained in her ring. Lysiart arrives at the castle and Euryanthe welcomes him.

Act II That night, Eglantine, coming out of Emma's tomb after removing the poisoned ring from the corpse, is surprised by Lysiart. They form an alliance. Back in the king's hall, Lysiart produces Emma's ring as proof of Euryanthe's love for him and claims victory in the wager. Adolar's estates are forfeit and he takes Euryanthe away, intending to kill her.

Act III Adolar and Euryanthe are in a mountain gorge. Suddenly a snake appears. Euryanthe tries to protect Adolar. He kills it, but, touched by her offer of self-sacrifice, he cannot bring himself to kill her and abandons her to the elements. She is found by the king and his hunting party; explaining Eglantine's deceit, she easily convinces the king of her innocence. Adolar returns to his castle and confronts Lysiart, who is about to marry Eglantine. The king arrives and clears up the misunderstandings about Euryanthe. Eglantine pours scorn on Lysiart; he stabs her to death and is led away. The opera ends with Euryanthe and Adolar happily united.

Weber's aim in *Euryanthe* to show that he could write opera in a much grander style than *Der Freischütz* succeeded, as far as the music is concerned. However, *Euryanthe* is fatally marred by the weakness of its libretto. Despite this and the dramatic deficiencies of the work as a whole, its influence on later composers, notably Marschner, Schumann, Liszt and Wagner, was considerable.

Oberon, or The Elf King's Oath

Romantic opera in three acts
Libretto by James Robinson Planché, after *Oberon* by Christoph Martin Wieland (1780) and the 13th-century French romance *Huon de Bordeaux*
PREMIERES 12 April 1826, Covent Garden, London; US: 20 September 1826, Park Theater, New York
CAST Oberon *t*, Puck *ms*, Reiza *s*, Sir Huon of Bordeaux *t*, Sherasmin *bar*, Fatima *ms*, 2 Mermaids 2 *ms*; *spoken roles*: Namouna, Haroun al Rachid, Babekan, Abdallah, Roshana, Almanzor; *satb* chorus of fairies, ladies, knights, slaves, mermaids, etc.

Weber was originally asked to write *Oberon* for the London season of 1825, but delays over the libretto led to a year's postponement. Weber quickly realized that he was dealing with a very different libretto from those he was used to, and he wrote to Planché in February 1825, 'The intermixing of so many principal actors who do not sing, the omission of the music in the most important moments – all these things deprive our *Oberon* the title of an Opera, and will make him unfit for all other Theatres in Europe; which is a very bad thing for me, but – *passons là dessus.*'

SYNOPSIS
Act I Oberon and Titania have quarrelled over whether man or woman is the more inconstant in love; they have vowed not to be reunited until they find a couple who are constant. Puck informs Oberon that Charlemagne has condemned Huon of Bordeaux to go to Baghdad, where he must kill the man on the caliph's right hand, then kiss the caliph's daughter and marry her. Oberon decides to use Huon as a means to win reconciliation with Titania. He conjures up a vision of the caliph's daughter, Reiza, and Huon falls instantly in love. Reiza is similarly smitten with Huon. Oberon gives Huon a fairy horn and a magic

goblet. He then dispatches Huon and his squire, Sherasmin, to Baghdad.

Act II After a number of adventures, they manage, through the power of the horn, to carry off Reiza and her maid, Fatima, with whom Sherasmin has fallen in love; they escape by ship. Later, all except Huon are carried off to Tunis by pirates.

Act III With the help of Oberon and his horn, Huon succeeds in rescuing his companions. Oberon, reunited with Titania, transports the lovers to Charlemagne's palace where the opera ends in general rejoicing.

Despite the circumstances of its composition, *Oberon* contains some of Weber's most delightful music (best known is Reiza's recitative and aria 'Ocean! thou mighty monster'). This has ensured it a permanent, if peripheral, place in the repertoire, even though its essentially undramatic structure is far from satisfactory. British audiences of the day were more anxious for spectacular stage effects (e.g. Oberon conjures up 'the interior of a Persian kiosk' to tempt Huon) and plentiful ballad-like songs than for the artistically unified concept that concerned Weber. To accommodate John Braham, the original Huon, the aria 'From boyhood trained' was replaced with 'Ah, 'tis a glorious sight to see', and an additional aria, 'Ruler of his awful hour', was inserted. Such practicalities meant that use of the unifying musical devices employed in Weber's earlier operas (tonalities, characterization through orchestral colouring, etc.) was impossible. However, Weber unified the opera by employing Oberon's horn call, which opens the overture, as a motif at various points in the work. Had he lived, he would certainly have revised *Oberon*, adding recitatives, to make it suitable for the German stage.

In 1860, Planché produced a revised version in Italian, which had recitatives by Weber's pupil Julius Benedict and incorporated some music from *Euryanthe*. There have been many other arrangements, including one with recitative by Franz Wüllner, and one by Gustav Brecher with sections of instrumental music by Gustav Mahler (based on material from the opera) to accompany the dialogue.

Other operas: *Die Macht der Liebe und des Weins*, 1798 (lost); *Das Waldmädchen* (fragments of 2 arias survive), 1800; *Peter Schmoll und seine Nachbarn*, 1803; *Rübezahl, oder Der Beherrscher der Geister* (3 numbers survive, 1805); *Silvana*, 1810; *Abu Hassan*, 1811; *Die drei Pintos*, (inc., 1824; completed by Gustav Mahler), 1888

C. A. B.

KURT WEILL
Kurt Julian Weill; *b* 2 March 1900, Dessau, Germany; *d* 3 April 1950, New York

Weill was the third child of the chief cantor at the Dessau synagogue. He received his musical education first from the conductor Albert Bing (a pupil of Hans Pfitzner) in Dessau and in 1918 from Humperdinck at the Berlin Hochschule für Musik. After a year's practical work at the opera house in his home town (where Hans Knappertsbusch was the music director) and as staff conductor at the Lüdenscheid opera in Westphalia, he returned to Berlin in 1920 to join Busoni's composition masterclass.

By the time he started to collaborate with Bertolt Brecht in 1927, Weill was established as one of the leading composers in Weimar Germany, with four successful stage works under his belt; it was indeed Weill who gave the unknown writer his first chance of fame with the sensational premiere of the *Mahagonny Songspiel* at Baden-Baden. Brecht continued to ride on Weill's coat-tails with *Die Dreigroschenoper* (1928), *Aufstieg und Fall der Stadt Mahagonny* (1930), *Happy End* (1929) and *Der Jasager* (1930), after which they drifted apart; as Lotte Lenya, whom the composer had married in 1926, was to put it later, her husband was not interested in setting the Communist Manifesto to music, and Weill resumed collaboration with the Expressionist playwright Georg Kaiser in *Der Silbersee* (February 1933). This was simultaneously premiered in three cities (which gives some idea of the composer's status), but was to be the last Weill premiere in Germany. Nazi thugs disrupted early performances, and nine days after the first night the Reichstag fire gave them the opportunity to assume power. Weill fled precipitately from Berlin to Paris in March, with few belongings and none of his music.

The Nazis seem to have feared him more than any other composer, and for years went to inordinate lengths through diplomatic channels worldwide to have his scores, orchestral parts and records destroyed. Weill himself believed that all his German works save for *Dreigroschenoper* were irretrievably lost, and reused some of the music in later pieces.

Weill spent 18 months in Paris, which saw a brief reunion with Brecht for *Die sieben Todsünden* and the incidental music for Jacques Deval's play *Marie Galante* (which included one of his greatest songs, 'J'attends un navire', later used as a signal by the French resistance), and went to the US in 1935 to complete the score for the Franz Werfel–Max Reinhardt pageant of Jewish history *Der Weg der Verheissung*, eventually staged as *The Eternal Road* (New York, 1937). He remained in the US for the rest of his life, composing for Broadway and Hollywood, and died from a heart condition in 1950 while embarking on a musical version of *Huckleberry Finn*.

Weill is beyond any doubt one of the most important composers for the theatre – a more accurate designation than 'opera composer' – of the 20th century. His precise place in the history of Western music in general and opera in particular is still impossible to assess. The cultural upheaval caused by the short-lived but still reverberating Nazi tyranny in the very heartland of European music; a generally left-wing political and critical stance, allied to knee-jerk anti-American sentiment in post-war Europe that bolstered accusations of a progressive composer 'selling out' to Broadway commercialism (his US works are loathed in Germany); Weill's tragically premature death aged only 50: all contribute to clouding a highly complex issue.

At the time, the end of the First World War seemed like a watershed, though today we may see it as only the first act of a European drama that is still being played out. But it afforded an opportunity for composers to grapple with the post-Wagnerian legacy. Wagner had pushed tonality as far as it could go: what next? Strauss largely wrote neo-Wagnerian operas; Schoenberg devised a new musical language, dodecaphony; Stravinsky and Busoni advanced – or retreated – into neo-classicism; Schreker, Zemlinsky and others nudged Wagnerianism over the edge into no-holds-barred Expressionism. Most composers embraced without question an aesthetic of linear progress: music could only get more complicated, more demanding, more remote from everyday audiences, more dependent on a state-subsidized system of presentation. The artificial separation of high art and popular art is still a very real problem, and it seems to be only in music that this linear progress has been accepted virtually without question: few would regard the path in painting from, say, Giotto to Raphael, as one of smooth, uninterrupted progress.

Though Weill's early works are conventionally Expressionist, there is a vitally important neo-classical element in *Dreigroschenoper* and *Mahagonny*. The latter was rejected by Otto Klemperer – later a leading exponent of the 'sell-out' school of Weill criticism – at the Kroll Oper, and Weill took it instead to Berlin's equivalent of Broadway, the Kurfürstendamm, for a commercial run. *Dreigroschenoper* and *Happy End* were commercial ventures, and, although there were still projects for subsidized theatres (*Die Bürgschaft* and *Der Silbersee*), Weill had taken the basic decision to write for a mass audience long before he went to America. In Germany he transformed into high art familiar song and dance idioms of the time and place, and the mass popularity of *Dreigroschenoper* cannot be overstressed. In America he naturally turned to the popular and folk idioms of his new homeland – to have done otherwise would have been senseless – and it is this that has stuck in sensitive European throats. But, as Weill wrote in 1949, 'The American popular song, growing out of American folk music, is the basis of the American musical theatre, just as the Italian song was the basis of Italian opera.'

The notion that a radical, left-wing composer 'sold out' to naked commerce does not bear serious examination. The people Weill collaborated with in the US were for the main part committed radicals of the kind who got into serious trouble in the McCarthy era, and *Johnny Johnson*, *Knickerbocker Holiday*, *Street Scene*, *Love Life* and *Lost in the Stars* are works brimming over with political and social concern. The collaboration with Brecht cannot be taken as evidence that Weill was in any sense a conventional left-winger: the break coincided with the playwright's conversion to orthodox communism. Weill, on the evidence in particular of his US output as well as his later German works, could best be described as a militant humanist, a man set on using popular theatre to combat intolerance, prejudice, deprivation and injustice wherever they were to be found.

His compositional aesthetic is neatly summed up in an interview he gave to the *New York Sun* in 1940. 'I have never acknowledged the difference between "serious" music and "light" music. There is only good music and bad music,' he said, and continued

with a direct challenge to critical orthodoxy: 'Schoenberg has said he is writing for a time 50 years after his death. But the great classical composers wrote for their contemporary audiences. They wanted those who heard their music to understand it, and they did. For myself, I write for today. I don't give a damn about writing for posterity.'

Weill was above all a great writer of tunes: The Ballad of Mack the Knife has become an authentic 20th-century folksong, and he composed many others worthy of that status. He was a tirelessly inventive orchestrator, varying the accompaniments to each verse of his songs and, almost uniquely on Broadway, insisted on scoring every bar of his works and writing his own dance sequences. Yet his melodic genius should not be taken to imply the smallest degree of facileness: David Drew's analysis of *Dreigroschenoper* in the Cambridge Opera Handbook suggests a personal, highly complex serialist technique.

An of-necessity interim report must credit Weill with at least four masterpieces: *Dreigroschenoper*, *Mahagonny*, and *Die sieben Todsünden* have never lost their hold on the repertoire, and after regular revival *Street Scene* has now been accepted as one of the great American operas, a work to set beside *Porgy and Bess* and one Weill considered to be his first complete technical success. A pleasing new critical stance holds that it was with *Street Scene* that he reached full maturity as a composer for the theatre.

When the rest of his output is investigated now that prejudice against his later works is fading, other masterpieces may emerge. As it is, his importance in having shown that popular theatre can – or rather must – be serious is now generally accepted, and his influence on later Broadway composers, from Bernstein to Sondheim, is incalculable.

Die Dreigroschenoper
The Threepenny Opera
Play with music in three acts (music: 1h 15m; full-length play)
Libretto and play text by Bertolt Brecht, based on the translation by Elisabeth Hauptmann of *The Beggar's Opera* by John Gay (1728), with interpolated ballads by François Villon and Rudyard Kipling
PREMIERES 31 August 1928, Theater am Schiffbauerdamm, Berlin; US: 13 April 1933, Empire Theater, New York; UK: 9 February 1956, Royal Court Theatre, London
CAST Jonathan Jeremiah Peachum *bar*, Mrs Peachum *ms*, Polly Peachum *s*, Macheath *t*, Tiger Brown/Streetsinger *bar*, Lucy *s*, Jenny Diver *s*, Macheath's gang; *satb* chorus of whores, beggars and police

Weill composed the score of *Die Dreigroschenoper* in the spring and summer of 1928 for the impresario J. E. Aufricht, who had unexpectedly come into money and taken a lease of the Theater am Schiffbauerdamm. Final rehearsals were chaotic – the piece did not find its final form until well after the premiere – and the theatre was not full on the first night. Those involved were half expecting a flop. But, despite mixed notices, word of mouth ensured a hit of near-unprecedented proportions (the triumph of *The Merry Widow* a quarter of a century earlier provides a nicely ironic parallel) and the piece was soon staged throughout Europe (save for Britain) and in the US. Only the advent of the Nazis in 1933 interrupted its near continuous run in Berlin and countless productions all over Germany.

SYNOPSIS

Act I In a prologue set in London's Soho, the Street-singer sings The Ballad of Mack the Knife, admiringly cataloguing the petty criminal's crimes. Mr and Mrs Peachum briefly interrupt the businesslike organiza-tion of the band of beggars and thieves they control to note the absence of their daughter Polly. It emerges that she has eloped with Mack, a highly unsuitable son-in-law. In the second scene Polly and Mack cele-brate their wedding in a stable surrounded by stolen goods and the gang. Polly entertains the company with a song she recently heard a bedraggled hotel chambermaid singing (Pirate Jenny). Among the guests is the police chief Tiger Brown, Mack's old schoolfriend. They reminisce over happy days in the Indian Army (Cannon Song). Left alone, the newly-weds sing a love duet of sickly sentimentality. Back with her parents, Polly seeks to explain her new liaison via the Barbara Song, but they are determined to force Brown to arrest Mack. In the First Threepenny Finale, the three comment on the intractability of human existence.

Act II In the stable, Mack and Polly sing a duet of farewell: he has 'business' to attend to. Mean-while, Mrs Peachum bribes the whore Jenny to betray Mack to the police (Song of Sexual Dependency), which Jenny duly does in a brothel in Turnbridge, having first joined with him in the Tango Ballad, in which they remember affectionately the good old days when he was her pimp. In the Old Bailey, Mack sings the Ballad of the Good Life (based on Villon). Brown's daughter Lucy, feigning pregnancy, reproaches Mack and sings a furious Jealousy Duet with Polly, but nevertheless helps her seducer to escape. The Second Threepenny Finale, sung by the entire company, re-turns to the problems of human existence: man sur-vives only by suppressing his humanity and exploiting his fellow man.

Act III Peachum blackmails Brown: if Mack is not rearrested, his army of beggars will disrupt the forthcoming coronation. Mack is found with another whore and returned to the Old Bailey. Polly and his gang are unable, or unwilling, to come up with the necessary bribe to prevent his hanging. He takes a bitter farewell of the world. But Peachum announces that the company has thought up a different ending (Third Threepenny Finale): the king's messenger (Brown) brings news that in honour of the coronation the queen grants Mack a reprieve, a peerage, a grace-and-favour castle and a pension. The company sings a mock-Bach chorale of ironic relief: 'Don't prosecute crime: it will die out of its own accord.'

The action was never intended to be in any way naturalistic: décor and acting style were non-represen-tational, and the plot came to a halt for the musical numbers, which were differently lit. This was 'epic theatre' after the manner of the day and, in Weill's words, 'the most consistent reaction to Wagner . . .

the complete destruction of the concept of music drama'. *The Beggar's Opera* satirized the 18th-century ruling classes by putting them in a low-life setting (Hogarth's painting shows the original cast still very grandly dressed); *The Threepenny Opera*'s target is the solid bourgeoisie of post-war Europe. It has become customary to play both works as low-life extravagan-zas, which weakens their impact: the characters should be instantly, inescapably recognizable as, and to, the audience.

Weill wrote the music not for opera singers but for artists from the fields of cabaret, musical comedy and (in the case of Macheath) operetta. The dart of his satire is poisoned by the beauty and catchiness of the tunes. As you hum or listen to them, the cheerful, subversive obscenity of the words inevitably sinks in, nowhere more devastatingly than in the Tango Ballad, the Song of Sexual Dependency (which the first Mrs Peachum refused to sing), or – more point-fully – the finales. The songs nevertheless need to be sung properly, not snarled or shouted as has become the custom in low-life productions: early recordings (hoarded and secretly played by liberal Germans under Nazi rule) reveal a sweetness and innocence of approach that makes their appeal all the more insinuating.

Brecht revised both the libretto and the lyrics after the premiere, bringing them into line with his own growing Marxist convictions and by 1931 establishing the text as usually played today. The original is shorter, funnier, more anarchic and less didactic, but is unlikely to be revived before Brecht's copyright runs out.

The New York revival of 1954, which ran for 2,611 performances in Marc Blitzstein's translation, marked a significant stage in the revival of interest in Weill's work – revivals and recordings of his other European scores followed – and confirmed *Dreigroschenoper* as one of the most important (and in the right circum-stances enjoyable) pieces of music theatre composed in the 20th century.

Happy End

Comedy with music in three acts (music: 40m; full-length play)
Book by 'Dorothy Lane' (Elisabeth Hauptmann); lyrics by Bertolt Brecht
PREMIERES 2 September 1929, Theater am Schiffbauerdamm, Berlin; UK: 14 August 1964, Traverse Theatre, Edinburgh; US: 6 April 1972, Yale Repertory Theater, New Haven, Connecticut
CAST Lilian Holliday s, Bill Cracker t or bar, Lady in Grey s, Dr Nakamura bar, Hannibal Jackson t, Sam Wurlitzer bar, spoken roles

To cash in on the unprecedented success of *Die Drei-groschenoper*, the impresario Aufricht solicited an-other play with music from Weill and Brecht. Brecht subcontracted the book to Elisabeth Hauptmann, one of his many long-suffering mistresses and collabora-tors (the true extent of her contribution to *Dreigroschen-oper* is only now being established). During the run-up to the premiere of *Happy End* she attempted suicide when Brecht suddenly married Helene Weigel; in the circumstances it is hardly surprising that the resulting text is less than coherent. Brecht wrote some new song texts and cannibalized others.

The cast, which included Carola Neher, Oskar Homolka, Helene Weigel, Peter Lorre and Kurt Gerron, was kept waiting until the last minute for the text of Act III, and one reason for this became obvious at the premiere: after two well-received acts, Weigel apparently stepped out of character to harangue the audience with socialist propaganda in the third, and the piece ended with an agitprop ensemble entitled 'Hosannah Rockefeller'. The evening was a fiasco, and there were only two further performances.

The action, loosely inspired by Shaw's *Major Barbara* and strikingly similar to Damon Runyon's *Guys and Dolls*, tells of a Salvation Army lass (Lilian) who falls for a criminal (Cracker); eventually Salvationists and criminals – in some versions the gang leader, the Lady in Grey, and the Salvationist general turn out to be the same – join forces in capitalist enterprise. The play is entertaining, if somewhat inconsequential; the 13 musical numbers, though only loosely connected to it, mark the apogee of Weill's Berlin song style and a significant musical advance on *Dreigroschenoper*. The melodies are longer-breathed and the instrumentation is more inventive and varied – each song verse is differently accompanied. The agitprop numbers are undeniably stirring, but it is the nostalgically sentimental songs that have entered the repertoire: the Bilbao Song, the Sailors' Tango and above all 'Surabaya Johnny'. The play has never enjoyed a commercial success, but a *Happy End Songspiel* devised by the Weill authority David Drew in 1975 has enjoyed wide currency.

Aufstieg und Fall der Stadt Mahagonny

Rise and Fall of the City of Mahagonny
Opera in three acts (2h 15m)
Libretto by Bertolt Brecht
PREMIERES 9 March 1930, Neues Theater, Leipzig; US: 23 February 1952, Town Hall, New York; UK: 16 January 1963, Sadler's Wells, London
CAST Leocadia Begbick *ms*, Fatty the Bookkeeper *t*, Trinity Moses *bar*, Jenny Smith *s*, Jim Mahoney *t*, Jakob Schmidt *t*, Bankroll Bill *bar*, Alaska Wolf Joe *b*, Tobby Higgins *t*; *satb* chorus of people of Mahagonny

The full-length *Mahagonny* opera, conceived early in 1927, received a preview in the form of the so-called *Mahagonny Songspiel*, a music-theatre setting of a group of loosely linked poems from Brecht's *Hauspostille* about an imaginary US city. God consigns its licentious citizens to hell, but they truculently reply that they are there already. The *Songspiel* fulfilled a commission to Weill from the Baden-Baden Deutsche Kammermusik festival, and the premiere there on 17 July 1927 was an enormous *succès de scandale* – an audience expecting respectable avant-garde experiment was regaled with raucous music-hall songs set in a boxing ring.

SYNOPSIS

Act I A desert in America. A battered truck drives on to the stage and breaks down. Its passengers are Begbick, Fatty and Trinity Moses, fugitives from justice on charges of white-slaving and fraud. Noting that it is easier to extract gold from men than from the dried-up riverbed they are stranded on, Begbick decides to found Mahagonny, a 'city of nets' given over to pleasure since life is so miserable everywhere else. Jenny and her friends – the first 'sharks' – enter: 'Oh show us the way to the next whisky bar' (Alabama Song). Fatty and Moses recruit emigrants from the industrial cities of the world, and Jimmy Mahoney and his friends Jake, Bill and Joe, four 'simple lumberjacks from Alaska', arrive to a sprightly parody of the Bridesmaids' Chorus from *Der Freischütz*. They are offered their choice of girls, and Jimmy buys Jenny Smith for 30 dollars. She asks him whether or not he would like her to wear knickers. He answers in the negative. Mahagonny suffers a recession, and Jimmy is only just dissuaded from leaving by his friends. In the saloon he rails (to a parody of 'The Maiden's Prayer') against too much peace and quiet. An approaching typhoon is the answer to his prayer. As they await its arrival, Jimmy protests that the city is hemmed in by too many regulations: society should be founded on total permissiveness, on *laissez-faire* and each man for himself – 'as you make your bed, so you lie on it' ('Wie man sich bettet so liegt man').

Act II Mahagonny is miraculously spared and its citizens follow Jimmy's precepts in four tableaux: gluttony, in which Jake eats himself to death; lechery, in which Begbick presides over a brothel; fighting, in which Jimmy puts all his money on Joe in a boxing match with Trinity Moses (Joe is killed); and drinking, in which Jimmy buys rounds of drinks for which he cannot pay. When Begbick demands payment, Jenny refuses his appeal for a loan and throws 'Wie man sich bettet' back at him. Imprisoned, he dreads the dawn of a new day.

Act III In the courts, Tobby Higgins is cleared of murder after handing money over to the bench. Jimmy asks Bill for a loan so that his case may similarly be heard fairly; Bill replies that he is fond of him, but money is something else. So Jimmy has no defence against accusations of subversion, the violation of Jenny, the death of Joe for financial gain and – the most serious crime of all in Mahagonny – inability to pay, for which he is sentenced to death. The remaining principals dream of another city, Benares, only to hear that it has been destroyed by an earthquake. Jimmy bids farewell to Jenny and exhorts the citizens to continue living life to the full: there is no afterlife, and he has no regrets. As he is strapped into the electric chair, they enact God's visit to Mahagonny. Following his execution, there are mass demonstrations and counter-demonstrations against the rising cost of living, while the city burns. Jimmy's relics are paraded, but there is no way of helping a dead man.

Following the Leipzig premiere and stagings in other German cities, *Mahagonny* was turned down by Klemperer at the Berlin Kroll Oper; Weill responded by organizing a commercial run on the Kurfürstendamm in December 1931, conducted by Zemlinsky. Revisions were made, and rehearsals saw the not-quite-final break with Brecht, who resented the dominance of the music and accused the composer of writing 'phoney Richard Strauss'. After the war, Brecht supervised a drastically cut, ideologically more acceptable version for performance in East Germany. Weill himself allowed substantial cuts for a Vienna production in 1932, and had performances not been interrupted by the Nazi regime would surely have worked to tighten the action more systematically and resolve the conflict between the need for operatically trained voices and decidedly unoperatic material.

Nevertheless, *Mahagonny* as it stands remains one of the great 20th-century operas, a beguiling mixture of lively neo-classical formulae and music-hall songs, melodically prodigiously rich. The expressionistically grotesque trial scene builds up unstoppable dramatic momentum, and the finale with its marches and counter-marches, in which all the hit tunes are brought back, has a pole-axing effect. This is in a way a 20th-century equivalent to *Die Zauberflöte*, a journey not from darkness to light, but from darkness to even greater darkness, one in which the eternal truths proposed are distinctly less comfortable than Mozart's and Schikaneder's. No easy answers are given (Brecht had not yet quite embraced Marxist fundamentalism), which makes the work all the more disturbing. At the final curtain the cast is, as it were, addressing the audience with the title of Weill's lost musical of 1927, 'Na und?' ('And so?'). The fact that that question remains unanswered 60 years later suggests that *Mahagonny* has by no means had its day.

Der Silbersee – Ein Wintermärchen

The Silver Lake – A Winter's Tale
Play with music in three acts (music: 1h 15m; full-length play)
Libretto and play text by Georg Kaiser (1932)
PREMIERES 18 February 1933, simultaneously in three cities: Altes Theater, Leipzig; Stadttheater, Magdeburg; and Stadttheater, Erfurt; US: 20 March 1980, New York City Opera (radically revised version by Hugh Wheeler (play and lyrics) and Lys Simonette (musical arrangement)); UK: 17 June 1982, Manchester University Theatre (amateur); 30 March 1987, Bloomsbury Theatre, London
CAST Fennimore *s*, Frau von Luber *ms*, 2 Shopgirls 2 *s*, Severin *t*, Lottery Agent *t*, Olim *bar*, Baron Laur *bar*; *spoken roles*; *satb* chorus

For his last theatre composition before being forced into exile, Weill resumed collaboration with Europe's leading Expressionist playwright Georg Kaiser, who had written the libretto for Weill's *Der Protagonist* (1926). The result was, in the words of the original Leipzig director Detlef Sierck (reborn as the Hollywood movie director Douglas Sirk), 'ten times tougher than any Brecht play'. By the time of the successful triple premiere Hitler was already chancellor, and Nazi thugs disrupted early performances. The Reichstag fire and suspension of civil liberties followed, and within a month Weill had fled to Paris.

SYNOPSIS
The allegorical action is clearly based on contemporary social and political circumstances.

Act I Severin and his comrades, unemployed and starving on the shores of the Silver Lake, raid a grocery store; while the comrades take bread, Severin steals a pineapple and is shot and wounded by the policeman Olim. Olim's liberal conscience (offstage voices) pricks him: if he were rich, he would devote his life to caring for the wounded looter. A lottery agent answers his prayer to a smoochy tango. Confined to a wheelchair, Severin agrees to move into the castle that his unknown benefactor has bought.

Act II Olim's housekeeper Frau von Luber and her seedy accomplice Baron Laur employ the former's niece Fennimore as a companion, and plot to reveal Olim's true identity to the vengeful Severin. But, thanks to Fennimore, the men are reconciled.

Act III Cheated out of his property by his bourgeois employees, Olim leads Severin to joint death in the Silver Lake, but the waters miraculously freeze over and bear them to a new life on the other side.

A hauntingly atmospheric and suggestive work, *Der Silbersee* is arguably the masterpiece of Weill's German period. Yet it is fraught with performance problems, composed as it was for the sort of municipal theatrical ensemble of singers and actors that scarcely exists any more (it was conceived for the Deutsches Theater in Berlin, but political pressures necessitated provincial premieres). Kaiser's play demands virtuoso acting; the role of Severin needs a robust operatic tenor with dramatic ability to match, and the genre of play-with-music has anyway not prospered. Yet this is no excuse for the New York City Opera version, musically a well-meaning travesty of Weill's intentions, dramaturgically a betrayal of Kaiser (Hugh Wheeler, on adapting the play, professed himself 'bored with that 1930-ish, pissy-assed socialism').

In contrast to the Brecht collaborations, the musical numbers are firmly integrated into the text rather than alienatory devices, save for the Ballad of Caesar's Death, a rousing march song sung by the mousy Fennimore and, with its message that those who live by the sword shall perish by it, aimed directly at Hitler. The despair of the starving workers, the prissiness of the shop assistants, the sleaze of the lottery agent, the cynical opportunism of the bourgeois intriguers, all are caught in music of spellbinding dramatic power.

Perhaps the main problem is the optimistic ending, in characteristically bittersweet waltz tempo: given the political situation of the time, the irony is hard to stomach – so much so that at the work's UK premiere it was set (not altogether convincingly) in the gas chamber of a concentration camp, just lest the audience miss the irony. Despite all its problems, *Der Silbersee*'s time will come.

Die sieben Todsünden

The Seven Deadly Sins
Ballet chanté in one act (35m)
Scenario by Edward James and Boris Kochno; choreography by George Balanchine; libretto by Bertolt Brecht
PREMIERES 7 June 1933, Théâtre des Champs-Élysées, Paris; UK: 28 June 1933, Savoy Theatre, London (as *Anna-Anna*); US: 4 December 1958, City Center, New York
CAST Anna I *s*, Anna II *dancer*, The Family 2 *t*, *bar*, *b*

Within a month of arriving in Paris in 1933 Weill had been commissioned to compose a ballet by the English philanthropist Edward James, who was funding the first season of Balanchine's and Kochno's dance company Les Ballets 1933, which had just broken away from Diaghilev's Ballets Russes. James insisted on a role for his estranged wife, the dancer Tilly Losch, in the hope that it would lead to a reconciliation (it didn't – they divorced spectacularly the following year), and when the basic idea of dividing a split personality between a dancer and a singer, between flesh and spirit, was established, James in turn suggested Lotte Lenya for the singing role, although Weill and Lenya were at the time in the middle of their own divorce proceedings (they remarried in the US in 1937). Lenya's lover at the time, Otto von Pasetti, was given one of the tenor roles in the family.

When Cocteau declined to write the libretto, James urged Brecht on a none-too-willing Weill: they had fallen out over the Kurfürstendamm *Mahagonny* 18 months earlier. Brecht was at first unenthusiastic about the scenario, but managed to feed enough social criticism into it to salve his conscience. When the libretto was included in his collected works after the war, he expanded the title to *Die sieben Todsünden der Kleinbürger* ('of the Petty-Bourgeois'), lest anyone miss the point.

SYNOPSIS
In the prologue the two Annas, sisters from Louisiana, introduce themselves. Anna I, the singer, is the practical, down-to-earth one; her dancing sister, Anna II, she warns us, is a bit dizzy ('etwas verrückt'). 'But we're really one person, not two, with one past and one future, one heart and one savings bank account.' Their mission is to travel to seven cities in America to earn enough money for their family to build a little house back in Louisiana, and the voices of the family quartet (the mother sung by the bass) are throughout heard singing biblical bromides warning them not to fall into sin. The basic joke is that the instinctive dancer Anna is tempted to give in to sin at each turn, but is prevented by the singer Anna: sin compromises their earning power. Thus, Anna II is too proud to take her clothes off in a striptease cabaret ('Pride is only for rich people,' warns Anna I); too wrathful over cruelty to an animal when working as a movie extra, and risking dismissal; too prone to gluttony when agents want only slim dancers; too much given to lust (a toy-boy), which upsets her sugar-daddy (named 'Edward', an obvious in-joke); and so on. Bourgeois morality is wittily turned on its head. In the epilogue the sisters return to the little house in Louisiana, the practical Anna I triumphant, Anna II's human spirit utterly crushed.

Weill here achieved a perfect synthesis of popular form and weightiness of content. The tunes beguile, the dance rhythms sparkle, yet the score is rigorously organized along traditional symphonic lines. The sardonic musical wit balances that in the text, but the composer triumphs decisively over the detached librettist in the compassion he shows for human, instinctive, near-wordless Anna II. The final bars are heart-rending.

The premiere, attended by the Parisian *beau monde*, was an artistic triumph, but the season as a whole was a financial disaster. Among those who attended the first run was Lincoln Kirstein, who recognized Balanchine's genius and was to lure the choreographer to the US and found the New York City Ballet for him. The company gave the US premiere (and first postwar performance) of Weill's ballet in 1958, with Lenya. It has been given numerous productions since. When Lenya was engaged for the premiere, Weill sanctioned downward transpositions of parts of the score to accommodate her limited resources. It has been recorded mostly in that form.

Johnny Johnson
Musical play in three acts (music: 1h; full-length play)
Libretto by Paul Green
PREMIERES   19 November 1936, 44th Street Theater, New York; UK: 6 August 1986, Almeida Theatre, London

Weill's first music-theatre work written wholly in the USA is apple-pie American in subject matter but distinctly German in musical outline. It gives the lie to the 'sell-out to Broadway' canard, being written near-collectively at the left-wing Group Theatre's summer camp to a text by the pacifist southern writer Paul Green. The cast at the Broadway premiere, directed by Lee Strasberg, included Elia Kazan, Lee J. Cobb and John Garfield (the last-named was a victim of the McCarthy purges).

The action opens in 1917. A peace rally is interrupted by the announcement of President Wilson's declaration of war (the march 'Peace, peace, peace' is repeated note for note to the words 'War, war, war', a distinctly worrying example of music's non-specific power). Johnny joins up, converses with the Statue of Liberty as he sails for Europe, is horrified by what he witnesses in the trenches, befriends a German sniper, and out of naïve, very American idealism seeks to promote peace. He releases laughing gas at a High Command conference and, disguised as a general, declares an armistice. He is arrested and shipped home to an asylum for the criminally insane, where he sets up a League of Nations for the inmates. After ten years, lobotomized, he is deemed safe to be released, and becomes an itinerant toy-seller, refusing to stock military wares.

Many of the musical numbers are acid parodies, some recycled from earlier scores: the recruiting officer's tango, the sour romantic number for Johnny's perfidious girlfriend Minny-Belle, a Wild West pastiche and a satirical Psychiatry Song (one verse accompanied by celesta and trombone). But the dialogue for Johnny and the Statue of Liberty, the Lament of the Cannons over the sleeping GIs doomed to die the next day, and the prayers of the German and American chaplains (words identical, languages different) have great theatrical power. Johnny's Song, heard in full only as the finale, is one of Weill's great tunes. While it is curious that Weill, who knew better than anyone the political horror engulfing Europe, should have subscribed to an idealist pacifist tract, this cannot diminish *Johnny Johnson*'s stark theatrical power. It demands revival.

Street Scene

'An American Opera' in two acts (2h 30m)
Book by Elmer Rice, based on his own play (1929); lyrics
by Langston Hughes
PREMIERES 9 January 1947, Adelphi Theater, New York;
UK: 6 June 1983, Royal Academy of Music, London
(semi-staged and much cut); 26 April 1987, Palace Theatre,
London
CAST Anna Maurrant s, Rose Maurrant s, Mrs Jones ms,
Mrs Fiorentino s, Mrs Olsen c, Sam Kaplan t, Frank
Maurrant b, Harry Easter bar, Mae Jones singer-dancer,
Dick McGann singer-dancer, Willy Maurrant boy s, Henry
Davis bar, Mr Buchanan t, Mr Fiorentino t, Jennie
Hildebrand ms, Mrs Hildebrand ms, Mr Jones bar,
Abraham Kaplan t, 2 Nursemaids s, ms, Steve Sankey, Shirley
Kaplan spoken roles, 5 other spoken roles; satb chorus of
neighbours

Weill had known the playwright Elmer Rice since his
earliest days in America – they met during rehearsals
of *Johnny Johnson* in 1936, and he wrote incidental
music for Rice's play *Two on an Island* in 1939 – and
the possibility of turning Rice's social-realist study of
life in a slum tenement block into an opera had been
at the back of his mind since seeing a performance of
Street Scene in Europe before being driven into exile.
'It seemed like a great challenge to me', he wrote
later, 'to find the inherent poetry in these people and
to blend my music with the stark realism of the play.'

Other composers had seen operatic possibilities in
Street Scene, but Rice was fiercely protective of his
material; he turned down Deems Taylor's projected
setting for the Met because it strayed too far from the
original. Weill secured the playwright's agreement in
1945, and the result is remarkably faithful; the composer from the land of *Fidelio* and *Freischütz* saw no
problem with long passages of spoken dialogue in
serious music drama, and his use of Hollywood rather
than traditional German-style melodrama helped bind
music and speech into an indissoluble whole. 'Not
until *Street Scene* did I achieve a real blending of
drama and music,' wrote Weill at the time of the
premiere.

The black poet Langston Hughes was engaged to
supply the lyrics, and the collaboration was close if
not always easy. Hughes took Weill to Harlem to
gather material for the Janitor's Song, and together
they roamed New York listening to vendors' cries and
children's street games. After a less than successful
try-out in Philadelphia, *Street Scene* ran in New York
for 148 performances (not bad for an opera – Gershwin's *Porgy and Bess* managed only 126). The leading
roles were taken by trained opera singers: Polyna
Stoska of the City Opera as Anna, Norman Cordon
of the Met as Frank, Anne Jeffreys as Rose, and
Brian Sullivan, a future Lohengrin, as Sam.

SYNOPSIS

Act I The sidewalk outside a tenement block in New
York City; early evening in June (the action is contained within 24 hours). The inhabitants of the block,
half-stifled by the humidity ('Ain't it awful, the heat'),
are introduced: the black janitor, Henry Davis ('I got
a marble and a star'); the tenement bitch, Mrs Jones,
who leads the gossip about Anna Maurrant's affair

with the milk collector, Mr Sankey; Sam Kaplan, a
shy, bookish boy in calf love with the Maurrant
daughter, Rose; Sam's father Abraham, an elderly
socialist firebrand, and his sister Shirley, a teacher;
Mr Buchanan, whose wife is about to give birth for
the first time; finally the Maurrants, Frank, an inarticulate, reactionary theatre electrician, and his wife Anna,
who expresses her disillusion in the extended aria
'Somehow I never could believe' – she contrasts her
romantic girlhood dreams with the bitter reality of
life. The solace of her affair with Mr Sankey is known
to all except her husband, who nevertheless starts to
suspect something during the course of Act I. Mr
Fiorentino – the block is authentically multiracial –
leads the Ice Cream Sextet, likening a cone to the
torch held by the Statue of Liberty glimpsed by all
European immigrants as they sail into New York.
Jennie Hildebrand returns from her graduation
ceremony to general rejoicing ('Wrapped in a ribbon');
the cheerful optimism of the concerted number is
tempered by the knowledge that the Hildebrand
family, deserted by the father, is to be evicted for non-
payment of rent the following day. Maurrant leaves
for an evening's drinking; gossip resumes; Sam attacks
the gossipers before singing of his misery in 'Lonely
house'. Rose Maurrant enters with Harry Easter, a
married man from her office with plans to set her up
as his mistress. He tempts her with the sleazy
'Wouldn't you like to be on Broadway?'; she counters
with 'What use would the moon be?'; like her mother
before her, she nurtures romantic ideals. Easter prudently withdraws when Maurrant returns drunk from
the bar. Buchanan's wife goes into labour; Anna Maurrant runs to help her. Mrs Jones's daughter Mae
enters with an admirer, Dick; their love is anything
but romantic ('Moonfaced, starry eyed', an energetic
jitterbug). In a long duet ('Pain! Nothing but pain')
Rose and Sam sing of the possibility of escape to a
better life, taking as a symbol Walt Whitman's Lilac
Bush ('In the dooryard fronting an old farmhouse')
before bidding each other a tender goodnight.

Act II Early the next morning. Raucous children's
street games carry a whiff of the class war. Buchanan
thanks Anna, who has been up all night with his wife.
Frank leaves for work, after gruffly rejecting Rose's
plea to him to be kinder to her mother (trio: 'You've
got no right'). Anna sends her son Willy off to school.
Rose tells Sam about Harry Easter's importunings,
and they sing of running away together. Easter arrives
to accompany Rose to an office funeral. Anna Maurrant invites Mr Sankey up to her apartment. City
marshals start to put the Hildebrands' belongings out
on the sidewalk. The suspicious Maurrant returns
unexpectedly, and Sam's shouted warning to Anna is
too late: shots ring out. Maurrant escapes, but Rose
returns with an excited crowd to see her dying mother
being carried out to the ambulance (ensemble: 'The
woman who lived up there'). Sankey is dead. The
eviction of the Hildebrands proceeds. Some hours
later, Scene 2 is launched by two nursemaids from
uptown gawking at the scene of the double murder
with their charges ('Sleep, baby dear') – the other side
of the class war. Maurrant is caught, and before being
led away by the police tells Rose he killed her mother

out of jealousy and panic at the thought of losing her. The crowd disperses, leaving Rose and Sam alone. She plans to go away to start a new life, and kindly but firmly refuses to let the lovelorn Sam go with her. The experience of her parents' tragedy makes her unwilling to enter any such commitment. She leaves. Two prospective tenants come to view the Hildebrands' empty apartment. The neighbours drift back to the sidewalk ('Ain't it awful, the heat'). Life goes on.

The technical brilliance of *Street Scene* cannot be overstressed, nor the way Weill sets Rice's intentionally flat prose to music of charm, colour and dramatic power. Some commentators have found Hughes's lyrics banal, but underprivileged, barely literate people tend to express themselves in cliché – they know no other way. To that extent, Hughes's verses are as social-realist as Rice's prose. The action is set among – to borrow a phrase from *Dreigroschenoper* – 'the poorest of the poor', which is rare enough in opera (Gustave Charpentier's *Louise* is one of the very few other operatic studies of working-class life). The tenement represents a trap, and the action examines various ways of coming to terms with or escaping from it. Mae and Dick resort to dope and sex; Anna to adultery; Sam to study and self-improvement; many of the others – including Frank Maurrant – to drink. For a moment Rose seriously considers Harry Easter's offer: anything to escape the grinding, cheerless spiritual and material poverty of the tenement. Otherwise Rose dreams with Sam of Whitman's Lilac Bush, which remains a dream, since *Street Scene*'s creators heroically declined to settle for the Broadway Happy End. The fact that it ends with two young lives irretrievably ruined – this is not a cheerful evening in the theatre – may account for its slow acceptance into the general operatic repertoire; Weill couldn't quite, like Janáček, turn physical disaster into spiritual triumph. On the other hand, Weill's musical treatment of all the inhabitants of the tenement trap (save perhaps for the monstrous Mrs Jones, a villain of Begbick or Frau von Luber proportions) is notable for its compassion, its anger and its total lack of condescension.

In *Mahagonny* Brecht's doggerel line 'Is here no telephone' has been proposed as the catch-phrase of 20th-century alienation; the last words of 'Ain't it awful, the heat', which opens and closes *Street Scene*, are 'Don't know what I'm gonna do' – just as powerful an image of the hopelessness of the 20th-century human condition. Nowhere else is the voice of Weill the militant humanist heard so clearly.

Lost in the Stars

A musical tragedy in two acts (music: 1h; full-length play)
Libretto by Maxwell Anderson, based on the novel *Cry the Beloved Country* by Alan Paton (1948)
PREMIERES 30 October 1949, Music Box Theater, New York; UK: 23 May 1991, Brighton Festival

For his last completed work Weill resumed collaboration with his lifelong friend Maxwell Anderson, who had previously written the libretto for *Knickerbocker*

Holiday (1938). In a faithful adaptation of Paton's popular novel set in South Africa, the Revd Stephen Kumalo goes to Johannesburg in search of his son Absalom, who has fallen into dubious company and become involved in the unpremeditated murder of a young, liberal white man. Absalom is given an unfair trial and executed, and the work ends with the black and white fathers reconciled and united by a vision of a new South Africa.

If good liberal intentions were all, *Lost in the Stars* could count as one of Weill's lasting successes, but time, not to mention South African history, has not been kind. Even at the start it was felt that the picture painted of racial conflict was too rosy, not to say tinged with Uncle Tom-ish condescension, one reason why Paul Robeson declined to sing the leading role. It was taken by Todd Duncan, the creator of Gershwin's Porgy, and the premiere was staged by *Porgy*'s original director, Rouben Mamoulian.

The only serious flaw in the work is the oversentimental, much-recorded title song, which sticks out both musically and dramatically from all that surrounds it with near-embarrassing prominence, and is arguably the only instance in which the composer bowed to commercial pressures. The rest of the music, scored with the utmost ingenuity for a chamber orchestra of twelve (Virgil Thomson wrote that instrumentally this was the composer's masterpiece), is top-drawer Weill, especially the elaborate choruses 'Fear', 'Murder in Parkwold', 'Cry the Beloved Country' and 'Train to Johannesburg' (another, the cynical and rather essential 'Gold', was cut before the premiere but has since been restored). The musical underpinning of the dialogue is as faultlessly achieved as in *Street Scene*.

The time for *Lost in the Stars*, like that for *Silbersee*, may yet come, but so far revivals have been few and unmarked by success, for reasons that have little to do with the quality of the music.

Other operatic works: *Der Protagonist*, 1926; *Royal Palace*, 1927; *Na und?* (lost, 1927); *Der Zar läßt Sich photographieren*, 1928; *Der Jasager*, 1930; *Die Bürgschaft*, 1932; *Der Kuhhandel*, (1934); *The Eternal Road*, 1937; *Knickerbocker Holiday*, 1938; *Davy Crockett* (inc., 1938); *Ulysses Africanus* (inc., 1939); *Lady in The Dark*, 1941; *One Touch of Venus*, 1943; *The Firebrand of Florence*, 1945; *Down in the Valley*, 1948; *Love Life*, 1948; *Huckleberry Finn* (inc., 1950)

JUDITH WEIR

b 11 May 1954, Cambridge, England

Weir studied first with John Tavener, then with Robin Holloway at Cambridge and Gunther Schuller at Tanglewood. *A Night at the Chinese Opera*, her first full-length opera, put her firmly on the map as a composer with a distinct theatrical aptitude and an accessible yet individual musical language. These qualities had been discernible in a string of earlier concert works that perhaps could be termed 'concert-theatre' or opera-in-embryo: works that involve narrative and dramatic techniques of an operatic kind but, for reasons of scale, inhabit a concert hall rather than a theatre. The most reductionist of these is *King Harald's Saga* (1979), a ten-minute 'grand opera in three acts' for unaccompanied soprano singing eight solo roles and one representing the Norwegian army. In all her works, Weir uses her own texts derived from a variety of sources. In *Harald*, she used an Icelandic saga, and something fundamental to all her texts is in the tone of this original source: a deadpan narrative style that enables fantastic or epic events to be recounted with economy and speed. *A Serbian Cabaret* (1984) intersperses improvisations on folksongs played by a piano quartet with the players narrating the song texts, presenting each as a tiny drama in its own right. In *The Consolations of Scholarship* (1985), described as a 'music drama' for mezzo-soprano and nine instruments, the Yüan dynasty tale (the same story as *A Night at the Chinese Opera*) unfolds through plain narration and relevant philosophical discourse. This work has been convincingly staged, further confounding any attempt to classify what counts as opera within her *oeuvre*.

Weir's musical language is aphoristic and understated, developing in early works from a quasiminimalist style to encompass more straightforwardly melodic ideas that can assimilate all sorts of ethnic flavouring, whether Scottish (as Weir is herself), Chinese, Spanish or Serbian, without resorting to parody and pastiche. Weir has cited Stravinsky's *Oedipus Rex* as a major influence on her work. Also similar to Stravinsky in his neo-classical phase is her emotional detachment from her material: she always prefers to depict rather than to psychologize. This has led her work to be dubbed witty and ironic, but, while these qualities are present, dark and sinister elements are pervasive, particularly in *The Black Spider* (1984), a children's opera, and *HEAVEN ABLAZE in his Breast* (1989), a retelling of E. T. A. Hoffmann's *The Sandman* for eight dancers, six singers and two pianos – an experimental mixture of dance, opera, extended vocal techniques and spoken theatre.

A Night at the Chinese Opera

Opera in three acts (1h 45m)
Libretto by the composer, based on the 13th-century Yüan dynasty drama *The Chao Family Orphan* by Chi Chun-Hsiang
PREMIERES   8 July 1987, Everyman Theatre, Cheltenham; US: 29 July 1989, Opera Theater, Santa Fe, New Mexico

The setting is late-13th-century China, under the military rule of Mongolia, the era of Khubilai Khan and of Marco Polo. It concerns Chao Lin, a Chinese collaborator with the Mongolian regime, who attends a performance of *The Chao Family Orphan*. He finds that the first half of the play mirrors his own life and strives to take steps to avoid his surmised fate. Acts I and III tell his story and origin, and Act II is an interrupted performance of the play, accompanied by a reduced orchestra (predominately flutes, violas, basses and percussion) imitating traditional Chinese music. This act adheres closely to the traditional style of Yüan drama in its mixture of speech and sung rhythmic declamation, and in its fast and furious pace. The two narratives, that of Chao Lin and that of the play, essentially the same story, entwine in the final act with a double conclusion, one tragic and one more optimistic.

The music is economical, pictorial, spacious and brilliantly coloured. One instantly identifiable stylistic trait – a naturalistic speech rhythm duplicated simultaneously by the orchestra – aptly both supports and undermines the text – a fitting musical metaphor for a work where so much is double-edged.

The Vanishing Bridegroom

Opera in three parts (1h 30m)
Libretto by the composer, drawn from J. F. Campbell of Islay (ed.), *Popular Tales of the West Highlands*, vol. 2 (1860), and Alexander Carmichael (ed.), *Carmina Gadelica*, vol. 2 (1900)
PREMIERES   17 October 1990, Theatre Royal, Glasgow; US: 2 June 1992, Loretto-Hilton Center, St Louis, Missouri

Three separate Highland tales concerning bridegrooms who vanish in one way or another are linked to give the semblance of a family saga. In *The Inheritance* a man dies and, to discover which of his three sons has stolen his legacy, the doctor tells a parable (enacted) of a bride sent by her rich husband back to her former lover, who then returns her; on her way home she is robbed. The doctor then asks the sons which man they most admire: the husband, the lover or the robbers. By admiring the robbers, the youngest gives himself away. In *The Disappearance*, the bride, now settled with her husband, has a child. On his way to fetch the priest for the christening, the husband is lured away by fairies. He reappears, still young, to find that 20 years have passed and his daughter has grown up. In *The Stranger*, the daughter is courted by a rich and handsome man, but she distrusts him. When the priest sanctifies the ground she stands on, the man is revealed as the devil. The sanctified ground blooms, and the girl is left alone and independent.

The use of story within a story is characteristic of Weir's work, but here takes on a new simplicity and directness. The music is very different from that of her previous opera, darker, more contrapuntal and with a deepening vein of lyricism, particularly in the bride's lament in Part 1 – and the whole of Part 2. This opens with a fabulously rapt meditation on one chord, which flavours the entire act, culminating in a magical scene where 20 years pass in five minutes of stage time. The chorus has a major role throughout, most memorably as mourners in the first part and as Gaelic-singing fairies in Part 2.

Blond Eckbert

Opera in two acts (1h 15m)
Libretto by the composer, after Ludwig Tieck's fairy-tale, *Der blonde Eckbert* (1796)
PREMIERES   20 April 1994, Coliseum, London; US: 30 July 1994, Opera Theater, Santa Fe, New Mexico

Eckbert lives with his wife Bertha in the Harz mountains. Bertha tells their one friend, Walther, the story of her life, her flight from cruel parents and her fostering by a strange old woman who had a magic bird and a dog, whose name she has forgotten. When Walther supplies the dog's name, the couple's lives are ruined by paranoia and suspicion. In Act II Eckbert kills Walther and Bertha falls ill and dies. Eckbert seeks solace in a city, but a new friendship with a knight, Hugo, founders through Eckbert's mistrust. He wanders into the wilderness and finds the old woman of Bertha's story, who reveals that she, Walther and Hugo were the same person, and that Bertha was Eckbert's sister.

This is Weir's most concise opera to date, but also the most theatrically problematic, because of the extreme laconicism of the libretto and the fact that the four singers almost never interact. Weir's now familiar obsession with a story within a story is further framed by the bird, who opens and closes the opera by telling the tale to the dog. Bertha's life story is a 20-minute monologue scored for chamber forces that contrasts with the rest of the piece. The score is less consciously modelled on folk music than its predecessors, though it is subtly tinged with devices from German Romanticism, such as Weberesque horn calls and evocations of lieder. A highly organized, motivic and symphonic work, it has some ravishingly lyrical passages which, in Act II, reveal depths of emotion that may herald a new departure in Weir's work.

Other operative works: *King Harald's Saga*, 1979; *The Black Spider* (children's opera), 1984; *The Consolations of Scholarship*, 1985; *HEAVEN ABLAZE in his Breast*, 1989; *Scipio's Dream* (Mozart adaptation), 1991

J.G.

ERMANNO WOLF-FERRARI
Ermanno Wolf; *b* 12 January 1876, Venice; *d* 21 January 1948, Venice

The surname that Wolf-Ferrari used after about 1895 brought together those of his Bavarian father and his Venetian mother – neatly symbolizing the uncertainty about his nationality that persistently haunted him. Born in Italy, he studied in Munich and spent much of his adult life in the German-speaking world. Moreover, his works were at first much more successful north of the Alps than in his native land. A crucial factor underlying this was his failure, until well after the First World War, to be taken up by an Italian publisher.

After initially concentrating mainly on instrumental music, Wolf-Ferrari first came before the opera public with *Cenerentola* (1900), which won success in Bremen after a disastrous premiere in Venice. Though eclectic, the work shows a promising inventiveness in (for example) its sometimes unexpectedly bold harmonies. It was, however, in his next two operas that Wolf-Ferrari created that special type of graceful,

gently satirical comedy which was to become distinctively his own: though first performed in German, *Le donne curiose* and *I quatro rusteghi* were originally composed to Italian libretti based on Goldoni. *I quatro rusteghi* in particular recaptures the spirit, rather than the letter, of 18th-century opera buffa with a charm and subtlety that place it among the best Italian operatic comedies since Verdi's *Falstaff*. *Il segreto di Susanna*, though slighter, has won even wider success, thanks partly to its conveniently small cast.

I gioielli della Madonna, by contrast, shows Wolf-Ferrari trying his hand at post-Mascagnian verismo, a genre to which his talents were ill suited. Then, after the unjustly neglected little Molière opera *L'amore medico* (1913), he went through a prolonged crisis under the impact of the First World War, during which he took refuge in Zurich. Since Italy and Germany were fighting on opposite sides, his mixed blood and background proved particularly problematical for someone of his hypersensitive yet childlike temperament: small wonder that he composed little during the war and the immediately post-war years. However, *Sly* has recently resurfaced after decades of neglect.

In the 1930s Wolf-Ferrari wrote three further comic operas, including two more adaptations of Goldoni. Of these, *Il campiello* is regarded by many in both Italy and Germany as fully equal to *I quatro rusteghi*. After 1940 only one more opera followed, and Wolf-Ferrari again became prolific in the field of instrumental music.

I quatro rusteghi
(*Die vier Grobiane*)
School for Fathers (literally, *The Four Curmudgeons*)
Comic opera in three acts (four scenes) (2h 15m)
Libretto by [Luigi Sugana and] Giuseppe Pizzolato, based on the play *I rusteghi* by Carlo Goldoni (1760)
PREMIERES 19 March 1906, Hoftheater, Munich; UK: 7 June 1946, Sadler's Wells, London; US: 18 October 1951, City Center, New York

Although the librettists made appropriate changes, they skilfully retained important features of Goldoni's famous comedy. Here as there, most of the characters use Venetian dialect: only Count Riccardo speaks standard Italian, thus identifying himself as an outsider and an aristocrat. The spirit of Wolf-Ferrari's music indeed seems so closely bound up with the racy idiosyncrasies of Venetian speech that something essential is inevitably lost in translation.

The *rusteghi* of the title (the Venetian word has very different overtones from its Italian counterpart) are crusty old pedants, hidebound by the mores of the society in which they live. One of them, Lunardo, has arranged for his daughter Lucieta to marry his friend Maurizio's son Filipeto; but custom dictates that the young couple may not see each other before their wedding. Naturally both youngsters rebel fiercely and, with the help of the older female characters and of Count Riccardo, Filipeto is smuggled into Lunardo's house disguised as a woman. The couple fall for each other at once. But, having discovered that Filipeto has anticipated marriage to the extent of actually meeting his bride-to-be, Lunardo decrees that the wedding must now be cancelled. Only after determined persuasion by the more enlightened characters – including a formidable tirade by Felice, the wife of one of the other *rusteghi* – do Lunardo and his friends relent.

This slender plot provides ample scope both for memorable comic characterization and for deft evocation of the 18th-century setting; and the music rises delightfully to the occasion. Using the old opera-buffa tradition as a creative starting-point rather than a rigid model, Wolf-Ferrari finds room for passing allusions to Wagner and Verdi, for mildly 'modern' touches of dissonance, and even for a Venetian popular melody which figures prominently in all three acts. Yet, far from being merely eclectic, the total effect is surprisingly unified and personal, so spontaneous is the melodic invention, so individual the delicately imaginative orchestration. An immediate success in Germany, *I quatro rusteghi* took considerably longer to convince the Italians, and reached the English-speaking world only after the Second World War. Edward Dent's witty translation contributed significantly to the opera's great success at its British premiere in 1946.

Il segreto di Susanna

(*Susannens Geheimnis*)
Susanna's Secret
Intermezzo in one act (45m)
Libretto by Enrico Golisciani
PREMIERES 4 December 1909, Hoftheater, Munich; US: 14 March 1911, Metropolitan, New York; UK: 11 July 1911, Covent Garden, London

Though too slight and eclectic to show Wolf-Ferrari's full stature as a composer, this amiable *jeu d'esprit* deserves its popularity. Not only is it cheap to produce (having only two singing characters), but its unaffected tunefulness and the disarmingly simple idea of the libretto have an immediate, undemanding appeal. Count Gil suspects that his young wife, Susanna, has a lover. How else can he explain the smell of tobacco smoke that pervades the house? Why else did he catch sight of her out and about without his permission? It eventually emerges – after a sustained build-up of misunderstanding – that Susanna herself is the smoker, and that the purpose of her furtive outing was to buy more cigarettes. Relieved, Gil agrees to take up smoking too, to keep her company.

The music's allusions range from almost literal pastiche of opera buffa in the vivacious little overture to free yet unmistakable references to Debussy's *Prélude à l'après-midi d'un faune* in the woodwind phrases representing cigarette smoke. Such stylistic waverings matter little in so unpretentious a piece; but the distinctive personal 'voice' of Wolf-Ferrari's best comic style, which was all-pervading in *I quatro rusteghi*, is here only intermittently audible.

Other operas: *Irene*, (1896); *La Camargo* (inc., c. 1897); *Cenerentola* (*Aschenbrödel*), 1900, rev. 1902; *Le donne curiose* (*Die neugierigen Frauen*), 1903; *I gioielli della madonna*, 1911; *L'amore medico* (*Der Liebhaber als Arzt*), 1913; *Gli amanti sposi* (1916), 1925; *Das Himmelskleid* (*La veste del cielo*), (1925), 1927; *Sly, ovvero La leggenda del dormiente risvegliato*, 1927; *La vedova scaltra*, 1931; *Il campiello*, 1936; *La dama boba*, 1939; *Gli dei a Tebe* (*Der Kuckuck von Theben*), 1943

J.C.G.W.

RICCARDO ZANDONAI

Riccardo Antonio Francesco Zandonai; b 28 May 1883,
Sacco di Rovereto, Trentino, Italy; d 5 June 1944, Pesaro,
Italy

Among the Italian composers born around 1880, Zandonai can on the whole be ranked as a traditionalist (he had studied for a time under Mascagni). However, he was never a mere imitator of his famous predecessors: he showed considerable enterprise in grafting aptly colourful details and piquant harmonic enrichments on to basically traditional stems.

His first opera to attract much attention was *Il grillo del focolare* (1908), which was well enough received to persuade Ricordi's publishing house to give him preferential treatment during the next few years – evidently regarding him as Puccini's natural successor. The firm even sent him to Spain to 'collect material' for his next opera, *Conchita*, which confirmed their hopes by gaining him his first major success. The peak of his operatic achievement was reached when *Francesca da Rimini* was launched in 1914, quickly winning worldwide fame.

None of Zandonai's later works succeeded in matching *Francesca*'s lasting popularity, and before long he showed dangerous signs of repeating himself: this is notably the case in *Giulietta e Romeo*, his second most frequently performed opera. *I cavalieri di Ekebù* is more interesting; and Zandonai's last completed opera, *La farsa amorosa* (1933), based on the same story as Falla's *The Three-Cornered Hat*, also deserves attention at its modest level: with two donkeys among its principal characters, the work revives aspects of the spirit of the old opera-buffa tradition.

Francesca da Rimini

Opera in four acts (five scenes) (2h 15m)
Libretto by Tito Ricordi, a shortened version of the play by Gabriele d'Annunzio (1901)
PREMIERES 19 February 1914, Teatro Regio, Turin; UK: 16 July 1914, Covent Garden, London; US: 22 December 1916, Metropolitan, New York

D'Annunzio's ornately colourful dramatic elaboration of the story from Dante's *Inferno* was heavily cut for operatic purposes. The resultant work captured the popular imagination to a greater extent than any other d'Annunzio opera: by 1976 it had been produced (or revived) well over 200 times in more than 20 countries.

Francesca has been promised in marriage to the lame and brutal lord of Rimini, Gianciotto Malatesta, whom she has never seen. To overcome her expected resistance to the idea, her family tricks her into thinking that Gianciotto's handsome younger brother Paolo – who arrives as ambassador from the Malatestas – is her husband-to-be: she falls in love with him in a remarkable 'silent love duet', which forms the serenely beautiful culmination of Act I. Their love develops throughout the opera, although the marriage to Gianciotto takes place: at first the lovers keep their emotions to themselves; but when Francesca finds Paolo slightly wounded while the castle of Rimini is being attacked she reveals her feelings to him and finds them reciprocated. Their love bursts fully into flower while they are reading together from a book about the love of Lancelot and Guinevere. But Paolo's evil, one-eyed younger brother Malatestino, also in love with Francesca, becomes aware of what is going on and arranges for Gianciotto to catch the pair together, killing them on the spot.

Zandonai's flair for picturesque colour is much in evidence: his wish to create a suitably 'medieval' atmosphere even led him to feature a lute in the orchestra. The ensembles of female voices include some of his most radiantly beautiful inventions, whereas the Act II battle music, though exciting enough, is undeniably crude in its unbridled rhetoric. The characterization is on the whole less original or persuasive than the evocation of context. But, despite the work's uneven quality, its merits are more than sufficient to justify its lasting success.

Other operas: *La coppa del re*, (before 1907); *L'uccellino d'oro* ('fiaba musicale'), 1907; *Il grillo del focolare*, 1908; *Conchita*, 1911; *Melenis*, 1912; *La via della finestra*, 1919, rev. 1923; *Guilietta e Romeo*, 1922; *I cavalieri di Ekebù*, 1925; *Giuliano*, 1928; *Una partita*, 1933; *La farsa amorosa*, 1933; *Il bacio* (inc.), (1944)

J.C.G.W.

ALEXANDER ZEMLINSKY

Alexander (von) Zemlinsky (Zemlinszky); b 14 October 1871, Vienna; d 15 March 1942, Larchmont, New York

Zemlinsky was a child of his time, his music eclectically reflecting the worlds in which he lived. He reached adulthood in Brahms-dominated Vienna and maturity during the turbulent *fin-de-siècle* period when art nouveau was the all-pervading artistic ambience, when Mahler (the greatest influence on his music) was director of the Vienna Court Opera and Viennese operetta was at its best. He reached his zenith during the First World War and the period of cultural turmoil that followed, and shared in the reaction against Expressionism and the demand for a 'new objectivity' characterized by Kurt Weill.

Zemlinsky was better known in his lifetime as a conductor than as a composer. In his early career the two paths ran parallel. He became conductor of Vienna's Carltheater in 1900, and the same year Mahler staged Zemlinsky's second opera, *Es war einmal*, at the Vienna Court Opera, after advising the young composer on revising it and indeed composing 50 bars himself. In 1904 Zemlinsky moved to the newly opened Jubiläumtheater (later to become the Volksoper) and the same year launched a society to foster new music in Vienna with his brother-in-law and one-time pupil, Schoenberg. Three years later he joined Mahler at the Vienna Court Opera as a conductor, but after Mahler's resignation later that season his successor, Felix Weingartner, cancelled plans to produce Zemlinsky's third opera, *Der Traumgörge*, although it was already in rehearsal, and Zemlinsky resigned too. He returned to the Volksoper, where he emulated Mahler's innovative repertoire planning, conducting the Viennese premieres of Dukas's *Ariane et Barbe-bleue* and Strauss's *Salome*. From 1911 to 1927 Zemlinsky was opera director at the Neues Deutsches Theater in Prague, and it was here that he wrote his most significant works, while continuing his championship of modern music – including the world premiere of Schoenberg's *Erwartung* and employing members of the Schoenberg circle on his staff – as well as conducting much of the standard repertoire. Stravinsky praised his Mozart conducting (some of Zemlinsky's 1920s performances have been reissued on CD). In 1927 he moved to Berlin to be Klemperer's deputy at the Kroll Opera, and he stayed there until its closure in 1931. However, he continued teaching at the Musikhochschule until 1933, when, in the wake of the Nazi takeover, he moved back to Vienna, where he had no permanent post. In 1938 Hitler's *Anschluss* drove Zemlinsky, at 67, out of Europe. He settled in the United States but made little impact. His music was virtually ignored from 1934 until the late 1970s, when German and British radio stations and a handful of German opera houses began reviving it. He suffered from being closely connected with three major figures, Mahler, Schoenberg and Klemperer; but his posthumous recognition has benefited from these connections.

Eine florentinische Tragödie

A Florentine Tragedy
Opera in one act (55m)
Libretto: the play by Oscar Wilde (1894), trans. Max Meyerfeld
Composed 1915–14 March 1916

PREMIERES 30 January 1917, Württembergisches Staatstheater, Stuttgart; US: 22 April 1982, Manhattan School of Music, New York; UK: 22 August 1983, King's Theatre, Edinburgh
CAST Bianca *ms*, Guido Bardi *t*, Simone *b*

With this opera, premiered by his fellow composer and opera-house director Max von Schillings, Zemlinsky achieved a modest international success and, together with his other Wilde opera (*Der Zwerg*), it re-established his reputation in the 1980s. The emotionally ambiguous plot is typically *fin de siècle*, the music capturing the hot-house atmosphere of the lovers' ardour. Zemlinsky stipulated that the opera be illuminated only by shadowy moonlight.

SYNOPSIS
Simone, a merchant in 16th-century Florence, returns home early and finds his wife, Bianca, with Guido, the duke of Florence's son. Initially he feigns innocence, fawningly tries to sell the aristocrat some of his fabulous fabrics, and drinks with him. Gradually Simone's comments become more barbed, Guido's less circumspect and Bianca's more reckless. When it becomes clear that Simone knows that they are having an affair, the two men duel. Bianca at first urges on Guido to kill her husband and liberate her love for him; but after Guido falls mortally wounded Bianca realizes that what she really needed was for her husband to assert himself. The couple are reconciled over the corpse of her lover.

The opera is dominated by Simone. Zemlinsky's edgy, atmospheric music heightens his barely repressed fury, the malevolence behind the volubility and the apparent sincerity of Wilde's character. Bianca and Guido are given few words, but her hatred for Simone and the contempt in which Guido holds him are portrayed through iridescent colours and searing nervous energy. As in Richard Strauss's *Der Rosenkavalier* (1911), their passionate love-making is depicted exhilaratingly in the orchestral prelude before the curtain rises, and its music returns briefly as part of their later love duet; Zemlinsky places this for maximum dramatic effect at the moment of maximum danger, as the likelihood of Simone discovering their affair increases with the lovers' every heedless moment. Guido's death occurs over a desperate, violent, descending scale – a simple device but here dramatically convincing and musically cathartic.

Der Zwerg

The Dwarf
Ein tragisches Märchen für Musik in one act (1h 30m)
Libretto by Georg C. Klaren, after the story *The Birthday of the Infanta* by Oscar Wilde (1888)
Composed 1920–4 January 1921
PREMIERES 28 May 1922, Theater am Habsburger Ring, Cologne; UK: 22 August 1983, King's Theatre, Edinburgh
CAST Donna Clara, the Infanta *s*, Dwarf *t*, Ghita *s*, Don Estoban *b*, 3 Ladies-in-waiting 3 *s*; *sa* chorus of the infanta's entourage (playmates, maids and ladies); beggars *silent*

With this opera Zemlinsky returned to a subject he had considered a decade earlier, the explosion that can result when physical deformity becomes a barrier to emotional fulfilment. *Der Zwerg* might sum up the predicament of Zemlinsky himself: a short, unattractive man who never recovered from the ending of his relationship with Alma Mahler and who constantly sought the company of young women. *Der Zwerg* was his most successful opera, with performances in Vienna, Prague and Berlin. It has been at the forefront of the Zemlinsky revival.

SYNOPSIS

The Spanish infanta's best birthday present is a proud but melancholy dwarf who is entirely unaware of his grotesque appearance. The infanta and her friends are ordered to cover the mirrors so he cannot see himself; the truth would kill him. He mournfully explains that he was an orphan, sold to a sultan, knowing neither mother nor homeland; everyone laughs at him and only God loves him. Although he is a court singer, he wants to sing only sad songs when he sees the infanta. They play together. In her childish way, she tells him she loves him, and he realizes he truly loves her. His passion grows; she is the first person not to mock him, and she gives him a present of a white rose. But the infanta selfishly remarks that he is different from her and orders her maid, Ghita, to show him a mirror. The kindly Ghita refuses, but eventually the dwarf sees his reflection and realizes the truth. He begs the infanta to tell him the image is not him. She cruelly tells him she will still play with him – but only as one would with an animal; one must love people. As the dwarf dies, his heart broken, he begs for the white rose.

This tragic story is matched by a characteristically eclectic score. The dance rhythms have a Spanish flavour, and the orchestration accompanying the girls is iridescent with clear, neo-classical textures. The infanta's music underlines her treatment of the dwarf as a toy. Her emotion is synthetic; whenever the games cease, her music matches her brittle, spoilt personality. The dwarf, however, is real. Growling, jerky trombones and tuba characterize his ugliness, while his claim to be the princess's knight in shining armour is set to Wagnerian mock heroics. But his love music has a radiant innocence, and the anguish of his self-awakening, rejection and death have a shattering, Mahlerian melancholy intensified at its catharsis by echoes of the rest of the world, unconcerned, outside.

For the production that relaunched the work, by the Hamburg State Opera in 1982, the text was rewritten by Adolf Dresen to correspond more closely to the original Oscar Wilde story, making the dwarf an abducted, uneducated and absurd peasant, not an innocent courtier used to royal palaces, and making several cuts. This version significantly changes the relationship between text and music.

C.B.

Der König Kandaules

King Candaules
Opera in three acts
Libretto by the composer after the German adaptation by Franz Blei of the play *Le roi Candaule* by André Gide (1901)

Composed 14 May 1935–29 December 1936 (short score, 137 pages orchestrated), orch. completed by Antony Beaumont
PREMIERE scheduled for 6 October 1996, Staatsoper, Hamburg
CAST König Kandaules (King Candaules) *dramatic t*, Gyges *dramatic bar*, Nyssia *dramatic s*, 3 *t*, 2 *bar*, 4 *b*, *silent*; *tb* chorus of guests, offstage voices; servants *silent*

In 1933, on leaving Nazi Germany, Zemlinsky decided to abandon his career as an opera conductor and return to his native Vienna to devote the greater part of his energies to composition. Works dating from this period include the Fourth String Quartet (1936) and *Der König Kandaules*. After Zemlinsky's death the manuscript remained in the Library of Congress, Washington, DC, until Antony Beaumont began work on it in 1989.

SYNOPSIS

In ancient Lydia the king, Candaules, throws a banquet at which his queen, Nyssia, is to appear for the first time in public unveiled. A magic ring is found embedded in the flesh of a fish that is served at the royal table. Gyges, an uncouth but honest fisherman, is called before the king to account for his catch. Candaules is fascinated by Gyges, dressing him in fine clothes and heaping riches upon him. Gyges unwillingly takes the magic ring, later exploiting its powers not only to see Nyssia naked but also to spend a night in her arms. Finally he murders Candaules and orders Nyssia to resume the veil; she refuses, saying, 'Candaules has torn it to shreds.'

In the death of the king, the opera can be seen as an allegory of the end of an epoch of Western music; the new dynasty founded by Gyges symbolizes the new music as advocated by Zemlinsky's friend Schoenberg. Zemlinsky himself described the music of this opera as 'ultra-modern': it moves logically and boldly from pentatonicism and diatonicism through bitonality and polytonality to the very threshold of atonality. The composer never previously achieved proportions so perfect, nor demonstrated his sense of theatre so tellingly, as in *Der König Kandaules*.

A.C.W.B.

Other operas: *Sarema*, 1897; *Es war einmal*, 1900; *Der Traumgörge*, (1906), 1980; *Kleider machen Leute*, 1910, rev. 1922; *Der Kreidekreis*, 1933
Incomplete operas: (all manuscripts in the Library of Congress, Washington DC) *Malwa*, (1913); *Der heilige Vitalis*, 1915; *Raphael, oder Das Chagrinleder*, (1918); *Circe*, (1939)

BERND ALOIS ZIMMERMANN

b 20 March 1918, Bliesheim, Cologne, Germany;
d 10 August 1970, Königsdorf, Cologne

Brought up under the Nazis, Zimmermann is the classic instance in music of the psychological instabilities of post-war Germany. A pupil of Philipp Jarnach during the war, and of Wolfgang Fortner and René

Leibowitz after it, he emerged as a composer at a time when a slightly younger generation of new composers was adopting extreme solutions to the problems of recent European history. Zimmermann was trained in serial method. He attended the Darmstadt Ferienkurse in 1948–50, and much of his early music shares the angular lines and intellectual schemes cultivated there. But there is always a feeling in these instrumental works that a tortured spirit is fighting to escape from mental prison. In his only opera, *Die Soldaten*, the spirit finally breaks out, and on its many levels this work is one of the most characteristic products of early 1960s Germany, with its desperate need to reject its own intellectual and military history while rummaging in that history for causes, explanations and scapegoats.

Die Soldaten established a pluralist, associative style which was to become Zimmermann's trade-mark, and was to serve him in several striking works during the last decade of his life. These works show increasing intellectual as well as stylistic anxiety. It could well be that the generous use of quotation in the *Requiem für einen jungen Dichter* shows too much faith in the artistic power of good credentials. It certainly looks, in any case, as if Zimmermann was personally overtaken by the menace of history. In August 1970 he took his own life, apparently in blank despair at the state of the world.

Die Soldaten

The Soldiers
Opera in four acts (1h 45m)
Libretto by the composer, after the play by Jakob Michael Reinhold Lenz (1776)
Composed 1958–60, rev. 1963–4
PREMIERES 15 February 1965, Opernhaus, Cologne; UK: 21 August 1972, King's Theatre, Edinburgh; US: 22 January 1982, Opera House, Boston
CAST Wesener *b*, Marie *very dramatic coloratura s*, Charlotte *ms*, Wesener's Old Mother *low c*, Stolzius *youthful high bar*, Stolzius's Mother *very dramatic c*, Obrist *b*, Desportes *very high t*, Pirzel *high t*, Eisenhardt *heroic bar*, Haudy *heroic bar*, Captain Mary *bar*, Countess de la Roche *ms*, Her Son *very high lyrical t*, 3 *very high t* (or *dramatic s*), 4 *actors, dancers*, 18 officers and cadets *spoken roles*; stage percussion

Lenz's play was based on an incident he himself had witnessed in Strasburg. A friend – an aristocratic soldier in the French garrison – had failed to honour a marriage contract with the daughter of a Strasburg jeweller. The play is a bitter attack on the tendency of an idle and peripatetic soldiery to ruin local girls in this way, but attributes the problem partly to the fact that the soldiers were on oath to remain unmarried. Zimmermann characteristically generalizes this plot into a rambling attack on soldiers everywhere, with the setting transferred to French Flanders.

SYNOPSIS

Act I Scene 1 (Strofe): After a long opening prelude, the curtain rises on the house of the fancy-goods dealer Wesener, in Lille. His daughter Marie is writing to the mother of her fiancé, the draper Stolzius, in Armentières. Scene 2 (Ciacona I). The letter is received

and Stolzius is teased by his mother. Scene 3 (Ricercari I): Back in Lille, Marie is courted by Desportes, a French officer. But Wesener refuses him permission to take Marie to the theatre. Later he lectures her on the dubious morals of soldiers. Scene 4 (Toccata I): On the old town moat in Armentières, French officers discuss their leisure activities. Captain Haudy defends the theatre and its attendant debauchery against the disapproval of the chaplain, Eisenhardt. Scene 5 (Nocturno I) returns us to Lille, where Wesener advises Marie to discourage neither the aristocratic Desportes nor Stolzius.

Act II Scene 1 (Toccata II): In the crowded Armentières coffee-house, Eisenhardt deplores Haudy's plot to lure Marie away from Stolzius. The officers tease Stolzius about Desportes's designs on his fiancée. Scene 2 (Capriccio, Corale and Ciacona II) has three simultaneous settings. In Lille Desportes seduces Marie, who has received a scolding letter from Stolzius; in the same place, but on a darkened stage, Marie's grandmother sings of her coming ruin; in Armentières Stolzius and his mother receive Marie's reply, written with Desportes's help.

Act III Scene 1 (Rondino): Eisenhardt remarks with concern to Captain Pirzel that Captain Mary has also taken lodgings in Lille. Scene 2 (Rappresentazione): Meanwhile, in Lille, Stolzius takes a post as Mary's batman. Scene 3 (Ricercari II): Mary arrives with Stolzius to take Marie for a drive. She only half-recognizes Stolzius. Scene 4 (Nocturno II) introduces the countess de la Roche, a philanthropic aristocrat. Her son, too, is involved with Marie, and the countess determines to save her. In Scene 5 (Tropi) she visits Marie and engages her as companion.

Act IV Scene 1 (Toccata III): Marie has run away and threatens to rejoin Desportes (who is now in prison); wanting to be rid of her, he offers Marie to his gamekeeper, who rapes her. This is shown on film, while a complex stage action, in the Armentières coffee-house, suggests various levels of interpretation, culminating in the question, 'Must those who suffer evil be afraid?' Scene 2 (Ciacona III): Mary and Desportes are at dinner, waited on by Stolzius. They discuss Marie contemptuously, but Stolzius has poisoned Desportes. As he dies, Stolzius walks on to Mary's sword. Scene 3 (Nocturno III): Wesener is accosted by a beggarwoman by the river Lys. He fails to recognize his own daughter. As he hands her a coin, she sinks to the ground.

In its montage of short scenes and savage anti-military satire, the play looks forward half a century to *Woyzeck* (whose author, Georg Büchner, wrote a novel about Lenz). Zimmermann took the hint, and the Berg of *Wozzeck* (as well as of *Lulu*) is an obvious father figure of *Die Soldaten*. Zimmermann uses not only film, but also various musical layering techniques. Berg's associative methods (dance music in *Wozzeck*, film in *Lulu*) are greatly extended, while his touches of quasi-cinematic montage become a standard device. Zimmermann uses film both to extend the scope of Lenz's action and to bring in newsreel associations. More interestingly, he has multi-level scenes depicting simultaneous or non-sequential actions. Finally he adopts Berg's device of associating each scene with a musical genre (chaconne, toccata, ricercar, etc.); moreover, by giving different scenes the same generic name, he suggests connections between them, a procedure not found in Berg. Bach chorales pop up in more or less straightforward arrangements to suggest an apocalyptic view of the action. Pop music and jazz accompany a ballet sequence in Act II, Scene 1. The dense overlaying of styles and texts comes to a climax in the final act, where Eisenhardt's voice intones the Lord's Prayer in Latin to the accompaniment of tapes of military commands, the sound of 'unrestrained weeping', 'hopeless moaning', and so forth. Pop music emanates (along with a crowd of drunken soldiers) from a dance hall, while film of military equipment, tanks, etc. reminds us that all evil is ultimately one: a valid if not startling observation.

Is *Die Soldaten* more than the sum of its parts? It hardly seems so now that its early vogue (especially in Germany) has subsided. Dramatically it is one-paced, and Zimmermann's own angular vocal style and undifferentiated orchestral textures convey little interest in the human significance of the actual plot. In a review of the British premiere, Winton Dean compared the work with Meyerbeer, quoting Wagner's dictum: 'effects without causes'. As a document of its time it certainly has importance, but that may not guarantee it a permanent place in the repertoire.

S.W.

Contributors

A.C.
Alfred Clayton read music at the universities of Oxford, Cambridge, Hamburg and Vienna. He has written articles and reviews and published numerous translations. These include Carl Dahlhaus, *Schoenberg and the New Music* (1987; translated jointly with Derek Puffett) and Paul Badura-Skoda, *Interpreting Bach at the Keyboard* (1992).

A.C.W.B.
Antony Beaumont, a Londoner (born 1949), read music at Cambridge. Since 1972 he has been resident in Germany, where he is active as a conductor but also broadcasts, lectures and writes about music. After several years of intensive research he wrote two books about Busoni and reconstructed the closing scene of the unfinished opera *Doktor Faust*. He has now turned his attention to Zemlinsky and is preparing several publications devoted to him.

A.H.
Amanda Holden studied at Oxford University with Egon Wellesz and (piano) at the Guildhall School of Music with James Gibb. After several years as an accompanist and on the Guildhall staff, she began (in 1985) planning the *Viking/Penguin Opera Guides* and translating libretti. Her many translations, which include several of Mozart, Rameau's *Les Boréades*, Wagner's *Lohengrin* and Verdi's *Falstaff*, are performed throughout the English-speaking world.

A.J.
Arthur Jacobs lectured at the Royal Academy of Music 1965–79, was head of the Department of Music at Huddersfield Polytechnic 1979–84, and has lectured at various US, Canadian and Australian universities. A member of the editorial board of *Opera* since 1962 and a translator of many operas for performance, his books include *Arthur Sullivan: A Victorian Musician* and the *Penguin Dictionary of Music* (five editions).

A.J.C.
Andrew Clements (born 1950) is chief music critic of the *Guardian*. He has written for the *Financial Times* and the *New Statesman*, was a contributor to the *New Grove Dictionary of Opera*, and is a member of the editorial board of *Opera* magazine.

B.D.
Basil Deane was born and educated in Northern Ireland. He has been professor of music in the universities of Sheffield, Manchester and Birmingham, and has held the posts of music director at the Arts Council of Great Britain and foundation director of the Hong Kong Academy for Performing Arts. His principal research interests are in French music, and music of the classical period. He has published books on Roussel, Cherubini and Hoddinott, and is currently working on a study of the French theatre from 1789 to 1815.

B.L.K.
Barbara L. Kelly is a Scottish musicologist specializing in French music of the early 20th century. After graduating from the University of Glasgow, she studied in America at the University of Illinois with Professor Alexander Ringer and is now at Liverpool University. She has written on Maeterlinck and French opera, and Milhaud and his collaboration with Paul Claudel. Her present research is focused on Milhaud and the concept of the French musical tradition.

C.A.B.
Clive Brown studied at Cambridge (M.A.) and Oxford (D.Phil.), and was lecturer in music at The Queen's College, Oxford (1981–9). He is at present senior lecturer in performance studies at Bretton Hall College, University of Leeds. Publications include a critical biography of Spohr (CUP) and articles on performing practice, opera and early Romantic music, as well as critical editions of Beethoven and Weber; he is preparing a book on classical and Romantic performing practice for OUP. He has conducted revivals of operas by Schubert, Mendelssohn, Spohr and Haydn.

C.A.P.
Curtis Price is a specialist on baroque and classical music and opera. He is the author of *Music in the Restoration Theatre*, *Henry Purcell and the London Stage*, the Norton Critical Score of *Dido and Aeneas* and numerous articles on English and Italian music. In 1985 he received the Dent Medal of

the Royal Musical Association. Among his other scholarly interests are the music of Handel and the history of theatre architecture. He is King Edward professor and head of the Department of Music at King's College, London, and a director of the Royal Academy of Music.

C.B.
Clive Bennett was for ten years in charge of opera broadcasts on BBC Radio 3, and is now executive producer, vocal productions, with Philips Classics.

C.F.
Christopher Fifield is a conductor, author and broadcaster. For many years he was on the staff at Glyndebourne, and, for a decade, director of music at University College, London. He wrote the first biographies of the composer Max Bruch and of Wagner's amanuensis, the conductor Hans Richter.

C.I.P.
Charlotte Purkis graduated in music from Leeds University in 1982, became a junior research fellow in literature at Wolfson College, Oxford, a tutor for the Open University, and lecturer in performing arts at the University of Southampton. Currently head of drama and television at King Alfred's University College, Winchester, she has written on Krenek and Max Brand for the *New Grove Dictionary of Opera* and published elsewhere on Rutland Boughton and Rudolf Laban, as well as on erotic literature and theatre, 1890–1914.

D.A.C.
David Cairns (born 1926) took a (first-class) degree in history at Oxford (1948). In 1950, with Stephen Gray, he founded the Chelsea Opera Group, singing in early performances (Leporello, Dr Bartolo) conducted by Colin Davis. He has worked at the House of Commons (as library clerk, 1951–3), *The Times Educational Supplement* (1955–8) and since 1958 as music critic on the *Spectator*, the *Financial Times*, the *Sunday Times*, etc. He was classical programme co-ordinator, Philips Records (1967–72), is founder/conductor of The Thorington Players (1983–), and was, in 1985, distinguished visiting professor, University of California, Davis. He became officier de L'Ordre des Arts et des Lettres in 1991. Publications include: as translator, Berlioz's *Memoirs* (1969); *Responses: Musical Essays and Reviews* (1973); *Berlioz: The Making of an Artist* (1989); and contributions to ENO Opera Guides on *Die Zauberflöte* (1980) and *Falstaff* (1982).

D.B.
David Brown was, after five years' school-mastering, music librarian of London University for three years before joining the music staff of Southampton University in 1962. He retired as professor of musicology there in 1989. He has published books on Thomas Weelkes, John Wilbye and Glinka; his four-volume study of Tchaikovsky was completed in 1990. He has also edited numerous editions of

English Renaissance music, contributed many articles to periodicals, and broadcast frequently.

D.J.B.
Donald Burrows is a senior lecturer in music at the Open University, and an internationally known Handel scholar, being a member of the Vorstand of the Händel-Gesellschaft and a member of the Advisory Board for the Maryland Handel Festival (USA) as well as a founding council member of the Handel Institute. He is author of the Master Musicians biography of Handel (Dent, 1995) and co-author of *A Catalogue of Handel's Musical Autographs* (OUP), and has written on many aspects of Handel's music, as well as editing *Messiah, Alexander's Feast* and Handel's violin sonatas for publication.

D.K.
David Kimbell, by birth a man of Kent, has spent the whole of his professional life in Scotland; he is currently professor of music and dean of the Faculty of Music at the University of Edinburgh. Author of *Verdi in the Age of Italian Romanticism* and *Italian Opera* (both CUP), he is also a contributor to the *New Oxford History of Music* and the Halle edition of the collected works of Handel.

D.L.-J.
David Lloyd-Jones has conducted over 100 different operas in Great Britain and abroad in his career as freelance conductor, assistant music director of English National Opera (1972–8) and artistic director of Opera North (1978–90). He has made critical editions of *Boris Godunov* (OUP and Muzika), *The Gondoliers* (Eulenberg) and *La jolie fille de Perth* (UMP). He is an acknowledged authority on Russian music, and has made widely used singing translations of operas by Musorgsky, Borodin, Tchaikovsky and Prokofiev.

D.M.
David Murray was born in Halifax, Nova Scotia. He studied music and philosophy in Canada (and played the piano professionally), then studied more philosophy at Oxford. He wrote many scores for radio plays and theatre and now lectures in philosophy at Birkbeck College, University of London, and reviews music for the *Financial Times*, the BBC and various journals. He has also contributed to several books about music.

D.O.-S.
David Osmond-Smith, born in 1946, completed his education at the universities of Cambridge and York. In 1970 he went to Milan to study with Umberto Eco, but also worked with Cathy Berberian and with Luciano Berio, of whose music he has made a special study. Since 1973 he has taught at the University of Sussex, where he is now professor of music. He has published two books on Berio, plus numerous other essays and translations. He broadcasts regularly, and lectures in Italy and France.

D.P.
David Pountney was director of productions at English National Opera (1982–93), where he directed over twenty operas, and previously at Scottish Opera. He was awarded the Janáček medal for the Janáček cycle he directed in collaboration with Welsh National Opera; his *From the House of the Dead* won a Laurence Olivier award. Productions elsewhere include Philip Glass's *The Voyage* at the Metropolitan, New York, and *Der fliegende Holländer* and *Nabucco* for the Bregenz Festival. In 1993 he became a CBE and a chevalier in the French Ordre des Arts et des Lettres. He has translated several libretti and written the libretto for Maxwell Davies's *The Doctor of Myddfai* (WNO, 1996).

D.W.-J.
David Wyn-Jones is a lecturer in the Department of Music, University of Wales College of Cardiff. He is the author with H. C. Robbins Landon of *Haydn, His Life and Music*. He has prepared critical editions of music by J. C. Bach, Haydn and Vanhal, and contributed to the *Heritage of Music* and *The Mozart Compendium*.

E.F.
Elizabeth Forbes is a musical journalist who specializes in opera. She has contributed to many encyclopedias, including the *New Grove Dictionary of Music* (1980) and the *New Grove Dictionary of Opera* (1992) and has published the following books: *Opera from A to Z* (1977), *The Observer's Book of Opera* and *Mario and Grisi: A Biography* (1985). She has also translated opera libretti from French, German and Swedish.

E.G.
Edward Garden is professor of music at Sheffield University. He has written many articles on Russian music; books include the definitive one in English on Balakirev (Faber, 1967), and the Master Musicians biography of Tchaikovsky (Dent, 2nd edn 1993), which has been translated into German and Spanish. He is also co-editor of *To My Best Friend: The Correspondence between Tchaikovsky and Nadezhda von Meck, 1876–8* (OUP, 1993).

E.H.
Elizabeth Hudson teaches at the University of Virginia and writes on various aspects of 19th-century Italian opera. She is an editor of the *Cambridge Opera Journal* and is editing *Il Corsaro* for the Verdi Critical Edition. She is preparing a book on women's narratives in 19th-century Italian opera.

E.S.
Erik Smith (M.A. Cantab, 1954) is the son of German conductor Hans Schmidt-Isserstedt but grew up in England. He has worked for Universal Edition (Vienna, 1957), as record producer for Decca (1968), head of A. & R. (until 1989) and record producer for Philips: his many recordings

include 80 operas. He was musical organizer of the 1991 Philips Complete Mozart Edition, for which he also orchestrated several sketches. His publications include many record-sleeve notes and articles (mainly on Mozart), the BBC Music Guide on Mozart serenades and dances and the music section of the CUP guide to *Die Zauberflöte*.

F.A.
Felix Aprahamian (born 1914, London), British music critic, writer and broadcaster, has been a familiar figure on the London scene since 1931, when he began his career as a musical journalist. He was deputy music critic of the *Sunday Times* (1948–89), and has also been for many years a leading reviewer for the *Gramophone*. He even appeared in a film (John Schlesinger's *Darling*, 1965) in the role of a critic. An authority on French music, he has also been adviser to the Delius Trust since 1961, and is vice-president of the Delius Society. He edited the essays of Ernest Newman, and was co-editor of the 20th-century volume of *The Heritage of Music* (1989).

G.B.
George Biddlecombe studied at the Royal Academy of Music and at Oxford University. He teaches at the Royal Academy of Music and specializes in 19th-century opera, particularly with regard to feminist aspects.

G.H.
Gwen Hughes read music at Oxford. After working as assistant editor of *Opera Now*, she joined BBC Radio 3 as a producer in 1992 and is now editor, opera.

G.S.
Graham Sadler was educated at the universities of Nottingham and London. Senior lecturer in music at the University of Hull, recordings reviews editor of *Early Music*, co-author of the *New Grove French Baroque Masters* (1986) and area adviser to the *New Grove Dictionary of Opera*, he has written numerous articles and broadcasts on Rameau and his period. Editions include music by Campra, Leclair, Lully and Rameau, many of which have been recorded and/or broadcast.

H.M.
Hugh Macdonald is Avis Blewett professor of music at Washington University, St Louis. He has taught at Cambridge, Oxford and Glasgow, where he was professor of music, 1980–87. He has been general editor of the New Berlioz Edition since its inception in 1967, and has published books on Berlioz and Skryabin. He has edited Berlioz's three operas and has made a number of opera translations, including Debussy's *Pelléas et Mélisande*.

I.B.
Ian Brunskill is a former editor of *Opera Now* who is now assistant arts editor of *The Times*. He has also written on music and opera for the *Guardian*,

The Times Literary Supplement, Opera, Classic CD and the Musical Times.

I.J.M.
Jonathan Mantle was born in England in 1954 and educated at Cambridge University. He is the author of several books, including a biography of Andrew Lloyd Webber.

I.K.
Ian Kemp recently retired as professor of music at the University of Manchester, having previously held appointments at the universities of Aberdeen, Cambridge and Leeds. In 1965 he edited the first book to be published on Tippett, and he is author of a major study, Tippett: The Composer and his Music. He has also written on Berlioz, Hindemith and Weill.

J.A.C.
Jon Alan Conrad teaches music theory and literature at the University of Delaware. He has been a contributing editor of Opus magazine, and has written articles and reviews for the Kurt Weill Newsletter, Opera Quarterly and the New York Times. He is a contributor to the New Grove Dictionary of Opera and the Metropolitan Opera Guide to Recorded Opera.

J.A.S.
Jan Smaczny studied at Oxford University and the Charles University in Prague. A specialist in the operas of Dvořák, he has written and broadcast on many aspects of Czech music. Since 1983 he has been a lecturer in music at the University of Birmingham. He also writes frequently for the Independent, Opera and the BBC Music Magazine.

J.C.G.W.
John C. G. Waterhouse (born 1939) studied at the University of Oxford, where in 1969 he was awarded a D.Phil. for his thesis The Emergence of Modern Italian Music (up to 1940). He has been a lecturer in music in the extramural departments of the universities of Belfast (1966–72) and Birmingham (from 1973), and has also spent much time in Italy. His many publications on 20th-century Italian music include the book La musica di Gian Francesco Malipiero (1990); an English version is in preparation.

J.C.S.
Jeremy Sams is a freelance accordionist, composer, translator and director.

J.G.
Julian Grant lives and works in London. Writings include 'A Foot in Bluebeard's Door' for ENO's Bartók opera guide and various articles on Russian music. Operas staged in London have been The Skin Drum (1990, ENO Studio), Out of Season (1991, Royal Opera House Garden Venture), The Queen of Sheba's Legs (1991, ENO Baylis programme) and A Family Affair (1993, Almeida Opera).

J.R.
Julian Rushton took his Mus.B. at Cambridge and D.Phil. at Oxford, his thesis being Music and Drama at the Académie Royale de Musique, Paris, 1774–1789 (1969). He taught at the universities of East Anglia and Cambridge until 1982 when he became professor of music at the University of Leeds. He has taught and lectured in Canada, the United States, and Israel. Publications include Cambridge Opera Handbooks on Don Giovanni (1981) and Idomeneo (1993), The Musical Language of Berlioz (1983), four volumes of the New Berlioz Edition (including La damnation de Faust) and two prefaces for the Pendragon French Opera edition. He is general editor of Cambridge Music Handbooks and is chairman of the editorial committee of Musica Britannica.

J.T.
John Tyrrell was born in Harare, Zimbabwe, and studied at the universities of Cape Town, Oxford and Brno. He worked at the New Grove Dictionary of Music and the Musical Times, and since 1976 has taught at the University of Nottingham, where in 1989 he became reader in opera studies. His books include Leoš Janáček: Kát'a Kabanová (1982), Czech Opera (1988), which has also been published in Czech (1992), and Janáček's Operas: A Documentary Account (1992).

J.W.B.
Jennifer Williams Brown (Ph.D., musicology, Cornell, 1992) specializes in 17th-century Venetian opera. Her dissertation examines the problems of aria-borrowing, revivals and revisions in the late 17th century; she has also presented papers on 17th-century source studies, opera production and harmonic organization. From 1987 to 1990 she taught part-time at the Eastman School of Music, where she prepared an edition of Cavalli's La Calisto for productions at Eastman and in New York. She is currently assistant professor of musicology at Louisiana State University.

J.W.D.
John Deathridge (born in 1944) is a fellow and director of studies in music at King's College, University of Cambridge. He has also been visiting professor at the universities of Princeton and Chicago and is an editor of the Richard Wagner-Gesamtausgabe in Munich. His recent publications include an enlarged edition of The Family Letters of Richard Wagner (1991), the English-language edition of Ulrich Müller's and Peter Wapnewski's Wagner Handbook (1992) and an article on Wagner and the post-modern (1992).

K.P.
Keith Potter is lecturer in music, Goldsmiths' College, University of London, and a writer on many aspects of contemporary music. He has particular interests in American and British composition since 1945, including John Cage, Morton Feldman, Philip Glass and Steve Reich, and the younger

generation of British composers. From 1971 to 1988 he was founding and chief editor of *Contact*, a journal of contemporary music; for eight years he wrote a regular new-music column and many reviews for *Classical Music* magazine. He is a regular contributor to the *Independent, The Times Literary Supplement* and the *BBC Music Magazine*.

L.A.W.
Lesley A. Wright is currently an associate professor of musicology at the University of Hawaii. After her doctoral dissertation on Bizet's compositional process (Princeton University), she has continued her research on Bizet and his contemporaries. She has prepared editions of Bizet's letters and musical works and has published articles both in dictionaries and in such journals as *19th-Century Music, Studies in Music* and *Current Musicology*.

L.F.
Lewis Foreman is known for his biography of Sir Arnold Bax, books on Rubbra, Grainger, Havergal Brian and Sir Arthur Bliss, and a chronological anthology of British composers' letters, *From Parry to Britten*. For over 20 years he has worked to devise enterprising concerts, typical being a historical conspectus of 'British Opera 1876–1916' at St John's, Smith Square, London, in 1982, issued on two LPs. Music trustee of the Sir Arnold Bax Trust, for 15 years he was a member of the City of Westminster Arts Council Music Committee.

L.H.
Leslie Howard, the British composer, pianist and musicologist (born in Melbourne in 1948) is himself the composer of the opera *Hreidar the Fool*, produced in Melbourne in 1975, as well as a good deal of chamber music. He is a regular writer and broadcaster on music, and especially the music of Liszt. He is president of the British Liszt Society, and is currently completing the mammoth project of recording that composer's complete piano music for Hyperion – some 80 compact discs in all. His repertoire includes over 80 concertos, and his recital programmes cover an enormous range of rare and familiar works, with special emphasis on Russian music and the complete works of Beethoven and Liszt.

L.S.
Lionel Sawkins, formerly principal lecturer in music, Roehampton Institute, London, and visiting professor, Groupe de Formation Doctorale (Musique et Musicologie) at the École Normale Supérieure, Paris, has contributed many articles on French baroque music to books, journals and dictionaries in France and Britain, and edited works by Lully, Lalande, Rameau and Royer. He is currently preparing the *catalogue raisonné* of Lalande's works, to be published by OUP with the assistance of the British Academy.

M.A.
Mark Audus studied at the University of Nottingham where his teachers included Nigel Osborne and John Tyrrell. Following postgraduate studies at King's College, London, he worked as an editor at Universal Edition, London, particularly on scores by Birtwistle and with Tyrrell and Charles Mackerras on editions of Janáček's operas. He now teaches at the University of Nottingham and is music director of the Bern Bach Soloists.

M.E.P.
Marvin E. Paymer received his Ph.D. from the City University of New York, where he has taught at York and Hunter Colleges. His interests have centred on the authenticity of the hundreds of works attributed to Giovanni Battista Pergolesi, and to this end he has received fellowships from the Andrew Melon Foundation and the National Endowment for the Humanities. Paymer is cofounder of the Pergolesi Research Center and of the new Pergolesi complete works.

M.F.R.
Michael Robinson, born in Gloucester in 1933, is professor of music and head of department at the University of Wales, Cardiff, chairman of the University of Wales Creative Arts subject panel, and chairman of the Welsh Music Information Centre. He is the author of *Opera Before Mozart* (Hutchinson, 1966), *Naples and Neapolitan Opera* (Clarendon Press, 1972), *A Thematic Catalogue of the Works of Giovanni Paisiello* (Pendragon Press, 1991) and numerous articles on opera. He is also a composer of chamber music and conductor of the Cardiff University chamber orchestra.

M.K.
Michael Kennedy, born in Manchester in 1926, has been a music critic for the *Daily Telegraph* since 1950 and latterly for the *Sunday Telegraph*. He has written biographical studies of Elgar, Vaughan Williams, Britten, Walton, Mahler and Strauss, histories of the Hallé Orchestra and the Royal Manchester College of Music, biographies of Sir John Barbirolli and Sir Adrian Boult, and the *Oxford Dictionary of Music*. He is a regular broadcaster and contributor to *Opera, Gramophone* and other periodicals. He is the author of the Strauss entry in the *New Grove Dictionary of Music* and the BBC Music Guide on the Strauss tone poems. He was appointed OBE in 1981 for services to music.

N.G.
Noël Goodwin is a member of the editorial board of *Opera* and a regular critic for *The Times*. He was music critic of the *Daily Express* 1956–78, London correspondent of *Opera News* (New York) 1975–90 and a council member and deputy chairman of the Music Advisory Panel, Arts Council of Great Britain 1979–81. He collaborated with Sir Geraint Evans on *A Knight at the Opera* (1984), was editor of the *Royal Opera Year-*

books 1978–80, and has contributed to the *New Grove Dictionary of Music* and the *New Grove Dictionary of Opera*, *Enzyklopädie des Musiktheaters* (Munich), *Encyclopaedia Britannica* and other works of reference.

N.K.
Nicholas Kenyon is controller, BBC Radio 3. He was born in Cheshire and read modern history at Balliol College, Oxford. He worked for the English Bach Festival and the BBC before becoming a music critic of the *New Yorker*, 1979–82. He returned to London as a music critic of *The Times* and music editor of the *Listener*; he joined the *Observer* in 1986 and was also editor of *Early Music*, 1983–92. He has been a member of the Music Advisory Panels of the Arts Council and the South Bank Centre, and he is author of *The BBC Symphony Orchestra, 1930–80* and *Simon Rattle: The Making of a Conductor*, and editor of *Authenticity and Early Music*.

N.M.
Noel Malcolm studied at Cambridge University, where he was awarded a starred first in English and a doctorate in history. From 1981 to 1988 he was a fellow of Gonville and Caius College. He was political correspondent of the *Spectator* from 1987 to 1991, when he became that paper's foreign editor. He has published a biography of Marc' Antonio de Dominis (1984), a study of the life and music of George Enescu (1990) and an edition of the complete correspondence of Thomas Hobbes (1993).

N.W.
Nicholas Williams studied at Cambridge University with Alexander Goehr. He works in music publishing and as a music critic for the *Independent*.

P.A.G.
Paul Griffiths (born 1947) was educated in Birmingham and at Oxford. In the 1970s he worked on the *New Grove Dictionary of Music* while also writing music criticism for the *Financial Times*, *The Times* and other papers. He is now music critic of *The New Yorker*. His publications include several books on music (including studies of Boulez, Cage, Bartók, Davies, Ligeti, Messiaen and Stravinsky), two novels and a libretto for Mozart, The Jewel Box.

P.B.B.
Patricia B. Brauner (Ph.D., Yale University, 1970) is a member of the editorial committee of the *Edizione critica delle opere di Gioachino Rossini* (Fondazione Rossini and G. Ricordi) and coordinator of the Center for Italian Opera Studies at the University of Chicago. She was a contributor to the *New Grove Dictionary of Music* and editor of Rossini's *Ermione* (with Philip Gossett), *Armida* (with Charles S. Brauner), and *La riconoscenza* for the critical edition.

P.D.
Peter Dickinson is a composer, writer, broadcaster and pianist. An emeritus professor of Keele University, where he started the Music Department with its Centre for American Music in 1974, he is now professor at Goldsmiths' College of the University of London. His recorded compositions involve some of the leading performers and include concertos for organ and for piano, a series of song-cycles with piano, and choral works such as *Outcry* and the *Mass of the Apocalypse*. His book *The Music of Lennox Berkeley* was published in 1989.

P.G.
Philip Gossett (Ph.D., Princeton University, 1970) is Robert W. Reneker distinguished service professor in the Department of Music and dean of the Division of Humanities of the University of Chicago. He is general editor of *The Works of Giuseppe Verdi* (University of Chicago Press and G. Ricordi) and direttore dell'edizione of the *Edizione critica delle opere di Gioachino Rossini* (Fondazione Rossini and G. Ricordi). He is the author of '*Anna Bolena*' and the Maturity of Gaetano Donizetti (OUP, 1985) and of numerous studies, articles and reviews, as well as the critical editions of Rossini's *Tancredi*, *Ermione* (with Patricia Brauner) and *Semiramide* (with Alberto Zedda).

P.J.
Peter Jonas is general director of the Bavarian State Opera. Previously, he was general director, English National Opera (1985–93); director of artistic administration, Chicago Symphony Orchestra and Orchestral Association of Chicago (1976–85); and assistant to music director, Chicago Symphony Orchestra (1974–6). He has been a fellow of the Royal College of Music since 1990 and a member of the council there since 1988; he was made a CBE in 1993. He was educated at the University of Sussex (which awarded him a D.Mus. in 1994), the Royal Northern College of Music (Northern School of Music) and the Royal College of Music.

R.G.H.
Robin Holloway was born in 1943 in the Midlands, but brought up in London as a chorister at St Paul's Cathedral, then as a schoolboy at King's, Wimbledon. At Cambridge he read English then music – the dual preoccupations of a lifetime. He has held a fellowship at Caius College since 1969 and a university lectureship since 1975. Compositions include two operas – *Clarissa* (1976, ENO 1990) and its buffa complement, inspired by the life and work of Cynthia Payne (1991) – and numerous orchestral works, ensemble pieces, concertos, songs, etc. He also contributes many articles to books and journals, most regularly a monthly music review in the *Spectator*.

R.H.C.
Ronald Crichton (born Scarborough, 1913) worked in London on Anglo-French cultural rela-

tions (1938–40). After war service (1940–46) and work for the British Council in Greece, Belgium, West Germany and London (1946–67) he joined the *Financial Times* as music critic in 1967, retiring in 1978. He was co-editor of *Dictionary of Modern Ballet* (1959) and has contributed to many publications. His work includes *Manuel de Falla – A Descriptive Catalogue of his Works* (1976), *Falla* (BBC Music Guides, 1982) and the abridged edition of *The Memoirs of Ethel Smyth* (1987).

R.J.S.
Robert Samuels studied English and music at Robinson College, Cambridge, including electronic music with Peter Zinovieff and a Ph.D. with Derrick Puffett. Interests include the works of Mahler, music analysis, and contemporary theory. He is currently on the staff of the Music Department at Lancaster University.

R.L.
Richard Luckett is Pepys librarian and precentor of Magdalene College, Cambridge, and a university lecturer in English. He has published *Handel's Messiah: A Celebration* (1992), and has edited, with Christopher Hogwood, *English Music in the Eighteenth Century*, a collection of essays; his contributions to *The Companion* to the Latham and Matthews edition of Pepys's *Diary* include the article on music and the biographies of musicians.

R.L.H.
Robert Henderson is the music critic of the *Daily Telegraph*. He studied at the universities of Durham and Oxford (with Egon Wellesz, the medievalist Frank Harrison and the art historian Edgar Wind). After graduating he worked for several years as a freelance writer and broadcaster, specializing in medieval and 20th-century music. He has written extensively on the music of Henze, is a regular contributor to *Opera*, and wrote the chapters on Monteverdi and Offenbach in Alan Blyth's *Opera on Record*.

R.M.
Rodney Milnes read history at Oxford, and after a short career in publishing moved into musical journalism. He has been associated with *Opera* magazine since 1971, and became editor in 1986. He was opera critic of the *Spectator* from 1970 to 1990, and after two years with the London *Evening Standard* was appointed chief opera critic of *The Times* in 1992. He has translated many operas, including *Rusalka* (Dvořák), *Osud* (Janáček) and *Tannhäuser* (Wagner). He was appointed knight of the Order of the White Rose of Finland in 1987.

R.P.
Roger Parker teaches music at Oxford University. He has written numerous articles on 19th-century Italian opera, and is co-author (with Arthur

Groos) of *Giacomo Puccini: La bohème* (CUP, 1986). He is the editor of *Nabucco* in the Verdi Critical Edition and *The Oxford Illustrated History of Opera* (1994) and is co-editor of the *Cambridge Opera Journal*.

R.T.
Richard Traubner is the author of *Operetta: A Theatrical History* (Gollancz) and a frequent contributor to the *New York Times*, *Opera News*, *The Economist*, *Stagebill*, *American Record Guide* and other publications. He has lectured and broadcast on operetta and film throughout the US and the UK, and has written notes for many opera and record companies. His four Offenbach translations have been produced around the US, and he has directed and designed several operettas. He restored material for the New York Shakespeare Festival *Pirates of Penzance*, and wrote new lyrics for the 1991 Houston Grand Opera production of Victor Herbert's *Babes in Toyland*.

S.H.
Steven Huebner holds a Ph.D. degree from Princeton University and is currently associate professor of music at McGill University in Montreal, Canada. His first book, *The Operas of Charles Gounod*, published in 1990, will be followed by one on *fin-de-siècle* French opera.

S.W.
Stephen Walsh was born in 1942 and educated at St Paul's School, London, and Gonville and Caius College, Cambridge. From 1963 to 1976 he worked as a music critic and broadcaster in London, writing regularly for *The Times, Daily Telegraph* and *Financial Times*. He was deputy music critic of the *Observer* from 1966 to 1985. Since 1976 he has been senior lecturer in music at Cardiff University. He is the author of several books on music, including *The Music of Stravinsky* (Routledge/OUP, 1988/1993) and *Stravinsky: Oedipus Rex* (CUP, 1993); he is now at work on a biography of Stravinsky.

T.C.
Tim Carter has worked extensively on early baroque opera – his doctoral dissertation was on Jacopo Peri – and on music in Florence during the 1600s, as well as being the author of the Cambridge Opera Handbook on Mozart's *Le nozze di Figaro* and *Music in Late Renaissance and Early Baroque Italy* (Batsford). He is currently reader in music at Royal Holloway and Bedford New College, University of London.

W.A.
William Ashbrook (born 1922, Philadelphia) was educated at the University of Pennsylvania and at Harvard. After a 40-year career of teaching humanities, mostly at Indiana State University, where he is distinguished professor emeritus of humanities, he continues to teach part-time, to lecture, and to write copiously on the subject of Italian opera of

the *ottocento*. His studies of Donizetti and Puccini are well known. He is the editor of *The Opera Quarterly*, and is also currently engaged on a critical biography of Arrigo Boito.

Z.C.
Zofia Chechlinska is a musicologist, and the author of books on Polish 19th-century music, including Chopin. She is head of the Music Department of the Institute of Art in Warsaw, the editor of a series devoted to 19th-century musical culture, and the editor of *Chopin Studies*, published by the Chopin Society in Warsaw. She contributed to the *New Grove Dictionary of Music*. She is currently preparing a book on the history of 19th-century musical culture in Poland.

Index of Librettists

Index of Titles